Najmieh takes us with her on an extraordinary culinary journey: from the daily fish market in Bushehr, on the Persian Gulf, where she and her host buy and cook a 14-pound grouper in a tamarind, cilantro, and garlic sauce, to the heart of historical Isfahan, in central Iran, where she prepares lamb necks in a yogurt, saffron, and candied orange peel sauce topped with caramelized barberries. Traveling north to the Caspian Sea, she introduces us to the authentic Gilaki version of slow-cooked duck in a pomegranate and walnut sauce, served over smoked rice; and the unique flavors of a duck-egg omelet with smoked eggplant and baby garlic. Lingering in the north, in tribal Kurdistan, she treats us to lamb-and-bulgur meatballs filled with caramelized onions and raisins in a saffron sauce. Dropping south, to Bandar Abbas on the coast, she teases our palate with rice cooked in date juice and served with spicy fish, while in Baluchistan she cooks spiced goat in a pit overnight and celebrates the age-old method of making bread in hot ashes.

At every village and off-the-beaten-track community, Najmieh unearths traditional recipes and makes surprising new discoveries, giving us a glimpse along the way of the places where many of the ingredients for the recipes are grown. She treks through the fields and orchards of Iran, showing us saffron being picked in Khorasan and pomegranates in Yazd, dates harvested by the Persian Gulf, pistachios in Kerman, and tea and rice by the Caspian.

With more than 250 recipes and 400 photographs, *Cooking in Iran* is packed with inspiring ideas and practical tips—everything you'll need for recreating these glorious dishes so that you can embark on a culinary journey of your own.

COOKING in IRAN
REGIONAL RECIPES & KITCHEN SECRETS

NAJMIEH BATMANGLIJ

MAGE PUBLISHERS

Copyright © 2018 Najmieh Batmanglij

Full credits on page 706

All rights reserved.
No part of this book may be reproduced
or transmitted in any manner whatsoever
without written permission from the publisher.

MAGE PUBLISHERS INC.
WASHINGTON, DC
WWW.MAGE.COM
AS@MAGE.COM

Library of Congress Cataloging-in-Publication Data
Available at the library

ISBN 13: 978-1933823-95-9
ISBN 10: 1-933823-95-X

Printed in China

Cooking *lavash* bread on a *saj* in tribal Iran.

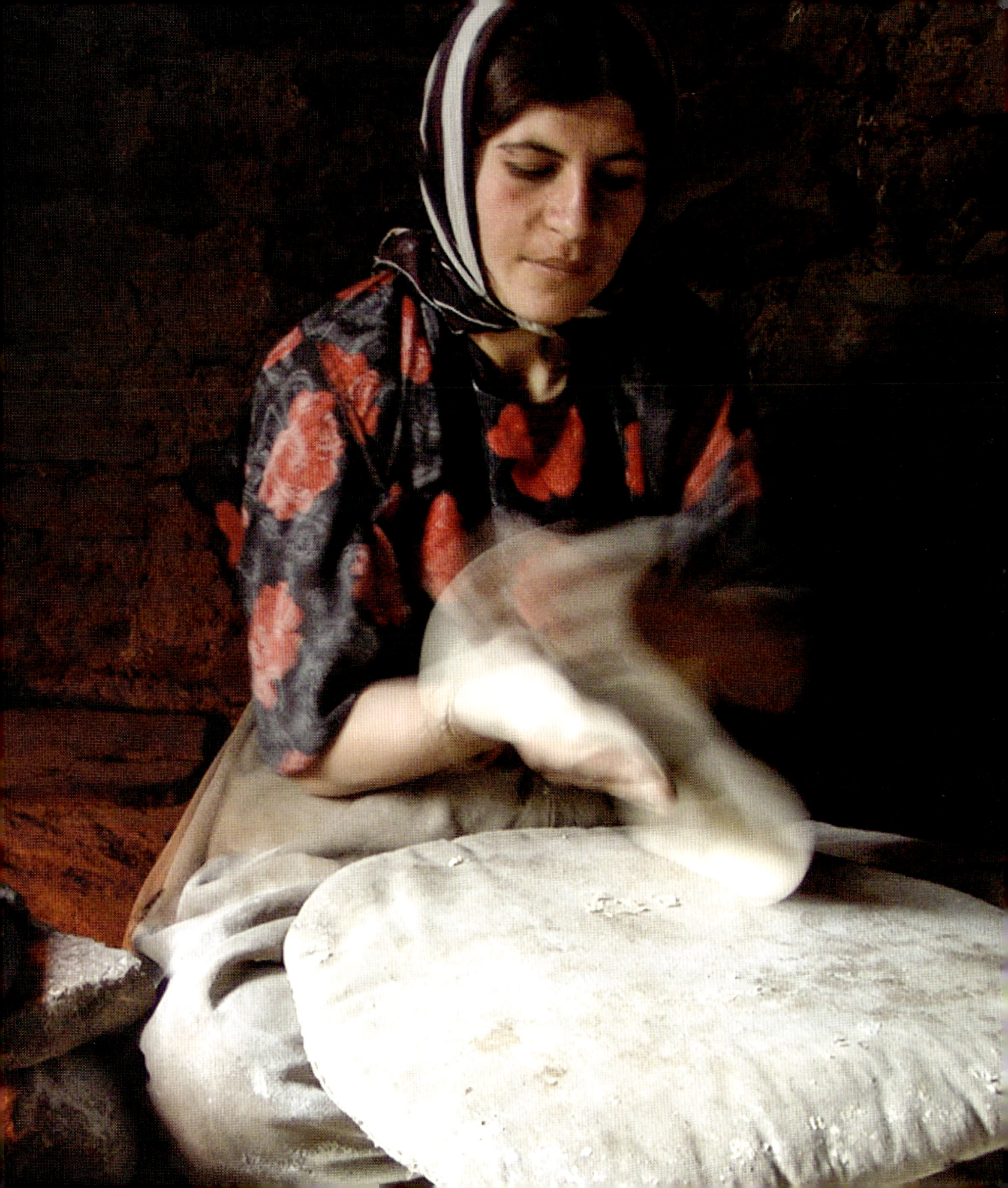

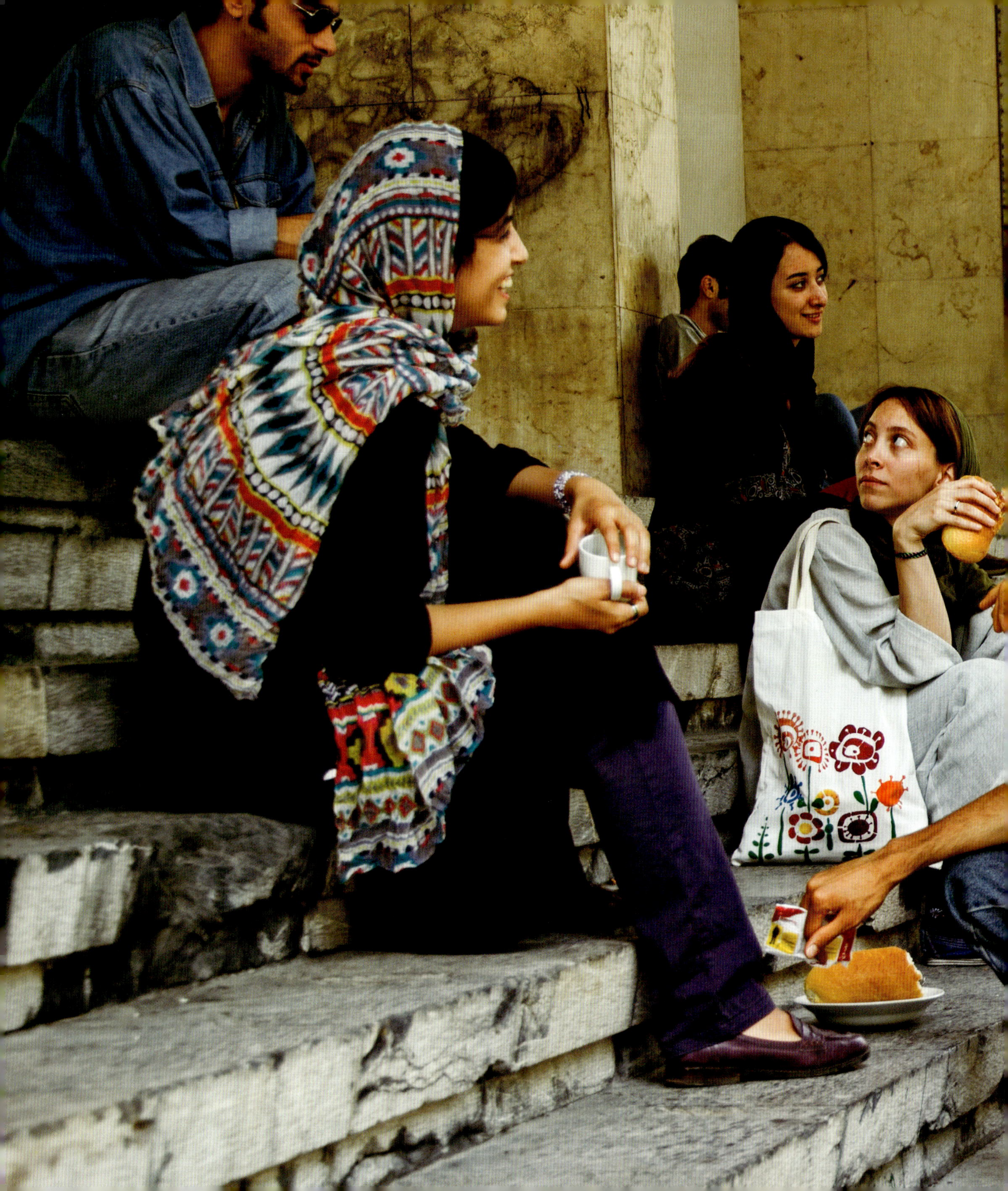

For young Iranians and the struggle for the soul of Iran

Pickled baby garlic/*gol-e sir* in Chaboksar by the Caspian. The red ones have been flavored with sour cherries.

Contents

Recipe contents are on page 708.

A Geography of Iran 11
Preface 13

Tehran 14
Arrival 17
Climate 18
A Little History 21
The Tajrish Bazaar 25
Downtown Tehran 33
Iranian Soups
  and the Kitchen 37
Ladies' Lunch 40
Tehran in the 1900s 42
Darband 50
Darakeh 56

The Caspian 68
A Little History 71
A Caspian Story 73
Cooking in Rasht 80
Masouleh 103
Harvesting Tea 166

Azarbaijan 172
A Little History 175
Ardabil 177
Tabriz 178
Cooking in Tabriz 183
The Story of Omaj 193
The National Dish:
  Chelow Kabab 208
The Story of Minced
  Kabab 215
Wine in an Ancient
  Kitchen 227

Qom 228
A Little History 229

Qazvin 232
A Little History 233
Dessert 241

Hamadan 244
A Little History 245
Iranian Jews 253

Arak 268
A Little History 269

Bread 284
A Flat Bread Story 287

Kurdistan and
Tribal Region 312
A Little History 313

Isfahan 352
A Little History 354
Iranian Armenians 379

Kashan 382
A Little History 383
Do Not Despair 385

Khorasan 388
A Little History 391
Saffron 393
Barberries 417

Yazd 428
A Little History 431
The Cypress at
  Abarkuh 435
Iranian Zoroastrians 437
Pomegranates 443
A Pastry Workshop 452

Kerman 461
A Little History 463
The Pistachio Journey 465
The Persian Garden 509

Fars / Shiraz 516
A Little History 518
Hafez 520
Sesame 555
Fill the Glass with Wine 559

Khuzestan 563
A Little History 565

The Persian Gulf 574
A Little History 577
Bushehr 579
The Bounty of the Sea 581
The Date Palm 585
A Conversation Between a
  Date Palm and a Goat 593

Sistan + Baluchistan 680
A Little History 682

A Visual Glossary of an
Iranian Pantry 702
Acknowledgements 704
Credits 706
Recipe Contents 708
Index 714

Three women weaving a carpet in a village in eastern Azarbaijan.

A Geography of Iran

Iran is divided into several plateaus separated by high mountain ranges running west to east and north to south, with the Caspian Sea in the north and the Persian Gulf in the south. These regions have distinctly different climates, and until the advent of modern transportation, each had its own local ingredients and food culture. Many of Iran's provinces, such as Tehran, Kerman or Isfahan, have the same name as their main city. For this book, some provinces have been combined into regions based on cooking styles and ingredients preferences.

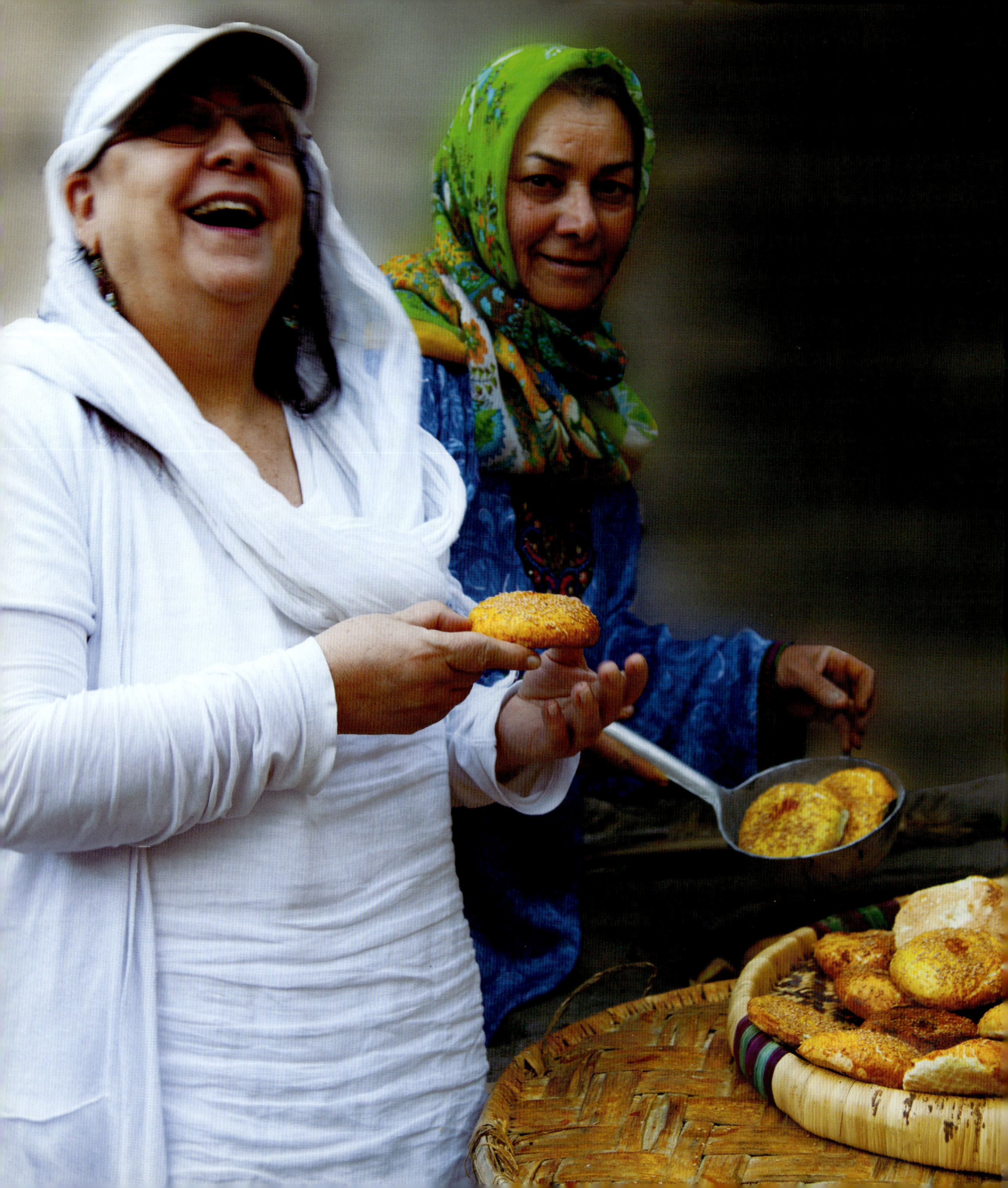

Preface

Every country expresses itself in food—the meals and casual delights created from what grows in its soil, swims in its seas, grazes on its fields. Food is so much more than sustenance. In ways both subtle and powerful, it maintains bonds of family, friends, communities, and entire societies.

Iran is the country of my birth, but I've lived away from it for much of my adult life. This book is about going back. For a long time, I have wanted to renew my ties directly: to wander in Iran's amazing markets; to meet its cooks and restaurateurs; to share kitchens and tables and tastes and scents that convey the very essence of the place.

It is a big country, highly diverse in climate and terrain, with mountain ranges, grasslands, and deserts. Seas lie to the north and south. Here and there are great cities where many cultures mingle. All this variety is reflected in the cooking, as is Iran's deep and fascinating past.

To capture the range of Iranian cuisine, I traveled for months, starting in the capital city of Tehran, where I spent my childhood, and then proceeding outward to regions that have their own distinctive culinary traditions. Accordingly, the book is organized as a journey. For each region that I visited, I have supplied recipes that highlight local tastes and techniques. In the pages that follow, you will also see some of the visual beauty of Iran, share some encounters that were especially meaningful to me, and even hear a few poetic voices of the past, for Iran has a great literary tradition that sometimes touched on the pleasures of food.

So come with me now and share my adventure of exploration. Here is Iran expressing itself in food and cooking, a diversity that is also one.

Tehran

An aerial view of Tehran at night from the Milad Tower.

Above and opposite: With my cousins in Tehran.

Arrival

I arrived in Tehran at 3 am. By the time I'd gone through customs and picked up my luggage it was 5 in the morning. But perhaps the real moment of arrival occurred when I was sitting in the back of a car taking me to my cousin's house in northern Tehran. I rolled down the window and all of a sudden smelled the earth after a sprinkling of rain. Oh my God! I was really home. This was the smell of Iran that I remembered from my childhood.

At last I was doing something I had wanted to do for a very long time: document, through first-hand observations and experiences, what food means in Iran. I wanted to share kitchens with old and young cooks who were keeping traditions alive around the country; photograph the bounty and the atmosphere of local markets and bazaars; visit the regions and cities that, in their varied ways, make Iranian cuisine one of world's greatest.

I was grateful to have my own apartment, which my dear cousin Mansoureh Manuchehrian, the matriarch of the family, and her daughter Ferdows had offered me. After a quick shower, I fell fast asleep. When I woke up around 4 in the afternoon, I wandered over to a family gathering organized for my benefit. It was a joyous occasion and lovely to see all the young and old members of the family. I received lots of hugs and told them about my project, and spent the next hour trying to answer their excited questions. But of course the real answers were lying in wait for me in the months ahead.

The next morning I visited my parents' tomb at Behesht-e Zahrah, on the outskirts of town. As soon as I closed the door of the entrance to the mausoleum, I became very emotional. The names on the gravestones conjured faces and moments in my life so vividly that this place almost seemed to exist outside of time. On each of the graves, I placed roses I'd bought on the way to the cemetery. Then I poured out my heart to my dear father/*aqa joon* and my dear mother/*madar joon* and asked them to help and guide me on the journey ahead. I knew the language and culture, but I could not function smoothly. I didn't know how to use the telephone, I didn't know what the money was or meant, and I didn't understand the psychology behind the way people spoke to each other—it was different from what I had known so well. It seemed I had to learn re-code and decode people's words and gestures. I really needed help to make my trip a success.

Climate

Tehran is situated in north-central Iran. It is a city on the foothills of a high, east-west mountain range called Alborz. On a clear day, its two highest mountains, Damavand and Tochal (18,000 and 13,000 feet respectively) are visible from the center of the city. On the north side of this mountain range are the lush coastal regions of the Caspian Sea. To the south and east is an arid desert. This geographical juxtaposition decides Tehran's semi-arid climate, which is also Mediterranean in its rainfall patterns. Spring and autumn can be very pleasant, while summers are hot (sometimes very hot) and winters can be cold and snowy—there are several good ski resorts less than an hour's drive from the city.

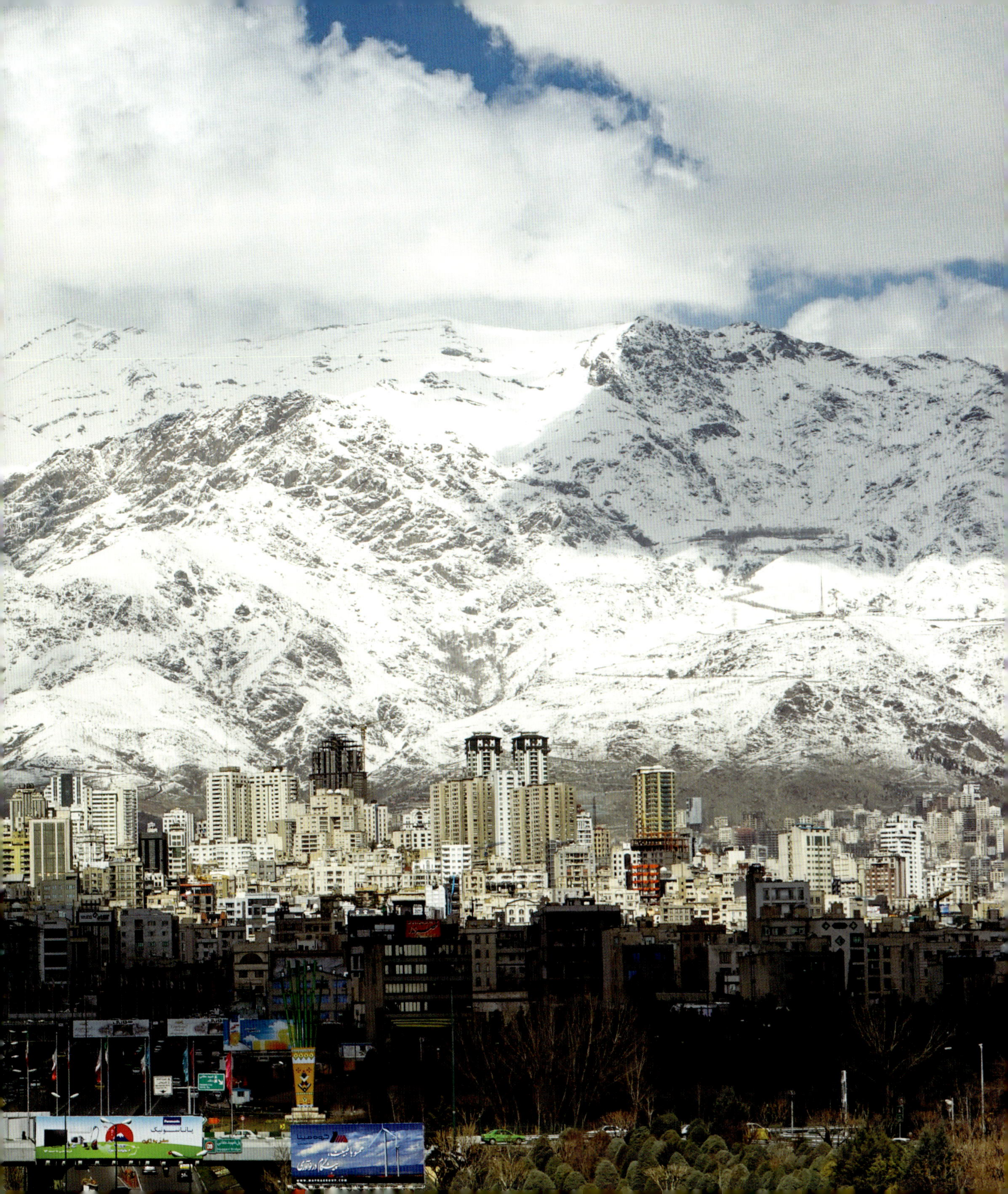

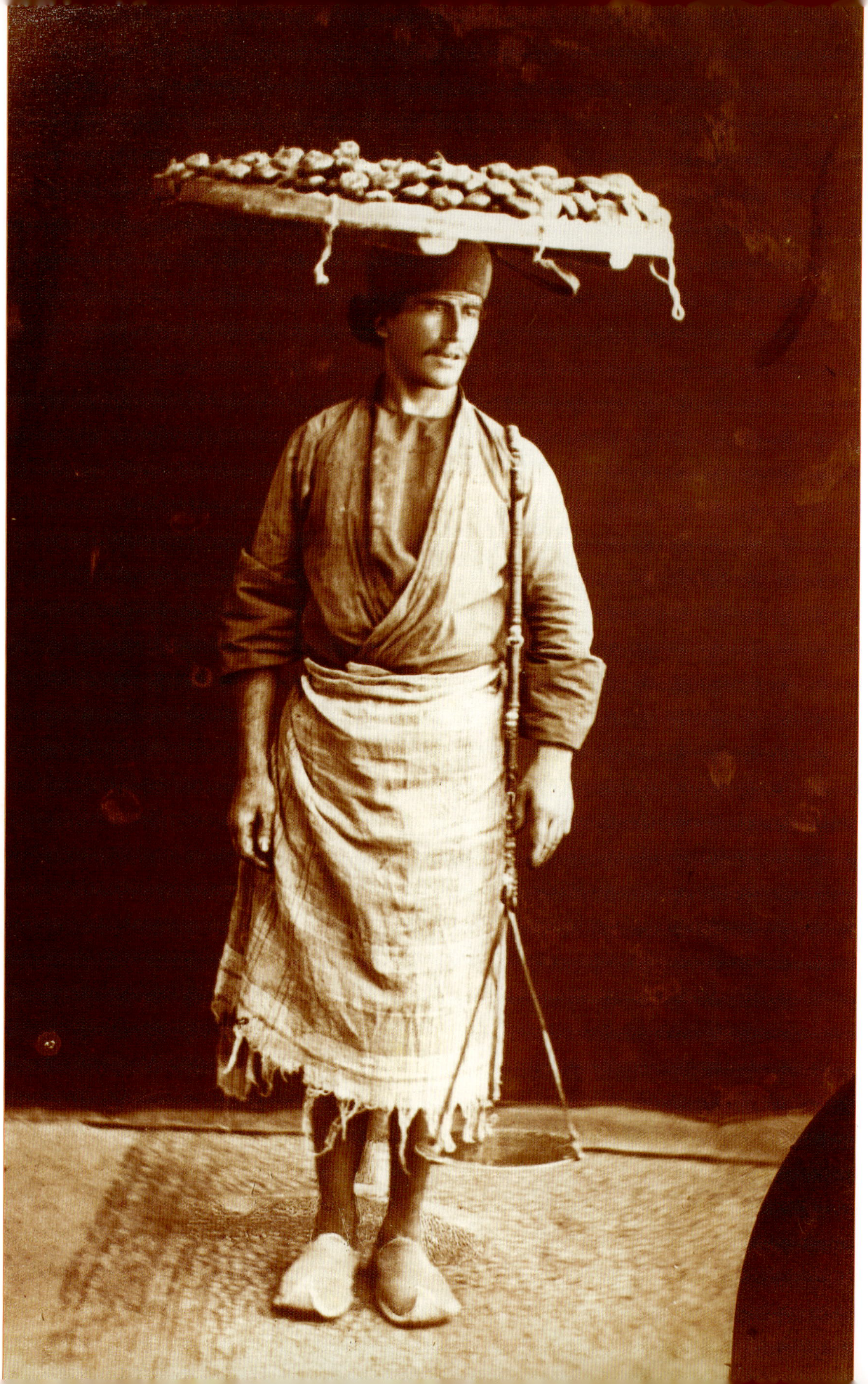

A Little History

Tehran was not always the capital of Iran. Once, it was just an obscure village whose inhabitants apparently lived in dugouts underneath their gardens. Some say that the name Tehran comes from "*tah*", meaning "the end of", or "below" in Persian. About 50 kilometers to the south was a much more impressive town called Ray (or Raghes or Ragha in European references). It a major stop on the Silk Road, a network of trade routes that connected China to Italy in medieval times. When Ray was attacked by Mongols around 1220, many people fled to Tehran and took refuge there.

In 1786, the founder of the Qajar dynasty, Aqa Mohammad Khan, moved his capital from Isfahan to Tehran as part of his efforts to subdue rival powers in the south and east of Iran and to unify the country under his tribe and family. Nevertheless, it remained a provincial town until Naser al-Din Shah launched a building and expansion program after his visit to European capitals in the 1870s. Today, greater Tehran is a cosmopolitan city with a population of sixteen million.

Opposite: Street vendor selling fresh figs in Tehran circa 1900.

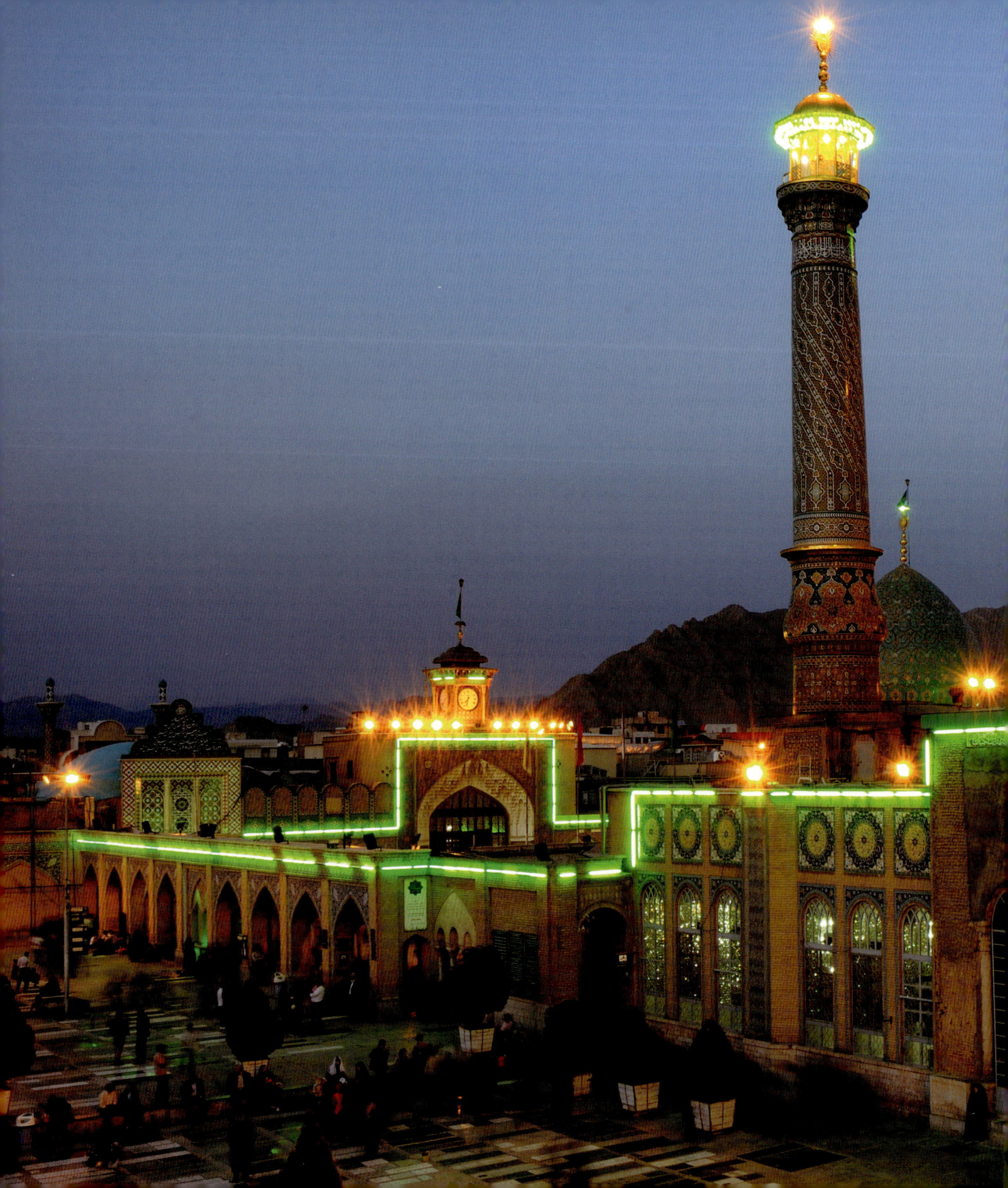

Shabdolazim Shrine in Ray, which was once a major city on the Silk Road but is now a part of greater Tehran.

آرامگاه صفا
ظهیرالدوله
۱۳۱۷
یا علی

بسم الله
...

۳

The Tajrish Bazaar

As soon as I stepped into Tehran's Tajrish bazaar, the atmosphere, aromas, people, and sights of all the fresh fruit and vegetables almost overwhelmed me, but in the most pleasant way imaginable. Here I was with my backpack, wearing a Nike hat and a light blue cotton scarf around my neck, iPhone camera in hand, talking like a mad person to every vendor and taking pictures of them and whatever they had to sell. When I asked an old lady with a purple scarf and a beautiful smile what she was going to do with the cardoon/*kangar* stalks she was buying (they taste somewhere between artichoke and celery, she smiled and said, "Cardoons are now in season, and they are local to this area; they grow in the foothills of the mountains." Then she patiently gave me a cardoon braise recipe in detail. I hugged her and thanked her.

What kind and warm people Iranians are. Everyone seemed to be happy to go out of their way in their busy lives to help and share their secrets with a total stranger.

Opposite: Entrance gate to the Zahir Dowleh cemetery in Darband, a mile north of the Tajrish bazaar. I went there to put some flowers on my mother-in-law Lila *joon*'s grave. The cemetery is run by Sufis, and many Iranian poets, such as Forough Farrokhzad and Malek-o Sho'ara Bahar, are buried there.

Above: Cardoons sold in the market in Tajrish.

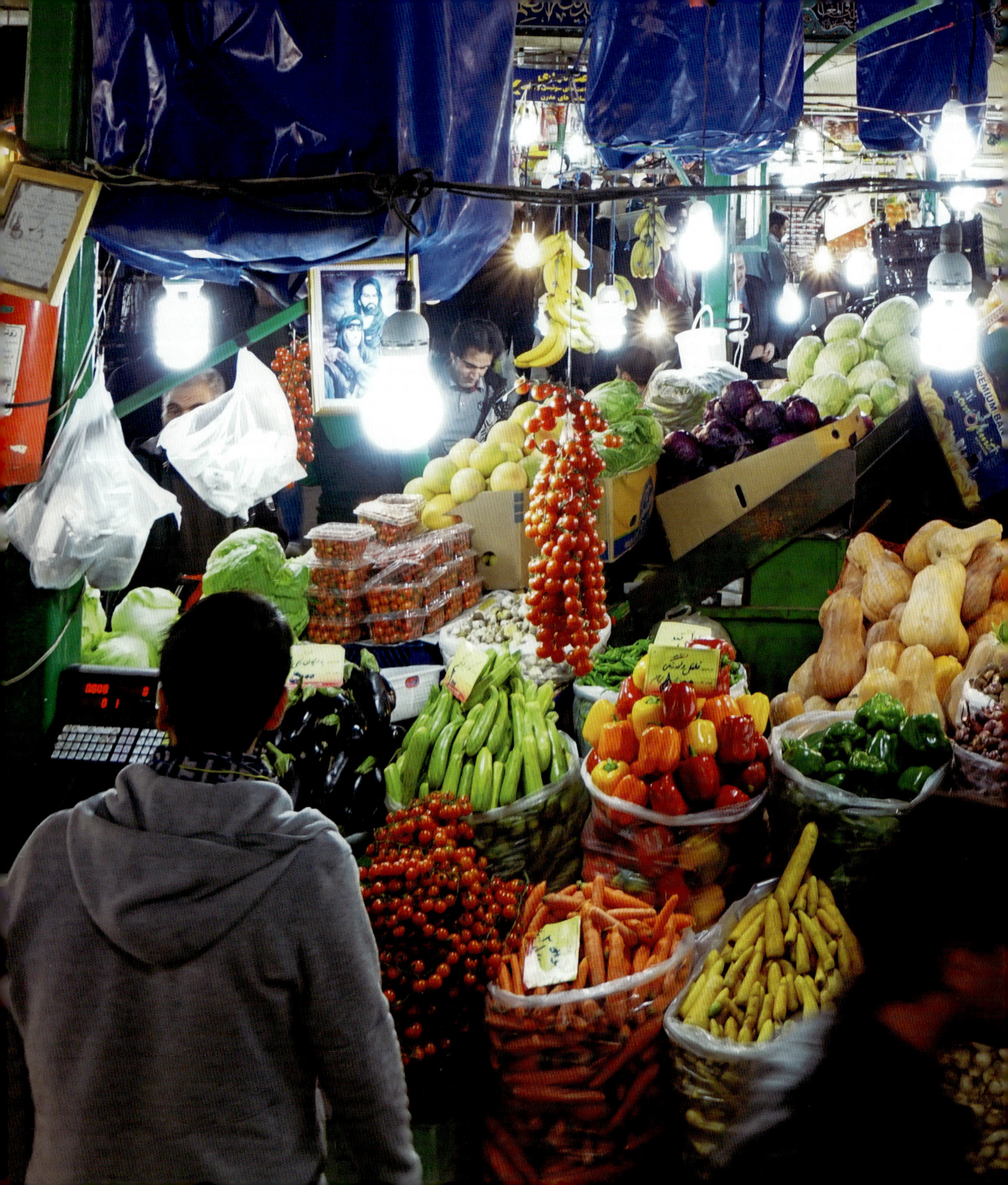

The daily market in the Tajrish bazaar

I had been writing about the food, ingredients, and ceremonies of Iran for the past thirty-nine years while living in France and America. Now I was here, in Iran, and I felt like a child in a candy store.

I started to buy all kinds of ingredients and delicacies that tempted me with their tasty freshness: softly sweet fresh white mulberries/*toot*, baby greengages sprinkled with salt/*gojeh sabz*, tiny green fresh almonds in their shells/*chaghaleh badam*, large Isfahani cherries, and tasty, thin barley bread sprinkled with delicious cumin, sesame, and poppy seeds. After a few hours, still excited but exhausted, I left the bazaar—but in my heart, I wanted to spend days there, basking in the abundance.

توت سفید
کی
۱۰۰۰۰
تومان
توت فرنگی بوته ای
نیم کیلو
سنندج
۶۰۰۰
تومان
Fresh Fruit

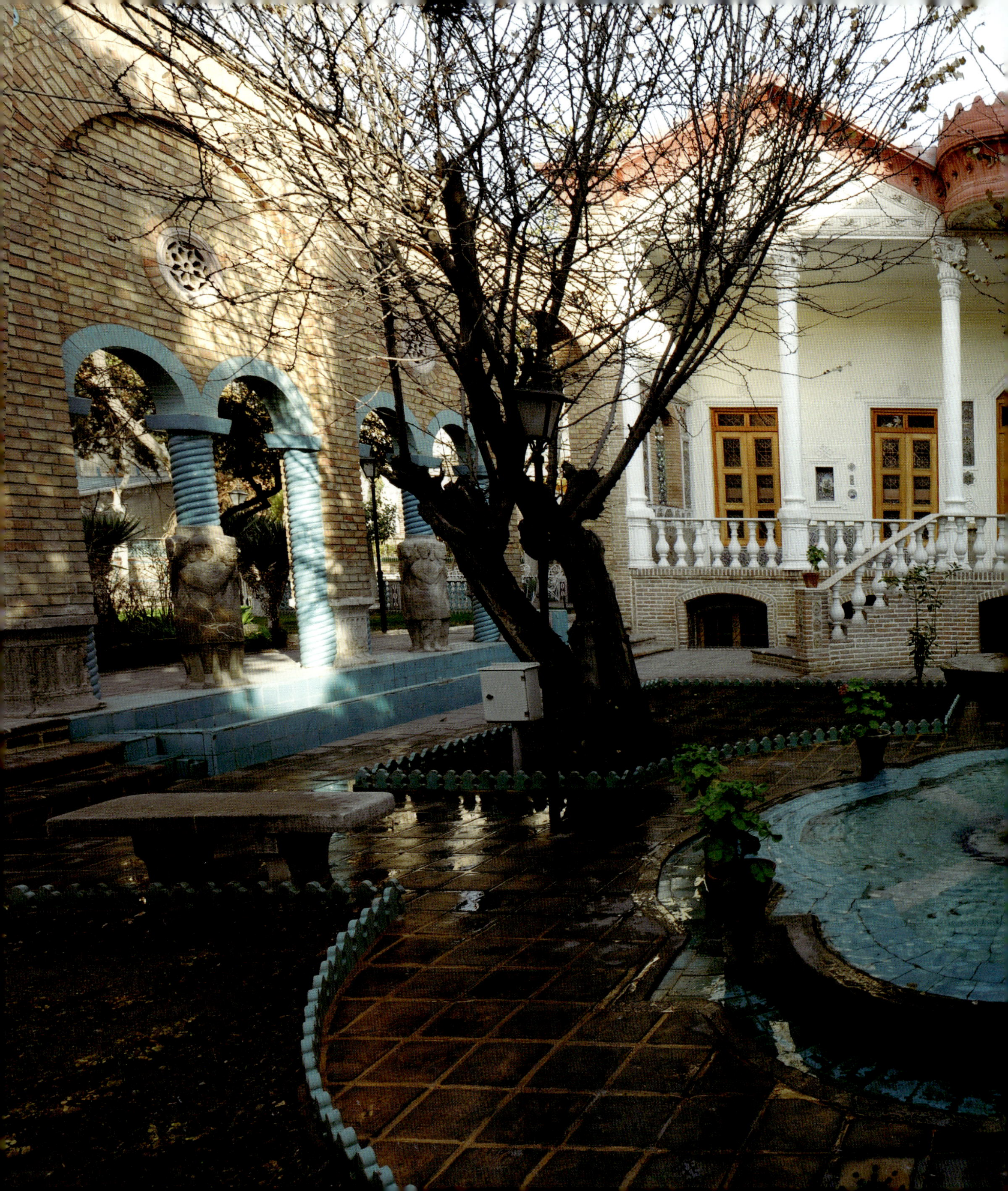

One of my favorite traditional houses in Tehran, Khaneh-ye Moghadam.

Downtown Tehran

The downtown Tehran of my childhood was full of trees. In those days Tehran had a population of about three million. Today, greater Tehran's population is five times more. But you don't feel that it is overcrowded. One reason might be that the city has more than a thousand parks.

Tehran is also much cleaner than many major cities—Istanbul, Athens, even New York. Another pleasant surprise for me was the traffic, which I found quite bearable, especially downtown where car entry was controlled.

Whenever I wanted to pay a cab driver and asked him what the fare had come to, he would say, "*qabeli nadareh*," meaning "it's not an amount worth paying." This is called "*ta'arof*" (politesse or courteous politeness). Some call it insincere politeness, but I find nothing insincere about *ta'arof*. For me it's a lovely gesture that is a hallmark of Iranian hospitality. *Ta'arof* is an elaborate, back-and-forth protocol about priority and hierarchy between people. It comes into play constantly in such things as who will go through the door first or who pays the bill. Keeping this in mind is not only a gesture of kindness but also an indication of good manners and politeness. It has nothing to do with insincerity; it is an adorable part of Iranian culture.

I grew up in a traditional Iranian family in an old house in what used to be the center of town but gradually became the old part of town as more and more Tehranis moved to the northern suburbs. On this trip, as soon as I found my bearings, I went back to the old neighborhood. Walking along Manuchehri Street, where antique shops are still thriving, I looked for a teapot like the one I remembered from my childhood. On Saadi Street, I was thrilled to see the Mignion pastry shop was still there. I remembered the Armenian family that had been running it for seventy years or so. And

An early-1960s photo of stacked trays of rice and fillet kababs/*chelow kabab* being delivered, under cloches, in Tehran by a very acrobatic bicycle delivery man.

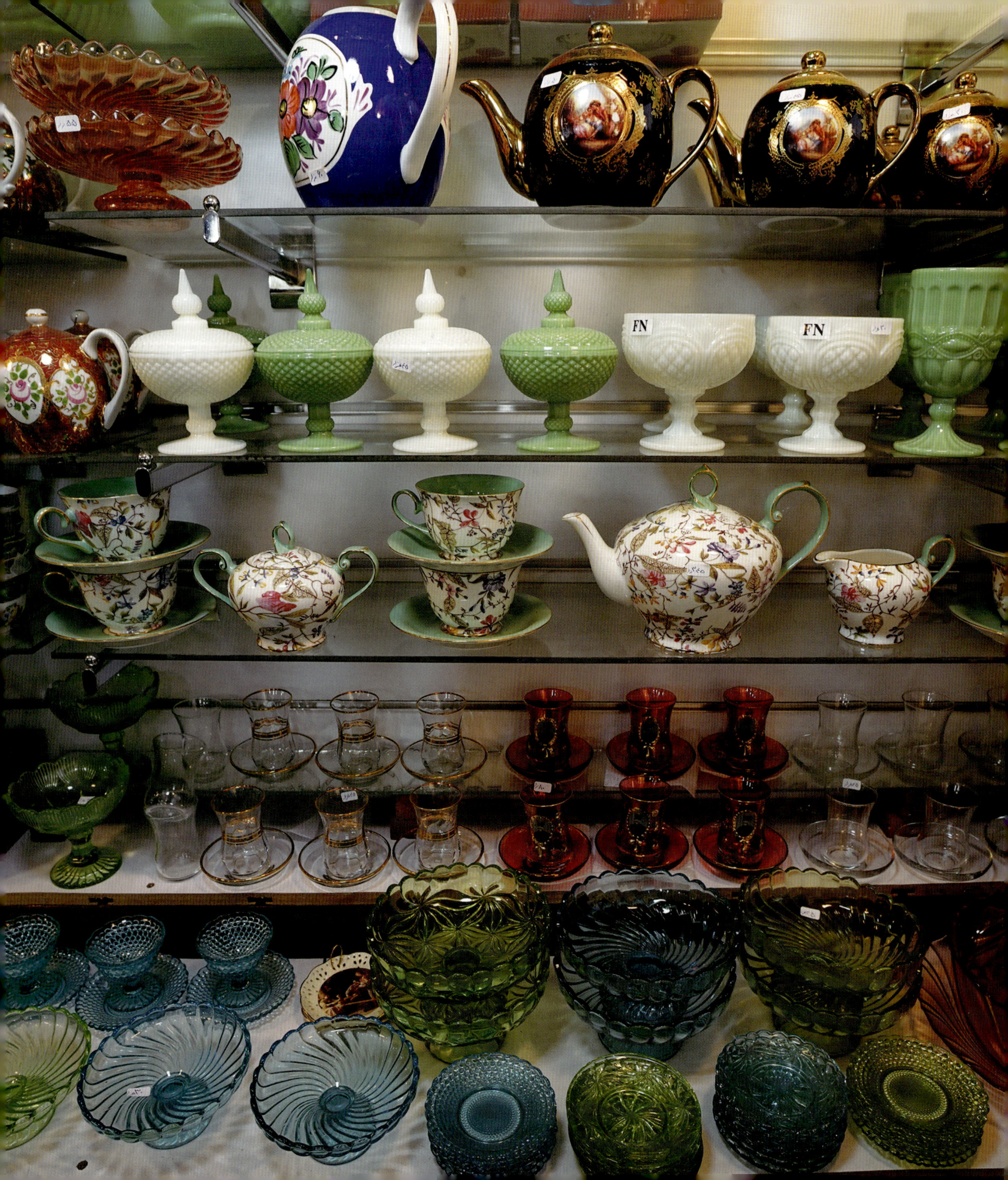
FN
FN

amazingly, Roben, the patriarch, also remembered me and my older sister, who had been a stunning beauty.

After a long walk, nothing is better than a slice of *gata*—a light, flaky pastry—and Armenian coffee, piping hot, foamy, rich, thick, and served in demitasse cups. A relative of Roben's made it, and, after drinking the coffee, she told me to place the saucer over the cup, invert the cup and saucer, and push them away with my left hand (the hand of the heart). We chatted as we let the inverted cup stand without disturbing it. She then took the cup and started to read my fortune in the viscous patterns the grounds left behind inside and around the cup. She gave me encouragement for my journey and said something about me being on a long journey, which would be successful.

The Armenian immigrants who started these pastry shops represented modernity for us children because they did not have the familiar Persian pastries such as *haj badumi*, *ghotab*, or baklava. My sisters and I would go to them after a movie. I can still recall the taste of candied orange peel dipped in chocolate, and the cold, creamy, strawberry ice-cream that we'd eat with bites of their specialty flaky pastry/*gata*. It was heavenly!

The Tehran of my childhood was ethnically diverse. It is less so today. Our neighbors were Armenians, Jews, Assyrians, and Georgians. And because, traditionally, most people came to Tehran from other parts of Iran as well as from other countries (there were several migrations at the turn of the nineteenth century from Russia, Poland, and Ukraine), the food of the city displays a great mixing of influences. Tehran today is thoroughly cosmopolitan, with restaurants from around the world. ☙

A shop window on Manuchehri Street.

I loved these girls, who were finishing their lunch at Dizzy Sara. My iPhone snapshot doesn't do them justice but catches the mood that I want to share with you.

Iranian Soups and the Kitchen

Iranians love their soups—watery-cold yogurt soup/*abdugh khiar*, onion and egg soup/*eshkeneh*, walnut and *kashk* soup/*kaleh jush*, flour and spinach soup/*omaj*; much thicker soups with legumes, herbs, and dried fruit/*osh*; thick porridges/*halim*; and more. These soups are made throughout Iran with similar or varying names, with each region changing some of the ingredients.

Just as in English, the word for supper comes from soup. In Persian, the cook is called the soup cook/*osh paz*, and the kitchen is called the house where the soup is cooked/*osh paz khaneh*.

The iconic Iranian lamb shank soup/*ab gusht*—literally water and meat—was traditionally called *dizzy*, from the name of the ceramic or stone dish in which the soup was often made. These days, the name *dizzy* and the traditional cooking method has become popular once again, and restaurants specializing in it as a kind of fast gourmet food have cropped up all over the country. *Dizzy* is always served with trimmings that include pickles, salads, and a fresh herb platter. (Recipe on page 39).

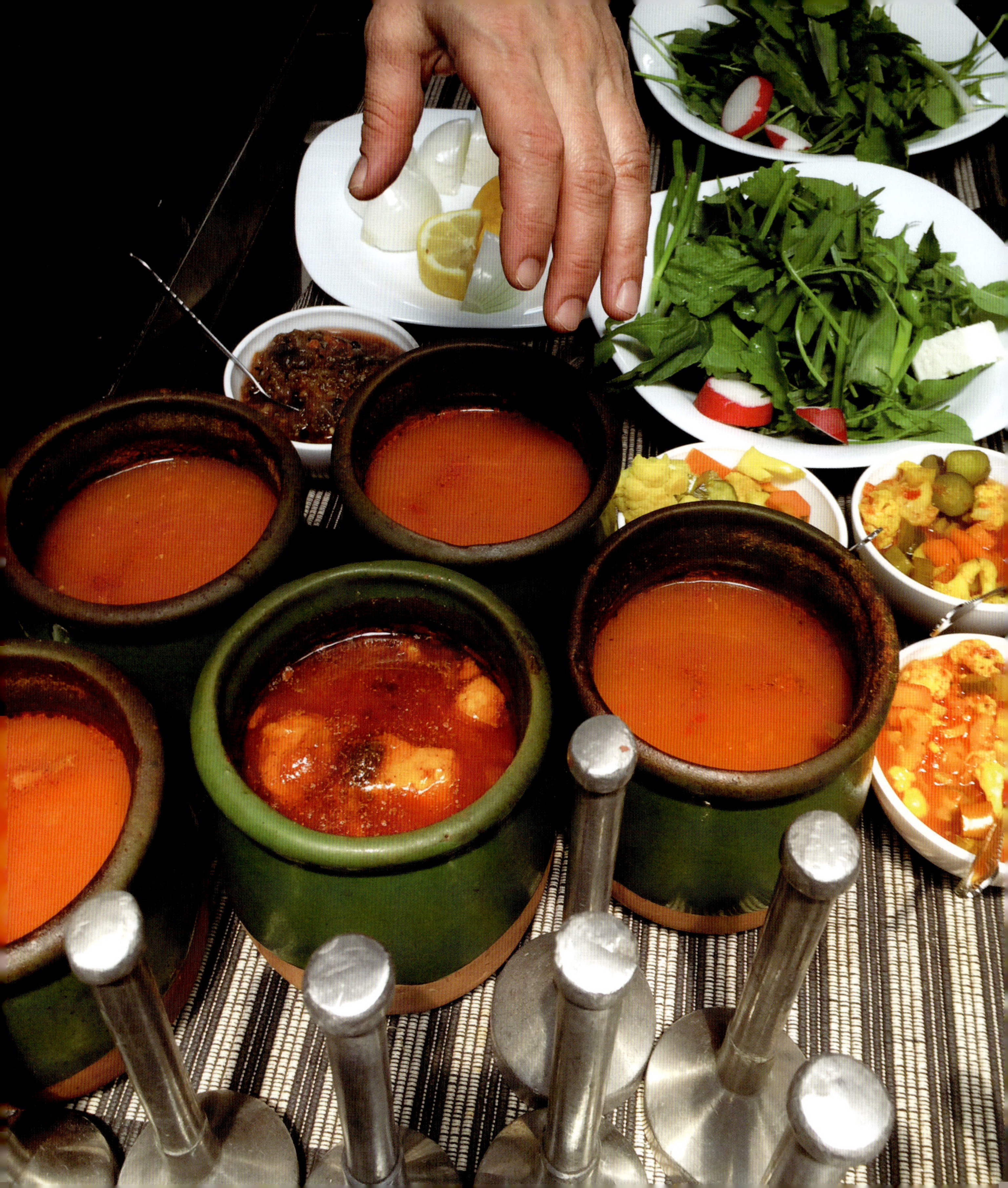

Lamb Shank, Chickpea + Kidney Bean Soup

Abgusht-e nokhod lubia, Dizzy

Serves 6
Prep: 10 minutes
Cooking: 2 hours 15 minutes

SOUP

½ cup/100g chickpeas soaked overnight, drained
½ cup/100g red kidney beans, soaked overnight, drained
2lb/900g lamb shanks
1lb/450g breast of lamb
2 large onions, peeled and quartered
8 cups/1.9l water
1 teaspoon turmeric
½ teaspoon freshly ground black pepper
3 large/1.3kg russet potatoes, peeled, cut into halves
2 teaspoons fine sea salt
4 medium tomatoes, peeled and sliced
1 tablespoon tomato paste
1 teaspoon ground cinnamon
4 whole dried Persian limes, pierced
½ teaspoon ground saffron dissolved in 2 tablespoons hot water

GARNISH

1 teaspoon ground cinnamon
1 large, white onion, peeled and sliced

TRIMMING

Pickled garlic
Shirazi-style tomato and cucumber salad
Sangak bread
Fresh herb platter
Yogurt dip

This soup, long popular as a teahouse favorite, is called dizzy, *from the name of the ceramic or stone pot in which it is traditionally cooked. Dizzy is popular throughout Iran but varies from region to region. Some use legumes in differing amounts, and in Qom they add kohlrabi and a mint garnish/na`na dagh, and call it abgusht-e qonbid. In downtown Tehran, I visited the renowned Dizzy Restaurant with friends, which inspired me to adapt this recipe.*

1. *To make the soup:* Place the meat, onions, and water in a large laminated cast-iron pot. Bring to a boil, skimming the froth as it forms. Add the chickpeas, beans, turmeric, and pepper. Cover and let simmer for 1½ hours over low heat.

2. Add the potatoes, salt, tomatoes, tomato paste, cinnamon, dried limes, saffron water, and *advieh*. Cover and continue to simmer for 45 minutes over low heat. Test, using the tip of a knife, to see if the meat and potatoes are tender. Adjust seasoning to taste.

3. Use a slotted spoon to remove all of the ingredients. Debone the meat (reserve the bones for later use). Mash the meat and vegetables together to make the paste called *gusht kubideh*. It should have the consistency of lumpy mashed potatoes. Iranian cooks would use a mortar and pestle to pound the meat to just the right consistency. A food processor may be used instead. Use the pulse feature of the processor, but do not overdo it and take care not to let the paste get too smooth.

4. Taste the meat paste and adjust seasoning to taste by adding more salt and pepper. Arrange on a serving platter. Pour 3 tablespoons of the hot soup over the paste. Garnish with cinnamon and fresh slices of raw onion.

5. Scoop or push out the marrow from the bones and reheat the broth. Mix the marrow with the broth and serve in bowls. Serve the meat paste separately with a Persian pickle/*torshi*, as well as Shirazi-style salad; a platter of spring onions, radishes, fresh tarragon, basil, and mint (*sabzi-khordan*). *Sangak*, lavash, or pita bread should accompany this soup. Pieces of bread can be used to scoop up the meat paste and garnish it with trimmings before putting it in your mouth. The bread can be toasted and broken up into the soup (*tilit* in Persian) like croutons. *Nush-e joon!*

Ladies' Lunch

When I was growing up in Tehran, *dizzy* used to be served in working-class neighborhoods from hole-in-the-wall type restaurants. I was fascinated to see that this fare is now available in upscale restaurants. Young and old gather at these restaurants to eat quite delicious traditional Iranian dishes served with all their trimmings. The restaurants usually have only one main dish, and when you sit down, everything is brought without too much fuss. The result is an organized and efficient service that has all the benefits of fast food combined with the pleasures of slow food: local, traditional, and community-oriented.

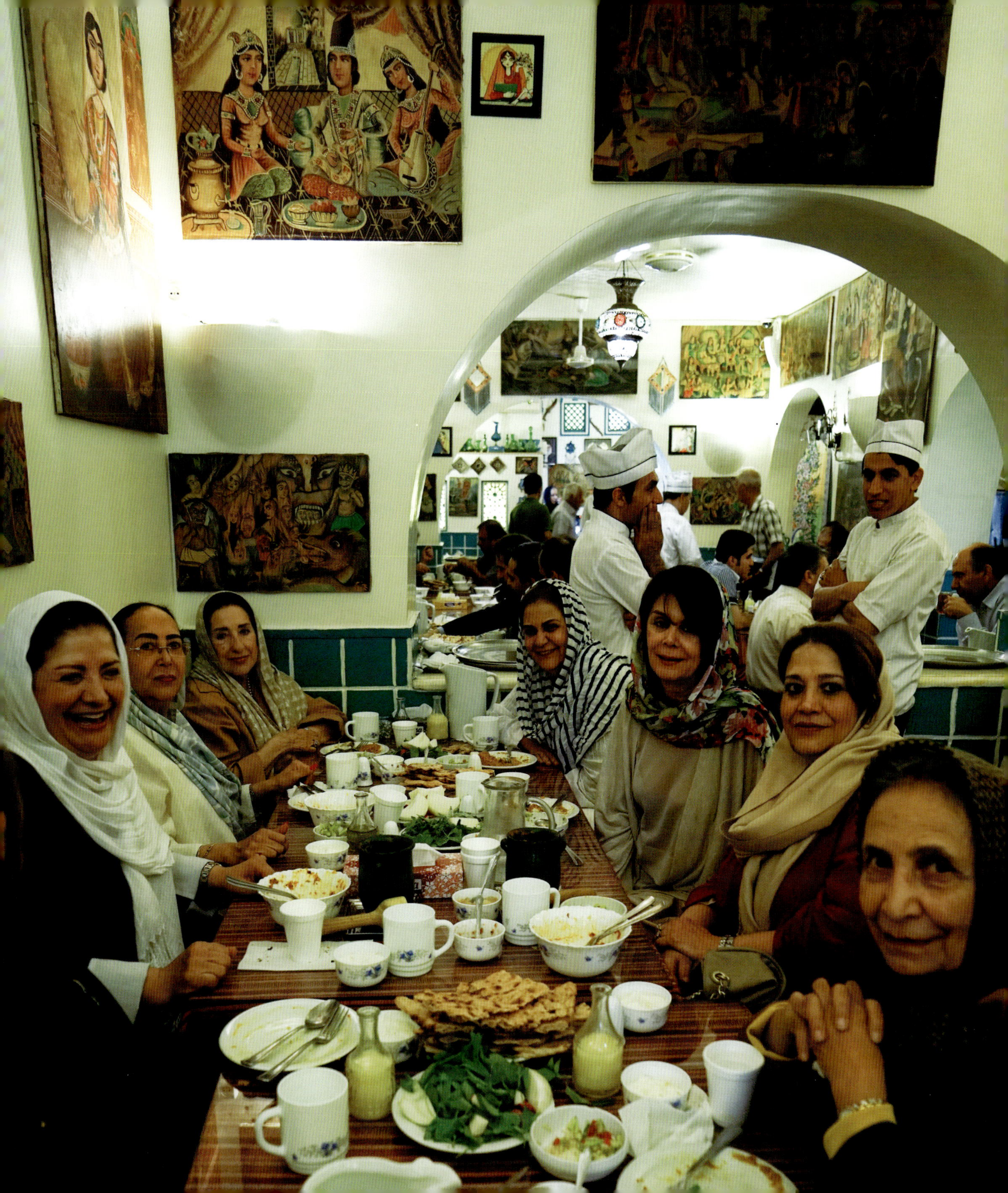

Tehran in the 1900s

This photograph of a *dizzy* seller with his pots and *sangak* bread was taken by Antoin Sevruguin, who ran a successful commercial photography studio first in Tabriz, and then in Tehran on what is now Ferdowsi Street. Sevruguin had grown up in Tiblisi, Georgia, where he trained as a painter. He was honored by Naser al-din Shah Qajar (late 1800s), but his photographs were confiscated by Reza Shah Pahlavi (1930s), because they did not represent the modern Iran that the shah was trying to portray.

43

Lamb's Head, Feet + Tripe Soup

kaleh pacheh-o sirab shirdun

Serves 6-8
Prep: 30 minutes
Cooking: 4½ hours'

- 1 mutton or lamb's head with the tongue
- 4 muttons' or lambs' feet (2 pounds/900g)
- 12 cups/3 liters water
- 1lb/450g calf or lamb tripe, dressed by your butcher and cut into small pieces
- 3 large onions, peeled and quartered
- 4 cloves garlic, peeled and crushed
- 4 bay leaves
- 2 teaspoons turmeric
- 1 tablespoon salt
- 1 teaspoon freshly ground pepper
- 1 teaspoon ground cinnamon
- Croutons of toasted *sangak* bread

In Iran, as in many other countries in the past, dressed head, feet, and tripe soup is a popular, nutritious, and cheap dish for the working class. Aqa-ye Aqdassy, a friend of my cousin, took us to a typical tripe restaurant in Tehran. It's always served very early in the morning. I was surprised I could enjoy this soup at 6 am, but I did. They served it with homemade, hot-from-the-oven sangak bread.

1. Sear mutton head and feet over an open flame to burn off hairs. Scrape and wash thoroughly. Remove the nose completely. Split the head in half vertically, with the tongue in one half, unless your butcher has already done so. Rinse with cold water.

2. Bring 12 cups of water to a boil in a large laminated cast-iron pot and add the head, tongue, feet, and tripe, as well as the onions, garlic, and bay leaves. Bring back to boil. Skim froth as it forms. When it stops forming, reduce the heat to low, add the turmeric, cover, and simmer for 4 hours or until the meat separates easily from the bones. Skim broth occasionally while cooking. Add more warm water if necessary to keep the water level at a minimum of 3 cups. (**Do not add salt** until soup has finished cooking. This prevents discoloration.)

3. Remove the head from the soup and peel the tongue and the skin off the bones. Separate the meat and brains from the skull. Cut into bite-size pieces. Remove bay leaves. Return meat to the broth. Add the salt, pepper, and cinnamon. Keep warm until ready to serve.

4. Adjust seasoning to taste. Pour the soup into a tureen. Place croutons in each soup bowl before ladling out the soup. Serve with lots of Persian pickles/*torshi*, fresh vegetables, and herbs/*sabzi-khordan*. *Nush-e joon!*

At the Tabbakhi-e Lux-e Talai restaurant.

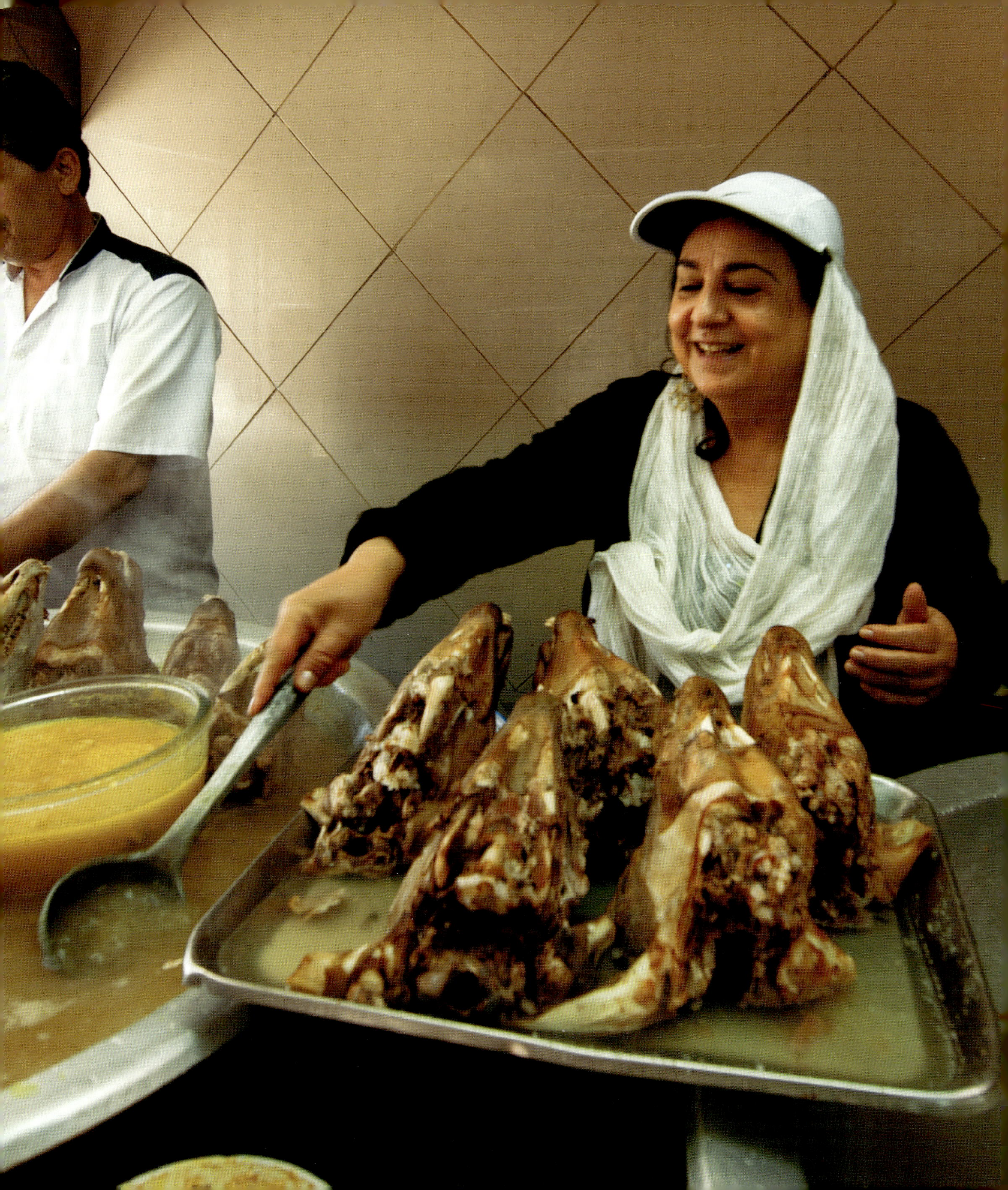

Onion, Egg + Spinach Soup
eshkeneh-ye tehrani

Serves 6
Prep: 20 minutes
Cooking: 1½ hours

SOUP

¼ cup/60ml oil
2 large onions, peeled and thinly sliced
1 teaspoon fine sea salt
½ teaspoon freshly ground pepper
1 teaspoon turmeric
2 tablespoons flour
2 tablespoons dried savory or fenugreek leaves
2 cups/110g chopped fresh spinach
6 cups/1.5l water
1 cup/150g dried pitted sour cherries (optional)
1 russet potato (about 1lb/450g), peeled and cut in halves (optional)
5 eggs

GARNISH

1 cup/240g drained yogurt
3 flat breads/lavash

When the Mongols invaded Ray in the thirteenth century, many of its inhabitants fled to Tehran, a village in the foothills full of gardens. Today, with a metro population of sixteen million, much of the city's best fruit and vegetables are still supplied by its surrounding gardens and farms. This is a simple winter soup also made in other parts of Iran, including Khorasan and Isfahan. In some regions, it is made without potatoes or sour cherries. I had it in Arak with unripe plums. In Azarbaijan, it's called ojez. Here, I am giving you a vegetarian version that is my favorite.

1. Heat the oil in a large laminated cast-iron pot over medium heat and sauté the onions until golden brown. Add the salt, pepper, turmeric, flour, fenugreek, and spinach. Sauté for 1 minute.

2. Add the water, cherries, and potato and bring to a boil. Reduce heat to medium, cover, and allow to simmer for 35 to 40 minutes until the potatoes are tender.

3. Add the eggs and stir for a few minutes to combine them with the soup. Bring back to boil. (An alternate method is to add the eggs one by one and allow them to poach in the soup gradually.) Adjust seasoning to taste.

4. Pour the soup into a tureen and serve with yogurt and bread. *Nush-e joon!*

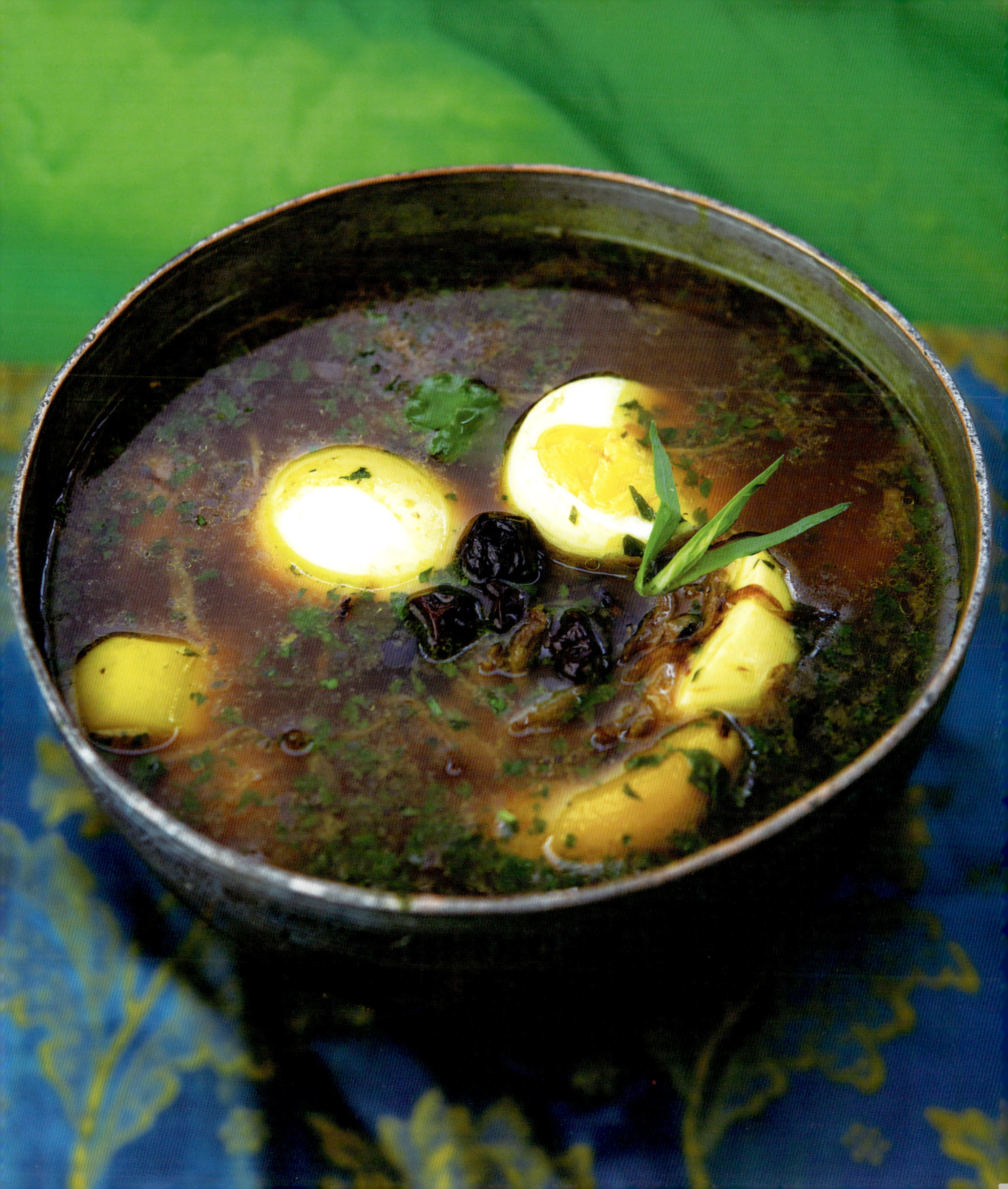

Ramp Polow
valak polow

Serves 6 to 8
Prep: 45 minutes
Cooking: 1 hour

3 cups/600g basmati rice
4 cups/340g ramps, trimmed, washed, and coarsely chopped
8 baby green garlics, trimmed, washed, and coarsely chopped
1 cup/240ml oil or ghee
1 teaspoon ground saffron dissolved in 4 tablespoons warm water
1 teaspoon ground cinnamon

Ramps, also known as wild leeks (valak in Persian), are wonderfully strong-flavored mountain bulbs that are available fresh in the late spring. They grow on the foothills of the mountains near Tehran. Nowadays they have become popular in the U.S. and are available at farmers' markets in the spring.

1. Wash the rice by placing it in a large container and covering it with water. Agitate gently with your hand, pour off the water, and repeat 3 times until the water is clear.

2. In a large non-stick pot, bring 8 cups/1.9l water and 2 tablespoons fine sea salt to a boil. Add the rice and boil briskly for 8 minutes, gently stirring twice to loosen any grains that may have stuck together or to the bottom of the pot. Add the ramps and garlic, and continue to boil for 2 minutes. Drain the rice mixture in a large fine-mesh colander and rinse with 3 cups water.

3. Place ½ cup/120ml oil, 2 tablespoons water, and a few drops of saffron water in the pot. Use a rubber spatula to mix thoroughly.

4. Use a spatula to gently place the rice mixture in the pot and form it into the shape of a pyramid (the shape allows room for the rice to expand and enlarge). Sprinkle the cinnamon on top. Cover and cook for 10 minutes over medium heat.

5. Pour the remaining oil, ½ cup/120ml water, and the rest of the saffron water over the rice pyramid. Wrap the lid with a clean dish towel and cover the pot firmly to prevent steam from escaping. Cook for 50 minutes longer over low heat.

6. Remove pot from heat and allow to cool for 5 minutes on a damp surface (I use a rimmed sheet pan with a moist towel on it) without uncovering it (this frees the crust from the bottom of the pot). Unmold the rice onto a serving platter. *Nush-e joon!*

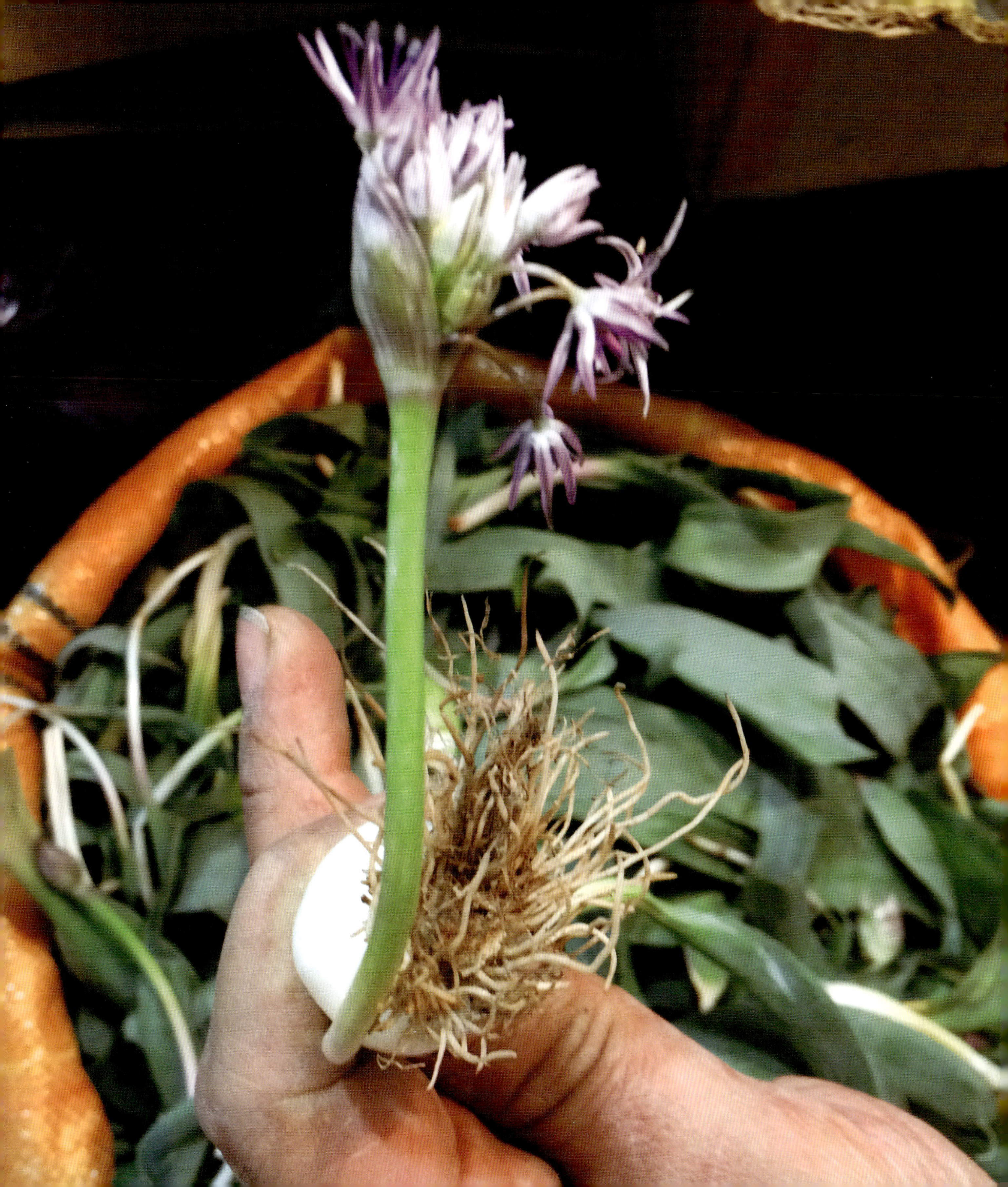

Darband

Until the 1920s the Tajrish and Shemran districts consisted of a collection of small villages in the foothills of the mountains above Tehran. Now they are very much part of the city. Darband used to be one of these villages. Its name literally means "door to the mountain." During my student days we would go there to begin a hike up to the peak of Tochal Mountain at about 13,000 feet/4,000 meters. Locals had a few stalls where the hikers could get breakfast or a snack before starting up the mountain. But all that has changed. The stalls are now restaurants where Tehranis go on summer evenings for a meal or just to snack on street food and enjoy the theater of all the people there. On this trip, my cousins took me there. We clambered up the trail, lined with vendors' stalls. They were selling hot steaming fava beans sprinkled with vinegar and Persian hogweed powder/*golpar* as well as red pepper flakes; and steaming roasted red beets that shone under the bright lights as if they were giant rubies. There was corn on the cob, roasted on wood charcoal. The corn sizzled as it was dropped into big jars of salted water before being handed to you. Another stall offered a variety of candied fruit. And for drinks there were stalls selling pomegranate juice that was freshly squeezed in front of you. My cousins and I sat on a carpeted platform-bed and enjoyed juicy chicken kababs marinated in saffron and lime, and tender lamb ribs marinated in yogurt and grilled on charcoal. After the meal, we drank tea, and a hookah was passed around. Around us, young Tehranis were all dressed up and talking on their cell phones. It suddenly dawned on me that Iran was mainly about a young generation no longer confronting modernity, but rather coming to terms with it.

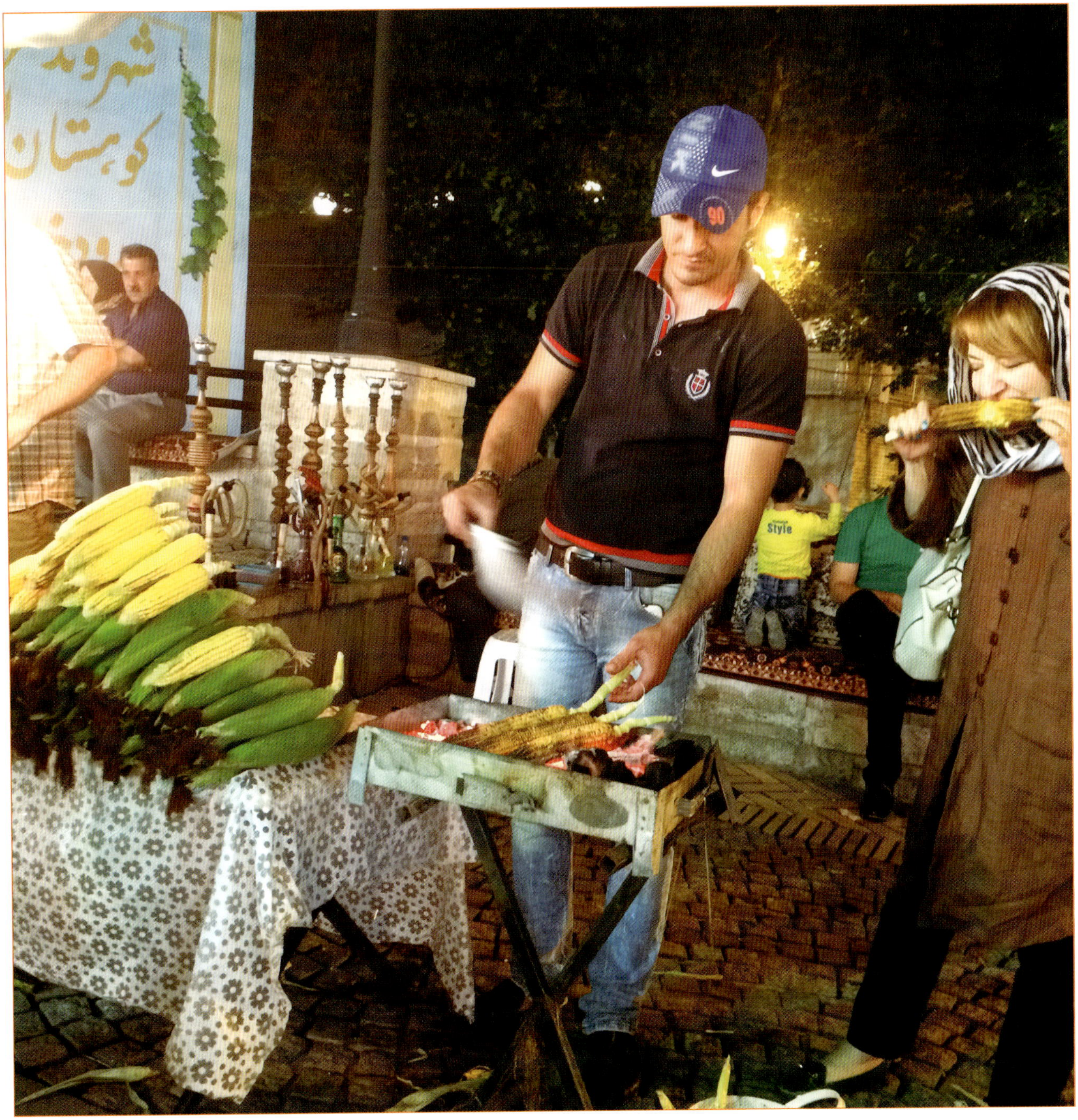
کوهستان
90
Style

Darbandi Chicken Kabab
Jujeh kabab-e darband

Serves 6 to 8
Prep: 20 minutes + 24 hours of marinating
Cooking: 15 minutes

MARINADE

- ¼ teaspoon ground saffron dissolved in 2 tablespoons water
- 1 teaspoon turmeric
- Zest of 2 limes
- ¼ cup/60ml fresh lime juice
- ½ cup/120g olive oil
- 2 large onions, peeled and thinly sliced
- 2 cloves garlic, peeled and crushed
- ¼ cup/60g whole plain yogurt
- 2 teaspoons fine sea salt
- 1 tablespoon freshly ground pepper

CHICKEN

- 6 Cornish hens, 4lb /2kg, each cut into 10 pieces, or 4 pounds/2kg of boneless chicken thighs cut into 3in/7.5cm cubes
- 12 cherry tomatoes
- 10 serrano or jalapeno peppers

BASTE

- ½ cup/110g butter
- Juice of 1 fresh lime

GARNISH

- 1 package/12 ounces lavash bread
- 2 limes, cut in half
- 3 bunches fresh basil leaves
- Sumac powder (optional)

SKEWERS

- 12 flat ½in/1cm sword-like metal skewers or 16 wooden skewers

This recipe is adapted from the chicken kabab we had in Darband in the foothills of Tehran's mountains. We feasted on it in May, al fresco, on carpeted, raised platforms, taking in the magnificent views of the mountains around us.

1. ***To marinate the chicken:*** In a 4-quart/3.8l non-reactive container with cover, combine all the ingredients for the marination. Beat well with a fork. Add the chicken and toss well. Cover and marinate for at least 24 hours and up to 3 days in the refrigerator. Turn the chicken twice during this period (best results are with 3 days of marination).

2. ***To grill the chicken:*** Start a bed of charcoal 30 minutes before you want to cook and let it burn until the coals glow evenly, or preheat the oven broiler. Keep in mind that the success of a good kabab depends on a very hot grill.

3. Meanwhile, skewer the tomatoes. Spear wings, breasts, and legs onto different skewers (they require different cooking times). Thread the peppers in between the pieces of chicken. Place the skewers on a sheet pan next to you.

4. ***To prepare the baste:*** In a small saucepan, heat the butter and lime juice over low heat. Keep warm.

5. Paint the tomatoes with the basting mixture. Grill the chicken and tomatoes 8 to 15 minutes, turning frequently until done. The chicken is done when the juice that runs out is yellow rather than pink.

6. Meanwhile, spread a whole lavash bread on a flat serving platter. Remove the chicken, peppers and tomatoes from the grill and place on the lavash bread. Paint the chicken with the basting mixture. Keep chicken on the skewers until just before serving—this helps to keep it warm. To remove the chicken from skewers steady them on the platter with a piece of bread and pull out the skewers. Garnish with limes and sprigs of basil. Cover the kababs with more bread.

7. Serve immediately with lime, basil, yogurt and cucumber dip/*mast-o khiar*, and, if desired, pinches of sumac. *Nush-e joon!*

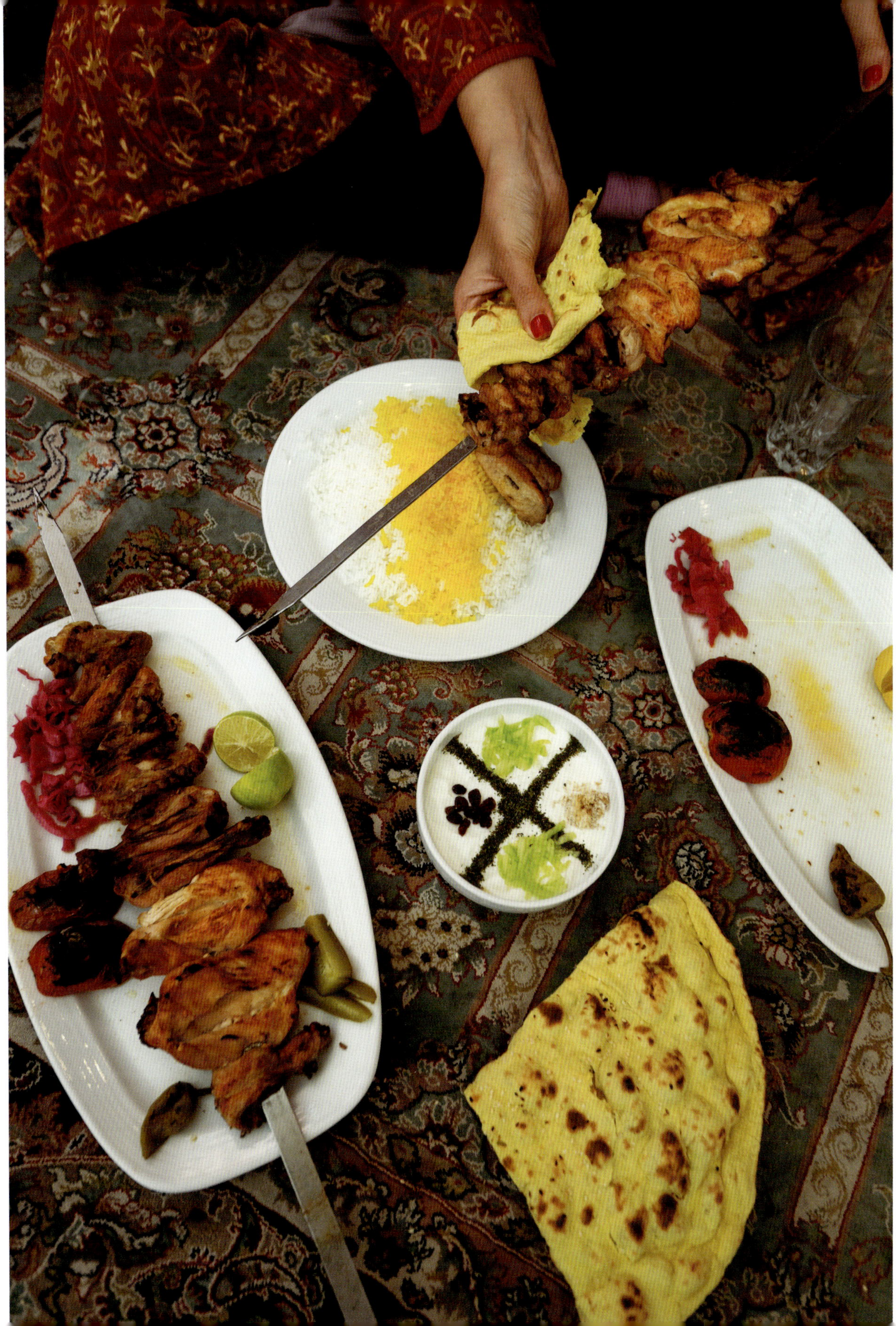

Fresh Herb Braise

khoresh-e qormeh sabzi

Serves 6
Prep: 25 minutes + soaking beans overnight
Cooking: 3 hours

LAMB

¼ cup/60ml oil or ghee
2 large onions, peeled and thinly sliced
2 clove garlic, thinly sliced
2 teaspoons fine sea salt
1 teaspoon freshly ground pepper
1½ teaspoons turmeric
1½lb/675g boneless lamb shoulder cut into 3in/7.5cm pieces
¾ cup/150g kidney beans, soaked in water overnight, drained and rinsed
6 whole dried Persian limes, pierced

HERBS

¼ cup/60ml oil or ghee
3 cups/250g finely chopped fresh parsley
1 cup/100g finely chopped fresh chives or spring onions
3 cups/250g finely chopped fresh cilantro
¼ cup/20g dried fenugreek leaves or 1 cup chopped fresh fenugreek

SPICES/*CHASHNI*

¼ cup/60ml freshly squeezed lime juice
1 teaspoon ground cardamom
½ teaspoon ground saffron dissolved in 1 tablespoon rose water (optional)

This dish was adopted by Tehranis in the early 1800s when the Qajars brought a variation of it from Azarbaijan. In Tabriz it is made with black-eyed beans instead of kidney beans, tarragon instead of fenugreek, and verjuice instead of dried Persian limes. Around the Persian Gulf it is made hot and spicy, and they add dill, spinach, and lots of garlic. In the photo opposite, this fruit and vegetable seller was very proud of his herbs. Others had been already washed and chopped—the most time consuming part of making this braise.

1. **To cook the lamb:** Heat ¼ cup/60ml oil in a medium-sized laminated cast-iron braiser or pot over medium heat and sauté the onions and garlic until lightly golden. Add salt, pepper, and turmeric, and sauté for 1 minute. Add the meat and sauté for 5 to 10 minutes until golden brown and all the juices have been absorbed.

2. Add the kidney beans and dried limes and stir-fry for 1 minute. Pour in 5 cups/1.2l water. Bring to a boil, reduce heat to low, cover, and simmer for 30 minutes, stirring occasionally.

3. **Meanwhile, to prepare the herbs:** In a wide skillet, heat ¼ cup/60ml oil over medium heat and sauté the parsley, chives, cilantro, and fenugreek for 20 to 25 minutes, stirring frequently until the aroma of the herbs rises (this stage is very important to the taste of the braise, but be careful not to burn the herbs).

4. Add the sautéed herbs, lime juice, cardamom, and saffron-rose water to the pot. Cover and simmer over low heat for another 1½ hours, stirring occasionally.

5. Check to see if meat and beans are tender. Taste the braise and adjust seasoning by adding more salt or lime juice to taste. Cover and keep warm until ready to serve.

6. Serve hot with saffron steamed rice/*chelow*. *Nush-e joon!*

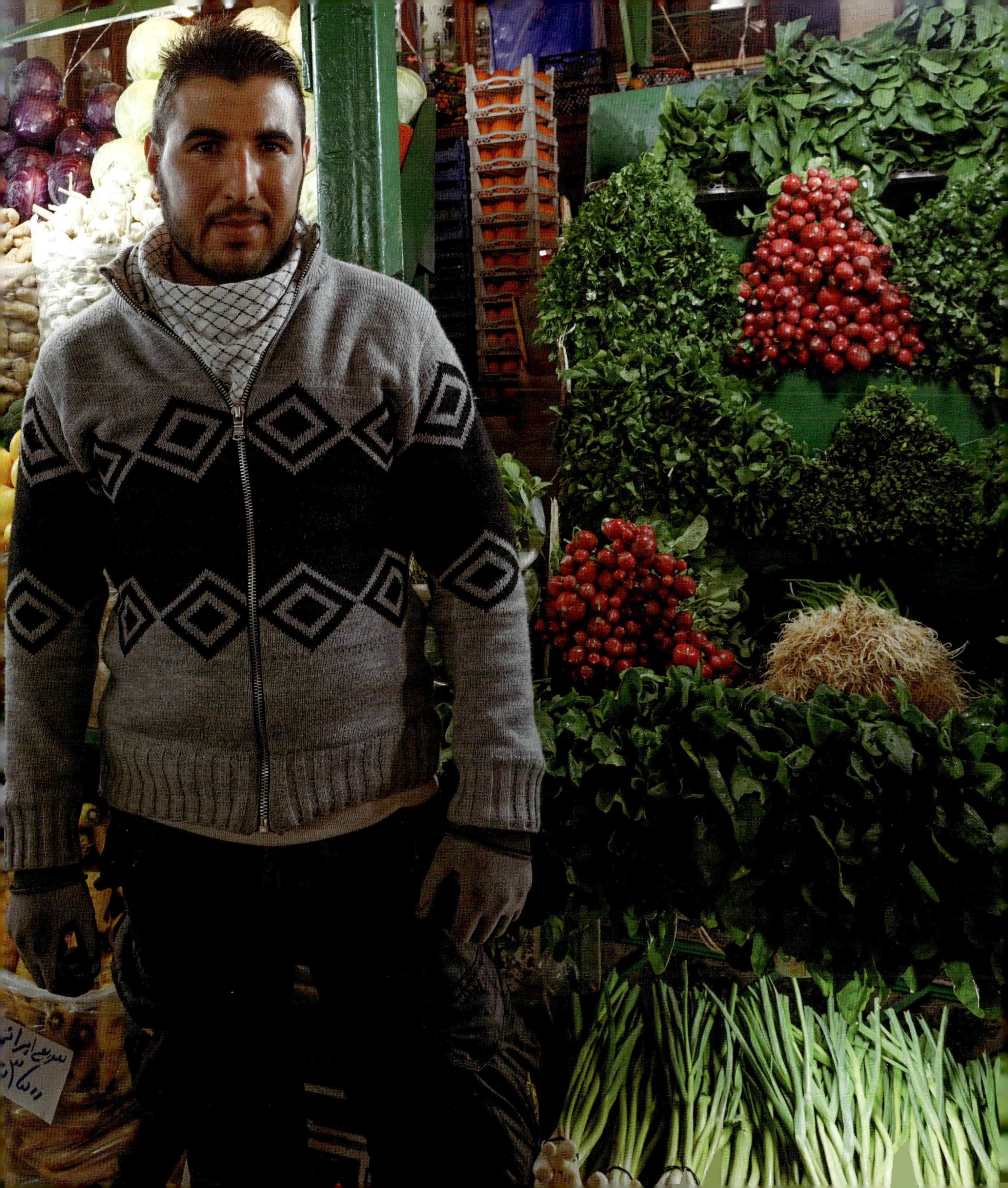

Darakeh

Darakeh is on the foothills of the mountains above Tehran, and used to be a small village. These days it is one of the most popular parts of town. My cousins took me to SPU restaurant there for lunch and I loved the place. They first served us a delicious barley soup, and then brought us a fava bean and aromatic spring dill rice/*baqali polow* flavored with saffron and cardamom. Finally, the server drizzled hot brown butter over the rice—wow! This was accompanied by fresh trout, sautéed in olive oil and served with a squeeze of sour orange/*narenj*, and lamb kababs. Sitting in an old garden on wooden benches covered with Persian carpets, with water bubbling in the stream and intoxicated with the aroma of hot fresh bread made in front of you in their outdoor oven while sitting next to my dear cousins, made me think for a moment that I was in paradise.

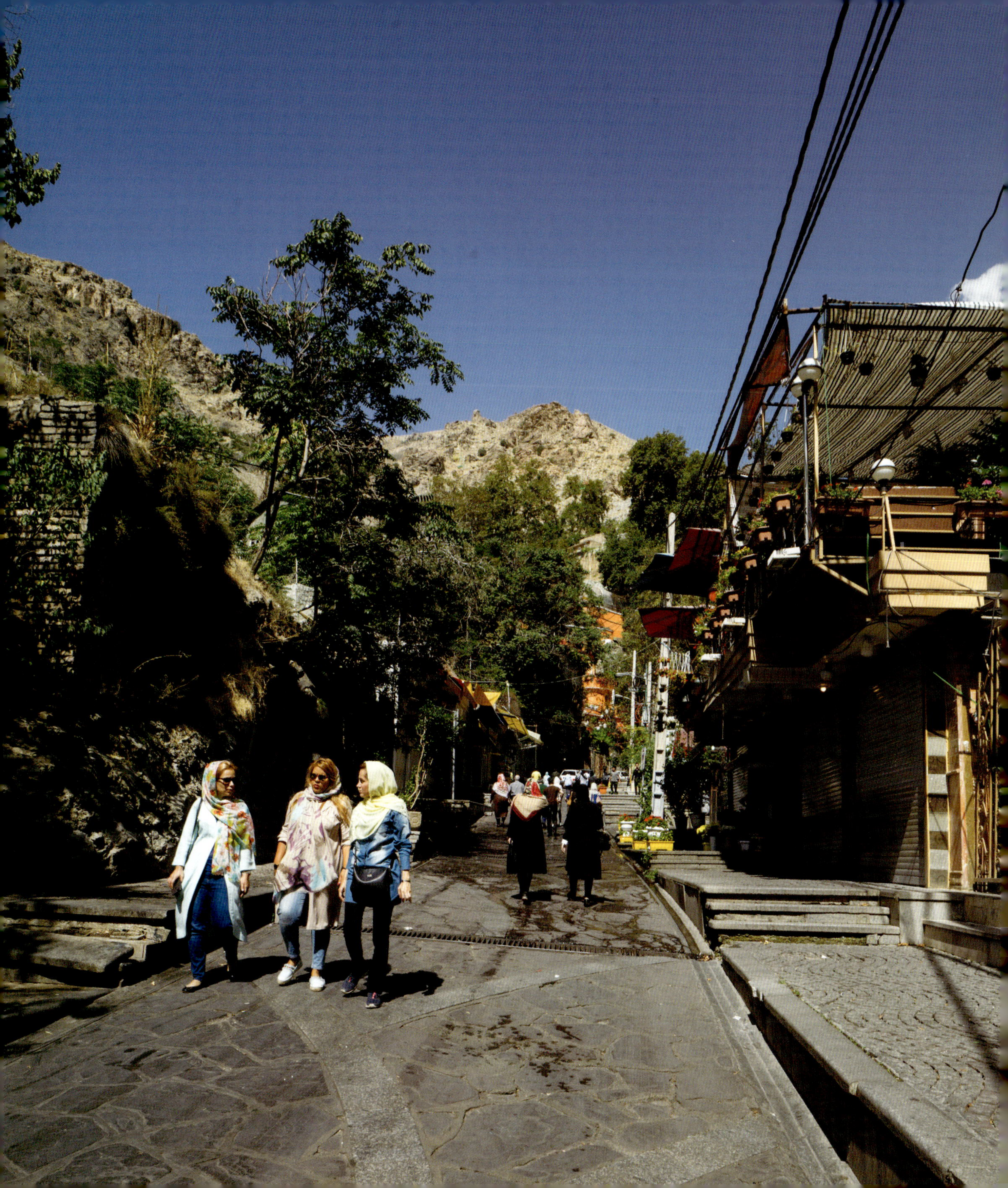

Wheat and Turkey Breakfast Porridge
halim-e gandom

Serves 6
Prep: 15 minutes + soaking beans and wheat berries overnight
Cooking: 3 hours

BROTH

2lb/900g turkey or shoulder of lamb (both with bone)
8 cups/1.9l water
2 onions, peeled and thinly sliced
1 tablespoon sea salt
1 teaspoon freshly ground pepper
1 teaspoon turmeric

WHEAT AND CHICKPEAS

1lb/450g (2 cups) whole wheat grain, soaked overnight and drained
½ cup/100g chickpeas, soaked overnight in water with ½ teaspoon baking soda, drained and rinsed

GARNISH

¼ cup/55g butter, melted
1 teaspoon cinnamon
2 tablespoons sugar

I was downtown one early morning and went to Halim- Ma'navi restaurant to have a wonderful, creamy, soft, warm bowl of porridge/halim for my breakfast. Halim is a favorite traditional breakfast in Iran. It is slow cooked for a long time—usually all night—then served in the early morning. Just before serving, it's flavored with a touch of cinnamon, sugar, and a little brown butter is drizzled over it. It's a hearty early morning meal and many Tehranis order it for takeout. By nine in the morning restaurants are usually sold out. This is a great dish to make with leftover turkey, including the bones for the broth.

1. **To cook the broth:** Place the turkey in a large heavy-bottomed pot, add the water, bring to a boil, skim the froth as it forms until it stops forming. Add onions, salt, pepper and turmeric. Bring back to a boil. Reduce heat, cover, and simmer over low heat for 2 to 2½ hours until the turkey is tender and falling off the bone. Add more warm water if needed. Stir occasionally to prevent sticking to the bottom of the pot.

2. *Meanwhile, to cook the wheat and chickpeas:* In a large saucepan, place the wheat, chickpeas, and 6 cups water. Bring to a boil, reduce heat to low, cover, and simmer for 2 hours or until the wheat and chickpeas are tender. Add more warm water if necessary.

3. **To assemble the porridge:** Place a large sieve over the pot containing the wheat and chickpeas. Drain the broth through the sieve. Separate the turkey from the bones and return it to the pot. Discard the bones and anything else left in the sieve.

4. Cover the pot and cook over low heat for 20 minutes.

5. Use a handheld mixer to puree the turkey, wheat, and chickpea until you have a homogenized, slightly elastic puree. Adjust seasoning to taste. Keep warm until ready to serve.

6. Spoon the porridge into individual serving bowls. Garnish to taste with a little melted butter, cinnamon, and sugar on the top. *Nush-e Joon!*

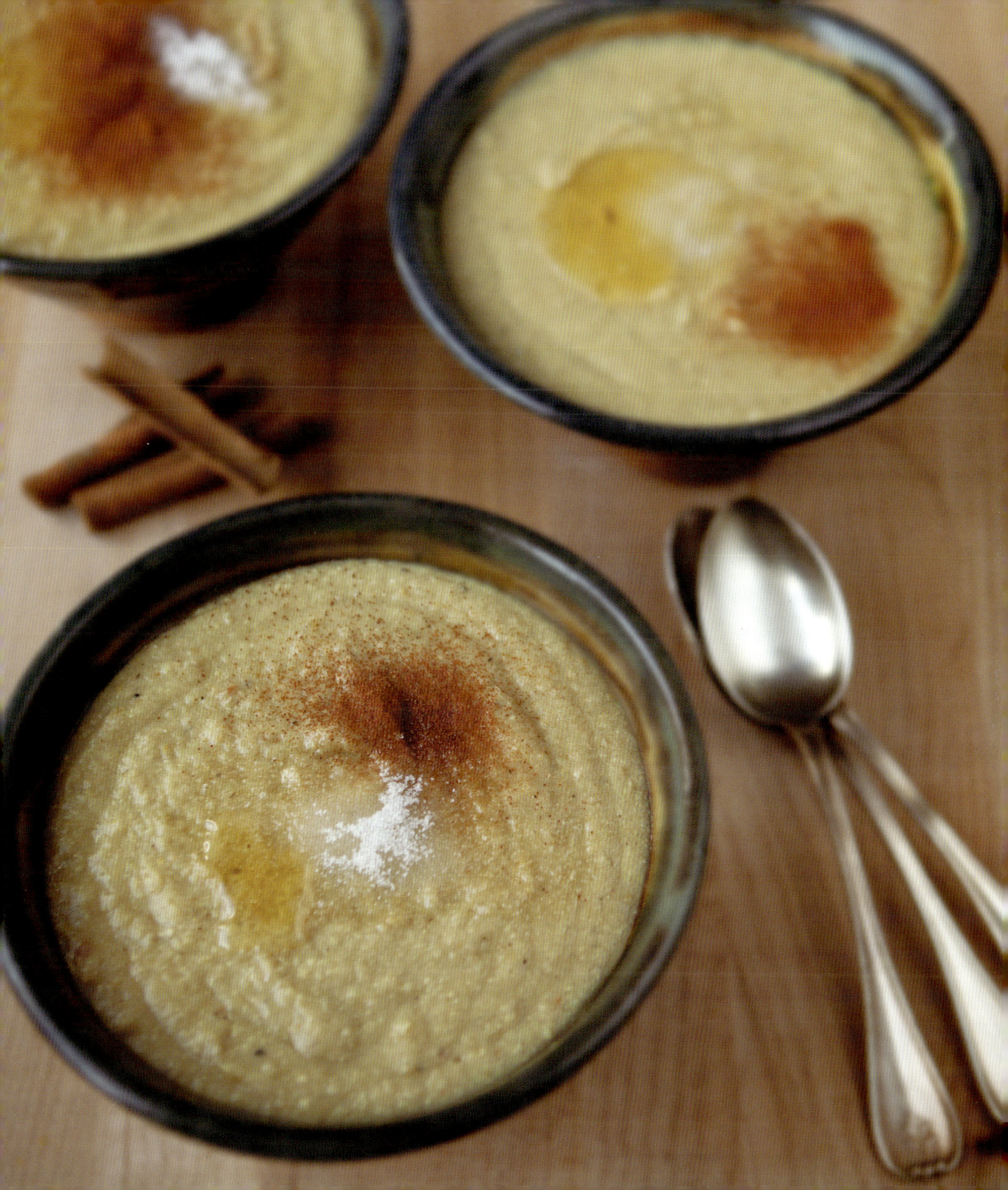

Savory Mushroom Pie
pirashki-e khosravi

Makes 10 to 12 pies, serves 4 to 6
Prep: 15 minutes, plus 2 hours resting
Cooking: 20 minutes

DOUGH

2 teaspoons active dry instant yeast
1 cup/240g thick plain yogurt
2 teaspoons sugar
3 eggs, lightly beaten
¼ cup/60 ml oil or ghee
4½–5 cups/500g all-purpose flour, sifted with ¼ teaspoon fine sea salt

MUSHROOM + HERBS FILLING

2 tablespoons oil
1 medium onion, sliced
2lb/900g cremini mushrooms, finely chopped
2 cloves garlic, grated
2 teaspoons ground cumin
2 teaspoons fine sea salt
1 teaspoon ground cinnamon
1 teaspoon freshly ground pepper
1 teaspoon cayenne
2 cups/170g chopped fresh parsley
1 cup/85g chopped fresh tarragon or 1 tablespoon dried
1 cup/85g chopped fresh mint or 1 tablespoon dried
1 cup/125g ground pistachio kernels

FOR DEEP-FRYING

2 cups/480ml sesame oil for deep-frying the pies

This Iranian variation on the Russian pirozhki (small pie) has many forms. It can be large or small, savory or sweet. As school kids in downtown Tehran we'd buy them to eat as snacks. We'd choose the sweet ones, usually custard filled. But more often pirozhkis are savory, and filled with meat, potatoes and mushrooms. Here, I am giving you a delicious, mushroom-filled one. The photograph is of the inside of the Khosravi Pirozhki Shop. The menu, which calls them "donuts" in English, lists the various fillings available, including: cream, meat, potato, spinach, and cabbage. Also interesting are the photos on the walls, including Charlie Chaplin in "Modern Times," as well as James Dean and Marlon Brando.

1. **To make the dough:** In a food processor bowl, combine the yeast with the yogurt. Add the sugar, eggs, and oil, and mix until creamy. Gradually add 4½ cups of the flour mixture. Mix for about 3 minutes (do not over-mix) until you have a dough. Transfer the dough to a lightly oiled bowl. Cover with plastic wrap and allow to rest for 2 hours.

2. **To make the filling:** Meanwhile, heat the oil in a large skillet over medium heat until very hot. Sauté the onions and mushrooms until golden. Add the rest of the ingredients for the filling and sauté for 1 minute. Remove from heat, transfer to a bowl and allow to cool. Cover and refrigerate for 20 minutes or until ready to use.

3. **To prepare the pies:** Place a wire rack in a sheet pan and set aside. On a cool, floured surface, knead the dough for 1 minute and shape it into a flat rectangle. Use a rolling pin to roll out the dough to a thin layer. Fold over and roll out again. Repeat this process 6 times. Finally, roll out the dough into a sheet with a thickness of ⅜in-thick/1cm (this process of creating layers helps to make the dough lighter).

4. Use a cookie cutter or the open end of a glass to cut out 3in/7.5cm-diameter discs of dough. Fill each disc with 1 tablespoon of the filling. Fold each disc into a half-moon shape and close the edges with your fingers. Use a fork to crimp around the edges of the dough to double seal the filling inside.

5. **To deep-fry the pies:** In a small shallow pot, heat 2 cups/480ml oil over medium heat until hot but not smoking. Carefully place batches of the turnovers in the hot oil (do not crowd the pot) and fry each side for 3 to 4 minutes until lightly golden brown. Use a slotted spoon to remove the turnovers and place them on the wire rack. Serve warm. *Nush-e joon!*

Donuts	
Cream	
Meat	
Potato	
HotDog	
Susage	
Special	

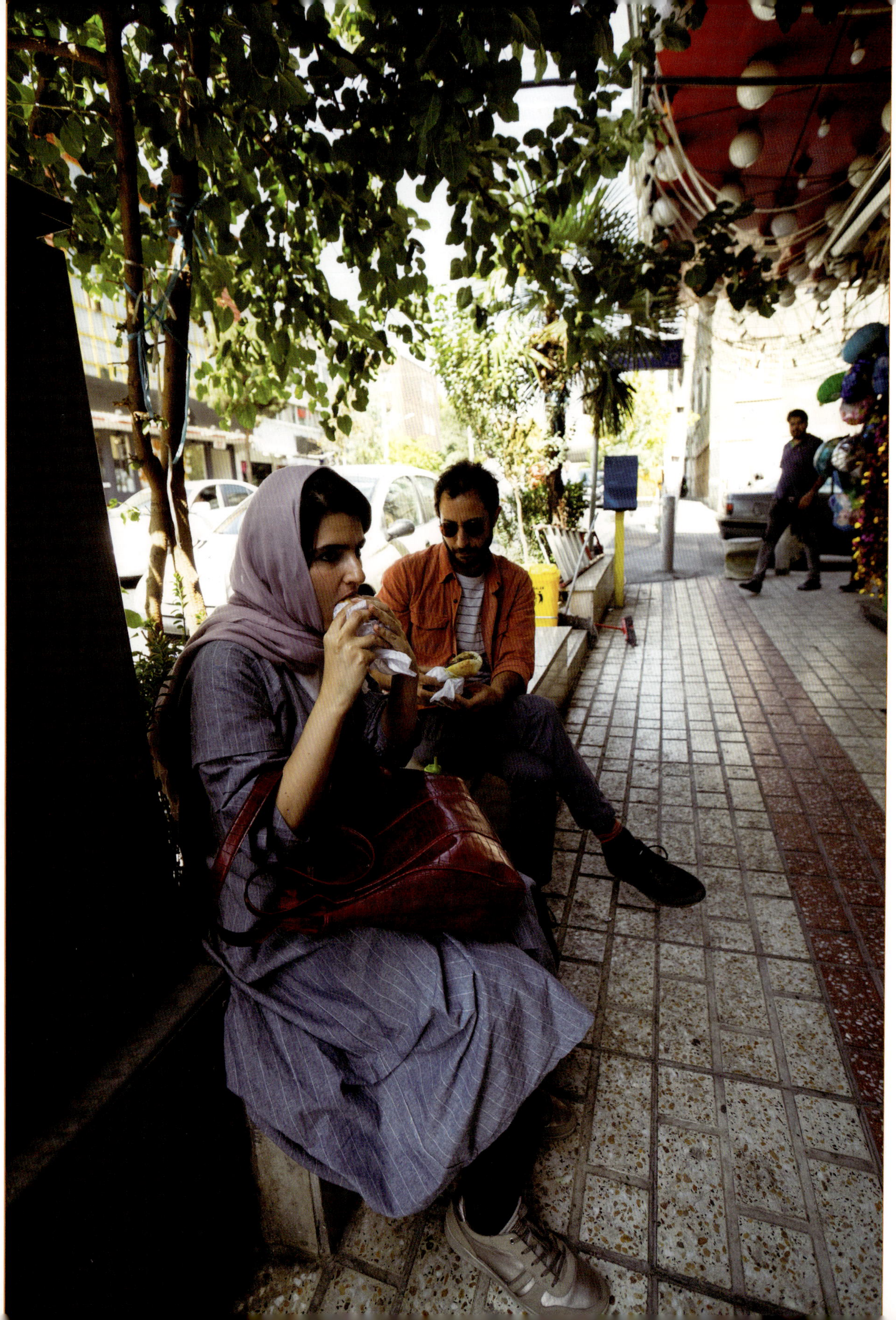

Tongue Sandwich

sandwich-e zaban-e André

Serves 4
Prep: 20 minutes
Cooking: 4 hours

TONGUE

5 lambs' tongues
2 medium onions, peeled and thinly sliced
2 cloves garlic, peeled and crushed
2 bay leaves
2 whole cloves
¼ teaspoon freshly ground pepper

SAUCE

2 tablespoons ghee or olive oil
1 medium onion, thinly sliced
2 cloves garlic
1 teaspoon salt
½ teaspoon freshly ground pepper
1 teaspoon turmeric
1 tablespoon flour
2 tablespoons tomato paste
2 tablespoons cream
2 tablespoons fresh lime juice

BREAD

2 baguettes or 4 ficelles

TRIMMINGS

1 cup/200g pickled cornichons or cucumbers
2 tomatoes, sliced
1 cup/85g chopped fresh parsley

André's (now days it's called Joseph's) was the Armenian sandwich shop/deli par excellence during my childhood in Tehran. Besides their renowned kielbasa (sausage in Polish), which was actually more like an Italian mortadella, they made the most delicious chicken sandwiches in a baguette. However, my favorite was their lamb's tongue sandwich. I have fond memories of sneaking off to the deli on my way home from school (my mother did not like us eating out), waiting in line, and ordering a tongue sandwich and a Coke. I can still taste those delicious sandwiches, which inspired me to make this recipe. Photograph opposite show's my relative, Maryam (with her husband Richie), biting into a tongue sandwich more than fifty years later.

1. **To cook the tongue:** Wash and rinse the tongues and place them in a large pot. Cover with water (1in above the tongues). Add the onions, garlic, bay leaves, cloves, and ¼ teaspoon pepper (do not add salt because it changes the color of the tongues). Bring to a boil, skimming off the foam. Cover and simmer over low heat for 3 to 3½ hours until cooked and tender.

2. Discard the bay leaves and remove the tongues from the broth and place on a cutting board. Allow the tongues to cool. Reserve the broth. Remove the skins and excess fat from the tongues and cut them into thin slices.

3. **To make the sauce:** In a wide skillet, melt the ghee over medium heat. Sauté the onion and garlic until golden brown. Add salt, pepper, turmeric, flour and the tomato paste. Stir-fry for 1 minute.

4. Add 1½ cups of the reserved broth, the cream, and lime juice to the skillet. Stir well. Bring to a boil. Reduce heat and simmer for 5 to 10 minutes over low heat until you have a smooth sauce. Adjust seasoning to taste.

5. **To make the sandwich:** Cut a well-cooked baguette in half lengthwise. Spread half the sauce on one side of the bread and arrange half the tongue slices along the length of the baguette. Place half the sliced cucumber pickles and the tomatoes on top. Sprinkle chopped parsley on top. Place the other half of the baguette on top and slice the baguette in half. Repeat all the steps for the second baguette. Serve hot. *Nush-e joon!*

Cream Puffs
nun-e khamei

Makes 12 pieces
Prep: 20 minutes
Cooking: 20 minutes

FILLING

1 cup/240ml heavy cream (8oz)
6 tablespoons powdered sugar
1 tablespoon rose water
½ teaspoon vanilla extract

DOUGH

1 cup/240ml cold water
¼ teaspoon fine sea salt
6 tablespoons/90g butter (unsalted), diced into small pieces
1 teaspoon vanilla extract
1 tablespoon rose water
1 cup/120g unbleached all-purpose flour, triple sifted
4 eggs (room temperature)

DUSTING

1 cup/130g powdered sugar
2 tablespoons ground pistachios (optional)
1 tablespoon rose petals (optional)

I have delicious childhood memories of biting into one of these fresh cream-filled puff pastries. The Yas bakery by the Majles also made pastry cones filled with the cream and topped with coarsely ground raw pistachio kernels—It's a treat even better than ice-cream. .

1. **To prepare the filling:** In a mixing bowl, combine the cream, sugar, rose water, and vanilla, and whip at high speed until soft peaks form. Cover and keep chilled.

2. **To make the dough:** Line 2 baking sheets with baking mats or parchment paper. Place the oven rack in the middle and preheat oven to 425°F/220°C.

3. In a heavy-bottomed medium saucepan over medium heat, combine the water, salt, and butter, and bring to a boil, stirring well with a wooden spoon. Add the vanilla and rose water. Reduce heat to very low and add the flour, all at once, stirring constantly (3 to 5 minutes) until you have a stiff paste.

4. Remove from heat and continue to stir for 4 to 5 minutes (to help the dough cool a little).

5. The temperature of the mixture at this stage is very important; use a candy thermometer to be sure it is around 150°F/65°C. Add 1 egg and stir for 1 minute. The dough becomes glossy and silky. Continue to stir for another minute until the egg has been absorbed and the dough is no longer glossy. Continue adding the eggs, 1 at a time, stirring each time an egg is added until the dough is no longer glossy. The dough should be light, smooth, and airy.

6. **To bake the cream puffs:** Use an ice-cream scoop to drop dollops of the dough onto the prepared baking sheets, leaving 2in/5cm between each dollop to allow for expansion. Bake for 20 minutes.

7. Without opening the oven door, reduce heat to 350°F/180°C and continue to bake for another 20 to 25 minutes or until the puff pastries are golden.

8. Remove from the oven, poke a whole in the pastries to allow steam to escape, and allow to cool thoroughly on a cooling rack.

9. Prior to serving, use a pastry bag or resealable storage bag to squeeze the chilled filling into the pastry until full. Repeat for all the pastry. Dust with powdered sugar, ground pistachios, and rose petals and chill until ready to serve. *Nush-e joon!*

Tehran

1890s photo of an ice-cream peddler with his customers. Although the Persians were one of the earliest civilizations to have ice houses and to make sorbets with various fruit flavors, ice-cream was a relative newcomer.

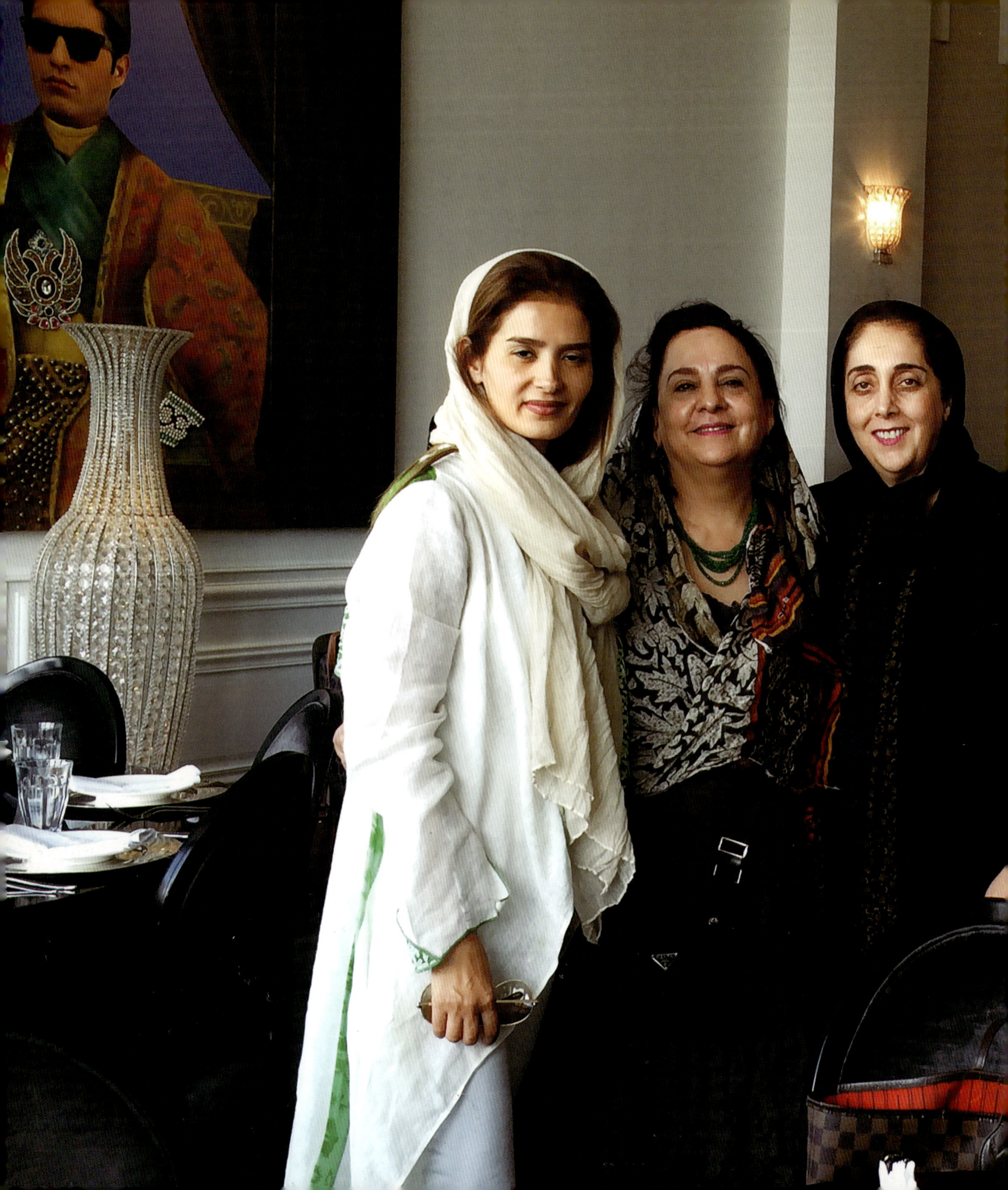

At the Divan restaurant with my cousin Mojdeh and the co-owner Rana Moavenian.

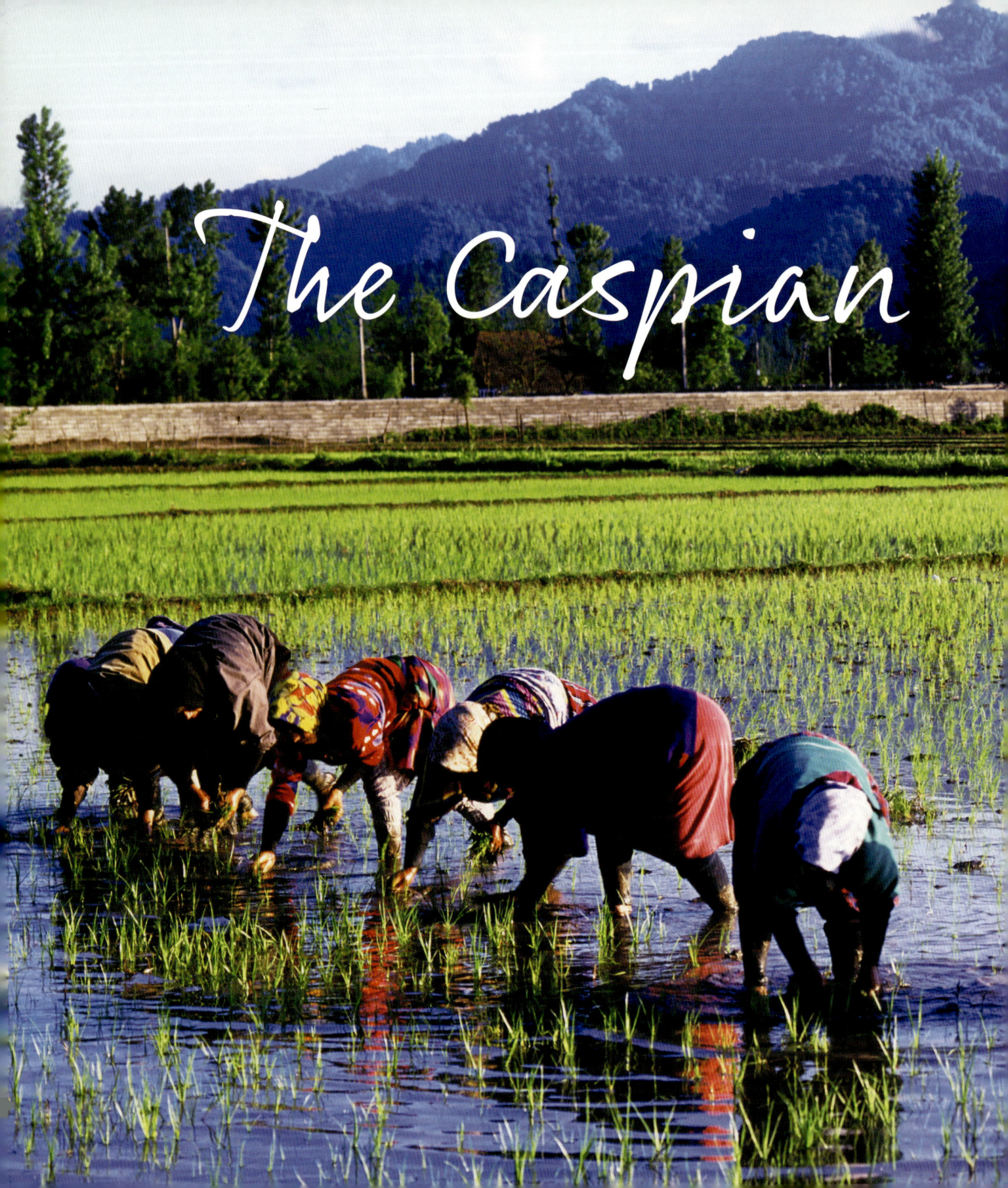

The Caspian

Gilani women tending to their rice fields.

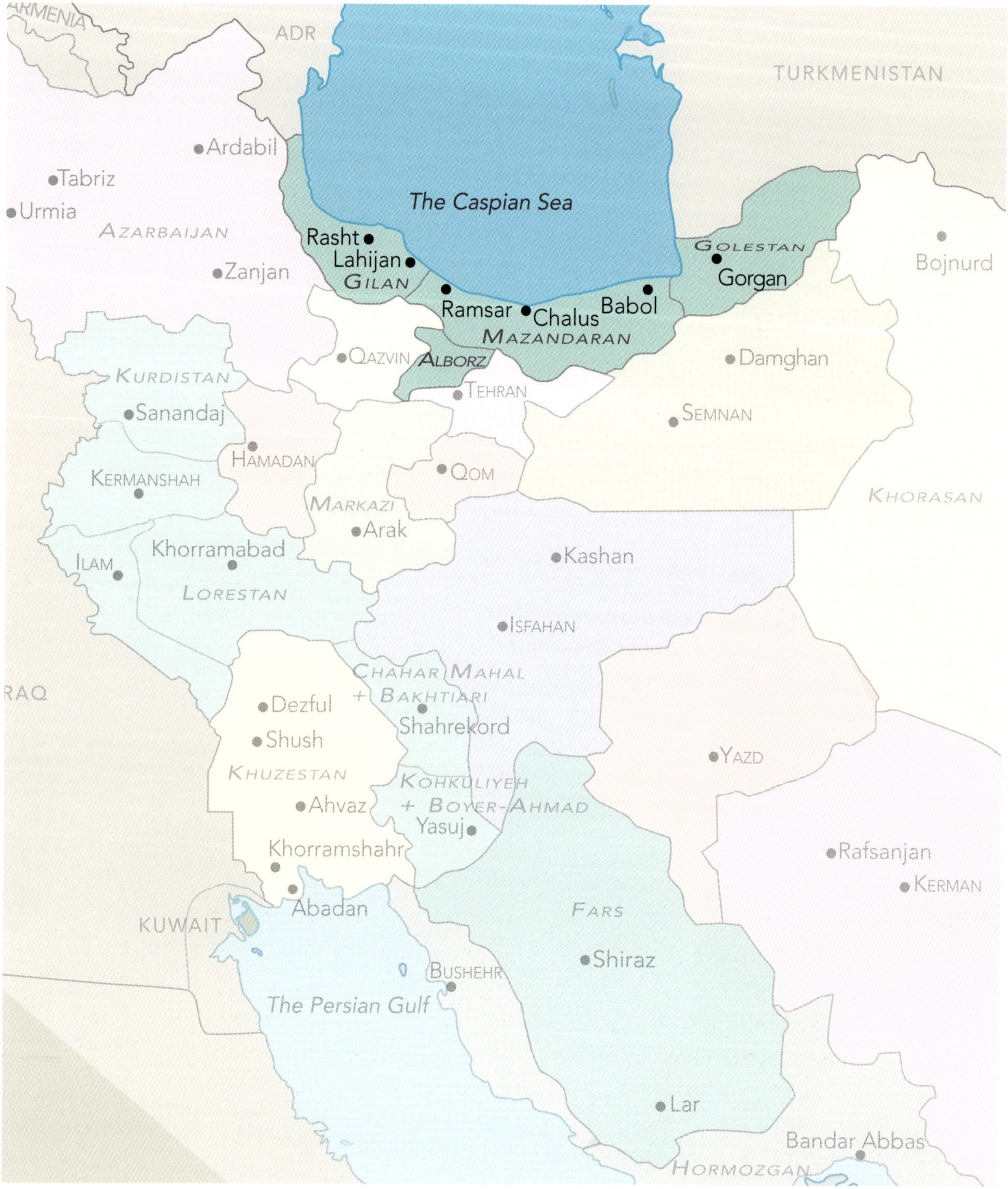

ARMENIA
ADR
TURKMENISTAN
Ardabil
Tabriz
Urmia
AZARBAIJAN
The Caspian Sea
Rasht
Lahijan
GILAN
Zanjan
GOLESTAN
Gorgan
Bojnurd
Ramsar
Chalus
Babol
MAZANDARAN
QAZVIN
ALBORZ
Damghan
KURDISTAN
TEHRAN
Sanandaj
SEMNAN
HAMADAN
KERMANSHAH
QOM
KHORASAN
MARKAZI
Arak
Khorramabad
Kashan
ILAM
LORESTAN
ISFAHAN
CHAHAR MAHAL
+ BAKHTIARI
IRAQ
Dezful
Shahrekord
Shush
YAZD
KHUZESTAN
KOHKULIYEH
+ BOYER-AHMAD
Ahvaz
Yasuj
Khorramshahr
Rafsanjan
KERMAN
Abadan
KUWAIT
FARS
Shiraz
BUSHEHR
The Persian Gulf
Lar
Bandar Abbas
HORMOZGAN

A Little History

We went over high mountain passes and descended through rice paddies and tea plantations before arriving at Rasht, the capital of Gilan province and the major city of the Caspian region of Iran.

The "Caspians/*Kaspia*" was the name of an ancient people living along the southwestern shore of the Caspian Sea. Known to the ancient Assyrians as the "great sea of the rising sun." Iranians commonly refer to the region simply as "the north/*shomal*" and to the sea as "The Sea of Mazandaran/*darya-ye mazandaran*." Hundreds of years before the formation of the first Persian Empire, the people of this region (Marlik, south of present-day Rasht) had wonderfully sophisticated cooking implements, as well as jewelry in fine gold depicting pomegranate buds and olive branches Pomegranates and olives remain some of this region's favorite cooking ingredients.

The provinces of Gilan and Mazandaran are spectacular, from the mild-weathered beaches of the Caspian Sea to the snow-capped Alborz Mountains—and the plains in between. This is where rice, tea, sturgeon, and caviar come from. The most exotic and medicinal wild herbs of any region in Iran are also to be found here. And this is where you will encounter the most delicious yet simple vegetarian dishes of the Iranian kitchen. Rice, which is the staple here, is even eaten for breakfast, and its flour is used for making bread.

The bounty of the region is reflected in its markets. Two distinguishing marks of what's popular are: the use of garlic and the love of sour rather than sweet dishes. Every meal has a little rice and fish, whether salted, smoked, fried, or roasted.

We had garlic in every dish: fresh, baby green garlic, sautéed garlic, garlic stuffed in the belly of the fish, garlic roasted with olive oil, and garlic as a pickle. It's delicious and, surprisingly, did not stay on our breath while we were there. Limes and sour oranges, and pomegranate in all its forms, are favorites for giving these dishes a tasty tang. ☙

We were heading to the Caspian Sea coast, a three-hour journey north of Tehran, but you have to cross the Alborz Mountains to get there. Once over the mountains, the climate becomes mild, almost Mediterranean, and the countryside verdant.

After a couple of hours driving, we were ready for a good breakfast. We picked a roadside rest stop called Parastu (swallow). I was impressed by its clean, efficient appearance. The food looked good too. We had the typical Iranian breakfast that I remembered from childhood: two sunny side up eggs fried in brown butter (runny yolks but crispy whites); hot, crispy lavash bread; jam, honey, yogurt, cheese; and of course sweet black tea at just the right temperature, served in small glasses so you could see its beautiful dark-red color. Iranian are fussy about their tea, and it's part of every meal or snack. I would have tea four or five times a day and became addicted to it during my stay in Iran.

This photograph of Mount Damavand (18,600ft/5600m) was taken from Rineh in Mazandaran. Damavand (originally called Dunbavant "mountain of many faces") is a volcano and has the highest elevation in the region. It has been a symbol of the Iranian homeland in Persian mythology and legends since ancient times, especially in Ferdowsi's *Book of Kings/Shahnameh*. Villagers living in the foothills around the mountain still recount legends particular to their village and tend to be quite superstitious.

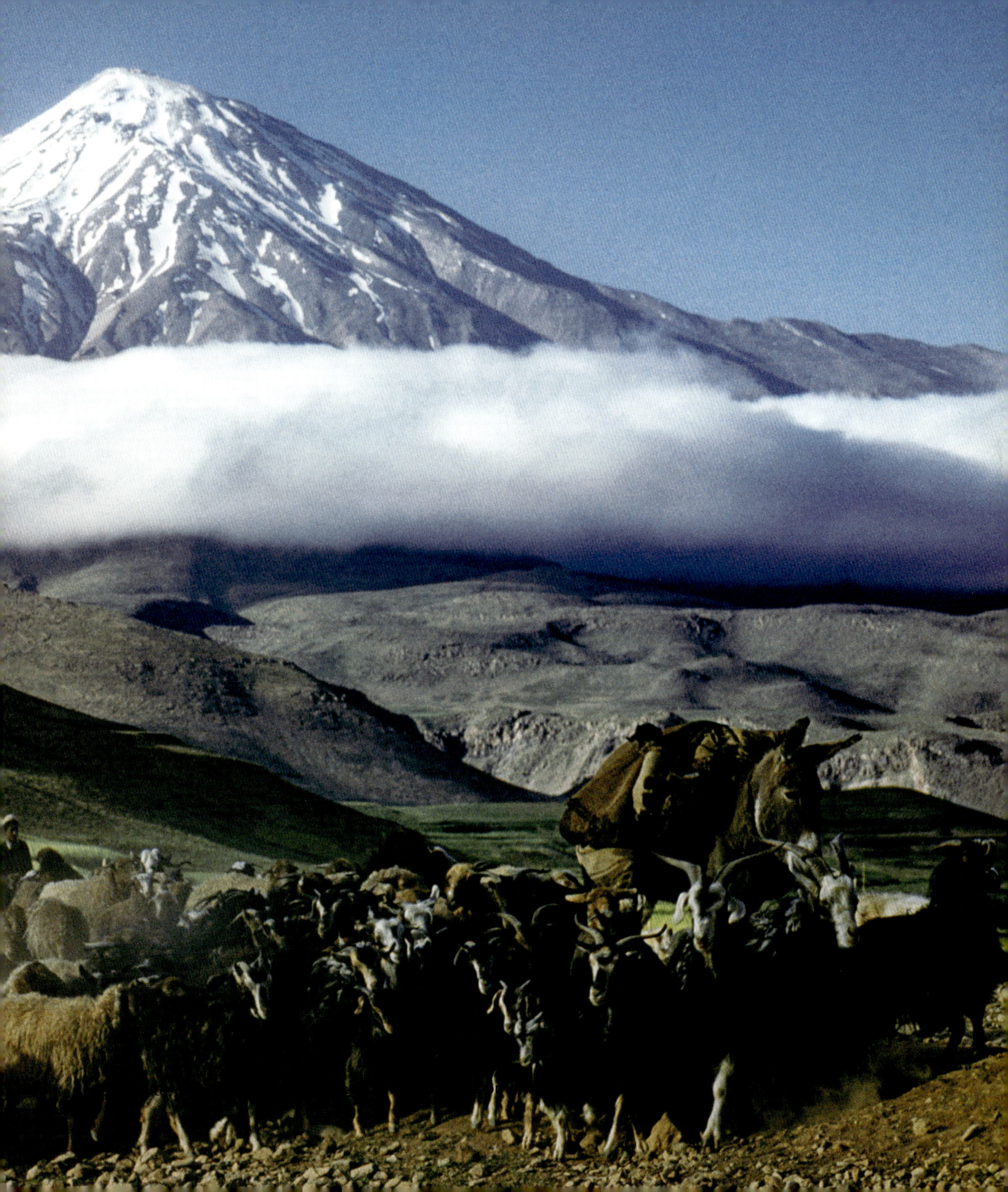

Om al-Kolsum Asadi Golshotori at the Rudbar olive shop, Zeytoun Sara-ye Saheli

A Caspian Story

On our way to Rasht, the capital of Gilan province and the main city of the Caspian region, we stopped at an olive shop in Rudbar. I bought some olive oil, pickled olives, and garlic to take back to my family in Tehran. When I asked the owner what he considered the tastiest local dish, he answered, "My mother's sweet and sour patties/*shami-e torsh*." I asked him where his mother lived, and he pointed upstairs. We climbed the stairs, and found a beautiful family: mother, daughter-in-law and her two children. The mother, Om al-Kolsum Asadi Golshotori served us tea and just-picked apricots from the one tree in their backyard. Then she explained how the patties/*shami* was an easy dish to make. The way she cooked and served us this simple lunch with some fresh local bread touched all of us. She made us feel part of her family. After lunch, she told me about the pain of losing one of her sons in the war with Iraq. I said she'd better count her blessings instead of her loss. All of a sudden she looked into my eyes and nodded her appreciation. We took photos and bought more olive oil. When we said goodbye, I could see in her face that we had truly communicated with one another—she by her hospitality and generosity and me by my encouragement. I found this to be a recurring theme throughout my trip: Iranians, and especially women, touched my heart again and again with their kindness and generosity of spirit toward total strangers. As the poet Sohrab Sepehri said, Iran has the finest mothers, the best food, but the worst intellectuals.

Sweet + Sour Patties
shami-e torsh-e rudbar

Serves 4
Prep: 20 minutes
Cooking: 25 minutes

PATTIES

1 lb/450g ground chicken thighs or ground leg of lamb
1 medium onion, peeled and grated
1 clove garlic, grated
¼ cup/20g chopped fresh mint or 2 teaspoons dried
1 cup/85g chopped fresh parsley
2 tablespoons chopped fresh basil
1 teaspoon dried *khalvash* (optional)
1 teaspoon fine sea salt
1 teaspoon freshly ground pepper
½ teaspoon turmeric
2 teaspoons ground Persian hogweed seeds/golpar
1 tablespoon rice or chickpea flour
1 egg

¼ cup/60ml oil for frying the patties

GLAZE

2 tablespoons pomegranate molasses mixed with 1 tablespoon water

I adapted this recipe from one demonstrated to me by Khanum-e. Om al-Kolsum in her small kitchen above the olive store in Rudbar. She said, "Just use any aromatic herbs you have, chopped with onion and garlic. Add a little ground meat or fish, salt, pepper, and turmeric and use a little rice flour and an egg to bind it all together." Then she started frying the patties in olive oil and flavored them with a drizzle of pomegranate molasses, which I think was the secret of this dish. Khalvash is a local Caspian herb. If you don't have any, you can replace it with a combination of mint and basil.

1. **To make the patties:** In a mixing bowl, combine all the ingredients for patties and knead lightly until you have a paste. Shape the paste into 3in/7½ cm patties.

2. In a wide skillet, heat ¼ cup oil over medium low heat. Cook the patties for about 5 minutes on each side until golden brown. Remove the patties and set aside.

3. Add the glaze to the skillet. Return the patties to the skillet, cover, and cook over low heat for 4 minutes. Turn the patties, cover, and cook for another 2 minutes. Serve with bread or plain rice/*kateh*. Nush-e Joon

The Caspian Region

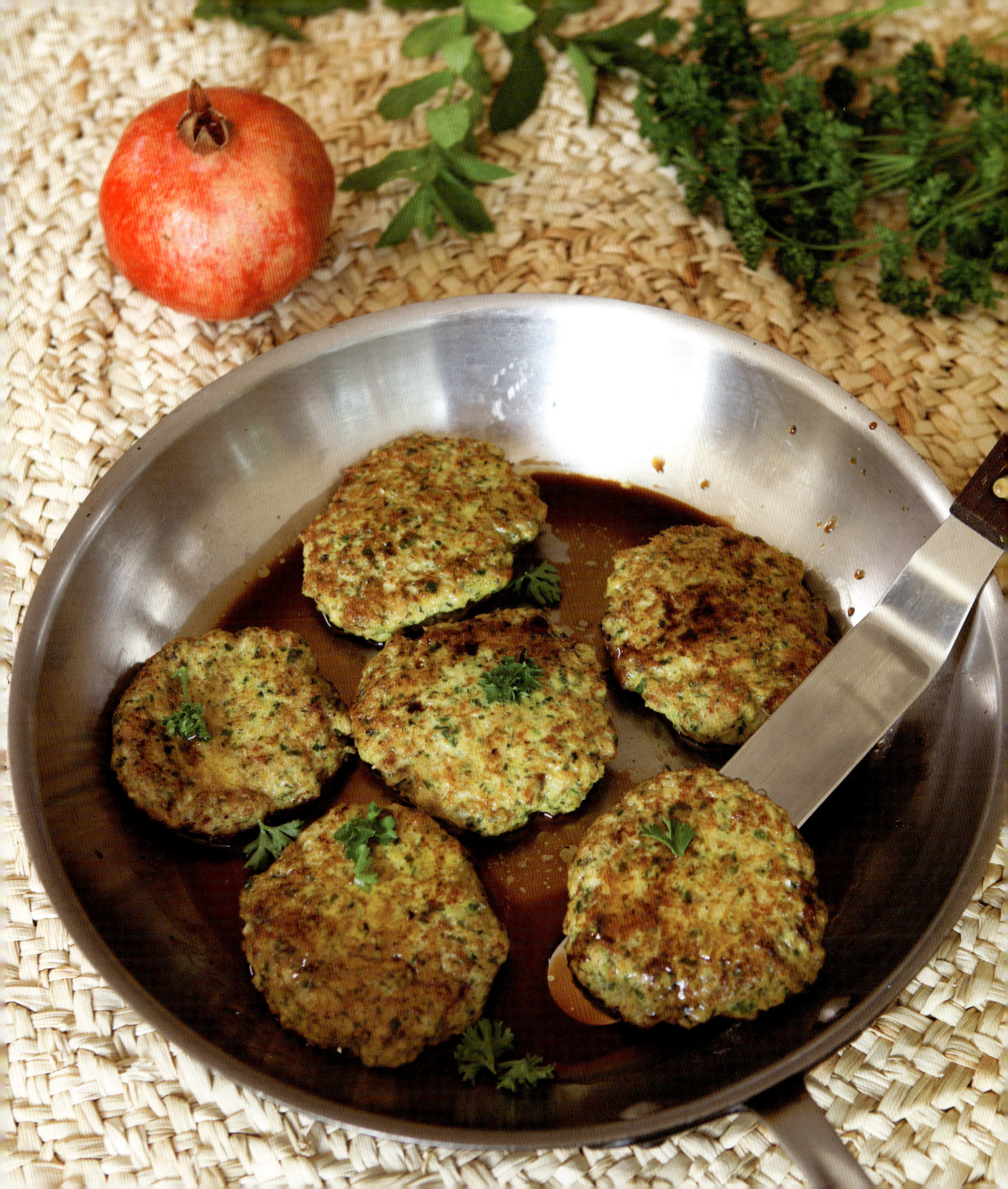

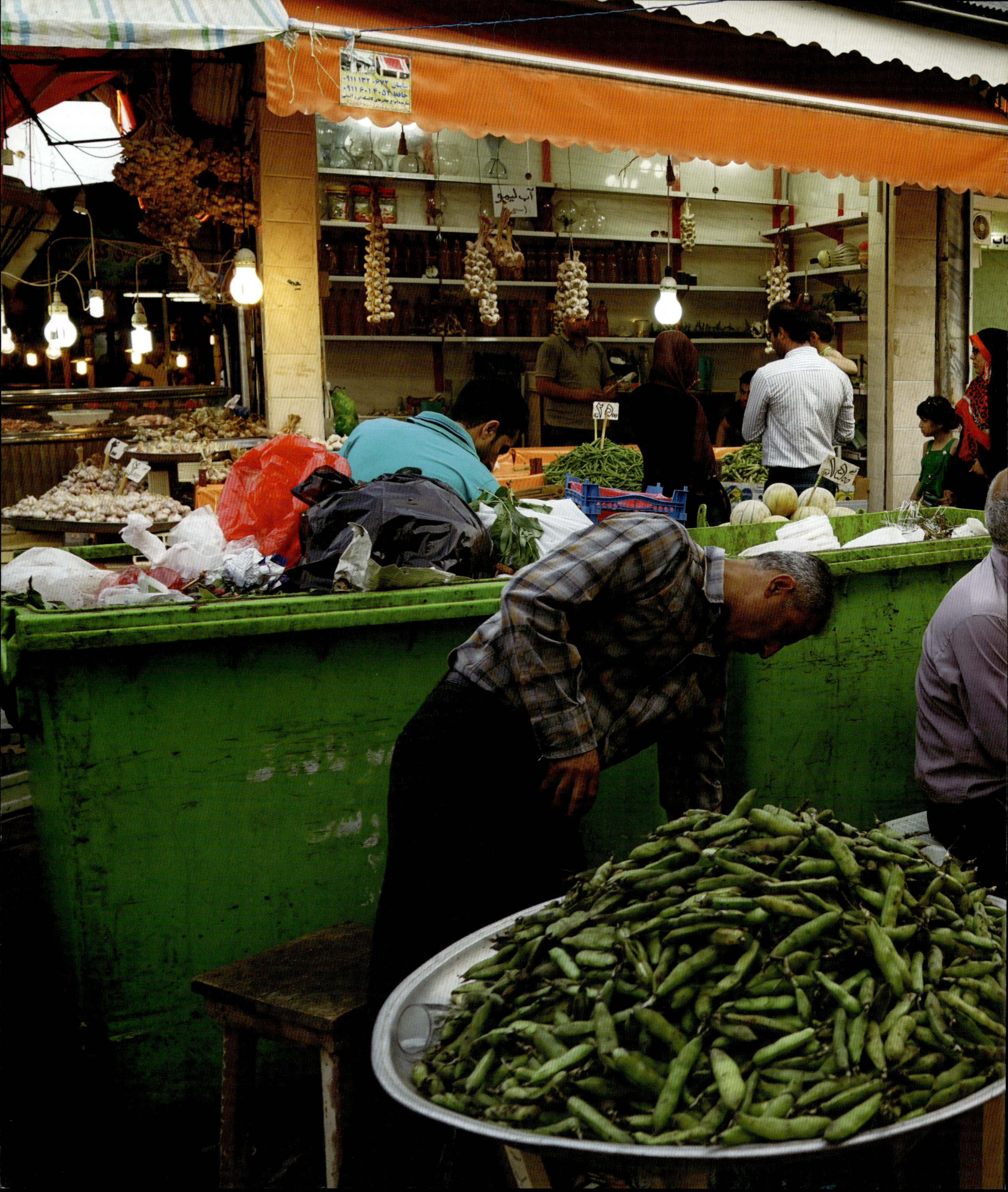
آب لیمو

We met up with Khanum-e Ashjari's daughter Mahdis at a tea house. She was to be our local guide in Rasht. Our first stop was the colorful Rasht market.

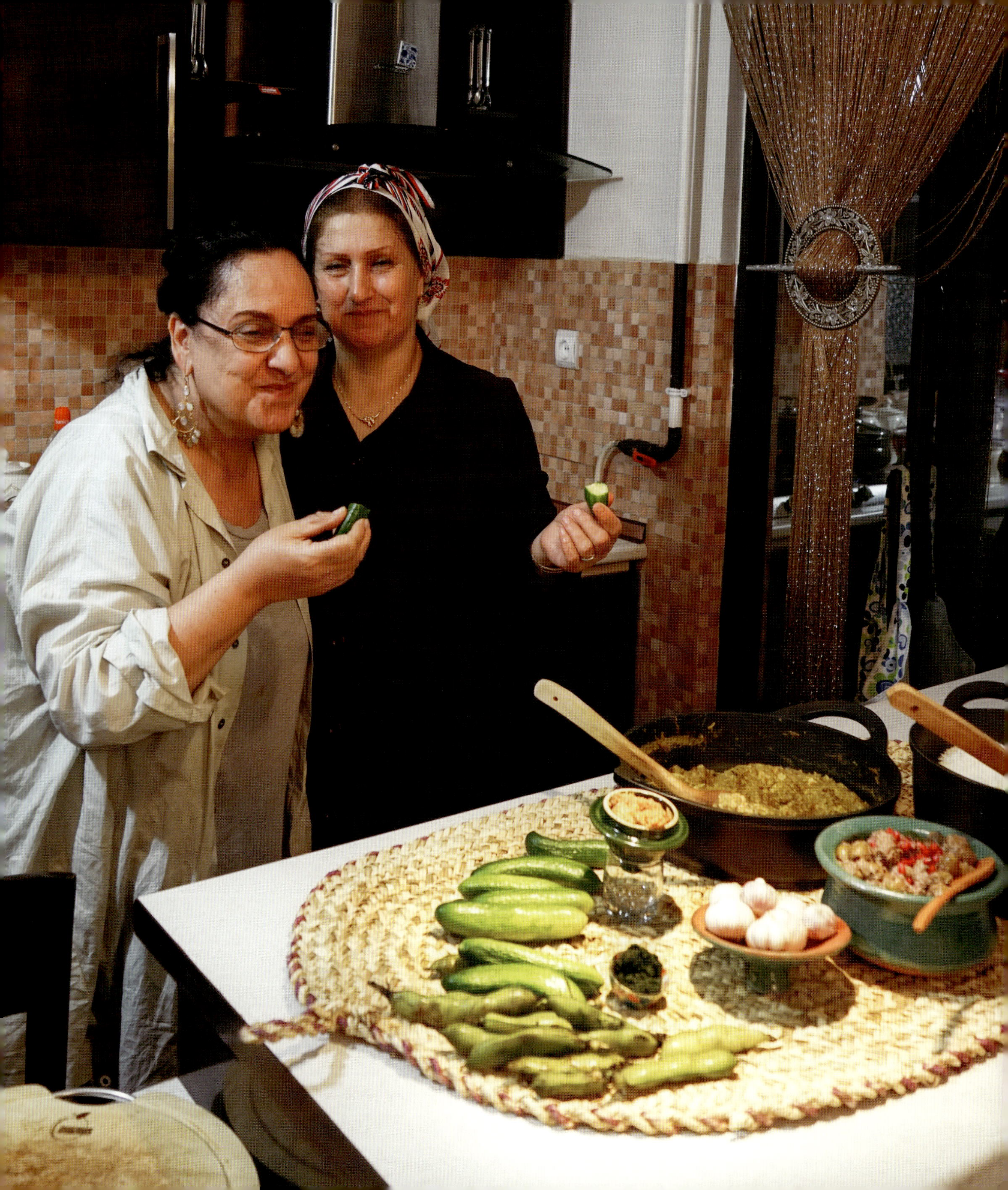

Cooking in Rasht

From a local market in Rasht, we bought 10 seedless eggplants and 4 fresh duck eggs with beautiful multi-colored shells of blue, salmon, and off-white. We also bought bunches of fresh garlic and basil, and a bottle of the local olive oil, as well as some smoked rice.

Khanum-e Ashjari (who was our guide's mother and a good home cook) and I put on our aprons and lit the coals in the little grill in the backyard of her house so we could roast the eggplants. Burning the skin of the eggplants on the open fire to get rid of any bitterness, and so they could develop an unforgettable smoky taste, was quite challenging. You had to turn them frequently until the eggplants became dark black and soft. While I was smoking the eggplant, Khanum-e Ashjari started peeling and pounding the garlic. Then she removed all the skins from the eggplant and chopped them on a wooden board. In a wide, beaten-up black skillet, she heated a good amount of olive oil and sautéed the garlic and eggplant until all the water from the eggplants had evaporated. She sprinkled on salt, pepper, and turmeric, gave it a stir, flattened the mashed eggplant, made four holes in it, then drizzled a little olive oil in each hole.

Next, she broke a duck egg in each hole, sprinkled a little salt and pepper on top, adding a little fresh garlic over the eggs. She covered the pan and allowed it to simmer for about 4 minutes. Then she stirred the eggs gently, using a long-handled wooden spoon. You could see that she was really enjoying her cooking. It was a simple menu of cooked, roasted eggplants with delicious garlicky duck eggs over a bowl of smoked rice, topped with basil.

Nonchalantly, she placed a bunch of tiny, raw fresh baby green fava beans, cucumbers, and garlic—just picked from her backyard—on the table. Then she took a clove of garlic, expertly peeled it, and offered it to me. I was surprised and at first hesitated (she was offering me a raw clove of garlic to go with dishes that already had lots of garlic in them), but I was intrigued by this gesture. I had never known that this tiny raw fresh baby green garlic combined with spoonfuls of smoked rice and roasted eggplant flavored with pomegranate could do so much to my senses. I felt very close to the earth. Seeing my delighted expression she offered me a raw, fresh green fava bean to taste, another springtime delicacy in this region. I suddenly realized that no matter where we are—at home, by the sea or a brook, or in the mountains—we Iranians like to set up a festive meal. It's like picnic time at every meal. Sharing food, drinking tea, telling stories and jokes. There was genuine warmth around the table because this family really had poured out their love for us: their guests. ⊗

A medieval castle in Fuman near Rasht.

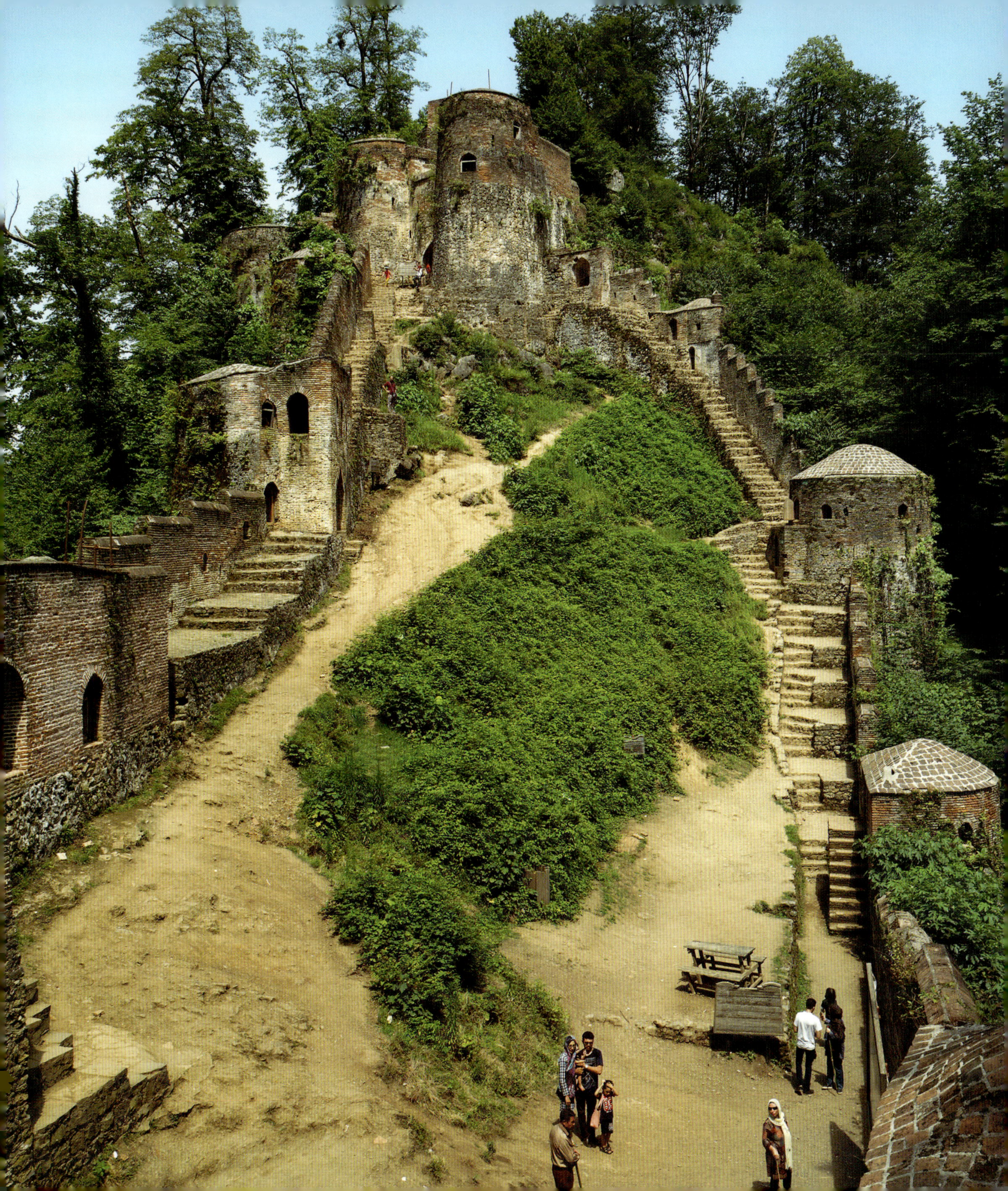

Caspian Green Salt

dalar

Makes 1 cup/120g
Prep: 40 minutes

- 4 cups/340g fresh mint leaves or 1 cup dried mint
- 8 cups/680g cilantro leaves
- 2 cups/170g basil leaves
- ¼ cup/20g fresh khalvash leaves or 1 teaspoon dried (optional)
- ¼ cup/20g fresh chochaq leaves or 1 teaspoon dried (optional)
- 1 tablespoon coarse sea salt
- Juice of 1 lime (2 tablespoons)
- ¼ cup/60ml olive oil (optional)

This is a very popular green herb salt called dalar. Traditionally it is made in a namak-yar, a stone mortar and pestle used for grinding the herbs with the salt. Dalar is used in place of salt to bring out the flavor in cucumbers or any sour fruit. Sometimes it is mixed with vinegar, lime, and sugar to make a sauce for dipping lettuce or to flavor a puree of sour plum/aloucheh feshkan. Dalar is also well known to be one of the cravings of pregnant women in this region. I adapted this, and many of the other recipes in this section, from Zari Khavar, a wonderful Gilaki cook. I like to add a little olive oil, which I've made optional here.

1. **To wash the herbs:** Place all the herbs in a large container and cover with water. Allow to soak for 10 minutes. Drain and rinse thoroughly. Use a salad spinner to thoroughly dry them.

2. Roughly cut all the herbs to facilitate grinding. Transfer the herbs to a food processor and pulse a few times. Add the salt and finely grind until you have a grainy green salty mixture. Add the lime juice, and olive oil and puree. Add more olive oil to taste. Store in an airtight glass container in the fridge. Use as you would use salt.

Apple + Caspian Green Salt Salad

sibtorsh dalar

Serves 6
Prep: 20 minutes

- 4 Fuji apples, peeled and diced into 1in/2.5 cm cubes
- 5 Persian cucumbers, diced into 1in/2.5 cm cubes
- 5 tablespoons green salt/*dalar* (made above)
- juice of 2 limes
- ½ teaspoon freshly ground pepper

This dish is traditionally made with sibtorsh, a local Caspian sour apple, or sour plum. If you don't have them, I particularly like the taste and texture of Fuji apples and cucumbers combined with a little lime juice.

1. In a large salad bowl, combine all the ingredients and toss well. Adjust seasoning to taste by adding more lime juice or green salt. *Nush-e joon!*

The Caspian Region

V VEGAN

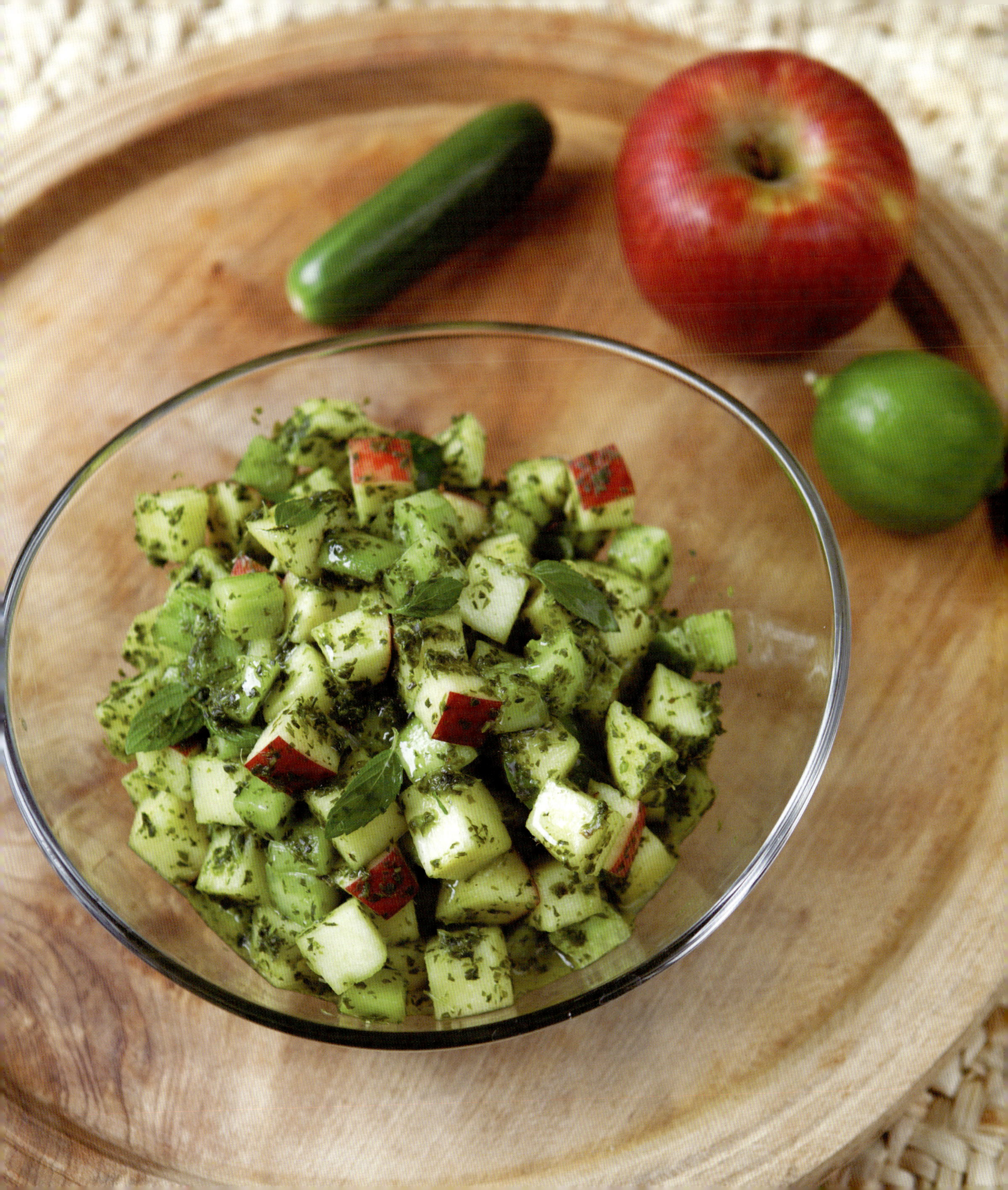

Olive Tapenade
zaytun parvardeh

Serves 6
Prep: 30 minutes

WALNUT PASTE

1 cup/125g walnuts

7 cloves garlic, smashed and peeled

2 tablespoons fresh khalvash leaves or 1 teaspoon dried (optional)

2 tablespoons fresh chochaq leaves or 1 teaspoon dried (optional)

½ cup/40g fresh basil leaves

2 tablespoons fresh cilantro leaves

½ cup/40g fresh mint leaves or 1 tablespoon dried

1 teaspoon ground Persian hogweed seeds/*golpar*

½ teaspoon fine sea salt

½ teaspoon freshly ground pepper

½ cup/110g pitted green olives

OLIVE MIX

¼lb/110g (about ½ cup) pitted green olives

½ cup freshly squeezed pomegranate juice

2 tablespoons fresh lime juice (if pomegranate juice is not sour enough)

1 cup pomegranate arils

Around the Caspian, especially north of Rasht by the Sefid Rud River, you can see olive groves everywhere. This olive tapenade is served as a condiment in many regions of Iran, but it's most common in the Caspian region and usually on every table, whether at home or in a restaurant. It can be eaten as a dip or as a salsa and works particularly well with some Caspian favorites such as baqala qataq and mirza qasemi.

1. In a food processor, place all the ingredients for the walnut paste and pulse until you have a smooth paste. Transfer to a serving bowl.

2. Add the olives, pomegranate juice, lime juice, and pomegranate arils and mix well.

3. Adjust seasoning to taste. Serve as a condiment.

4. If you don't plan to use this tapenade immediately, store in an airtight container in the refrigerator for up to 3 days. *Nush-e joon!*

The Caspian Region

VEGAN

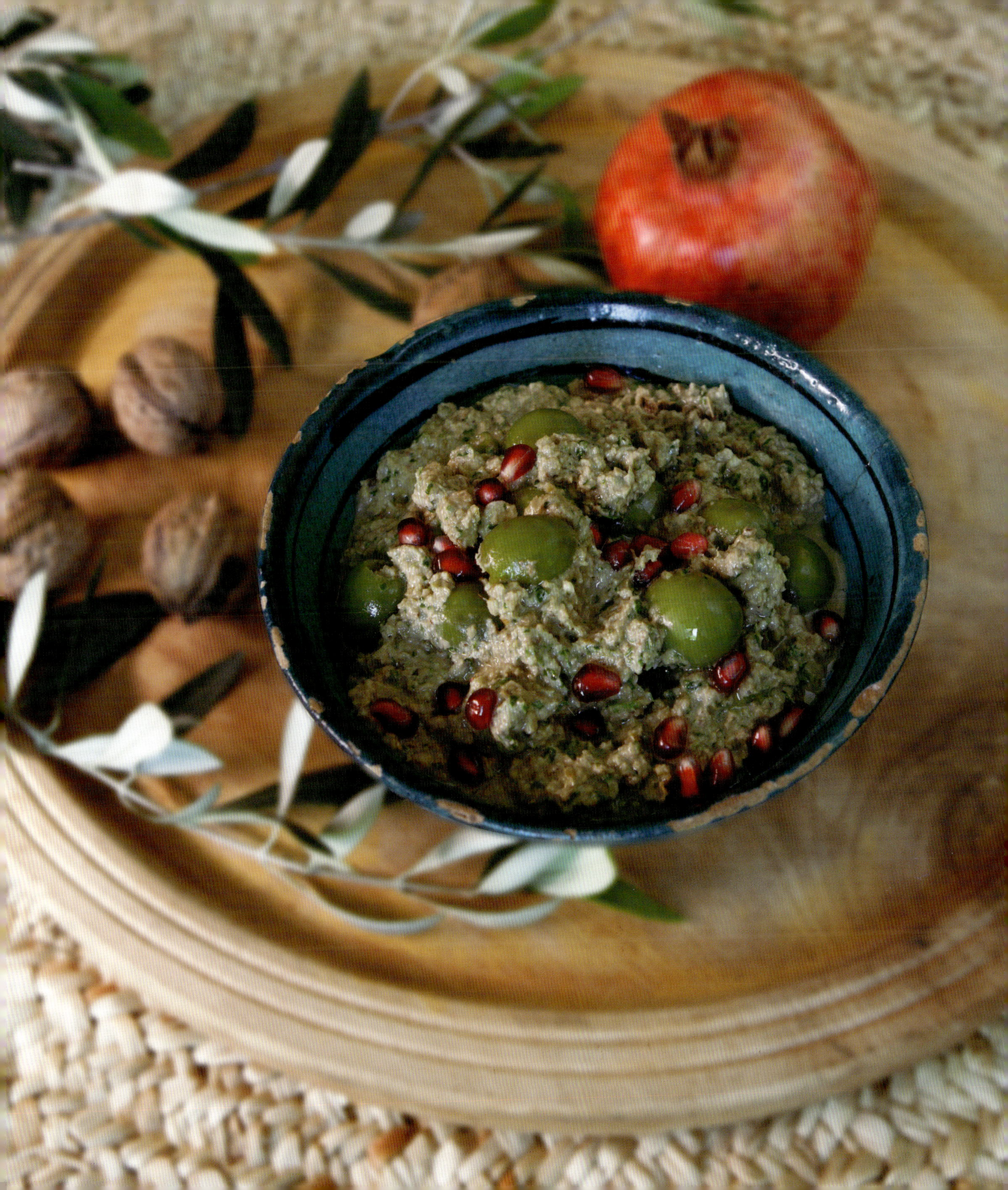

Tomato, Egg + Garlic Omelet
cheghertemeh-ye pomodor gilaki

Serves 4
Prep: 20 minutes
Cooking: 1¼ hours

ONION AND TOMATO SAUCE

3 medium onions, peeled and quartered
2lb/900kg tomatoes
½ cup/120ml olive oil
4 cloves garlic, peeled and grated
2 teaspoons fine sea salt
½ teaspoon freshly ground pepper
1 teaspoon turmeric
1 teaspoon dried khalvash or a mixture of 1 teaspoon dried mint and 1 teaspoon dried basil

EGGS

2 tablespoons olive oil
6 eggs

GARNISH

1 cup/85g fresh basil leaves

I love to make this dish when tomatoes are in season and full of flavor. I prefer it with sangak bread but locals eat it with plain rice. It's interesting that in northern Iran, because of Russian influence, they call tomatoes "pomador" whereas in southern Iran because of Portuguese influence, they call it "tamata."

1. *To dice the onions:* Place the onions in a food processor and pulse to create small pieces. Remove from the food processor and set aside.

2. *To blanche the tomatoes:* Cut out the tomato stems and score cross hairs at the base. Drop them into boiling water for 1 minute or until the skins lift up slightly. Remove with a slotted spoon and place it in a bowl of ice water.

3. Remove the tomato skins and puree the tomatoes in the food processor.

4. *To cook the onion and tomato sauce:* Heat the oil in a wide, deep skillet over low heat and sauté the onions for 30 minutes or until golden brown. Add the garlic, salt, pepper, turmeric, and the herbs, and stir-fry for 2 minutes. Add the tomato puree and sauté for 20 minutes or until most of the juices have been absorbed.

5. *To cook the eggs:* Just before serving, reduce heat to low and spread out the onion and tomato mixture evenly in the skillet. Make 6 holes with the handle of a wooden spoon. In each hole, drizzle a little oil and an egg on top. Cook over low heat for 15 to 20 minutes until the eggs are softly set.

6. Stir the mixture gently with a wooden spoon and transfer to a serving platter. Garnish with fresh basil and serve with plain rice/*kateh*. *Nush-e joon!*

The Caspian Region

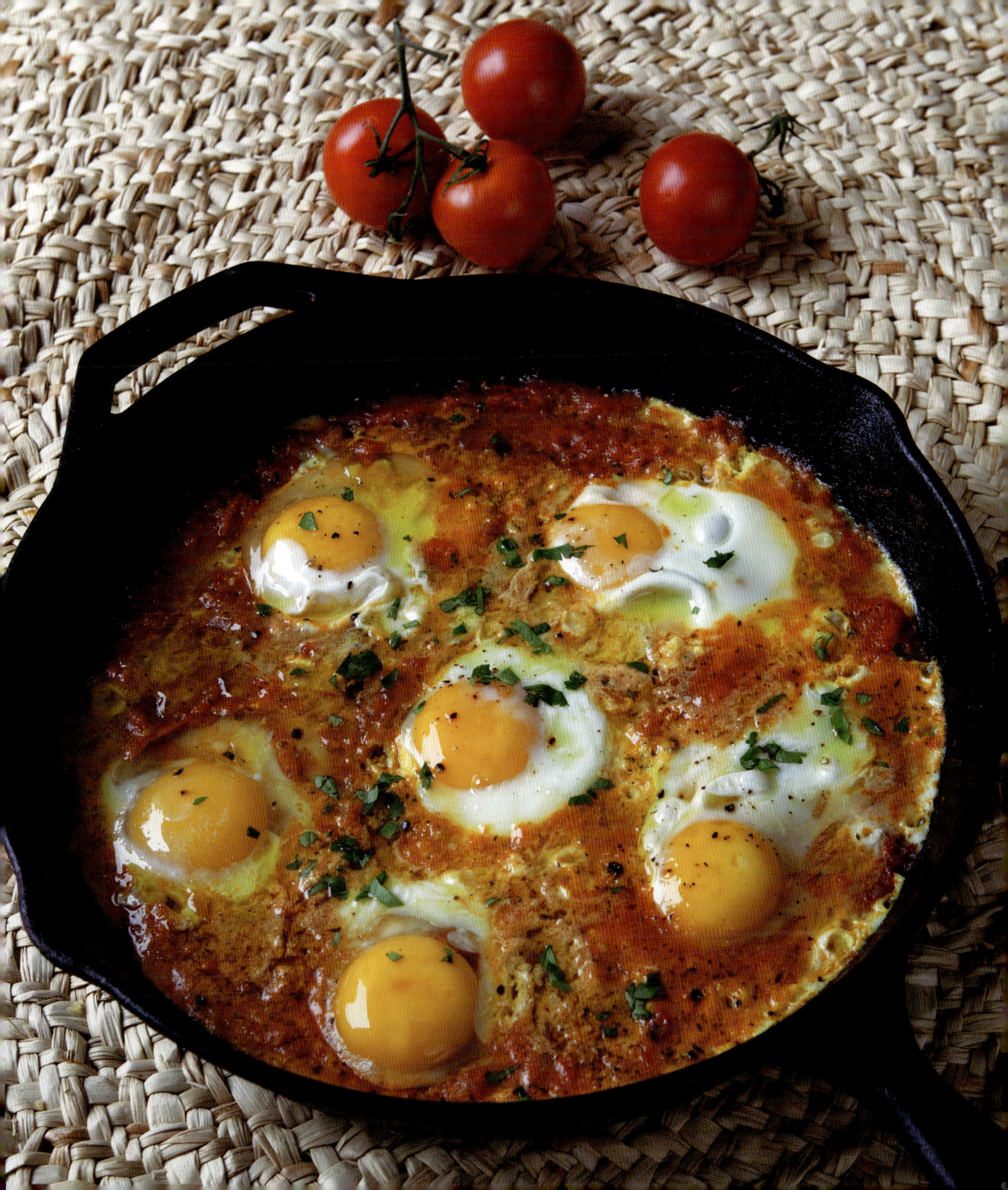

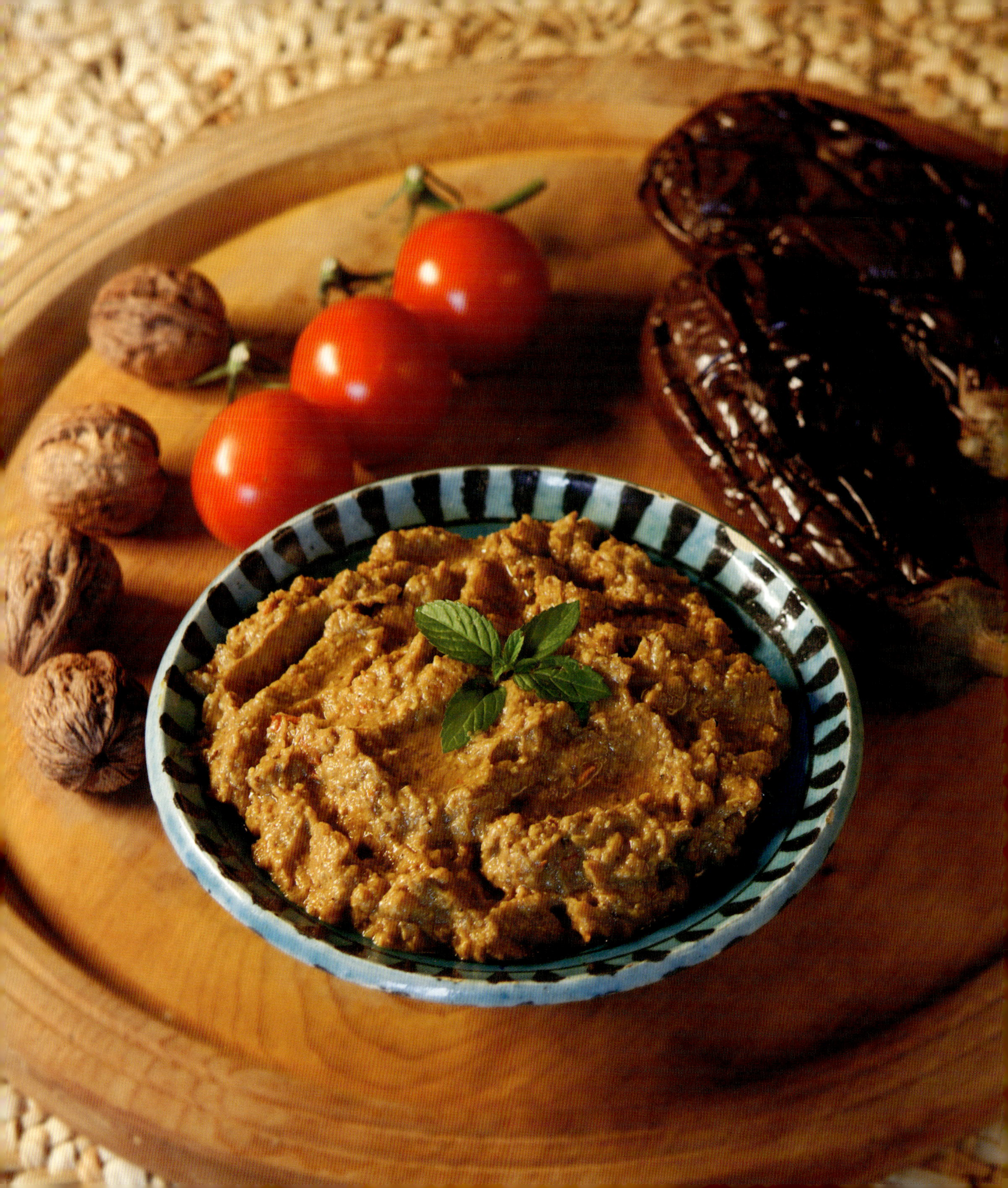

Smoked Eggplant, Tomato + Walnut Spread

aghuz tareh

Serves 4 to 6
Prep: 30 minutes
Cooking: 30 minutes

- 9 seedless eggplants (about 3 pounds/1.3kg)
- ¼ cup/60ml olive oil
- 1 medium onion, peeled
- 6 cloves garlic, peeled
- 1 cup/125g walnuts
- 2 medium tomatoes, peeled and cut into quarters
- 1 tablespoon fine sea salt
- ½ teaspoon fresh ground pepper
- 1 teaspoon turmeric
- ½ teaspoon dried wild cumin seeds/*gav zireh* or 1 tablespoon regular cumin

I have adapted this recipe from a young passionate cook, Hanif Sadr. He grew up with his grandparents in Tonekabon by the Caspian and learned this dish from Abji Khanum, the family cook.

1. Roast the eggplants on all sides over a stovetop flame until the entire outer skin is burnt black and the eggplants are tender.

2. Transfer the eggplants to a cutting board, cut off the crowns, and remove all the skins.

3. In a medium-sized pot, heat the oil and sauté the onion and garlic for 10 minutes.

4. Place the onion mixture, the eggplant, walnuts, tomatoes, and spices in a food processor and pulse until pureed.

5. Transfer this mixture to the pot. Cover and cook over low heat for 45 to 50 minutes until you have a thick paste. Adjust seasoning to taste.

6. Garnish with 1 tablespoon shredded fresh mint.

7. Serve spread on bread or with plain rice/*kateh*. *Nush-e joon!*

Eggplant Tapenade

kaleh kabab

Prep: 30 minutes

- 4 seedless eggplants (about 1 ½ pound/675g)
- 3 cloves garlic, peeled
- 2 cups/250g walnuts
- 1 teaspoon fine sea salt
- ¼ teaspoon fresh ground pepper
- ½ teaspoon ground coriander
- 1 teaspoon ground *golpar*
- 1 teaspoon dried khalvash or basil
- 1 cup fresh mint leaves or 2 tablespoons dried
- 1 cup fresh cilantro leaves
- 2 tablespoons olive oil
- 1 cup pomegranate juice

VEGAN

I adapted this recipe from Parivash Shafi`i, a wonderful cook from the Golsar neighborhood of Rasht. For the locals, this dish is considered to be one of the essential condiments/mazzehs on a Caspian table/sofreh. Its name, kaleh, means raw. Only the eggplant is grilled/kabab. The rest of the ingredients are used fresh and raw.

1. Roast the eggplants on all sides over a stovetop flame until the entire outer skin is burnt black and the eggplants are tender. Transfer the eggplants to a cutting board, cut off the crowns and remove all the skins.

2. Transfer the eggplants to a food processor and add the rest of the ingredients. Pulse until you have a grainy paste. Adjust seasoning to taste. *Nush-e joon!*

VARIATION

Eggplant with Garlic + Verjuice
dokhtar naz

Eliminate the walnuts from the Eggplant Tapenade ingredients and add 2 tomatoes, diced into ¼in/6mm cubes. Increase the garlic to 6 grated garlic, increase the olive oil to ¼ cup/60ml, and replace the pomegranate juice with verjuice. Everything else remains the same.

The Caspian Region

Smoked Eggplant with Eggs + Garlic

mirza qasemi

Serves 4
Prep: 10 minutes
Cooking: 30 minutes (if using a gas flame for eggplants)

EGGPLANTS

6 Italian eggplants (about 3½ pounds/1.6kg)
½ cup/120ml olive oil
5 cloves garlic, peeled and grated
2 teaspoons fine sea salt
½ teaspoon freshly ground pepper
1 teaspoon turmeric

EGGS

2 tablespoons olive oil
2 cloves garlic, grated
4 eggs

GARNISH

1 cup/85g fresh basil leaves

Mirza qasemi is made throughout the Caspian region, but each town has its own variation: some add tomato; others cook the eggs and eggplants separately and mix them together at the end. But the result is always a deliciously smoky taste. As we went from town to town, each believed their mirza qasemi was the best.

1. Roast the eggplants on all sides over the flame of a charcoal grill or a gas cooktop until the skin is burnt and completely blackened. If you don't have a gas cooktop, preheat the oven to 450°F/230°C. Prick the eggplants in several places with a fork to prevent them from bursting during cooking. Place them on a rack in a rimmed sheet pan and roast in the oven for 50 minutes.

2. Place the eggplants on a chopping board and leave until cool enough to handle. Use your hands to remove and discard the skins. Finely chop the eggplants.

3. Heat the oil in a wide, deep skillet over medium heat and sauté the garlic for 20 seconds until golden. Add the salt, pepper, turmeric, and chopped eggplants, and stir-fry for 5 to 10 minutes until all the juices have been absorbed.

4. Just before serving, reduce heat to low and spread out the eggplant mixture evenly in the skillet. Make 4 holes with the handle of a wooden spoon. In each hole, drizzle a little oil, a little grated garlic, and an egg on top. Cover and cook over low heat for 15 to 20 minutes until the eggs are softly set.

5. Stir the mixture gently with a wooden spoon and transfer to a serving platter. Garnish with fresh basil and serve with plain rice/*kateh*. *Nush-e joon!*

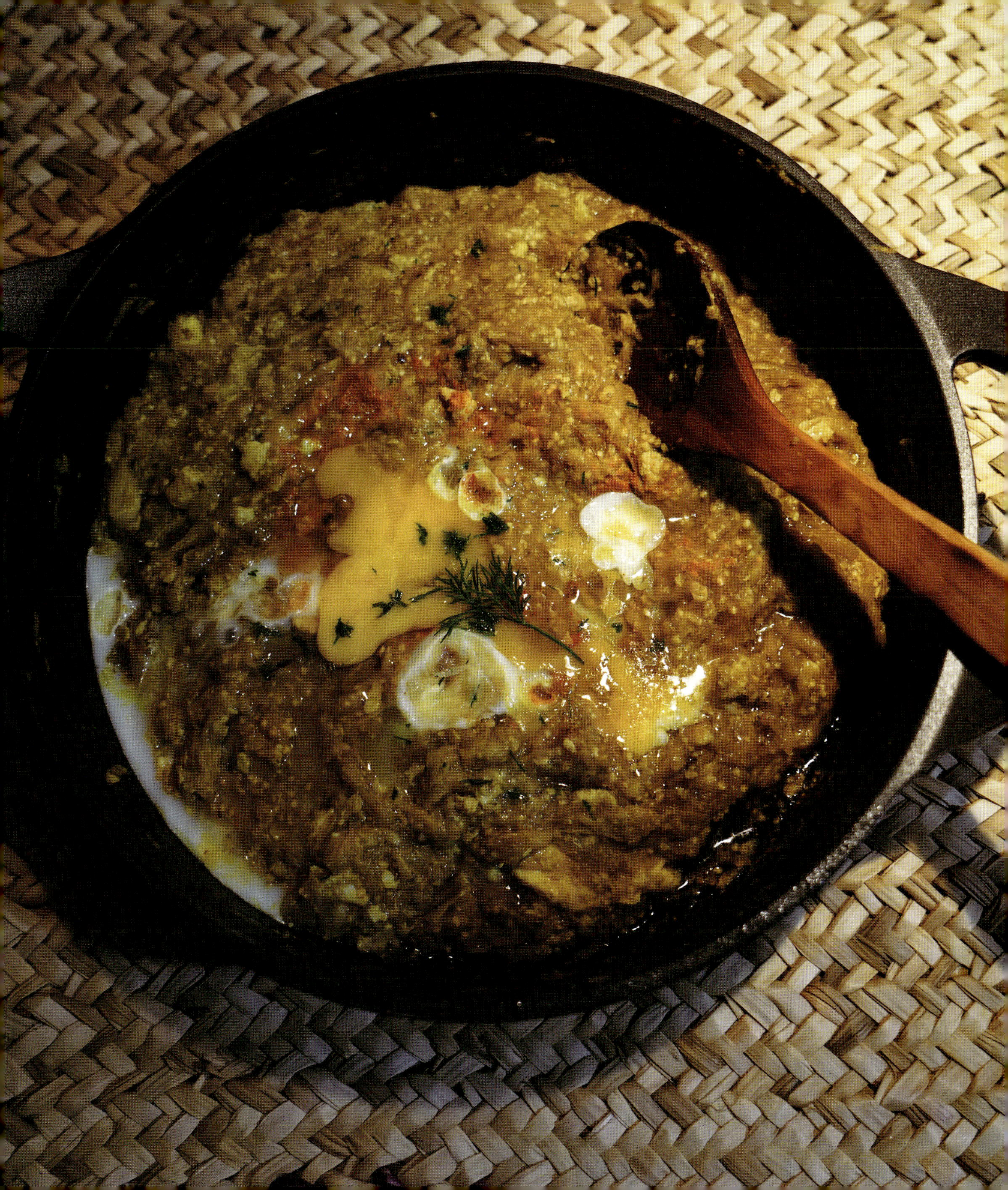

In Ramsar, we met up with Mohammad Kouchakpour, a renowned photographer, who took us to his son's restaurant next door. We had a delicious meal of deep-fried trout, smoked eggplant/*aghuz tareh*, fava beans in the pod, an olive pickle, and a tomato salsa.

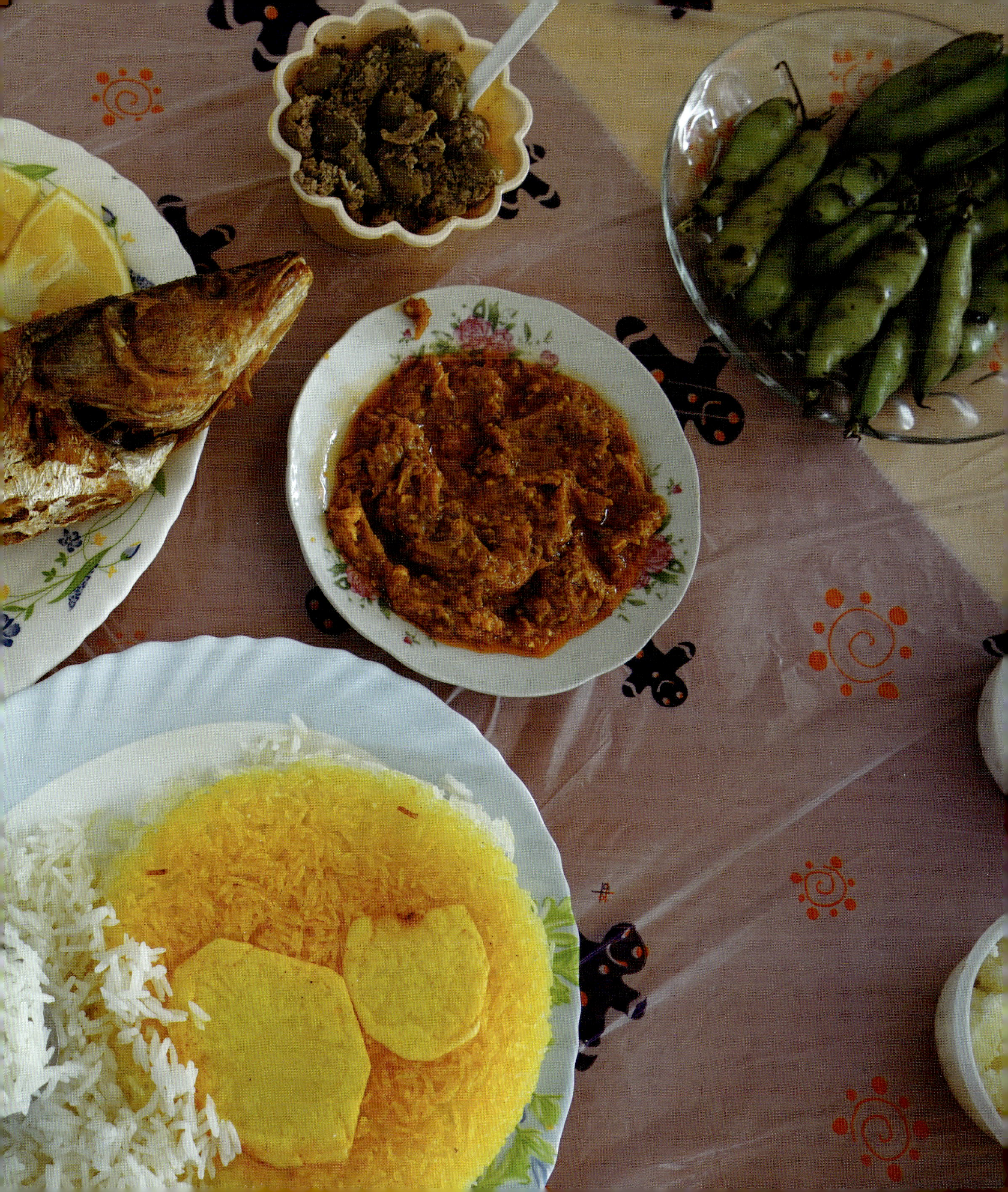

Garlic-Chive Omelet
sir-abij

Serves 4
Prep: 10 minutes
Cooking: 10 minutes

½ cup/120ml raw sesame oil
3 cups/255g garlic chives, wash and chop into 1/4in/6mm lengths
6 eggs
1 teaspoon fine sea salt
1 teaspoon freshly ground pepper
2 teaspoons turmeric

Around the Caspian, they love to use fresh green garlic shoots (allium tuberosum), which is a perennial bulbous plant with strap-shaped leaves unlike either onion or garlic. It has straight, thin white-flowering stalks that are much taller than the leaves. The flavor is more like garlic than chives. Locally, they add this omelet to a chicken and split pea broth to make a very flavorful dish called qaliyeh-ye sir. *The photo shows the dish in the skillet before stirring in step 3.*

1. In a wide skillet, heat the oil over medium heat and add the garlic shoots. Sauté for 5 to 7 minutes until lightly golden.

2. Break the eggs into a mixing bowl and add the salt, pepper, and turmeric, and beat lightly with a fork.

3. Add the egg mixture to the garlic and allow to cook undisturbed for 5 to 7 minutes until the eggs are almost set. Give it a stir with a wooden spoon to combine the egg and garlic shoots. Adjust seasoning to taste.

4. Remove from heat. Serve with plain rice/*kateh*, smoked fish, and yogurt. *Nush-e joon!*

Cheese + Dill Omelet
panir abij ba shivid

Serves 4
Prep: 10 minutes
Cooking: 10 minutes

¼ cup/60ml raw sesame oil
1lb/450g feta-like cheese, crumbled
1 cup/85g chopped fresh dill or 2 tablespoons dried
6 eggs
¼ teaspoon fine sea salt
1 teaspoon freshly ground pepper
½ teaspoon turmeric or ¼ teaspoon ground saffron threads.

1. In a wide skillet, heat the oil over medium heat and add the cheese and dill. Sauté for a few minutes until the cheese is lightly golden.

2. Break the eggs into a mixing bowl, add the salt, pepper, and turmeric, and beat lightly with a fork.

3. Add the egg mixture to the skillet. Give it a stir with a wooden spoon to combine the egg and cheese. Allow to cook for a few minutes until the egg is set. Adjust seasoning to taste.

4. Remove from heat. Serve immediately over plain rice/*kateh* or flat bread. *Nush-e joon!*

The Caspian Region

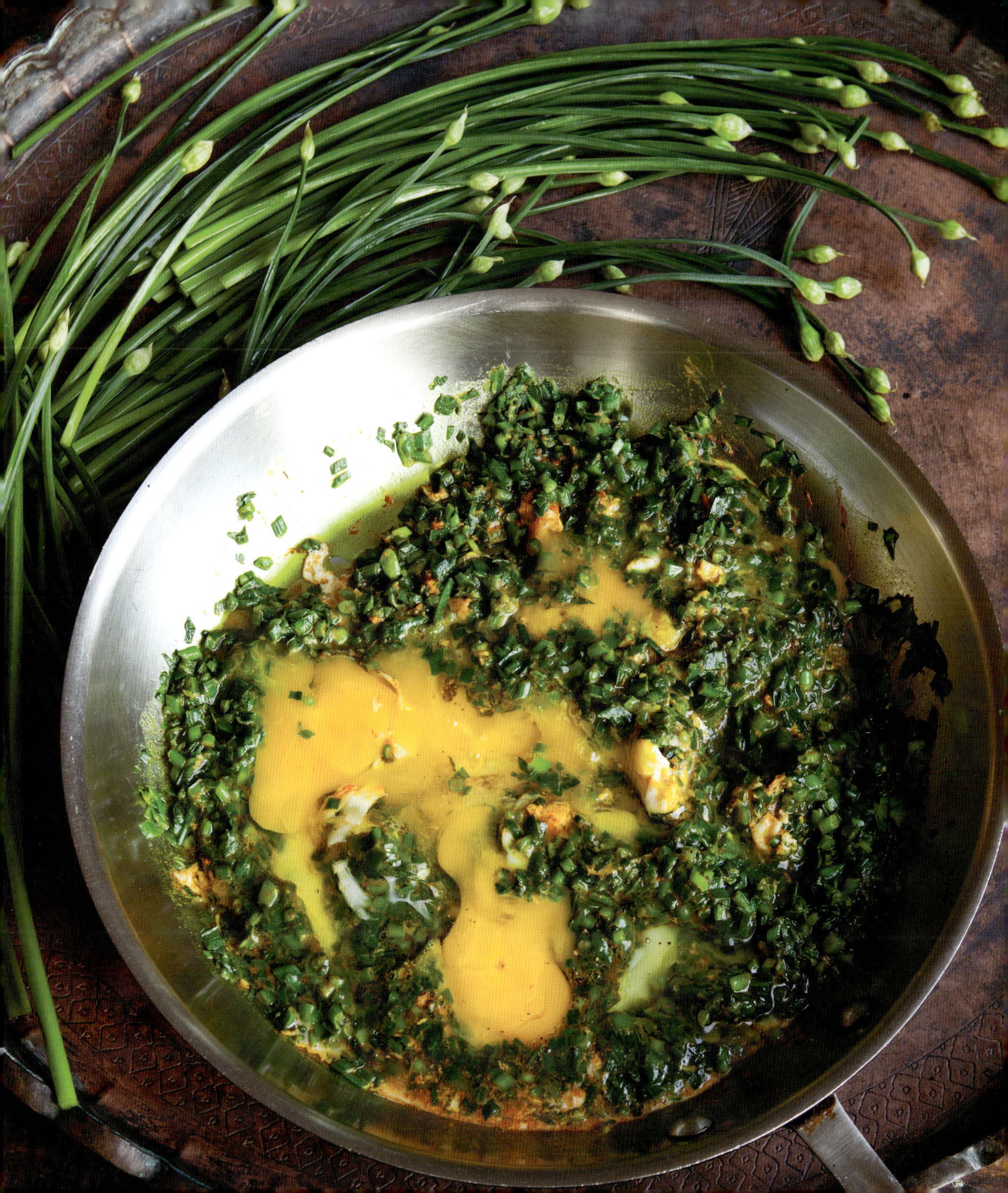

Butternut Squash with Rice Flour Patties
kui kaka

Makes 20 patties, serves 6 to 8
Prep: 30 minutes + 30 minutes resting
Cooking: 20 minutes

BATTER

3lb/1.3kg butternut squash peeled and diced into 2 inch/5cm pieces (about 5 cups)
2 tablespoons sugar
¾ cup/90g walnuts
3 cups/450g rice flour mixed with 1 teaspoon salt
½ teaspoon ground saffron dissolved in 2 tablespoons rose water
1 tablespoon yogurt
½ teaspoon ground cardamom
1 teaspoon ground cinnamon
1 teaspoon baking powder
1-inch/2.5cm fresh ginger, peeled and grated (optional)
3 eggs

FOR COOKING

¼ cup oil

1. **To make the batter:** In a medium saucepan, place the butternut squash and 1 cup water. Cover and cook over medium heat for 20 to 30 minutes until soft. Drain.

2. Transfer the butternut squash, while still hot, to a food processor. Add the rest of the ingredients, except the eggs, and puree.

3. Add the eggs and mix until you have a thick batter. Transfer to a mixing bowl, cover, and allow to rest for 30 minutes or overnight in the fridge.

4. **To make the patties:** Heat 2 tablespoons oil in a wide iron skillet over low heat until hot but not smoking. Use an ice-cream scoop to place dollops of the thick batter in the skillet. Cook for 5 to 10 minutes, over low heat. Flip over and cook for another 5 to 7 minutes until the patties are cooked through completely.

5. Remove from the skillet and place on a serving platter. Repeat for all the batter. Serve warm. *Nush-e joon!*

NOTE

You can also make these patties without sugar and glaze them with grape molasses after cooking.

The Caspian Region

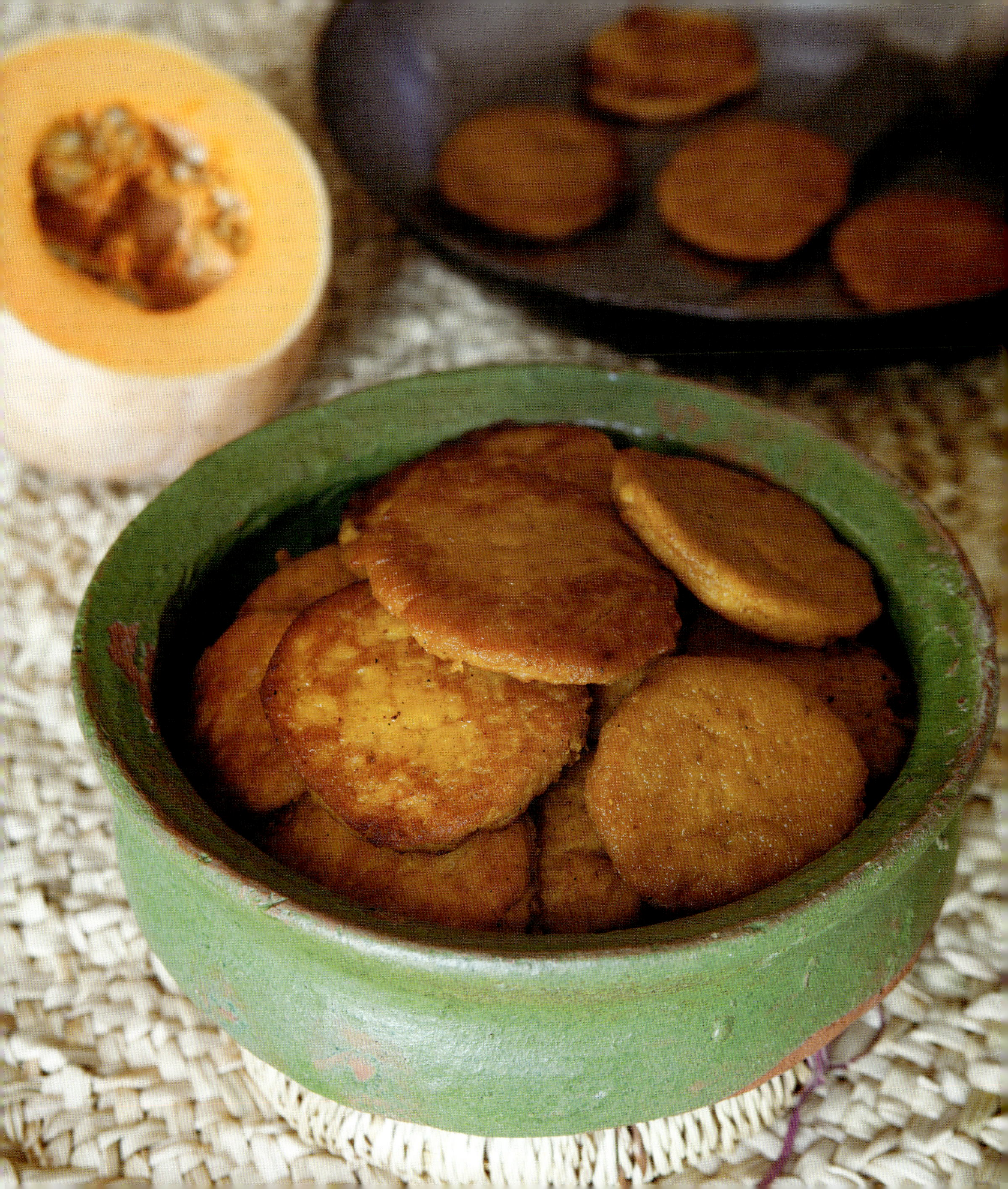

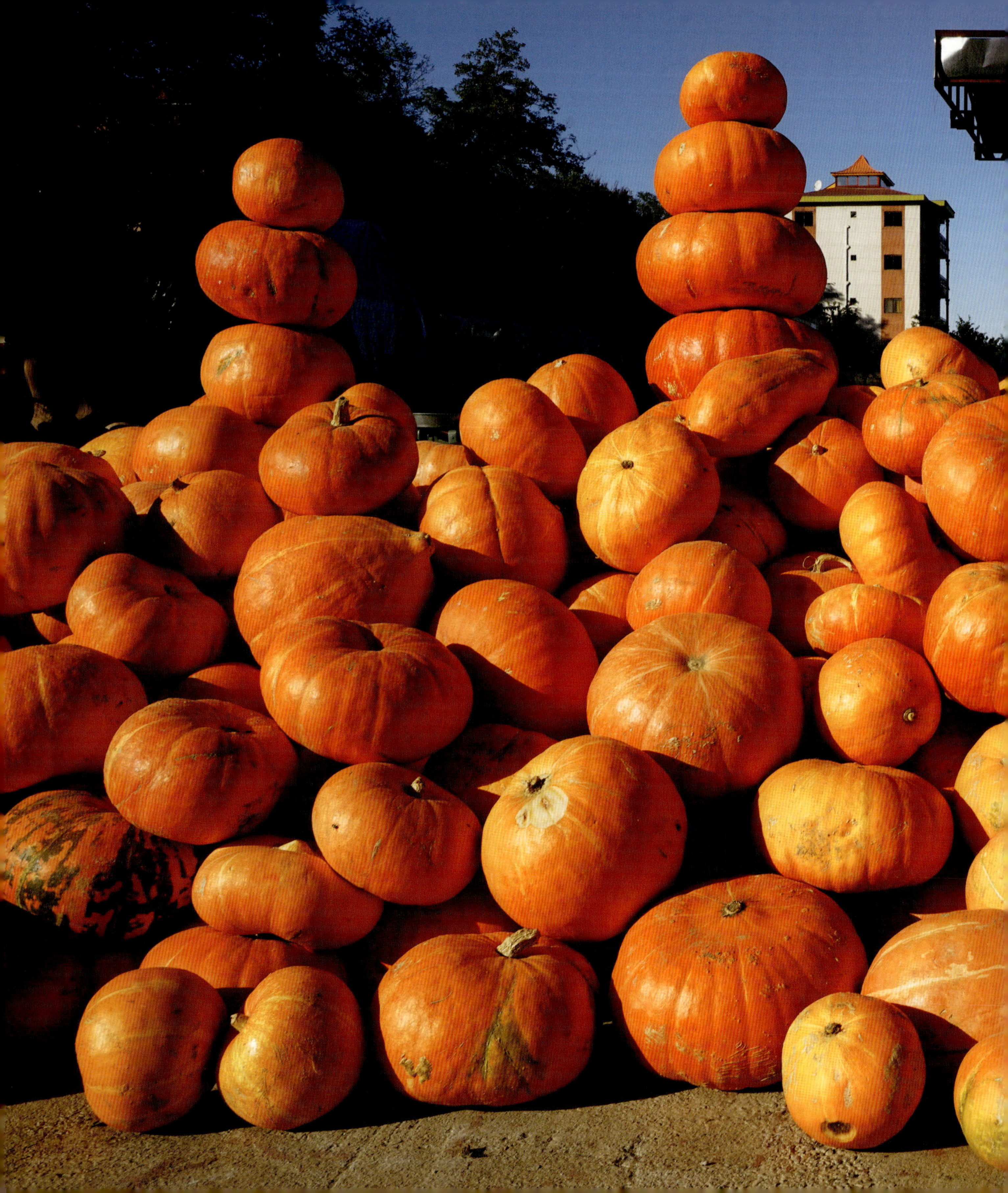

Butternut Squash Osh
osh-e kuhi

Serves 6 to 8
Prep: 20 minutes
Cooking: 1 hour

1 tablespoon oil or ghee
2lb/900g peeled butternut squash or pumpkin cut into 1 inch/2.5cm cubes
½ teaspoon fine sea salt
½ cup brown lentil, rinse, and drain
½ cup/100g rice, rinsed and drained
3 cups/720ml water
1 cup/240ml almond milk, or milk
1 tablespoon sugar
½ teaspoon cinnamon
½ cup/40g ground walnuts

GARNISH

2 tablespoons chopped fresh parsley
2 tablespoons fresh lime juice

1. Heat the oil in a medium-sized heavy pot over medium heat. Add the butternut squash and stir-fry for 5 minutes. Add the salt, lentils, and rice, and stir-fry for 20 seconds.

2. Pour in the water and bring to a boil. Reduce heat to medium, cover, and simmer, stirring occasionally, for about 40 minutes or until the butternut squash and lentils are tender.

3. Add the milk, sugar, cinnamon, and walnuts, and bring back to a boil. Reduce heat to low and simmer for another 15 minutes, stirring occasionally.

4. Use a handheld mixer to partially puree the solids.

5. Keep covered and warm until ready to serve. Just before serving, add the parsley and lime juice. Adjust seasoning to taste. *Nush-e joon!*

The Caspian Region

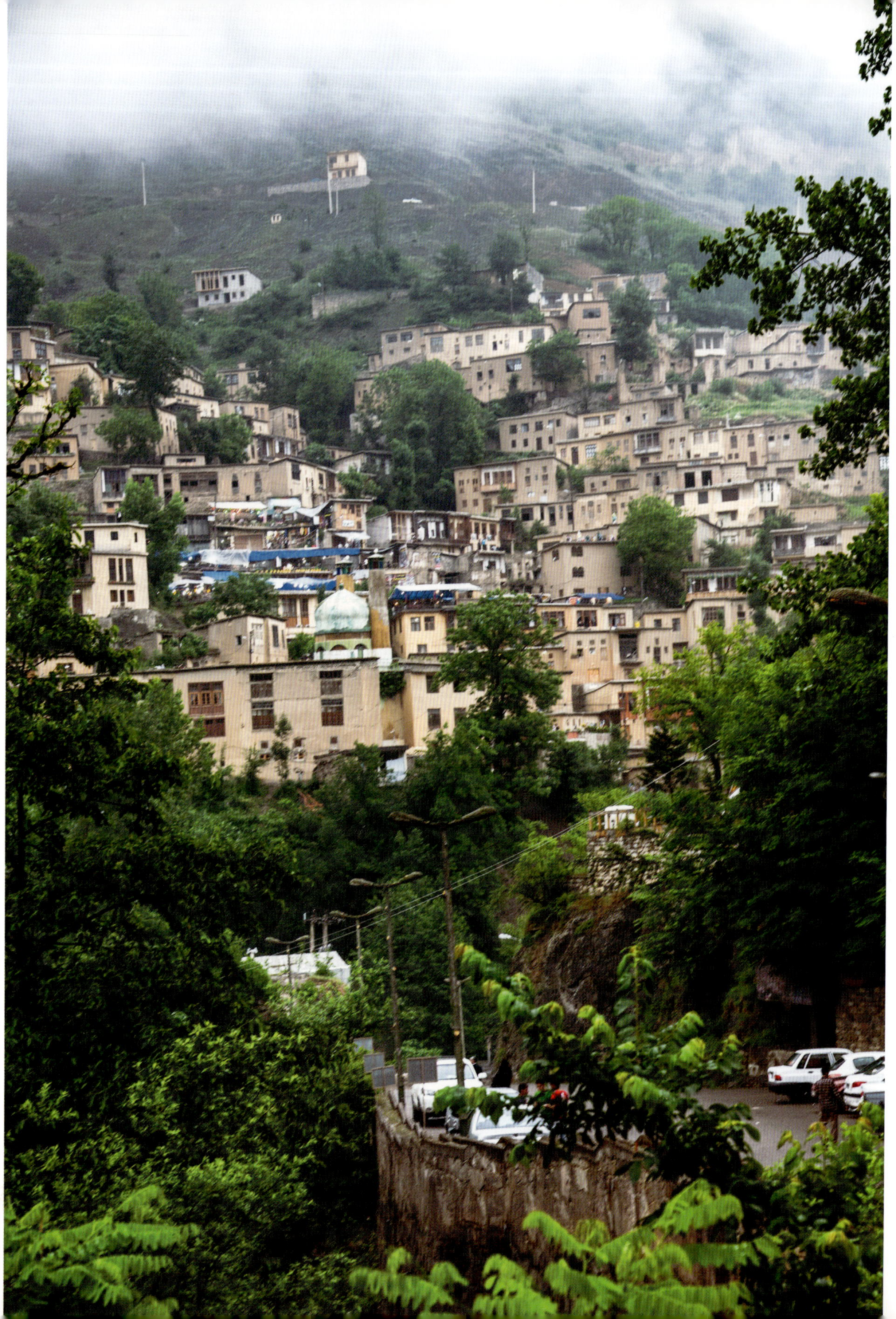

Masouleh

Masouleh is a hilltop village at the foot of the Alborz Mountains and is 60 kilometers southwest of Rasht. The terrace of one house is the roof of the house below. Its architecture is unique in Iran and reminiscent of some European hill towns. The atmosphere is laid back and, as you might notice in the photo of the cafe below, not much different from a cafe in Provence. I bought a large basket of whole Persian hogweed seeds/*golpar* there. Unfortunately, and surprisingly, when I was returning home, the U.S. Customs officer at the airport asked if I had brought back any *golpar* with me. When I didn't answer immediately, he said, "I can smell it" and confiscated the whole lot. The seeds are not allowed in the U.S., but you can buy the ground powder at Iranian stores.

As you enter the market, it's the fish that first impress—fresh caught Caspian salmon/ *kutum*, salted and smoked fish, and pink and brown fish roe, which locals use in their omelets. The people of Rasht, called *Rashtis* in Persian, are really fond of their fish, so much so that they are teasingly called fish-head-eaters (*kaleh-mahi khor*). Of course, we know that the most delicate and tastiest parts of the fish are the little pieces of delicious meat just behind the eyes and around the jaw bones.

105

Caviar

khaviar

Caviar is the unfertilized, processed roe of the sturgeon. The name for caviar comes from the Persian, *mahi-e khayeh dar*, literally meaning "fish bearing eggs." The best caviar is from the Caspian Sea. There are four main types of caviar, each from a different species of sturgeon. The largest eggs, known by the Russian name beluga, are from the *fil-mahi*, literally "elephant fish." The average-sized roe, *osetra*, comes from tas-mahi, or the "bald fish"; and the smallest eggs, *sevruga* and *sterlet*, are those from the *uzunbrun*, or the "long-nosed fish." Besides the size, each type has its own particular flavor, and you have to try each one to see which you prefer. The most important step in the production of caviar is the salting. The different brands available vary in quality.

I have often been asked, "How does one know if the caviar is fresh or not?" The best answer I can give is that it should smell of the sea but not fishy.

Caviar has not been widely appreciated by Iranians except by the local inhabitants of the provinces Gilan and Mazandaran, which are around the Caspian. Historically, this was mainly because of the difficulty of refrigerated transport. In 2009, Iran was the world's largest producer and exporter of caviar, with annual exports of more than 300 tons, followed by Russia. Iranian expertise helped China produce 10 tons of farmed caviar in 2013. With the depletion of Caspian Sea caviar, production of farmed or "sustainable" caviar has greatly increased (photograph on facing page shows a sturgeon farmed in Iran). Northern California is reported to account for 70% to 80% of U.S. production. In addition, a "no-kill" caviar harvesting technique has been developed in Germany and implemented in California.

Unfortunately, around the Caspian itself, you don't have easy access to caviar, except on the black market. The official production is mostly for export.

There are various recipes from this region that include the roe of the sturgeon. One that I like is with garlic chives in an omelet. The Russians also like to garnish their caviar with onion and egg white, but I believe good-quality caviar should be eaten simply. Place a good-sized dollop on a thin piece of lightly buttered toast (*sangak* bread is my favorite) and squeeze a little fresh lime over it (pomegranate can also enhance the flavor of the caviar). *Nush-e joon!*

Serves 4

4 ounces/120g Caspian Sea caviar
Toasted *sangak* bread or thin toast
2 tablespoons butter
2 fresh limes cut into halves, or pomegranate arils

The Caspian Region

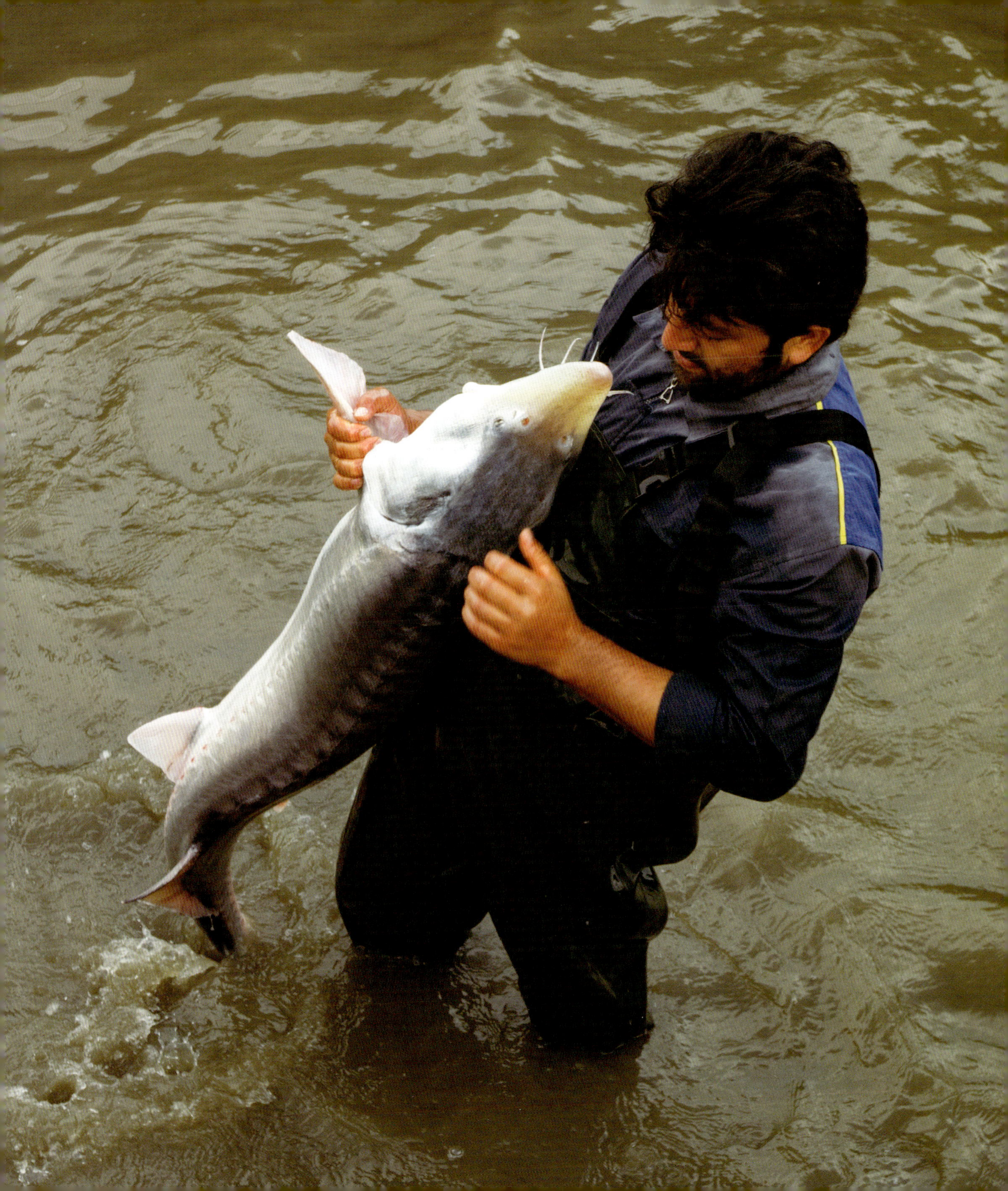

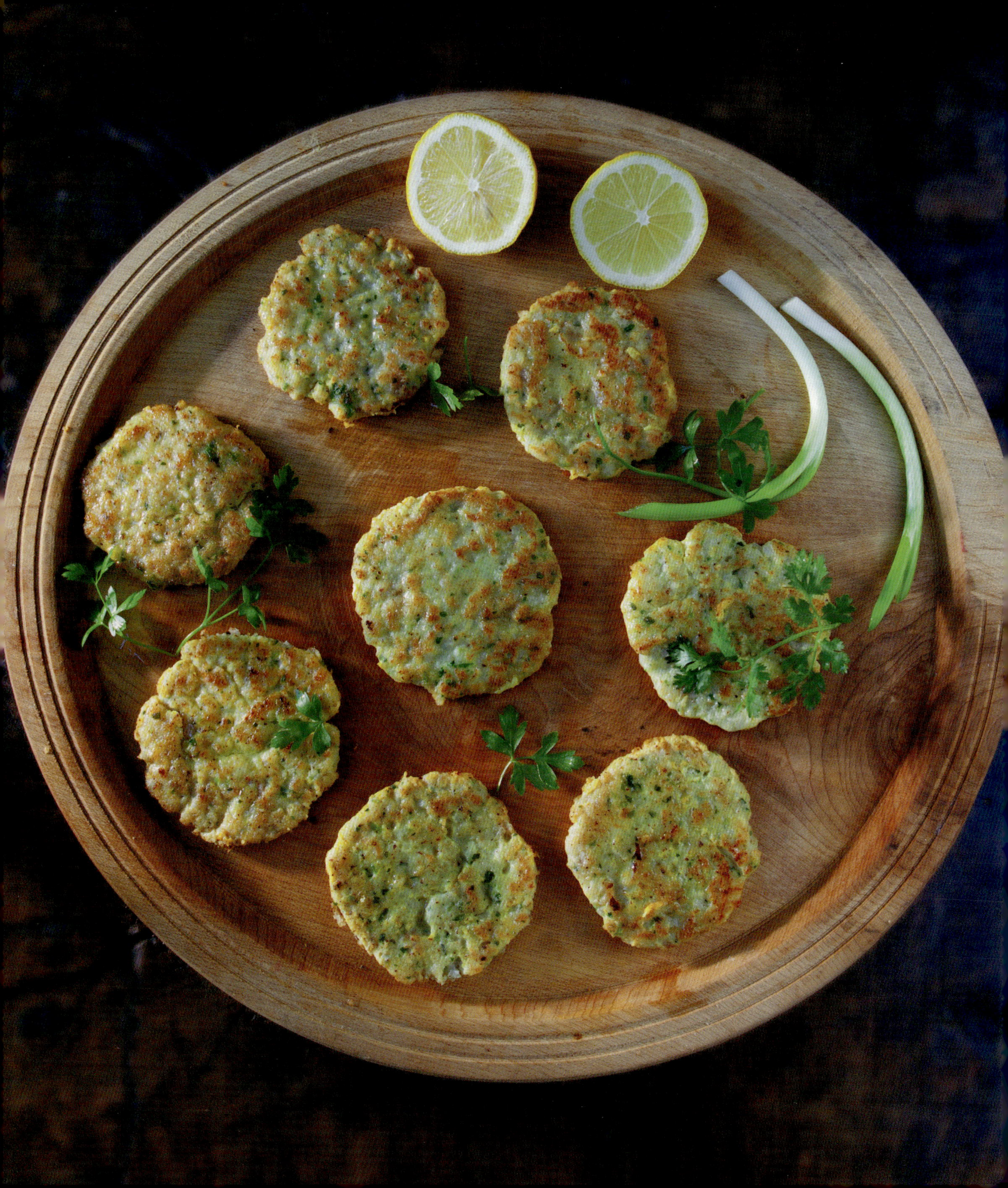

Sturgeon Patties

kotlet-e uzunburun

Makes 20 patties, serves 4 to 6
Prep: 10 minutes + 30 minutes chilling the paste
Cooking: 20 minutes

PASTE
1 lb/450g sturgeon or cod fillets, skin removed, cut into 2 inch/5cm pieces
1 small onion, quartered
1 spring onion, cut up
2 tablespoons fresh parsley leaves
2 teaspoons fine sea salt
½ teaspoon freshly ground pepper

2 eggs (lightly beaten)

BREAD CRUMBS
1 cup/60g bread crumbs

OIL FOR COOKING
4 tablespoons oil or ghee

GARNISH
2 sour oranges/*narenj* or limes, halved
¼ cup chopped fresh parsley
6 spring onions, washed and trimmed
6 radishes, washed and trimmed

Sturgeon, besides its distinctive taste, is good for making patties (and kababs) because it is a firm-fleshed fish and doesn't have any small bones.

1. *To make the paste:* In a food processor, place the fish, onions, parsley, salt, and pepper, and pulse until you have a thick, soft paste. Transfer to a mixing bowl. Add the eggs. Knead lightly, cover, and chill in the fridge for 30 minutes and up to 24 hours.

2. *To make the patties:* Heat the oil in a wide skillet over medium-low heat until hot but not smoking.

3. Scoop the paste, using an ice-cream scoop, into walnut-sized lumps. Flatten each lump between your palms into round patties, 3 inch/8cm across. Turn the patties in the bread crumbs, covering both sides.

4. Fry the patties, as you make them, for 3 to 4 minutes on each side until golden brown (add more oil if necessary).

5. Carefully arrange the patties in a serving platter and squeeze the sour orange over it. Keep warm until ready to serve.

6. Garnish, according to your fancy, with fresh parsley and radishes, and serve with rice/*kateh* or bread, and pickles. *Nush-e joon!*

Fish Roe Omelet

ashpal-e gilaki

Serves 4
Prep: 10 minutes
Cooking: 15 minutes

2 tablespoon oil or butter
½ pound/225g fish roe, cleaned
1 clove garlic, peeled and grated
½ teaspoon fine sea salt
½ teaspoon freshly ground pepper
½ teaspoon turmeric
¼ cup/25g fresh chopped spring onions
4 eggs, lightly beaten
¼ cup/20g fresh dill weed or 1 tablespoon dried dill weed

Around the Caspian, fish roe is called "ashpal." In the West, we associate Iran with caviar, which is salted and cured sturgeon roe, but Iranians of this region love roe from other fish as well. Some favorite roes are from the renowned Caspian white fish, kutum, others from bream, roach, and cod. The roe is cured or smoked, and usually served with rice/kateh and garlic pickle (sometimes for breakfast) or mixed with other ingredients such as eggs to make this omelet.

1. *To make the omelet:* Heat the oil in a wide skillet over medium-low heat until hot but not smoking. Add the fish roe and garlic and sauté for 1 minute. Add the salt, pepper, turmeric, and spring onions, and sauté for another minute.

2. Reduce heat to low, add the eggs, and allow to cook for 5 to 10 minutes until softly set.

3. Add the dill, give it a gentle stir, and allow to cook for 1 more minute. *Nush-e joon!*

The Caspian Region

Fish Head Soup
mahi kaleh ab

Serves 4 to 6
Prep: 20 minutes
Cooking: 1 hour

FISH

5 branzino or 3 rockfish heads, gills removed and rinsed thoroughly
½lb/225g branzino or rockfish fillets, skins removed, rinsed, and patted dry

BROTH

2 tablespoons olive oil
10 cloves garlic, peeled and grated
½ teaspoon turmeric
Zest of ½ an orange
3 cups/720ml water
¾ cup sour orange juice or ½ cup orange and 2 tablespoons lime juice
1½ teaspoons fine sea salt
½ teaspoon fresh ground pepper
¼ teaspoon saffron threads dissolved in 1 tablespoon warm water (optional)

GARNISH

2 spring onions (white and green parts) sliced

People from Rasht are known in Iran as "fish head eaters" because they love fish so much they eat even the fish heads. This soup, beside being delicious, is also an inexpensive way, when combined with a pot of rice, to feed 6 people. In Rasht they use the white fish of the Caspian, which is similar to a striped bass/rockfish or branzino. But salmon heads also work well for this soup. If using salmon heads, just two heads will be enough.

1. **To prepare the fish:** Heat the oil in a medium-sized laminated pot over medium heat and sauté the fish heads and the fillets until golden on both sides. Add the garlic and turmeric, and sauté for 1 minute.

2. **To make the broth:** Add the orange zest and water, and bring to a boil. Reduce heat to low, cover, and cook for 30 minutes.

3. Add the sour orange, salt, pepper, and saffron, and bring back to a boil. Remove from heat and adjust seasoning to taste.

4. Garnish with spring onions and serve with plain rice/*kateh*. Nush-e joon!

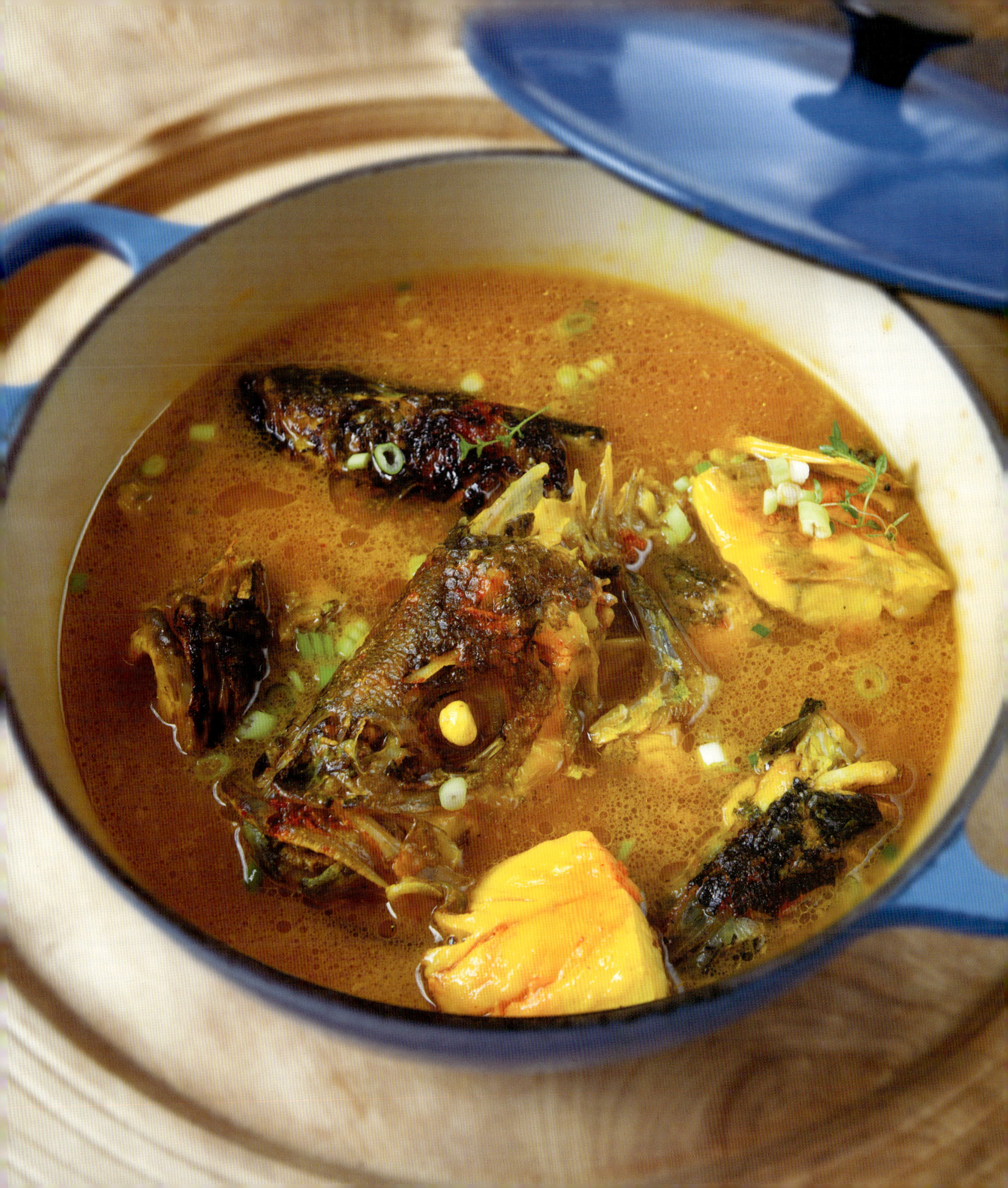

Seared Fish with Garlic + Vinegar Glaze
mahi-e kapur-e torsh-o shirin

Serves 4 to 6
Prep: 30 minutes
Cooking: 10 minutes

DUSTING

1½ teaspoons fine sea salt
½ teaspoon freshly ground black pepper
1 teaspoon ground turmeric
1 tablespoon all-purpose flour
1 tablespoon ground Persian hogweed seeds/*golpar*

FISH

¼ cup raw sesame oil
4 thick fish fillets (about 2 pounds/900g), catfish or striped bass, all skins and bones removed
10 cloves garlic, grated

SAUCE

1 cup wine vinegar mixed with 2 tablespoons sugar

GARNISH

2 tablespoons chopped fresh parsley

This dish is also wonderful with fresh sour orange, when in season, instead of vinegar. I was taken by the sight of this couple on their moped in the photo on the facing page. When I asked if we could take a photo of them, they invited us to lunch. We followed them to their cottage. They'd cooked this dish in a clay pot/gamaj. It was a memorable lunch full of love.

1. **To prepare the dusting:** In a sheet pan lined with parchment paper, mix together all the dusting ingredients and set aside.

2. **To prepare the fish:** Rinse the fish and pat dry. Dredge both sides in the dusting and arrange on the sheet pan. Keep cool until ready to cook.

3. **To cook the fish:** Heat the oil in a wide sauté pan over high heat until very hot. Sear the fish until brown on both sides (about 1 minute on each side).

4. Reduce heat to low and add the garlic. Sauté the garlic for 1 minute until golden brown.

5. Add the vinegar mixture and simmer for 8 minutes over low heat until the fish is tender. Adjust seasoning to taste.

6. Garnish with parsley and serve with plain rice/*kateh*. *Nush-e joon!*

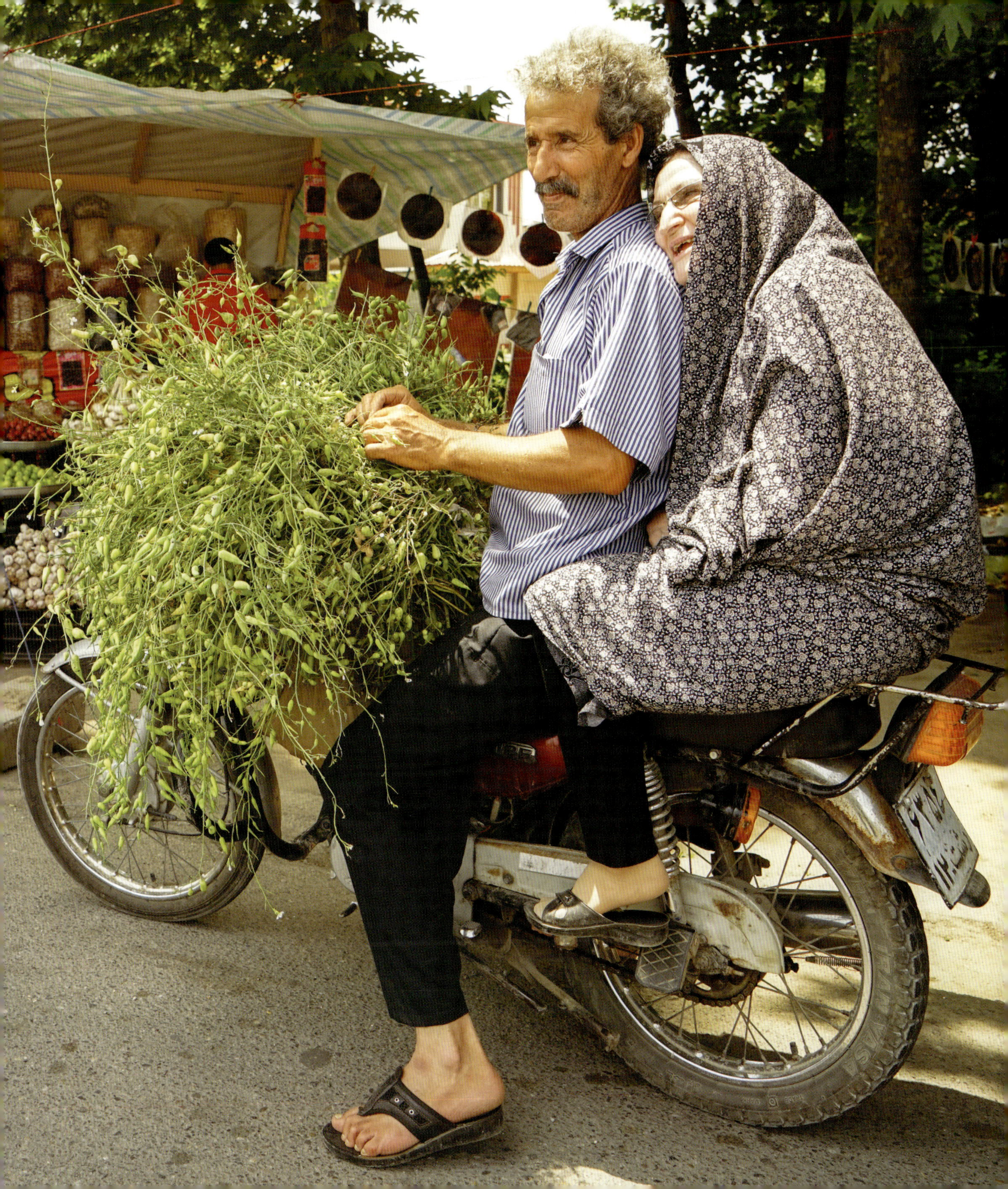

Sturgeon Kabab with Sour Orange
kabab-e uzunburun ba narenj

Serves 4
Prep: 10 minutes + 8 hours of marinating
Cooking: 6 minutes

FISH

2lb/900g sturgeon, skin removed, rinsed and cut into 2 inch/5cm cubes

MARINADE

2 medium onions, sliced
1 cup/240ml fresh lime juice
2 teaspoons fine sea salt
½ teaspoon freshly ground black pepper
1 teaspoon ground Persian hogweed seeds/*golpar* (optional)
½ cup oil

BASTE

¼ cup sour orange juice
2 tablespoons butter
2 tablespoons tomato past
½ teaspoon fine sea salt

GARNISH

¼ cup/20g chopped fresh parsley
1 sour orange, cut in half

SKEWERS

6 flat, ½ inch/1cm wide sword-like skewers

Sturgeon does not have small bones and its flesh is firm and uniquely tasty; it's a perfect fish for kababs. But the skin is very tough and must be removed for any kind of cooking. Be sure not to overcook it, as with shrimp or tuna, it can quickly become tough and dry. Once upon a time sturgeon came mainly from the Caspian, but these days it is often farmed, including in Iran and the U.S. If you can't find sturgeon fillets through your local fishmongers, try the Internet.

1. **To make the marinade:** In a mixing bowl whisk together all the ingredients for the marinade. Add the fish, toss well, cover, and refrigerate for 8 hours and up to 24 hours.

2. Start a bed of charcoal 30 minutes before you want to cook and let it burn until the coals are glowing evenly. Meanwhile, thread the cubes of fish onto the skewers.

3. **To make the baste:** In a saucepan, combine all the ingredients for the baste and bring to a boil. Keep warm.

4. **To grill the fish:** Once the coals are evenly lit, grill the fish for 1 minute on each side (do not overcook). The fish should be seared on the outside, juicy and tender on the inside. Transfer on a serving platter, sprinkle parsley on top, and add a squeeze of fresh sour orange. Serve hot with rice/*kateh* and garlic pickles. *Nush-e joon!*

Opposite: View of Ramsar from the Lotfi Restaurant in Chaboksar.

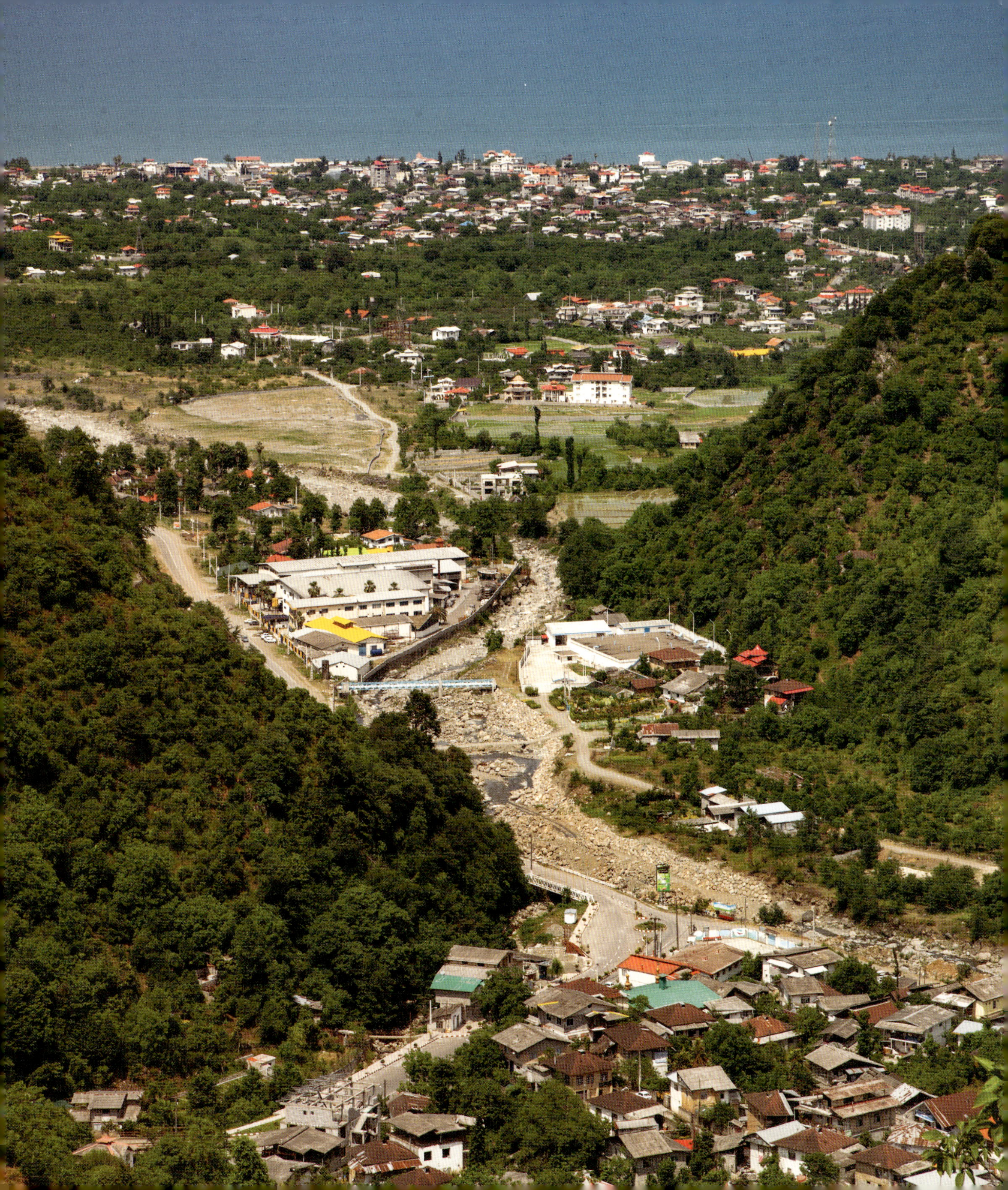

Sweet + Sour Kabab
kabab-e torsh

Makes 6 skewers, serves 4
Prep: 25 minutes + 8 hours of marinating
Cooking: 8 minutes

MEAT

2lb/900g boneless chicken thighs, lamb or beef tenderloin cut into 2½ inch/6 cm pieces

MARINADE

1 large onion, peeled and quartered
4 cloves garlic, peeled
1 cup/125g walnuts
2 tablespoons fresh basil leaves
2 tablespoons fresh mint leaves
2 tablespoons chopped fresh cilantro
½ teaspoon dried *khalvash* (optional)
½ teaspoon dried *chochaq* (optional)
2 cups/480ml pomegranate juice
¼ cup/60ml fresh lime juice
¼ cup/55g olive oil
1 teaspoon fine sea salt
1 teaspoon freshly ground pepper
1 teaspoon Persian hogweed seeds/*golpar*

SWEET + SOUR GLAZE

1 tablespoon pomegranate molasses
¼ teaspoon freshly ground pepper
1 teaspoon fine sea salt
½ teaspoon red pepper flakes
1 teaspoon ground Persian hogweed seeds/*golpar*
¼ cup/55g butter or ¼ cup/60ml olive oil

GARNISH

½ cup pomegranate arils
1 cup/100g chopped fresh spring onions

SKEWERS

6 flat, ½ inch/1cm-wide sword-like skewers

My cousins Naz and Raz took us to the Lotfi Restaurant in Chaboksar near Ramsar (photo on the facing page). I had the best sweet and sour kabab there They served it with an eggplant/miraza qasemi side dish and golden crusted rice/polow ba tah dig.

1. **To make the marinade:** Place all the ingredients for the marinade in a food processor and pulse until you have a grainy mixture. Place the chicken in a non-reactive container or bowl and pour marinade over chicken. Toss well. Cover (use plastic wrap if container doesn't have a cover) and allow chicken to marinate in the fridge for at least 8 hours and up to 48 hours.

2. **To make the glaze:** In a saucepan, combine all the ingredients for the glaze. Stir well and keep warm on very low heat until ready to use.

3. **To prepare the grill:** Start the barbecue 30 minutes before you want to cook and let it burn until the coals are glowing evenly. If you are using the oven broiler or an indoor grill make sure it is preheated and very hot.

4. In the meantime, **to skewer the kababs:** thread 4 or 5 pieces of chicken on each skewer, leaving at least 2in/5 cm free at the top of the skewers.

5. **To grill the kababs:** Place the skewers on the grill and cook for 2 to 4 minutes on each side, turning frequently. When done, baste both sides immediately, while still on the grill, with the glaze.

6. Place the skewers on a serving platter and sprinkle the pomegranate arils and spring onions over them. Serve immediately with plain rice/*kateh* and olive tapenade/*zaytun parvardeh*. Nush-e joon!

The Caspian Region

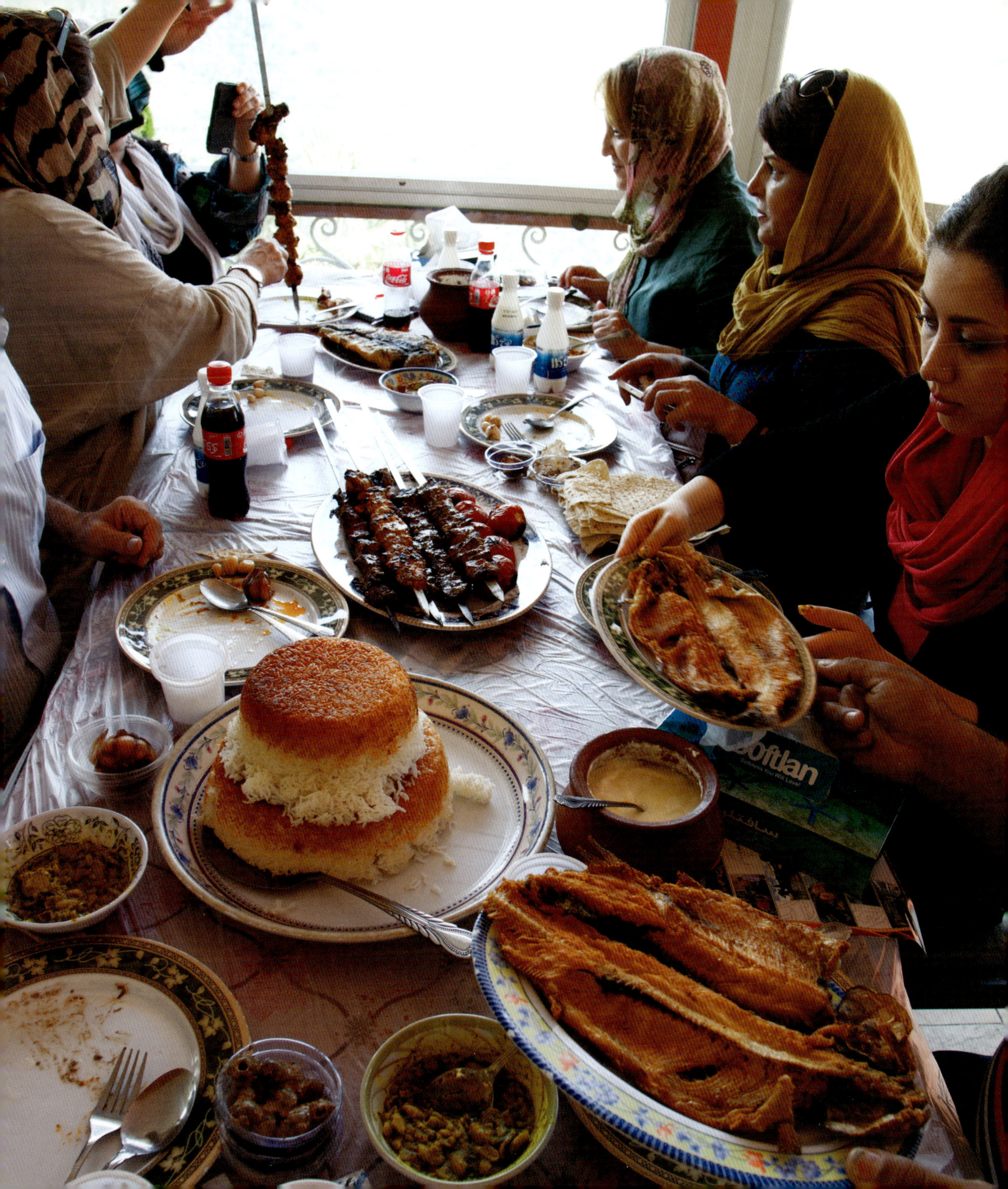

Duck Kabab
kabab-e ordak

Serves 4
Prep: 1 hour + 8 hours of marinating
Cooking: 1¼ hours

BROTH/BRINE

2 onions, thinly sliced
2 bay leaves
2 celery stalks and their leaves, coarsely chopped
1 tablespoon fine sea salt
1 teaspoon turmeric
4 cups/960ml water

DUCK

1 duck (4.5 to 5.5lb/2 to 2.5kg, Muscovy or Peking), thawed if frozen and rinsed

MARINADE

1 cup/240ml fresh lime juice
1 cup/240ml oil
1 teaspoon fine sea salt
1 teaspoon freshly ground black pepper
¼ teaspoon ground saffron threads dissolved in 1 tablespoon warm water

BASTE

2 tablespoons lime juice
2 tablespoons pomegranate molasses (optional)
1 cup butter or olive oil
¼ teaspoon fine sea salt
¼ teaspoon freshly ground pepper

In the U.S. the only way to eat a wild duck is to shoot it yourself or to get some from a duck-hunting friend. The marshes around the Caspian are migratory duck heaven. The locals hunt and sell them at the Rasht market. Teal, called khodka, is a small migratory duck, particularly popular during the autumn when they are in season. The kabab is quite delicious, especially when basted with a little pomegranate molasses.

1. **To prepare the broth:** In large pot, place the onions, bay leaves, celery, salt, and turmeric. Add the water and bring to a boil. Add the duck, including neck and giblets, and bring back to a boil. Reduce heat to low, cover, and cook for 1 hour (duck will be about half cooked).

2. Remove the duck from the broth and place it on a large cutting board. Cut out the spine bone and return it to the broth. Save the broth for a wonderful duck soup later. Cut the duck, with the bone, into 8 pieces.

3. **To prepare the marinade:** In a large glass container, whisk together all the ingredients for the marinade. Add the duck pieces to the marinade. Toss well, cover, and refrigerate for at least 8 hours and up to 24 hours.

4. Start a bed of charcoal 30 minutes before you want to cook and let it burn until the coals are glowing evenly. Meanwhile, thread the pieces of duck onto the skewers and place them on sheet pans.

5. **To prepare the baste:** In a saucepan, combine all the ingredients for the baste and keep warm.

6. **To grill the kababs:** Once the coals are glowing evenly, place the skewers on the grill, turning frequently until the duck is seared on the outside, and it is juicy and tender inside (keep in mind duck needs more cooking than chicken). Baste on all sides. Serve hot with plain rice/*kateh* and garlic pickles. *Nush-e joon!*

VARIATION

This is also how goose/*kabab-e ghaz* is cooked in Rasht.

Birds at the daily market in Rasht

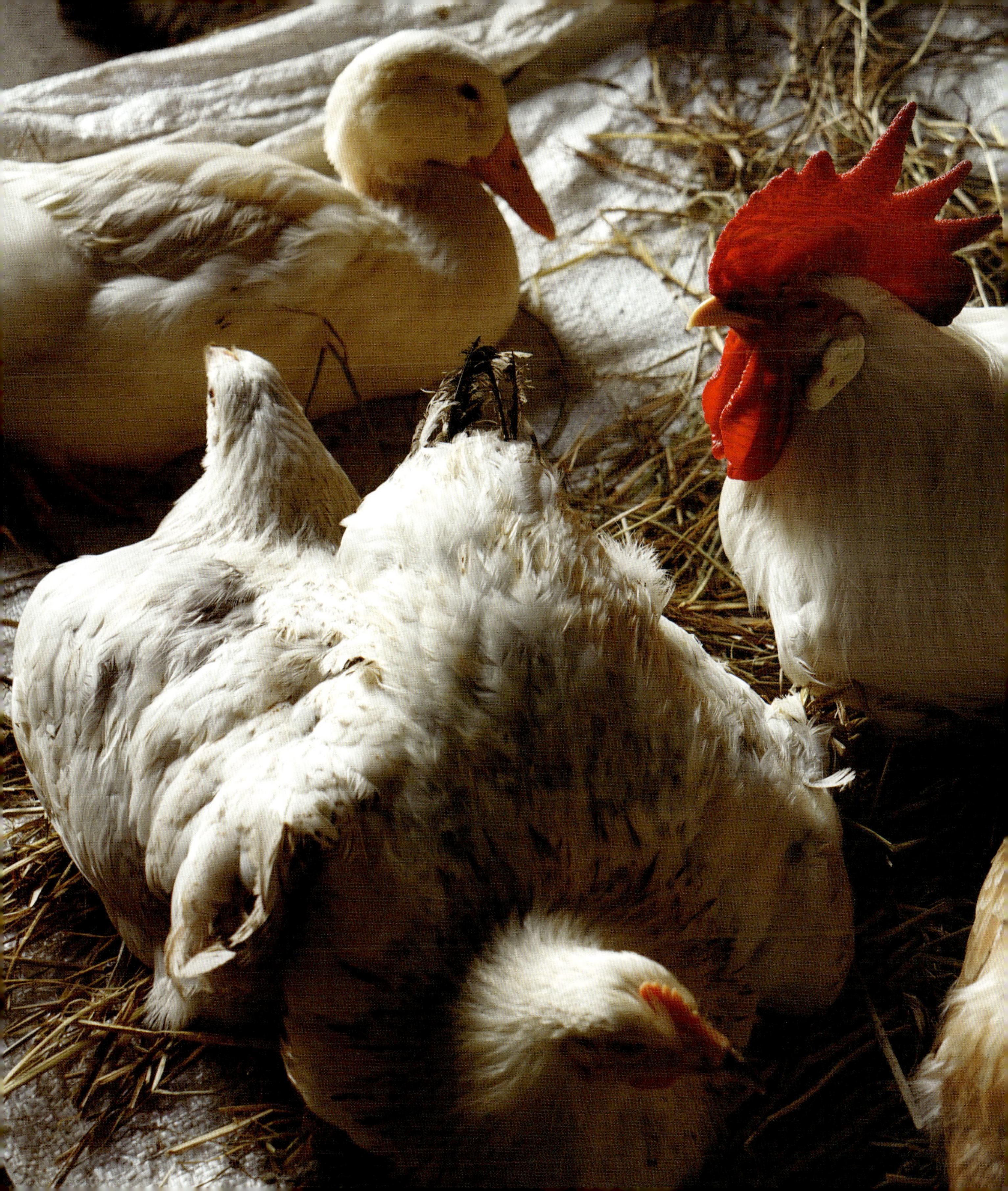

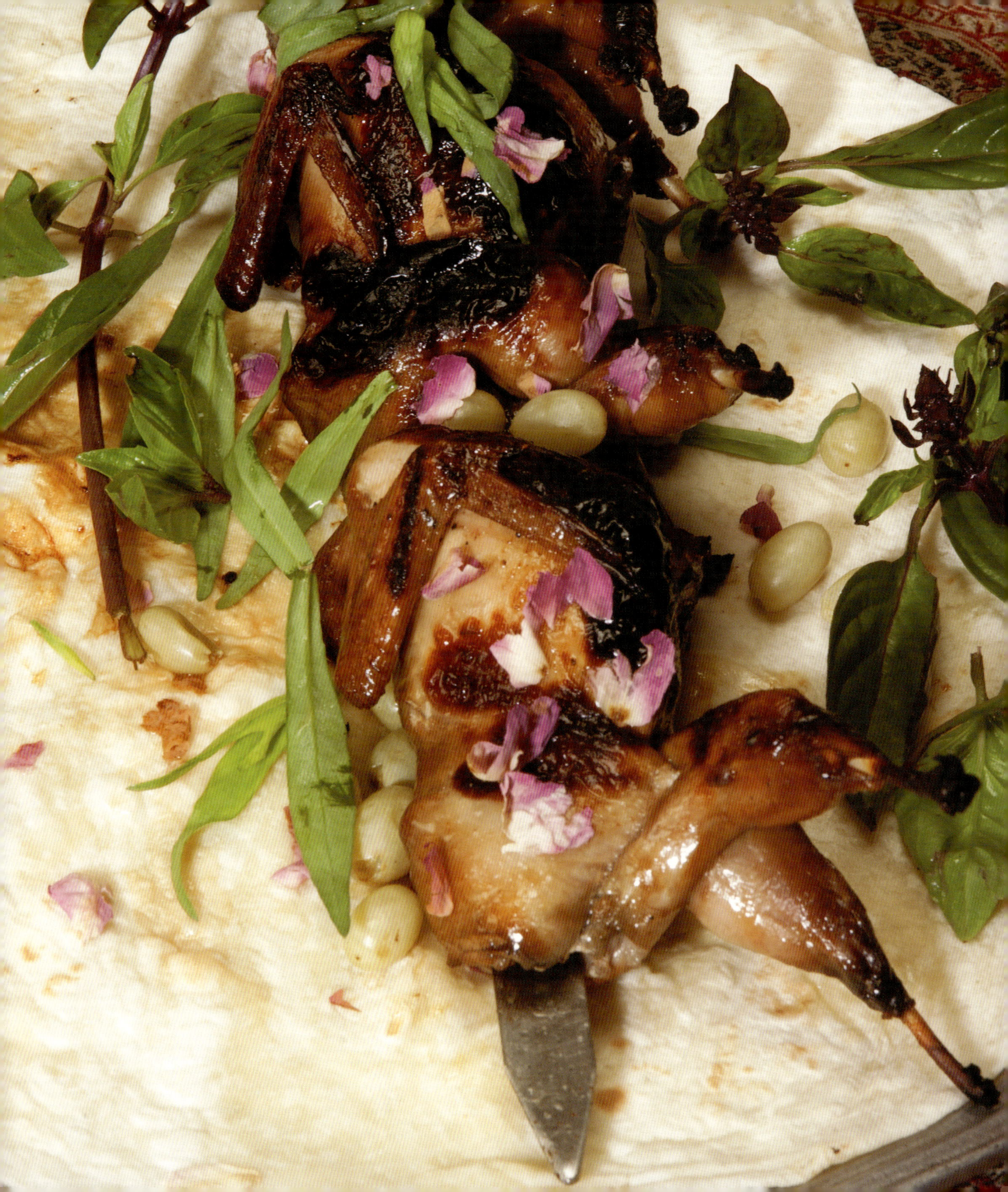

Quail Kabab

kabab-e belderchin

Serves 6
Prep: 20 minutes + 8 to 24 hours of marinating
Cooking: 20 minutes

QUAIL

12 semi-boned quails (leg and wing intact)

MARINADE

1 cup olive oil
2 cups/480ml cream
½ teaspoon ground saffron dissolved in 2 tablespoons rose water
½ cup/120ml verjuice (unripe grape juice/ab-ghureh) or ¼ cup (60ml lime juice
2 teaspoons fine sea salt
2 teaspoons freshly ground black pepper

BASTE

2 tablespoons butter
1 tablespoon fresh lime juice
1 teaspoon grape molasses (optional)

GARNISH

1 cup chopped fresh basil and tarragon leaves
¼ teaspoon coarse salt
¼ teaspoon freshly ground pepper
2 tablespoons ground dried rose petals

Quail kabab is very popular around the Caspian. In the U.S. you can find semi-boneless quail as well as whole bone-in. Both work well for this kabab, as well as for the pan-roasted and deep-fried variations.

1. *To marinate the quail:* Rinse the quails and pat dry. Make an incision through the spine of each quail and cut in half. In a non-reactive container, whisk together all the ingredients for the marinade. Rub inside and outside of the quails thoroughly with the marinade mixture.

2. Cover and allow to marinate in the refrigerator for 8 to 24 hours. Turn the quails in the marinade once during this period.

3. *To prepare the grill:* Start a bed of charcoal at least 30 minutes before you want to cook and let it burn until the coals are glowing, or turn on the grill until very hot. Spread a piece of lavash or other flat bread on a serving platter and set aside.

4. *To make the baste:* Melt the butter in a saucepan and add the rest of the ingredients for the baste. Stir well.

5. *To cook the quail:* Remove the birds from the marinade and skewer on metal skewers.

6. Cook each side 7 to 10 minutes, turning frequently. The quails are cooked when they are crisp and golden on the outside and the juices that run out are yellow and not pink (do not overcook the bird). Paint the quail with the baste just before removing from the grill.

7. Place the skewers onto the lavash bread and cover with more bread. When ready to eat, press the palm of your hand down on the bread over the kabab, pull out the skewers and garnish. *Nush-e joon!*

VARIATIONS

Pan-Roasted Quail

In a baking pan, heat 2 tablespoons butter and 1 tablespoon oil over medium-high heat and brown all sides of the quails. Remove from heat, cover, and set aside. Just before serving preheat oven to 500°F/260°C, uncover the quails, and bake in the same pan for 1 to 2 minutes until done. Paint the quails with the baste.

Deep-Fried Quail

Before marinating in step 1, parboil the quail, drain, and then marinate. Remove the quail from the marinade. Place on a sheet pan lined with parchment paper. In a wide saucepan, heat 4 cups oil until hot but not smoking. Deep-fry all side of the quails, remove with a slotted spoon, and paint with the baste.

Plain Rice
kateh

Serves 6
Prep: 5 minutes
Cooking: 1 hour

3 cups/600g white basmati rice
2 teaspoons fine sea salt
5 cups/1.2l water
¼ cup/60ml oil
¼ cup/55g ghee or butter, melted

Around the Caspian they smoke rice after harvesting and before husking. The harvested sheaves of rice are hung in a smokehouse over a smoldering mixture of rice chaff and wood, and then smoked in large containers called kalevi. The distinctive flavor of this rice is heavenly. It's hard to obtain outside Iran. If you can find smoked rice, use this recipe to make it; otherwise, this is a wonderful, simple recipe for quick and easy basmati rice.

1. Wash the rice by placing it in a large container and covering it with water. Agitate gently with your hand and pour off the water. Repeat 2 to 3 times until the water is clear.

2. Place all the ingredients except the oil and ghee in a 5qt/4.75l non-stick pot. Bring to a boil over high heat. Gently stir the rice with a wooden spoon a few times while it boils. Reduce heat to medium and cook for 10 to 15 minutes, uncovered until all the water has been absorbed.

3. After all the water has been absorbed, swirl the oil and ghee over the rice, and reduce heat to medium-low. Wrap the lid with a clean dish towel and cover the pot firmly to prevent steam from escaping. Cook for 40 minutes over medium-low heat.

4. Gently taking one spatula full of rice at a time, mound the rice on a serving platter. Separate the golden crust/*tah-dig* and serve it on the side. *Nush-e joon!*

VARIATION

Smoked Rice
kateh-ye berenj-e dudi

If you have some Caspian smoked rice, then use it; otherwise, when using regular basmati rice, to achieve a smoky taste similar to smoked rice, add 4 cloves of grated garlic in step 2 above.

Brown Basmati Rice

For brown basmati rice, use 7 cups water instead of 5 cups and increase the cooking time in step 2 to 20 to 25 minutes.

Varieties of rice at the market, where I bought some hard to find smoked rice.

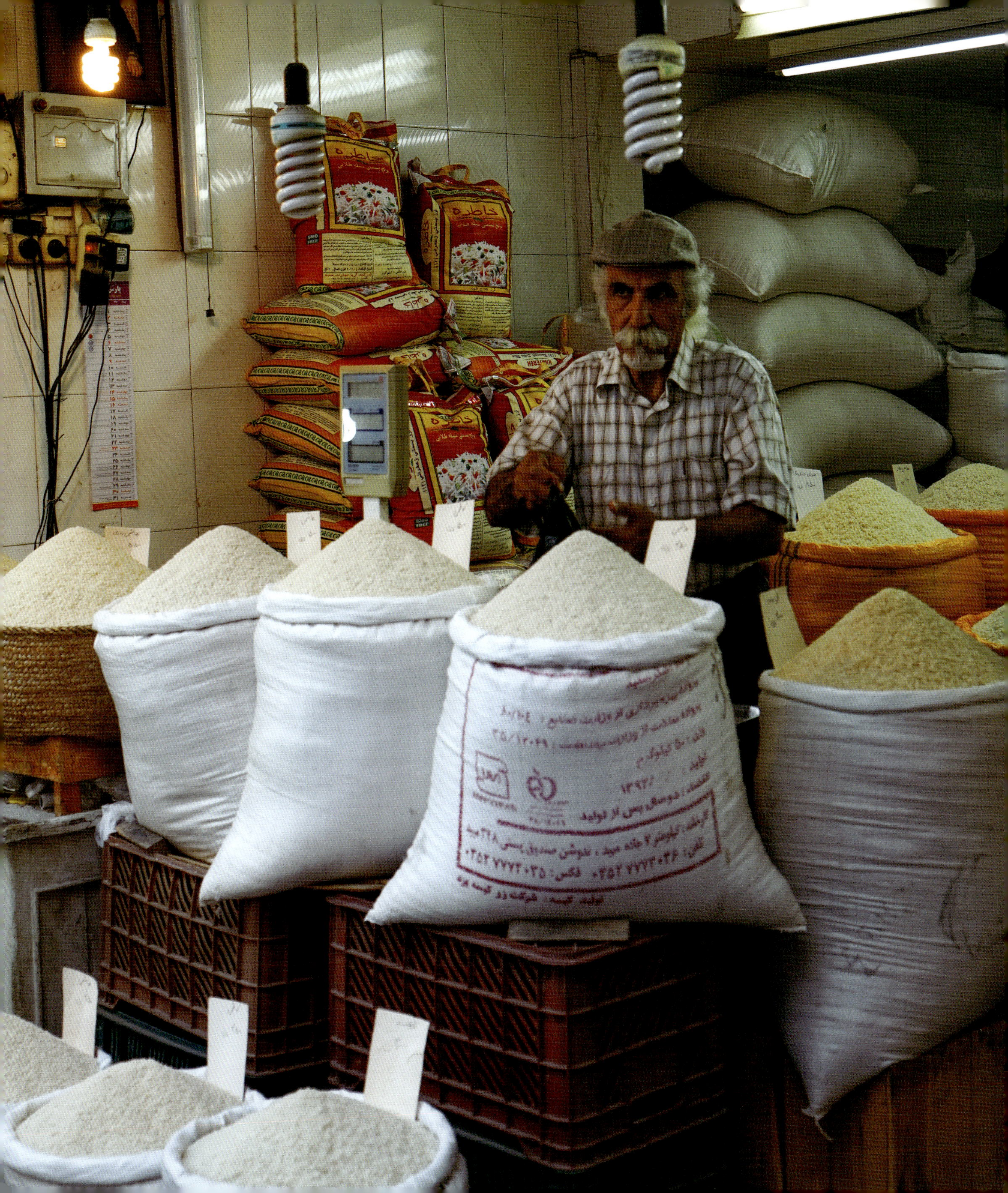

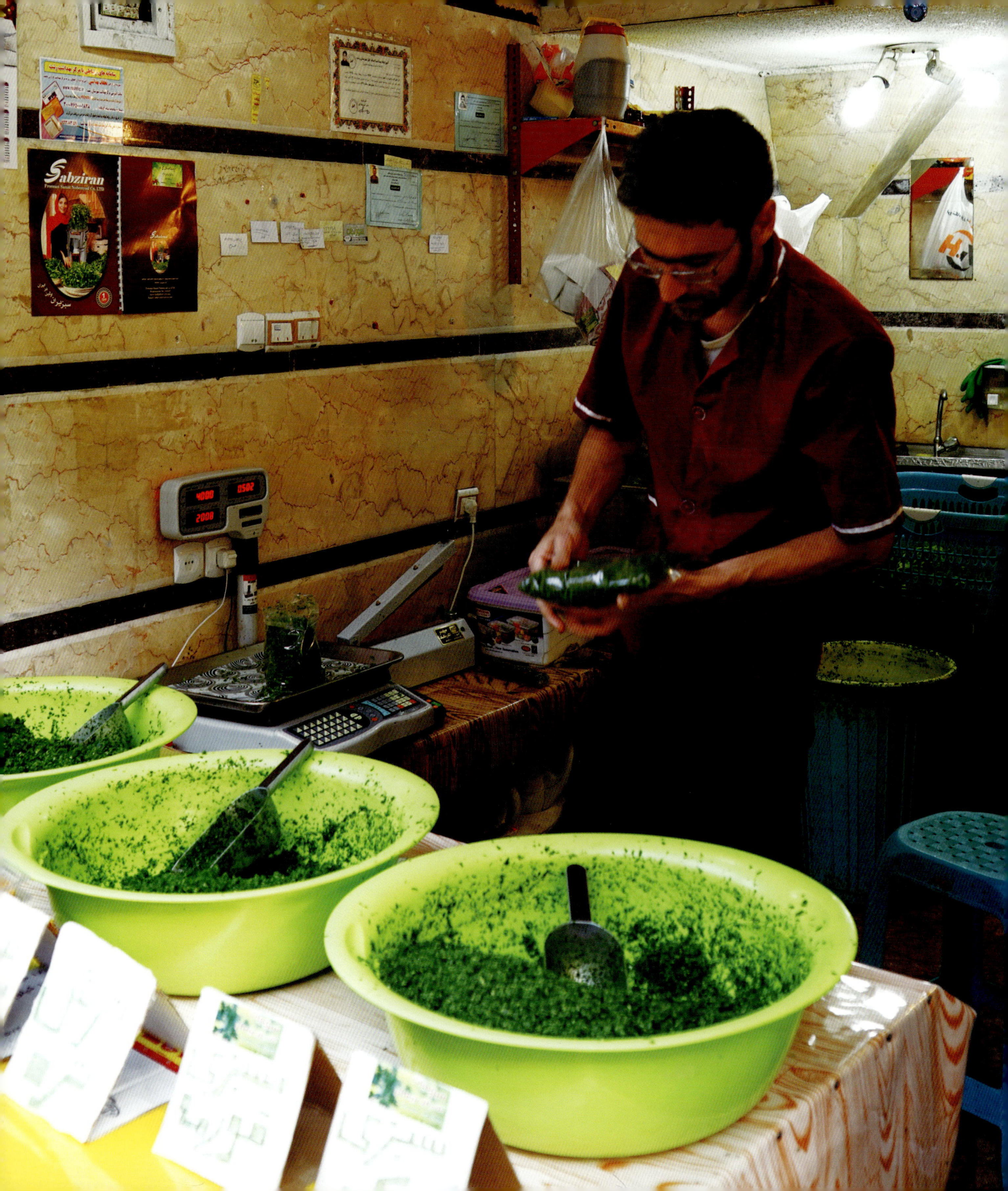
Sabziran

Opposite: A young vendor selling pre-prepared herbs for cooking dishes like Eggs, Herbs, Garlic + Sour Orange Braise/*torshi tareh*. Above: Fresh, unshelled and shelled *patch baqala*, a local, delicate, and very tasty fava bean used for the braise/*baqal qataq* (recipe on the next page). It's interesting that both around the Caspian and by the Persian Gulf, there are fish dishes that use a great amount of herbs, and in both places the markets sell the herbs already prepared. .

Duck Eggs + Fava Beans Braise
baqala qataq

Serves 6
Prep: 25 minutes
Cooking: 25 minutes

BRAISE

3lb/1.3kg fresh fava beans in the pod, or 1lb/450g frozen fava, second skins removed

½ cup/120 ml olive oil

10 cloves garlic, peeled and grated

2 teaspoons fine sea salt

½ teaspoon freshly ground pepper

1 teaspoon turmeric

½ teaspoon sugar

2 cups/170g chopped fresh dill weed or ¼ cup/20g dried

2½ cups/600ml water

EGGS

3 duck eggs

NOTE

Frozen fava beans with the second skins removed are available in Iranian markets.

Around the Caspian they refer to a braise as "qataq" instead of "khoresh," which is what a braise is called in other regions of Iran. They have small delicate fava beans called *pach baqala*, which I have not been able to find in the U.S. However, this braise, which is a perfect vegetarian dish when served over rice, is equally delicious when made with fresh fava beans, lima beans, or even edamame. The photo shows the braise slow cooked in a clay pot (*gamaj*), which I bought in the Rasht bazaar. On the table, the pot sits on its own wicker base/*gamaj daneh*.

1. **To make the braise:** If you are using fresh fava beans in pods, shell them and remove second skins.

2. In a medium-sized laminated cast-iron pot or *gamaj*, heat the oil over medium low heat. Add the garlic, fava beans, salt, pepper, and turmeric, and sauté for 1 minute.

3. Add the sugar, dill, and the water, and bring to a boil. Reduce heat. Cover and cook for 15 to 20 minutes, over low heat until the beans are tender.

4. Add the eggs. Cover and simmer over medium heat for 2 to 5 minutes or until the eggs are set. Give the mixture a stir and adjust the seasoning to taste.

5. Serve warm over smoked rice/*berenj-e dudi*. In the Caspian region, they serve this dish with salted fish and olive tapenade. *Nush-e joon!*

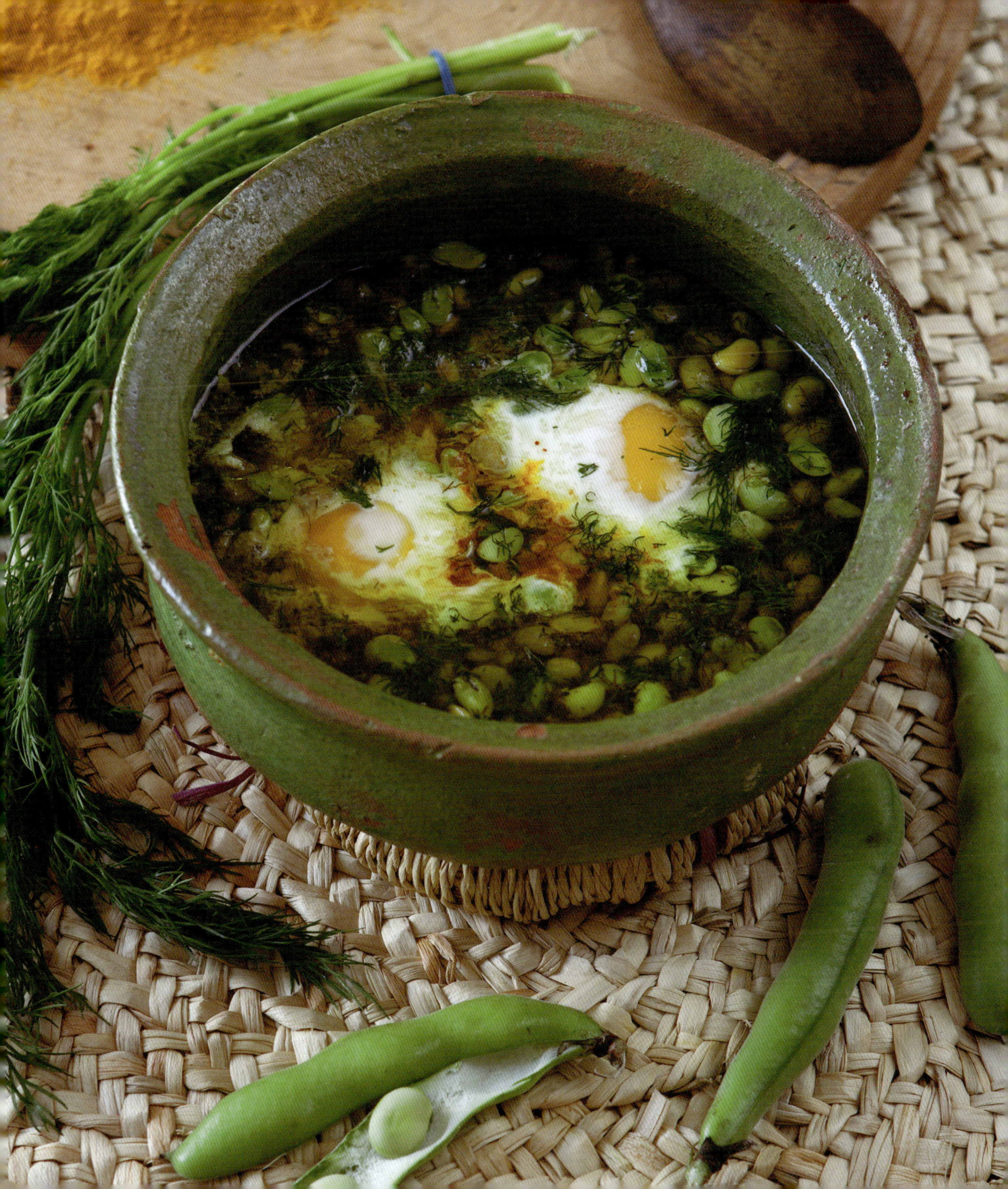

Zari Azarpira teaches cooking at her school in Rasht. We arrived at eleven o'clock with a basket of ingredients I'd bought at the market: fresh herbs, sour oranges, duck eggs, and smoked rice. We made an herb, egg, and garlic braise/*torsh tareh* served over smoked rice. ☙

A traditional, thatch-roofed, Caspian region house.

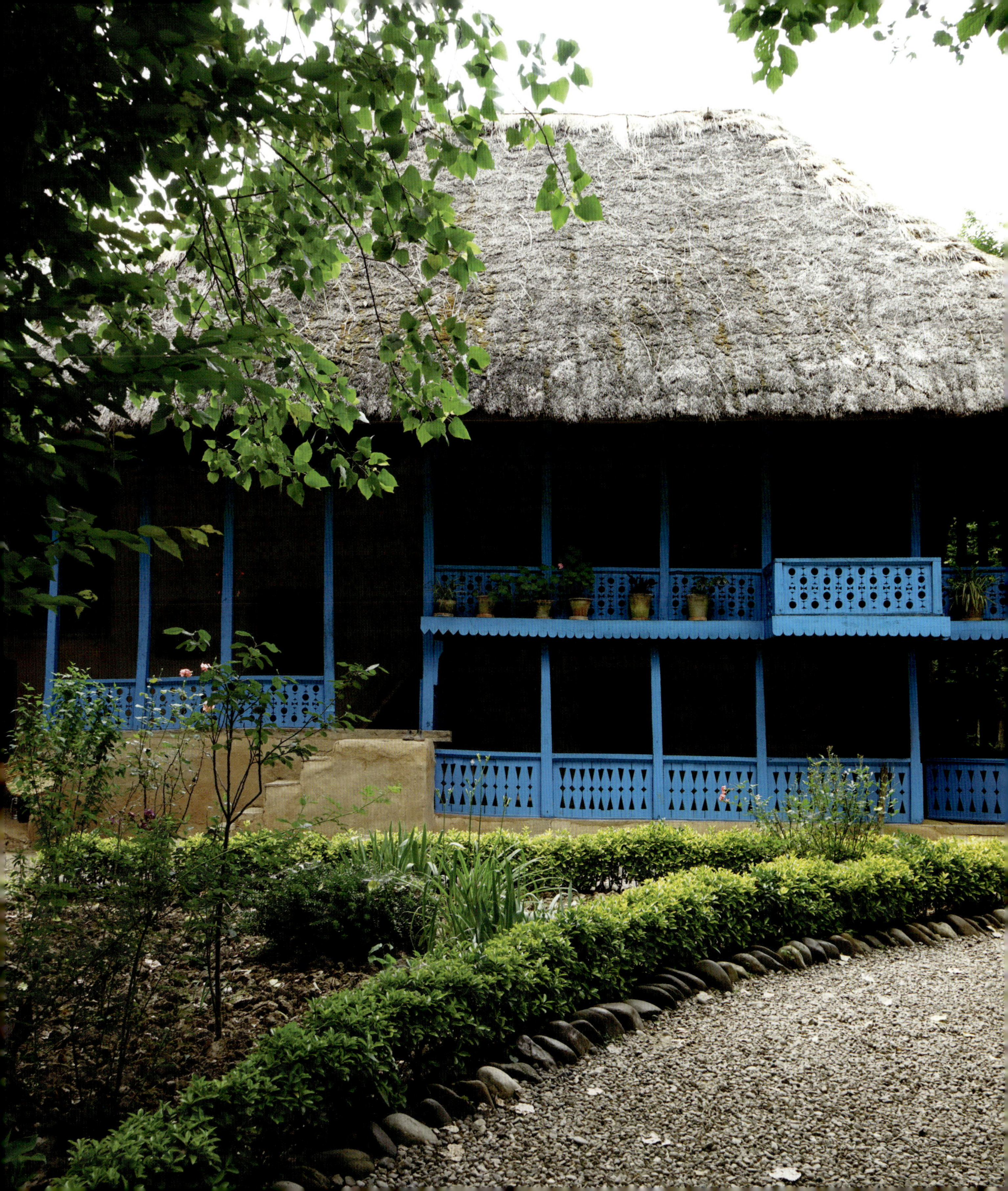

Eggs, Herbs, Garlic + Sour Orange Braise
torsh tareh

Serves 6
Prep: 20 min.
Cooking: 1¼ hours

GREEN SAUCE

2 cups/175g fresh spinach, washed and coarsely chopped, or 1 cup frozen spinach

2 cups/175g roughly chopped fresh parsley

2 cups/175g roughly chopped fresh cilantro

2 cups/175g roughly chopped fresh chives or spring onions

½ cup/40g roughly chopped fresh mint, or 2 tablespoons dried

½ cup/40g roughly chopped fresh basil or 2 tablespoons dried

½ cup/40g chopped fresh khalvash or 1 teaspoon dried (optional)

2 cloves garlic, peeled

¼ cup/60ml olive oil

1 teaspoon fine sea salt

½ teaspoon ground turmeric

1½ cups/360ml water

2 tablespoons rice flour dissolved in 1 cup/240 ml water

EGGS

½ cup/120ml oil or butter
8 cloves garlic, peeled and grated
6 eggs
1 teaspoon fine sea salt
¼ teaspoon freshly ground pepper
½ teaspoon turmeric
½ teaspoon cinnamon
1 cup/240ml fresh sour orange/narenj or ½ cup/120ml lime juice

Torsh tareh, which we made with Zari Azarpira, was one of the most delicious vegetarian braises I've ever had. And the smoked rice brought out the unique taste of this dish. The braise is traditionally made with khalvash (a local wild mint), which is not available in the U.S. In this recipe, I have replaced it with a mixture of basil and mint to approximate that taste.

1. **To make the green sauce:** Place all the herbs and garlic in a food processor and pulse until finely chopped.

2. Heat ¼ cup/60ml olive oil in a medium-sized cast-iron pot (I use le Creuset pots). Transfer the herb mixture to the pot and sauté over medium heat for a few minutes.

3. Add salt, turmeric, and 1½ cups/360ml water, and bring to a boil. Reduce heat to medium, cover, and cook for 30 minutes. Add the diluted rice flour and give it a stir. Cover, reduce heat to medium-low, and allow to simmer for another 30 minutes.

4. **To make the garlic scrambled eggs:** Heat the oil in a wide skillet over low heat until hot. Add the garlic and sauté for 20 to 30 seconds or until caramelized.

5. Break the eggs in a mixing bowl and add the salt, pepper, turmeric, and cinnamon, and lightly whisk.

6. Just before serving, add the egg mixture to the garlic and stir-fry for a few minutes until you have soft scrambled eggs.

7. Add the eggs and the sour orange juice to the green sauce in the pot. Bring back to a boil and reduce heat to low. Give it a stir. Adjust seasoning to taste. It should be a little sour.

8. Serve with plain rice/*kateh*. *Nush-e joon!*

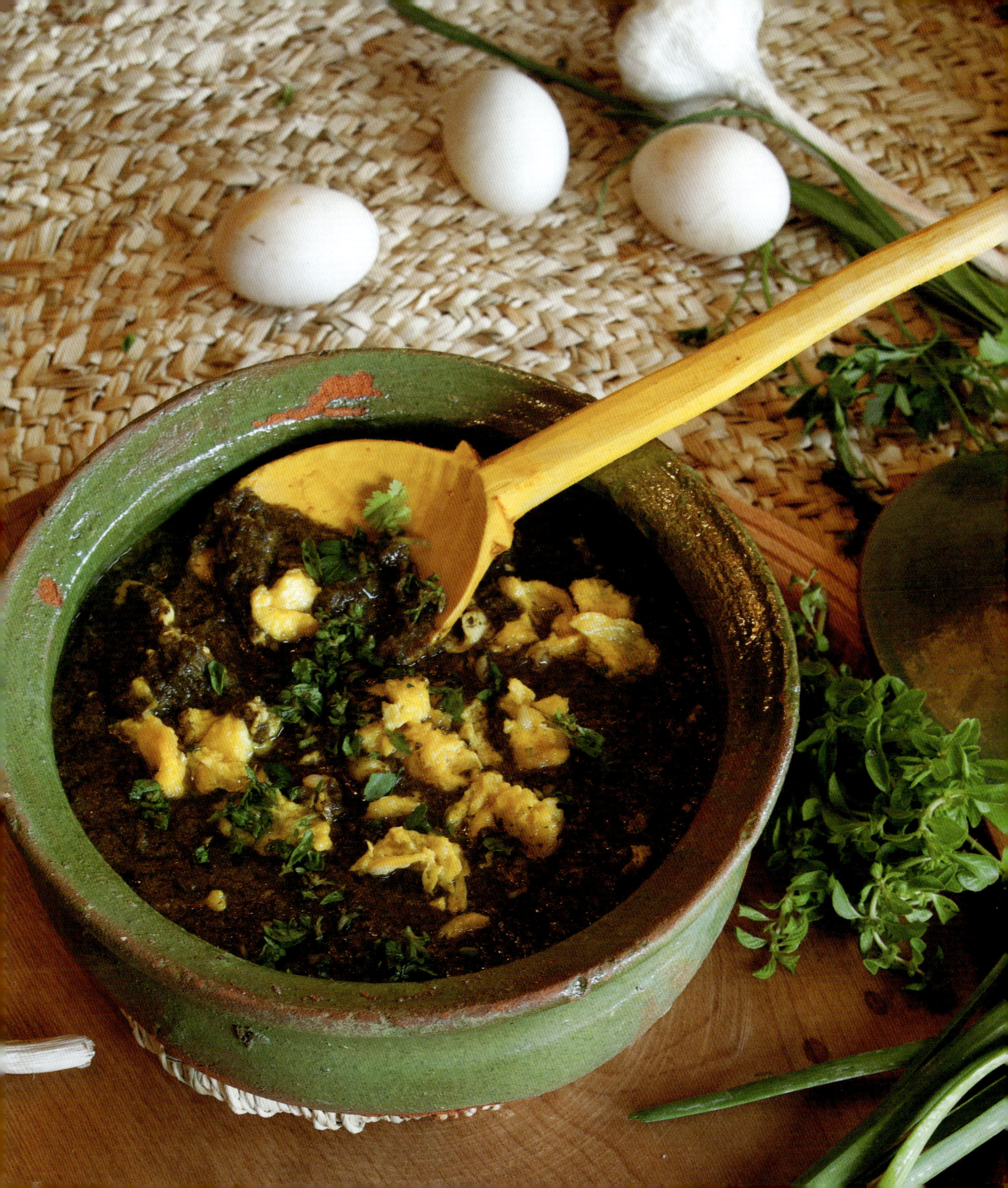

Duck + Pomegranate Braise
khoresh-e fesenjun-e gilaki ba morqabi

Serves 4
Prep: 30 minutes
Cooking: 4 hours

DUCK

1 duck about 5lb/2kg (or wild teal/*khodka*) or turkey
4 cups/960ml water
1 tablespoon fine sea salt
1 tablespoon black pepper
1 tablespoon turmeric

WALNUT PASTE

1 cup/240ml duck fat (from the duck broth)
2 large onions, coarsely chopped
4 cloves garlic, peeled
3 cups/375g walnuts
4 cups/960ml pure pomegranate juice
2 tablespoons pomegranate molasses
2 teaspoons fine sea salt
½ teaspoon freshly ground pepper
1 teaspoon cinnamon
1 tablespoon ground Persian hogweed seeds/*golpar*

GARNISH

Arils of 1 pomegranate

FESENJUN VARIATIONS

Raisin Fesenjun
Add 1 cup raisins to step 6.

Date Fesenjun
Add 10 pitted dates to step 6.

Sour Cherry Fesenjun
Replace the pomegranate juice and molasses with sour cherry juice.

Sesame Fesenjun
Replace the walnuts with raw sesame seeds

Around the Caspian they like their fesenjun sour. They also prefer it almost black, which they achieve by dropping a horseshoe/na'l-e asb into the pot (Perhaps the iron helps the oxidation. They remove the horseshoe once the braise is done and keep it handy in the kitchen for the next time). The walnuts are ground using a mortar and pestle/namak-yar. The classic combination of pomegranate and duck, loved by Iranians reflects the plenitude of both in this region since ancient times.

1. *To cook the duck:* Rinse the inside and outside of the duck thoroughly. Remove the spine and discard. Cut the duck into 6 pieces. Place the duck pieces in a large cast-iron pot and add the water, salt, pepper, and turmeric. Bring to a boil, reduce heat to low, cover, and cook for 1 hour.

2. Remove the duck from the pot and set aside. Use a spoon to draw 1 cup/240ml of duck fat from the top of the broth and set aside.

3. Remove the skin from the duck, separate the small bones from the cavity, and discard. Return the duck pieces to the pot.

4. *Meanwhile, to make the walnut paste:* In a wide skillet, heat the 1 cup duck fat over low heat until very hot and sauté the onions for 20 to 25 minutes, stirring occasionally with a wooden spoon until lightly golden brown. Add the garlic and walnuts and sauté for 1 minute longer.

5. Transfer the onion and walnut mixture to a food processor and finely grind. Add 1 cup pomegranate juice, the pomegranate molasses, salt, pepper, cinnamon, and *golpar*. Mix well to create a creamy, smooth paste.

6. Transfer the walnut paste to the pot. Add the remaining pomegranate juice (3 cups), cover, and simmer over very low heat for 2 hours, stirring occasionally with a long wooden spoon to prevent the walnut sauce on the bottom of the pot from burning. Uncover and cook for another 30 minutes over medium-low heat.

7. This braise should be sweet and sour and have the consistency of heavy cream. Adjust to taste by adding more pomegranate molasses for sourness.

8. Cover and place in a warm oven until ready to serve. Just before serving, sprinkle with fresh pomegranate arils. In the Rasht, I had this braise with smoked rice and thin slices of peeled white radishes. *Nush-e joon!*

VARIATION

fesenjun-e kashk-e tafresh
Replace the pomegranate juice with 4 cups/960ml water and replace the pomegranate molasses with 2 cups/480g liquid kashk, added in step 7.

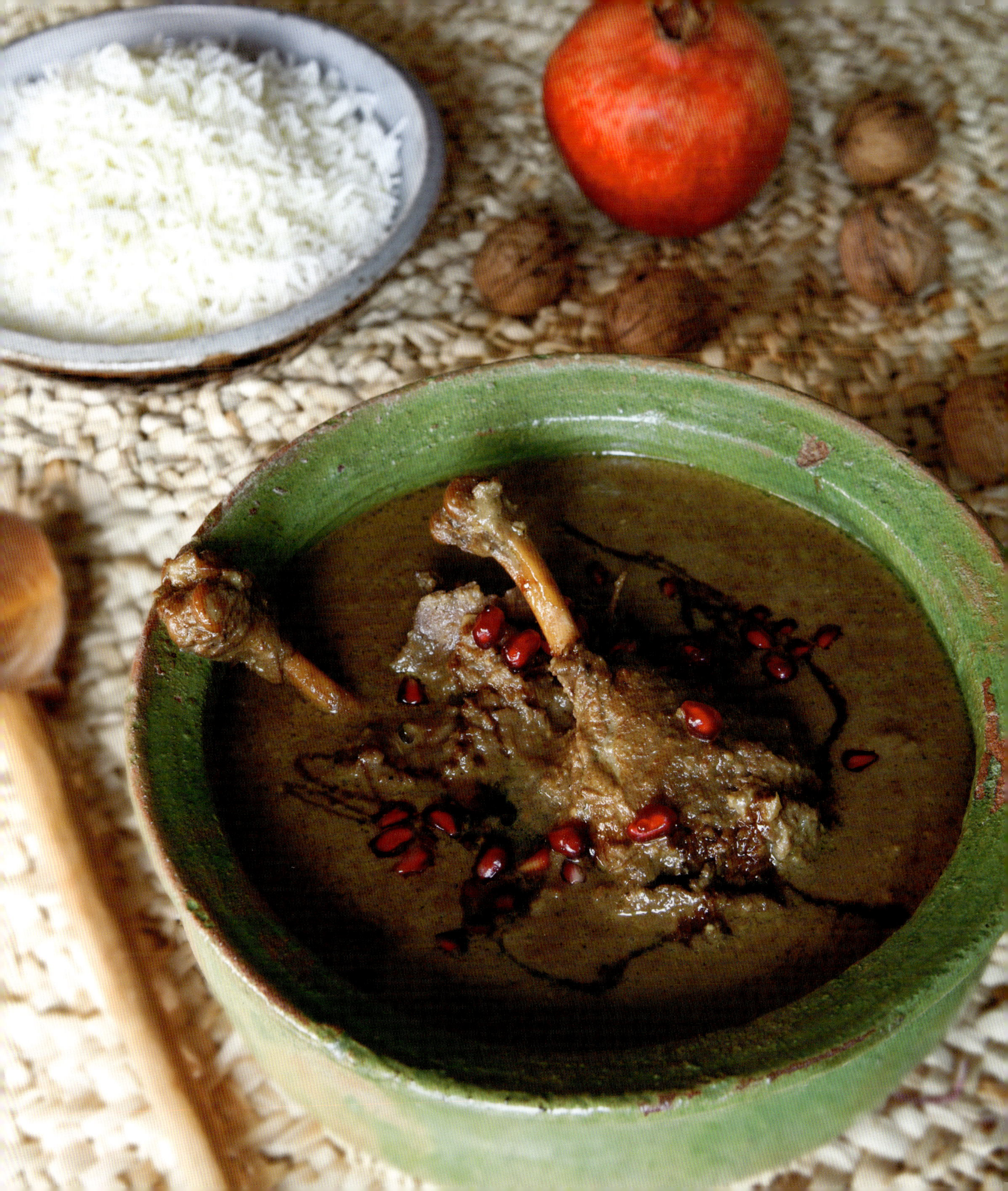

Eggplant, Walnut + Herb Braise with Meatballs

khoresh-e anar abij/sangeh khoresh

Serves 4
Prep: 25 minutes
Cooking: 1 hour

WALNUT SAUCE

4 cups/960ml pomegranate juice
1½ cups/180g walnuts

HERBS

5 cloves garlic, peeled
2 cups/170g chopped fresh parsley
2 cups/170g chopped fresh cilantro
1 tablespoon dried mint
½ cup/40g chopped fresh basil
¼ cup/20g chopped fresh *khalvash* or 1 teaspoon dried (optional)
¼ cup/20g chopped fresh *chochaq* or 1 teaspoon dried (optional)
½ cup/40g chopped spring onions
½ teaspoon ground cinnamon
1 teaspoon fine sea salt
1 teaspoon freshly ground pepper
½ teaspoon turmeric
½ cup sour orange juice or molasses

EGGPLANTS

¼ cup/60ml oil
4 Chinese eggplants (2lb/900g) peeled and sliced

MEATBALLS

1lb/450g ground chicken, turkey or lamb
1 small onion, grated
1 teaspoon fine sea salt
½ teaspoon freshly ground pepper
1 teaspoon turmeric
1 teaspoon dried mint
2 tablespoons panko bread crumbs

GARNISH

½ cup pomegranate arils (optional)
½ cup/40g chopped fresh cilantro

1. **To prepare the walnut sauce:** Place 1 cup of the pomegranate juice and the walnut in a food processor. Pulse until you have a smooth paste. Transfer to a medium-sized cast-iron pot and add the remaining pomegranate juice. Bring to a boil, reduce heat to *low*, cover, and allow to simmer for 15 minutes.

2. **To prepare the herbs:** In a food processor puree all the ingredients for the herbs until you have a smooth, green sauce. In a wide skillet, heat ¼ cup/60ml oil over low heat and sauté the eggplants for 5 minutes. Add the herbs and sauté for another 7 minutes. Transfer to the pot. Bring to a boil, reduce heat to low, cover and simmer for 30 minutes.

3. **Meanwhile, to prepare the meatballs:** In a mixing bowl, combine all the ingredients for the meatballs and lightly knead and shape the paste into walnut-sized balls. Add them gently to the pot as you make them and bring back to a boil. Cover and simmer over low heat for 40 minutes. Adjust to taste; It should be sweet and sour.

4. Garnish with pomegranate arils and cilantro, and serve with plain smoked rice/*kateh-ye berenj-e dudi* (page 122). *Nush-e joon!*

Fresh *chochagh* and *kholvash*—types of mint particular to this region—are picked daily and sold at the market.

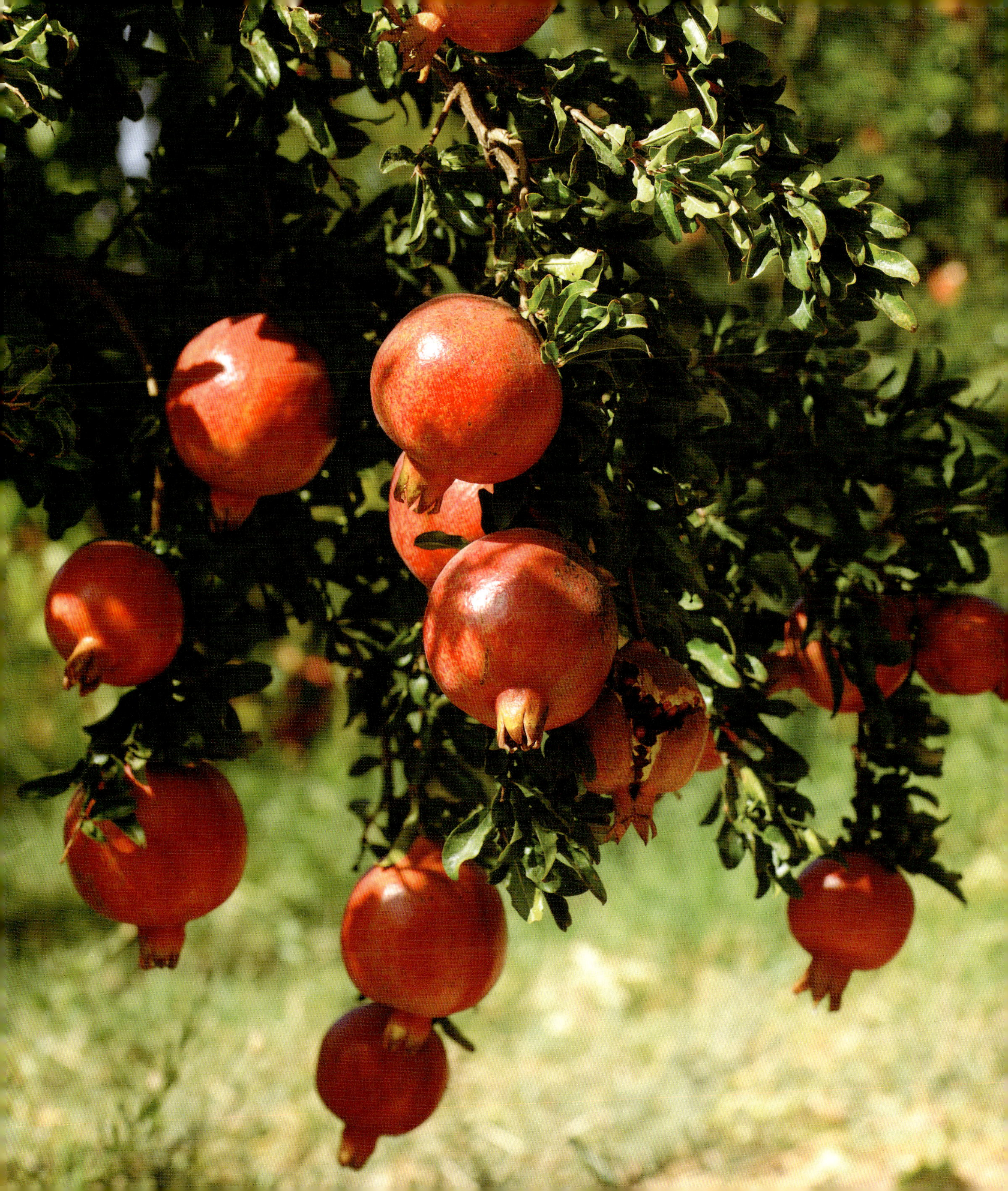

Butternut Squash, Walnut + Pomegranate Braise

khoresh-e kui-e tar

Serves 6
Prep: 45 minutes
Cooking: 45 minutes

3 tablespoons olive oil
2 medium onions, peeled and thinly sliced
1 teaspoon fine sea salt
½ teaspoon freshly ground pepper
½ teaspoon turmeric
1 tablespoon ground Persian hogweed seeds/*golpar*
3 cups/375g walnuts
4 cups/960 ml fresh pomegranate juice
1 teaspoon pomegranate molasses

ROASTING BUTTERNUT SQUASH

1 large butternut squash, about 3 pounds/1.35kg, peeled and cut into 2in /5cm cubes
½ teaspoon fine sea salt
½ teaspoon freshly ground pepper
1 tablespoon olive oil

GARNISH

½ cup/75g pomegranate arils
Sprigs of cilantro

This is a deliciously nutritious vegan braise/fesenjun. It is made throughout Iran with various nuts and fruit. The walnuts can be replaced with almonds, pistachios, hazelnuts, cashews, pecans, raw sesame seeds, or peanuts. The butternut squash can be replaced with sweet potatoes or quince.

1. In a medium-sized enameled cast-iron pot, heat 2 tablespoons oil over medium heat. Add the onions and sauté for 10 to 15 minutes until golden brown. Add the salt, pepper, turmeric, and *golpar*, and sauté for 20 seconds.

2. Transfer the walnut and the onion mixture to a food processor and finely grind. Add 1 cup of the pomegranate juice, and the pomegranate molasses, and mix well to create a smooth, creamy sauce.

3. Transfer the walnut sauce to the pot, add the remaining pomegranate juice (3 cups) and bring to a boil. Reduce heat to low, cover, and simmer for 45 minutes, stirring occasionally with a wooden spoon to prevent any sticking to the bottom of the pot and burning.

4. **Meanwhile, to roast the butternut squash:** Preheat the oven to 450F°/230C°. In a rimmed sheet pan, place the butternut squash cubes and add ½ teaspoon salt, ½ teaspoon pepper, and 1 tablespoon olive oil. Toss well with your hands, and spread evenly on the pan. Roast in the preheated oven for 15 to 20 minutes until tender.

5. Add the butternut squash to the walnut sauce, reserving some it for the garnish. Cover and cook for 15 minutes. Adjust seasoning to taste.

6. **Just before serving:** Garnish with the reserved roasted butternut squash, pomegranate arils, and sprigs of cilantro on top. Serve hot with plain rice/*kateh*. *Nush-e joon!*

The Caspian Region

VEGAN

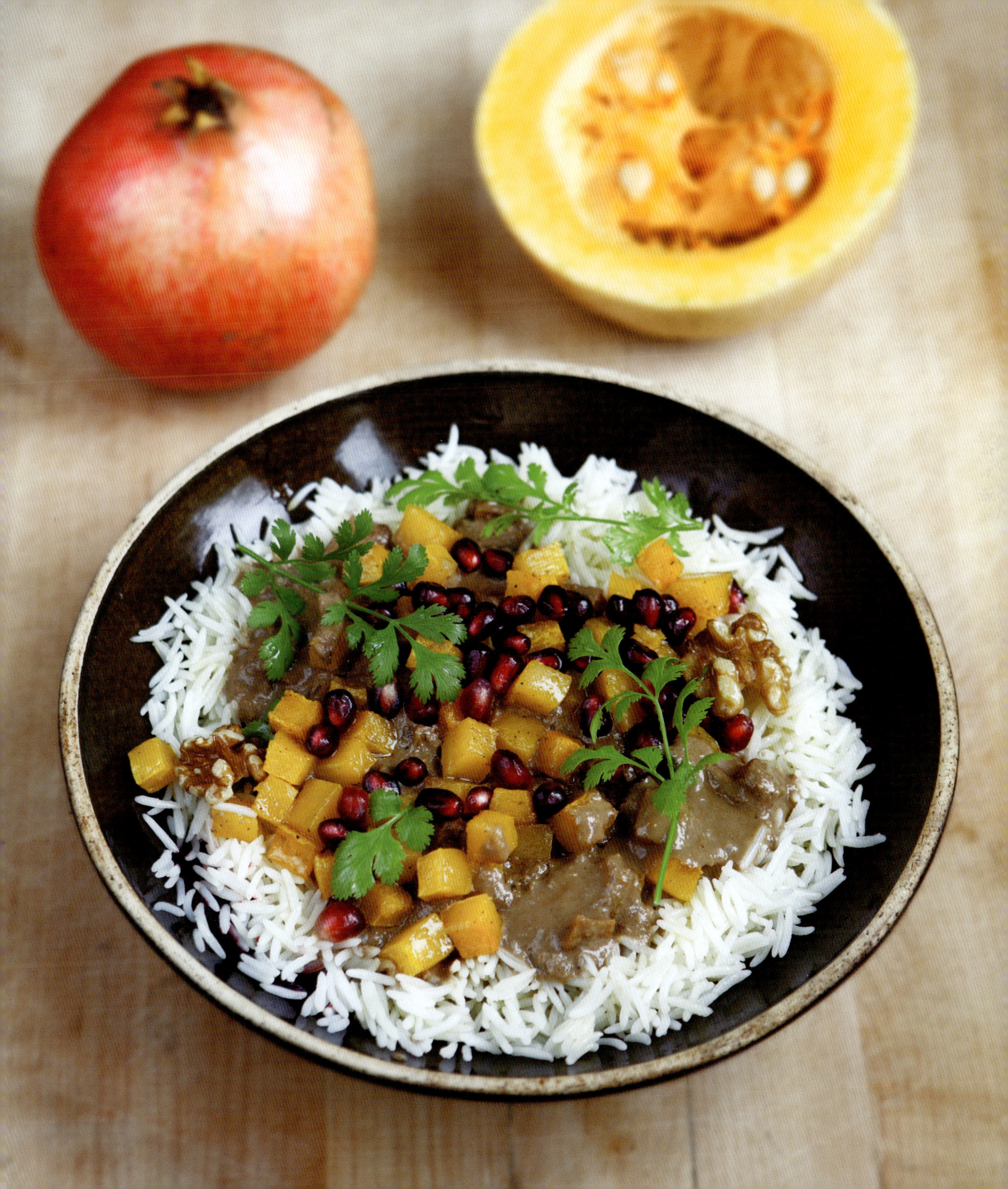

Medlar, Walnut, Pomegranate + Chicken Casserole
lavangi

Serves 6
Prep: 20 minutes
Cooking: 1½ hour

2 tablespoons oil

DUSTING

2 teaspoons fine sea salt
1 teaspoon freshly ground pepper
2 teaspoons turmeric
1 tablespoon ground Persian hogweed seeds/*golpar*

CHICKEN

1 whole chicken (3½–4lb/1.8kg), cut up

MEDLAR + WALNUT SAUCE

2 medium onions, peeled and quartered
1 cup walnuts
1 cup/85g chopped fresh cilantro
1 tablespoon dried fenugreek leaves
3 tablespoons medlar molasses
1 tablespoon pomegranate molasses
2 tablespoons oil

GARNISH

½ cup pomegranate arils (optional)
½ cup/40g chopped fresh cilantro leaves

This is a simple and delicious casserole made in the oven. I adapted the recipe from Parivash Shafi`i.

1. Place the oven rack in the center and preheat the oven to 350°F/180°F

2. Use your hands to thoroughly oil the bottom and all sides of an enameled stoneware baking dish with cover.

3. ***For the dusting:*** In a small bowl, combine all the ingredients and mix well.

4. ***To prepare the chicken:*** Dust the chicken pieces thoroughly and arrange them in the baking dish.

5. ***To prepare the medlar and walnut sauce:*** In a food processor, place all the ingredients for the sauce and pulse until you have a grainy mixture.

6. Spread the sauce over the chicken. Cover and bake for 90 minutes.

7. Adjust seasoning to taste. Garnish and serve with rice/kateh or bread. *Nush-e joon!*

A rice field near the Caspian.

The Caspian Region

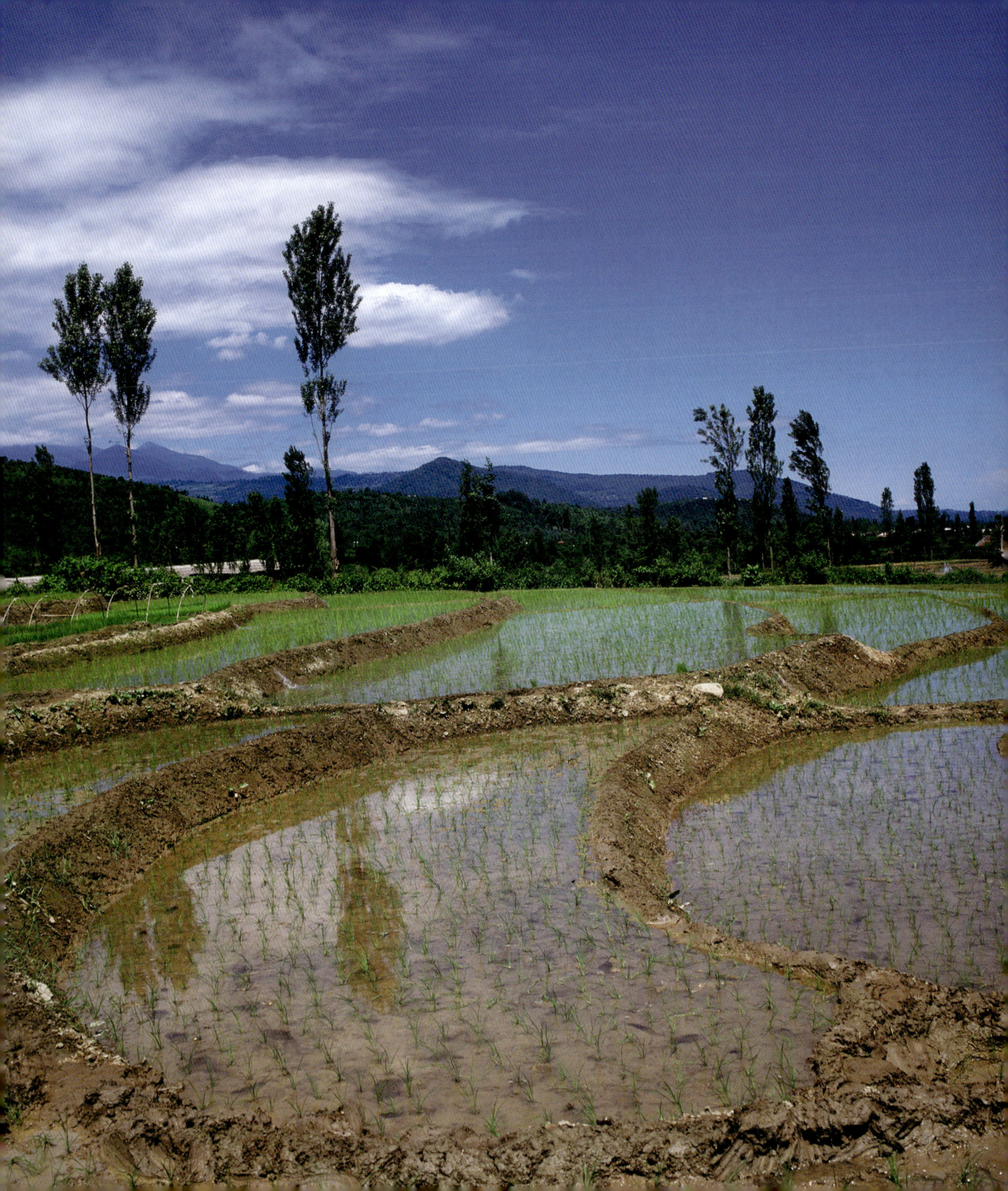

Sour Cherry Braise
khoresh-e albalu-ye gorgani

Serves 4 to 6
Prep: 30 minutes
Cooking: 1¼ hours

MEATBALLS

1lb/450g ground chicken thighs
1 small onion, grated
1 teaspoon fine sea salt
½ teaspoon freshly ground pepper
½ teaspoon turmeric
½ teaspoon ground cardamom
½ teaspoon cinnamon
2 tablespoons rice flour
3 tablespoons oil

KHORESH

2 tablespoons oil or ghee
2 medium onions, peeled and thinly sliced
1 teaspoon fine sea salt
½ teaspoon freshly ground pepper
½ teaspoon turmeric
½ teaspoon ground cinnamon
1½ cup/360ml chicken broth or water
1lb/450g fresh or frozen pitted cherries
½ teaspoon ground saffron dissolved in 2 tablespoons water
1 teaspoon cayenne (optional)
¼ cup sugar (if cherries too sour)
2 tablespoons fresh lime juice (if sour cherries are not sour enough)

GARNISH

1 tablespoon oil
½ cup/60g slivered almonds
½ cup/60g sliver pistachios

I adapted this earthy, tangy caramelized sour cherry braise with tiny meatballs/kufteh-ye kaleh gonshiki from Khanum-e Farideh Gorgani.

1. **To make the meatballs:** Place all the ingredients for the meatballs except the oil in a mixing bowl. Knead lightly, cover and allow to rest in the fridge for 10 minutes.

2. In a wide skillet heat 3 tablespoons oil over low heat until very hot. Shape the paste into hazelnut-sized meatballs and add them carefully to skillet as you make them. Swirl and shake the skillet back and forth to brown the meatballs all over. Set aside.

3. **To make the braise:** In an enameled cast-iron pot, heat 2 tablespoons oil over medium-low heat and sauté the onions until golden brown. Add salt, pepper, turmeric, and cinnamon, and sauté for 1 minute. Add 1½ cups/360ml water and bring to a boil. Add the meatballs. Reduce heat to low, cover, and simmer for 45 minutes until the meatballs are tender.

4. Add the cherries, saffron, cayenne, and sugar or lime juice (depending if you need to make it more or less sweet), and simmer over medium heat for 30 minutes. Reduce heat and keep warm.

5. **Meanwhile, to make the garnish:** Heat 1 tablespoon oil in a wide skillet over medium-low heat. Add the nuts and stir-fry for 20 seconds. Remove the nuts from the skillet and set aside.

6. Just before serving, adjust seasoning to taste. Add the nuts and serve with plain rice/kateh. Nush-e joon!

The Caspian Region

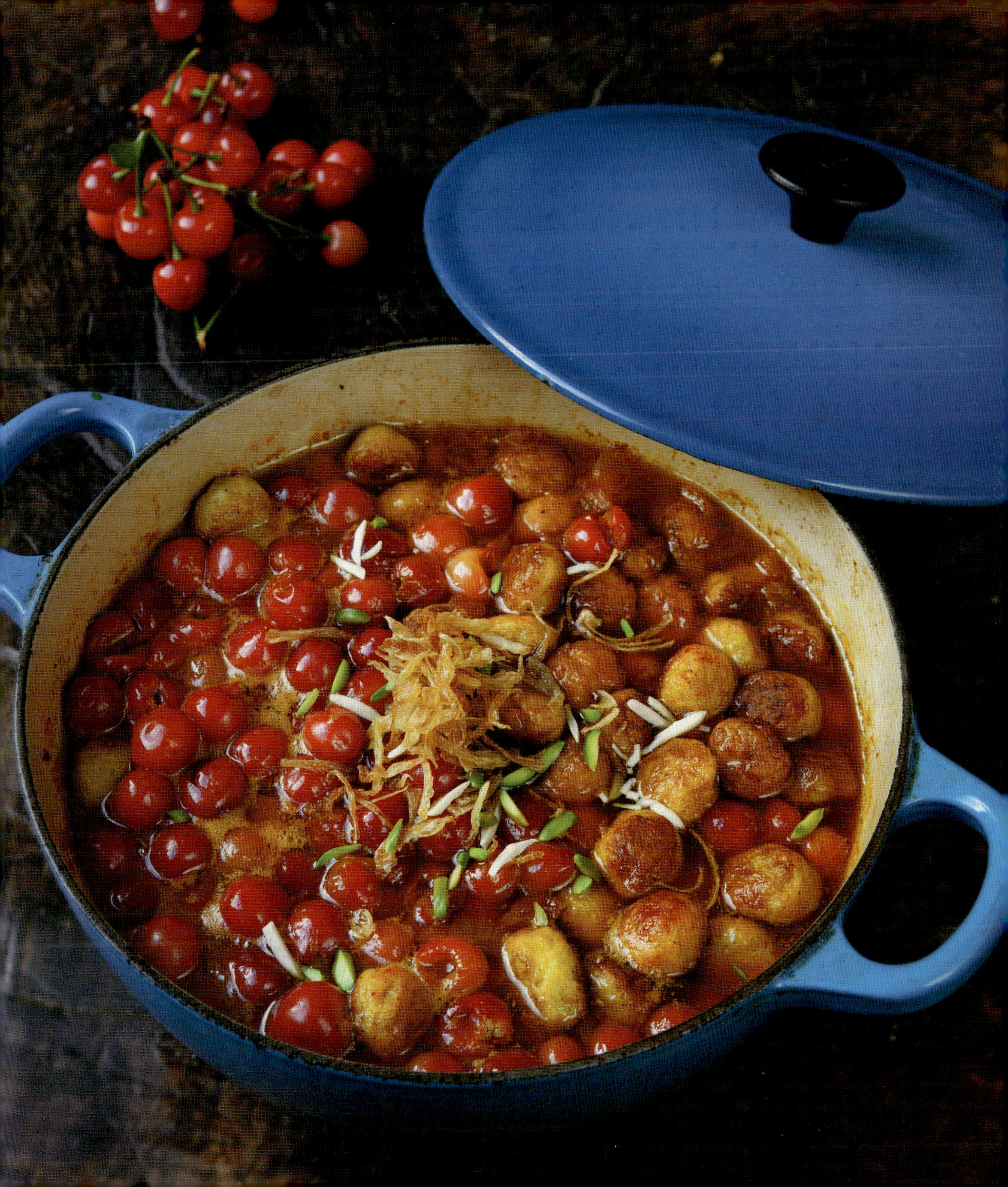

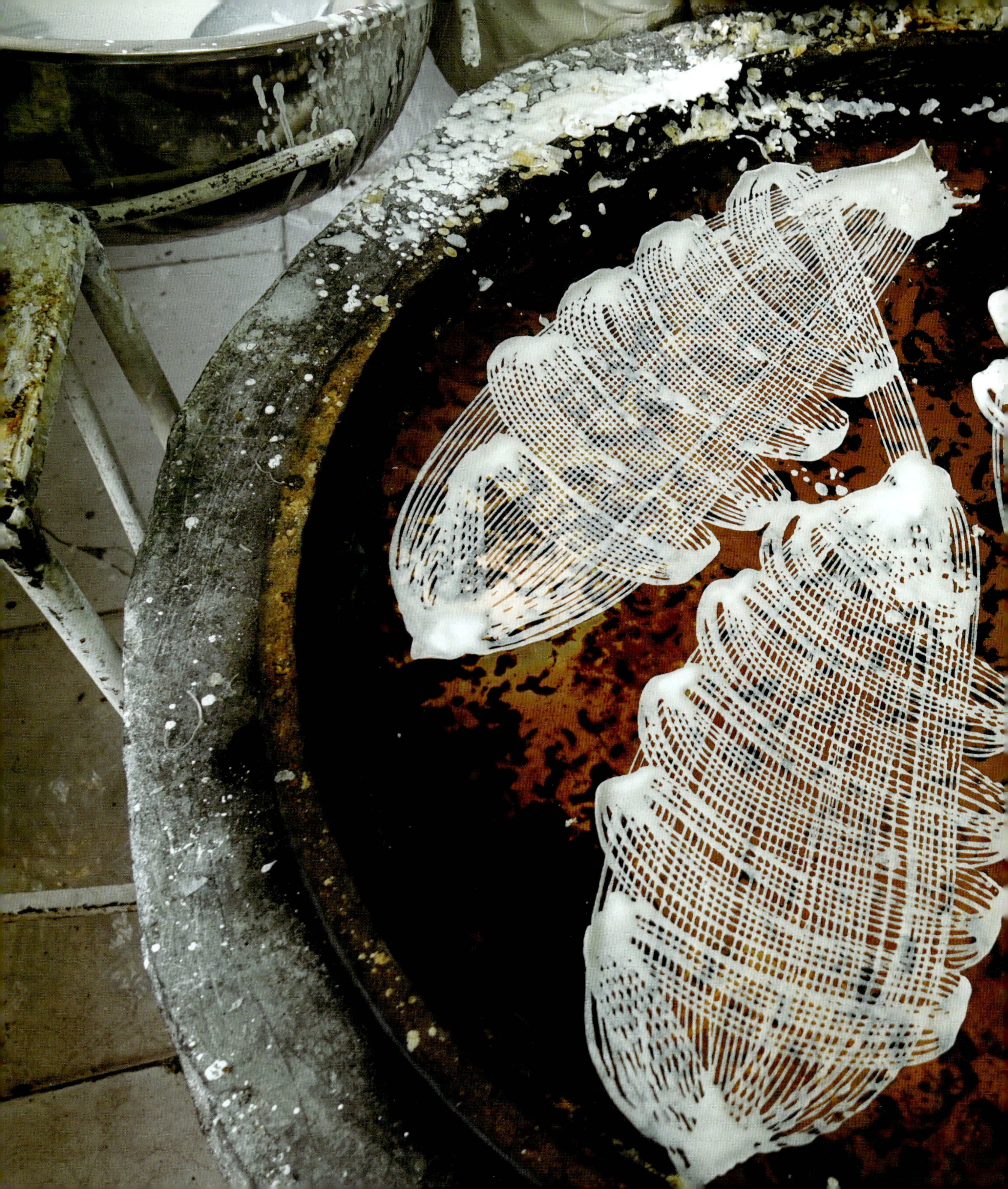

An aroma drew me to a man who was making rice pancakes. They didn't look like regular pancakes or crepes, but rather lacy works of art. A filigree of rice dough was then filled with a mixture of ground walnuts and sugar, and folded into a neat, artistic parcel. I bought a bunch of them to take to our host for our dessert. She told us we should fry them in a little brown butter and drizzle some sugar syrup on top. They were delicious! Recipe is on the next page.

Rice Lace Pancakes

reshteh-ye khoshkar

Makes 6 pancakes, serves 4 to 6
Prep: 30 minutes
Cooking: 10 minutes

SYRUP

½ cup/100g sugar
1 cup/240ml water
¼ cup/60ml rose water
½ teaspoon ground cardamom

BATTER

1 cup + 2 tablespoons/170g rice flour dissolved in 1 cup boiling water
¼ cup/30g all-purpose flour

FOR COOKING

1 egg yolk, at room temperature, whisked with 2 tablespoons butter

FILLING

1 cup/125g ground walnuts
2 tablespoons sugar
½ teaspoon ground cardamom
½ teaspoon ground cinnamon

GARNISH

4 tablespoons ground pistachio kernels

TRADITIONAL STYLE

Traditionally in Rasht, they start with rice instead of rice flour for making the batter: Soak 3 cups/600g rice overnight and drain in a fine-mesh colander. Allow to sit for 10 minutes. Transfer to a food processor and grind until smooth. Pass through a sieve. Continue with step 2.

Reshteh-ye khoskar is a popular street snack in Gilan. It's associated with Ramadan (the month of fasting), served as a dessert for the iftar (breaking the fast) dinner. Locals generally buy them ready-made in the market as a lace pancake and, then, just before serving, cook them in a little butter, drizzle some syrup over them, and sprinkle ground pistachio on top. They are usually served warm. I am sharing this homemade recipe so you can make it either as a thin pancake or as a lace, which is a little more exacting. Traditionally, they have a metal device that is used to spread the batter onto the skillet. I have adapted this recipe from Aqa Soleyman, a vendor at the market. Photo on the previous page shows him making the pancakes in the bazaar, and below are some of the finished lace pancakes.

1. *To make the syrup:* Combine all the ingredients in a small saucepan. Stir well until the sugar dissolves completely. Bring to a boil (be careful not to overboil), remove from heat, and set aside to cool. Use this syrup at room temperature.

2. *To make the batter:* Place the dissolved rice flour in a food processor, add the all-purpose flour, and mix for about 5 minutes until you have a batter that has a thick yogurt-like texture. Pass through a sieve so you have a smooth batter. Fill a clean squeeze bottle or pastry bag with the batter.

3. *To make the filling:* Place all the ingredients for the filling in the food processor and pulse until you have a smooth powder.

4. *To cook the pancakes:* Heat a wide skillet over low heat. Paint the skillet with a little of the egg yolk and butter mixture.

5. Hold the squeeze bottle perpendicular over the skillet and squeeze batter into the skillet by twirling it fast left and right into a 3 x 6in/6 x 10cm rectangular lace pancake. Use an offset spatula to remove the pancake from the pan and place it on a sheet pan lined with parchment paper.

6. Sprinkle a spoonful of the filling over the pancake and then roll and fold it like a parcel. Set aside.

7. *When you are ready to serve:* Heat 2 tablespoons butter in the skillet over medium heat and fry each side of the parcels until golden.

8. Remove from the skillet with an offset spatula and gently drop it into the syrup. Allow to soak for 30 seconds. Remove it from the syrup and place it on a serving platter. Repeat for the remaining pancakes. Garnish with the ground pistachio. *Nush-e joon!*

Fuman Bun

kolucheh-ye fuman

Makes 24 scones (3in/7.5cm each)
Prep: 20 minutes plus 4 hours resting
Cooking: 22 minutes

DOUGH

- 1 package (1 tablespoon) active dry yeast
- ½ cup/120ml warm water (100°F/38°C)
- 1 tablespoon sugar
- 2 eggs
- ½ cup/110g melted butter or oil
- ½ cup/120g yogurt
- ½ cup/120ml milk
- 4 to 5 cups/400 to 500g unbleached all-purpose flour, sifted with 1 teaspoon baking powder, ¼ teaspoon salt and 4 tablespoons powder sugar

FILLING

- 2 tablespoons butter or oil
- 2 tablespoons all-purpose flour
- 1 tablespoon ground nutmeg (or 1 whole nutmeg, grated)
- 1 teaspoon ground cinnamon
- 1 teaspoon ground cardamom
- 3 cups/375g walnuts
- 2 cups/260g powder sugar
- ½ cup/120ml rose water

EGG WASH

- 1 egg yolk, beaten with the mixture of ¼ teaspoon ground saffron 2 tablespoons of rose water, and 2 tablespoons milk

GARNISH

- 2 tablespoons raw poppy or sesame seeds

1. *To make the dough:* In a food processor, dissolve the yeast in the warm water. Add 1 tablespoon sugar and allow to rest for 10 minutes.

2. Add the eggs, one at a time, butter, yogurt, and milk. Mix until creamy.

3. Gradually add 4 cups of the sifted flour mixture to the food processor and mix for 4 to 5 minutes until you have a soft, sticky dough.

4. Remove dough from the food processor and turn it in a generously oiled, wide bowl to ensure it is evenly coated. Cover with plastic wrap and allow to rest at room temperature for at least 4 hours or overnight.

5. *To make the filling:* Heat the butter in a medium-sized skillet over medium heat. Add the flour and stir-fry for 1 minute until the color of the flour changes slightly. Transfer it to the food processor. Add the rest of the ingredients for the filling and pulse until you have a soft paste. Divide paste into 24 portions.

6. Place the oven rack in the center and preheat the oven to 375°F/190°C. Line 2 sheet pans with parchment paper.

7. On a cool, floured surface, transfer the dough and make a 48in/120cm long rod (add more all-purpose flour if necessary) and divide it into 24 sections. Shape into balls. Roll out each ball into a 4in/10cm diameter disc.

8. Place one portion of the filling in the center of each disc. Gently lift the disc, gather, and pinch the edges to seal the filling inside, then twist to create a knot on top. Turn the disc over and gently press it down using a rolling pin to flatten it out.

9. Lay the scones on the lined baking sheets 2in/5cm apart.

10. Use a stamp to decorate the top. If you don't have the Fuman stamp just use the edge of any round cookie cutter and decorate according to your fancy (keep in mind that the stamp should lightly go through the dough to prevent the scone from rising).

11. Brush each scone generously with the egg wash. Sprinkle poppy seeds on top.

12. Bake for 15 to 20 minutes until the scones are lightly brown and a tester comes out clean.

13. Remove from the oven and allow to cool. Arrange in a basket and serve with tea. To keep for later use, store in the refrigerator in a covered glass container. *Nush-e joon!*

Baking the famous Fuman scones in the village of Fuman near Rasht.

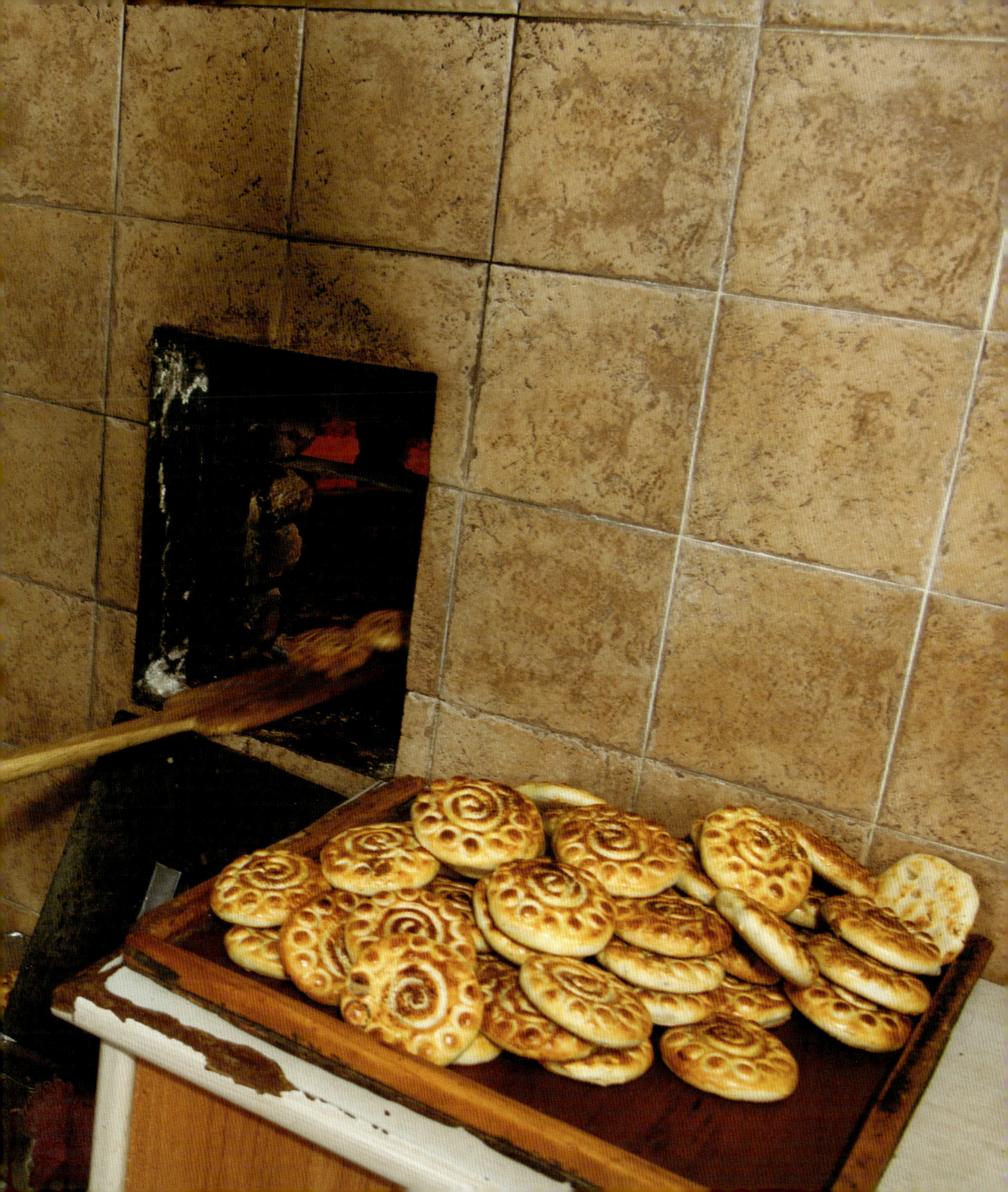

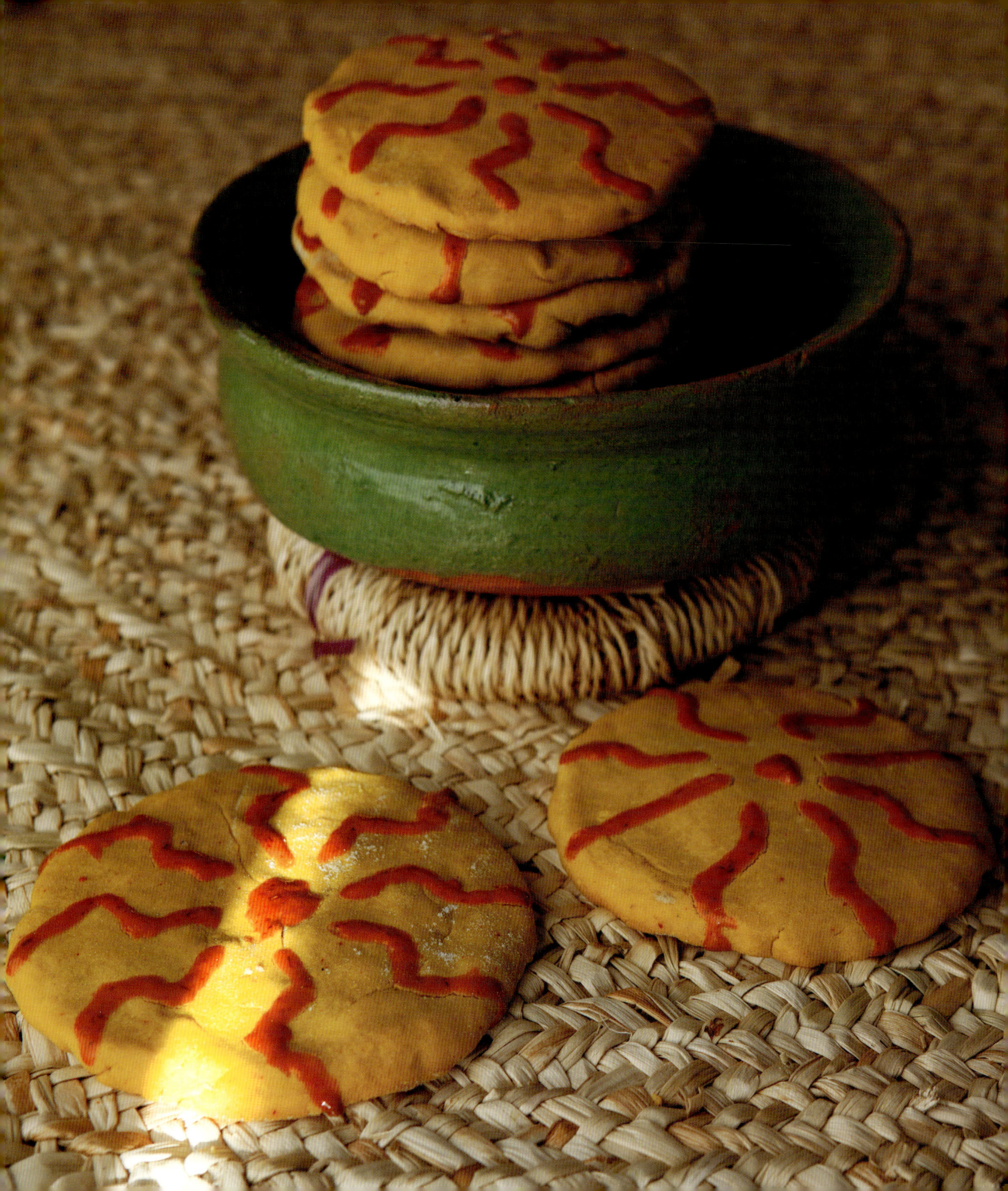

Saffroned Rice Flour Cookies with a Walnut + Cardamom Filling

shekam por/shirini-e sam-e pusteh

Makes eight 5in/12.5cm cookies
Prep: 15 minutes + 2 hours of resting dough
Cooking: 20 minutes

DOUGH

3 cups/450g rice flour
1 cup water, boiling
1 cup/130g powdered sugar
1 cup/225g butter or oil (240ml)
½ teaspoon ground saffron dissolved in 2 tablespoons rose water
5 egg yolks

FILLING

1 cup/125g walnuts
½ cup/65g powdered sugar
2 teaspoons ground cardamom
2 tablespoons rose water

EGG WASH

1 egg yolk
¼ teaspoon ground saffron threads

1. **To make the dough:** In a mixing bowl, whisk together the rice flour and boiling water until you have a grainy paste. Set aside.

2. In a food processor, mix the sugar and butter until creamy. With the mixer on, add the saffron-rose water and the egg yolks (one by one as they get absorbed).

3. Gradually add the rice flour paste and mix for 5 minutes until you have a soft dough that does not stick to your hands. Transfer to the mixing bowl, cover with plastic wrap, and allow to rest in the fridge for 2 to 24 hours.

4. **To make the filling:** Combine all the ingredients for the filing in the food processor and pulse until you have a soft paste. Divide paste into 8 portions.

5. **To make the egg wash:** Beat the egg yolk and ground saffron until smooth.

6. Place the oven rack in the center and preheat the oven to 350°F/180°C. Line 2 baking sheets with parchment paper. On a cool, floured surface, roll the dough into a log and divide log into 16 balls. Roll out each ball of dough into a ½in thick x 5in/1cm thick x 12cm diameter disks. Add more rice flour if needed.

7. Place 1 portion of filling in the center of a disk. Gently place another disc on top and pinch the edges to seal the filling inside.

8. Place the filled disks on the lined baking sheets, 2in/5cm apart. Keep chilled until ready to bake. Use a brush to paint a sun and rays on each bun with the saffron egg wash.

9. Bake in the preheated oven for 15 to 20 minutes or until the bases of the cookies are lightly brown.

10. Remove from the oven and allow to cool. Arrange in a basket and serve with tea. To keep for later use, store in the refrigerator in a covered glass container. *Nush-e joon!*

The Caspian Region

Rose Petal Rice Pudding
gol-e paludeh

Serves 6 to 8
Prep: 5 minutes + soaking of rice overnight
Cooking: 45 minutes

- 1 cup white rice/200g, soaked overnight
- 2 cups/170g organic fresh rose petals or 1/3 cup/30g dried
- 2 tablespoons butter or oil
- 3 cups/720ml water
- ½ teaspoon fine sea salt
- 1 cup/200g sugar
- 3 cups/720ml whole plain milk or almond milk

GARNISH
- 2 tablespoons ground pistachio kernel
- ¼ cup/20g fresh organic rose petals, ground (use a spice grinder to grind)

NOTE
If you use dried rose petals, in step 2, just rinse and toast them. Dried damask rose petals are available at Iranian markets.

This is a spring dish usually made with fresh damask rose petals, which grow in abundance in Gilan. Everyone in this region was very specific about making this dish only with damask rose petals from around the Caspian, but I think any of the more delicate damask rose petals will work equally well.

1. Drain the rice in a fine-mesh colander, rinse, and set aside.

2. Place the rose petals in a colander, rinse, and chop finely on a cutting board. In a wide skillet, heat the butter over medium heat and stir-fry the rose petals for 1 minute. Set aside.

3. In a food processor, place the moist rice, 3 cups/720ml water, and the salt, and mix until you have a smooth paste. Transfer it to the pot and cook over low heat, whisking constantly for 10 minutes until smooth and creamy.

4. Add the sugar and milk, and continue to cook over low heat, stirring frequently for 20 minutes.

5. Add the rose petals and continue to whisk over low heat for 5 to 10 minutes until it has thickened to a pudding consistency and you can draw lines on the surface of the pudding.

6. Remove from the heat and immediately spoon into individual bowls. Garnish with pistachio and rose petals. Chill. *Nush-e joon!*

VARIATION

Rose Petal Sugar
gol-e qand

1. Line a sheet pan with parchment paper.

2. Place 1lb/450g organic dried rose petals in a sieve and rinse with cold water.

3. In a food processor, finely grind the rose petals with 1 cup/130g powdered sugar. Spread the paste on a sheet pan and allow to dry at room temperature for 24 hours.

4. Once again, transfer the rose petal and sugar paste to the food processor and add 1 cup/130g powdered sugar and mix until you have a fine powder. Transfer to the sheet pan and allow to air dry at room temperature for 24 hours. Store in an airtight glass container and use as needed.

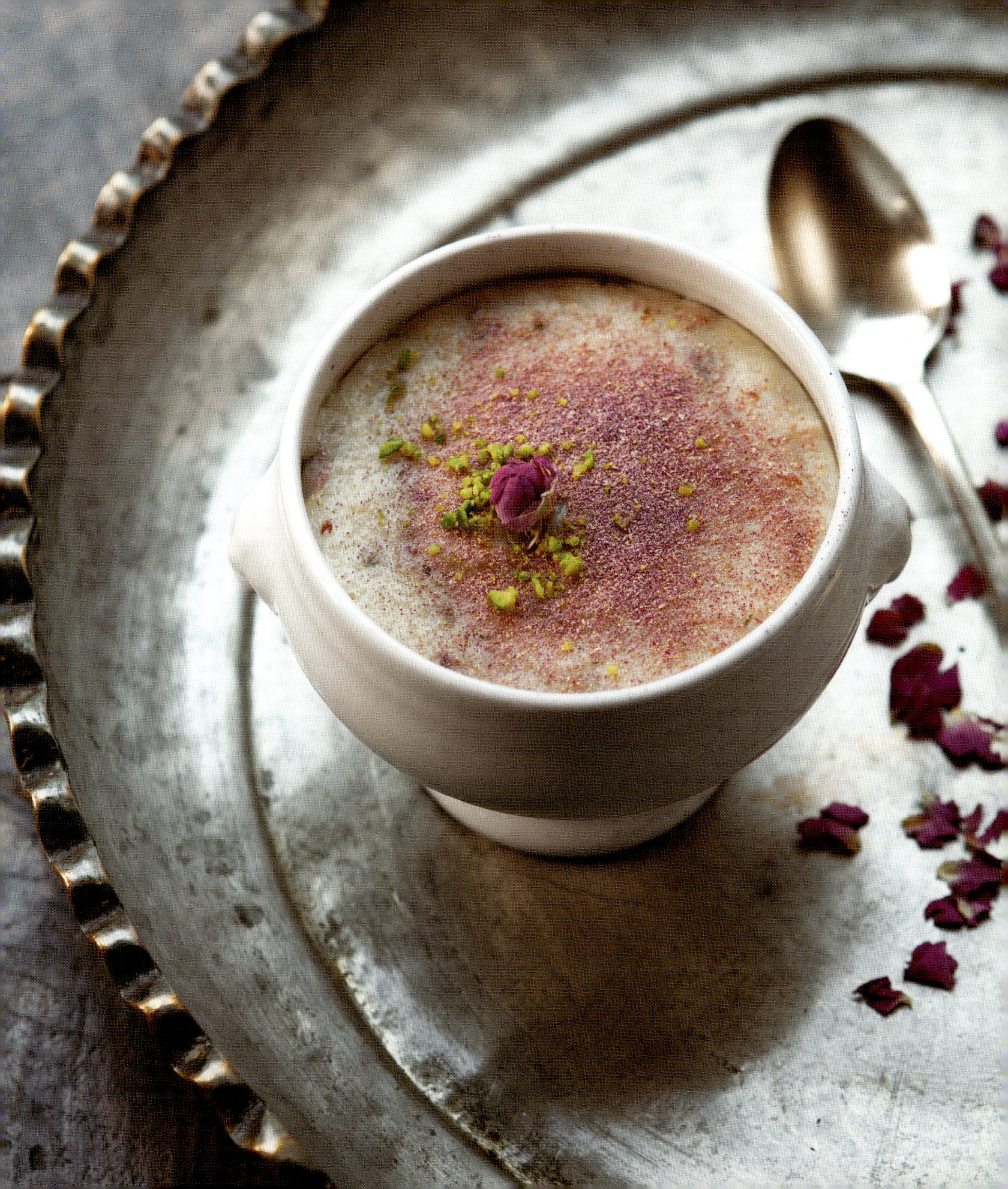

Grape Molasses
dushab-e angur

Makes ½pt/240g
Prep: 40 minutes
Cooking: 3 hours

10lb/4.5kg grapes

1. Remove the individual grapes from the clusters. Rinse thoroughly.

2. Place in a large large saucepan, cover, and cook over low heat for 30 to 40 minutes until soft.

3. Pass through a sieve into a large laminated pot, squeezing out all the juice. Discard the solids.

4. Reduce the grape juice by cooking, uncovered, over low heat for a few hours or until you have the consistency of molasses. This is one of the oldest sweetening agents that continues to be popular in Iranian cooking. *Nush-e joon!*

Verjuice Molasses
rob-e ab ghureh

Makes ½pt/240g
Prep: 20 minutes
Cooking: 1 hour

10lb/4.5kg unripe baby green grapes
1 tablespoon fine sea salt

1. Remove the individual grapes from the clusters. Rinse thoroughly. Juice the grapes in the juicer, pass through a sieve, and squeeze out all the juice. Discard the seeds and pulps.

2. In a large laminated pot, pour in half of the juice and bring to a boil over high heat. Reduce heat to medium and simmer uncovered for 30 minutes. Add the rest of the juice and bring back to a boil. Add the salt. Reduce heat to medium, gently stir occasionally, and simmer until the syrup has thickened (about 30 minutes). Remove from the heat and allow to cool.

3. Sterilize jars in boiling water, drain, and allow to dry thoroughly. Fill the jars with the verjuice molasses. Seal and keep in a cool, dark place. *Nush-e joon!*

Sour Apple Molasses
rob-e sib-e torsh

Makes 1pt/480g
Prep: 20 minutes
Cooking: 1 hour

20lb/9kg sour apples

1. Remove the stems of the apples and rinse. Core and cut into 4 pieces. Juice the apples and transfer half of the juice to a medium-sized laminated pot.

2. Bring the apple juice to a boil over high heat. Reduce heat to medium and simmer uncovered for 30 minutes. Add the rest of the juice and bring back to a boil. Gently stir with a long spoon, reduce heat to medium, and continue to simmer for 30 to 50 minutes until the syrup has thickened. Remove from heat and allow to cool.

3. Sterilize a 1pt/480g jar in boiling water. Drain and allow to dry thoroughly. Fill the jar with apple molasses. Seal and keep in a cool, dark place. *Nush-e joon!*

153

Rose Petal Preserve
moraba-ye gol-e mohammadi

Makes ½pt/240g
Prep: 20 minutes
Cooking: 1 hour

2lb/900g fresh organic damask rose petals
5 cups (2lb/900g) sugar
3 cups/720ml water
2 tablespoons lime juice
½ cup/60g slivered pistachio kernels

This preserve is very nutritious and good for the stomach, but it should be used in small quantities.

1. Rinse the rose petals in a colander, drain, and set aside.

2. Place the sugar and water in a medium-sized heavy bottom laminated pot and bring to a boil over high heat. Reduce heat to medium and simmer for about 40 to 45 minutes until the syrup is thick enough to coat the back of a spoon.

3. Meanwhile, place the rose petals in a wide skillet and toast for a few minutes, over low heat, stirring occasionally.

4. Transfer the rose petals to the pot, and add the lime juice and pistachio kernels. Stir gently and immediately remove from heat.

5. Fill a sterilized ½pt/240g jar with the hot preserve and seal. *Nush-e joon!*

Fig Jam
khams-e anjir

Makes ½pt/240g
Prep: 5 minutes plus overnight macerating
Cooking: 1 hour

4lb/1.8kg ripe, fresh green/yellow figs
1 cup/120g sugar
2 cups/480ml water
½ teaspoon ground cardamom
1 tablespoon lime juice

Khams-e anjir is made from large, ripe figs that grow wild around the Caspian region. Some of these figs are so large they are called "anjir-e se vaght," meaning triple-sized.

1. Snip the fig stems and rinse thoroughly in a colander.

2. Transfer the figs to a heavy-bottomed laminated pot. Cook over low heat, stirring frequently with a long wooden spoon until the figs are soft.

3. Dissolve the sugar in the water and add it to the pot. Bring to a boil. Reduce heat to low. Use a handheld mixer to puree the figs. Continue cooking over low heat for 30 to 45 minutes until it has thickened enough to coat the back of a spoon. Add the cardamom and lime juice, and give it a stir.

4. Sterilize the jelly jar in boiling water, drain, and allow to dry.

5. Fill the jar with the hot jam and then seal. Store in a cool, dark place. *Nush-e joon!*

The Caspian Region

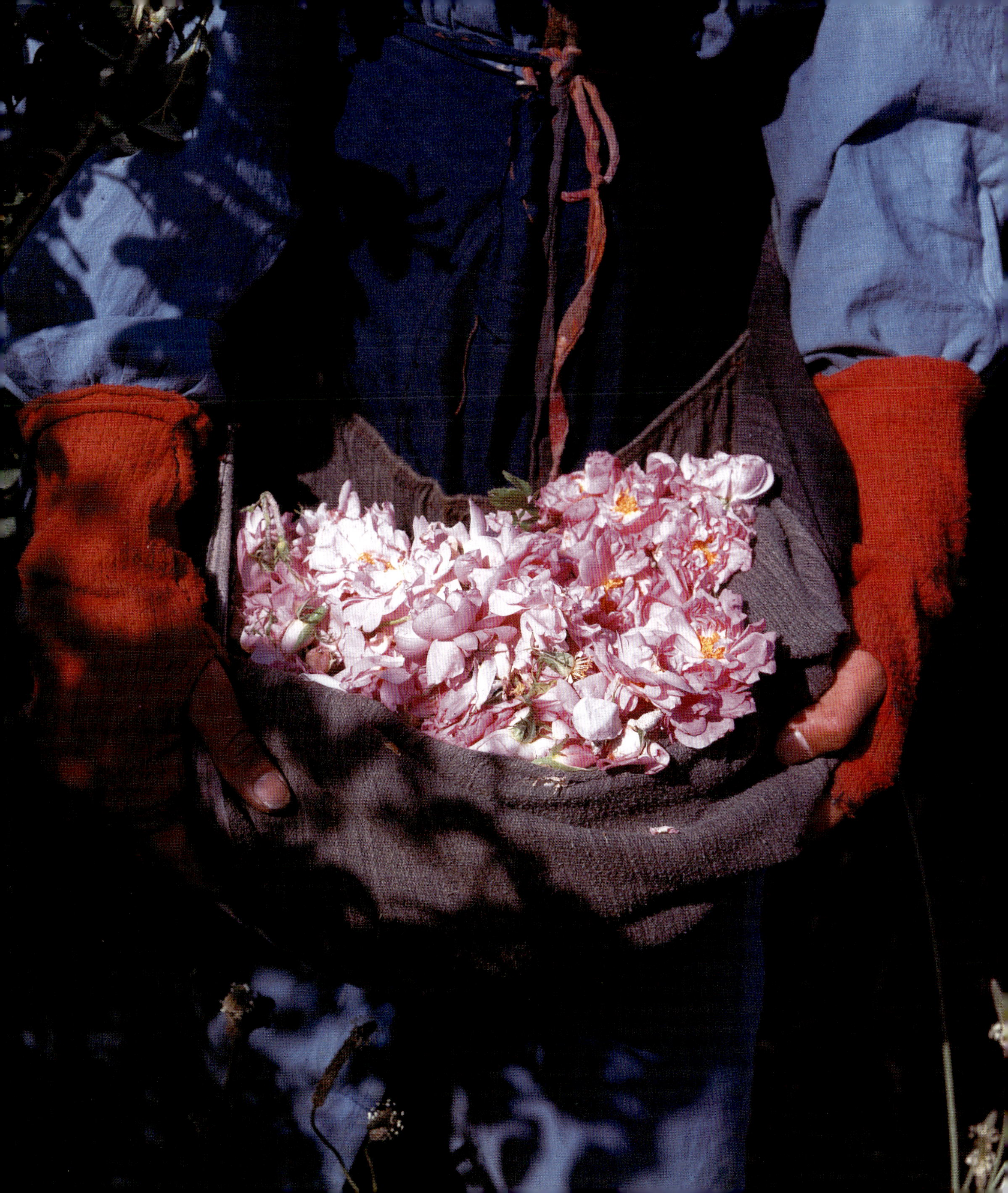

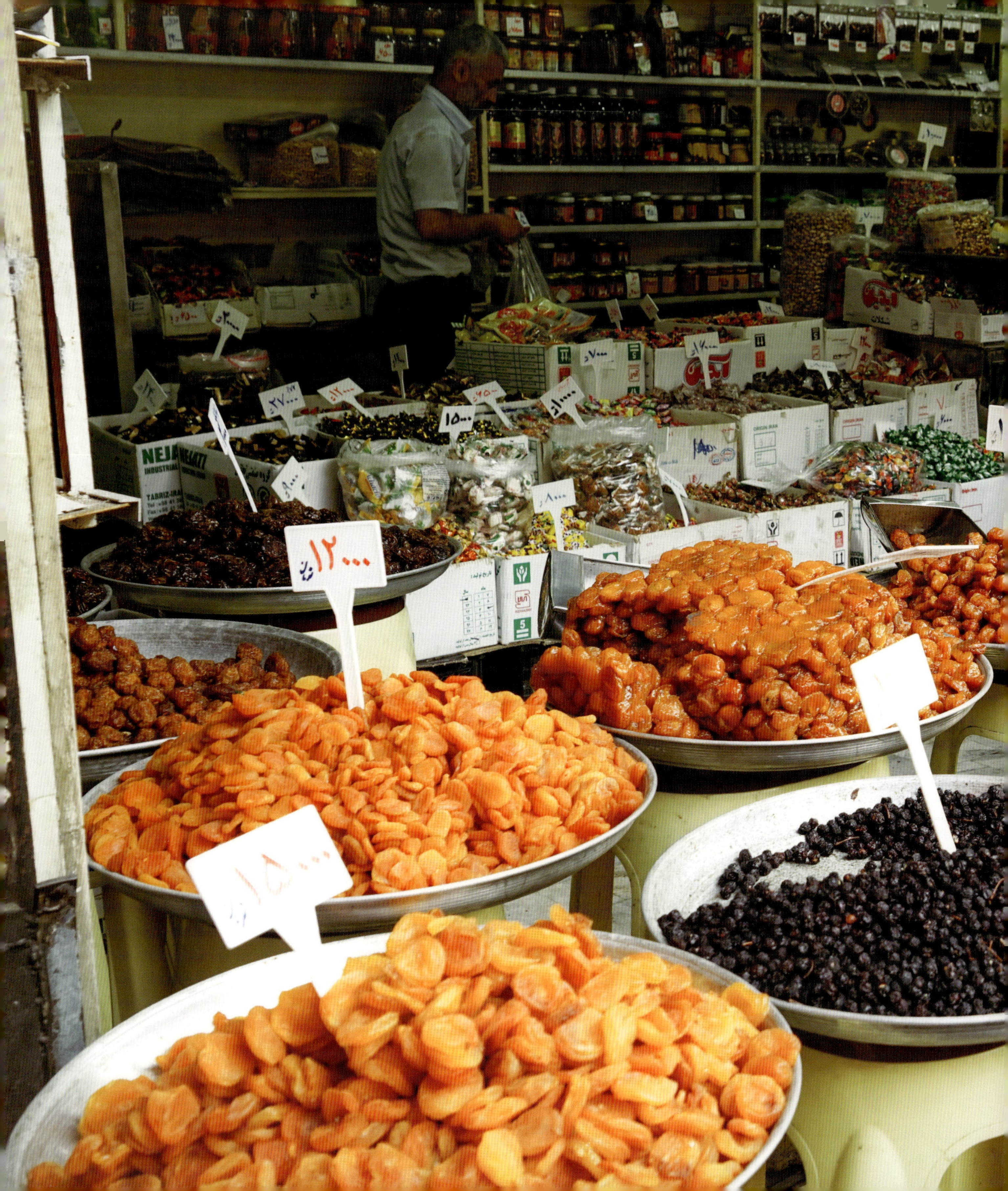

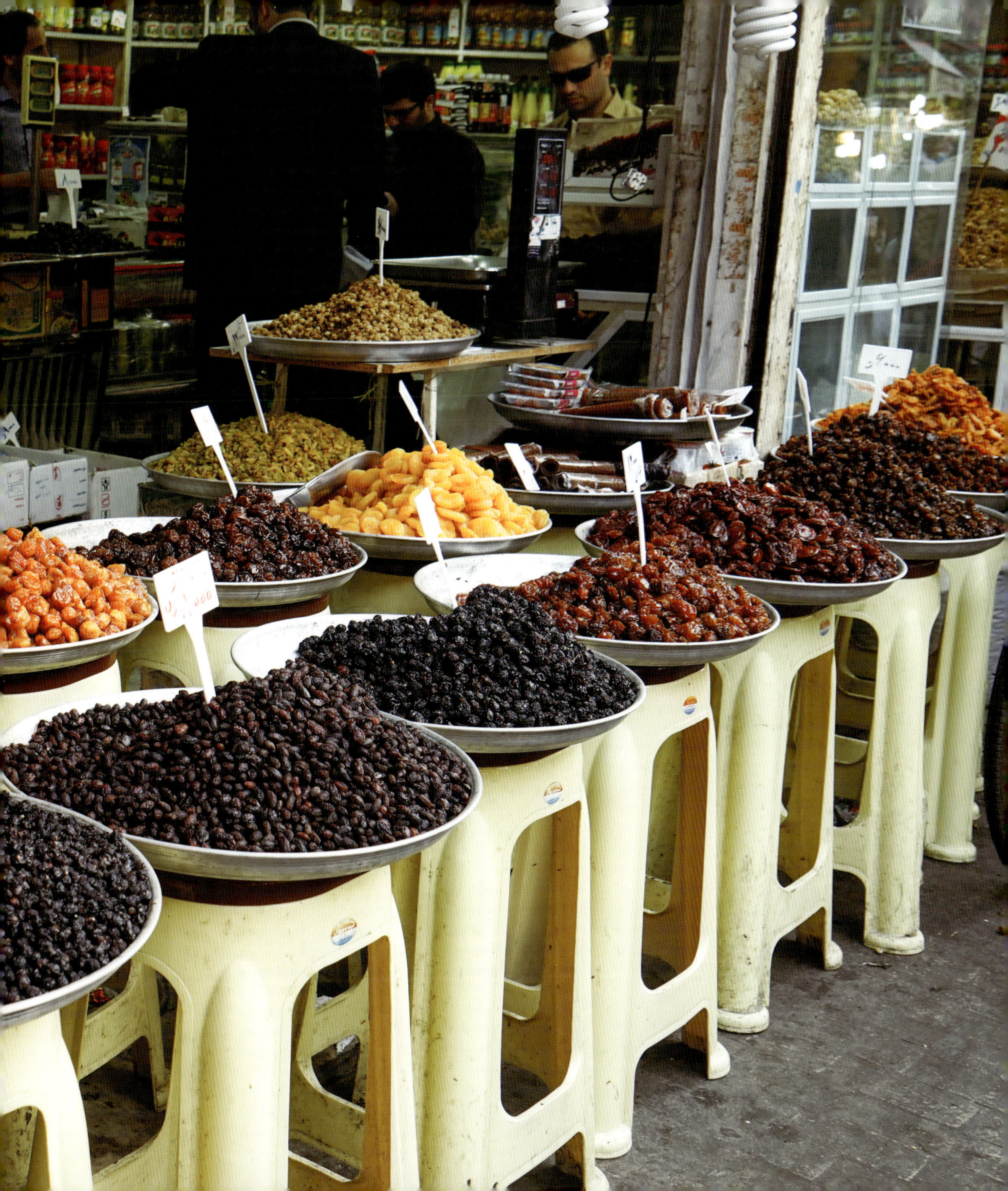

عسل کنار
زیتون با هسته
عالی
زیتون بی هسته
عالی
زیتون شکسته
چرب عالی

Wild Parsnip Preserve
moraba-ye shaqaqol

Makes ½pt/240g
Prep: 5 minutes + overnight macerating
Cooking: 1 hour

2lb/900g parsnips
4½ cups/900g sugar
3 cups/720ml water
2 tablespoons rose water
2 tablespoons lime juice
Seeds of 5 cardamom pods

These wild parsnip roots/shaqagol local to the Caspian region have the color of carrots but the shape of ginger. Their nutritious and medicinal preserve does wonders for settling the stomach. It should be eaten in small quantities.

1. Rinse the parsnips thoroughly in a colander. Transfer them to a large container, cover with water 1in/2.5cm above the parsnip, and allow to soak in a cool place overnight. When the skins are softened, drain.

2. Peel and cut the parsnips into 2in/5cm lengths and julienne them.

3. In a heavy-bottomed laminated pot, bring 8 cups/1.9l water to a boil and add the parsnips. Bring back to a boil, reduce heat to medium and cook for 15 minutes. Drain.

4. In the same pot, bring 3 cups water and the sugar to a boil. Reduce the heat to medium and simmer for 30 minutes.

5. Add the parsnips, rose water, lime juice, and cardamom. Simmer for 10 to 15 minutes over medium heat until syrup has thickened enough to coat the back of a spoon.

6. Sterilize jelly jar in boiling water, drain, and allow to dry.

7. Fill the jar with the preserve and seal. Store in a cool, dark place. *Nush-e joon!*

Greengage Molasses
rob-e alucheh

Makes ½pt/240ml
Prep: 20 minutes
Cooking: 1 hour

10lb/4.5kg baby greengages/*jojeh sabz*
1 tablespoon fine sea salt

1. Remove the stems of greengages and rinse thoroughly in a colander.

2. Place the greengages in a medium-sized saucepan and bring to a boil over high heat. Reduce heat to medium, cover, and simmer for 10 minutes or until the they are soft. With a long wooden spoon stir for a few minutes to loosen the pits and skins from the flesh.

3. Drain in a large fine-mesh colander into a medium-sized laminated pot. Use a masher to push the greengages through the colander, leaving the pits and skin behind and all the pulp and juice squeezed through to the pot. Discard the pits and skins.

4. Bring to a boil over high heat. Reduce the heat to medium and simmer, uncovered, for 30 minutes.

5. Add the salt, give it a gentle stir, and simmer for 30 to 50 minutes over medium heat until the syrup has thickened. Remove from heat and allow to cool.

6. Sterilize the jar in boiling water. Drain and allow to dry thoroughly. Fill the jar with the greengage molasses. Seal and keep it in a cool, dark place. *Nush-e joon!*

Opposite: Shop in Chaboksar selling homemade jams and pickles as well as sour orange molasses, olives and olive oil.

The Caspian Region

Cornelian Cherry Chutney

khams-e akhteh

Makes ½pt/240g
Prep: Soak overnight + 20 minutes
Cooking: 10 minutes

4lb/1.8kg fresh or 2lb/900g dried cornelian cherries
1 teaspoon fine sea salt
1 teaspoon ground Persian hogweed seeds/*golpar*

The fruit of the cornelian cherry is red and oblong and has medicinal properties. This chutney/khams-e akhteh is a sticky, sweet and sour paste eaten as a snack in a similar way to a fruit roll-up. It is wrapped in paper and sold by street vendors around the Caspian. Kids eat them with their fingers.

1. Rinse the cornelian cherries thoroughly in a colander and transfer to a large laminated pot. Cover with water to about 1in/2.5cm above the fruit. Bring to a boil. Remove from the heat, cover, and allow to soak overnight.

2. Stir with a long-handled wooden spoon for a few minutes to loosen the pits and the skin from the flesh of the fruit.

3. Drain through a fine-mesh colander on a laminated pot and use a masher to push as much of the fruit through as possible. Discard the pits and skins. Bring to a boil over medium heat.

4. Sprinkle the salt and *golpar* on top. Use a handheld mixer to puree the fruit. Adjust the salt and *golpar* to your taste.

5. Transfer to a sterilized ½pt/240g jar. Cover tightly and store in the refrigerator. *Nush-e joon!*

Blackberry Preserve

moraba-ye tameshk/velash

Makes ½pint/240ml
Prep: 10 minutes + overnight macerating
Cooking: 1 hour

2lb/900g fresh blackberries
4½ cups/900g sugar
2 tablespoons rose water
2 tablespoons fresh lime juice

Blackberries grow wild in the woods around the Caspian.

1. In a large colander thoroughly rinse the blackberries.

2. Place the berries and sugar in alternating layers in a medium size laminated pot. Cover and macerate overnight.

3. Bring the berries to a boil. Reduce heat to medium and simmer for 35 minutes.

4. Add rose water and lime juice and simmer for 5 to 10 minutes until the syrup has thickened enough to coat the back of a spoon.

5. Sterilize jelly jar in boiling water, drain, and allow to dry.

6. Fill the jar with the preserve and seal. Store in a cool, dark place. *Nush-e joon!*

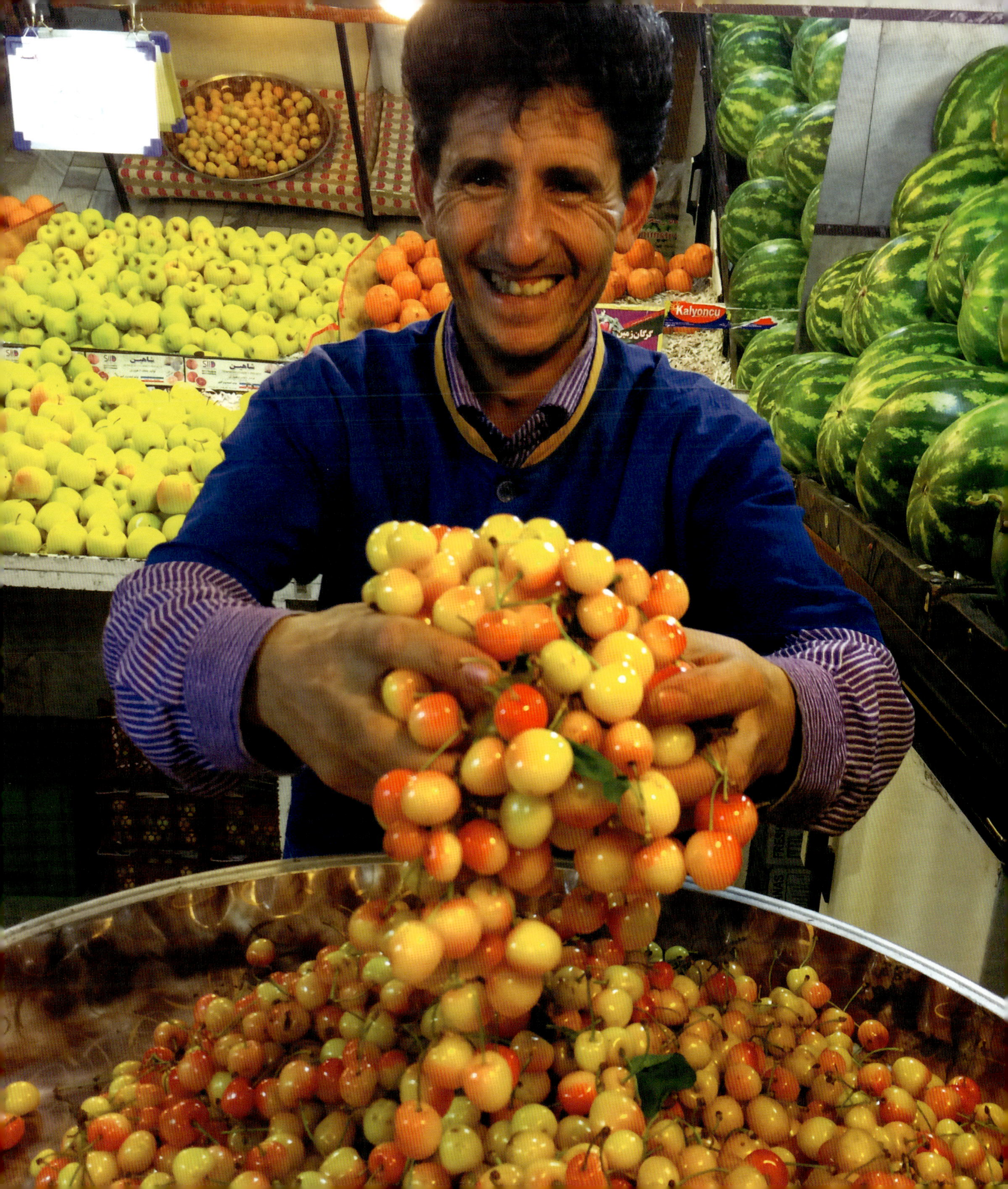
Kalyoncu

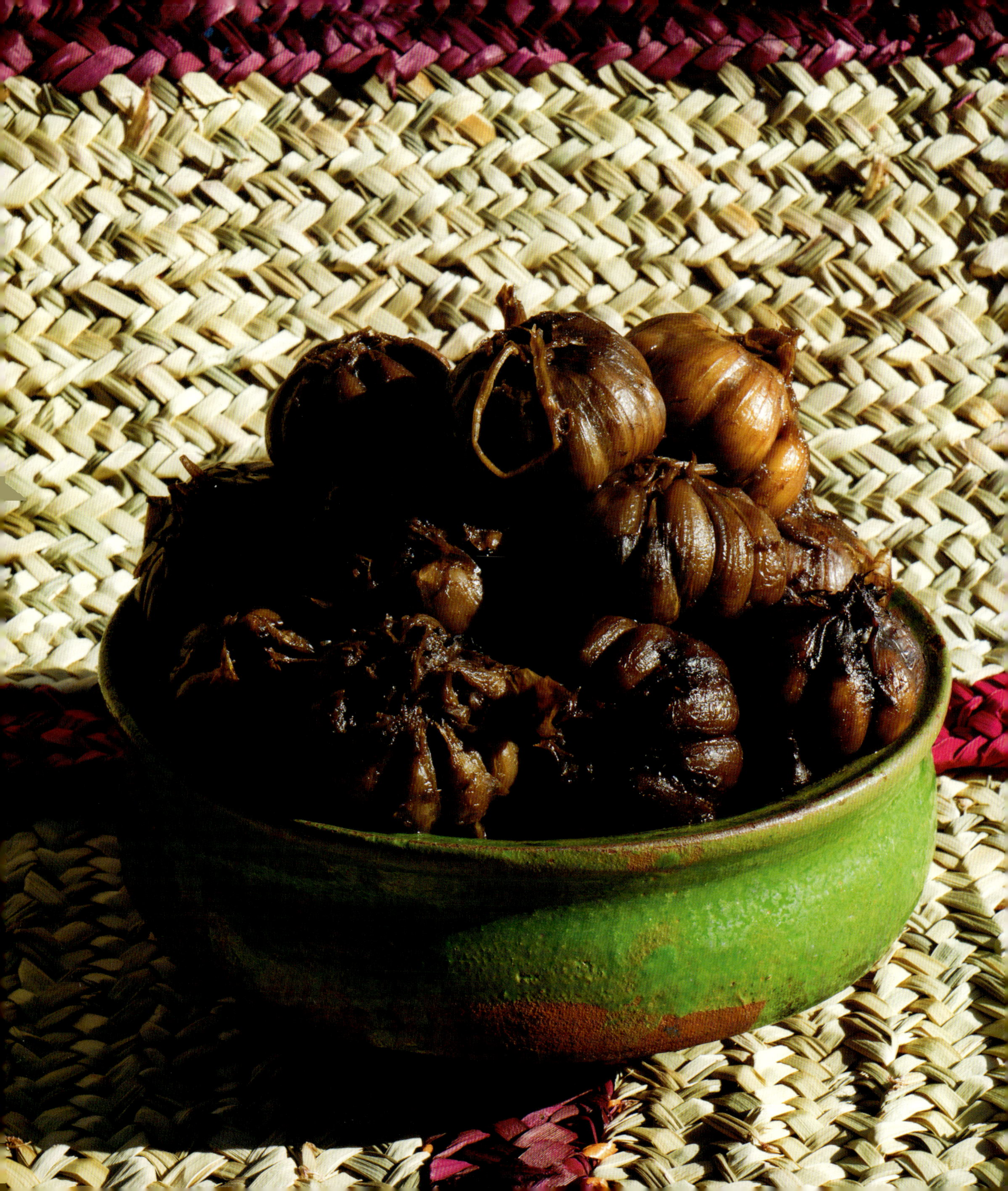

Black Garlic Pickle
sir torshi-e shomali

Makes 1pt /480g
Prep: 20 minutes
Storage: at least 6 weeks minimum before using

1lb/450g garlic bulbs

BRINE

1 cup/240ml sour cherry juice
1½ cups/360ml malt vinegar or apple cider vinegar
1 tablespoon fine sea salt
¼ cup/50g sugar

This is a delicious pickle that you can find on every Caspian table. It's best when it has aged about 7 years and has become black and sweet. The great Iranian savant Mulla Nasruddin related a story involving the renowned pickles. One day, he was asked, "Is it true that you have some seven-year-old garlic pickle?" "Yes, it is," said Mulla. "Would you please give me a dish of it?" asked the stranger. "No," said Mulla. "If I were to give everyone who asked for some, it wouldn't have become even a month old."

1. Sterilize a wide-opening jar in boiling water, drain, and allow to dry thoroughly.

2. Peel off just one outside layer of the garlic bulbs. Trim extra roots with the point of a paring knife.

3. **To make the brine:** Combine all the ingredient for the brine in a saucepan. Stir well, bring to a boil, and remove from heat.

4. Fill the jar with garlic bulbs.

5. Fill the jar to within ½in/1cm of the top with the brine.

6. Store the jars in a cool, dark place for at least 6 weeks up to a year before using. *Nush-e joon!*

Medlar Pickle
ab konus-e azgil

Makes ½pt/240g
Prep: 20 minutes
Store for at least 2 weeks before serving

MEDLAR

1½lb/675g firm unripe medlars
1 teaspoon ground Persian hogweed seeds/*golpar*

BRINE

2 cups/480ml water
1 tablespoon fine sea salt

Medlar was one of my favorite childhood fruits. It is the size of a walnut and usually light brown, as shown in the photo on the facing page. It has a unique sour flavor, something between a persimmon and a blueberry. I bought some of the pickle in Masouleh. In Gilan they serve this pickle, sprinkled with golpar powder, during the winter festival/shab-e yalda.

1. Place the medlars in a colander, rinse thoroughly, and pat dry completely.

2. In a clean mason jar alternately arrange layers of the fruit and sprinkles of the *golpar* seeds up to near the top of the jar.

3. **To make the brine:** In a small saucepan, combine the water and salt and bring to a boil. Stir well until the salt has dissolved completely. Remove from heat.

4. Fill the jar to within ½in/1cm of the top with the warm brine (not hot). Close tightly, turn upside down, and allow to sit for 10 to 15 minutes until cool.

5. Store the jar in a cool, dark place for at least 2 weeks before serving. *Nush-e joon!*

The Caspian Region

ازگیل یک کیلو ۶۰۰۰

Harvesting Tea

Tea is the most popular drink, by far, throughout Iran. Nothing of consequence is ever done without small glasses of tea being passed around. But no one really knows how it managed to replace coffee as the stimulant drink of choice in Iran. Tea started to become more prevalent in northern Iran during the Russian occupation of Tabriz and parts of the Caspian region in the 1830s. Some say this happened after the Russians presented a samovar to the governor of Gilan, which he sent to the court in Tehran. Others say it was after a merchant gave a tea set and a samovar as a gift to Amir Kabir, the chief minister of Naser al-Din Shah in 1850.

By the 1880s plantations (tea gardens/*bagh-e chai*) of Assam tea, which is black and preferred by Iranians, started to appear on the foothills of the Alborz Mountains, usually on steep hills above the rice fields of the valleys below. Sometimes these tea gardens are interspersed among citrus groves and mulberry orchards. As their name suggests, tea gardens have remained small family operations in Iran despite the tremendous demand for tea, much of which is still imported. The Iranian-grown teas I tried had a very delicate flavor and aroma, and reminded me of some of the best Ethiopian coffees.

Herbal teas, such as borage and hogweed seeds, have a much longer history and still remain popular in Iran (see the pages that follow).

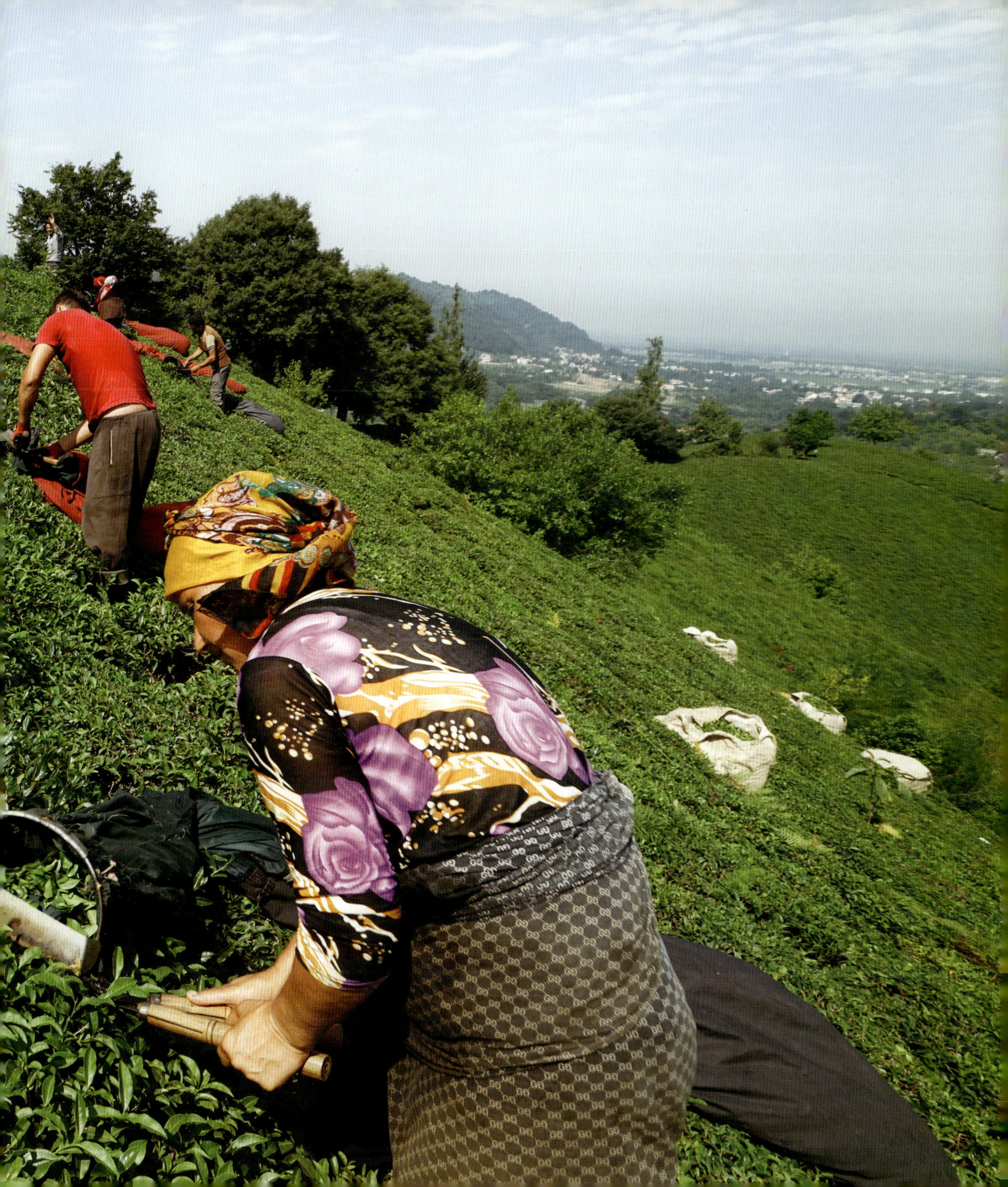

A family picking borage flowers in their fields near Tonekabon.

Borage + Valerian Tea
dam nush-e gol gav zabun va sombolative

Serves 4 cups
Prep: 25 minutes

4 cups/960ml water
2 dried Persian limes, pierced
1 cup/85g fresh organic borage or 2 tablespoons dried
1in/2.5cm dried valerian root
2 tablespoons sugar or rock candy

1. Bring the water to a boil in a medium saucepan. Add the limes, borage, valerian, and sugar, and bring back to a boil. Reduce heat to low, cover, and allow to simmer for 20 minutes. Keep warm until ready to serve.

2. Before serving, pour a glassful of tea and return it to the saucepan to be sure the tea is evenly mixed.

3. Serve the tea in small tea glasses. Add more sugar to taste. *Nush-e joon!*

Jujub Panacea Tea
dam nush-e annab

Serves 4 cups
Prep: 20 minutes

4 cups/960ml water
1 cup/100g fresh or ½ cup dried jujubes (Chinese dates)
1in/2.5cm rock candy or 1 tablespoon sugar

This tea, perhaps originally from Khorasan, was popular in our household during my childhood. My mother would often serve it for various ailments, from the common cold to a stomach ache.

1. Bring the water to a boil in a medium saucepan. Add the jujubes and bring back to a boil. Reduce heat to low, add the rock candy, cover, and allow to simmer for 20 minutes. Keep warm until ready to serve.

2. Before serving, pour a glassful of tea and return it to the saucepan to be sure the tea is evenly mixed.

3. Serve the tea in small tea glasses. Add more sugar to taste. *Nush-e joon!*

Saffron Love Tea
dam nush-e zaferun

Serves 4 cups
Prep: 20 minutes

4 cups/960ml water
2 whole cardamom pods, bruised
½ teaspoon saffron threads, ground
½ teaspoon rose water
2in/5cm rock candy or 2 tablespoons sugar

This tea is traditionally served in Shushtar by the bride-to be to the groom's family after she and her family have accepted a marriage proposal. This subtle way of saying "yes" might be related to the belief that saffron has aphrodisiac qualities

1. Bring the water to a boil in a medium saucepan. Add the cardamom, saffron, rose water and sugar. Reduce heat to low, cover, and allow to simmer for 15 minutes.

2. Before serving, pour a glassful of tea and return it to the saucepan to be sure the tea is evenly mixed.

3. Serve the tea in small tea glasses. Add more sugar to taste. *Nush-e joon!*

The Caspian Region

Hogweed Seed Tea
dam nush-e golpar

Serves 4 cups
Prep: 10 minutes

4 cups/960ml water
1 teaspoon ground Persian hogweed seeds/*golpar*
1 tablespoon honey or sugar

1. Bring the water to a boil in a medium saucepan. Add the ground *golpar* and bring back to a boil. Reduce heat to low, add the honey, cover, and allow to simmer for 10 minutes. Keep warm until ready to serve.

2. Before serving, pour a glassful of tea and return it to the saucepan to be sure the tea is evenly mixed.

3. Serve the tea in small tea glasses. Add more sugar to taste. *Nush-e joon!*

Chabahar Milk Tea
shir chai-ye chabahar

Serves 6 cups
Prep: 20 minutes

3 cups/720ml water
2 tablespoons black tea
2 tablespoons sugar
½ teaspoon ground cardamom
½ teaspoon ground cinnamon
3 cups/720ml milk

Solmaz Khanezaei served us this deliciously satisfying tea in Chabahar by the Pink River. It was a cold December day and the tea hit the spot.

1. Bring the water to a boil in a medium saucepan. Add the tea, sugar, cardamom, and cinnamon. Give it a stir.

2. Reduce heat to low, add the milk, cover, and allow to simmer for 10 minutes.

3. Serve and add more sugar to taste. *Nush-e joon!*

Dried Persian Lime Tea
dam nush-e limu omani

Serves 4 cups
Prep: 20 minutes

4 cups/960ml water
6 dried Persian limes, pierced
1in/2.5cm rock candy or 1 tablespoon sugar

I had this tea in Shiraz. You can also make it into a delicious and thirst quenching ice tea by allowing it cook and adding ice to taste.

1. Bring the water to a boil in a medium saucepan. Add the dried Persian limes and the rock candy, and bring back to a boil. Reduce heat to low, cover, and allow to simmer for 20 minutes. Keep warm until ready to serve.

2. Before serving, pour a glassful of tea and return it to the saucepan to be sure the tea is evenly mixed.

3. Serve the tea in small tea glasses. Add more sugar to taste. *Nush-e joon!*

The Caspian Region

Various herbal teas for sale in the market, including dried borage/*gol gav zabun*, (bottom left) as well as whole Persian hogweed seeds/*golpar* (bottom right).

Azarbaijan

A view of Tabriz with the mountains in the background.

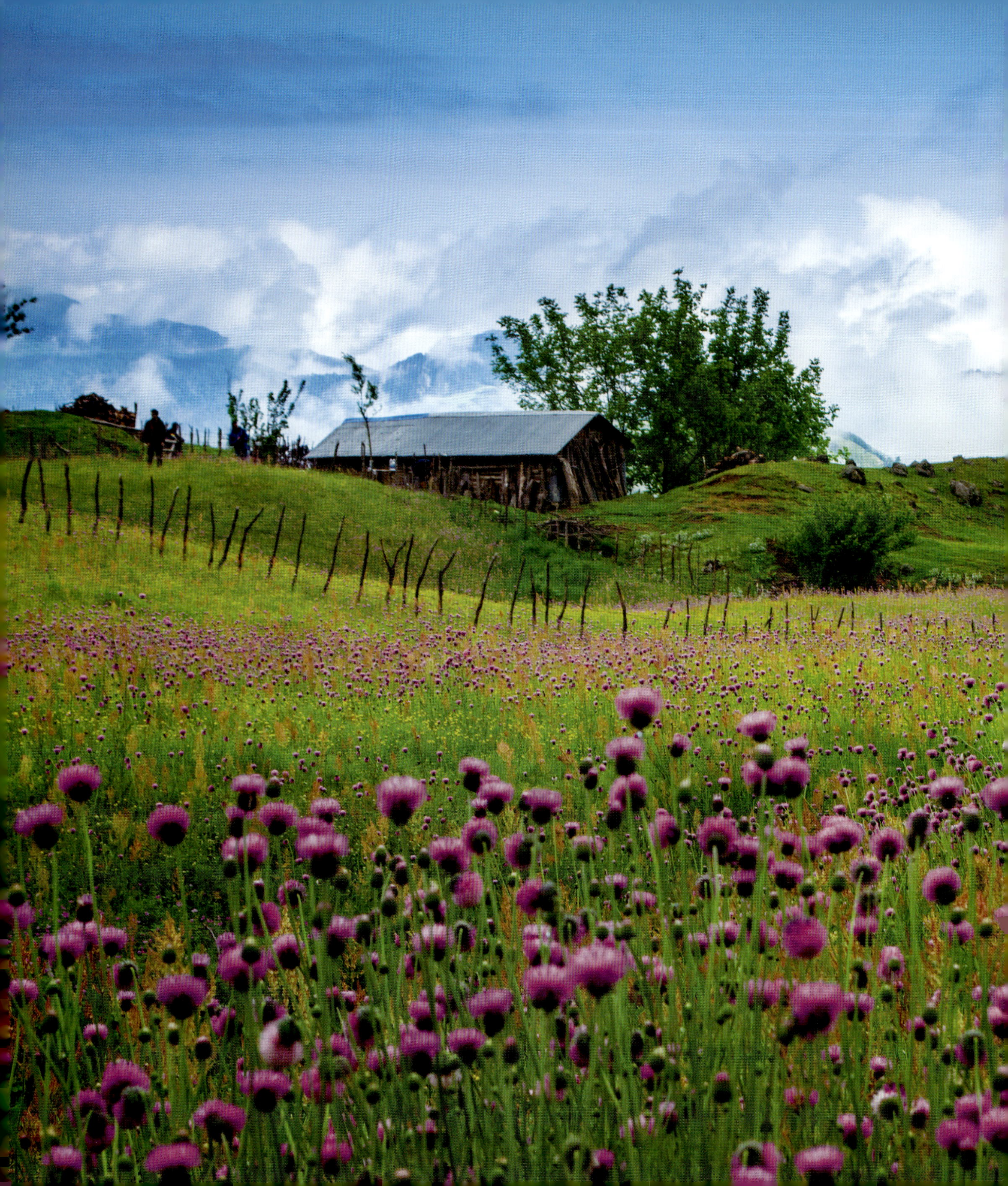

A Little History

In the early 1800s, after intense military and economic pressure, Iran was forced to cede its former lands in the Caucasus to Russia. The Russians initially called the region Eastern Transcaucasia. After the Bolshevik takeover, however, they divided the region and renamed it Georgia, Armenia, and Azerbaijan—a historically questionable name for what is now the Republic of Azerbaijan.

Iranian Azarbaijan is the land that originally bore the name Azarbaijan, and I will be using it to refer to the four Iranian provinces of West and East Azarbaijan, Ardabil, and Zanjan.

Leaving the lush green Caspian region and heading to Tabriz, we had two choices: Go south through Zanjan or go north through Ardabil. We chose the latter. This route took us past some of the most beautiful landscapes I have ever seen, including fields aflame with wild poppies. Along the way were small stalls serving delicious thick soups/*osh* and kababs (made with lamb butchered in front of you from carcasses hanging at the side of the road).

An early-1970s photograph at "The Brothers Cafe" in Ahar.

Ardabil

Ardabil was where the Safavids dynasty that ruled Iran from 1495 to 1720 was founded. We visited Sheikh Safi's tomb, and took a detour to the foothills of the magnificent Sabalan Mountain, where we bought some of the area's famous honey.

Tabriz

The construction of the Tabriz Bazaar goes back to the eighth century. By 1500, Tabriz was among the five largest cities in the world with a population of around 300,000, but this was also the period when control of the city passed back and forth between the Iranian Safavids and Turkish Ottomans. Today it is only the sixth largest city in Iran.

Tabriz is also a summer resort with many thermal springs in its vicinity. The population is mostly Azarbaijanis, who speak a Turkish dialect called Azari, though the official language is Persian.

Tabriz has been a major city for trade and a gateway to Iran from the West—Marco Polo passed through on his way to China in 1275. Nonetheless, it is also one of the more religiously conservative cities of Iran. I was touched by the Tabrizi people's welcoming attitude in the bazaar. We stopped at every food stall, where I tasted all kinds of halvas. My favorite was the carrot, saffron, and walnut halva (recipe on page 222). And I cooked with some wonderful Tabrizi women who welcomed me into their homes and showed me some of their specialized techniques, especially for making their famous meatballs.

At the copper section of the bazaar, I bought a calligraphed friendship bowl (the traditionally shared wine bowl) and a tin-lined copper pot for making rice.

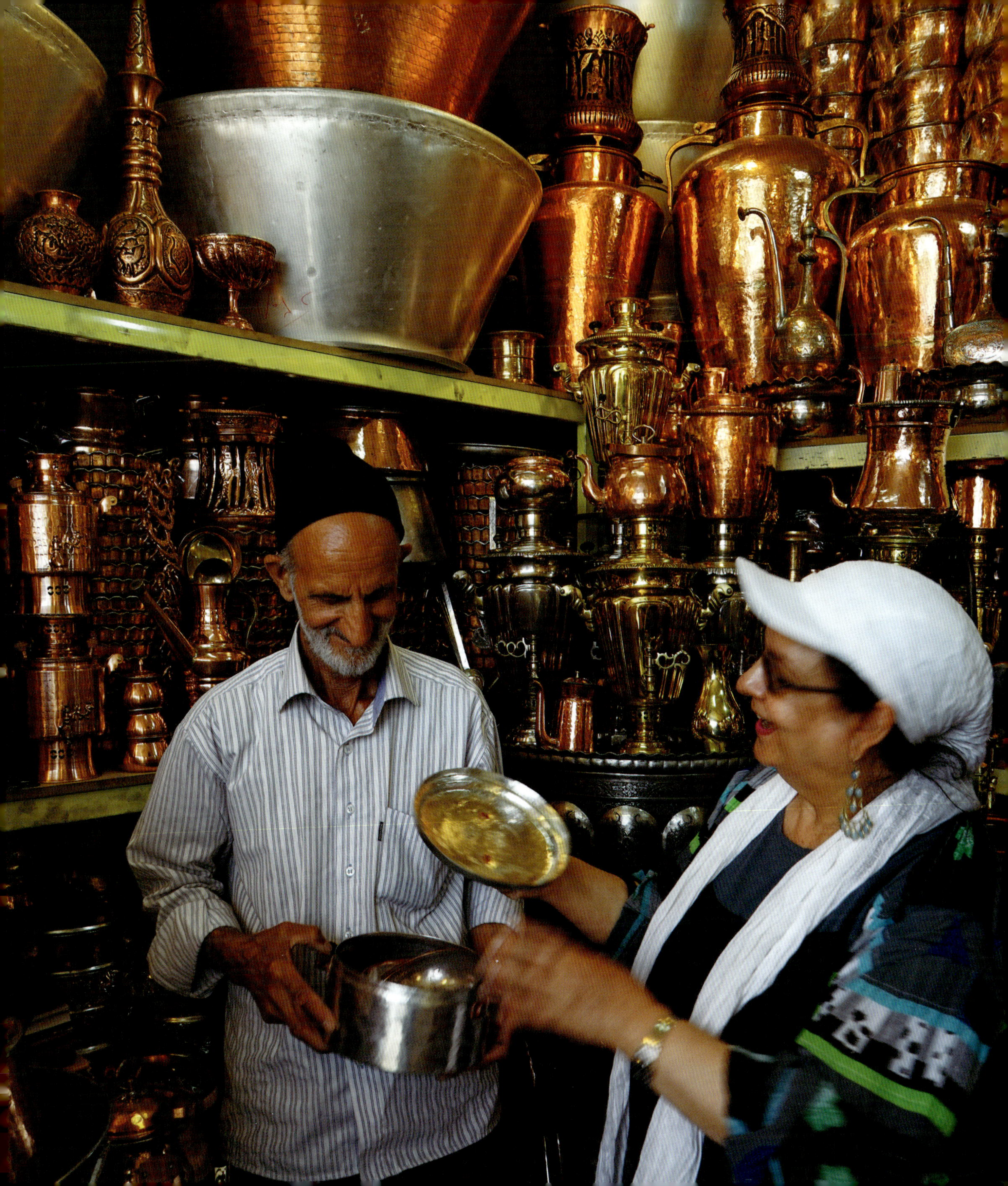

Stalls in the Tabriz Bazaar.

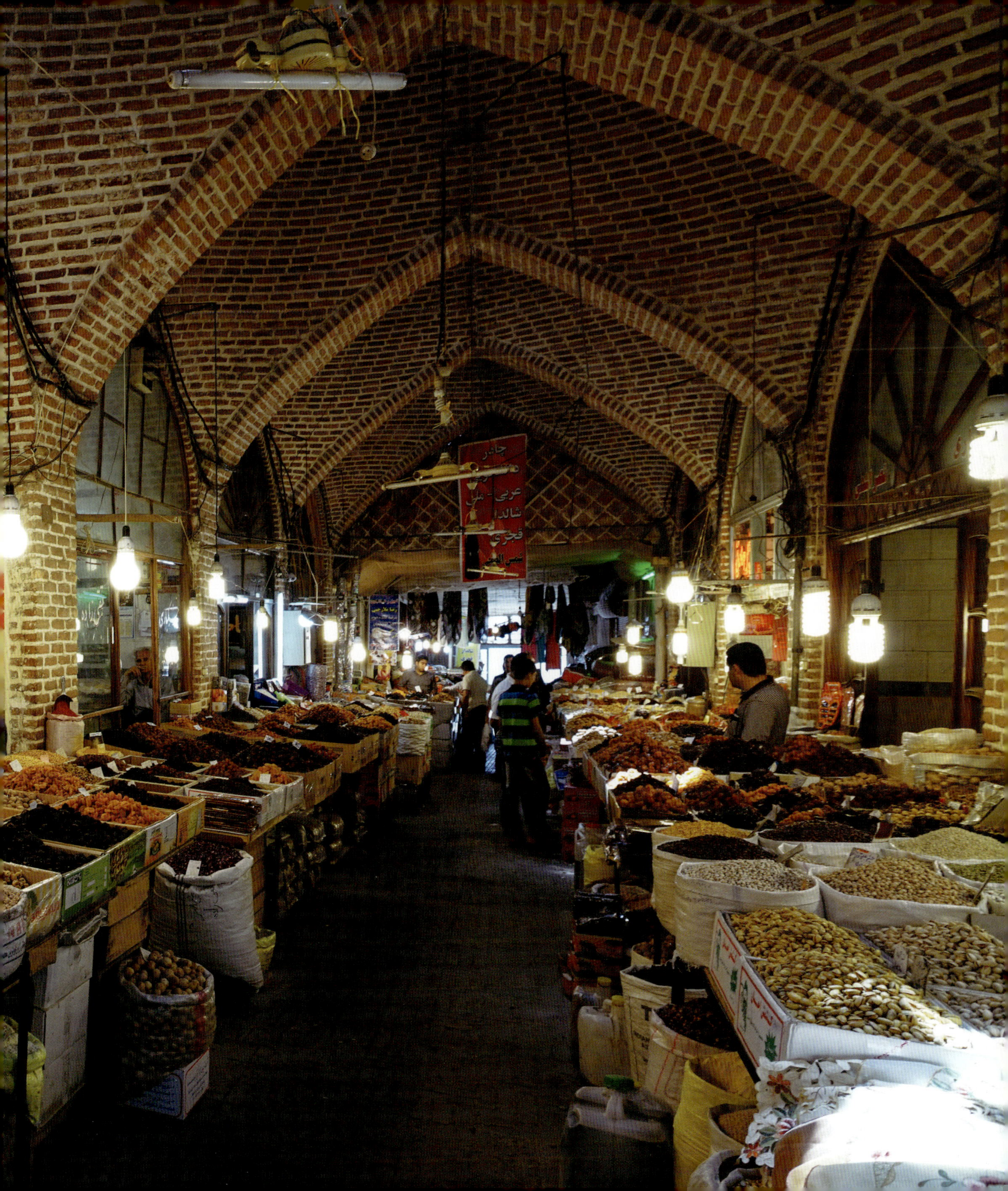

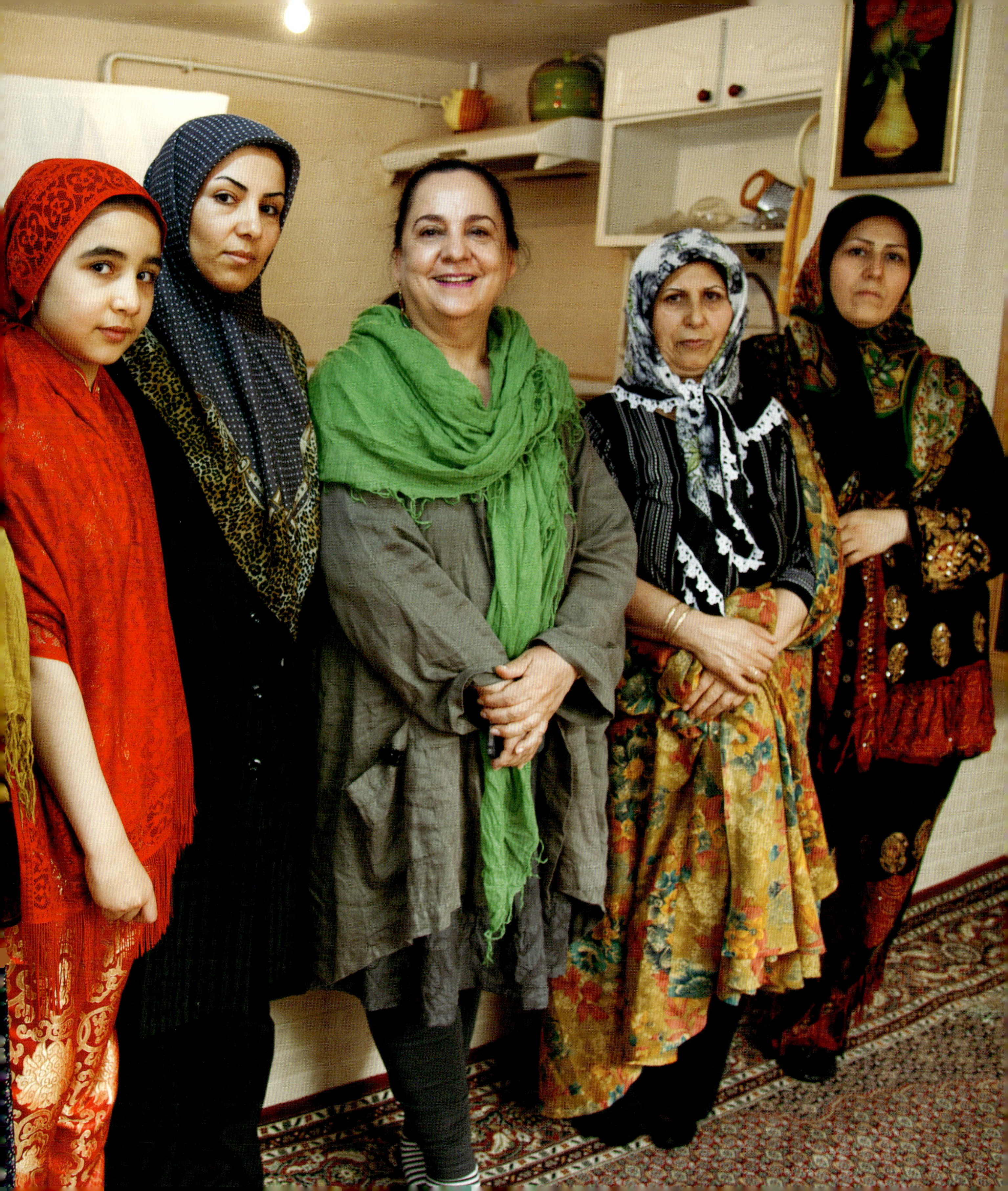

Cooking in Tabriz

Some of Iran's most sophisticated cooking is that of Azarbaijan. Tabriz, Ardebil, Zanjan, and Urmia have wonderful kababs, meatballs, dumplings, and vine leaves with delicious fillings. And for dessert, the variety of their halvas is matchless.

A brilliant young Tabriz University student was our guide. He took us to his grandmother, Rahman Khanum, who made me feel welcomed in her house. They were a religious family and the women covered their heads not because of government edicts but because that had been their tradition. Their tiled yard with a fig tree at its center was no more than the size of a large room. The family spread a beautiful Tabriz carpet under the fig tree, placed a tablecloth on top, and placed the dishes we had prepared together on the spread. I loved the very simple soup/*osh-e omaj*. I was enthralled by the fresh herb platter of basil, chives, summer savory, and radishes, and was surprised that they used summer savory in the fresh herb platter, as I had not seen it used elsewhere in Iran's iconic herb platters/*sabzi khordan*. See the recipes we made in the pages that follow.

Azari Three-Spice Advieh
advieh-ye azari

Makes 1 cup/125g
Prep: 20 minutes

Four 4in cinnamon sticks, broken up
¼ cup/50g black cumin seeds
½ cup/8g dried rose petals

I use this simple three-spice advieh *for the wonderful aroma it imparts to both braises and rice dishes. I've adapted it from one suggested by Nosratallah Tarighi's mom, a wonderful cook from Tabriz.*

1. Grind the cinnamon, cumin, and rose petals, each separately in a spice grinder.

2. Transfer them to a small bowl as you grind them and mix well.

3. Transfer to an airtight glass jar and keep in a cool place to use as needed. *Nush-e joon!*

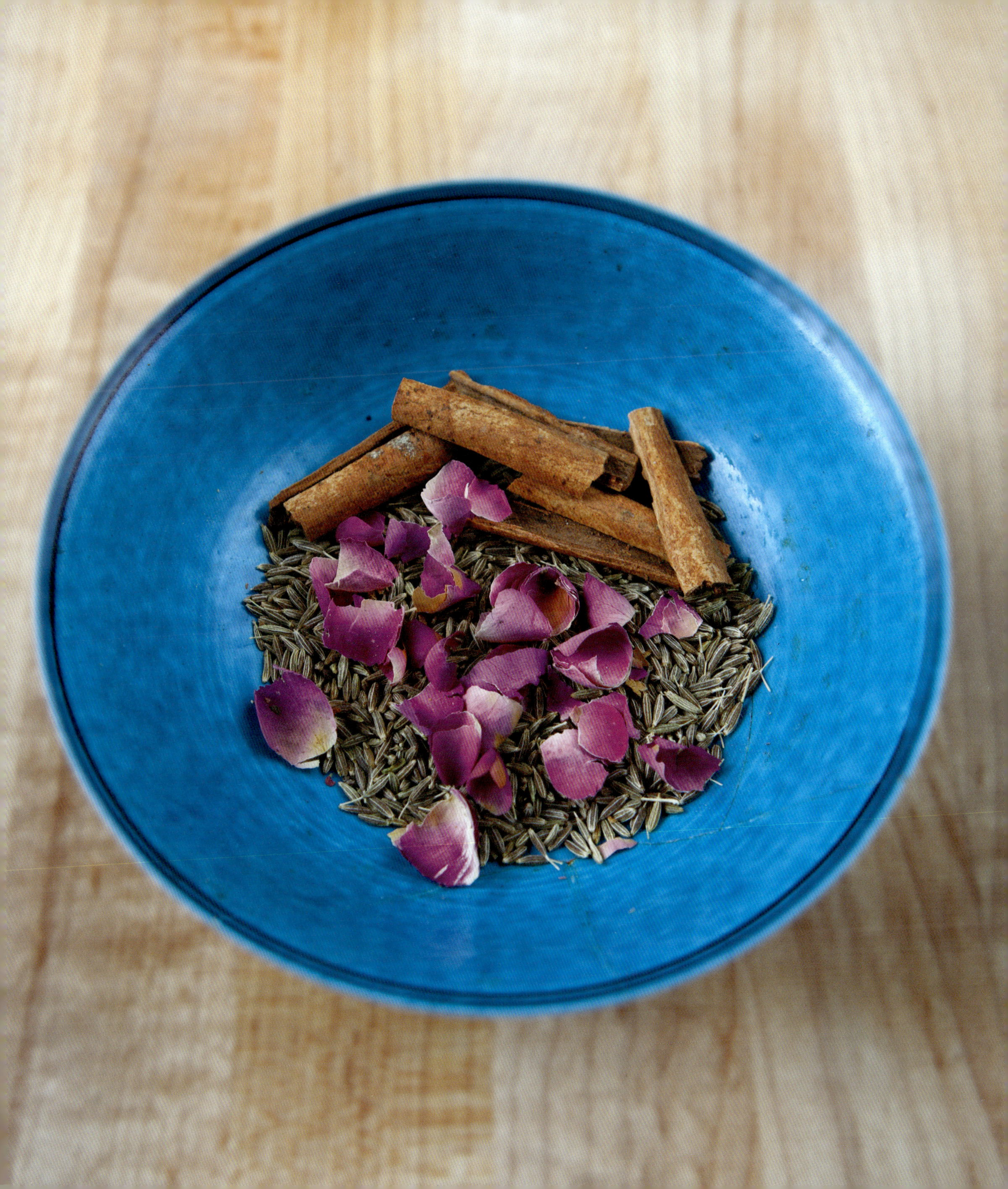

Tabrizi Cheese, Walnut + Herb Balls
doymaj

Makes 10 to 14 balls, serves, 4 to 8
Preparation time: 30 minutes

2 cups/250g walnuts
2 fresh spring onions, roughly chopped (green and white parts)
2 cups/170g fresh basil leaves
1 cup/85g fresh tarragon leaves
2 cups/170g fresh mint leaves
½ teaspoon fine sea salt
½ teaspoon freshly ground pepper
½lb/225g white, feta-type goat cheese, rinsed and drained
½ cup/120g thick plain whole yogurt
8in/20cm round of Persian or pita bread, toasted and cut up into 1in/2.5cm squares

In Tabriz, these aromatic, nutritious egg-shaped cheese balls are eaten as a snack or taken by children to eat for breakfast on their way to school. This same dish is called qut *in Hamadan.*

In a food processor, place all the ingredients and pulse until you have a grainy paste (if the paste becomes too thick, add 2 tablespoons water). Place the paste in a bowl and take a tablespoon of it at a time and form it into a small egg-shaped ball. Place the balls on a serving platter, cover, and keep chilled until ready to serve. *Nush-e joon!*

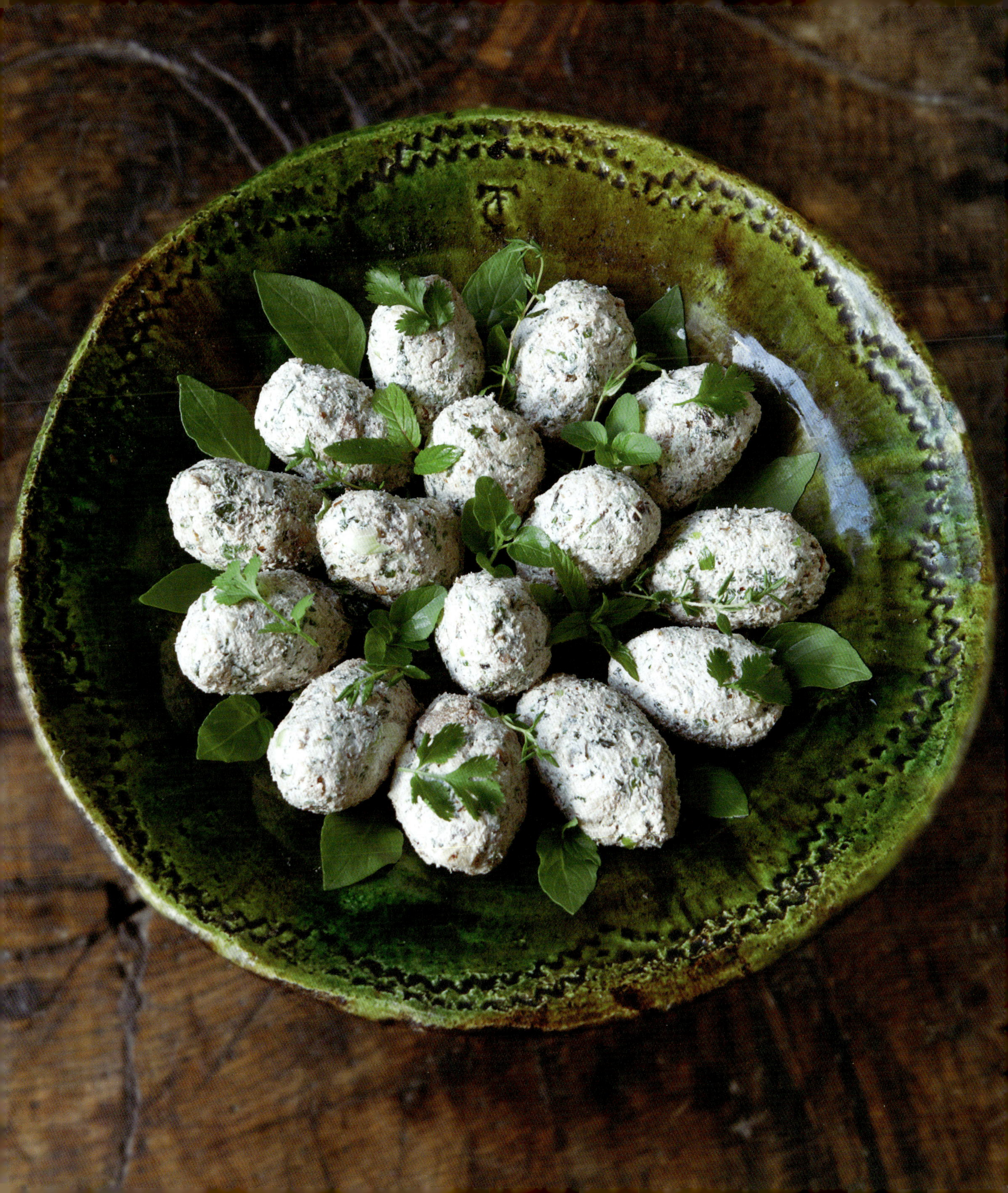

Saffron Omelet with Rose Petals
khagineh-ye tabrizi

Serves 4
Prep: 15 minutes + 5 minutes of resting
Cooking: 15 minutes

SYRUP

¼ cup/50g sugar
¼ cup/60ml water
½ teaspoon zest of orange
¼ teaspoon saffron dissolved in 2 tablespoons rose water

BATTER

4 eggs
1/3 cup/80g plain whole yogurt
1 teaspoon baking powder
1/3 cup/40g unbleached all-purpose flour mixed with ½ teaspoon salt and ½ teaspoon pepper

¼ cup/60ml oil, butter, or ghee for cooking

GARNISH

1 teaspoon dried rose petals, ground
2 tablespoons coarsely chopped walnuts or pistachios
¼ teaspoon ground cinnamon

Azaris love yogurt and add it to many dishes. I adapted this delicious breakfast omelet from a recipe told to me by Khanum-e Rahman in Tabriz.

1. **To make the syrup:** In a small saucepan mix together the sugar, water, zest of orange, and saffron-rose water, and bring to a boil. Reduce heat to low and simmer for 4 minutes. Remove from heat.

2. **To make the batter:** In a mixing bowl, whisk together the eggs, yogurt, and baking powder. Gradually add the flour mixture and whisk until you have a thick, smooth batter (do not over-mix). Allow to rest for 5 minutes.

3. **To cook the omelet:** Heat the oil in an 8in/20cm frittata pan until hot but not smoking, pour in the batter, cover, and cook for 8 to 9 minutes over low heat until somewhat firm. Flip over, cover, and cook for 5 to 6 minutes until the pancake is cooked through.

4. Transfer to a serving dish, drizzle the syrup over the omelet, and sprinkle the rose petals, walnuts and cinnamon on top.

5. Serve with bread, basil, and Onion, Cucumber + Coriander Pickle (page 675). *Nush-e joon!*

Azarbaijan

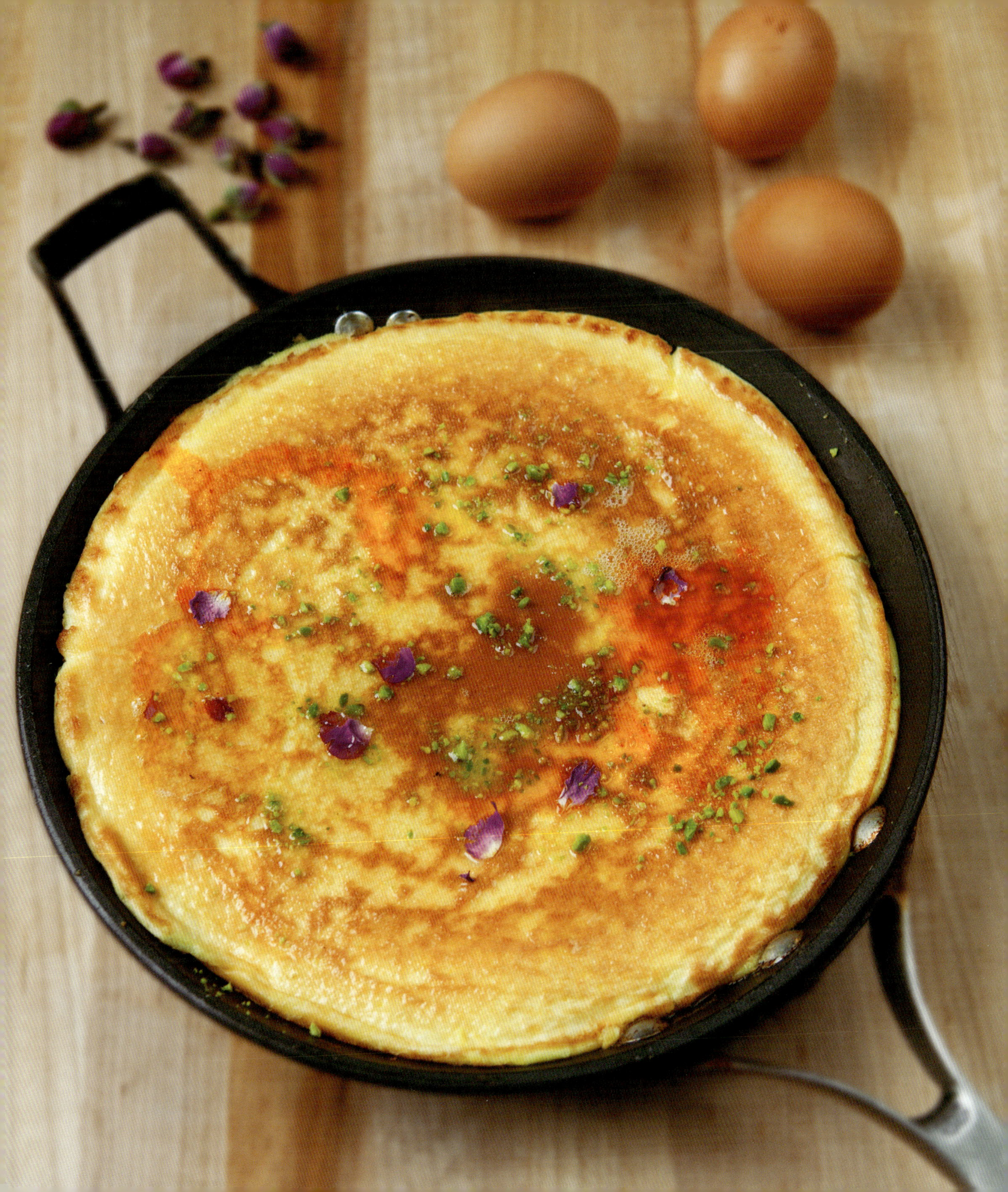

Stuffed Grape Leaves
dolmeh-ye balg-e mo-tabrizi

Serves 6 to 8
Prep: 1 hour
Cooking: 2 hours

VINE LEAVES

50 fresh grape leaves (in season)

FILLING

½ cup/100g rice
½ cup/90g bulgur
2 teaspoons fine sea salt
½ cup/120ml olive oil
1 onion, peeled and thinly sliced
2 cloves garlic, peeled and grated
2 cups/200g chopped spring onions
¼ cup/20g fresh summer savory or
  1 tablespoon dried
½ cup/40g chopped fresh dill or
  2 tablespoons dried
¼ cup/20g chopped fresh tarragon or
  1 tablespoon dried
¼ cup/20g chopped fresh mint or
  1 tablespoon dried
3½ cups/300g chopped fresh parsley or
  1 cup/80g dried
½ cup/75g raisins
½ teaspoon ground black pepper
½ teaspoon red pepper flakes
1 teaspoon ground cinnamon
2 tablespoons dried rose petals, ground
2 tablespoons lime juice

BROTH

2 cups/480ml water

SYRUP/CHASHNI

¼ cup/50g sugar
¼ cup/60ml wine vinegar
1 teaspoon fine sea salt
¼ cup/60ml fresh lime juice

GARNISH

1 medium tomato, chopped

1. Pick fresh and tender grape vine leaves, tie them together in batches, and blanch them in boiling water for 2 minutes. Drain in a colander and rinse with cold water.

2. *To make the filling:* In a small saucepan, place the rice, bulgur, and salt with 3 cups/420ml water and bring to a boil over medium heat. Cover and cook over low heat for 10 minutes. Drain thoroughly and set aside to cool.

3. In a wide skillet, heat ¼ cup/60ml oil over medium heat and sauté the onion and garlic until caramelized. Add the rice and bulgur mixture, and the remaining ingredients for the filling. Knead thoroughly, using your hands.

4. Place three layers of grape leaves on the bottom of a well-oiled medium-sized laminated cast-iron pot.

5. *To assemble the stuffed grape leaves:* Place a grape leaf on top of a wooden board with the vein side up and nip off the little stem. Top with 1 tablespoon filling. Roll up the leaf, folding in the ends to prevent the filling from leaking out while cooking. Place in the pot. Repeat, filling all the leaves and placing them in the pot side by side.

6. Pour 1 cup/240ml water and ¼ cup/60ml oil over the stuffed leaves in the pot. Set a small ovenproof plate on top of the stuffed grape leaves. Cover and cook over medium-low heat for 1 hour.

7. *To make the syrup:* In a bowl, thoroughly mix all the ingredients for the syrup. Uncover the pot and drizzle the syrup over the top. Cover and continue to cook over low heat for another hour until the leaves are tender.

8. Taste sauce and adjust seasoning. The sauce should be quite reduced. Garnish and serve in the same pot with bread and yogurt. *Nush-e Joon!*

Azarbaijan

VEGETARIAN

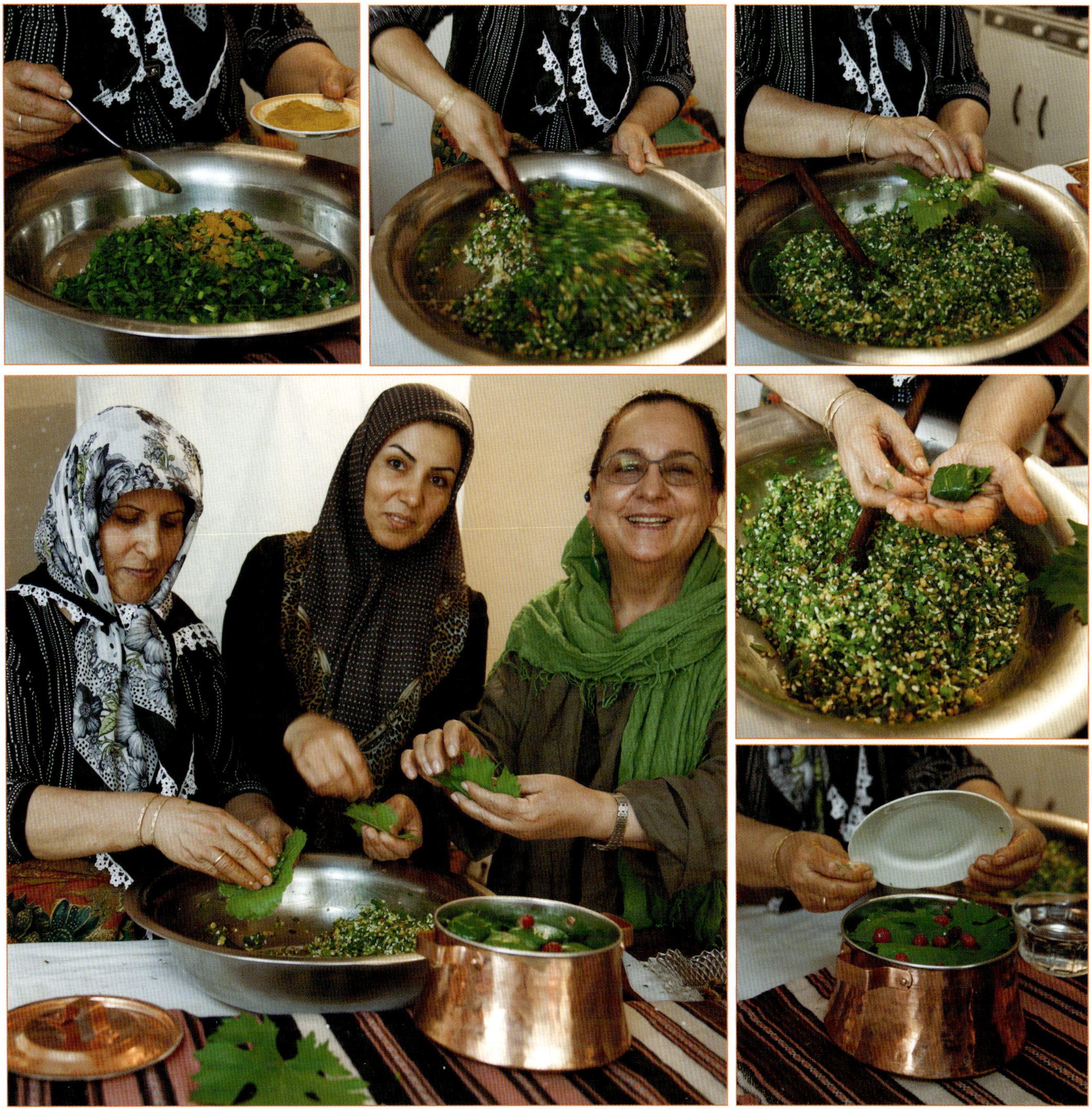

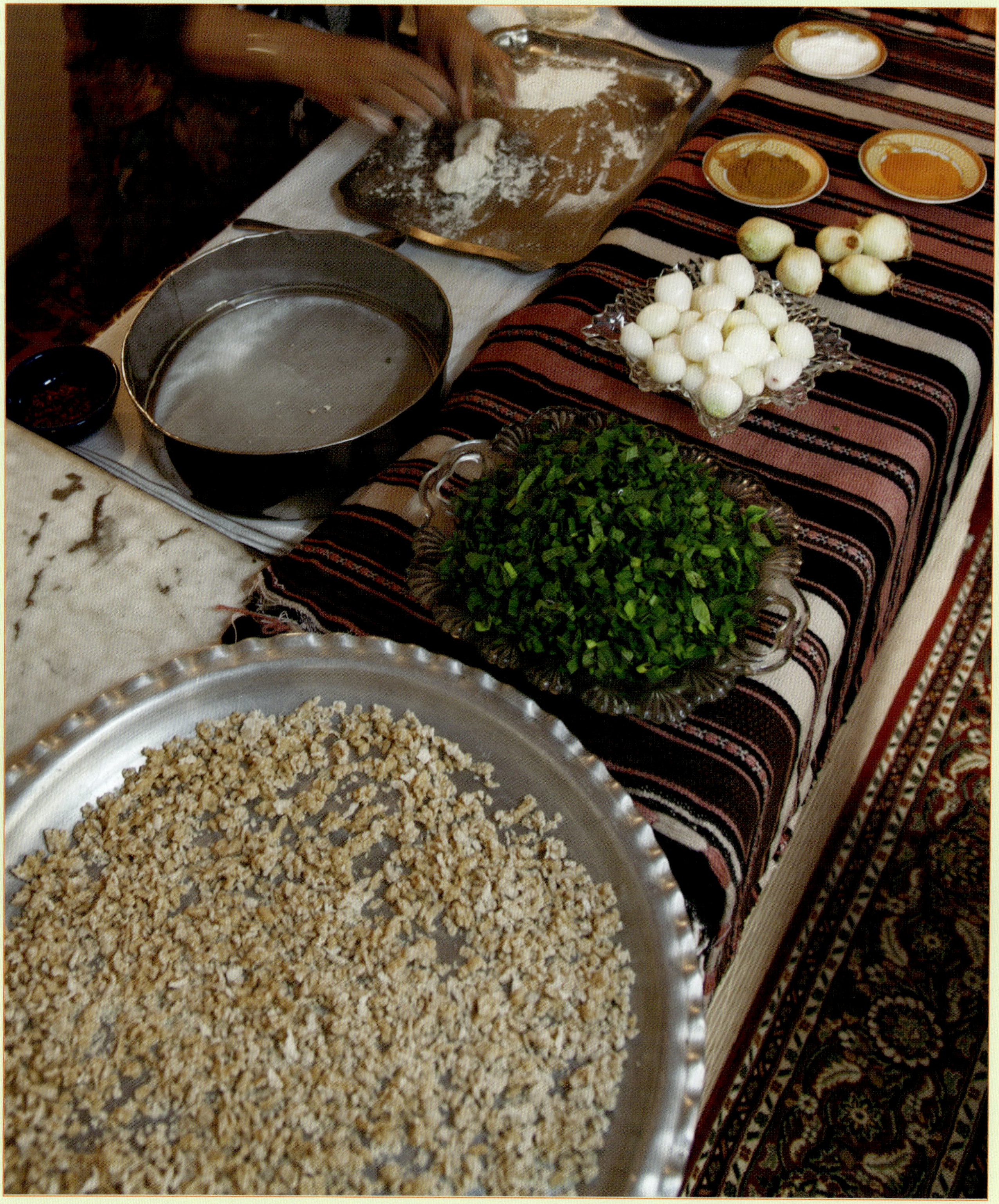

The Story of Omaj

Osh-e omaj, the name of this soup in Persian, is made in many parts of Iran, with variations in the ingredients used, but I especially like this Tabrizi version because it uses only a few ingredients and is easy to make. And, of course, it's delicious. "Omaj" refers to the small pellets of dough made by mixing wheat flour, salt, and water. Ashkenazi Jews make similar small dough pellets for Passover and call it "matzah farfel." You can see the pasta pellets at the bottom of the photo on the facing page. The recipe for making the soup is on the pages that follow.

Pasta Pellet Osh
osh-e omaj-e tabrizi

Serves 4 to 6
Prep: 20 minutes
Cooking: 55 minutes

DOUGH

½ cup/60g unbleached all-purpose flour mixed with ½ teaspoon fine sea salt
2 to 3 tablespoons water

OSH

2 tablespoons oil
1 medium onion
1 teaspoon fine sea salt
½ teaspoon fresh ground pepper
1 teaspoon turmeric
1 cup/85g chopped fresh summer savory or 1 tablespoon dried
8 cups/1.9l water

HERBS

½ cup/125g chopped fresh mint or 2 tablespoons dried
1½ cup/125g chopped fresh spring onions
1½ cup/125g chopped fresh parsley
1½ cup/125g chopped fresh cilantro
½ teaspoon red pepper flakes (optional)

EGGS (OPTIONAL)

2 eggs, beaten (optional)

I have adapted this recipe based on what Rahman Khanum showed me. Keep in mind that traditionally the herbs are added in step 3 with the osh, but I prefer to add them in step 6 at the end of the cooking process. This results in a greener, fresher osh. In Hamadan, they make the same osh but add legumes—red beans and lentils.

1. **To prepare the dough:** In a mixing bowl, combine the flour mixture with 2 to 3 tablespoons water and knead to create a firm dough. Shape it into a small ball.

2. Line a sheet pan with parchment paper. Use the largest side of a grater to grate the dough into tiny ball-shaped bits of dough. Spread the dough bits on a sheet pan. Set aside to dry out

3. **To make the osh:** In a medium-sized laminated cast-iron pot, heat the oil over medium heat and sauté the onion for 15 to 20 minutes until golden brown. Add the salt, pepper, turmeric, and savory, and sauté for 1 minute.

4. Add the water and bring to a boil. Reduce heat to medium, cover, and simmer for 15 minutes.

5. Add the dough bits to the simmering *osh* and bring back to a boil, giving it a gentle stir. Reduce heat to low, cover partially, and simmer for 15 minutes.

6. **For the herbs:** Add the mint, spring onions, parsley, cilantro, and red pepper flakes. Cover and simmer for another 5 minutes.

7. Add the egg gradually while stirring. Bring back to a boil. Reduce heat to low. Adjust seasoning to taste and keep warm until ready to serve. *Nush-e Joon*

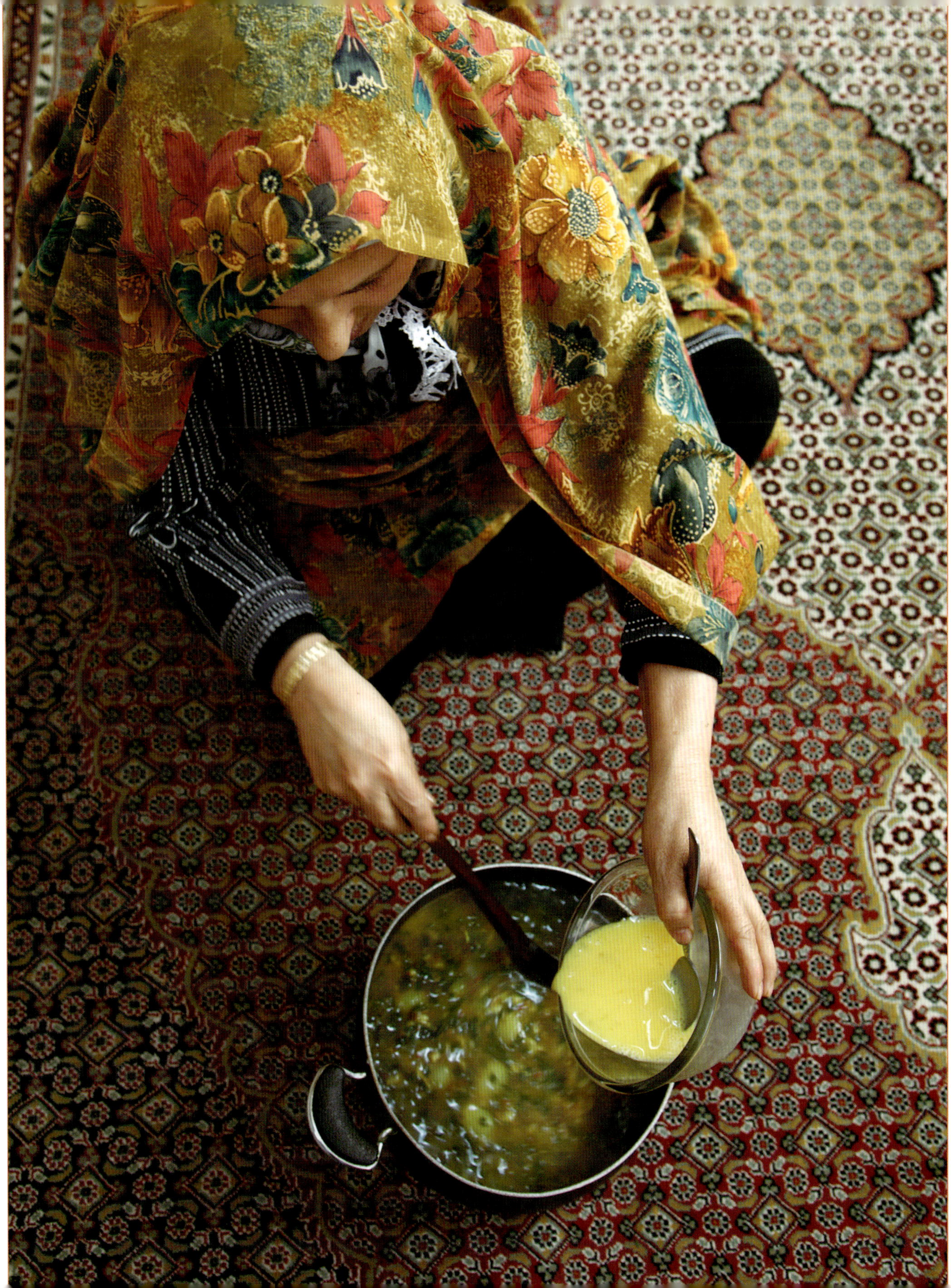

Yogurt + Chickpea Osh
osh-e dugh-e ardebili

Serves 8 to 10
Prep: 20 minutes + soaking of chickpeas overnight
Cooking: 2 hours

BROTH

½ cup/100g chickpeas, soaked overnight, drained, and rinsed
¼ cup/60ml oil
2 large onions, peeled and thinly sliced
½ teaspoon freshly ground pepper
5 cups/1.2l water
½ cup/100g rice, soak 20 minutes, drain
1 tablespoon fine sea salt

YOGURT MIX/DUGH

4 cups/940g whole plain yogurt
1 egg
2 tablespoons all-purpose flour
4 cups/960ml water

MEATBALLS

½ small onion, peeled and grated
2 cloves garlic, grated
½lb/225g ground lamb or chicken thighs
½ teaspoon fine sea salt
¼ teaspoon freshly ground pepper
¼ teaspoon turmeric
1 tablespoon dried mint flakes

HERBS

½ cup/40g chopped fresh parsley
½ cup/40g chopped fresh cilantro
½ cup/50g chopped spring onions
1 cup/85g chopped fresh spinach or beet leaves
½ cup/40g chopped fresh dill weed
5 cloves garlic, peeled and grated

GARNISH

1 teaspoons red pepper flakes (optional)
1 teaspoon dried thyme

At every stop on the road in western Iran, we came across stalls serving this osh, with and without meatballs, along with lamb kababs grilled in front of you. The osh is popular in many parts of Iran. Some make it without legumes, while others make it without bulgur.

1. **To make the broth:** Heat the oil in a large laminated cast-iron pot over medium heat until hot. Sauté the onions until golden brown. Add the chickpeas and pepper and sauté for 1 minute. Pour in the water. Bring to a boil. Reduce heat to low, cover, and simmer for 45 minutes. Add the rice and salt. Cover and cook for another 15 minutes.

2. **To make yogurt mixture:** In a large mixing bowl, first whisk the yogurt with the egg and flour for 5 minutes (beating the yogurt prevents curdling), then add the water and continue to whisk until you have a smooth, yogurt liquid.

3. Add the yogurt mixture to the pot, stirring constantly for 1 minute. Reduce heat to low, cover, and simmer for 25 minutes.

4. **To make the meatballs:** In a mixing bowl, combine the grated onion, garlic, ground lamb, salt, pepper, turmeric, and mint. Knead lightly and, with moist hands, take pieces of the paste and shape them into chestnut-sized meatballs. Gently add them to the *osh* as you make them. Bring the *osh* back to a boil. Reduce heat to low and simmer for 15 minutes, stirring occasionally.

5. Add the herb and garlic mixture, and give it a stir. Cover and simmer over low heat for 15 minutes longer. Check to see if chickpeas are tender. Adjust seasoning to taste.

6. Pour the hot *osh* into a tureen. Sprinkle red pepper flakes and thyme on top. Serve with flat bread. *Nush-e joon!*

Azarbaijan

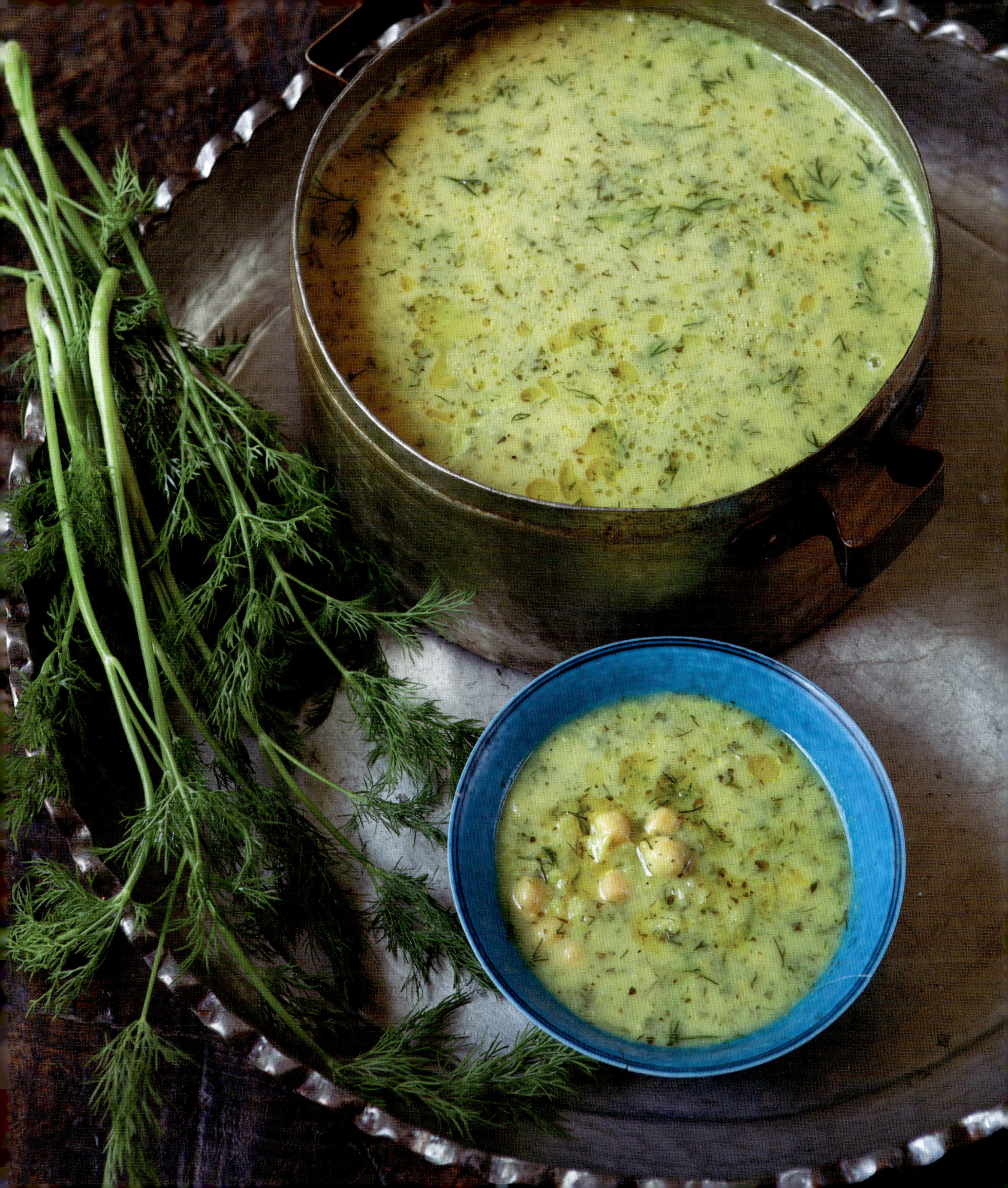

Azarbaijani Dumpling Soup
gush bareh-ye azarbaijani

Serves 6
Preparation time: 1 hour
Cooking: 1 hour

DOUGH

2 cups/240g unbleached all-purpose flour
½ teaspoon fine sea salt
1 teaspoon baking powder
½ cup/120ml water
½ cup/120ml oil

BROTH

8 cups/1.9l chicken broth or water
1 cup/225g tomato puree
2 teaspoons fine sea salt
½ teaspoon freshly ground pepper
½ teaspoon red pepper flakes
2 dried Persian limes, pierced
½ teaspoon ground saffron
½ teaspoon dried thyme
½ teaspoon Azari three-spice *advieh*

FILLING

1 small onion, peeled and quartered
2 cloves garlic, peeled and quartered
½ teaspoon salt
½ teaspoon freshly ground pepper
½ teaspoon turmeric
1 teaspoons Tabrizi three-spice *advieh*
½ teaspoon dried thyme
¼ cup/40g raisins
2 tablespoons oil
½lb/225g ground lamb or chicken

YOGURT SAUCE

1½ cups/360g thick yogurt
4 cloves garlic, grated

GARNISH

½ cup/40g chopped fresh cilantro
¼ teaspoon dried thyme

Gush bareh *and* dush bareh *literally mean the dumplings are shaped like lamb ears, as can be seen in this photo.*

1. *To make the dough:* In a food processor bowl, place the flour, salt, and baking powder, and pulse. Add the rest of the ingredients and continue to pulse for about 5 minutes until you have a dough. Remove the dough, wrap in plastic and place in the fridge for at least 30 minutes.

2. *To make the tomato broth:* In a wide pot, combine all the ingredients for the broth and bring to a boil. Reduce heat to low, cover, and simmer for 30 minutes.

3. *To make the filling:* In a food processor bowl, combine all the ingredients for the filling and pulse until you have a paste. Transfer to a small mixing bowl and set aside.

4. *To assemble the dumplings:* Place a sheet pan lined with parchment paper next to you. On a cool, floured surface, knead the dough until soft and pliable. Use a rolling pin to roll it out as thin as you can.

5. Cut the dough into 3in/7.5cm diameter discs using a cookie cutter dipped in flour (or the open end of a glass). Fill each disc with 1 tablespoon of the filling. Dab the edges with water, fold each circle into a crescent shape, seal with your fingers, and arrange on the sheet pan.

6. Carefully transfer the dumplings to the simmering broth. Bring back to a simmer, stirring gently with a wooden spoon once or twice to avoid any dumplings sticking to the bottom of the pan. Cover and cook over low heat for 1 hour.

7. *To make the yogurt sauce:* In a mixing bowl, whisk together the yogurt and garlic for 5 minutes (this prevents curdling when it's added to the hot soup), and transfer to a small serving dish.

8. Just before serving add the cilantro and thyme. Ladle the soup into individual serving bowls and spoon some of the yogurt sauce on top. *Nush-e joon!*

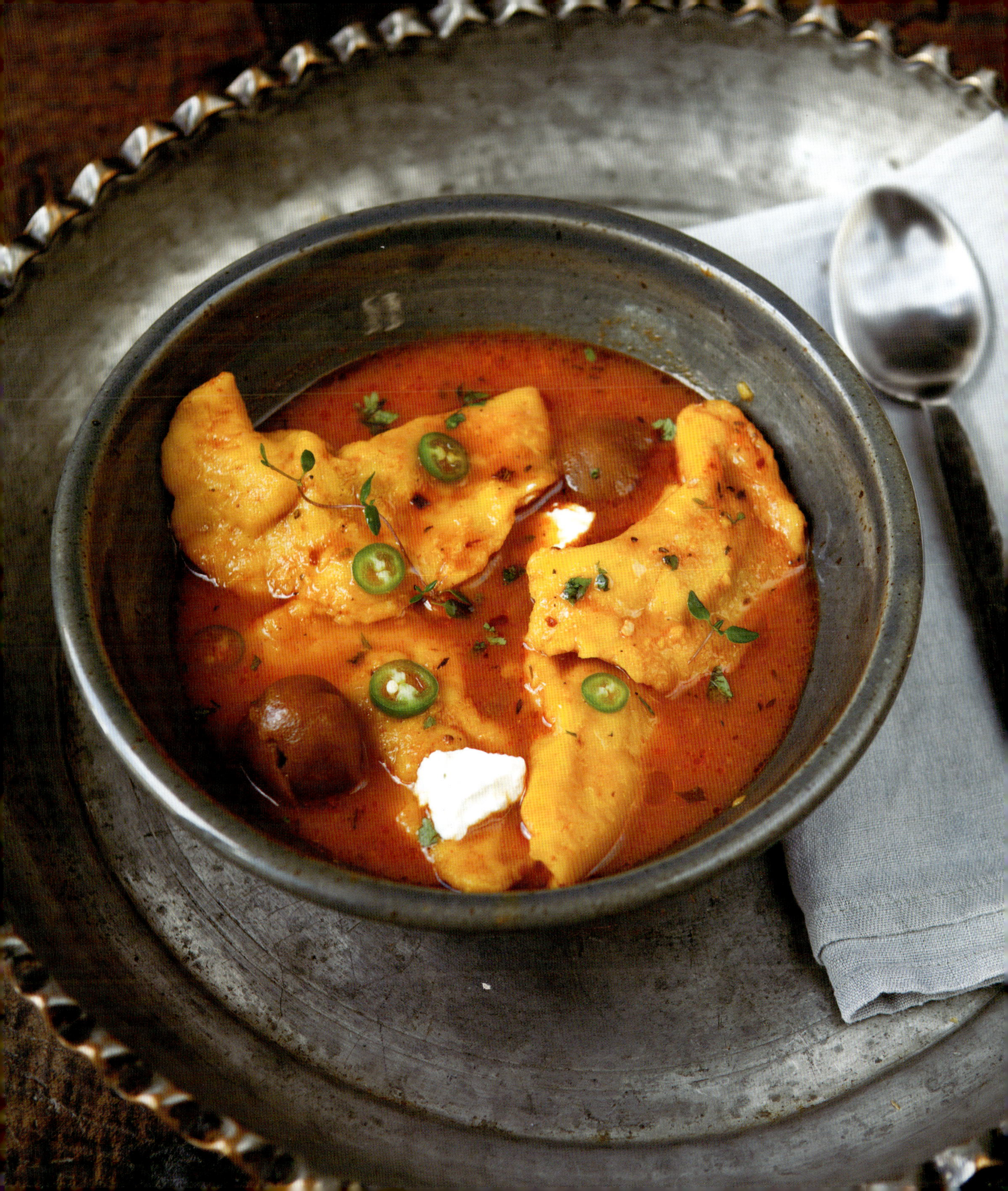

Barley Soup
sup-e jow

Serves 6 to 8
Prep: 10 minutes
Cooking: 1 hour 10 minutes

BARLEY

½ cup/100g barley
8 cups/1.9l water or broth

ROUX

2 tablespoons oil or butter
1 medium onion, peeled and thinly sliced
2 cloves garlic, peeled and thinly sliced
1 tablespoon fine sea salt
1 teaspoon freshly ground black pepper
2 tablespoons unbleached all-purpose flour or rice flour

YOGURT

2 cups/480g plain, thick whole yogurt

GARNISH

½ cup/40g chopped fresh dill weed or 2 tablespoons dried

When we sat down at the Jalai Restaurant in Tabriz for a lunch of chelow kabab (the classic Iranian fluffy, saffroned white rice with fillet kababs, see page 208), The waiter appeared carrying a large tray with bowls full of warm, light, and delicious barley soup. No one had requested it, but it was a perfect starter after a long day. I prefer to make the soup with water instead of broth because of how light it becomes, especially if you are eating it as an appetizer for chelow kabab.

1. **To cook the barley:** In a large heavy-bottomed pot, place the barley and water, and bring to a boil. Reduce heat to medium, cover, and simmer for 20 minutes, stirring occasionally.

2. **Meanwhile, to make the roux:** In a wide skillet, heat 2 tablespoons oil over medium heat until hot. Sauté the onion and garlic until lightly golden. Add the salt, pepper, and flour, and sauté for 1 minute. Transfer to the pot, stirring gently for 1 minute.

3. In a mixing bowl, whisk the yogurt for 5 minutes to prevent from curdling. Transfer it to the pot. Stir constantly for 2 minutes as you bring back to a boil. Reduce heat to low, cover, and simmer for 30 minutes. Adjust seasoning to taste.

4. Just before serving, garnish with dill and give it a stir. *Nush-e joon!*

Opposite: Roasted sweet potato vendor in the Tabriz bazaar.

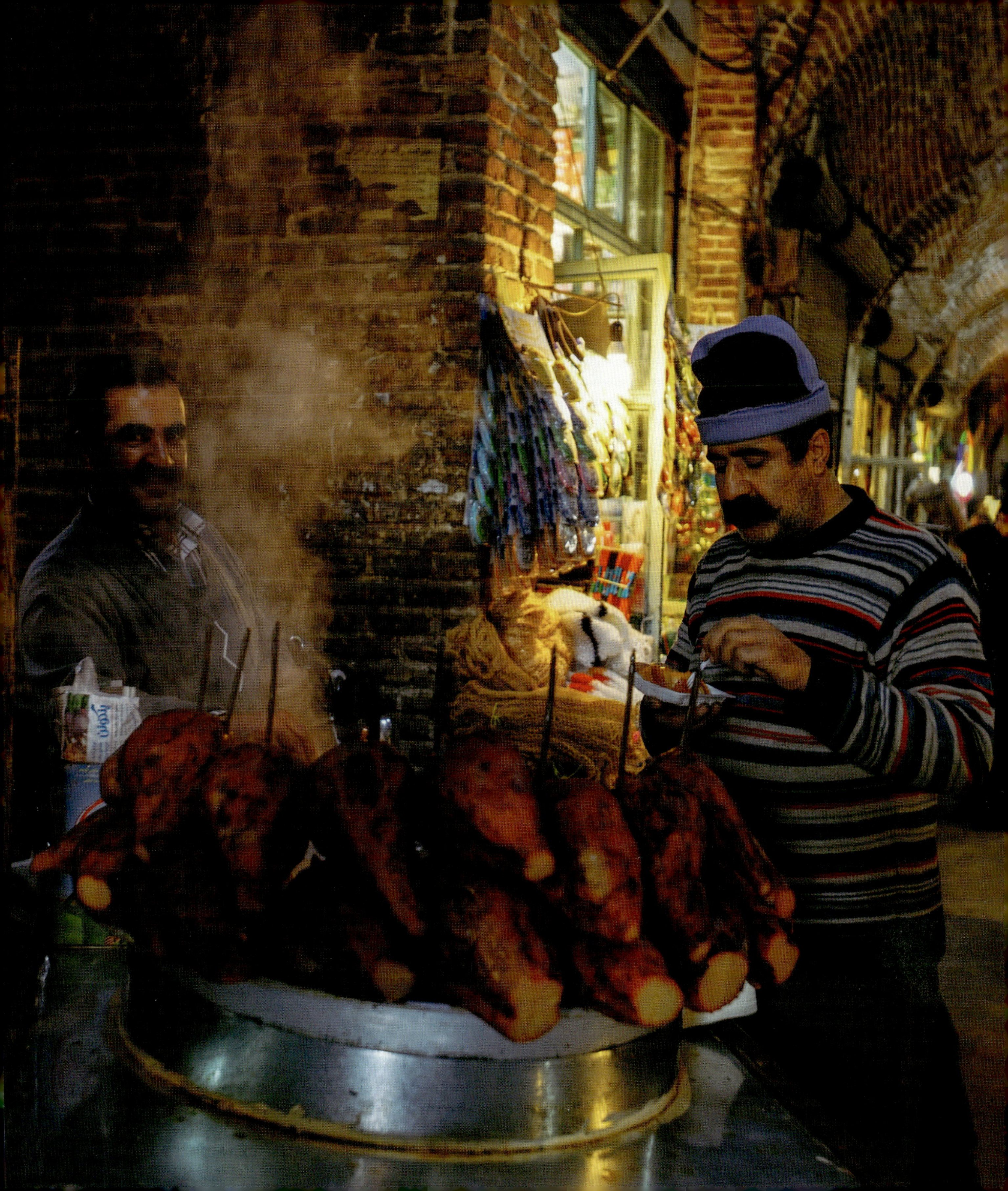

Tabrizi Meatballs with Split Peas + Tomatoes
kufteh tabrizi

Serves 4
Prep: 40 minutes + 30 minutes of resting
Cooking: 1 hour

LAMB PASTE

1¼ cups/250g dried yellow split peas
1 cup/200g rice
1 russet potato, peeled and diced
2 teaspoons fine sea salt
1 large onion, peeled and grated
1 teaspoon freshly ground black pepper
1 teaspoon turmeric
1 cup/85g chopped fresh summer savory or 2 tablespoons dried
1 cup/85g chopped spring onions
1 cup/85g chopped fresh tarragon or 2 tablespoons dried
1lb/450g ground lamb
2 eggs, lightly beaten

BROTH

¼ cup/60ml oil or ghee
1 small onion, thinly sliced
2 teaspoons fine sea salt
1 teaspoon freshly ground pepper
1 teaspoon turmeric
1 tablespoon tomato paste
3 cups/675g tomato puree
3 cups/720ml water

FILLING

¼ cup/60ml oil
2 medium onions, thinly sliced
6 tablespoons dried barberries, rinsed
2 tablespoons walnuts, chopped
2 hard-boiled eggs, halved

I had these meatballs under the fig tree in Rahmani Khanum's backyard in Tabriz. It's traditionally made on the stovetop, but here I'm making it in the oven. In Hamadan, they make a very similar meatball except that they use chickpeas instead of split peas and use a combination of vinegar and grape molasses instead of tomatoes in the broth. For the filling, they replace the barberries with prunes.

1. *To make the lamb paste:* In a large saucepan, place the split peas, rice, and potatoes. Pour in 8 cups/1.9l water and bring a boil. Reduce heat to medium and cook for 30 minutes. Drain and set aside to cool.

2. In a food processor, place the split peas, rice, and potato mixture, and pulse until you have a smooth puree. Transfer it to a large mixing bowl and add the rest of the ingredients for the paste. Knead with your hands for 4 minutes. Cover and allow to rest in the refrigerator for at least 30 minutes.

3. *To make the broth:* In a large saucepan, heat the oil and sauté the onion until golden brown. Add the rest of the ingredients for the broth and bring to a boil. Reduce heat to low, cover, and allow to simmer.

4. *To make the filling:* Heat the oil and sauté the onions over medium heat until caramelized. Add the rest of the ingredients for the filling, except the boiled eggs, and sauté for 20 seconds. Remove from heat and allow to cool.

5. *To cook the meatballs:* Preheat the oven to 400°F/200°C. Generously oil a wide non-reactive baking dish (12 x 14in/30 x 35cm) large enough to fit 4 orange-sized meatballs. Set aside.

6. Divide the paste into 4 equal portions and shape each portion into an orange-sized ball.

7. Use a small bowl to help you fill and form the meatballs. Evenly spray it with oil and place a meatball in it. Use your thumb to make a deep, wide indentation in the center. Place half a hard-boiled egg and 2 tablespoons of the filling in the indentation. Close the indentation and shape it back to a large, smooth ball. Repeat for the remaining 3 meatballs. Gently place the meatballs, as you make them, in the oiled baking dish, leaving space between them. Generously oil each meatball with a brush.

8. Bake in the preheated oven for 10 minutes. Pull out the oven rack and gently spoon the simmering broth over the meatballs. Cover with oiled parchment paper and bake for 50 minutes, basting the meatballs once again during this time. Serve with bread, a herb platter, and yogurt. *Nush-e joon!*

203

A tea house in the Tabriz bazaar. The older men are smoking their hookahs while the younger ones are busy with their cell phones.

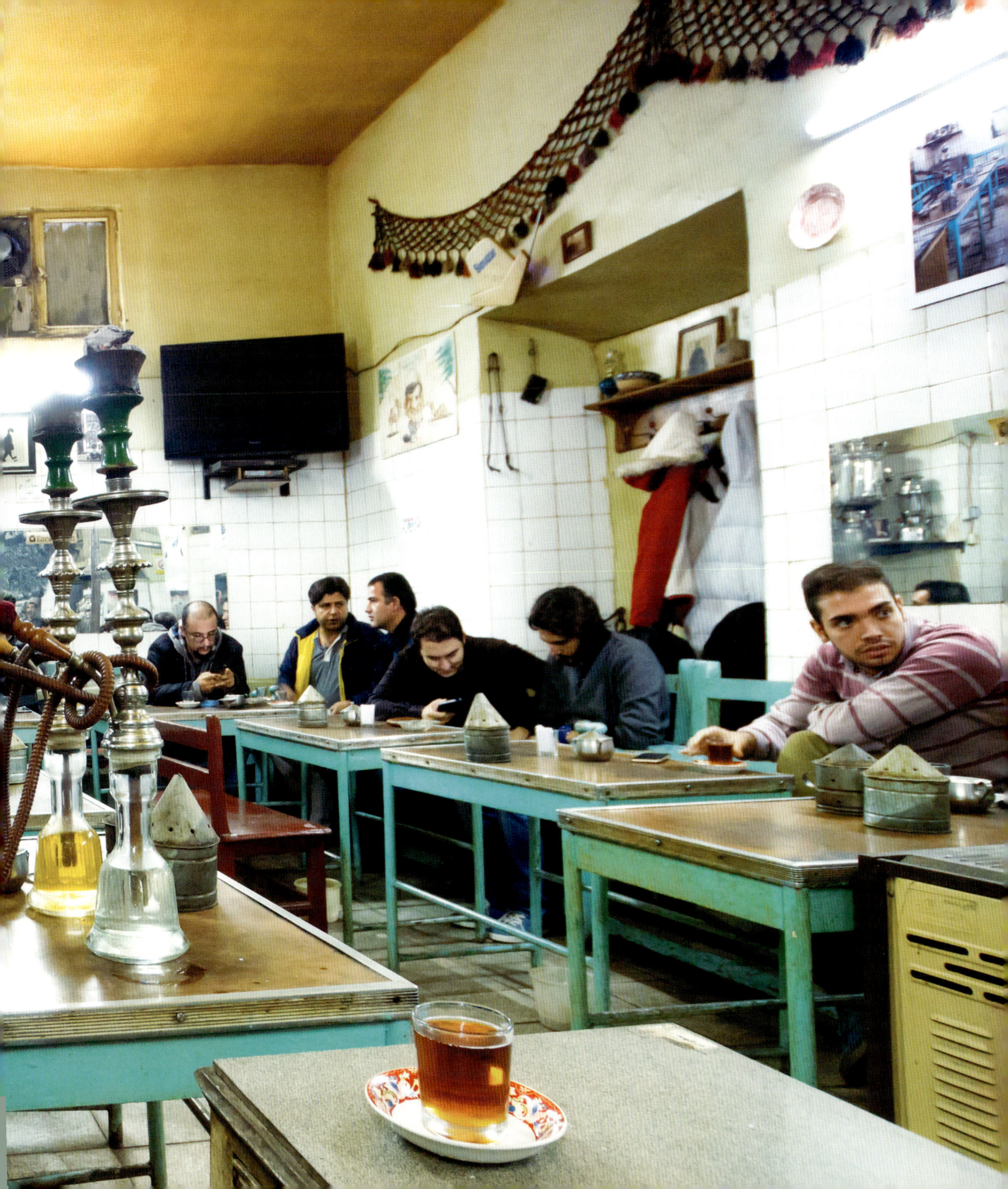

Vegetable + Fruit Casserole
tas kabab-e ardabil

Serves 6
Prep: 15 minutes
Cooking: 2½ hours

SPICE MIX

1 tablespoon fine sea salt
1 teaspoon freshly ground pepper
1 teaspoon turmeric
2 tablespoons dried Persian lime powder
2 teaspoons Azari three-spice *advieh*

CHICKEN AND VEGETABLES

¼ cup/60ml oil or 55g butter
2 large onions, peeled and thinly sliced
4 chicken leg quarters with the bone (3 pounds/1.2kg), or 2lb/900g boned leg of lamb, thinly sliced
2 cloves garlic, peeled and sliced
2 quinces, or apples, cored, hard parts removed and sliced into wedges
2 Chinese eggplants, peeled and sliced (1in/2.5cm thick)
2 carrots, peeled and sliced (1in/2.5cm thick)
2 tomatoes, peeled and sliced (1in/2.5cm thick)
2 large russet potatoes (1.3 pounds/600g), peeled and sliced (1in/2.5cm thick)
1 cup/175g pitted prunes
1 cup/175g dried apricots
5 medjool dates/85g, pitted and halved

BROTH

½ teaspoon ground saffron threads
1 cup/240ml water

This dish is traditionally made on the stovetop with thin slices of boned leg of lamb. Here I am using chicken on the bone and cooking it in the oven, because I find it much easier, and the result is tastier. However, if you'd like to use lamb, just replace the chicken. Everything else remains the same.

1. Preheat oven to 350°F/180°C.

2. *To make the spice mix:* In a small bowl combine all the spices and mix well.

3. *To cook the chicken and vegetables:* Pour 2 tablespoons oil into a 4 quart/3.7l ovenproof casserole dish, and layer the ingredients in the following order (sprinkling some of the spice mixture between the layers): onion, chicken, garlic, quince, eggplant, carrot, tomato, and potato. Use the palms of your hands to press down. Top with a layer of prunes, apricots, and dates. Pour the remaining oil on top.

4. Combine the saffron and water and pour it over the chicken and vegetables.

5. Cover tightly and cook in the oven for 2 to 2½ hours until chicken and potatoes are tender. Adjust seasoning to taste.

6. Serve right out of the casserole dish with bread, yogurt, salad, and fresh herbs. *Nush-e joon!*

NOTE

This casserole may also be cooked on the stovetop in a laminated cast-iron braiser or pot over low heat for 2½ hours or until the meat and potatoes are tender.

You can also use 2lb/900g boneless chicken thighs.

If you have whole dried Persian limes, cut in half, discard the seeds and grind the rest to make the powder.

Azarbaijan

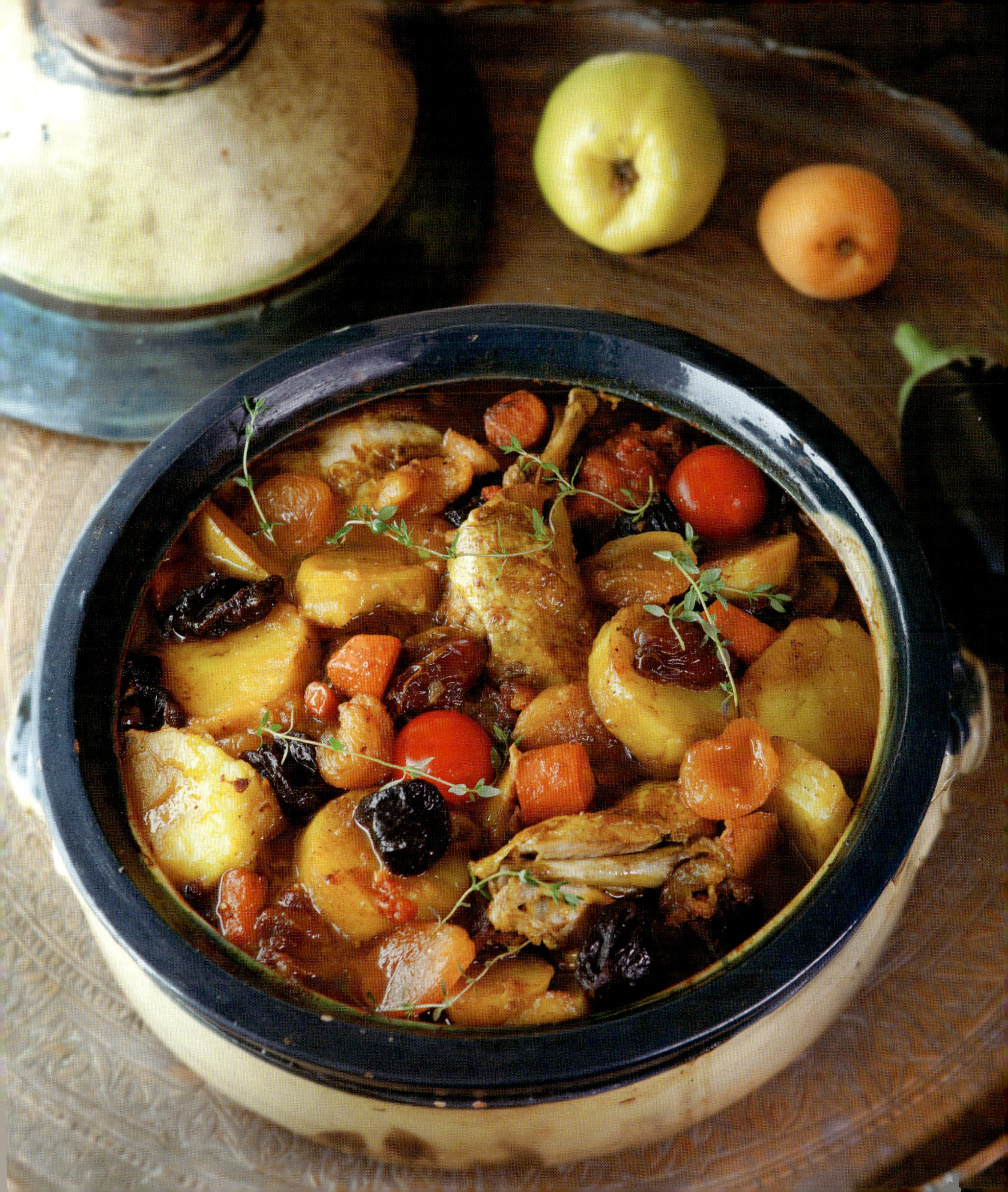

The National Dish: Chelow Kabab

Chelow kabab is Iran's national dish, the equivalent of a burger and fries in the United States. It is served everywhere, from palaces to roadside stalls, but the best *chelow kababs* are probably those sold in the bazaars, where the rice is served with a tin cloche covering the plate to keep it warm, and the kababs are brought to the table by the waiter, who holds 5 or 10 skewers in his left hand and a piece of bread in his right hand. He places a skewer of meat directly on the rice and, holding it down with the bread, dramatically pulls out the skewer, leaving the sizzling kababs behind.

No one really knows where this dish originated, but it is thought that Naser al-Din Shah Qajar brought it from Tabriz to Tehran around the 1840s, when he went there to be crowned king. Some have said it was his favorite dish.

Chelow kabab consists of saffron steamed rice/*chelow* and kabab/*kabab-e barg* (skewers of lamb, veal, or beef strips marinated in saffron, onions, and lime juice). Skewers of ground lamb/*kabab-e kubideh* can also be added. When both types of skewered lamb are included, the dish is called *chelow kabab-e soltani,* which literally means "fit for a sultan". Grilled tomatoes and raw onions are also an integral part of chelow kabab. The traditional way to serve chelow kabab is as follows:

Heap a pyramid of *chelow* on each plate. Add a dab of butter and sprinkle with a teaspoon of powdered sumac. Mix well.

Serve hot with trimmings such as a fresh herb platter/*sabzi-khordan*, yogurt and cucumber/*mast-o khiar*, yogurt and Persian shallots/*mast-o musir*, and pickles/*torshi*. The trimmings often also include powdered sumac, quartered onions, and raw egg yolks in the shell (for mixing with the rice; this was standard in the past but less common these days). *Chelow kabab* is often washed down with a minty yogurt drink/*dugh*. In my childhood, it was a treat to have it with a "Pepsi" instead of the traditional *dugh*.

Saffron Steamed Rice

chelow

Serves 6
Prep: 5 minutes of marinating
Cooking: 1½ hours

RICE

4 cups/800g white basmati rice
8 cups/1.9l water
3 tablespoons fine sea salt
2 tablespoons cardamom seeds (not the pods. Optional)
2 tablespoons rose water (optional)

GOLDEN CRUST/*TAH-DIG*

1¼ cups/300ml olive oil or ghee
2 tablespoons plain whole milk yogurt
½ teaspoon ground saffron dissolved in 4 tablespoons hot water

RICE POT

Non-stick pots make unmolding the rice much easier. For the ultimate Persian rice with a good crust/*tah-dig*, I use a 5-quart/4.7l pot (11¼ in/28.5cm in diameter and 3¼ in/8cm deep). The best are hard-anodized and non-stick. They are available at kitchen equipment stores, Iranian markets, or via the Internet.

NOTE FOR RICE WITHOUT GOLDEN CRUST/*TAH-DIG*

If, for any reason, you don't want the rice to have a golden crust/*tah-dig*, in step 4, reduce the oil to 2 tablespoons, and in step 7, reduce the cooking time to just 15 minutes.

When I asked if I could meet the cooks and photograph some of the dishes at the Jalali Restaurant, I was surprised to hear the manager say she was familiar with my cookbook Food of Life *and that I was welcome to visit their kitchen. I have adapted the rice and kabab recipes that follow in consultation with their chef/kababi.*

1. *To cook the rice:* Wash the rice by placing it in a large container and covering it with water. Agitate gently with your hand, then pour off the water. Repeat 4 to 5 times until the water is clear. Set aside.

2. Fill a large non-stick pot with 8 cups/1.9l of water, add the salt, cardamom, and rose water, and bring to a boil. Add the rice and boil briskly for 6 to 10 minutes (depending on the type of rice), gently stirring twice with a wooden spoon to loosen any grains that stick to the bottom. Once the rice rises to the top of the pan, it is done.

3. Drain the rice in a large fine-mesh strainer and rinse with water (about 3 cups/700ml).

4. *To make the golden crust/tah-dig:* In the same pot, combine 2 spatulas of the cooked rice (about 2 heaped cups) with 1 cup oil, the yogurt, ¼ cup/60ml water, and 1 tablespoon saffron water. Stir well, using a rubber spatula until the mixture is smooth and no longer lumpy, then spread out evenly in the pot—this will form the golden crust/*tah-dig*.

5. Gently heap the remaining rice, 1 spatula at a time, onto the *tah-dig* layer. Shape the rice into a pyramid to allow it to expand.

6. Cover the pot and cook the rice for 10 minutes over medium heat.

7. Mix ½ cup water with ¼ cup/60ml oil and pour over the rice. Sprinkle the remaining saffron water on top. Wrap the lid in a clean dish towel and then place on the pot to absorb condensation and prevent any steam from escaping. Reduce heat to low and cook for 70 minutes longer.

8. Remove the pot from the heat and leave it to cool, still covered, on a damp surface (a damp dish towel on a rimmed sheet pan) for 5 minutes to loosen the crust.

9. There are two ways to serve the rice. The first is to hold the serving platter tightly over the uncovered pot and invert the two together, unmolding the entire mound onto the platter. The rice will emerge as a golden-crusted cake, traditionally served in wedges. Or serve the rice straight from the pot and the crust/*tah-dig* separately. *Nush-e joon!*

Azarbaijan

RICE CRUST VARIATIONS

Plain Crust—For this crust, in a mixing bowl, whisk together 1 cup/240ml oil, ¼ cup/60ml water, a few drops of saffron water, and 3 spatulas of the parboiled rice (about 2 cups). Spread the mixture in the bottom of the pot and mound the rest of the rice over it. In step 8 cover and cook over medium-high heat for 10 minutes. Then, in step 9 cover and cook over low heat for 70 minutes.

Yogurt Crust—In a mixing bowl, whisk together 1 cup/240ml oil, ¼ cup/60ml water, a few drops of saffron water, 2 tablespoons yogurt, and 3 spatulas (about 2 cups) of the parboiled rice. Spread the mixture in the bottom of the pot and mound the rest of the rice over it. In step 8 cover and cook over medium heat for 10 minutes. Then, in step 9 cover and cook over low heat for 70 minutes.

Milk Crust—In a mixing bowl, whisk together 1 cup/240ml oil, ½ cup/120ml milk, a few drops of saffron water, and 3 spatulas (about 2 cups) of the parboiled rice. Spread the mixture in the bottom of the pot and mound the rest of the rice over it. In step 8 cover and cook over medium heat for 10 minutes. Then, in step 9 cover and cook over low heat for 60 minutes.

Egg Crust—In a mixing bowl, whisk together ½ cup/120ml oil, ¼ cup/60ml water, a few drops of saffron water, 2 tablespoons yogurt, 2 egg yolks, and 3 spatulas (2 cups) of the parboiled rice. Spread the mixture in the bottom of the pot and mound the rest of the rice over it. In step 8 cover and cook over medium heat for 20 minutes. In step 9 cover and cook over low heat for 60 minutes.

Lavash Crust—In a mixing bowl, whisk together ½ cup/120ml oil, ½ cup/120ml water, and a few drops of saffron water, and spread in the pot. Place a layer of **lavash** bread on top to fit the bottom of the pot and mound the rest of the rice over it. For this crust, in step 8 cover and cook over medium heat for 10 minutes. Then, in step 9 cover and cook over low heat for 50 minutes.

Potato Crust—In a mixing bowl, whisk together ½ cup/120ml oil, 2 tablespoons water, and a few drops of saffron water, and spread in the pot. Arrange slices of peeled ¼in/6mm thick rounds of russet potatoes (do not wash the potatoes, the starch helps to bind the *tah-dig*) to fit the bottom of the pot. Place a thin layer of rice over the potatoes and press down firmly with your hands. Mound the rest of the rice on top. For this crust, in step 8 cover and cook over medium heat for 10 minutes. Then, in step 9 cover and cook over low heat for 70 minutes. Photo on facing page.

Quince Crust—In a mixing bowl, whisk together ½ cup/120ml oil, ¼ cup/60ml water, and a few drops of saffron water, and spread in the pot. Arrange ¼in/6mm thick rounds of cored quinces to fit the bottom of the pot. Place a thin layer of rice over the quinces and press down firmly with your hands. Mound the rest of the rice on top. For this crust, in step 8 cover and cook over medium heat for 10 minutes. Then, in step 9 cover and cook over low heat for 50 minutes.

> **NOTE**
> I am giving you guidelines and proportions for making your favorite golden crust/*tah-dig*. However, you should experiment and practice using your stovetop and the type of basmati rice you have (I am using a gas flame and an aged Indian basmati). Making good rice with a perfect golden crust is all about the combination of the temperature and the cooking time. Traditionally, Iranians use a ready-made padded lid/*damkoni* to cover the rice pot to absorb condensation and prevent steam from escaping during long-term steaming. You can buy one or make your own. Otherwise, wrap a clean dish towel over the lid of the pot.

211

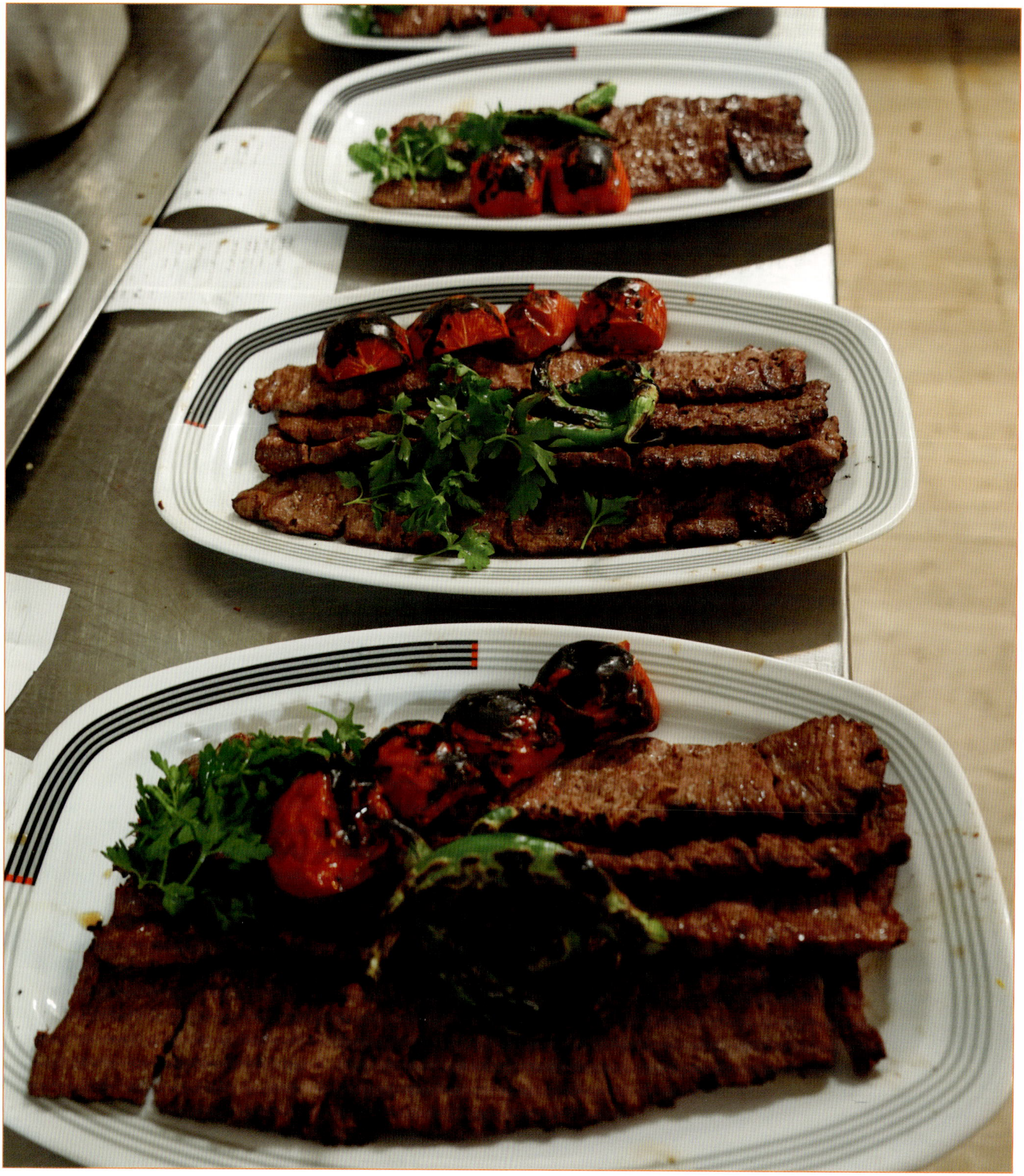

Fillet Kabab
kabab-e barg

Serves 4
Prep: 20 minutes + 24 hours of salting + 20 minutes marinating
Cooking: 3 to 4 minutes

LAMB

2½lb/1.1kg lean lamb loin (fillet), or beef (tenderloin) or veal (veal tender) rubbed with 1 tablespoon fine sea salt all over and allowed to sit in a sheet pan, cover, and refrigerator for 24 to 48 hours, remove and pat dry.

MARINADE

2 large yellow onions, peeled, grated, and juice squeezed out through a fine-mesh sieve
1 cup/240ml olive oil
1 teaspoon freshly ground pepper
¼ teaspoon ground saffron threads dissolved in 1 tablespoon warm water

BASTE

1 cup/110g butter
1 tablespoon fresh lime juice

COOKING + GARNISH

4 flat, thin ½in/1cm wide skewers
1 package/12oz/340g lavash bread
2 tablespoons sumac powder (optional)
12 capri tomatoes or 4 large tomatoes, cut in quarters

On entering the Jalali Restaurant in Tabriz, we were surprised by the shiny plastic tablecloths and a decor that seemed inauthentic for such a traditional place. But the food was so good that we soon forgot about the table setting and decor. The chef/kababi told me that the secret for making this kabab was to rub the lamb loin with salt all over and allow it to sit in the fridge for 24 to 48 hours before cutting the fillets. The salt, he said, will draw out the water in the meat, making it much tastier.

1. *To prepare the lamb loin:* Place the salted loin on a cutting board, open it up on one side, turn, and open on the other side to form a flat piece of meat. To tenderize and give the meat the particular texture and delicacy of this kabab, use the blunt edge of a cleaver to gently pound the flattened loin vertically with the grain (about 3 minutes).

2. Cut the loin lengthwise into 3 strips. Moisten the cutting board and press one of the pieces down firmly and cut it, across the grain, into 2½in/6cm pieces. Repeat for the rest of the meat.

3. Thread each piece of meat, *against the grain*, onto a flat, swordlike skewer, leaving 2in/5cm at the top of the skewer. Use the cleaver to trim and straighten the edges of the skewered meat. Arrange the skewers side by side on a large, rimmed sheet pan. Spear tomatoes on separate skewers.

4. *To make the marinade:* In a mixing bowl, combine all the ingredients for the marinade and pour over the skewered kababs. Cover with another sheet pan (inverted) and allow to marinate for 20 minutes at room temperature. Turn the skewers in the marinade once during this period.

5. Start a bed of charcoal at least 30 minutes before you want to cook until the coals glow. The secret to a good kabab is a very hot fire.

6. *To prepare the baste:* In a small saucepan, place the ingredients for the baste, melt the butter, mix, and keep warm.

7. When coals are ready, brush the tomatoes lightly with the baste and place them on the grill first (they take longer to cook). A few minutes later arrange the skewered meat on the grill. Cook for 3 to 4 minutes, turning frequently. The meat should be seared on the outside and pink and juicy on the inside.

8. Place the kabab and grilled tomato skewers on the serving platter and pour the baste over them (keep them on the skewers until ready to serve). Cover with lavash bread to keep warm.

9. Sprinkle the kababs with sumac powder. Serve immediately with saffron steamed rice/*chelow*, lavash bread, pickles/*torshi*, and a dish of fresh herbs, especially spring onions and basil. Remove the meat from each skewer by placing a piece of lavash bread to hold down several pieces of meat as you pull them off the skewer. *Nush-e joon!*

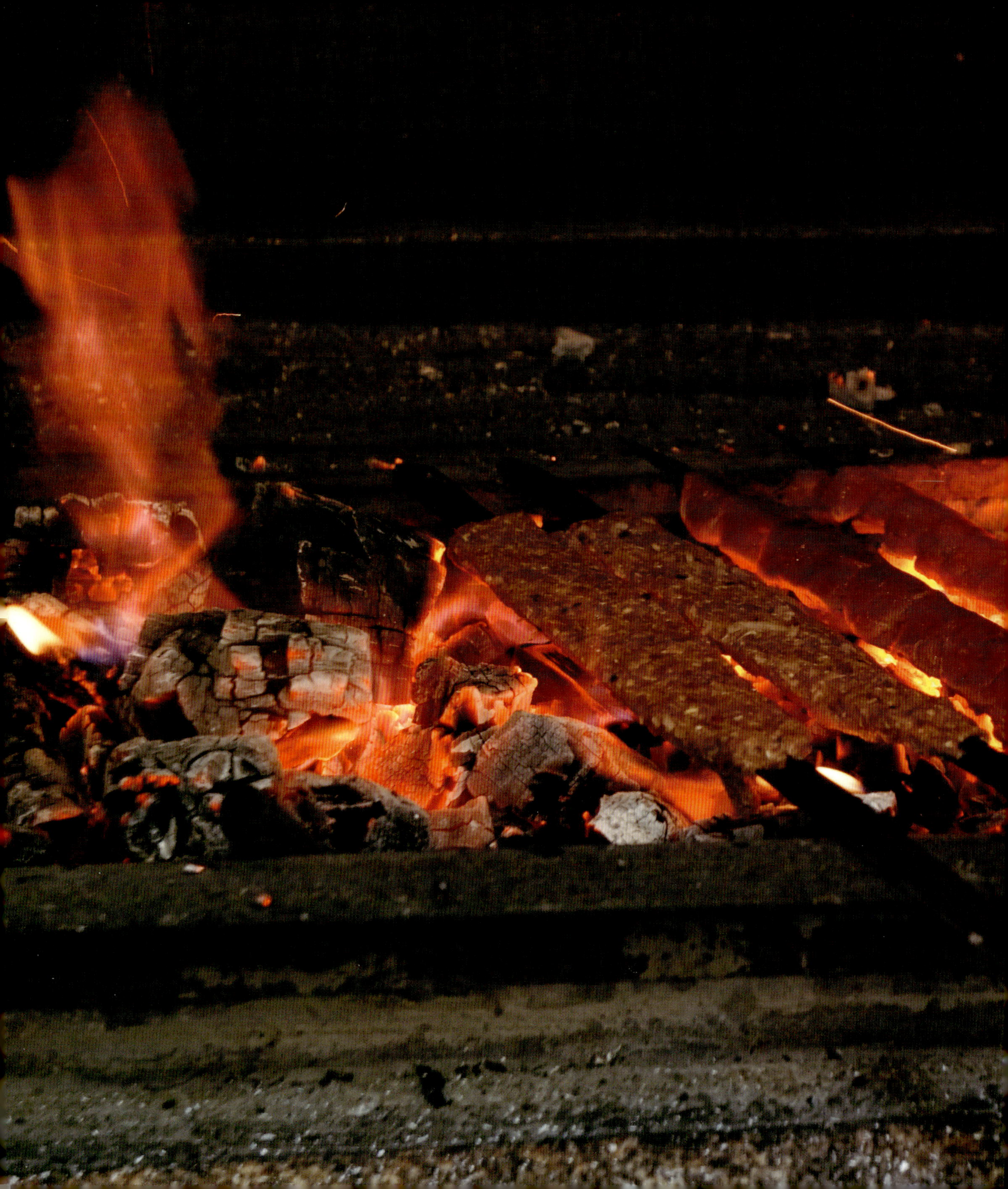

The Story of Minced Kabab
kabab-e bonab

Bonab is a small town east of Lake Urmia in western Azarbaijan. It is famous for its minced kabab/*kabab-e bonab*, which has become popular in restaurant chains in other cities in Iran. Instead of ground lamb, they use shoulder of lamb, place it on a chopping board, and use 2 sharp cleavers to mince the lamb (this takes some practice). They then sprinkle the onion on top and continue to chop until the onion and lamb are minced together. Everything else is the same as for ground lamb kabab (page 216) except that they add 2 egg yolks to help with the bonding of the paste. This kabab also needs extra-wide skewers (it is said that the first person to make this kabab used his sword as a skewer).

Ground Lamb Kabab
kabab-e kubideh-ye gusfand-e tabrizi

Serves 6
Prep: 30 minutes + 30 minutes of resting
Cooking: 10 minutes

LAMB PASTE

2lb/900g twice-ground lamb shoulder, or beef (85% lean)
2 teaspoons fine sea salt
2 teaspoons fresh ground black pepper
½ teaspoon ground saffron dissolved in 1 tablespoon rose water, or ½ teaspoon turmeric
½ teaspoon baking soda
2 medium yellow onions, grated
2 cloves garlic, peeled and grated
2 tablespoons fresh parsley leaves
2 tablespoons slivered pistachio kernels

BASTE

1 cup/225g butter or olive oil
1 teaspoon fresh lime juice

COOKING AND GARNISH

14 flat ¼in/6mm skewers
1 package (12oz/340g) lavash bread
½ cup/50g sumac powder
2 limes, cut in half
Persian basil

1. *To make the meat paste:* In a warm, wide skillet, combine all the lamb paste ingredients. Knead with your hands for a few minutes. Cover the paste and let stand for at least 30 minutes and up to 24 hours in the refrigerator.

2. Start charcoal at least 30 minutes before you want to cook and let it burn until the coals are glowing evenly. For this kabab, you want the coals to be as high as possible, close to the meat, and at their hottest. Do not spread the charcoal thin. If you are using an indoor grill make sure it is preheated and very hot.

3. Using damp hands (keep a bowl of water next to you), divide the lamb paste into equal lumps about the size of small oranges. Shape each into a 5in/12.5cm long sausage and mold it firmly around a flat, sword-like skewer. Pinch the two ends ensuring that the meat is firmly attached to the skewer. Arrange on a sheet pan, separated from each other. Cover and keep in a cool place.

4. *To make the baste:* Melt the butter in a small saucepan and add the lime juice. Keep warm.

5. *To grill the meat:* Arrange the skewers on the fire 3in/7.5cm above the coals (bricks on either side make good platforms; keep in mind that the ground meat should not touch the grill). After a few seconds, turn the meat gently to help it attach to the skewers and to prevent it from falling off (these first few seconds are important for cooking skewered ground kababs).

6. Grill the meat for 3 to 5 minutes, turning frequently. Baste just before removing from the fire. Avoid overcooking. The meat should be seared on the outside, juicy and tender on the inside.

7. Place all the kabab skewers on a platter. Keep on skewers until ready to serve, pour the baste on top, and cover with an upside-down rimmed sheet pan to keep warm. Use a piece of lavash bread to loosen and slide the meat off each skewer. Sprinkle with sumac and lime juice to taste. Serve with fresh basil and a yogurt and cucumber dip. *Nush-e joon!*

VARIATION
Ground Chicken Kabab

In a food processor, place 2lb/900g chicken thighs cut up into 2in/5cm pieces, 1 small onion (peeled and chopped), 3 cloves garlic (peeled), zest of 2 limes, 2 teaspoons fine-grind sea salt, 1 teaspoon freshly ground black pepper, ¼ teaspoon ground saffron dissolved in 1 tablespoon rose water, and 1 tablespoon olive oil. Pulse for a few minutes until you have a thick paste. Do not over-mix. Transfer to a glass container. Cover and allow to rest in the refrigerator for 30 minutes. Continue with step 2.

Caucasian Fillet Kabab

kabab-e qafqazi-e urumia

Serves 4 to 6
Prep: 20 minutes + 24 hours of marinating
Cooking: 3 to 4 minutes

LAMB

2lb/900g lamb loin (fillet), or beef (tenderloin) or veal (veal tender)
1 tablespoon fine sea salt

MARINADE

2 large yellow onions, thinly sliced
½ cup/120ml olive oil
¼ teaspoon ground saffron dissolved in 1 tablespoon rose water (optional)
½ teaspoon fresh ground pepper

VEGETABLES

1 large onion, quartered vertically, layers separated
2 bell peppers sliced vertically into 3x2in/75x50mm strips, soaked in hot water for 10 minutes
8 cocktail tomatoes
8 serrano peppers

BASTE

¼ cup/55g butter
2 tablespoons fresh lime juice

COOKING AND GARNISH

6 flat, thin ½in/6mm wide skewers
1 package (12oz/340g) lavash bread
2 cups fresh Persian basil leaves

1. **To prepare and salt the meat:** Ask your butcher to remove the backbone from the loin and trim all gristle from the main muscle (or do it yourself). Place the lamb fillet on a plate and rub it all over with 1 tablespoon fine sea salt and allow to sit in the fridge for at least 2 hours or overnight.

2. Place loin on a cutting board and cut it into 3in wide by 1in by ½in/7.5cm wide by 2.5cm by 1.2cm strips, cutting against the grain of the meat.

3. **To marinate the meat:** In a non reactive container place the meat pieces, add the onion, and toss well using your hands. Add the olive oil, saffron, and pepper, and toss well. Cover and marinate for at least 2 hours and up to 24 hours in the fridge.

4. Thread 2 pieces of meat, against the grain, onto a flat, sword-like skewer, and alternate with strips of onion and bell pepper. Be sure to leave some space at the top of the skewer.

5. Spear tomatoes and serrano peppers on separate skewers.

6. Start a bed of charcoal at least 30 minutes before you want to cook and let it burn until the coals glow. The secret to a good kabab is a very hot fire.

7. To make the baste: In a small saucepan over very low heat, melt the butter and add the lime juice. Keep warm.

8. When coals are ready, brush the tomatoes lightly with the baste. Place tomatoes on the grill first and then arrange the skewered meat on the grill. Cook for 3 to 4 minutes, turning frequently. The meat should be seared on the outside and pink and juicy on the inside. Brush both sides the kababs with the baste.

9. Spread lavash bread on a serving platter. Place the kabab and grilled vegetables skewers on the bread (keep them on the skewers until ready to serve). Cover with lavash bread to keep warm.

10. Serve immediately with saffroned steamed rice/*chelow*, lavash bread, and a platter of fresh herbs, including spring onions and basil.

11. Remove the meat from each skewer by using a piece of lavash bread to hold down several pieces of meat as you pull them off the skewer. *Nush-e joon!*

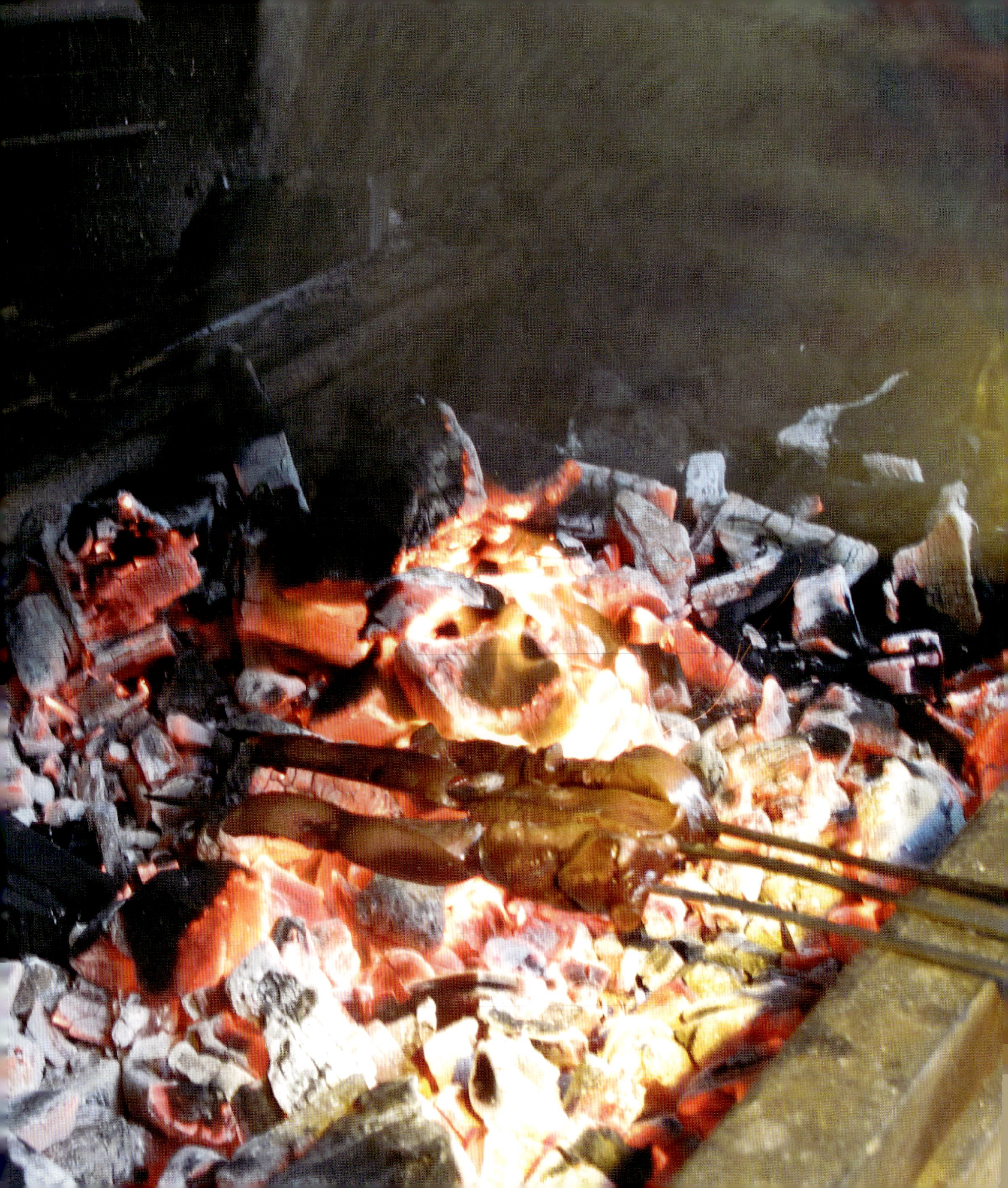

Lamb Liver Kabab

kabab-e jigar

Serves 2 to 4
Prep: 20 minutes
Cooking: 6 minutes

LIVER

1 lamb liver

BASTE

¼ cup/55g butter or 60ml olive oil
1 teaspoon dried thyme
1 tablespoon sumac powder
1 teaspoon fine sea salt
1 teaspoon freshly ground pepper
Juice of 2 fresh limes

BASTE 2

¼ cup/60g pomegranate molasses
½ teaspoon salt
½ teaspoon freshly ground pepper

Lamb liver kabab is a popular street snack available from morning to late night in most cities in Iran, but those of the street stalls in Tabriz are some of the best I've had. Lamb liver is smaller and tastier than calf liver (though you can substitute the latter). It's a little harder to find in the U.S., but you can order it from specialty butchers. Here I am giving you two popular bastes that you can use according to your fancy.

1. Rinse the liver, pat it dry, and cut it into 1in/2.5cm strips.
2. Light a bed of charcoal and let it burn until the coals glow evenly or preheat the broiler or grill.
3. **To make the baste:** In a saucepan over very low heat, combine all the ingredients for the baste and keep it warm.
4. **To grill the liver:** Skewer strips of liver onto ⅜in/1cm wide skewers. Grill over hot coals for 4 to 6 minutes. Turn the skewers frequently while grilling.
5. When the liver is cooked to your liking, baste it all over and remove from the grill. Serve hot with lavash bread, spring onions, and garlic pickles. *Nush-e joon!*

Lamb Fries Kabab

kabab-e donbalan

Serves 4
Prep: 10 minutes
Cooking: 6 minutes

8 lamb fries (testicles)
2 tablespoons melted butter
½ teaspoon fine sea salt
½ teaspoon freshly ground pepper

Wherever lamb is raised for meat, the fries/testicles are considered a great delicacy. They are usually referred to by terms such as rocky mountain or prairie oysters, or swinging steak in the United States, or caprices de femme (lady's whims) in France. Whatever you call them, they are excellent as an appetizer served with drinks.

1. Cleaned and prepared lamb fries are available at good butchers, especially halal ones.
2. **To prepare the lamb fries:** If they have not been already prepared, remove the thin outer membranes. Place them in a large bowl of cool water; wash, drain, and cut each one in half (vertically).
3. Light a bed of charcoal and let it burn until the coals glow evenly, or preheat the broiler or grill.
4. Thread the fries onto ⅜in/1cm wide skewers. Paint them with melted butter, sprinkle with salt and pepper, and grill over hot coals for 4 to 6 minutes, turning them over often and quickly.
5. Serve hot them hot off the grill. *Nush-e joon!*

Azarbaijan

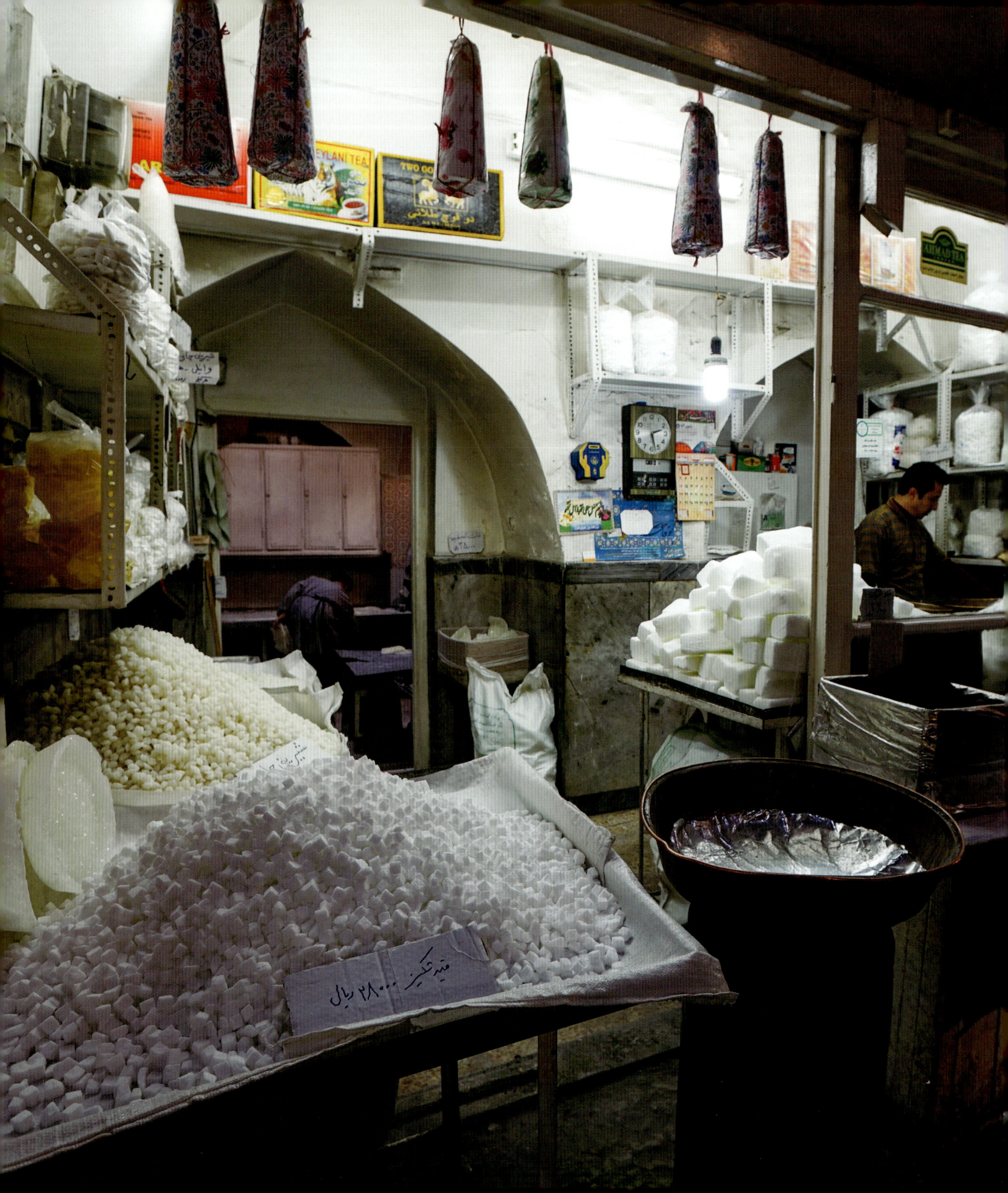
قند شکن ۲۸۰۰۰ ریال

I was fascinated to see that in the Tabriz bazaar there was a workshop for making sugar cones/*kaleh qand*. Above, you can also see the old-style scales as well as an abacus for calculations.

Carrot + Walnut Halva

halva-ye havij-e urmia

Serves 12
Prep: 15 minutes + 1 hour maceration
Cooking: 40 minutes

HALVA

2lb/900g carrots, peeled and cut to 1in/2.5cm slices
2 cups/400g sugar
1 cup/240ml grape molasses
2 cups/250g ground walnuts
½ teaspoon ground saffron dissolved in 2 tablespoons rose water
1 tablespoon ground cardamom
½ teaspoon ground cinnamon

GARNISH

2 tablespoons chopped pistachio kernels
¼ cup/40g coarsely chopped walnuts

This nutritious, gluten-free and comforting halva is associated with the Winter Festival/shab-e yalda in Azarbaijan.

1. **To make the halva**: Puree the carrots and sugar in a food processor. Transfer to a medium-sized laminated cast-iron pot. Cover and allow to macerate for 1 hour.

2. Place the pot over low heat, cover and cook, stirring occasionally with a wooden spoon for 30 to 40 minutes, until the carrots are tender..

3. Add the grape molasses, cover and cook for another 10 minutes over low heat, stirring occasionally.

4. Add the walnuts, saffron-rose water, cardamom, and cinnamon, stirring constantly for 2 to 4 minutes, until you have a thick, grainy halva.

5. Transfer to a serving platter, and garnish with pistachios and walnuts. Allow to cool and serve either as a main dish with lavash bread or alone as a dessert. *Nush-e joon!*

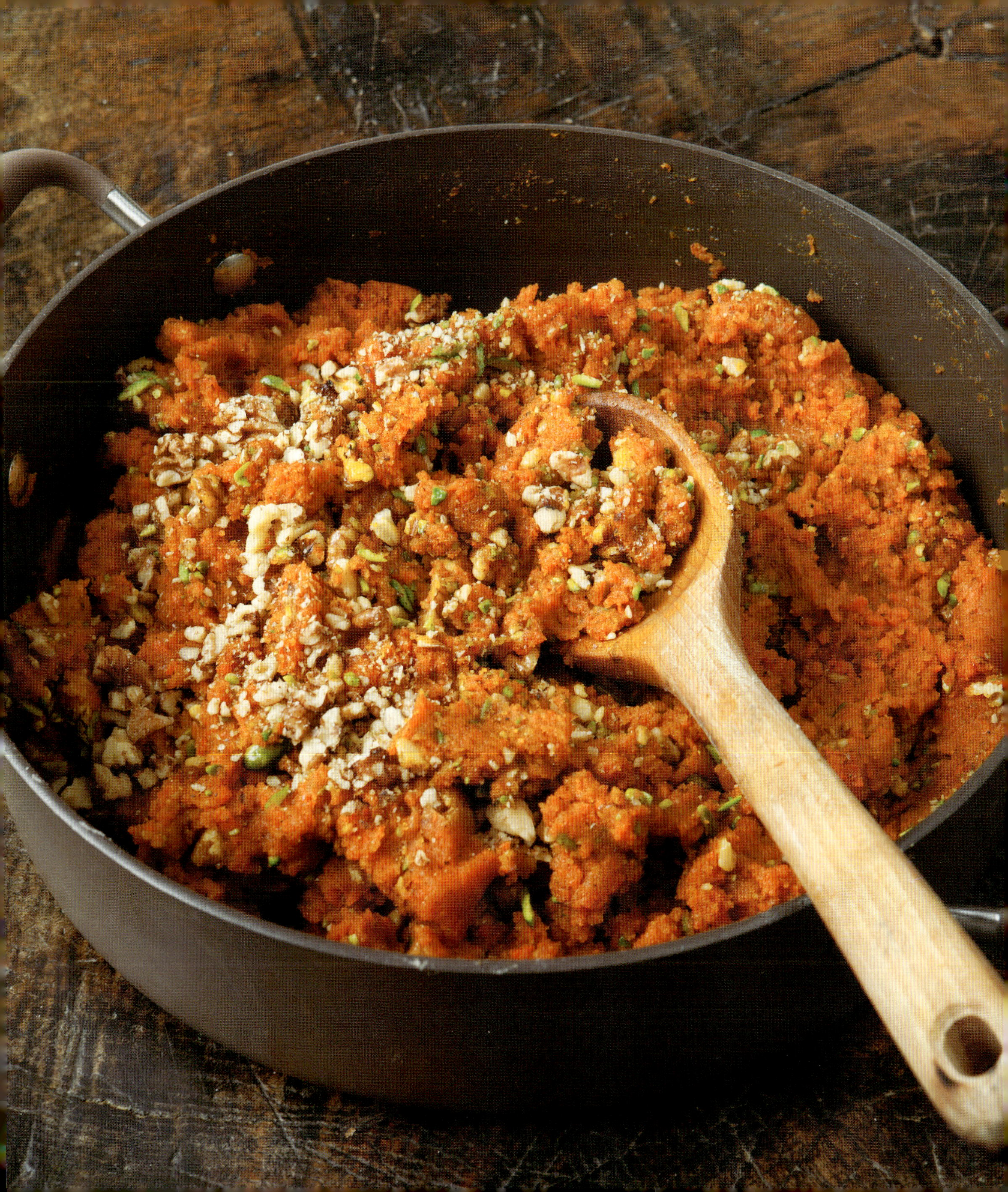

Black Walnut Halva

halva-ye siah-e ardebili

Serves 12
Prep: 15 minutes
Cooking: 40 minutes

HALVA

1 cup/240ml oil
2 cups/200g all-purpose flour
1 cup/125g walnuts, coarsely chopped
½ teaspoon ground saffron dissolved in ½ cup rose water
1 tablespoon ground cardamom
1½ cups/360g grape molasses

GARNISH

1 tablespoon ground pistachio kernels
1 tablespoon ground walnuts
1 tablespoon dried rose petals, crushed
¼ teaspoon ground cinnamon

Halva means "sweet." In Iran it refers to wheat flour (or rice flour) lightly caramelized in oil, butter or ghee and blended in a sweet syrup of sugar, honey, or grape or date molasses, to create a sweet soft paste. In the West "halva" refers to tahini paste, which in Iran is called "halvardeh." Ardeh is the Persian term for sesame paste. This halva is made with grape molasses instead of sugar. Besides being healthy and nutritious, it's delicious.

1. **To make the halva:** In a wide, shallow laminated cast-iron pot, heat the oil over medium-high heat and gradually add the flour, stirring constantly with a long wooden spoon. Cook for 20 to 25 minutes until the mixture turns golden.

2. Reduce heat to very low, and carefully add the walnuts, saffron-rose water, and cardamom, stirring constantly for 1 minute.

3. Wear oven mitts and gently add the grape molasses to the hot flour mixture. Cook over low heat for 3 to 5 minutes, stirring quickly and constantly with a long wooden spoon to make a thick, smooth black paste.

4. Transfer to a serving platter. Garnish with pistachios, walnuts, rose petals, and cinnamon. Allow to cool.

5. Serve either as a main dish with lavash bread or alone as a dessert. *Nush-e joon!*

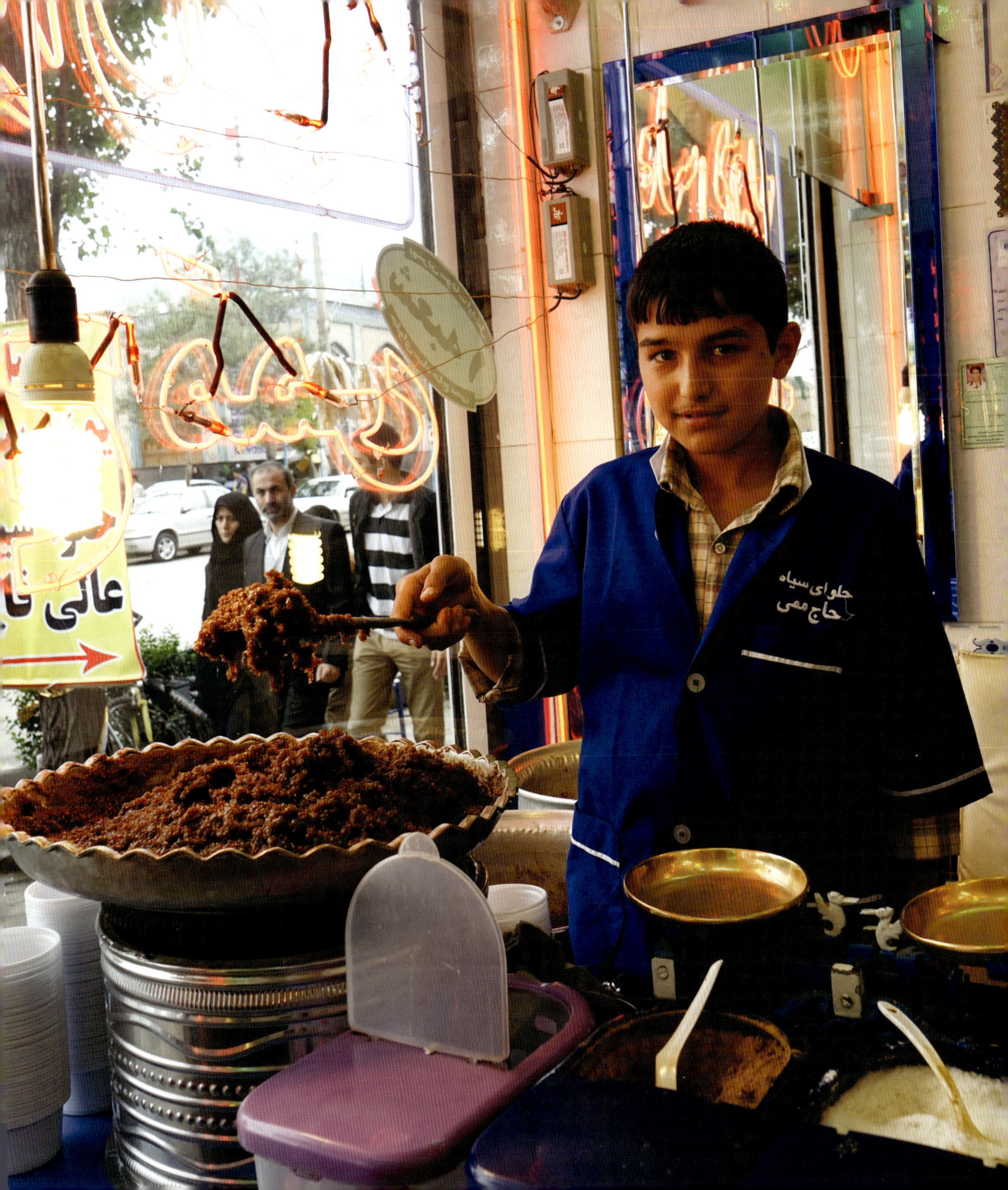
حلوای سیاه
حاج ممی

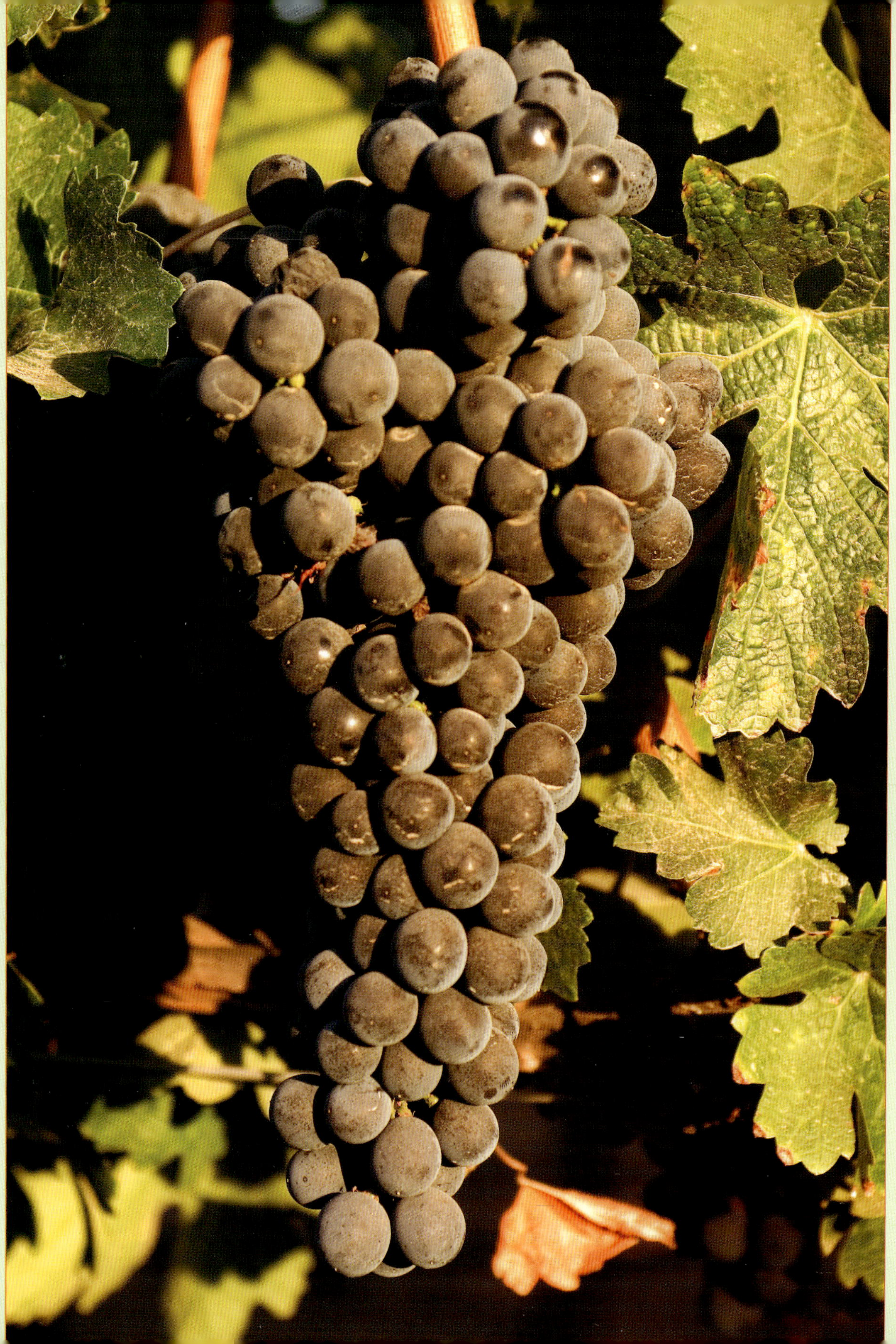

Wine in an Ancient Kitchen

Chemical analysis of a residue in a jar (opposite)—one of six found in the kitchen of a Neolithic house in the village of Hajji Firuz Tepe, south of Lake Urmia in Azarbaijan—revealed that it held wine seven thousand years ago.

Above: Archeologist Mary Voigt (orange shirt on the left) of the University of Pennsylvania Museum supervises the excavation of the room where the jars were set in the floor along one wall. Remnants of a fireplace and other vessels that were evidently used for storing and preparing foods indicate that this space served as a kitchen. The house also included two storage rooms and a large room that probably doubled as living and sleeping quarters for an extended family.

Qom

A Little History

Qom is a holy city 125 kilometers southwest of Tehran. It is famous for its religious schools, its kohlrabi soup (dizzy)/abgusht-e qonbid (p. 39), spicy meatballs/*kufteh-ye qom*i, and caramel brittle/*sohan-e qom*. The city was ruled by Yemeni Arabs when Islam first came to Iran, but the Mongols totally destroyed it several times in the thirteenth century. It was later rebuilt by Fath Ali Shah Qajar in the 1800s. More recently, Qom has thrived both economically and as a center of Shia Islam.

Spicy Meatballs with Verjuice
kufteh-ye qomi

Serves 4 to 6
Prep: 25 minutes
Cooking: 50 minutes

FOR THE PASTE

½ cup/100g rice, washed and drained
2 cups/300g fresh or frozen green peas
1 teaspoon fine sea salt
1 small onion, peeled and quartered
2 cloves garlic, peeled
1 teaspoon freshly ground pepper
1 teaspoon red pepper flakes
1 teaspoon ground cumin
1 teaspoon ground cinnamon
1 teaspoon ground fennel seeds/ *raziyaneh*
¼ cup/20g roughly chopped fresh parsley
¼ cup/20g roughly chopped fresh cilantro
¼ cup/20g roughly chopped fresh dill
¼ cup/20g dried tarragon
½ cup/50g roughly chopped spring onions
¼lb/110g ground lamb or chicken thighs

BROTH

¼ cup/60ml oil
2 onions, peeled and thinly sliced
2 teaspoons fine sea salt
½ teaspoon freshly ground pepper
1 teaspoon ground cardamom
2 tablespoons tomato paste
1 tablespoon dried fenugreek leaves
¾ cup/180ml verjuice
1 cup/240ml water

GARNISH

2 tablespoons peas
½ cup/40g chopped fresh parsley

The combination of spices, herbs, and verjuice gives these meatballs a unique taste. I have adapted this recipe from Bibi Khanum, who lives in Qom.

1. **To make the paste:** In a saucepan place the rice and 4 cups water. Cover and cook for 10 minutes over medium heat. Add the peas and ½ teaspoon salt, cover, and cook for another 5 minutes. Drain (do not rinse) and allow to cool completely.

2. In a food processor, add the cooled rice and peas mixture and all the ingredients for the paste, except the lamb, and pulse until finely ground. Transfer to a mixing bowl, add the lamb, and knead with your hands until you have a smooth paste (about 3 minutes; do not over-mix). Shape into walnut size meatballs and place in a wide sauté pan side by side.

3. **To make the broth:** Heat the oil in a medium saucepan over medium heat and sauté the onions until golden brown. Add the salt, pepper, cardamom, tomato paste, and fenugreek and sauté for 1 minute. Add verjuice and water. Bring to a boil.

4. Pour the broth over the meatballs in the sauté pan and bring to a boil. Reduce heat to low, cover, and simmer for 40 minutes. Adjust seasoning to taste, cover and keep warm.

5. Just before serving, garnish and simmer for another 5 minutes. *Nush-e joon!*

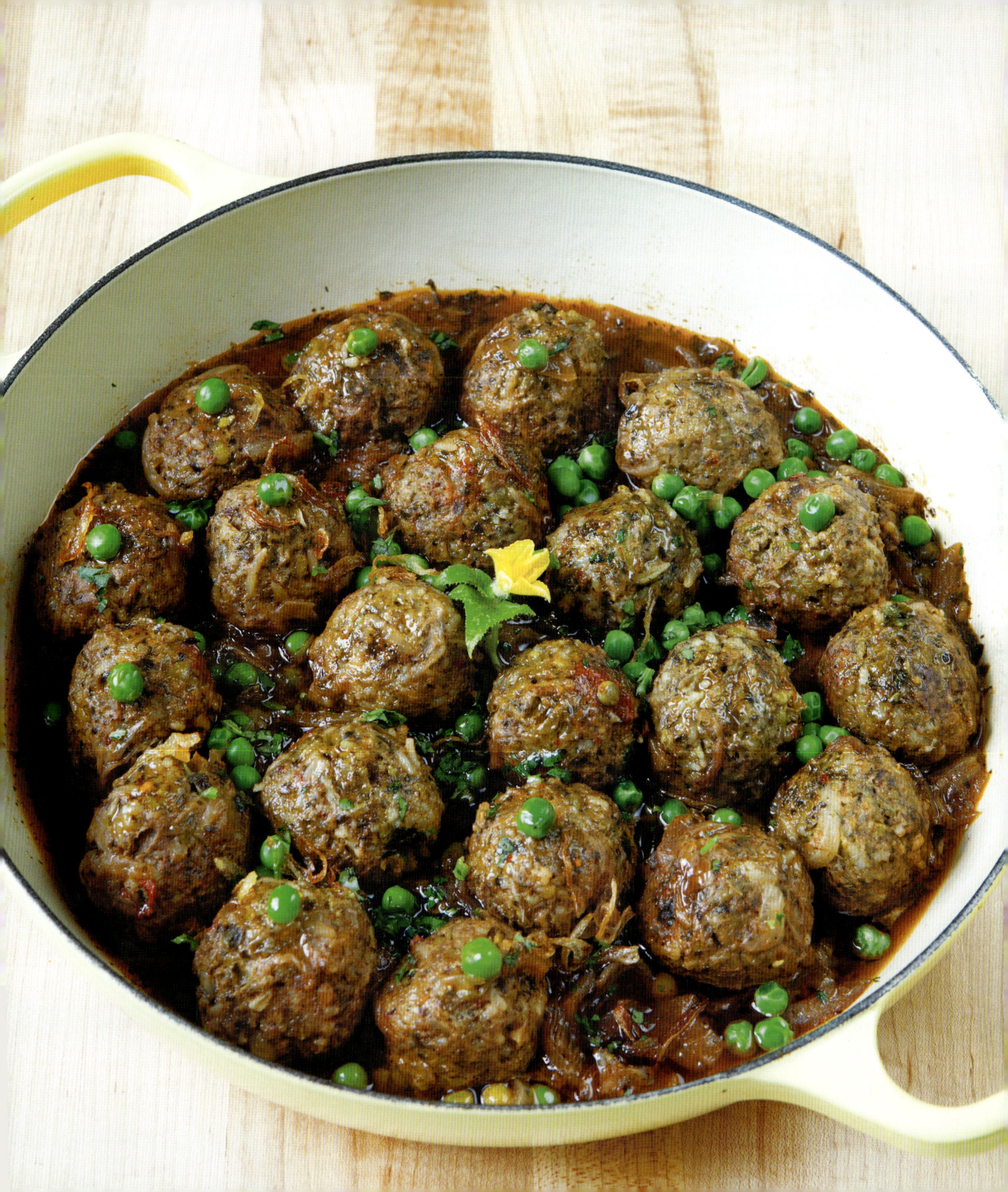

Qazvin

A Little History

Qazvin is a city about 150 kilometers northwest of Tehran. The name may be a variation on "Caspian" as it lies at the junction of several roads leading to that region through the easiest pass across the Alborz Mountains. It was the capital of Iran for about 50 years in the 1500s, and several sophisticated, traditional Iranian dishes, attributed to Qazvin, are thought to have originated in its royal court kitchens. The region is also renowned for its raisins, dried fruit, and almonds. The photograph here was taken in Takestan, a small village near Qazvin, surrounded by vines and orchards. It shows grapes spread in a field getting dried into raisins by the sun.

Qazvini Four-Spice Advieh
advieh-ye gheymeh nesar

Makes 1½ cups/150g
Prep: 20 minutes

4 tablespoons black cumin seeds
Two 4in/10cm cinnamon sticks, broken into pieces to make grinding easier
4 tablespoons green cardamom pods
1/2 cup/40g dried organic rose petals

I adapted this recipe, which is especially used for the renowned wedding dish Rice, Lamb, Rose Petals + Barberries/gheymeh nesar (page 236), from Pooya Alaedini's aunt, who lives in Qazvin.

1. Grind the cumin seeds, cinnamon sticks, cardamom pods, and rose petals separately in a spice grinder.

2. Transfer them to a small mixing bowl as you grind them. Mix well.

3. Transfer to an airtight glass jar, label, and keep in a cool place to use as needed. *Nush-e joon!*

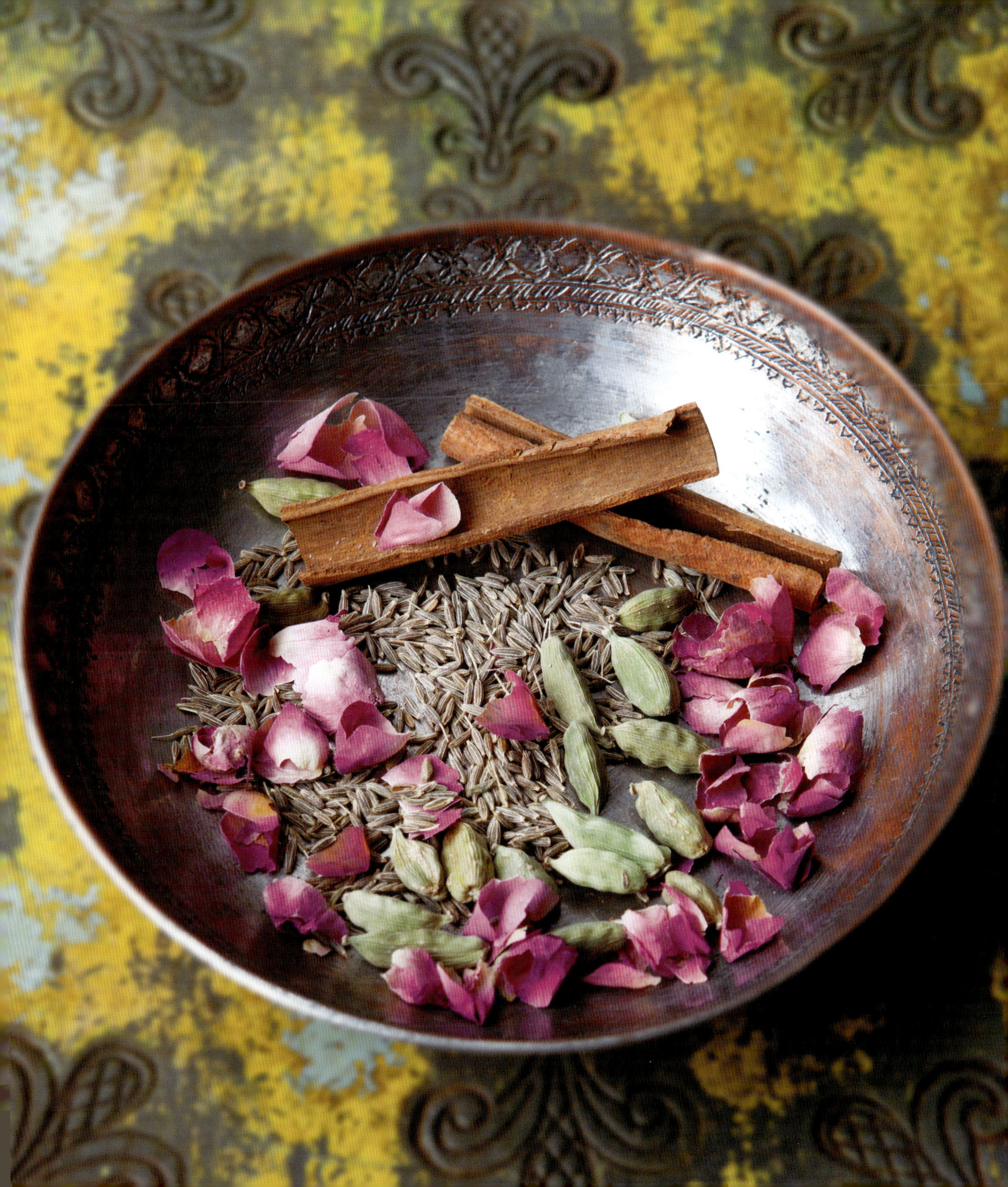

Rice, Lamb, Rose Petals + Barberries

qeymeh nesar-e qazvini

Serves 6 to 8
Prep: 30 minutes
Cooking: 1 hour

FOR THE LAMB BRAISE

2 tablespoons oil
1lb/450g boned leg of lamb or chicken thighs, cut into 1in/2.5cm pieces
2 medium yellow onions, thinly sliced
2 teaspoons fine sea salt
1 teaspoon freshly ground pepper
½ teaspoon turmeric
1 tablespoon Qazvini four-spice *advieh*
2 tablespoons tomato paste
1 teaspoon ground saffron dissolved in 2 tablespoons rose water

FOR THE CANDIED ORANGE PEEL

½ cup oranges peels (no pith), slivered
½ cup/100g sugar
½ cup/120ml water

FOR THE BARBERRIES

1 cup/75g dried red barberries, soaked in cold water for 20 minutes, rinsed and drained
1 tablespoon sugar
½ teaspoon ground saffron dissolved in ¼ cup orange blossom water
2 tablespoons oil

FOR THE RICE

2 cups/400g white basmati rice
½ cup/110g butter or oil

FOR THE GARNISH

½/60g cup slivered pistachios
½/60g cup slivered almonds
2 tablespoons dried rose petals, crushed

This is a popular, traditional dish in Qazvin. It was probably developed in the royal court kitchens in the late 1400s when Qazvin was the capital of Iran. These days it's usually served at weddings and other celebratory occasions. It even has its own spice mix, advieh-ye qeymeh nesar, which is comprised of and equal portion of cardamom, cinnamon, cumin, and rose petals.

1. *To cook the lamb braise:* Heat the oil in a medium-sized laminated cast-iron pot over medium heat. Add the lamb and onions, and sauté for 10 to 15 minutes until golden brown and all the juices have been absorbed. Add the salt, pepper, turmeric, *advieh*, tomato paste, and saffron rose water, and sauté for 2 minutes.

2. Add 2 cups water and give it a stir. Bring to a boil, reduce heat to low, cover, and cook for 45 to 60 minutes until the lamb is tender.

3. *Meanwhile, to make the candied orange peel:* Remove the bitterness from the orange peels by placing them in a small saucepan. Cover with water and bring to a boil. Drain and rinse with cold water. Return the orange peel to the saucepan, add the sugar and water, and bring to a boil. Reduce heat to medium-high and cook for 7 to 10 minutes until the orange peels are caramelized. Transfer the orange peel with its syrup to the lamb. Give it a stir, cover, and keep warm.

4. *To caramelize the barberries:* In a wide skillet, place the barberries, sugar, saffron orange blossom water, and 2 tablespoons oil. Stir-fry for 4 to 5 minutes over medium-high heat until the barberries are caramelized (beware, barberries burn easily). Set aside.

5. *To cook the rice:* Wash the rice by placing it in a large container and covering it with water. Agitate gently with your hand, pour off the water, and repeat 2 to 3 times until the water is clear.

6. In a large non-stick pot bring 8 cups/1.9l water and 2 tablespoons fine sea salt to a boil. Add the rice and boil for 8 minutes. Drain and rinse with 2 cups water. In the same pot pour 2 tablespoons water and 2 tablespoons oil. Add the rice on top. Pour ¼ cup oil and ¼ cup water over the rice. Cover tightly and cook for 15 minutes over medium heat. Keep warm until ready to serve.

7. *To Serve:* On a serving platter, gently place layers of rice, lamb, and barberries according to your taste to form a pyramid.

8. Garnish on top with the nuts and rose petals. *Nush-e joon!*

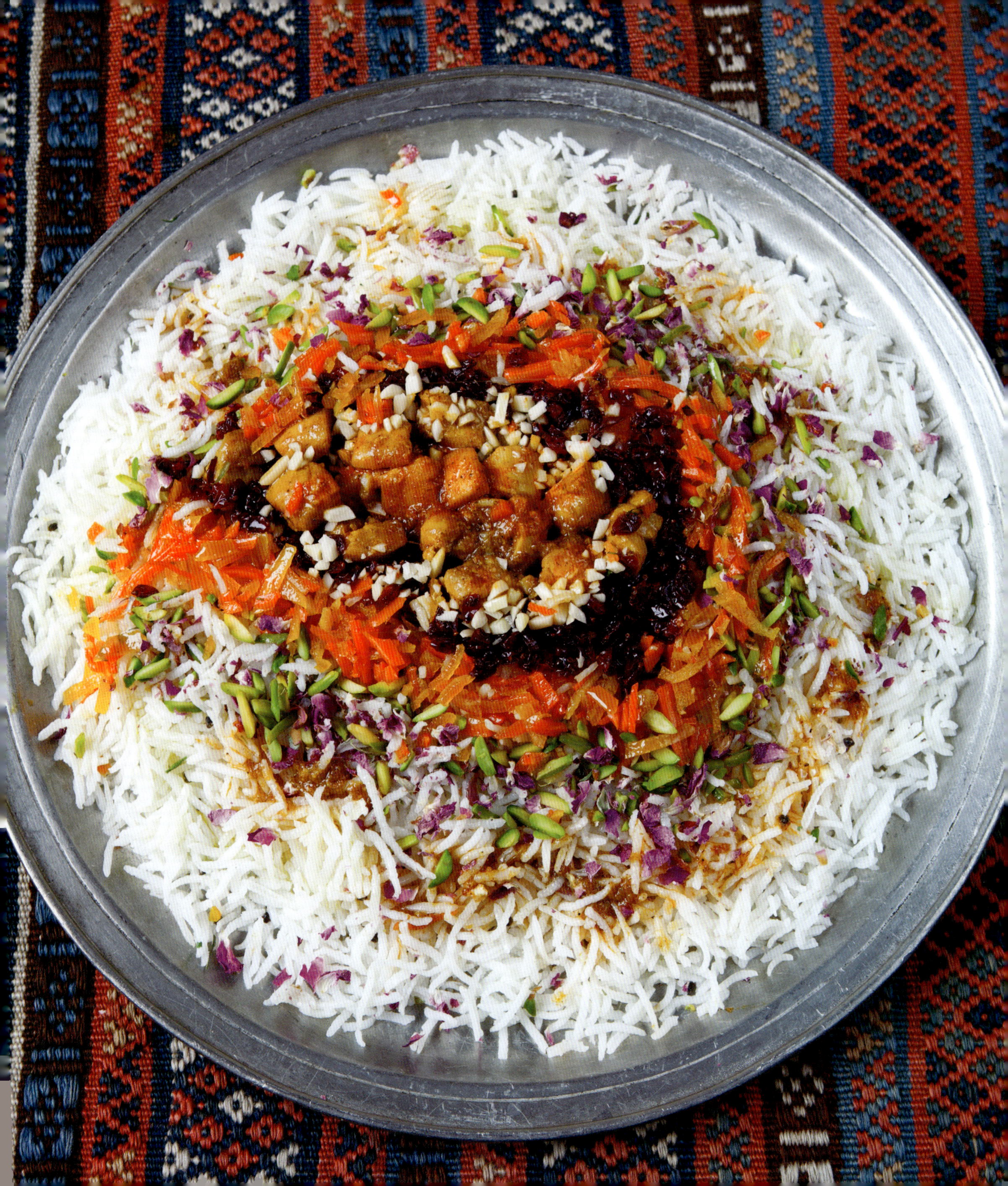

Lentil, Lamb + Prune Braise
marju khoresh-e qazvini

Serves 6
Prep: 20 minutes
Cooking: 2¼ hours

- 2 cups/400g brown lentils, soaked for 1 hour or overnight, drained and rinsed
- 2 tablespoons oil or ghee
- 2 large onions, peeled and thinly sliced
- 1lb/450g stewing lamb
- 4 teaspoons fine sea salt
- 1 teaspoon freshly ground pepper
- 1 teaspoon turmeric
- 1 tablespoon Qazvini seven-spice *advieh*
- 1 teaspoon red pepper flakes
- 2 tablespoons tomato paste
- 1 russet potato (1lb/450g), peeled and cut into 1in/2.5cm cubes
- 1 large tomato, peeled and chopped
- 1 cup/125g pitted prunes
- ¾ cup/120ml verjuice
- ½ teaspoon ground saffron dissolved in 2 tablespoons water (optional)

FOR THE GARNISH
- 2 tablespoons chopped fresh parsley

I tasted this braise in Qazvin. The combination of prunes and verjuice in a spicy sauce is unique. This dish is also made on the other side of the Alborz Mountains in Taleqan. You can eliminate the lamb, make it a very tasty vegetarian dish, and reduce the cooking time from 1 hour to 10 minutes in step 2.

1. Heat 2 tablespoons oil in a medium-sized laminated cast-iron pot over medium heat and sauté the onions and lamb until golden brown. Add the salt, pepper, turmeric, *advieh*, and red pepper flakes, and sauté for 1 minute longer. Add the tomato paste and sauté for 2 minutes.

2. Pour in 6 cups water and bring to a boil. Reduce heat to low. Cover and simmer over low heat for 1 hour, stirring occasionally.

3. Add the lentils, potato, and fresh tomato, and bring back to a boil. Reduce heat to low, cover, and simmer for 25 minutes.

4. Add the prunes, verjuice, and saffron water. Cover and cook over low heat for another 25 minutes.

5. Check to see if lentils and potato are tender. Adjust seasoning to taste and garnish.

6. Serve with plain rice or bread and a fresh herb platter. *Nush-e joon!*

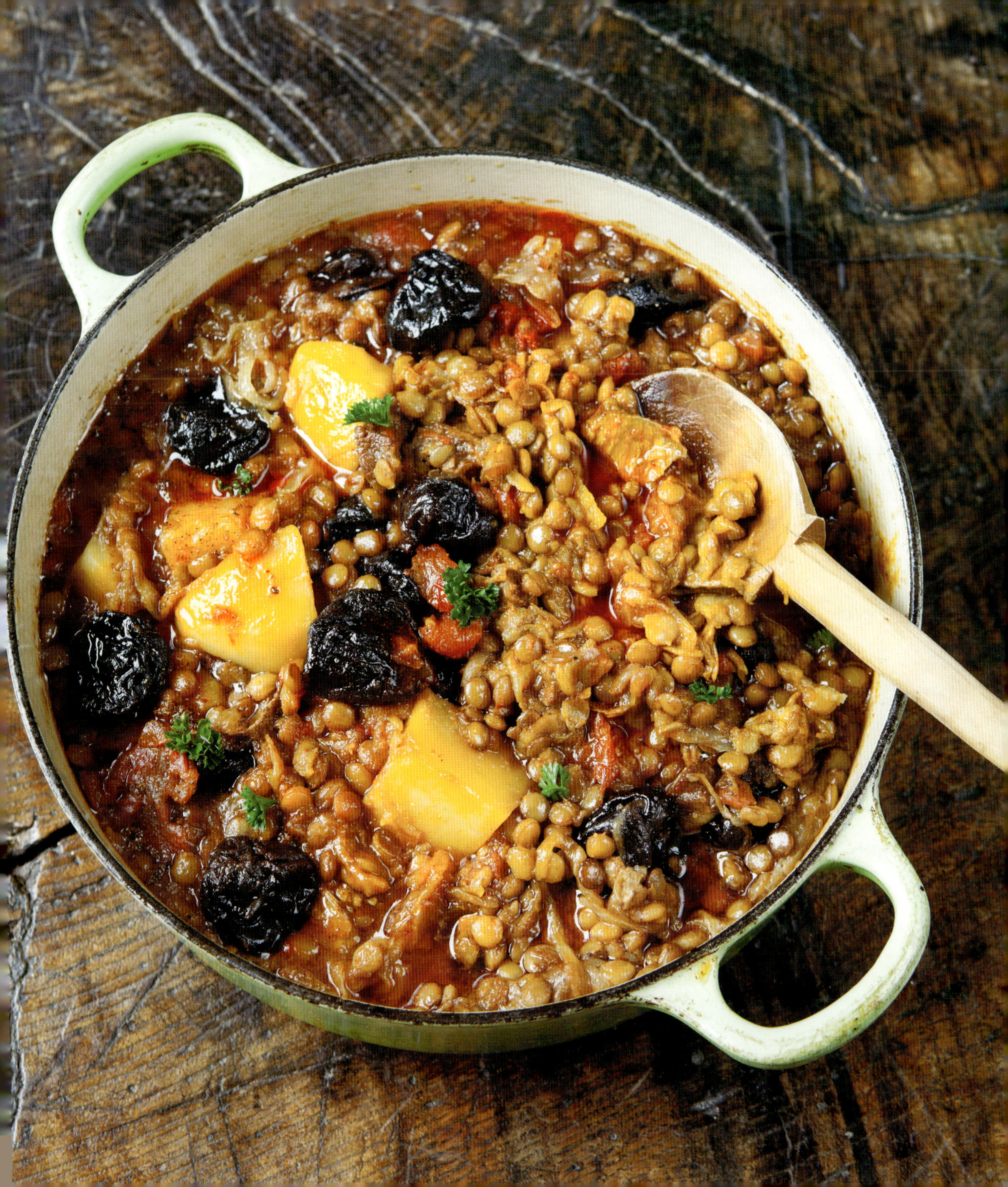

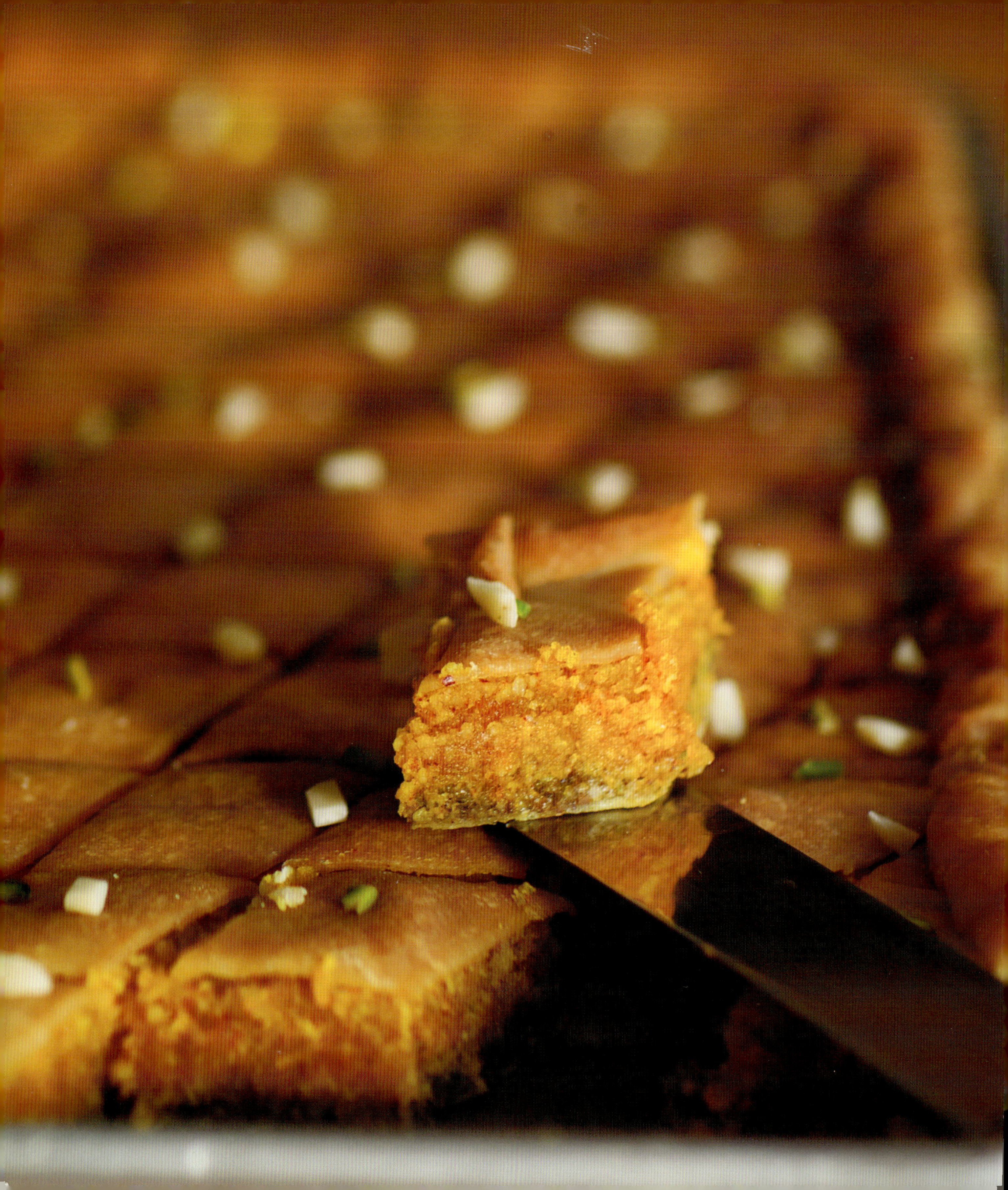

Dessert

The word "dessert," referring to a sweet dish usually eaten at the end of the meal, was first used by the French in the sixteenth century. However, the tradition of eating a sweet course at the end of the meal goes back at least 2,500 years to the ancient Persians. This is documented by Herodotus in his famous work *The Histories*. He writes that the dessert-loving Persians mocked the Greeks for not having any proper desserts. Iranians believed that finishing a meal with sweets helped the digestion. At the end of a meal they would clear away the *sofreh* (everything laid out on the table) and prepare a new setting, usually outside in the garden, where they would then serve wine together with many light sweets and small dishes/*noghl-e mey* such as fresh or candied dried fruits, nuts, *dragées* (nuts coated in sugar), and baklava. This is the same practice that the French adopted in the sixteenth century, calling it "dessert" from the French *de-servir* meaning "to clear the table."

It is said that the sixth-century Persian king Khosrow considered baklava/*lausinaj* to be the best dessert and liked to serve it at Nowruz, the Persian New Year. Made of almonds ground together with sugar and rose water in a delicate pastry, it would have been somewhat similar to my baklava (recipe on page 242). Macarons, so popular these days, are the descendants of this baklava. As late as the seventeenth century, recipes for macarons showed their heritage by including rose water and musk for flavoring. Ladurée, the famous French pastry shop established in the 1800s in Paris, still calls their rose-water-flavored macaron Ispahan.

Saffroned Almond + Pistachio Baklava
baqlava-ye do rangeh-ye qazvini

Makes one 17 x 11 x 1in/43 x 28 x 2.5cm sheet pan (60 full pieces)
Prep: 45 minutes
Cooking: 35 minutes

FOR THE SYRUP

1 cup/340g honey
½ cup/120ml water
1 cup/240ml rose water
2 tablespoons fresh lime juice

FOR THE DOUGH

¼ cup/60ml milk
½ cup/120ml oil
1 tablespoon syrup (prepared in step 1)
¼ cup/60ml rose water
1 egg
2½ cups/250g unbleached all-purpose flour, sifted

FOR THE PISTACHIO FILLING

2lb/900g pistachio kernels
1 cup/200g sugar
1 tablespoon ground cardamom

FOR THE ALMOND FILLING

2lb/900g blanched almonds
1 cup/200g sugar
½ teaspoon ground saffron dissolved in 2 tablespoons rose water
1 tablespoon ground cardamom

FOR BAKING

½ cup/120ml oil

FOR DECORATING

4 tablespoons ground pistachios
4 tablespoons slivered almonds
1 tablespoon dried rose petals

This baklava tastes somewhere between a baklava and saffron pudding/sholeh zard. It is made with a layer of saffroned almonds and a layer of pistachios. I adapted this recipe from Pooya Alaedini's aunt, who lives in Qazvin.

1. *To make the syrup:* Combine the honey and water in a saucepan, stir well, and bring to a boil (do not overboil). Add the rose water and lime juice and remove from heat. Set aside.

2. *To make the dough:* Combine the milk, oil, syrup (from step 1), rose water, and egg in the mixing bowl of a food processor. Pulse for 20 seconds. Add the flour, gradually, and mix well for 5 minutes to create a dough that does not stick to your hands. Divide the dough into 2 balls of equal size and immediately wrap in plastic. Set aside.

3. *To make the pistachio filling:* In the food processor, finely grind together the pistachio kernels, sugar, and cardamom. Transfer to a bowl and set aside.

4. *To make almond filling:* In the same food processor, finely grind together the almonds, sugar, saffron-rose water, and cardamom. Transfer to a bowl and set aside.

5. Brush a 17 x 11 x 1in/43 x 28 x 2.5cm rimmed sheet pan with ¼ cup/60ml oil. Place the oven rack in the center and preheat oven to 350°F/180°C.

6. Prepare a large, wide surface for rolling out the dough and dust it with flour. Unwrap 1 ball of dough and roll it out into a very thin rectangular layer using a thin wooden rolling pin (roll dough from the center to the outside edge in all directions). Dust the dough with flour as necessary. The finished dough should be larger than the sheet pan all around.

7. Roll the thin layer of dough around the wooden rolling pin and transfer it to the oiled sheet pan and unroll the dough until it covers the whole sheet pan. Do not cut off the excess dough; let the dough hang over the edge of the sheet pan (1in/2.5cm on all sides).

8. Spread the pistachio mixture on top of the dough. Press down and smooth it out using your hands, then use a small rolling pin to even it out and to pack it down firmly (this is important to achieve a tight, firm baklava when baked).

9. Repeat the same process spreading the almond filling on top of the pistachio layer and pack it down firmly.

10. As with step 7, roll out the second ball of dough into a very thin rectangular layer. Transfer the dough sheet on top of the filling, allowing

it to hang over on all sides, as you did with the bottom layer of dough. Use your hands to press down on the dough to smooth it and even it out.

11. Fold and turn the overhanging dough from the top layer under the dough from the bottom layer. Press together, pinching the top and bottom edges together to seal like a pie, and form a rim of dough around the edge of the baking pan.

12. Press down the dough with your palm while cutting the dough with a sharp knife (all the way through) into diamond shapes. Use a brush to paint the dough with ¼ cup oil.

13. Place the sheet pan in the preheated oven and bake for 30 to 35 minutes (depending on your oven) until the baklava is golden or pinkish in color.

14. Spread a damp towel on the counter. When the baklava is pinkish, remove it from the oven and place it on the moist towel. Evenly pour the syrup all over the baklava.

15. Decorate the baklava with pistachios, almonds, and rose petals. Cover immediately with a layer of plastic wrap and a layer of aluminum foil and seal tightly. Let stand at room temperature for at least 2 hours. It is important that the baklava be covered at all times because it dries out very easily.

16. When ready to serve, use a sharp knife to lift 2 of the diamond pieces out of the sheet pan (to create an opening), then carefully lift 1 diamond at a time and arrange on a serving dish. Alternatively, transfer to a covered glass container for storing in the refrigerator. *Nush-e joon!*

Qazvin

Hamadan

A Little History

Hamadan/Ahmatan/Ecbatana—all are various spellings through time for the same town, which literally means "the gathering place." Hamadan is one of the oldest and coldest cities of Iran. It was the capital of the Median Empire and the summer residence of the Achaemenids 2,500 years ago. The tombs of the Bible's Jewish-Iranian queen Esther and her cousin Mordechai are in Hamadan. Here too is the burial place of Avicenna/Ibn Sina, considered the father of medicine.

The city sits on the eastern slopes of the Alvand massif (11,700 feet/3,570 meters) in the Zagros mountain range. The region has 1,500 *qanats*—man-made subterranean canals that carry water from the mountainside to villages and farms—that irrigate its orchards, and wheat and barley fields.

Hamadani cuisine is quite distinctive, perhaps because of its long winters. Cooks there use less fresh ingredients and more of the dried and preserved forms. The region is renowned for making the best pickles and preserves, using traditions that have been passed down over many centuries.

Some Hamadani families still use an earthenware container called *lanjeen*, in which they make dough, and a big, woven basket called *tevijeh*, used to hold dried bread for long periods. The bread is prepared for eating by simply sprinkling it with water and reheating it. *Nan-e gerdeh* (literally "round bread")—made with whole-wheat flour, painted with an egg wash, and sprinkled on top with ground fenugreek, sesame, and nigela seeds—is very popular.

Hamadani Seven-Spice Advieh
advieh-ye hamadani

Makes 1½ cups/150g
Prep: 20 minutes

1 tablespoon red pepper flakes
2 tablespoons whole cloves
4 tablespoons black cumin seeds
4 tablespoons coriander seeds
Two 4in/10cm cinnamon sticks, broken into pieces to make grinding easier
4 tablespoons green cardamom pods
4 tablespoons ginger powder

I have adapted this advieh and many of the Hamadani recipes in this section from Shabnam Shahbazian, a wonderful and generous cook in Hamadan.

1. Grind the red pepper, cloves, cumin seeds, coriander seeds, cinnamon sticks, and cardamom pods separately in a spice grinder.

2. Transfer them to a small mixing bowl as you grind them. Add the ginger powder and use a spoon to mix well.

3. Transfer to an airtight glass jar and keep in a cool place to use as needed. *Nush-e joon!*

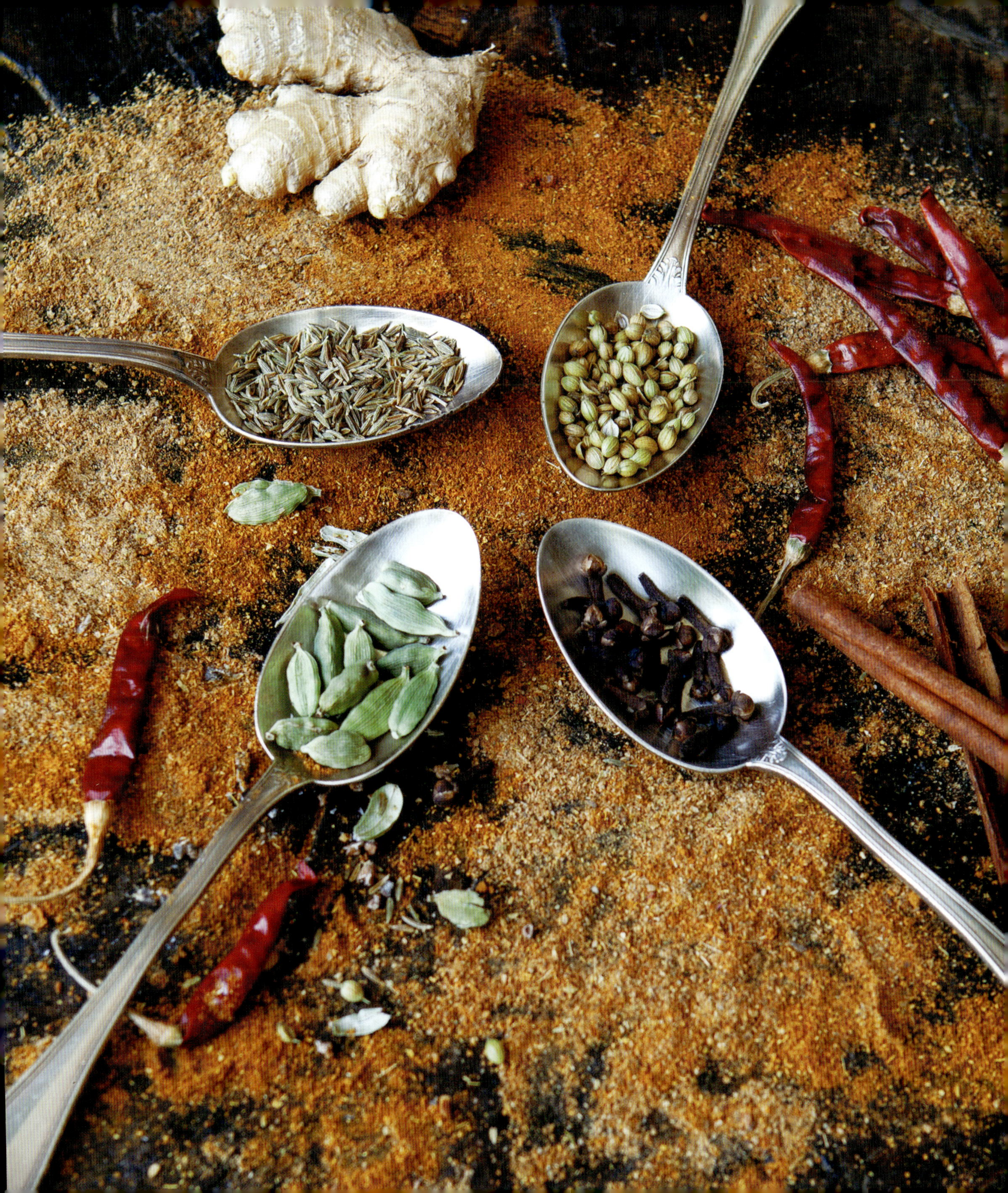

Cheese, Walnut + Herb Balls
qut-e hamadani

Serves 6
Prep: 30 minutes

- ½lb/225g feta-type goat cheese, rinsed, drained, and cut up
- 2 cups/250g walnuts or pistachios, toasted
- 2 fresh spring onions, chopped (white and green parts)
- 1 small onion, peeled and quartered
- 1 cup/85g fresh basil leaves
- ½ cup/40g fresh tarragon leaves
- 2 cups/170g fresh mint leaves
- ½ teaspoon fine sea salt
- ¼ teaspoon freshly ground pepper
- 1 russet potato (about 1lb/450g), peeled, cooked, and quartered
- ½ cup goat butter
- 6in/15cm square piece of flat bread such as *sangak* or lavash, cut up and moistened with water

Qut, shown in the photo on the lower left, is often prepared for the family's afternoon tea in Hamadan. A variation on this dish is popular throughout northwest Iran. Each region and even each household in a region have their own mix of flavors and ingredients. I had one version that included caramelized onions, which gave it a quite distinctive taste.

1. Place all the ingredients in a food processor and pulse until you have a grainy paste. Adjust seasoning to taste. Make bite-sized oval-shaped balls and arrange on a serving platter. *Nush-e joon!*

Hamadan

VEGETARIAN

Opposite: Shabnam Shahbazian tries some of her butternut squash preserve at a traditional Hamadani lunch setting/*sofreh*.

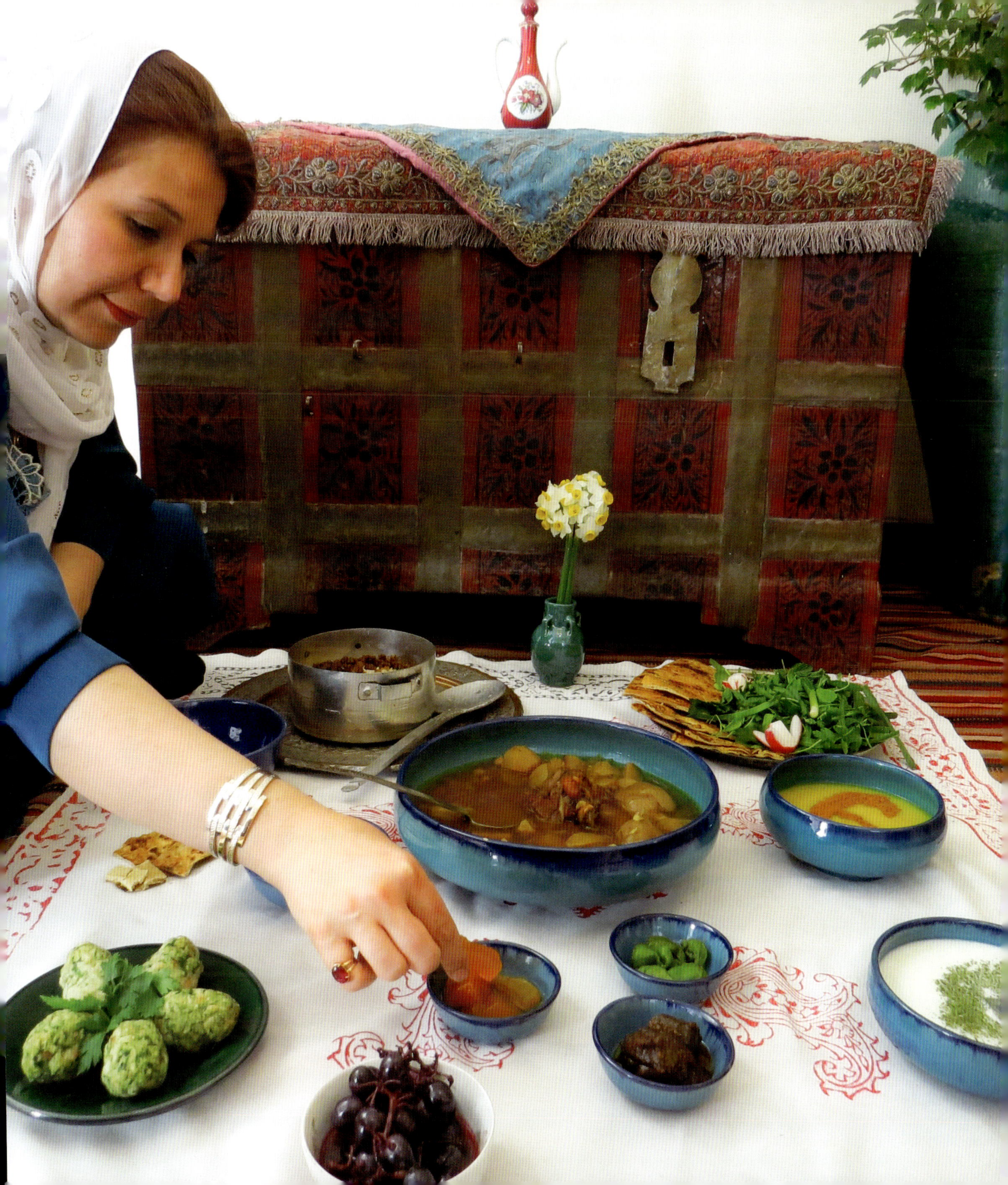

Dried Fruit + Noodles Osh

osh-e khoshkbar-e hamadani

Serves 6 to 8
Prep: 30 minutes + soaking of legumes overnight
Cooking: 1½ hours

LEGUMES SOAKED OVERNIGHT AND DRAINED

½ cup/100g brown lentils
⅛ cup/25g red beans
⅛ cup/25g chickpeas

BROTH

¼ cup/60ml oil or ghee
2 onions, peeled and thinly sliced
1 tablespoon fine sea salt
½ teaspoon freshly ground pepper
1 teaspoon turmeric
2 tablespoons Hamadani *advieh*
10 cups/2.4l broth or water
1 tablespoon rice
¼ cup/40g dried pitted tart cherries
¼ cup/40g dried apricots
¼ cup/40g dried peaches
½ cup/75g dried prunes
½lb/225g Persian noodles

SWEET + SOUR HERBS

2 tablespoons grape molasses
2 tablespoons red wine vinegar
1 cup/85g chopped fresh parsley
1 cup/100g chopped spring onions
¼ cup/20g chopped fresh dill
1 tablespoon dried mint
1 cup/85g chopped fresh cilantro

GARNISH/NA`NA DAGH

2 tablespoons oil
10 cloves garlic, peeled and grated
½ teaspoon turmeric
4 tablespoons dried mint flakes

In Shiraz they make this osh without the dried fruit.

1. **To make the broth:** Heat the oil in a large laminated cast-iron pot over medium heat until hot. Add the onion and sauté until golden brown. Add the salt, pepper, turmeric, *advieh*, and legumes, and sauté for 1 minute. Pour in the broth and bring to a boil. Reduce heat to medium-low, cover, and simmer for 45 minutes, stirring occasionally.

2. Add the rice and dried fruits to the pot. Cover and simmer for 15 minutes longer.

3. Add the noodles and bring back to a boil. Reduce heat to low, cover, and simmer for 15 minutes longer.

4. **To cook the sweet and sour herbs:** Add the grape molasses, vinegar, and the herbs to the *osh*. Simmer, uncovered, for 10 minutes longer, stirring occasionally. Season to taste, adding more molasses or vinegar if needed. Keep warm until ready to serve.

5. **To cook the garnish:** Heat 2 tablespoons oil in a medium-sized skillet over medium heat. Add the garlic and sauté until golden brown. Add the turmeric, give it a stir, and remove from the heat. Crumble the dried mint flakes in the palm of your hand and add them to the skillet. Stir well and set aside.

6. Pour the *osh* into a tureen or individual bowls and garnish on top. Stir the garnish in just before serving. *Nush-e joon!*

Nuts and dried fruit for sale on the of the road to Hamadan.

Hamadan

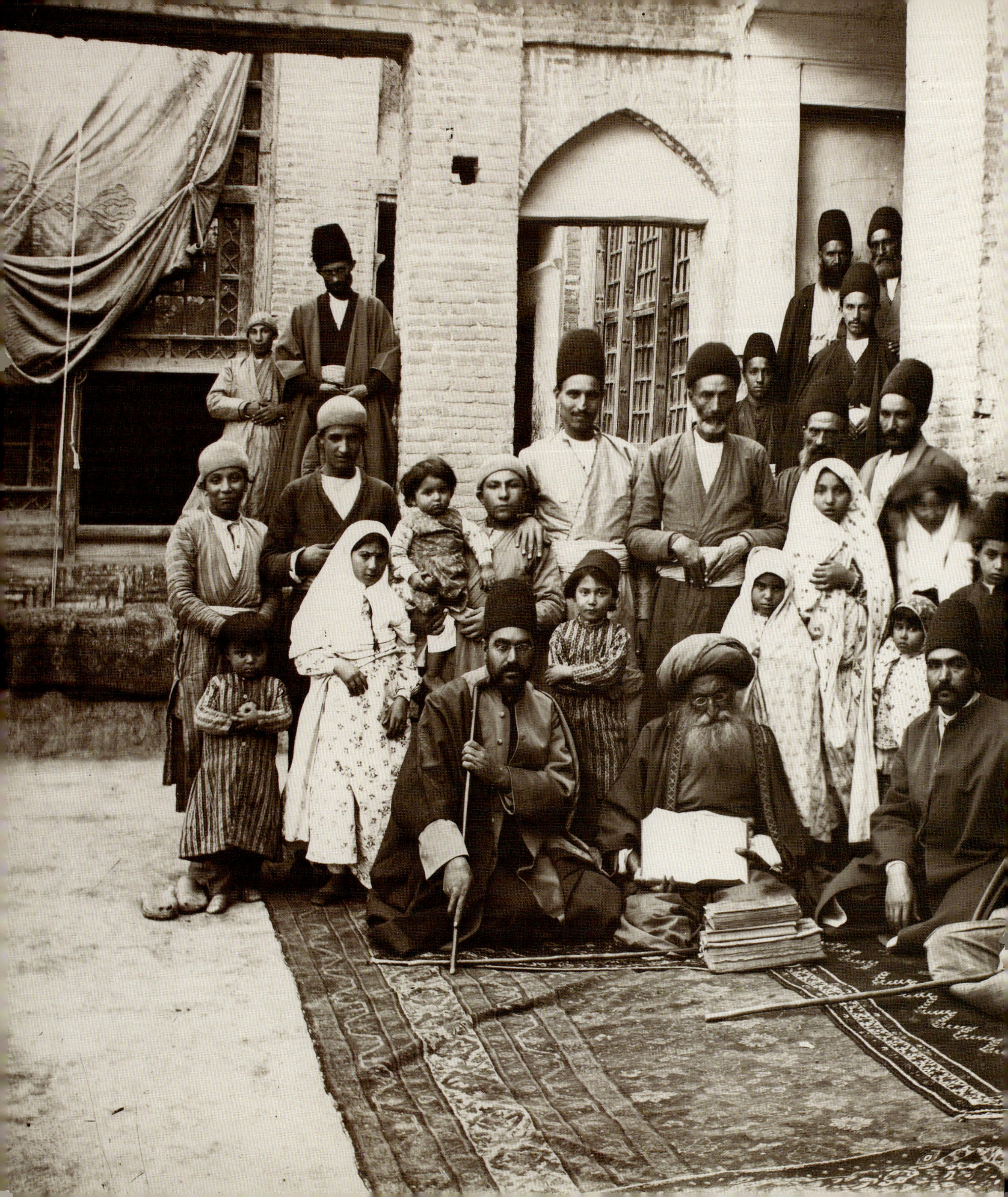

Iranian Jews

In the early eighth century BCE many Jews of Samaria were deported by the Assyrians to where Iranian tribes had just started to settle, around present-day Hamadan. More than a hundred years later, the Babylonian king Nebuchadrezzar reduced Jerusalem to ruins and exiled much of the population to Babylon. A few decades after that, Cyrus the Great conquered Babylonia and decreed that the exiled Jews could return to their homeland and rebuild their Temple in Jerusalem. (The Hebrew Bible calls Cyrus the "messiah" meaning "savior.") Some Jews stayed on, some went back to Jerusalem, while others went to Iran, living freely and prosperously. A few, like the biblical figures Ezra and Nehemiah, attained influential positions in the government of the Persian Empire.

The ancient Iranian religions and Zoroastrianism influenced the Jewish concepts of creation, the nature of God, heaven and hell, and purity. And a millennium later, Jewish dietary laws exerted a strong influence on Islamic dietary laws.

The Jews of Iran—today numbering perhaps 25,000—have been so intertwined with Persian culture for so long that little difference is seen in their food—except perhaps that, to be kosher, butter is not mixed with meat. A few dishes have religious symbolism: One, linked to Passover, is charoset/*halegh*, a sweet combination of dates, nuts, and fruit; it is a variation on *ranginak* (page 659), popular throughout southern Iran. A favorite among Jewish Iranians is the Caspian's walnut and pomegranate braise/*fesenjun* (page 132), to which dried fruit is added. Another is a basic chicken soup with chickpea meatballs/*gondi*; generally, Iranians, depending on the region they come from, flavor it with sumac, pomegranates, dates, verjuice, or tomatoes.

A 1890s photo of Hakim Nur-Mahmud (center with book in hand) with his family, patients, and servants. He was said to have been Naser al-Din Shah's Jewish doctor.

Carrot + Bulgur Osh

osh-e halim-o havij-e hamedani

Serves 6 to 8
Prep: 20 minutes + soaking of legumes overnight
Cooking: 2½ hours

LEGUMES SOAKED OVERNIGHT + DRAINED

1 cup/200g brown lentil
⅛ cup/25g kidney beans
⅛ cup/25g chickpeas

BROTH

¼ cup/60ml oil or ghee
2 onions, peeled and thinly sliced
1 tablespoon fine sea salt
1 teaspoon freshly ground pepper
1 teaspoon turmeric
2 teaspoons Hamadani seven-spice *advieh*
1½ cup/270g bulgur
1lb/450g carrots (about 6 medium carrots), peeled and diced into ½in/12mm cubes
10 cups/2.4l broth or water

1 cup/240g liquid *kashk* or almond milk

GARNISH/NA`NA DAGH

2 tablespoons oil or ghee
10 cloves garlic, peeled and grated
1 teaspoon turmeric
2 tablespoons dried mint flakes

Bulgur is the hulled kernels (berries) of durum (hard) wheat, which are steamed, dried, and cracked. It's an ancient way of preparing wheat that is popular throughout the Middle East. Bulgur was a staple of the Iranian diet before rice took over in the fifteenth century. It remains popular, however, in certain regions of Iran, particularly in Hamadan and the tribal areas. Traditionally, this osh is made with 1lb/450g lamb, cut up and sautéed with the onions in step 1, but I prefer it meatless. I am suggesting using broth here, but you can also make it completely vegan by using water instead and almond milk instead of kashk.

1. **To cook the osh:** Heat 2 tablespoons oil in a large laminated cast-iron pot over medium heat and sauté the onions until golden brown. Add the salt, pepper, turmeric, *advieh*, legumes, bulgur, and carrots. Sauté for 1 minute.

2. Add the broth and bring to a boil. Cover and simmer over medium heat for 1½ hours, stirring occasionally until the beans and carrots are tender.

3. Add ¾ cup of the *kashk* to the *osh*. Use a handheld mixer to partially puree the *osh*. Adjust seasoning to taste, cover, and keep warm.

4. **To cook the garnish:** Heat 2 tablespoons oil in a skillet until hot, add the garlic, and sauté until golden brown. Add the turmeric and stir-fry for 1 minute. Remove from heat and add the crushed mint flakes, stir well, and set aside.

5. Just before serving, transfer the *osh* to a serving bowl and garnish with the mint and garlic mixture and the remaining *kashk*. Serve with bread and fresh herbs. *Nush-e joon!*

VEGAN VARIATION

Bulgur, Legumes + Verjuice Soup
osh-e ghurabeh-ye hamadani

In step 1, replace the carrots and lentils with pinto beans. In step 3, replace the *kashk* with ½ cup/120ml verjuice. Add 2 cups/170g chopped fresh beat leaves, 1 cup/85g each of chopped fresh dill, cilantro, and parsley. Everything else remains the same.

Bulgur + Curly Cucumber Osh

osh-e khiyar chambar-e hamadani

Serves 6
Prep: 20 minutes
Cooking: 1¼ hours

LENTILS SOAKED OVERNIGHT + DRAINED

1 cup/200g dried lentils

BROTH

½ cup/120ml oil
2 medium onions, peeled and chopped
2 teaspoons fine sea salt
½ teaspoon freshly ground pepper
1 teaspoon turmeric
1 teaspoon Hamadani adiveh
2 cups/360g bulgur
8 cups/1.9l broth or water

CUCUMBER GARLIC MIXTURE

2 tablespoons oil
1lb/450g Armenian cucumbers (available in asian supermarkets) or Persian cucumbers, peeled, seeded and sliced into 2-in /5cm lengths
6 cloves garlic, grated
2 tablespoon Panko bread crumbs
½ cup/120g liquid *kashk*

GARNISH/NA`NA DAGH

1 tablespoon oil
½ teaspoon turmeric
2 tablespoons dried mint flakes

Curly cucumbers, known as Armenian cucumbers (khiyar chambar in Persian), are not in fact cucumbers or in the gourd family, but actually are in the melon family (C. melo). However, they look like long cucumbers, 12 to 18in/40cm long, pale green and slender. This osh is a specialty of Hamadan but is also popular in Arak. In Khorasan, it is made with lots of spinach instead of the curly cucumbers, and the kashk is replaced with yogurt. I prefer the vegetarian version of this osh, but traditionally it's made with 1lb/450g lamb, cut up and sautéd with the onions in step 1.

1. **To make the broth:** Heat 2 tablespoons oil in large laminated cast-iron pot over low heat and sauté the onions until golden brown. Add the salt, pepper, turmeric, *adviéh*, lentils, and bulgur and stir-fry for 1 minute.

2. Add the broth and bring to a boil. Reduce heat to medium, cover, and simmer for 50 to 55 minutes until lentils and bulgur are cooked.

3. **To make the cucumber and garlic mixture:** Heat 2 tablespoons oil in a wide skillet and sauté the cucumbers and garlic for 2 minutes. Add the bread crumbs and sauté for 1 minute. Transfer to the *osh* in the pot.

4. Cover and cook over medium heat for 15 minutes. Add the *kashk*, stir gently, adjust seasoning to taste, and keep warm until ready to serve.

5. **To prepare the garnish:** Heat 2 tablespoons oil in a medium-sized skillet over medium heat. Add the turmeric and stir-fry for 1 minute. Remove from heat. Crumble the dried mint flakes in the palm of your hand and add them to the skillet. Stir well and set aside.

6. Pour the *osh* into individual serving bowls, garnish with a dollop of *kashk* and the mint garnish. *Nush-e joon!*

Bulgur, Noodle + Currant Pilaf
petleh polow-ye hamadani

Serves 6 to 8
Prep: 25 minutes
Cooking: 1 hour

LAMB + BULGUR

¼ cup/60ml oil or ghee
4 medium onions, peeled, thinly sliced
½lb /225g ground lamb
2 teaspoons fine sea salt
½ teaspoon pepper
1 teaspoon turmeric
1 tablespoon Hamadani *advieh*
1 cup/180g coarse bulgur
1 teaspoon ground saffron dissolved in ¼ cup/60ml rose water
1½ cups/250g currants

RICE

2 cups/400g basmati rice
½lb/220g toasted Persian noodles/reshteh, cut in 3in/75mm lengths
½ cup/120ml oil or ghee
1 teaspoon Hamadani seven-spice *advieh*

CRUST/TAH-DIG

¼ cup/60ml oil
¼ cup/60ml water
¼ teaspoon ground saffron dissolved in 2 tablespoons hot water
Lavash bread to fit the bottom of pot

NOTE

If you don't have toasted noodles, toast regular noodles in a wide skillet over medium heat for a few minutes until golden.

This rice is mentioned by Jean Chardin in his Travels in Persia *in 1673.*

1. **To cook the lamb:** Heat 2 tablespoons oil in a medium-sized laminated cast-iron pot and sauté the onion and lamb until golden brown. Season with the salt, pepper, turmeric, and *advieh*. Add the bulgur and sauté for 1 minute longer.

2. Pour in 2 cups/480ml water. Cover and simmer for 30 to 40 minutes over medium heat until the bulgur is tender and all the water has been absorbed. Add 2 tablespoons of the saffron-rose water and the currants, and give it a stir. Cover and keep warm.

3. **Meanwhile, to cook the rice:** Wash the rice by placing it in a large container and covering it with water. Agitate gently with your hand, pour off the water. Repeat 4 to 5 times until the water is clear. Bring 8 cups/1.9l water and 2 tablespoons fine sea salt to a boil in a large non-stick pot. Pour the rice into the pot and add the noodles. Boil briskly for 6 to 10 minutes, gently stirring twice with a wooden spoon to loosen any grains that may have stuck to the bottom. Bite a few grains of the rice; if it feels soft and all of it has risen to the surface, it is ready. Drain the rice and noodle mixture in a large fine-mesh colander and rinse with 2 cups water.

4. **To make the bread crust/tah-dig-e nuni:** In the non-stick pot, mix together ¼ cup oil, ¼ cup water, and 2 tablespoons of the saffron-rose water. Place a layer of lavash bread, cut to fit the bottom of the pot, on top of this mixture.

5. Place several spatulas of the rice and noodle mixture in the pot, and sprinkle some *advieh* over it. Repeat this process, arranging the layers in the shape of a pyramid. Cover and cook for 10 minutes over medium heat. Mix the remaining oil and ½ cup water, and pour over the rice. Wrap the lid of the pot with a clean dish towel/*damkoni* and cover firmly to prevent condensation and steam from escaping. Cook for 50 minutes over low heat.

6. Remove rice from heat and allow to cool for 5 minutes on a damp surface without uncovering; this helps free the crust from the bottom of the pot.

7. Gently mound the rice on a serving platter without disturbing the crust. Garnish on top with the lamb and bulgur mixture. Detach the layer of crust from the bottom of the pot using a wooden spatula. Place the pieces of crust on a small platter and serve on the side. Serve with a green herb platter/*sabzi khordan* and walnut pickles. *Nush-e joon!*

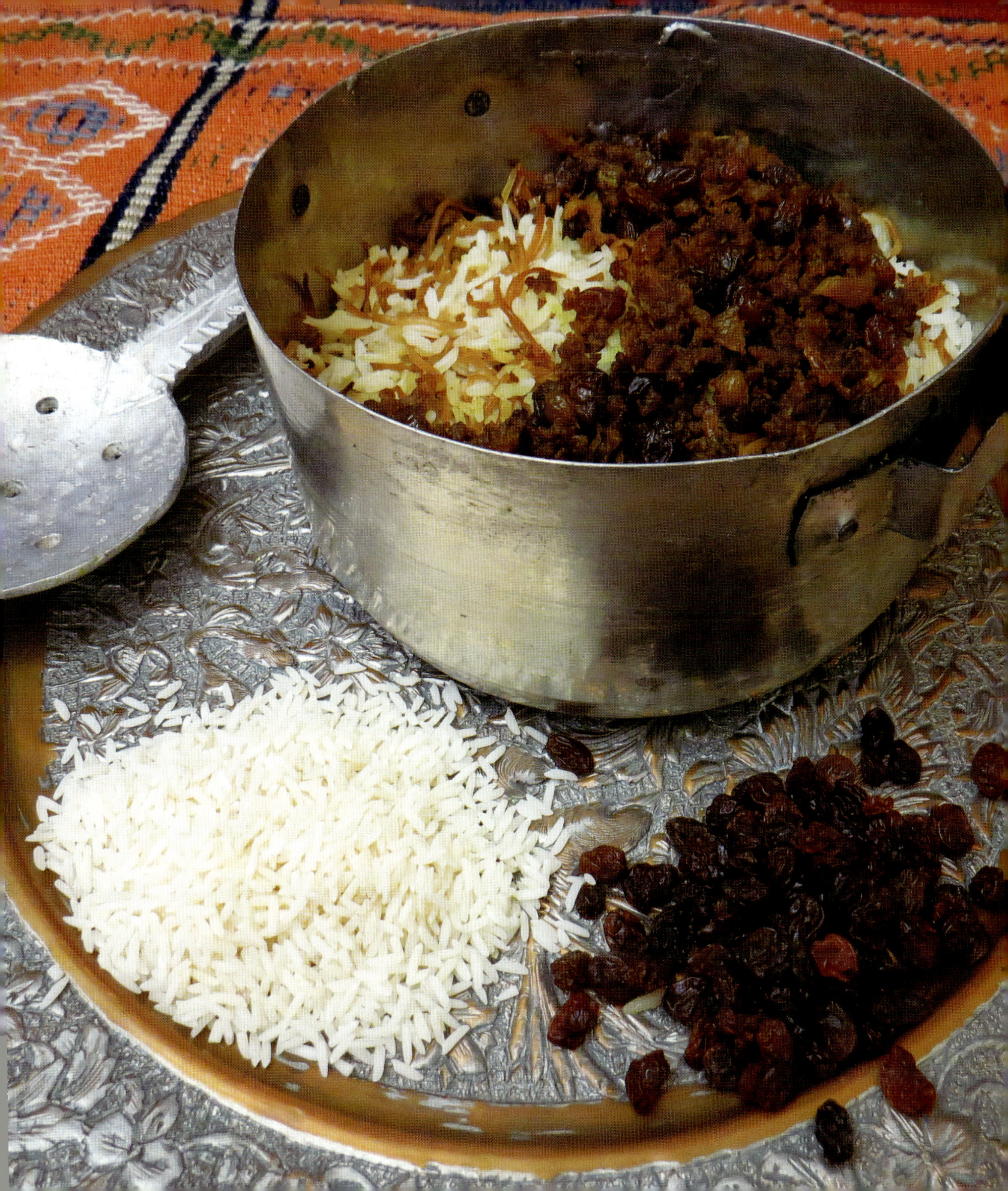

Pumpkin Preserve
moraba-ye kadu halvai-ye hamadani

Makes three ½pt/240g jars
Prep: 30 minutes + 48 hours soaking
Cooking: 1 hour

PUMPKIN

2lb/900g pumpkin flesh
¼ cup/60g pickling lime

SYRUP

3 cups/720ml water
5 cups/1kg sugar
¼ cup/30g pistachio kernels
2 tablespoons fresh lime juice
¼ cup/60ml rose water
Seeds of 10 cardamom pods

NOTE

Pickling lime or slaked lime is calcium hydroxide and the food grade powder is available at some drugstores and through the Internet (http://www.canningpantry.com/pickling-lime.html). It is used to keep pickled fruit and vegetables crisp.

This preserve is also popular in other parts of Iran, including Tabriz, but I had it in Hamadan.

1. Sterilize the jelly jars in boiling water, drain, and allow to dry completely.

2. *To prepare the pumpkin:* Peel the shiny, hard orange rind off the pumpkin and discard it. Cut the pumpkin into 2in/5cm rings. Use a spoon to remove the seeds and fibers while keeping the flesh. Place the flesh on a flat surface. Stamp out shapes using your favorite cookie cutters or cut into 1in/2.5cm diameter pieces.

3. In a laminated pot (do not use aluminum pots), dissolve ¼ cup/60g pickling lime in 8 cups/1.9l water, stir well, and allow to sit for 10 minutes. Add the pumpkin flesh to the pickling lime and allow to soak overnight (this helps to keep the pumpkin crisp). Remove the pumpkin using a slotted spoon and discard the lime water. Rinse pumpkin, cover with water, and soak in the fridge overnight to remove any trace of lime. Drain and rinse in cold water.

4. In the same laminated pot, bring 8 cups/1.9l water to a boil. Add the pumpkin, reduce heat to medium, and boil for 15 minutes. Drain, rinse thoroughly with cold water, and set aside.

5. *To make the syrup:* In the same pot, combine 3 cups/720ml water and 5 cups sugar, stir well, and bring to a boil. Simmer for 10 minutes over medium heat until the sugar has dissolved completely.

6. Add the pistachio and pumpkin and bring back to a boil. Reduce heat to medium and simmer, uncovered, for 45 minutes. Add the lime juice, rose water, and cardamom seeds, and continue to cook for 5 to 10 minutes until the syrup has thickened enough to coat the back of a spoon. Remove from heat.

7. Fill the sterilized jars with the hot preserves leaving ½in/12mm of head space. Seal the jars and store in a cool, dark place. *Nush-e Joon!*

VARIATION

Azari Tomato Preserve

Replace the pumpkin flesh with 2lb/900g firm, medium-sized tomatoes in season. Peel and halve the tomatoes. Proceed with step 3 above and eliminate step 4. Everything else remains the same.

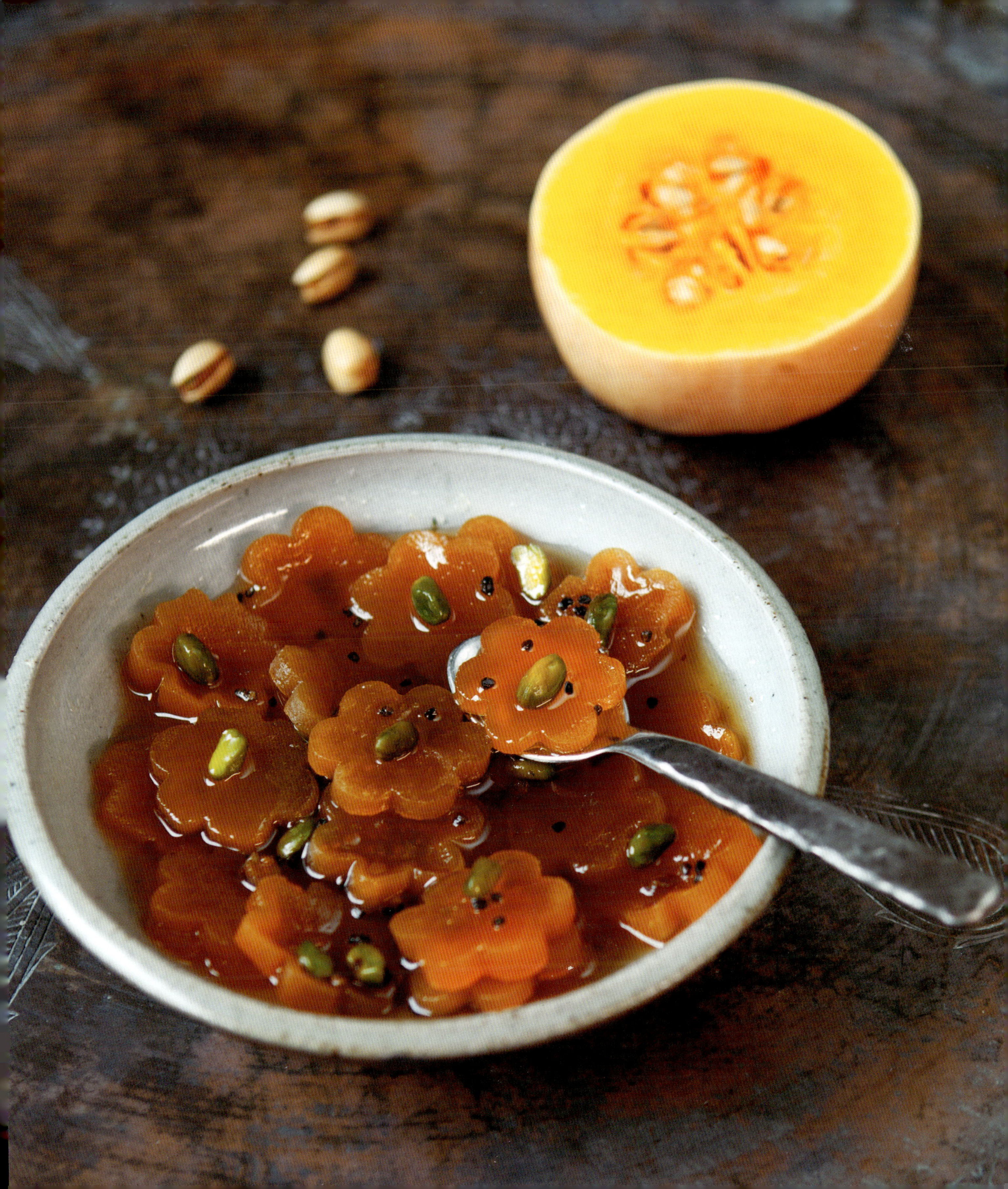

Roasted Butternut Squash + Grape Molasses

kadu halvai-o gerdu-o shireh-ye angur-e hamadani

Serves 6 to 8
Prep: 15 minutes
Cooking: 55 minutes

SYRUP

½ teaspoon ground saffron threads dissolved in ½ cup/120ml water
⅓ cup/80g grape molasses
One 4in/10cm cinnamon stick

SQUASH

1 butternut squash or pumpkin (about 3lb/1.5 kg)

GARNISH

½ cup/75g fresh pomegranate arils (optional)
½ cup/60g toasted walnuts
Thick yogurt, or vanilla ice-cream, or whipped cream (optional)
Sprigs of mint

This is a very tasty dessert, and if you add whipped cream or thick yogurt to it, it's even more delicious.

1. Preheat oven to 350°F/180°C.

2. **To make the syrup:** In a deep laminated cast-iron sauté pan, combine the saffron-water, grape molasses, cinnamon, and stir well.

3. Cut the squash into ½in/12mm wide rings (slice horizontally). Peel and remove the seeds.

4. Place the squash rings, side by side, in the sauté pan.

5. Cover and bake for 45 to 55 minutes until done.

6. Remove from the oven, baste, and allow to cool. Transfer to individual serving dishes. Garnish according to your fancy. *Nush-e joon!*

STOVETOP COOKING VARIATION

Cover the pan tightly and cook over low heat for 45 to 50 minutes until the squash is cooked through.

VARIATION

Roasted Beets with Grape Molasses + Walnuts
choghondar-o gerdu-ye shirazi

Replace the butternut squash with 2lb/900g beets. Everything else remains the same.

NOTE

To toast the walnuts: Preheat the oven to 350°F/175°C. Spread the walnuts on a sheet pan lined with parchment paper. Bake in the oven for 7 to 10 minutes until nicely toasted.

1917 postcard sent from Shahrud to Mashhad depicting a roasted beets peddler.

Hamadan

Sweet Sesame Bun

nan-e komaj-e hamadani

Makes 8 loaves
Prep: 15 minutes + 6 hours of resting
Cooking: 40 minutes

DOUGH

1 package or 1 tablespoon active dry yeast
2 cups/480ml warm milk (100°F/38°C)
1 cup/130g powdered sugar
2 eggs, lightly beaten
¼ cup/60ml oil or butter
4½ to 5 cups/600g unbleached all-purpose flour, sifted with 1 teaspoon baking powder and ¼ teaspoon fine sea salt

EGG WASH

1 egg yolk mixed with 1 tablespoon milk

DECORATION

2 tablespoons sesame or poppy seeds

In Hamadan, these buns are usually served with one of their popular spreads: angusht pich *or* halva zardeh *(page 264).*

1. **To make the dough:** In the bowl of an electric mixer, dissolve the dried yeast in the warm milk. Add the sugar and allow to rest for 10 minutes undisturbed.

2. Gradually add the eggs and oil, and mix until creamy.

3. Sift together the flour, baking powder and salt into a bowl. Gradually add it, one cup at a time, to the yeast mixture, and knead on low speed for about 10 minutes until 4¼ cups/425g of flour have been added and you have sticky dough (adding more flour if necessary).

4. Transfer the dough to a lightly oiled, wide bowl and turn the dough to ensure it is evenly coated with oil. Cover with plastic wrap and allow it to rise in a warm, dark place for 4 to 24 hours.

5. Preheat the oven to 325°F/160°C and line 2 sheet pans with parchment paper.

6. Turn the dough out onto a floured work surface and punch down. Divide it into 8 tangerine-sized equal balls using a dough scraper. Use your hands to flatten each ball to a 4in/10cm diameter disk. Place 4 loaves on each sheet pan. Cover with a dish towel and allow to rest for another 2 hours.

7. **To prepare the egg wash:** In a small bowl, beat together the egg yolk and milk with a fork until smooth.

8. **To cook the buns:** Generously paint the loaves with the egg wash. Sprinkle on top with sesame seeds.

9. Bake in the preheated oven for 35 to 40 minutes until golden brown.

10. Remove from the oven and allow to cool briefly on a cooling rack. Keep covered to prevent drying. Serve with the finger twist spread/ *angusht pich. Nush-e joon!*

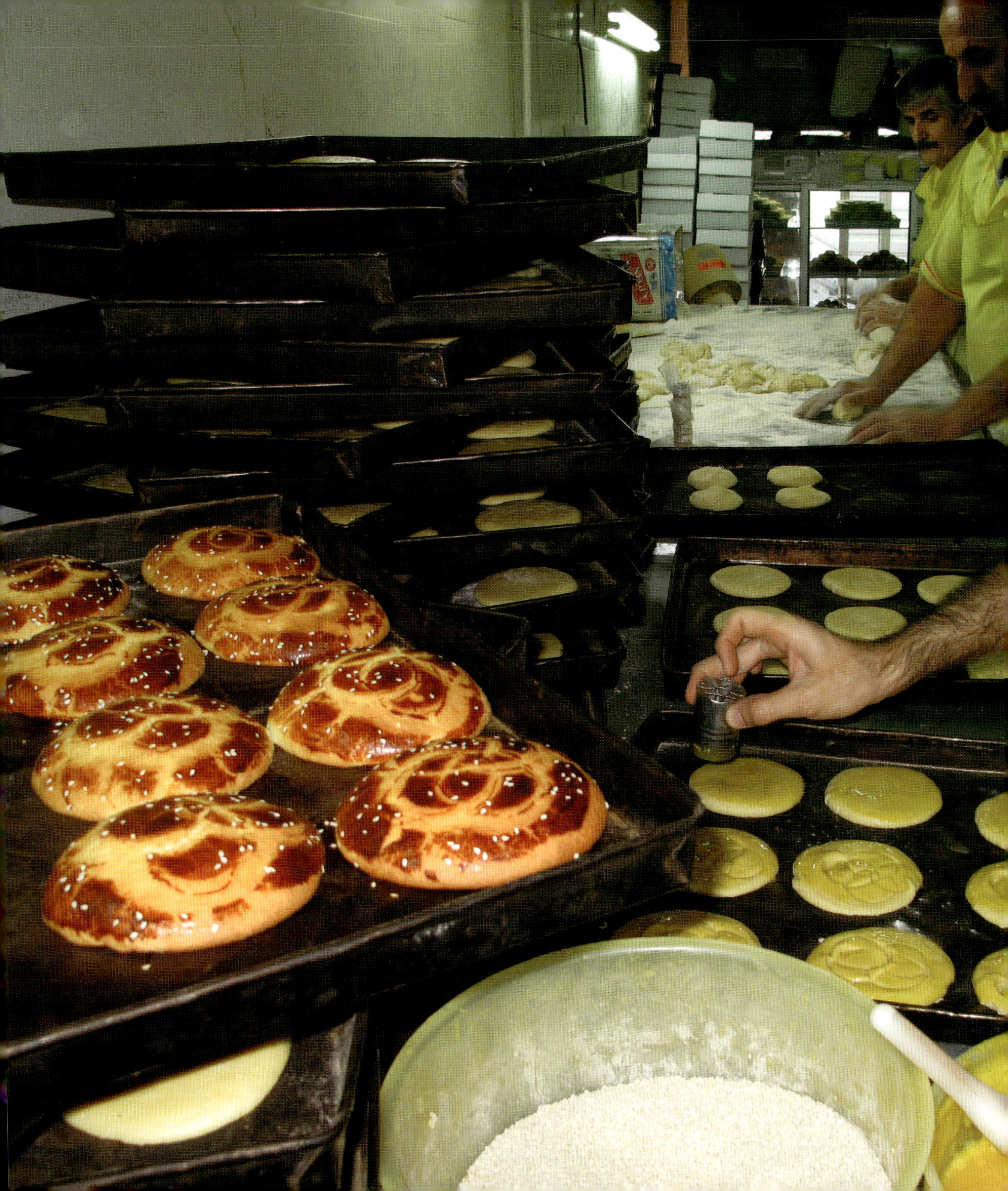

Finger Twist Spread
angusht pich-e hamadani

Makes ½pt/240g
Prep: 15 minutes
Cooking: 50 minutes

3 cups/390g powdered sugar
2 cups/480ml rose water
3 egg whites
½ teaspoon tartaric acid or
   1 tablespoon lime juice

This is a sweet, white stretchy paste. In Hamadan you can buy jars of it at pastry shops. It is often used as a spread over a komaj bun for breakfast or as a snack.

1. Heat a medium-sized saucepan over low heat. Add the sugar and rose water, and stir well. Allow the sugar to melt and lightly change color (about 30 minutes). You want a syrup that has the consistency of honey and sticks to your hand.

2. In the mixing bowl of an electric mixer, beat the egg whites and tartaric acid until stiff.

3. Select a low speed for the mixer and gradually add the syrup, while the machine is running until swirls appear on the top and you have a white, stretchy, light paste that you can twist around your finger. Store in an airtight glass container and use as a spread. *Nush-e joon!*

Egg + Saffron Spread
halva zardeh-ye hamadani

Serves 4
Prep: 15 minutes
Cooking: 10 minutes

2 egg yolks
1 cup/130g powdered sugar
½ teaspoon ground saffron dissolved in
   ¼ cup/60ml rose water
3 tablespoons oil or ghee

This sweet, yellow spread, on its own or combined with finger twist, is also a favorite with fresh-baked sesame buns/nan-e komaj.

1. In the bowl of an electric mixer, beat the egg yolks and sugar until white and creamy.

2. Add the saffron-rose water and oil and continue to beat until thick and yellow.

3. Pour the egg mixture into a wide, non-stick skillet over low heat, stirring constantly (about 10 minutes) with a long wooden spoon until you have a thick, yellow paste that separates and rolls easily in the skillet.

4. Use as a spread on bread. Store in an airtight glass container in the refrigerator. *Nush-e joon!*

Pouya joon, my cousin's son, enjoying a finger twist in a bakery in Hamadan.

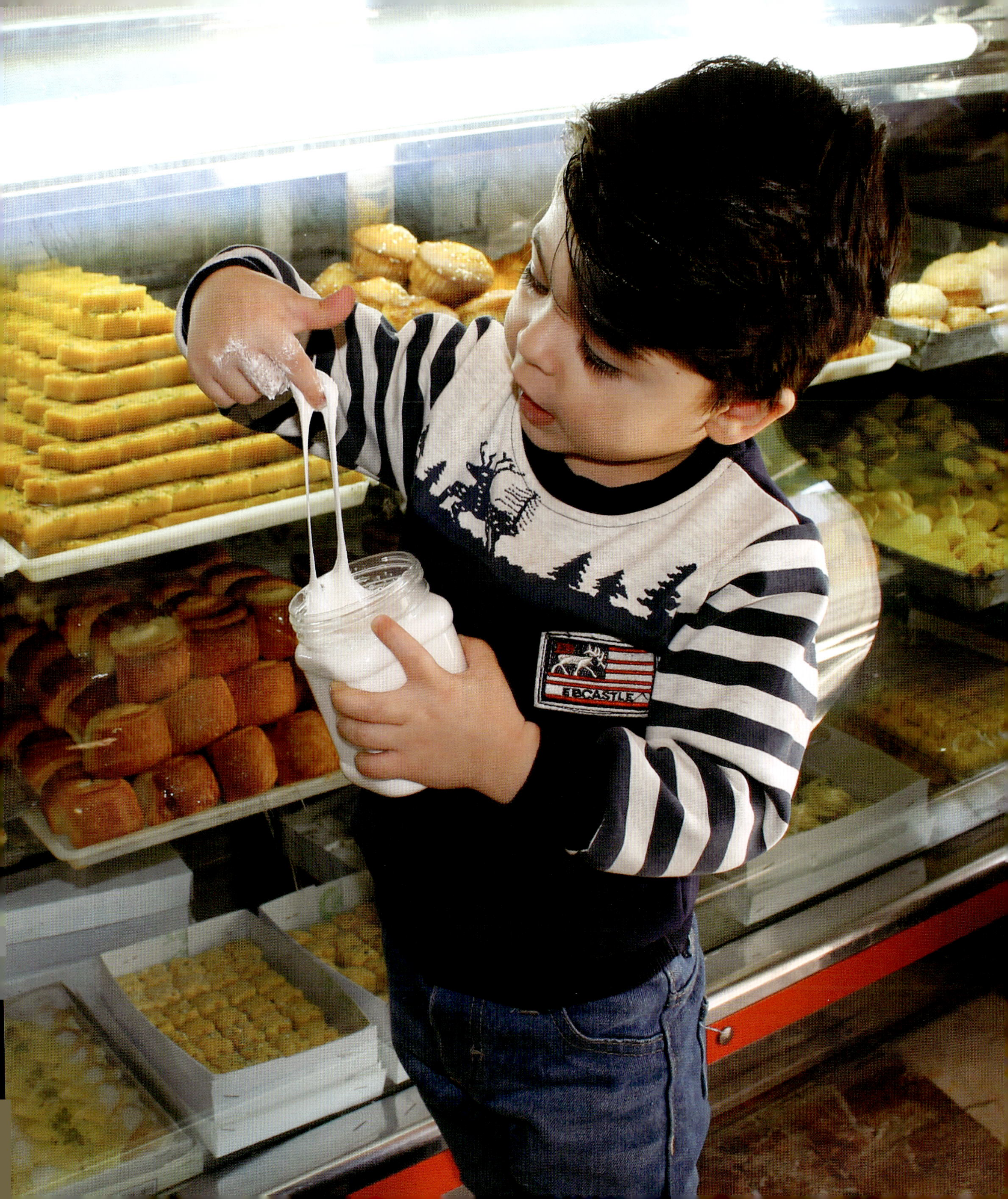
EBCASTLE

Apricot + Nut Pickle
torshi-e ajil-e hamadani

Serves 4 to 6
Prep: 10 minutes + overnight soaking
Cooking: 5 minutes

APRICOT

1lb/450g dried apricots
4 cups/960ml apple cider vinegar
2 tablespoons honey

NUTS

1 tablespoon blanched almonds
1 tablespoon shelled hazelnuts
1 tablespoon pistachio kernels
1 tablespoon walnuts
2 teaspoons Hamadani seven-spice *advieh*
2 teaspoons salt

This is a unique pickle. It's particularly good with lamb. You can also chop the apricots to make it a little more delicate.

1. **For the apricots:** Place the apricots in a medium-size glass container, add the vinegar, and toss well. Cover and allow to soak overnight in the fridge.

2. Drain the apricots, discard the vinegar, and return the apricots to the glass container.

3. **To toast the nuts:** Heat a wide skillet over medium heat and toast the nuts for 1 minute, stirring constantly. Add the *advieh* and salt, and toast for 1 to 2 minutes until the aroma rises and the nuts are lightly golden.

4. Add the nuts and honey to the apricots. Toss well and adjust seasoning to taste, adding more honey if necessary. *Nush-e joon!*

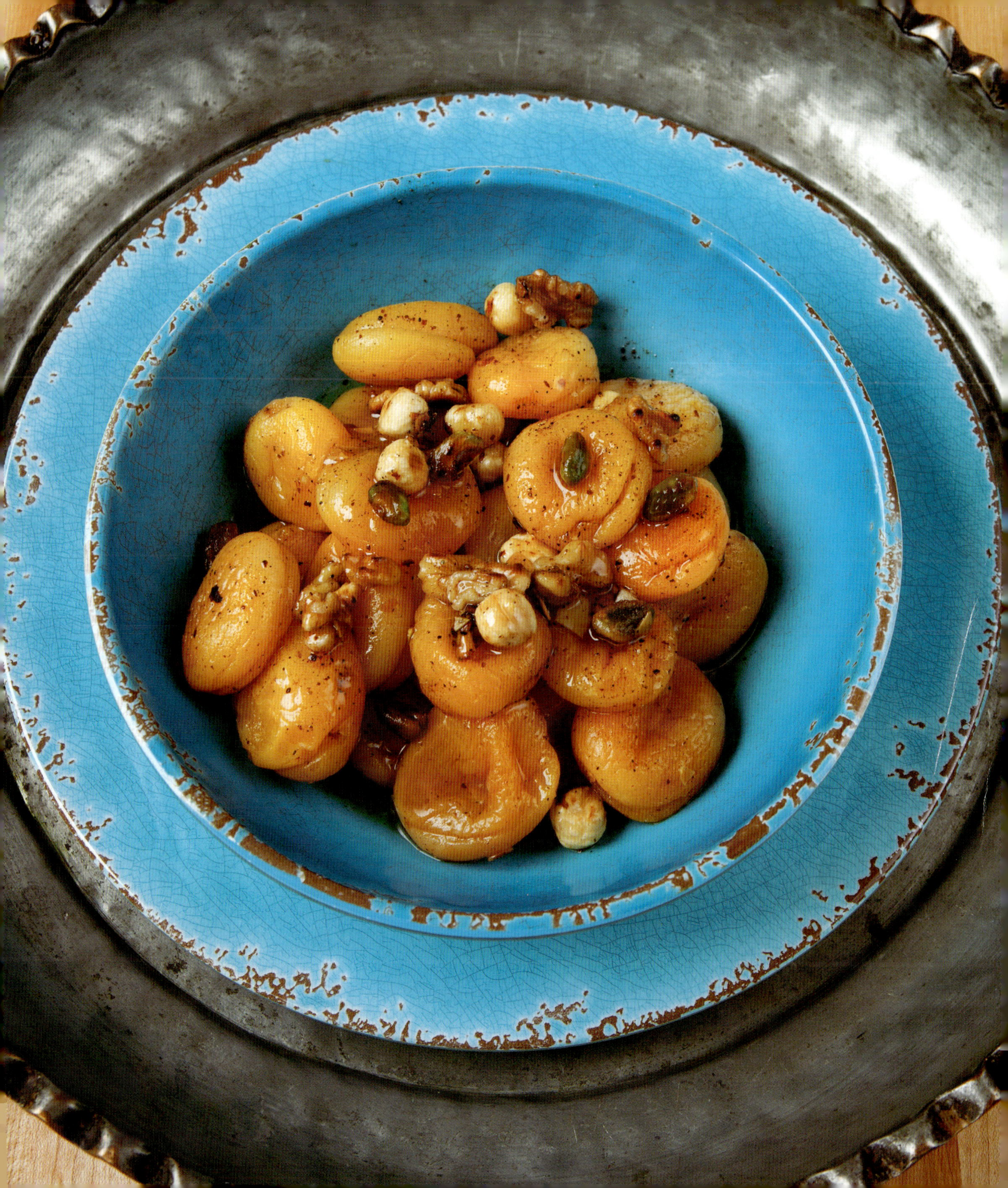

Arak

A Little History

Arak is the main city of the Markazi Province of central Iran. It's located in the plain of Farahan (famous for its carpets) on the edge of the Zagros Mountains. The name comes from the medieval Arabic designations of Araq-e Ajam to refer to ancient Media in northwestern Iran (while Araq-e Arab referred to Mesopotamia). The cuisine of this region is similar to Kurdish cooking. Legumes, bulgur, and yogurt and its by-products such as, *kashk*, and black *kashk/qareh qurut* (used as a souring agent, page 276), are popular.

Tomato + Lime Broth with Tiny Meatballs

gushtabeh/kufteh-ye kaleh gonjishki-e araki

Serves 4 to 6
Prep: 15 minutes
Cooking: 1 hour

BROTH

2 tablespoons oil, butter, or ghee
2 medium onions, peeled and thinly sliced
2 teaspoons fine sea salt
½ teaspoon fresh ground pepper
1 tablespoon turmeric
1 tablespoon tomato paste
2 fresh tomatoes, peeled and finely chopped
1 teaspoon dried Persian lime powder
½ cup fresh orange juice
¼ cup fresh lime juice
5 cups/1.2l water

MEATBALLS

1 small onion, peeled and finely chopped
1 pound/450g ground lamb
1 teaspoon sea salt
1 teaspoon freshly ground pepper
½ teaspoon ground turmeric
½ teaspoon ground cinnamon
½ teaspoon smoked paprika

1lb/450g small golden potatoes, peeled

My mother learned to make this soup from her mentor, my father's sister Ameh Fatemeh. Their family had originally come from Arak. During my childhood, I had this soup often; it's quick, delicious, and very easy to make.

1. **To make the broth:** Heat the oil in a medium-sized laminated cast-iron pot over medium heat and sauté the onions until golden brown. Add the salt, pepper, turmeric, and tomato paste, and sauté for another 2 minutes. Add the fresh tomatoes and the rest of the ingredients for the broth, and bring to a boil. Reduce heat to medium and allow to simmer.

2. Combine all the ingredients for the meatballs and knead lightly to create a paste. Shape the paste into hazelnut-sized meatballs and add them to the broth as you make them.

3. Reduce heat to low, add the potatoes, cover, and simmer for 40 to 45 minutes until the potatoes are tender. Adjust seasoning to taste. Serve with bread and a fresh herb platter. *Nush-e joon!*

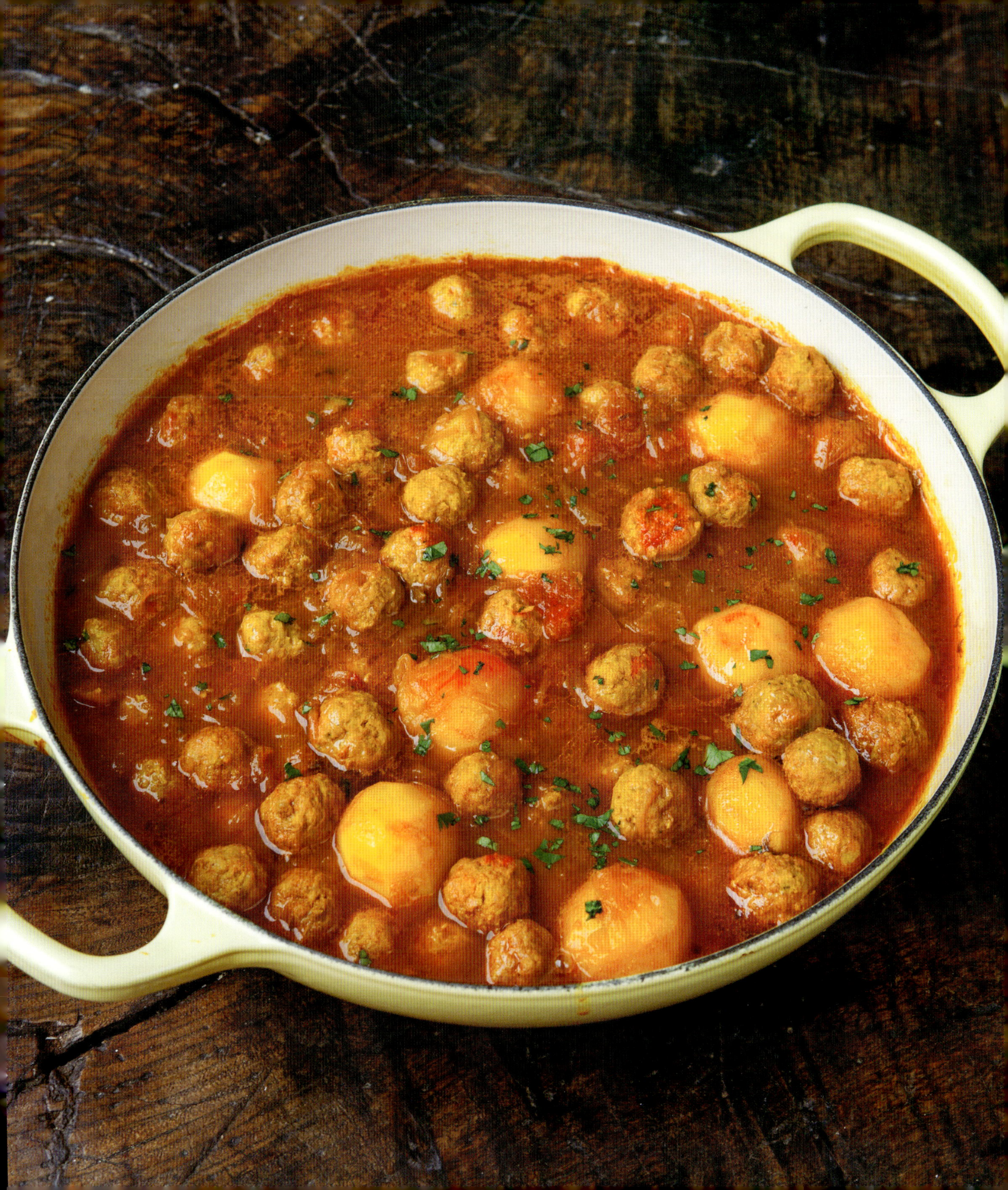

Split Pea, Bulgur + Yogurt Osh
osh-e mast-e araki

Serves 6 to 8
Prep: 10 minutes
Cooking: 1¾ hours

BROTH

¼ cup/60ml oil
2 large onions, peeled and thinly sliced
1 tablespoon fine sea salt
1 teaspoon freshly ground black pepper
2 teaspoons turmeric
1 teaspoon ground coriander
½ cup/50g split peas, soaked in water for 10 minutes and drained
2 cups/360g bulgur, rinsed thoroughly
10 cups/2.4l broth or water
½ cup/100g rice, rinsed and drained
1 cup /85g chopped fresh parsley or 1 tablespoon dried
2 cups/170g chopped fresh cilantro or 2 tablespoons dried
½ cup/50g chopped fresh spring onions
2 cups/480g plain yogurt

GARNISH/NA`NA DAGH

2 tablespoons oil
10 cloves garlic, peeled and grated
½ teaspoon turmeric
3 tablespoons dried mint flakes

Some say yogurt was first accidentally made in ancient times in the deserts of greater Iran. Iranians love yogurt and have been using it in their cooking ever since. This yogurt osh is made throughout Iran, with each region using their own particular legumes, herbs, and spices. I was served it in the village of Saruq (of magnificent carpet fame), where Fakhri Khanum made the broth using lamb on the bone. This osh is also delicious using water or vegetable broth instead of a meat broth.

1. *To make the broth:* Heat the oil in a large pot over low heat until hot. Sauté the onions until golden brown. Add the salt, pepper, turmeric, coriander, split peas, and bulgur, and sauté for 1 minute. Pour in the water and bring to a boil. Reduce heat to low, cover, and simmer for 35 minutes.

2. Add the rice, cover, and simmer for 25 to 35 minutes until the split peas are tender.

3. Add the herbs, give it a stir, and simmer for another 5 minutes.

4. In a mixing bowl, whisk the yogurt for 5 minutes, then stir in a few spoonfuls of hot soup (to temper the yogurt). Add it to the pot, gently stirring constantly for 2 minutes to prevent curdling. Adjust seasoning to taste.

5. *To make the garnish:* Heat 2 tablespoons oil in a wide skillet, add the garlic and turmeric, and sauté for 1 minute. Remove from heat, crush the mint flakes in the palm of your hand, and add them to the skillet. Stir well.

6. Pour the soup into a tureen and garnish on top according to your fancy. *Nush-e joon!*

VARIATION

Araki Barley Osh
osh-e jow-e araki

Replace the split peas and bulgur with chickpeas and pinto beans. Add ½ cup/100g lentils and 2 cups/400g barley. Replace the yogurt with 2 cups/480g liquid *kashk*. Everything else remains the same. If you replace the bulgur with 2 *tarkhineh* patties, you'll make it an Araki-style *tarkhineh osh*, which is different from the Kurdish *tarkhineh* osh (page 320).

Opposite: Churning butter in the traditional tribal way.

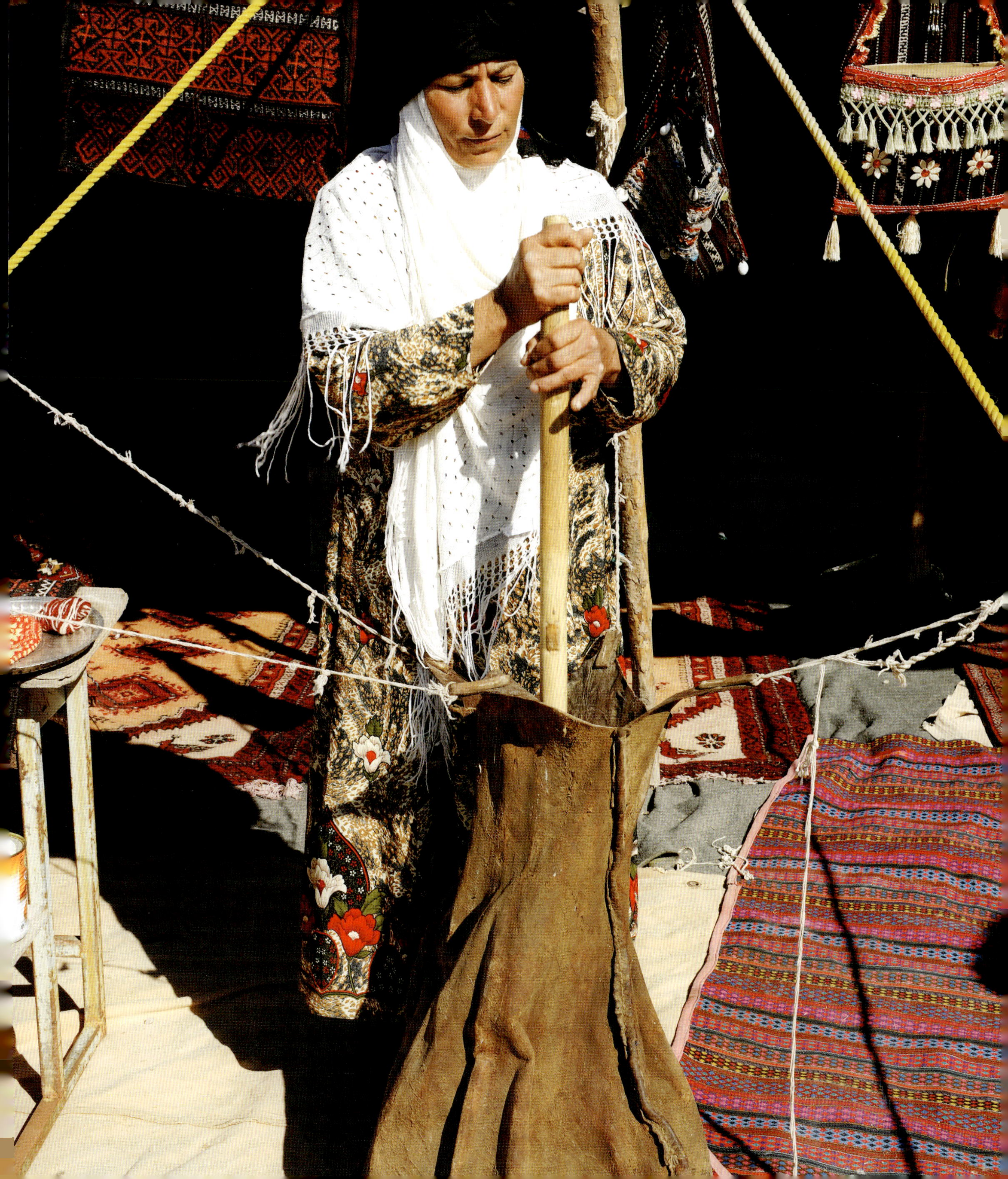

Sautéed Liver + Kidney with Black Kashk

jaghurbaghur-e araki ba qareh qurut

Serves 4
Prep: 15 minutes
Cooking: 30 minutes

- 1 lamb liver, rinsed and patted dry
- 2 hearts, rinsed and patted dry
- 8 kidneys, rinsed and patted dry
- 3 tablespoons oil
- 2 medium onions, chopped
- 4 cloves garlic, grated
- 2 teaspoons fine sea salt
- ½ teaspoon freshly ground pepper
- 1 teaspoon dried thyme
- 1 russet potato (about 1lb/450g), peeled and diced into 1in/2.5cm cubes
- 2 tablespoons tomato paste
- 1oz/30g black *kashk/qareh qurut* dissolved in 2 cups/480ml boiling water
- 2 tablespoons verjuice
- 1 teaspoon grape molasses

GARNISH

- 1 tablespoon chopped fresh parsley
- ½ cup/70g pickled cucumbers, thinly sliced

1. Cut the liver and hearts lengthwise into ½in/12mm thick strips. Cut kidneys into 1in/2.5cm cubes.
2. In a medium-sized sauté pan, heat the oil over medium-high heat and add the liver, hearts, and kidneys. Sauté for 2 minutes. Add the onions and garlic, and sauté for 3 to 5 minutes until brown.
3. Add the potatoes, salt, pepper, and thyme, and sauté for 2 minutes. Add the tomato paste and sauté for 1 minute.
4. Add the dissolved black *kashk*, verjuice, and grape molasses, and bring to a boil. Reduce heat to low, cover, and simmer over medium heat for 15 to 20 minutes until the potatoes are tender.
5. Adjust seasoning to taste. Remove from the heat and transfer to a serving dish. Garnish with parsley and pickled cucumbers. Serve immediately; this dish should be served hot with bread and a green herb platter or salad. *Nush-e Joon!*

An 1880s photo of a dervish on the road to Isfahan.

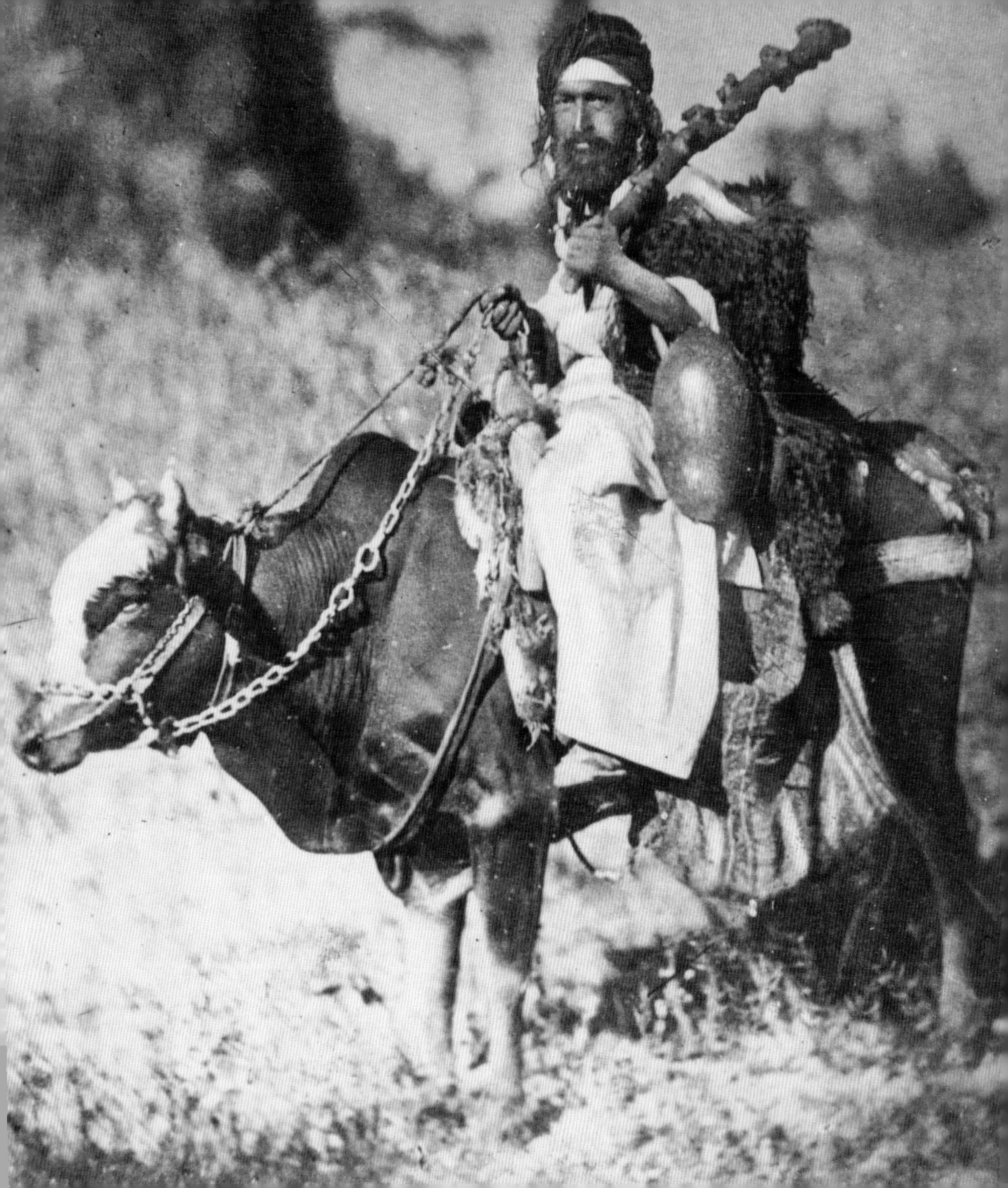

Kashk
kashk

Serves 4
Prep: 15 minutes
Cooking: 2 hours

4½ cups/1l plain yogurt
2 cups/480ml water
1 tablespoon fine sea salt
2 tablespoons vinegar

You can buy kashk *and black* kashk/gareh gurut *at Iranian markets, but you can also make them quite easily at home. The photo on the facing page shows women at a stall in the bazaar buying* kashk *and black* kashk *(some of which have different colors due to their various flavorings).* Kashk *is used in cooking as a liquid; however, traditionally, for convenience of storage, it was formed into balls or patties and left out to dry. These would then be diluted as needed and used for cooking.*

To make kashk: You need to start with sour yogurt (plain yogurt that has been left out of the fridge for a couple of days). However, some store-bought yogurts won't go sour (due to preservatives); you can remedy this by making your own yogurt or by adding a little vinegar.

1. In a large mixing bowl or food processor, blend 4¼ cups/1l yogurt with 2 cups/480ml water, 1 tablespoon fine sea salt, and 2 tablespoons vinegar for 5 minutes.

2. Transfer to a saucepan and bring to a boil over medium-high heat, stirring frequently. Reduce heat to low and allow to simmer, stirring frequently for 2¾ hours until reduced to the consistency of a heavy cream.

3. Place three layers of cheese cloth over a sieve in a bowl, pour in the yogurt, and allow to drain. The longer you allow it to drain the harder the *kashk* becomes. As we usually use *kashk* in liquid form, you can store the liquid *kashk* in a tightly covered glass container in the fridge. Or, you can allow some of it to firm up at which time you can shape it into balls and allow it to dry on a sheet pan lined with parchment paper, in the sun, or in an oven overnight with just the oven light on. Do not discard the leftover liquid in the bowl as it can be used to make black *kashk/qareh qurut*, which is a distinctive-tasting souring agent.

Black Kashk
qareh qurut

1. Pour the yogurt-water left over from the *kashk*-making process into a saucepan and cook over medium heat, stirring frequently, until the liquid has reduced to about 1 cup/480ml (about 15 minutes).

2. Meanwhile, dissolve 2 tablespoons corn starch in ½ cup/120ml cold water.

3. Add the dissolved corn starch to the saucepan, stirring frequently, and continue to cook over medium heat for about 10 minutes until the liquid thickens, turns dark, and solidifies. The black *kashk* (which may well be more brown than black) is very sour and only a small amount goes a long way. Store in a covered glass container and use as needed.

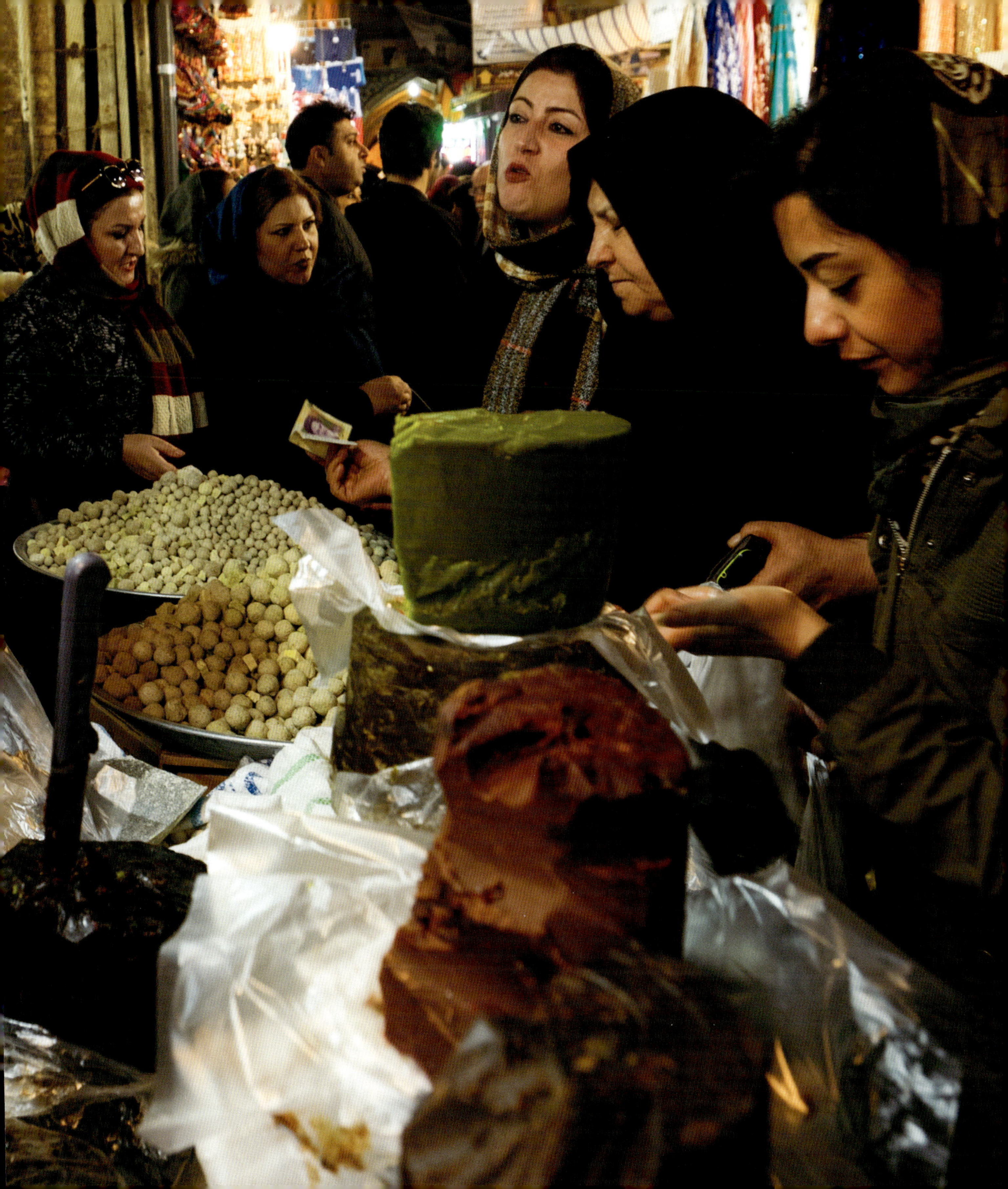

Rice with Mung Beans + Caramelized Onions
dami-e mash-e araki

Serves 6
Prep: 15 minutes
Cooking: 1½ hours

- 2 cups/400g dried mung beans, soaked in water for 30 minutes and drained
- 2 cups/400g long-grain rice, soaked in water for 30 minutes and drained
- 1 cup/240ml oil
- 2 medium onions, peeled and thinly sliced
- 1 tablespoon fine sea salt
- ½ teaspoon freshly ground pepper
- 2 teaspoons turmeric
- 2 teaspoons ground cumin
- 6 cups/1.5l broth or water

GARNISH/*PIYAZ DAGH*

- ¼ cup/60ml oil
- 2 medium onions, thinly sliced
- ¼ teaspoon fine sea salt
- 1 teaspoon turmeric
- ½ cup/85g pitted dates, sliced
- ½ cup/75g raisins, soaked for 30 minutes and drained
- 1 cup fresh chopped cilantro

OPTIONAL

- 2 tablespoons oil
- 6 eggs
- ½ teaspoon salt
- ¼ teaspoon fresh ground pepper

I love mung beans. Besides being delicious, they are very nutritious. My mother used to cook this dish with chicken, but I'm giving you a vegan version here.

1. In a deep non-stick pot, heat ½ cup/120ml oil over medium heat and sauté the onions until golden brown. Add the salt, pepper, turmeric, cumin, and beans, and sauté for 1 minute.

2. Add 6 cups/1.5l broth and bring to a boil, stir with a wooden spoon, reduce heat to medium, cover, and simmer for 20 minutes or until the beans are almost tender.

3. Add the rice to the pot. Bring back to a boil, give it a gentle stir with a wooden spoon, cover, and simmer for 20 minutes over medium heat. As soon as the water has evaporated, drizzle the rest of the oil on top.

4. Wrap the lid of the pot with a clean dish towel and cover the pot firmly to prevent steam from escaping. Cook for 20 minutes over low heat. Remove the pot from heat and allow to cool for 5 minutes on a damp surface without uncovering it.

5. **Meanwhile, to make the garnish/*piyaz-dagh*:** Heat the oil in a wide skillet over low heat. Add the onions and sauté until golden brown. Add the salt, turmeric, dates, and raisins, and sauté for 1 minute. Transfer to a plate and set aside.

6. Just before serving, heat 2 tablespoons oil in the same skillet and fry the eggs, sprinkle with salt and pepper.

7. **To serve the rice:** Gently taking 1 spatula full at a time, place the rice in a serving dish without disturbing the crust. Mound the rice in the shape of a cone. Garnish with raisins, dates, cilantro, and fried eggs. Serve the crispy bottom of the pot/*tah-dig* on the side. *Nush-e joon!*

VARIATIONS

Bushehri-Style Mung Bean Rice
polow mashak

Eliminate the garnish and add 8 finely chopped baby green garlic shoots to step 3. Everything else remains the same.

Yellow Fava Bean Rice
dampokhtak-e baqali zard

Replace the mung beans with dried yellow fava beans. Everything else remains the same.

Shirazi-Style Pinto Beans and Rice
dami-e cheshm bolboli

Replace the mung beans with pinto beans, and in step 3, add 3 cups/255g chopped fresh dill weed and 1in/2.5cm fresh ginger, peeled and grated. Everything else remains the same.

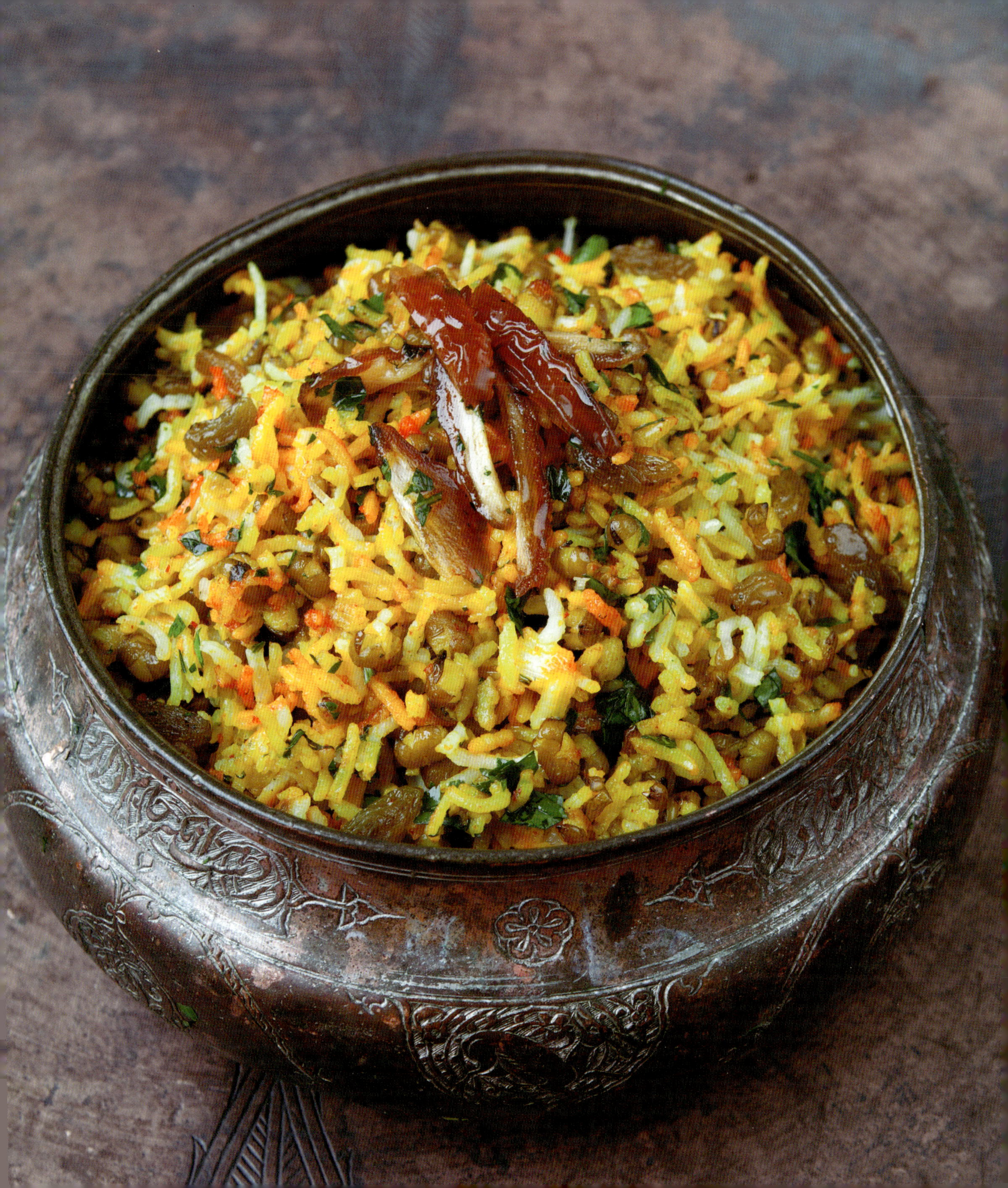

Walnut + Sumac Meatballs
kufteh-ye somaq-e araki

Serves 8 to 10, makes 24 meatballs
Prep: 30 minutes
Cooking: 55 minutes

SUMAC JUICE

1 cup/120g sumac powder
5 cups/1.2l water

MEATBALLS

½ cup/100g split peas or mung beans, rinsed thoroughly
½ cup/100g rice, rinsed thoroughly
1 large onion, peeled and quartered
1½ cups/180g walnuts
½ cup/30g plain panko bread crumbs
3 cups/250g chopped fresh parsley
1 cup/85g chopped fresh tarragon
1 cup/85g chopped fresh cilantro
1 tablespoon fresh lime juice
2 teaspoons fine sea salt
1 teaspoon red pepper flakes
1 teaspoon freshly ground pepper
1 teaspoon turmeric
1 tablespoon ground cumin
1 teaspoon cinnamon
1lb/450g ground lamb, turkey thigh, or deboned fish fillets
1 egg
¼/60ml cup oil to brush meatballs

BROTH

2 tablespoons oil
2 medium onions, peeled and thinly sliced
1 teaspoon salt
½ teaspoon freshly ground pepper
1 teaspoon turmeric
½ teaspoon red pepper flakes
2 tablespoons grape molasses
2 tablespoons pomegranate molasses

GARNISH

½ cup/75g pomegranate arils/seeds
½ cup/40g fresh chopped parsley

Traditionally this meatball is cooked on the stovetop but I am making it in the oven because it is simpler. These meatballs can be the size of tangerines or walnuts according to your fancy.

1. **To make the sumac juice:** In a small saucepan, combine the sumac powder and 5 cups/1.2l water. Cover and cook over low heat for 30 minutes. Pass through a sieve. Reserve the sumac juice and discard any solids.

2. **To make the meatballs:** Place the split peas and rice in a small saucepan, add 4 cups/960ml water, and cook over medium heat for 20 minutes. Drain and allow to cool.

3. Place all the ingredients for the meatballs, except the ground lamb and egg, in a food processor and pulse until you have a grainy paste. Transfer to a large mixing bowl and add the lamb and egg. Lightly knead with your hands for a few minutes (do not over-mix). Cover and chill in the fridge for at least 10 minutes or up to 24 hours.

4. **Meanwhile, to prepare the broth:** In a medium saucepan, heat the oil and sauté the onions until golden brown. Add the salt, pepper, and turmeric, and sauté for 1 minute. Add the sumac juice and the rest of the ingredients for the broth. Bring to a boil, reduce heat to low, cover, and allow to simmer over low heat.

5. Preheat the oven to 400°F/200°C. Generously oil a wide, non-re-active baking dish (about 12 x 14in/30 x 35cm) that is large enough to fit 24 walnut-sized meatballs and set aside.

6. Remove the lamb paste from the fridge and use an ice-cream scoop to pick up some paste. Shape it into walnut-sized meatballs with your hands. Place the meatballs in the baking dish and brush generously with oil. Bake in the oven for 15 minutes.

7. Pull out the oven rack and use a ladle to gently pour all of the broth over the meatballs. Cover with oiled parchment paper and bake for another 30 minutes. Baste once during this time.

8. Garnish and serve warm with its sauce. You can also use flat bread or green leaf lettuce as a wrapper. *Nush-e joon!*

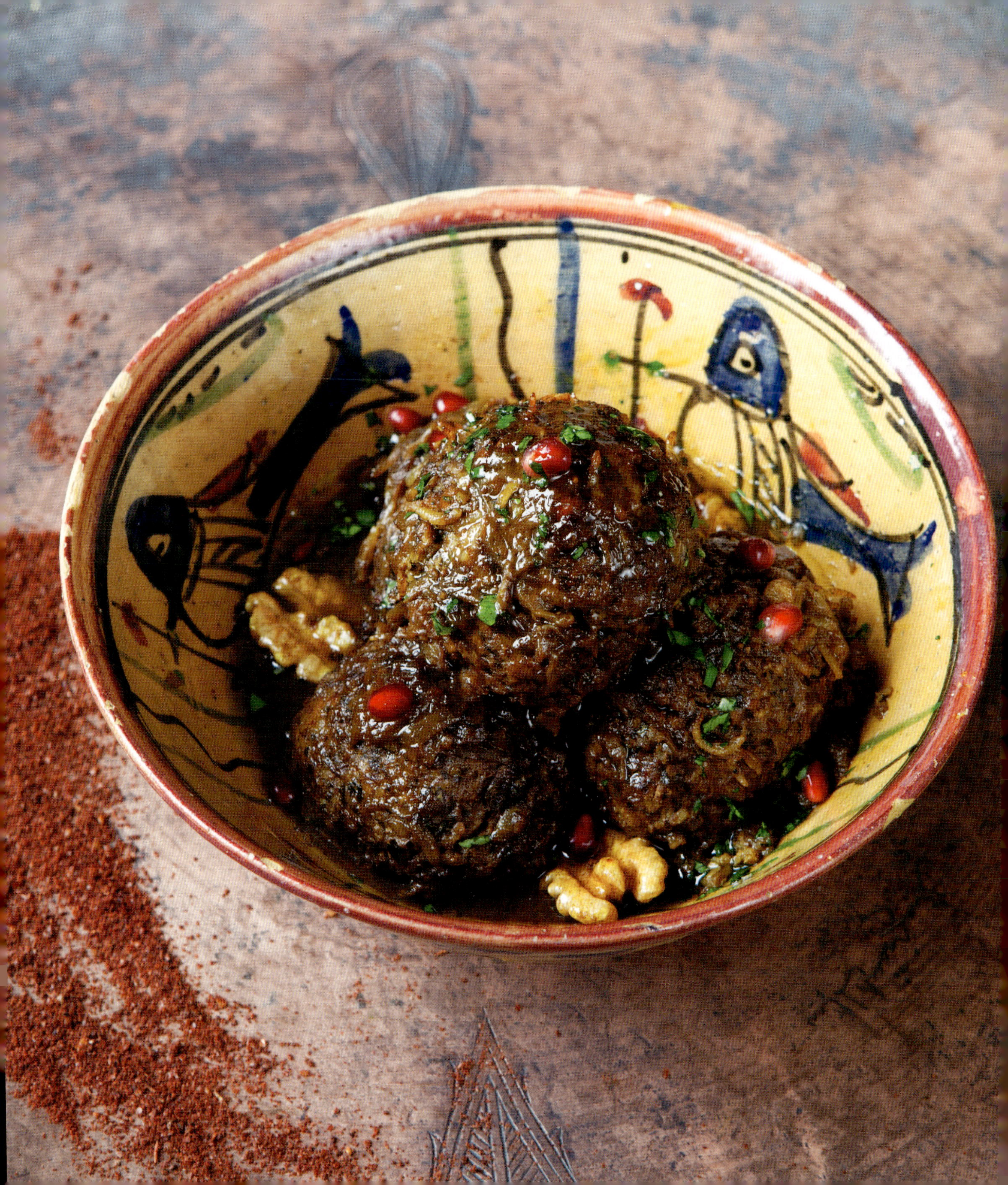

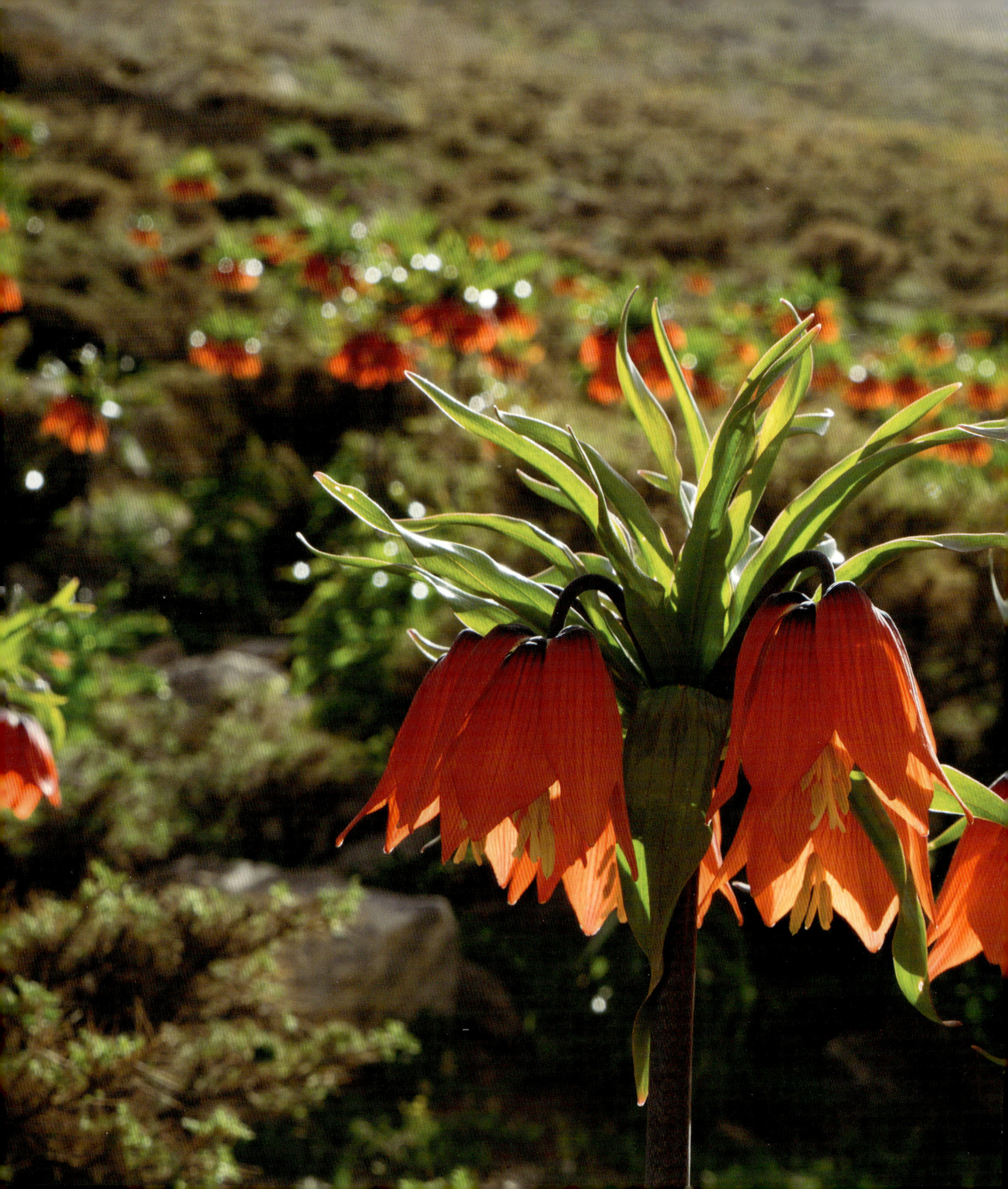

Rare wild upside-down tulips on the road from Khansar to Arak. Dutch growers still visit the mountains of Iran looking for wild tulips to use for their cultivars.

Bread

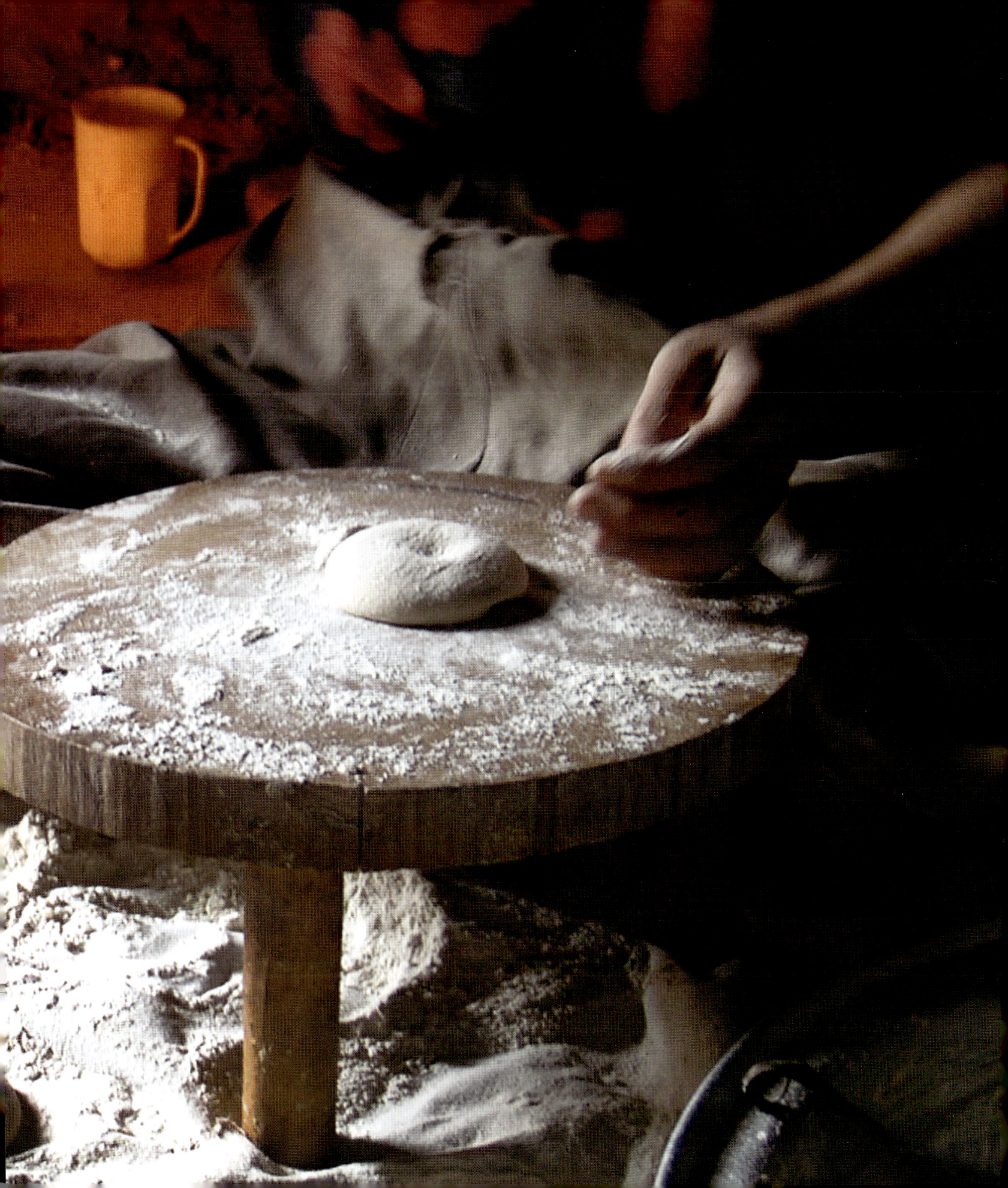

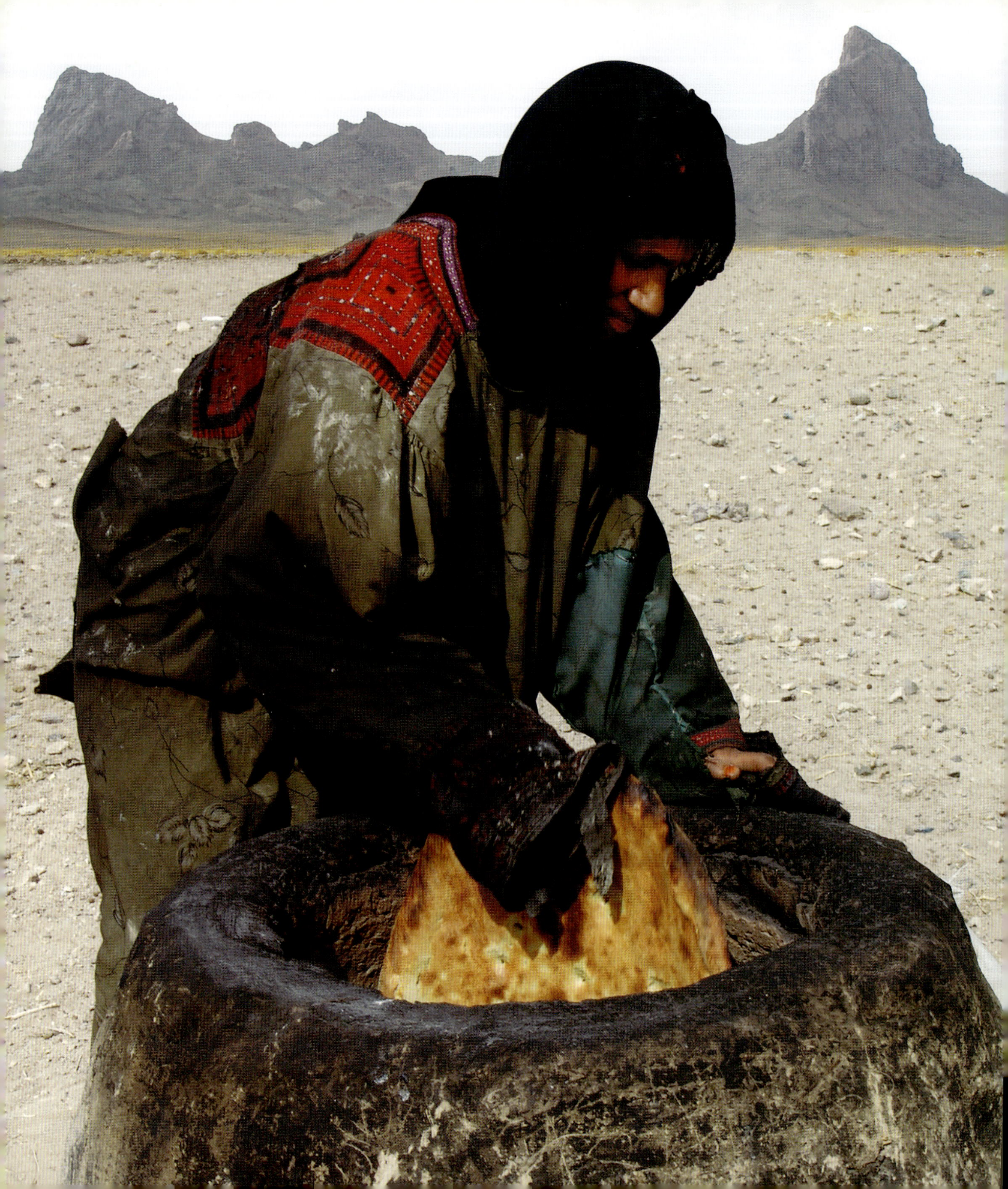

A Flat Bread Story

My mother's picking basil.
Bread and basil and cheese, a cloudless sky, wet petunias.
Salvation is near, amidst the flowers in the courtyard.
What caresses the light pours into a copper goblet!

                              Sohrab Sepehri

Bread, called *nan* in Persian, is the staple food of Iran. *Nan* is a Persian word first used in Achaemenid Iran (550–330 BCE), from which other languages borrowed it.

The main Iranian breads are flat breads, but they are well leavened and light and usually eaten fresh daily. Leftover bread is often used like croutons in soups, or with milk as if a cereal, or ground with cheese, nuts, and herbs and eaten as a snack.

Traditionally, bread and salt were treated with great respect in Iran. As children, my sisters and I were taught not to consider bread as a food but rather as a gift from god. If we saw a piece of bread lying on the ground, we'd pick it up and place it on high ground, because stepping on bread was considered disrespectful, and throwing bread away was also frowned upon. To this day I find it hard to throw away stale bread.

Priests in ancient Iran would make a round, flat wheat bread called *dron* as a ritual offering to the divine. We know that the Achaemenids continued the practice, as did the Sasanian kings (224–651 CE). This ritual is still practiced by Zoroastrians today. The Manicheans, a mostly vegetarian religious sect started in Iran during this period, considered bread to be full of light and thought that by eating it you would become enlightened.

In Iranian cities, four types of bread are prepared fresh daily—*barbari*, *sangak*, *lavash*, and *taftun*—and every neighborhood has its own specialized bakers for each of these breads. Each type of bread is cooked at a different time of the day. Light and fluffy *barbari* (somewhat similar to an Italian *foccacia*), for example, is usually made in the early mornings and is a favorite breakfast bread, eaten with butter and quince or fig jam, or with cheese, and hot, sweet tea (perhaps only the *baguette parisienne* can

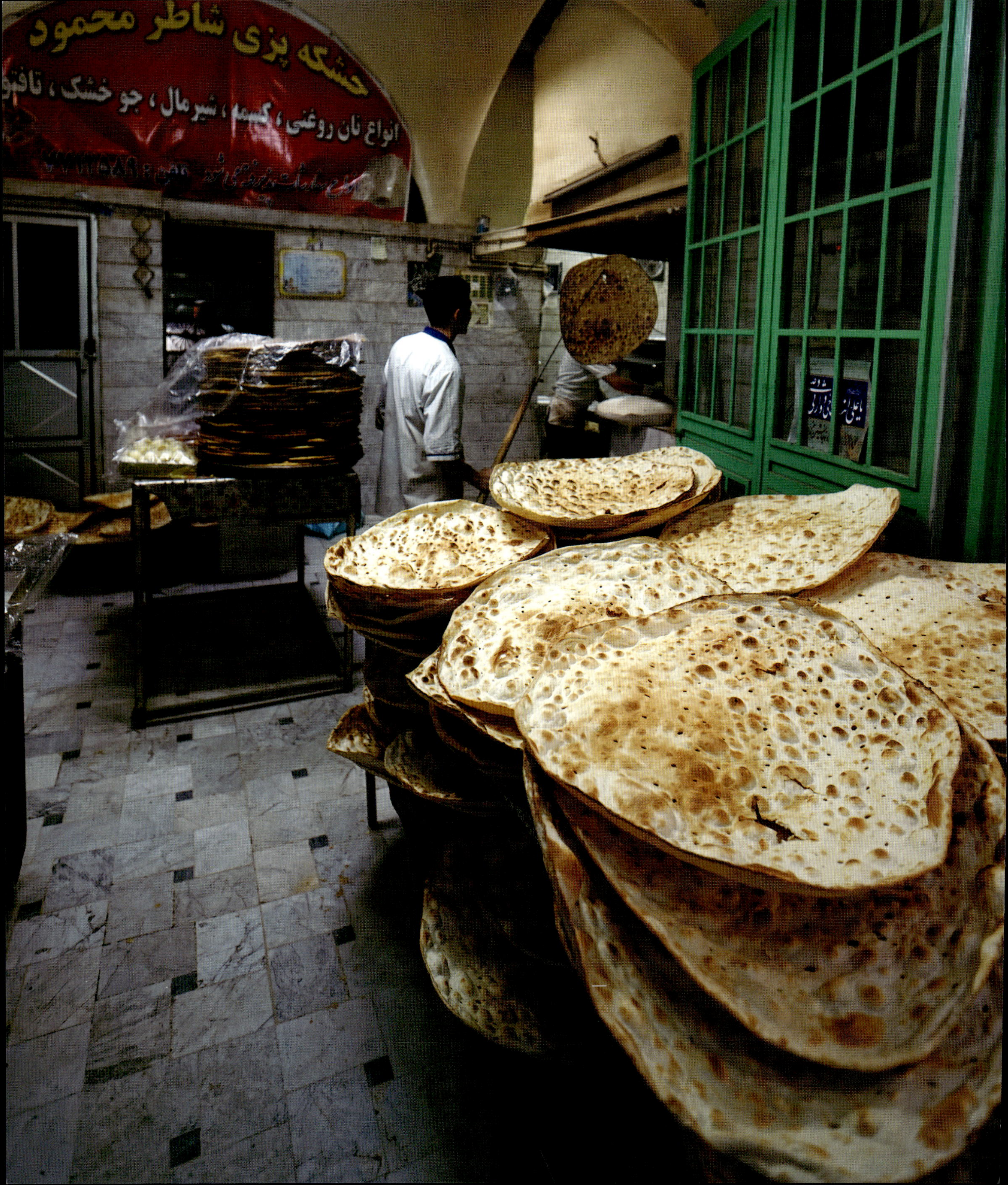
خشکه پزی شاطر محمود
انواع نان روغنی، کسمه، شیرمال، جو خشک،

compete with *nan-e barbari*). Barbari bread (top right) is popular in Tehran and people think it originated there, but it actually originated in Khorasan, where it was made by the Hazaras, an ethnic group of possibly Mongol origin from central Afghanistan. Iranians used to call them *Barbars*. The Hazaras themselves call the bread *nan-e tandoori* (*tandoor* is the name for an oven in that region; in Persian it is pronounced as *tanur*).

Crispy *sangak* bread (bottom right), on the other hand, is made throughout the day and is most popular for the evening meal. It is long and oval-shaped, and made with mostly whole-wheat flour. The starter yeast for *sangak* bread is a guarded secret and handed out to the specialized bakers by the bread-makers union. It is baked on pebbles in a very hot oven/*tanur* by indirect heat. Its name comes from *sang* (meaning a stone or pebble in Persian).

Lavash bread (opposite) is paper-thin, round, and pliable, and usually eaten at lunch time. In the seventeenth century, lavash bread was often used as a plate, a spoon to scoop up food, and as a napkin. It is often placed under and over, kababs to help keep them warm. The bread under the kababs, soaked with all the juices from the kababs, is considered a delicacy/*nun-e zir-e kabab*. In cities, *lavash* is made on the walls of clay or stone ovens by bakers, always men, but in villages it is made usually by women on a *saj* or *taveh* (a heated, flat, or domed iron griddle). This is the main bread of the tribal and nomadic regions of Iran, where the best *lavash* breads are made.

Taftun, made similarly to *lavash*, is thicker and the easiest bread to make. *Lavash* and *taftun* are often used as spoons for picking up rice or meats, or as wrappers for making mini sandwiches/*loghmeh* to pop in your mouth (making wraps or sandwiches has very ancient roots in Iran). Bread and cheese/*nan-o panir*, bread and yogurt/*nan-o mast*, or bread and onion/*nan-o piaz* (similar to farmers' meals in southern France) were until quite recently the main meal of the majority of the Iranian people.

There are also many other sweet and semi-sweet breads made throughout Iran. Spiced and deep-fried breads are popular in various regions (see recipes that follow). One of the most popular of these breads is a sweet, crunchy, unleavened bread/*nan-e qandi*, a favorite in Shiraz. Another is a thick, sweet, saffron-glazed bread/*nan-e shirmal*, a specialty of Qom, usually eaten at tea time. Another similar semi-sweet, almost bun-like bread called *nan-e komaj* is made in Mahan, near Kerman, with a dough flavored with turmeric and cumin, and filled with dates. It is then topped with cumin seeds. In Hamadan, the dough is slightly sweetened with sugar, but there's no filling, and it's topped with sesame seeds. Fried breads/*chozmeh* and *nan-e roghan jush* are popular in both Khorasan and Kerman. Around the Persian Gulf they make a bread sweetened with date juice and flavored with sesame (recipe on page 307).

Bread in Iran was not only made from wheat (a luxury) and a variety of grains such as barley, millet, rice, and sorghum, but also from dried fruits such as mulberries and wild olives; nuts and seeds such as walnuts, almonds, hemp seeds, and acorns; as well as from dried fish and legumes. The preferred grain, however, was wheat, except around the Caspian, where rice was the main grain and wheat bread was considered unhealthy (there's a popular children's story from the 1900s about a girl who is going to leave the Caspian region and head south to gain her independence, even if it means she has to eat wheat bread). The poorer you were the less likely you would be to eat wheat or rice bread. Often the only flour for making bread among the nomads of Iran came from dried, ground acorns (sometimes called the staff of life). Acorn flour, which is purported to be very nutritious, is available in the U.S. and I'm giving you a recipe for a flat bread made with it.

Up to the early twentieth century, well-to-do households had their own bakers, and they baked bread twice a day. Middle-class, urban families bought a year's supply of wheat at harvest time and baked some of their bread needs themselves. They would take their grains to a local stone mill for grinding. The common bread oven in Iran was usually an earthenware jar sunk in the ground at floor level. A fire would be made in the oven and flat dough would be stuck to the interior walls. An interesting side use of the oven was that after all the bread had been baked, in cold winter nights, the oven would continue to provide heat.

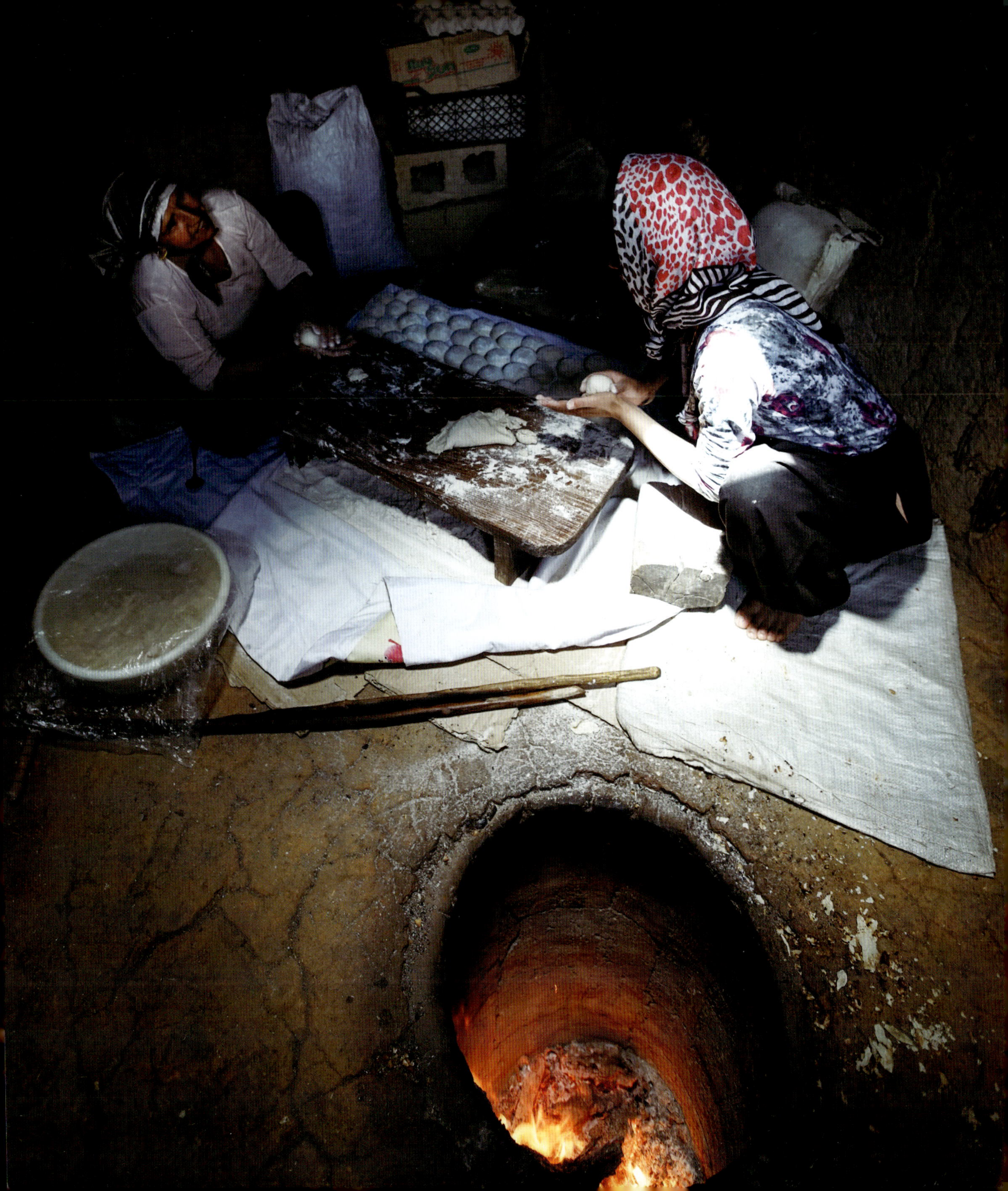

Russians introduced European-style white bread in the form of small baguettes (*nan-e sefid* or *nan-e bulki*) to Tehran in 1931. Later, Armenian bakeries made this type of bread and delis serving sandwiches became a craze. I remember in my childhood the joy my sisters and I felt at going to one of these delis near our house and ordering a mortadella sandwich with pickled cucumbers in a white baguette. Looking back, I think these white baguette sandwiches represented modernity for us.

In contemporary Iran, the traditional four breads are still being made but usually in commercial bakeries using mechanized systems. It's sad to say that many of the artisanal bakeries have shut down. And unfortunately, as I traveled through Iran, many of the hotels served sliced white loaf bread for breakfast. I craved some good, hot fresh flat Persian bread. But on a good note, I was touched by a recent community movement in northern Iran where bakeries have set up a voucher system called kindness bead/*nan-e mehrabani*. Those who can afford it buy vouchers for a few extra loaves. They hang them on a board in front of the bakery. The vouchers can then be picked up and used by those who cannot afford to pay for their bread.

In America these days, you can find wonderful artisanal, daily-made *lavash* and *taftun* bread in the Washington, DC area, or in California and New York. Great-tasting *sangak* and barbari breads too are being made and distributed on both coasts. I visited Alidad Hakimi at his Lyon Bakery in DC. He's an Iranian-American who loves what he's doing, and though his bakery makes mostly Western breads to satisfy the needs of local restaurants and markets, he follows all the old principles of using only flour, salt, water, and yeast. No extra gluten, fillers, or any other additives. During my visit, he cooked us an excellent *barbari* bread.

In the pages that follow, I am giving you recipes for breads from the various regions of Iran where the best versions are made. The wonderful thing about Persian breads is that, for the most part, they are easy to make at home.

A baker in Hamadan wears a homemade arm band to protect him from the oven.

Urmia Chorayi Bread
yaghli al choraki/nan-e roghani-e urumia

Makes one 12in/30cm loaf
Prep: 20 minutes + 2 hours of resting dough
Cooking: 30 to 35 minutes

DOUGH

½ cup/120ml milk
¾ cup/180ml water
1 package yeast
1 tablespoon sugar
3 cups/300g all-purpose flour
1 teaspoon fine sea salt
2 tablespoons oil or ghee

EGG WASH

1 egg yolk
½ teaspoon milk
⅛ teaspoon ground saffron threads dissolved in 1 tablespoon rose water

GARNISH

1 teaspoon sesame seeds
1 teaspoon nigella seeds

Here's what Nosratallah Tarighi, a friend from Urumia remembers about yaghli al choraki (locally pronounced chorayi), a specialty of the city. "It was one of the most delicious breads I'd ever had in my life: soft, delicate, delicious, and fresh. It also had an aroma of sheep grazing in the meadow in the early morning. It's a luxury Friday (equivalent of Sunday in Iran) morning breakfast bread served with local cream/sar shir, honey, cheese, butter and jam, and walnuts! Tea was, of course, mandatory. My father would stand in line to get two or three of them very early in the morning, while we were all asleep. After breakfast, my mother would put whatever remained of the bread in the fridge, and even after several weeks it would still be fresh after she heated it up on the stove. This bread was so popular it was usually sold out by 8 am. This bread was also baked especially on Ramadan for the eftar. I also remember people taking their own local fat, saffron, and sesame, a day or two in advance, for the baker to make this bread for them."

1. **To make the dough:** In a small saucepan combine the milk and water, and heat to 100°F/38°C (cooks who don't have a thermometer dip their little finger in and if it's hot but does not burn after counting to 10, it's a good temperature). Add the yeast and sugar and allow to sit for 10 minutes.

2. Combine the flour, salt, and oil in a food processor and mix for 20 seconds. Gradually add the milk mixture to the flour and pulse until you have a sticky dough. Transfer the dough to an oiled mixing bowl, cover with a plastic wrap, and allow to rest at room temperature for 2 hours and up to 8 hours.

3. **To cook the bread:** Preheat oven to 350F°/180C° and line a rimmed sheet pan with parchment paper. Transfer the dough to a lightly floured surface, shape it into a ball, and place it on the lined sheet pan. Use your hands to flatten it (12in/10cm diameter round). Indent all around it 1in/2.5cm from the outside edge. Use a knife to lightly draw strokes that score the middle into diamond shapes.

4. In a small container, place all the ingredients for the egg wash and stir well. Paint the loafs with egg wash and sprinkle on top with seeds.

5. Bake in the preheated oven for 30 to 35 minutes until a tester comes out clean and top is golden. *Nush-e joon!*

Azarbaijan

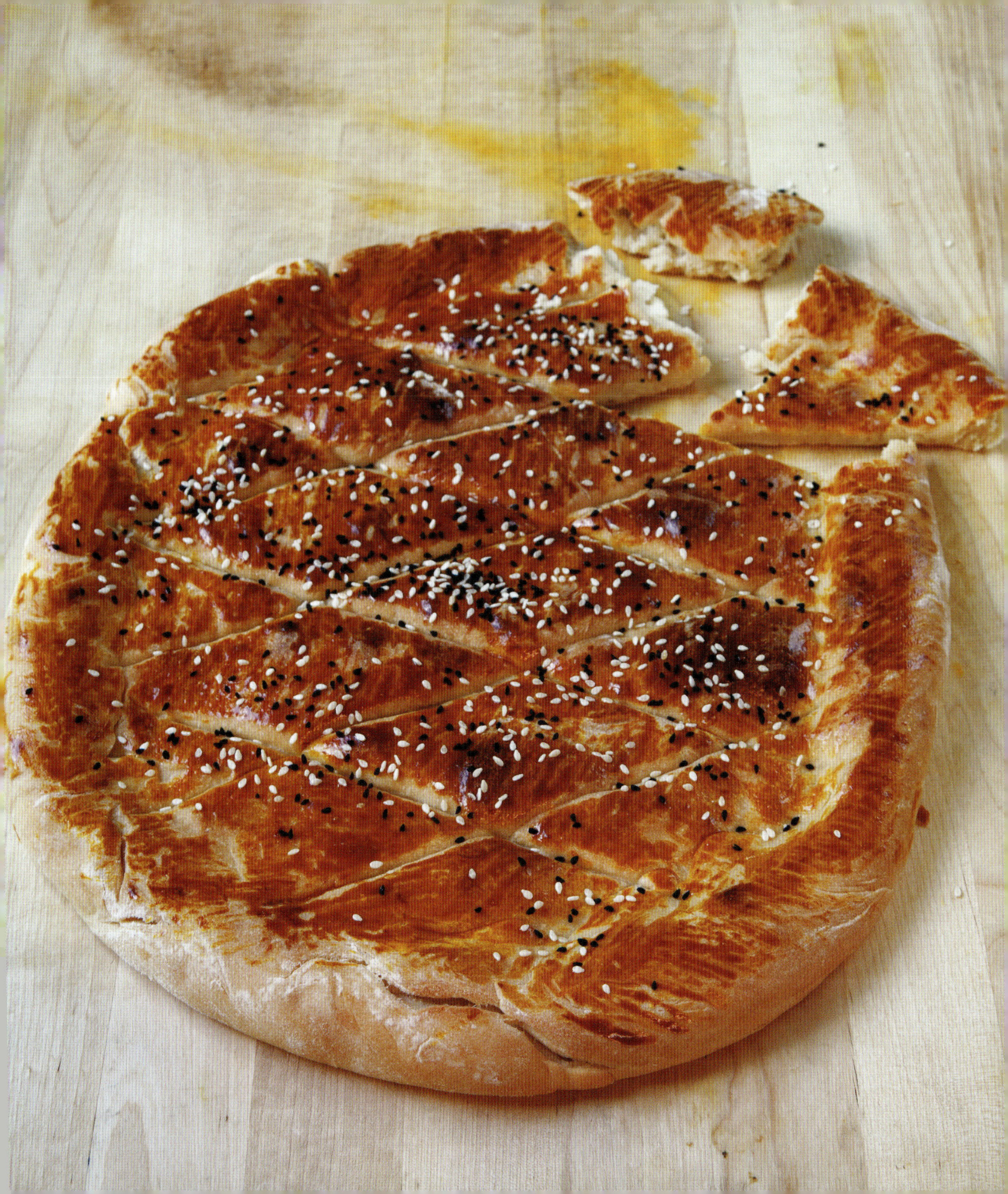

Tribal Pan-Flat Bread
nan-e saj-e kordi

Makes 8 loaves
Prep: 5 minutes + 30 minutes of resting dough
Cooking: 2 minutes per loaf

DOUGH

2¾ cups/275g all-purpose flour and ½ cup/60g flour dusting
1 tablespoon oil
½ teaspoon fine sea salt
½ teaspoon sugar
1¼ cups/300ml warm water (100°F/38°C)

GARNISH

1 tablespoon nigella or anis seeds

1. **To make the dough:** In a wide mixing bowl, combine the flour, oil, salt, and sugar. Add the water and stir well with a wooden spoon. Knead with your hands to make a sticky dough. Cover with plastic wrap and place a towel on top. Allow to rest at room temperature for at least 30 minutes.

2. Meanwhile, heat a lightly oiled *saj* (cast-iron griddle that can be flat or convex) or an upside down wok over a gas flame on high heat.

3. Divide the dough into 8 balls. Place each ball on a floured, flat surface, sprinkle with seeds, and use a thin rolling pin to roll out until it is about 8in/20cm in diameter. Flip the dough across the back of your hands to stretch it a little and to shake out any extra flour.

4. Slide the dough onto the hot *saj*. Cook for 1 minute. Use an offset spatula to flip the bread to cook the other side for another minute.

5. Use the spatula to remove the bread from the *saj* and immediately place it in a plastic storage bag to keep it soft. Continue until all the loaves have been cooked. *Nush-e joon!*

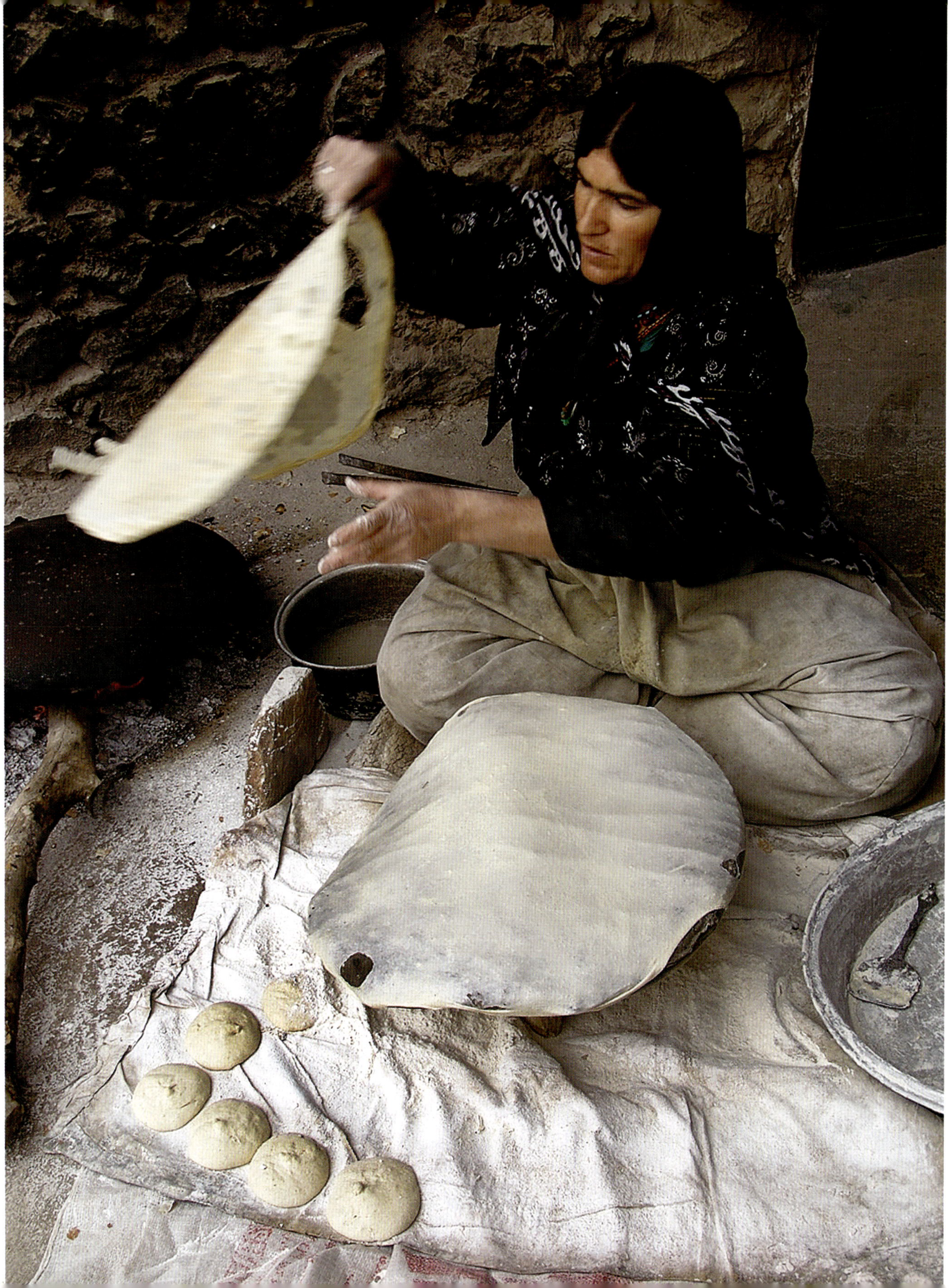

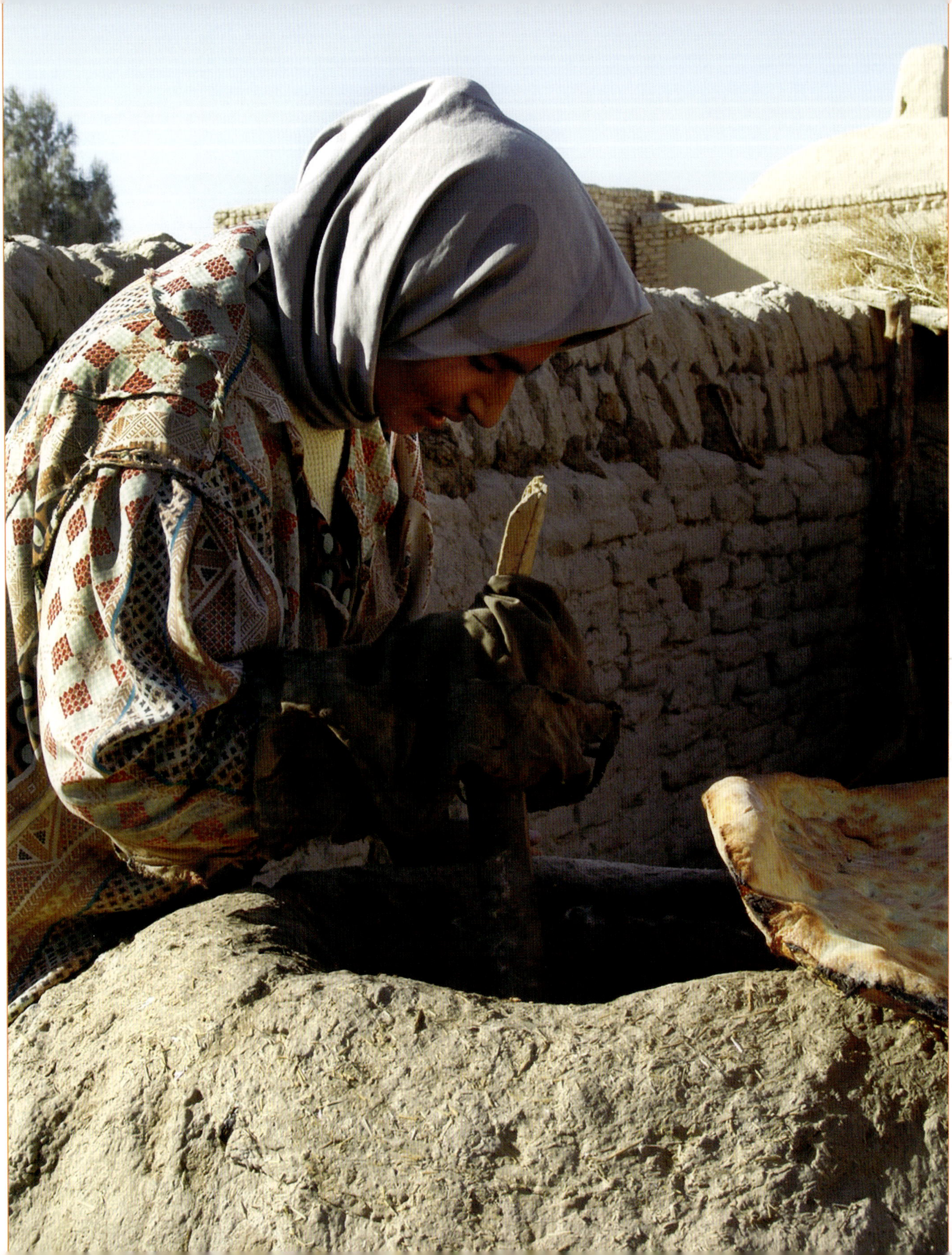

Khorasani Taftun Bread

nan-e taftun-e khorasani

Makes 2 loaves
Prep: 25 minutes + 4 hours for dough to rise
Cooking: 24 minutes

DOUGH

- 1 envelope or 2½ teaspoons active dry yeast
- 1 cup/240ml warm milk or water (100°F/38°C)
- 2 teaspoons sugar or honey
- ¼ cup/60g plain yogurt, beaten with 1 egg
- ¼ cup/60ml vegetable oil
- 3 to 3½ cups/360g unbleached all-purpose flour mixed with 1½ teaspoons fine sea salt and 1 teaspoon baking powder, sifted into a bowl

Taftun is an everyday medium-thick flat bread. It's ideal for dunking into soups or using for croutons. In Hamadan, they call it gerdeh *(meaning "the round one"). They paint it with an egg wash and sprinkle seeds over it—fenugreek, sesame, and nigella—before cooking.*

1. **To make the dough:** In the mixing bowl of an electric dough maker, dissolve the yeast in the warm milk, add the sugar, and allow to rest for 10 minutes undisturbed.

2. Add the yogurt and egg mixture, and 2 tablespoons oil. Mix well.

3. Gradually add 3 cups of the flour mixture, while the machine is running, kneading for 5 minutes. Allow the dough to rest in the machine for 2 minutes, then continue to knead for another minute, adding more flour if needed until you have a sticky dough.

4. Turn the dough in a well-oiled bowl to ensure it is coated evenly with oil all over. Cover with plastic wrap or a dish towel, and allow it to rise at room temperature for at least 4 hours (or overnight) until it doubles in size (the dough should spring back when pushed in with your finger).

5. Turn out the dough onto a floured work surface and knead for a few minutes, adding more flour if needed until you have a soft dough that does not stick to your hands. Divide the dough into 2 equal balls. Cover and allow to rest.

6. **To cook the bread:** Preheat the oven to 450°F/230°C.

7. Flatten 1 ball into a 16in/41cm disc and place it on an oiled baking sheet. Stripe the dough using a fork. Bake for 11 to 12 minutes until golden brown on top. Repeat for the remaining dough.

8. Make a pile and cover with a clean kitchen towel. Eat hot or wrap in plastic to eat later. *Nush-e joon!*

Deep-Fried Flat Bread
chozmeh-e bojnurdi

Makes 24 loaves
Prep: 15 minutes plus 2 hours for dough to rise
Cooking: 16 minutes

DOUGH

2 teaspoons active dry yeast
1 cup/240ml warm water (100°F/38°C)

SEEDS

2 teaspoons sesame seeds
2 teaspoons cumin seeds
2 teaspoons nigella seeds

FLOUR MIXTURE

3½ cups/350g all-purpose flour mixed with 1 teaspoon fine sea salt and 1 teaspoon turmeric
¼ cup/60ml oil

BAKING SODA

1 teaspoon baking soda dissolved in 1 tablespoon water

4 cups/960ml raw sesame oil for deep-frying the bread

GARNISH

1 cup/130g powdered sugar

VARIATION DOUGH WITHOUT YEAST)

Mix 2 cups/200g all-purpose flour, 2 cups/200 bread flour, 2 teaspoons fine sea salt, and ¼ cup/60ml oil until grainy. Gradually add 1 cup/240ml water. Allow to rest for 30 minutes. Proceed with step 5.

I adapted this recipe from Saeed Jahed, who told me his recollections of his grandmother Farah Banu Mozafar cooking this fried bread in Bojnurd: "She'd make it on cold, snowy days. Her kitchen was the biggest room in the house and covered with beautiful, colorful Persian carpets around which the family would gather, interact, and watch television. All of a sudden, she'd bring us all a towering pile of hot chozmeh sprinkled with powdered sugar. She made the bread often for her children and grandchildren with such easy artfulness, and with so much love that it has remained engraved in my mind as a beautiful memory." This bread is also made in Kerman. Shohreh Amin mentioned that her grandmother would often make it on special occasions for giving away as alms to the poor. They used clarified butter instead of sesame oil and call it nan-e roghan jush.

1. **To make the dough:** In the mixing bowl of a dough maker, dissolve the yeast in the warm water add allow to rest for 10 minutes undisturbed.

2. Add all the seeds and mix well. Gradually add 3 cups of the flour mixture, while the machine is running, and knead for 5 minutes. Add more flour if needed until you have a smooth, sticky dough.

3. Turn the dough in a well-oiled bowl to ensure it is coated evenly with oil. Cover with plastic wrap and a dish towel, and allow it to rise at room temperature for at least 2 hours (or overnight) until double in size (the dough should spring back when pushed in with your finger).

4. Return the dough to the mixing bowl and add the dissolved baking soda. Knead for another 2 minutes. Cover and allow to rest for another 15 minutes at room temperature.

5. Line a sheet pan with paper towels.

6. Divide the dough into 24 balls. Roll out each ball into 4in/10cm diameter by ⅛in/3mm thick discs of dough. Make a few holes in the dough using a fork. Stack the discs on top of each other with layers of parchment paper between them.

7. **To fry the bread:** Heat a deep skillet with 4 cups/960ml oil over medium heat until hot but not smoking. Gently drop each disc into the hot oil and cook for 1 to 2 minutes on each side until it puffs up and is golden. Use tongs to remove from the oil, give it a shake, and place on the lined sheet pan. Allow to cool before dusting both sides with powdered sugar. *Nush-e joon!*

Khorasan

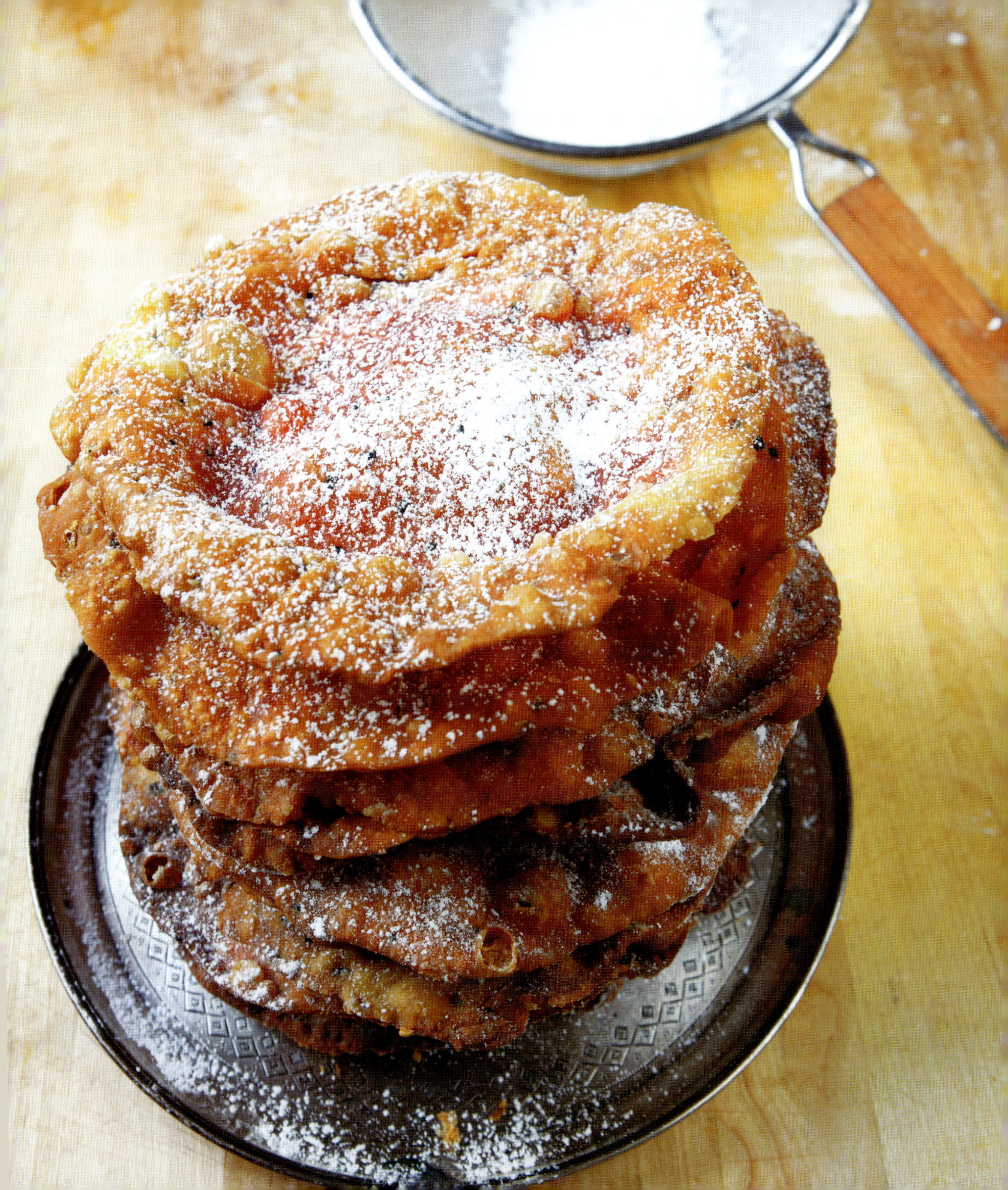

Sweet Gingerbread Crackers
nan-e qandi

Makes 6 loaves
Prep: 15 minutes + 30 minutes of resting dough
Cooking: 20 to 25 minutes per loaf

DOUGH

¾ cup/180ml warm water
¾ cup/180ml vegetable oil
⅓ cup/110g honey
¾ cup/150g brown sugar
1 teaspoon baking soda
5¼ to 6 cups/660 to 720g unbleached all-purpose flour
1 teaspoon sea salt
2 teaspoons grated fresh ginger or 1 tablespoon dried ginger powder

EGG WASH

1 egg yolk, lightly beaten

TOPPING

1 tablespoon white sesame seeds
1 tablespoon black sesame seeds

This is a delicious gingerbread with just the right amount of sweetness. It's perfect with butter, jam, and a glass of hot tea. It was one of our favorite after-school snacks. I prefer the crackers crunchy, when baked slightly more, but they can be comfortably soft and chewy if baked slightly less. These gingerbread crackers are also popular in Saveh and Shiraz.

1. Preheat the oven to 400°F/200°C and line 4 baking sheets with parchment paper.

2. **To make the dough:** In a wide mixing bowl, combine the water, oil, honey, sugar, and baking soda. Whisk well.

3. In another bowl, combine 5 cups/600g flour, salt, and ginger powder. Gradually add the flour mixture to the oil mixture. Whisk until all the water has been absorbed.

4. Transfer the dough to a floured surface and knead for a minute, adding more flour if needed until you have a soft dough that does not stick to your hands. Divide the dough into 6 equal balls. Cover and set aside.

5. Roll out 1 ball on a floured surface to form a 14 x 4 x ¼in/350 x 10 x .60mm thick oval loaf.

6. Transfer the rolled out dough onto a baking sheet, stripe the surface with a fork, and paint it with the egg wash. Sprinkle the top with ½ teaspoon of each of the sesame seeds.

7. **To cook the bread:** Bake for 10 to 15 minutes until lightly golden (depending on how chewy you'd like it). Remove from the oven and allow to cool. Repeat for all the loaves. This bread should be oval and brittle, and taste sweet and spicy. *Nush-e joon!*

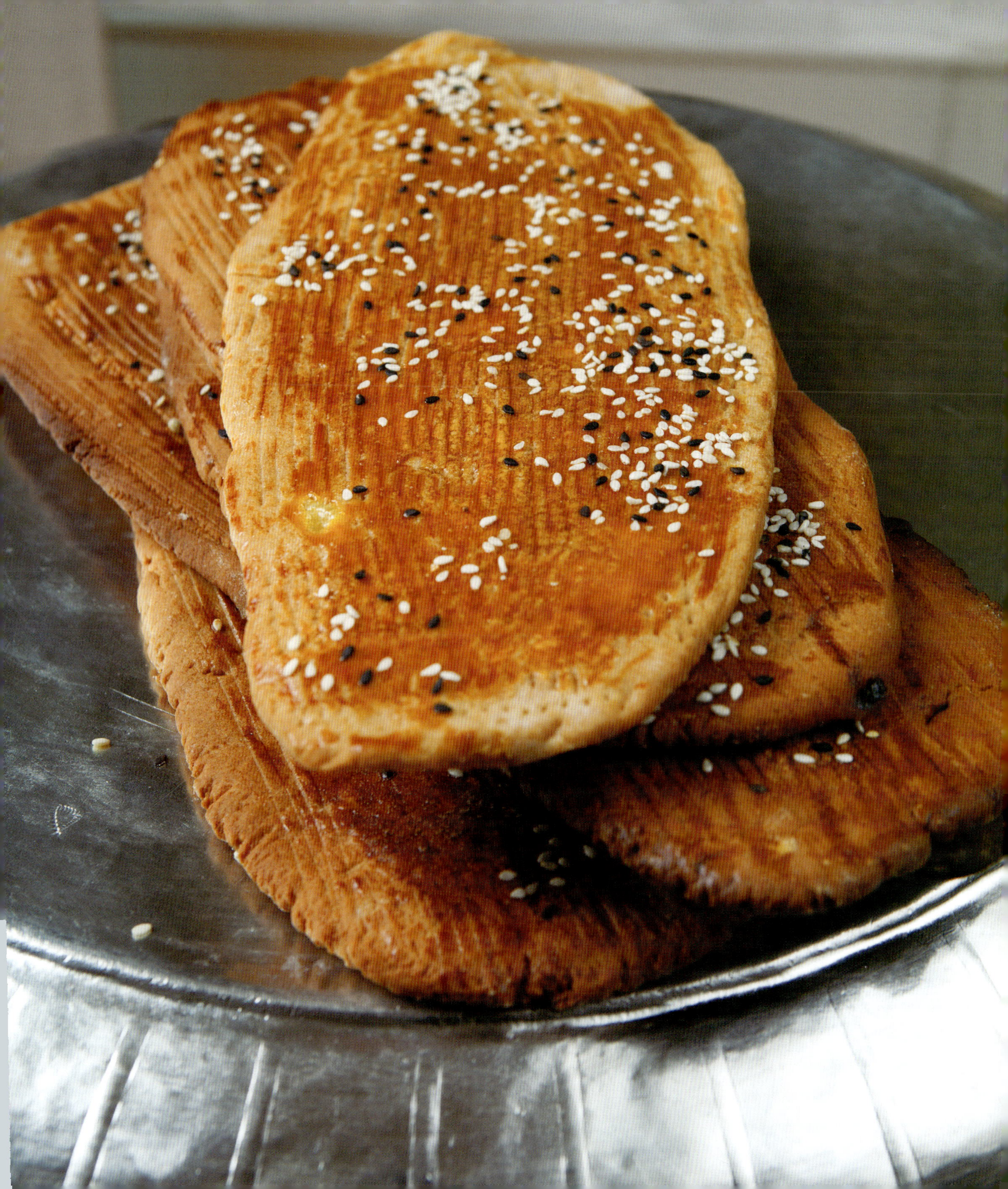

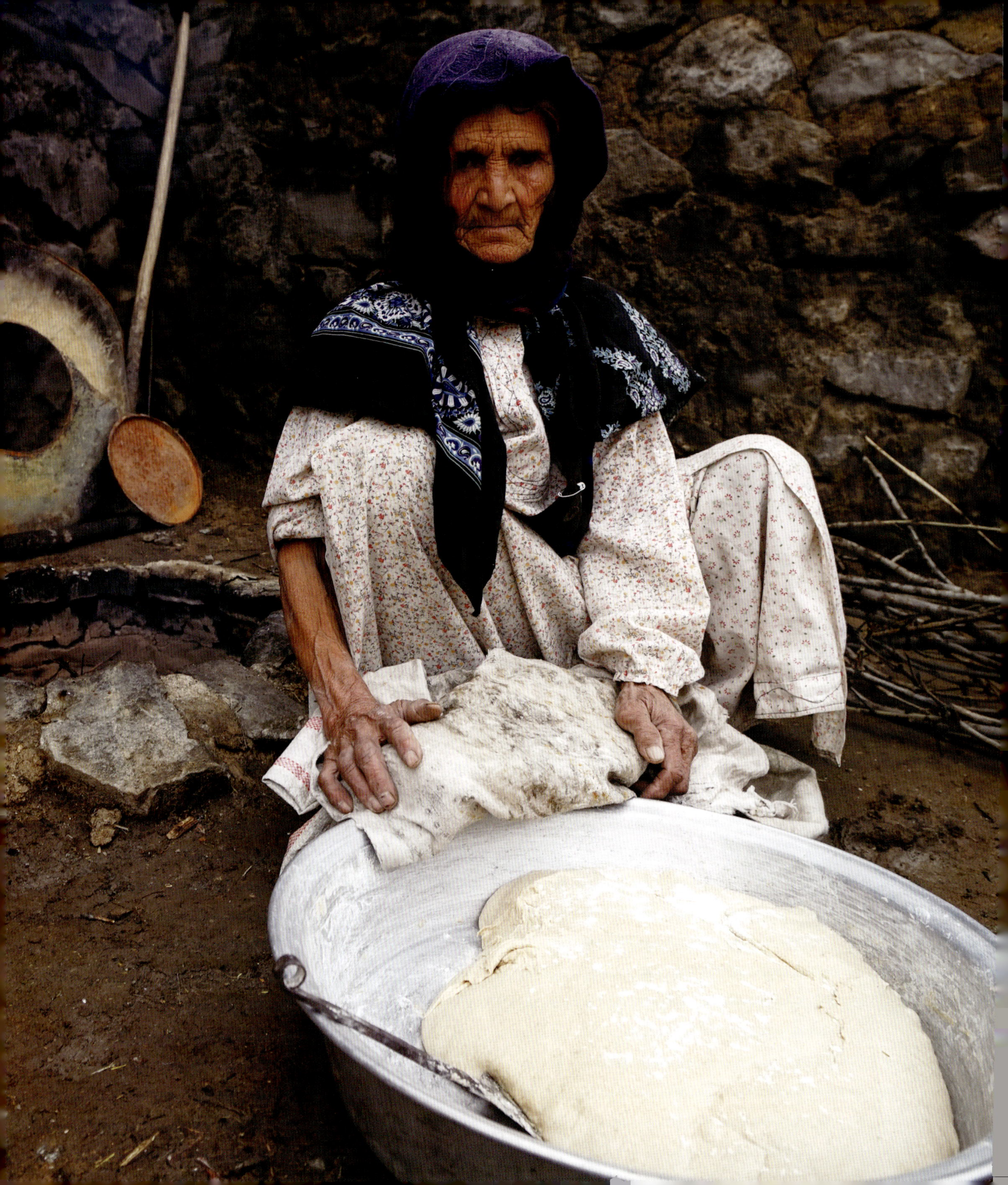

Twice-Cooked Semi-Sweet Bread

nan-e sokhari

Makes 10 slices
Prep: 15 minutes + 2 hours of resting dough
Cooking: 80 minutes

DOUGH

- 1 tablespoon or one envelope instant yeast
- ½ cup/120ml warm water
- ½ cup/100g sugar
- 4 eggs
- 1 teaspoon vanilla extract
- ½ cup/120 oil
- ¼ cup /60g heavy cream
- 1 tablespoon lime juice
- 5 cups/600g all-purpose unbleached flour mixed with 1 teaspoon salt

EGG WASH

- 1 egg yolk
- 1 tablespoon powdered sugar

This twice-cooked bread was one of our childhood favorites for dunking in our afternoon tea. A British doctor working in Tehran and Shiraz in the 1860s mentions a very dry twice-fired bread that was specially made for travelers.

1. **To make the dough:** In the bowl of an electric mixer, dissolve the yeast in the warm water. Add the sugar and allow to rest for 10 minutes undisturbed.

2. Add the eggs, vanilla, oil, heavy cream, and lime juice, and mix until creamy.

3. Sift together the flour and salt, and gradually add it, one cup at a time, to the egg and cream mixture. Knead for 5 minutes until you have a sticky dough

4. Turn the dough in a lightly oiled mixing bowl to ensure it is evenly coated with oil. Cover with plastic wrap and allow to rise in a warm, dark place for 2 hours (I use my oven with just the oven light turned on)

5. Preheat the oven to 350°F/180°C. Line a sheet pan with parchment paper.

6. Turn the dough out onto a floured work surface. Punch down and shape the dough into a 10in/25cm long by 3in/7.5cm wide rectangular block and place it on the sheet pan.

7. **To make the egg wash:** In a small bowl, mix together the egg yolk and powdered sugar, and paint the dough.

8. **To make the bread:** Bake in the preheated oven for 40 to 45 minutes until lightly brown, and a tester comes out clean. Remove from the oven and allow to cool.

9. Cut the bread into diagonal slices using a large sharp knife. Arrange the slices, flat side down, back on the baking sheet.

10. Reduce oven temperature to 325°F/150°C and bake for 30 to 35 minutes longer until the slices are golden brown and crispy.

11. Remove from the oven and allow to cool. Store in an airtight glass container. *Nush-e joon!*

306

Date + Sesame Bread

gerdeh-ye bushehr

Makes 8 loaves
Prep: 15 minutes + 6 hours of resting
Cooking: 40 minutes

DATE JUICE

2 cups/350g pitted dates
3¼ cups/780ml water

DOUGH

1 package or 1 tablespoon active dry yeast
2 cups/480ml warm date juice prepared above (100°F/38°C)
¼ cup/60ml raw sesame oil
4¼ to 4½ cups/540g unbleached all-purpose flour, sifted with 1 teaspoon baking powder and ½ teaspoon fine sea salt

GARNISH

¼ cup/40g sesame seeds

GLAZE

¼ cup/60ml toasted sesame oil

I made this deliciously semi-sweet bread with Layla Khanum in her backyard in a half-sunken earthenware oven/tanur under an old lime tree in Bushehr. Her face was full of dignity, her hands and movements showed years of practice and talent, and the bread, hot out of the tanur, was to die for.

1. **To make the date juice:** Place the dates and 3¼ cups/780ml water in a saucepan, cover and cook over low heat for 1 hour. Drain into a sieve over a bowl, pushing down as much juice as possible. Discard the pulp and reserve the date juice. Allow it to cool to 100°F/38°C.

2. **To make the dough:** In the bowl of an electric mixer, dissolve the dried yeast in the warm date juice and allow to rest for 10 minutes undisturbed.

3. Gradually add the oil and mix until creamy.

4. Sift together the flour, baking powder and salt into a bowl. Gradually add it, one cup at a time, to the yeast mixture, and knead on low speed for about 10 minutes until 4¼ cups/425g of flour have been added and you have sticky dough (adding more flour if necessary).

5. Transfer the dough to a lightly oiled, wide bowl and turn the dough to ensure it is evenly coated with oil. Cover with plastic wrap and allow it to rise in a warm, dark place for 4 to 24 hours (I use the oven with just the oven light on).

6. Preheat the oven to 350°F/200°C and line 4 sheet pans with parchment paper.

7. Turn the dough out onto a floured work surface and punch down. Divide it into 4 equal-sized balls using a dough scraper. Cover with a dish towel and allow to rest for another 30 minutes.

8. **To prepare the garnish:** Place a bowl of water and a plate with the sesame seeds next to your work area.

9. **To cook the bread:** Dip 1 side of each ball of dough into a bowl of water and then dip that side in sesame seeds. Transfer each ball to the middle of one of the lined sheet pans, sesame seed side up, and use your hand to flatten each loaf to a 9in/24cm disc.

10. Bake each loaf in the preheated oven for 25 to 30 minutes until golden brown.

11. Remove from the oven and place on a cooling rack. Drizzle some toasted sesame oil over it, and allow to cool briefly. Cover with plastic wrap or aluminium foil to prevent drying. *Nush-e joon!*

Bread Cooked in Ashes
nan-e purani

This ancient method of cooking bread in ashes continues in Baluchistan today. The thick unleavened dough is made with only salt, water, and wheat flour, and rolled out into a 15in/38cm disk. It is placed in a pit and covered with hot coal ashes. After 1 hour, the ashes are pushed aside, the bread lifted, and a palm branch is used to brush off any remaining ash. The result is an earthy and tasty hot bread. Photos are from the day we cooked this bread with Usta Musa in a village outside Chabahar.

Sistan + Baluchistan)

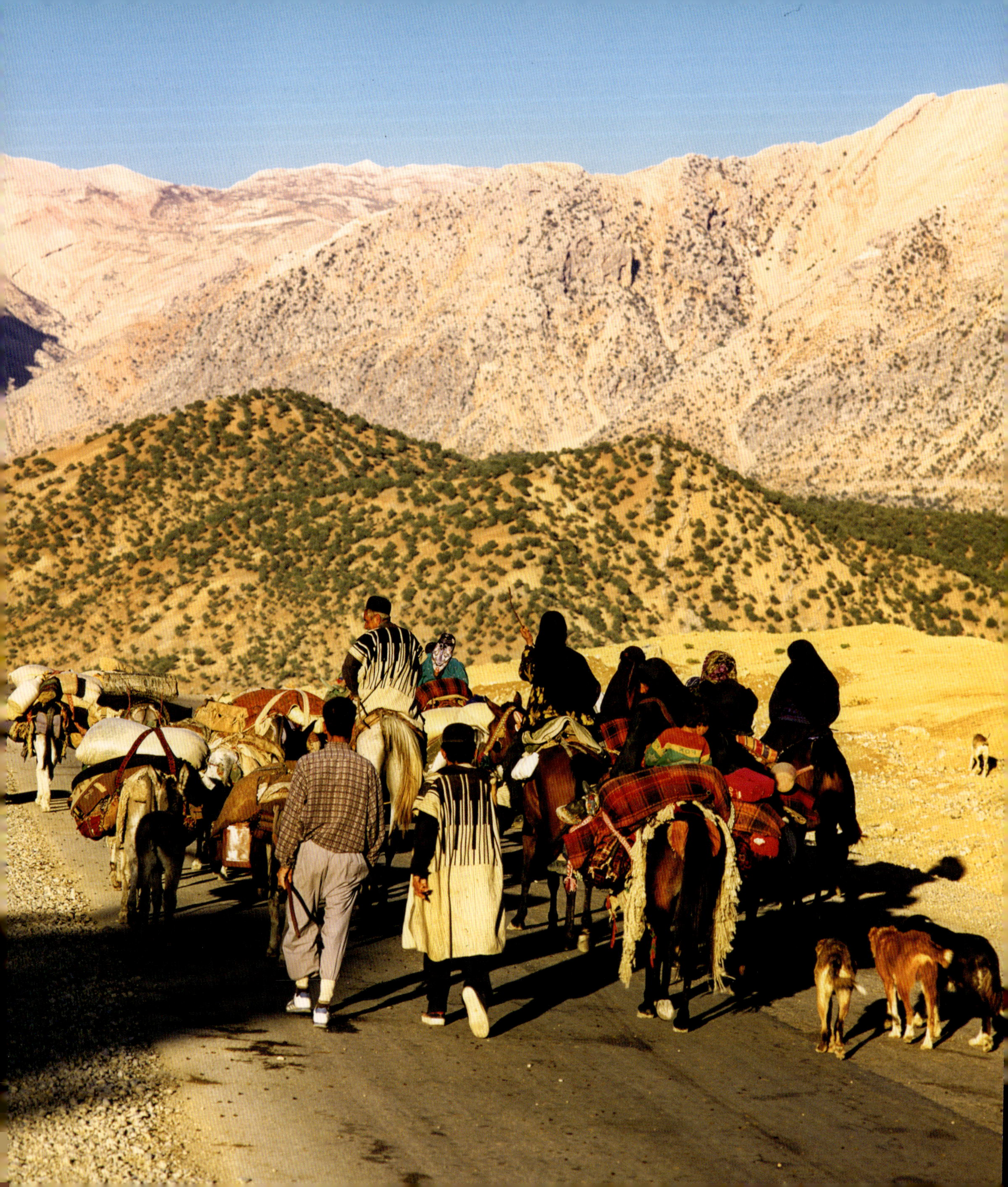

Acorn Pan Bread

nan-e balut/kalak-e chahar mahal-e bakhtiari

Makes 2 pan breads
Prep: 5 minutes + 30 minutes resting
Cooking: 2 minutes

DOUGH

1 cup/100g acorn flour
½ teaspoon fine sea salt
½ cup/120ml warm water (100°F/38°C)

Women of the nomadic tribal Bakhtiari region cook this dark brown, delicious, and mineral-rich bread (a little of it goes a long way—eat only small quantities of this bread). It's one of the oldest breads known. The acorns are gathered at the end of autumn. The green outer shell is removed, the brown shell broken and the hearts allowed to dry. They are then ground to flour, and sometimes mixed with a little wheat lour to make the bread. The Bakhtiaris call this bread "kalagy."

1. **To make the dough:** Place the flour in the mixing bowl of an electric mixer and, with the machine running on low, gradually add the warm water until you have a soft dough. Transfer to a mixing bowl, cover, and allow to rest for 30 minutes or up to 24 hours in the fridge.

2. **To cook the bread:** Heat an 8in/20cm non-stick skillet or pancake pan over medium heat until very hot. Use a brush to paint the skillet with oil.

3. Place a thin layer of dough and cook for 30 seconds, flip over and cook another 30 seconds until you have a brown and crispy bread. *Nush-e joon!*

Opposite: A nomadic family on the road outside Isfahan.
Right: Acorns from the oak-rich Bakhtiari tribal region.

Kurdistan + Tribal Region

Kurdistan + The Tribal Region

A Little History

The western Iranian provinces of Kurdistan, Kermanshah, Ilam, Lorestan, Chahar Mahal + Bakhtiari, and Kohkuliyeh + Boyer Ahmad run north-south parallel to the Zagros Mountains. They form the main tribal and nomadic region of Iran. According to Ferdowsi's *Shahnameh*, recounting the myths of the first kings, the Kurds were Iranians who had escaped to the mountains when King Zahhak needed to feed their brains to the snakes that had grown on his shoulders after he made a pact with the devil.

Yogurt and bulgur are the favorite ingredients in the cuisine of this region, which also utilizes mulberries, walnuts, and wild pistachios/*baneh* (terebinth). Every part of these trees contributes, from the molasses of the sweet white mulberries to the oil of the wild pistachios and the sap/*saghez* of its bark.

A view from Bazoft in the Bakhtiari tribal region

Kurdish Seven-Spice Advieh
advieh-ye haft chanshni-e kordi

Makes ¾ cup/75g
Prep: 20 minutes

Two 4in/10cm cinnamon sticks, broken up
1 tablespoon cloves
2 tablespoons black pepper corns
2 tablespoons cumin seeds
2 tablespoons mustard seeds
1 tablespoon nutmeg
2 tablespoons ground turmeric

Kurds use various spice mixes, but this one is my favorite. I have adapted it from Layla Kordbacheh, a passionate Kurdish cook. Several of the recipes in this section have also been adapted from her.

1. Grind the cinnamon, cloves, pepper corns, cumin seeds, mustard seeds, and nutmeg each separately in a spice grinder.

2. Transfer them to a small mixing bowl as you grind them. Add the ground turmeric and use a spoon to mix well.

3. Transfer to an airtight glass jar and keep in a cool place to use as needed. *Nush-e joon!*

Layla Kordbacheh and I after a day of cooking together.

Kurdistan + Tribal Region

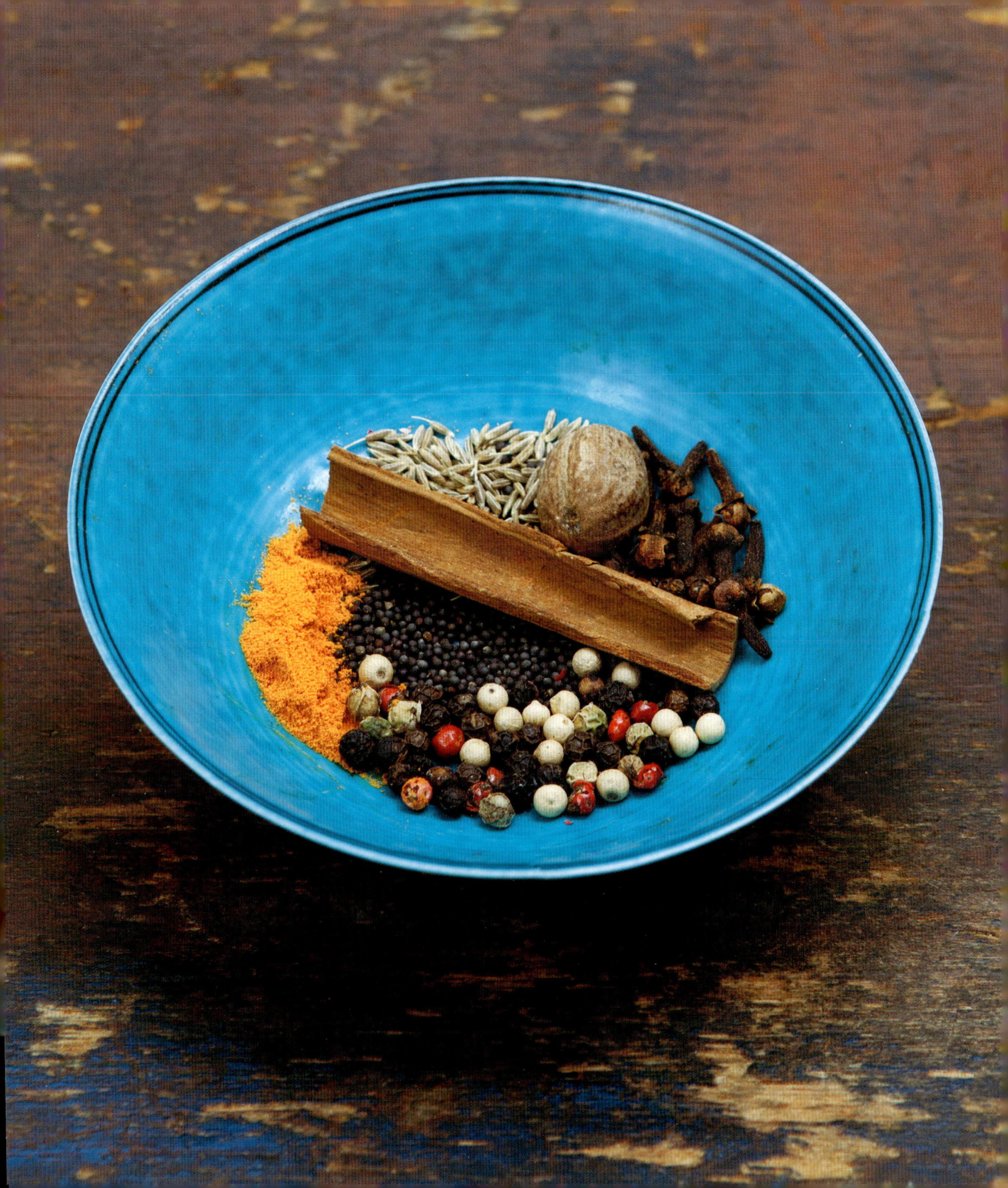

Lettuce + Yogurt Salad
borani-e kahu-ye kordi

Serves 4
Prep: 15 minutes

3 hearts of romaine lettuce, shredded

DRESSING

2 garlic cloves, peeled and grated
2 tablespoons dried mint flakes
2 tablespoons fresh lime juice
¼ cup/60ml olive oil
1 teaspoon fine sea salt
½ teaspoon freshly ground pepper
2 cups/480g plain thick yogurt

This simple salad is delicious by itself, or with meatballs or kababs.

1. Place the lettuce in a large container of water. Add 2 tablespoons vinegar and allow to soak for 10 minutes. Drain, rinse and dry thoroughly. Shredded thinly.

2. In a mixing bowl, combine all the ingredients for the dressing and mix well with a fork. Add the lettuce and toss thoroughly. Adjust seasoning to taste. *Nush-e joon!*

VARIATIONS

Celery, Walnut + Yogurt Salad
borani-e karafs

Replace the lettuce with 7 stalks of the heart of celery, diced, and add ½ cup/40g of ground walnuts. Everything else remains the same.

Cucumber, Sumac + Yogurt Salad
borani-e khiar-o somaq

Replace the lettuce with 7 Persian cucumbers, peeled and sliced. Add 1 tablespoon sumac powder. Everything else remains the same.

Kurdistan + Tribal Region

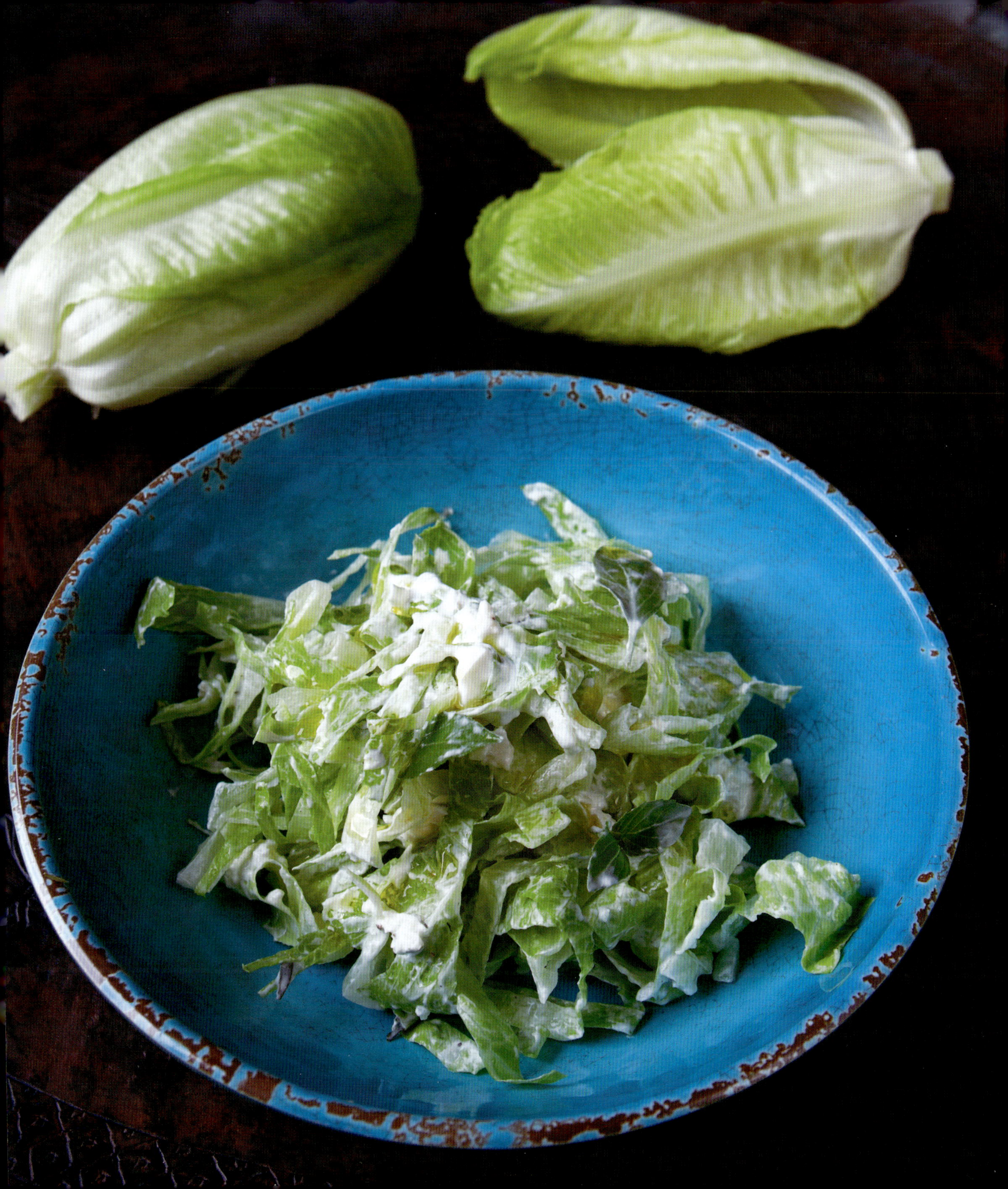

Barley, Nettle, Yogurt + Kashk Osh
osh-e gazing

Serves 6 to 8
Prep: 20 minutes
Cooking: 1¼ hours

OSH

¼ cup/60ml oil
2 onions, peeled and thinly sliced
½lb/225g boned leg of lamb or chicken thighs cut into ½in/12mm cubes (optional)
2 teaspoons fine sea salt
½ teaspoon freshly ground pepper
½ teaspoon turmeric
8 cups/1.9l broth or water
1¼ cups/250g barley
½lb/225g chopped fresh nettles/*gazaneh* or 1 cup/85g dried
1 cup/240g yogurt
½ cup/120g liquid *kashk*
½ teaspoon ground saffron threads dissolved in 2 tablespoons water

GARNISH/NA`NA DAGH

2 tablespoons oil
1 onion, peeled and thinly sliced
½ teaspoon turmeric
2 tablespoons dried mint flakes

Stinging nettle/gazaneh is a popular local herb that grows in the mountain regions of Kurdistan. Nettles are available at farmers' and Asian markets. You can replace them with either beet leaves or spinach. To make a vegetarian version, eliminate the lamb in step 1 and reduce cooking time to 10 minutes.

1. **To make the osh:** Heat the oil in a large laminated cast-iron pot over medium heat until hot. Sauté the onions and lamb until golden brown. Sprinkle with the salt, pepper, and turmeric, and sauté for 1 minute. Pour in the water and bring to a boil. Add the barley, reduce heat to low, cover, and simmer for 50 minutes, stirring occasionally.

2. Add the nettles and give it a stir. Cover and simmer for 20 minutes longer, stirring occasionally.

3. In a mixing bowl whisk together the yogurt, *kashk*, and saffron for 5 minutes (beating the yogurt prevents curdling).

4. Add the *kashk* mixture and continue stirring for 1 minute using a long wooden spoon. Bring back to a boil. Reduce heat to low and simmer for 10 minutes. Adjust seasoning to taste, cover, and keep warm until ready to serve.

5. **To prepare the garnish:** Heat 2 tablespoons oil in a wide skillet over medium-low heat and sauté the onion until golden. Add the turmeric and stir-fry for 1 minute. Remove from heat. Crush the mint flakes in the palm of your hand and add it to the skillet. Stir well.

6. Pour the simmering *osh* into a tureen and add the garnish. *Nush-e joon!*

Opposite: 1950s photo of a Kurdish woman at her hearth.

Kurdistan + Tribal Region

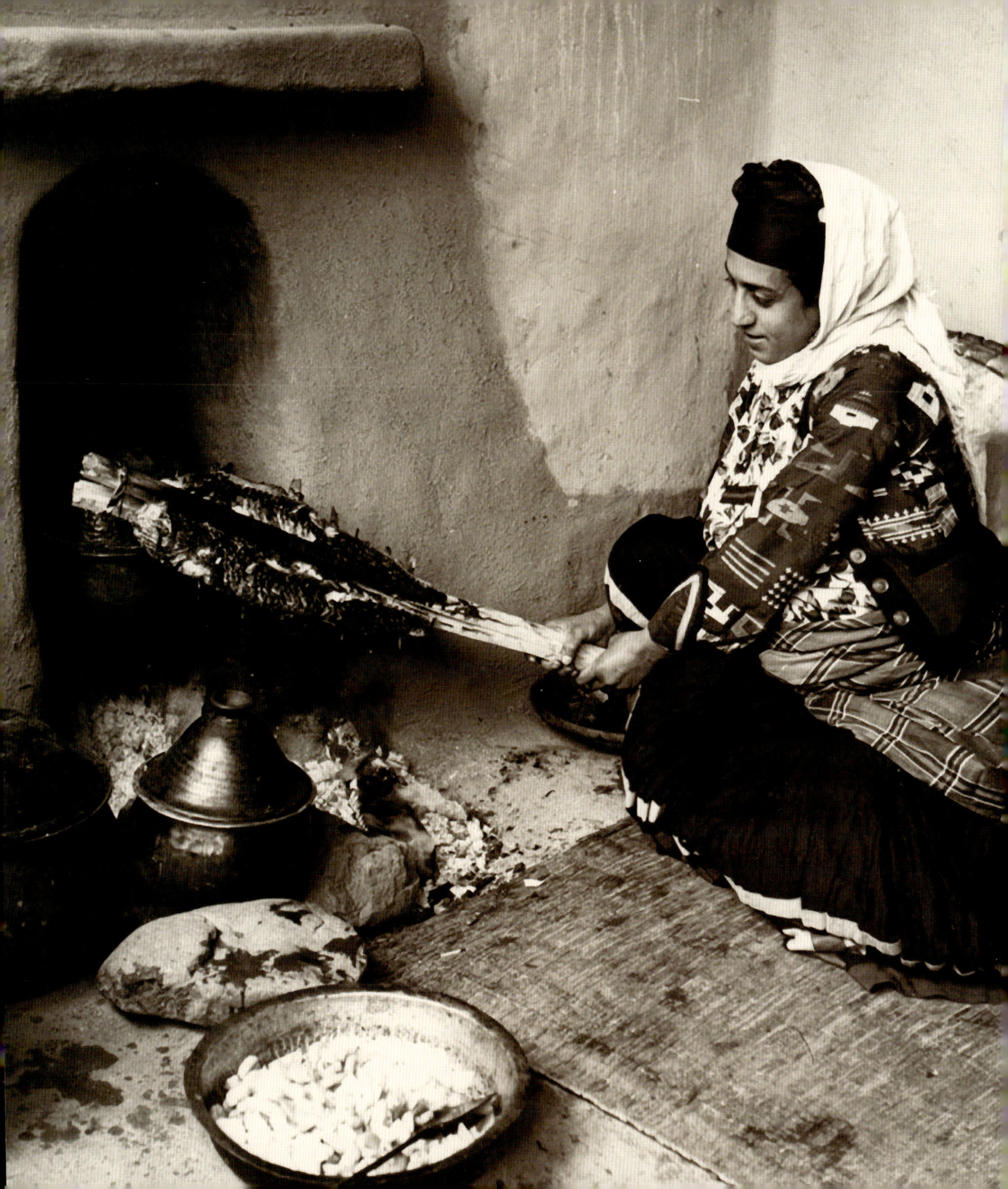

Tarkhineh Osh
osh-e tarkhineh-ye kordi

Serves 6 to 8
Prep: 20 minutes
Cooking: 2 hours

OSH

¼ cup/60ml oil, butter, or ghee
2 large onions, peeled and thinly sliced
1 teaspoon fine sea salt
1 teaspoon freshly ground black pepper
½ cup/100g white beans, soak overnight, drain, rinse
½ cup/100g chickpeas soak in water with ½ teaspoon baking soda overnight, drain and rinse
8 cups/1.9l broth or water
3 tarkhineh patties (½lb/225g)
½ cup/40g chopped fresh parsley
½ cup/40g chopped fresh cilantro
2 cups/170g chopped fresh spinach

GARNISH

¼ teaspoon ground saffron dissolved in 1 tablespoon hot water
1 cup/125g ground walnuts
½ cup/75g raisins

BULGUR + YOGURT PATTIES

Makes 6 doughnut-sized patties
Prep: 20 minutes + soaking bulgur overnight
Cooking: 40 minutes

1 cup/180g raw bulgur
2 cups yogurt/480g whole, plain thick yogurt beaten with 1 cup/240ml water for 5 minutes
1 teaspoon fine sea salt
1 teaspoon freshly ground pepper
1 tablespoon turmeric
1 tablespoon dried mint
1 tablespoon dried tarragon

VEGETARIAN

I adapted this recipe from Sahar Sepehri's mother, Fatemeh Zangeneh. For her garnish, she used fried onion and mint (na`na daq), page 318. *Tarkhineh is a fermented yogurt and bulgur preparation dried into patties (for adding to a broth later to create a thick soup). It is popular throughout Kurdistan (variations of this soup are also popular in Arak and Khorasan). Ready-made tarkhineh patties can be found at some Iranian markets in the U.S. You can also make your own simple versions using the recipe below. Traditionally, the patties are sun-dried, which is why store-bought ones should be rinsed.*

1. **To make the osh:** Heat the oil in a large laminated cast-iron pot over medium heat. Add the onions and sauté for 15 minutes until onions are golden brown. Add the salt, pepper, beans, and chickpeas, and stir-fry for 20 seconds. Add the broth and bring to a boil. Reduce heat to medium, cover, and simmer for 45 minutes, stirring occasionally.

2. Meanwhile place the bulgur patties in a mixing bowl. Add 2 cups of boiling water and allow to sit for 40 minutes until soft. Use your hands to form a soft paste and add it to the pot. Stir constantly for a few minutes until the *osh* becomes thick and smooth. Cover and cook over medium heat for 20 to 25 minutes until the legumes are tender.

3. Add the herbs and use a handheld mixer to partially puree the *osh*. Reduce heat to very low. Adjust seasoning to taste. Cover and keep warm until ready to serve.

4. Just before serving, transfer the osh to a serving bowl and garnish with saffron, walnuts, and raisins. *Nush-e joon!*

Homemade Bulgur + Yogurt Patties
tarkhineh

1. Place the bulgur in a medium-sized saucepan, cover with 8 cups/1.9l water, and allow to soak overnight. Drain in a fine-mesh colander.

2. Transfer the bulgur to a saucepan, add the yogurt and salt, pepper, turmeric, and dried herbs, and mix well. Cook over low heat for 30 to 40 minutes until all the water has evaporated.

3. Line 2 sheet pans with parchment paper. Shape the paste into doughnut-sized patties with a hole in the center and arrange on the sheet pans. Allow to dry overnight or place in a 200°F/95°C oven for 3 hours to dehydrate.

4. Store the patties in resealable plastic bags in the freezer and use as needed.

Kurdistan + Tribal Region

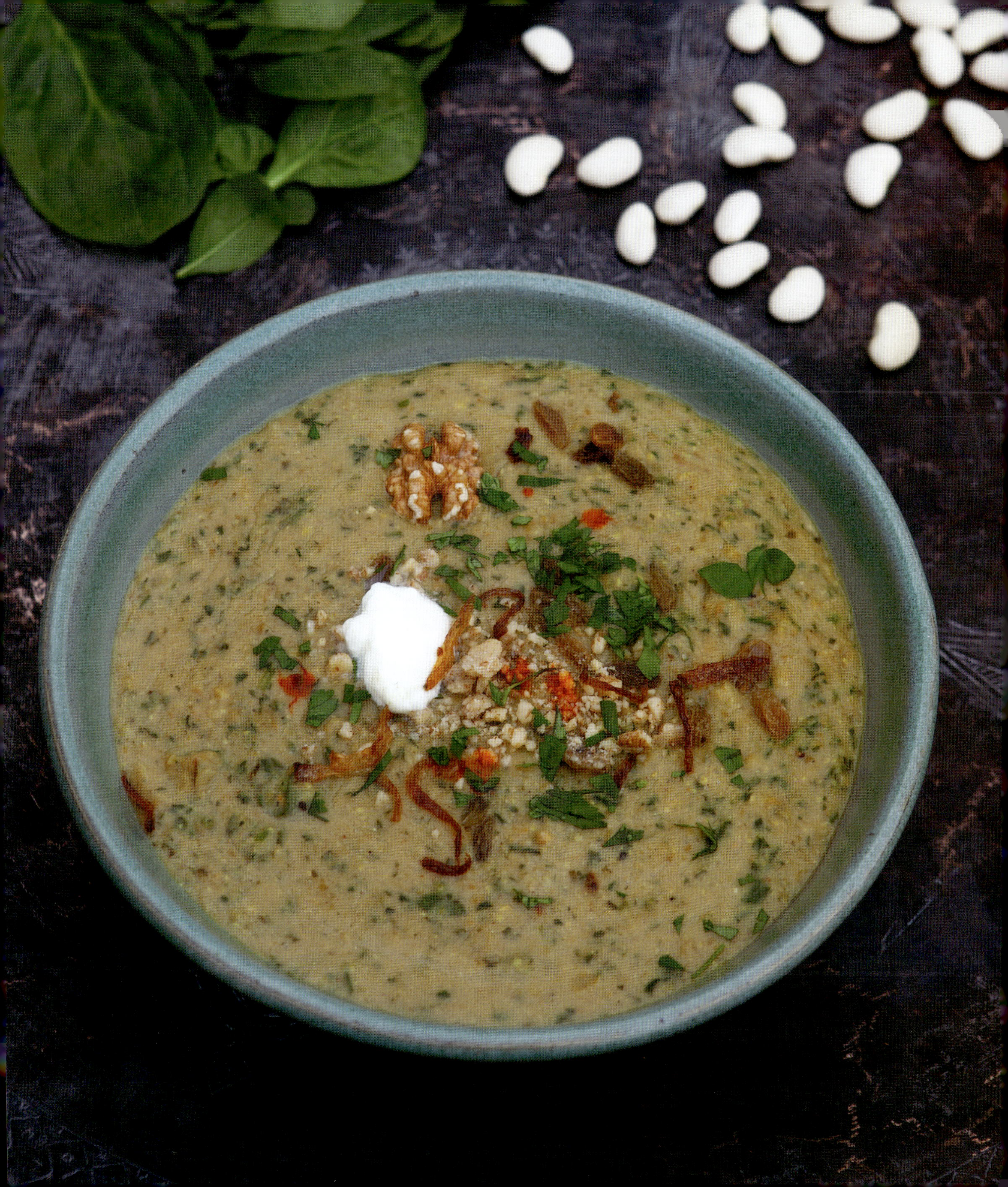

Baked Onions Filled with Rice + Herbs
dolmeh-ye piaz-e kordi

Serves 4–5
Prep: 45 minutes
Cooking: 2 hours

4 to 5 large even-sized yellow or white onions

FILLING
1/3 cup/70g rice, rinsed and drained
1/2 cup/120ml oil
1/2 lb/225g ground lamb, or chicken thighs, or fish fillets
1 teaspoon fine sea salt
1 teaspoon freshly ground pepper
1 teaspoon red pepper flakes (optional)
1 teaspoon Kurdish seven-spice *advieh*
1 tablespoon tomato paste
1/2 cup/40g chopped fresh parsley
1/4 cup/40g chopped fresh mint or 1 tablespoon dried
1/4 cup/20g chopped fresh summer savory or 1 tablespoon dried
1 cup/240ml broth or water

BROTH
2 cups/480ml broth or water
1 teaspoon salt
1 teaspoon turmeric

GLAZE
2 tablespoons sugar
1/4 cup/60ml fresh lime juice

GARNISH
1/4 cup/20g chopped fresh tarragon

NOTE
You can replace the lime juice with pomegranate juice mixed with 1 tablespoon pomegranate molasses.

Kurdistan + Tribal Region

Kurds love stuffing vegetables and have many recipes for that. This one is one of my favorites.

1. **To prepare the onions:** Remove the 2 outer layers of onions and cut off the tops 1/2in/1cm from the crown. Set the crowns aside to use later. Slice off the bottoms of the onions so they can sit flat in the dish. Hollow out the onions using the tip of a knife or a melon baller to scoop out the pulp, leaving a shell about 1in/2.5cm thick. Save the pulp to use later in the filling. Place the onion shells in a large pot of water, bring to a boil, reduce heat to low, and simmer for 10 minutes. Drain in a colander.

2. **To make the filling:** In a medium-sized saucepan, heat the oil and sauté the reserved onion pulp and the lamb for 5 minutes. Add the salt, pepper, red pepper flakes, *advieh*, tomato paste, herbs, and rice, and stir-fry for 1 minute. Add 1 cup/240ml broth. Stir well, cover, and cook for 10 to 15 minutes over low heat until all the juice has been absorbed. Remove from heat and set aside.

3. **To stuff the onions:** Preheat the oven to 350°F/180°C.

4. In a well-greased laminated cast-iron pot or a baking dish that is large enough for the onions to sit side by side, place the onions and stuff them with the filling. Pack down the filling and replace the crown. Pour in 2 cups/480ml broth (add any leftover filling to the pot around the onions). Cover tightly and bake for 1 hour.

5. **To make the glaze:** In a small bowl, combine the sugar and lime juice, stir well until the sugar is dissolved. Remove the crowns from the onions and drizzle the glaze over the onions. Replace the crowns, cover the pot, and return it to the oven. Bake for 30 to 45 minutes until the onions are tender.

6. Adjust seasoning to taste. Garnish with the fresh tarragon and serve hot, or at room temperature, in the same pot, with bread, yogurt, and fresh herbs. *Nush-e joon!*

VEGETARIAN VARIATION
Baked Onion Stuffed with Bulgur
dolmeh-ye piaz ba balghur

Replace the meat with 1 cup bulgur (soaked in 1 cup hot water, covered and allowed to rest for 30 minutes. Squeeze out the water). Everything else remains the same. Proceed with the recipe.

VO VEGAN OPTION

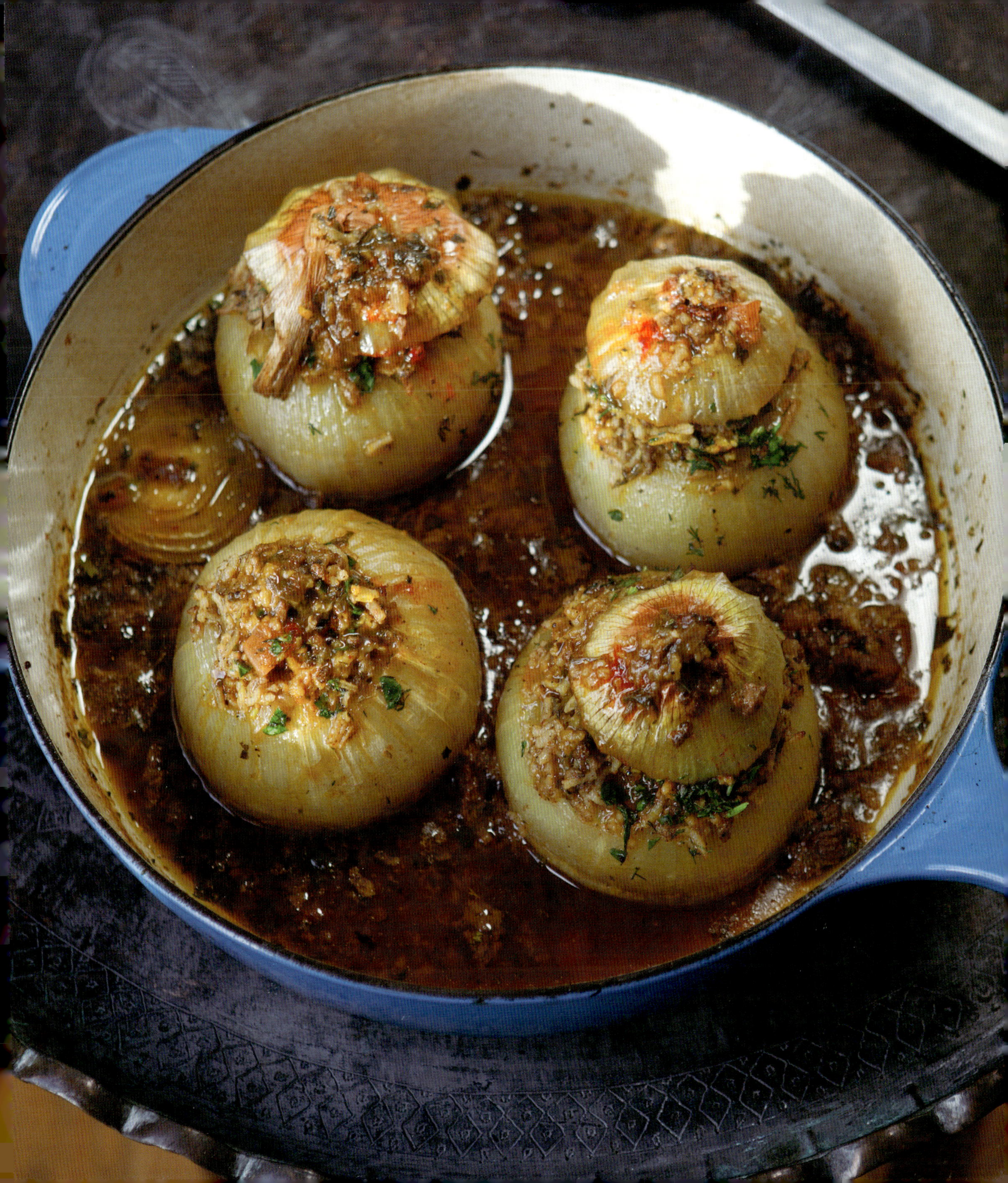

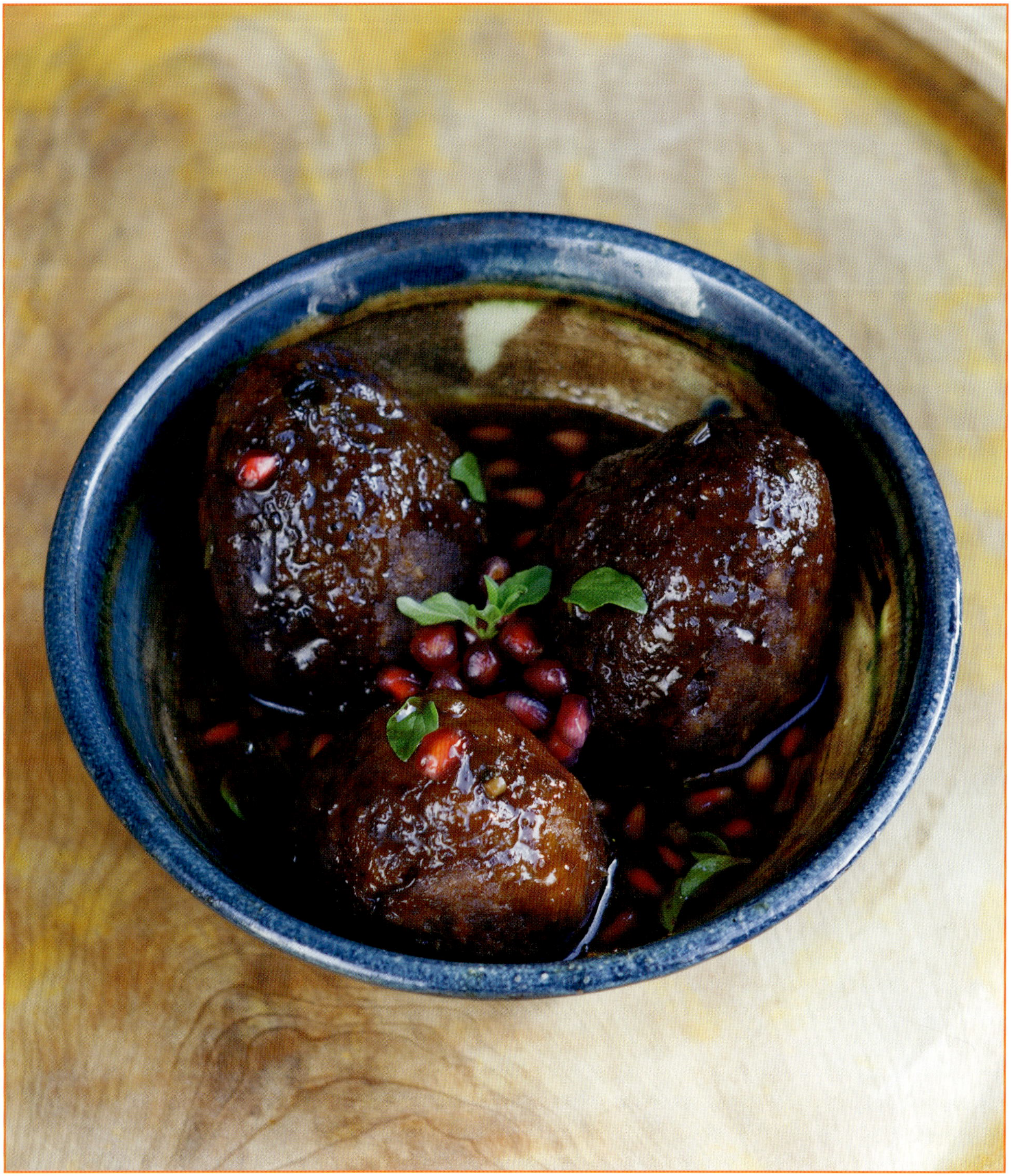

Bulgur Meatballs Filled with Caramelized Onion + Barberries
kabab-e balghur-e kordi

Makes 8 oval-shaped meatballs
Prep: 40 minutes + 2 hours of soaking bulgur
Cooking: 50 minutes

SHELL

2½ cups/450g bulgur
1 lb/450g ground lamb or chicken
2 teaspoons fine sea salt
1 teaspoon Kurdish seven-spice *advieh*
½ teaspoon ginger powder
½ teaspoon ground cinnamon
1 small onion, peeled and quartered

FILLING

2 tablespoons oil
2 small onions, finely chopped
¼ teaspoon fine sea salt
¼ teaspoon freshly ground pepper
¼ teaspoon ground cinnamon
¼ teaspoon Kurdish seven-spice *advieh*
¼ cup/30g walnuts, finely ground
2 tablespoons raisins
2 tablespoons barberries, rinsed
2 tablespoons chopped fresh parsley

POMEGRANATE SAUCE

2 tablespoons oil
1 medium onion, thinly sliced
1 teaspoon salt
½ teaspoon freshly ground pepper
1 tablespoon chickpea flour
2 cups/480ml broth or water
¼ cup/60ml pomegranate molasses (or tomato paste)
1 teaspoon grape molasses

EGG WASH

2 egg yolks, lightly beaten

½ cup/120ml oil for frying

1. *To make the shell:* Place the bulgur in a large mixing bowl, add 4 cups boiling water, cover, and allow to soak for 2 hours. Drain through a fine-mesh colander, place on a dish towel, and squeeze out any water.

2. Transfer the bulgur to a food processor, add the rest of the ingredients for the shell, and pulse until you have a sticky paste. Transfer to a mixing bowl, cover, and chill in the fridge for 20 minutes.

3. *To make the filling:* Heat 2 tablespoons oil in a wide skillet and sauté the onions and lamb until golden brown. Add the rest of the ingredients for the filling and sauté for 1 minute. Remove from heat and allow to cool.

4. *To make the pomegranate sauce:* Heat 2 tablespoons oil in a laminated cast-iron pot large enough to fit 8 large, egg-shaped meatballs. Sauté the onion until golden brown. Add salt, pepper, and chickpea flour, and sauté for 1 minute. Add the water, pomegranate molasses, and grape molasses, and bring to a boil. Reduce heat to low and simmer for 10 minutes.

5. Heat ½ cup/60ml oil in a wide skillet until hot but not smoking.

6. With damp hands, divide the paste into 8 equal balls. Place each ball in the palm of your hand and use your fingers to make a deep, wide indentation in the center of the ball. Place 2 teaspoons of the filling in the opening. Close up the meatball, smooth, and shape it into a large egg. Paint the meatballs with the egg wash as you make them and fry them on all sides until crispy and golden brown.

7. Transfer the meatballs to the pomegranate sauce and bring it back to a boil. Reduce heat to low, cover, and cook for 50 minutes. Adjust the seasoning of the broth to taste. Serve hot with a green salad. *Nush-e joon!*

VARIATION

Split Pea Meatballs
halow kabab

Eliminate step 1. In step 2, for making the shell, replace the bulgur with 2 cups/400g split peas cooked in 8 cups water for 30 minutes and drained—do not rinse. Everything else remains the same.

Bulgur Meatballs in a Vegetable Broth
kufteh savara-ye kordi

Serves 6
Prep: 40 minutes + 30 minutes of resting
Cooking: 2 hours

PASTE

1 cup/180g bulgur
¼ cup/50g rice
1 large onion, peeled and quartered
2 teaspoons fine sea salt
1 teaspoon freshly ground black pepper
½ teaspoon red pepper flakes
½ teaspoon Kurdish Seven-spice *advieh*
2 tablespoons fresh parsley leaves
½lb/225g ground lamb or boneless chicken thigh
1 egg, lightly beaten
1 tablespoon rice flour

BROTH

¼ cup/60ml oil or ghee
2 medium onions, peeled and thinly sliced
2 teaspoons fine sea salt
½ teaspoon freshly ground pepper
1 teaspoon Kurdish Seven-spice *advieh*
2 tablespoons tomato paste
1 carrot, peeled and diced
1 zucchini, diced
¼ cup/40g fresh or frozen peas
2 bay leaves
1 tablespoon lime juice
1 large tomato, peeled and diced
6 cups/1.5l broth or water

EGG WASH

1 egg lightly beaten with 1 tablespoon water

Of the many Kurdish meatballs, this one is my favorite. It's simple and quite delicious.

1. **To make the paste:** In a medium saucepan, place the bulgur and rice, add 4 cups/960ml water and ½ teaspoon salt, cover, and cook for 15 minutes over medium heat. Strain, squeeze out the liquid, and set aside to cool.

2. In a food processor, place, the bulgur and rice mixture, add the rest of the ingredients for the paste, and pulse until you have a sticky paste. Cover and allow to rest in the refrigerator for at least 30 minutes and up to 24 hours.

3. **To make the broth:** Heat the oil in a laminated cast-iron pot wide enough to fit 6 large oval shaped meatballs the size of tangerines. Brown the onions over-medium heat, add the salt, pepper, *advieh*, tomato paste, carrots, zucchini, and peas, and sauté for 1 minute Add the bay leaves, lime juice, diced tomato, and broth, and bring to a boil. Reduce heat to low, cover, and allow to simmer while you prepare the meatballs.

4. Place a bowl of water next to you. Using damp hands, divide the meatball paste into 6 equal parts, and shape each meatball into a large, smooth oval ball and paint it with the egg wash. Gently slip each meatball, as you make it, into the simmering broth. Be sure to leave some space between the meatballs. Bring back to a boil.

5. Reduce heat to medium and cook, uncovered, for 15 minutes. Reduce heat to low, cover, and cook for 45 minutes. Baste once with pan juices to prevent drying out. Adjust the broth seasoning to taste. Remove the bay leaves and serve with yogurt. *Nush-e joon!*

Kurdistan + Tribal Region

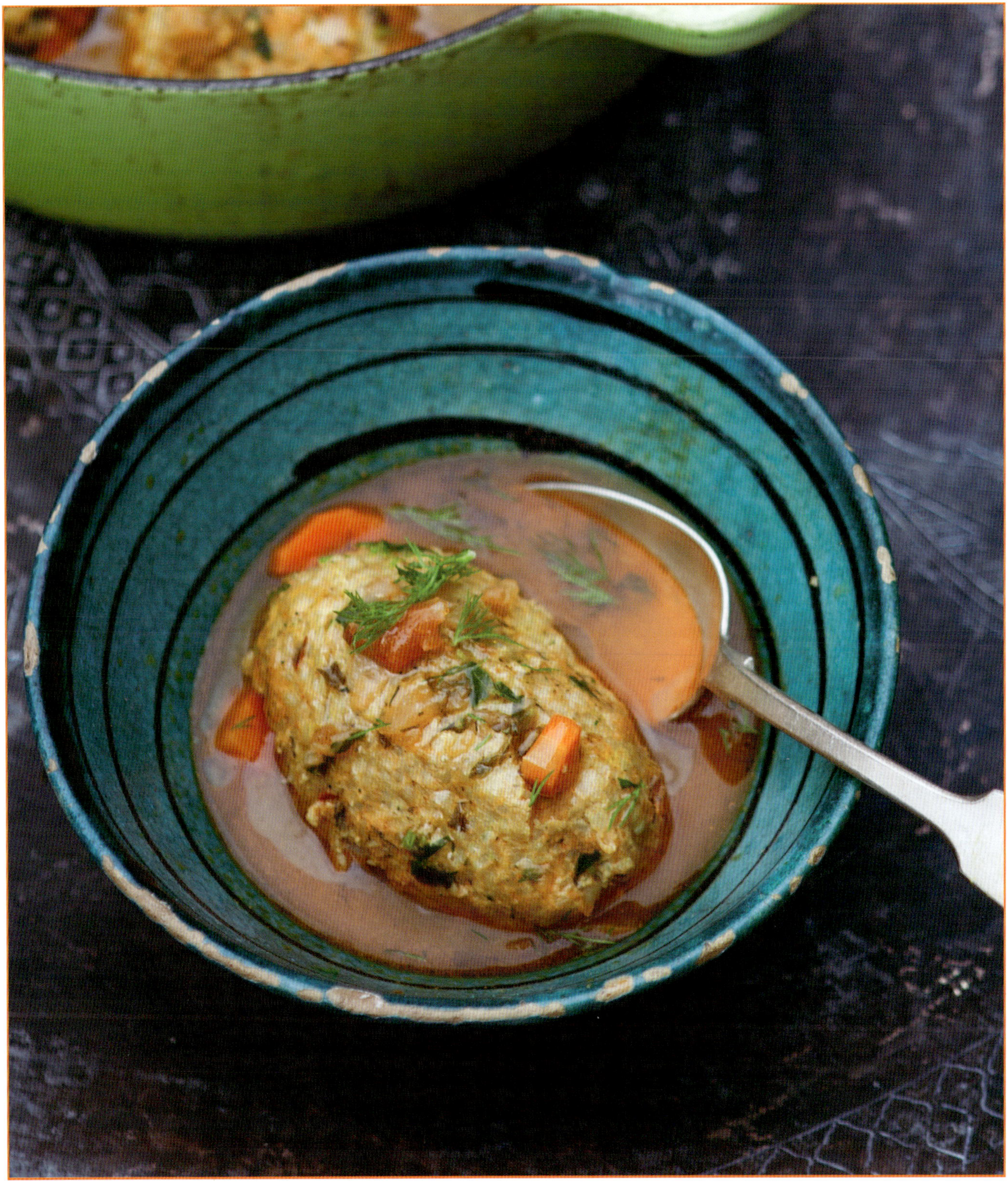

Saffron Rice + Potato Croquettes

kobeh-ye kordi/ kefteh halab

Makes 10 croquettes
Prep: 40 minutes
Cooking: 30 minutes

SHELL

½lb/225g small russet potatoes, peeled, cut into 2in/5cm cubes
1¼ cups/250g rice
2 teaspoons fine sea salt
1 teaspoon freshly ground pepper
½ teaspoon ground saffron threads
1 egg lightly beaten
½ cup/75g rice flour

FILLING

2 tablespoons oil
1 medium onion, finely chopped
¼lb/110g ground lamb or chicken thighs
½ teaspoon fine sea salt
¼ teaspoon freshly ground pepper
½ teaspoon turmeric
1 teaspoon red pepper flakes
2 teaspoons tomato paste
2 tablespoons barberries, rinsed thoroughly
¼ cup/35g raisins
2 tablespoons chopped fresh parsley
2 tablespoons walnuts, ground

GARNISH

1 tablespoon oil
¼ cup/40g barberries, rinsed thoroughly
1 teaspoon grape molasses
1 tablespoon water

Traditionally, according to Khanum-e Kordestani, these potato croquettes are deep-fried and not baked. If you want to try them that way, heat 2 cups oil in a small saucepan over medium heat until hot but not smoking. Fry in batches, 5 at a time until golden on all sides. These croquettes are also popular around the Persian Gulf, probably from the Indian dish batata chaat, which are made with more potato than rice and rolled in bread crumbs. For a vegan version, just eliminate the meat.

1. *To make the shell:* Place the potatoes in a medium saucepan, add 4 cups/960ml water, bring to a boil, reduce heat to medium, cover, and cook for 10 to 15 minutes until the potatoes are tender. Drain (do not rinse) and set aside to cool.

2. In another medium saucepan, place the rice, add 4 cups/960ml water, bring to a boil, reduce heat to medium, cover, and cook for 10 minutes. Drain (do not rinse) and set aside to cool.

3. Transfer the potato and rice to a food processor. Add the rest of the ingredients for the shell and pulse until you have a smooth paste. Transfer to a mixing bowl. Set aside.

4. *To make the filling:* Heat the oil in a wide skillet over medium heat and sauté the onion and lamb until golden brown. Add the rest of the ingredients for the filling and stir-fry for 3 to 4 minutes until all the juices have been absorbed. Remove from heat and allow to cool.

5. Preheat oven 450F°/230C°. Line a sheet pan with parchment paper and spray evenly with olive oil.

6. Place a bowl of cold water next to you for moistening your hands. Use an ice-cream scoop to take a walnut-sized scoop of the paste. Place a ball of paste in the palm of your hand and flatten it. Place 1 teaspoon of the filling on the paste and fold over to to close it up, smooth it out, and shape it into a ball or an egg-shaped oval. Repeat for all the potato balls and arrange on a sheet pan. Generously spray each croquette with olive oil and bake for 20 to 25 minutes until crispy.

7. *To make the garnish:* In a small skillet over medium heat, place the oil, barberries, grape molasses, and water and stir-fry for 4 minutes.

8. Serve with caramelized barberries and a green salad. *Nush-e joon!*

Kurdistan + Tribal Region

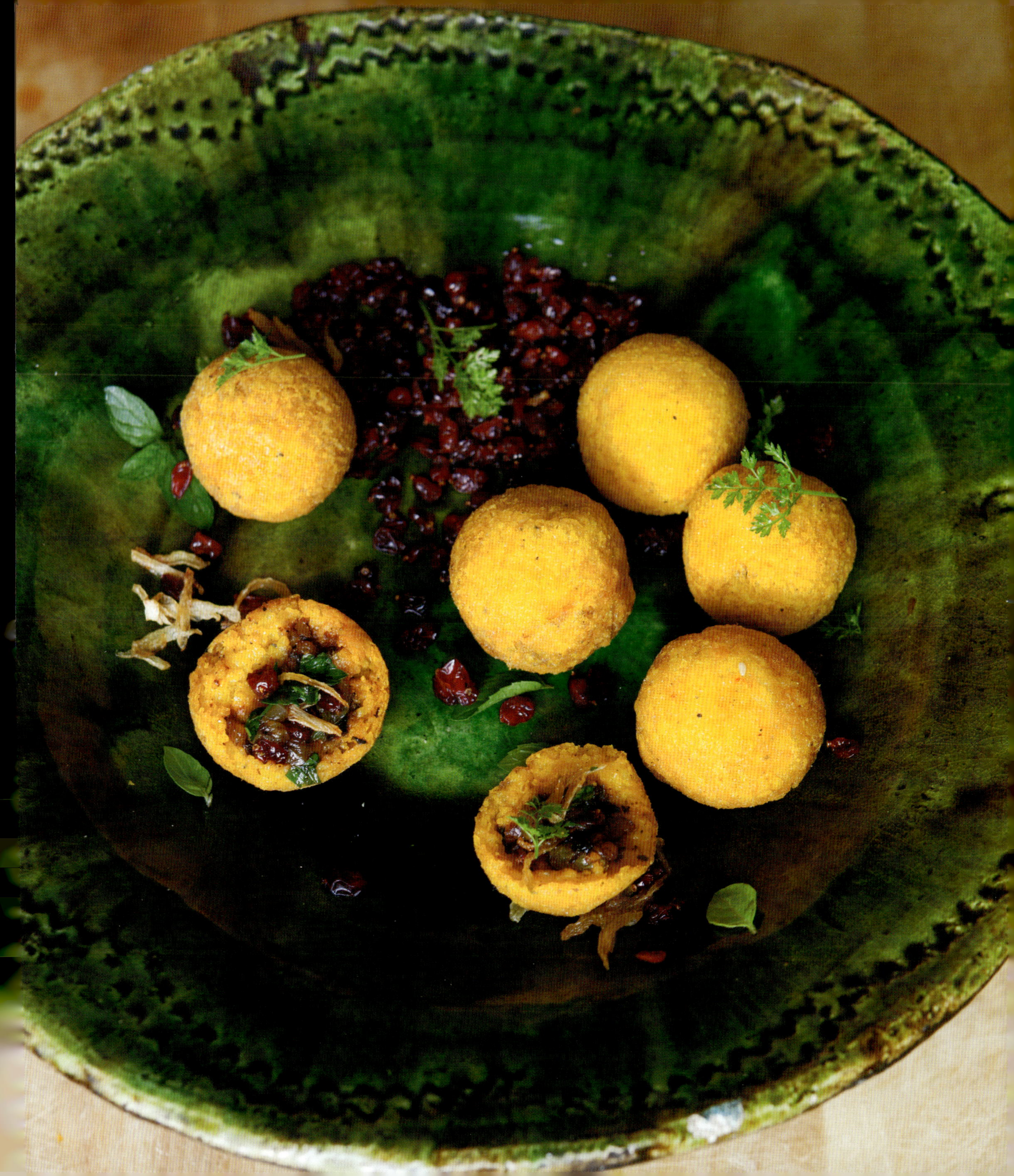

Chive + White Bean Braise
khoresh-e tareh-ye kordi

Serves 6
Prep: 25 minutes
Cooking: 2½ hours

SOAKING OVERNIGHT

2 cups/400g dried white beans, soaked overnight, drained

BRAISE

2 tablespoons oil, butter, or ghee
2 large onions, peeled and thinly sliced
1½lb/675g boned leg of lamb or chicken thighs cut into 2in/5cm pieces
1 teaspoon freshly ground black pepper
1 teaspoon turmeric
1 tablespoon Kurdish seven-spice *advieh*
3 whole dried Persian limes, pierced
6 cups/1.4l water

CHIVES

2 tablespoons oil
8 cups/800g finely chopped fresh chives or spring onions
2 tablespoons tomato paste
1 tablespoon fine sea salt
½ cup/120ml freshly squeezed lime juice

GARNISH (OPTIONAL)

1lb/450g large potato (1 large russet potato), peeled and cut into ½in/12mm cubes, and soaked in cold water for 20 minutes, drain and pat dry thoroughly
¼ cup/60ml oil for frying the potatoes
¼ teaspoon Kurdish seven-spice *advieh*
½ teaspoon fine sea salt
1 medium tomato, peeled and diced

This is a very popular traditional dish in Kurdistan. It's both hearty and delicious with bread or rice. I cooked this recipe with Layla Kordbache.

1. **To make the braise:** Heat 2 tablespoons oil in a laminated cast-iron braiser or pot over medium heat, and sauté the onions and meat until golden brown. Add the pepper, turmeric, *advieh*, and dried lime, and sauté for 1 minute.

2. Add 6 cups/1.4l of water and the beans, and bring to a boil. Reduce heat to low, cover, and simmer for 1 hour, stirring occasionally.

3. Meanwhile, in a wide skillet, heat 2 tablespoons oil over medium heat and sauté the chives for 10 minutes, stirring frequently. Add the tomato paste, and salt, and sauté for 1 minute longer.

4. Add the chives and lime juice to the pot. Cover and simmer for 1 to 1½ hours over low heat, stirring occasionally, until the lamb and beans are cooked.

5. Adjust seasoning to taste by adding more salt or lime juice. Cover and keep warm until ready to serve.

6. **To make the garnish:** In a wide iron skillet, heat the oil until hot and sauté the potatoes over medium heat until golden brown and crispy. Sprinkle the *advieh* and salt over them and give it a stir. Remove from the skillet and set aside.

7. In the same skillet sauté the tomatoes.

8. Just before serving the braise, garnish with the potatoes and tomatoes. Serve with plain rice/*kateh*. Nush-e joon!

VEGAN VARIATION

Eliminate the meat from the ingredients and proceed with the recipe.

Chive + Split Pea Khoresh
khoresh-e tareh ba lapeh

Replace the white beans with 2 cups/400g split peas (only soaked in water for 10 minutes and drained) and add them with the chives in step 4. Everything else remains the same.

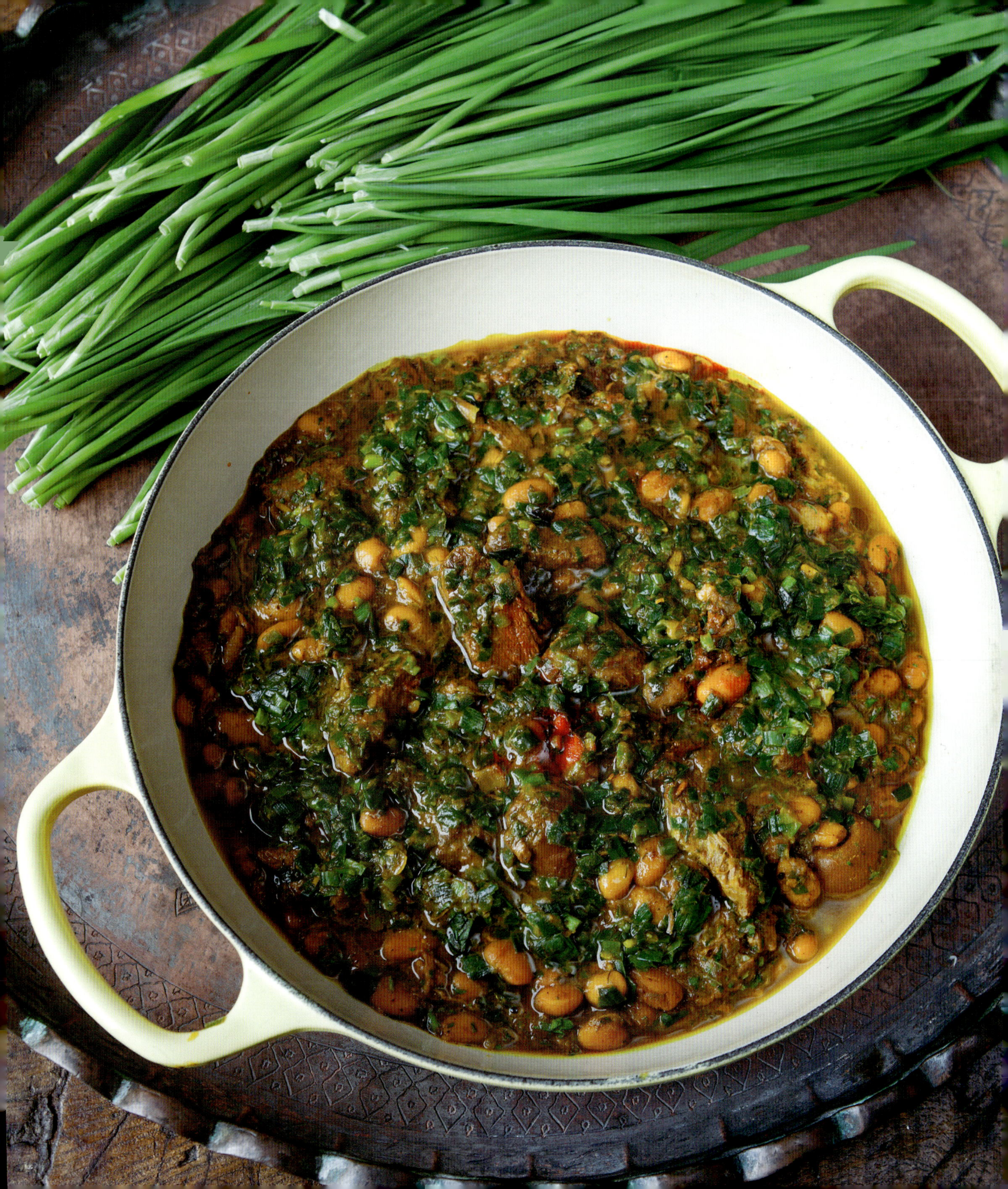

1900s photo of food being delivered under cloches, probably rice with lamb kababs.

Rice with Lamb Rib Chops

dandeh polow-ye ilamati

Serves 4 to 6
Prep: 20 minutes + 30 minutes of marinating
Cooking: 1½ hours

RICE

2 cups/400g basmati rice

½ teaspoon ground saffron dissolved in 2 tablespoons rose water

ONION + RAISIN MIXTURE

½ cup/110g sheep tail fat (for the traditional way) or ghee

4 medium onions, peeled and thinly sliced

½ cup/75g seedless green raisins

1 teaspoon cinnamon

1 tablespoon ground cumin

LAMB

¼ cup/55g sheep tail fat (for the traditional way) or ghee

1 teaspoon fine sea salt

1 teaspoon freshly ground pepper

2 teaspoons turmeric

8 lamb rib chops with bone, individually cut (about 1½lb/675g)

This simple way of cooking rice and lamb has a long history here, where the Elamites once ruled before the Persians in the first millennia BCE. These days, rice is mostly grown in the Caspian region in Iran, but in ancient times it is thought to have originated in this region, east of the Tigris river. I was fascinated to also see the same dish cooked by women outdoors on an open flame in a very large, black pot in Sarakhs, Khorasan on the Turkmenistan/Afghanistan border.

1. Wash the rice by placing it in a large container and covering it with water. Agitate gently with your hand and pour off the water. Repeat 2 to 3 times until the water is clear.

2. **To cook the rice:** In a large non-stick pot, bring 8 cups water and 2 tablespoons fine sea salt to a boil. Add the rice and boil briskly over high heat for 6 to 10 minutes (depending on the kind of rice you are using), gently stirring twice with a wooden spoon to loosen any grains that may have stuck to the bottom. Bite a few grains. If the rice feels soft and all the rice has risen to the top, it is ready. Drain in the fine-mesh colander and rinse with 2 cups water. Keep in the colander and set aside.

3. **To make the onion and raisin mixture:** Heat ½ cup tail fat in a wide skillet and sauté the onions until golden brown. Add the raisins, cinnamon, and cumin, and stir gently. Transfer this mixture to the rice and toss well. Set aside.

4. **To assemble the rice and lamb:** Heat ¼ cup tail fat in a 5qt/4.7l non-stick pot over low heat. In a small bowl, combine the salt, pepper, and turmeric, and dust the lamb on all sides. Arrange the lamb on the bottom of the pot and place the rice and onion mixture on top.

5. Use the palms of both hands to firmly press the rice down, compacting it evenly throughout (this will help the unmolding later). Pour 1 cup/240ml water and the saffron-rose water over the rice. Wrap the lid of the pot in a dish towel, cover tightly to prevent steam from escaping, and cook for 2 hours over low heat.

6. Line a sheet pan with a wet dish towel. Place the pot on the damp towel and allow to cool for 10 minutes without uncovering it. Uncover the pot and place a large serving platter, a little wider than the pot, over the pot. Hold both the serving platter and the pot firmly together with two hands and turn them upside down. Allow to rest for 5 minutes. Tap the pot and gently unmold the rice by lifting up the pot.

7. Serve hot with fresh herbs, yogurt, and Persian pickles/*torshi*. *Nush-e joon!*

Saffroned Lamb + Barberry Braise

qeymeh zereshk-e kordi

Serves 6
Prep: 30 minutes
Cooking: 2 hours

BRAISE

2 tablespoons oil, butter, or ghee

2 medium onions, peeled and thinly sliced

1½ lb/675g boneless leg of lamb or chicken thighs, cut into 1in/2.5cm cubes

1½ teaspoons fine sea salt

½ teaspoon freshly ground pepper

1 teaspoon turmeric

1 teaspoon ground cinnamon

1 tablespoon ground cumin

3 tablespoons tomato paste

GARNISH

1 tablespoon oil

2 tablespoons blanched almonds

2 tablespoons pistachio kernels

1 tablespoon ground rose petals

BARBERRIES

¼ cup/60ml water

2 tablespoons oil

½ cup/120g grape molasses or sugar

½ teaspoon ground saffron dissolved in 2 tablespoons rose water

2 cups/300g dried barberries, cleaned, soak in water for 20 minutes, and drained and rinsed thoroughly (see page 418)

This is a popular Kurdish dish that I first tasted in Kermanshah.

1. **To prepare the lamb:** Heat 2 tablespoons oil in a laminated cast-iron pot over medium heat, and brown the onions and lamb. Add the salt, pepper, turmeric, cinnamon, cumin, and tomato paste, saffron rose water, and sauté for 1 minute.

2. Add water—3½ cups/840ml for lamb and 2½ cups/600ml for chicken—and bring to a boil. Reduce heat, cover, and simmer over low heat for 1½ hours for lamb and 1 hour for chicken.

3. **Meanwhile, to make the garnish:** Heat 1 tablespoon oil in a wide skillet over medium-low heat, add the almonds, and stir-fry for 20 seconds (beware that almonds burn easily). Remove the almonds from the skillet. Add the pistachio kernels and set aside.

4. **To caramelize the barberries:** Wipe the skillet and add ¼ cup/60ml water, 2 tablespoons oil, the grape molasses, saffron water, and barberries, and stir-fry for 4 minutes over medium-high heat (beware that barberries burn easily; do not overcook). Remove from heat.

5. Add half of the caramelized barberries to the lamb (reserve the rest of the barberries for garnish). Give it a gentle stir. Cover and cook for 15 minutes.

6. Check to be sure the lamb is tender. Adjust seasoning to taste. Cover and keep warm until ready to serve.

7. Just before serving, garnish with the reserved barberries, nuts, and rose petals. Serve with plain rice. *Nush-e joon!*

VEGAN VARIATION

Eliminate the meat from step 1. In step 2 reduce the water to 1 cup/240g and the cooking time to 5 minutes. In step 3 increase the nuts to ½ cup/60g each. Proceed with the recipe.

Barberry Lamb + Split Pea Khoresh

Cook ½ cup/75g split peas with 4 cups/960ml water and ½ teaspoon fine sea salt for 20 to 30 minutes until almost tender. Drain and add in step 5.

Kurdistan + Tribal Region

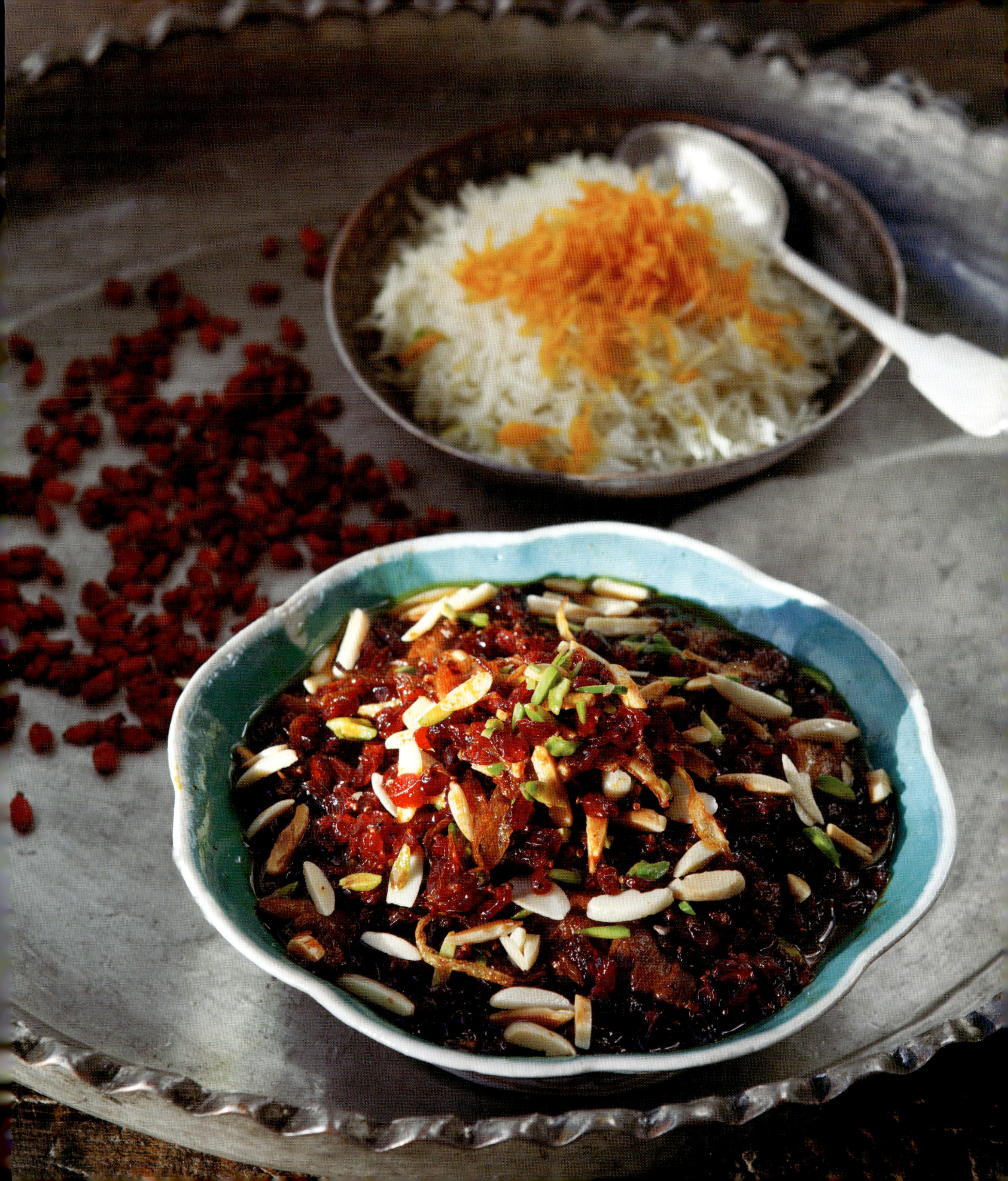

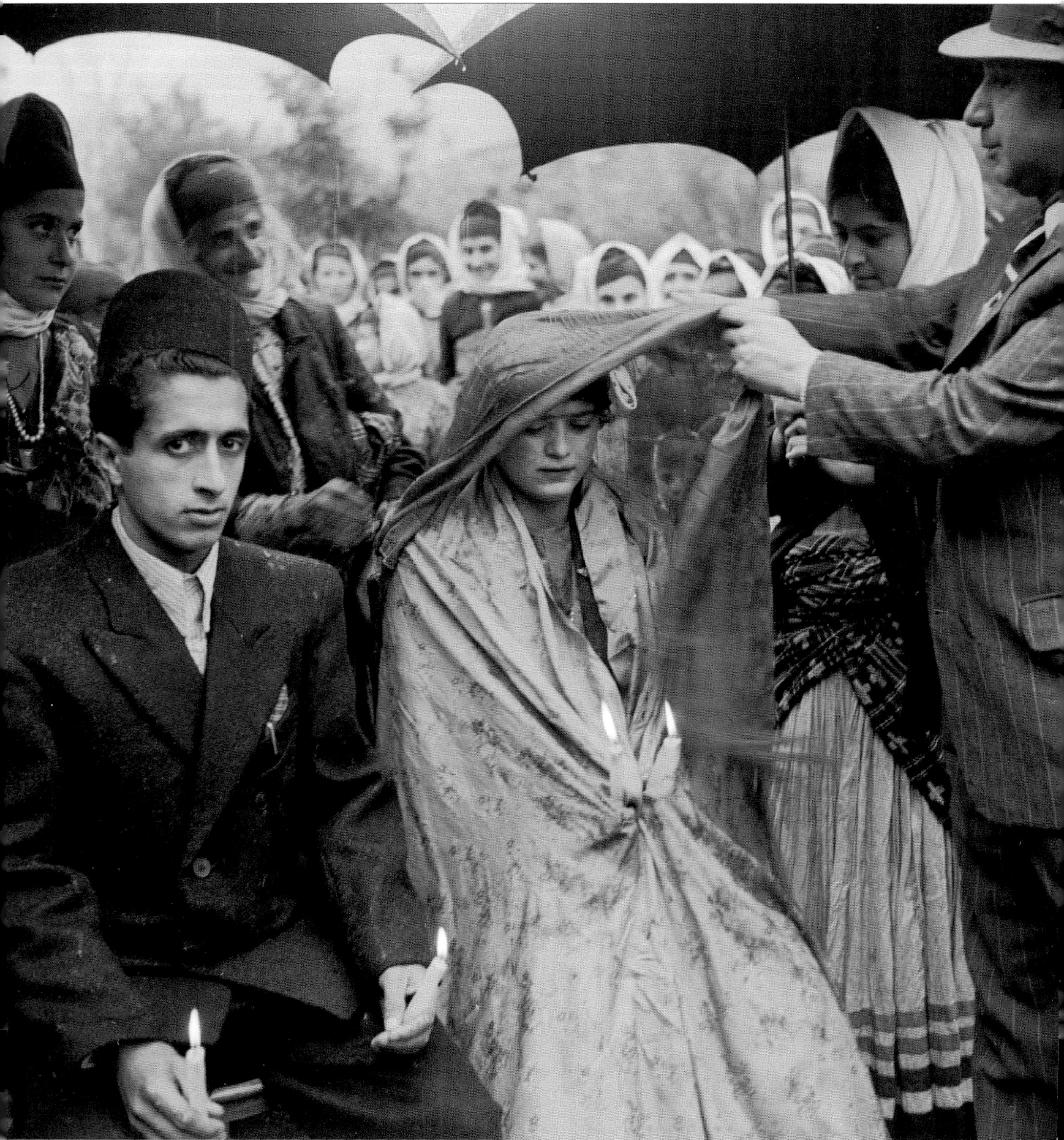

Almond, Lamb, Saffron + Rose Water Braise

khoresh-e khalal-e badam-e kermanshahi

Serves 6
Prep: 30 minutes
Cooking: 2 hours

LAMB

¼ cup/120ml oil, butter, or ghee

2 onions, peeled and thinly sliced

1lb/450g boneless leg of lamb or chicken thighs cut into 1in/2.5cm pieces

1 teaspoon fine sea salt

½ teaspoon freshly ground pepper

½ teaspoon turmeric

1 teaspoon Kurdish seven-spice *advieh*

1 tablespoon tomato paste

3 dried limes, pierced

ALMONDS

2 tablespoons oil

3 cups/360g blanched almonds, soaked for 1 hour and drained

½ teaspoon ground saffron dissolved in 1 tablespoon rose water

2 tablespoons fresh lime juice

GARNISH

2 tablespoons slivered pistachio kernels

2 tablespoons barberries, picked over and rinsed thoroughly

1 tablespoon ground dried rose petals

The photograph on the facing page is from a Kurdish wedding in the 1940s, and coincidentally, I first tasted this dish at a Kurdish wedding in Kermanshah. This braise is similar to the renowned Yazdi qeymeh, but it develops its own nutty taste because here they use almonds instead of potato fries. In Azarbaijan, they make a similar dish called qeymeh pechaq. They use cinnamon instead of the Kurdish advieh, reduce the almonds to 1 cup, and add 2 eggs in step 4.

1. **To cook the lamb:** Heat the oil in a laminated cast-iron braiser or pot over medium heat, and sauté the onions and lamb until golden brown and all juices have been absorbed. Add the salt, pepper, turmeric, *advieh*, tomato paste, and dried limes, and sauté for 1 minute longer.

2. Pour in water—4 cups/960ml for lamb and 3 cups/720ml for chicken. Bring to a boil. Give it a gentle stir. Reduce heat to low, cover, and simmer for 1½ hours for lamb and 1 hour for chicken.

3. **To prepare the almonds:** In a wide skillet heat 2 tablespoons oil over medium heat and stir-fry the almonds, over medium heat until lightly golden (beware that almonds burn easily).

4. Transfer the almonds to the pot with the lamb. Add the saffron-rose water and the lime juice, and give it a stir. Cover and simmer over low heat for 30 minutes longer.

5. Check to see if the lamb is tender. Adjust seasoning to taste.

6. Cover and keep warm until ready to serve. Garnish and serve hot from the same dish with saffron steamed rice/*chelow*. *Nush-e joon!*

Rice with Mushrooms + Barberries
qarchak/qarch polow-ye kordi

Serves 4–6
Prep: 30 minutes
Cooking: 70 minutes

MUSHROOM SAUCE

½ cup/120ml oil
2 large onions, peeled and thinly sliced
1lb/450g cremini mushrooms, thinly sliced
1 tablespoon ground cumin
2 teaspoons fine sea salt
1 teaspoon freshly ground pepper
1 teaspoon Kurdish seven-spice *advieh*
1 teaspoon cayenne
1 teaspoon cinnamon
2 tablespoons tomato paste
¼ cup/50g sugar
1 cup/150g dried barberries, rinsed thoroughly

RICE

1½ cups/300g long-grain basmati rice
6 tablespoons oil, butter, or ghee
½ teaspoon ground saffron dissolved in 2 tablespoons hot water

GARNISH

1 cup/85g chopped fresh parsley

Besides being a delicious combination of barberries and mushrooms, this rice dish is wonderfully nourishing for vegetarians.

1. **To make the mushroom sauce:** In a wide skillet, heat the oil and sauté the onions over low heat until golden brown. Add the mushrooms, cumin, salt, pepper, *advieh*, cayenne, and cinnamon, and sauté for 2 minutes. Add the tomato paste and sauté for 1 minute. Add the sugar, ¼ cup/60ml water, and the barberries, and sauté for 4 minutes. Remove from heat and set aside.

2. **To make the rice:** Wash the rice by placing it in a large container and covering it with water. Agitate gently with your hand and pour off the water. Repeat 2 to 3 times until the water is clear.

3. In a large non-stick pot, bring 8 cups/1.9l water and 2 tablespoons fine sea salt to a boil. Pour the rice into the pot. Boil briskly for 6 to 10 minutes, gently stirring twice to loosen any grains that may have stuck to the bottom. Bite a few grains. If the rice feels soft and all of it has risen to the surface, it is ready to be drained. Drain rice in a large fine-mesh colander and rinse with 3 cups water.

4. **To steam the rice and mushrooms:** Pour ¼ cup/60ml oil and 2 tablespoons water in the same pot. Place 2 spatulas full of rice over it; then a spatula of the mushroom sauce. Repeat, alternating layers in the shape of a pyramid. Cover and cook for 10 minutes over medium heat.

5. Pour 2 tablespoons oil, ½ cup/120ml water, and the saffron water over the rice. Wrap the lid of the pot with a clean dish towel and cover pot firmly to prevent steam from escaping. Cook for 30 minutes over low heat.

6. Remove the pot from heat and allow to cool for 5 minutes on a damp surface without uncovering it.

7. Gently taking 1 spatula full of rice at a time, place it on a serving platter. Mound the rice in the shape of a cone. Garnish with parsley. *Nush-e joon!*

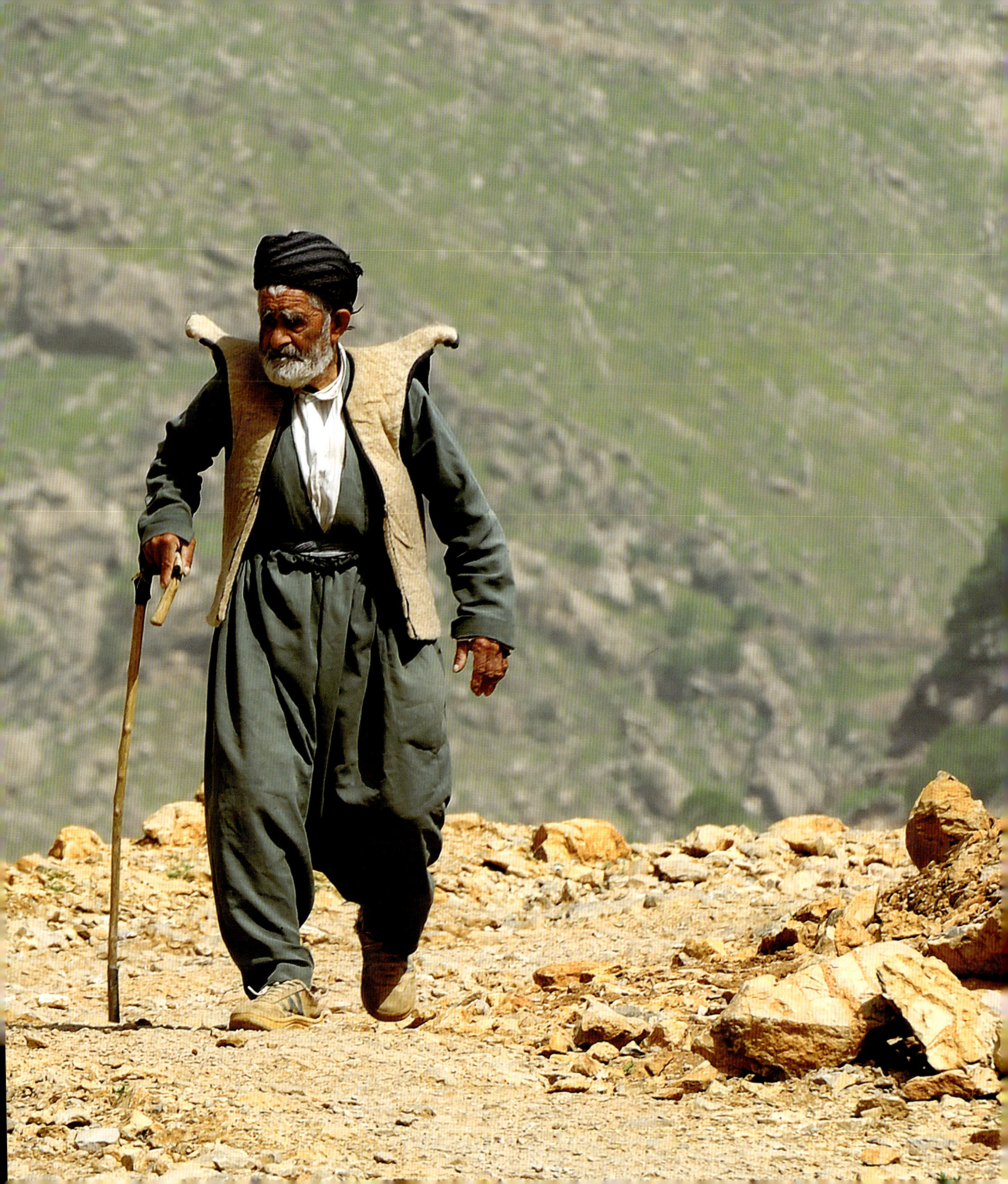

Bulgur + Lamb Pilaf
savar pilau-ye kordi

Serves 6
Prep: 20 minutes
Cooking: 30 minutes

BULGUR

2 cups/360g coarse bulgur
½ cup/120ml oil or ghee
3 medium onions, thinly sliced
½lb/225g ground lamb or chicken thighs
1 tablespoon fine sea salt
1 teaspoon freshly ground black pepper
½ teaspoon red pepper flakes
1 teaspoon turmeric
1 teaspoon Kurdish Seven-spice *advieh*
2 tablespoons tomato paste
2 cups (400g, 2 large tomatoes), peeled and finely diced
3 cups/720ml broth or water

GARNISH

½ cup/75g seedless raisins
1 cup/85g chopped fresh dill weed (optional)
2 tablespoons oil

I'm calling this a pilaf because the combination makes it quite different from the classic Persian polow. Bulgur was very popular in medieval Persian cooking, but over time it was replaced with rice. Bulgur is created by removing the wheat husk, then steaming, drying, and crushing the berries. Do not confuse bulgur with cracked wheat. Bulgur is pre-steamed and needs very little cooking, whereas cracked wheat must be cooked in broth or water. Cooking with bulgur continues to be popular in the Kurdish and tribal regions of Iran. In the photo I am serving it with a little cooked plain rice.

1. In a large mixing bowl soak the bulgur in 6 cups/1.5l water for 20 minutes, drain and set aside

2. Meanwhile, heat ½ cup/120ml oil in a medium-sized laminated cast-iron pot over medium heat, and sauté the onion and lamb until golden brown. Add the salt, peppers, turmeric, *advieh*, tomato paste, and bulgur, and sauté for 1 minute.

3. Add the fresh tomatoes and broth, give it a gentle stir, and bring to a boil. Reduce heat to medium, cover, and cook for 15 minutes.

4. Add the raisins and dill, and drizzle with 2 tablespoons oil. Fluff with 2 forks. Cover the pot tightly and cook for another 10 minutes over low heat.

5. Remove the pot from heat and allow to cool for 5 minutes on a damp surface without uncovering it. Serve with a green herb platter and pickles. *Nush-e joon!*

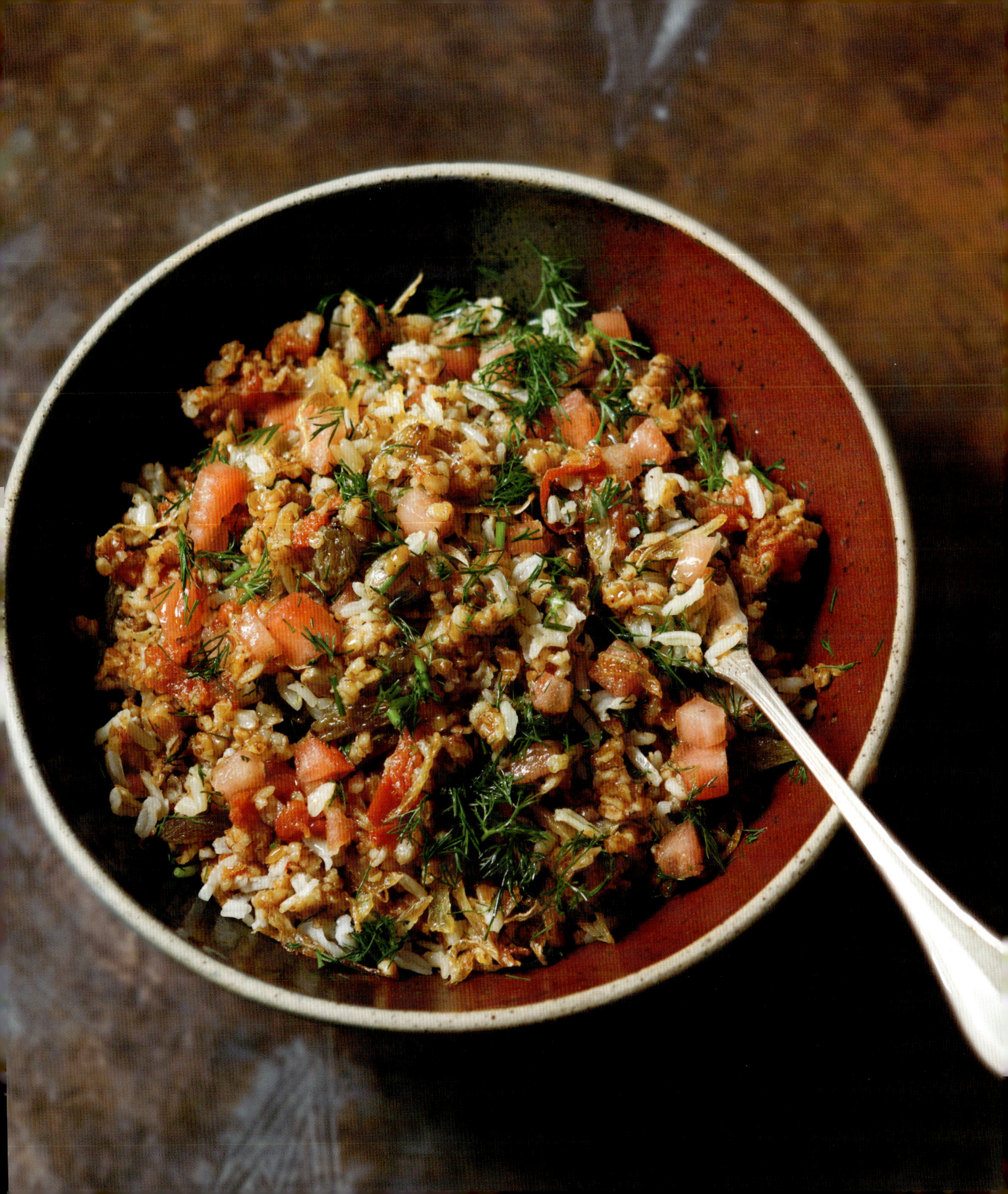

Walnut, Pomegranate + Herb Patties
shami kabab-e khorramabad/lori

Serves 6 to 8
Prep: 25 minutes
Cooking: 2 hours

BROTH

2 tablespoons oil
1 medium onion, peeled and sliced
1 tablespoon fine sea salt
1 teaspoon fresh ground black pepper
1 teaspoon turmeric
2 tablespoons all-purpose wheat flour
2 cups/250g walnuts, ground
5 cups/1.2l water
1 cup/240g pomegranate molasses
1 tablespoon grape molasses

PATTIES/SHAMI

1 medium onion, peeled and quartered
2½lb/1.1kg russet potatoes (about 3 potatoes), peeled and cut into 2in/5cm pieces
2½ cups/310g walnuts
1 tablespoon fine sea salt
½ teaspoon fresh ground black pepper
1 teaspoon turmeric
½ cup/40g fresh mint or 1 tbsp dried
½ cup/40g fresh chives or 1 tbsp dried
½ cup/40g fresh tarragon or 1 tbsp dried
½ cup/40g fresh savory or 1 tbsp dried
1 cup/85g fresh parsley or 2 tbsp dried

½lb/225g ground lamb or chicken thighs
3 eggs, lightly beaten

½ cup/120ml oil for frying

GARNISH

2 tablespoons pomegranate seeds or chopped fresh parsley

Lorestan, an Iranian province south of Kurdistan and north of Khuzestan, is the land of the Lors and in the heart of the Zagros Mountains. The Lors were nomads, and some continue to be so to this day. This recipe, a Lori specialty, has a very distinctive taste and is little known outside the region. All the grinding is traditionally done with pounding, but I am giving you a food processor option here. Try this recipe. You will be delighted by its tastiness. I adapted it from Khanum-e Moradi.

1. *To make the broth:* In a large laminated cast-iron pot, heat the oil over medium heat. Sauté the onion until golden brown. Add the salt, pepper, turmeric, flour, and walnuts, and sauté for 1 minute. Pour in 5 cups water and bring to a boil. Reduce heat to low, cover, and cook for 20 minutes, stirring occasionally. Add the pomegranate and grape molasses, cover, and cook for 30 minutes longer.

2. *To make the patties:* In a food processor, combine all the ingredients for the patties except the lamb and eggs. Mix until you have a soft paste. Transfer to a mixing bowl, add the lamb and eggs, and knead with your hand until you have a soft paste that does not stick to your hands.

3. Heat 2 tablespoons oil in a wide skillet over medium heat. Shape the paste into 2in/5cm patties and fry each side of the patties for 4 to 5 minutes until brown. Arrange the patties on a platter as they are done and continue until they have all been fried.

4. Gently add the patties to the simmering broth. Bring the broth back to a boil and reduce heat to low. Cover and simmer for 1 hour.

5. Adjust seasoning to taste and garnish. Serve directly from pot with plain rice/*kateh* or bread. *Nush-e joon!*

Kurdistan + Tribal Region

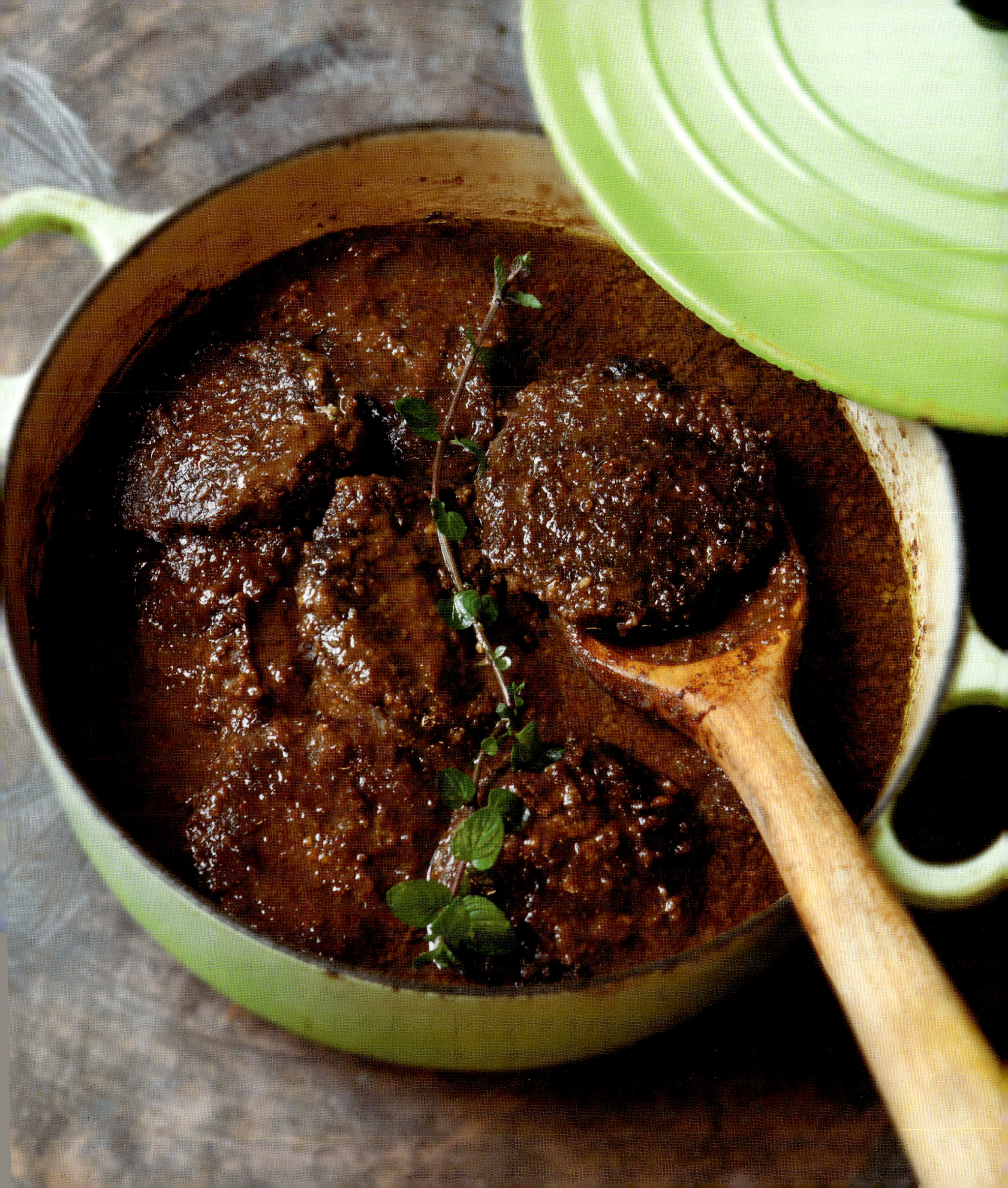

Lace-Fat-Wrapped Lamb Liver Kabab

jigar vaz-e lorestan

Serves 4
Prep: 20 minutes
Cooking: 6 minutes

2 lamb livers
Caul (lace fat)/*vaz*
1 teaspoon fine sea salt
1 teaspoon freshly ground pepper
1 onion, horizontally sliced into 1in/2.5cm wide strips

Sheep are the main livestock of the Lorestan region and lamb's liver is a favorite. However, the caul or lace fat casing is what's distinctive in this recipe because of the taste and texture it gives the liver. Iranians have used caul for making dumplings since ancient times. Caul fat, also known as lace fat, mesentery, crépine, or fat netting, is the thin membrane that surrounds the stomach and internal organs of some animals, such as cows, sheep. It is used as a casing for sausages, roulades, pâtés, and various other meat dishes. I buy my caul from Rockville Gourmet Halal Meat, Agha Reza is a great butcher in this area.

1. Clean the livers and cut into 1 x 3in/2.5 x 7.5cm strips.

2. Cut the stomach fat into 4 x 4in/10 x 10cm squares.

3. Place a strip of liver on the lace fat, and sprinkle with a little salt and pepper. Add some strips of onion and wrap the lace fat around the liver. Set aside.

4. Light a bed of charcoal and let it burn until the coals glow evenly or preheat the broiler in your oven.

5. Place the wrapped liver pieces in a grill basket side by side and lock the basket. Grill over hot coals for 4 to 6 minutes, turning frequently.

6. Serve immediately with lavash bread, spring onions, and garlic pickles. *Nush-e joon!*

Kurdistan + Tribal Region

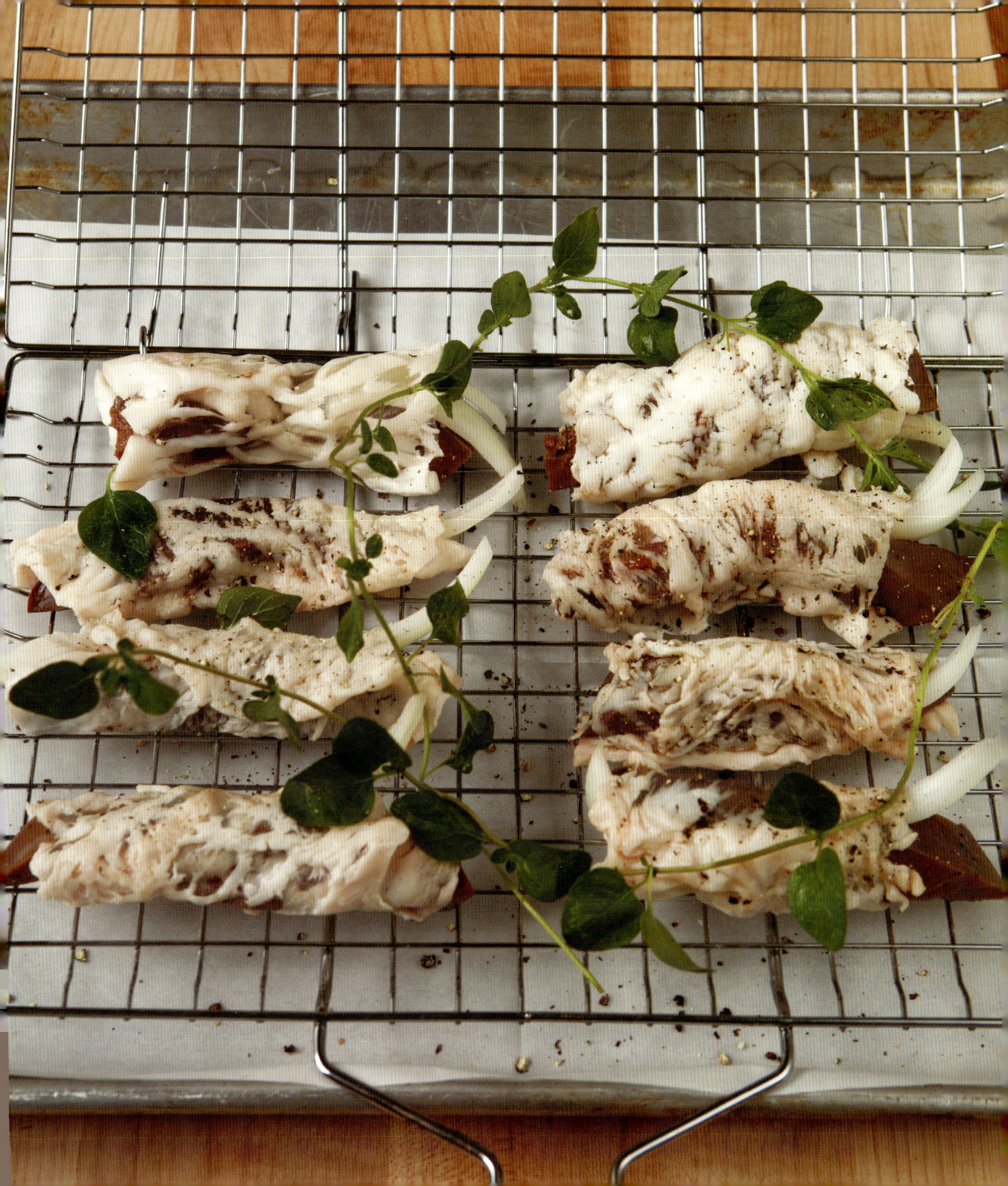

Saffron Rice Cookies
nan-e berenji-e kordi/qors-e khorshidi

Makes 40 pieces
Prep: 30 minutes + 30 minutes of resting
Cooking: 20 minutes

BATTER/FLOUR MIXTURE

3 cups/450g rice flour
⅛ teaspoon fine sea salt
1 tablespoon ground cardamom
1 cup/240ml oil or soft butter

EGG MIXTURE

3 egg yolks at room temperature
1½ cups/200g powdered sugar
2 tablespoons milk
½ teaspoon ground saffron dissolved in ½ cup/120ml rose water

GARNISH

2 tablespoons purslane or poppy seeds

The bakers in Sanandaj in the photo on the facing page gave me this recipe in murmurs as they were making the cookies.

1. **To make the dough:** Sift together the rice flour, salt, and ground cardamom into a mixing bowl. Add the oil and whisk together until you have a soft dough. Set aside.

2. In another mixing bowl, whisk together the egg yolks, sugar, milk, and saffron-rose water until creamy. Fold in the rice flour mixture and mix until you have a thick batter (do not over-mix). Cover with plastic wrap and chill in the refrigerator for 30 minutes and up to 24 hours.

3. **To bake the cookies:** Place the oven rack in the center and preheat oven to 300°F/150°C. Line 3 sheet pans with baking mats or parchment paper.

4. Use an ice-cream scoop to scoop up a walnut-sized amount of dough. Place it on the baking mat. Flatten slightly using an offset spatula. Repeat, leaving 2in/5cm between each cookie. Sprinkle with purslane seeds.

5. Place a sheet pan (one in the oven at a time) in the preheated oven and bake for 27 to 30 minutes until the bottom of the cookies are lightly brown.

6. Remove the sheet pan from the oven and allow the cookies to cool on a cooking rack. These cookies crumble very easily; remove them carefully from the baking mat using an offset spatula. Arrange the cookies on a serving dish. If you are not serving them immediately, store in an airtight glass container. You can keep in the fridge for up to 1 week and in the freezer for up to 3 weeks. *Nush-e joon!*

Kurdistan + Tribal Region

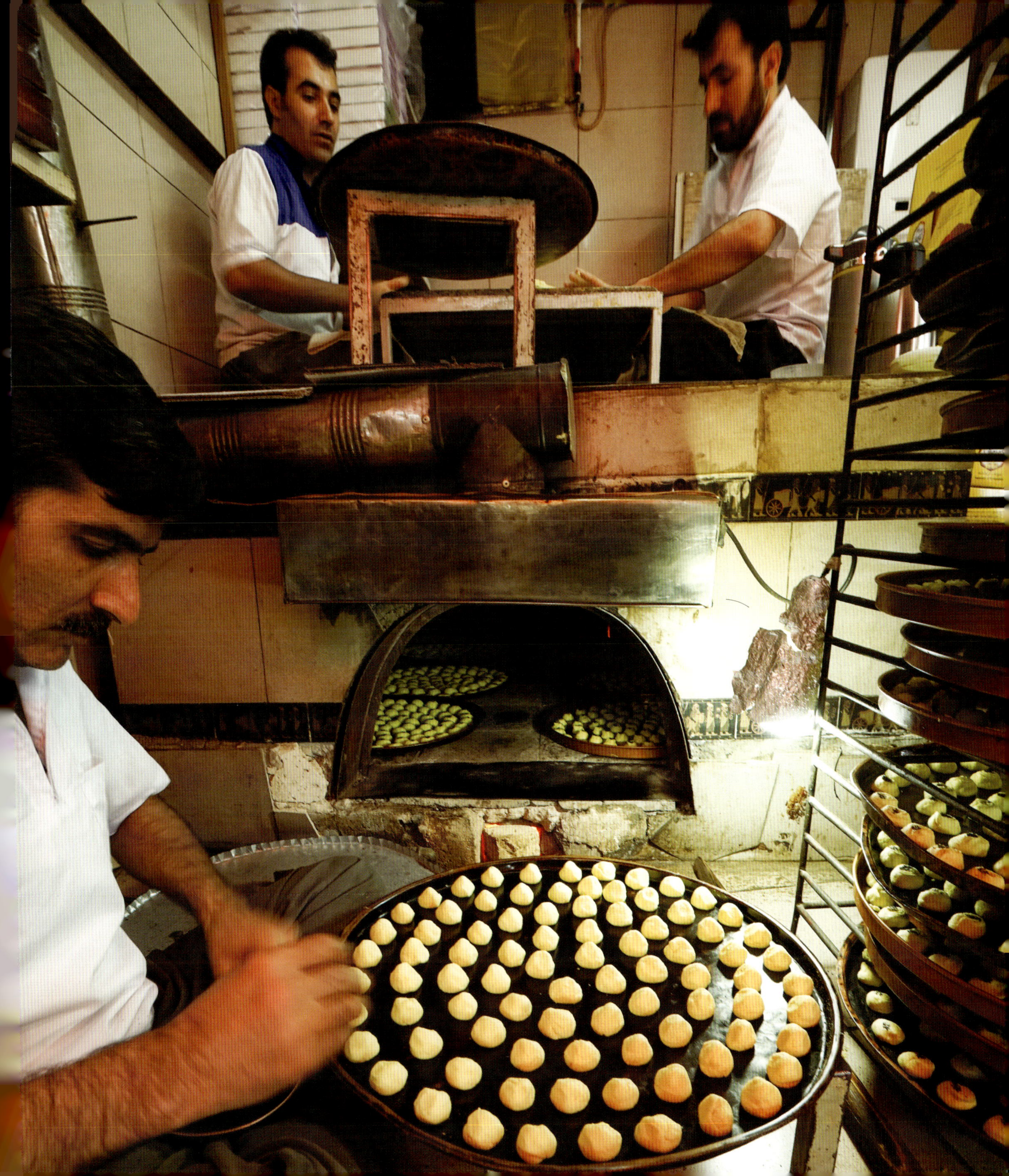

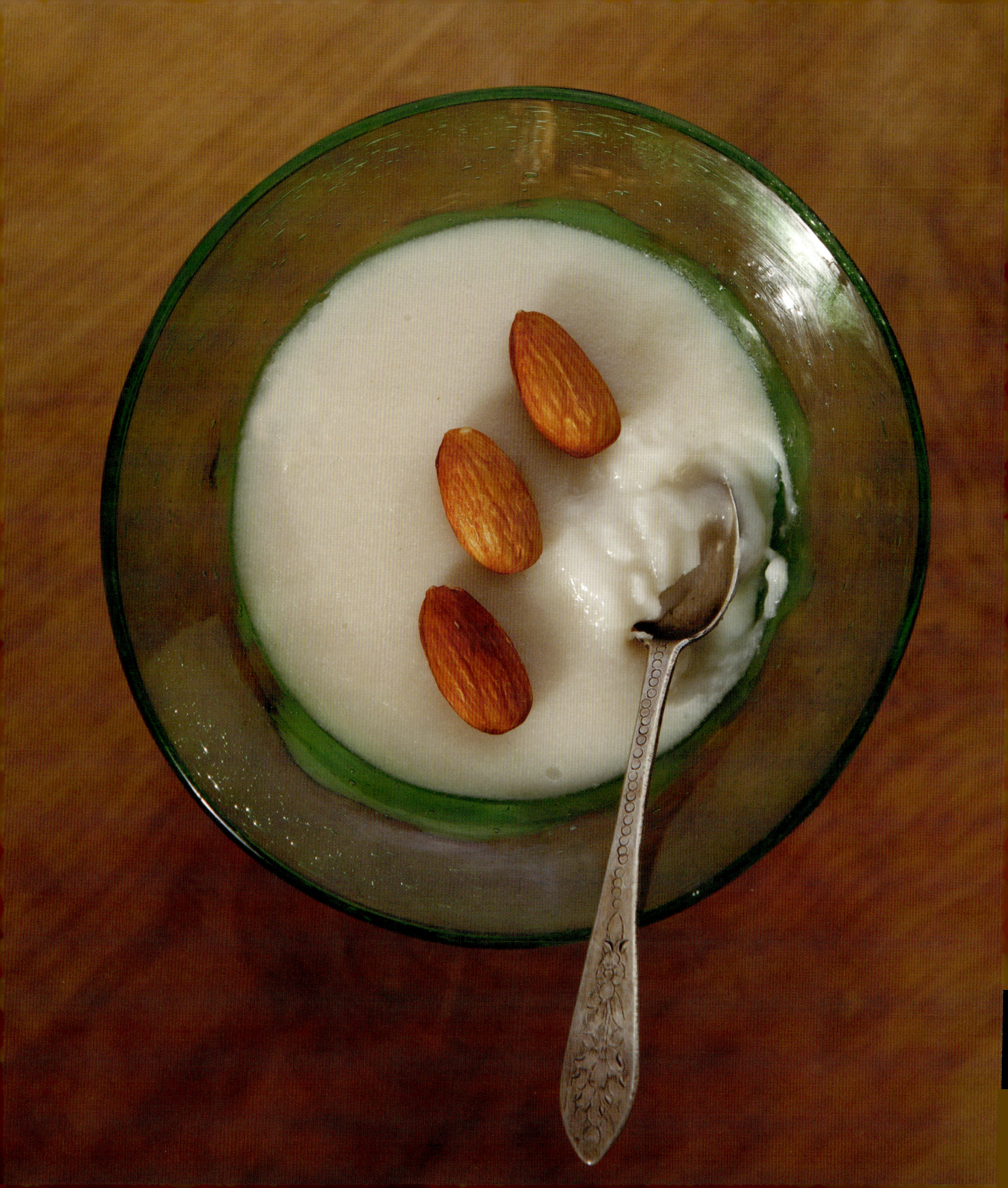

Almond Pudding
fereni-e badum/kashkul-e kordi

Serves 6
Prep: 10 minutes
Cooking: 25 minutes plus 4 hours of chilling time in the refrigerator

½ cup/75g rice flour
1 cup/240ml water
2 cups/480ml almond milk
½ cup/65g powdered sugar
¼ teaspoon fine sea salt
1 tablespoon rose water
½ teaspoon orange blossom water
1 teaspoon vanilla extract
⅛ teaspoon ground saffron threads (optional)

BLOOMED GELATIN

1 envelope unflavored gelatin soaked in ½ cup/120ml water

GARNISH

¼ cup/60g date molasses
2 tablespoons sliced almonds, toasted or 2 tablespoons ground pistachio kernels

Traditionally this recipe is made by mixing milk and ground almonds, but I'm using just almond milk here (it's tastier and easier to make).

1. In a medium-sized heavy-bottom saucepan, whisk together the rice flour and the water until smooth. Cook for 4 minutes over low heat, stirring frequently.

2. Add the almond milk, sugar, salt, rose water, orange blossom water, vanilla, and saffron, and bring to a boil over low heat.

3. Add the bloomed gelatin and cook over low heat for about 15 to 20 minutes, stirring quickly and constantly until the mixture reaches the consistency of a smooth pudding (and you are able to draw a line on the surface). Remove from heat.

4. Immediately transfer to a serving dish or to individual ramekins while the pudding is hot. Garnish, allow to cool at room temperature, then chill in the refrigerator for at least 4 hours. Serve cold. *Nush-e joon!*

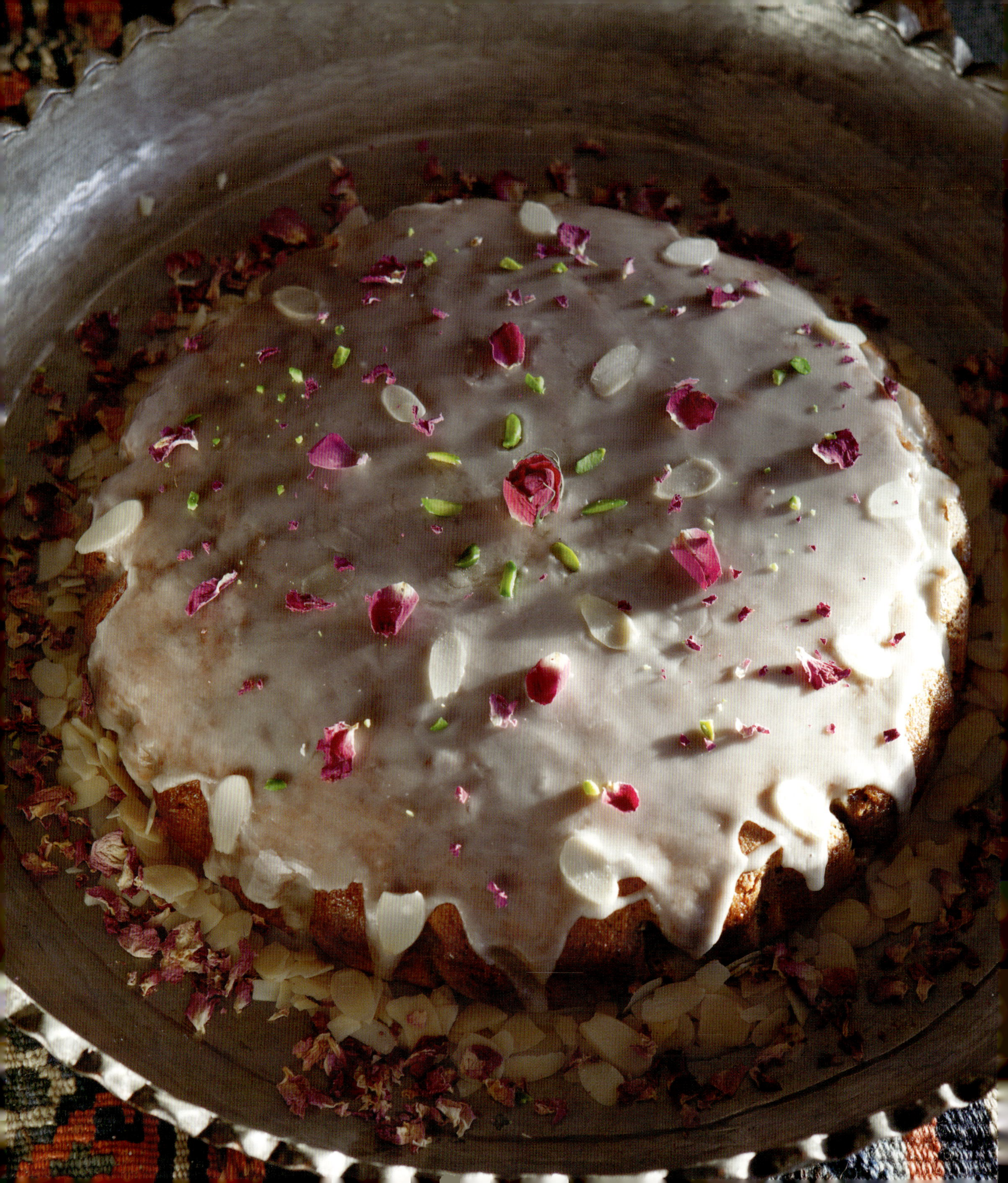

Rose + Yogurt Love Cake
cayk-e eshq-e kermanshahi

Makes one 8in/20cm diameter cake
Prep: 20 minutes
Cooking: 40 to 45 minutes

This delicious cake represents Kermanshahi cooking perfectly because it combines yogurt, almonds, saffron, and rose water, all favorite ingredients. You can make this cake gluten-free by replacing the ½ cup wheat flour with ¼ cup rice flour and ¼ cup potato starch.

BATTER

- ¾ cup/150g granulated sugar
- 4 eggs, separated (room temperature)
- Zest of 1 lime
- 2 tablespoons fresh lime juice
- 2 teaspoons ground cardamom
- ½ teaspoon ground saffron threads dissolved in 4 tablespoons rose water
- 1 cup/240g plain yogurt
- ½ cup/120ml olive oil
- 3 cups/240g almond flour
- ⅛ teaspoon fine sea salt
- 2 teaspoons baking powder
- ½ cup/60g unbleached all-purpose flour

GLAZE

- ¼ cup/85g honey
- 2 tablespoons fresh lime juice

ICING

- 1 cup/125g powdered sugar
- 1 tablespoon fresh lime juice
- 2 tablespoons rose water

DECORATION

- 2 tablespoons slivered pistachio kernels (available in Iranian stores)
- 2 tablespoons dried organic rose petals
- 1 tablespoon sliced blanched almonds

1. **To make the cake:** Place the oven rack in the center and preheat oven to 350°F/180°C.

2. Oil an 8in spring form cake pan and line the base with parchment paper. Oil and dust the parchment paper with flour.

3. In a mixing bowl, whisk together the sugar, egg yolks, lime zest, lime juice, cardamom, saffron-rose water, yogurt, and oil for 3 to 4 minutes until creamy. Add the almond flour and use a rubber spatula to fold in.

4. On a sheet of parchment paper, sift together the salt, baking powder, and all-purpose flour. Fold into the egg yolk mixture.

5. In a separate mixing bowl, whisk the egg whites until they form soft peaks. Fold into the egg yolk mixture until you have smooth batter.

6. Gently pour the batter into the cake pan and bake in the preheated oven for 40 to 45 minutes until a tester comes out clean.

7. **To make the glaze:** Place all the ingredients for the glaze in a small saucepan and bring to a gentle boil over low heat while stirring (do not overboil). Reduce heat to very low and keep warm.

8. **To make the icing:** In a mixing bowl beat all the ingredients for the icing until you have a smooth icing.

9. Remove the cake from the oven and transfer it to a cooling rack. Drizzle the glaze on top while the cake is still warm. Allow to cool for 15 minutes.

10. Unlock the pan to release the cake, remove it from the mold, and place it on the cooling rack until completely cool. Transfer to a serving platter. Pour the icing over the cake and decorate according to your fancy. *Nush-e joon!*

Isfahan

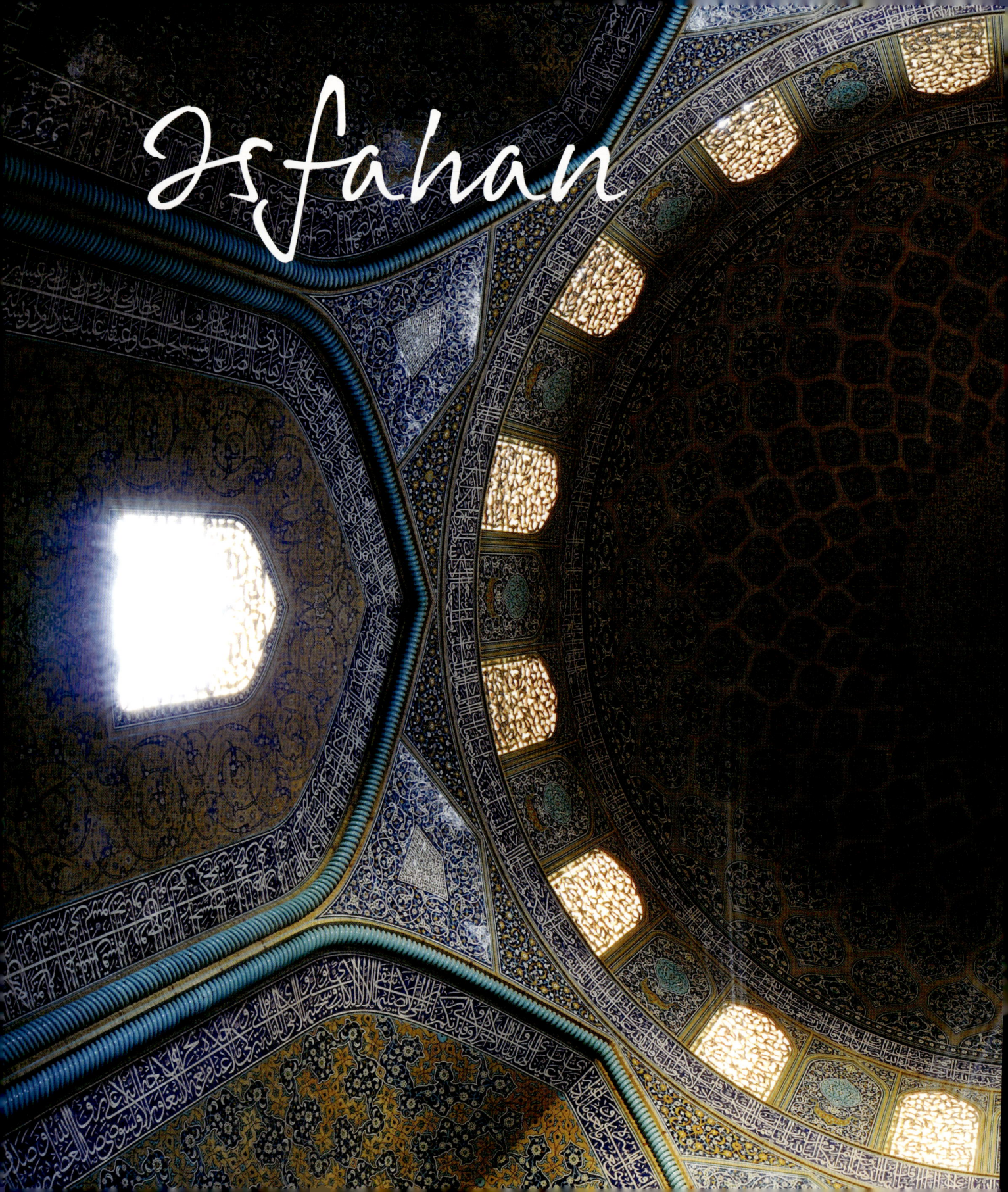

View of the ceiling of the Sheikh Lotfollah Mosque built in the early 1600s.

A Little History

Isfahan lies more or less in the center of Iran, on the north-south road linking the Caspian to the Persian Gulf. Straddling the Zayandeh River, it is a historical treasure-house. Twice it has been the capital of Iran—first in the eleventh century during the highly Persianized culture of the Seljuk Empire, and then again during the sixteenth and seventeenth centuries under the Safavids, when it was embellished with some of the most magnificent architecture in all of Iran. Isfahan suffered in the eighteenth century when the Afghans invaded, looted, and burned the city. It did not begin to revive as a great city again until the 1920s.

Since its inception Isfahan has been ethnically diverse—embracing a mix that includes two important enclaves, one Jewish and the other Armenian/Christian. Both communities are still there but in lesser numbers than before the Islamic Republic. The food of Isfahan was greatly influenced by the ethnic communities and also by the refinements of Safavid court cuisine—influences that have never lost their hold. It has been said that Shah Abbas encouraged Christian missionaries to come to the city in the hope that Isfahan's winemaking would improve and surpass that of Shiraz, which from ancient times was known for its wine. The seventeenth-century French traveler Jean Chardin considered it the cleanest city he'd been to and wished that the people of London or Paris would take baths as regularly as the Isfahanis.

View inside one of the hallways of the Shah Mosque/*masjed-e shah* of Isfahan.

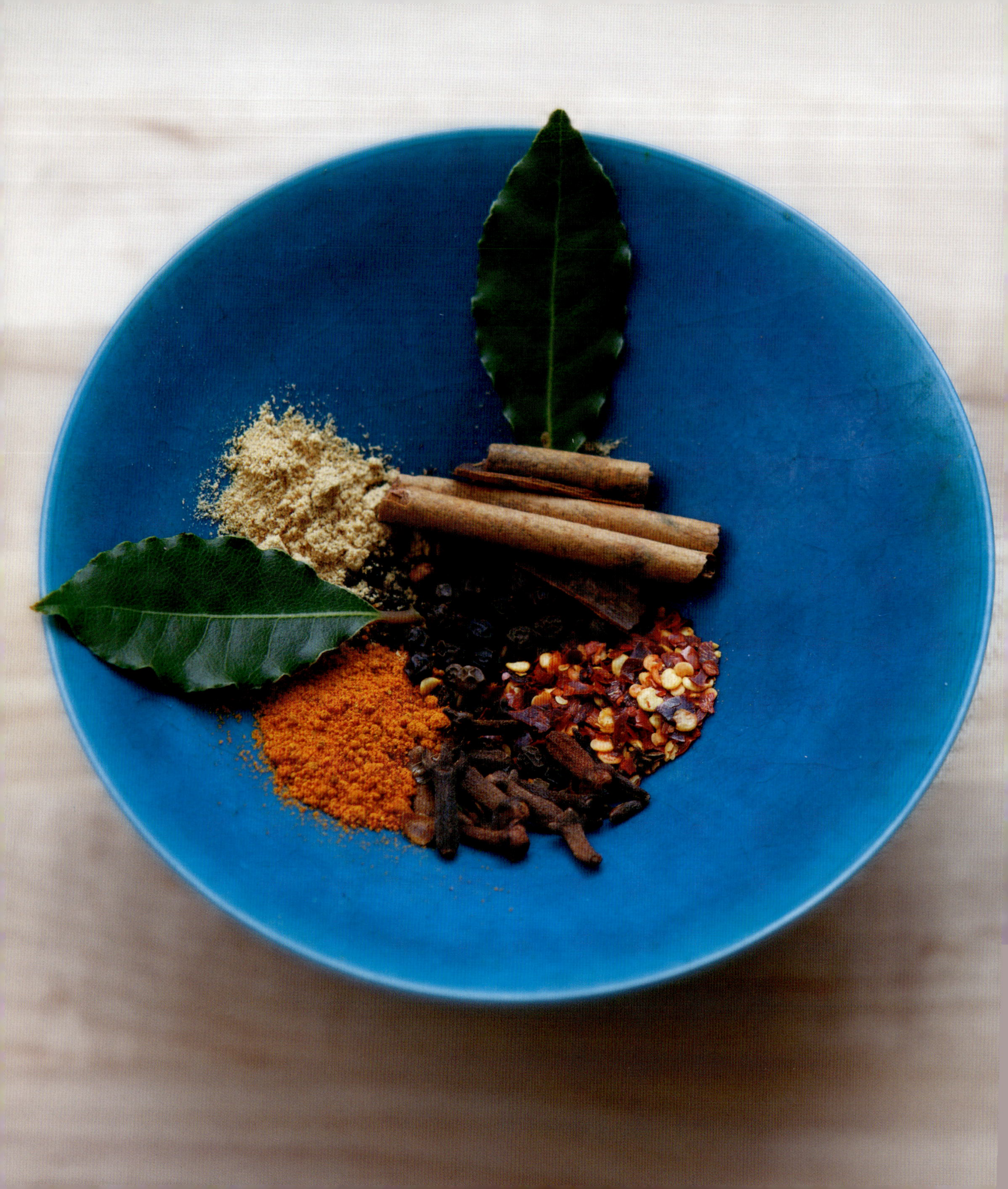

Isfahani Seven-Spice Advieh

advieh-ye esfahani

Makes 1¾ cups/175g
Prep: 20 minutes

¼ cup/6g dried bay leaves, crushed
2 tablespoons dried ginger
¼ cup/40g turmeric powder
¼ cup/40g red pepper flakes
Four 4in/10cm cinnamon sticks broken up
2 tablespoons whole cloves
2 tablespoons red pepper flakes

I have adapted this spice mix from Shahin Solaymani, an excellent cook from Isfahan. I adapted many of the other recipes in this section from Khanum-e Esfahnian.

Grind the spices, each separately, in a spice grinder. Transfer them to a small bowl as you grind them and use a spoon to mix well. Transfer to an airtight glass jar and keep in a cool place to use as needed. *Nush-e joon!*

Preparing the soup for the day of remembrance/*ashura*, in Natanz, north of Isfahan on the road to Kashan.

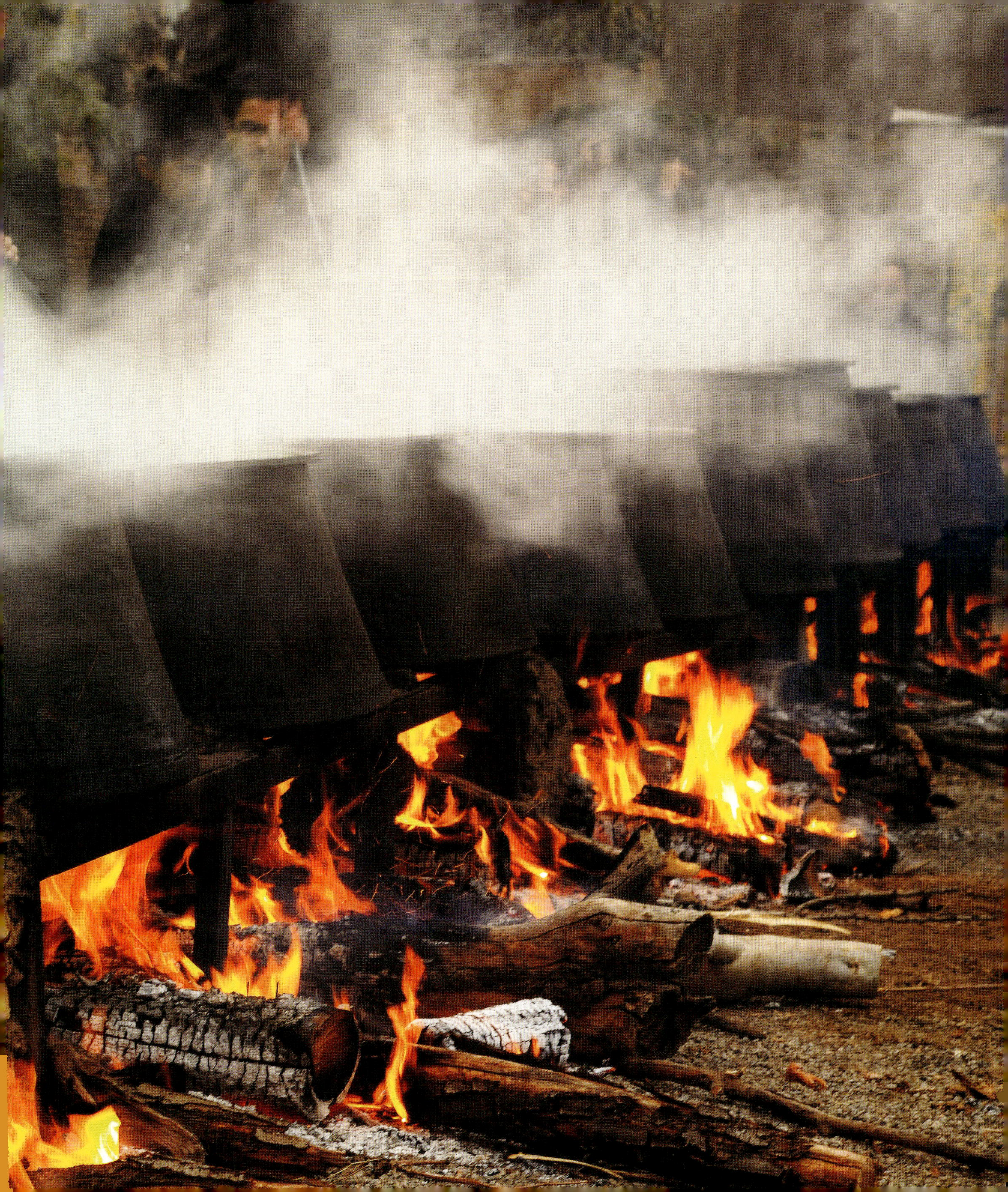

Sumac Soup
sup-e somaq-e esfahani

Serves 6 to 8
Prep: 20 minutes + 2 hours of soaking
Cooking: 2 hours 40 minutes

SUMAC BROTH

3 cups/300g sumac powder, dissolved in 6 cups/1.5l water
3 tablespoons oil
2 medium onions, thinly sliced
1 tablespoon fine sea salt
1 teaspoon freshly ground pepper
1 teaspoon turmeric
2 cups/400g rice
8 cups/1.9l water

MEATBALLS

1 onion, grated
1lb/450g ground lamb or chicken
1 teaspoon fine sea salt
½ teaspoon freshly ground pepper
½ teaspoon turmeric
1 teaspoon dried tarragon
2 tablespoons chopped fresh parsley
2 tablespoons sumac powder
¼ cup/20g ground walnuts
1 teaspoon ground cumin
1 tablespoon grape molasses or sugar

HERBS

2 cups/170g chopped fresh parsley or ¼ cup/20g dried
2 cups/170g chopped fresh cilantro or ¼ cup/20g dried
1 cup/85g chopped fresh mint or 2 tablespoons dried
1 cup/85g chopped fresh tarragon or 2 tablespoons dried

GARNISH/NA`NA DAGH

2 tablespoons oil
5 cloves garlic, peeled and sliced
½ teaspoon turmeric
1 tablespoon dried mint flakes

Fresh ground sumac, earthy and slightly sour, brings out the flavor of many dishes—including kababs—in unique ways. Here, however, it's the main flavor. Traditionally, this soup is made with sumac berries, but as they are hard to find outside Iran, I am using sumac powder, readily available at Iranian markets in the U.S.

1. ***To prepare the sumac broth:*** Place the sumac water in a large laminated cast-iron pot and bring to a boil. Reduce heat to medium and simmer for 35 minutes. Strain through a fine-mesh sieve set over a bowl, reserving the sumac water and discarding the solids.

2. Heat the oil in the same pot over medium heat and sauté the onions until golden brown. Add the salt, pepper, turmeric, and rice. Sauté for 1 minute. Add the water and bring to a boil. Reduce heat to low, cover, and cook for 20 minutes.

3. Add sumac water, cover, and simmer for 15 minutes.

4. ***Meanwhile, to make the meatballs:*** In a mixing bowl, combine all the ingredients for the meatballs. Knead lightly (do not over-mix) and shape into chestnut-sized meatballs. Gently add them to the pot and bring back to a boil. Add the grape molasses, reduce heat to low, partially cover, and simmer for 30 minutes.

5. Add the herbs. Cover and cook for 15 minutes.

6. ***Taste the soup:*** It should be sweet and sour. Add more grape molasses if the soup is too sour. Cover and keep warm until ready to serve.

7. ***To make the garnish:*** Heat 2 tablespoons oil in a skillet and brown the garlic. Add the turmeric and sauté for 1 minute. Remove from heat. Crumble the dried mint flakes in the palm of your hands and add them to the garlic mixture. Mix well. Pour the soup into a tureen and garnish. *Nush-e joon!*

A late 1800s photo of a tea house/*ghahveh khaneh* in Isfahan, where they may well have also served this soup.

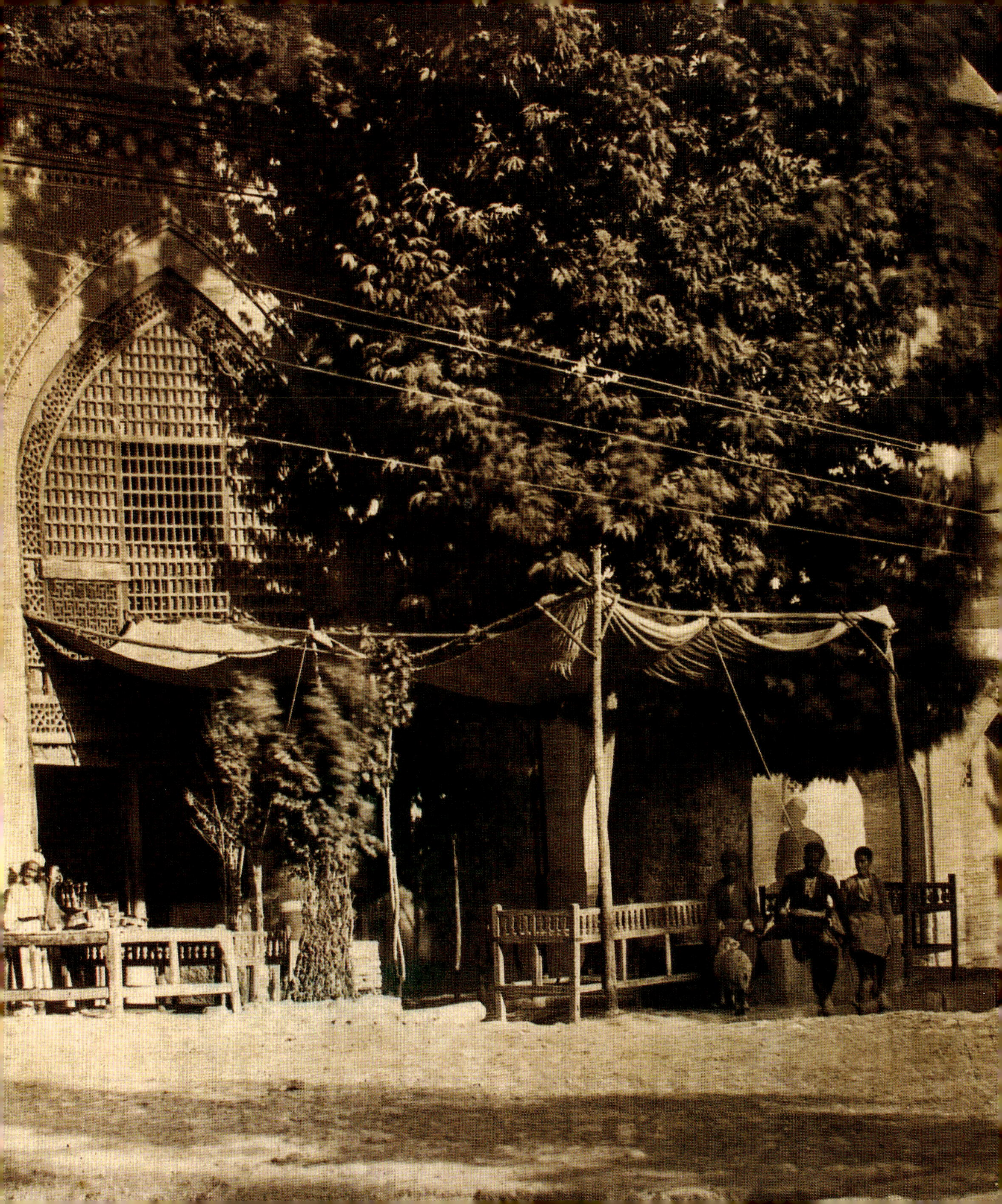

Lamb, Prune, Apricot + Quince Spread
yakhmeh-ye torsh-e esfahani

Serves 6 to 8
Prep: 20 minutes
Cooking: 2½ hours

LAMB

2 tablespoons oil
½lb/225g ground lamb
1 onion, peeled and thinly sliced
1 teaspoon fine sea salt
½ teaspoon freshly ground pepper
½ teaspoon turmeric
4 cups/960ml water
1 cup/200g rice, rinsed thoroughly
16 pitted dried prunes (3.5oz/100g) pitted prune
16 dried apricots (3.5oz/100g)
2lb/900g quinces (about 2 quinces) or Fuji apples, cored, and diced to ½in/12mm cubes

CARAMELIZED ONION + MINT/NA`NA DAGH

2 tablespoons oil
1 onion, peeled and thinly sliced
½ teaspoon turmeric
2 tablespoons dried mint leaves, crushed

This spread, containing both lamb and dried fruit, has a deliciously unusual flavor, almost like a lamb jam.

1. **To cook the lamb:** Heat 2 tablespoons oil in a medium-sized laminated cast-iron braiser or pot, and sauté the ground lamb and onions until golden brown. Add the salt, pepper, and turmeric, and sauté for 1 minute.

2. Add the water and rice, and bring to a boil. Reduce heat to low and add the prunes, apricots, and quinces. Cover and simmer over low heat for 50 to 60 minutes until the rice is cooked and the water has been absorbed.

3. Use a handheld mixer to puree to a thick paste.

4. **To caramelize the onion and mint:** Heat 2 tablespoons oil in a wide skillet over medium heat until hot. Add the onion and sauté until golden brown. Add the turmeric and stir-fry for 1 minute. Remove from heat. Add the crushed mint flakes, stir well, and set aside.

5. Transfer the spread to a serving platter and garnish. Serve with bread. *Nush-e joon!*

A wonderfully well-stocked dried herbs, nuts and fruit store in Khansar.

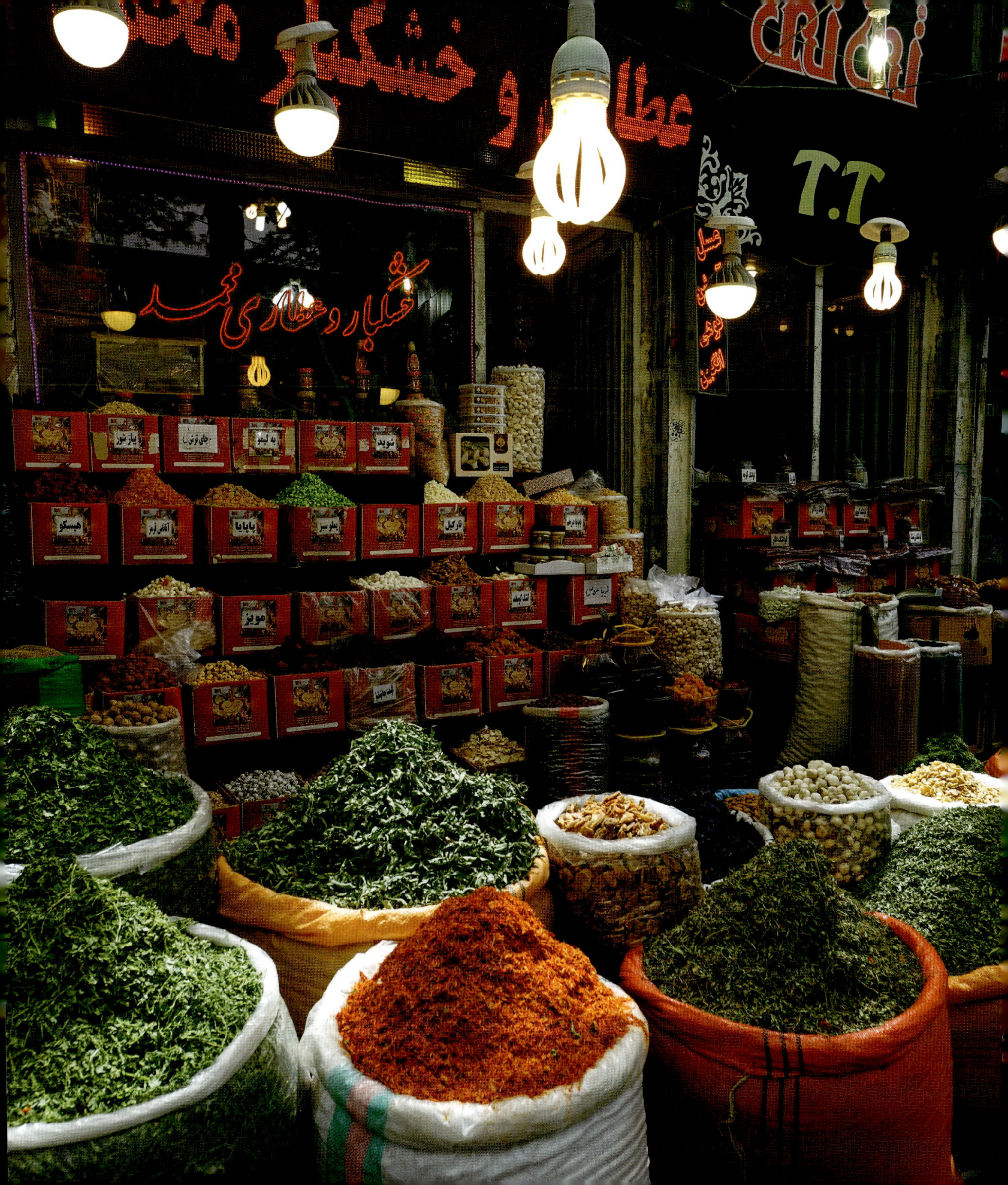
خشکبار و عطاری محمد
T.T

Mung Beans + Kohlrabi Spread
halim-e maush qomry-e esfahani

Serves 6 to 8
Prep: 20 minutes
Cooking: 2½ hours

LAMB

- ½lb/225g boned lamb shoulder, cut into 2in/5cm pieces
- 1 medium onion, peeled and thinly sliced
- 1 clove garlic, grated
- 1 tablespoon fine sea salt
- 1 teaspoon freshly ground pepper
- 1 teaspoon turmeric
- 4 cups/960ml water

MUNG BEANS + KOHLRABI

- 1 cup/200g mung beans
- ¾ cup/150g rice
- 2 kohlrabies (2lb/900g), peeled and grated
- 2 cups fresh roughly chopped parsley
- 5 spring onions, chopped
- 1 cup/85g fresh or 1 tablespoon dried tarragon leaves
- 1 tablespoon dried fenugreek leaves
- 1 tablespoon dried summer savory
- ½ cup/120g liquid *kashk*

CARAMELIZED ONION + MINT/NA`NA DAGH

- 2 tablespoons oil
- 2 onions, peeled and thinly sliced
- 2 cloves garlic, peeled and grated
- ½ teaspoon turmeric
- 2 tablespoons dried mint leaves, crushed

GARNISH

- ½ cup/120g liquid *kashk*
- ½ teaspoon ground saffron dissolved in 2 tablespoons warm water

*Isfahanis love spreads and porridges/*halim *and have a considerable variety of them. They rarely use garlic with lamb, but in the U.S., I find the garlic brings out the taste. This dish is traditionally made with lamb necks, which—surprisingly—is often available at my local Whole Foods. But cooking lamb necks is labor-intensive, so I am using boned lamb shoulder here. You can also eliminate the kashk, which some Isfahanis also do.*

1. **To prepare the lamb:** Heat 2 tablespoons oil in a large pot over medium heat and sauté the lamb and onion until golden brown. Add the garlic, salt, pepper, and turmeric, and sauté for 1 minute.

2. Add 4 cups/960ml water and bring to a boil. Reduce heat to low, cover, and simmer for 30 minutes.

3. Add the mung beans, rice, kohlrabi, and herbs. Cover and cook over low heat for 1½ to 2 hours until the lamb and mung beans are tender.

4. Add the *kashk* and use a handheld mixer to puree to a thick paste. Adjust seasoning to taste, cover, and cook over low heat for 10 minutes.

5. **To caramelize the onion and mint:** Heat 2 tablespoons oil in a wide skillet over low heat until hot. Add the onions and sauté until golden brown. Add the garlic and turmeric, and stir-fry for 2 minutes. Remove from heat. Add the crushed mint flakes, stir well, and set aside.

6. Just before serving, transfer the spread to a serving platter. Garnish with caramelize onions, *kashk*, and saffron water. Serve with bread. *Nush-e joon!*

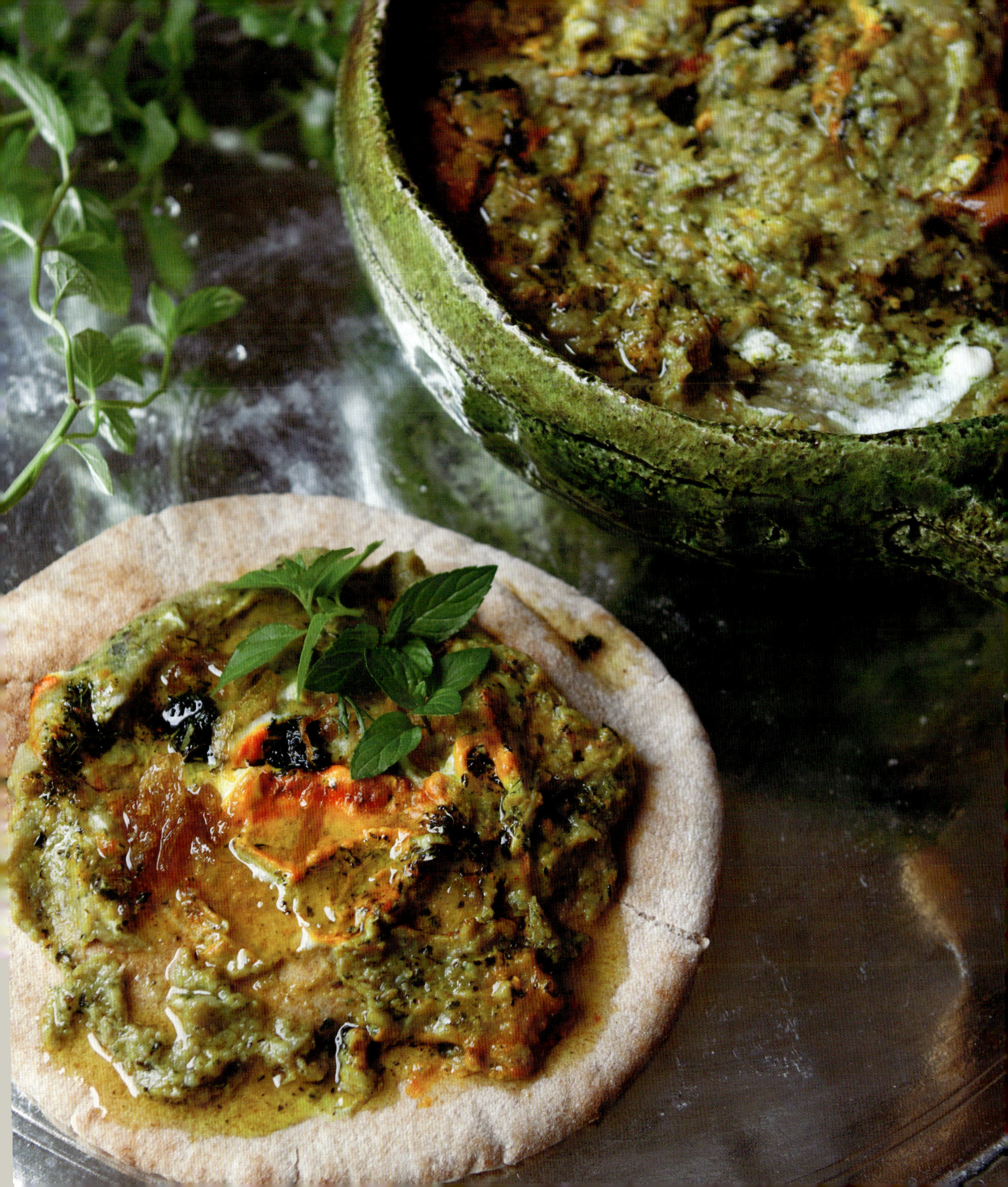

Chickpea Meatballs in Aromatic Tomato Sauce
khoresh-e ghermez-e nokodchi-e esfahani

Serves 6
Prep: 15 minutes
Cooking: 1½ hour

PASTE FOR MEATBALLS

½lb/225g ground lamb, chicken thighs, or fish fillets (all small bones removed)
1 onion, peeled and grated
2 teaspoons salt
½ teaspoon fresh ground pepper
½ teaspoon turmeric
1 teaspoon Isfahani seven-spice *advieh*
1 teaspoon dried mint
½ teaspoon dried thyme
1 tablespoon tomato paste
1 cup/100g chickpea powder
2 to 3 tablespoons warm water

BROTH

¼ cup/60ml oil
1 medium onion, thickly sliced
2 teaspoons fine sea salt
½ teaspoon fresh ground black pepper
½ teaspoon turmeric
1 tablespoon dried mint
1 teaspoon thyme
2 dried bay leaves
1 tablespoon tomato paste
2 fresh tomatoes (2 cups/400g), peeled and finely chopped
3 cups/720ml water

GARNISH

Sprigs of fresh thyme leaves or 1 teaspoon dried thyme

Khanum Kuchick in Isfahan inspired me to make this recipe. I particularly like its simplicity.

1. **To make the paste for meatballs:** In a wide mixing bowl, combine the lamb, grated onion, salt, pepper, turmeric, *advieh*, dried mint, thyme, tomato paste, and chickpea powder, and mix for 1 minute. Add 2 to 3 tablespoons warm water, while kneading with your hand until you have a soft paste that does not stick to your hands (beware not to over-mix). Cover and refrigerate for 30 minutes.

2. **To make the broth:** In a medium-sized laminated cast-iron pot, heat the oil over medium heat. Sauté the onion until golden brown. Add the salt, pepper, turmeric, mint, thyme, bay leaves, and tomato paste, and sauté for 1 minute. Add the fresh tomatoes and 3 cups water. Bring to a boil, reduce heat to low, cover, and allow to simmer for 30 minutes.

3. Place a small bowl of water next to your work area. With moist hands, shape the paste into walnut-sized balls and gently add them to the simmering broth as you make them. Bring the broth back to a boil, reduce heat to low, and simmer uncovered for 5 minutes. Cover and simmer for another hour.

4. Adjust seasoning to taste and garnish. Serve directly from pot over plain rice/*kateh* or bread with a herb platter on the side. *Nush-e joon!*

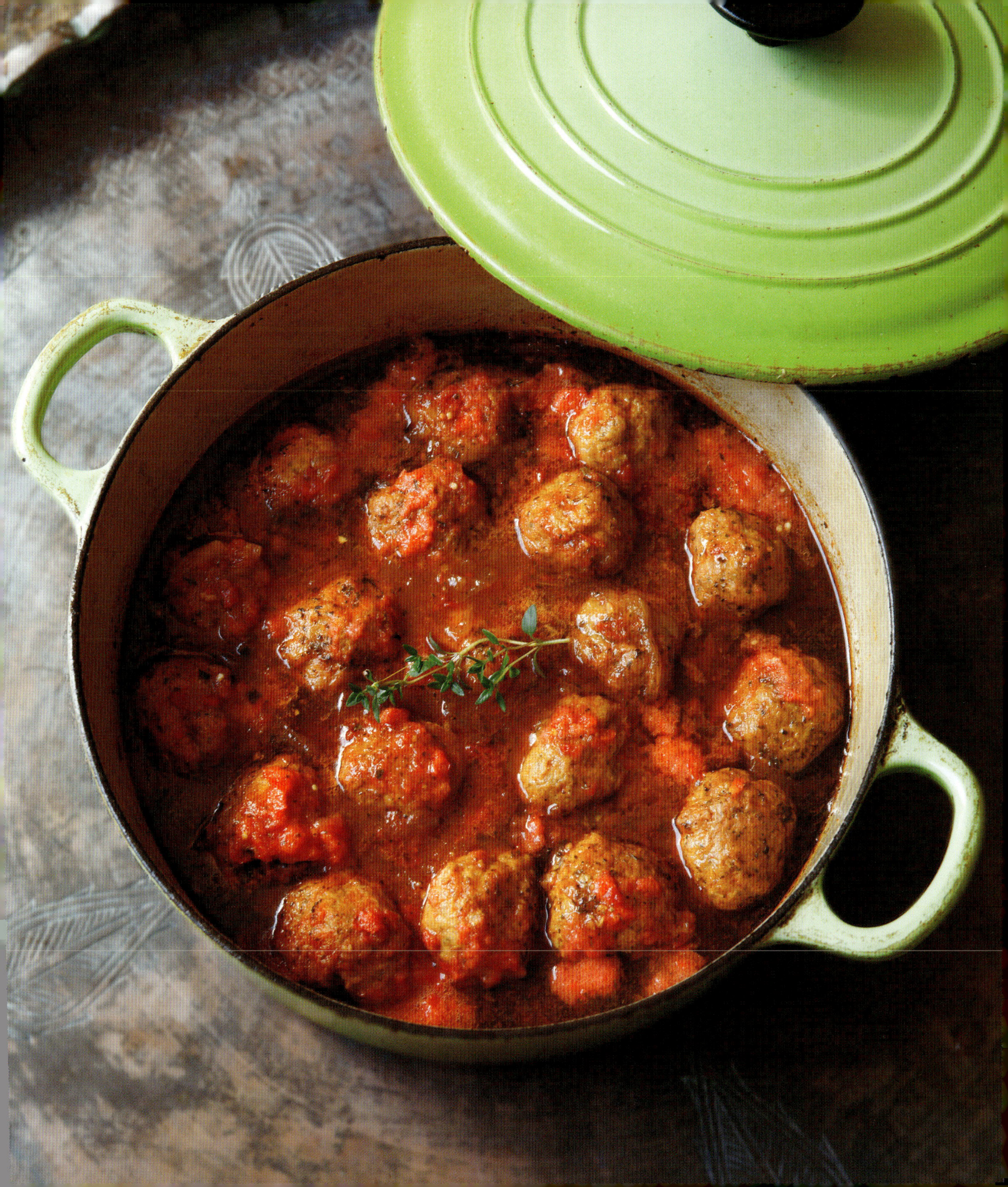

Isfahani Lamb Briyani Wrap
kabab-e beriyani-e esfahan

Makes 10 patties, serves 4 to 6
Prep: 20 minutes
Cooking: 2 hours

LAMB SHOULDER

3¼lb/1.5kg lamb shoulder with bone, rinsed
4 cups/960ml water
2 medium onions, peeled and thinly sliced
2 teaspoons fine sea salt
1 teaspoon freshly ground pepper
2 teaspoons turmeric
2 bay leaves

PASTE

1 teaspoon fine sea salt
1 teaspoon freshly ground pepper
2 tablespoons dried mint flakes
¼ teaspoon ground saffron dissolved in 2 tablespoons warm water

LAMB LUNG (OPTIONAL)

1 lamb lung (2 to 2½lb/1kg)
2 cups water
1 medium onion, peeled and sliced
1 teaspoon fine sea salt
½ teaspoon pepper
2 tablespoons oil

FOR COOKING

3 tablespoons oil
1 tablespoon ground cinnamon

GARNISH

2 *sangak* bread loaves, cut into 8in/20cm squares, or tortilla
¼ cup/40g slivered almonds
¼ cup/40g ground walnuts
2 cups/170g chopped fresh parsley or basil leaves

This popular Isfahani street food traditionally includes the lung, but you can regard it as optional. The taste is delicious and remarkable, especially with plenty of fresh herbs and a green salad, or served as a wrap—a very satisfying dish. I adapted this recipe from a the cook in a stall in the bazaar in Isfahan.

1. **To cook the lamb shoulder:** Place the lamb in a large pot, add the water, and bring to a boil. Remove any froth as it rises. Add the onions, salt, pepper, turmeric, and bay leaves. Reduce heat to medium-low, cover, and cook for 1½ hours until the lamb is tender. Discard the bay leaves.

2. **To make the paste:** Remove the pot from heat and allow to cool enough to handle the lamb. Place a sieve over a large bowl and drain the lamb. Return the broth to the pot, cover, and keep warm.

3. Separate the lamb from the bones and discard the bones (be sure to **remove all the little bones**). Place the lamb and onion in a food processor and grind until you have a puree. Add the salt, pepper, mint, and saffron water, and mix for 1 minute. Adjust seasoning to taste and transfer to a large mixing bowl. Form the paste into ten 3½in/9cm diameter patties and arrange on a sheet pan lined with parchment paper. Cover and keep cool in the fridge until ready to cook the patties.

4. **To cook lamb's lung (optional):** On a cutting board, pound the lung with a mallet to release any air. Use a knife to remove any bronchi or cartilaginous parts. Rinse and cut into 2in/5cm pieces. Place in a medium saucepan, cover with the water, and add the onions, salt, pepper, and oil. Bring to a boil. Reduce heat to medium-low, cover, and cook for 2 hours until tender. Once all the water has been absorbed, continue to cook for a few minutes longer until the lung is lightly golden. Transfer to a food processor and pulse until you have a paste. Set aside.

5. **To cook the patties:** Heat 1 tablespoon oil in a wide cast-iron skillet over high heat until hot. Sprinkle a pinch of cinnamon on top of each patty and sear each side for 1 to 2 minutes until brown. Continue for the remaining patties.

6. **To serve:** Place a piece of bread on a plate and pour ¼ cup/60ml of the reserved lamb broth over it. Place a patty on the bread and add a tablespoon of lung paste. Garnish on top with 1 tablespoon of the nuts and parsley. Fold the bread over to make a wrap. *Nush-e joon!*

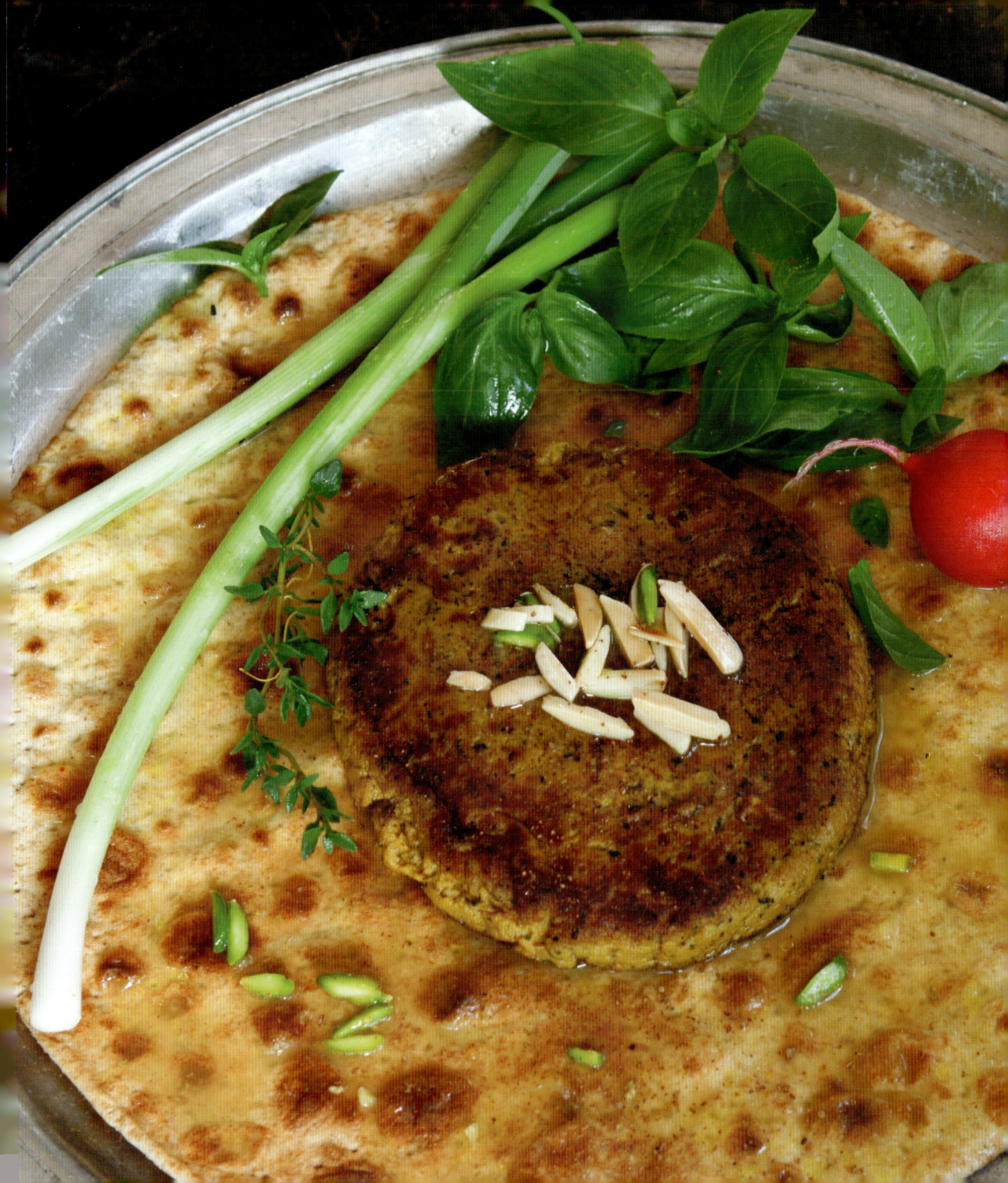

Sweet + Sour Glazed Chickpea + Carrot Patties
kabab-e moshti-e esfahani

Serves 4 to 6
Prep: 20 minutes + 30 minutes of resting
Cooking: 45 minutes

PASTE

1lb/450g ground lamb, chicken, or fish fillets
1 medium onion, peeled and quartered
1½lb/675g carrots (about 4 large), peeled and grated
2 teaspoons fine sea salt
1 teaspoon freshly ground pepper
1 teaspoon turmeric
2 teaspoon Isfahani seven-spice *advieh*
½ cup/50g chickpea flour

¼ cup/60ml oil or butter for frying

LIME + SAFFRON GLAZE

¼ cup/60ml water
¼ cup/50g sugar or grape molasses
¼ cup/60ml lime juice
½ teaspoon ground saffron dissolved in 1 tablespoon water
½ teaspoon fine sea salt

ALTERNATE VINEGAR + GRAPE MOLASSES GLAZE

2 tablespoons tomato paste
½ cup/120ml vinegar
¼ cup/60g grape molasses
½ teaspoon fine sea salt

GARNISH

¼ cup/20g chopped fresh cilantro

I have given you an option to use two different glazes: one with sugar, lime juice, and saffron, and the other with tomato paste, vinegar, and grape molasses. Try these patties both ways—you won't be disappointed.

1. Line a sheet pan with parchment paper.

2. *To prepare the paste:* Place the lamb in a large mixing bowl.

3. In a food processor, place the onion, carrots, salt, pepper, turmeric, and *advieh*, and pulse until you have a grainy paste. Transfer to the mixing bowl, add the chickpea flour a little at a time, and knead with your hands until all of it has been absorbed (do not over-mix). Cover and allow to rest for 30 minutes.

4. *To cook the patties:* Heat 2 tablespoons oil in a medium-sized sauté pan over medium-low heat until hot but not smoking. Shape the paste into 3in/7.5cm patties. Gently, place them in the pan and cook for 5 to 7 minutes on each side until golden.

5. *To make the glaze:* In a small bowl, combine all the ingredients for the glaze and stir well. Pour it over the patties. Reduce heat to very low, cover, and allow to simmer for 3 to 5 minutes until all the sauce has been absorbed.

6. Garnish with cilantro and serve. I like to use green leaf lettuce and basil to make a wrap with these patties inside. *Nush-e joon!*

VARIATION

For a traditional *shami*, add 3 eggs to the lamb in step 2.

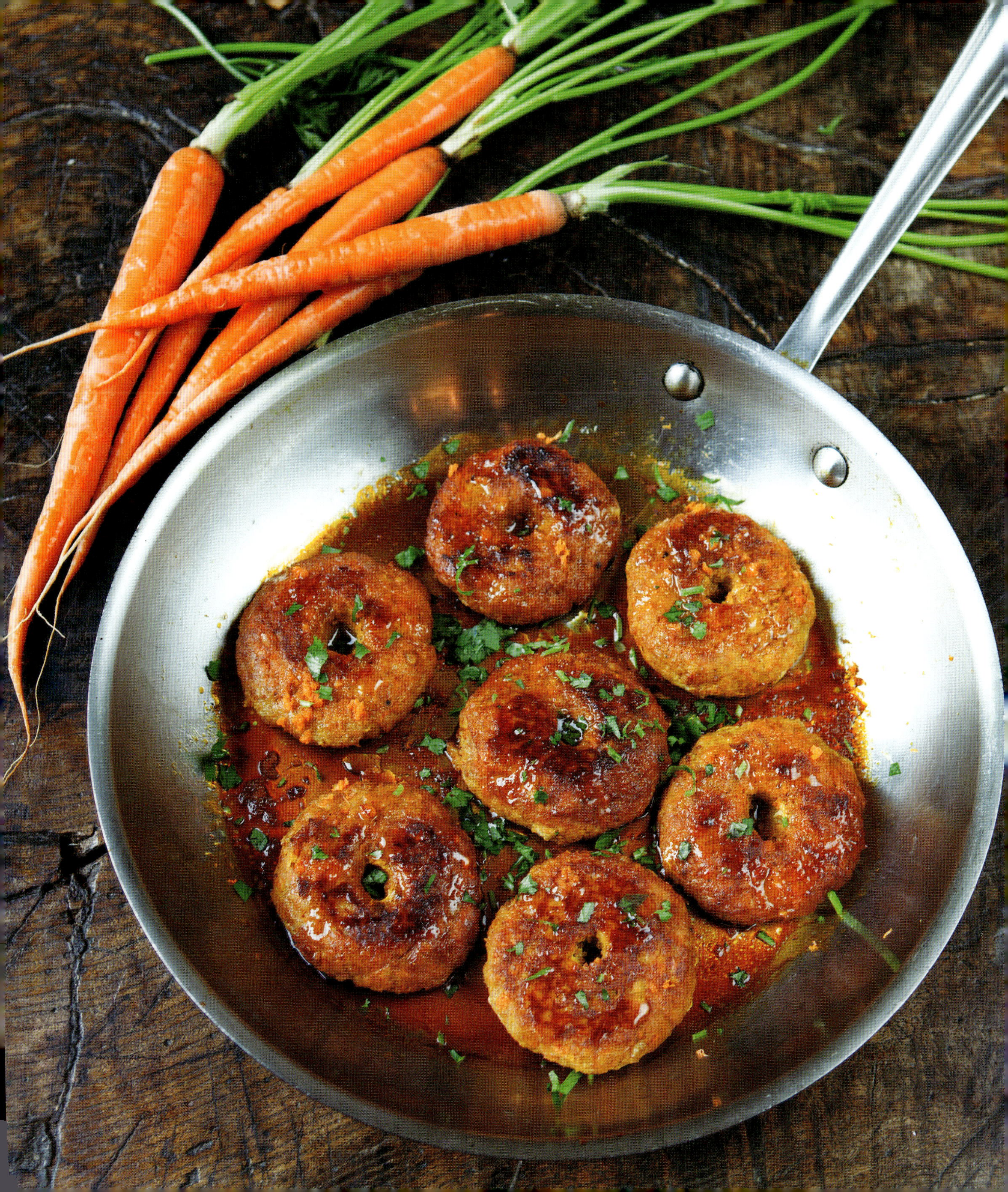

Lamb, Quince + Plum Braise
khoresh-e beh-o alu

Serves 6
Prep: 20 minutes
Cooking: 2 hours

LAMB

- ¼ cup/60ml oil, butter, or ghee
- 2 medium onions, peeled and thinly sliced
- 1lb/450g boneless leg of lamb, or chicken thighs cut into 3in/7.5cm cubes
- 2 teaspoons fine sea salt
- ½ teaspoon freshly ground pepper
- ½ teaspoon turmeric
- ½ teaspoon ground cinnamon

QUINCE

- 3 medium quinces (about 2lb/900g)
- ½ teaspoon ground saffron dissolved in 2 tablespoons water
- 1 cup/150g dried plums or prunes
- 2 tablespoons fresh lime juice
- 2 tablespoons wine vinegar
- 2 tablespoons sugar

Many regions in Iran have their own variation on this braise. We made it in Yazd using vinegar, lime juice, and sugar to achieve the desired sweet and sour flavor. In Kerman they use dried greengages. In Arak they add tomato paste and split peas. In Isfahan they make it with prunes/alu baraghuni, but I prefer it, as shown in the photograph on the facing page, with dried golden plums (available at Iranian markets). All versions are delicious, especially over saffroned rice/chelow.

1. **To cook the lamb:** Heat 2 tablespoons oil in a laminated cast-iron braiser or pot over medium heat and sauté the onions and lamb until golden brown. Add salt, pepper, turmeric, and cinnamon, and sauté for 1 minute longer.

2. Pour in 3½ cups of water. Cover and simmer over low heat for 1¼ hours for lamb, 45 minutes for chicken, stirring occasionally.

3. **Meanwhile, to prepare the quince:** Wash and core the quinces (do not peel them). Cut them into quarters, removing any remaining seeds. Cut them into cubes.

4. Heat 2 tablespoons oil in a wide skillet over medium-low heat. Sauté the quinces, for 15 to 20 minutes, shaking the skillet back and forth until golden brown. Add 1 tablespoon saffron-rose water and stir-fry for 1 minute until the quince is coated with saffron.

5. Add the quince, plums, saffron-water, the lime juice, vinegar and sugar to the pot. Cover and simmer for 30 to 45 minutes over low heat until the quince is tender.

6. Adjust seasoning to taste, adding sugar if too sour. Cover and keep warm until ready to serve.

7. Serve hot over rice/chelow. *Nush-e joon!*

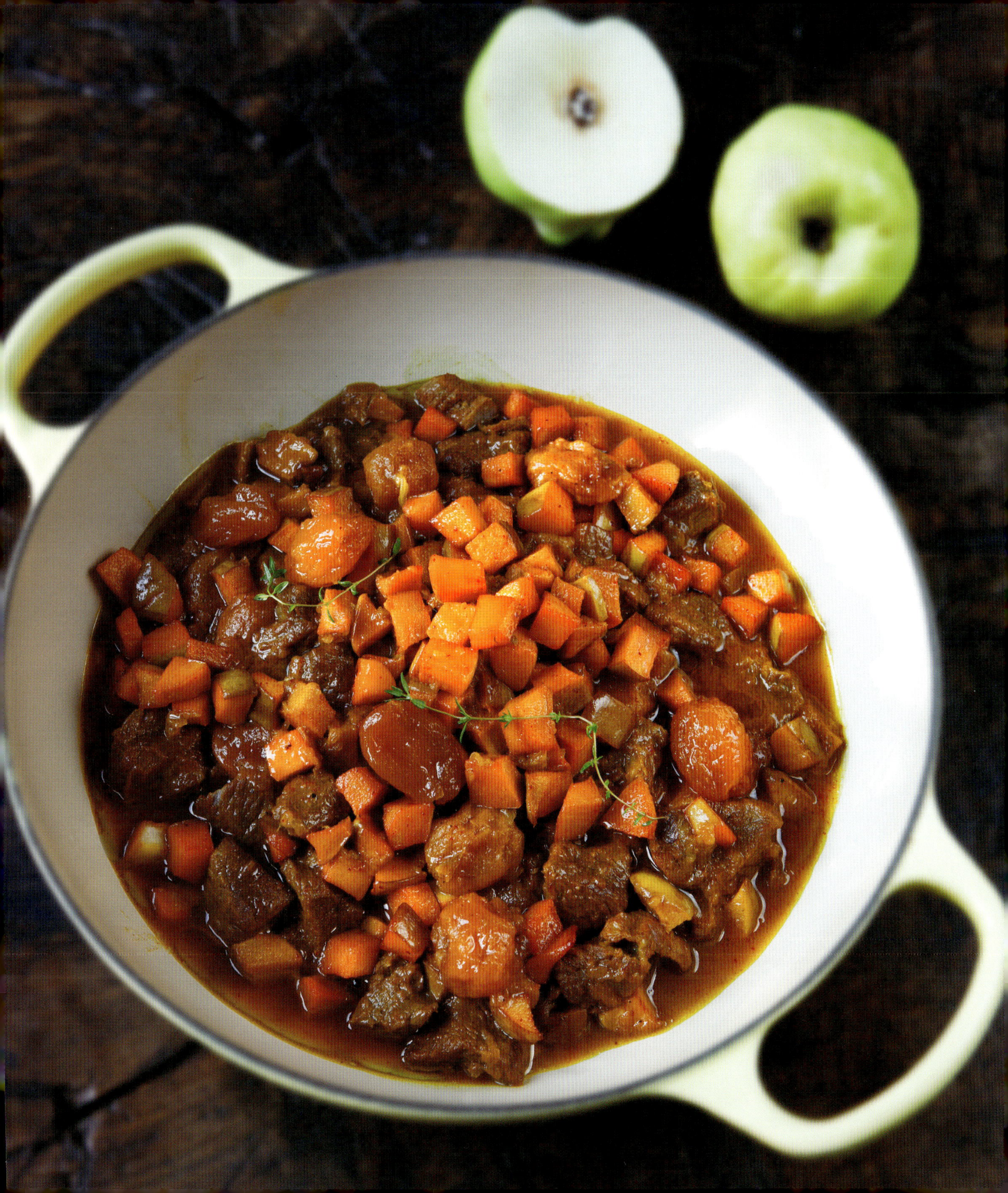

Saffroned Yogurt + Lamb Neck Braise with Barberries
khoresh-e mast-e esfahani ba garden-e gusfand

Serves 6
Prep: 15 minutes
Cooking: 2¾ hours

LAMB NECKS

2 lamb necks (about 2lb/900g) or 1lb/450g boned lamb shoulder
1 medium onion, peeled and thinly sliced
2 teaspoons fine sea salt
½ teaspoon freshly ground pepper
1 teaspoon turmeric
1 teaspoon cinnamon

NUTS

1 tablespoon oil
¼ cup/30g slivered almonds
¼ cup/30g coarsely chopped walnuts
¼ cup/30g slivered pistachios

BARBERRIES

2 cups/300g barberries/*zereshk*, picked over and rinsed thoroughly
2 tablespoons sugar
2 tablespoons oil
¼ cup/60ml water

YOGURT SAUCE

2 tablespoons orange zest
1 teaspoon ground saffron threads, dissolved in ¼ cup rose water
½ cup/80g raw almonds
¼ cup/35g raisins
2 cups/480g strained plain yogurt or *labneh* (a creamy yogurt strained until thick. Available at Iranian stores and some grocers—our Whole Foods carries it for example, but not Safeway.)

Isfahan

I have eaten this braise in Isfahan both as a sweet, cold dessert on its own and as a stretchy, warm braise over rice/chelow. Both versions are particular to Isfahani cuisine. I prefer the warm braise, which is how I have given it here for you. Using raisins for sweetening (instead of sugar) and almonds for thickening (instead of eggs) goes back to ancient Persian cuisine.

1. **To cook the lamb necks:** In a medium-sized laminated cast-iron pot, place the lamb and 3 cups/720ml water to cover the lamb. Bring to a boil. Remove the froth as it rises. Reduce heat to low, add the onion, salt, pepper, turmeric, and cinnamon. Cover and simmer for 2 hours.

2. **To prepare the nuts:** In a wide skillet, heat 1 tablespoon oil over medium heat until hot. Add the almonds and stir-fry for about 2 minutes until slightly golden. Add the walnuts and pistachios, and give it a stir (be careful not to burn the nuts, especially the almonds). Transfer to a small serving bowl and set aside. Wipe the skillet.

3. **To caramelize the barberries:** In the same skillet, combine the barberries, sugar, oil, and water, and stir-fry for 4 minutes over medium-high heat (be careful, barberries burn easily; do not walk away). Set aside.

4. Remove the pot from heat and allow to cool enough to handle the lamb. Place a sieve over a large bowl and drain the lamb. Return the broth to the pot. Separate the lamb meat from the bones (be sure to remove all the little bones and any fat) and return the meat and onions to the pot. Discard the bones. Cover and allow to simmer over low heat.

5. **To make the yogurt sauce:** In a food processor, place the orange zest, saffron-rose water, almonds, raisins, and yogurt. Mix for 5 minutes (beating yogurt will prevent it from curdling). Gradually add this mixture to the lamb and cook over low heat, stirring clockwise for 5 minutes.

6. Adjust seasoning to taste. Cover and simmer over very low heat for 55 minutes, stirring occasionally.

7. Use the handheld mixer to puree the mixture until it becomes thick and elastic with the consistency of a porridge. Cover and simmer over **very low heat** for 15 minutes.

8. **To serve:** In individual serving bowls of cooked rice (page 122), top with a ladle of the yogurt braise, 2 tablespoons of barberries, 1 tablespoon of the nut mix, and few sprigs of basil. Serve with an Onion, Cucumber + Coriander Pickle (page 675). *Nush-e joon!*

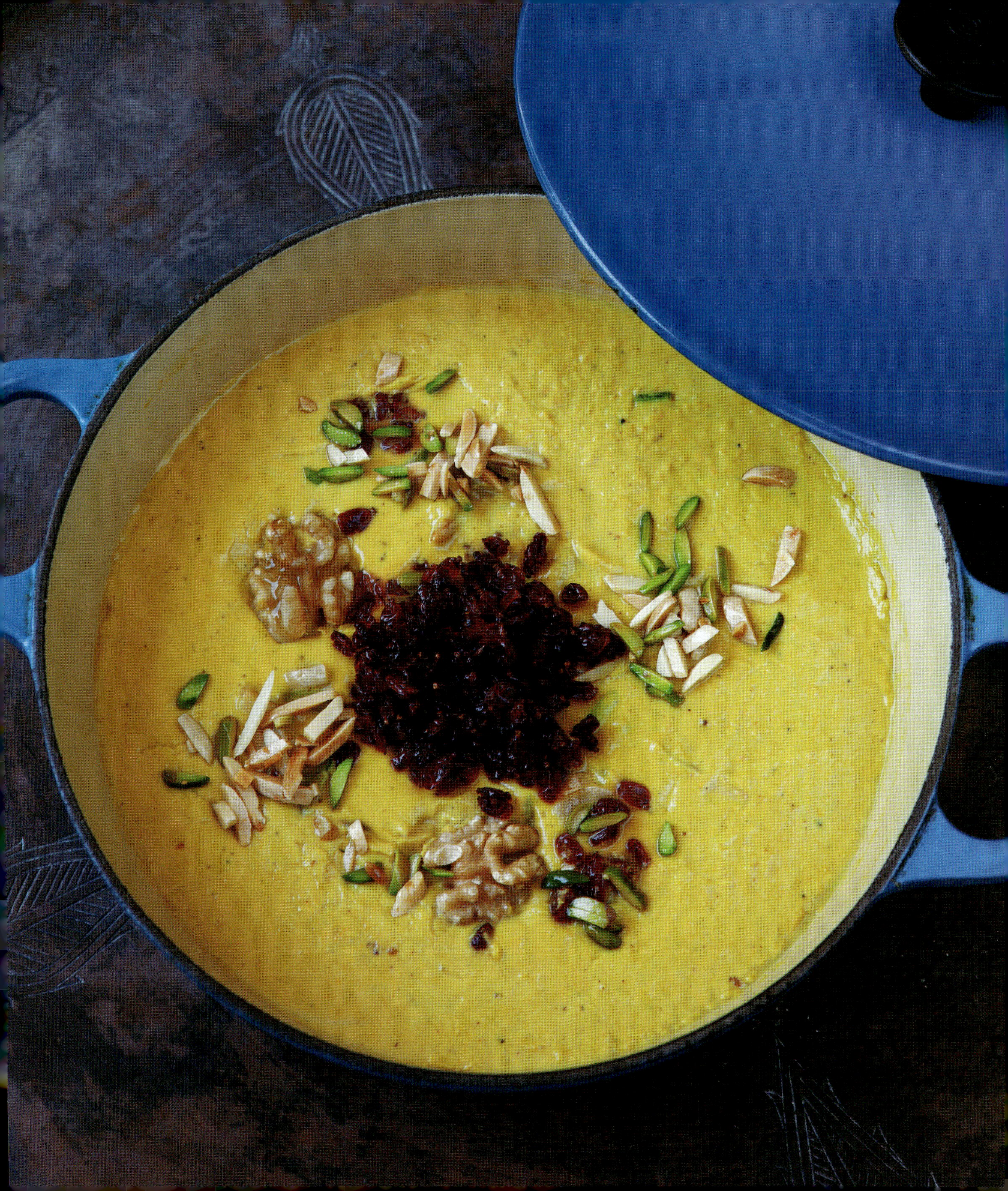

Saffroned Chicken + Yogurt Braise
khoresh-e mast-e esfahani ba morgh

Serves 4 to 6
Prep: 25 minutes
Cooking: 1½ hours

CHICKEN

- 2 tablespoons oil, butter, or ghee
- 2 medium onions, thinly sliced
- 2lb/900g boneless chicken thighs cut into 4in/10cm pieces
- 2 teaspoons fine sea salt
- ½ teaspoon freshly ground pepper
- 1 teaspoon ground saffron threads dissolved in ¼ cup/60ml rose water
- Zest of 2 oranges or 2 tablespoon dried slivered orange peel
- 6 kaffir lime leaves, crushed

YOGURT

- 2 cups/480g strained plain whole yogurt or *labneh*
- ½ cup/80g raw almonds
- ¼ cup/35g raisins

NUTS

- 1 tablespoon oil
- 1 cup/170g whole raw almonds
- ¼ cup/30g coarsely chopped walnuts
- ¼ cup/30g slivered pistachios

CARAMELIZED BARBERRIES

- 1 cup barberries/*zereshk*, cleaned and rinsed thoroughly
- 2 teaspoons sugar
- 2 tablespoons oil or ghee
- 2 tablespoons water

GARNISH:

- Bowl of fresh Persian basil leaves
- Tomato, Cucumber + Herb Salad (page 523)

In my Food of Life, *I have the spicy chicken version of this braise attributed to the fourteenth-century Mughal court. This version is a sixteenth-century Safavid Court variation.*

1. *To cook the chicken:* Heat 2 tablespoons oil in a medium-sized laminated cast-iron braiser or pot until hot. Add the onions and sauté for 5 to 10 minutes until the onion is translucent. Add the chicken and sauté for another 5 minutes. Add the salt, pepper, saffron-rose water, orange zest, and lime leaves and sauté for 10 to 15 minutes until all the juice has been absorbed.

2. Meanwhile, in a food processor, puree the almonds and raisins then add the yogurt and mix for 5 minutes (beating the yogurt prevents it from curdling when cooked). Add this mixture to the pot and give it a gentle stir.

3. Cover and simmer over low heat for 45 to 55 minutes until the chicken is tender. Remove the lime leaves and adjust seasoning to taste. Keep covered and warm until ready to serve.

4. *To roast the nuts:* Heat 1 tablespoon oil in a wide skillet over medium heat until hot. Add the almonds and stir-fry for about 1 minute or until slightly golden. Add the walnuts and pistachios and give it a stir. Transfer to a small serving bowl and set aside. Wipe the skillet.

5. *To caramelize the barberries:* In the same skillet, combine the barberries, sugar, oil, and water, and stir-fry for 4 minutes over medium-high heat. Set aside.

6. *To serve:* In individual serving bowls of cooked rice (page 122) top with a ladle of the yogurt and chicken braise, 2 tablespoons of barberries, 1 tablespoon of nuts, and a few sprigs of basil. Serve with an Onion, Cucumber + Coriander Pickle (page 675). *Nush-e joon!*

Ali Qapu/lofty gateway is a five-storied building from the early 1600s overlooking the great square/maydan-e shah of Isfahan. The photo on the right is of the ceiling of the fifth floor, traditionally used for entertainment and known as the music room. The magnificent saffron-pigmented plasterwork depicts plates, bowls, vases, and bottles. We know that the walls of Shah Abbas's wine cellar was similarly decorated with an inscription that read: Life is a series of intoxicating states/ Pleasure passes, hangovers remain.

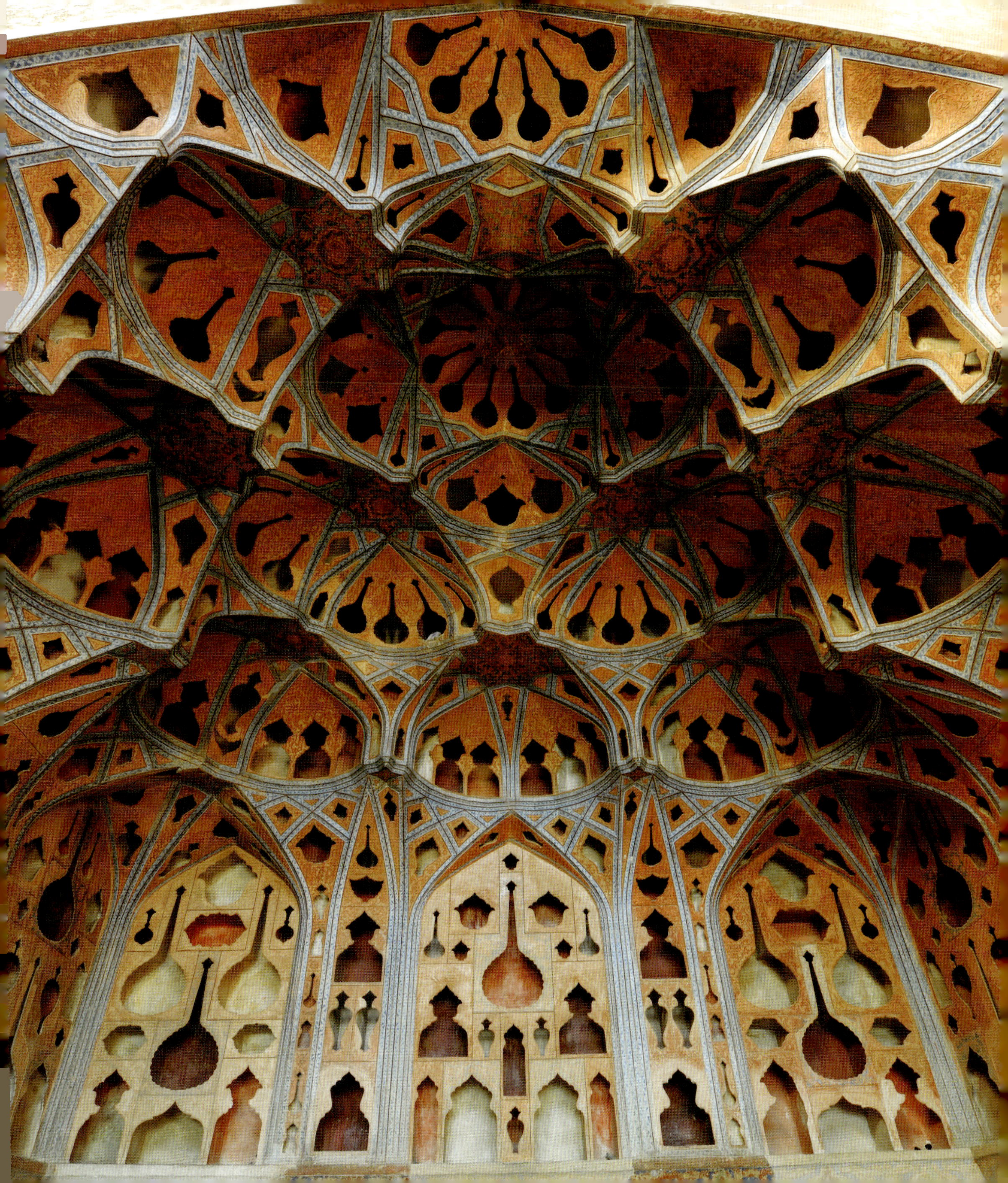

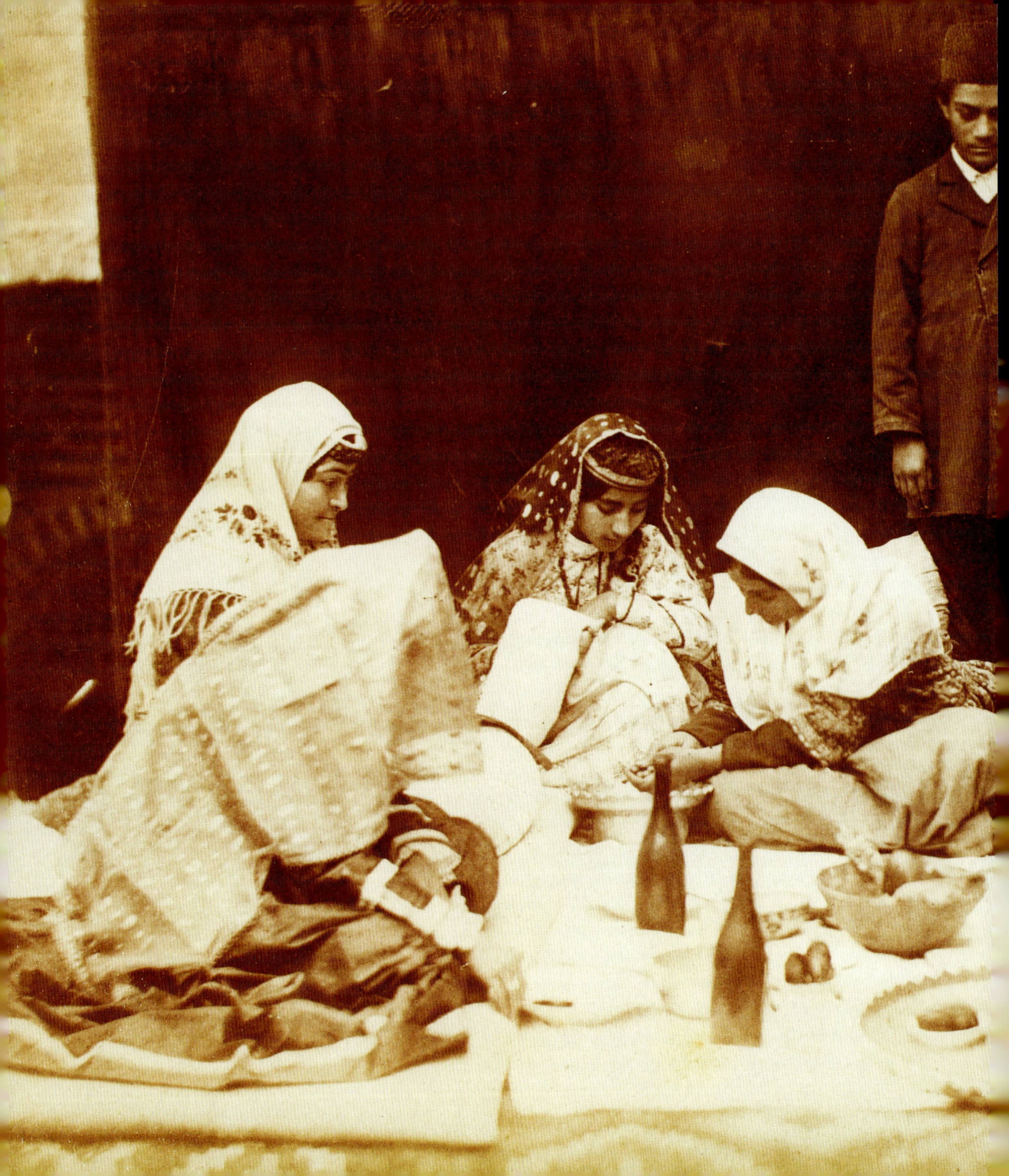

Iranian Armenians

Iranians and Armenians have been close since ancient times and often fought next to each other in the vast Persian Empire. Today, many ethnic Armenians—upwards of 150,000—still live in Iran, mostly in Tehran, Isfahan, and Azarbaijan, forming the country's largest Christian minority.

Iranian-Armenians have long had their own churches as well as the first Westernized school systems, with music and dance education. During the Iranian Constitutional Revolution of 1905 to 1909, they played an important role in the movement toward a more democratic government. They were pioneers in photography, theater, and film and opened the first cinema in Tabriz in 1916. The extensive list of their contributions to Iranian society even includes fast food. I can still taste the mortadella sandwiches of my childhood from the Armenian deli next to our house in old Tehran. The sandwiches were made with small baguettes spread with butter, slices of mortadella, tomatoes, and pickled cucumbers, and sprinkled with salt, pepper, and chopped fresh parsley. Mortadella was forbidden because it contained pork, but my sisters and I ate it anyway and enjoyed it all the more. What delicious memories!

A photograph of an Iranian-Armenian family in Isfahan from the late 1800s.

Isfahani Nougat
gaz-e esfahani

Persian nougat is called gaz. The gaz of Isfahan is renowned because it was traditionally made with gaz-angebin, the sap/manna of the honeydew from the anus of a nymph (insect) that lives on the tamarisk tree (found on the outskirts of Isfahan). Gaz-angebin is collected during the year and mixed with various ingredients including rose water and pistachios to make the gaz of Khansar (a village outside Isfahan). This type of gaz is delicious but hard to find. The usual nougat /gaz sold in stores is not made from gaz-angebin. Aqa-ye Maqsudi (photo on the left), who kindly and proudly invited us into his workshop, is the fifth generation of gaz makers of the Meli Gaz Company of Isfahan.

Makes 20 pieces
Prep: 20 minutes
Cooking: 1½ hours

DUSTING

1 cup/120g unbleached all-purpose wheat flour

NUTS

1 cup/175g pistachio kernels
2 tablespoon coriander seeds

SYRUP

1¼ cups/250g sugar
¾ cup/180ml water
¾ cup/225g glucose or corn starch

EGG WHITE

5 egg whites (6oz/175g)
2 tablespoons rose water

1. **To prepare the dusting:** Line a sheet pan with parchment paper and dust it with 1 cup/120g flour.

2. **To toast the pistachio kernels and coriander seeds:** In a wide skillet, toast the pistachio kernels and coriander seeds by shaking the pan back and forth until the aroma of the coriander starts to rise (about 30 minutes). Cover and keep warm until ready to use.

3. **To make the syrup:** Place the sugar and water in a saucepan and bring it to a simmer over low heat until all the sugar has dissolved. Add the glucose, give it a stir with a wooden spoon. Increase the heat to medium and bring to a boil. Reduce heat to low, and allow to cook, undisturbed, for 30 minutes until a candy thermometer shows a temperature of 293°F/145°C and you have a thick, stretchy, and lightly caramelized syrup.

4. **Meanwhile, to prepare the egg white:** In the bowl of an electric mixer, add the egg white and rose water, and beat until you have soft peaks. Add 2 tablespoons of the hot syrup and continue to mix for 1 minute.

5. Add the egg white mixture to the syrup. Use a handheld mixer to mix for 5 to 10 minutes over low heat until stiff.

6. Use a rubber spatula to fold in the warm pistachio and coriander seeds until they have been incorporated in the paste. Remove from heat and allow to cool for 10 minutes.

7. Transfer the paste onto the prepared sheet pan and knead for 1 minute to release any air pockets. Roll the paste into a long cylindrical log. Cut the paste into 1in/2.5cm pieces. Allow to dry overnight.

8. Store in an airtight glass container until ready to serve. *Nush-e joon!*

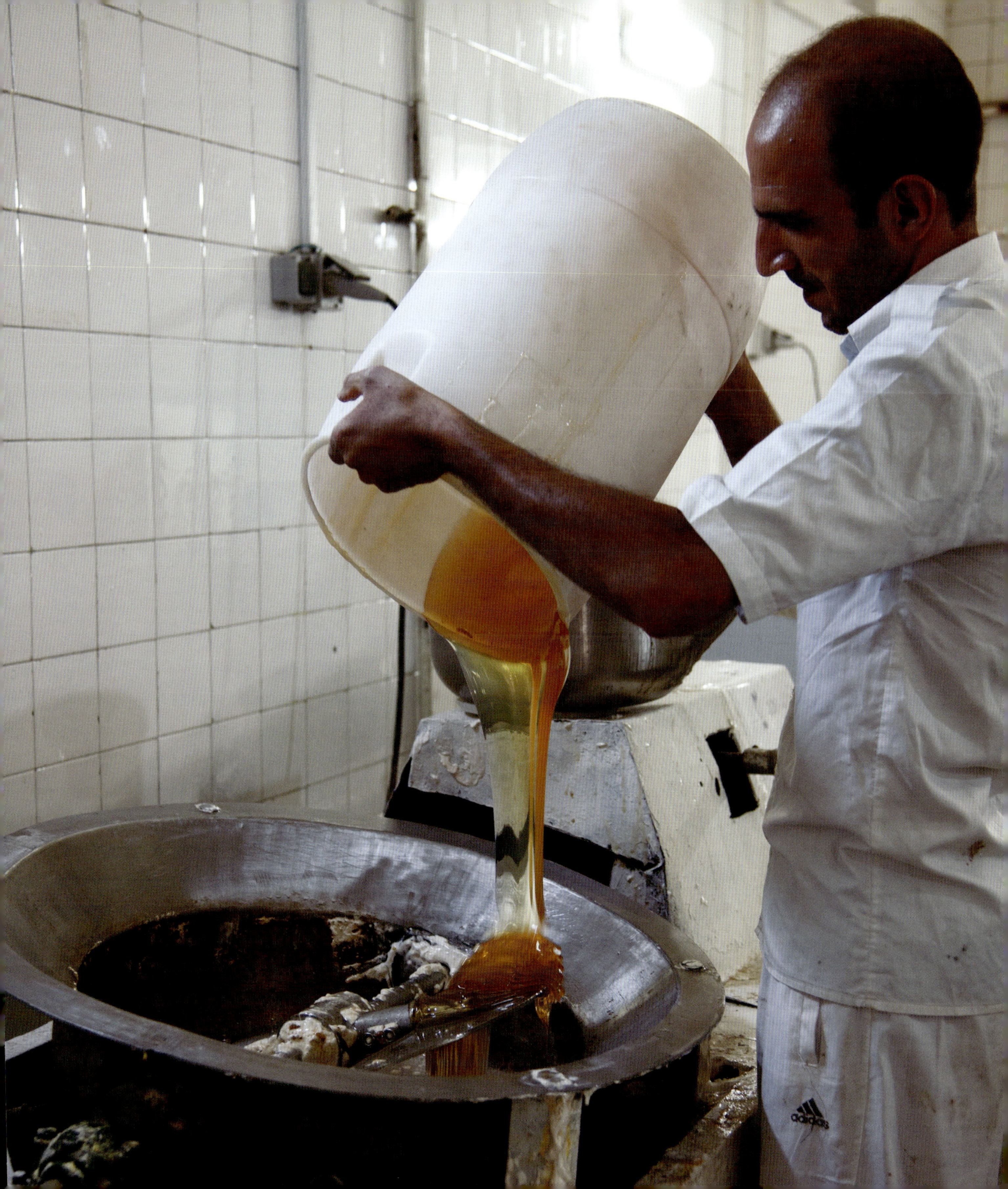

Kashan

A Little History

Kashan, a two-hour drive northeast of Isfahan, is an oasis of gardens on the edge of a vast desert. But because of the mountains to its southwest, plenty of water is brought down to the city and environs. Kashan is known for its magnificent carpets, silk, and textiles, as well as for its fine tiles. In fact, *kashi* (the Persian word for "tile") comes from Kashan. Because of trade, especially the silk trade, Kashan developed a rich ethnic tradition, which is reflected in its recipes and dishes.

In its architecture and city planning, Kashan also demonstrates how much care the inhabitants took to be in harmony with nature and the arid environment. Buildings and alleyways were oriented to take advantage of favorable winds and to provide shade. And to conserve water, they transport it through subterranean aqueducts.

One of the most distinctive ingredients in the Persian kitchen (and a signature element in my own cooking) is the damask rose/*gol-e mohammadi* and its rose water. The two villages of Ghamsar and Neyasar, just outside of Kashan, are where most of Iran's artisanal rose water is produced.

One of my favorite modernist Iranian poets is Sohrab Sepehri. He was born and raised in Kashan and his poems are full of emotions and images that intertwine his hometown with food.

> I saw a woman pounding light with a mortar and pestle
> There was bread on their spread at noon,
> There were greens, a plate of dew, and a piping
>   hot bowl of affection.
>
>   Sohrab Sepehri

Opposite: An embroidered silk cloth from Kashan.

Bringing in the rose petals for making rose water in the traditional artisanal way in Kashan.

Do Not Despair

Lost Joseph will return to Canaan's land again
    —do not despair
His grieving father's house will fill with flowers again
    —do not despair

O sorrow-stricken heart, your fortunes will revive,
Order will come to your distracted mind again
    —do not despair

And if the heavens turn against us for two days
They turn, and will not stay forever in one place
    —do not despair

Sweet singing bird, survive until the spring, and then
You'll tread on grass again, deep in the flowers' shade
    —do not despair

Don't give up hope, you have no knowledge of Fate's lore;
Behind the veil who knows what hidden turns still wait?
    —do not despair

When, if you long to tread the pilgrims' desert trail
To Mecca's distant shrine, sharp thorns beset your path
    —do not despair

For God, who solves all sorrows, knows the sorrows of
Our absence and desire, the guardian's scornful rage
    —do not despair

O heart, if nothingness should wash away the world,
Since Noah guides your craft, when you encounter storms
    —do not despair

And though the journey's filled with dangers, and its goal
Is all unknown, there is no road that has no end
    —do not despair

O Hafez, in night's darkness, alone, in poverty,
While the Qur'an remains to you, and murmured prayer
    —do not despair.

HAFEZ/DAVIS

Lamb + White Bean Braise with Dill Rice
gusht-o lubia-o shivid polow-ye kashani

Serves 6
Prep: 25 minutes
Cooking: 2½ hours

SOAKING OVERNIGHT
2 cups/400g dried white beans, soaked overnight and drained,

BRAISE
2 tablespoons oil, butter, or ghee
2 large onions, peeled and thinly sliced
5 cloves garlic, peeled and sliced
1½lb/675g boned leg of lamb or chicken thighs cut into 3in/7.5cm pieces
1 teaspoon freshly ground pepper
1 tablespoon turmeric
2 teaspoons ground cinnamon
1 tablespoon ground cumin
4 whole dried Persian limes, pierced
6 cups/1.4l water
½ cup/120ml verjuice or ¼ cup/60ml fresh lime juice
1 tablespoon fine sea salt

POTATOES
1½lb/675g russet potatoes (about 2 large ones), peeled and cut into ½in/12mm cubes and soaked in cold water for 20 minutes, drained and thoroughly patted dry
¼ cup/60ml oil for frying the potatoes
¼ teaspoon turmeric
½ teaspoon salt

RICE
2 cups/400g basmati rice
2 cups/170g chopped fresh dill weed
½ cup/120ml oil
1 teaspoon ground saffron threads dissolved in ¼ cup/60ml water

I was inspired to adapt this traditional dish by Shifteh Matini, who is from Kashan. It's made with varying ingredients. Some Kashanis use potatoes and dried limes, and serve the broth separately as a soup together with croutons. Others mash the beans and lamb and serve it as a porridge with rice.

1. **To make the braise:** Heat 2 tablespoons oil in a laminated cast-iron braiser or pot over medium heat, and sauté the onions, garlic, and lamb until golden brown. Add the beans, pepper, turmeric, cinnamon, cumin, and dried limes, and sauté for 1 minute.

2. Add 6 cups/1.4l of water and bring to a boil. Reduce heat to low, cover, and simmer for 2 to 2½ hours, stirring occasionally, until the lamb and beans are tender.

3. Add the salt and verjuice, give it a gentle stir, and adjust seasoning to taste. Cover and keep warm until ready to serve.

4. **Meanwhile, to cook the potatoes:** In a wide iron skillet, heat the oil until hot and sauté the potatoes over medium heat until golden brown and crispy. Sprinkle the turmeric and salt over them and give it a stir. Remove from the skillet and set aside.

5. **To cook the rice:** Wash the rice by placing it in a large container, cover it with water, agitate gently with your hand, then pour off the water. Repeat 2 to 3 times until the water is clear.

6. In a large non-stick pot, bring 8 cups/1.9l water and 2 tablespoons fine sea salt to a boil. Add the rice and boil briskly for 6 to 10 minutes, gently stirring twice to loosen any grains that may have stuck to the bottom. Bite a few grains. If the rice feels soft, it is ready to be drained. Drain rice in a large fine-mesh colander and rinse with 3 cups water. Set aside.

7. Place 2 tablespoons oil and 2 tablespoons water in the non-stick pot and use a rubber spatula to mix thoroughly.

8. Place 2 spatulas full of rice in the pot and 1 spatula full of the dill and potato mixture. Repeat, alternating layers and mound in the shape of a pyramid.

9. Pour the remaining oil and ½ cup/120ml of the broth over the rice. Drizzle the saffron water over the top. Wrap the lid of the pot with a clean dish towel and cover the pot firmly to prevent steam from escaping. Cook for 15 minutes over medium heat. Keep warm until ready to serve.

10. **To serve:** On a large serving platter, gently mound the rice. Use a slotted spoon to arrange the lamb and beans on top. You can serve the broth in a bowl on the side for those who might want more juice. *Nush-e joon!*

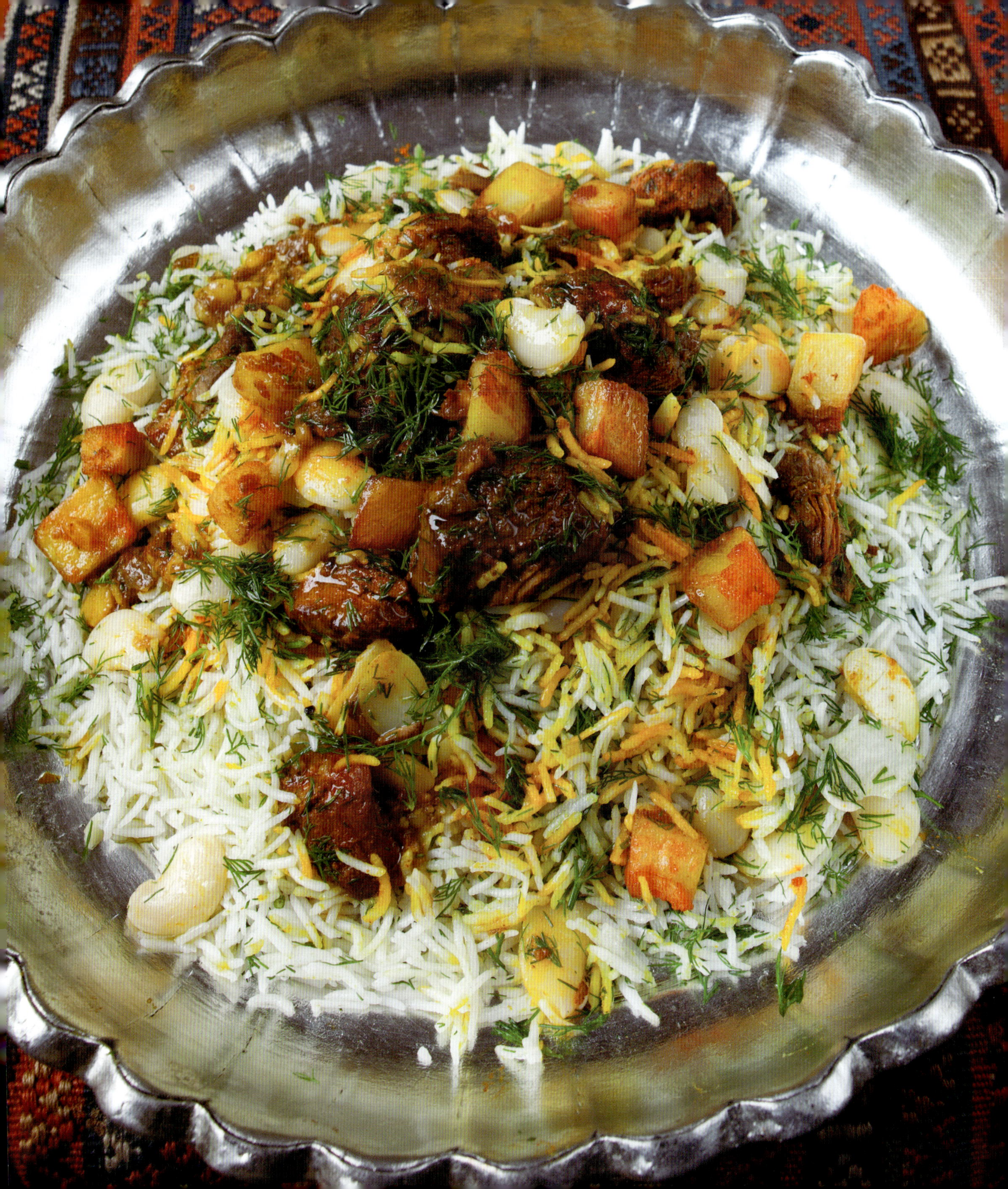

Khorasan

TURKMENISTAN
Caspian Sea
Bojnurd
Golestan
Gorgan
Ramsar
Chalus
Babol
Mazandaran
Mashhad
Damghan
Tehran
Khorasan
Semnan
Qom
Qaen
Kashan
Birjand
Afghanistan
Isfahan
Yazd
Zabol
Rafsanjan

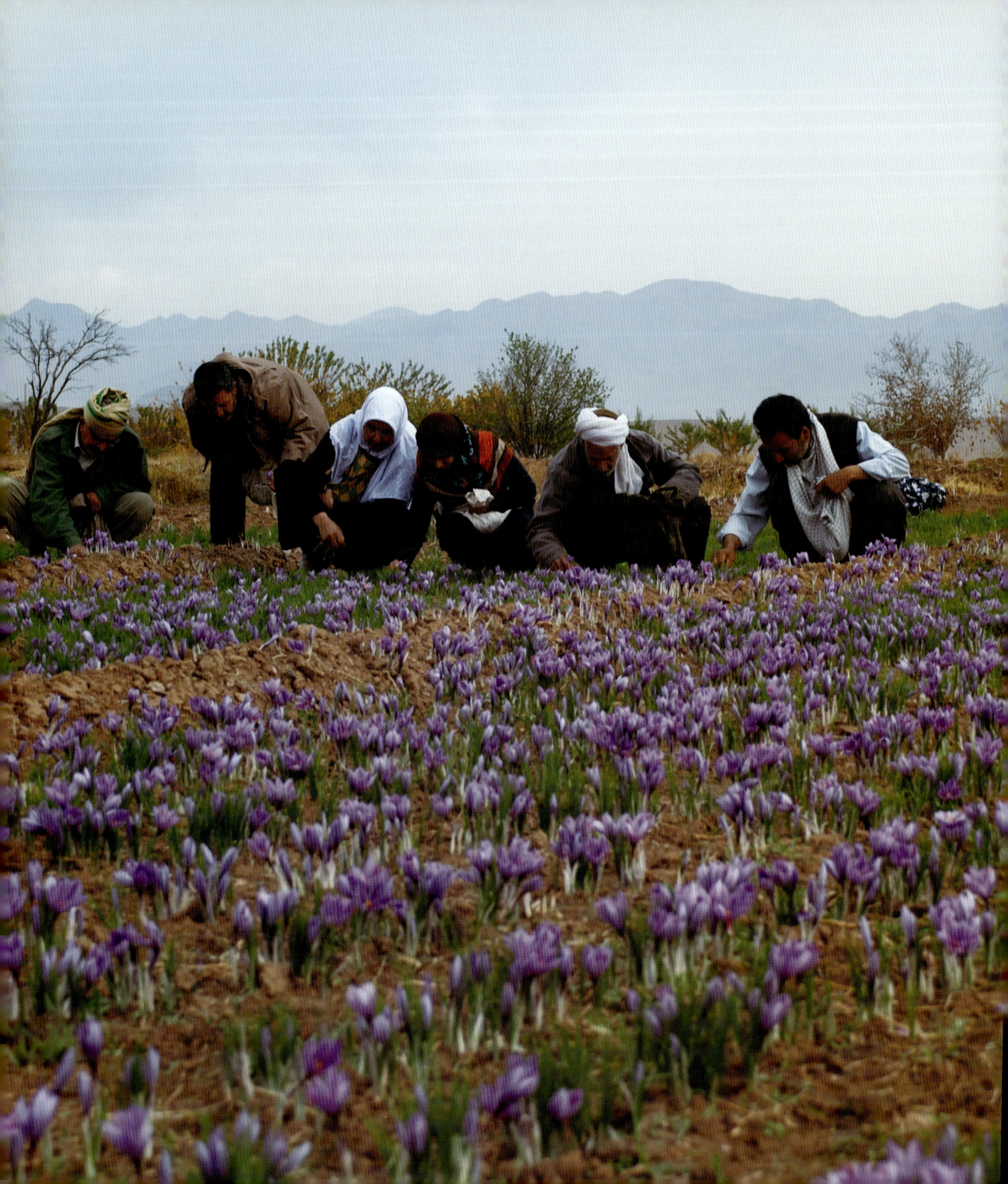

A Little History

In pre-Islamic Persia, Khorasan included all of Afghanistan, Uzbekistan, and Tajikistan, and bordered China. For many centuries, in medieval times, Khorasan was Iran's cultural center par excellence. It is where the great poets such as Ferdowsi and Rumi were born; where the mathematician, astronomer, and poet Omar Khayyam practiced; where scientists like Avicenna/Ibn Sina, Farabi, and Biruni delved into medicine, physics, and geography. Today, its connection to some great poets and musicians remains strong, but it is mostly known as a city where millions of Muslims come as pilgrims to visit the shrine of Imam Reza—a descendant of Prophet Mohammad and the eighth Shiite Imam.

This province's most important city is Mashhad, known for its wonderfully gentle climate in summers and its fruits and vegetables, especially the melon/*shakhteh-ye mashhad*. Mashhad also has some of the tastiest cherries and peaches in the world.

This region is also where most of Iran's saffron and barberry production comes from. It is said that one of the reasons Mashhad's famous Shandiz Restaurant's lamb chops are so delicious is because their sheep are fed the pulp of the saffron flower after the stamens have been plucked.

Villagers picking saffron flowers early in the morning.

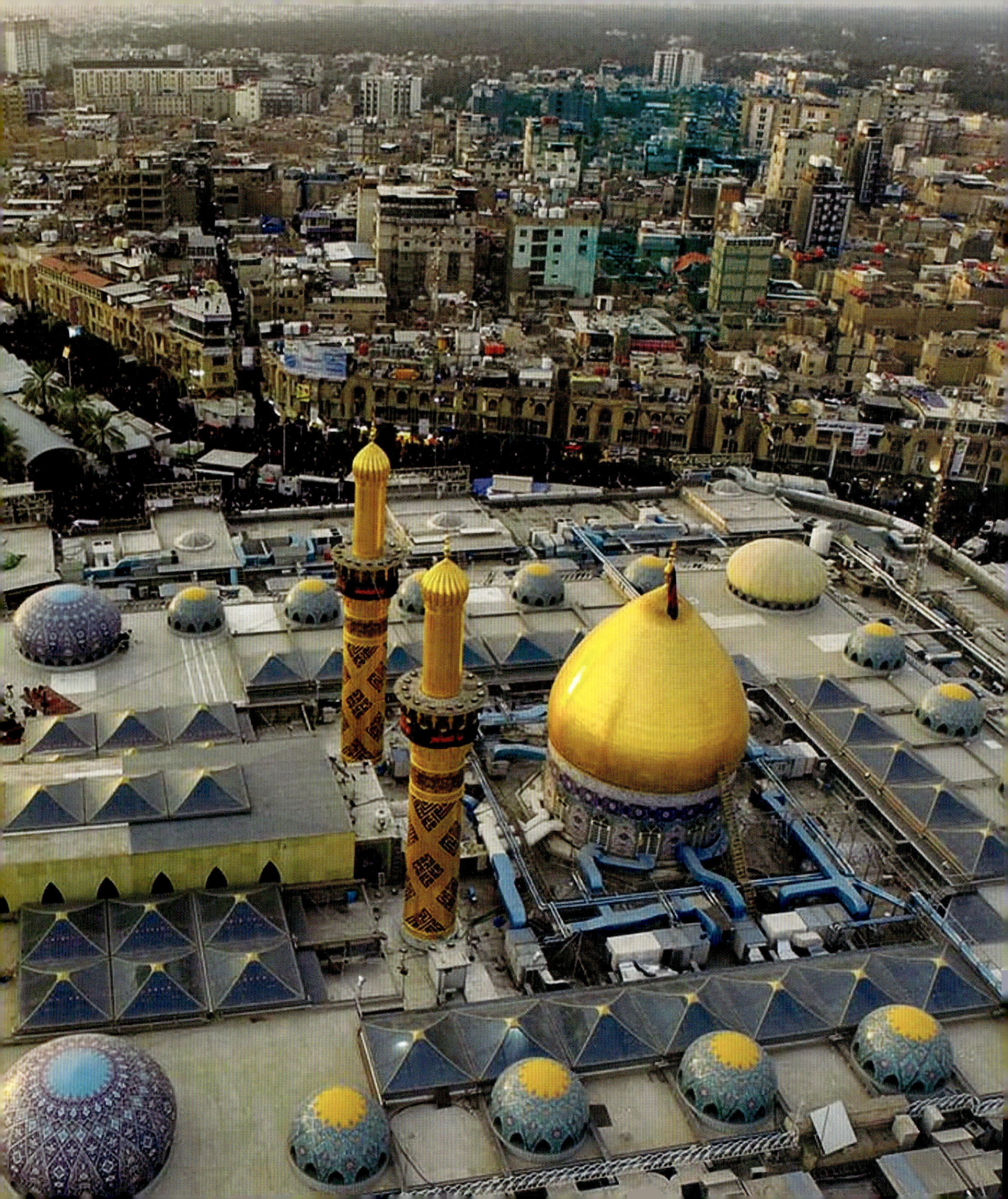

A few hours' drive south of Mashhad, just before reaching the town of Birjand, is a group of villages known collectively as Qaenat, which is the source of much of the world's best saffron. The people of these villages have been engaged in its production for several thousand years—a long time to keep a tradition passing down through families. To see the harvesting, we had to get up with the sunrise, which is when the saffron flower-picking begins. By nine in the morning all the saffron for that day has been picked and the flowers are brought inside. They are left to air for a few hours (they shouldn't be too dry) and then the separation of the stigma from the flowers gets underway. The stigmas/threads are tied together and hung to dry (this is the artisanal way). Saffron is the most expensive spice in the world for a reason: A great deal of dedicated human labor yields only tiny amounts of product. But it's well worth it, because when you know how to use the stigmas of the purple crocus in cooking, it imparts a heavenly color and flavor that's hard to achieve in any other way.

Opposite: Aerial view of Mashhad. Above: Saffron stamens/threads tied into clusters

Khorasani Seven-Spice Advieh

advieh-ye haft qalami-e khorasan

Makes 1 cup/100g
Prep: 15 minutes

2 tablespoons dried ginger
2 tablespoons black pepper corns
2 tablespoons red pepper flakes
Two 4in/10cm cinnamon sticks (broken up to help grinding)
2 tablespoons ground turmeric
3 tablespoons ground sumac berries (optional)
3 tablespoons ground Persian hogweed seeds/*golpar*

I adapted this and several other recipes in this section from Khanum-e Razavi, a great cook from Mashhad. Whole golpar/Persian hogweed seeds, shown on the right in the photo on the facing page, are not available in the U.S., but you can find already ground golpar in Iranian stores, sometimes under the name golpar/angelica. I was surprised by the inclusion of sumac in this mix, but it works very well, especially for soups and meatballs.

1. Grind all the whole spices, each separately, in a spice grinder. Transfer them to a small bowl as you grind them.

2. Add the pre-ground spices and use a spoon to mix well.

3. Transfer to an airtight glass jar and keep in a cool place to use as needed. *Nush-e joon!*

Khorasani Seven-Spice Rice Advieh

advieh-ye haft qalami-e khorasan

Makes 1 cup/100g
Prep: 15 minutes

2 tablespoons ground ginger
2 tablespoons coriander seeds
3 tablespoons cumin
3 tablespoons ground golpar/Persian hogweed
2 tablespoons nigella seeds
2 tablespoons black pepper corns
2 tablespoons ground turmeric

I adapted this spice mix from Behjat Shahverdiani. It's an excellent mix for rice.

1. Grind all the whole spices, each separately, in a spice grinder. Transfer them to a small bowl as you grind them.

2. Add the pre-ground spices and use a spoon to mix well.

3. Transfer to an airtight glass jar and keep in a cool place to use as needed. *Nush-e joon!*

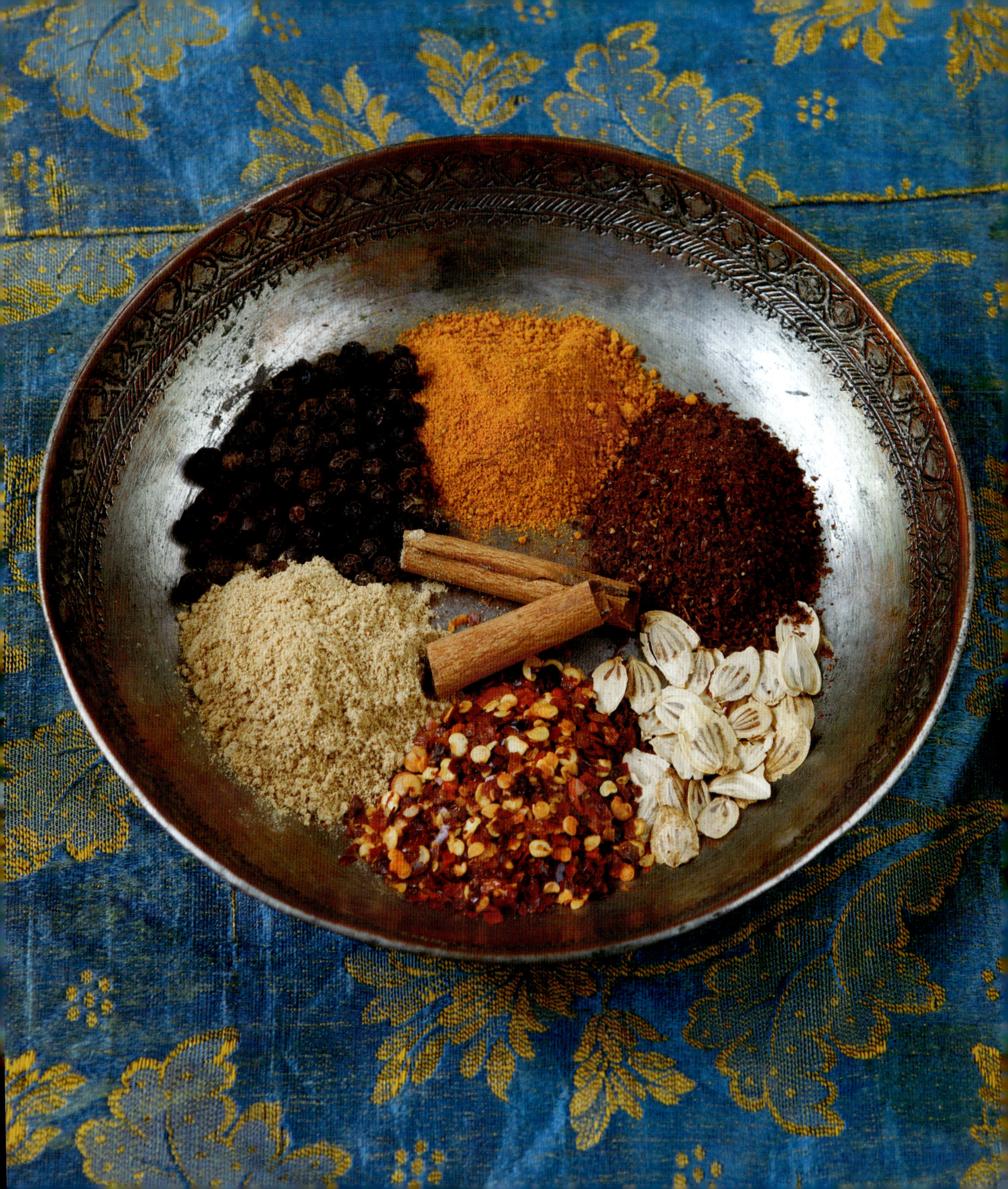

Potato Kuku with Saffron Syrup Glaze
kuku-ye shirin-e mashhadi

Serves 4
Prep: 35 minutes
Cooking: 40 minutes

BATTER

2 medium russet potatoes (2lb/900g)
2 eggs
1 teaspoon baking powder
1 tablespoon potato starch
1 teaspoon fine sea salt

½ cup oil, butter, or ghee

GLAZE

½ cup/100g sugar
½ cup/120ml water
¼ teaspoon ground saffron threads dissolved in 2 tablespoons rose water

1. *To make the batter:* In a medium saucepan, bring 4 cups water to a boil. Score around the middle of the potatoes and add them to the boiling water. Cook for 15 to 20 minutes until potatoes are almost tender. Drain, allow to cool, and peel.

2. Use the large holes of a grater to grate the potatoes.

3. Break the eggs into a mixing bowl. Add the baking powder, potato starch, and salt, and beat thoroughly with a fork.

4. Add the potatoes and use a rubber spatula to fold in until you have a thick batter.

5. *To cook the kuku:* Heat the oil in an 8in/20cm frittata pan over low heat. Pour in the potato mixture and cook for 20 to 30 minutes until golden brown. Flip over and cook for another 15 to 20 minutes until lightly golden

6. *Meanwhile, to make the glaze:* In a small saucepan whisk together all the ingredients for the glaze and bring to a boil. Remove from heat immediately.

7. When the kuku is lightly golden, remove from heat and pour the glaze over it. Cover and allow to cool at room temperature for 5 minutes. *Nush-e joon!*

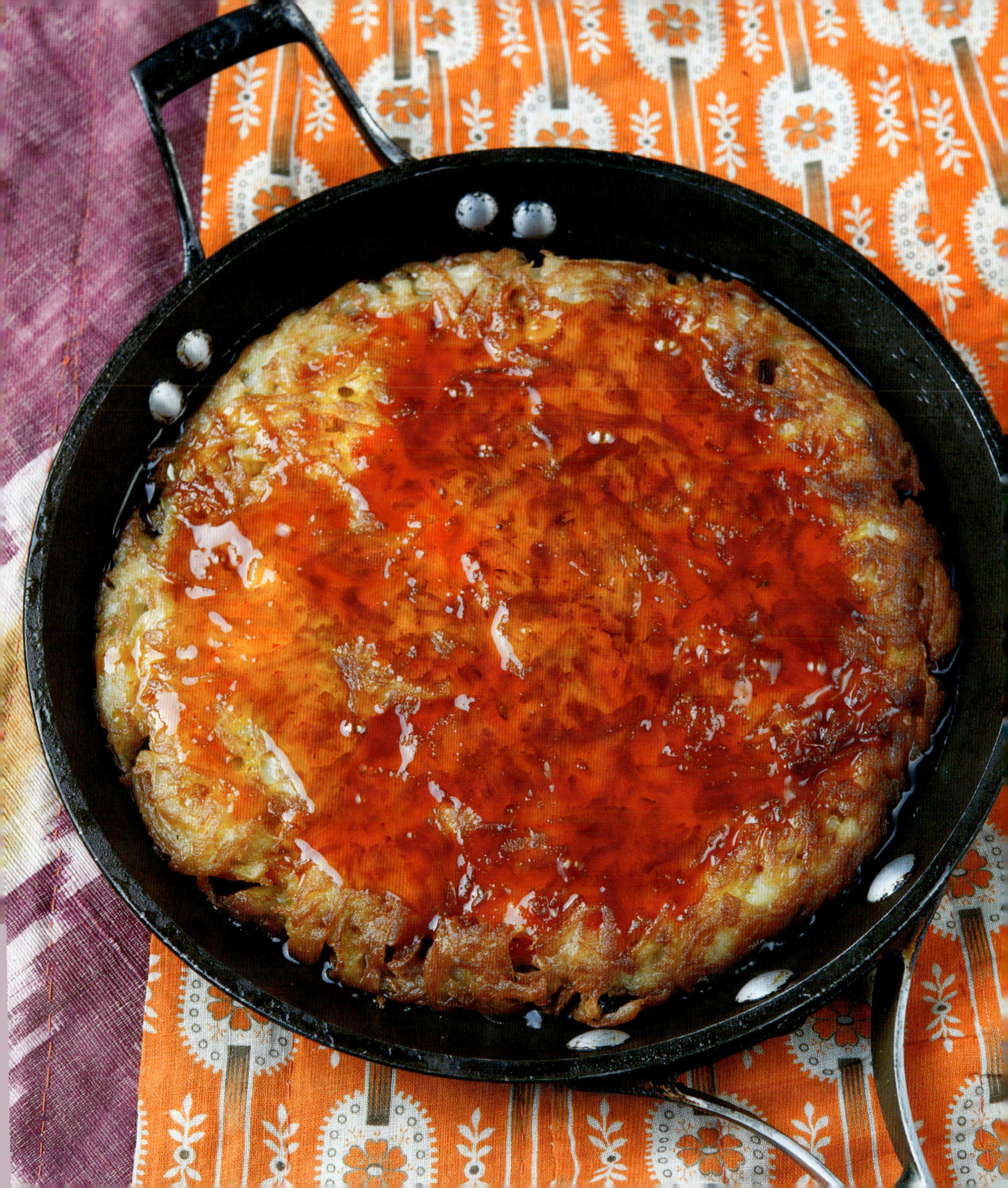

Barberry Osh
osh-e zershk-e khorasani

Serves 6
Prep: 20 minutes + soaking of legumes + rice overnight
Cooking: 1½ hours

LEGUMES + RICE

½ cup/100g chickpeas
½ cup/100g brown lentils
½ cup/100g barley
½ cup/100g rice

BARBERRIES

2 cups/300g barberries, picked over

BROTH

2 tablespoons oil
2 large onions, peeled and thinly sliced
4 teaspoons fine sea salt
1 teaspoon freshly ground black pepper
1 teaspoon turmeric
½ teaspoon red pepper flakes
8 cups/1.9l water or broth

HERBS

2 cups/170g chopped fresh parsley
2 cups/170g chopped fresh spinach
1 cup/85g chopped fresh mint or 2 tablespoons dried
1 cup/85g spring onions, chopped
1 cup/85g chopped fresh cilantro
1 tablespoon Persian hogweed seeds/ *golpar*
1 teaspoon grape molasses or sugar (if the barberries are too sour)

GARNISH NA`NA DAGH

2 tablespoons oil
5 cloves garlic, peeled and grated
½ teaspoon turmeric
2 tablespoons dried mint flakes

I first had this delicious osh during the barberry harvest in Ghaen in Khorasan, but when I was in Shiraz, the cooks I worked with claimed that it originated in their city. This may be so, though barberries are mainly cultivated and harvested in Khorasan.

1. Place the legumes and rice in a large mixing bowl, cover with cold water, and allow to soak overnight. Drain, rinse, and set aside.

2. Soak the barberries in cold water for 20 minutes. Drain in a fine-mesh colander and rinse thoroughly with cold water.

3. *To make the broth:* Heat the oil in a large laminated cast-iron pot over medium heat and sauté the onions until golden brown. Add the salt, pepper, turmeric, red pepper flakes, legumes, and rice, and sauté for 1 minute. Add the water and bring to a boil. Reduce heat to low, cover, and simmer for 45 minutes.

4. Add the barberries, cover, and continue to simmer over low heat for 20 minutes.

5. Add the herbs, *golpar*, and grape molasses. Use a handheld mixer to partially puree the legumes. Cover, and simmer for 15 minutes longer. Adjust seasoning to taste—the *osh* should be sweet and sour.

6. *To make the garnish:* Heat 2 tablespoons oil in a skillet and sauté the garlic until golden. Add the turmeric and stir-fry for 1 minute. Remove from heat. Crumble the dried mint flakes in the palm of your hand and add them to the garlic. Mix well.

7. Pour the *osh* into a tureen and garnish. Just before serving, stir in the garnish. *Nush-e joon!*

Khorasan

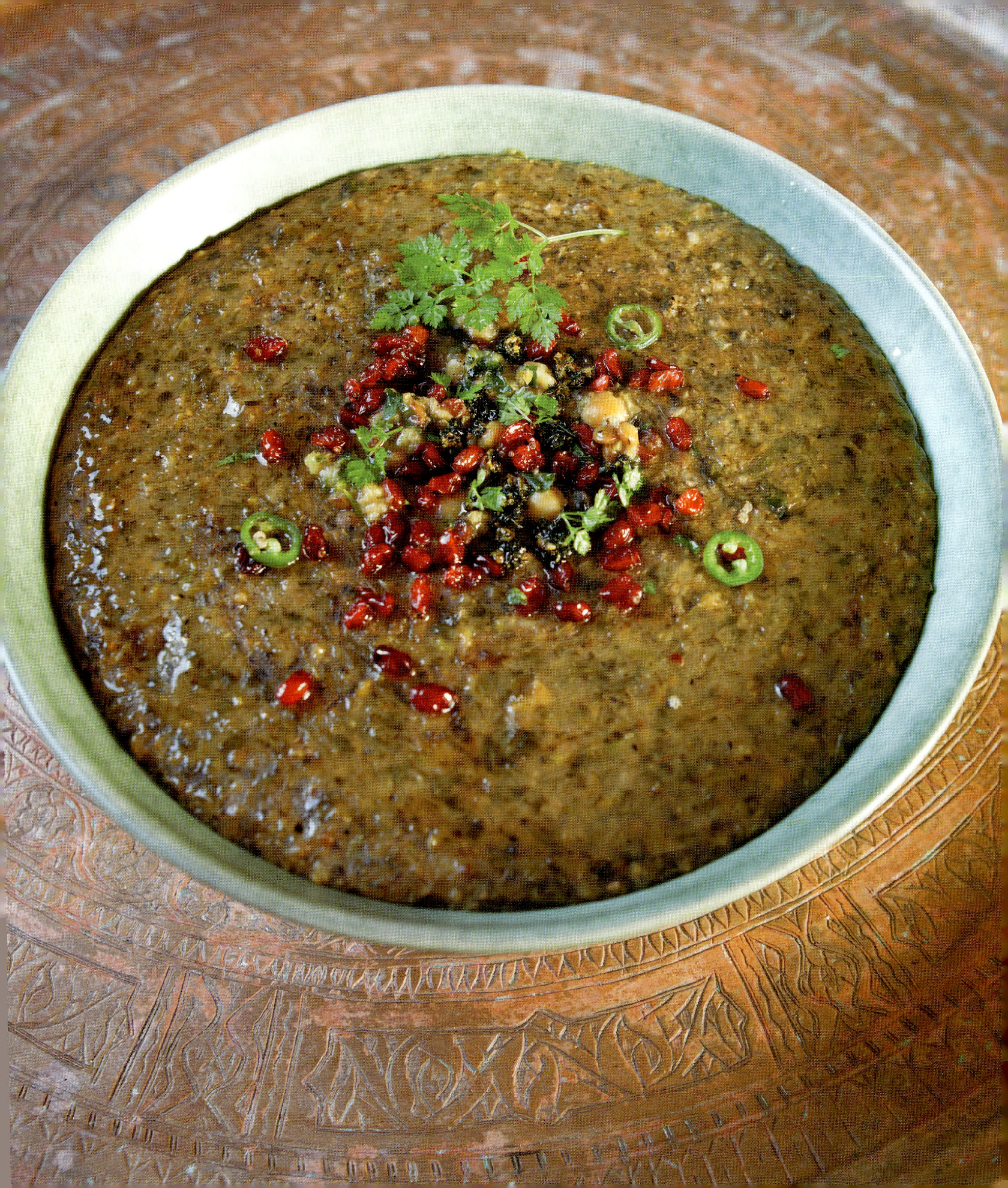

Wild Pistachio + Cucumber Soup
pesteh baneh-ye birjandi

Serves 4 to 6
Prep: 10 minutes plus 4 hours of chilling and soaking
Cooking: 5 minutes

GARNISH

8 pieces dried Persian shallots/*musir*, soaked for 4 hours and drained
5 Persian cucumbers, peeled and cut up
½ cup/50g fresh spring onions, cut up
¼ cup/20g fresh basil leaves
¼ cup/20g fresh mint leaves
¼ cup/20g fresh tarragon leaves

SOUP

1 cup/120g pistachio kernels, picked over and rinsed
½ cup/60g shelled walnuts, picked over and rinsed
2 cloves garlic, peeled
2 teaspoons fine sea salt
½ teaspoon freshly ground pepper
4 cup/960ml water

CROUTONS + RAISINS

8in/20cm flat bread/lavash cut into 1in/2.5cm squares
1 cup/150g golden seedless raisins (optional)

Birjand, in the hills by the desert, used to be a caravan town on the Silk Road. It has kept many of the traditions of Iran's village cuisine (as opposed to those developed in royal courts), which also has much in common with bordering Afghan cuisine. This recipe, adapted from the Sepehri family, is traditionally made as a cold soup with the tiny fruit of the terebinth tree (Pistacia terebinthus), also known as wild pistachios/pesteh baneh. The pistachios are first ground and mixed with water and then passed through a fine-mesh colander. This juice is used and the pistachio solids are discarded. Since it's hard to find these wild pistachios outside their local regions, I have adjusted the recipe to use regular pistachio kernels. Keep in mind that this soup should be served chilled.

1. *To make the garnish:* Place all the ingredients for the garnish in a food processor and pulse until they are finely chopped. Transfer to a glass container. Cover and chill in the fridge.

2. *To make the soup:* Place all the ingredients for the soup, but only 1 cup/240ml of water in a food processor. Mix until you have a smooth sauce. Transfer to a large serving bowl. Add the rest of the water (3 cups/720ml) and stir well. Cover and keep chilled.

3. *To toast the croutons:* Preheat the oven to 400°F/200°C. Line a sheet pan with parchment paper. Spread out the bread pieces on the lined sheet pan and toast in the oven for 5 minutes. Transfer to a serving bowl.

4. Just before serving, add the garnish to the chilled soup in the serving bowl. Stir well and adjust seasoning to taste. Serve with croutons and raisins. *Nush-e joon!*

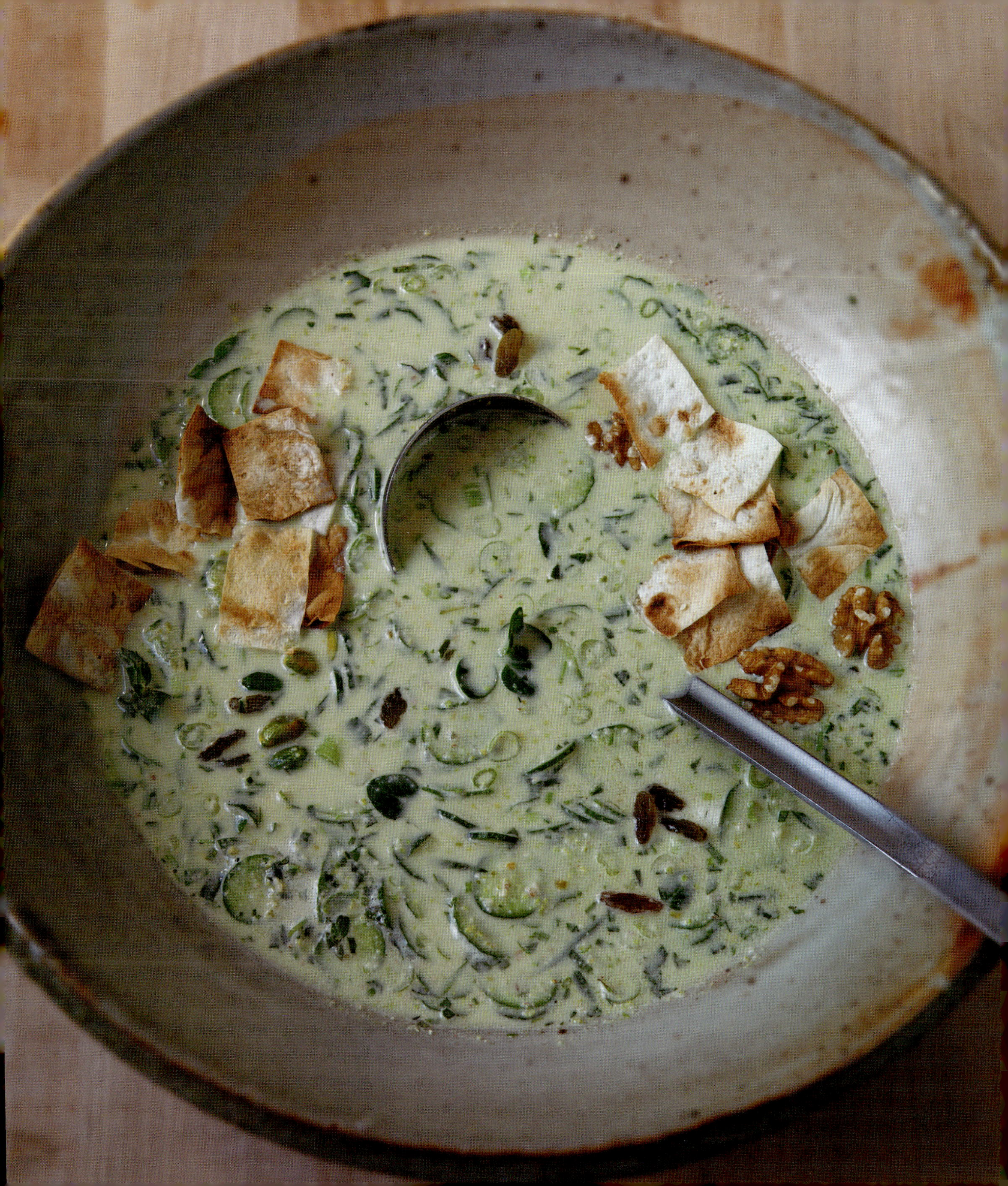

Spinach + Dumpling Osh
osh-e jushvareh-ye sabzevari

Makes 24 dumplings, serves 6 to 8
Prep: 20 minutes
Cooking: 1 hour

DOUGH

1¼ cups/125g unbleached flour
½ teaspoon fine sea salt
½ cup/120ml soda water
1½ teaspoons white vinegar
1½ teaspoons oil

FILLING

½ cup/100g lentils, rinsed
¼ cup/60ml oil
1 medium onion, thinly sliced
1 teaspoon fine sea salt
½ teaspoon freshly ground pepper
1 teaspoon turmeric
½ teaspoon ground coriander
1 teaspoon ground fennel
½ teaspoon ground nutmeg
2 tablespoons fresh parsley leaves
1 cup/110g chopped baby spinach

BROTH

2 tablespoons oil
1 onion, peeled and sliced
½ teaspoon turmeric
6 cups/1.5l water
2 teaspoons fine sea salt
½ teaspoon freshly ground pepper
1 star anise

YOGURT SAUCE

1 cup/240g plain yogurt
2 cloves garlic, peeled and grated
1 tablespoon dried mint
½ teaspoon fine sea salt
½ teaspoon freshly ground pepper
1 teaspoon red pepper flakes

Osh-e jushvareh, also called jush pareh, is a traditional vegetarian dumpling osh. In Sabzevar, they serve this osh for ceremonies such as the Wednesday eve of the new year/shab-e chahar shanbeh suri. I have adapted this recipe from Maryam Yassavoli, who is from Sabzevar and runs a home food cooking school.

1. *To make the dough:* Place the flour and salt in a food processor, and pulse. Gradually add the soda water, vinegar, and oil. Continue to pulse for 5 minutes until you have a soft dough. Transfer to a bowl, cover, and allow to rest at the room temperature, for at least 30 minutes.

2. *To make the filling:* Place the lentils and 3 cups water in a saucepan and bring to a boil. Reduce heat to medium, cover, and cook for 30 to 45 minutes until lentils are tender. Drain and transfer to the food processor.

3. Meanwhile, heat ¼ cup/60ml oil in a wide skillet and sauté the onion until golden brown. Add the spices and herbs and sauté for 2 to 5 minutes until all the juices have been absorbed. Transfer to the food processor and pulse until you have a grainy paste. Transfer to a bowl, cover, and set aside.

4. *To prepare the broth:* Heat the oil in a medium-sized laminated cast-iron pot over medium heat and sauté the onion. Add the turmeric and sauté for 1 minute. Add the water, salt, pepper, and anise, and bring to a boil. Reduce heat to low and simmer for 15 minutes.

5. *To assemble the dumplings:* On a cool, floured surface, knead the dough until soft and pliable. Use a rolling pin to roll it out into a very thin rectangular layer. Cut into twenty-four 3 x 3in/7.5 x 7.5cm squares.

6. Fill each square with 1 tablespoon of the filling. Fold each square from corner to corner into a triangle. Gently press the corners together. Pinch and seal the edges with your fingers. Slip the dumplings into the simmering broth as you make them. Bring back to boil. Reduce heat to low, cover partially, and cook for 20 minutes, stirring gently once or twice to avoid any dumplings sticking to the bottom of the pot.

7. *To make the yogurt sauce:* In a mixing bowl, whisk all the ingredients for the yogurt sauce for 5 minutes to prevent the yogurt from curdling. Transfer it to the pot. Bring back to a boil. Remove from heat and adjust seasoning to taste by adding more salt or pepper. Spoon the *osh* into individual serving bowls. *Nush-e joon!*

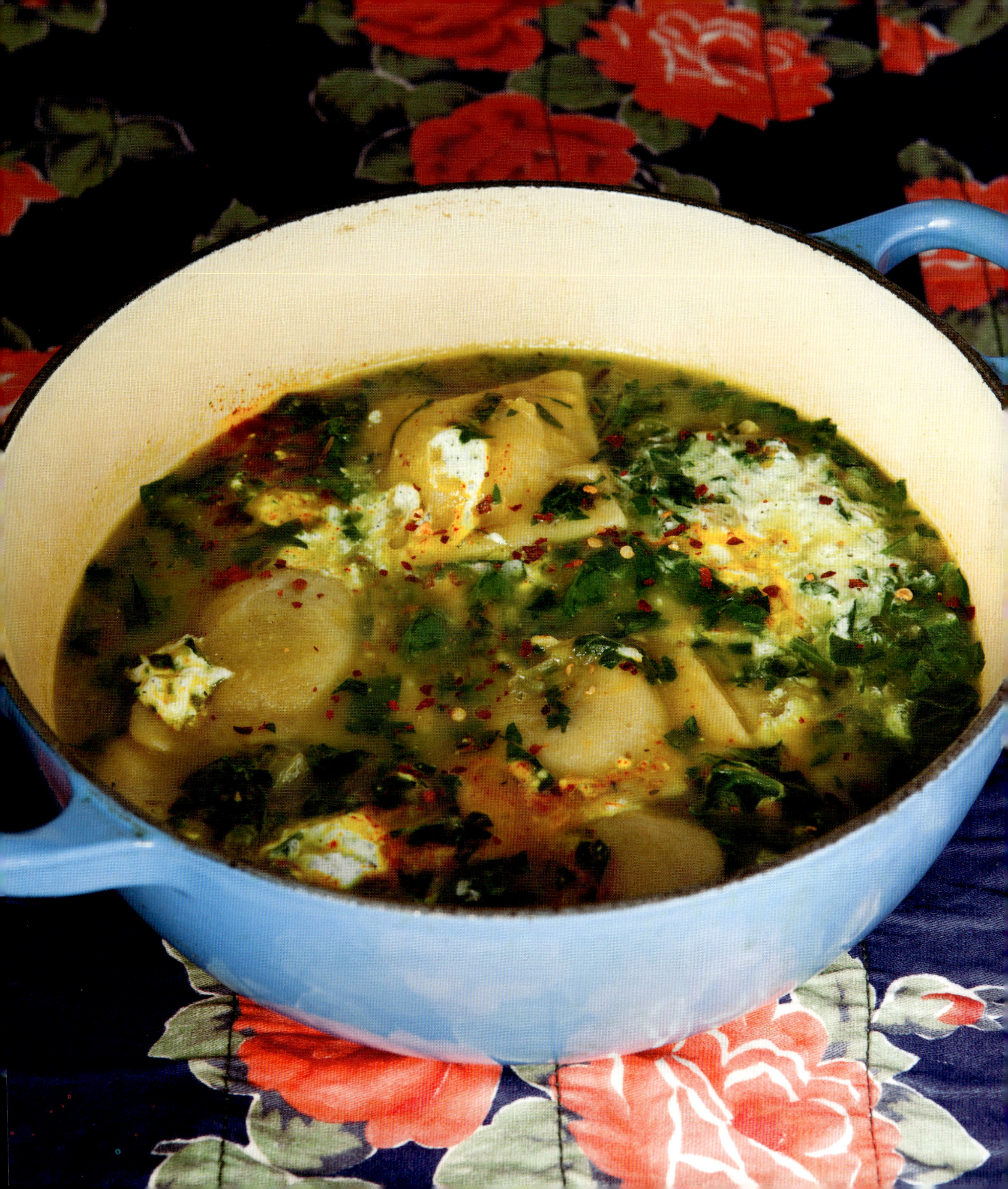

Turnip Osh
osh-e shalqam-e khorasani

Serves 6
Prep: 20 minutes
Cooking: 2 hours

OSH

- ½ cup/120g sheep tail fat or oil
- 4 medium onions, peeled and thinly sliced
- 5 cloves garlic, peeled and crushed
- 1 tablespoon fine sea salt
- 1 teaspoon freshly ground black pepper
- 2 teaspoons turmeric
- 1 teaspoon ground coriander
- 1½ cups/300g mung beans
- ½ cup/100g rice
- 10 cups/2.4l broth or water
- 2lb/900g turnips, peeled and diced

HERBS

- 2 cups/110g chopped fresh spinach
- 1 cup/85g chopped fresh cilantro
- 1 cup/85g chopped fresh tarragon
- 1 cup/85g chopped fresh chives
- 1 cup/240g liquid *kashk* or verjuice (optional)

GARNISH/NA`NA DAGH

- 2 tablespoons sheep tail fat or oil
- 5 cloves garlic, peeled and grated
- 1 teaspoon turmeric
- 2 tablespoons dried mint flakes

Elamite tablets from Khuzestan 3,500 years ago include a recipe for turnip soup. But these days in Iran, turnip osh is attributed to Mashhad, the city of pilgrimages, shrines, and beautiful gardens. It is thought that this combination of turnips and mung beans does wonders in curing a cold. I am holding a bowl of this osh in the photo taken in Mashhad.

1. **To make the osh:** Heat the tail fat in a large heavy pot over medium heat and brown the onions and garlic. Add the salt, pepper, turmeric, mung beans, and rice, and stir-fry for 1 minute. Pour in the broth and bring to a boil. Reduce heat to medium-low, cover, and simmer for 20 minutes, stirring from time to time.

2. Add the turnips, cover, and simmer over low heat for another 55 minutes, stirring occasionally.

3. **To prepare the garnish:** Heat 2 tablespoons sheep tail fat in a medium-sized skillet over medium heat. Add the garlic and sauté until golden brown. Add the turmeric, give it a stir, and remove from heat. Crumble the dried mint flakes in the palm of your hand and add it to the skillet. Stir well and set aside.

4. Check to see if beans and vegetables are done. Add the spinach, cilantro, tarragon, chives, and *kashk*. Use a handheld mixer to partially puree the *osh*. Simmer, over low heat, for 15 minutes. Adjust seasoning to taste. Keep warm until ready to serve.

5. Pour the *osh* into a tureen. Decorate the surface with the garnish. Stir in the garnish just before ladling *osh* into individual bowls. *Nush-e joon!*

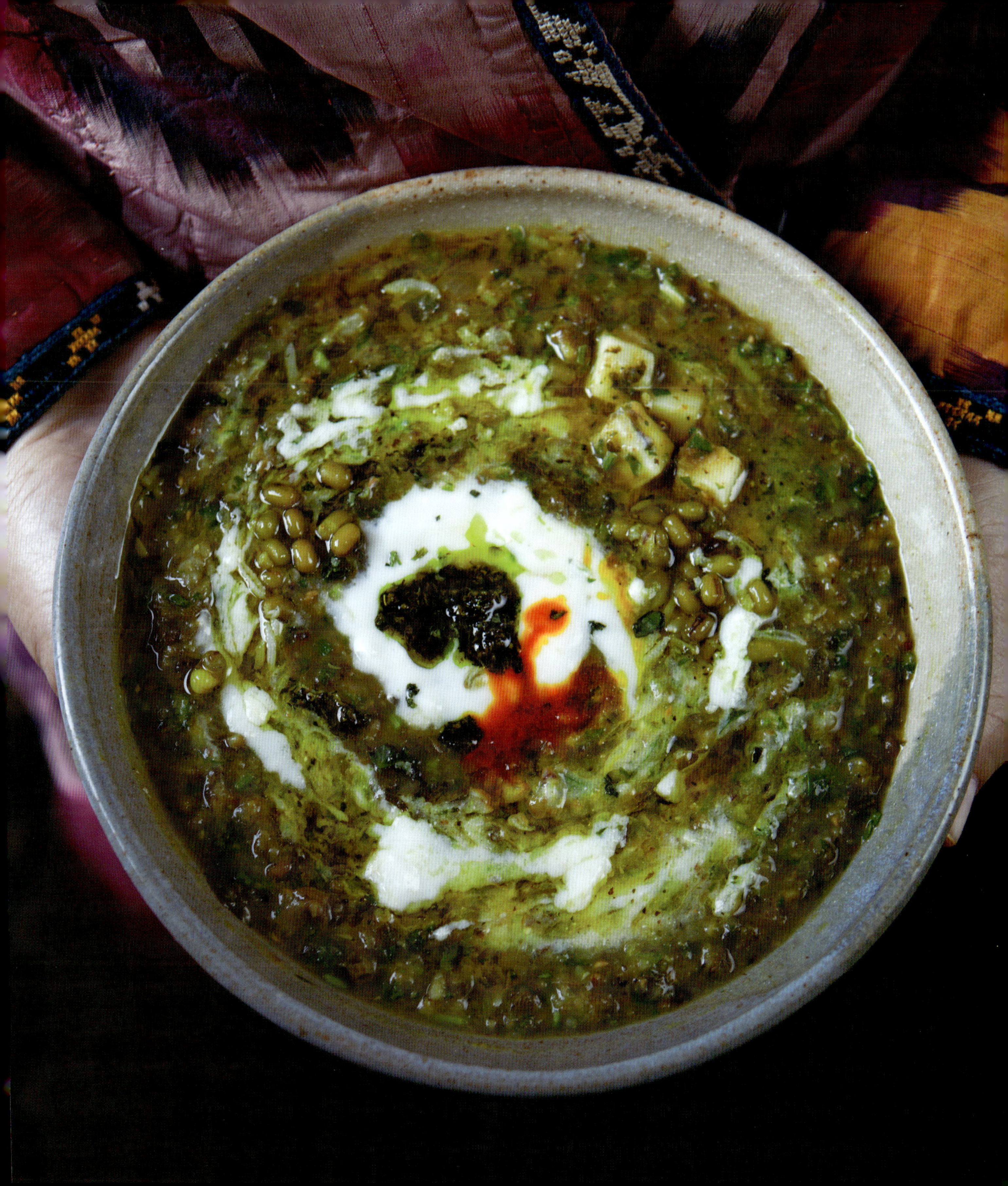

Walnut + Kashk Soup
kaleh jush-e khorasan

Serves 4
Prep: 15 minutes
Cooking: 35 minutes

CROUTONS
1 flat bread

SOUP
2 cups/240g walnuts
1 tablespoon fennel seeds
2 tablespoons oil
2 large onions, peeled and thinly sliced
1 tablespoon flour
2 teaspoons fine sea salt
½ teaspoon freshly ground pepper
1 teaspoon ground turmeric
1 teaspoon ground anise seeds
3 cups/720ml water
2 cups/480g liquid *kashk*

GARNISH
2 tablespoons oil
¼ teaspoon turmeric
2 tablespoons dried mint flakes

In Persian, kaleh jush literally means "at the boiling point." That may be because once the kashk is added, the soup should not boil. It is made in many parts of Iran with various names. When I cooked it in Kerman, we used pistachios instead of walnuts.

1. *To make the croutons:* Preheat oven to 400F°/200°C. Cut the flat bread into ½in/1cm squares. Spread evenly on a sheet pan lined with parchment paper and toasted in the oven for 5 minutes until crispy. Transfer to a serving bowl and set aside.

2. Place the walnuts and fennel seeds in a food processor and pulse until coarsely chopped.

3. *To make the soup:* Heat the oil in a medium-sized laminated cast-iron pot over medium heat. Add the onions and sauté for 5 to 10 minutes until the onions are golden brown.

4. Add the walnut and fennel mixture and stir-fry for 2 minutes (be careful, as the walnuts will burn quickly). Add the flour, salt, pepper, turmeric, and ground anise, and stir for 1 minute.

5. Add the water and bring to a boil. Reduce heat to low and simmer for 10 minutes.

6. Add the *kashk* and stir for 5 to 10 minutes over low heat. As soon as it begins to boil, immediately remove from heat. Adjust seasoning to taste.

7. *To prepare the garnish:* Heat 2 tablespoons oil in a skillet over medium heat, add the turmeric, and sauté for 1 minute. Remove from heat and add the mint flakes. Stir well.

8. Pour the soup into individual serving bowls and garnish. Place a bowl of the croutons on the side for everyone to add croutons to the soup as they please. *Nush-e joon!*

VARIATION
Yogurt Walnut + Tomato Soup
kaleh jush-e sabzevari/komeh jush ba gojefarangi

In step 5, reduce the water to 1 cup/240ml and add 3 cups/720ml fresh tomato puree. In a mixing bowl, whisk together 2 cups/480g plain yogurt, 2 tablespoons *kashk*, and 2 eggs for 5 minutes (to prevent from curdling). In step 6, slowly stir it into the broth using a wooden spoon. Keep stirring and bring it back to a boil. Remove from heat. Adjust seasoning and continue with step 7.

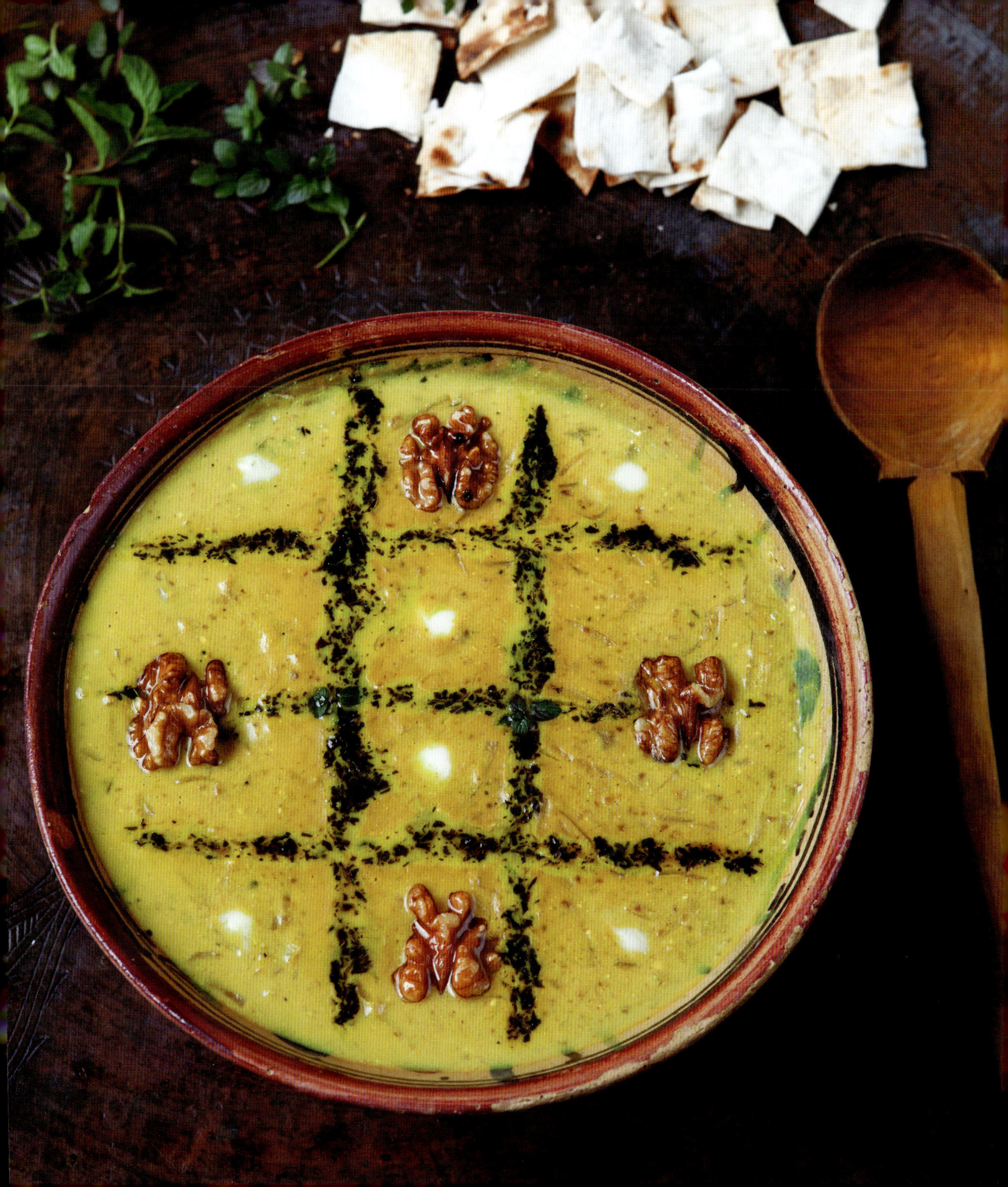

Lamb Neck, Bulgur + Bean Porridge
sholeh-ye mashhadi

Serves 8 to 10
Prep: 15 minutes + soaking of legumes overnight
Cooking: 4½ hours

SOAKING LEGUMES

Place all the legumes in a large container and soak overnight. Drain and rinse.
¼ cup/50g mung beans
¼ cup/50g chickpeas
¼ cup/50g pinto beans
¼ cup/50g white/navy beans

BROTH

2lb/900g lamb necks (available at good butchers or at Middle Eastern markets)
8 cups/1.9l water

BULGUR + RICE

½ cup/100g rice, washed and drained
1 cup/180g bulgur

ONION + SPICES

1 cup/240g lamb tail fat
4 medium onions, peeled and thinly sliced
1 tablespoon fine sea salt
1 teaspoon freshly ground black pepper
1 teaspoon turmeric
1 tablespoon ground cardamom
1 tablespoon ginger powder
1 tablespoon ground nutmeg

Sholeh falls somewhere between a porridge and a thick soup. It's a specialty of Mashhad and a favorite in the region. This unique-tasting brothy, meaty dish is full of umami. And although it takes a long time to cook, it's well worth trying. I adapted this recipe from Sedigheh Shams, given to me by her daughter Fatemeh, one of Iran's wonderful contemporary poets.

1. *To cook the legumes:* Place the legumes in a medium-sized saucepan, add 6 cups/1.5l water and bring to a boil. Reduce heat to low, cover, and simmer until the legumes are tender (about 1 hour). Remove from heat and set aside.

2. *Meanwhile, to make the broth:* Place the lamb necks in a large laminated cast-iron pot, add 8 cups/1.9l water and bring to a boil. Skim off any froth as it forms until the frothing stops. Reduce heat to low, cover, and simmer for 2 hours or until the meat is tender and falling off the bone (add more warm water if necessary). Stir occasionally to prevent any sticking to the bottom of the pot.

3. Drain the contents of the pot through a fine-mesh sieve into a large bowl. Pour the strained stock back into the pot. Separate the meat from the bones and return the meat to the pot. Discard the bones and anything else left in the sieve.

4. Add the cooked legumes, rice, and bulgur to the pot. Give it a stir, cover, and simmer over low heat for 30 minutes.

5. In a wide skillet, heat the tail fat over medium-low heat and sauté the onions until golden brown. Add the spices and sauté for 1 minute. Transfer the onion mixture to the pot. Cover and cook over low heat for another 30 minutes.

6. Use a handheld mixer to puree the meat and legumes in the pot (a few minutes) until you have a homogenized mixture. Cover tightly and simmer over low heat for 30 minutes, stirring occasionally. Adjust seasoning to taste. Spoon the porridge into individual serving bowls and serve with fresh herbs on the side. *Nush-e joon!*

Khorasan

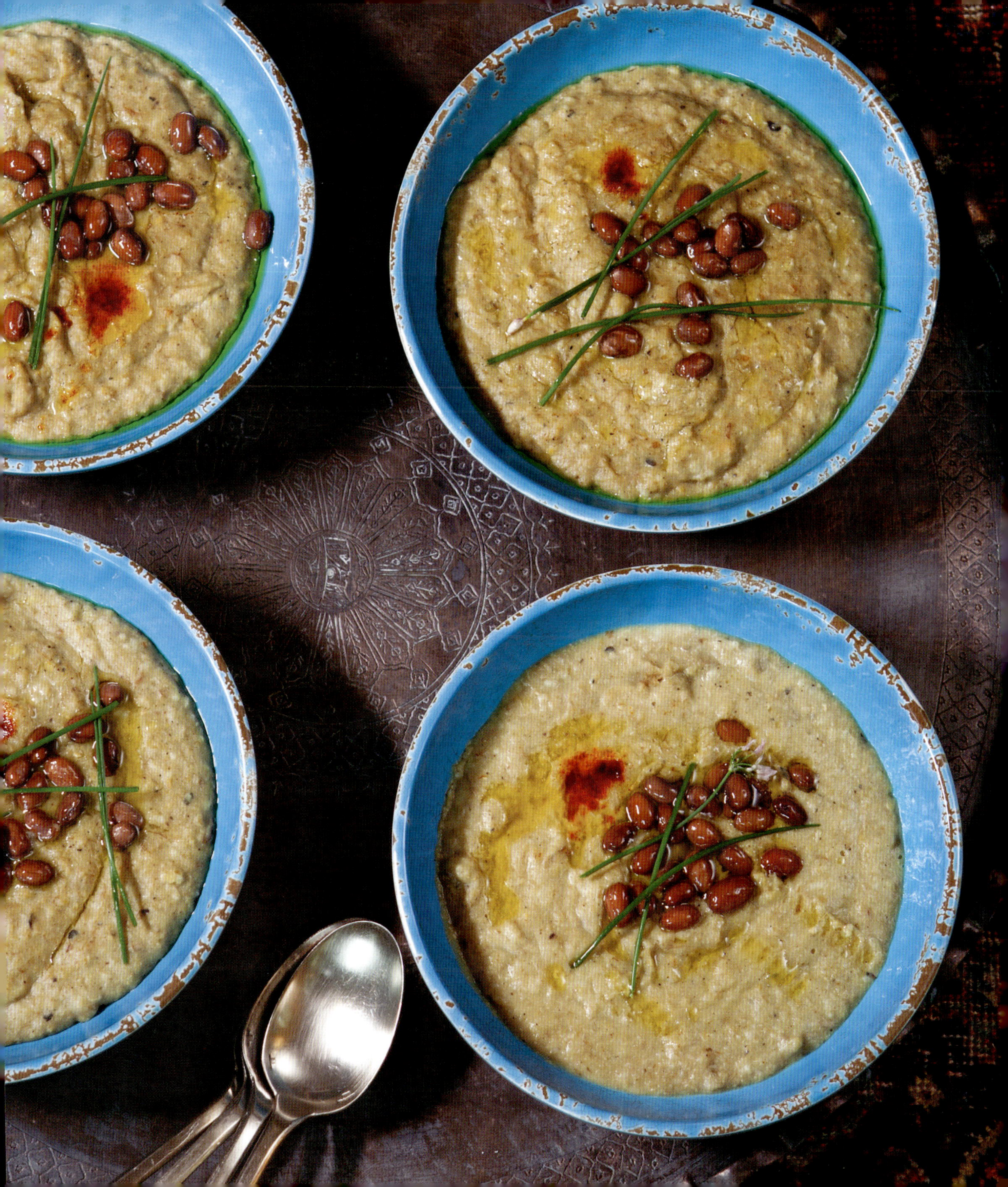

Roasted Vegetables with Garlic Kashk
quruti-e birjand

Serves 2 to 4
Prep: 10 minutes
Cooking: 20 minutes

CROUTONS

2 small pitas or 1 *lavash* cut into 1in/2.5cm squares

VEGETABLES

1 onion, quartered
1 zucchini, sliced into 1in/2.5cm rounds
2 chinese eggplants, peeled and sliced into 1in/2.5cm rounds
1lb/450g butternut squash, peeled and diced into 1in/2.5cm cubes
½ teaspoon fine sea salt
½ teaspoon freshly ground pepper
2 tablespoons oil

SPINACH

2 tablespoons oil
1 onion, peeled and sliced
½lb/225g baby spinach leaves

KASHK SAUCE

2 tablespoons oil
5 cloves garlic, peeled and sliced
½ cup/40g ground walnuts
½ teaspoon salt
1 teaspoon freshly ground pepper
½ teaspoon turmeric
1 tablespoon dried mint
1 cup/240g liquid *kashk* dissolved in 1 cup water

GARNISH

1 cup/85g fresh mint leaves

I adapted this recipe from the Sepehri family in Birjand. It's simply a combination of roasted vegetables and sautéed spinach with a very tasty garlic and kashk sauce. The kashk, which is a tangy and nutritious by-product of drained yogurt, adds a magical flavor to the vegetables.

1. Preheat oven 400F°/200°C. Line 2 sheet pans with parchment paper.

2. *To toast the croutons:* Spread the bread on one of the lined sheet pans and toast in the oven for 5 minutes. Remove from the oven and transfer to a small serving bowl.

3. *To roast the vegetables:* Place the onion, zucchini, eggplant, and butternut squash on the lined sheet pan. Sprinkle on top with ½ teaspoon salt, ½ teaspoon pepper, and 2 tablespoons oil. Toss well with your hand and spread evenly. Roast for 20 to 25 minutes until the vegetables are roasted.

4. *To cook the spinach:* Heat the oil in a medium-sized braiser over medium heat until hot, and sauté the onion until golden brown. Add the spinach and sauté for 5 to 10 minutes until the juices have been absorbed. Remove from braiser and set aside.

5. *To make the kashk sauce:* Heat the oil in the same braiser over medium heat until hot and sauté the garlic until golden brown. Add the walnuts, salt, pepper, turmeric, and mint and stir-fry for 1 minute. Add the diluted *kashk*, bring to a boil, reduce heat to low, and cook, stirring frequently for 1 minute (you want everything blended). Adjust seasoning to taste.

6. Arrange the roasted vegetables in the braiser with the spinach and garlic sauce. Garnish with croutons and fresh mint. *Nush-e joon!*

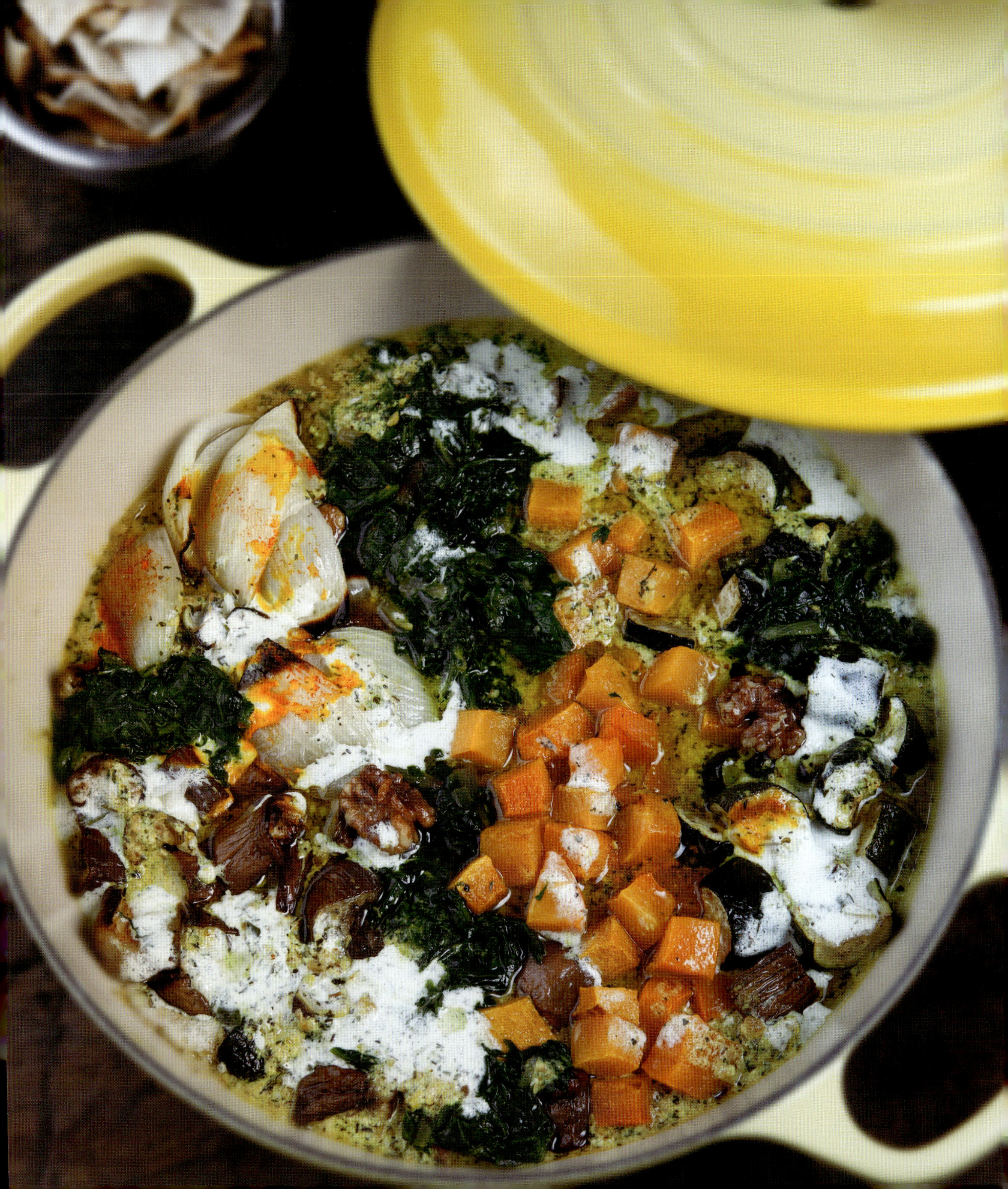

Twice-Cooked Lamb in Tail-Fat with Fried Bread
Bojnordi qormeh ba nan-e roghani

Serves 6
Prep: 20 minutes
Cooking: 30 minutes

2lb/900g leg of lamb, thinly sliced in 1 x 2in/2.5 x 5cm strips
¾ cup/180ml water
One 6in/15cm lamb leg bone (optional)
½ cup/120ml sheep tail fat (available at Iranian or halal butchers) or ghee
2 teaspoons fine sea salt
½ *taftun* bread or 2 small pitas cut into 2in/5cm wedges

GARNISH

1 cup/85g fresh mint leaves
1 cup/85g fresh basil leaves

Qormeh is traditionally made with sheep tail fat, rendered in large quantities during the cold winters of northern Khorasan and wrapped and hung from the ceiling of the coldest room in the house. It is refried and used as needed. School kids of this region also often take some of it to school with them as a snack or for lunch. I adapted this recipe from my friend Saeed Jahed's granda, Farah Banu Mozafar, in Bojnurd

1. In a deep, wide skillet, place the lamb strips, ¾ cup/180ml water and the lamb bone. Cook uncovered over medium heat for 20 to 25 until all the juices have been absorbed. Use tongs and turn around each piece of lamb until it's cooked.

2. Add the sheep tail fat and salt, and sauté over medium heat for 4 to 5 minutes until lamb is seared and brown on all sides.

3. Add the bread to the skillet and stir-fry, for 1 to 2 minutes until the bread is crispy.

4. Use tongs to first transfer the bread to a serving platter, then arrange the lamb on top. Garnish with basil and mint. *Nush-e joon!*

A nineteenth-century lithograph from Jane Dieulafoy's *La Perse, la Chaldée, et la Susiane*, showing the very large fat-tailed sheep of northeastern Iran. In 1684 German doctor and astute observer Engelbert Kaempfer, who spent some years in Iran, wrote:

> "These sheep are as much as three feet taller than other sheep and closer to the size of a small donkey. They are different from our sheep [in Europe], because of a very large piece of fat to which adheres a kind of tail, hanging from their rump. The fat is so heavy that sometimes it breaks off by itself. You will not believe me, though it is the truth, if I say that sometimes this mass of fat weighs 40 pounds. This sheep's meat is superior to that of all other animals'; and its tail fat is by far the tastiest; it replaces butter because of its agreeable taste for cooking rice and all kinds of dishes, and it is much better. This sheep is also covered with a particularly noteworthy fleece, which distinguishes itself above all by the fineness of its hair and is beautiful curls."

In the U.S., you can find fat-tailed karakul sheep at Checkmate Farms in Bluemont, Virginia.

Rice with Legumes + Butternut Squash
qaboli polow-ye bojnurdi

Serves 6 to 8
Prep: 10 minutes + soaking of legumes overnight
Cooking: 1¾ hours

LEGUMES

½ cup/100g black-eyed peas
¼ cup/50g chickpeas
½ cup/50g brown lentils

LAMB

½ cup/120ml oil
2 medium onions, thinly sliced
½lb/225g leg of lamb cut into 1in/2.5cm cubes (optional)
4 teaspoons fine sea salt
1 teaspoon freshly ground pepper
1 teaspoon turmeric
1 teaspoon ground nutmeg
1 teaspoon cinnamon
3 tablespoons tomato paste
4 cups/960ml water

RICE

2 cups/400g basmati rice, washed and drained
1 cup/175g dates, pitted (about 10 dates)
1lb/450g butternut squash, peeled and cut into 1in/2.5cm cubes (about 3 cups)

I adapted this recipe from Farah Banu Mozafar in Bojnurd. You can eliminate the meat in step 1 to produce a perfectly delicious vegetarian dish.

1. **To prepare the legumes:** Soak the legumes in a large bowl of water overnight. Drain, rinse, and set aside.

2. **To cook the lamb:** Heat the oil in a large non-stick pot over medium heat and sauté the onions and lamb until golden brown. Add the salt, pepper, turmeric, nutmeg, cinnamon, tomato paste, and legumes. Sauté for 1 minute longer.

3. Add 4 cups/960ml water and bring to boil. Reduce heat to medium-low, cover, and cook for 1 hour or until the lamb and legumes are almost tender.

4. Add the rice to the pot. Give it a gentle stir and bring to a boil. Add the dates and squash (do not stir). Reduce heat to low, cover tightly, and cook for 30 to 35 minutes until the rice and squash are cooked and all the liquid has been absorbed.

5. Gently transfer the rice to a serving platter and serve with fresh green herbs on the side. *Nush-e joon!*

Khorasan

VEGETARIAN

1900s photo of a men's lunch gathering.

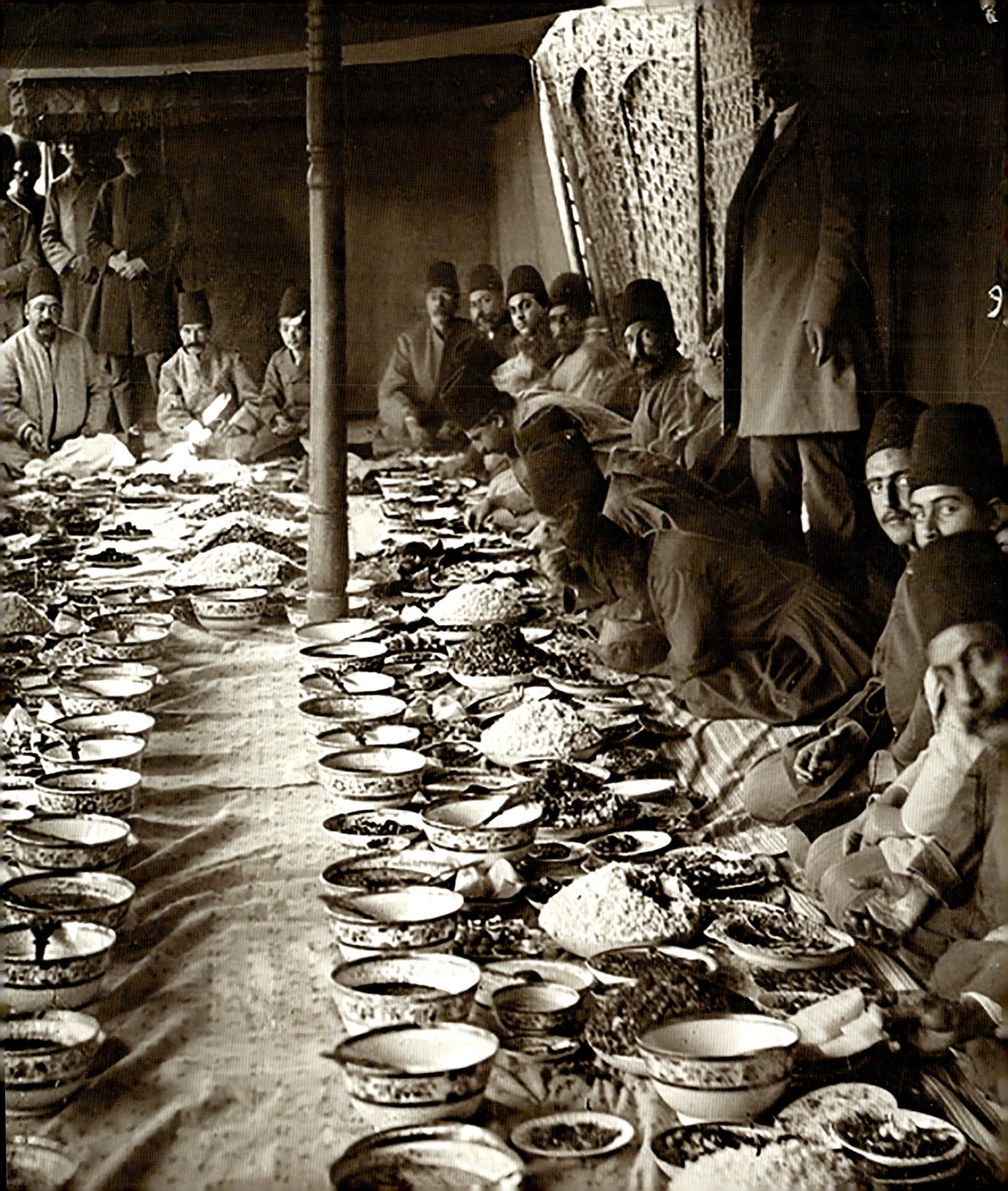

A barberry tree full of ripe berries.

Barberries

Saffron fields and barberry groves/*zereshkestan* are often right next to each other and they are both harvested around the same time in October.

Barberry bushes are thorny and produce a tart red fruit high in malic and citric acids. The berries are usually too sour to be eaten raw, although as children we often enjoyed dried barberries as a snack. In medieval Europe, barberries were pickled or made into syrups, jam, or wine. But by 1918, it was discovered that the barberry bush harbored the spores of a wheat blight (stem rust), and a barberry bush eradication program began. Since then, commercial planting has been prohibited in the West.

These days, barberries are mostly produced in Iran, where they continue to be used distinctively in cooking to impart a tart flavor to soups, braises, chicken, and rice dishes/*zereshk polow*, for example. Fresh barberry juice is also often sold by street vendors in Iran and is thought to lower blood pressure and cleanse the system. In a small farm in Qaen, we were lucky to be treated to some fresh-picked barberry juice—you've tasted nothing like it—sour but delicious. Iranians also make tasty roll-ups and preserves from barberries.

Dried barberries are available from Iranian markets in the U.S., but be sure to choose red ones. Dark brown colored berries may be those leftover from earlier seasons.

Barberry Rice
zereshk polow-ye khorasani

Serves 6
Prep: 15 minutes
Cooking: 1½ hours

CHICKEN

- 2 young chickens, cut up (about 3 to 4 lb/1.8kg) or 2lb/900g boneless, skinless chicken thighs
- 2 teaspoons fine sea salt
- 1 teaspoon freshly ground black pepper
- 1 teaspoon turmeric
- ¼ cup/60ml lime juice
- 2 medium onions, peeled and thinly sliced
- 2 cloves garlic, peeled
- ½ teaspoon ground saffron dissolved in 2 tablespoons rose water

RICE

- 3 cups/600g long-grain basmati rice
- 1 cup/240ml oil or ghee
- 2 tablespoons yogurt
- 3 tablespoons cumin seeds, toasted
- ¼ cup/30g slivered, blanched almonds
- ¼ cup/30g slivered pistachio kernels

BARBERRIES

- 2 tablespoons oil or ghee
- 2 cups/300g dried barberries/zereshk, cleaned, washed, and drained
- ½ cup/100g sugar
- ¼ cup/60ml water
- 1 teaspoon ground saffron dissolved in 2 tablespoons rose water

NOTE

Clean the barberries by removing their stems and placing the berries in a sieve. Place the sieve in a large container full of cold water and allow barberries to soak for 20 minutes. The sand will settle to the bottom. Take the sieve out of the container and run cold water over the barberries. Drain and set aside.

I had this rice during the barberry harvest in late October in a village in Qaenat. Just-picked barberries make this dish divine. When using dried barberries, be sure to look for red ones rather than brown ones, which usually means they are leftover from the previous year's harvest.

1. *To cook the chicken:* In a medium pot, place the chicken and the rest of the ingredients. Cover tightly and cook over low heat for about 1½ hours. Adjust seasoning, debone, cover, and set aside.

2. *To cook the rice:* Wash the rice by placing it in a large container and covering it with water. Agitate gently with your hand and pour off the water. Repeat 4 to 5 times until the water is clear. Bring 8 cups/1.9l water and 2 tablespoons fine sea salt to a boil in a large non-stick pot. Add the rice and boil briskly for 6 to 10 minutes, gently stirring twice to loosen any grains that may have stuck together or to the bottom of the pot. When the rice feels soft, bite a few grains to be sure, and all of it has risen to the top, it is ready to be drained. Drain the rice in a large fine-mesh colander and rinse with 2 to 3 cups cold water.

3. *For the golden crust/tah-dig:* In a mixing bowl, whisk together ½ cup oil, ¼ cup water, yogurt, a few drops of saffron-rose water, and 3 spatulas of rice. Spread the mixture evenly over the bottom of the pot.

4. Place 1 spatula full of rice in the pot, then sprinkle the cumin over the rice. Repeat these steps, arranging the rice in the shape of a pyramid. This shape allows room for the rice to expand and enlarge. Cover and cook for 10 minutes over medium-high heat.

5. Mix the remaining oil with ½ cup/120ml water and pour over the pyramid. Pour the remaining saffron-rose water over the rice. Add the slivered almonds and pistachios on top. Wrap the lid of the pot with a clean dish towel and cover firmly to prevent steam from escaping. Cook for 70 minutes longer over low heat.

6. *To cook the barberries:* In a wide skillet combine the oil, barberries, sugar, water, and 2 tablespoons saffron-rose water, and stir-fry, over medium-high heat for 5 minutes (beware that barberries burn very easily). Set aside.

7. Remove the rice from heat and allow to cool, covered, for 5 minutes on a damp surface to free the crust from the bottom of the pot.

8. *To assemble the rice:* Gently take 1 spatula full of rice at a time and place it on a serving platter in alternating layers with the barberry mixture. Arrange the chicken around the platter. Detach the crust and serve on the side. *Nush-e joon!*

A cluster of barberries.

420

Barberry Preserve
moraba-ye zereshk

Makes ½pt/240g
Prep: 30 minutes plus drying the barberries overnight
Cooking: 50 minutes

1½ cups/225g dried barberries
1 cup/240ml water
1⅛ cups/225g sugar
½ teaspoon vanilla
¼ teaspoon ground saffron threads dissolved in 2 tablespoons rose water
2 tablespoons fresh lime juice

Barberry preserve is not only delicious as a spread with bread and butter, it also makes a wonderful condiment with kukus, roast chicken, or plain rice.

1. **To clean the barberries:** Spread the barberries on a sheet pan and pick over and remove any stems or grit. Place the barberries in a sieve and place the sieve in a large container full of cold water. Allow them to soak for 20 minutes. Any sand will settle to the bottom. Take the sieve out of the container and run cold water over the barberries. Drain and spread on a sheet pan lined with a layer of parchment. Allow to dry overnight.

2. Sterilize a ½pt/240g Mason jar in boiling water. Drain and dry thoroughly.

3. **To make the syrup:** In a medium-sized laminated cast-iron pot, place the sugar and water, and bring to a boil over high heat.

4. **To make the preserve:** Add the barberries and bring back to a boil. Reduce heat to low and simmer for 30 minutes.

5 Add the vanilla, saffron-rose water, and lime juice, and continue to simmer over low heat for 10 to 15 minutes until the syrup is thick enough to coat the back of a spoon. Allow to cool.

6. Fill the jar with preserve and then seal tightly. Store in a cool, dark place. *Nush-e joon!*

A 1900s photo of a barberry juice peddler.

Khorasan

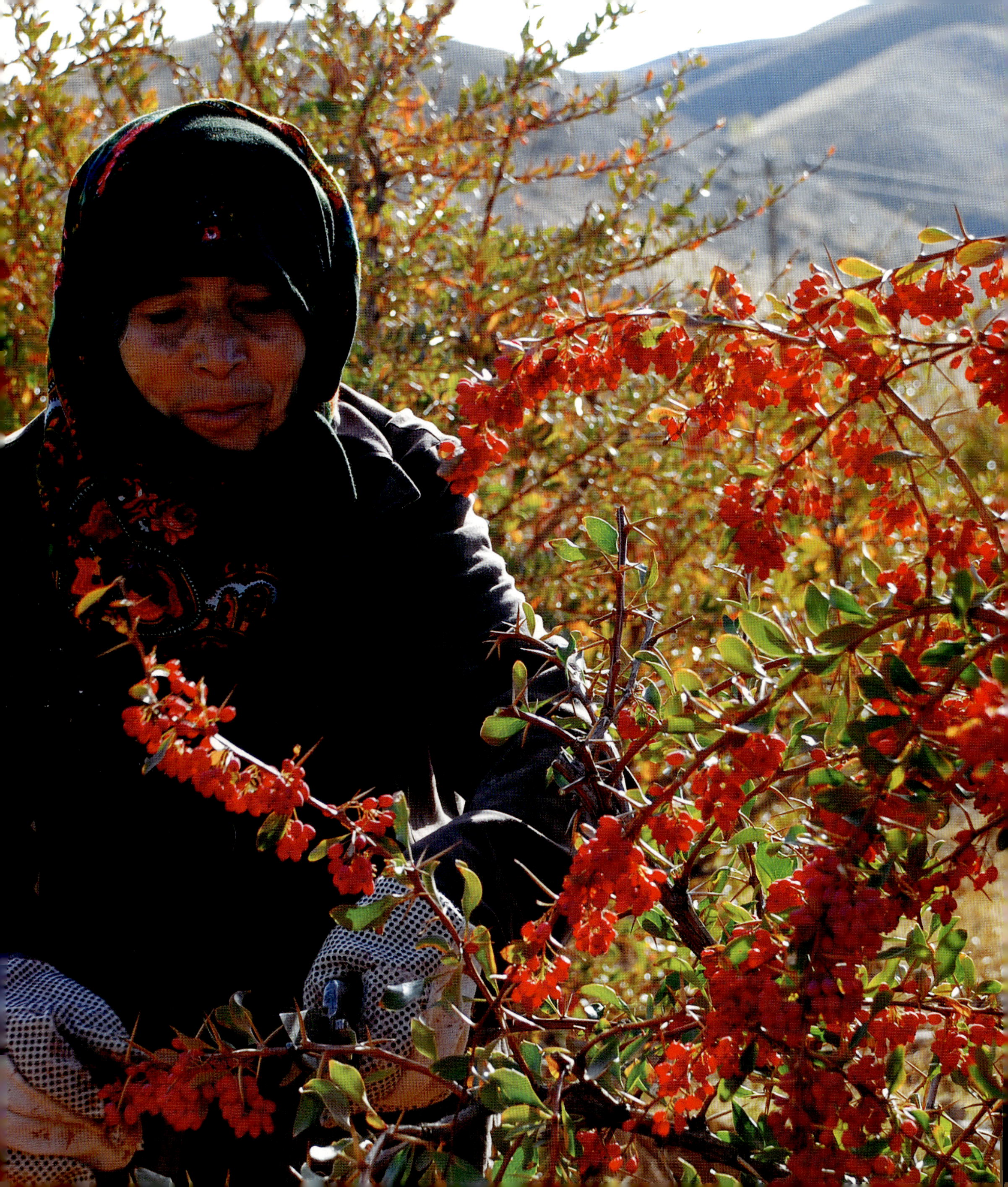

Barberry Pickle
torshi-ye zereshk

Makes ½pt/240g
Prep: 30 minutes plus drying the barberries overnight
Cooking: 10 minutes

BRINE

1 cup/240ml apple cider vinegar
1 tablespoon fine sea salt

PICKLE

1½ cups/225g dried barberries
1 clove garlic, peeled
1 teaspoon ground Persian hogweed seeds/*golpar*

1. Clean, wash, and dry the barberries as on page 421. Sterilize a ½pt/240g Mason jar in boiling water. Drain and dry thoroughly.

2. **To make the brine:** In a small saucepan, place the vinegar and salt and bring to a boil over high heat. Give it a stir to be sure the salt has dissolved. Remove from heat.

3. **To make the pickle:** Place the barberries, garlic, and golpar in the Mason jar. Fill the jar to the top with the brine and seal tightly. Store in a cool, dark place. *Nush-e joon!*

Barberry thorns are sharp as needles and protective gloves are needed for picking them.

Saffroned Rice Flour Pudding with Cumin
zireh katchi-e bojnurdi

Serves 6 to 8
Prep: 10 minutes
Cooking: 25 minutes

SYRUP
5½ cups/1.3l water
2¼ cups/450g rock candy, coarsely chopped
1 teaspoon ground saffron threads dissolved in ¼ cup/60ml rose water

ROUX
1 cup/225g ghee or oil
2 cups/300g rice flour
1 tablespoon ground black cumin
1 tablespoon ground fenugreek seeds

GARNISH
2 tablespoons slivered pistachios

Katchi is given to new mothers during breast-feeding to restore their strength. It's basically halva in liquid form and best served warm. You can use sugar or honey in place of rock candy. I have adapted this recipe from Mahbubeh Nateghi.

1. ***To make the syrup:*** Bring the water and rock candy to a boil in a saucepan. Add the saffron-rose water. Remove from heat and set aside. Be sure the rock candy has dissolved completely.

2. ***To make the roux:*** Heat the ghee in a large non-stick pot over medium heat. Gradually add the flour stirring constantly with a wooden spoon. Cook for about 10 to 15 minutes until golden brown. Add the spices and give it a stir.

3. Reduce heat to low and add the saffron syrup, stirring quickly and constantly with a wooden spoon. Allow to simmer until the mixture reaches a creamy consistency. Add more warm water if too thick.

4. Transfer the pudding to a serving bowl and garnish. Serve warm. *Nush-e joon!*

Saffron crocuses showing their orange-colored stamens.

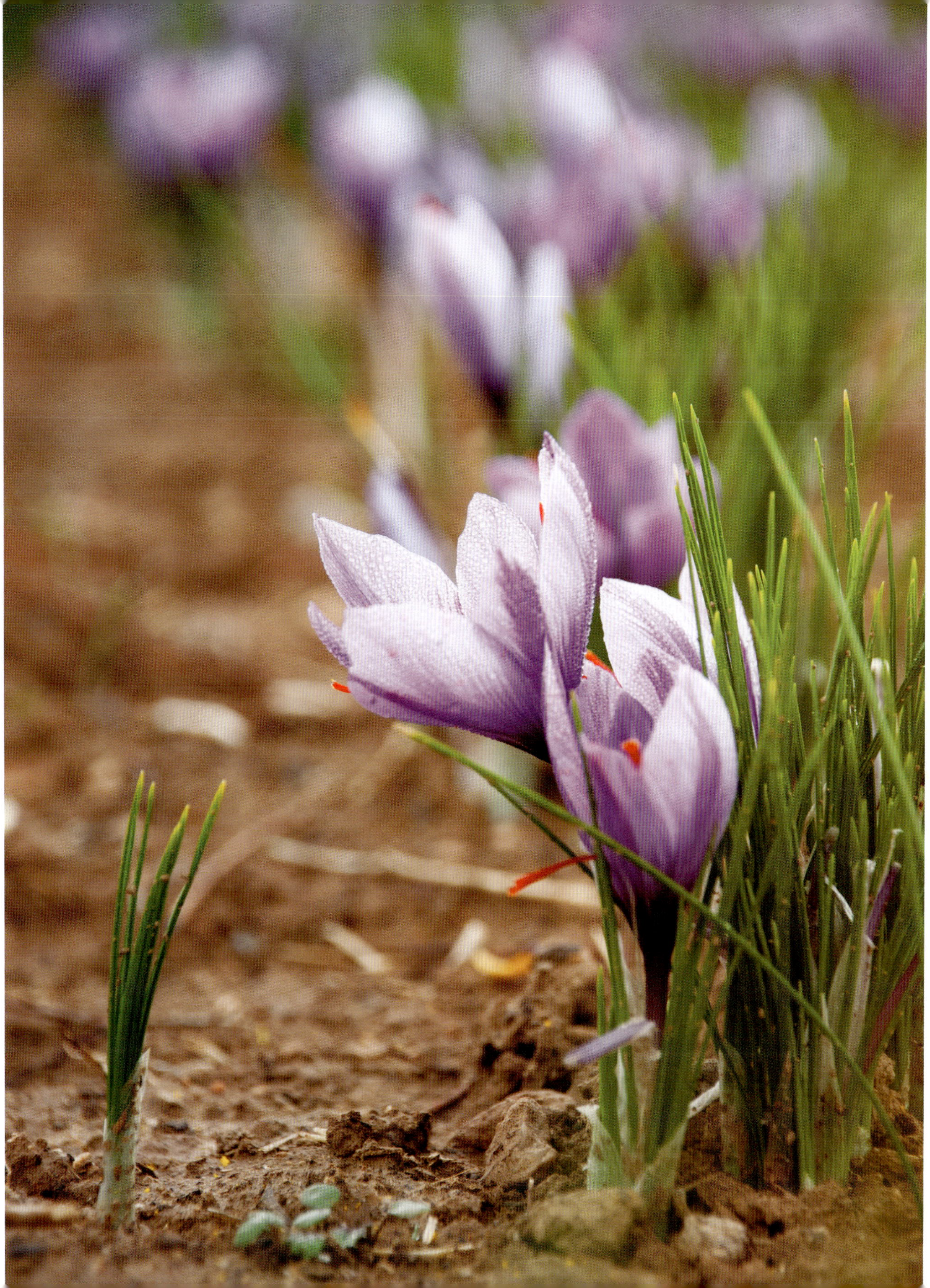

Mashhadi Rice + Milk Cake
digcheh-ye mashhadi

Serves 6
Prep: 5 minutes
Cooking: 1½ hours

- ¾ cup/150g white rice, cleaned, washed, soaked overnight, drained, and rinsed
- 2 cups/480ml water
- ¼ teaspoon fine sea salt
- 3 cups/720ml whole plain milk
- ¾ cup/150g sugar
- 2 envelopes unflavored gelatin dissolved in ¼ cup cold water
- ¼ cup/60ml rose water
- 2 teaspoons ground cardamom

GARNISH

- ¼ cup/20g ground raw pistachios
- ¼ teaspoon ground saffron threads dissolved in 1 tablespoon rose water (optional)

This traditional and nourishing rice cake is usually prepared for religious ceremonies in the region. It is also a favorite for breaking the fast during Ramadan. Traditionally, the dish is made without adding gelatin, but I find the gelatin improves the texture considerably. I adapted this recipe from Behjat Shahverdiani.

1. Place the rice in a medium-sized saucepan with 2 cups/480ml water and ¼ teaspoon salt. Cook over low heat for 15 to 20 minutes, stirring occasionally until the water has been absorbed and the rice is tender.

2. Add the milk and sugar, and bring to a boil. Reduce heat to low and cook for 55 minutes, stirring occasionally.

3. Add dissolved gelatin, the rose water, and cardamom, and give it a stir. Cook over low heat for 15 to 20 minutes longer, stirring frequently until the mixture has thickened to the consistency of a pudding.

4. Butter all over the inside of an 8in/20cm diameter by 4in/10cm deep non-stick mold.

5. Remove from heat and spoon into the buttered mold. Allow to cool, then cover and chill in the fridge for at least 4 hours.

6. Remove from the fridge and separate the cake from the mold by going around between the mold and rice cake using a rubber spatula. Turn over onto a platter. Garnish with the pistachios and saffron-rose water. Serve by cutting into wedges as you would a cake. *Nush-e joon!*

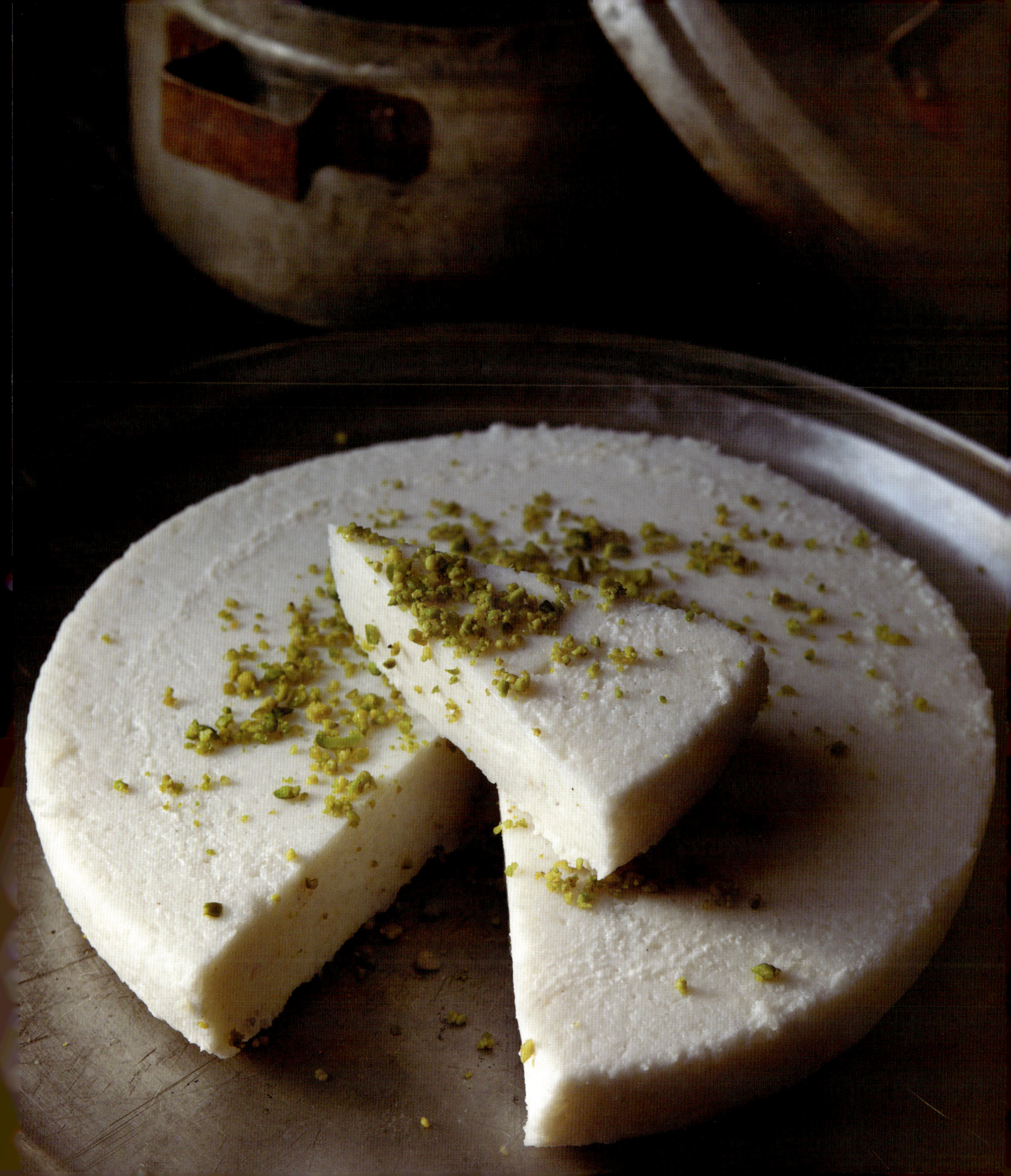

Yazd

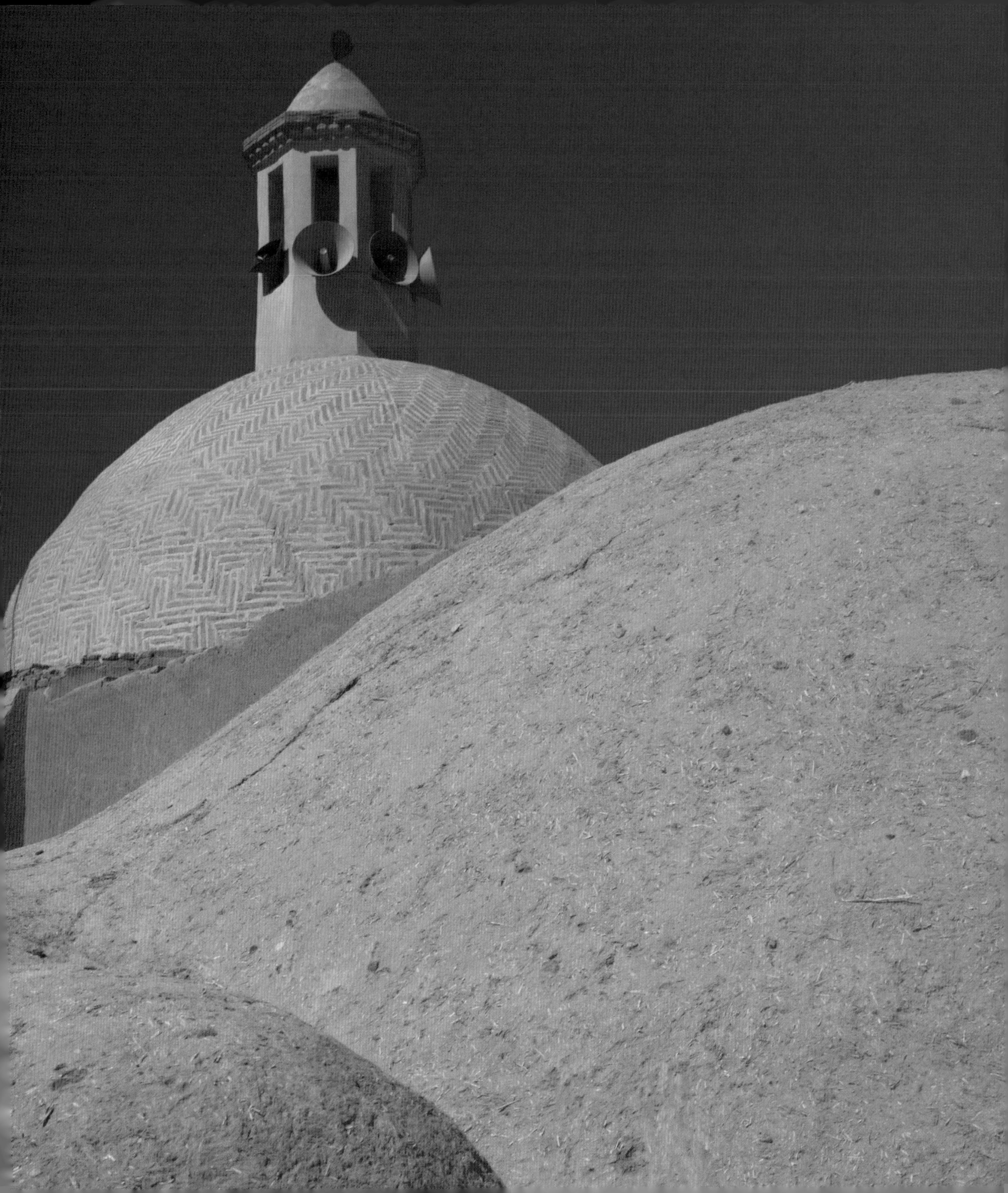

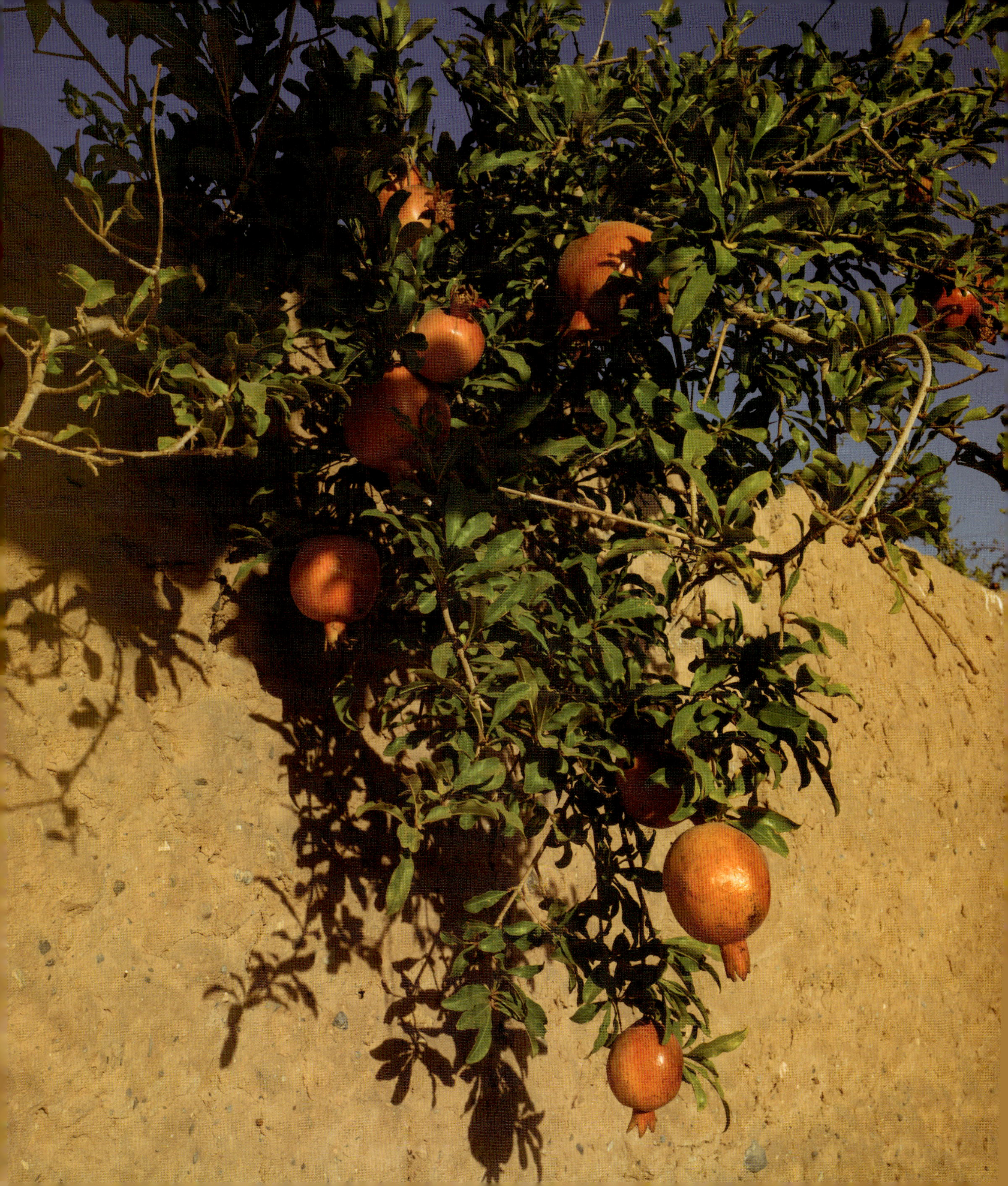

A Little History

The people of Yazd are hard-working, peaceful, clever, and extremely family-oriented. It is an ancient city that for centuries remained the center of Zoroastrian culture. The name of the city is probably derived from King Yazdegerd, a Sasanid ruler in the fifth century CE.

Yazd was one of the stops on the Silk Road and was visited by Marco Polo. The city is famous for its stitch work and silk weaving, as well as for its pomegranates, pastries, candies, and sweets.

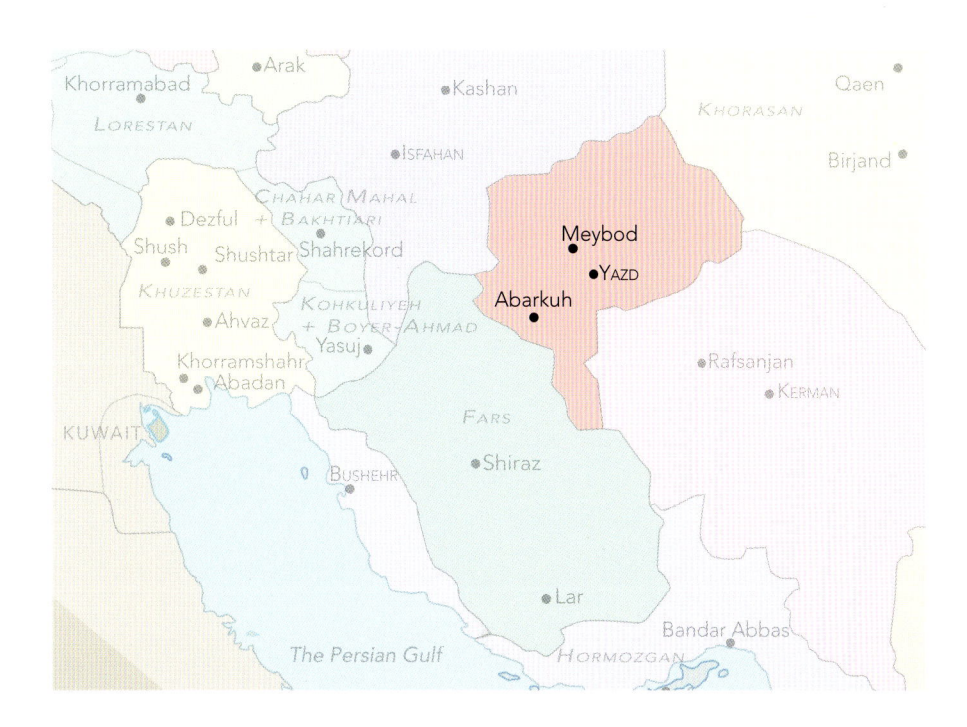

Spinach + Beet Osh
osh-e shuly-e yazdi

Serves 6
Prep: 20 minutes
Cooking: 1½ hours

SOAKED OVERNIGHT + DRAINED

1 cup/200g brown lentils

BROTH

2 tablespoons oil
2 medium onions, peeled and finely chopped
4 teaspoons fine sea salt
1 teaspoon fresh ground pepper
2 teaspoons turmeric
1 teaspoon nigela seeds
1lb/450g white or red beets, peeled and finely chopped
1 cup/120g all-purpose flour dissolved in 2 cups/480ml water

HERBS

1lb/450g chopped fresh or frozen spinach
1 cup/85g chopped fresh beet leaves
1 cup/85g chopped fresh dill weed
1 cup/85g chopped fresh parsley leaves
1 cup/85g chopped spring onions
1 teaspoon dried fenugreek leaves

VINEGAR

⅔ cup/160ml apple cider vinegar
1 tablespoon sugar

GARNISH/NA`NA DAGH

2 tablespoons oil
1 onion, peel and thinly sliced
½ teaspoon turmeric
¼ cup/20g dried mint

There's a friendly competition between the Yazdis and Kermanis (who have a similar osh, which they call omajoo*) about which of them came up with the dish first. I have adapted this recipe from Sarah Alavi's mom in Yazd. For variations, you can replace the lentils with split peas and the beets with turnips. Traditionally this osh is made with white beets, but I made it with red beets because they're prettier. Also, you can replace the vinegar with black* kashk/qareh qorut.

1. **To make the broth:** Heat the oil in a large pot over medium heat and sauté the onions until golden brown.

2. Add the salt, pepper, turmeric, nigela seeds, and lentils, and stir-fry for 1 minute. Add 5 cups water and the beets, and bring to a boil. Reduce heat to low, cover, and simmer for 40 to 45 minutes until the lentils and beets are cooked.

3. In a mixing bowl, whisk together the flour with 2 cups waters. Add it to the broth and continue to stir until the flour has been completely absorbed by the *osh*. Simmer for 15 minutes.

4. Add the herbs and simmer for 5 minutes. Add the vinegar and simmer for another 10 minutes. Adjust seasoning to taste. Cover and keep warm.

5. **To make the garnish:** Heat 2 tablespoons oil in a wide skillet over medium heat and sauté the onion until golden brown. Add the turmeric and sauté for 1 minute. Remove from the heat. Add the mint and stir well.

6. **To serve the** *osh:* Pour the *osh* into a tureen and garnish on top. Stir in the garnish just before serving in individual bowls. *Nush-e joon!*

Yazd

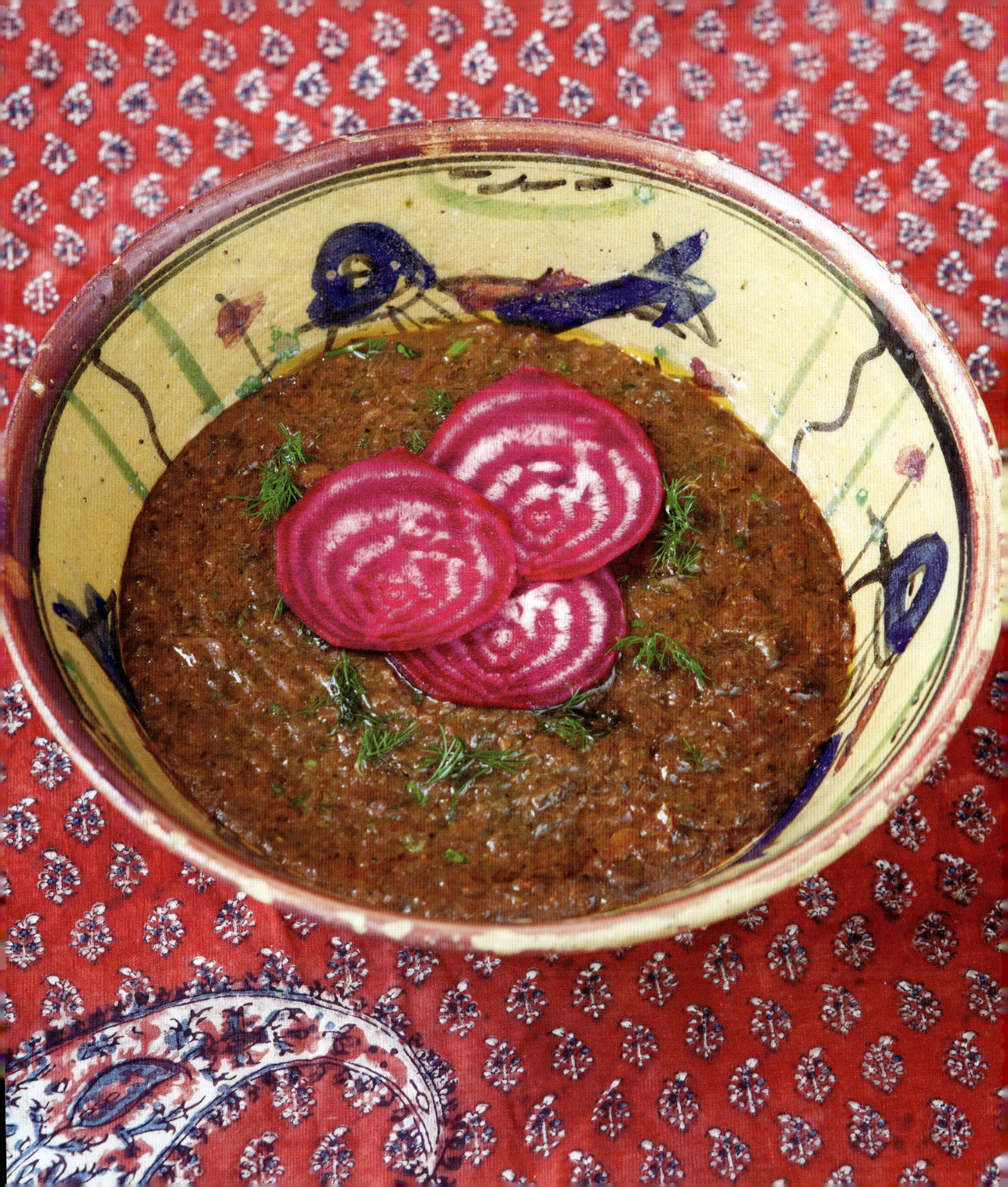

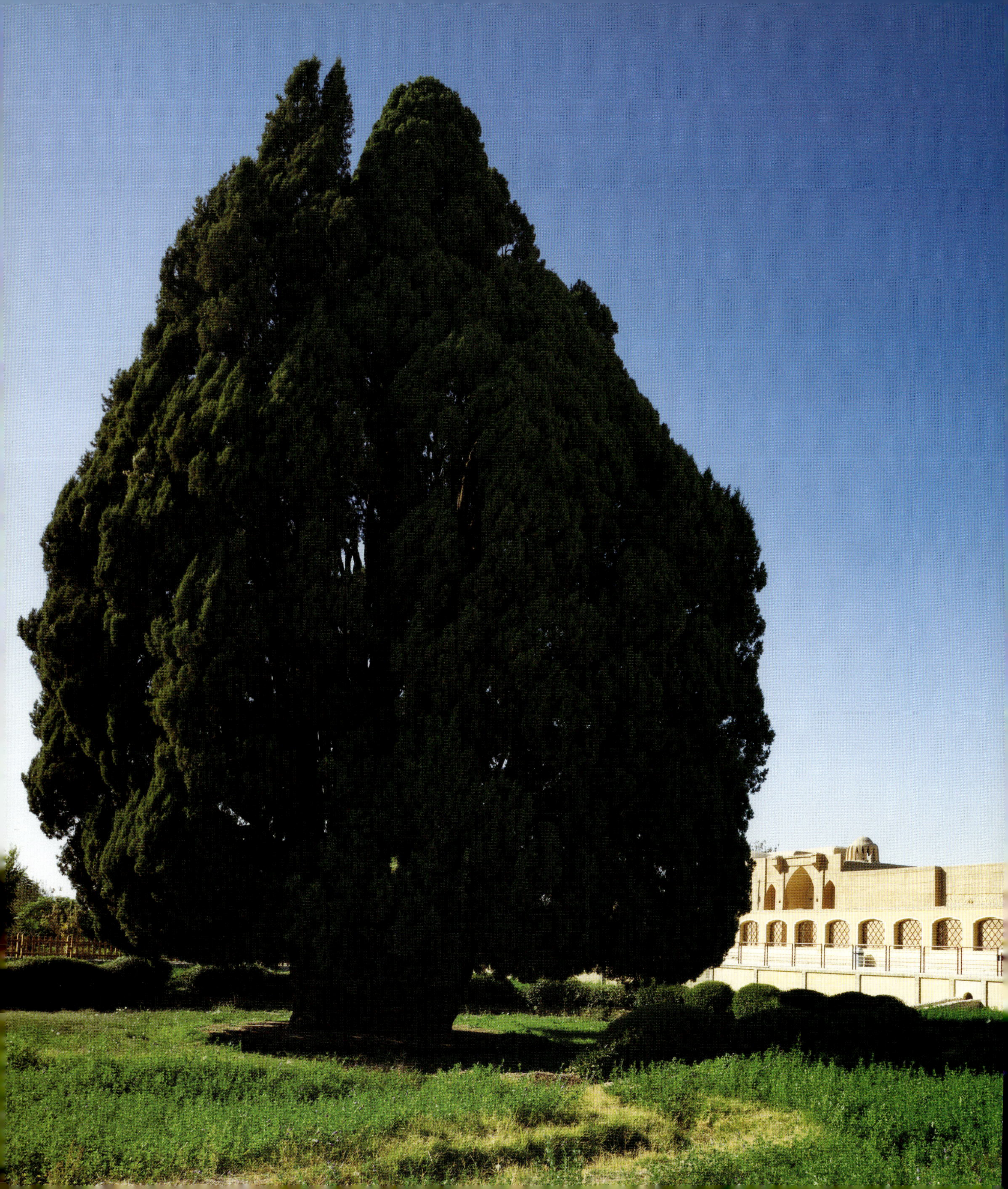

The Cypress at Abarkuh

This cypress at Abarkuh/*sarv-e abarkuh* near Yazd is one of the most venerable living trees in the world. It is estimated to be 4,500 years old. The cypress tree has had symbolic significance in Iran since ancient times. It is often mentioned in Persian poetry as exemplifying the graceful stately gait of the belovéd. The famous paisley motif/*boteh jeqqeh*, which is used on shawls/*termeh*, carpets and textiles, is believed by some to be the stylized top of the cypress bent by the wind.

According to a Zoroastrian tradition, a sapling of the "noble cypress/*sarv-e azadeh*" was brought from paradise by Zoroaster and given to the Persian king, who planted it near the first fire temple as a symbol of his conversion to Zoroastrianism.

436

Iranian Zoroastrians

Zoroastrianism coexisted and intermingled with other ancient Iranian religious practices for many centuries before it became the official religion of Iran in the fifth century BCE. Among those practices was an elaborate festive meal to which deities were invited as honored guests. They were offered sacrificial food and a sacred drink/*haoma*, and entertained with the recitation of poetry. Zoroaster, the founding prophet, was himself both a priest and a poet.

The religion had complex beliefs about the purifying power of fire and water, and the nature of the soul, death and the afterlife. According to Zoroastrianism, the world was divided between the followers of Truth/*artavan* and the followers of the Lie/*drugvant*. This was related to the concept of light as good and darkness as evil. Judaism, Christianity, and Islam were all influenced by Zoroastrianism to some degree.

Today, even though the majority of Iranians have been Moslems for over a thousand years, many of the ancient ceremonies continue to be practiced in everyday life throughout the country. These include the Spring Festival/*nowruz* (the Persian New Year); the Summer Festival of Water/*tirgan*; the Autumn Festival/*mehregan*; and finally the Winter Festival/*yalda* (the birthday of the sun on the longest night of the year).

Yazd and Kerman remain centers of the Zoroastrian minority in Iran, where they still have fire temples for worship. Those Zoroastrians who emigrated to India—the majority of followers today—are known as Parsis.

The ancient Iranian philosophy of duality is reflected in the harmonizing of ingredients in Persian cooking—the complementary duality of hot- and cold-natured foods/*garmi o sardi*, known as yin yang in China and Ayurveda in India.

Opposite, top: The primary symbol of Zoroastrianism/*foruhar* (believed to depict the guardian angel) with its maxim, "good deeds, good thoughts, good words," on a building in Yazd.
Bottom: An 1870s photo of three Zoroastrian-Iranian women.

Saffroned Lamb Braise with Potato Fries
qeymeh-ye yazdi

Serves 6
Prep: 20 minutes
Cooking: 2¼ hours

FOR THE BRAISE

4 tablespoons oil, butter, or ghee
2 large onions, peeled and thinly sliced
1lb/450g leg of lamb or chicken thighs cut into ½in/1cm cubes
4 whole dried Persian limes, pierced
2 teaspoons fine sea salt
½ teaspoon freshly ground pepper
½ teaspoon turmeric
1 teaspoon cinnamon
1 large tomato, peeled and chopped
1 tablespoon sugar or honey
Zest of 2 oranges
½ teaspoon ground saffron dissolved in 2 tablespoons orange blossom water
¼ cup/55g yellow split peas

POTATO FRIES

1½lb/675g russet potatoes, peeled, cut into matchsticks, and soaked in cold water
2 cups/480ml oil for deep-frying

GARNISH

¼ teaspoon coarse sea salt
1 teaspoon dried Persian lime powder

NOTE

You can replace split peas with ¼ cup/50g chickpeas, soaked overnight, drained, and rinsed.

Qeymeh *refers to diced meat sautéd with onion in a braise. There are various kinds of* qeymeh *in Iran, made with fried potatoes, eggplants, zucchini, or rhubarb. In some regions they don't use tomatoes or split peas. Our guide in Yazd was Aqa-ye Shir Gholami. He was young, kind, and knowledgable. He took us to his mother-in-law Khanum-e Mehry-e Assan's house, where we cooked this braise shown (top right) in the photo on the facing page. Yazdis use chickpeas, but I prefer split peas and tomatoes. Mixing the flavors of tomato, saffron, orange zest, and dried Persian lime creates a delectable taste combination.*

1. **To make the braise:** Heat 2 tablespoons oil in a medium-sized laminated cast-iron pot over medium heat. Sauté the onions and lamb until golden brown and all the juice has been absorbed. Add the dried limes, salt, pepper, and turmeric, and sauté for 2 minutes longer.

2. Pour in 3 cups/720ml water and bring to a boil. Reduce heat to low, cover, and simmer for 55 minutes, stirring occasionally.

3. Add the cinnamon, tomato, sugar, orange zest, and saffron-orange blossom water. Cover and cook over low heat for another 45 minutes.

4. In a saucepan, cook the yellow split peas in 3 cups/720ml water and ½ teaspoon salt for 30 minutes. Drain, rinse, and add to the pot. Give it a gentle stir. Check to see if lamb and split peas are tender. Adjust seasoning to taste by adding lime juice or salt. Cover and keep warm until ready to serve.

5. **To make the potato fries:** Drain rinse, and dry the potatoes thoroughly. Heat 2 cups oil in a skillet over medium heat, add the potatoes, and deep-fry until golden. Use a slotted spoon to remove the potatoes and place them on paper towels. Sprinkle with coarse sea salt and dried Persian lime powder, and set aside.

6. Just before serving place the potato fries on top of the braise. Serve with saffron steamed rice/*chelow*, pickles/*torshi*, and a fresh herb platter/*sabzi khordan*. *Nush-e joon!*

VARIATION FOR BAKING POTATOES

To bake the potatoes instead of frying them, preheat oven to 350°F/180°C. Place the potato slices in a resealable plastic bag with 1 tablespoon oil and ½ teaspoon salt, seal, and shake the bag to evenly coat potatoes. Line a baking sheet with parchment paper and spread potatoes over it. Bake in the oven for 40 to 45 minutes. Dust with salt and dried Persian lime powder.

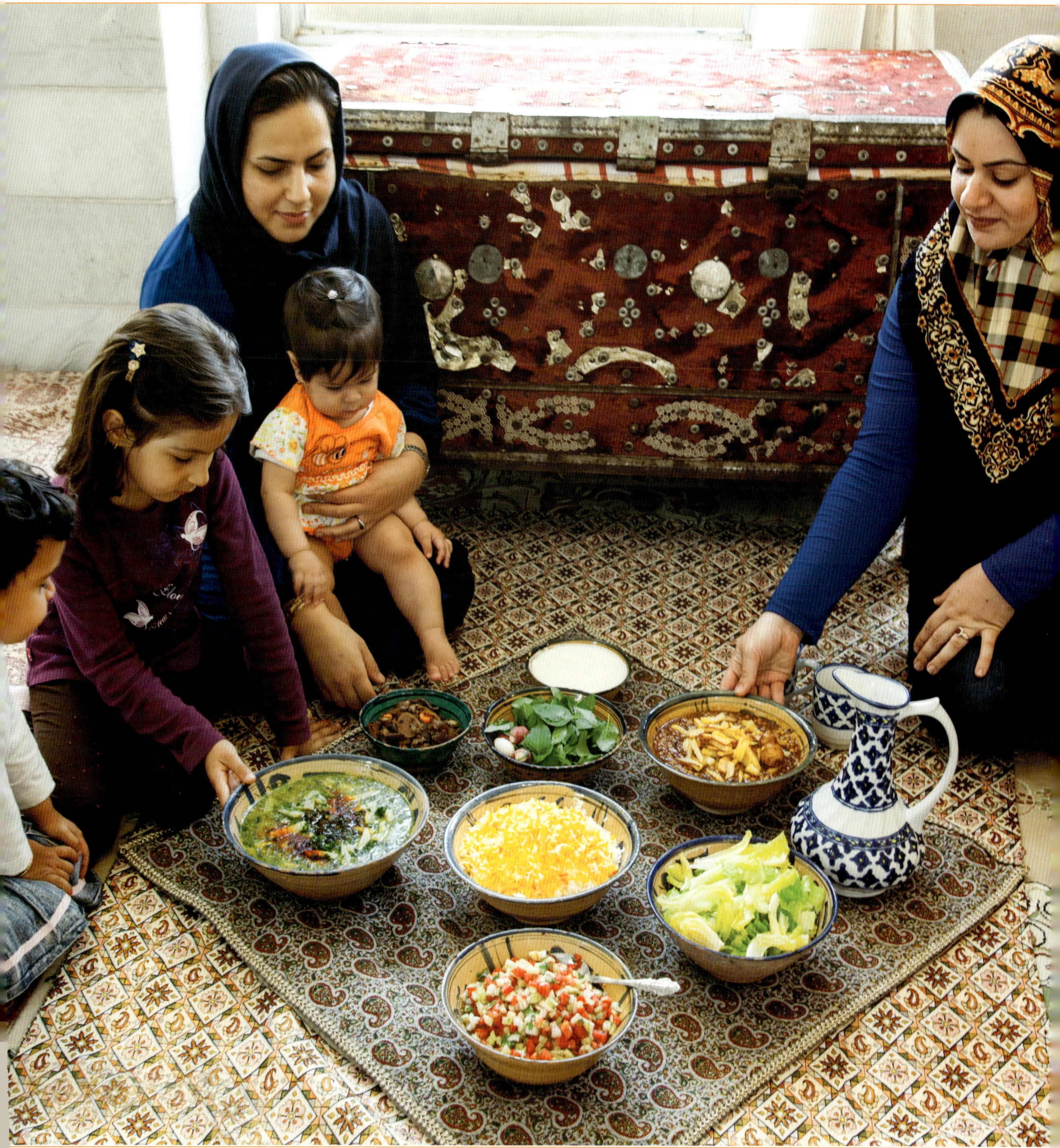

A view of Yazd and its walled gardens.

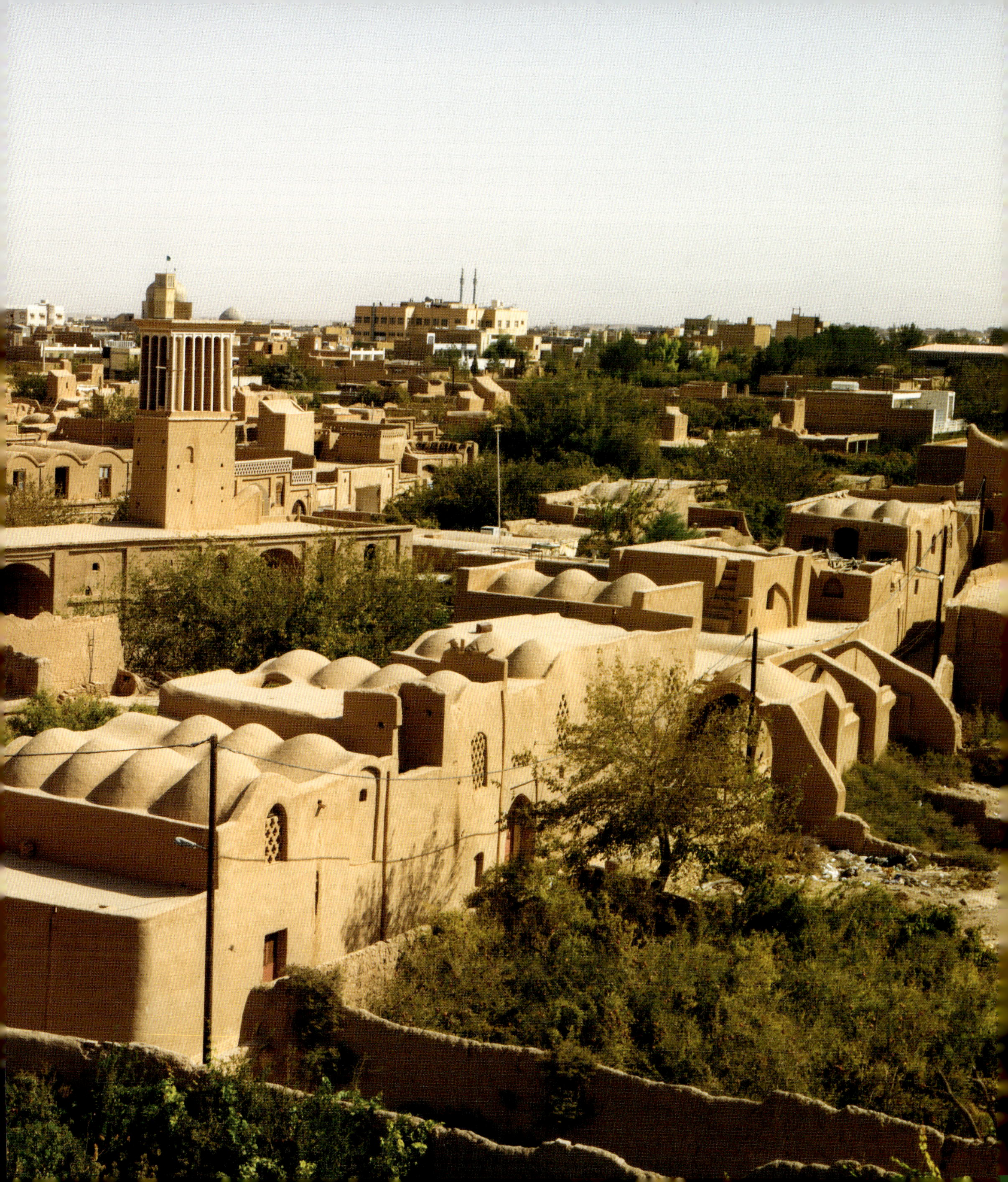

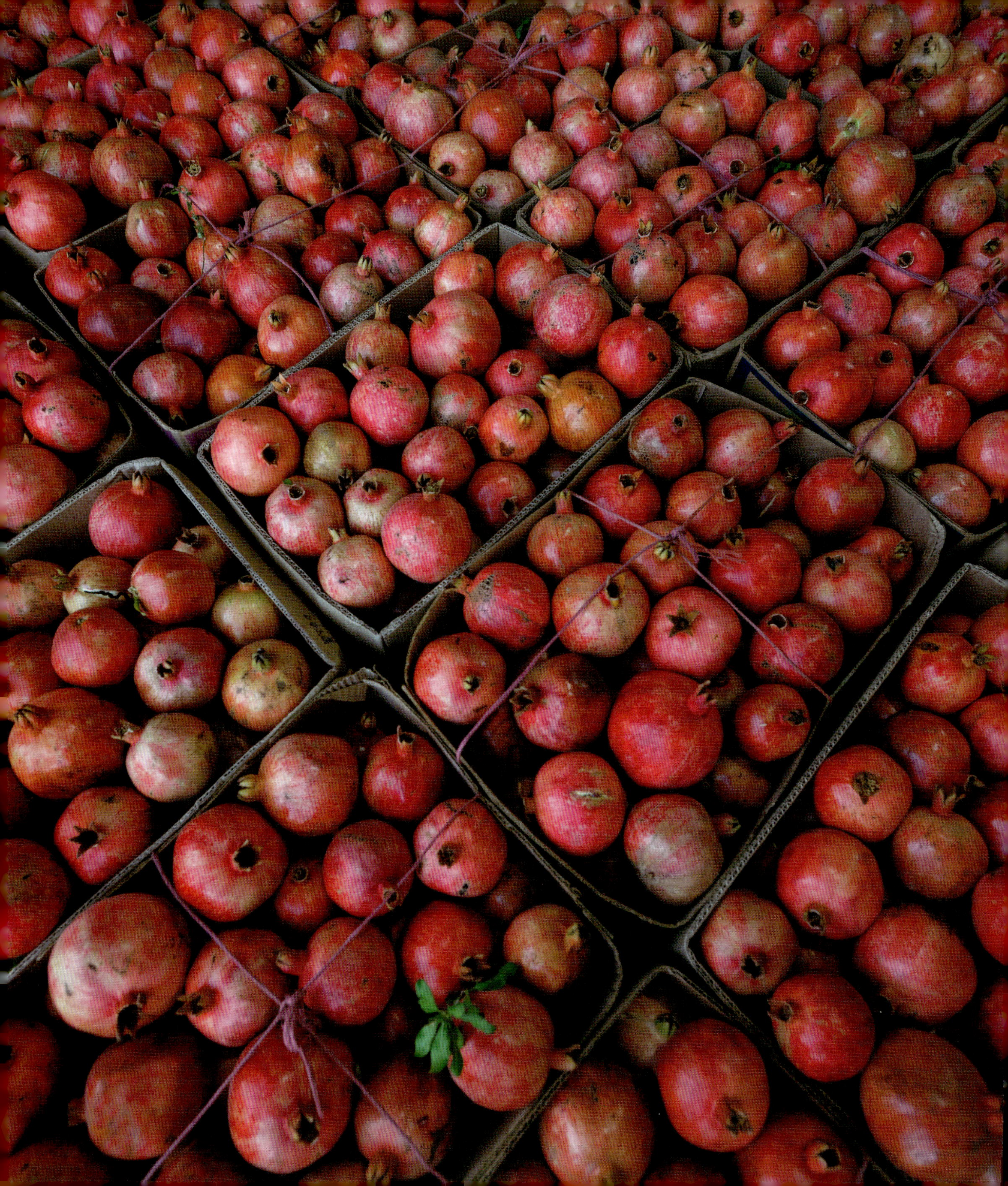

Pomegranates

The red pomegranate, native to Iran and cultivated there for at least 4,000 years, is considered the fruit of heaven; in fact, it was probably the real "apple" in the Garden of Eden. The ancients commended it. Among them was King Solomon, who had a pomegranate orchard. And Prophet Mohammad said, "Eat the pomegranate, for it purges the system of envy and hatred."

The fruit grows on large bushes or small trees, whose masses of crimson flowers brighten the pale mud walls of villages in Yazd, Isfahan, Qom, and around the Caspian. In Persian folk medicine, every part of the plant is believed to have virtue.

Pomegranates, ranging in taste from sweet to sour, have a special place in Iranian cookery. The fresh seeds, or arils (the edible part of the fruit), sprinkled with a little salt and powdered hog weed seeds/*golpar*, make a tart appetizer, and they add a bright note to green salads. Pomegranate juice is a popular street vendor drink as well. Or the juice may be reduced to a paste, a favorite souring agent, particularly around the Caspian, and in central and southern Iran. Most recipes that include pomegranate, which is classified as a cold food, also include hot foods like walnuts or ginger for balance.

Pomegranates are available in supermarkets in the fall and winter. Choose deep red fruits without blemishes. They will keep at home for about a week at room temperature. I have been able to keep them fresh at the end of the season for 3 weeks or more by wrapping them in newspaper and keeping them in the refrigerator drawer.

To seed a pomegranate easily, use a sharp knife to cut the pomegranate in half. Hold each half, 1 at a time, seed side down over a bowl and tap the skin with a heavy wooden spoon to dislodge the arils from the membrane that holds them. The arils will fall through your fingers into the bowl.

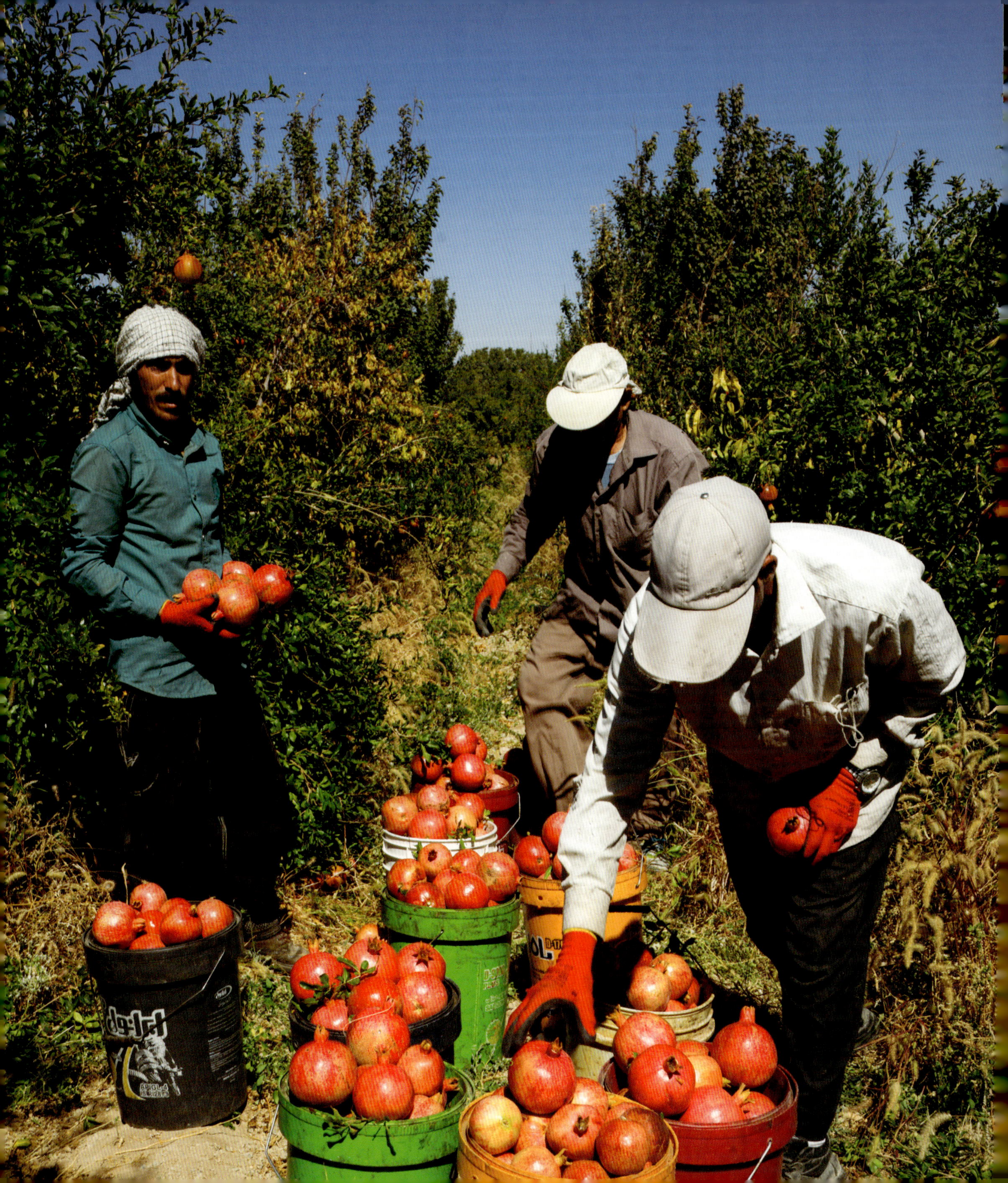

Iranians also love to juice a pomegranate in its skin/*ablambu*. It allows one to drink the juice of a pomegranate without fuss or mess. Choose a good-looking pomegranate with no blemishes or holes in the skin. Then, holding it in both hands with one thumb over the other, start by gently squeezing one of the raised parts of the fruit (there are usually 4 or 5 hills and valleys). The idea is to squeeze the seeds inside the skin without bursting the skin. This needs to be done gently and systematically, going around the pomegranate until the whole fruit is soft and squishy. Then press it to your mouth, bite into the skin, making a small hole in it with your teeth, while you suck with your mouth and squeeze gently with your hands. You will get a very refreshing burst of juice in your mouth that is both delicious and sensual. Continue working around the fruit, squeezing and sucking, until you have drunk all the juice. It is an art that you will perfect with practice, and once you know how, you will never again see a good-looking pomegranate without wanting to *ablambu* it.

To make pomegranate molasses/*rob-e anar*, in a large, heavy-bottomed, non-reactive saucepan, pour in 8 cups/1.9l pomegranate juice. Bring to a boil over high heat. Reduce heat to medium, add 1 tablespoon salt, and let simmer uncovered for about 1 hour or more. Gently stir occasionally until the syrup has thickened, then remove the pan from heat. Store in an airtight glass container in the fridge and use as needed.

Pomegranate harvest/*zapt-e anar* in Yazd in early October.

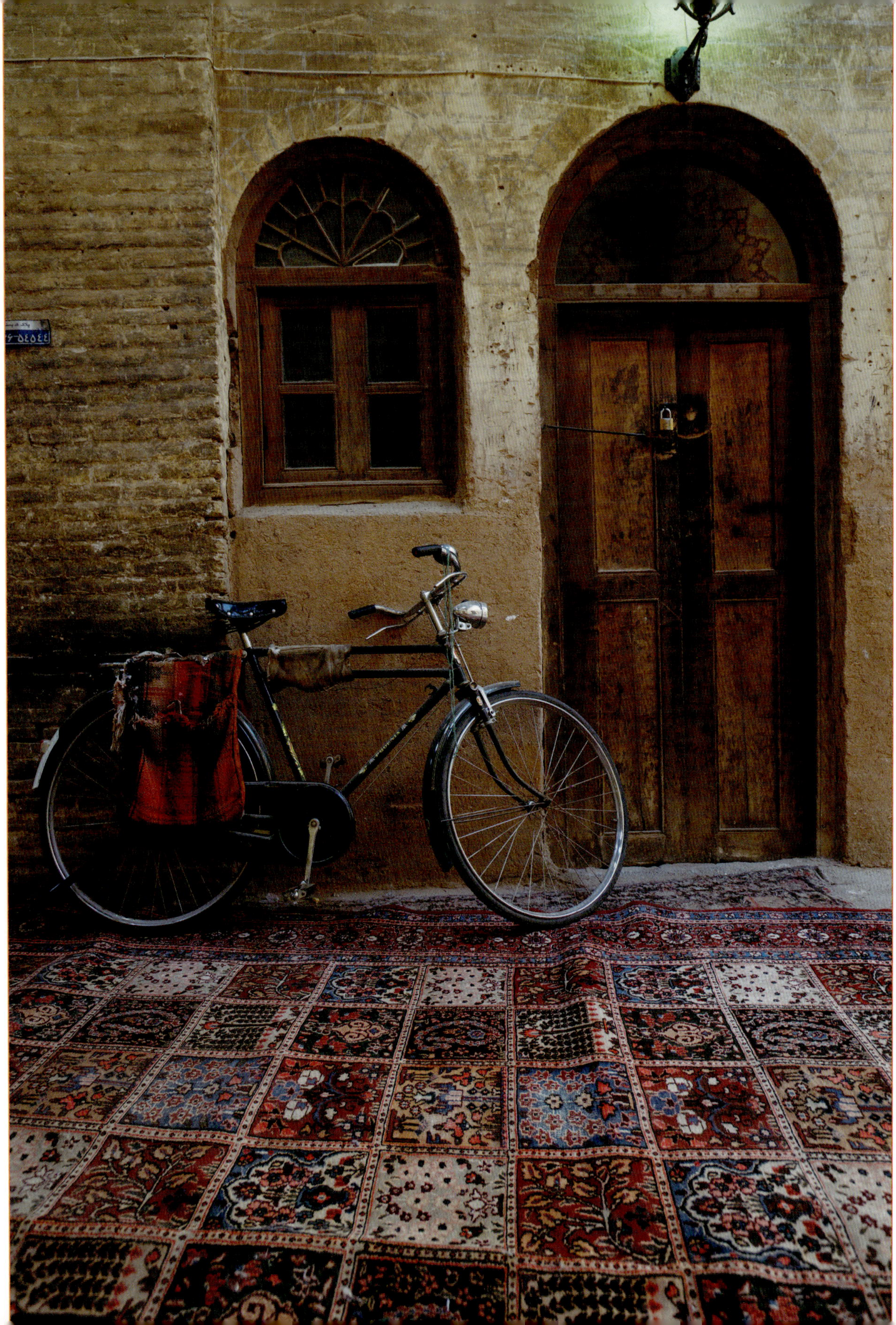

Iced Starch Drops Sorbet
faludeh/paludeh-ye yazdi

Serves 6
Prep: 10 minutes + 4 hours setting
Cooking: 20 minutes

FOR THE SYRUP

1 cup/200g sugar
1 cup/240ml water
2 tablespoons mint water
1 tablespoon fresh lime juice

STARCH BALLS

1 cup/150g wheat starch or corn starch
8 cups/1.9l water

GARNISH

2 tablespoons ground pistachios
2 limes, halved

Faludeh/paludeh-ye Yazdi varies from that of Shiraz. It uses wheat or corn starch to make starch balls instead of rice vermicelli.

1. **To make the syrup:** In a saucepan, place all the ingredients for the syrup and simmer for 5 to 10 minutes, stirring occasionally until thick enough to coat the back of a spoon. Allow to cool.

2. **To make starch balls:** In a medium saucepan over medium heat, bring 8 cups/1.9l water to a boil.

3. In a small mixing bowl, dissolve the starch in 1 cup water and add it to the boiling water. Stir well and boil for 15 to 20 minutes until it thickens and small bubbles appear on the surface. Remove from heat.

4. Fill a large container with ice and place a mesh sieve with a stand on it.

5. Pour the hot starch through the sieve and press down with a large spoon. As the starch hits the ice it turns into little starch balls.

6. Use a slotted spoon to transfer the iced starch balls to the syrup. Place in the freezer for about 4 hours.

7. **To serve:** Spoon into an individual serving bowl and garnish with some ground pistachios and a squeeze of lime. *Nush-e joon!*

Saffroned Almond Paste
loz-e badam-e yazdi

Makes one ¼ sheet pan (25 diamond-shaped pieces)
Prep: 20 minutes
Cooking: 10 minutes + setting overnight

SYRUP

2 cups/400g sugar

1 cup/240ml water

½ teaspoon ground saffron dissolved in ¼ cup/60ml pussy willow water/ *araq-e bidmeshk*

2lb/900g ground blanched almonds

GARNISH

¼ cup/20g ground pistachios mixed with 1 teaspoon ground cardamom or cardamom seeds

I've adapted this recipe from Sara Alavi's mother, Shayesteh Khanum, who is from Yazd. Sara says that in spring her mom would spread almonds on a clean sheet and cover them with pussy willow flowers, leaving them overnight for the perfume of the flowers to infuse the almonds. She can still remember the aroma that filled the whole house. I'm using pussy willow water with the saffron to achieve that aroma.

1. Line a quarter-sized rimmed sheet pan (9½ x 13in/24 x 33cm) with parchment paper.

2. **To make the syrup:** Place the sugar and water in a saucepan, stir well, and bring to a boil. Remove from heat, add the saffron and pussy willow water, and allow to cool for 2 minutes.

3. In a mixing bowl, beat the warm syrup for 4 to 5 minutes until pale.

4. Add the ground almonds and mix until you have a thick paste.

5. Spread the paste evenly in the pan. It should be about 4in/10cm thick. Spread a sheet of parchment paper on top of the almond paste and pack down well using your hands. Use a rolling pin to even out the surface; it should be compact and evened out.

6. Leave out at room temperature for 24 hours to dry out.

7. Cut into diamond shapes and garnish with the pistachios and cardamom mixture. Cover tightly with plastic wrap to prevent drying. Store in the fridge. *Nush-e joon!*

VARIATION

Make the almond past and shape it into 20 balls. Stuff each ball with ground pistachios and roll in powder sugar.

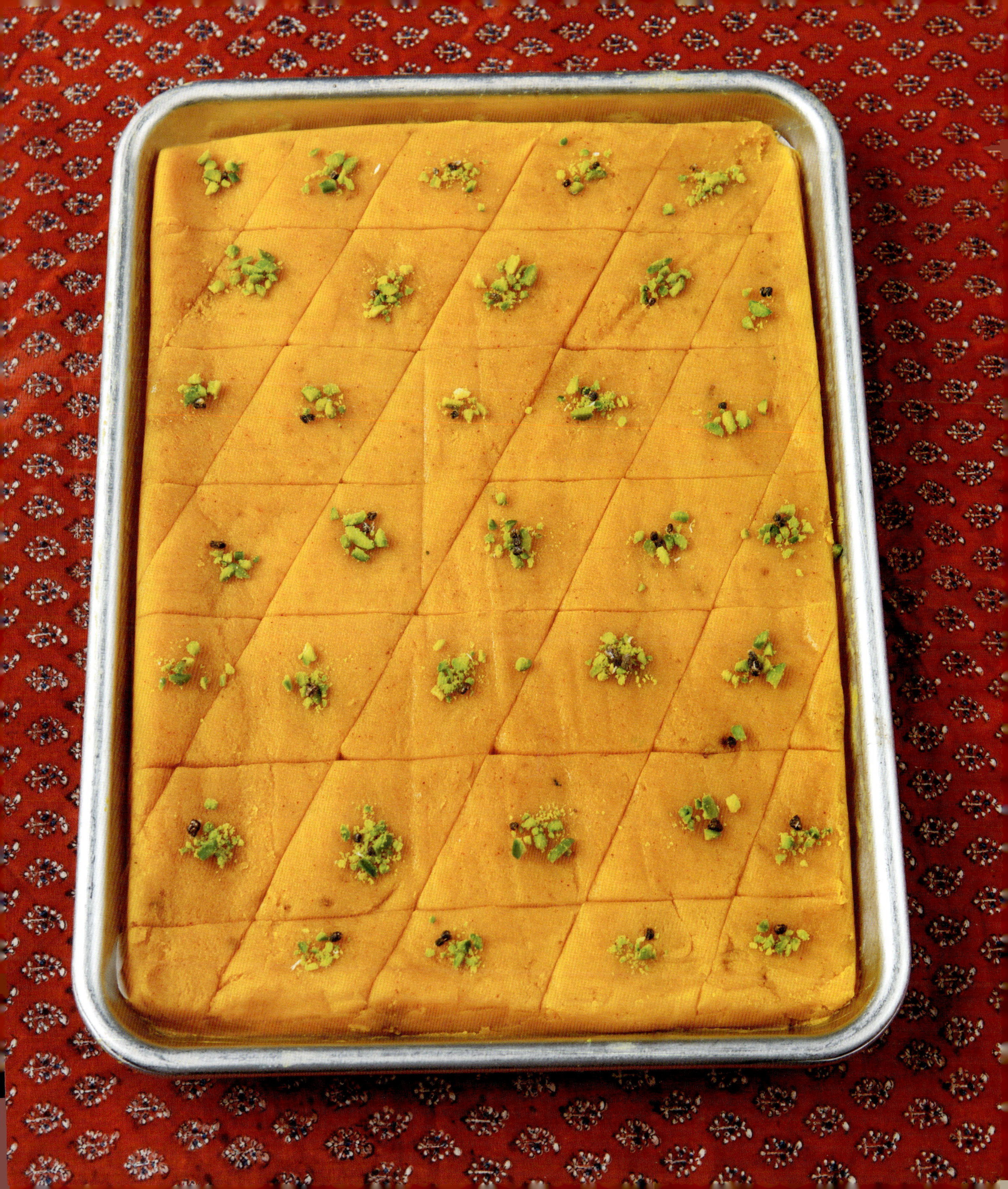

Mint, Vinegar + Flixweed Shrub
khak-e shir-o sekanjebin/yakhmal-e yazdi

Makes 1pt/480ml
Prep: 10 minutes
Cooking: 35 minutes

VINEGAR SYRUP/SEKANJEBIN

3 cups/600g sugar
1 cup/240ml water
¾ cup/180ml wine vinegar
2 sprigs fresh mint, washed and patted dry

FLIXWEED DRINK

½ cup/80g flixweed seeds
½ cup/120ml vinegar syrup (above)
4 cups/960g crushed ice

GARNISH

Sprigs of mint

Flixweed/Descurainia sophia is a member of the mustard family. This drink is served at street stalls in Kerman and Yazd. It is considered a wonderful thirst quencher. It is also thought to cool the metabolism/sardi to balance all the sweets and pastries they eat in this region, which are thought to heat the metabolism/garmi. The seeds are available as khak-e shir in Iranian markets, or you can find them at health food stores. The store-bought seeds can have sand and grit in them, so be sure to wash them thoroughly, changing the water several times until it runs clear.

1. **To make the vinegar syrup:** Bring the sugar and water to a boil in a medium-sized laminated pot. Reduce heat to medium and simmer for 10 minutes, stirring occasionally until the sugar has thoroughly dissolved.

2. Add the vinegar and boil for 15 to 20 minutes over medium heat until you have a thick syrup. Remove from heat, add the mint sprigs, and allow to cool.

3. Remove the mint from the syrup and discard. Pour the syrup into a clean, dry bottle. Cork tightly and use as needed.

4. Place the flixweed in a bowl, and cover with cold water, stirring gently. Pour off the water. Repeat 3 to 4 times until water is clear.

5. **To make the drink:** Place the flixweed seeds in a pitcher. Add ½ cup/120ml vinegar syrup/*sekanjebin* and 4 cups crushed ice and stir well. Adjust to taste by adding more syrup or ice. Stir, pour into individual glasses, and garnish with sprigs of mint. *Nush-e joon!*

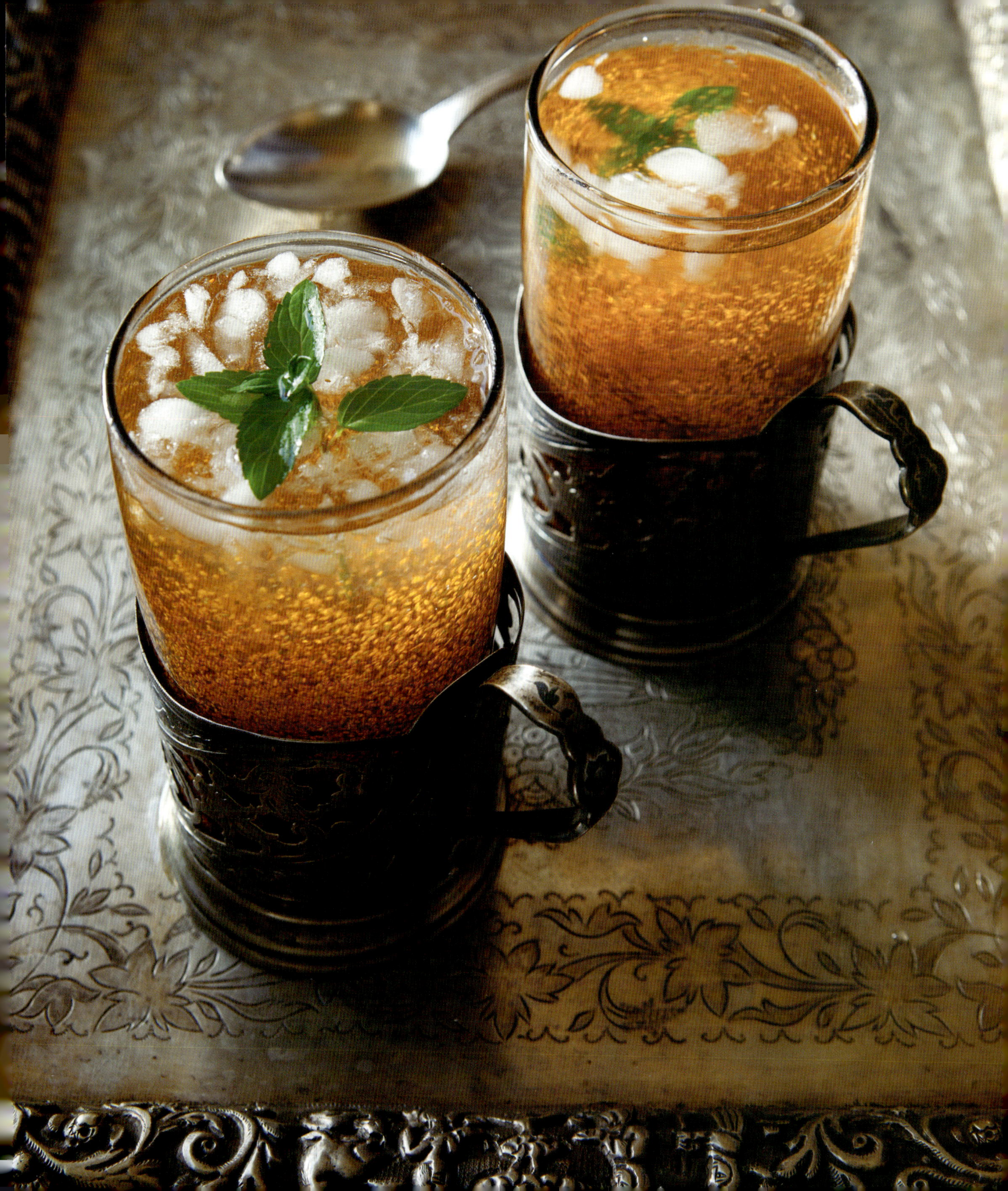

A Pastry Workshop

At the Haj Khalifeh Workshop in Yazd, they make irresistible traditional Iranian pastries. Fifth-generation owner Ali Rahbar was kind enough to welcome us there. It was interesting that the men were the cooks and the women took care of the packaging. On the facing page, the cooks are preparing a caramel brittle for making cotton candy/*pashmak*. They make a roux of flour and butter and add it to the caramel. It takes a special talent and practiced technique to handle the hot caramel and to stretch the roux to form long threads of the cotton candy. This process seems very similar to the way the Chinese make noodles, except that here they are doing it with hot caramel. On the pages that follow, you can see the cotton candy threads, which are then wrapped and packaged for sale.

453

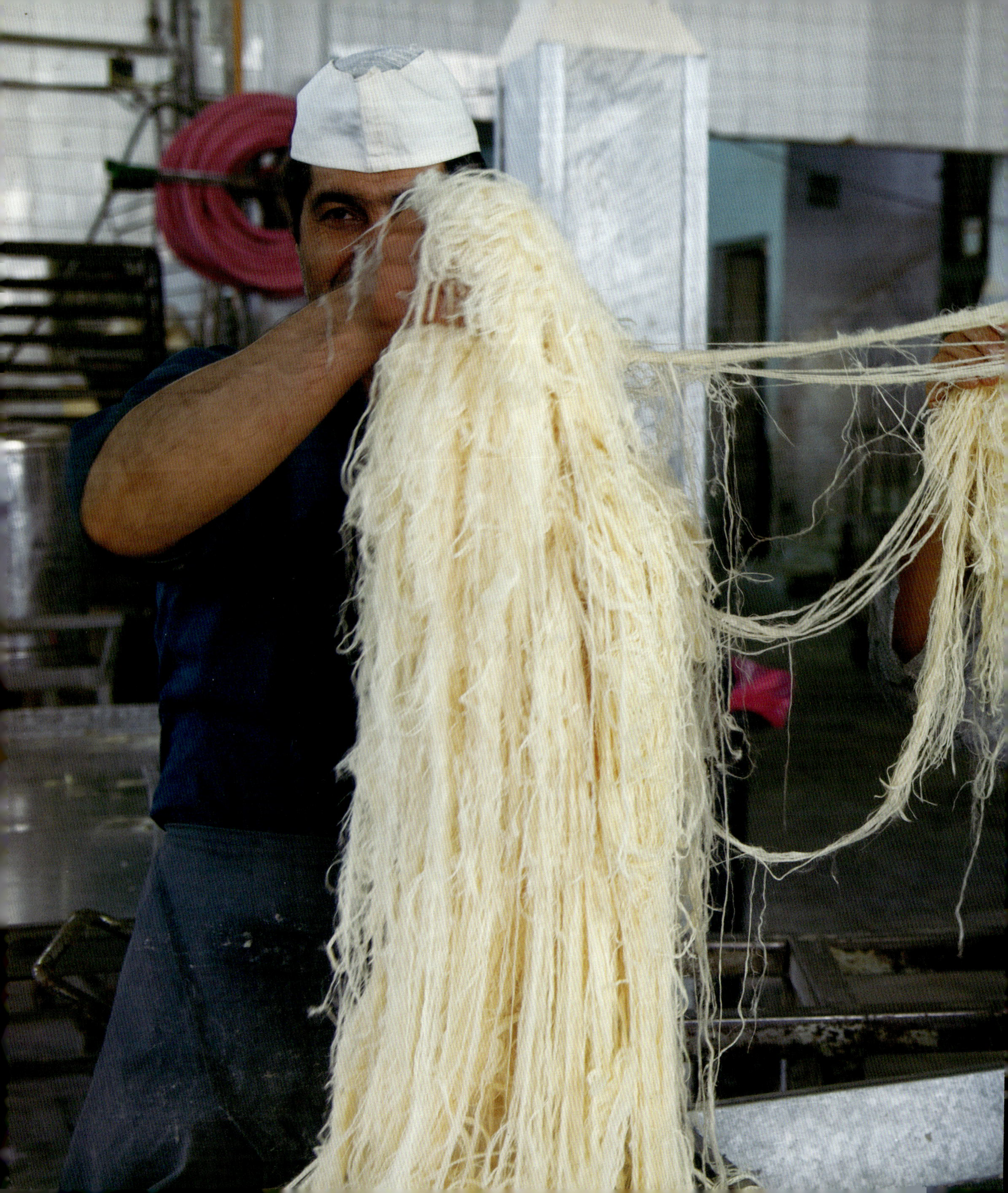

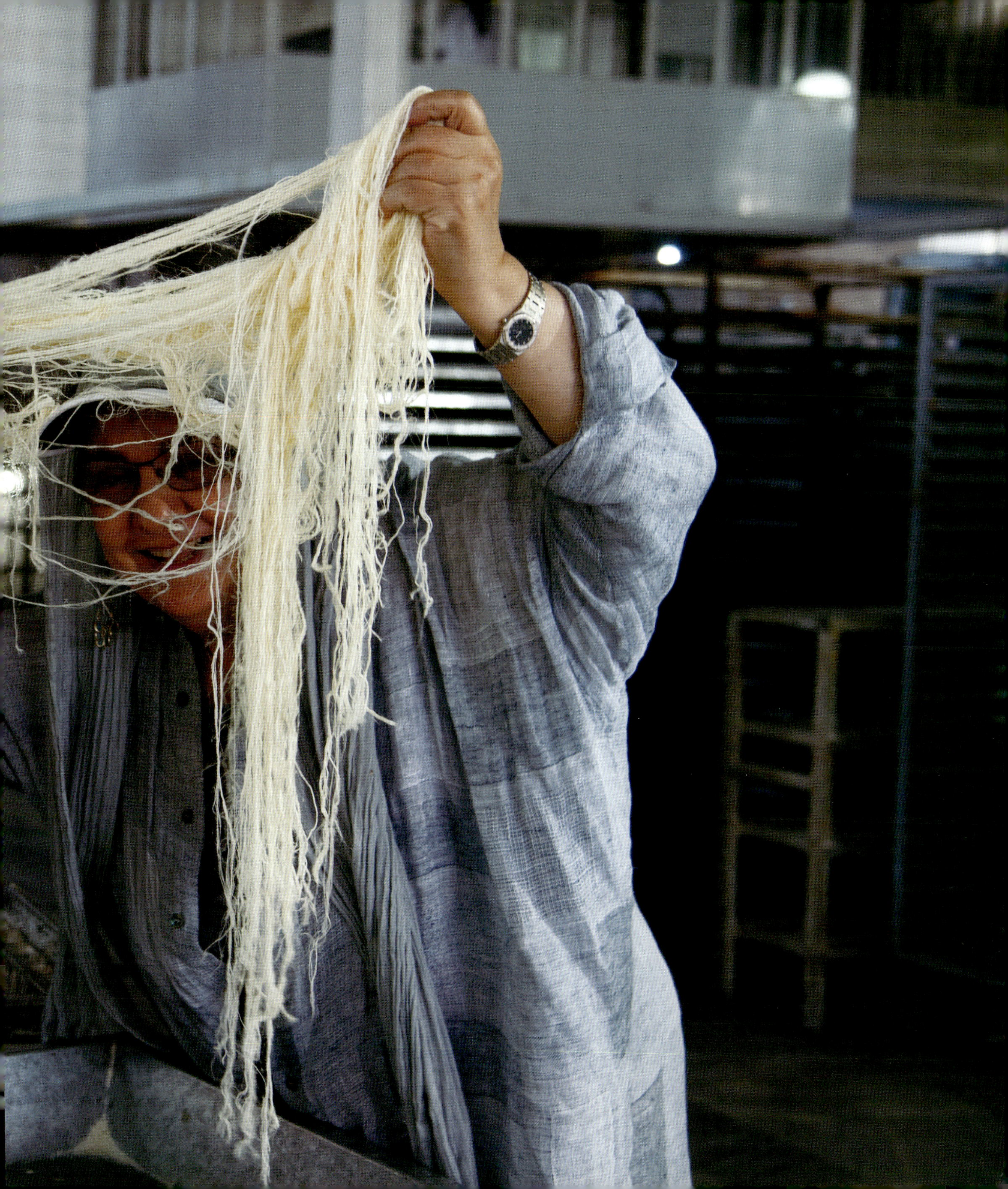

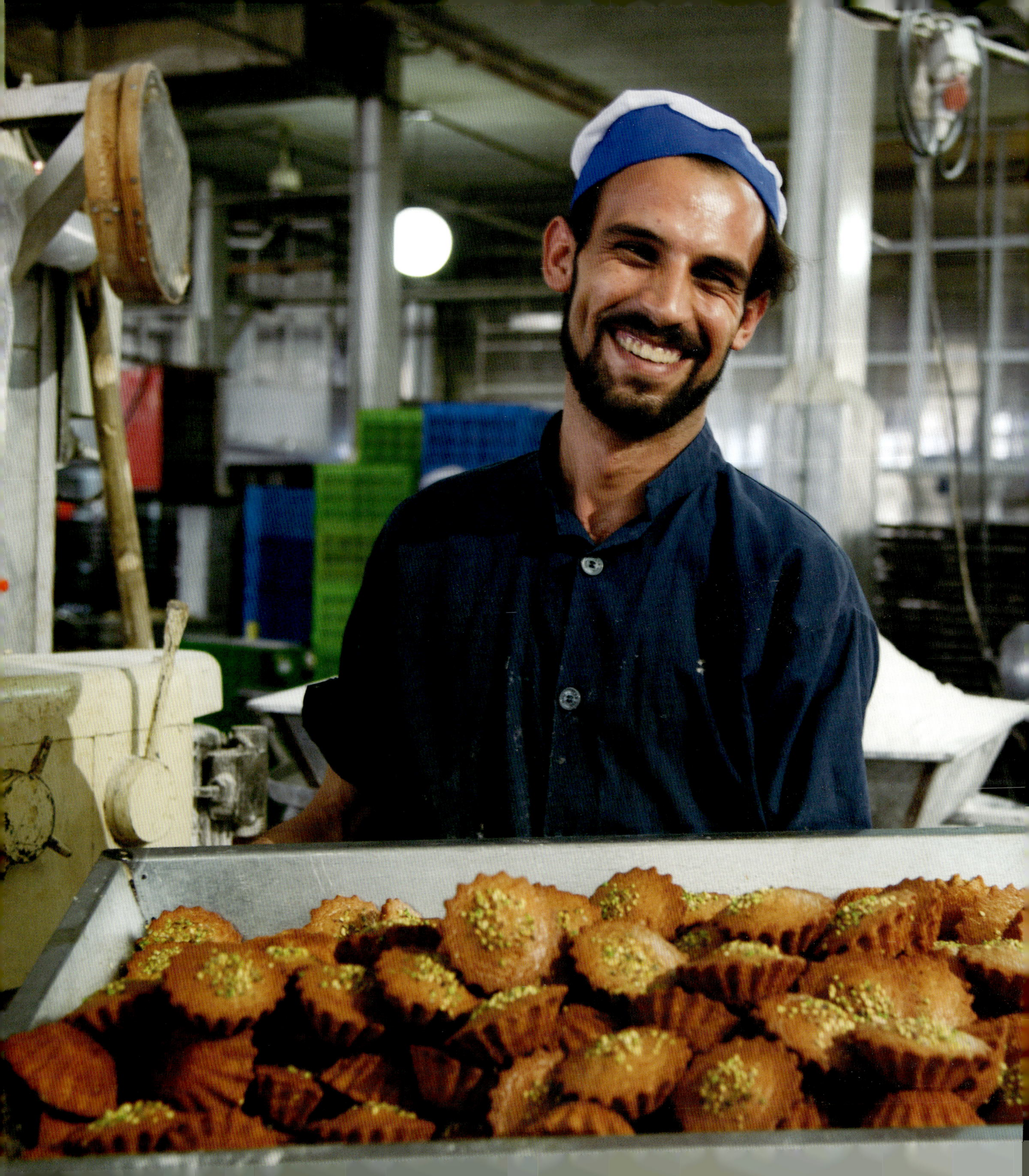

Yazdi Cupcakes
cayk-e yazdi

Makes 12 to 15 cupcakes
Prep: 15 minutes
Cooking: 15 minutes

BATTER

½ cup/110ml oil or ghee
¾ cup/150g cup sugar
¼ cup/60ml rose water
½ teaspoon vanilla extract
2 tablespoons honey
3 eggs (room temperature)
½ cup/120g whole plain yogurt
1 teaspoon baking soda
2 teaspoons baking powder
¼ teaspoon fine sea salt
1 tablespoon ground cardamom
2 cups/240g unbleached all-purpose flour

DECORATION

¼ cup/20g ground pistachios

OPTIONAL

¼ teaspoon ground saffron dissolved in ¼ cup/60ml rose water added in step 2

1. Place the oven rack in the center and preheat oven to 400°F/200°C. Line 2 muffin pans (capable of holding 12 muffins each) with paper cups.

2. *To make the batter:* In the mixing bowl of a electric mixer, blend the oil, sugar, rose water, vanilla, and honey. While mixer is running, add the eggs one by one. Add the yogurt and continue to blend until creamy.

3. Sift together the baking soda, baking powder, salt, cardamom, and the flour, and gradually add to the egg mixture. Blend for a few minutes—do not over-mix.

4. Pour the batter into lined molds, leaving ¼ in/6mm on top. Decorate each cupcake with some ground almonds.

5. Bake for 15 to 20 minutes or until golden brown and a tester comes out clean.

6. Remove the pan from the oven and allow to cool on a cooling rack. Remove the cupcakes from the pan and allow to cool *completely* before serving. Store in airtight glass containers. *Nush-e joon!*

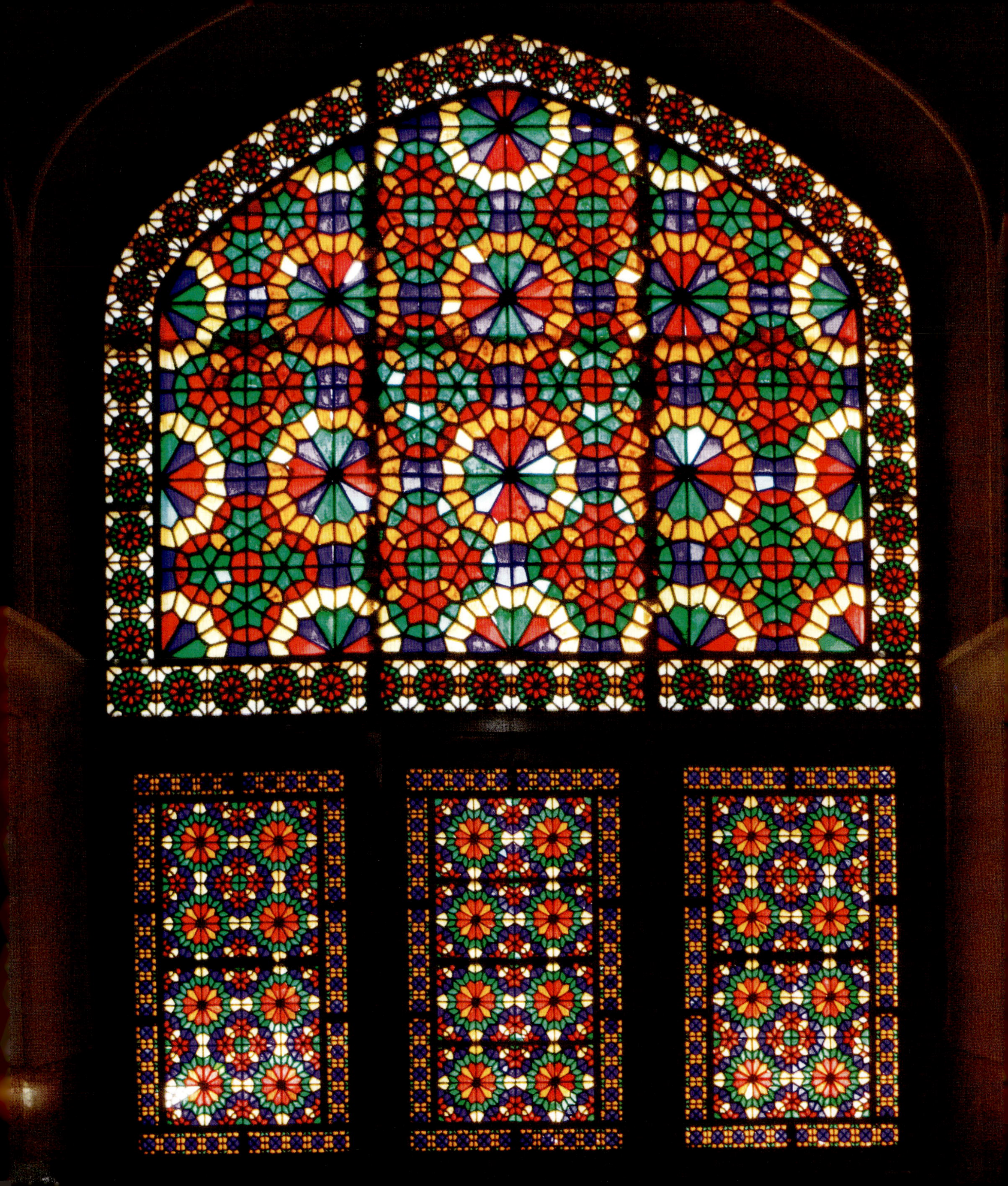

Opposite: A stained glass window in the wind-catcher of the
Dowlat Abad Garden in Yazd, built in 1747.
Above: Making saffron brittle at Haj Khalifeh's workshop.

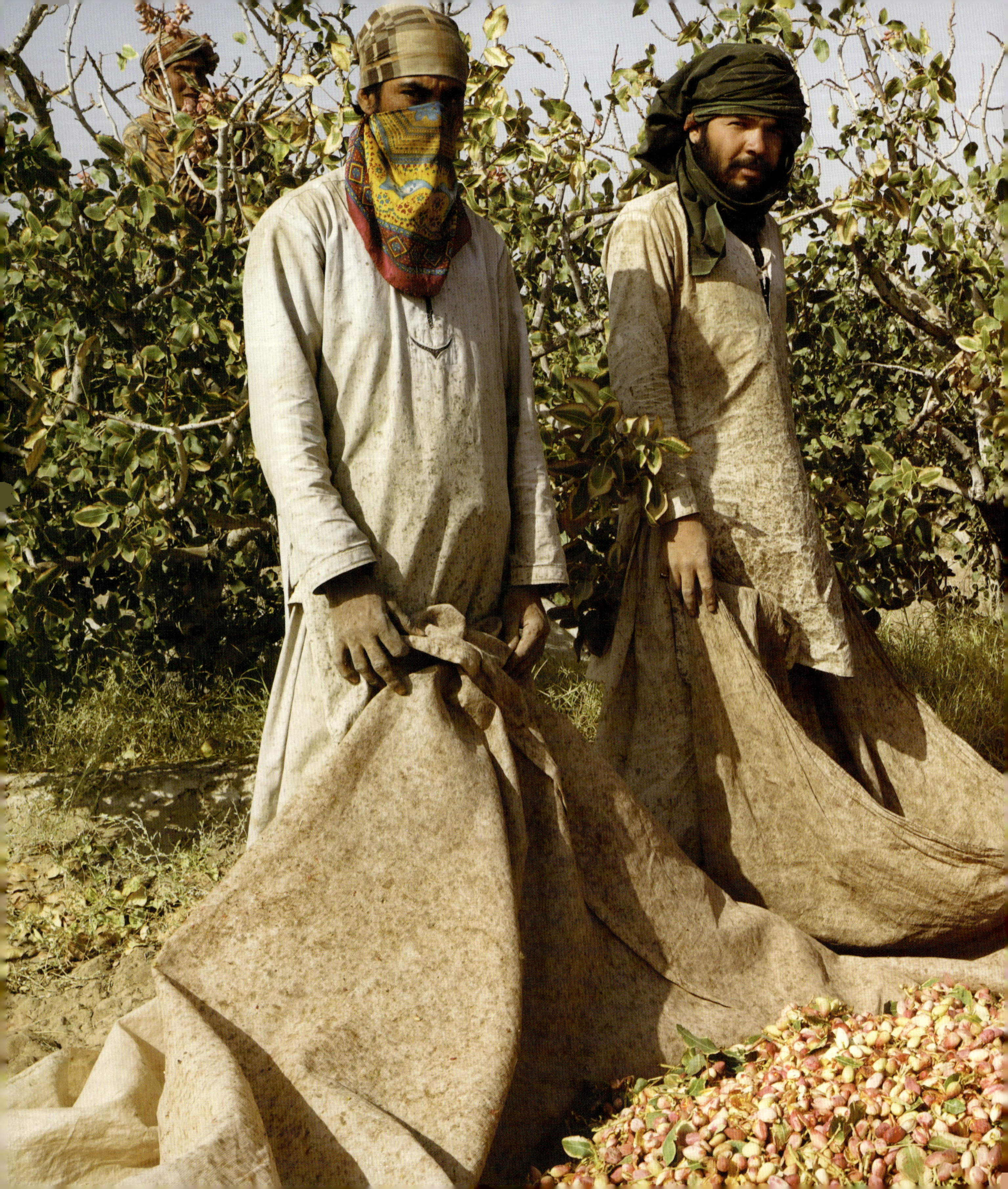

Kerman

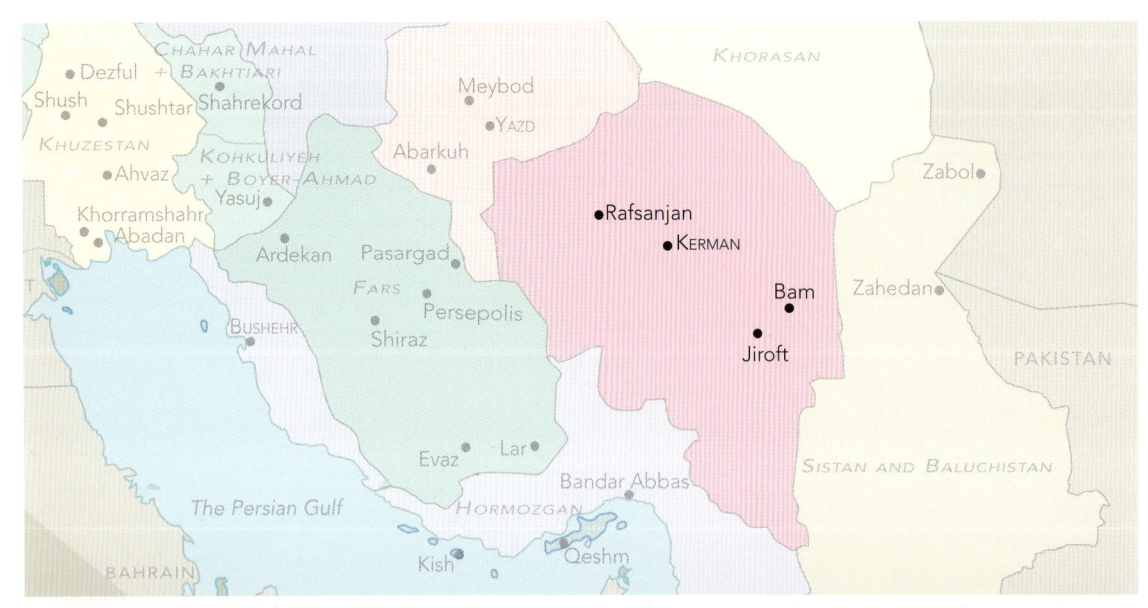

A typical interior courtyard of a Kermani house with a platform for sitting or sleeping set over a small pool.

A Little History

Kerman (the city and province go by the same name) is one of the cleanest cities in all of Iran, and its people are kind and hospitable. They opened their homes and their hearts to us with great dignity.

The city lies on the edge of a barren desert/*Dasht-e lut* but is surrounded by mountains. The most important city of southeast Iran, it has a long history and was mentioned in ancient inscriptions. In the time of Darius (550–486 BCE) the rosewood/*jag* used to build the palace at Susa was brought from there. At that time it was a part of Parsa (present day Pars Province, where Shiraz is the capital). The province continues to be rich in natural resources, especially copper. The city is home to many ancient Zoroastrian fire temples and historic mosques, and was an important stop along the Silk Road.

Antique Kerman carpets are some of the finest of all Persian carpets because of the quality of their wool (known as Carmania wool, the ancient Greek name for the province), the natural dies used, the range of their palette, and their lovely designs.

Kerman is perhaps most famous for its cumin, which mostly comes from Baft, a few hours' drive south of the city toward the Persian Gulf. Kermani cooks use cumin/*zireh* in almost every dish, including in their delicious breads. The Persian expression *"zireh be kermun bordan"* is similar to the English "taking coal to Newcastle."

Kerman and its neighboring town of Rafsanjan are where most of Iran's pistachios are produced. This is also the region where the traditional Iranian cuisine that incorporates pistachios has evolved over centuries. In the pages that follow, I am going to tell you about pistachios and give you several popular regional recipes that use them.

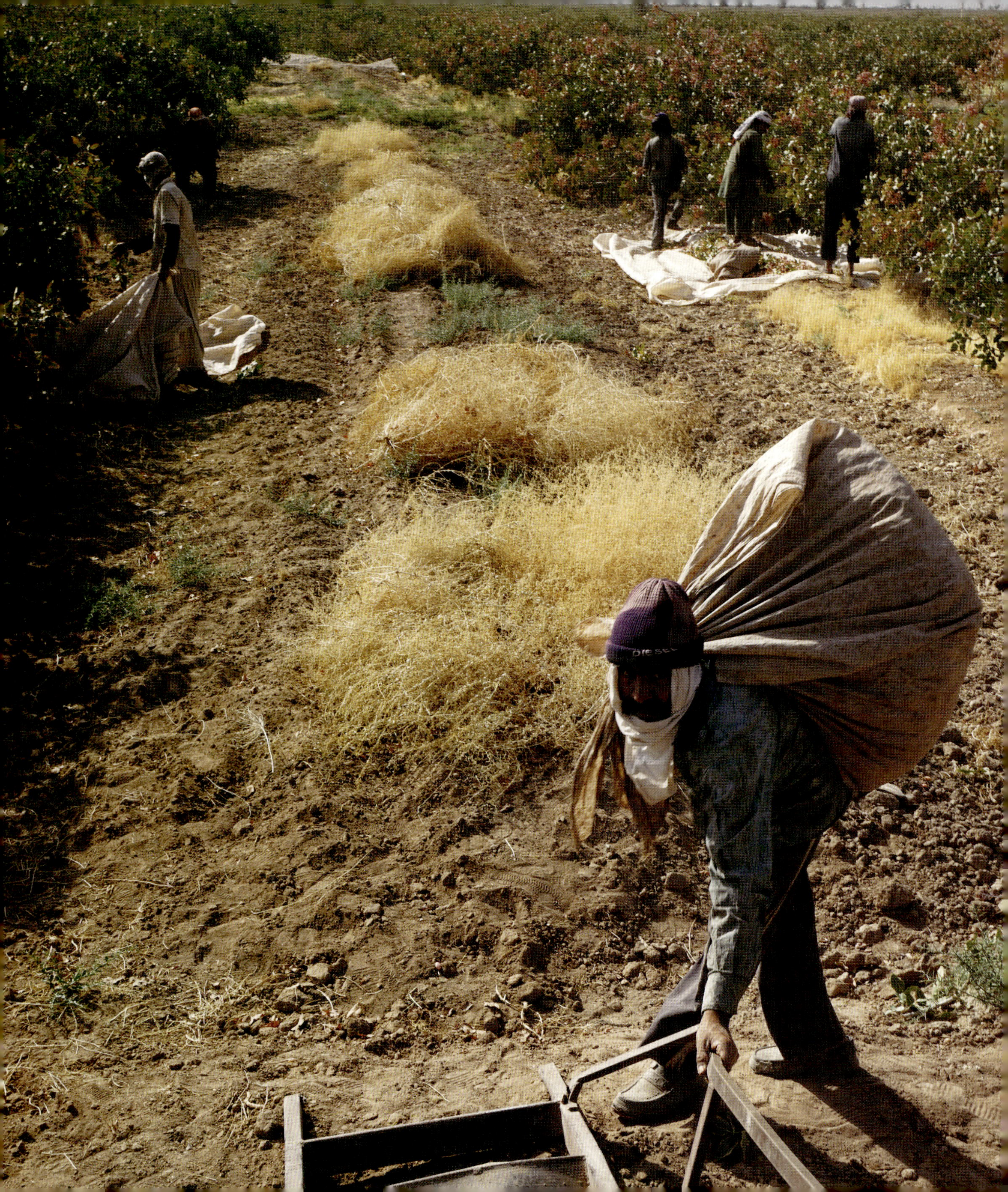

The Pistachio Journey
From Kerman to California

The word "pistachio" comes from the Persian "pesteh" via the Latin "pista." According to an ancient Greek chronicler, when King Astyages of the Medes gazed over his army after its defeat by Cyrus the Great, he exclaimed, "Woe, how brave are these pistachio-eating Persians!" And so Persians became known as "pistachio-eaters."

The oldest archeological evidence of pistachios was found at Jarmo, a site located in southern Kurdistan in the foothills of the Zagros Mountains. Jarmo was one of the earliest agricultural communities in the world, dating back to about 7000 BCE. Ancient written references to the nut are numerous. One mention appears in the Hebrew Bible: Genesis 43:11 speaks of honey, pistachios, and almonds.

In modern times, Iranians transformed the pistachio from a little-known local treat into a globally recognized snack, now one of their country's largest exports. A key role in this expansion was played by the Amin family, prominent merchants based in the town of Rafsanjan in the province of Kerman. Late in the nineteenth century, the family bought extensive agricultural lands around Rafsanjan and, along with growing cotton, began experimenting with pistachio farming. Pistachio trees proved well suited to the desert-like climate and salty soil of the area, and they required less water than cotton, pomegranates, or other crops. Soon Iran was exporting pistachios to places as far away as Bombay and Baku.

The first step toward pistachio-farming in the U.S. was taken in 1929, when a plant specialist at the Department of Agriculture, William E. Whitehouse, was sent to the Middle East to collect pistachio seeds. He returned with 20lb/9kg of seeds from various regions of Iran and elsewhere. Field tests were then conducted in the Central Valley in California to determine how well trees grown from his gatherings would do in their new environment. The best performers were those from Kerman seeds. They thrived beyond all expectation, yielding an abundance of nuts whose kernels are large, sweet, and tender. Today, U.S. pistachio production, consisting predominantly of the Kerman variety, surpasses the total output of Iran. Interestingly, the Amin family that fostered the rise of pistachio farming in Iran followed their Kerman seeds westward: Members of the family left Iran after the 1979 revolution there and are now heavily involved in the U.S. pistachio business.

Most American pistachio orchards are in California, although there are also some in Arizona and New Mexico. The trees are drought-tolerant and thrive in long, hot, and dry summers and cold winters. They start to yield nuts after 7 to 10 years and, with proper care, can remain productive for 100 to 150 years. Pistachio trees are divided into male and female, which are pollinated by wind (not insects). One male tree can pollinate 8 to 24 female trees. The trees bloom in April. Development of the nut eventually forces its hard shell to split—which will allow for the roasting, salting, and spicing of the nuts without first removing the shells,

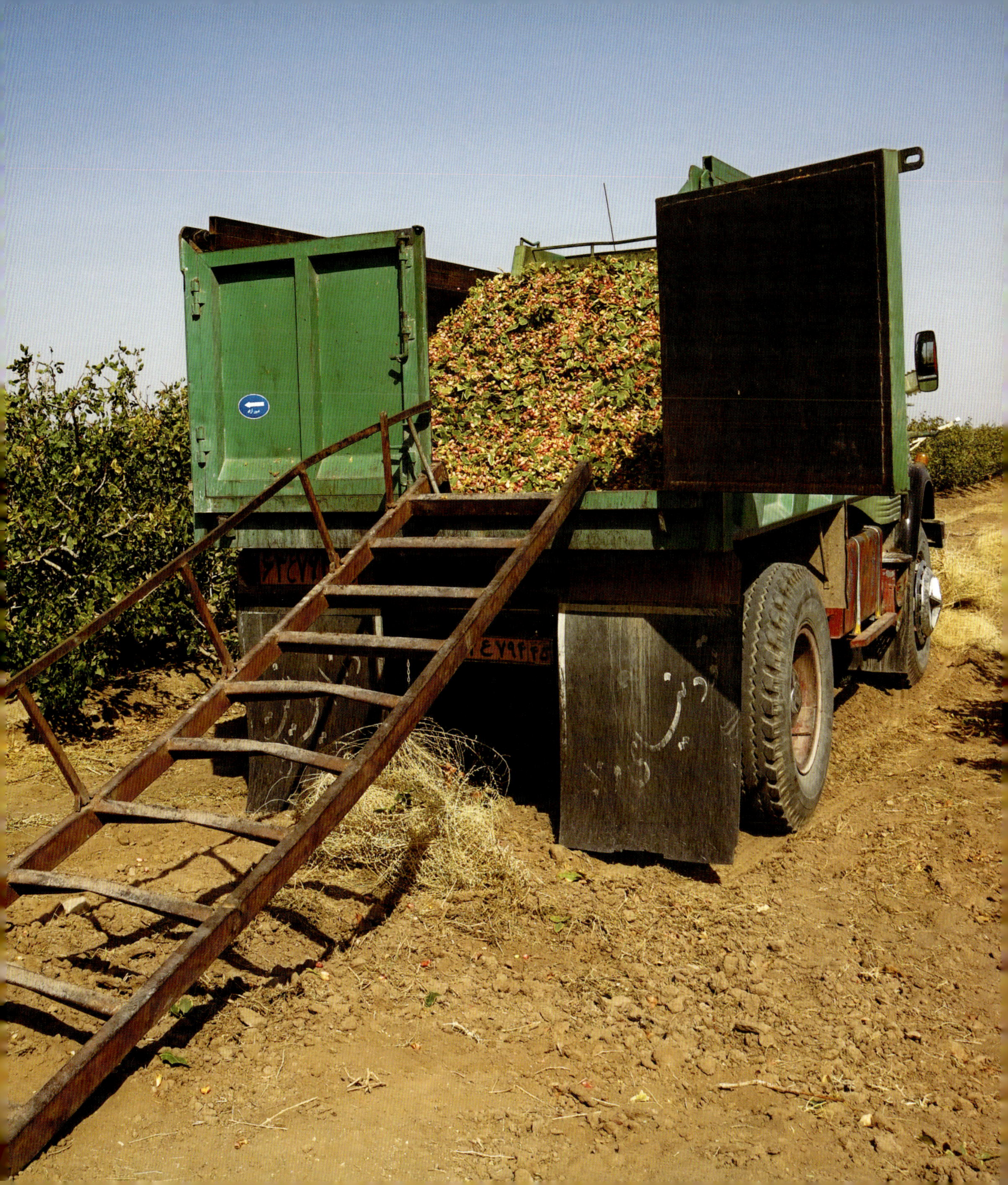

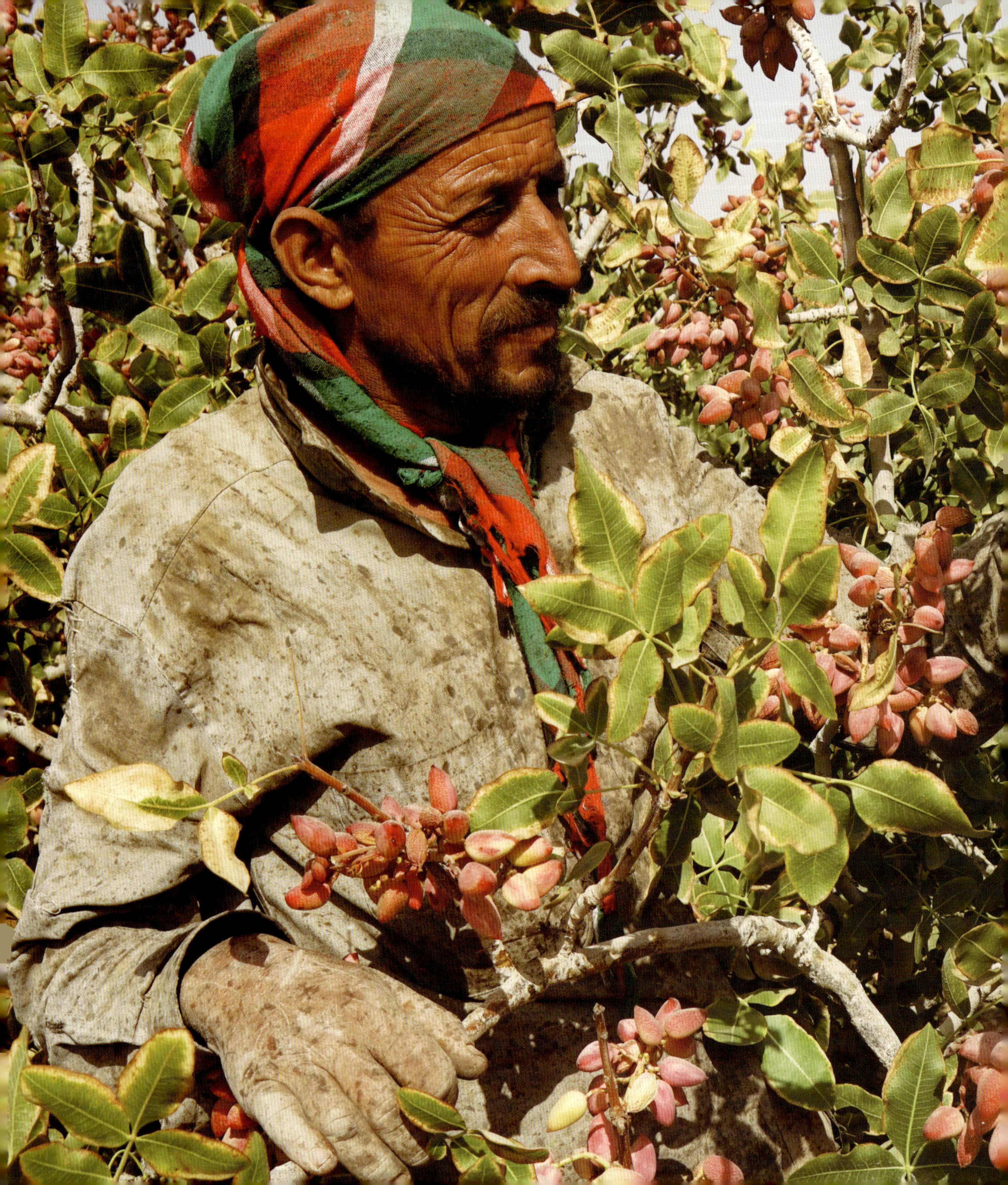

resulting in an easy-to-eat snack. The trees are trimmed and pruned to grow as much as 30 feet tall. At that size, they can be harvested by powerful machines that grab the trunks and shake the trees for several seconds, sending the nuts raining down into fabric-covered frames. The harvest takes place from early September to mid-October.

In Iran, a number of pistachio varieties flourish. They bear names like "long," "round," and "jumbo." One variety, shaped like the head of a wild sheep/*kaleh ghouchi*, is long and slender and very tasty. Pistachio trees are allowed to grow naturally in Iran—like bushes—and are traditionally harvested by hand.

Pistachios have a wide range of roles in Iranian cuisine. In late spring—when they are young, tender, and green, resembling small oval grapes—they are picked for making pickles and preserves. In Birjand and parts of Kurdistan, cooks use the wild nut/*pesteh baneh* at this stage for making a delicious yogurt soup (recipe on page 400). Over the summer, the skins/hulls (these are the soft skins protecting the hard shell) gradually become pinkish red. When they start to open at the seams, and as the harvest begins, they are carefully removed by hand and used for making jam. The hulls are so delicate and perfumed that no further spices or aromatics are used.

Pistachios can be eaten fresh (raw) in season as a snack, but more commonly they are roasted in the shell and salted, and sometimes flavored with lime juice, saffron, garlic, onion, or even jalapeño. As an ingredient in cooking, pistachio kernels are used raw. I incorporate them in a variety of dishes, ranging from salads and soups to meatballs and desserts. Some Kurdish cooks use pistachio oil to make very tasty rice.

In the U.S. we are familiar with almonds, walnuts, and peanuts in cooking, but less so with pistachios. Hopefully, in time, U.S. producers will start making raw pistachios available not only as kernels but also in sliced, slivered, and powdered form to expand their roles in the kitchen. The possibilities are endless. A Kermani delicacy, for example, is a slow-cooked pistachio braise made with pieces of lamb and whole pistachio kernels, which are sautéed in ghee and flavored with saffron, rose water, and verjuice. Pistachios serve to embellish and flavor rice dishes. And they are used extensively in pastries: The famous Persian baklava, for example, is made with thin layers of dough stuffed with ground pistachios and almonds flavored with saffron, and is soaked in honey, cardamom, and rose water. As for vegetarians, pistachios provide both proteins and vitamins along with a distinctive, seductive taste.

One of my favorite childhood snacks was a sweet powder made from ground raw pistachio kernels sweetened with powdered sugar. We would scoop it into the palms of our hands, throw back our heads, and pour it into our mouths. My friend Shohreh Amin, who grew up in Kerman, has shared some of her family's recipes with me. She recounts a wonderful childhood memory of their pistachio orchards in the village of Farahzad. They would use pistachio branches to make a bonfire, let it burn to ashes, and roast the fresh pistachios in their hulls while the ashes were still hot. Then they would peel them, sprinkle on some salt, and shell and eat them immediately—warm, smoky, and aromatic. What delicious childhood moments!

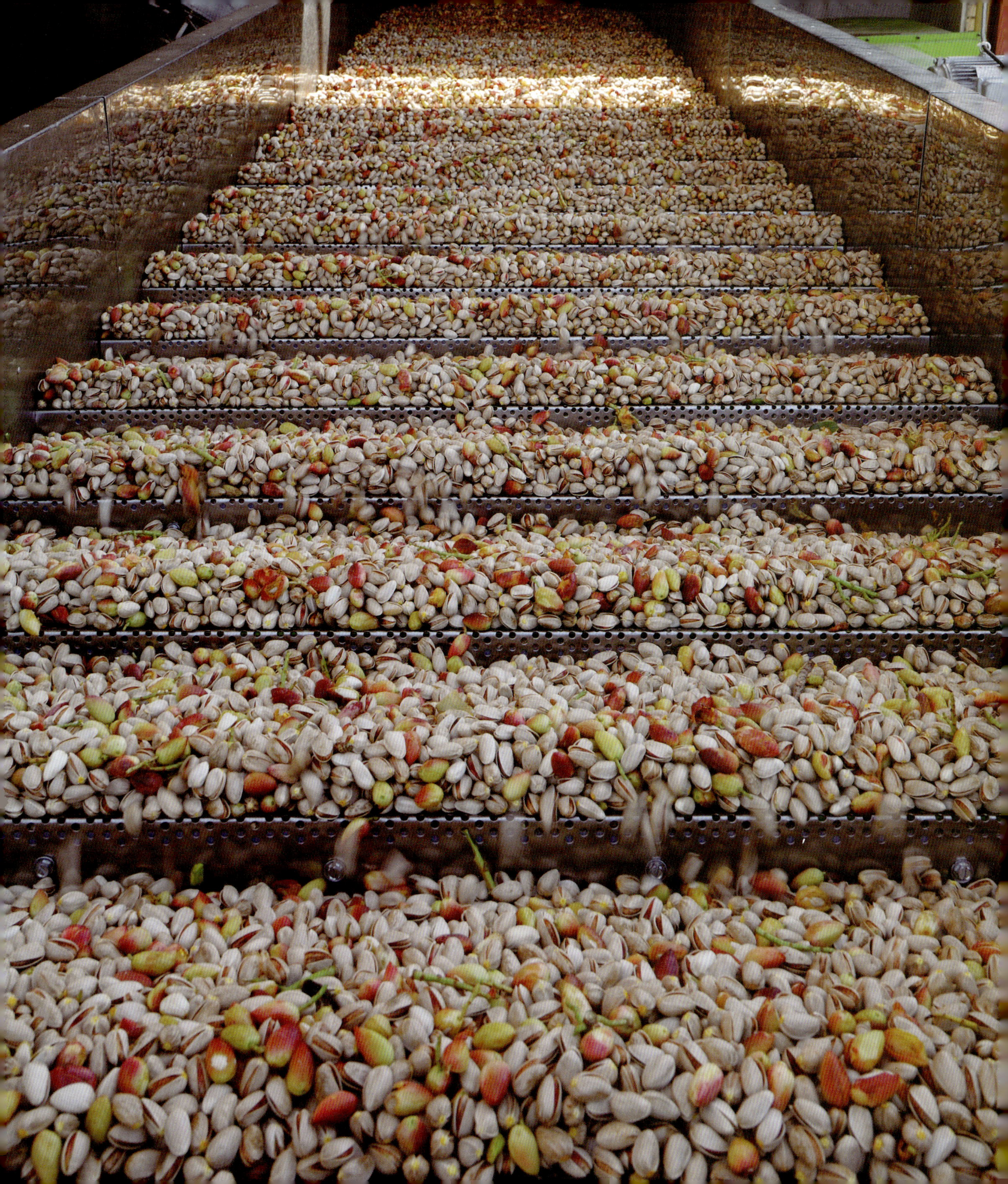

Kermani Seven-Spice Bread Advieh

advieh-ye nan-e kermani

Makes 1 cup/100g
Prep: 20 minutes

2 tablespoons safflowers/*gol-e rang*
2 teaspoons dried fenugreek leaves
2 tablespoons dried spring onions
2 tablespoons nigela seeds
3 tablespoons sesame seeds
3 tablespoons cumin seeds
2 tablespoons coriander seeds

Black cumin is the spice par excellence in Kermani cooking for all savory dishes. For bread they use a seven-spice advieh that is renowned, but I also use it in my kitchen for many dishes because it's so distinctive, unlike any of the other Iranian regions' adviehs. I adapted this recipe and most of the recipes in this section from Shohreh's Amin's family in Kerman and Rafsanjan. For pastries, Kermanis use a five-spice advieh.

1. Grind the spices, each separately, in a spice grinder.

2. Transfer them to a small bowl as you grind them and use a spoon to mix well.

3. Transfer to an airtight glass jar and keep in a cool place to use as needed. *Nush-e joon!*

Kermani Pastry Advieh

advieh-ye shirini-e kermani

Makes ¾ cup/75g
Prep: 20 minutes

2 tablespoons anise seeds
2 tablespoons cloves
2 tablespoons cinnamon
2 tablespoons cardamom
3 tablespoons green cumin seeds
3 tablespoons nutmeg

This is a specifically Kermani pastry spice mix.

1. Grind the spices, each separately, in a spice grinder.

2. Transfer them to a small bowl as you grind them and use a spoon to mix well.

3. Transfer to an airtight glass jar and keep in a cool place to use as needed. *Nush-e joon!*

Brown Butter/Ghee

masskeh/roghan-e gusfand-e kermani

Makes 1lb/450g
Prep: 2 minutes
Cooking: 15 minutes

1lb/450g sheep or goat butter
1 tablespoon all-purpose flour

In Kerman, they mostly cook using sheep or goat ghee, which is the clarified or browned butter from the milk of those animals. It gives their dishes a unique taste.

1. Place the butter in a wide skillet over low heat and bring to a boil.

2. Sprinkle 1 tablespoon all-purpose flour and continue simmering until the flour is golden brown. Remove from heat and allow to cool for 1 minute. Pass through a fine-mesh sieve into a bowl. Discard any solids and keep the clarified butter in the bowl. This is the favored oil for Kermani cooking. *Nush-e joon!*

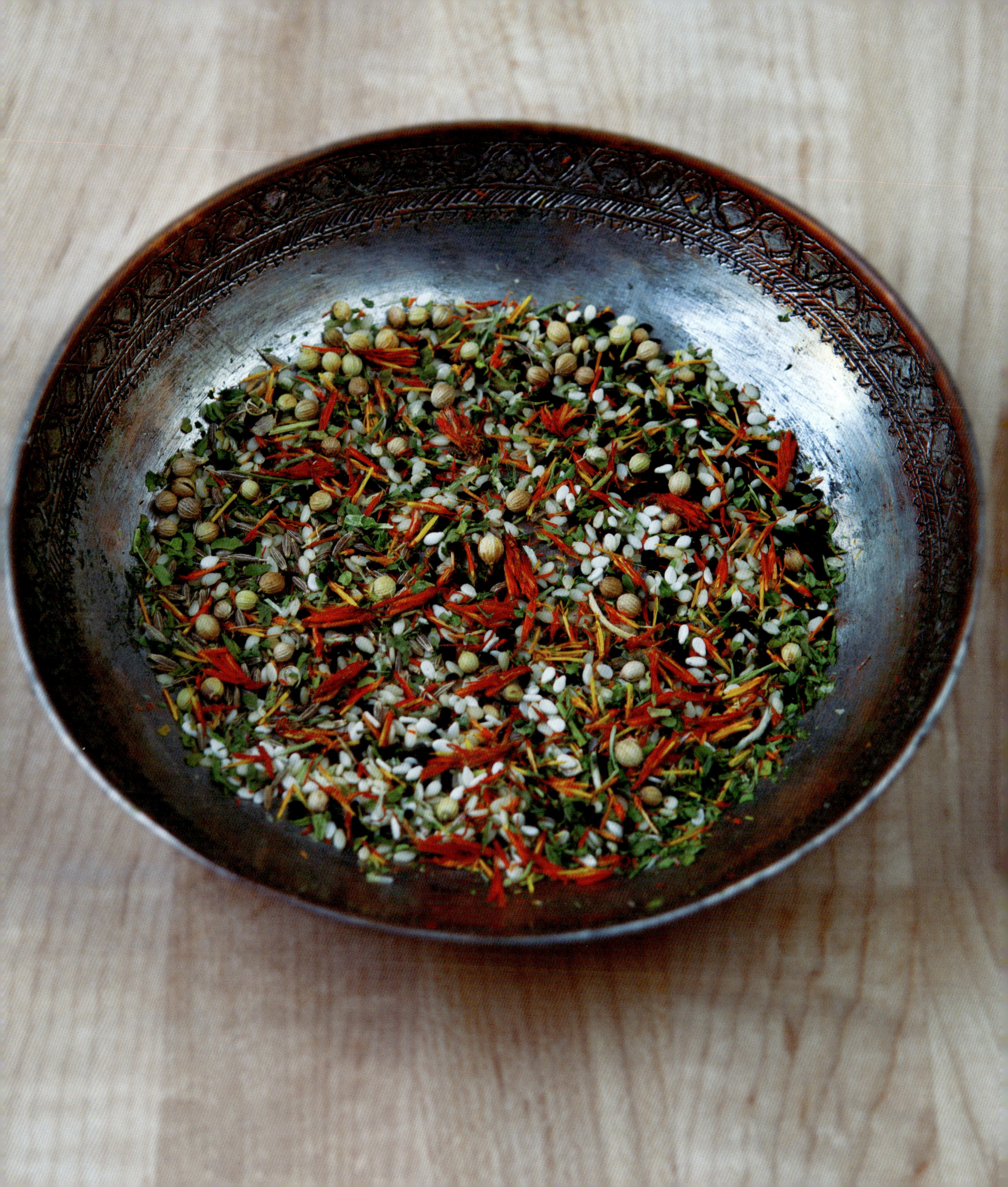

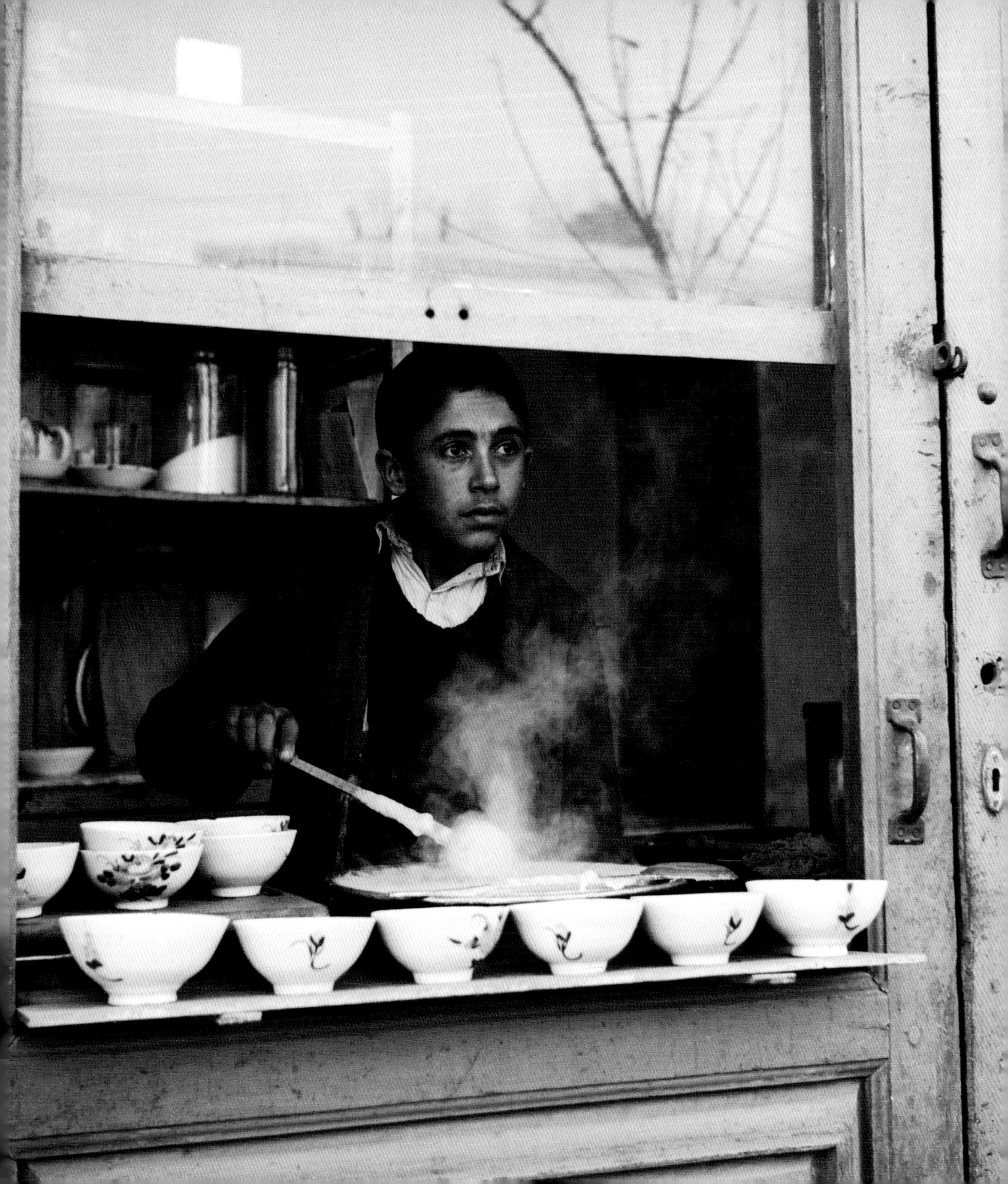

Pistachio, Saffron + Sour Orange Soup

sup-e pesteh ba za'ferun-o narenj-e kermani

Serves 4
Prep: 25 minutes
Cooking: 1 hour

SOUP

1 cup/120g raw pistachio kernels
2 tablespoons oil or ghee
1 small onion, finely chopped
2 cloves garlic, peeled and grated
2 teaspoons fine sea salt
½ teaspoon freshly ground pepper
½ teaspoon turmeric
1 tablespoon ground black cumin seeds
1 teaspoon ground coriander seeds
½ teaspoon ground ginger
½ teaspoon cayenne
2 tablespoons rice flour
8 cups/1.9l chicken broth or water
½ cup/120ml sour orange juice/*narenj* or combination of ¼ cup/60ml fresh orange juice and ¼ cup/60ml fresh lime juice
½ teaspoon ground saffron dissolved in 2 tablespoons water

GARNISH

2 tablespoons chopped raw pistachio kernels and/or organic edible flower petals

I adapted this recipe from a traditional pistachio soup made by the Amin family in Rafsanjan. The cover photo of this book shows the soup.

1. **To make the soup:** Pick over the shelled pistachios to be sure there are no broken shells or other particles in them. Grind the pistachios in a food processor or grinder until very smooth. Set aside.

2. Heat the oil in a medium-sized laminated cast-iron pot over medium heat. Add the onion and garlic, and sauté for 5 minutes. Add the salt, pepper, turmeric, cumin, coriander, ginger, cayenne, and rice flour, and sauté for 1 minute.

3. Add the broth and the pistachios, stirring constantly until it comes to a boil. Reduce heat to low, cover and simmer for 55 minutes, stirring occasionally.

4. Add the sour orange juice and saffron water, and use a hand-held mixer to create a creamy mixture. Cover and allow to simmer for another 5 minutes. Keep warm until ready to serve.

5. Adjust seasoning to taste. Pour the soup into a tureen and garnish. Serve with hot flat bread. *Nush-e joon!*

Camomile Flowers, Egg + Onion Soup

eshkeneh-ye gol-e babuneh-ye kermani

Serves 4
Prep: 10 minutes + 1 hour soaking flowers
Cooking: 1½ hours

½ cup/25g dried camomile flowers, soaked in water for 1 hour and drained
¼ cup/60ml oil
2 large onions, peeled and thinly sliced
1 tablespoon fine sea salt
½ teaspoon freshly ground pepper
1 teaspoon turmeric
2 tablespoons cumin seeds
2 tablespoons flour
1 tablespoon dried mint
6 cups/1.5l water
1 russet potato (1lb/450g), peeled and quartered
4 eggs

GARNISH

1 cup/240g drained yogurt
3 flat breads/lavash

As children, our mother would give me and my sisters camomile infusions and sometimes she'd wash our hair with a mixture of camomile and henna to give our hair a special glow, but I'd never imagined you could have camomile flowers in a soup. The taste is quite distinctive, and like the tea, the soup has a calming effect.

1. Heat the oil in a large laminated cast-iron pot over medium heat and sauté the onions until golden brown. Add the salt, pepper, turmeric, and cumin seeds, and sauté for 2 minutes. Add the flour, mint, and camomile, and sauté for 20 seconds.

2. Add the water and potato, and bring to a boil. Reduce heat to medium, cover, and allow to simmer for 35 to 40 minutes until the potatoes are tender.

3. Add the eggs and stir for a few minutes to combine them with the soup. Bring back to boil (an alternate method is to add the eggs one by one and allow them to poach in the soup gradually). Adjust seasoning to taste.

4. Pour the soup into a tureen and serve with yogurt and bread. *Nush-e joon!*

Kerman

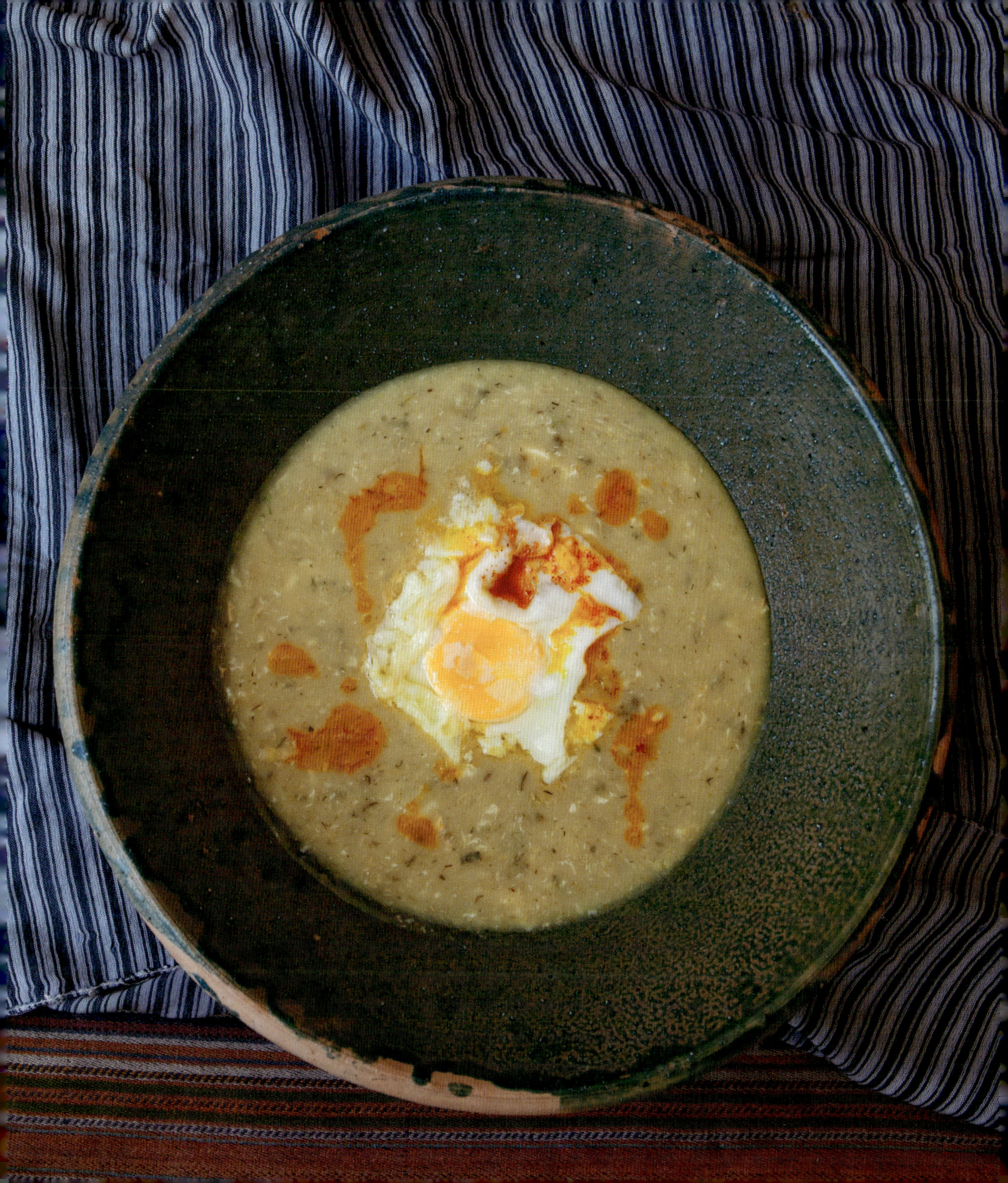

Kermani Wheat Osh
osh-e gandom-e kermani

Serves 6
Prep: 15 minutes + soaking overnight
Cooking: 2 hours

BROTH

2lb/900g lamb neck or turkey with the bone
4 medium onions, peeled and thinly sliced
2 cloves garlic, peeled and sliced
2 teaspoons fine sea salt
1 teaspoon freshly ground pepper
2 teaspoons turmeric
1 tablespoon ground black cumin

LEGUMES

1 cup/200g whole wheat grain, soaked overnight, drained, and rinsed
¼ cup/50g chickpeas, soaked overnight, drained, and rinsed
¼ cup/50g red beans, soaked overnight, drained, and rinsed
1 cup/240g liquid *kashk*

GARNISH/NA`NA DAGH

2 tablespoons oil
1 teaspoon turmeric
2 tablespoons dried mint
2 tablespoons liquid *kashk*
2 tablespoons ground walnuts

Both osh *and* halim *can be called porridge in English, but an* osh *is generally lighter than a* halim. *We were served this* osh *in Kerman in an old traditional house.*

1. **To cook the lamb:** Place the lamb neck in a large heavy-bottomed pot, add 8 cups/1.9l water, and bring to a boil. Skim the froth as it forms until it stops forming. Add the onions, garlic, salt, pepper, turmeric, and cumin. Bring back to a boil. Reduce heat to low, cover, and simmer for 1½ to 2 hours until the meat is tender and falling off the bone. Stir occasionally to prevent sticking to the bottom of the pot.

2. **Meanwhile, to cook the legumes:** In a large saucepan, place the wheat, chickpeas, beans, and 6 cups/1.5l water. Bring to a boil, reduce heat to low, cover, and simmer for 1 to 1¼ hours until the wheat and legumes are tender. Add more warm water if necessary.

3. **To assemble the osh:** Drain the meat through a fine-mesh colander and pour the broth back into the pot. Separate the meat from the bones and return it to the pot (discard the bones and any fat). Add the legumes with the juice and the *kashk* to the pot. Use a handheld mixer to partially puree the meat and legumes.

4. Place the pot over low heat, cover, and simmer for 10 minutes. Adjust seasoning to taste.

5. **Meanwhile, to make the garnish/na`na dagh:** Heat 2 tablespoons oil in a wide skillet over medium heat. Add the turmeric and sauté for 1 minute. Remove from heat. Add the dried mint and mix well.

6. Transfer the *osh* into a tureen and decorate with the garnish, *kashk*, and walnuts. Just before serving, give the *osh* a stir. *Nush-e joon!*

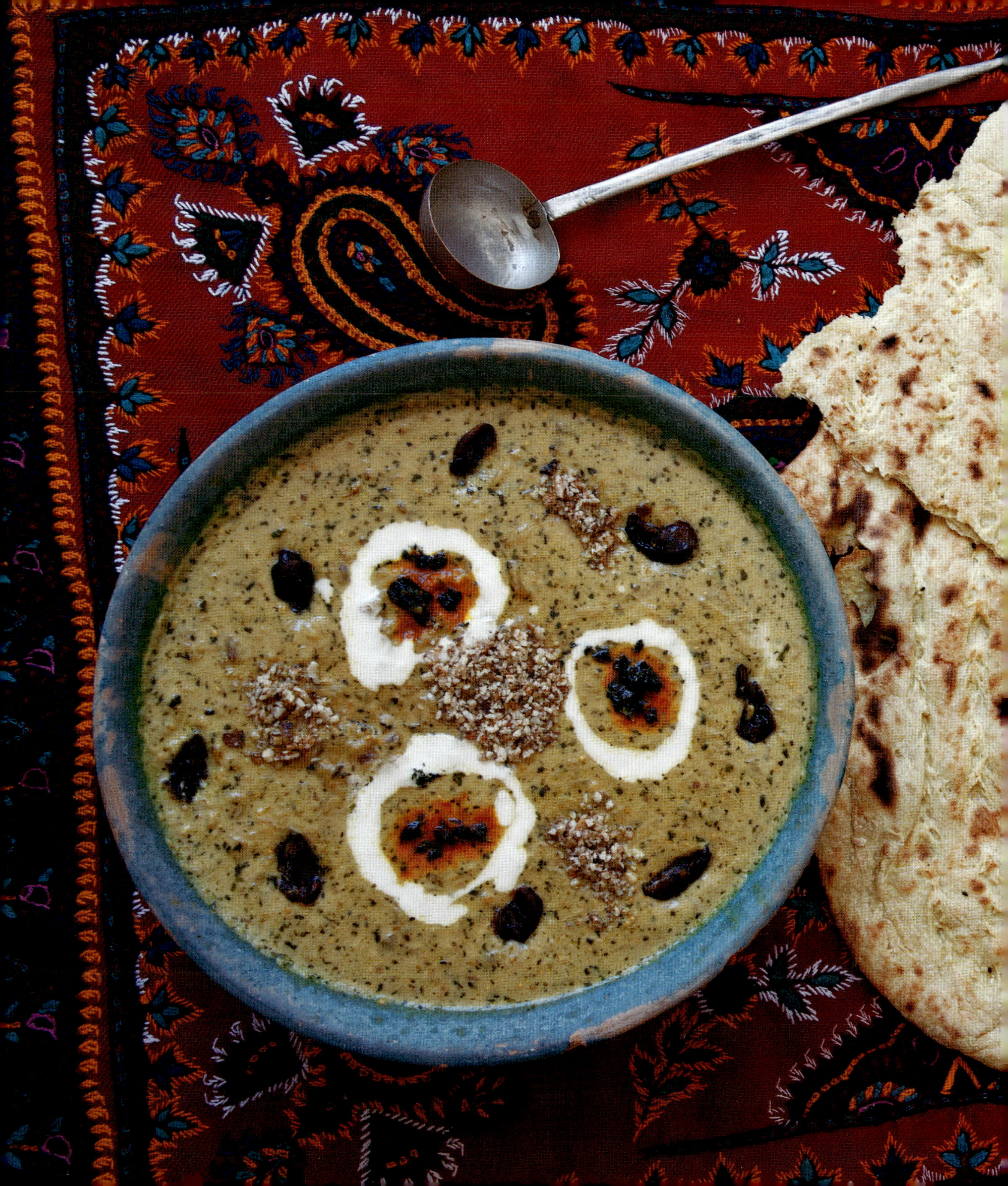

Pistachio, Fresh Herbs + Cardamom Kuku
kuku-ye pesteh-ye kermani

Serves 6 to 8
Prep: 40 minutes
Cooking: 40 minutes

CARAMELIZED ONIONS
2 tablespoons oil
1 medium onion, peeled and thinly sliced

PISTACHIO AND HERBS MIXTURE
1½ cups/180g pistachio kernels
2 cups/170g fresh roughly chopped dill weed
2 cups/170g fresh roughly chopped cilantro
1 cup/100g roughly chopped spring onions, (white and green parts)

EGGS AND SPICES
6 eggs
½ teaspoon baking powder
2 teaspoons fine sea salt
½ teaspoon freshly ground pepper
½ teaspoon turmeric
1 teaspoon ground cardamom
2 teaspoons ground cumin

6 tablespoons oil or ghee

GARNISH
1 tablespoon fresh dill weed

Another version of this kuku is made around the Caspian with walnuts instead of pistachios. For the Caspian version, use 1 cup walnuts instead of pistachios in the herb mixture, reduce the dill to 1 cup, and add 1 cup cilantro, 1 cup parsley, 1 tablespoon dried fenugreek leaves, and garnish with caramelized barberries.

1. **To caramelize the onions:** Heat 2 tablespoons oil in a fritata pan over low heat and sauté the onion for 20 to 30 minutes until golden brown.

2. **To prepare the pistachio herbs mixture:** In a food processor, pulse the pistachios, caramelized onions, and herbs until grainy.

3. **To prepare the eggs and spices:** Break the eggs into a large mixing bowl. Add the rest of the ingredients and beat lightly with a fork.

4. Transfer the pistachio and herbs mixture to the eggs and fold in using a rubber spatula (do not over-mix).

5. Heat 6 tablespoons oil in a frittata pan over low heat until hot but not smoking. Pour in the egg mixture, cover, and cook until it has set (about 20 minutes). Simply flip over and cook for another 15 to 20 minutes until cooked through.

6. Transfer to a serving dish, cut into diamond shapes, and garnish. Serve with bread and green salad. *Nush-e joon!*

COOK IN THE OVEN VARIATION

Preheat the oven to 400°F/200°C and line a quarter-sized (9½ x 13 in/ 24 x 33 cm) rimmed sheet pan with parchment paper. **To cook the kuku:** Paint the lined sheet pan with oil. Pour in the egg mixture from step 5, and gently shake the pan to even out the batter. Bake in the preheated oven for 15 to 20 minutes.

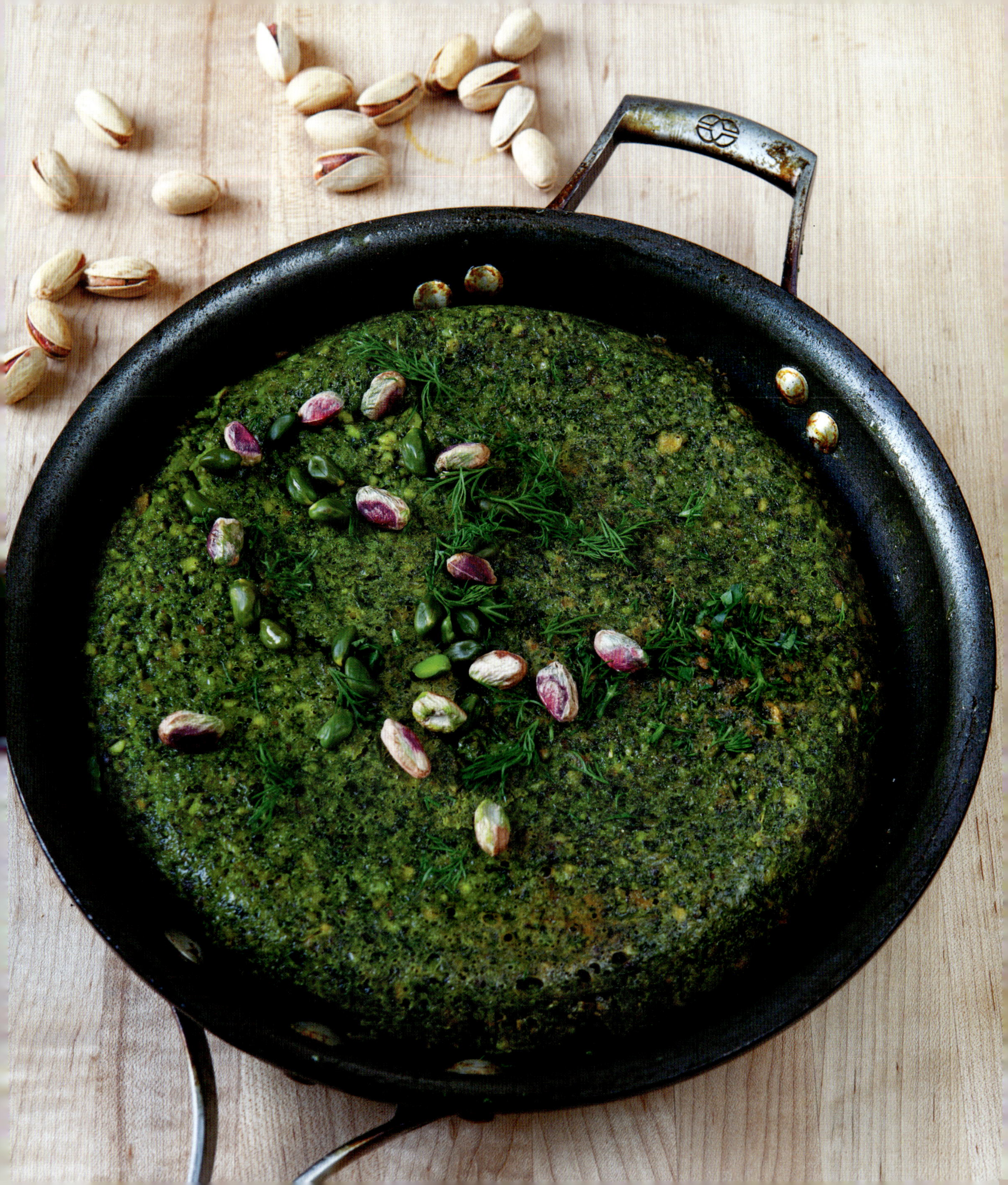

Skillet Kabab
kabab-e tabe'-ye kermani

Serves 4
Prep: 15 minutes
Cooking: 35 minutes

LAMB PASTE

1lb/450g ground lamb, beef or chicken thigh
1 medium onion, finely grated
2 cloves garlic, peeled and finely grated
1 teaspoon fine sea salt
½ teaspoon fresh ground pepper
1 teaspoon turmeric
1 tablespoon sumac
½ teaspoon red pepper flakes
1 teaspoon grape molasses or honey

2 tablespoons oil for frying

TOPPING

1 large tomato, peeled and sliced
½ teaspoon fine sea salt
½ teaspoon fresh ground pepper
3 tablespoons oil
1lb/450g russet potatoes, peeled thinly and sliced (optional)

This dish is popular throughout Iran under various names. In Hamadan, they grate the potato and mix it into the lamb paste (in step 1), use slices of bell peppers on top of the tomatoes, and call it kabab-e sardash.

1. **To make the lamb paste:** In a mixing bowl, combine all the ingredients for the lamb paste, except the oil. Knead lightly, using your hands, to create a soft paste (do not over-mix).

2. Oil a heavy-based 8in/20cm skillet. Moisten your hands and shape the paste into a large meatball and place it in the center of the skillet.

3. Press down with a spatula so the meat covers the base of the entire skillet. Raise the meat around the edges of the skillet by 1in/2.5cm to form a well.

4. Cook over medium heat for 15 minutes. Cut the meat into pie wedges. Arrange the tomato slices on top, sprinkle with salt and pepper, and drizzle 1 tablespoon oil evenly on top.

5. Cover and cook over low heat for another 15 minutes or until cooked through.

6. Meanwhile, heat 2 tablespoons oil in a wide skillet over medium heat and sauté the potatoes on both sides until golden brown.

7. Uncover the skillet with the lamb and place it under a broiler. Cook for 1 to 2 minutes until brown.

8. Arrange the potatoes on top. Transfer the kabab to a serving platter, and drizzle some of the pan juices on top. Serve hot with bread, green salad, and fresh herbs. *Nush-e joon!*

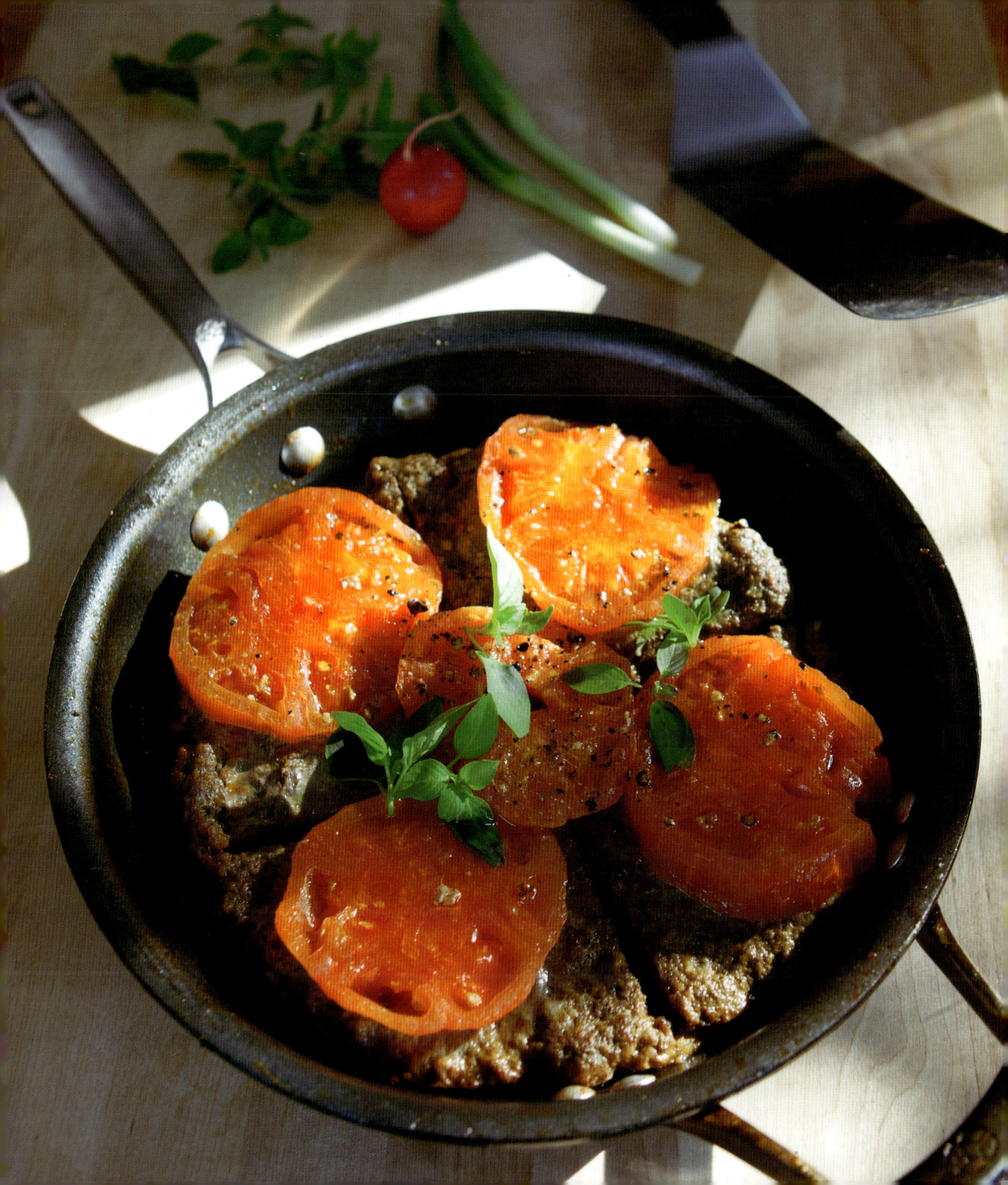

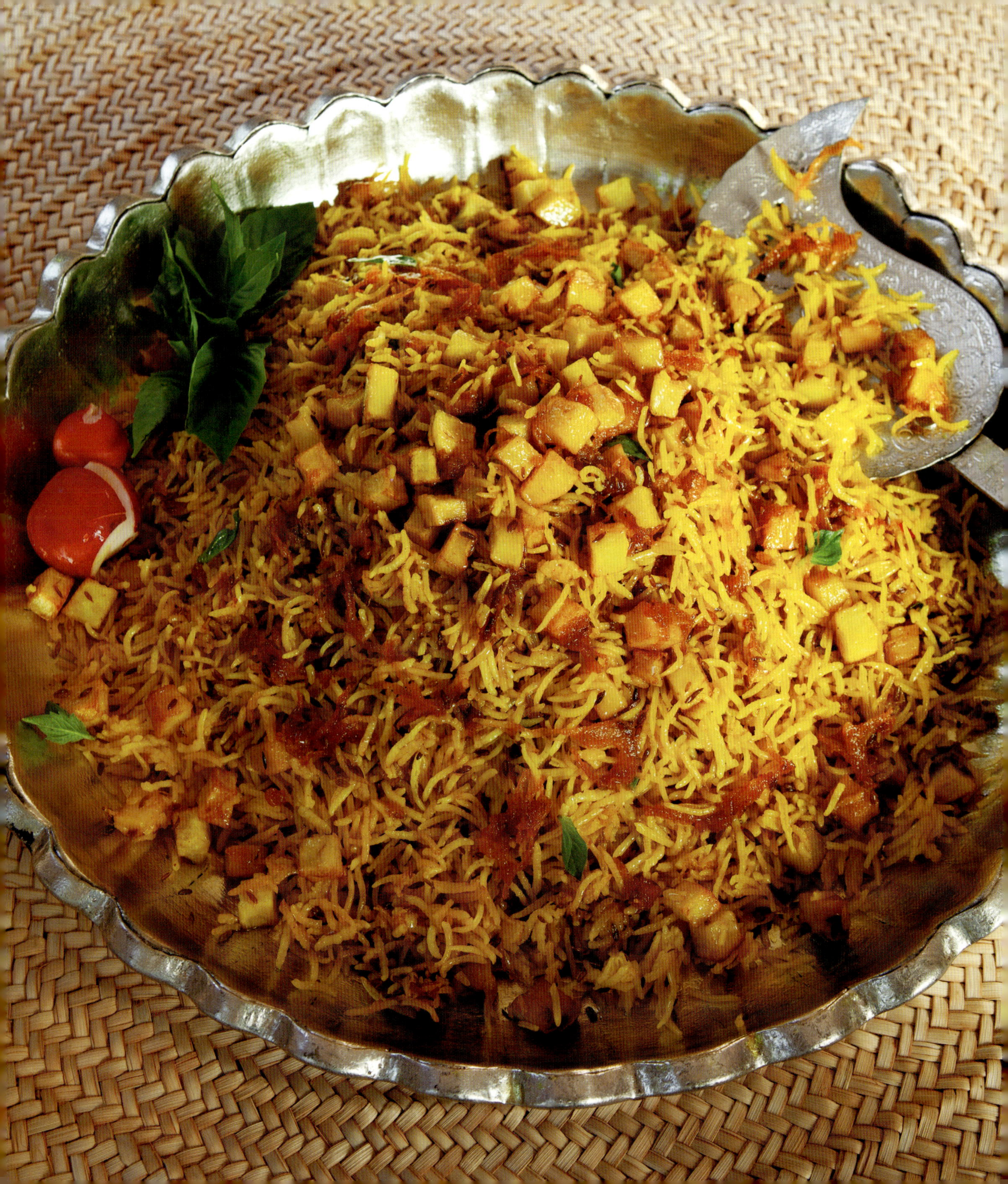

Steamed Rice with Cumin + Potatoes

zireh polow-ye kermani

Serves 6
Prep: 15 minutes
Cooking: 1 hour

2 cups/400g white basmati rice
½ cup/120ml oil or ghee
2 medium onions, peeled and thinly sliced
1lb/450g potatoes, peeled and diced into 1in/2.5cm cubes
4 tablespoons black cumin seeds
1 tablespoon fine sea salt
2 teaspoons turmeric or ½ teaspoon ground saffron
4 cups/960ml homemade chicken broth or water

I adapted this recipe from Mah-Gol Bagherpour, a wonderful cook at Shahin and Homayoun Sarlati's house in Kerman.

1. Wash the rice by placing it in a large container and covering it with lukewarm water. Agitate gently with your hand, then pour off the water. Repeat 4 to 5 times until the water is clear. Drain.

2. Heat ¼ cup/60ml oil in a large non-stick size pot over medium heat and sauté the onions until lightly golden brown. Add the potatoes, cumin, salt, and turmeric, and sauté for 2 minutes.

3. Add the rice and broth and bring to a boil over high heat. Gently stir the rice with a wooden spoon a few times while it boils.

4. Reduce heat to medium, cover and simmer for 20 minutes over medium heat.

5. When the rice has absorbed all the water, swirl the remaining oil over the rice. Reduce heat to low. Wrap the lid of the pot with a clean dish towel and cover firmly to prevent steam from escaping. Cook 30 minutes longer.

6. Remove the pot from heat and allow to cool for 5 minutes on a damp surface without uncovering it.

7. Gently taking one skimmer or spatula full of rice at a time, place it on a serving platter without disturbing the crust. Mound rice in shape of a cone. Serve with a fresh herb platter and a Tomato, Cucumber, and Herb Salad (page 523) *Nush-e joon!*

VARIATION

To make Persian Gulf Rice and Tomatoes/*sholeh-ye tamata-ye junubi*, replace the broth in step 3 with 5 medium tomatoes, pureed (about 2¼ lb/1kg); 2in/5cm fresh ginger, peeled and grated, and 1 tablespoon dried ground rose petals. Everything else remains the same.

Milk-Steamed Rice with Dates + Raisins
shir pilau-e kermani

Serves 6 to 8
Prep: 5 minutes
Cooking: 45 minutes

RICE

3 cups/600g white basmati rice
1 cup/240ml water
4 cups/960ml milk or almond milk
1 tablespoon fine sea salt
½ teaspoon saffron dissolved in 2 tablespoons rose water
3 tablespoons black cumin seeds

TOPPING

1 cup/175g dates, pitted and diced into ½ inch/1cm cubes
1 cup/150g raisins
¼ cup/60ml oil or ghee

This rice dish is cooked throughout Iran. Around The Caspian they call it shir pilaw *and add 1 teaspoon turmeric, 1 teaspoon cinnamon, and ½ cup/60g chopped walnuts. In Ardebil they call it* suti polow, *and add 2in/5cm grated fresh ginger to the above as well as adding slices of smoked fish to the rice in step 5*

1. Wash the rice by placing it in a large container and covering it with lukewarm water. Agitate gently with your hand, then pour off the water. Repeat 4 to 5 times until the water is clear. Drain.

2. Place the rice, water, milk, salt, saffron-rose water, and cumin seeds in a large non-stick pot. Bring to a boil over high heat. Gently stir the rice with a wooden spoon a few times while it boils.

3. Reduce heat to medium-low, cover, and simmer for 20 minutes.

4. Add the dates and raisins, and swirl the oil over the rice. Fluff with a fork.

5. Wrap the lid of the pot with a clean dish towel and cover firmly to prevent steam from escaping. Cook for 20 minutes over low heat.

6. Remove the pot from heat and allow to cool for 5 minutes on a damp surface without uncovering.

7. Gently taking one spatula full of rice at a time, place it on a serving platter without disturbing the crust. Mound rice in shape of a cone.

8. Detach the crust from the bottom of the pot using a wooden spatula. Place it around the rice. *Nush-e joon!*

Kerman

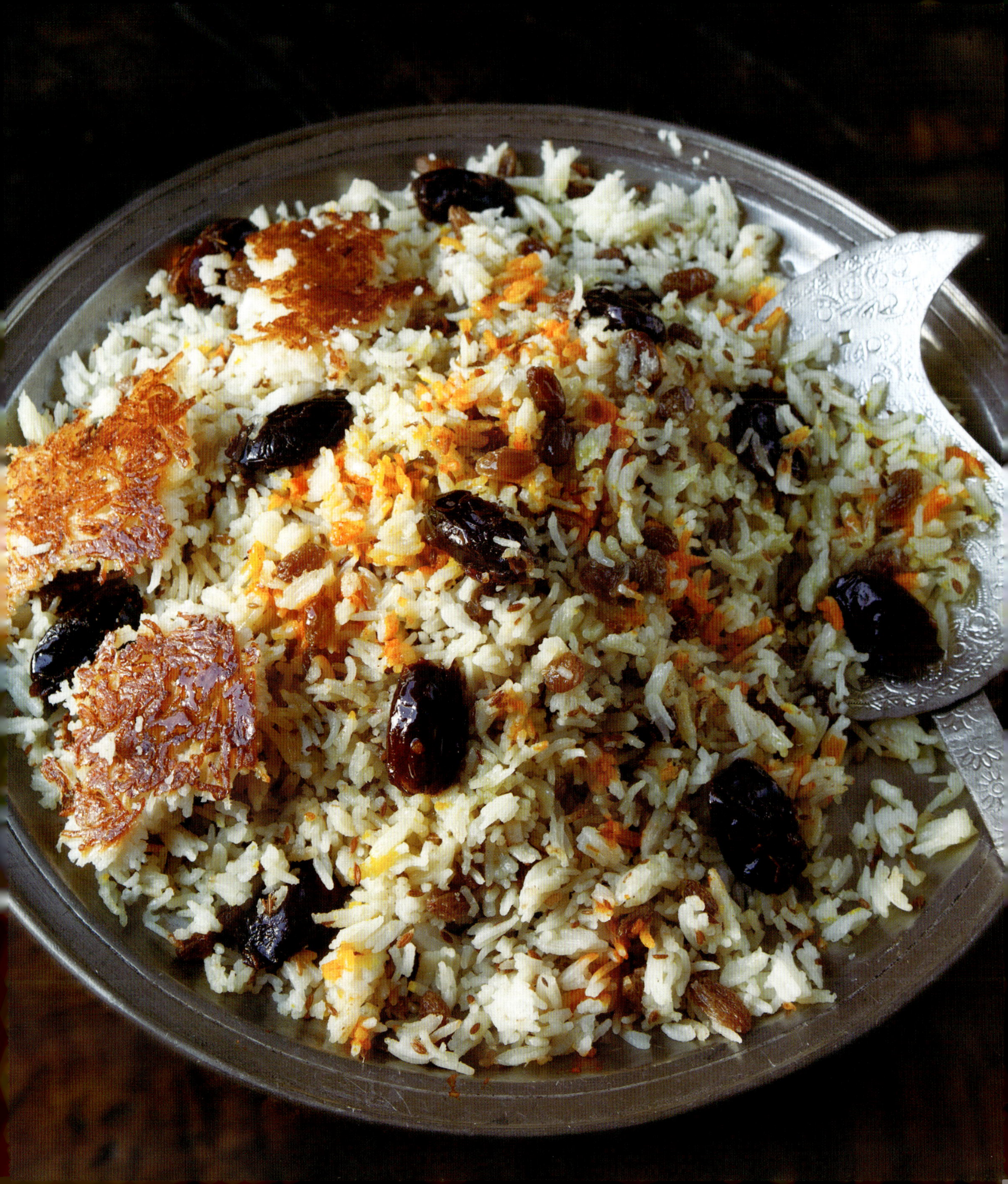

Pistachio + Dill Rice with Lamb Poached in Saffron-Rose Water
pesteh polow ba bareh

Serves 6
Prep: 35 minutes + soaking of pistachios overnight
Cooking: 1¾ hours

PISTACHIOS

2 cups/340g pistachio kernels

LAMB

2 tablespoons oil, clarified butter, or ghee
2lb/900g boned leg of lamb or chicken thighs cut into 3in/7.5cm cubes
2 yellow onions, peeled and sliced
1½ teaspoons fine sea salt
1 teaspoon freshly ground pepper
2 teaspoons turmeric
1 teaspoon cardamom
1 teaspoon ground cinnamon
1 tablespoon ground black cumin
½ teaspoon ground saffron dissolved in ¼ cup/60ml water
2 tablespoons fresh lime juice
3 cups/720ml water

RICE

3 cups/600g basmati rice
¾ cup/180ml oil, butter, or ghee
1 teaspoon ground saffron dissolved in ¼ cup/60ml rose water
1½ cups/125g fresh dill weed, washed and finely chopped
2 teaspoons ground cardamom
2 tablespoon dried organic rose petals

VARIATION

You can replace the pistachios with 1 lb/450g fresh or frozen fava beans, second skins removed, to make this dish into a fava bean rice/baqali polow

VO VEGAN OPTION

This is also a wonderful vegan dish if you eliminate the meat. In Shiraz they garnish it with 1 cup pomegranate arils and call it anar polow.

1. **To prepare the pistachios:** Place pistachio kernels in a bowl and pour in water to 1in/2.5cm above the pistachios. Cover and allow to soak in the fridge overnight. Drain and rub with a dish towel to remove second skin (eliminate this step if you find kernels with second skins removed).

2. **To cook the lamb:** Heat the oil in a medium-sized laminated cast-iron pot over medium heat. Add the lamb and onions, and sauté for 5 minutes. Add salt, pepper, turmeric, cardamom, cinnamon, cumin, saffron water, and lime juice, and sauté for about 10 to 15 minutes until all the juices have been absorbed. Add the water, give it a stir, and bring to a boil. Reduce heat to low, cover, and cook for 1½ hours. Adjust seasoning to your taste and keep warm until ready to serve.

3. *Meanwhile, to cook the rice:* Wash the rice by placing it in a large container and covering it with water. Agitate gently with your hand, and then pour off the water. Repeat 4 to 5 times until the water is clear.

4. Bring 10 cups/2.4l water and 3 tablespoons fine sea salt to a boil in a large non-stick pot. Pour the rice into the pot and boil briskly for 8 minutes. Add the pistachios, stirring gently with a wooden spoon to loosen any stuck grains. Bite a few grains. If rice feels soft and all of it has risen to the surface, it is ready to be drained. Drain in a large fine-mesh colander and rinse with 3 cups water.

5. *For the crust/tah-dig:* Using a rubber spatula, mix together ¼ cup/60ml oil, ¼ cup/60ml water, a few drops of saffron-rose water, and 3 spatulas of rice (about 2 cups/200g) in the pot.

6. Taking a spatula full of rice and pistachio mixture, place alternating layers of rice with the dill weed, cardamom, and rose petals in the pot. Cover and cook over medium-high heat for 10 minutes.

7. Mix the remaining oil and ¼ cup warm water and swirl it over the rice. Drizzle the remaining saffron-rose water on top.

8. Wrap the lid of the pot with a clean dish towel and cover firmly to prevent steam from escaping. Cook for another 50 minutes over low heat. Remove from heat and allow to cool for 5 minutes on a damp surface without uncovering.

9. **To serve:** In a wide serving platter, place a few spatulas of rice and a layer of lamb, and continue alternating layers to form a pyramid.

10. Detach the crust from the bottom of the pot with a wooden spatula. Unmold onto a small platter and serve on the side. *Nush-e joon!*

Kerman

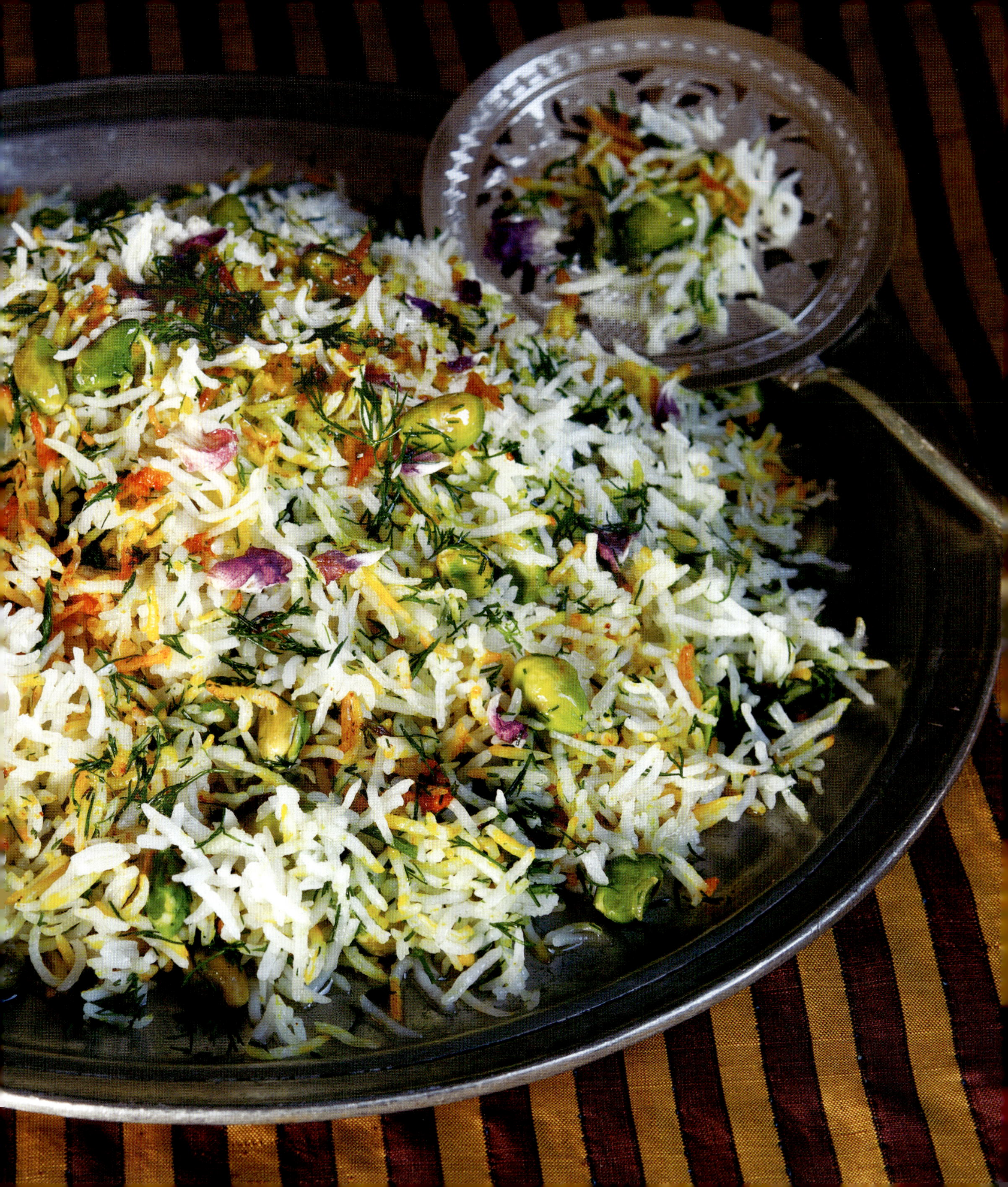

Pistachio + Pomegranate Braise with Meatballs
fesenjun-e pesteh-o kufteh-ye kermani

Serves 6
Prep: 30 minutes
Cooking: 2 hours

PISTACHIO PASTE

2 tablespoons oil, butter, or ghee
2 large onions, peeled and sliced
2½ cups/210g pistachio kernels, picked over for any bits of broken shells
1 teaspoon fine sea salt
¼ teaspoon freshly ground pepper
¼ teaspoon turmeric
½ teaspoon ground cinnamon
1 teaspoon ground cardamom
1 teaspoon ground cumin
1⅓ cups/450g pomegranate molasses dissolved in 4 cups/960ml broth or water
½ teaspoon ground saffron dissolved in 1 tablespoon rose water
1 teaspoon date molasses

MEATBALLS

1 medium onion, quartered
½ cup/40g ground pistachio kernels
1 clove garlic, peeled
1 teaspoon fine sea salt
½ teaspoon pepper
½ teaspoon turmeric
½ teaspoon cinnamon
2 teaspoons ground cumin
½ teaspoon baking powder
2 tablespoons roughly chopped parsley
2 tablespoons roughly chopped cilantro
2 tablespoons roughly chopped fresh or 1 tablespoon dried tarragon flakes
1 lb/450g ground lamb or turkey

GARNISH

Arils of 1 pomegranate
2 tablespoons pistachio kernels

We met Aqa-ye Alizadeh and his son in Kerman and drove together toward Rafsanjan. After a long drive, we arrived in their beautiful garden, which they had converted to a restaurant called Pomegranate. We sat on wooden benches covered with gorgeous kermani carpets under pomegranate trees. All of a sudden, a few large trays appeared with an array of delicious dishes. I especially enjoyed this braise, made by Khanum-e Alizadeh. She served it over a saffron steamed rice/chelow.

1. **To make the pistachio paste:** Heat 2 tablespoons oil in a medium-sized laminated cast-iron pot over medium heat and sauté the onions until golden brown. Add the pistachio and spices and sauté for 1 minute longer. Remove the onion and pistachio mixture from the pot and transfer to a food processor.

2. Finely grind the onion and pistachio mixture. Add 1 cup/240ml dissolved pomegranate molasses, saffron-rose water, and date molasses, and mix well until you have a creamy paste.

3. Add the paste and remaining dissolved pomegranate molasses to the pot, stirring gently. Bring to a boil. Reduce heat to low, cover, and simmer for 30 minutes, stirring occasionally with a wooden spoon to prevent any pistachio paste from sticking to the bottom and burning.

4. **To make the meatballs:** In the food processor, combine all the ingredients, except the lamb, for the meatballs and pulse until you have a fine paste. Transfer to a mixing bowl. Add the lamb, knead lightly, and shape into walnut-sized meatballs. Add them to the pot as you make them. Bring to a boil, reduce heat to low, cover, and cook for 1½ hours, occasionally stirring gently.

5. The braise should be sweet and sour and have the consistency of heavy cream. Adjust to taste by adding pomegranate molasses for sourness or date molasses for sweetness. If the sauce is too thick, thin it by adding a little more warm water.

6. Cover and keep warm in the oven until ready to serve. Just prior to serving, sprinkle with fresh pomegranate arils and pistachio kernels. Serve with saffron steamed rice/*chelow*. *Nush-e joon!*

Kerman

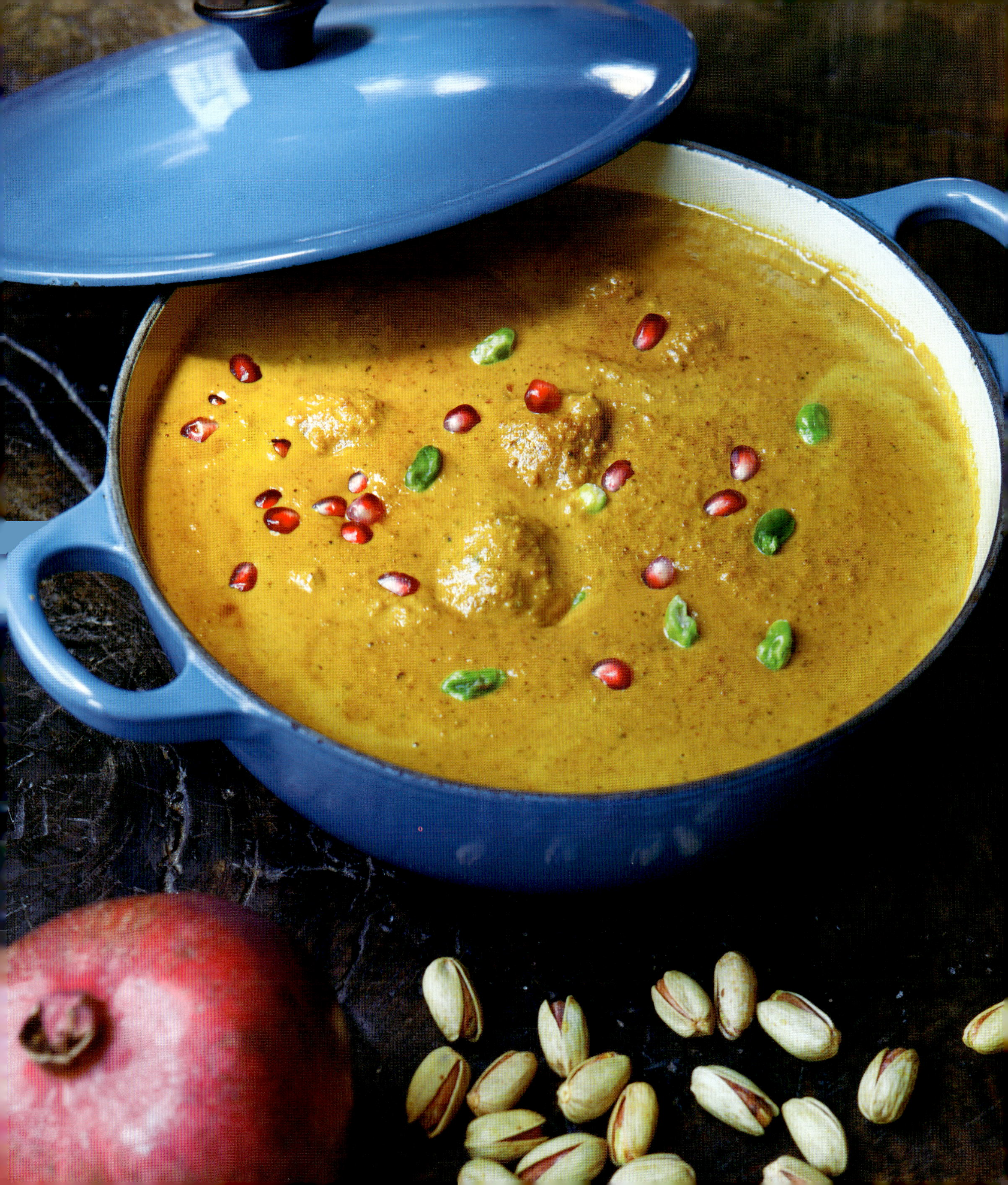

Lamb, Pistachio, Dill + Verjuice Braise

khoresh-e pesteh-o ab ghureh

Serves 6
Prep: 15 minutes + soaking for 24 hours
Cooking: 2 hours

PISTACHIOS

2 cups/240g raw pistachio kernels

LAMB

3 tablespoons oil, butter, or ghee
2 medium onions, thinly sliced
1lb/450g boneless leg of lamb cut into 3in/7.5cm pieces
2 teaspoons fine sea salt
½ teaspoon ground black pepper
1 teaspoon turmeric
1 tablespoon ground black cumin
¼ cup/30ml verjuice/*ab ghureh* or 2 tablespoons fresh lime juice
½ teaspoon ground saffron dissolved in 2 tablespoons rose water

GARNISH

2 cups/170g chopped fresh dill weed

This is a renowned Kermani dish.

1. **To prepare the pistachios:** Soak the pistachios in a container of cold water in the fridge for 24 hours, changing the water twice. Drain, spread on a clean kitchen towel, pat dry, and remove any skins that remain stuck to the kernels (if you use pistachio kernels that already have the second thin brown skins removed, eliminate this step).

2. **To cook the lamb:** Heat 2 tablespoons oil in a medium-sized laminated cast-iron pot over medium heat. Brown the onions and lamb. Add the salt, pepper, turmeric, and cumin, and sauté for 1 minute.

3. Pour in 4 cups/960ml water and bring to a boil. Cover and simmer over low heat for 1½ hours, stirring occasionally.

4. Add the verjuice, saffron-rose water, and pistachios. Give it a gentle stir. Cover and cook over low heat for 30 to 40 minutes until the pistachios are tender.

5. Adjust seasoning to taste and add the dill weed. Give it a gentle stir. Serve with saffron steamed rice/*chelow*. *Nush-e joon!*

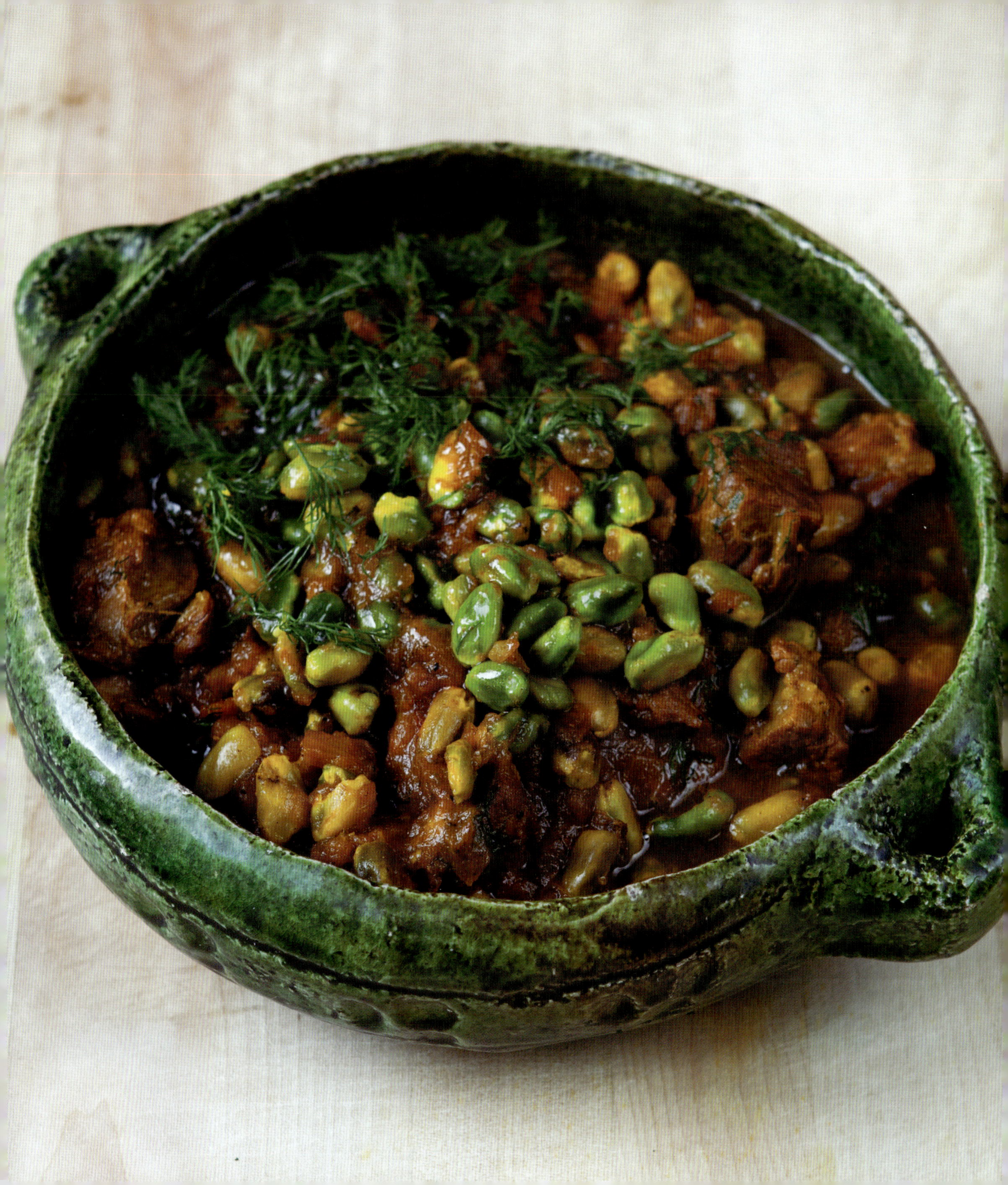

Goat Braised in Kashk + Served with Flat Bread Croutons
boz qormeh-ye kermani

Serves 4 to 6
Prep: 25 minutes + soaking of chickpeas overnight
Cooking: 3 hours

GOAT

- 1 cup/200g dried chickpeas, soaked in water with ½ teaspoon baking soda overnight, drained and rinsed
- 2 tablespoons oil or ghee
- 5 medium onions, peeled and thinly sliced
- 2lb/900g boned leg of goat, or lamb, or skinless and boneless turkey thighs, cut into 3in/8cm pieces
- 2 teaspoons fine sea salt
- 1 teaspoon freshly ground black pepper
- 2 teaspoons turmeric
- 1 tablespoon ground black cumin seeds
- 5 cloves garlic, peeled and sliced
- 1 tablespoon dried tarragon

KASHK

- 1½ cups/360g liquid *kashk*
- 5 cloves garlic, peeled and grated
- ½ teaspoon ground saffron dissolved in 2 tablespoons rose water

CROUTONS

- ½ a *sangak* bread cut in 1in/2.5cm squares
- 1 clove garlic, grated
- ½ cup/40g fresh tarragon leaves
- 2 tablespoons olive oil

This is a renowned Kermani dish. It's easy to make and satisfying to eat. I have adapted a traditional Amin family recipe here. You can make it the day before, and warm it up and garnish just before serving. The dish is perfect with lots of greens on the side (such as a platter of fresh herbs and a green salad). Boz qormeh is made in Tabriz as well, but theirs is somewhat different: they don't use chickpeas and usually make it with lamb shanks, which you can do too, if you prefer.

1. **To cook the goat:** Heat 2 tablespoons oil in a laminated cast-iron braiser or pot over medium heat and sauté the onions and meat until golden brown. Add salt, pepper, turmeric, cumin, garlic, tarragon, and the chickpeas, and sauté for 1 minute.

2. Pour in 4 cups/960ml water and bring to a boil, reduce heat to low, cover, and simmer for 2½ to 3 hours, stirring occasionally until the meat and chickpeas are tender.

3. **To prepare the kashk:** In a small saucepan over low heat, add the *kashk*, garlic, and saffron-rose water, and give it a gentle stir. Cover and simmer for 5 to 10 minutes until the *kashk* has warmed through (it should not come to a boil).

4. Add the *kashk* mixture to the pot. Cover and keep warm until ready to serve.

5. **To make the croutons:** Preheat the oven to 350F°/180C°. Cut the bread into 1in/2.5cm squares. Spread on a sheet pan lined with parchment paper. Add the garlic and tarragon, pour the oil over the bread, and toss well. Toast in the oven for 7 to 10 minutes until the bread is toasted. Transfer to a serving bowl.

6. Serve the braise in individual bowls and top with a few croutons. Accompany with a fresh herb platter/*sabzi khordan* and a green salad on the side. *Nush-e joon!*

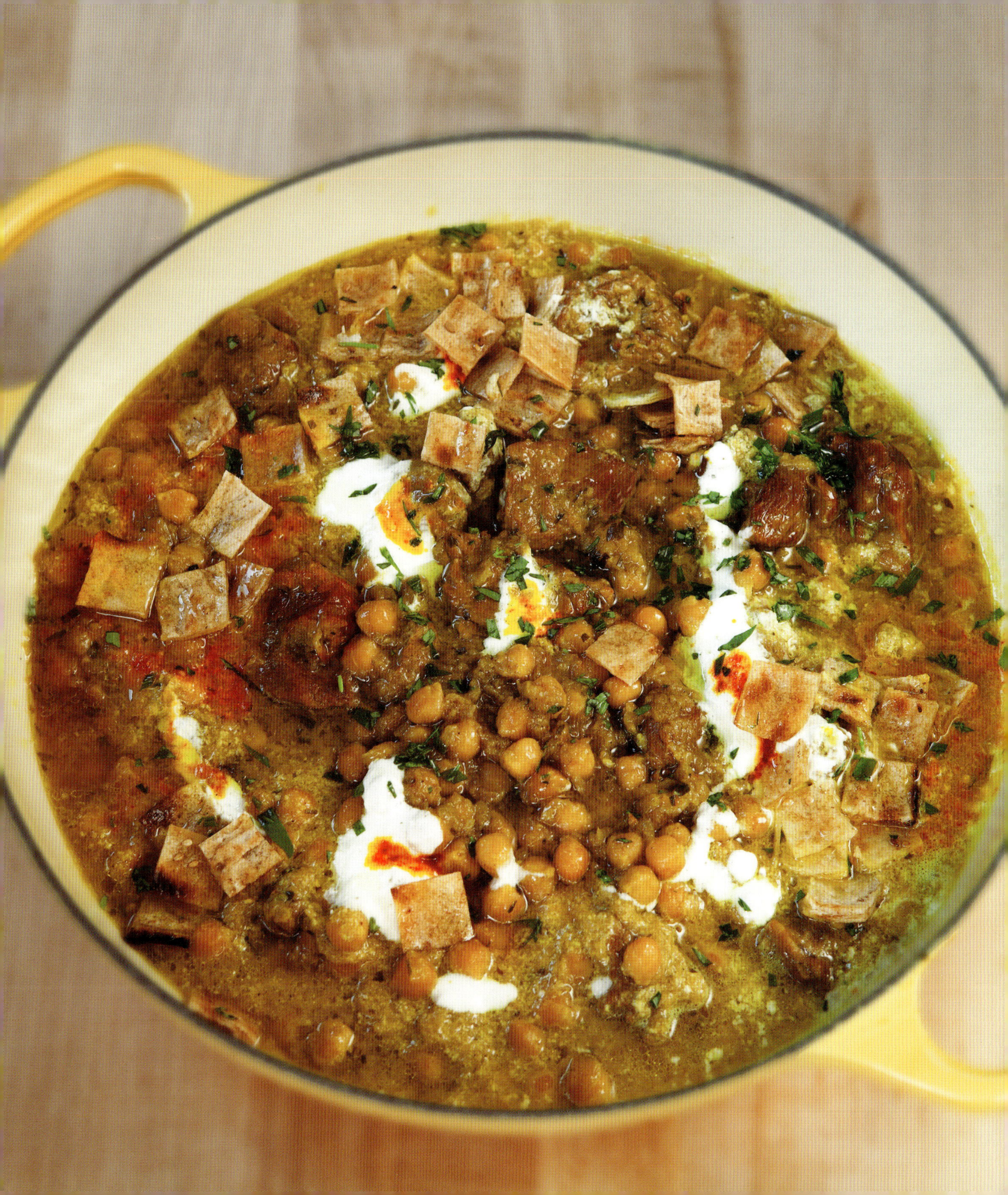

Pistachio Cake
cayk-e pesteh-ye kermani

Makes one 8in/20cm cake
Prep: 20 minutes
Cooking: 40 minutes

BATTER

1 cup/200g sugar
2½ cups/300g raw pistachios kernels
4 eggs (room temperature)
½ teaspoon saffron dissolved in ¼ cup/60ml rose water
1 cup/240g plain yogurt
½ cup/110g oil or ghee
½ teaspoon fine sea salt
2 teaspoons baking powder
1 teaspoon baking soda
1 teaspoon ground cardamom
1 cup/120g unbleached all-purpose flour

GARNISH

¼ cup/20g ground raw pistachio kernels
½ teaspoon cardamom powder
2 tablespoons powdered sugar for dusting (optional)

I love this light and fluffy pistachio cake. It's perfect with sour cherry jam and a hot glass of well-brewed black tea.

1. Place the oven rack in the center and preheat oven to 350°F/180°C.

2. Butter an 8in/20cm spring form cake pan and line the base with parchment paper. Butter and dust the top of the parchment paper.

3. **To make the batter:** Place the sugar and pistachios in a food processor and pulse until finely ground.

4. In a mixing bowl, whisk together the eggs, saffron-rose water, yogurt, and oil for about 5 minutes until creamy. Fold in the sugar and pistachio mixture using a rubber spatula.

5. Sift together the salt, baking powder, baking soda, ground cardamon, and flour onto a piece of wax paper. Fold into the egg and flour mixture.

6. Gently pour the batter into the cake pan and bake in the preheated oven for 40 to 45 minutes until a tester comes out clean.

7. Remove from the oven and allow to cool on a rack for 10 minutes. Tap the pan to release the cake. Turn the cake out onto the rack and remove the mold, peel off the parchment paper, and turn the cake over.

8. Sprinkle the top with ground pistachios, and dust with cardamom powder and powdered sugar. Allow to cool completely, uncovered, to air-dry. Transfer to a serving platter. *Nush-e joon!*

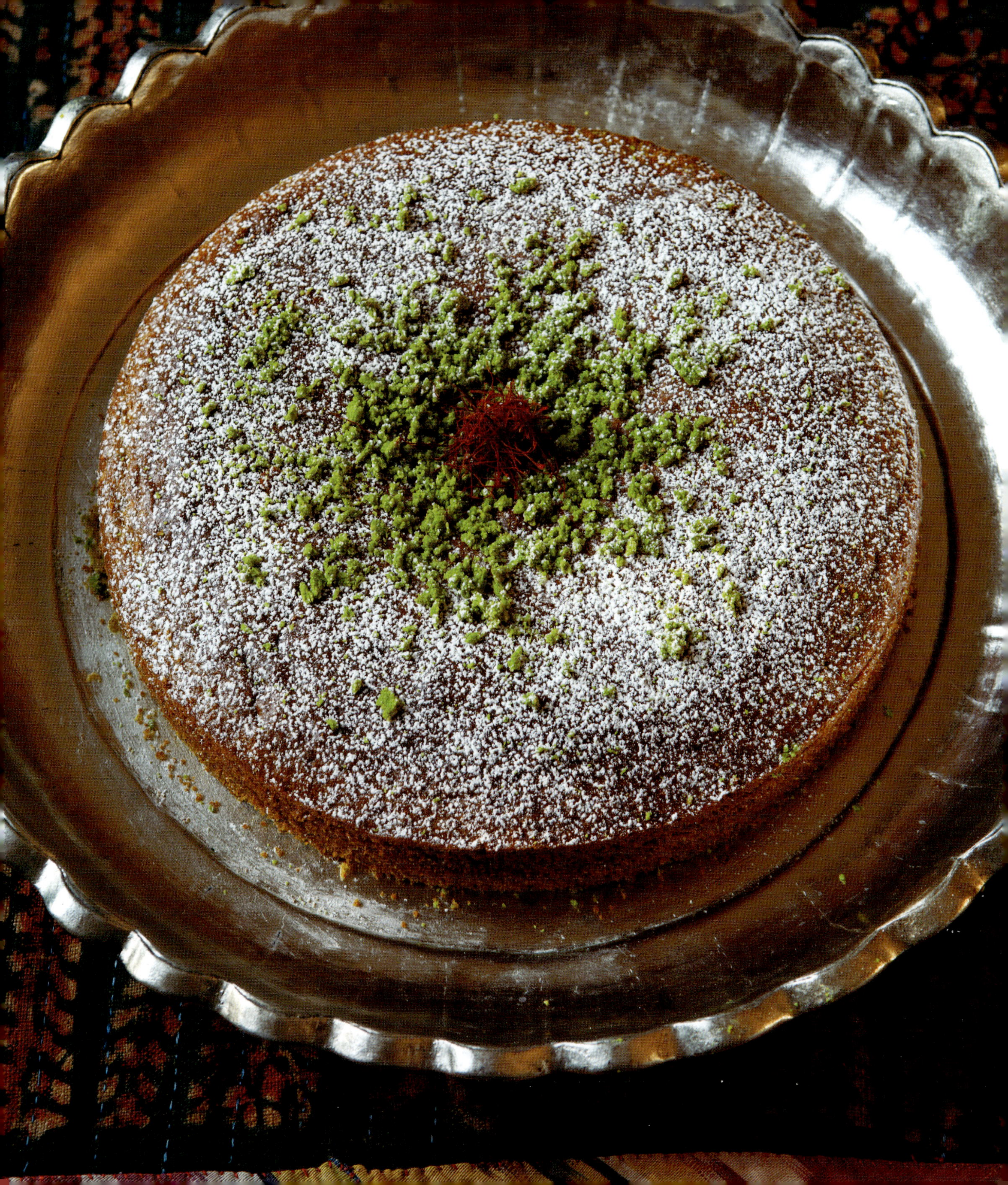

Wheat Sprout Flour Date + Walnut Pie
komaj-e sen-e kermani

Makes 50 pieces
Prep: 30 minutes
Cooking: 40 minutes

DOUGH

2 cups/240g wheat sprout flour/*sen*
2 cups/240g unbleached all-purpose flour
1 teaspoon baking powder
1 teaspoon ground turmeric
2 teaspoons ground anise seeds
1½ to 1¾ cups/360 to 420ml lukewarm water

FILLING

4 cups/480g raw pistachio kernels
3 cups/525g pitted dates

½ cup/120ml oil for brushing the sheet pan

GARNISH

1 cup/120g shredded coconut or ground pistachio kernels

We tasted this delicious pie at a local bakery in Kerman. They make it in a pie dish, but I prefer to use a sheet pan and store the pie in the fridge to serve as a nutritious snack with tea or coffee.

1. Preheat oven to 350°F/180°C. Oil a 17 x 11in/43 x 28cm baking sheet, line it with parchment paper, and oil the parchment paper.

2. *To make the dough:* In a food processor, pulse together, the wheat sprout flour (sen), all-purpose flour, baking powder, turmeric and anise. Gradually add 1¾ cups/420ml lukewarm water and mix well for about 5 minutes until you have dough that does not stick to your hands. Divide dough into 2 balls of equal size. Wrap each ball in plastic and set aside.

3. *To make the filling:* In the same food processor, pulse the pistachio kernels for 1 minute, then add the pitted dates, and continue to pulse until you have a grainy paste.

4. On a lightly floured surface, roll out 1 ball to a thin rectangle to fit the sheet pan and transfer it to the lined sheet pan.

5. Spread the filling evenly on top. Press down and smooth out.

6. Roll out the second ball of dough and use the rolling pin to pick it up and transfer on top of the filling. Use a rolling pin to pack down firmly and evenly.

7. Pinch the top and bottom edges together to seal them like a pie. With a sharp knife cut through the dough to create 2in/5cm squares. Use a brush to paint the top with oil.

8. *To cook the pie:* Bake for 35 to 40 minutes until lightly brown on top and you can see the crust separating from the baking dish. Garnish, cover, and allow to cool. *Nush-e joon!*

Kerman

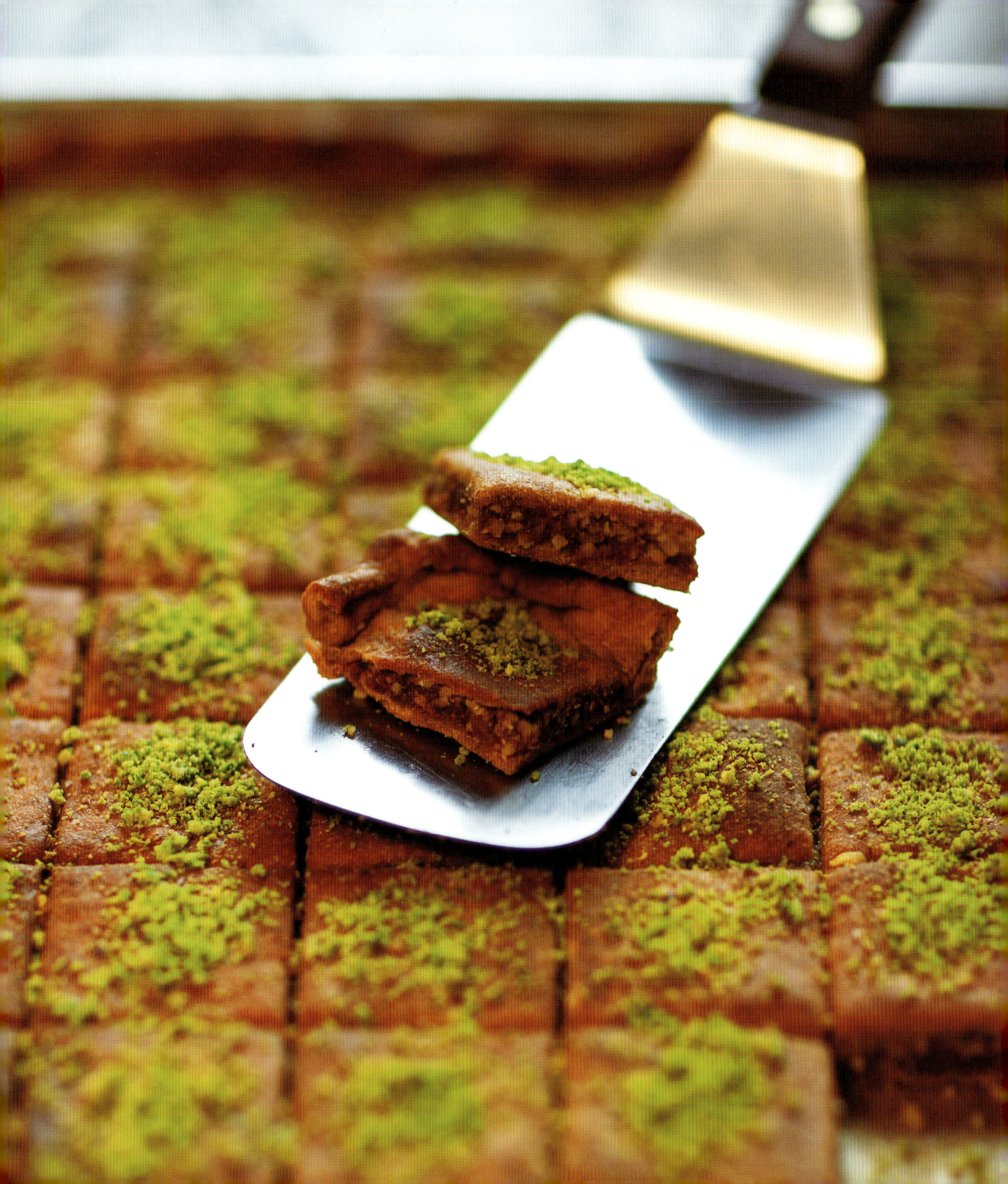

Date + Walnut Cookies
kolombeh-ye kermani

Makes thirty 3in/7.5cm cookies
Prep: 20 minutes
Cooking: 15 minutes per sheet

DOUGH

1 cup/225g butter, goat or sheep ghee, or oil
½ cup/120ml whole plain milk
1 egg yolk
2 to 2½ cups/240g unbleached all-purpose flour, sifted with 1 teaspoon baking powder

DATE FILLING

2 cups/350g pitted dates
2 cups/250g walnuts
1 teaspoon ground cloves
1 teaspoon ground nutmeg

This delicate Kermani cookie is filled with nuts and dates, and stamped with a traditional design. It is much sought after by the locals. I have adapted it here from an Amin family recipe.

1. **To make the dough:** Place the butter, milk and egg yolk in a bowl of food processor and mix until creamy. Add 2 cups sifted flour mixture and mix for 5 minutes until you have soft dough that does not stick to your hands (add more flour if necessary)

2. Transfer to a large mixing bowl, cover with plastic wrap, and set aside.

3. **To make the filling:** Combine all the ingredients for the filling in the food processor and mix until you have a soft paste. Divide the paste into 30 hazelnut-sized balls.

4. Place the oven rack in the center and preheat the oven to 350°F /180°C. Line 4 sheet pans with parchment paper.

5. On a cool, floured surface, roll out the dough into a ⅜in/1cm thickness. Use a 3in/7.5cm diameter cookie cutter and cut out 60 discs of dough.

6. Spread 1 ball of the filling over each of 30 discs of dough. Gently place another disc of dough on top of each of them, gather, and pinch the edges of each of the filled discs to seal the filling inside. Use a *kolombeh* stamp, if you have one, to stamp the top.

7. Lay the filled cookies on the lined baking sheets 1in/2.5cm apart. Place the baking sheet in the center rack of the preheated oven. Bake for 12 to 15 minutes until the cookies are lightly golden.

8. Remove from the oven and allow to cool. Store in the refrigerator in a covered glass container. *Nush-e joon!*

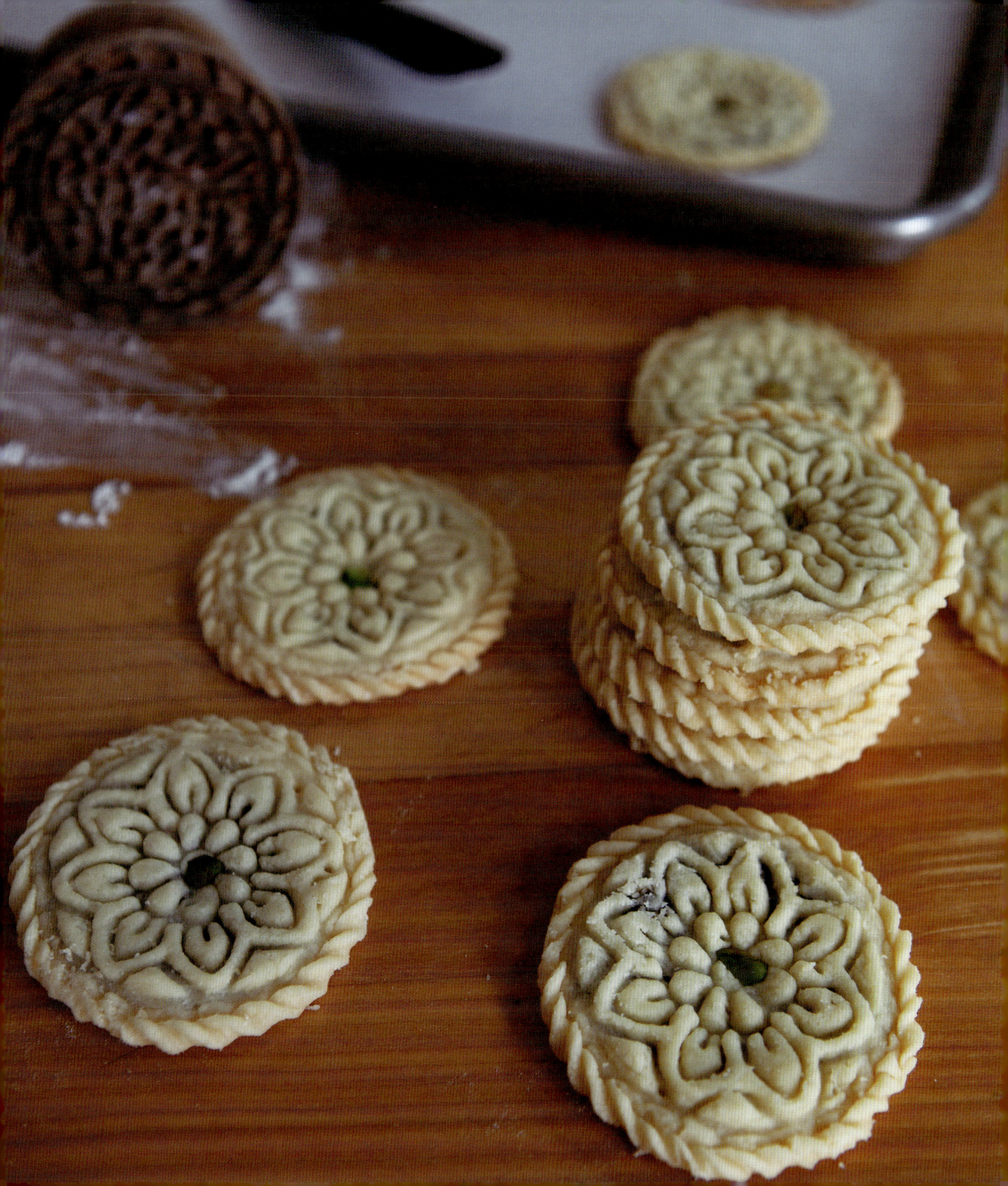

Bread + Date Paste
changmal

Makes one ¼ sheet pan (9½ x 13in/24 x 33cm)
Prep: 25 minutes
Cooking: 15 minutes

- 1 cup/240ml oil or ghee
- 1 *sangak* bread, or 6 sliced whole wheat bread (about 6 cups/225g), cut into 1in/2.5cm pieces
- 2½ cups/450g pitted dates, coarsely chopped
- 1 teaspoon ground cardamom
- 1 teaspoon coriander seeds
- 1 teaspoon ground fennel seeds
- ¼ teaspoon ground saffron dissolved in 2 tablespoons rose water
- 1 cup/120g raw pistachio kernels

In Kerman, this dish is served as a dessert or with afternoon tea. Most Kermanis have fond childhood memories of it. Traditionally, the paste is kneaded with your fingertips (which is what changmal *means in Persian). In Yazd, they call it* moshtack. *In Baluchistan they make a similar dish called* chingal, *but they use hot fresh bread and only fennel seeds.*

1. Line a quarter-sized (9½ x 13in/24 x 33cm) rimmed sheet pan with parchment paper.

2. In a wide skillet, Place the oil, bread, and dates, and stir-fry over low heat for 10 to 15 minutes until the bread is soft. Add the spices and saffron-rose water, and stir-fry for another minute. Remove from heat and set aside.

3. In a food processor, place the pistachio kernels and pulse until grainy. Add the warm bread and date mixture. Pulse until you have a soft paste.

4. Spread the paste on the sheet pan. Place an oiled sheet of parchment paper on top so your hand does not stick to the paste and pat down. Use a rolling pin to evenly spread and compact it. Cut the paste into diamond shapes and allow to cool completely. *Nush-e joon!*

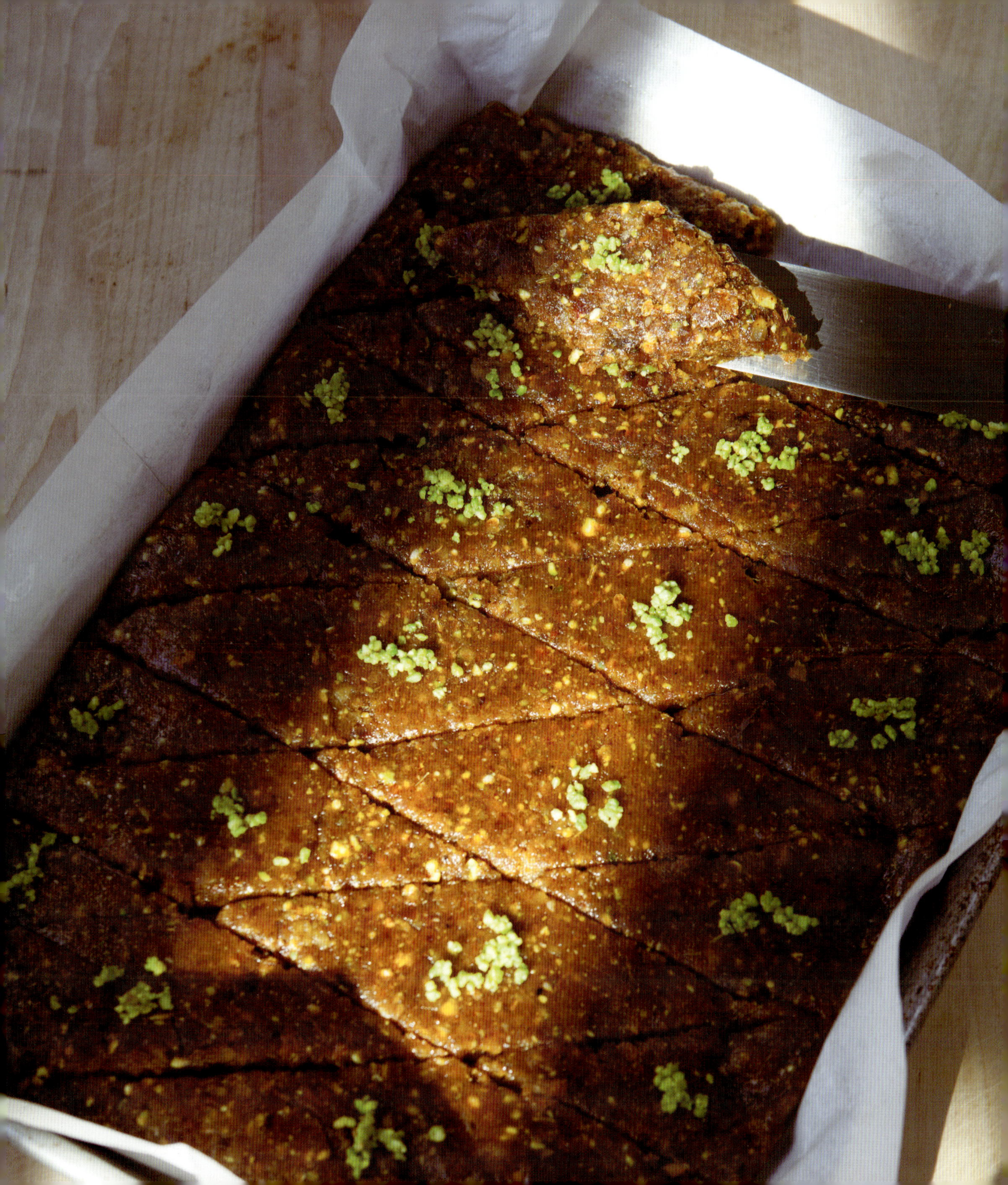

Turmeric, Cumin + Date Bun

nan-e komaj-e mahan

Makes 10 buns
Prep: 15 minutes plus 6 to 24 hours of resting
Cooking: 30 minutes

DOUGH

2 teaspoons active dry yeast
2 cups/480ml warm water (100°F/38°C)
¾ cup/150g sugar
¼ cup/60ml oil or butter
1 egg
5¼ to 6 cups/630 to 720g unbleached all-purpose flour sifted together with 2 teaspoons ground turmeric, 2 teaspoons ground cumin, and 1 teaspoon fine sea salt

FILLING

2 cups/350g dates, pitted and chopped
¼ cup/60ml oil or ghee

EGG WASH

1 egg yolk, lightly beaten with 1 tablespoon milk

GARNISH

2 tablespoons cumin seeds
1 tablespoon poppy or sesame seeds

All over Iran, there are variations of a similar bun or bread called komaj. *They all use either saffron or turmeric and their own locally abundant seeds and spices.*

1. *To make the dough:* In a food processor, dissolve the yeast in the water, add the sugar, and allow to rest for 10 minutes undisturbed. Add the oil and egg, and mix until creamy.

2. Whisk together the flour, turmeric, cumin and salt. Gradually add it to the yeast mixture while the machine is running until you have added 5¼ cups/525g. Mix for about 5 minutes until you have sticky dough.

3. Turn the dough in a generously oiled bowl to ensure it is evenly coated with oil. Cover with plastic wrap or a wet dish towel and allow to rise, undisturbed, at room temperature for at least 2 hours.

4. *To make the filling:* Place the dates and oil in the food processor and mix until you have a paste. Divided the paste into 10 balls.

5. *To make the buns:* Preheat the oven to 400°F/200°C. Line 2 sheet pans with parchment paper.

6. Punch the air out of the dough while still in the bowl. Turn the dough out onto a floured work surface and shape it into a log. Divide the dough into 10 balls and roll out each ball into a ½in/1.2cm thick by 8in/20cm diameter disc.

7. Place 1 portion of the filling on each of the 10 disks. Gently lift up each disc, gather, and pinch the edges to seal the filling inside. Turn disc over and gently press it down using a rolling pin to flatten it out, making a round flat loaf.

8. Lay the loaves on the lined sheet pan, 2in/5cm apart. Brush each bun generously with the egg wash. Sprinkle cumin and poppy seeds on top of each loaf

9. Bake for 8 to 10 minutes until the buns are lightly brown.

10. Remove the buns from the oven and allow to cool on a rack. *Nush-e joon!*

Power Shake

qovat'tu

Makes 8 cups/620g
Prep: 30 minutes

SPICE + CHICKPEA MIXTURE

½ cup/70g fennel seeds
½ cup/70g coriander seeds
½ cup/70g sesame seeds
½ cup/70g hemp seeds
½ cup/70g dill seeds
½ cup/70g purslane seeds
½ cup/70g flax seeds
¼ cup/35g green cardamom pods
½ cup/70g roasted chickpeas

SPROUTED WHEAT FLOUR MIXTURE

½ cup/60g sprouted wheat flour/*sen*
2 tablespoons powdered sugar (optional)

This recipe comes from Parvin Amin. When in Kerman, she goes to a communal stone mill, taking her own whole spices or choosing from those at the mill's workshop. At the mill, the spices are ground to a powder and put in airtight glass jars while she waits. Here, I am using a spice grinder, which works well too.

1. In a spice grinder, separately grind the spices and chickpeas until you have a powder (do not over-grind into a paste).

2. Mix all the ground spice powder together with sprouted wheat flour and sugar.

3. Eat the powder on its own or mix 1 tablespoon of it with a glass of your favorite milk: regular dairy milk, rice milk or almond milk. *Nush-e joon!*

Shohreh Amin and her daughter Leyla in Kerman. It was their family pistachio orchard that we visited and photographed. She was instrumental in helping me collect many of the Kermani recipes in this section from various members of her family, for which I am grateful.

Kerman

Rose Water + Apple Shrub
faludeh-ye sib-e kermani

Serves 4
Prep: 15 minutes
Cooking: 35 minutes

ROSE WATER SYRUP
1¼ cups/300ml water
2 cups/260g sugar
2 tablespoons fresh lime juice
2 tablespoons rose water

APPLE SHRUB
4 cups/960ml ice water
2 cups/280g crushed ice
1 large Fuji apple, sliced or grated
¾ cup/90ml rose water syrup (above)

GARNISH
½ cup/40g fresh mint leaves
thin slices of lime (optional)

1. **To make the rose water syrup:** In a small saucepan, bring the water and sugar to a boil. Reduce heat to low and allow to simmer for 10 minutes. Add the lime juice and rose water, and simmer 10 minutes longer, stirring occasionally. Remove from heat and allow to cool.

2. Pour the syrup into a clean, dry bottle and cork tightly. Use as needed.

3. **To make the apple shrub:** In a pitcher, mix together ¾ cup/180ml of the rose water syrup with 4 cups/960ml ice water and mix well.

4. Peel and grate the apples, them to the pitcher, and mix well using a long wooden spoon.

5. Add fresh mint leaves and slices of lime, and stir well. Adjust to taste by adding more syrup. Keep chilled until ready to serve.

6. **To serve:** Place ¼ cup/35g of crushed ice in each glass and fill with the apple shrub. *Nush-e joon!*

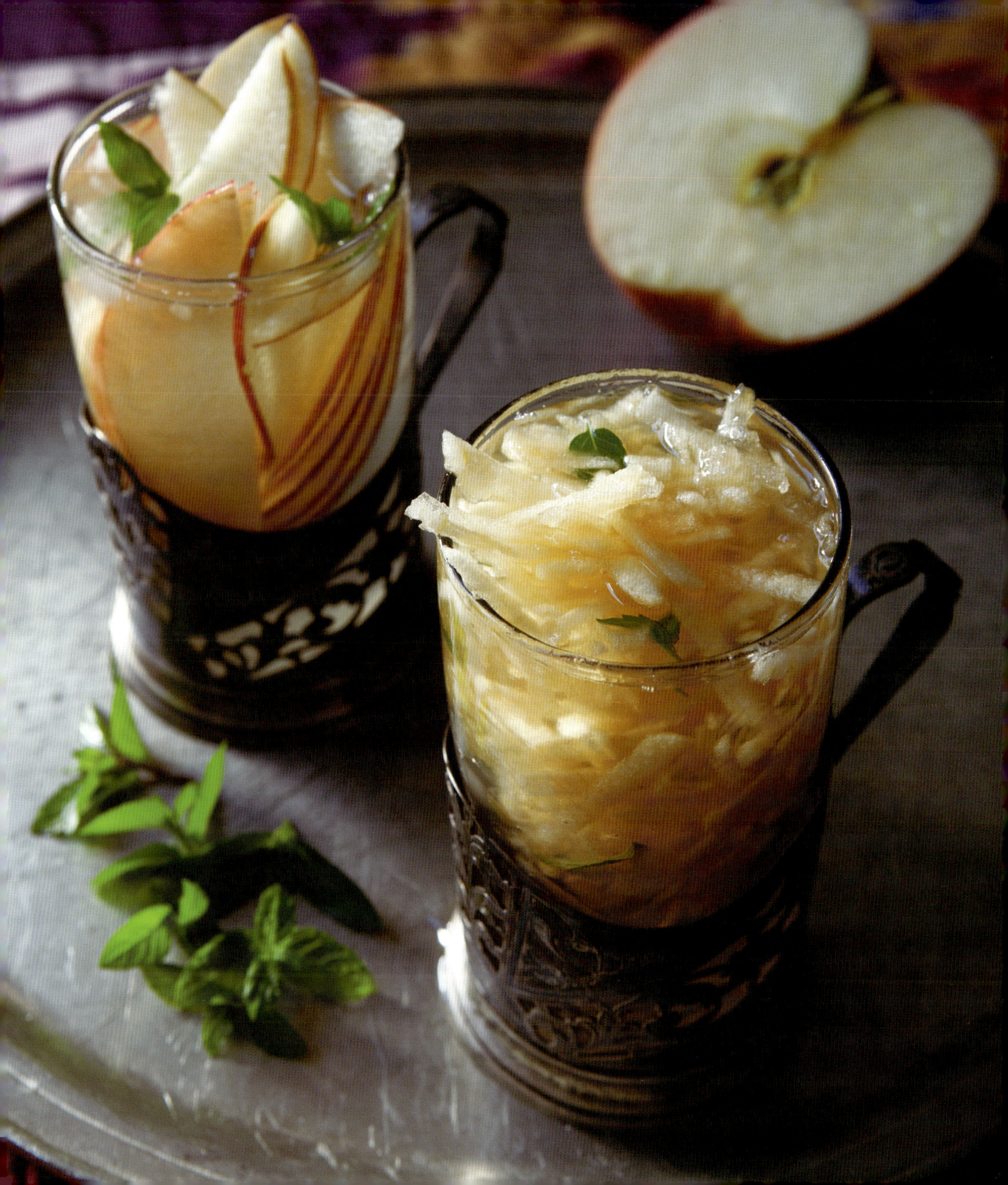

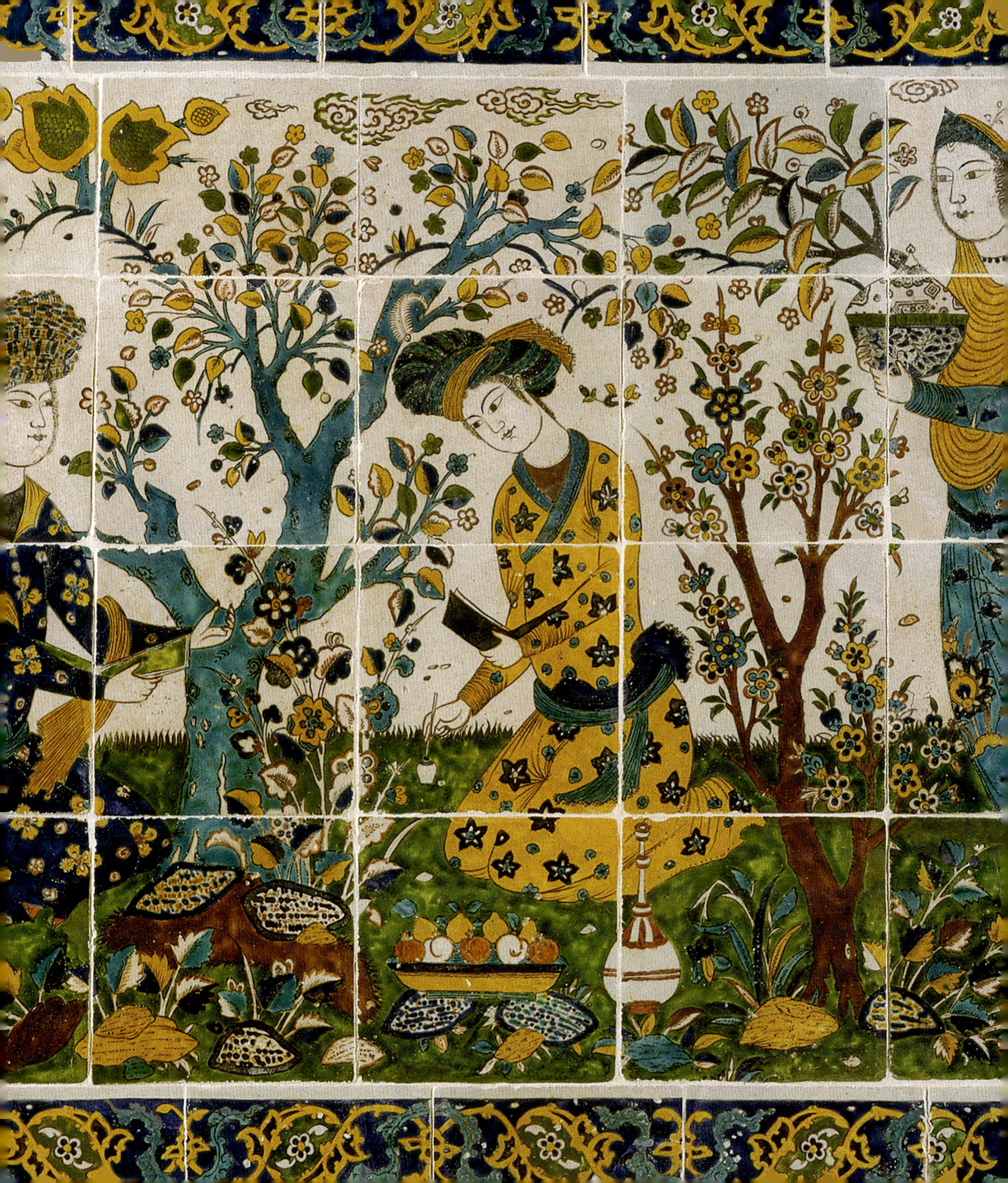

The Persian Garden

سیب چو پستہ ہای عقیق   نار بشکر درج ہای عقیق
بہ کوہی برگ کشیدہ بہ رنگ   پستہ یا خندہ تر از لب خشک
رنگ شقائق لوازنش بہای شاخ   کردہ یاقوت سرخ وزرد فراخ

The laden fruit trees that were growing there
Bent to the ground as if prostrate in prayer—

The fruit they bore was of a wondrous size
Filling the soul with rapturous surprise;

The apples were like goblets red with wine,
The pomegranates were so firm and fine

They seemed like agate boxes made to hold
Their little treasuries of jewels and gold;

Quinces seemed stuffed with musk, pistachios smiled
Like laughing lips sweet juices have beguiled;

Rubies and saffron's golden yellow vied
In parti-colored peaches side by side;

Bananas were fit for kings, dates as sweet
As three long bitten kisses when lips meet;

Pears as if crammed with sugar, figs as though
They'd make the garden's goblet overflow;

A grapevine there, its leaves a cap askew,
Surveyed the colors where its children grew,

The white and black, next to a noble stand
Of orange trees, trained by the gardener's hand.

Nezami Ganjavi/Dick Davis

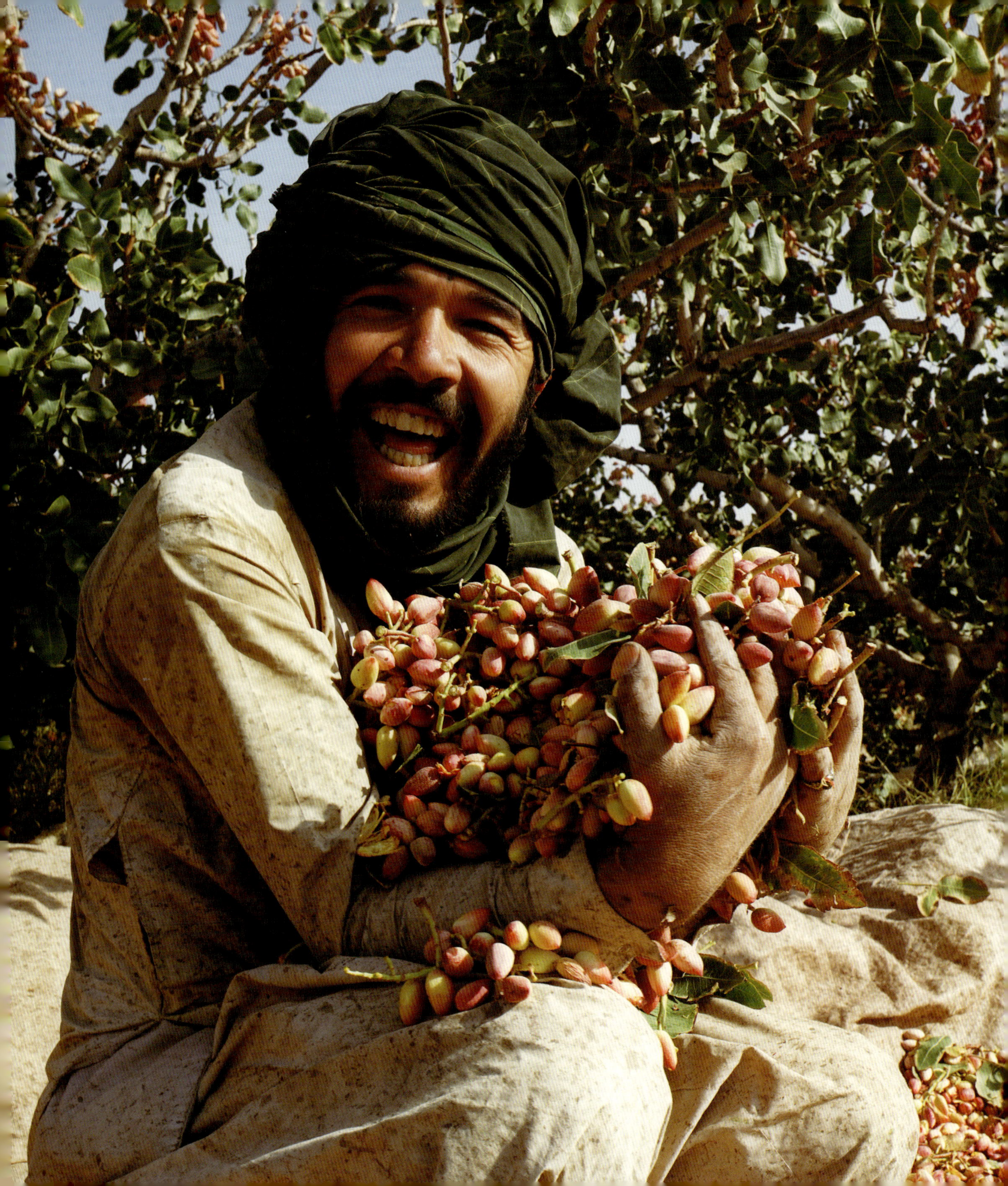

Pistachio Skin Jam
moraba-ye pust surati-ye pesteh

Makes ½pt/240g
Prep: 35 minutes plus 24 hours of soaking
Cooking: 1 hour

1lb/450g fresh pistachio skins (hulls) that cover the white shell
3 cups/720ml water
5 cups/1kg sugar
2 tablespoons fresh lime juice

In Kerman, in mid-August as the pistachio harvest begins, some locals select fresh, spotless pistachios that have no blemishes and carefully remove their hulls. California pistachio growers may soon be doing this immediately after harvest as well, freeze-dry the hulls, which are very nutritious and could have many uses besides making jam. This jam, which I have adapted from an Amin family recipe, is delightfully perfumed and doesn't need any additional aromatics.

1. Sterilize jelly jars in boiling water. Drain and allow to dry thoroughly.

2. Place the hulls in a large container and cover with cold water. Place in the refrigerator for 24 hours (changing the water twice to remove any bitterness). Drain and rinse thoroughly. Set aside.

3. Meanwhile, place the water and sugar in a medium-sized laminated pot and bring to a boil. Reduce heat to medium and simmer for about 5 minutes, stirring a few times until the sugar has dissolved.

4. Add the pistachio hulls to the syrup and simmer for 30 to 40 minutes until the syrup is thick enough to coat the back of a spoon. Add the lime juice, remove from the heat, and allow to cool.

5. Fill the jars with the hot preserve and seal. Store in a cool, dark place. *Nush-e joon!*

Baby Green Pistachio Pickle

torshi-e chaghaleh-ye pesteh-ye kermani

Makes 1pt/480g
Prep: 35 minutes

1lb/450g baby pistachios, stems removed

SPICE + HERBS

1 tablespoon ground Persian hogweed seeds/*golpar*
5 cloves garlic, peeled
5 sprigs of fresh tarragon

BRINE

1 tablespoon pickling salt
1¾ cups/420ml apple cider vinegar

Baby green unripe pistachios are picked in May in Rafsanjan, Kerman, and California. At this stage pistachios are unripe and their shells are greenish red, soft, and a little bitter. They make a distinctive pickle.

1. **To remove the bitterness from the baby pistachios:** In a large saucepan bring 8 cups/1.9l water to boil. Add the baby pistachios and bring back to a boil. Reduce heat to medium and boil for 5 minutes. Drain, rinse, and shake the colander to remove as much of the water as possible.

2. Spread the pistachios on a sheet pan lined with paper towels and allow to dry completely.

3. Fill the jar almost to the top with pistachios, and add the *golpar*, garlic, and tarragon.

4. **To make the brine:** In a measuring bowl, dissolve the salt in the vinegar.

5. Fill the jar to the top with the brine. Seal and store in a cool, dark place. *Nush-e joon!*

Baby Pistachio Preserve

moraba-ye chaghaleh-ye pesteh

Makes two ½pt/240g jars
Prep: 30 minutes
Cooking: 55 minutes

1lb/450g baby pistachios, stems removed
3 cups/720ml water
5 cups/1kg sugar
5 cardamom pods
2 tablespoons fresh lime juice

1. Sterilize the canning jars in boiling water. Drain and allow to dry thoroughly.

2. **To remove the bitterness from the baby pistachios:** In a large laminated pot, bring 8 cups/1.9l water to a boil over high heat. Add the pistachios and bring back to a boil, reduce heat to medium, and continue boil for 10 minutes. Drain and rinse the pistachios.

3. In the same pot, place the pistachios, 3 cups/720ml water, and sugar. Bring to a boil, reduce heat to medium, and simmer for 35 minutes.

4. Add the cardamom and lime juice and simmer another 10 to 15 minutes until the syrup has thickened enough to cover the back of a spoon. Remove from heat and allow to cool.

5. Fill the jars and seal. Store in a cool, dark place. *Nush-e joon!*

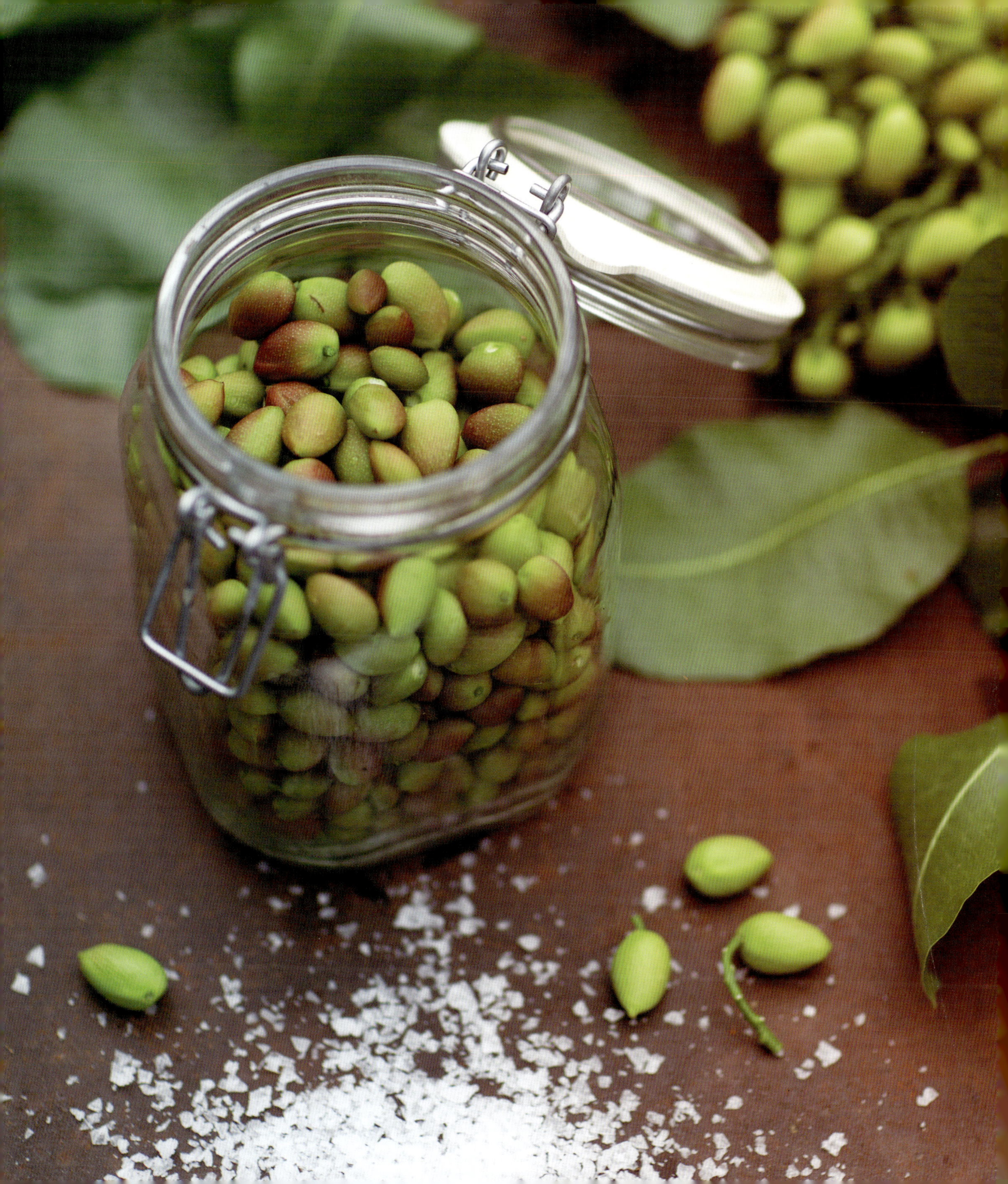

Saffron + Lime Roasted Pistachios
pesteh-ye bu dadeh ba zaferun-o limu-ye kermani

Makes 1lb/450g
Prep: 1 hour of soaking
Roasting: 5 hours in the oven at 200°F/95°C

1lb/450g raw pistachios in the shell
1½ cups/360ml fresh lime juice
1 tablespoon fine sea salt
½ teaspoon ground saffron dissolved in 2 tablespoons hot water

I love the taste of saffron, lime, and salt in these roasted pistachios. The treat is not normally available in markets, it's well worth the effort.

1. Place all the ingredients in a mixing bowl and toss well. Allow to soak for 1 hour.

2. Preheat the oven to 200°F/95°C. Line a rimmed sheet pan with parchment paper.

3. Toss the pistachios in the bowl once again and then spread them, along with the juices, evenly on the lined sheet pan.

4. Roast in the preheated oven for 2 hours. Pull out the oven rack and shake or use a rubber spatula to turn the pistachios. Return to the oven and allow to roast for another 3 hours, turning the pistachios once again halfway through until they are thoroughly dry, but not overly so.

5. Remove sheet pan from the oven and allow to cool on a cooling rack. Transfer pistachios to a bowl or store in a covered glass container. *Nush-e joon!*

Spicing + Roasting Nuts

In a large mixing bowl, combine ½ teaspoon each of cayenne, paprika, cardamom, cinnamon, cumin, and turmeric. Then add 1 tablespoon fine sea salt. Mix well. Add 4 tablespoons olive oil and ½ cup/120ml lime juice. Add 1lb/450g raw pistachios in the shell and toss. Allow to marinate for 1 hour. Proceed with toasting as above.

NOTE

You can also use a skillet for roasting the nuts.

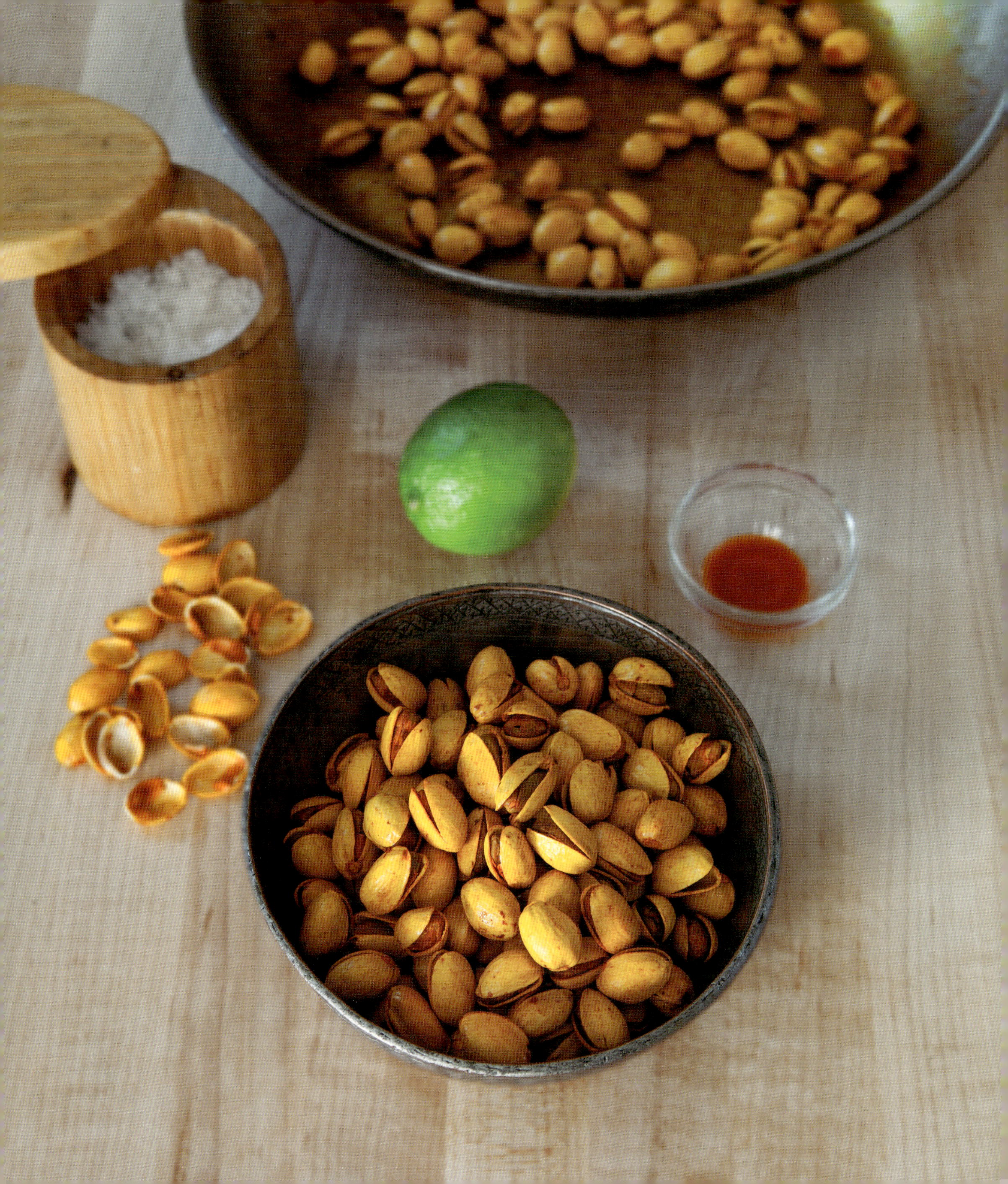

Fars / Shiraz

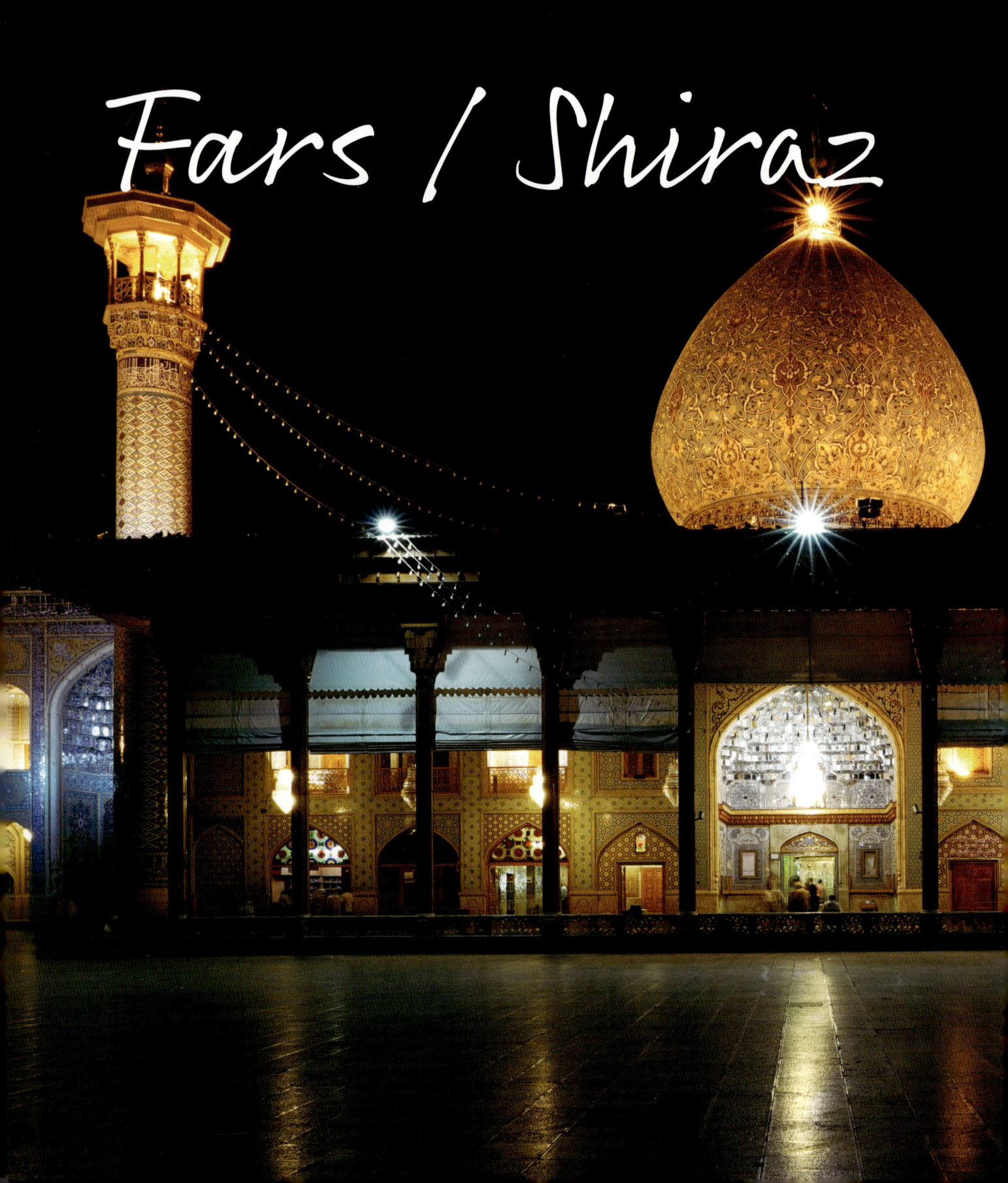

Shah Cheragh Mosque illuminated at night.

A Little History

Shiraz is the iconic, laid-back, cultural center of southern Iran. It is an ancient city known for its gardens, its poets (Hafez and Sa'di), and its wine. It is the capital of Fars Province, succeeding Persepolis (an hour's drive away), which was an important capital of the Achaemenids (550–330 BCE). At times the city has had titles such as the Seat of Government/*dar al-molk*, the Abode of Knowledge/*dar al-elm*, and the Tower of Saints/*borj-e awlia*. But Shiraz was sacked by the Afghans and suffered much internal turmoil during the 1700s.

The cuisine of Shiraz uses great quantities of aromatic herbs, and it is highly creative in its use of flower extracts such as orange blossoms and pussy willow buds. Shirazis also like sour flavors provided by lime juice and verjuice. The spice mix (*advieh*) in this region is similar to that of the Persian Gulf (Bandari Seven-Spice Advieh, page 594) except that Shirazis replace the hot pepper flakes with black pepper corns.

"Oh man, whoever you are and from wherever you come (for I know that you will come), I am Cyrus, who founded the empire of the Persians. Grudge me not, therefore, this little earth that covers my body."
Inscription at Cyrus' tomb (below) in Pasargadae according to Plutarch

Hafez

Hafez, one of the greatest Persian poets, was probably born in Shiraz in 1315 and lived to be 75. By the time of his death, his work was known far and wide. These days Hafez is perhaps most popular in Iran because, besides everything else, his poems are an antidote to hypocrisy.

درخت دوستی بنشان که کام دل به بار آرد

Plant friendship's tree – the heart's desire

    Is the fruit it bears;

And uproot enmity – which brings

    Sorrows and cares.

…

Your heart is so tired! You feel caught

    In the weary world's snares

But sip at your wine, and hear in your heart

    The hope it declares:

That Hafez will sit in his orchard

    By the stream that he shares

With his cypress-slim love, God willing,

    In the place that is theirs.

Hafez/Davis

At Hafez's tomb.

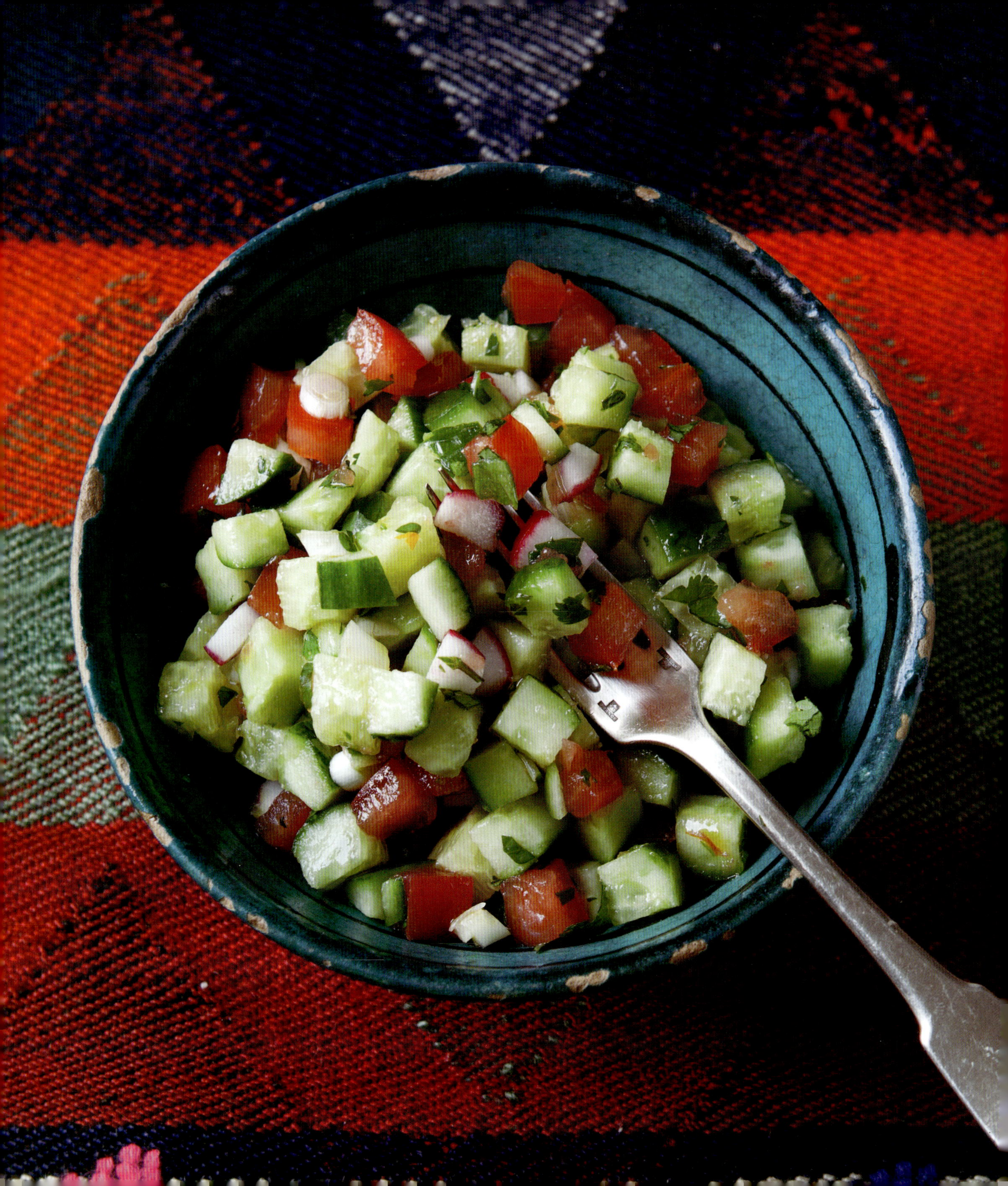

Tomato, Cucumber + Herb Salad
salad-e gojeh khiar-e shirazi

Serves 4
Prep: 15 minutes

- 2 medium ripe, firm tomatoes
- 6 Persian cucumbers or 1 long seedless cucumber
- 2 spring onions, chopped
- 3 radishes, thinly sliced
- 2 tablespoons chopped fresh parsley leaves
- 2 tablespoons chopped fresh mint leaves
- 2 tablespoons chopped fresh cilantro leaves

DRESSING

- 1 clove garlic, peeled and grated
- ½ cup (120ml) verjuice or ¼ cup (60ml) fresh lime juice
- ½ teaspoon fine sea salt
- ½ teaspoon freshly ground pepper
- 2 tablespoons olive oil (optional)

In Shiraz, this salad is on every table setting for lunch or dinner. They make it without oil, but you can try it both ways to see which you prefer. The dressing should be added just before serving, otherwise the salad becomes soggy and looses its freshness.

1. ***To blanche the tomatoes:*** Cut out the tomato stems and score cross hairs at the base. Drop them into boiling water for 1 minute or until the skins lift up slightly. Remove with a slotted spoon and place it in a bowl of ice water. Peel and cut into 1in/2.5cm cubes.

2. Peel and cut cucumber into 1in/2.5cm cubes.

3. ***To make the dressing:*** In a small bowl whisk together all the ingredients for the dressing and set aside.

4. In a salad bowl, place the tomatoes, the cucumbers, and the rest of the vegetables and herbs. Cover and keep in the fridge.

5. Just before serving, add the dressing and gently toss. Serve immediately. *Nush-e joon!*

VARIATION

For a Kurdish variation on this salad, replace the lime juice in the dressing with 1 tablespoon pomegranate molasses and add 2 teaspoons sumac powder. Everything else remains the same.

Red Onion + Pomegranate Salad
omar piyaz-e ahvazi

I have adapted this recipe from Farideh Afshar Penelton who grew up in Ahvaz.

- 2 red onions, peeled and thinly sliced (use a mandolin)
- 5 limes, juice and pulp
- 2 cups/300g pomegranate arils (2 pomegranates)
- 2 tablespoons dried mint
- 2 teaspoons ground Persian hogweed seeds/golpar
- 2 teaspoons fine sea salt
- ¼ teaspoon freshly ground pepper

In a salad bowl, combine all the ingredients and toss well. Adjust seasoning to taste. *Nush-e joon!*

VEGAN

Fars/Shiraz

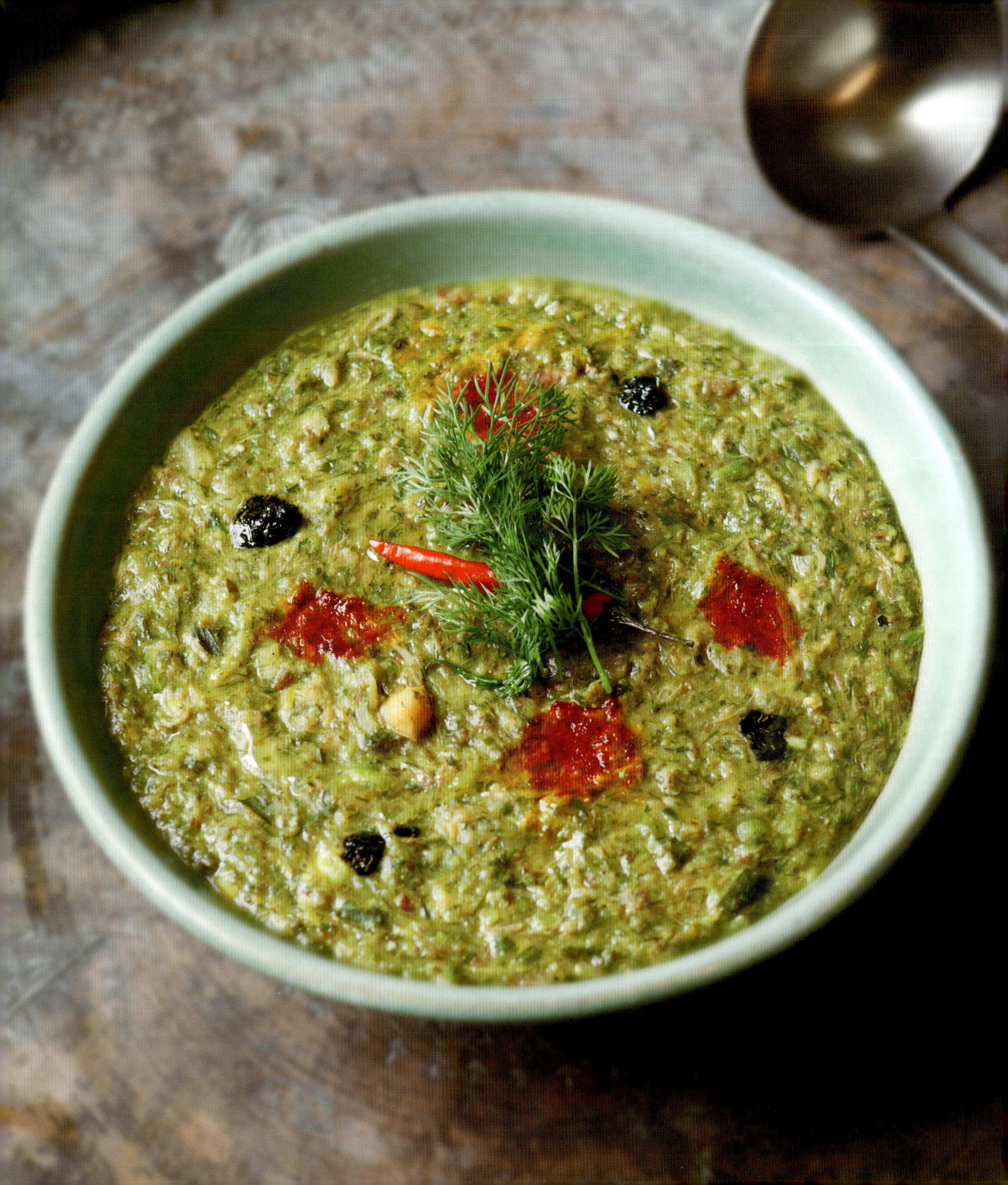

Green Herb Osh

osh-e sabz-e shirazi

Serves 6 to 8
Prep: 40 minutes plus soaking of the legumes + rice overnight
Cooking: 3¾ hours

LEGUMES + RICE

Soaked overnight, drained and rinsed
¼ cup/50g chickpeas
¼ cup/50g red beans
½ cup/100g brown lentils
¼ cup/50g rice

LAMB

1 lamb shank and one lamb neck (about 1¼lb/560g combined), thoroughly rinsed and drained
10 cups/2.4l water
1 tablespoon fine sea salt
1 teaspoon freshly ground black pepper
2 teaspoons turmeric

BROTH

¼ cup/60ml oil
4 medium onions, thinly sliced
1 teaspoon red pepper flakes

HERBS

2 cups/170g chopped fresh basil leaves or ¼ cup/4g dried basil
2 cups/170g chopped fresh spring onion or ¼ cup/4g dried chives
2 cups/170 chopped fresh tarragon or ¼ cup dried

¼ cup/60ml fresh lime juice

GARNISH/NA`NA DAGH

2 tablespoons oil
½ teaspoon turmeric
2 tablespoons dried mint
1 teaspoon freshly ground black pepper

This osh is usually served in the early mornings and during Ramadan for breaking the fast. Several neighboring regions have variations of in which, instead of the usual herbs, they use the leaves of a wild herb called kardin (biarum bovei). *This hard-to find herb is local to these regions and gives the* osh *an intensely aromatic and distinctive flavor. In Shiraz, where I tried the* osh *at a popular street stall, they call it* osh-e kardeh. *The Bakhtiaris and Isfahanis, as well as some Khuzestanis call it* osh-e kardin. *And in Behbahan it's called* osh-e horeh.

1. In a large laminated cast-iron pot, place the lamb shank and the neck, and cover with 10 cups/2.4l water. Bring to a boil. Remove any foam as it rises to the surface. Reduce heat to medium-low and add the salt, pepper, and turmeric. Cover, and simmer for 2 hours or until lamb comes off the bone easily, stirring occasionally.

2. Remove the meat from the broth, separate it from the bones and remove any fat, discard the bones and fat, and return the meat to the broth.

3. Meanwhile, in a wide skillet, heat the oil over medium heat. Add the onions and sauté for 10 to 15 minutes until golden brown. Add the red pepper flakes and legumes, and sauté for 1 minute. Transfer the onion and legume mixture to the pot. Bring to a boil. Reduce heat to medium, cover, and simmer for 55 minutes, stirring occasionally.

4. Add the herbs, reduce heat to low and continue to simmer for 15 minutes. Check to see if the beans and chickpeas are cooked. Use a handheld mixer to partially puree the *osh*. Add lime juice. Give a stir and adjust seasoning to taste.

5. **To make the garnish:** Heat the oil in a skillet, add the turmeric, and sauté for 1 minute. Remove from heat and immediately add the mint and pepper. Mix well and keep warm until ready to serve.

6. Pour the *osh* into a tureen. Garnish with *na`na dagh* on top. Stir in the garnish just before ladling *osh* into individual bowls. *Nush-e joon!*

VARIATIONS

Osh-e ghureh: Replace the beans with 1 cup/100g split peas, Increase the rice to ½ cup/100g, and replace the herbs with 2 cups/170g chopped fresh cilantro and 2 cups/170g chopped fresh mint. Replace the lime juice with 1 cup/240ml verjuice.

Osh-e ghur abeh: Make as in *osh-e ghureh* variation above except eliminate the split peas. This version should not be too thick.

Fars/Shiraz

Lemony Potato Snack

dopiyazeh alu-ye shirazi

Serves 6
Prep: 15 minutes
Cooking: 45 minutes

POTATOES

2lb/900g russet potatoes (about 3 potatoes)

TOMATO SAUCE

½ cup/120ml oil
4 medium yellow onions, peeled and thinly sliced
4 teaspoons fine sea salt
1 teaspoon freshly ground black pepper
1½ teaspoons turmeric
1 tablespoon dried fenugreek leaves
2 tablespoons dried Persian lime powder
3 large tomatoes, peeled and grated
1 tablespoon tomato paste

GARNISH

2 limes cut into wedges
Flat bread cut into 4in/10cm pieces and kept warm
1 cup/85g tarragon leaves, washed and dried
1 cup/85g basil leaves, washed and dried

I have adapted this recipe from Farideh Bahari in Shiraz. Dopiazeh alu, which means "two onion potatoes," is a popular snack. Vendors selling it used to be a familiar sight outside cinemas in Shiraz. But these days, Shirazis mostly make it at home in memory of the past. Fast food, however, is more prevalent than ever, with Iranian variations on burgers and pizza. Some outlets even call themselves "fastfood" written out in Persian script. The photo shows one of them in Shiraz.

1. **To cook the potatoes:** Place the potatoes in a saucepan and cover with water. Bring to a boil, reduce heat to medium-low, and cook for 20 to 30 minutes until tender. Drain, peel, and dice the potatoes into ½in/1cm cubes. Set aside.

2. **To make the tomato sauce:** Heat the oil in a large wide skillet over low heat until hot. Add the onions and sauté until golden brown. Add the potatoes, salt, pepper, turmeric, fenugreek, and lime powder, and sauté for 2 minutes. Add the grated tomatoes and the tomato paste and give it a gently stir. Cook for 10 to 15 minutes until all the juices have been absorbed.

3. Adjust seasoning to taste by adding more salt or dried lime powder. Reduce heat to low and keep warm until ready to serve.

4. When ready to serve, transfer to a serving platter and garnish with the limes, fresh tarragon, and basil leaves. Spread a tablespoon on a piece of the flat bread (sangak bread is best), add a squeeze of lime, and garnish with a handful of fresh herbs. *Nush-e joon!*

Fars/Shiraz

ایران برگر
IRAN BURGER

ساعات کار پارکینگ
۸ صبح الی ۲۲/۳۰
در صورت بسته بودن با شماره
۰۹۹۰۴۰۴۸۳۶۳
تماس حاصل فرمایید.

Desert-Truffle Kuku
kuku-ye aghar/donblan-e zamini

Serves 4
Prep: 10 minutes
Cooking: 20 minutes

½lb/225g truffle, cleaned, peeled and thinly sliced
½ cup/120ml oil or butter
2 medium onions, thinly sliced
1 teaspoon fine sea salt
½ teaspoon freshly ground black pepper
1 teaspoon turmeric
3 eggs

Desert truffles, faqqa *in Arabic and* donbalan-e zamini *in Persian (literally "testicles of the earth"), were known as a precious delicacy in ancient times, particularly among the Romans. Found on the southern foothills of the Zagros Mountains, they are still prized as a treat during the rainy season. After the rains, locals in Evaz, make it a day of picnics for the whole family and collect these truffles. I adapted the recipe from Halimeh Jonaybi in Evaz.*

1. Heat 6 tablespoons oil in a 10in/25cm skillet (or frittata pan) over medium-low heat until hot but not smoking, and sauté the truffles until translucent.

2. Add the onions and sauté for 10 to 15 minutes until golden brown. Add the salt, pepper, and turmeric and stir-fry for 1 minute.

3. Break the eggs into a bowl and beat lightly with a fork. Pour the eggs into the skillet and cook, covered until the eggs have set (7 to 10 minutes).

4. If you have a frittata pan, simply flip over and cook for another 5 to 10 minutes until golden. If you do not have a frittata pan, instead of flipping, you can cook the top under a hot broiler for 1 minute until lightly golden and a tester comes out clean. Transfer to a serving dish and cut into wedges. Serve with a green salad. *Nush-e joon!*

Opposite: A spread of local dishes prepared with Halimeh in her house in old Evaz.

Fars/Shiraz

Fars/Shiraz

All Green Shirazi Meatballs
kufteh-ye sabzi-e shirazi

Makes 6 meatballs, serves 4 to 6
Prep: 40 minutes + soaking of chickpeas + rice overnight
Cooking: 1½ hours

MEAT PASTE

¾ cup/150g dried chickpeas
2 cups/400g rice
1 small onion, peeled and grated
2 cloves garlic, peeled and grated
1 tablespoon fine sea salt
1 teaspoon freshly ground black pepper
1 teaspoon turmeric
2 teaspoons ground cumin
1 teaspoon red pepper flakes
½ cup/40g chopped fresh parsley
½ cup/40g chopped fresh dill
½ cup/40g chopped basil
½ cup/40g chopped fresh tarragon or 1 tablespoon dried
2 tablespoons dried mint
½ cup/40g chopped fresh basil
½lb/225g ground lamb

FILLING

¼ cup/60ml oil
2 medium onions, thinly sliced
½ cup/60g coarsely chopped walnuts
½ cup/75g barberries, picked over, washed, drained, and rinsed
½ cup/75g raisins
½ teaspoon fine sea salt
½ teaspoon turmeric

BROTH

½ cup/120ml oil
1 medium onion, finely chopped
1 cup/85g chopped fresh mint or 2 tablespoons dried
1 cup/85g chopped fresh dill
1 cup/85g chopped fresh tarragon or 2 tablespoons dried (BROTH CONTINUED)

I adapted this recipe from Farangis Shahab, our host and our guide's mother. We cooked the meatballs in the broth on a cooktop, but I much prefer my method of cooking them in the oven.

1. **To make the meat paste:** In a large bowl, place the chickpeas and rice, cover with water and allow to soak overnight. Drain thoroughly.

2. In a food processor, puree the chickpeas and rice. Transfer to a large mixing bowl. Add the rest of the ingredients for the meatballs and knead for 10 minutes until the mixture has the consistency of a smooth paste. Cover and allow to rest in the refrigerator for at least 10 minutes and up to 24 hours.

3. **To make the filling:** Heat the oil in a wide skillet over medium-low heat and sauté the onions until golden brown. Add the walnuts, barberries, raisins, salt, and turmeric, and sauté for 1 minute. Remove from heat and allow to cool.

4. **To cook the broth:** Heat the oil in a medium-sized laminated cast-iron pot over medium heat and sauté the onion until golden brown. Add the herbs and sauté for 2 minutes. Add the water, rice, and remaining ingredients for the broth, and bring to a boil. Reduce heat to low, cover and allow to simmer.

5. **To cook the meatballs:** Preheat the oven to 400°F/200°C. Generously oil a wide, non-reactive baking dish wide enough to fit 6 meatballs the size of tangerines with space between them.

6. Place a bowl of water next to you. Using damp hands, divide the meatball paste into 6 equal pieces and shape each into a tangerine-sized ball. Place a meatball in a small, moist bowl, and using your thumb make a deep, wide indentation in the center of each ball. Place 2 tablespoons of filling into each indentation. Close up the meatball and shape into a smooth ball.

7. Place the meatballs as you make them in the baking dish (be sure to leave some space between the meatballs as they will expand) and brush them generously with oil.

8. Bake in the oven for 20 minutes. Pull out the oven rack and use a ladle to gently pour all of the broth over the meatballs. Cover with oiled parchment paper and bake for another 30 minutes. Baste once during this time. Serve with garlicky yogurt and crispy Persian flat bread. *Nush-e joon!*

BROTH (CONTINUED)

1 cup/85g chopped parsley
8 cups/1.9l broth or water
¼ cup/50g rice
1 tablespoon fine sea salt
1 teaspoon freshly ground pepper
1 teaspoon turmeric
1 teaspoon red pepper flakes
2 tablespoons raisins
¼ cup/60ml fresh lime juice (2 limes)

GARNISH

2 cups/480g thick plain yogurt or *labneh* beaten with 2 cloves of grated garlic

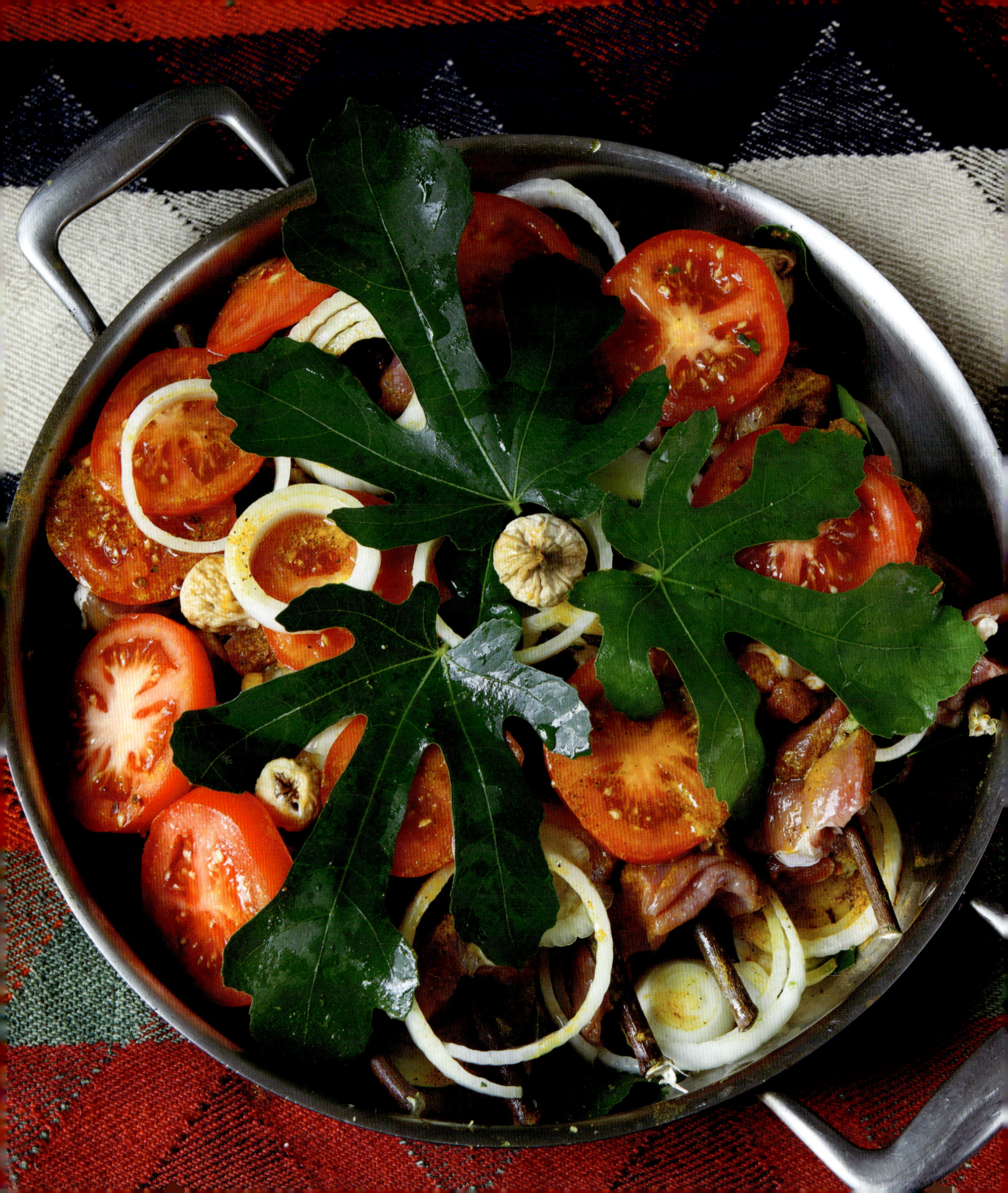

Pan-Cooked Lamb Kababs Shirazi-Style

kabab digi-e shirazi

Serves 4 to 6
Prep: 30 minutes + salting of lamb overnight
Cooking: 2 hours

SALTING THE LAMB

3lb/1.3kg boned leg of lamb cut into 2in/5cm cubes
1 tablespoon fine sea salt

SPICE MIX

½ teaspoon fine sea salt
1 teaspoon freshly ground pepper
1 teaspoon turmeric
½ teaspoon red pepper flakes

SKEWERS

6 fig-branch or small wood skewers

COOKING THE LAMB

½ cup/120ml oil, butter or ghee
6 baby fig leaves, washed thoroughly and patted dry (optional)
2 medium onions, peeled and thinly sliced
4 cloves garlic, peeled and grated
4 kaffir lime leaves, crushed
1 teaspoon ground saffron dissolved in 2 tablespoons rose water
2 large tomatoes, peeled and sliced into rings
Zest of 2 limes
8 dried Shirazi figs (available at Iranian markets), or fresh figs if available

GARNISH

Juice of 1 lime (about 4 tablespoons)
1 cup/240g plain drained yogurt/labneh
1 package (12-ounce/360g) lavash bread
1 cup/85g fresh spring onions
1 cup/85g fresh basil leaves

We bought dried fig leaves and branches at the Shiraz bazaar to make this kabab. Cooks make a similar kabab in Azarbaijan, called kabab-e hoseyni, *but they use pomegranate branches instead of fig skewers and add tail fat and bell peppers between the lamb chunks. In the photo on the facing page of the dish, I used fig leaves from the fig tree in our backyard in Washington, DC.*

1. *To salt the lamb:* Rinse the lamb thoroughly, drain, and pat dry. Place lamb in a bowl, sprinkle 1 tablespoon salt over it, and toss. Cover and refrigerate overnight.

2. *To prepare the spice mix:* In a small bowl, combine the spice mix ingredients, mix, and set aside.

3. *To cook the lamb:* Generously oil a large, shallow sauté pan (13½in/34cm diameter with cover) with ¼ cup/60ml oil and arrange 3 fig leaves on the bottom of the pan.

4. Arrange a layer of onion on top of the fig leaves to fit the bottom of the pan. Sprinkle with 1 teaspoon of the spice mix and a few drops of saffron-rose water on top.

5. Thread each fig branch with 7 pieces of lamb. Place the kabab skewers side by side on top of the onion rings and sprinkle with 1 teaspoon of the spice mix and the grated garlic. Place the lime leaves on top.

6. Arrange the tomato slices on top, and sprinkle with the rest of the spice mix and the remaining saffron-rose water. Add the zest of lime and figs.

7. Spread 3 fig leaves on top. Cover tightly (if you don't have a cover, seal with a layer of oiled parchment paper and a layer of aluminum foil on top). Cook over medium-low heat for 1½ to 2 hours until the lamb is tender and all the juice has been absorbed.

8. Serve directly from the pan or line a serving platter with the fig leaves and arrange the kabab skewers on top. Pour the pan juices and a squeeze of lime juice over the kababs. Serve with drained yogurt, bread (or plain rice/*kateh*), and fresh herbs. *Nush-e joon!*

OVEN-BAKED VARIATION

In step 7, cover, and bake in a 350°F/180°C oven for 2 hours.

Fars/Shiraz

Bakhtiari Mixed Grill
kabab-e bakhtiari

Serves 4
Prep: 20 minutes plus 8 hours of marinating
Cooking: 3 to 5 minutes

MARINATION FOR LAMB AND CHICKEN

- 2 large yellow onions, peeled and thinly sliced
- 1 tablespoon fine sea salt
- 2lb/900g lamb loin (fillet), or beef (tenderloin), rinsed, patted dry, and cut against the grain into 3 x ½in/7.5 x 1cm wide strips
- ½ cup/60g olive oil
- ¼ teaspoon ground saffron threads dissolved in 1 tablespoon warm water
- 1 teaspoon freshly ground pepper
- 2 cloves garlic, grated
- 2 bay leaves
- 2lb/900g, boneless, skinless chicken breast, rinsed, patted dry, and cut into 3 x 2in/7.5 x 5cm strips

VEGETABLES

- 2 large onions, peeled, quartered and layers separated
- 2 bell peppers, cut into 3 x 2in/7.5 x 5cm strips and soak in boiling water for 10 minutes to help with skewering
- 12 small tomatoes, campari/cocktail
- 8 serrano peppers

BASTE

- ½ cup/55g butter or 60ml oil
- 2 tablespoons fresh lime juice

COOKING AND GARNISH

- 4 flat, ½in/1cm wide metal skewers
- 1 package (12oz/340g) lavash bread
- 2 tablespoons sumac powder (optional)

1. *To marinate the lamb and chicken:* In a non-reactive container, place the onions, add the salt, and use your hands to toss well. Allow to sit for 20 minutes to release the juices of the onion. Add the oil, saffron water, pepper, and lamb and toss well. Cover and allow to marinate in fridge for 4 hours. Add the chicken, toss well, and allow to marinate for another 4 hours.

2. Thread 2 pieces of lamb, against the grain, onto a skewer, alternating with layers of onion, bell pepper, and 2 strips of chicken, leaving 2in/5cm at the top of the skewer. Follow the same steps with the other skewers and then arrange them side by side on a sheet pan.

3. Spear the tomatoes and serrano peppers, alternately, on other skewers.

4. *To grill the kababs:* Start a bed of charcoal at least 30 minutes before you want to cook and let it burn until the coals glow. The secret to a good kabab is a very hot fire or broiler.

5. For basting, in a saucepan, melt the butter and add the lime juice. Keep warm.

6. Spread a lavash bread on a serving platter.

7. When ready to cook, brush the tomato and pepper skewers lightly with the baste. Place them on the grill first, and then arrange the skewered lamb and chicken on the grill. First cook for 1 minute on each side, then turn frequently until done. The meat should be seared on the outside and juicy on the inside. Use a brush to paint them with the baste while still on the grill.

8. Transfer the kababs and tomato and pepper skewers to the serving platter. Cover with another layer of lavash bread to keep warm (keep everything on the skewers until ready to serve).

9. Serve immediately with saffron-flavored steamed rice/*chelow*, lavash bread, Persian pickles/*torshi*, and a platter of fresh herbs/*sabzi khordan*, be sure to include spring onions and fresh Persian or Thai basil. *Nush-e joon!*

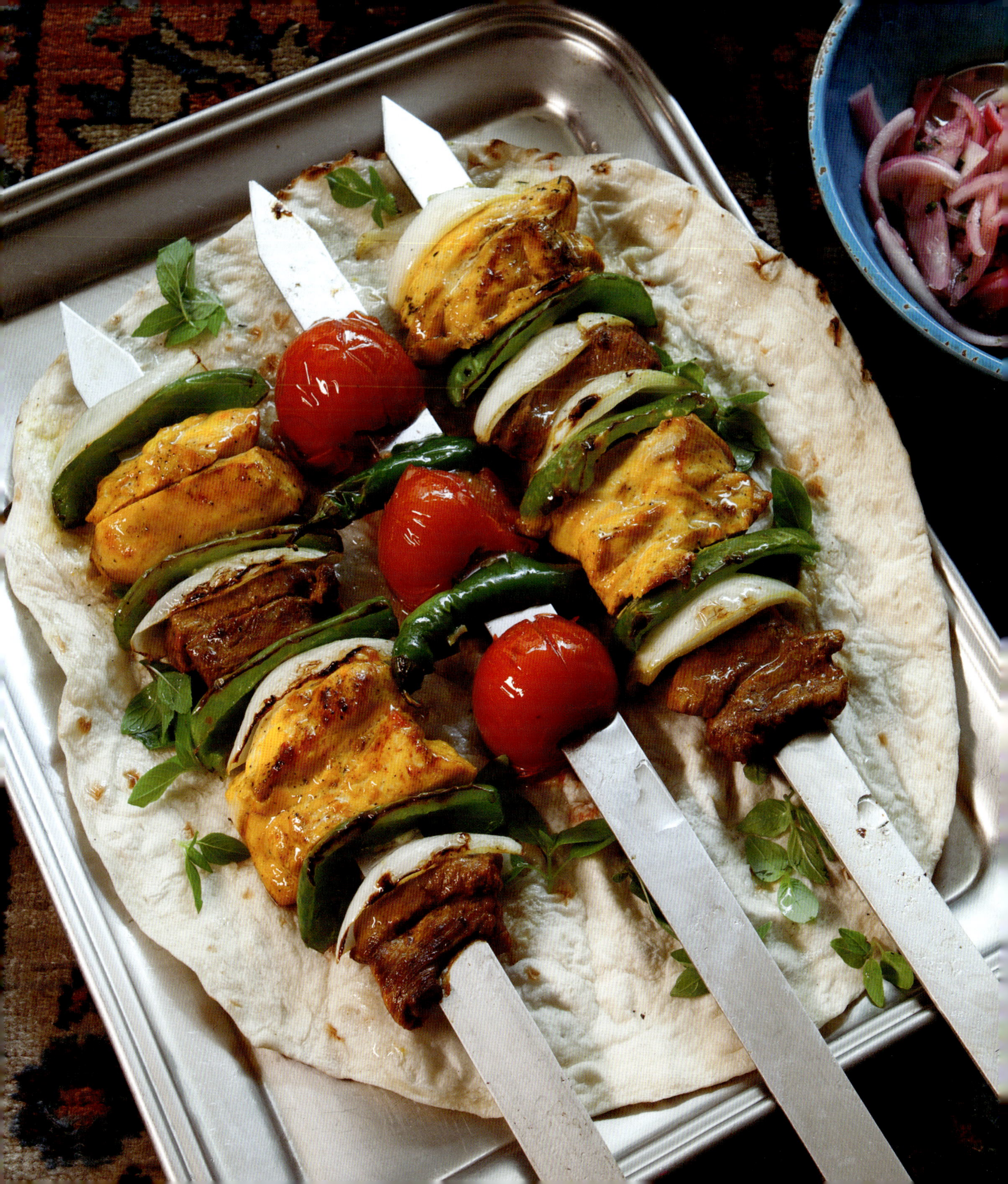

Lari Kabab
kabab-e kenjeh-ye lari

Serves 4 to 6
Prep: 20 minutes + 8 hours of marinating
Cooking: 15 minutes

MARINADE

- 2lb/900g boneless, skinless chicken thighs, or lamb or beef tenderloin, cut into 2in/5cm piece, rinsed with cold water and patted dry
- 2 teaspoons fine sea salt
- 2 large onions, peeled, coarsely sliced
- 2 cups/400g whole plain thick yogurt/*labneh*
- 2 tablespoons olive oil
- 2 teaspoons freshly ground pepper
- 1 teaspoon red pepper flakes (optional)
- 2 tablespoons coriander seeds, crushed

BASTE

- ½ cup/120g olive oil or melted butter

GARNISH

- 1 package (12 ounces/340g) lavash bread
- 2 limes, cut in half
- 2 onions, peeled and quartered
- 3 cups/255g fresh basil leaves
- Sumac powder (optional)

SKEWERS

- 12 flat ½in/1cm metal skewers, or 16 wood skewers, soaked overnight (prevents burning on the grill)

Lar is a small town on the road from Shiraz to the Persian Gulf. This delicious kabab, one of their specialties, is usually served at weddings and religious occasions. It is traditionally made with lamb, goat or beef loin, but I prefer it with chicken thighs. I adapted this recipe from Ghasem Haydari, the chef at Fulad Restaurant, one of the oldest restaurants in old town Lar. He was wonderfully generous with his knowledge and time.

1. *To marinate the chicken:* In a large non-reactive container, preferably with cover, combine the chicken, salt and onion. Mix well and allow to rest for 1 hour in the fridge. Add the rest of the ingredients, toss well, cover, and marinate for at least 24 hours (and up to 2 days) in the fridge. Turn the chicken in the marinade twice during this period.

2. *To grill the chicken:* Start a bed of charcoal 30 minutes before you want to cook and let it burn until the coals glow evenly, or preheat the oven broiler. Line a sheet pan with parchment paper.

3. Meanwhile, skewer the chicken thighs and place them on the sheet pan.

4. In a small saucepan, melt the butter over very low heat and keep warm. Spread a lavash bread on a flat serving platter.

5. Grill the chicken for 10 to 15 minutes, turning frequently until golden and slightly charred (chicken should not be pink inside). Paint the chicken with the baste. Remove from the flame, and place on the lavash bread.

6. Keep the chicken on the skewers until just before serving—this helps to keep them warm. To remove the chicken from skewers steady them on the platter with a piece of bread and pull out the skewers. Garnish and serve immediately. Traditionally this kabab is served with a yogurt drink/*dugh*. *Nush-e joon!*

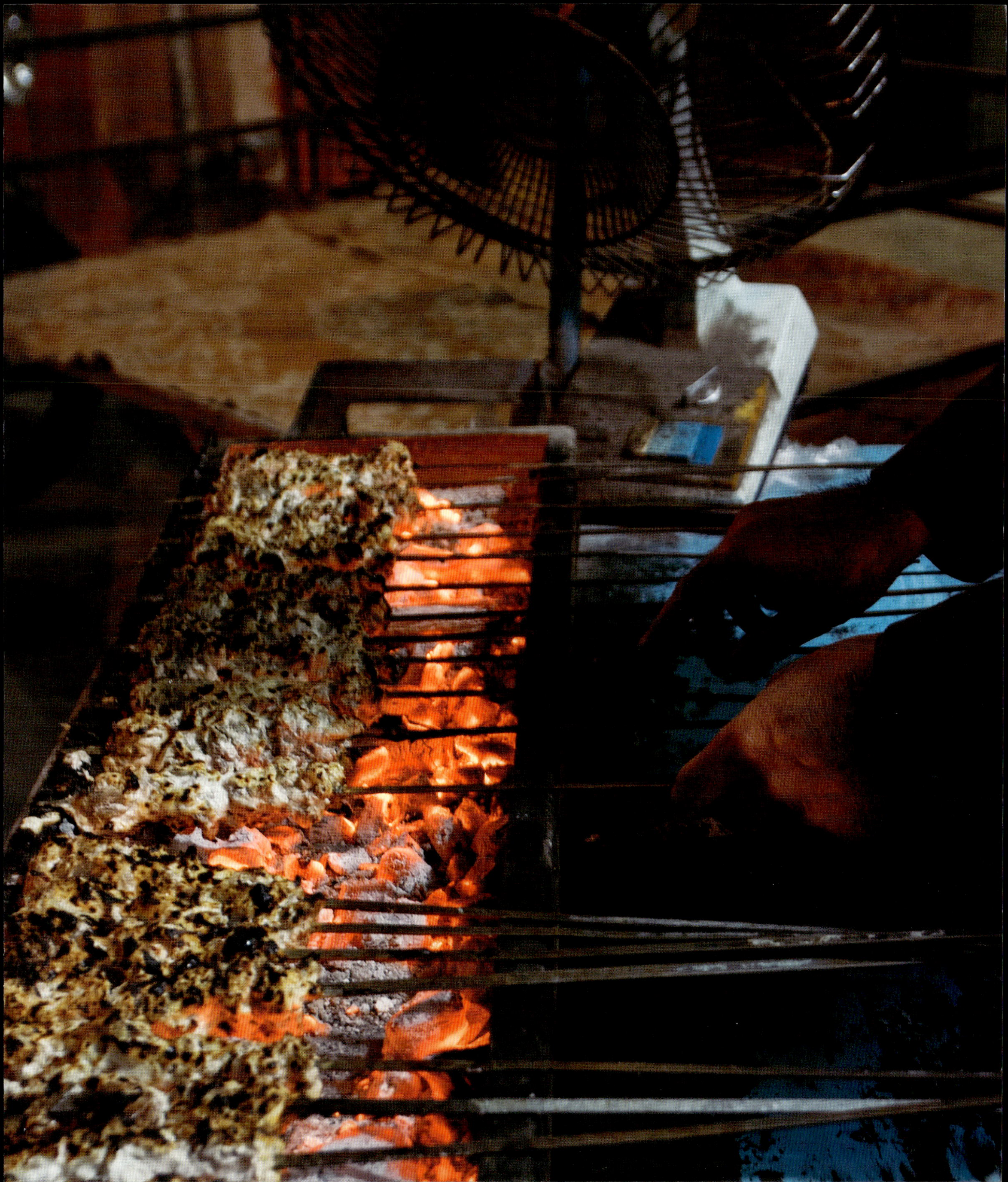

Rice with Sugar, Rose Water, Saffron + Tangerine

shekar polow-ye shirazi

Serves 6
Prep: 20 minutes
Cooking: 1¼ hour

CHICKEN

2 tablespoons oil
2 medium onions, peeled and thinly sliced
2lb/900g chicken thighs cut into 3in/7.5cm strips
1 teaspoon fine sea salt
½ teaspoon freshly ground pepper
½ teaspoon turmeric
2 tablespoons fresh lime juice

CARAMELIZED TANGERINE AND PISTACHIOS

1 cup/100g tangerine peels, slivered
¼ cup/60ml oil, melted butter, or ghee
1 cup/200g sugar
1 cup/240ml rose water
1 teaspoon ground saffron dissolved in 4 tablespoons hot water
1 cup/170g slivered pistachio kernels

RICE

3 cups/600g basmati rice

GOLDEN CRUST/ TAH-DIG

1¼ cups/300ml oil
2 tablespoons plain whole yogurt
¼ teaspoon ground saffron dissolved in 1 tablespoon rose water

VEGAN OPTION

Eliminate the meat, and the yogurt for the golden crust. These sweet rice variations work perfectly when combined with Red Lentil Soup/*dal* (page 611).

This dish is often served at weddings together with Saffroned Lamb Braise (without the fries) khoresh-e qeymeh, page 438. I adapted these recipes from Laila Jafari from Shiraz. They were her favorite childhood dishes.

1. *To cook the chicken:* In a medium-sized sauté pan over low heat, place the oil, onions, chicken, salt, pepper, turmeric, and lime juice. Cover and simmer for 1 hour. Make sure chicken is tender and adjust seasoning to taste. Keep covered until ready to serve.

2. *To caramelized the tangerine peels:* Remove any bitterness by placing the tangerine peels in a small saucepan, covering with water and bringing to a boil over high heat. Drain and rinse with cold water.

3. Return the peels to the same saucepan and add the oil, sugar, and rose water, and bring to a boil. Reduce heat to low and allow to simmer for 5 minutes. Add the saffron and pistachios, give it a gentle stir, and set aside.

4. *To cook the rice:* Wash the rice by placing it in a large container and covering it with water. Agitate gently with your hand, then pour off the water. Repeat 4 to 5 times until the water is clear.

5. In a large non-stick pot, bring 8 cups/1.9l water and 2 tablespoons fine sea salt to a boil. Add the rice and boil briskly for 8 to 10 minutes, gently stirring twice with a wooden spoon to loosen any grains that may have stuck to the bottom. Bite a few grains of the rice. If the rice feels soft and all of it has risen to the surface, it is ready. Drain the rice in a large fine-mesh colander and rinse with 3 cups/720ml water.

6. *For the golden crust/tah-dig:* In the same pot, using a rubber spatula, mix together 1 cup oil, ¼ cup water, 2 tablespoons yogurt, 1 tablespoon saffron-rose water, and 2 spatulas of rice. Spread the mixture evenly over the bottom of the pot. Gently place the rest of the rice in the pot. Cover, and cook for 10 minutes over medium heat. Reduce heat to low, wrap the lid with a dish towel, cover tightly and cook for 50 minutes.

7. Uncover the rice and spoon the caramelized tangerine peel mixture (reserving a little of it for decoration) with its syrup over the rice. Swirl the remaining oil on top. Cover tightly and cook over low heat for 20 minutes longer.

8. Remove the rice from heat and allow to cool (do not uncover) for 5 minutes on a damp surface to free the crust from the bottom of the pot. Hold the serving platter tightly over the uncovered pot and invert the two together, unmolding the entire mound onto the platter. The rice will emerge as a golden-crusted cake. Decorate on top with the reserved caramelized orange peel and serve with the chicken. *Nush-e joon!*

VARIATION

Caramelized Onion, Walnut + Raisin Rice with Pomegranate Syrup
rob polow-ye shirazi

Cook the chicken as above. ***To cook the caramelized onion, walnut and raisin sauce:*** In a wide skillet heat ¼ cup/60ml oil over low heat and caramelize 2 thinly sliced onions. Add 1 cup/170g coarsely chopped walnuts, 1 cup/150g raisins (soaked for 30 minutes, drained), and sauté for 1 minute. Set aside.

To make the pomegranate syrup: In a small saucepan, combine ½ cup/100g sugar, 1 cup/240g pomegranate molasses, and ¼ cup/60ml oil, stir gently and bring to a boil over low heat. Simmer for 4 minutes. Set aside. Cook the rice as above and continue with step 7, except replace the tangerine mixture with the caramelized walnut mixture and drizzle pomegranate syrup over it. Reduce the cooking time to 20 minutes. Everything else remains the same.

Kohlrabi + Herb Rice with Meatballs
kalam polow-ye shirazi

Serves 6 to 8
Prep: 30 minutes
Cooking: 1 hour

MEATBALLS

- 1lb/450g ground lamb or chicken thighs
- 1 onion, peeled and grated
- 1 teaspoon fine sea salt
- 1 teaspoon freshly ground pepper
- 1 teaspoon turmeric
- ½ teaspoon red pepper flakes
- ¼ cup/20g chopped fresh basil
- ¼ cup/60ml oil

CARAMELIZED ONION AND KOHLRABI

- ¼ cup/60ml oil
- 2 onions, thinly sliced
- 3 tablespoons cumin seeds
- 1 teaspoon fine sea salt
- 2lb/900g kohlrabi, peeled, hard parts removed and cut into ½in/1cm cubes

HERBS

- 1 cup/85g chopped fresh basil
- 1 cup/85g chopped fresh tarragon
- 1 cup/85g chopped fresh parsley
- 1 cup/85g chopped fresh cilantro
- 1 cup/85g chopped spring onion (white and green)

RICE

- 2 cups/400g basmati rice
- ½ cup/120ml oil
- 1 teaspoon ground saffron tread dissolved in 2 tablespoons hot water

1. *To cook the meatballs:* Combine all the ingredients for the meatballs except the oil and knead lightly to form a paste.

2. In a wide skillet, heat ¼ cup/60ml oil over low heat. With damp hands form the paste into meatballs the size of hazelnuts and, as you make them, carefully add them to the skillet. Swirl and shake the pan back and forth until meatballs are golden brown all over—if you use a spatula it might break up the meatballs. Use a slotted spoon to gently remove the meatballs and set aside.

3. *To caramelized onion and kohlrabi:* Heat ¼ cup/60ml oil in the same skillet over medium-low heat and sauté the onions until golden brown. Add the cumin seeds, salt and kohlrabi, and sauté for 5 minutes. Remove from heat and set aside.

4. Wash the rice by placing it in a large container and covering it with water. Agitate gently with your hand, then pour off the water. Repeat 4 to 5 times until the water is clear.

5. *To cook the rice:* In a large non-stick pot, bring 8 cups/1.9l water and 3 tablespoons fine sea salt to a boil. Add the rice. Boil briskly for 6 to 10 minutes, gently stirring twice to loosen any grains that may have stuck to the bottom. Bite a few grains. If the rice feels soft and all of it has risen to the surface, it is ready to be drained. Drain the rice in a large fine-mesh colander and rinse with 3 cups/720ml water.

6. Heat ¼ cup/60ml oil and 2 tablespoons water in the pot. Place 2 spatulas full of the rice and 1 spatula full of the caramelized onion and kohlrabi mixture in the pot, then add a layer of the herbs, and a layer of meatballs. Repeat, alternating layers. Mound the rice in the form of a pyramid. Cover and cook for 10 minutes over medium heat.

7. Pour ¼ cup/60ml oil, ½ cup/120ml water, and the saffron water over the rice. Wrap the lid of the pot with a clean dish towel and cover the pot firmly to absorb condensation and prevent steam from escaping. Cook for 50 minutes over low heat.

8. Remove the pot from heat and allow to cool for 5 minutes on a damp surface without uncovering it. Gently transfer the rice to a serving platter. *Nush-e joon!*

NOTE

This much-liked Shirazi rice dish is traditionally made with meatballs, but you can replace them with 1lb/450g stewing lamb or chicken thighs cut into ½inch/1cm cubes. Sauté them with the ingredients for meatballs until golden brown. Add them to the rice in step 6 in lieu of meatballs.

VARIATION

Carrot + Mung Bean Rice
qanbar polow-ye shirazi

I have adapted this well-known regional recipe from Khanum-e Soroosh, who lives in Shiraz. It is made in the same way as the kohlrabi and herb rice above, but you replace the kohlrabi and herbs with caramelized onions, carrots and mung beans.

Make the meatballs as above and set aside. In a small saucepan, cook 2 cups/400g mung beans with 6 cups water over medium heat for 30 minutes, drain and set aside. To cook the caramelized onion and carrots: In the wide skillet heat ¼ cup/60ml oil over low heat and caramelize 2 thinly sliced onions, add 1 pound/450g julienned carrots, 1 teaspoon fine sea salt, 1 teaspoon red pepper flakes, 1 teaspoon ground saffron, 1 cup/240g fresh lime juice, and 2 tablespoons date molasses, and sauté for 4 minutes. Add the mung beans and set aside. Continue with step 4 above. In step 6 replace the kohlrabi mixture with the caramelized onion, carrots and mung beans mixture. Everything else remains the same.

Oven-Baked Chicken, Eggplant + Barberry Rice
tachin-e shirazi/polow qalebi

Serves 6
Prep: 1 hour 40 minutes
Cooking: 3½ hours

CHICKEN

2lb/900g boneless, skinless chicken thighs, or leg of lamb, cut into 1in/2.5cm cubes
1 large onion, peeled and thinly sliced
2 cloves garlic, peeled and sliced
2 teaspoons fine sea salt
1 teaspoon freshly ground pepper
1 teaspoon turmeric
2 tablespoons fresh lime juice

RICE

3 cups/200g long-grain basmati rice

EGGPLANTS + ONIONS

4 tablespoons oil
2lb/900g Chinese eggplants
2 large onions, peeled and thinly sliced

BARBERRIES

2 tablespoons oil
2 teaspoons cumin seeds
¼ cup/60ml water
3 tablespoons sugar
1 cup/150g dried barberries, picked over and rinsed thoroughly

GOLDEN CRUST/*TAH-DIG*

3 eggs
2 cups/480g plain thick yogurt or labneh
1 teaspoon ground saffron dissolved in 2 tablespoons orange blossom water
¼ cup/60ml oil
2 teaspoons fine sea salt
1 teaspoon freshly ground pepper
1 teaspoon ground cinnamon
Zest of 1 orange
½ cup/55g butter or ghee (room temperature)

1. *To cook the chicken:* In a deep, wide skillet, place all the ingredients for the chicken (do not add water). Cover and cook for 1 hour over low heat. Uncover, raise the heat to medium, and continue to cook, uncovered until all the juices have been absorbed. Set aside.

2. *To cook the rice:* Wash the rice by placing it in a large container, cover it with water, agitate gently with your hand, then pour off the water. Repeat 2 to 3 times until the water is clear.

3. In a large non-stick pot, bring 8 cups/1.9l water and 2 tablespoons fine sea salt to a boil. Add the rice and boil briskly for 8 minutes, gently stirring once. Drain rice in a large fine-mesh colander and rinse with 3 cups/720ml water. Set aside.

4. *To caramelize the eggplants and onions:* Peel and cut eggplants into 3 x ½in/7.5 x 1cm thick slices. Heat 2 tablespoons oil in a wide skillet over medium heat and brown eggplant slices on both sides. Remove eggplant from the skillet and set aside. Add 2 tablespoons oil to the same skillet and sauté the onions until golden brown. Remove from the skillet and set aside.

5. *To caramelize the barberries:* Heat 2 tablespoons oil in the same skillet over medium heat and add the cumin. Stir-fry for 1 minute. Add ¼ cup/60ml water, the sugar, and barberries, and stir-fry for 4 minutes (beware, barberries burn easily; do not overcook). Set aside.

6. *To make the golden crust/tah-dig:* In a large mixing bowl, whisk the eggs, yogurt, saffron-orange blossom water, ¼ cup oil, salt, pepper, cinnamon, and zest of orange until smooth. Add the rice and fold.

7. Place the oven rack in the middle. Preheat oven to 375°F/190°C. Brush ½ cup/55g butter evenly and thoroughly all over the base and sides of a 4qt/3.7l ovenproof Pyrex dish.

8. Spread half the rice mixture evenly in the dish. Arrange chicken pieces on top. Spread the barberry mixture over the chicken. Arrange the eggplants and onions on top. Cover with the remaining rice and pack down using the palms of your hands. Cover with a layer of oiled parchment paper and a layer of aluminum foil on top, and once again press down evenly with your hands (this will help the unmolding process later). Seal tightly around the rim and pierce several holes on top so steam can escape.

9. Bake in the preheated oven for 2 to 2½ hours until the crust is golden brown (a glass ovenproof dish allows you to see through). Spread a wet dish towel on the counter or on a rimmed sheet pan.

10. Remove the dish from oven (do not uncover) and allow to cool for

15 minutes on the wet dish towel. Uncover and loosen the rice around the edges of the dish with the point of a knife. Place a serving platter (larger than the ovenproof dish) on top. Hold the dish and platter firmly together and turn over in a single motion with a jolt to unmold the rice. Allow to rest for a moment, then gently lift the ovenproof dish. Serve hot. *Nush-e joon!*

VARIATION

Stovetop-Style: In step 7, replace the Pyrex baking dish with a large (5qt/4.7l) non-stick pot. In step 9, and cook for 20 minutes over medium heat. Reduce heat to low and continue to cook for another 60 minutes. Proceed with step 10.

NOTE

Chinese eggplants (purple) are not bitter, but regular eggplants (black) need to have their bitterness removed. Place slices in a container, cover with water, sprinkle with 1 tablespoon salt, let stand for 20 minutes, drain, and rinse with cold water. Blot dry thoroughly.

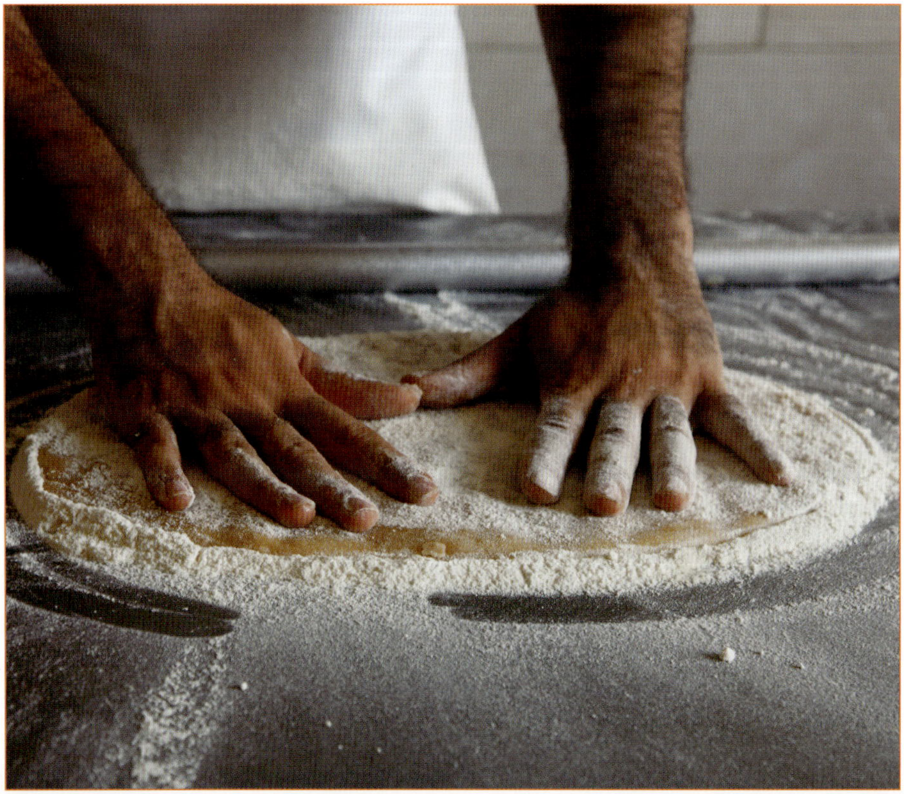

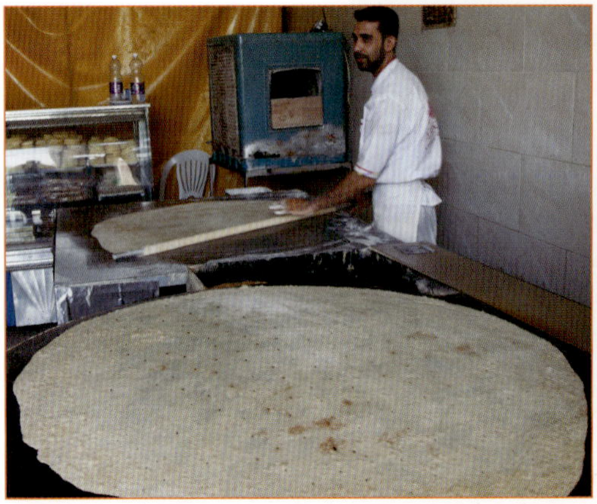

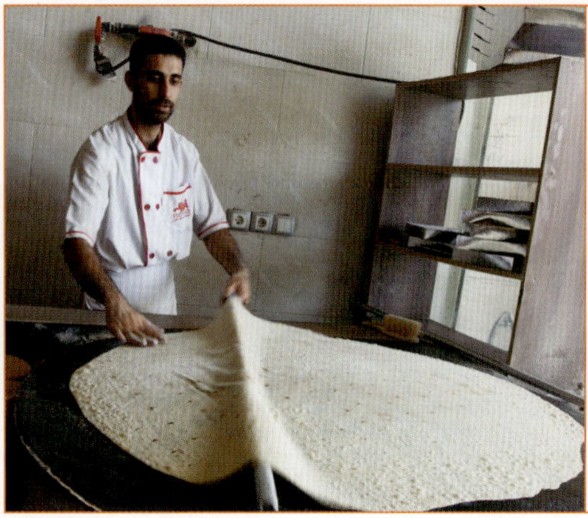

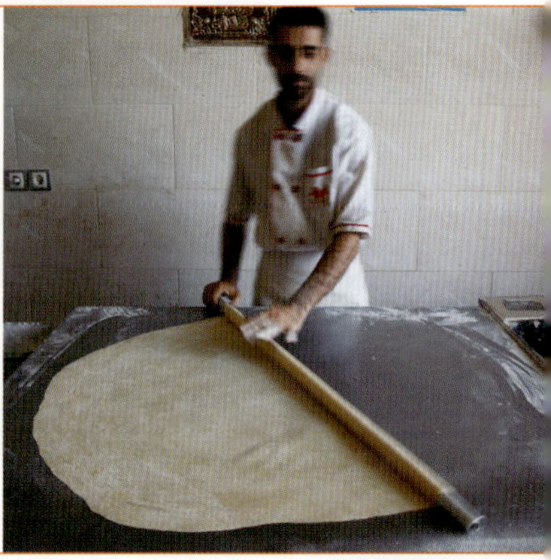

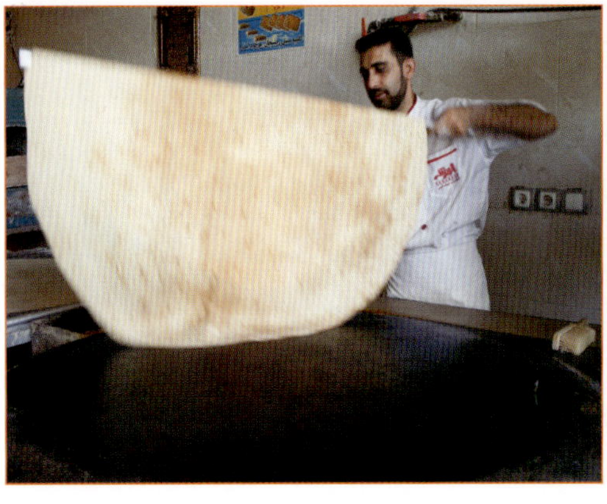

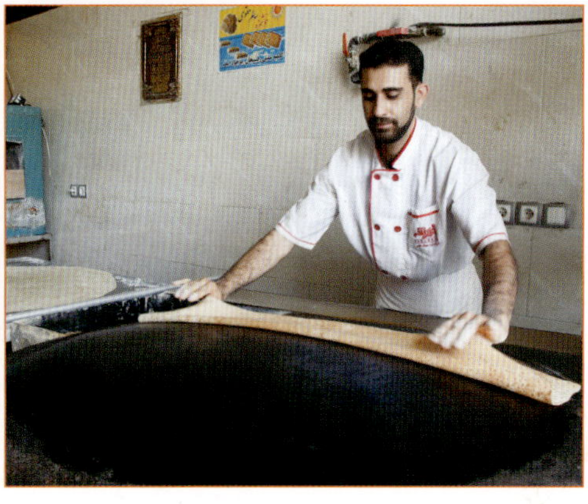

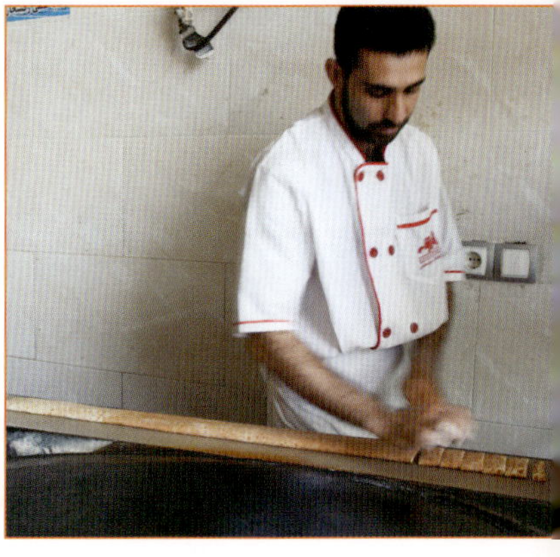

Pastry Roll Filled with Almond + Cardamom
kaak /yokheh-ye shiraz

Makes 5 rolls
Prep: 1 hour + 2 hours of resting
Cooking: 4 minutes for each roll

DOUGH

1 teaspoon yeast
½ cup/120g sugar
¼ cup/60ml warm water (100°F/38°C)
¼ cup/60ml oil
1 egg yolk (room temperature)
3 cups/300g all-purposed flour mixed with ¼ teaspoon fine sea salt

FILLING

½ cup/50g almond flour
1 tablespoon ground cardamom
2 tablespoons powdered sugar

I enjoyed my visit to the Yokhneh Workshop in Shiraz. It was thrilling to see their mastery in making this delicate pastry.

1. **To make the dough:** In the mixing bowl of an electric mixer, place the yeast, sugar, and warm water and allow to sit for 10 minutes. Add the oil and egg and mix for 1 minute. Gradually add the flour mixture and knead until you have a stiff dough that does not stick to your hands. Cover and allow to rest at room temperature for 2 hours.

2. On a floured surface, punch down and divide the dough into 5 walnut-sized balls. Cover and allow to rest for another 15 minutes.

3. **To make the filling:** In a small bowl, mix together the almond flour, cardamom, and powdered sugar. Set aside.

4. **To cook the thin pastry sheets:** Heat an iron skillet or *saj* until hot. On a floured surface, roll out each ball of dough to a very thin disc (about 8in/20cm). Use a thin rolling pin to pick up and transfer the disc to the hot skillet. Cook for 20 seconds on each side.

5. **To assemble the roll:** Remove the pastry from the skillet and place it on a clean surface. Spread a thin layer of the filling over it and fold it several times. Use the rolling pin to go over the pastry to flatten it. Use a sharp knife to cut the pastry diagonally into 3in/7.5cm pieces. Repeat for the remaining dough. *Nush-e joon!*

Fars/Shiraz

Shirazi Rose Water Custard
masqati-ye kasehi

Serves 6
Prep: 10 minutes plus 4 hours of setting time
Cooking: 35 minutes

1 cup/110g wheat, rice or corn starch
6 cups/1.5l water
1 cup/200g sugar
½ cup/120ml rose water
1 cup/120g sliced almonds
2 tablespoons slivered pistachios
¼ cup/55g butter or 60ml oil
⅛ teaspoon saffron dissolved in 1 tablespoon water (optional)

GARNISH

2 tablespoons sliced almonds, toasted
1 teaspoon slivered pistachios

I adapted this recipe from Farangis Shahab, our host and our guide's mother.

1. **To make the custard:** Dissolve the starch in the water and allow to sit for 5 minutes. Pass it through a sieve into a medium-sized heavy-bottomed saucepan.

2. Bring to a boil over low heat, whisking constantly to prevent curdling.

3. Add the sugar and continue to whisk until sugar has dissolved (about 2 minutes).

4. Add the rose water, almonds, and pistachios, whisking constantly (about 15 minutes) until the mixture reaches the consistency of a thick custard.

5. Heat the butter in a small saucepan and gradually add it to the saucepan, stirring until it has all been absorbed and the mixture is thick, smooth, and glossy (about 10 minutes).

6. Immediately transfer the custard to a large glass serving bowl, or to individual serving dishes while the custard is hot, and garnish. Allow to cool at room temperature, then cover and chill in the refrigerator for at least 4 hours. Serve cold. *Nush-e joon!*

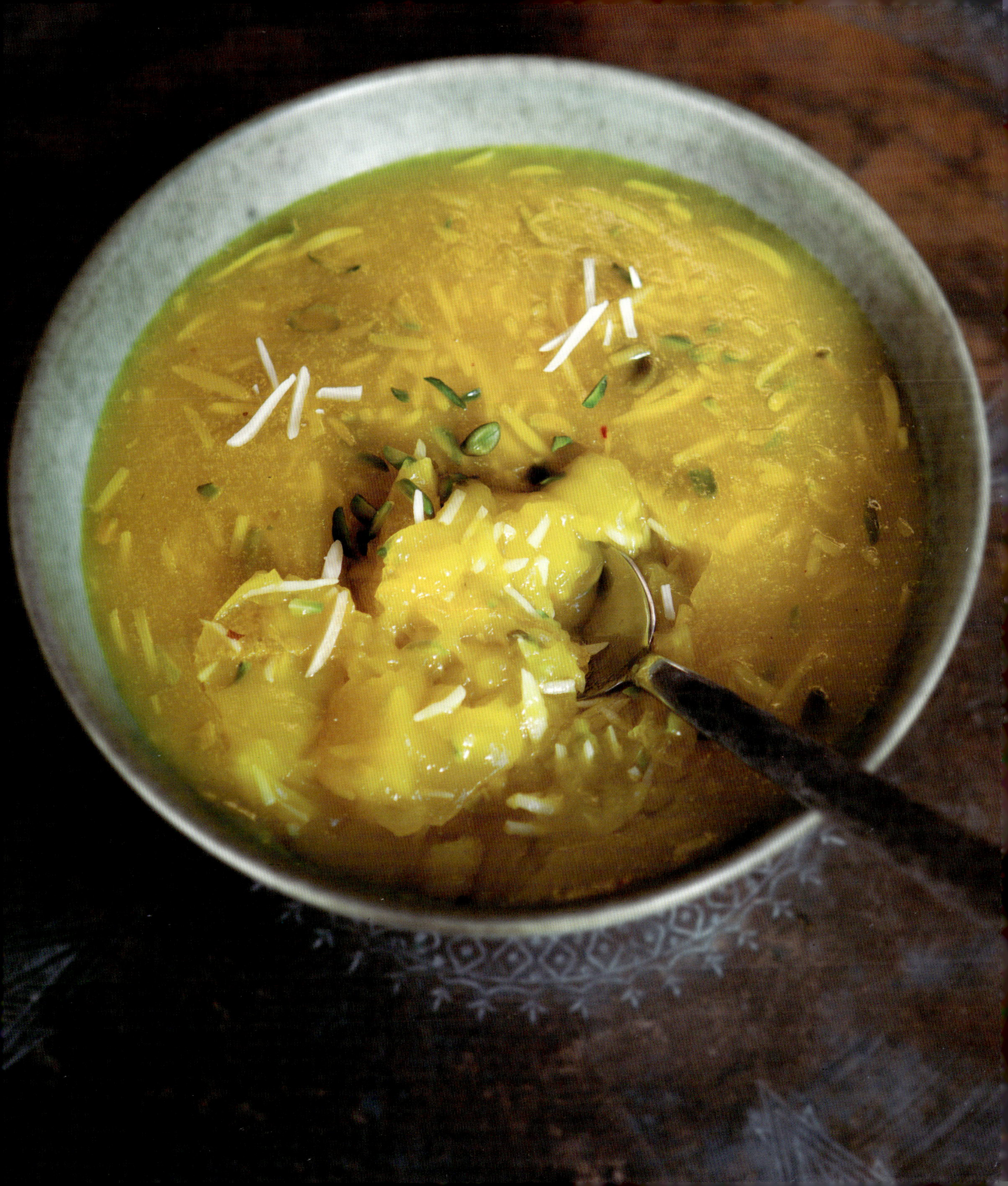

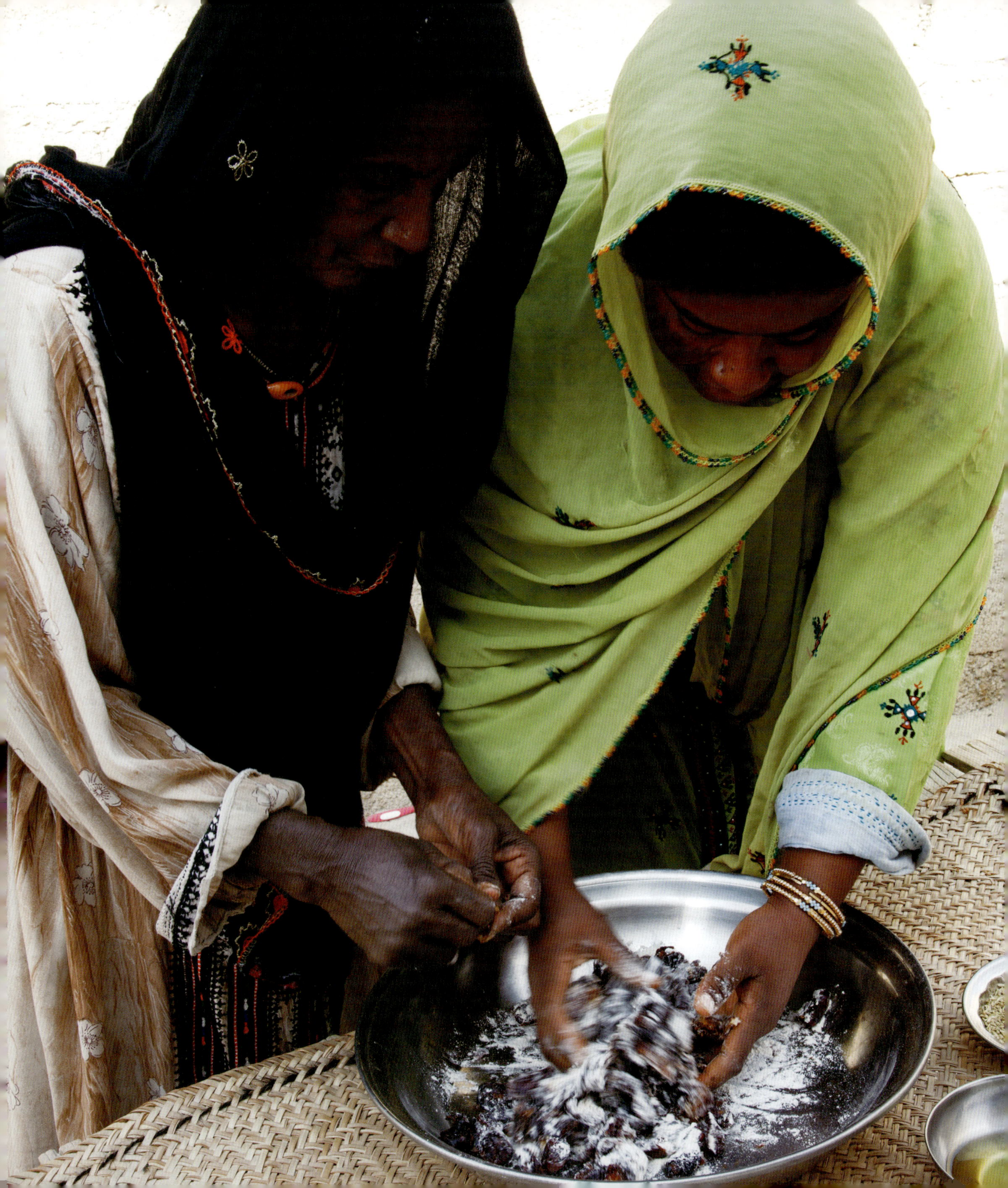

Date + Walnut Pie
ranginak-e shirazi

Makes a 9in/23cm pie
Prep: 30 minutes
Cooking: 20 minutes

FILLING

1 cup/125g walnut or pistachio kernels, coarsly chopped
3 cups/525g medjool dates, pitted

ROUX

1 cup/225ml oil or unsalted butter
1½ cups/150g sifted unbleached all-purpose flour

DUSTING

1 teaspoon ground cinnamon
2 teaspoons ground cardamom
½ cup/65g powdered sugar

GARNISH

1 cup/120g ground pistachio kernels
½ cup/30g shredded coconut, toasted

VARIATION

Crustless Date + Walnut Pie
qisava-ye khorma

Preheat the oven to 350°F/180°C. Oil the pie dish and proceed with steps 1 to 3. Eliminate steps 4 and 5. Bake in the oven for 5 minutes until the dates are soft. Whisk together 4 eggs, ½ cup/120ml milk, ½ teaspoon cinnamon until smooth. Pour it over the dates and return to the oven. Bake for another 6 to 10 minutes until the egg has set. Proceed with step 6 to dust and garnish.

Opposite: Two Baluchi women mashing dates and flour for making *khorma beriz*.

1. *To make the filling:* In a wide skillet, toast the walnuts over medium heat for 2 to 5 minutes, shaking the skillet back and forth. Set aside and allow to cool.

2. Place a few walnut pieces inside each date.

3. Arrange the dates, packed next to each other, in a flat 9in/23cm pie dish. Set aside.

4. *To make the roux:* In a large deep skillet, heat the oil over medium heat, and add the flour. Stir-fry with a long wooden spoon for 15 to 20 minutes until the mixture develops a golden caramel color (beware to neither undercook nor overcook the flour).

5. Spread the hot roux over the dates, pack down, and smooth out with the back of a spoon to create an even surface.

6. *Meanwhile, to make the dusting:* In a small bowl, mix together the cinnamon, cardamom, and powdered sugar. Sprinkle evenly over the hot pie.

7. Sprinkle the ground pistachios and coconuts evenly over the surface. Allow to cool thoroughly.

8. Just before serving, cut in small pieces (traditionally diamond shaped). Carefully arrange these on a serving platter or serve directly from the pie dish. *Nush-e joon!*

VARIATIONS

khorma beriz-e baluchi: Knead together the flour, dates, and 2 tablespoons fennel seeds until you have a grainy paste. Heat the oil in a wide skillet over medium heat and stir-fry the paste until caramelized (about 20 minutes). Garnish as above.

halva-ye khorma: In a food processor, puree the dates with ¼ cup/60ml warm water. Heat the oil in a wide skillet over medium heat until hot. Add the flour and stir-fry for 20 minutes until golden. Add the pureed dates and continue to stir-fry for 5 to 10 minutes until you have a smooth paste. Garnish as above.

chingal: Proceed as with *halva-ye khorma* but replace the flour with 3 cups/180g warm fresh bread croutons. Garnish as above.

halegh/charoset: Replace the flour in *halva-ye khorma* with 3 cups of your favorite dried fruits and nuts, sautéing for just 1 minute in step 4. The result should be a sweet and sour grainy paste.

The Persian Gulf

Three-Nut Starch Halva

halva-ye masqati-e lari

Serves 6
Prep: 20 minutes
Cooking: 1½ hours plus cooling overnight

NUTS

¼ cup/30g blanched slivered almonds
¼ cup/30g slivered pistachio kernels
¼ cup/30g chopped walnuts

SYRUP

2 cups/400g sugar
½ cup/120ml water
1 teaspoon cardamom
½ cup/120ml rose water
½ teaspoon ground saffron threads dissolved in 1 tablespoon water

STARCH

1 cup/240g wheat or corn starch
6 cups/1.4l water

OIL

½ cup/120ml sesame oil

I adapted this recipe from Abdolhasan Khalilian, a talented and generous man, who has been cooking this halva in a small artisanal workshop in Lar for more than a decade.

1. Line a quarter-sized (9½x13in/24x33cm) rimmed sheet pan with plastic wrap.

2. *To toast the nuts:* Place all the nuts in a wide skillet over low heat, shaking the pan until the aroma starts to rise. Remove from heat and set aside.

3. *To make the syrup:* In a medium-sized saucepan, whisk together the sugar and water until the sugar has dissolved. Bring to a boil. Remove from heat and add the cardamom, rose water, and saffron. Set aside.

4. *To prepare the starch:* dissolve the starch in water and pass it through a sieve over a large saucepan. Place the saucepan over low heat and cook, stirring constantly for 15 to 20 mintues until you have a thick paste.

5. Gradually stir in the syrup and oil, alternating between them, and continue to cook over low heat, stirring frequently, for 30 to 40 minutes until it has the consistency of a thick honey.

6. Gradually stir in the nuts and cook for another minute.

7. Transfer to the lined sheet pan and allow to cool overnight at room temperature. Cover with plastic wrap and keep in the fridge. *Nush-e joon!*

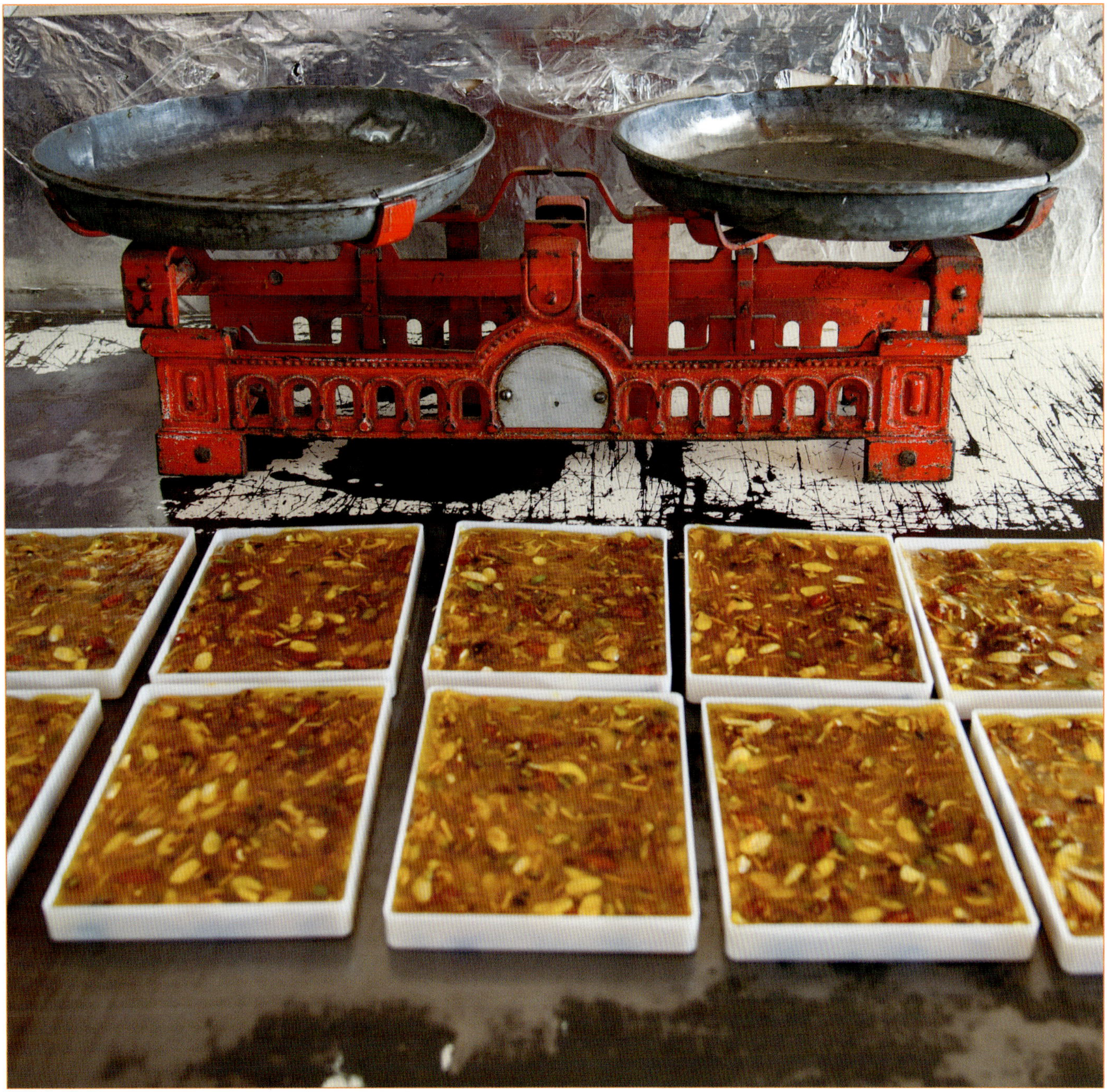

Tahini Halva
halvardeh

Makes 20 pieces
Prep: 5 minutes
Cooking: 5 minutes

1 cup/175g pistachio kernels
½ teaspoon ground cardamom
½ teaspoon ground cinnamon

SYRUP

2 cups/400g sugar
2 cups/480ml water

TAHINI

3 cups/675g tahini paste
2 tablespoons rose water

I was fascinated by how popular sesame products are throughout Iran, but I shouldn't have been surprised because I knew that sesame had been cultivated in Iran for several thousand years. In southern Iran, the sesame halva/halvardeh or pashmak-e ardeh versions are the most popular. I visited workshops in Shiraz, Evaz and Lar, where they still make it in the artisanal manner.

1. Use an 8½ x 2in/21 x 5cm square silicone mould.

2. **To toast the pistachio kernels:** In a wide skillet, toast the pistachio kernels by shaking the pan back and forth until the aroma of the coriander starts to rise (about 30 minutes). Add the cardamom and cinnamon, give it a stir, cover and keep warm until ready to use.

3. **To make the syrup:** Place the sugar and water in a saucepan over low heat and simmer until all the sugar has dissolved. Increase the heat to medium and bring to a boil. Reduce heat to low, and allow to cook, undisturbed, for 30 minutes until a candy thermometer shows a temperature of 293°F/145°C and you have a thick, stretchy, and lightly caramelized syrup.

4. Meanwhile, in the bowl of an electric mixer, beat the tahini paste, rose water, and 2 tablespoons of the syrup, for 5 minutes.

5. Add the remaining syrup and mix for 5 to 10 minutes until stiff.

6. Use a rubber spatula to fold in the pistachio and cardamom mixture until they have been incorporated in the paste.

7. Transfer the paste to the mould and allow to dry at room temperature overnight.

8. When completely dry, cover with plastic wrap. *Nush-e joon!*

VARIATION

Date Tahini Halva
halvardeh-ye khorma

Replace the syrup with date molasses.

Combining the tahini paste and syrup in the final stage of making sesame halva/halvardeh.

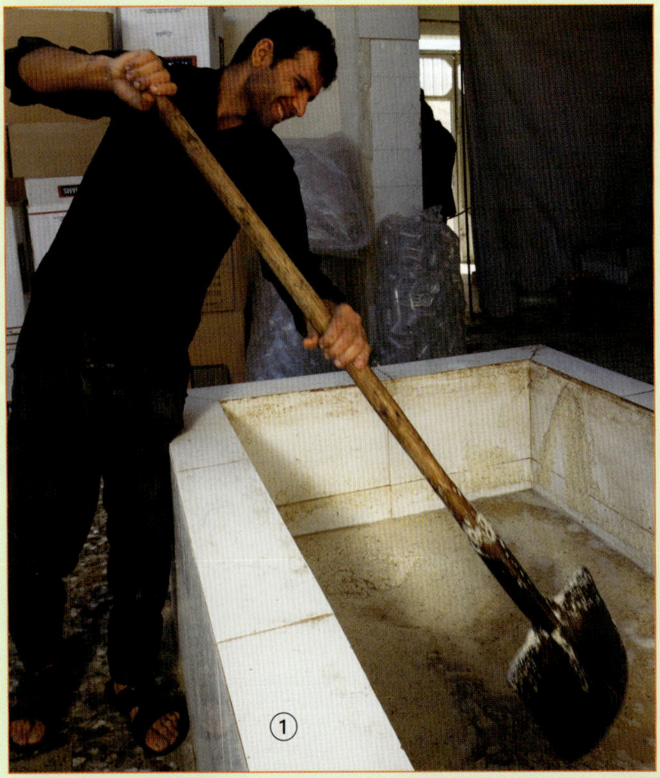

①

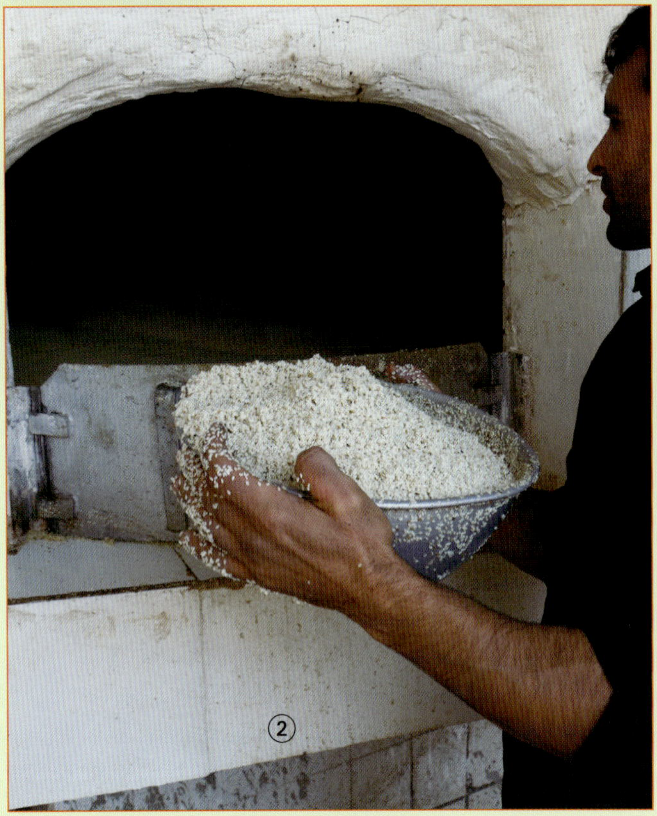

②

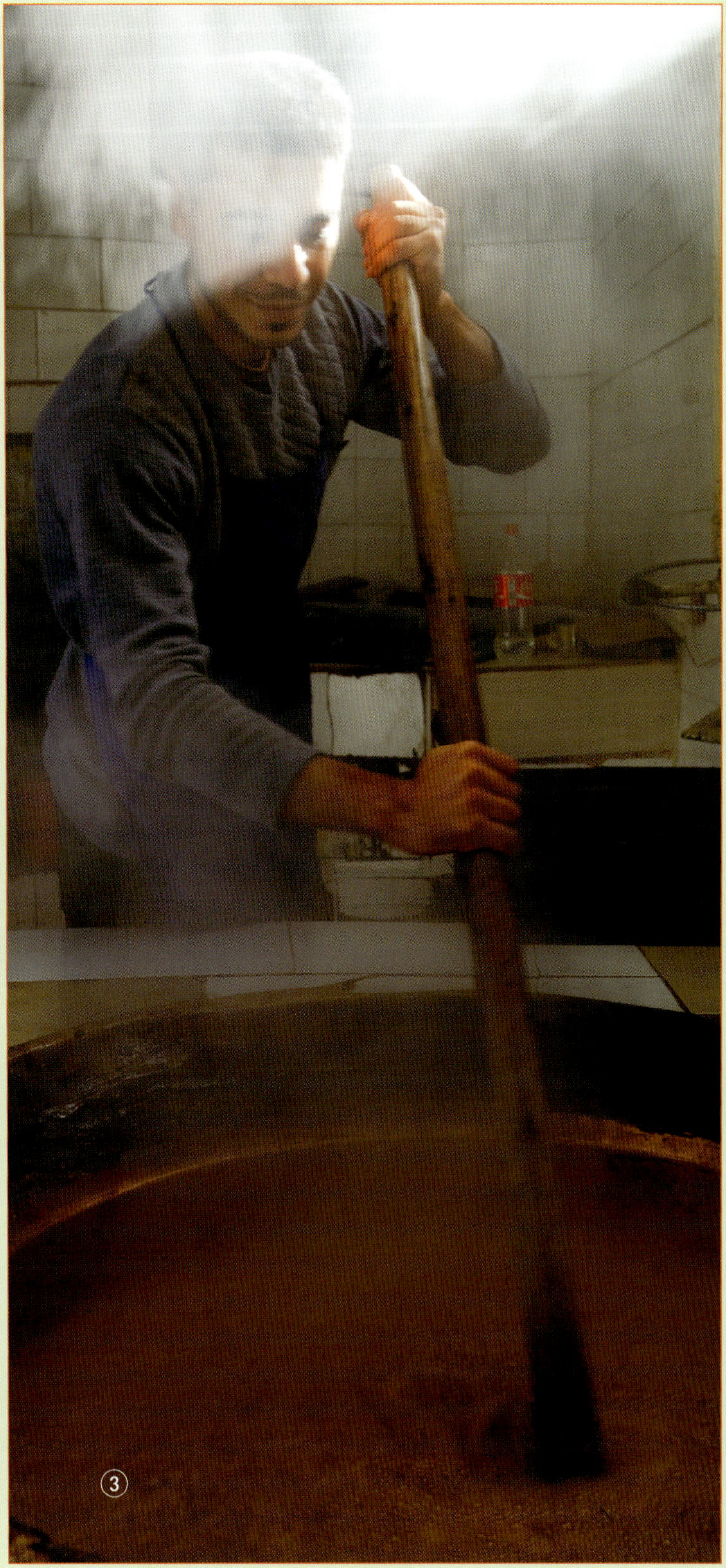

③

Sesame

Sesame is an annual flowering plant that can be up to 3ft/1m tall. Sesame seeds come from the elongated pods of the plant. In Iran, the seeds, and the ground form, tahini, are both called "ardeh" (tahini comes from the Arabic verb for "grind"). Their role in Iranian cooking is mentioned in millennia-old cuneiform tablets about Elam (ancient Khuzestan). Sesame plant cultivation goes back at least 3,000, years and its seeds are one of the oldest oil seeds known to man. To make tahini, sesame seeds are soaked in salt water overnight to be able to remove the skins. Next they are rinsed, drained, dried, and toasted in ovens. The toasted seeds are then ground. The best tahini in Iran comes from Ardekan near Shiraz, where they also make the most renowned tahini paste called halva in the West but *halvardeh* in Iran (also *pashmak ardeh* in southern Iran). The tahini halvardeh workshops in Shiraz, Lar and Evaz have been making artisanal halvardeh for many generations, passing skills down from father to son. Each claim to have the best *halvardeh*. There are two main types: one is dense and the other is soft and stretchy. They are also variously made either with a sugar syrup or a date syrup, and can be flavored with cinnamon, cardamom, and rose water. Some include pistachios, almonds and walnuts in the halvardeh.

Left:
1. Soaking sesame seeds in salt water.
2. Placing seeds in the oven for tasting.
3. Making the syrup.

Right from top:
4. Adding cardamom and cinnamon to flavor the halva.
5. Mixing the halva.
6. Halva in tin boxes lined with parchment paper.

فالوده لیمویی موجود میباشد؟ کاسه ای
عرقی و ساده نداریم؟
لطفاً سوال نفرمایید؟

Rice Noodle Sorbet with a Squeeze of Lime

paludeh-ye shirazi

Serves 6
Prep: 40 minutes
Freezing: Time based on sorbet machine

NOODLES

3oz/85g thin rice stick noodles or rice vermicelli, or you can make your own noodles (see below)

SYRUP

2½ cups/600ml water
2 cups/400g sugar
2 tablespoons light corn syrup
⅛ teaspoon fine sea salt
¼ cup/60ml fresh lime juice (2 limes)
1 tablespoon rose water

GARNISH

3 fresh limes, halved

HOMEMADE RICE NOODLES

To prepare your own noodles, slowly blend 1 cup rice starch with 9 cups/2.2l water in a saucepan. Stir well until smooth, pass through a metal colander, then bring to a boil over medium heat, stirring constantly until the mixture reaches the consistency of rich, smooth white cream and small holes appear on the surface (or until thick enough to coat the back of a spoon). Let it stand for a few minutes. Gently strain it through a metal sieve over a bowl of ice water, drain, and then proceed with step 3.

This ice dessert, a specialty of Shiraz and a favorite in their ice-cream parlors, is called paludeh *(or* faludeh*).*

1. **To prepare the noodles:** Snip them into 3in/75mm lengths using scissors. In a medium saucepan bring 8 cups/1.9l water to a boil and add the noodles. Boil for 3 to 5 minutes until tender. Drain immediately in a fine-mesh colander and rinse thoroughly with cold water to give the noodles a shock and to stop cooking.

2. **To make the syrup:** In the same saucepan, combine water and sugar, stir well, and bring to a boil to dissolve the sugar. Remove from heat and add the corn syrup, salt, lime juice, and rose water. Stir well.

3. Pour the syrup into an ice-cream maker or sorbet machine and start the machine. When the syrup has a white, icy consistency, add the noodles a little at a time, allowing them to freeze before adding the next batch. When the noodles freeze properly, they will not have a rubbery texture.

4. Scoop some rice noodle sorbet into individual dishes and place half a lime on the side for a last-minute fresh squeeze of lime juice. *Nush-e joon!*

NOTE

If you don't have a sorbet machine, pour the syrup into a wide, rimmed tray that will fit in the freezer. Freeze for 1 hour then fluff the ice with a fork and add the noodles. Replace in the freezer and fluff again twice more every hour until you have the consistency of a sorbet.

Gelatin + Walnut Roll

basloq-e shirazi

Makes 32 pieces
Prep: 15 minutes
Cooking: 45 minutes + 20 minutes chilling

DUSTING

2 cups/100g coconut powder
1 tablespoon powder sugar
½ teaspoon ground cardamom
2 tablespoons ground pistachios

GELATIN PASTE

1 cup/110g corn starch
2 cups/480ml water
2 cups/400g sugar
½ cup/120ml rose water
1 teaspoon vanilla extract

FILLING

1 cup/125g walnut or pistachio kernels

1. **To make the dusting:** In a small bowl, combine all the ingredients for the dusting, spread evenly on a rimmed sheet pan lined with parchment paper. Set aside.

2. Oil another rimmed sheet pan and set aside.

3. **To make the gelatin paste:** In a medium-sized non-stick pot, dissolve the corn starch in the water.

4. Cook over low heat, mixing constantly with a long-handled wooden spoon until the mixture thickens (about 10 minutes).

5. Add the sugar, rose water, and vanilla, and continue to mix for 30 to 35 minutes until you have a thick gelatinous paste that easily separates from the saucepan.

6. Add the walnuts and mix for 1 minute. Remove from heat and allow to cool, then chill in fridge for 20 minutes.

7. Remove from the fridge and transfer to the oiled sheet pan. With oily hands, knead the gelatin paste for 5 minutes. Divide into 4 balls and shape them into 2in/5cm diameter logs. Roll in the dusting.

8. Cut the gelatin rolls into 1½in/4cm pieces using a sharp, oiled knife. Serve immediately or store in an airtight glass container in the fridge. *Nush-e joon!*

Fill the Glass with Wine

Come, so that we can scatter flowers
        and fill the glass with wine,
And split the ceiling of the skies
        and try a new design!

If Sorrow sends her soldiers here
        and wants a bloody fight,
My serving boy and I will put
        them one and all to flight.

We'll add rose water to our wine
        and sugar will augment
The pungent aloes wood we burn,
        and sweeten its fierce scent.

A fine lute's in your hand, my friend,
        so give us a fine song—
We'll wave our hands and stamp our feet,
        and dance, and sing along!

Sweet breeze, convey the dust of our
        existence to that place
Where Splendor reigns—perhaps that way
        we'll see Him face to face . . .

One boasts about his intellect,
        one's all puffed up with pride;
Let's bring these arguments before
        our Judge—let Him decide.

Come join me in the wine-shop, friend,
        if you want paradise;
I'll tip you from the wine-cask to
        Kosar's stream in a trice.

Since in Shiraz poetic skill,
        Hafez, goes unrequited,
It's time to try another town
        whose court is less benighted.

HAFEZ/DAVIS

Shrubs
sharbat-ha

Shiraz is Iran's city of flower extracts and distillates. Here, I am giving you a base syrup that you can mix with your favorite extracts.

1. **To make the syrup:** In a saucepan bring 2½ cups/600ml water and 2½ cups/500g sugar to a boil. Reduce heat to medium and stir until liquid is clear (not cloudy), about 5 minutes. Add 2 tablespoons fresh lime juice, give it a stir, remove from heat and allow to cool. Pour the syrup into a clean, dry bottle and cork tightly.

Rose Water Shrub: In a pitcher, mix 1 part syrup, 3 parts water, 2 tablespoons rose water, 1 teaspoon dry organic rose petals. Stir and serve well chilled.

Saffron Shrub—Add ½ teaspoon ground saffron threads diluted in 2 tablespoons hot water and 2 crushed cardamom pods to the rose water shrub.

Basil Seed Shrub—Soak 1 cup/160g of basil seeds/*tokhm-e sharbati* in 2 cups/480ml water for 2 hours, then add soaking seeds to the Rose Water Shrub. This syrup is often served to the mother of a newborn baby.

Mint Leaf Shrub—Add 1 teaspoon mint water to the Rose Water Shrub.

Orange Blossom Shrub—Replace the rose water in the Rose Water Shrub with 2 teaspoons orange blossom water, 4 lemon verbena leaves, and ¼ teaspoon ground saffron threads.

Palm Shrub—Replace the rose water in the Rose Water Shrub with palm water.

Willow Shrub—Replace rose water in the Rose Water Shrub with willow water.

Barberry Shrub—To make barberry juice, pick over and thoroughly wash 1 cup/150g dried red barberries. Combine with 2 cups/480ml water and boil for 15 minutes over high heat. Allow to cool and pass the juice through 2 layers of cheesecloth into a pitcher. In a pitcher, mix 1 part syrup, 3 parts water, and the barberry juice. Stir and serve well chilled.

Tamarind Shrub—Replace the barberries with ½lb/225g dried tamarind pods. Everything else remains the same as for barberry shrub.

Nush-e joon!

Opposite: Kambiz Sowdagar at his Brentin Restaurant (a Shirazi pronunciation of *berin tu*, which means "go on in"). The restaurant, opened with his mother, serves delicious, traditional southern Iranian food in a contemporary setting.

561

Cuneiform script from the second millennium BCE is inscribed into the brick at the Elamite ziggurat dedicated to "The Lord of Shush" at Chogha Zanbil/basket mound, 40 kilometers south of Shush.

Khuzestan

Shush and its environs contain superimposed urban settlements in a continuous succession from the fifth millennium BCE until the thirteenth century CE. It is a testimony to Iran's Elamite, Persian, and Parthian traditions.

A Little History

Shush/Susa is located in the northern part of Khuzestan, the Iranian province that borders Iraq on the west and the top of the Persian Gulf in the south. This region was first settled at least six thousand years ago by the Elamites, a pre-Iranian civilization that made Susa their capital from about 2700 to 539 BCE (in classical literature, Elam was known as Susiana). We know a little about the cuisine of the region from Babylonian clay tablets that were deciphered during the past 30 years by Jean Bottero, a French archeologist who also happened to be a gourmet cook. They reveal that the region had at least 18 kinds of cheese, 100 soups, and 300 breads. Their cooks dried grains, beans, dates, grapes, and figs; they preserved fruits in honey; they flavored their various braises/*khorehses* with garlic, onions, leeks, and possibly mint, mustard, cumin, and coriander (much as we do now in Persian cooking).

This was the cuisine that the Persians inherited when the Achaemenids under Cyrus the Great came to power in 539 BCE and made Susa one of their four capitals in various parts of the Empire. And perhaps this was what Xenephon meant when he wrote, "The Persians kept recipes from their past and had special cooks for devising new ones."

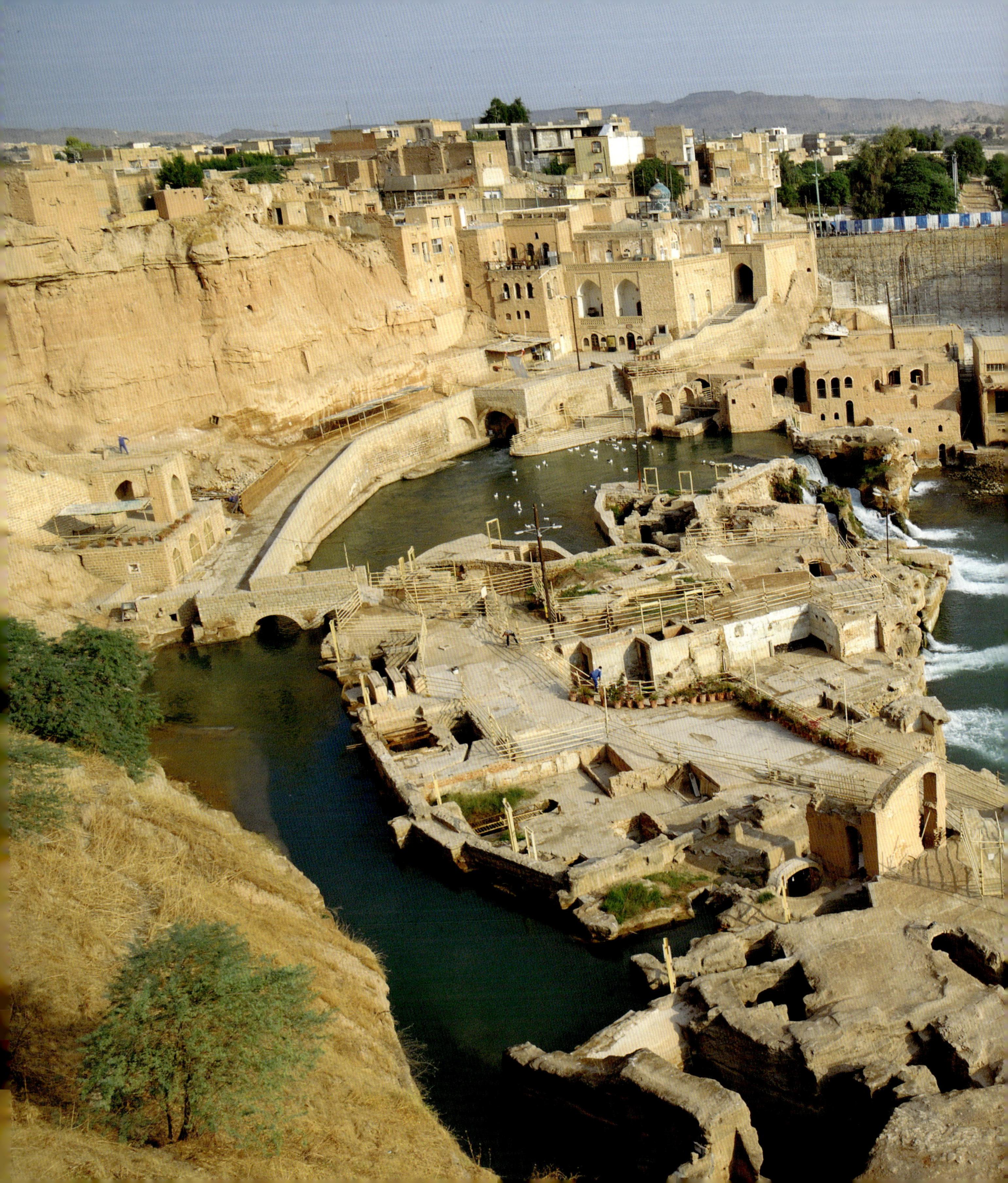

This is a view of the town of Shushtar and the Karun River, the longest river in Iran (and the only navigable one). It flows from the Zagros Mountains in Iran's Bakhtiari tribal region 300 miles north of here down to the mouth of the Persian Gulf. Caesar's dam/*band-e kaisar*, seen in this photo, is said to have been built by captured Roman soldiers after the Sasanian king Shahpur defeated the Roman emperor Valerian in 260 CE. But long before that, this was one of the earliest hydraulic irrigation systems in the world and included water mills, dams, tunnels, and canals. It dispersed water to a region that used to be both the breadbasket and the rice bowl of Iran. One theory is that the biblical Garden of Eden was located at the confluence of the Karun (Gihon), Pishon, Tigris, and Euphrates Rivers at the top of the Persian Gulf a few hundred miles south of here.

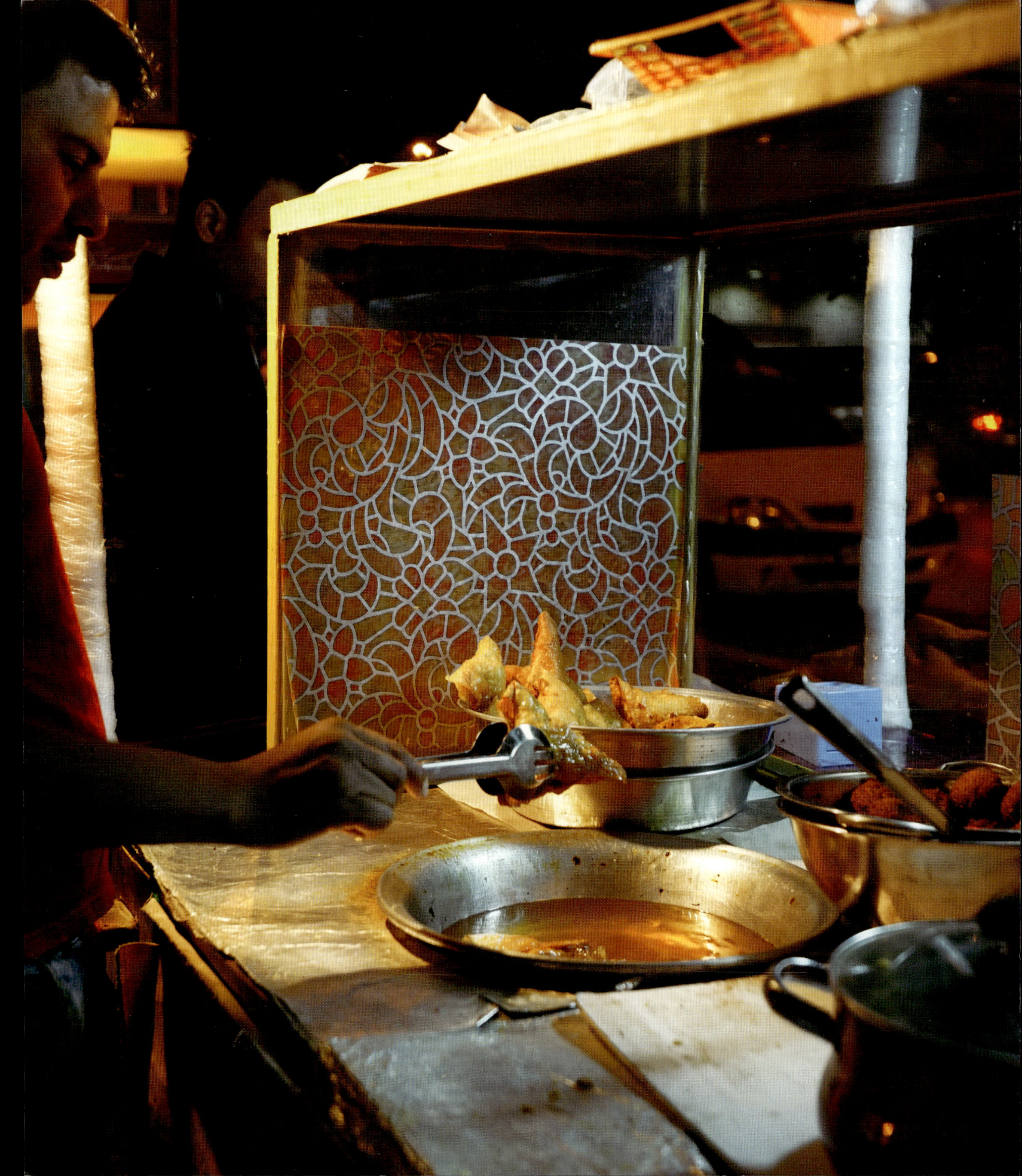

Crispy Falafel with Garlicky Tahini Sauce
falafel-e abadani

Makes 6 to 8 falafels, serves 2 to 4
Prep: 10 minutes + 30 minutes of refrigeration
Cooking: 1 hour

PASTE
- 1 cup/100g dried chickpeas, soaked overnight in water with 1 teaspoon baking soda, drained, and rinsed
- 2 tablespoons chickpea flour
- 4 cloves garlic, peeled
- ½ teaspoon baking powder
- 2 teaspoons fine sea salt
- ¼ teaspoon freshly ground pepper
- ½ teaspoon ground coriander
- 2 teaspoons ground cumin
- 1 teaspoon cayenne
- 2 eggs, lightly beaten
- ½ cup/40g chopped fresh dill
- ½ cup/40g chopped fresh cilantro
- ½ cup/40g chopped fresh parsley
- ½ cup/50g chopped spring onions

TAHINI SAUCE
- 1 clove garlic, peeled and grated
- ½ cup/120g tahini paste
- ¼ cup/60ml water
- ¼ cup/60ml lime juice
- 1 teaspoon fine sea salt
- ½ teaspoon ground cumin

GARNISH
- 1 heart of romaine lettuce

DUSTING
- ½ cup/80g raw sesame seeds
- 2 cups/480ml oil for frying

Pita bread, tortillas, or green leaf lettuce to use as a wrap

NOTE
Instead of 1 cup dried chickpeas, you can use a combination of 1/2 cup dried chickpeas and 1/2 cup dried yellow fava beans second skins removed.

Falafels are particularly popular around the Persian Gulf. This is my favorite falafel because it's full of fresh herbs. The photo on the facing page shows a local street vendor in Abadan making falafels, in the bowl on the right, and turnovers/dast pich wrapped in lavash bread (an Abadani specialty), being removed from the fryer.

1. **To make the paste:** Place the chickpeas in a medium saucepan, add 8 cups/1.9l water, and bring to a boil. Reduce heat to medium, cover, and simmer for 45 to 50 minutes until tender. Drain and set aside.

2. In a food processor, place the chickpeas, the chickpea flour, and all the ingredients for the paste and pulse until you have a soft paste (do not over-mix). Cover and refrigerate for at least 30 minutes or up to 24 hours.

3. **To make the tahini sauce:** In a mixing bowl, place all the ingredients for the sauce and whisk until you have a thick sauce. Set aside.

4. **To make the garnish:** Thinly shred the lettuce, place in a bowl, and set aside.

5. **To prepare the dusting:** Line a sheet pan with parchment paper and spread the sesame seeds evenly over it.

6. Use an ice-cream scoop to scoop out lumps of paste the size of walnuts (or use a falafel mold). Oil the palms of your hands and roll each lump between them into fat egg-shaped ovals. Roll them in the sesame seeds.

7. **To deep-fry the falafels:** Place a wire rack in a sheet pan for catching any drippings.

8. Heat 2 cups/480ml oil in a small saucepan over medium heat until hot but not smoking (test by dropping in a small piece of bread, if it sizzles the oil is hot enough). Add the falafels, in batches, and fry for 3 to 4 minutes, turning occasionally until golden brown on all sides. Using tongs, remove the falafels and place them on the wire rack.

9. **To serve:** Arrange the falafels on a platter, and garnish with tahini sauce and the lettuce. Serve hot as a wrap in pitas, tortillas, or green leaf lettuce.

Khuzestan

V VEGETARIAN

Turnip + Cilantro Braise
khoresh-e shalgham-o gishniz-e khoramshahr

Serves 4 to 6
Prep: 30 minutes
Cooking: 1¾ hours

CHICKEN

2 tablespoons oil
2 medium onions, thinly sliced
1 tablespoon fine sea salt
½ teaspoon freshly ground pepper
1 teaspoon turmeric
½ teaspoon red pepper flakes (optional)
1lb/450g skinless, boneless, chicken thighs cut into 3in/7.5cm strips
3 tablespoons ready-made tamarind paste dissolved in 3 cups/720ml water
1 teaspoon date molasses

TURNIPS

2 tablespoons oil
1½lb/675g turnips, peeled and thinly sliced

HERBS

2 tablespoons oil
5 cups/450g chopped fresh cilantro, (leaves and stems)
2 tablespoons dried fenugreek leaves
5 cloves garlic, grated
¼ teaspoon ground saffron dissolved in 1 tablespoon hot water (optional)

I adapted this recipe from Shari Lak. She told me this was her favorite dish growing up in Khoramshahr.

1. **To cook the chicken:** Heat 2 tablespoons oil in a medium-sized laminated cast-iron pot over medium heat, and sauté the onions until lightly golden. Add the salt, pepper, turmeric, red pepper flakes, and chicken, and sauté for 10 minutes.

2. Pour in the tamarind water and date molasses. Bring to a boil and give it a stir. Reduce heat to low, cover, and simmer for 15 minutes, stirring occasionally.

3. *Meanwhile, to cooks the turnips:* In a wide skillet heat 2 tablespoons oil over medium heat until hot. Sauté the turnips for 5 minutes stirring occasionally until lightly golden. Transfer them to the braise, cover and cook over medium heat for 10 minutes.

4. *To sauté the herbs and cook the braise:* In the same skillet, heat 2 tablespoons oil over medium heat, add the cilantro, fenugreek, and garlic, and sauté for 10 minutes. Transfer them to the pot and add the saffron water. Cover and simmer over low heat for 1¼ hours or until the chicken and turnip are tender.

5. Taste the braise and adjust the seasoning by adding more tamarind paste or salt. Serve with plain rice. *Nush-e joon!*

Khuzestan

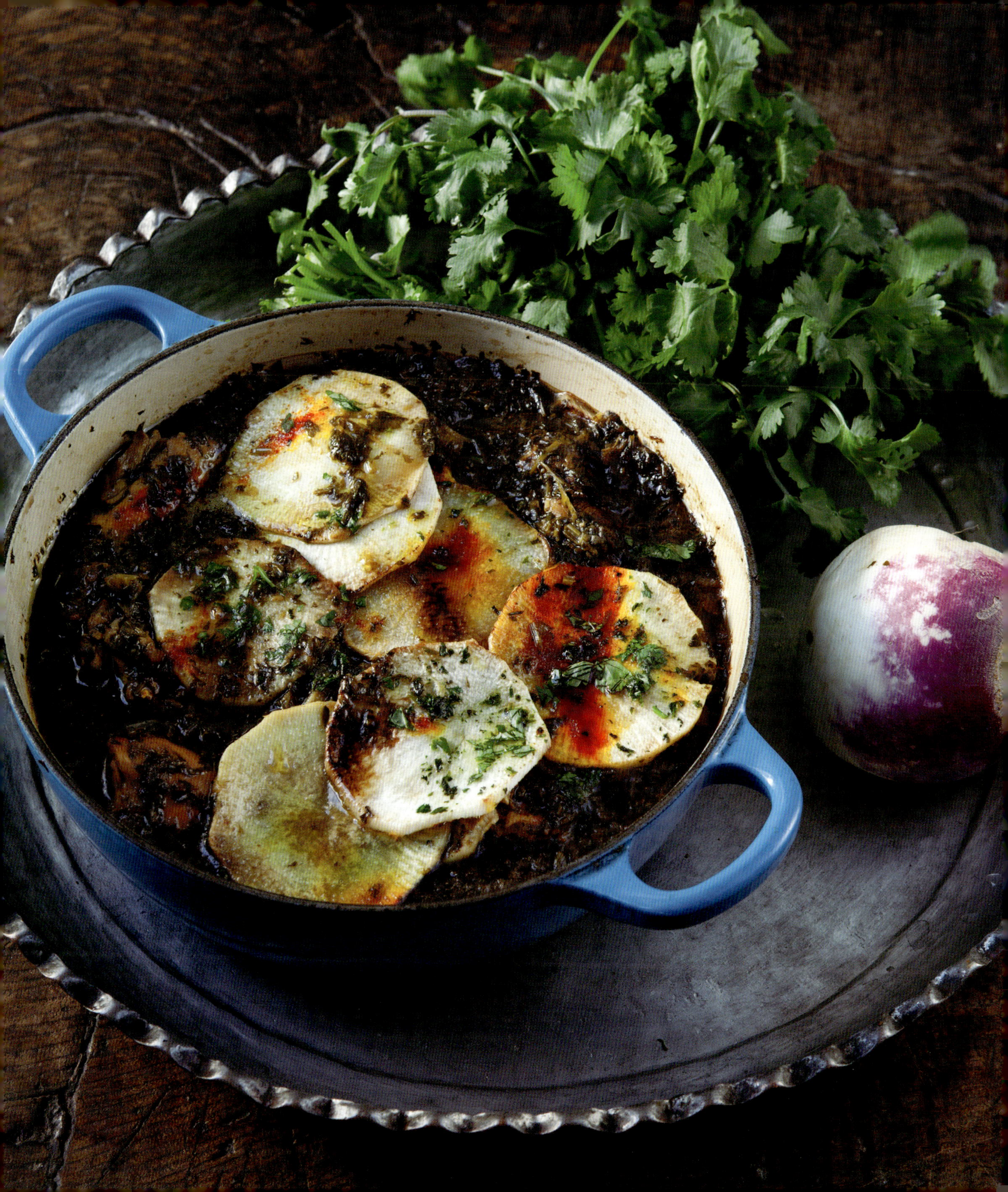

Grilled Saboor Fish with Tamarind + Cilantro Stuffing

mahi-e tanuri-e saboor

Serves 4
Prep: 20 minutes plus 15 minutes of chilling
Cooking: 10 to 12 minutes

FILLING

- ¼ cup/60ml oil
- 1 small onion, peeled and finely chopped
- 4 cloves garlic, peeled and grated
- 2 spring onions, chopped (white and green parts)
- 1 cup/85g chopped fresh cilantro
- 1 cup/85g chopped fresh parsley
- 1 cup/85g chopped fresh dill
- ½ cup/40g chopped fresh fenugreek leaves or 2 tablespoons dried
- 1 tablespoon tomato paste
- 1 tablespoon tamarind paste
- 1 teaspoon fine sea salt
- ½ teaspoon freshly ground pepper
- 1 teaspoon turmeric

FISH

- 4 whole saboor or branzino (striped bass/*loup de mer*), or 1 shad, cleaned and fins trimmed but scales not removed

RUB FOR FISH OUTER SKIN

- 4 teaspoons date molasses

DUSTING FOR INSIDE THE FISH

- ¼ cup/60g tamarind paste
- 4 teaspoons fine sea salt
- 2 tablespoons turmeric

BASTE

- ¼ cup/60g olive oil or melted butter

In Iran, saboor is especially popular where the gulf meets Arvand Rud at the confluence of the Euphrates and the Tigris. Saboor is in the same herring family as shad. The mature fish swims from the ocean back up to the fresh water rivers to spawn. Hamid Dabashi, who grew up in Ahwaz, told me his mother would give him a prepared dish of uncooked saboors to take to the baker to cook in a wood-burning oven. Hamid still remembers the intoxicating aroma of the tamarind and herbs as the fish baked, and the story his mother told him. Saboor means "patient" in Persian. It got its name, according to the story, because when the fish complained to the queen of fish that it had no bones, she told it to be patient and ask each of the other fish to give it one of their bones—as a result, it's a very bony fish. I prefer to use a grill for this recipe rather than cooking it in the oven.

1. **To make the filling:** In a wide skillet, heat the oil over medium heat and sauté the onion, garlic, and spring onions until lightly golden. Add the herbs and sauté for 1 minute. Add the rest of the ingredients and sauté for another minute. Remove from heat.

2. **To prepare the fish:** Rinse the fish and pat dry with a paper towel. Arrange them on a sheet pan lined with parchment paper. Rub the outer skin of each fish, on both sides, with 1 teaspoon date molasses (this helps to prevent the skin from burning and facilitates its removal once the fish is cooked).

3. **To make the dusting for inside the fish:** In a small bowl, combine all the ingredients. Rub the inside of each fish with ¼ of the dusting. Spread ¼ of the filling inside each fish. Cover and chill for 15 minutes or up to 8 hours.

4. **To cook the fish:** When ready to serve, start a bed of charcoal and let it burn until the coals glow or turn on the broiler and allow it to get hot.

5. Spray two stainless steel grill baskets with oil and place 2 stuffed fish, side by side, in each basket. Lock the basket and grill the fish for 4 to 5 minutes on each side until the skin is blackened.

6. Remove the fish from the baskets, remove the skins on 1 side, and drizzle with olive oil. Serve whole with grilled tomatoes. *Nush-e joon!*

Khuzestan

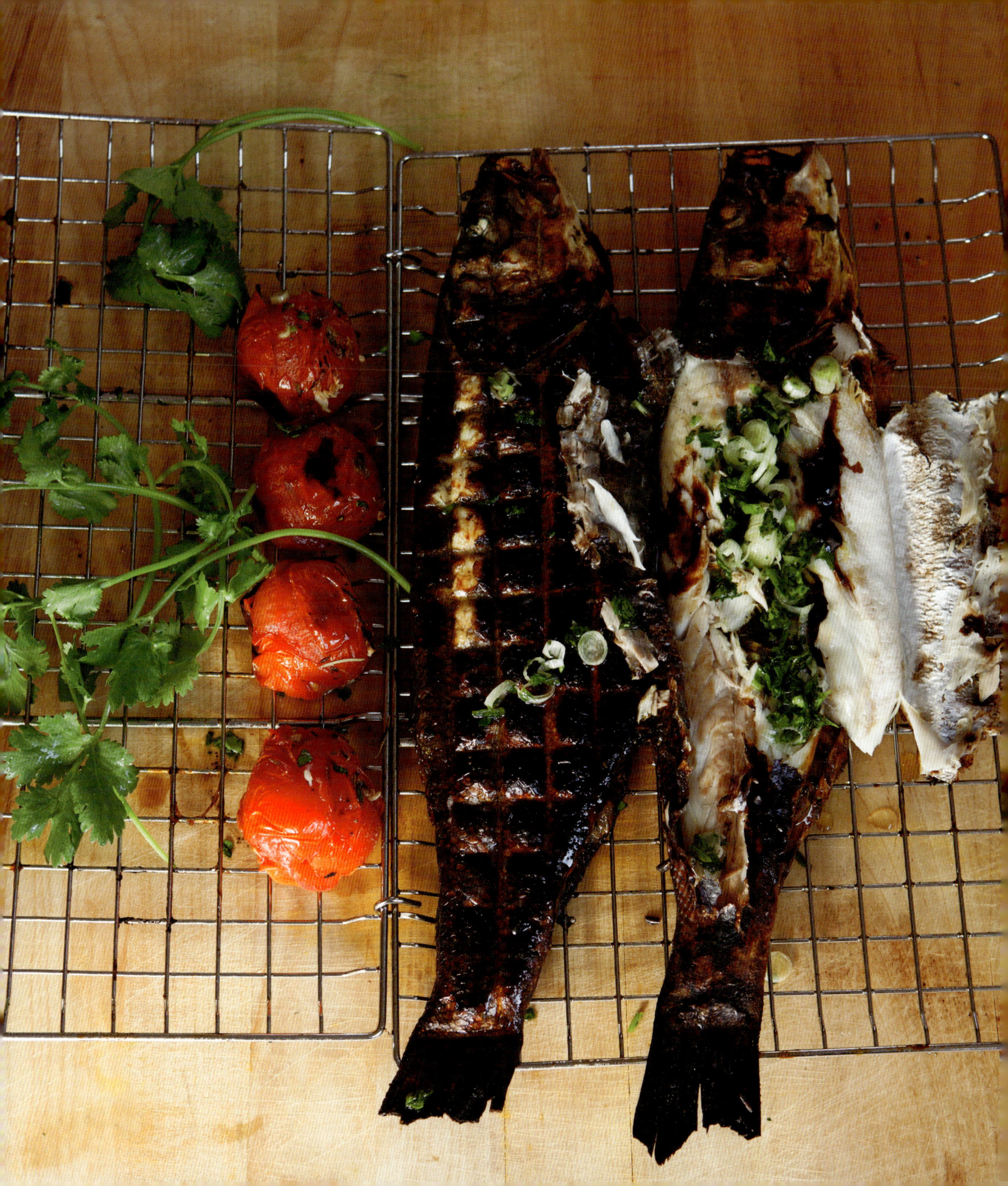

The Persian Gulf

Khuzestan
Ahvaz
Abarkuh
Zabol
Yasuj
Khorramshahr
Abadan
Rafsanjan
Kerman
Fars
Zahedan
Bushehr
Shiraz
Lar
The Persian Gulf
Hormozgan
Bandar Abbas
Kish
Qeshm
Chabahar

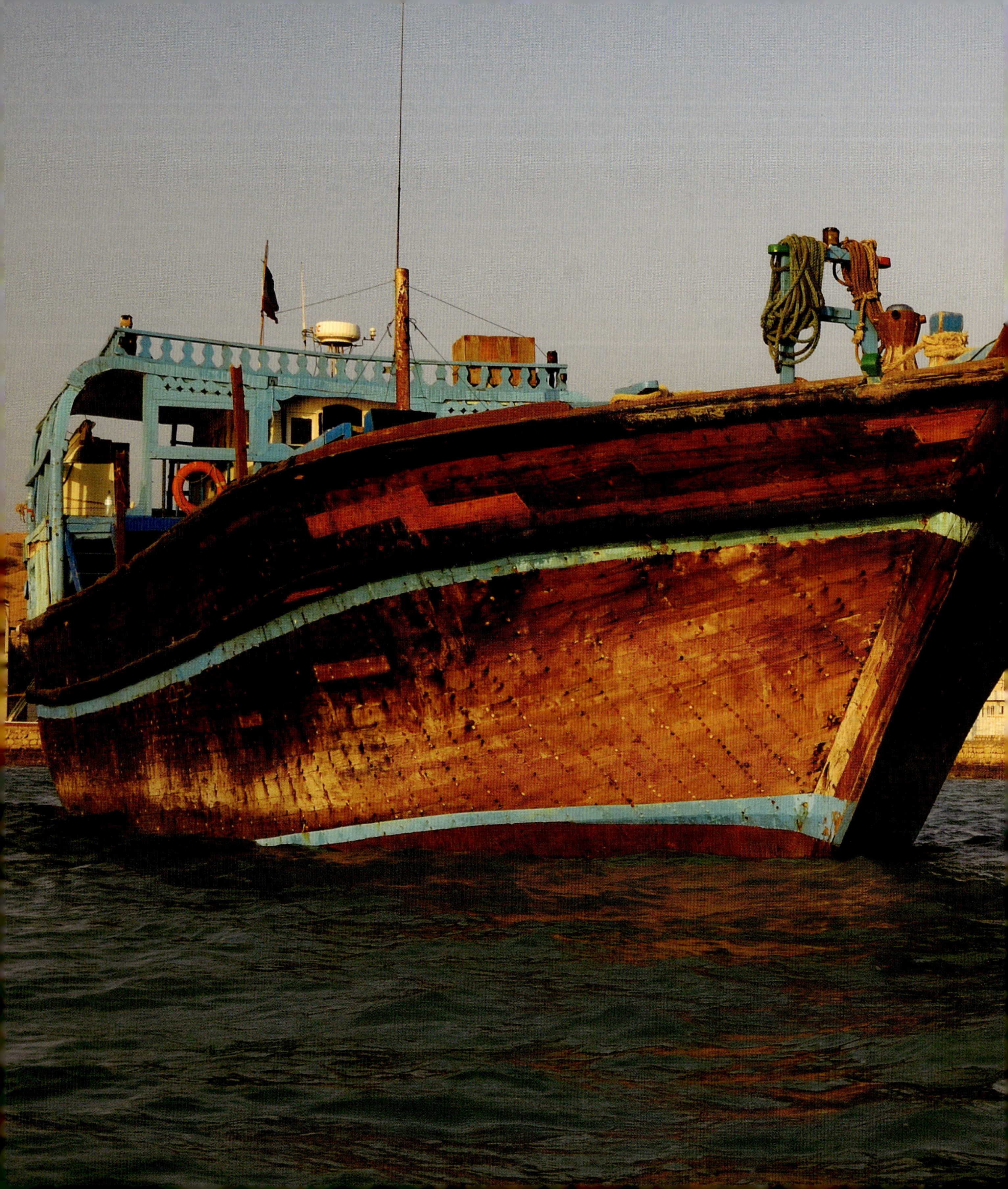

A Little History

The port cities of the Persian Gulf have a long history. There is some evidence that as far back as the sixth century BCE, Cyrus the Great wanted to revitalize trade in the Persian Gulf and built a palace at Taoce, near the present-day Bushehr. These ports were also the starting points of Darius the Great's explorations of the Red Sea and beyond around 500 BCE. Today, Bandar Abbas is named after Shah Abbas, who took it back from the Portuguese in 1622. Bandar Abbas was known as Gameroon, and it's tempting to think that the name is somehow related to the Persian/Portuguese name for shrimp, *kamrun/camarao*. The seventeenth-century jeweler and traveler Jean Chardin mentions that the Persian Gulf had the tastiest shrimp in the world. In the nineteenth century, the Omanis ruled Bandar Abbas for 90 years. Most of the trade through Bandar Abbas—including wheat, barley, and fruit—was coming from, or going to, Shiraz, Kerman, Yazd or Baluchistan.

Iranians call the people of the Persian Gulf region "Bandari," meaning "those who live by a (Persian Gulf) port/*bandar*." This region of Iran has an amazingly diverse ethnic mix of Persians, Arabs, Baluchis, Kurds, East African blacks, Armenians, and Jews, many of whom intermarried over the centuries.

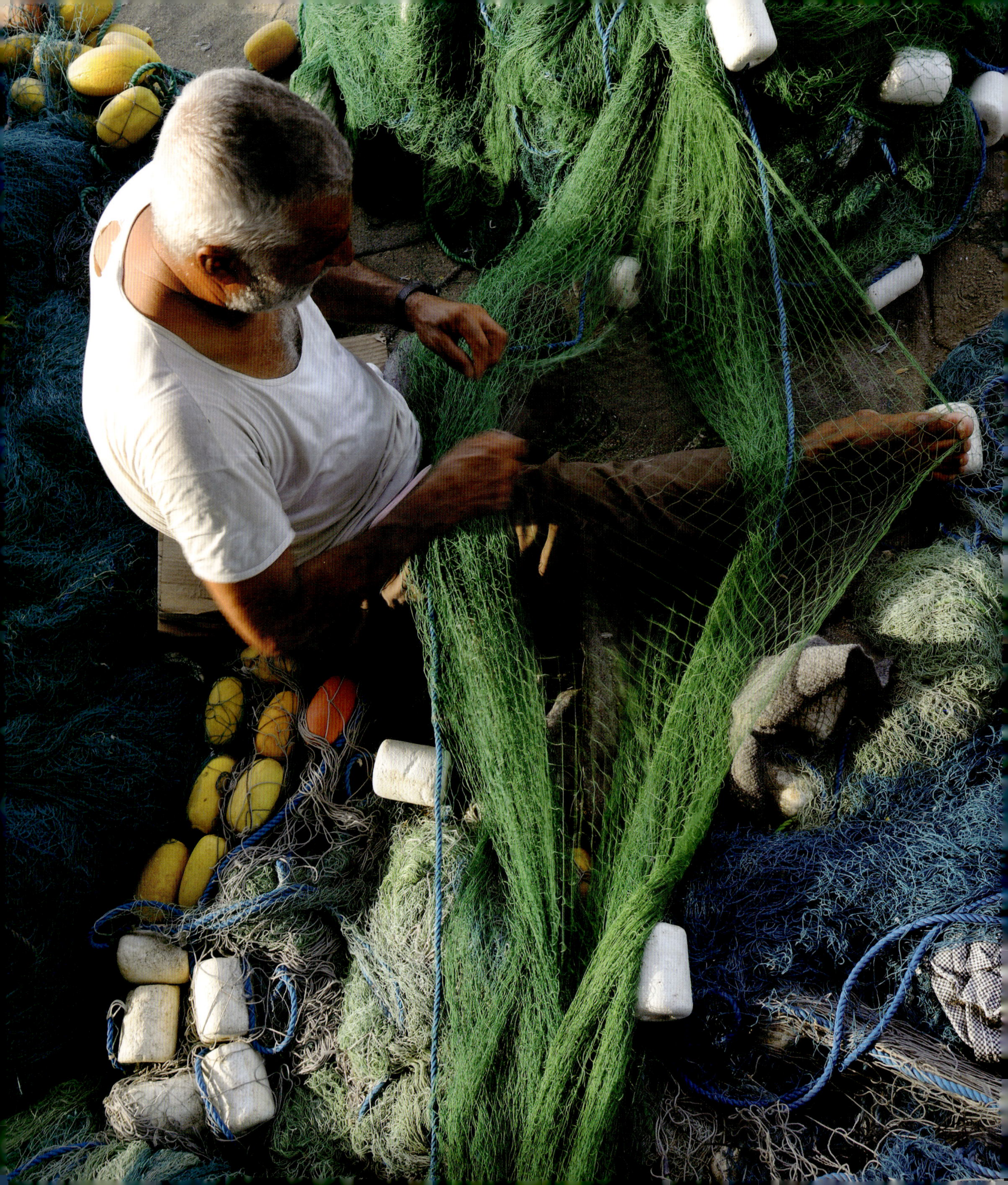

Bushehr

Bushehr was a port city at the center of East-West trade in ancient times. Later, because of its important commercial position on the Persian Gulf, Bushehr was twice occupied by the British, once in 1857 and again from 1915 to 1918.

Besides the cuisine of the Tangestani tribes in the region, one can also see considerable influence of Indian cooking and the use of spices from around the world. Fish and shrimp are the basis for the locale's favorite dishes. Our guides in Bushehr were Hossein and Golnessa Mozaffari, a wonderfully kind and educated couple, who introduced us to the culture of Bushehr and took us to their aunt Dowlat Khabarkhosh, with whom I cooked several local dishes, including my favorite braise/*qaliyeh* of fish and shrimp with cilantro, fenugreek, and garlic in a red peppery tamarind sauce (page 620).

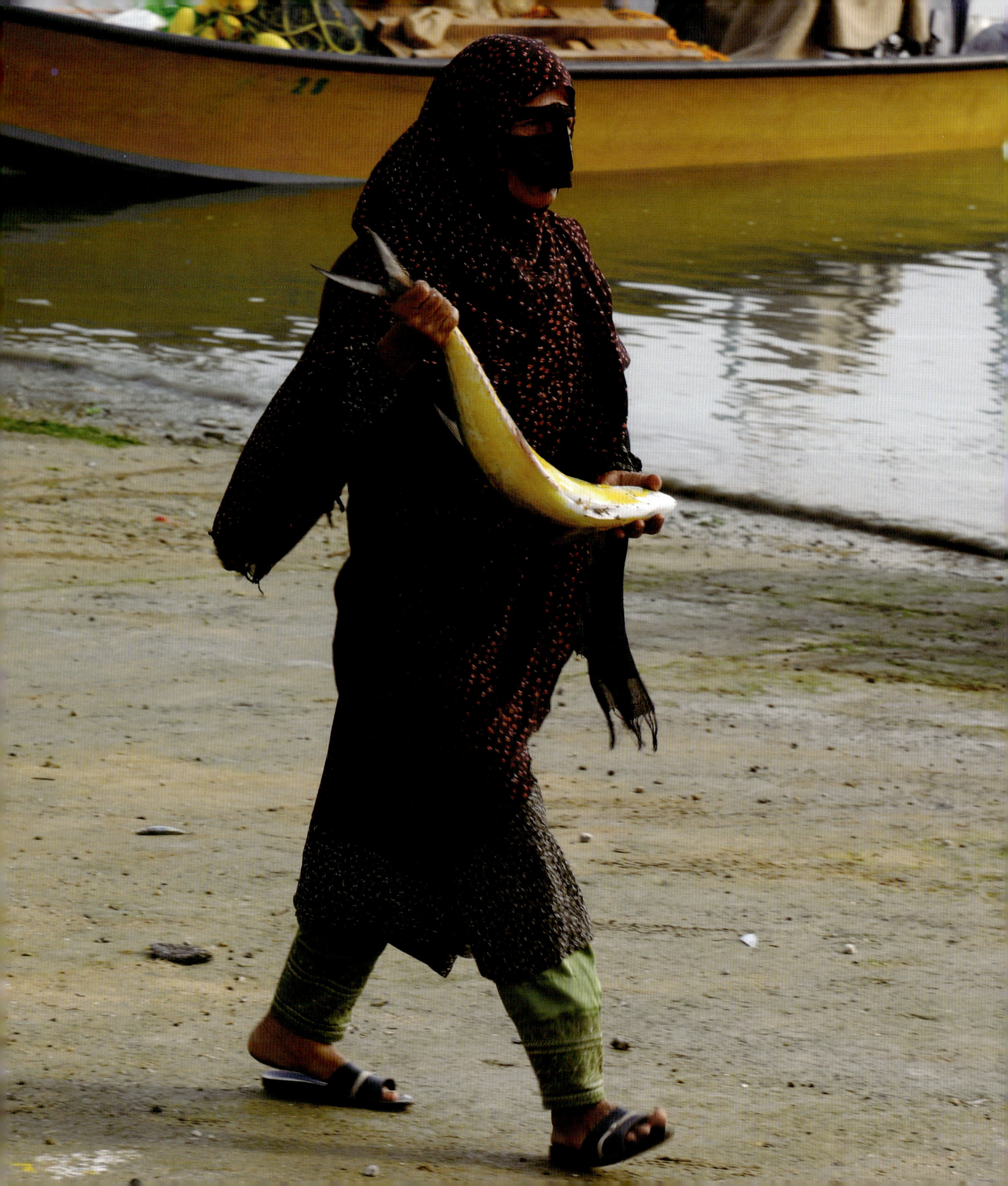

The Bounty of the Sea

The most interesting dishes of the Persian Gulf reflect the incredible variety of seafood in the region: tuna, mackerel, sardines, anchovies, barracuda, snapper, octopus, squid, shrimp, calamari, lobster, and crab. Locals eat all of these, cooked in many ways: salted, pickled, poached, fried, and grilled. Fish is served with bulgur/cracked wheat or rice together.

Dishes are sweetened with date molasses and powdered dates, and soured with tamarind, dried limes, sour orange, sumac powder, and tomato paste. They are spiced with turmeric, cilantro, fennel seeds, sour orange rind, and hot chili peppers. Other popular ingredients are chickpeas and chickpea flour as well as fruit such as pineapple, mango, date, and guava.

Hospitality, food, and music bring this region to life. On street corners you can often see bands with drums/*dohol* and tambourines/*dayereh*, playing a rhythmic type of dance music both fast and slow using quarter tones. It is often vocalized *a cappella* during celebrations such as weddings.

I love the way women of this region dress, with their colorful floral wrappings and tight embroidered leggings and variously shaped face masks (the younger women no longer use face masks). Their fingertips and the soles of their feet are often dyed with henna, and the older women may have tattoos all over. And they enjoy puffing on their hookahs. When you see them on the streets, you might think you are at a carnival, but as you get to know them, you'll find them warm, friendly, and hard-working. It's lovely to see them weaving beautifully designed baskets from date leaves/*pesh*, or sitting on the street corner preparing a local delicacy—wafer-thin crepes coated with fermented anchovies/*mahyabeh* or a sardine-and-red-earth (mineral-rich volcanic dust) sauce called *suraq*. Many of the traditional dishes of the region have grown rare these days—among them, fried grasshopper, sparrow soup, and bread made from the pits of dates.

I had the opportunity to shop, cook, and spend time with the women of the region. They were tolerant, calm, and hard-working. They didn't say much, but the expressions of their faces told me the story of their lives. I really connected with them and realized that we, as women, may dress or appear differently, but we have more similarities than differences.

Getting ready for a boat trip around Qeshm.

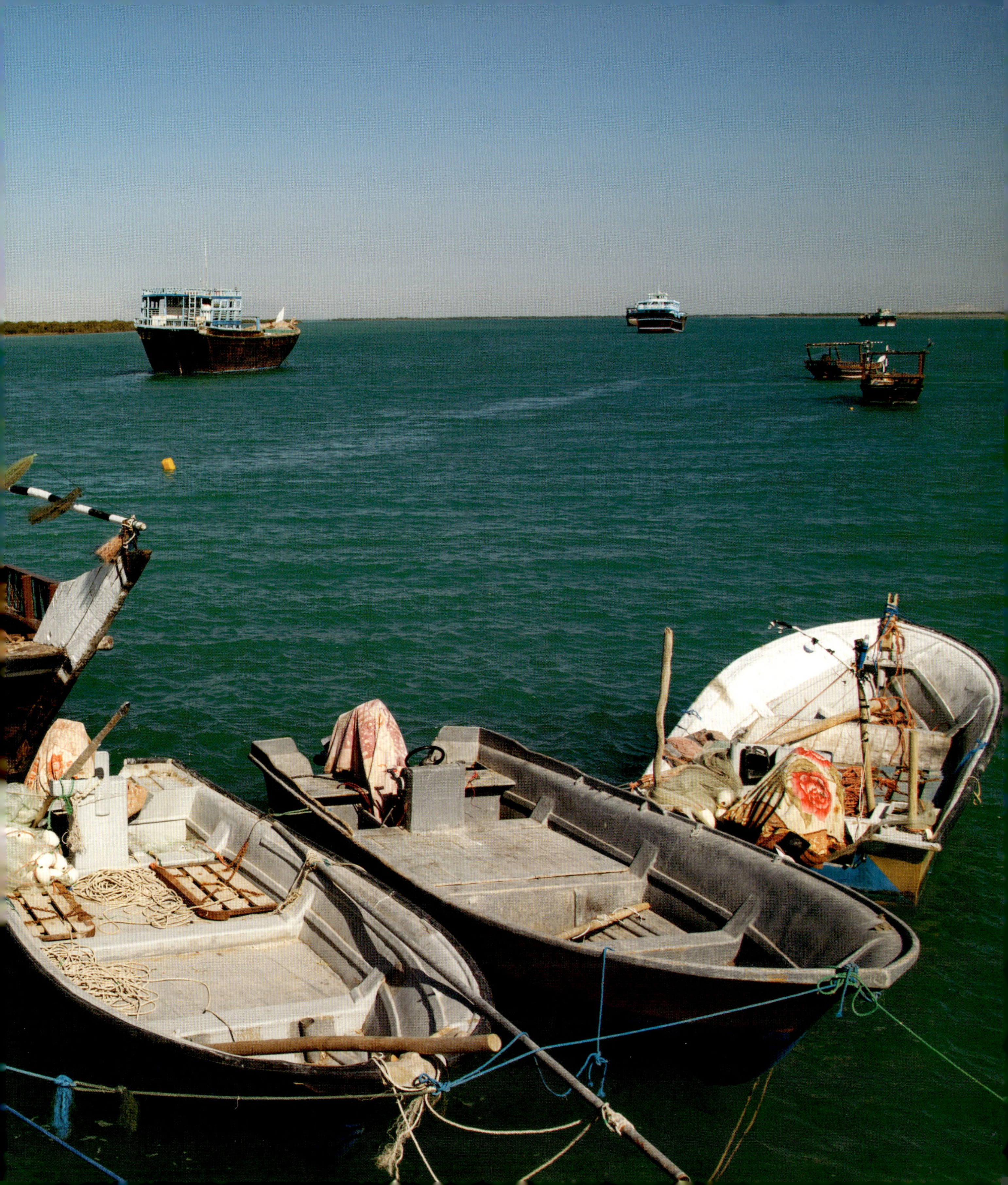

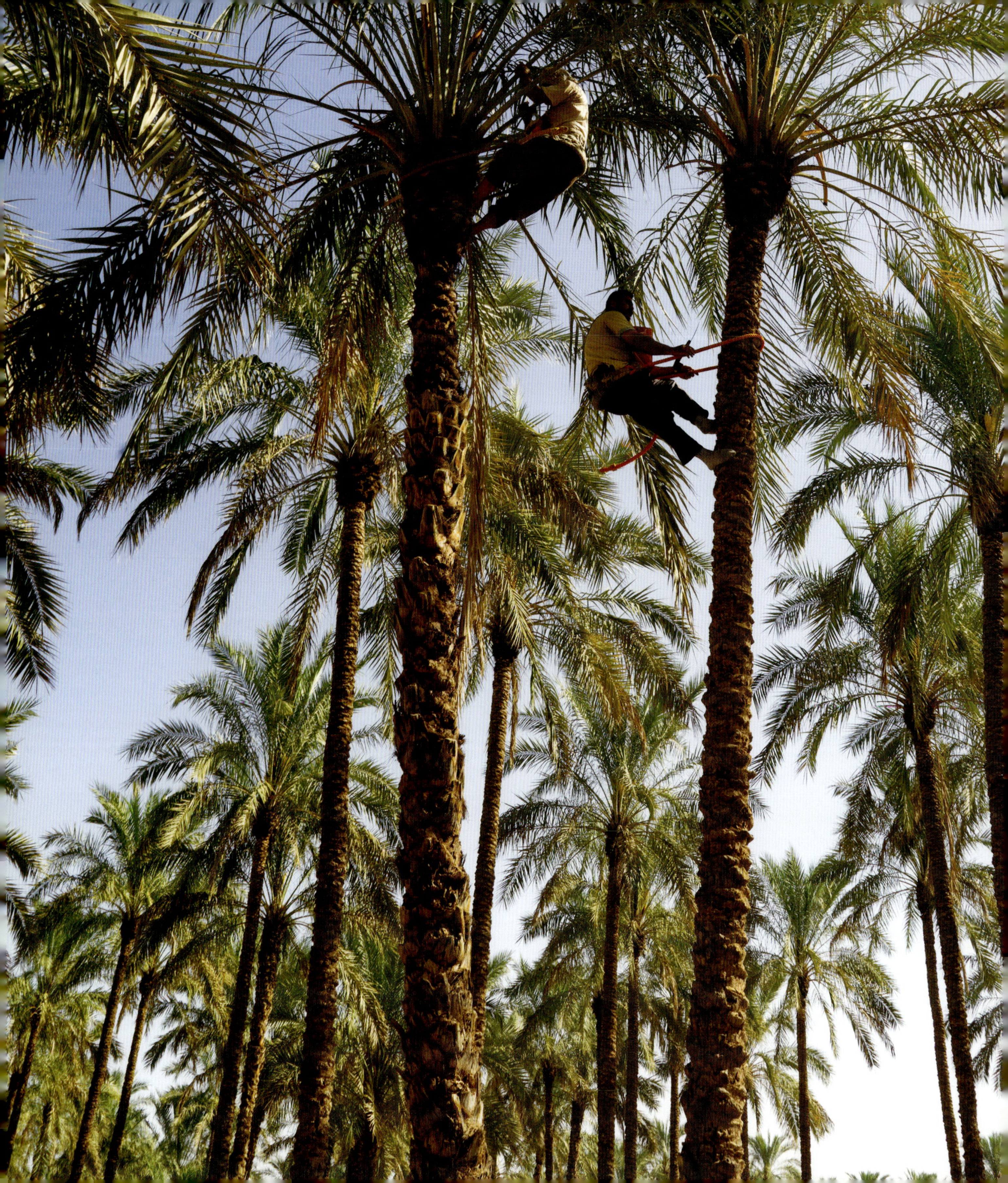

The Date Palm

During my travels around southern Iran, I was struck by the attitude of the locals toward the date palm and its fruit—integral to all Persian cooking but held in near reverence there. Dishes that include dates and date products abound in the region's cuisine. One of my favorites was a surprisingly simple yet tasty dessert: A black date/*kabkab* is dipped in a sesame sauce/*ardeh* and popped in your mouth, where it bursts with delicious and complex flavors, especially after a main course of fish. Pleasures like that stirred my curiosity about the date palm: I found myself wanting to know everything about this pillar of Iranian cooking.

Not surprisingly, the date palm/*nakhl* is native to the Persian Gulf region; some scholars even say it originated on Kharg Island near Bushehr (where I had just visited). Its economic importance for this part of Iran stretches back thousands of years. Marco Polo, a relative latecomer, mentioned plantations in Yazd, Kerman, and Hormoz (an old name for Bandar Abbas) and said that the inhabitants of Hormoz lived "chiefly upon dates and salted fish."

The tree and its fruit have figured large in cultural matters, too. In ancient times, the attributes of the sun god Mithra—well-built, lofty, and strong—were said to be jointly represented by the date palm and the cypress (page 435). For millennia, songs have been sung in praise of the palm. According to the Greek geographer and historian Strabo, during the Achaemenid period (550 to 330 BCE) there was a Persian song about 360 uses of the tree (I'd like hear that one). The date palm is a subject of many folktales, as well. One of them that focuses on the supposed similarities between the palm and humans: the existence of males and females (as well as hermaphrodites); the similarity between the scents of date pollen and semen; the susceptibility of the female palm to fall in love with the nearby male palm; comparable longevity; and they both have erect postures. Another—a wonderful Parthian story from the second century BCE—tells of a contest between a female date palm and a female goat; it is retold on page 593.

I was amazed to learn that in this region killing a date palm is compared to killing a person and is considered very unlucky. Those palms that become terminally diseased are cut down, but this is usually postponed until the religious mourning days of Moharram. If, however, a male palm tree is found to be sterile during the pollination period, it may be felled to gain access to its crisp, sweet white center—heart of palm/*panir*, literally "cheese." In such a case, the deed is usually done while celebrating a holiday

The generic name for date in Persian is *khorma* (*tamr* in Arabic). More than a hundred varieties are grown in Iran, and some among them rank with the best in the world. However, even though Iran is the second-largest exporter of dates after Egypt, the bulk of the country's production is not suitably harvested and preserved for export. The *shahani* variety from Jahrom in Fars and the *mozaffati* from Bam in Kerman are especially delicious, but they are generally best eaten fresh.

Date palms are propagated by replanting shoots that have developed roots at the foot of a female palm. When water is plentiful, the palm bears fruit within 4 to 5 years. When water is scarce, it can take 12 years. Depending on conditions and the variety, a female date palm can produce up to 550lb/250kg of dates a year and can live from 20 to 100 years.

In February, when the heat of the sun starts to increase, date palms become aroused, and sometime in March they begin to show their blossoms/*tareh*. The male blossoms have a reddish tinge; the female's are milky white. Several male palms can pollinate up to 100 females. Although the wind can do this, it's not reliable. For centuries, the process of pollination—called *bu dadan*, literally "scenting"—has been done artificially by experts, who climb the palm with the aid of a strong belt (a rope fashioned from palm leaflets) encircling the trunk. They pollinate the female flowers either by sprinkling the male pollen/*garda* onto the female blossoms or by loosely tying a group of male blossoms (inflorescence) to the female ones.

For the fruit to fully mature takes six months, from March to September. In May the fruit is conically shaped, shiny green, dry, and tough. At this stage, the fruit/*khumal* has an acidy taste. Locals eat them, but they are hard to digest. From June to July, the fruit/*kharak* is either red or yellow but is edible. In early August, the fruit is half ripe and half

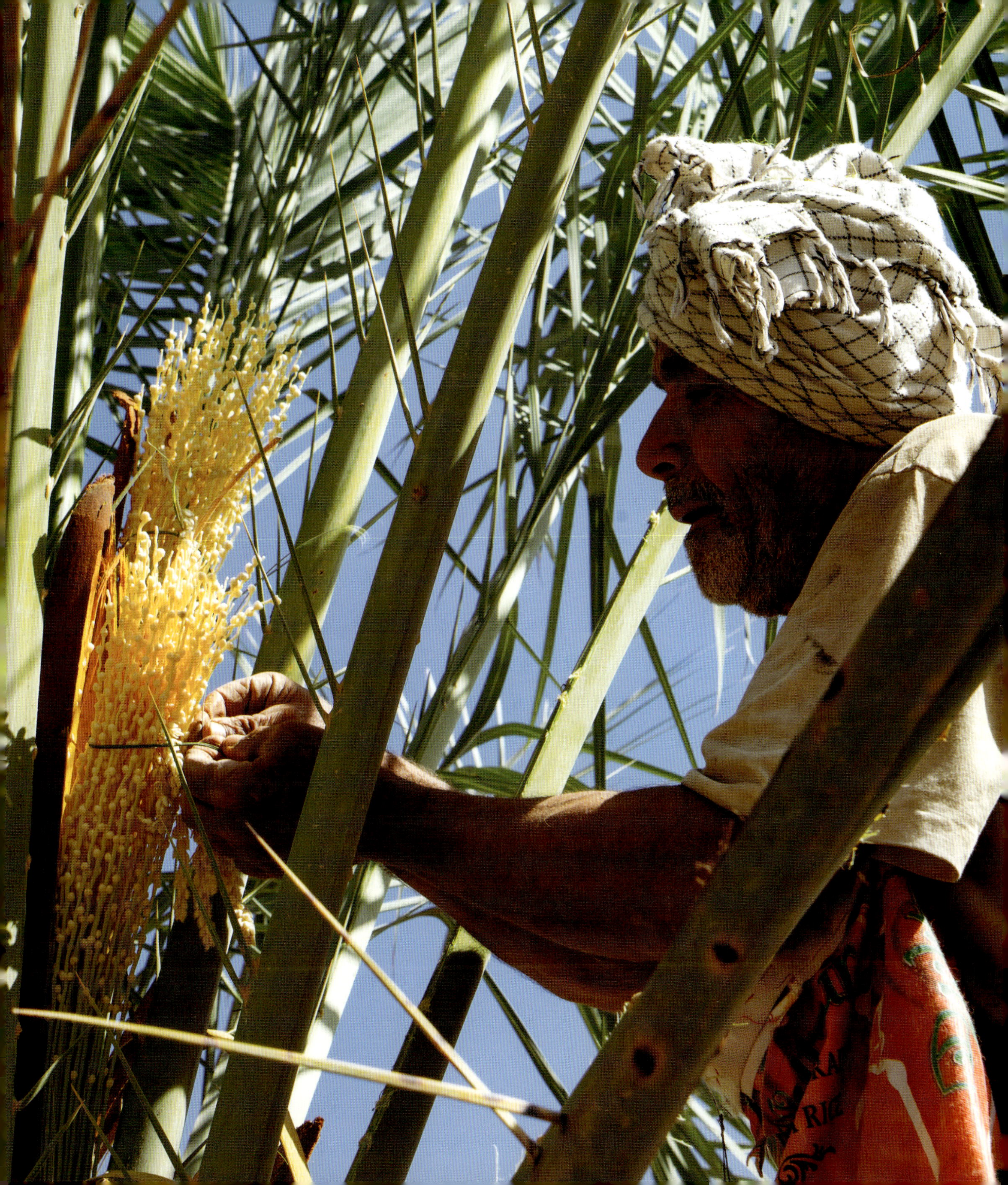

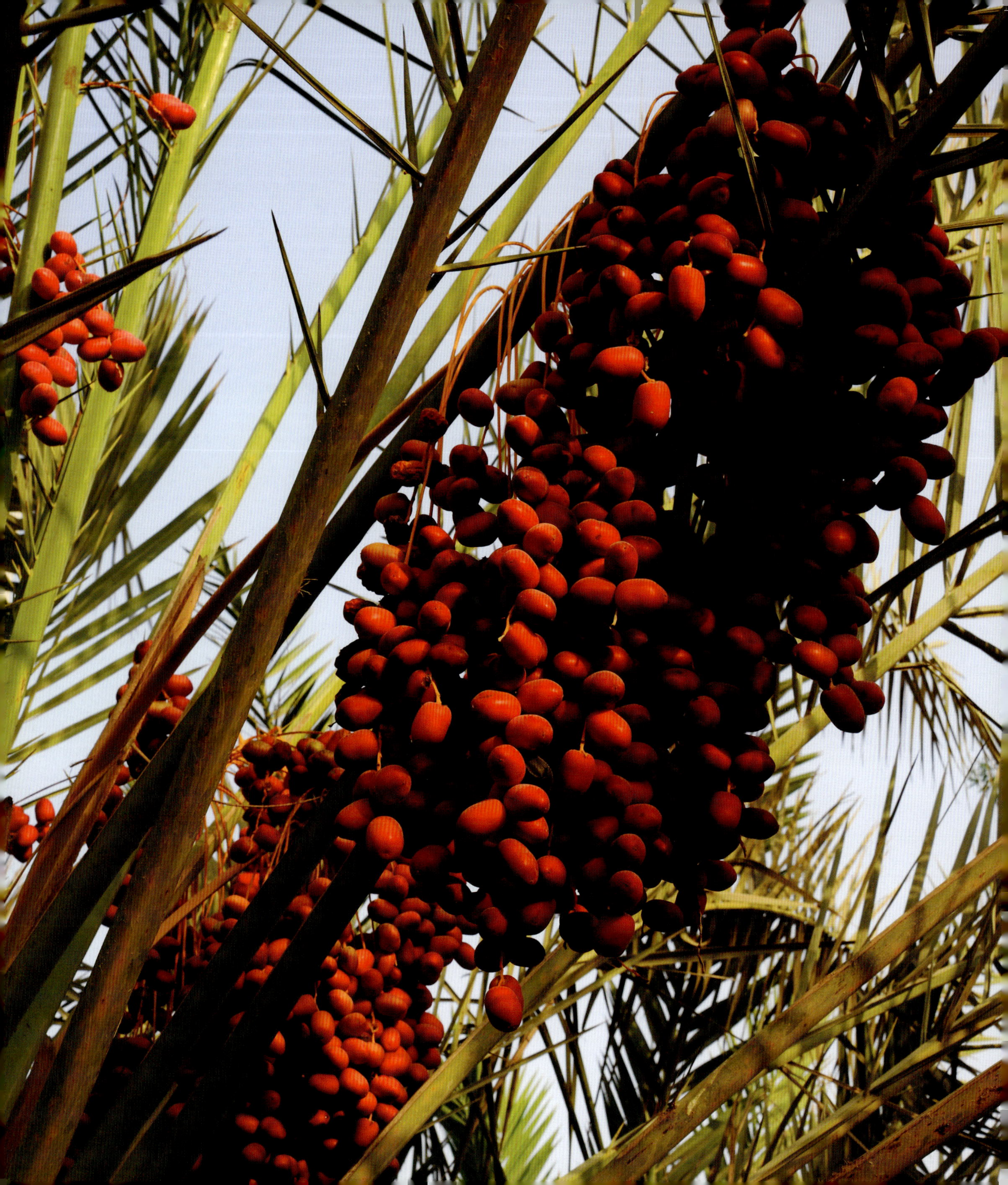

unripe/*rotab-e dombaz*. Locals consider it a gourmet delicacy at this stage. The unripe end has light orange, hard, dry flesh, a bit like crumbly flour, and tastes sweet and sour. The ripe tip is translucent, soft, and very sweet and, depending on the variety, has a shiny brown pastel color. By late August, the whole fruit is soft and juicy. These are fresh dates—called *rotab* in Persian—and very desirable, but they cannot be preserved at this stage; within a few days of picking, they will become rotten and ferment. (Happily, you can sometimes find fresh dates in the U.S. at Iranian and Asian markets during the season.) Finally, in September fruit left on the tree has dried somewhat in the sun. At this stage the date/*khorma* can be harvested and it can be easily preserved for distribution. This is what we normally buy in markets as dates.

Date syrup/*dushab* is made either by pressing fresh dates (which is expensive because 250lb/110kg of dates are needed to produce 4½lb/2kg of syrup) or by boiling poor-quality dates to the consistency of a syrup and then straining it. The residue of this process is fed to cattle. The syrup itself is used as a sweetener, replacing sugar in many dishes in southern Iran. In addition, it is drizzled over rice pudding or ice cream like chocolate syrup, or spread over bread like honey. It may also be used as a preservative for packing choice dates in earthenware jars.

In Pakistan, the sap of the date palm is routinely collected to make date sugar. In Iran, by contrast, only sterile male date palms and female trees that produce low-quality dates are sometimes tapped for their syrup/*shireh*. After the date clusters have been cut off, a container is fixed under the tip of each severed stalk to collect the sap, which continues to rise for weeks or, in the case of female palms, for months. This is then boiled down to molasses, which is used both as a sweetener in recipes and also fermented to make wine or vinegar. A popular alcoholic drink called *araq-e khorma*, was the wine of this region for thousands of years.

Amazingly, every part of the date palm can be put to good use. The date pit may be ground to a meal and fed to cattle or, during famines, made into bread. I even saw some beautiful jewelry created from date pits by locals. The trunk of the palm is used for construction. Each branch—the large branch or leaf of the palm is called a frond/*shakheh*—is 12 to 15ft/4 to 5m long. When the fronds are cut, the bases are left on the tree for footholds. The fronds themselves may be dried and used as fuel or as floats for fishing nets. Their many strong fibers are used to manufacture ropes, doormats, and sandals. The spines on the fronds are removed for threshing and for beating laundry. The leaflets are woven or braided into beautifully colorful baskets and mats/*toviz*. (I bought several in Bandar Abbas.) Locals also use these leaflets to make lids, bags, caps, brimmed hats, and fans, and bundle them together to make brooms.

Even in cooking, the date palm's uses seem endless. For me, it was thrilling to be able to enjoy a kabab of marinated goat threaded on palm skewers and, in Chabahar, to use the leaves of the wild date palm to wrap fish and grill it over charcoal made from palm branches. This is a marvelously versatile tree.

Heart of palm vendor on the roadside in Jahrom.

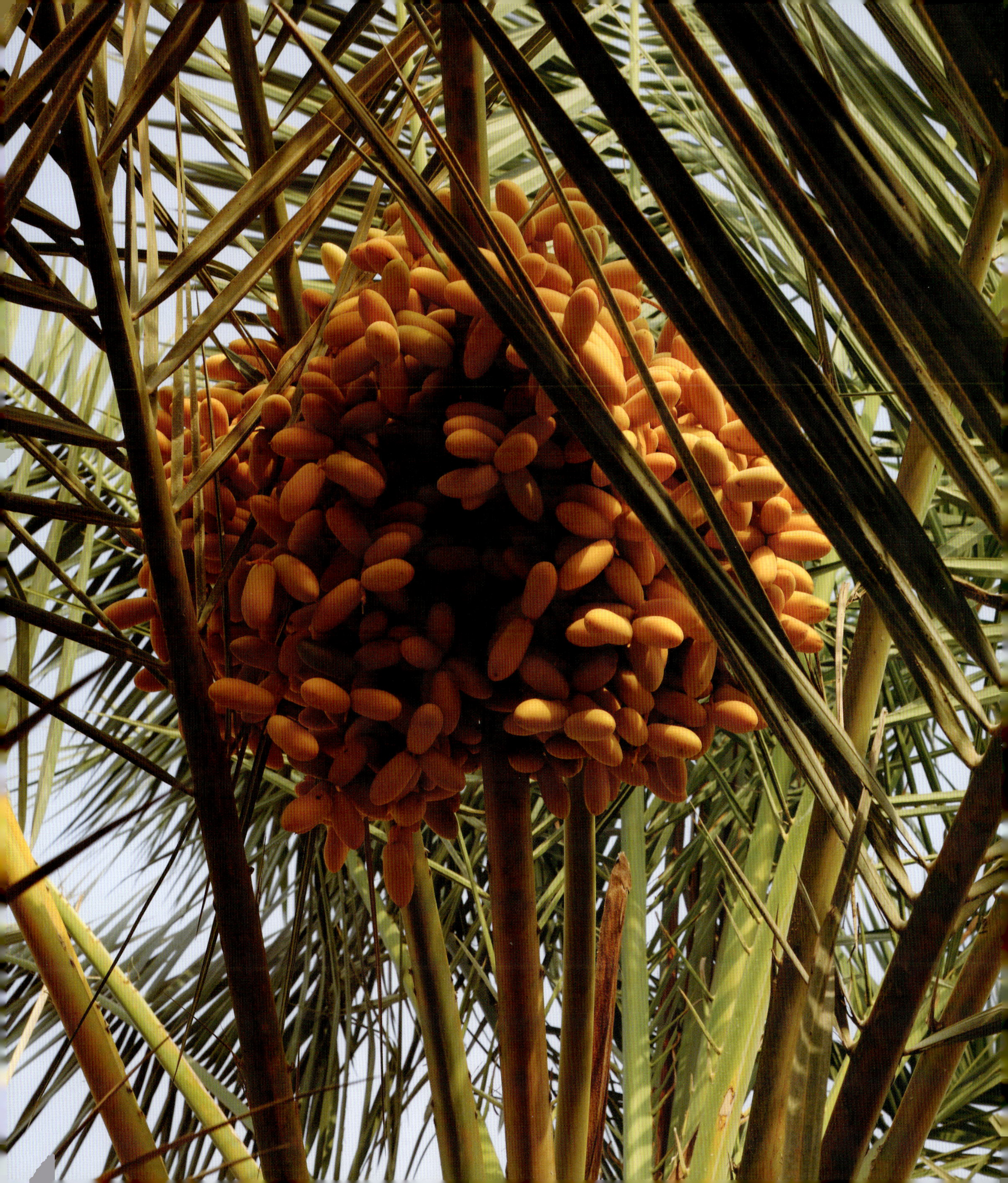

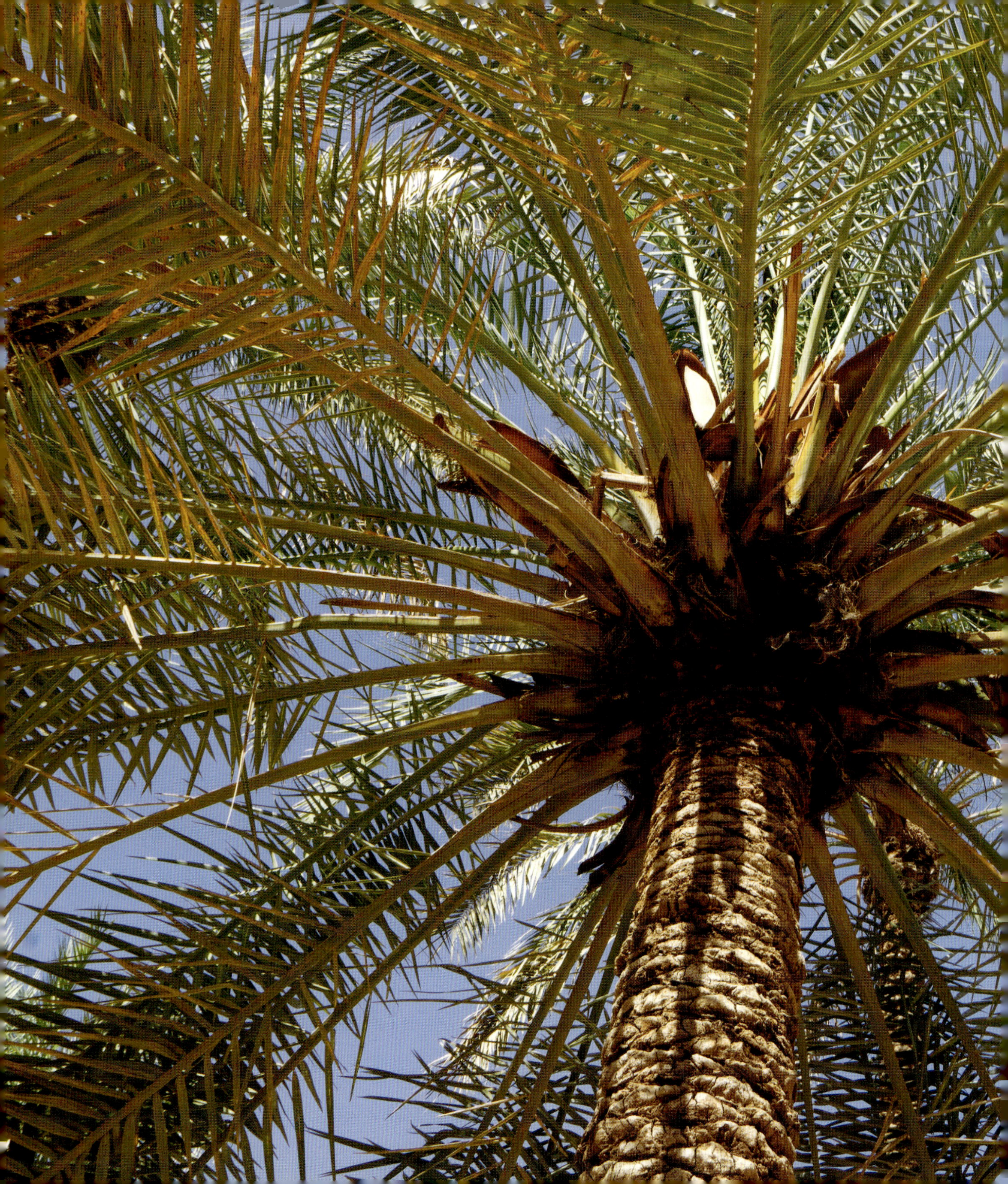

A Conversation Between a Date Palm and a Goat

As early as the second century BCE Iranians were considering the benefits of a sedentary agricultural life versus a nomadic pastoral one—and possibly vegetarianism versus meat-eating. This is played out in a poem (which starts as a riddle) written in the Parthian language (an Iranian language preceding Middle Persian) by an anonymous poet, who sets up a verbal dialogue between a palm tree and a goat. The tree lists for the goat all the benefits it provides:

A female palm tree in the land of Assyria:

"My trunk is dry; my top is moist; my leaves resemble canes; my fruits resemble grapes; and I bear sweet fruits for a people. In summer I am shade over the heads of rulers. I am vinegar for farmers, honey for noblemen; I am a nest for little birds and shade for travelers, who eat fruit from me until they become full."

The female goat challenges and ridicules it, listing its own benefits:

"They make my skin into water bags; in the plain and desert, on a hot day and at noon, cold water is from me. They make tablecloths of me, on which they arrange meals. The opulent great feast they adorn with my meat. They make trimmings from me for beer, kumis, and wine. I am milk and cheese; they dry my yogurt for palaces. Harp and lyre and lute and zither, every instrument they play, they play on me. Since the beginning that is primeval creation I go pasturing on the mountains, the sweet-smelling mountains; I eat fresh grass and drink cool water from springs."

In the end, the poet proclaims the goat the winner.

Many of the words for the food items remain the same or close to those used in Persian today: milk/*shir*, cheese/*panir*, churned sour milk/*dugh*, yogurt/*mast*, dried buttermilk/*kashk*, honey/*angabin*, vinegar/*sik*, bread/*nan*, appetizers/*pish parag*, pastries/*royn khowrag*, beer/*washag*, wine/*mey*.

From "*Drakht-e Asurik*," circa second century BCE

Bandari Seven-Spice Advieh
haft advieh-ye bandari/abzar

Makes 1¼ cups/125g
Prep: 20 minutes

¼ cup/40g green cardamom pods
2 tablespoons ground ginger
¼ cup/40g coriander seeds
¼ cup/40g red pepper flakes
Four 4in/10cm cinnamon sticks broken into small pieces
2 tablespoons whole cloves
¼ cup/40g black cumin seeds

I am calling this Persian Gulf spice mix "Bandari Seven-Spice Advieh." Iranians call the people of the Persian Gulf region "Bandari," meaning "those who live by a port/bandar." And spice mixes in Iran are generally called "advieh" from the Arabic for medicines. Locals in this region, however, call their advieh "abzar" meaning "ingredients" (it's interesting that the Indian spice mix garam masala comes from the Persian, "garm" meaning "hot" and "masaleh" meaning "ingredients"). This Bandari spice mix is different from those of the other regions of Iran, where the spicing tends to be more delicate both in flavor and aroma. The Bandaris like their spice mix hot, with red pepper and ginger being dominant. However, in Bandar-e Lengeh, they make theirs more aromatic, adding rose petals and pepper corns. I have adapted this and several of the recipes in this section from Mona Pourdaryai, a young and talented cook from this region.

1. Grind the spices, each separately, in a spice grinder.

2. Transfer them to a small bowl as you grind them and use a spoon to mix well.

3. Transfer to an airtight glass jar and keep in a cool place to use as needed. *Nush-e joon!*

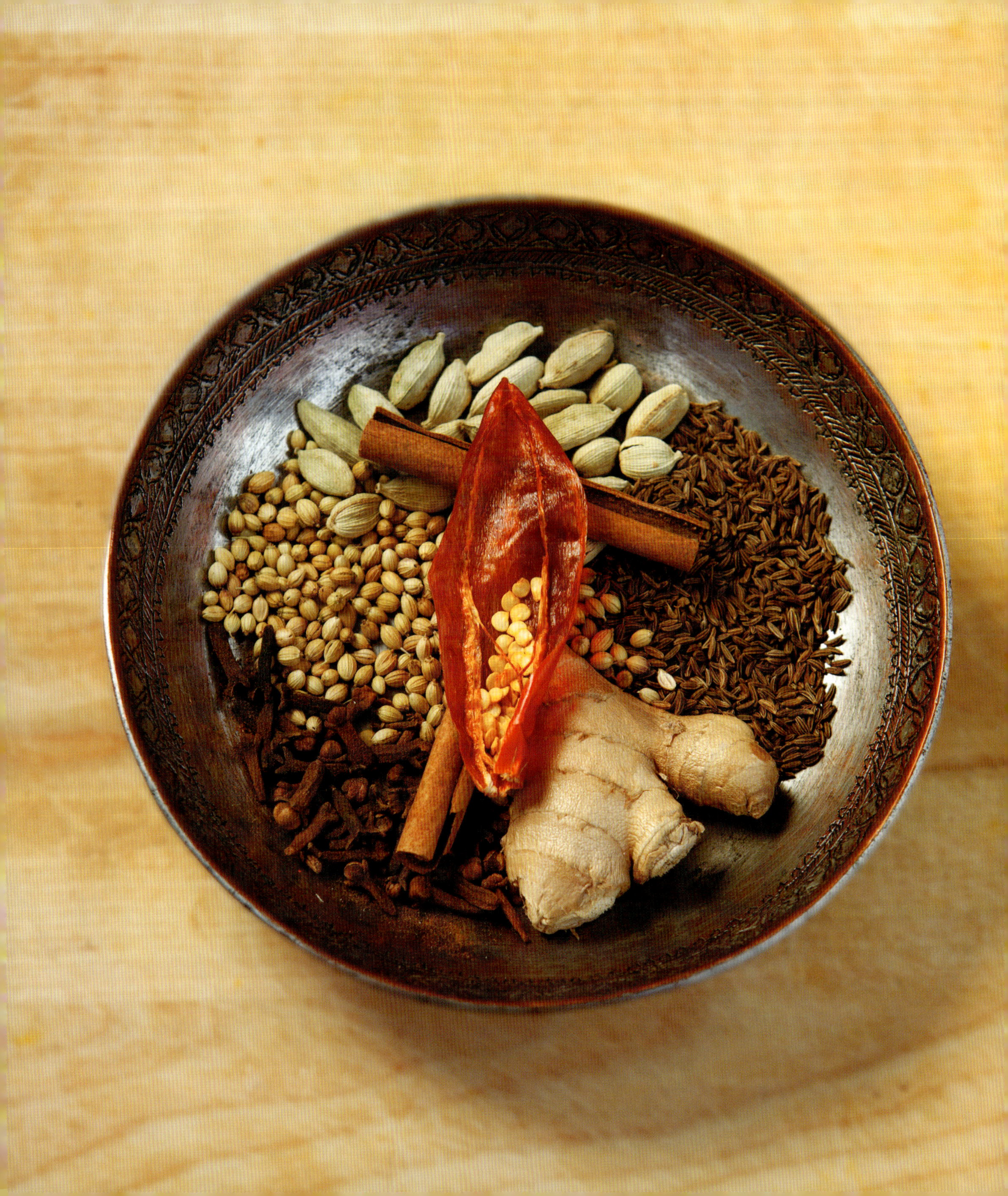

Spicy, Lemony Shrimp with Caramelized Onions
dopiyazeh maygu-e bushehri

Serves 4
Prep: 20 minutes
Cooking: 1 hour

SHRIMP

1lb/450g shrimp, peeled, deveined, butterflied, rinsed, and patted dry
1 teaspoon fine sea

TOMATO SAUCE

½ cup/120ml raw sesame oil
4 medium yellow onions, peeled and thinly sliced
5 cloves garlic, peeled and grated
1 teaspoon fine sea salt
1 teaspoon freshly ground black pepper
2 teaspoons turmeric
1 jalapeño pepper, finely chopped or 1 teaspoon red pepper flakes
2 tablespoons ground hearts of dried Persian limes
2 tablespoons tomato paste
5 medium tomatoes, peeled and finely chopped

GARNISH

1 jalapeño pepper, sliced
2 limes cut in half
2 cups/170g Persian or Thai basil leaves, washed and dried

FOR A WRAP

Flat bread cut into 4in/10cm pieces and kept warm
1 green leaf lettuce, leaves separated, washed and patted dry (or use a salad spinner to dry the leaves)

We arrived in Bushehr late at night tired and hungry. Our hosts took us to the Rais Restaurant, where we were served this dish with lots of basil and hot flat bread. It was quite delicious and an impressive introduction to the tastes we would encounter in this port city—a kind of Persian Gulf New Orleans, except that its traditions were much, much older.

1. *To prepare the shrimp:* Place the shrimp in a bowl and sprinkle 1 teaspoon salt over them. Toss well, cover and set aside in the fridge.

2. *To make the tomato sauce:* Heat the oil in a large wide skillet over low heat until hot. Add the onions and sauté until golden brown. Add the garlic, salt, pepper, turmeric, jalapeño, and dried lime hearts, and sauté for 2 minutes. Add the tomato paste and sauté for 1 minute.

3. Add the fresh tomatoes, cover, and cook medium-low heat for 20 to 25 minutes until the juices have been reduced

4. Heat 2 tablespoons oil in a wide skillet over medium-high heat until hot. Add the shrimp and stir-fry for 2 minute. Transfer it to the tomato sauce, give it a gentle stir, cover and cook over low heat for 10 minutes.

5. Adjust seasoning to taste. Reduce heat to low and keep warm until ready to serve.

6. When ready to serve, transfer to a serving platter and garnish with limes and basil leaves. Spread a tablespoon on a piece of bread (sangak bread is best), add a squeeze of lime, and place a some basil leaves on top. You can also make a wrap using lettuce leaves instead of bread. Be sure to include plenty of Persian or Thai basil inside. *Nush-e joon!*

In the backyard of the Rais Restaurant in Bushehr, where they are playing music and reciting Omar Khayyam poetry/*khayyam khuni*.

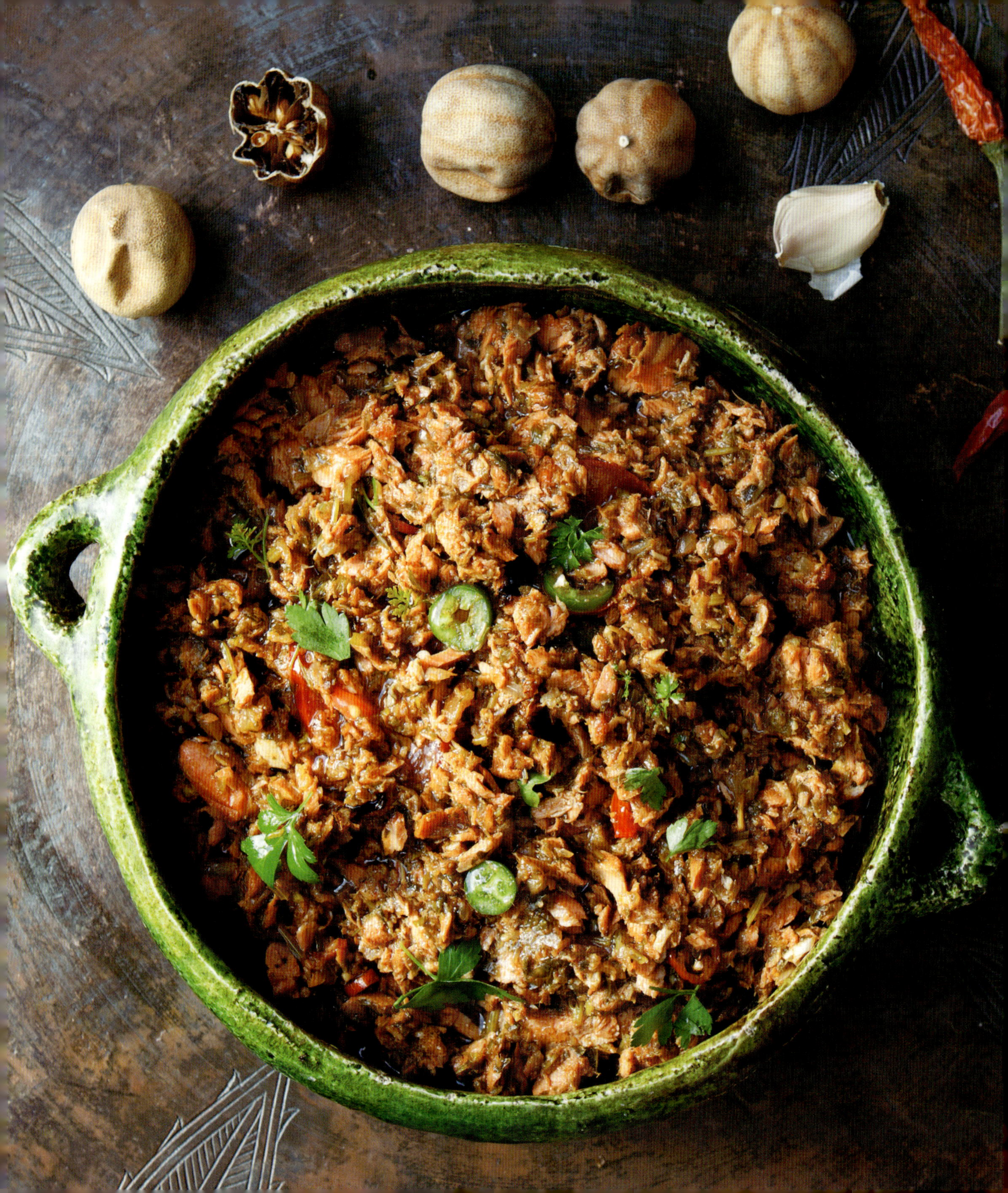

Fish with Fenugreek + Tomato Spread
pudini

Serves 4
Prep: 30 minutes
Cooking: 20 minutes

FISH

1lb/450g fish fillets (shark, tuna, or salmon), all small bones and skin removed, cut into 1in/2.5cm pieces
1 teaspoon fine sea salt
½ teaspoon freshly ground pepper
1 teaspoon turmeric
2 cups/480ml water

ONION-SPICE MIXTURE

¼ cup/60ml oil or ghee
2 medium onions, quartered
5 cloves garlic, peeled
1 tablespoon Bandari seven-spice *advieh*
2 serrano chilli peppers, stems removed, or ½ teaspoon red pepper flakes
1 tablespoon ground hearts of dried Persian limes

HERBS

2 tablespoons tomato paste
3 cups/255g roughly chopped fresh cilantro leaves
2 tablespoons dried fenugreek leaves
2 fresh tomatoes, peeled and quartered

I adapted this and several other dishes in this section from Raviyeh Daryanavardi, who was our guide Omid's mother. She used shark fillets and served it over plain rice. Fried onions and dried limes combined with fish gives this dish an earthy, tangy taste. You can use any type of fish. I used salmon and spread it over toasted sangak bread (available at Iranian markets)—delicious!

1. ***To cook the fish:*** In medium-sized saucepan, place the fish, salt, pepper, and turmeric and 2 cups water. Bring to a boil. Reduce heat to medium, cover, and cook for 5 minutes. Remove from the heat and set aside.

2. ***To make the onion-spice mixture:*** In a food processor, place all the ingredients for the onion spice mixture and pulse until you have a grainy paste.

3. Heat ¼ cup/60ml oil in a medium-sized laminated cast-iron braiser or pot over medium heat. Add the onion-spice mixture and stir-fry for 5 to 10 minutes until all the juices have been absorbed.

4. Add the tomato paste and sauté for 1 minute. Add the fish (including its juice) to the pot and cook over medium heat for 2 minutes.

5. Add the cilantro, fenugreek, and fresh tomatoes and give it a stir. Cover and cook over low heat for 15 minutes. Adjust seasoning to taste and serve with bread or rice. *Nush-e joon!*

NOTE

For deboning shark or similar firm fish slices, in a saucepan, cover the fish with 2 cups water and cook until soft. Drain, reserving the broth to use later, and debone the fish.

Pickled Sardine + Red Earth Sauce

suraq

Makes 1pt /480g
Prep: 25 minutes
Pickling: 5 weeks in sunlight

4lb/1.8kg sardines/*momagh*
4lb/1.8 kg coarse sea salt
3 tablespoons red earth (gilak, a specialty of Hormozgan region)
1 cup dried sour orange rind

Suraq is a salty reddish local relish attributed to the island of Hormoz in the Persian Gulf. Locals recall a legend attributing the sauce to the Portuguese conquerors of Hormoz in the sixteenth century. It is made with sardines pickled in salt and flavored with sour orange rind and the local red earth ocher/gilak. Small amounts of the mineral-rich ocher are believed to give the body strength. I have adapted this recipe from Halimeh Jonaybi, a talented cook from nearby Evaz.

1. Sprinkle 1 tablespoon of salt in a medium-sized earthenware jar.

2. Place the fish in a large colander. Remove the heads and empty the stomachs of the sardines and discard. Rinse, drain, and pat dry thoroughly.

3. Rub the fish, inside and outside, with the remaining salt. Transfer the fish to the jar.

4. Cover tightly. Allow the fish to pickled in the sun for 2 weeks. Stir with a long-handled spoon several times to ensure that the fish are always covered with salt (to prevent spoiling).

5. Transfer the fish from the jar to a mixing bowl and rub all over with the red earth.

6. Return the fish back to the jar and sprinkling sour orange rind between layers of the fish.

7. Cover tightly and allow to pickle for another 3 weeks in the sun. *Nush-e joon!*.

The naturally pigmented clay earth/red ocher on the island of Hormoz in the Persian Gulf. Wind blows the pigment onto the trees.

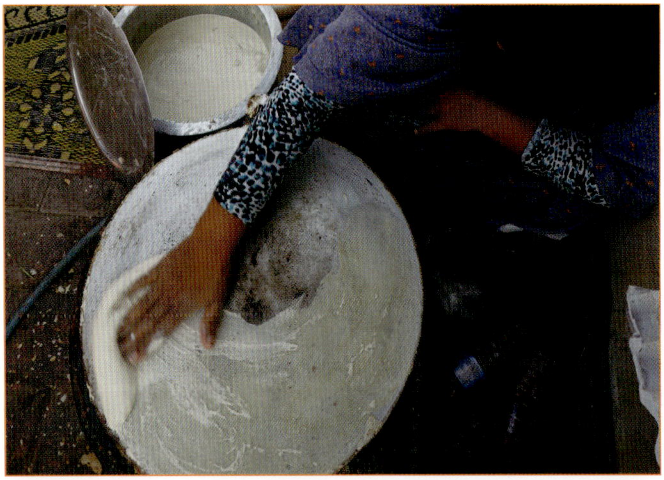

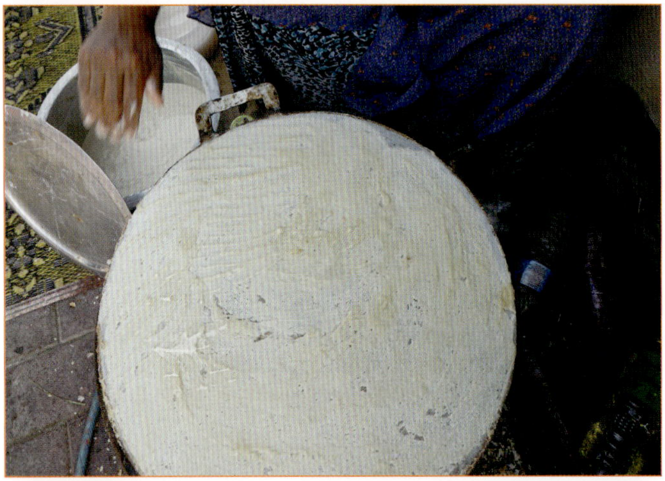

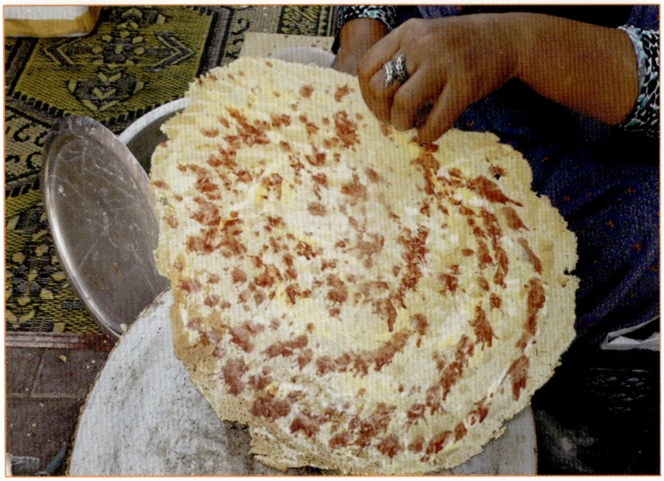

Fist Pancakes

nan-e tu moshi/tu moshti

Makes 2 to 4 pancakes
Prep: 10 minutes + 30 minutes of resting
Cooking: 2 minutes for each pancake

SOFT DOUGH

1½ cups/150g unbleached all-purpose wheat flour
½ teaspoon fine sea salt
1 cup/240ml warm water (100°F/ 38°C)

Our guide in Qeshm was a young architect called Omid. He took me to his mom Raviyeh Daryanavardi's house in nearby Dargahan. Raviyeh is a tall, beautiful cook and mother of three, with whom I made several local dishes, including these pancakes. She made the pancakes with nonchalant ease. She first moistened hand with a little cold water, then picked up a fistful of soft dough and spread it on the hot skillet with quick motions to even it out in a couple of seconds. I tried it too but burnt my hand the first time. You need practice to be able to do it without burning your hand. I suggest you use a rubber spatula to spread the soft dough. Even the younger local cooks use a metal device for pouring and spreading the batter. The old traditions are dying out.

1. **To make the soft dough:** In a large mixing bowl, place the flour and salt and whisk well. Gradually add 1 cup/240ml warm water and whisk for 3 to 5 minutes until you have a soft, smooth dough with the consistency of thick yogurt (add more water if needed). Cover and allow to rest at the room temperature for at least 30 minutes.

2. **To cook the pancakes**: Heat a 16in/40cm *saj* or a wide non-stick skillet over medium-low heat until hot.

3. Spread ½ cup/120g of the dough, using a rubber spatula in a circular motion to quickly, and lightly spread the batter evenly over the hot *saj*. Allow to cook for 1 minute. Season with toasted sesame oil and mahyaveh (recipe on page 605) on top and remove from the skillet. *Nush-e joon!*

Opposite: Woman making thin pancakes/*tu moshi* in the market at Qeshm. She has garnished it with spicy pickled fish sauce/*mahyaveh*. If requested, she'd add oil and cook an egg on top as well.

VEGAN

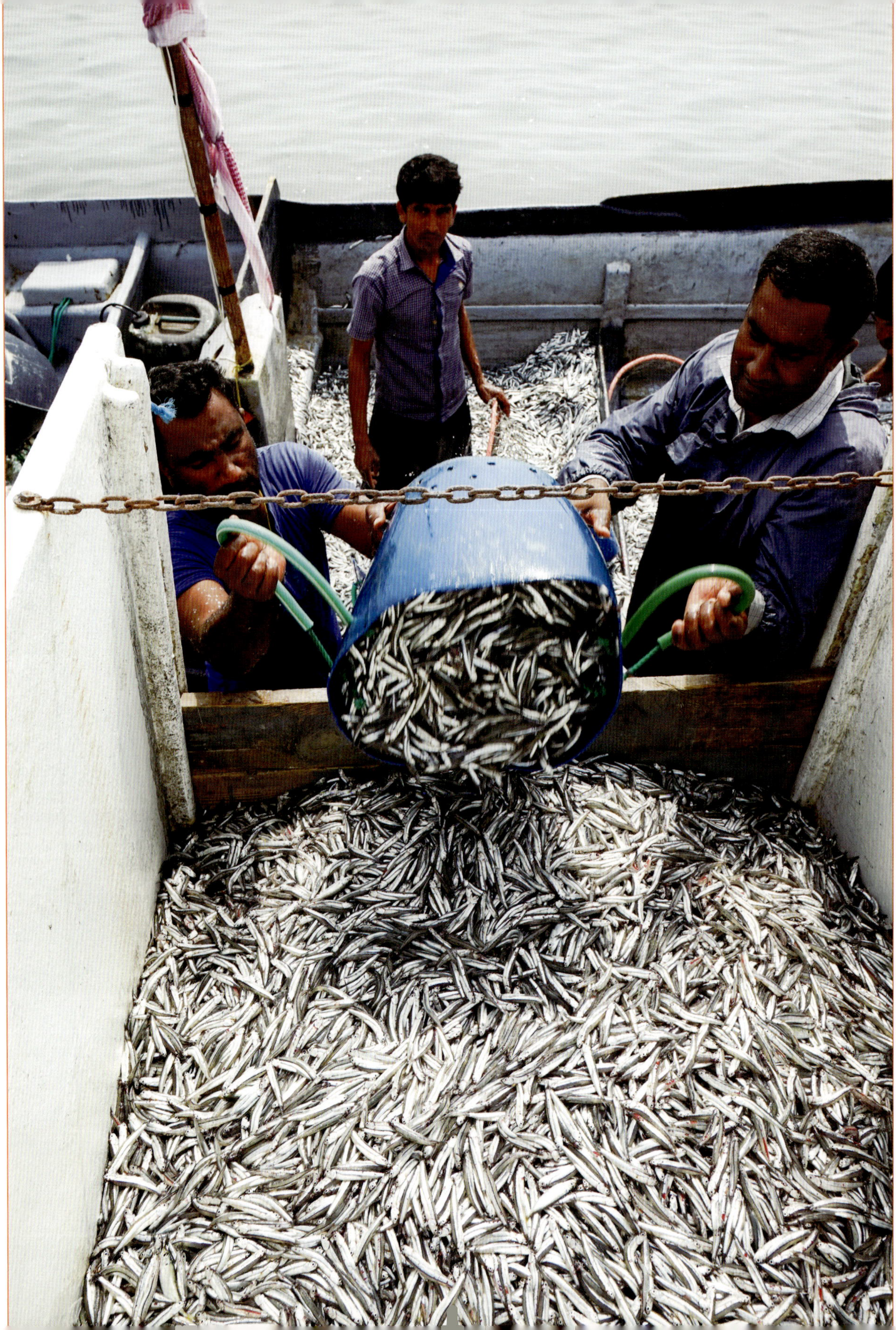

Spiced Pickled Fish Sauce

mahyaveh/mahi abeh

Makes 1pt/480g
Prep: 20 minutes
Pickling: 5 weeks fermentation

1lb/450g dried anchovies/*motu*
1lb/450g fine sea salt

SPICES

1lb/450g mustard seeds
½lb/225g fennel seeds
½lb/225g coriander seeds
2 tablespoons dried sour orange rind

This sauce is made from dried fish. It is a dark brown, salty, fishy, smooth sauce used in small amounts to enhance the flavor (somewhat similar to sriracha, the Thai hot sauce). It is used with various dishes: eggs, kuku, rice, or a braise as well as on bread. I adapted this recipe from Halimeh Jonaybi in Evaz. These days the sauce is locally available ready-made at markets in Hormozgan. Packets of dried powdered fish already mixed with salt and spices are also available as a short cut for making it.

1. Remove the the fish heads and discard. Soak the fish in a container of cold water for 30 minutes to remove any sand that might be there. Drain and rinse thoroughly.

2. Transfer the fish to an earthenware jar. Add the salt and cover with boiling water (the fish should be totally covered with water). Stir well, using a long wooden spoon, to dissolve the salt.

3. Cover with 3 layers of cheesecloth and allow the fish to ferment in a sunny spot for 3 to 4 weeks until the fish is soft. During this time, use the wooden spoon to stir twice a day to ensure the fish is coated with salt all over to prevent spoiling.

4. Transfer the fish from the jar to a fine-mesh colander over a container. Use your hands or a masher to mash the fish, reserving the sauce and discarding the solids. Return the fish juice to the earthenware jar.

5. In a wide skillet, place the mustard, fennel, coriander seeds, and orange rind, and toast over low heat, moving the skillet back and forth until the aroma rises. Grind the toasted spices, add them to the fish and stir well using a wooden spoon (Halimeh used a long, trimmed date branch).

6. Cover tightly and allow to ferment for another 2 weeks. Use as needed. *Nush-e joon!*

Fried Eggs with Fresh Ginger, Dates + Saffron

khagineh-ye khorma

Serves 4
Prep: 10 minutes
Cooking: 15 minutes

DATE

12 dates, pitted and sliced
¼ cup/60ml water
½ teaspoon cinnamon
½ inch fresh ginger, grated, or
 ¼ teaspoon dried ginger powder

EGGS

4 tablespoons coconut or sesame oil
6 eggs
1 teaspoon fine sea salt
½ teaspoon freshly ground pepper
⅛ teaspoon ground saffron dissolved in
 ½ teaspoon orange blossom water

GARNISH

Flat bread
Fresh basil

I was served this with zaatar bread for breakfast on the road from Shiraz to Bandar Abbas. It's simple and surprisingly delicious with a cup of tea in the morning.

1. **To make the date mixture:** In a wide skillet place the dates, water, cinnamon, and ginger, and cook over medium heat for 4 to 5 minutes until the dates are soft.

2. **To cook the eggs:** Spread the date mixture evenly in the skillet and drizzle the oil on top. Break in the eggs, sprinkle with the salt and pepper. Cook for 5 to 10 minutes over medium heat until the egg yolks have your preferred consistency—I like mine just right, not too hard nor too runny.

3. Drizzle the saffron-orange blossom water on top and serve hot with flat bread and fresh basil. *Nush-e joon!*

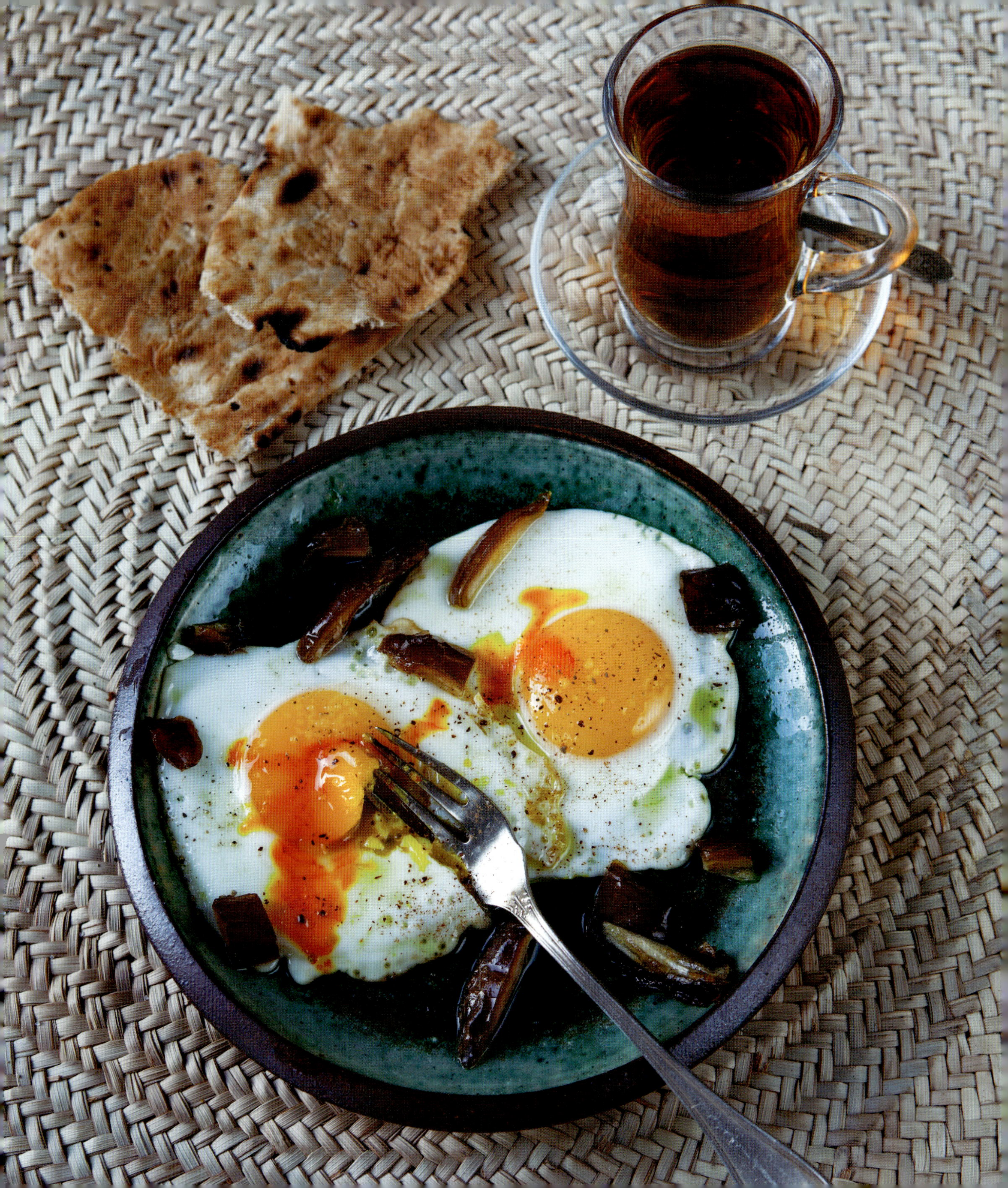

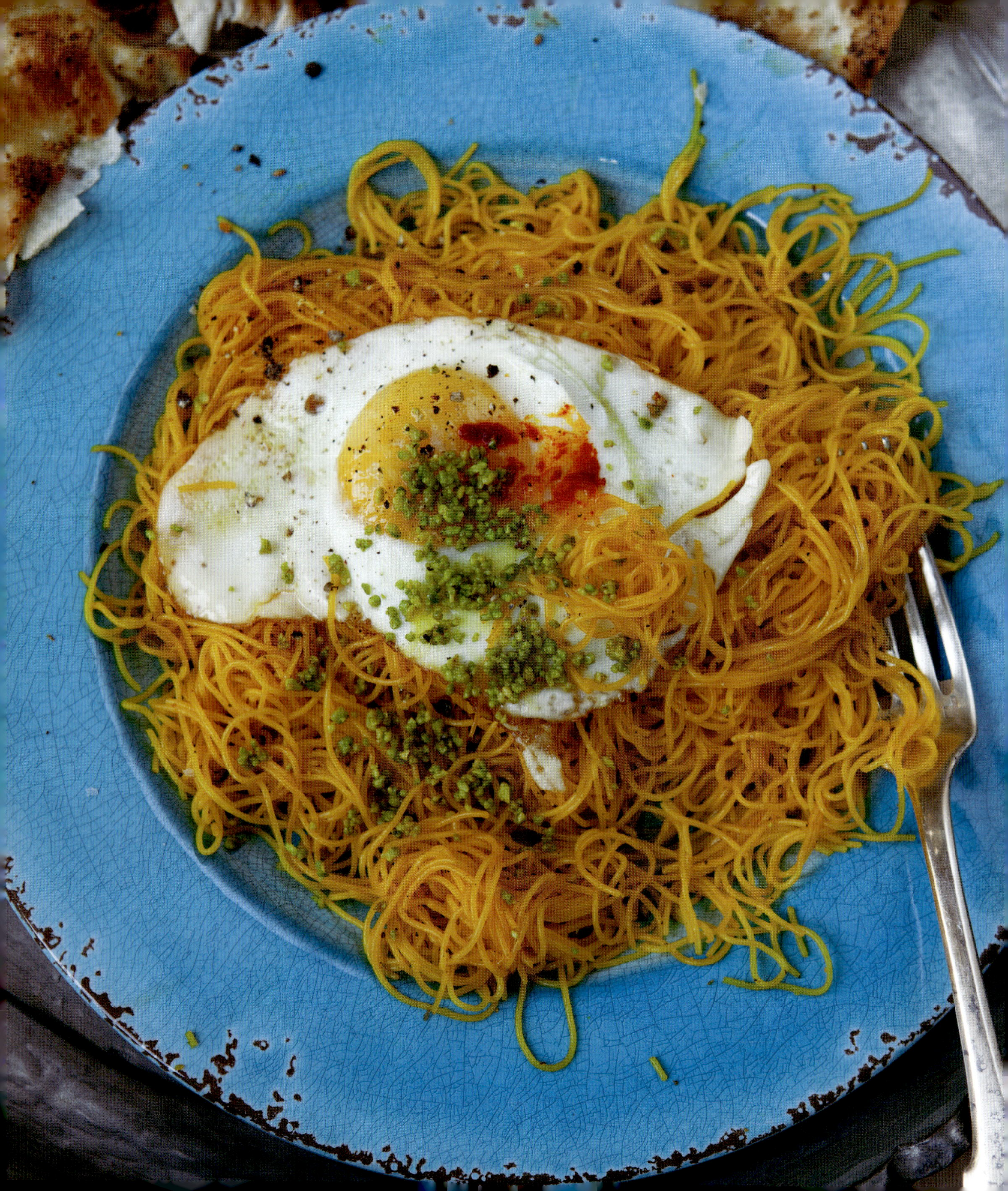

Angel Hair Noodles, Egg, Saffron + Cardamom
ballalat

Serves 2 to 4
Prep: 10 minutes
Cooking: 15 minutes

NOODLES

½lb/225g angel hair noodles
1 tablespoon fine sea salt

SAFFRON SAUCE

2 tablespoons coconut oil or butter
½ teaspoon ground cardamom
¼ teaspoon ground saffron dissolved in 2 tablespoons rose water
¼ cup/50g sugar

EGGS

¼ cup/60ml coconut oil or butter
4 eggs
½ teaspoon fine sea salt
¼ teaspoon freshly ground pepper

GARNISH

1 tablespoon ground pistachio kernels

This dish is served at traditional Persian Gulf breakfasts, but it can also be a main dish. Locals consider it comfort food. I adapted the recipe from Samieh Chamani, a sweet young cook from Bandar Abbas.

1. **To cook the noodles:** In a medium saucepan bring 6 cups/1.5l water to a boil. Add noodles and salt, and boil for 3 minutes, stirring occasionally until the noodles are al dente. Drain and set aside.

2. **To make the saffron sauce:** In the same saucepan, add 2 tablespoons oil, the cardamom, saffron rose water, and sugar and stir until the sugar has dissolved. Add the noodles and toss well. Cover and steam over low heat for 10 minutes.

3. **To cook the eggs:** In a wide skillet, heat the coconut oil over medium heat and break in the eggs. Sprinkle with salt and pepper and allow to cook for 2 to 3 minutes, spooning the oil over the eggs until they are crispy around the edges.

4. In a serving platter place some of the noodles and top with an egg (or 2). Garnish with the pistachio kernels. Serve with *zaatar*-flavored bread. *Nush-e joon!*

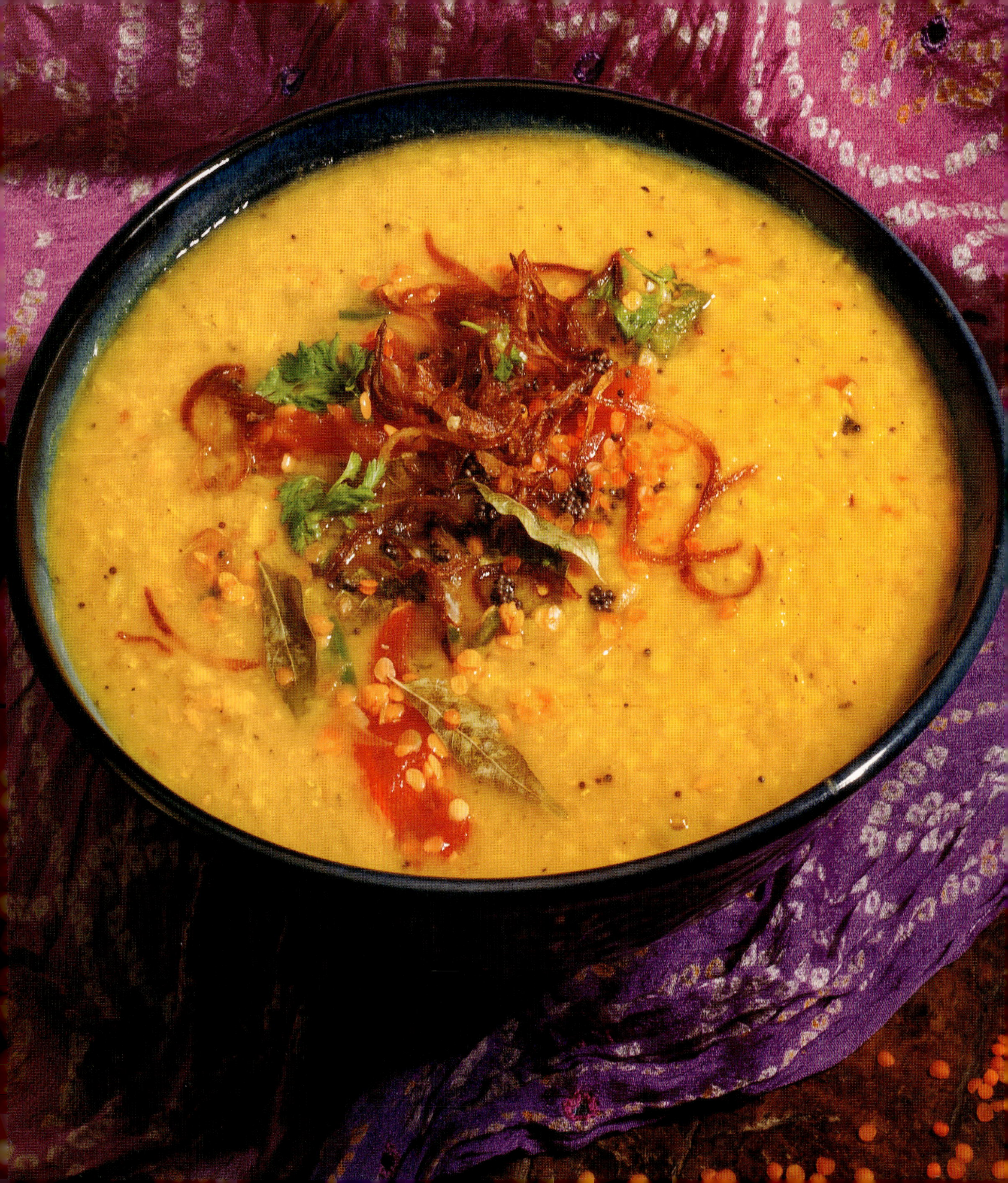

Red Lentil Soup
dal

Serves 6 to 8
Prep: 20 minutes
Cooking: 1¼ hours

2 cups/400g red lentils
4 tablespoons vegetable oil or ghee
1 onion, peeled and thinly sliced
2 tablespoons Bandari seven-spice advieh
½ teaspoon turmeric
1 tablespoon fine sea salt
½ teaspoon freshly ground pepper
8 cups/1.9l water
2 tablespoons rice flour dissolved in ½ cup/120ml water
2 cups/400g fresh tomatoes, peeled and chopped, or canned tomatoes
1 teaspoon tamarind paste

GARNISH
1 cup/85g chopped fresh cilantro

This soup shows the influence of Indian cooking on the cuisine of the region—red lentil flavored with tamarind and spices. It is an excellent vegan soup that can also be served over plain rice to make a complete meal. I adapted this recipe from Dowlat Khoshkhabar in Bushehr.

1. Place the red lentils in a container, cover with water, agitate with your hands, and pour off the water. Repeat 2 or 3 times until the water is clear. Drain and set aside.

2. Heat 4 tablespoons oil in a medium-sized laminated cast-iron pot over medium heat. Add the onion and sauté for 5 to 10 minutes until the onions are translucent. Add the advieh, turmeric, salt, and pepper, and stir-fry for 1 minute.

3. Add the red lentils and 8 cups/1.9l water, and bring to a boil. Reduce heat to medium, cover, and simmer for 45 minutes or until the lentils are tender.

4. Add the diluted rice flour, tomatoes, and tamarind paste. Partially mash the lentils with a handheld mixer. Bring back to a boil, reduce heat to low, cover, and simmer for another 15 minutes. Adjust seasoning to taste. Cover and keep warm until ready to serve.

5. Just before serving, garnish with the cilantro. Give it a stir and serve. *Nush-e joon!*

VEGAN

Barley + Tahini Soup
sup-e ardeh

Serves 6 to 8
Prep: 20 minutes + soaking overnight
Cooking: 2 hours

SOUP

¼ cup/50g chickpeas, soaked overnight in water with ½ teaspoon baking soda, drained and rinsed
½ cup/100g brown lentils, picked over, soaked overnight drained and rinsed
¾ cup/150g barley, rinsed and drained
2 tablespoons oil or ghee
1 large onion, thinly sliced
2 cloves garlic, crushed, peeled, and chopped
2 leeks, finely chopped (white and green parts)
1 fresh serrano chili, finely chopped, or ½ teaspoon red pepper flakes
1 teaspoon freshly ground black pepper
1 teaspoon ground turmeric
8 cups/1.9l broth or water

TAHINI SAUCE

½ cup/20g tahini paste, stirred well before using
1 tablespoon fine sea salt
2 teaspoons tamarind paste
½lb/225g tomato (1 large one), peeled and finely diced

HERBS

½ cup/40g chopped fresh dill
½ cup/40g chopped fresh parsley
½ cup/40g chopped fresh cilantro

It's interesting that barley soup is popular throughout Iran but only in this region is tahini added to it.

1. **To make the soup:** Heat the oil in a large laminated cast-iron pot over medium heat. Add the onion, garlic, leeks, and chili, and sauté for 10 minutes. Add the chickpeas, lentils, barley, pepper, and turmeric, and sauté for 1 minute.

2. Add the broth and bring to a boil. Reduce heat to low, cover, and simmer for 1½ hours until the legumes are cooked.

3. Add the tahini paste, salt, tamarind paste, and tomato. Using a handheld mixer, plunge it into the pot and partially puree the soup. Cover and simmer for 15 minutes.

4. Add the herbs and give it a stir. Cover and simmer for 5 minutes longer over low heat.

5. Adjust seasoning to taste. Cover and keep warm until ready to serve.

6. Just before serving, pour the soup into a tureen or individual serving bowls. *Nush-e joon!*

The Persian Gulf

VEGAN

An early 1900s photo of two Iranian-Armenian girls using a hand stone mill to make flour.

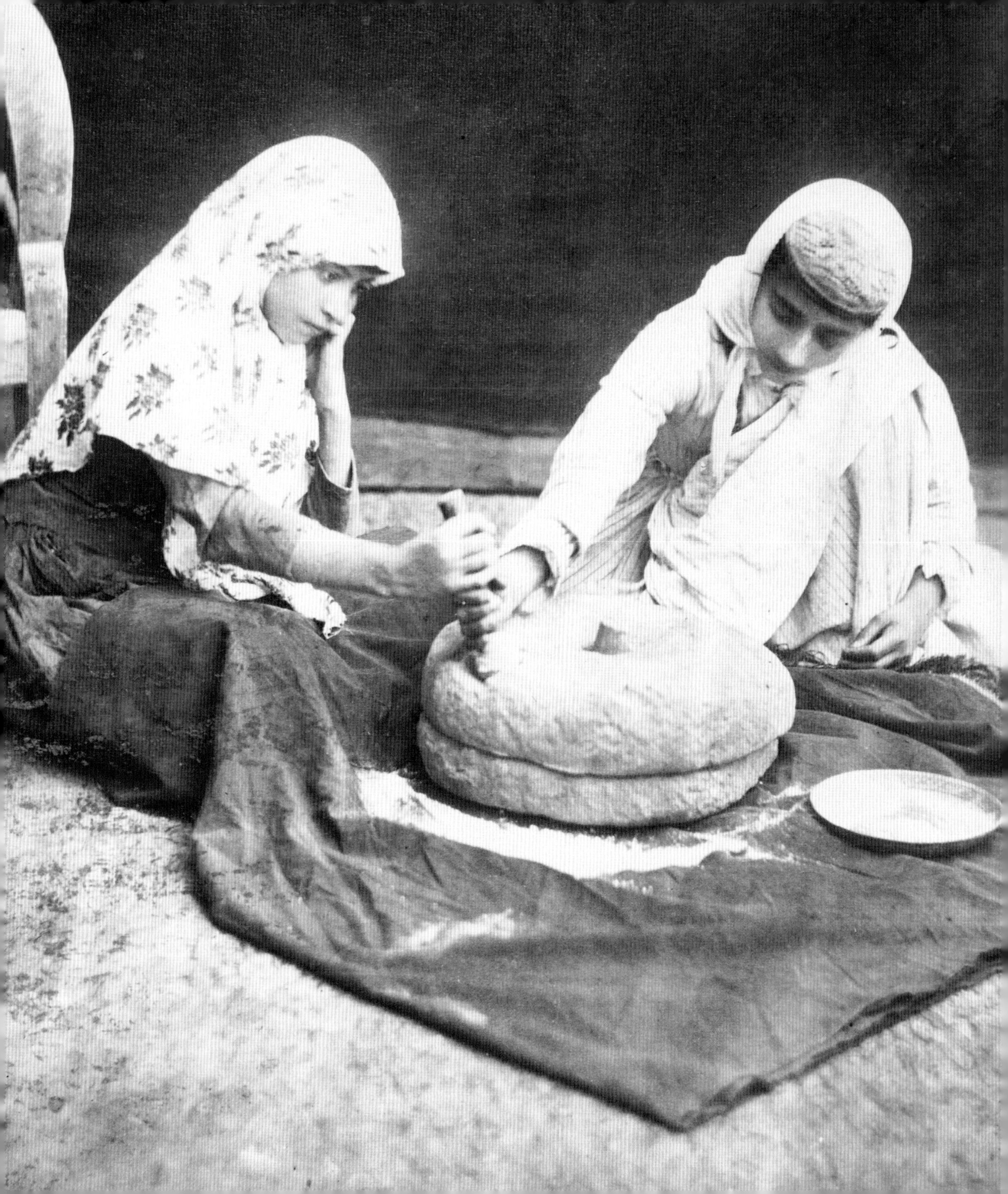

Fisherman's Soup
sup-e daryai-e bandari

Serves 4 to 6
Prep: 30 minutes + soaking overnight
Cooking: 1 hour 40 minutes

BROTH

- ¾ cup/150g chickpeas soaked overnight in water with ½ teaspoon baking soda, drained, and rinsed
- ¼ cup/60ml oil
- 2 medium onions, peeled and finely sliced
- ½lb/225g carrots, peeled and cut into 1in/25mm cubes
- 2 stalks celery, cut into ½inch/12mm lengths
- 1 serrano pepper, finely chopped
- ½ teaspoon fresh ground black pepper
- ½ teaspoon ground turmeric
- 1 tablespoon Bandari seven-spice *advieh*
- 1 tablespoon fennel seeds
- 2 tablespoons tomato paste
- 2 medium tomatoes, peeled and diced
- 4 cups/960ml water
- 1 cup clam juice
- Juice of 1 orange
- Zest of 1 orange
- ½ teaspoon ground saffron
- 1 large russet potato (about 1lb/450g, peeled and cut into 1in/25mm cubes

FISH + SHRIMP

- 1 tablespoons fine sea salt
- 1lb/450g cat fish, rock fish, or cod fillets cut into 4in/10cm pieces, any small bones removed with tweezers, rinsed and patted dry
- 1lb/450g shrimps deveined, butterflied, rinsed, and patted dry

GARNISH

- ½ cup/40g chopped fresh cilantro
- 1 fresh lime

This basic sea food soup is an everyday dish around the ports of the Persian Gulf. They were no doubt early adopters of New World ingredients such as sweet oranges (brought over by the Portuguese from China), tomatoes, potatoes, and peppers. The sea food, of course, was strictly local, and some of the best in the world.

1. **To cook the broth:** Heat the oil in a large laminated cast-iron pot over medium heat, and add the onions, carrots, celery, and serrano pepper. Sauté for 10 to 15 minutes until onions are golden brown.

2. Add the chickpeas, pepper, turmeric, *advieh*, fennel seeds, and tomato paste, and stir-fry for 1 minute.

3. Add the fresh tomatoes, water, clam juice, orange juice, orange zest, and saffron. Give it a stir and bring to a boil. Reduce heat to low, cover, and cook for 1 hour until chickpeas are tender.

4. Add the potatoes. Cover and cook for 25 minutes or until potatoes are tender.

5. **To cook the fish:** Add the salt and fish, and bring back to a boil. Reduce heat to low and allow to cook for 5 minutes.

6. **To cook the shrimp:** Gently add the shrimps and cook for another 2 to 3 minutes until the color of the shrimps starts to change.

7. Adjust seasoning to taste. Garnish with cilantro and a squeeze of fresh lime juice on top. Serve with plain rice or bread. *Nush-e joon!*

Onion Soup with Salted Fish

shur piyaz

Serves 4
Prep: 20 minutes + 1 hour of soaking
Cooking: 30 minutes

½lb/225g salted fish (bacala)
¼ cup/60ml oil
4 medium onions, peeled and sliced
1 teaspoon red pepper flakes or ½ small jalapeño pepper, thinly sliced
½ teaspoon turmeric
2 teaspoons Bandari seven-spice *advieh*
4 cups/960ml water
2 tablespoons fresh lime juice

They make soup with salted fish both in the Caspian and around the Persian Gulf, and the difference in the spicing is a measure of the amazing range of Persian cooking.

1. Soak the salted fish in a medium-sized container in cold water for at least 1 hour. Change the water several times.

2. Drain the fish in a colander and cut into 1in/2.5cm pieces. Remove any bones that may have remained.

3. Heat the oil over medium heat in a medium-sized saucepan and sauté the onions until lightly golden. Add the red pepper, turmeric, and *advieh* and stir-fry for 2 minutes. Add the fish and sauté for 1 minute.

4. Add the water and bring to a boil. Reduce heat to low, cover, and simmer for 10 minutes. Use a handheld mixer to partially puree. Cover and cook for another 10 minutes. Add the lime juice and give it a stir. Adjust seasoning to taste. *Nush-e joon!*

Opposite: Popular local pony fish (Leiognathus equulus). Around Bandar Abbas it is called "shengu" or "arus" meaning "bride".

The Persian Gulf

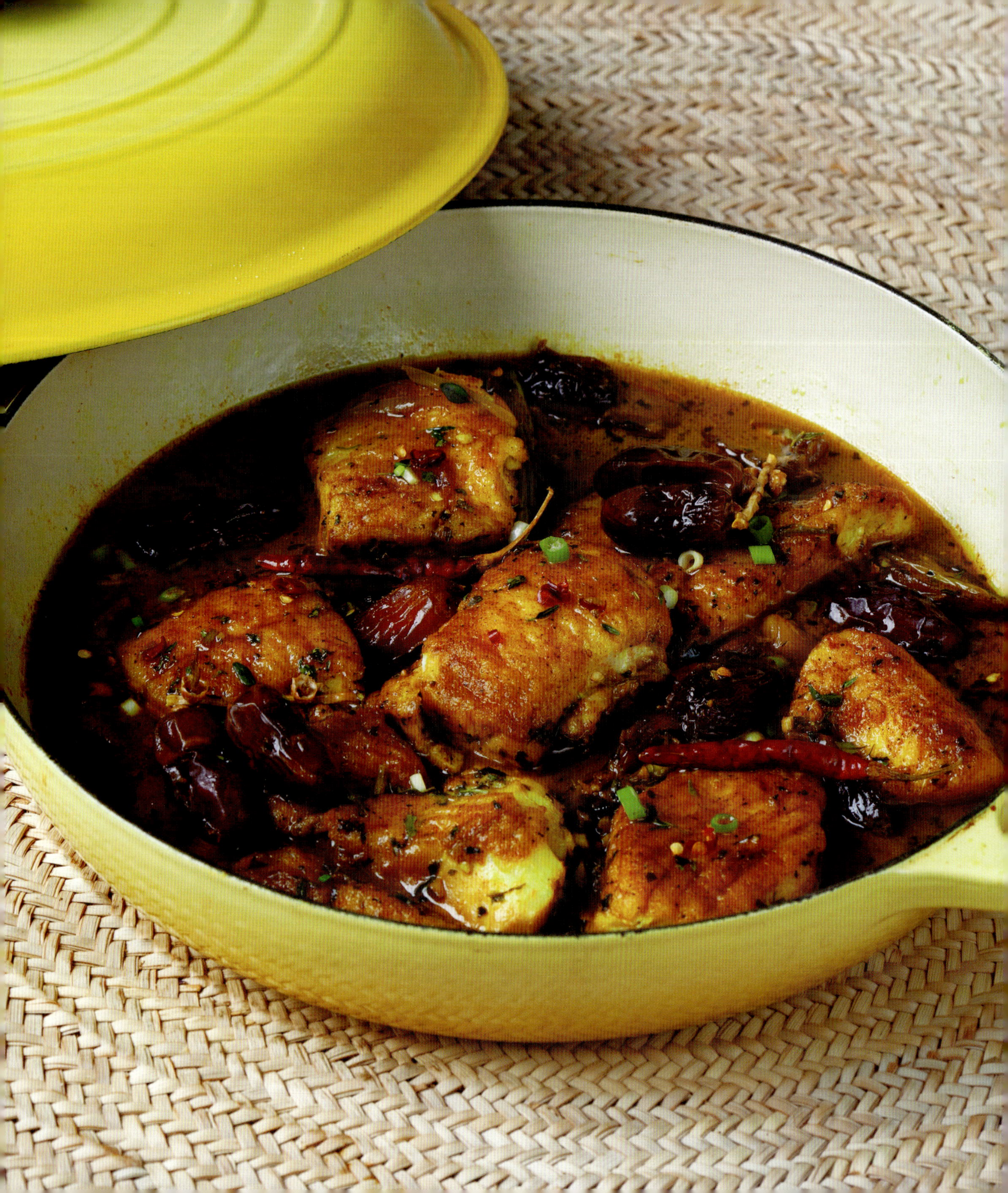

Spicy Sweet + Sour Fish with Dates

qaliyeh-ye khorma

Serves 4 to 6
Prep: 30 minutes
Cooking: 10 minutes

DUSTING

2 teaspoons fine sea salt
½ teaspoon freshly ground black pepper
1 teaspoon ground turmeric
1 tablespoon all-purpose flour

FISH

¼ cup/60ml oil
4-6 thick fish fillets (about 3 pounds/1.2kg), salmon, grouper, or halibut, all skins and bones removed
5 cloves garlic, grated

SAUCE

1 cup/240ml apple cider vinegar mixed with 2 tablespoons date molasses
1 scant teaspoon cayenne or 2 red Thai bird chilies, thinly sliced
1 tablespoon dried fenugreek leaves

GARNISH

5 medjool dates, pitted and halved
1 cup/100g chopped fresh spring onions
1 cup/85g fresh basil leaves

NOTE

You can replace the vinegar with fresh lime juice. In Bushehr, where there is an abundance of sour orange trees, they use fresh sour orange juice, which is a wonderful addition to the complex flavors in this dish.

Locals make this dish with grouper/hamour, but I've found it works very well using fresh Atlantic salmon fillets.

1. *To prepare the dusting:* In a small bowl, mix together all the dusting ingredients and set aside.

2. *To prepare the fish:* Rinse the fish and pat dry. Place them on a sheet pan lined with parchment paper.

3. Dust both sides of the fish fillets and arrange on the sheet pan. Keep cool until ready to cook.

4. *To cook the fish:* Heat the oil in a medium-sized sauté pan over high heat until very hot. Sear the fish until brown on both sides (about 1 minute on each side). Remove the fish and set aside.

5. *To make the sauce:* Reduce heat to low. Add the garlic and sauté for 1 minute until golden brown.

6. Add the vinegar and molasses mixture, cayenne and fenugreek, and give it a stir. Return the fish to the pan and simmer for 8 minutes over low heat until the fish is tender. Adjust seasoning to taste.

7. *To garnish:* Add the dates and spring onions. Serve with plain rice/kateh page 122, Onion, Cucumber + Coriander Pickle, page 675, Black Carrot Pickle, page 671, and fresh basil leaves. *Nush-e joon!*

TAHINI VARIATION

Spicy Sweet + Sour Fish with Dates + Tahini
qaliyeh-ye ardeh

In step 5, sauté 4 thinly sliced shallots with the garlic and replace the fenugreek leaves with ground cumin. Add ½ cup/120g tahini paste dissolved in ¼ cup/60ml water. Everything else remains the same.

The Persian Gulf

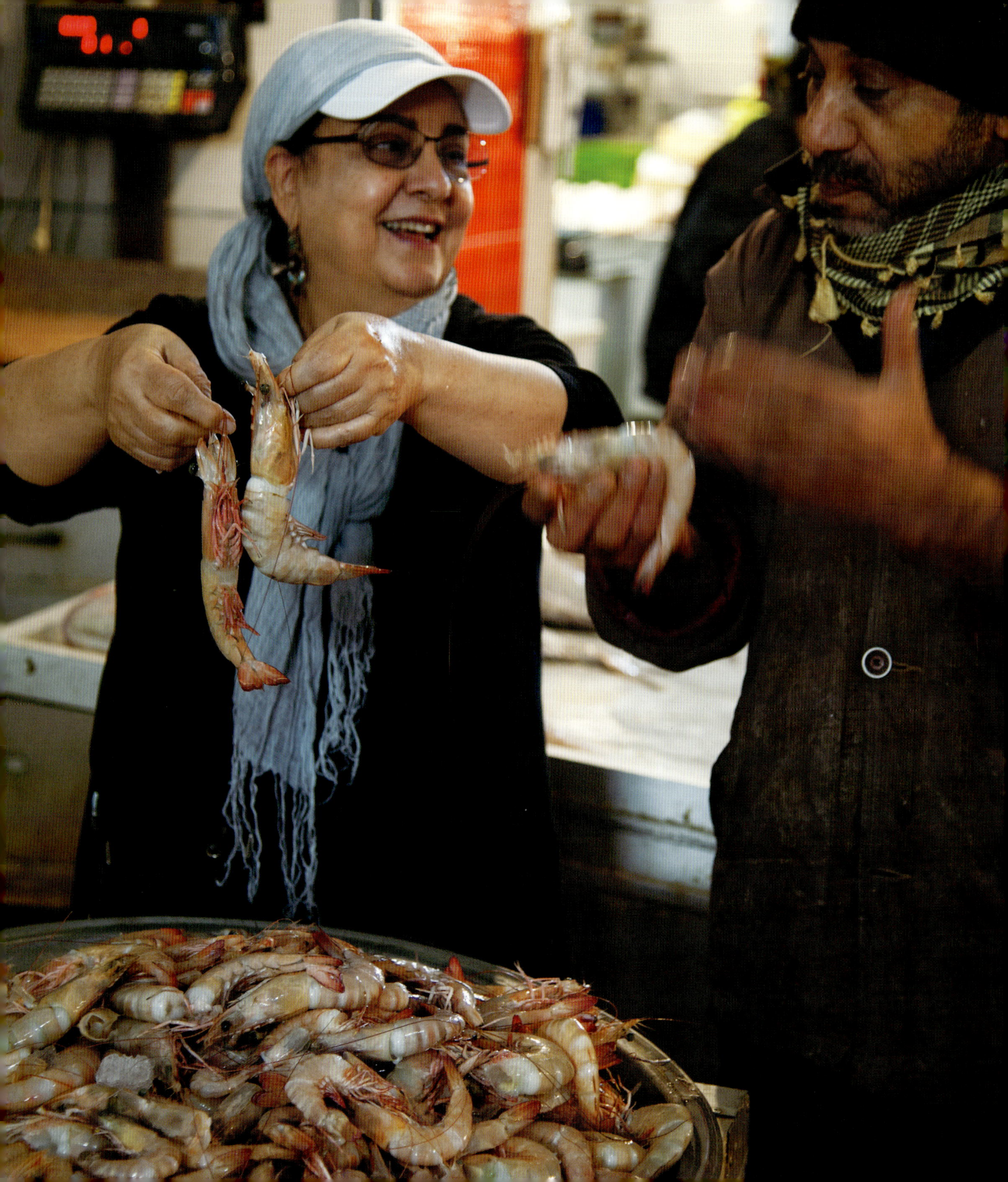

Tiger Prawn Tempura in Spicy Chickpea Batter
maygu-e pofaki

Serves 6
Prep: 30 minutes + 30 minutes of resting
Cooking: 1 hour

SHRIMP

2lb/900g tiger prawns, deveined, butterflied, rinsed, and patted dry. Rub with 1 teaspoon fine sea salt. Allow to macerate for 30 minutes.
oil for deep-frying

BATTER

1 teaspoon fine sea salt
½ teaspoon freshly ground pepper
1 teaspoon Bandari seven-spice *advieh*
½ teaspoon chili flakes
1 clove garlic, grated
2 tablespoons corn starch
½ cup/60g all-purpose flour
¾ cup/75g chickpea flour
1 cup/240ml sparkling water
½ teaspoon baking powder

GARNISH

½ cup/40g chopped fresh cilantro
1 sour orange halved

These days we mostly know "tempura" as a Japanese cooking technique. However, the name actually comes from a Portuguese dish. The Portuguese had a long history with Persian Gulf ports, so it makes sense that this style of cooking should be popular there. In the photo on the facing page, the fishmonger in Bushehr is giving me his own recipe. He suggested I should stuff the prawns with a puree of cilantro and garlic before dipping them in the batter. We did so and they were delicious.

1. **To make the batter:** Line a sheet pan with parchment paper. In a mixing bowl, combine all the ingredients for the batter and whisk well until you have a smooth batter. Cover and allow to rest at room temperature for 30 minutes.

2. **When you are ready to serve:** In a small saucepan, heat 2 cups oil over medium heat until hot but not smoky.

3. Give the batter a stir and dip the prawns, one by one, in the batter. Give the prawns a shake and gently drop in the oil for 3 to 4 minutes until they are crispy and golden brown. Cook in batches; do not crowd the saucepan. Transfer to the sheet pan.

4. Place the prawns in a serving platter, garnish with cilantro, and squeeze drops of sour orange juice on top. *Nush-e joon!*

Fish Kabab with Dried Lime + Coriander
kabab-e mahi bushehri

Serves 4 to 6
Prep: 20 minutes + 1 hour of marinating
Cooking: 10 minutes

FISH

2lb/900g fish fillets, (tuna or swordfish), boned, and skins removed, and cut into 2in/5cm cubes
1 teaspoon fine sea salt

MARINADE

¼ cup/60ml oil
1 medium onion, peeled and quartered
4 cloves garlic, peeled
2 tablespoons sour orange juice
½ teaspoon fine sea salt
½ teaspoon freshly ground pepper
1 tablespoon coriander seeds
1 tablespoon ground hearts of dried Persian limes
1 teaspoon turmeric
1 fresh serrano pepper, stemmed or 1 teaspoon red pepper flakes
1 cup/85g roughly chopped fresh cilantro

BASTE

¼ cup/60ml oil or butter, heated
¼ cup/20g chopped fresh cilantro
¼ cup/60ml sour orange juice

It's to be expected that grilled fish is popular both in northern Iran by the Caspian and in the south by the Persian Gulf. However, what makes them different is their marination and the type of local fish. In Bushehr, we made this marination with Dowlat Khoshkhabar and used it on tiger prawns, which we grilled—quite delicious.

1. **To marinate the fish:** Place the fish in a glass container and toss with 1 teaspoon salt. Cover and allow to rest in the fridge for 1 hour.

2. In a food processor, place all the ingredients for the marinade and pulse until you have a grainy paste. Add it to the fish, toss well, cover, and allow to marinate for 1 to 2 hours in the fridge.

3. **To cook the fish:** Start a bed of charcoal 30 minutes before you want to cook and let it burn until the coals glow evenly, or preheat the oven broiler.

4. **To prepare the baste:** In a small saucepan over very low heat, add all the ingredients for the baste and keep warm.

5. Thread the fish onto skewers or use an iron basket to arrange the fish inside.

6. Once the coals are evenly lit, grill the fish on one side for 1 to 2 minutes, baste, turn, and grill the other side for another 1 to 2 minutes. Avoid overcooking. The fish should be seared on the outside, juicy and tender on the inside. Serve hot. *Nush-e joon!*

VARIATION

Tiger Prawn Kabab
kabab-e maygu-e bushehri

Replace the fish with 2lb/900g large tiger prawns, peeled, deveined, tail kept intact, rinsed and patted dry. Stuff each prawn with the marinade. Everything else remains the same.

Opposite: Shopping for mackerel/*shurideh* (a favorite in the region) and tiger prawns at the market in Bushehr with Dowlat Khabarkhosh and Golnessa Mozaffari.

The Persian Gulf

Fish Patties Glazed with Tamarind + Date Molasses
kotlet-e mahi ba khorma-o tamr-e hendi

Makes 12 patties, serves 4 to 6
Prep: 30 minutes
Cooking: 20 minutes

POTATO

12oz/340g russet potato (about 1 potato)

PASTE

1lb/450g boneless, skinless fish fillets (tuna, grouper, salmon or catfish), cut into small pieces
2 cloves garlic, peeled
1½ teaspoons fine sea salt
½ teaspoon freshly ground pepper
1 serrano pepper or ½ teaspoon red pepper flakes
1 teaspoon turmeric
2 teaspoons ground cumin seeds
½ teaspoon baking powder
4 spring onions roughly chopped (white and green parts)
1 cup/85g roughly chopped fresh cilantro
2 teaspoons dried fenugreek leaves
2 tablespoons chickpea flour
2 eggs, lightly beaten

Cooking oil spray

TAMARIND AND DATE GLAZE

2 tablespoons tamarind paste dissolved in 2 tablespoons water
½ cup/170g date molasses
¼ teaspoon fine sea salt
¼ teaspoon cinnamon

1. *To cook the potato:* In a small saucepan place the potato, cover with water, and bring to a boil. Reduce heat to medium, cover, and cook for 20 to 25 minutes until tender. Drain, allow to cool, peel, and cut into quarters.

2. *To make the paste:* In a food processor, place the potato and pulse until grainy. Transfer to a large mixing bowl and set aside.

3. Ensure all small bones have been removed from the fish fillets and place them with the rest of the ingredients for the paste, except the eggs, in the food processor and pulse until you have a creamy mixture. Transfer it to the mixing bowl with the potatoes, add the eggs and fold, using a rubber spatula, until you have a smooth paste. Cover and chill in the fridge for at least 15 minutes and up to 24 hours.

4. *To make the patties:* Preheat the oven to 450°F/230°C. Generously spray the surface with oil.

5. Scoop up the fish paste using an ice-cream scoop. Use oily hands to mold 12 walnut-sized balls.

6. Gently arrange them side by side in the sheet pan. Gently flatten each ball into patties. Spray with oil and bake in the oven for 15 to 20 minutes until lightly golden.

7. Meanwhile, *to make the glaze:* In a small saucepan, combine all the ingredients for the glaze, stir well, and cook over low heat for 5 minutes. Keep warm until ready to serve.

8. Remove patties from the oven and drizzle the glaze on top. Garnish according to your fancy. I like to use lettuce leaf and some herbs to make a delicious wrap with these patties. *Nush-e joon!*

STOVETOP VARIATION

In a wide skillet, heat 6 tablespoons oil over medium heat until hot but not smoking. Fry the patties on both sides until golden brown.

VARIATION

Shrimp Patties
kotlet-e maygu

Replace the fish with 1lb/450g, cleaned and deveined shrimp. Everything else remains the same.

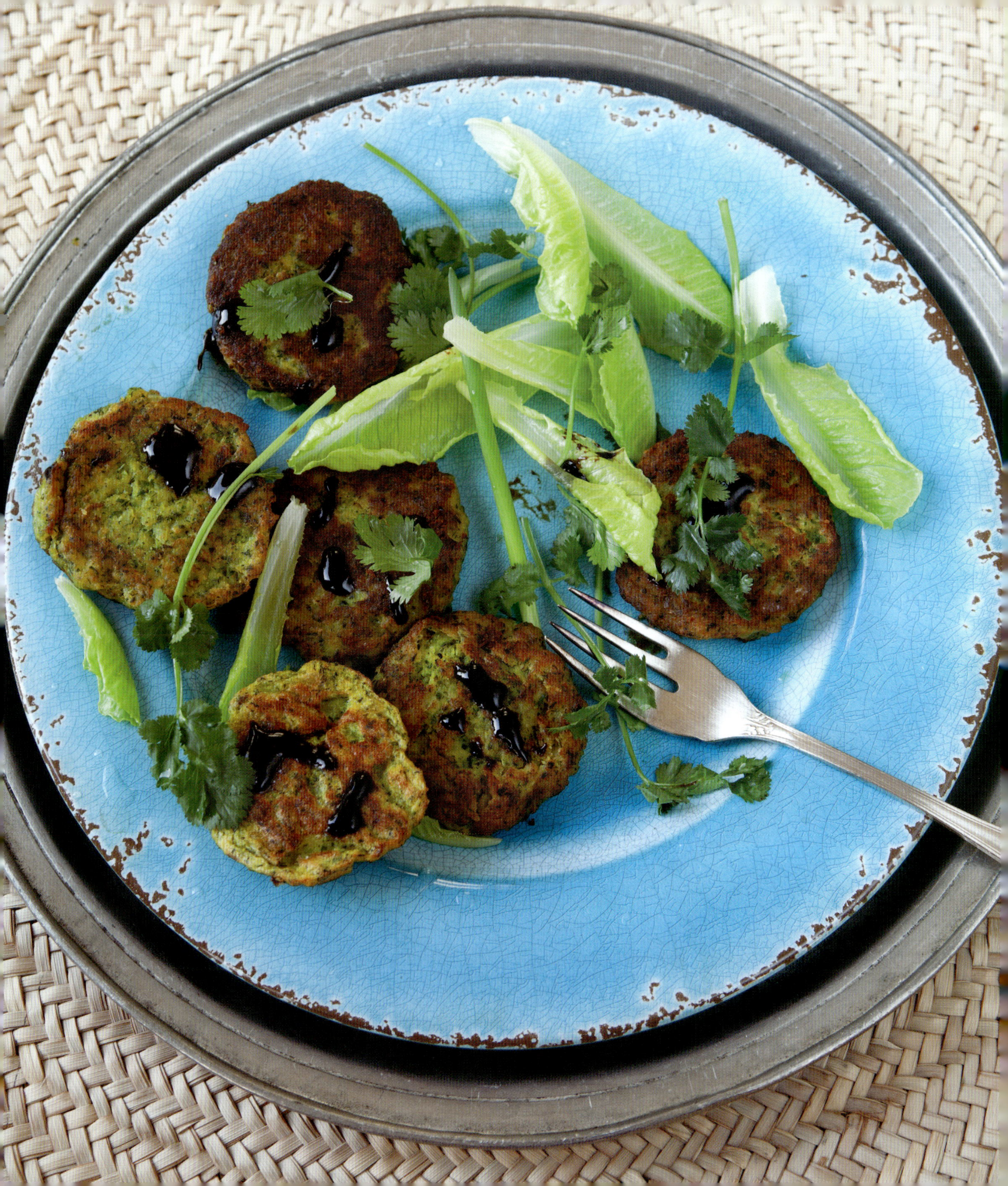

Spicy Chickpea + Wheat Flour Balls
pakurah

Makes 20 balls, serves 4 to 6
Prep: 30 minutes + 1 hour of resting
Cooking: 30 minutes

YEAST

1 tablespoon/1 envelope active dry yeast
1 tablespoon sugar
1½ cups/360ml warm water (100°F/38°C)

BATTER

1 medium onion, quartered
2 cloves garlic
2 serrano peppers, stemmed
1 cup/100g unbleached all-purpose flour
2 cups/200g raw chickpea flour
1 teaspoon turmeric
1 tablespoon ground cumin
1 tablespoon fine sea salt
½ teaspoon freshly ground pepper
2 cups/170g chopped fresh cilantro
1 egg

2 cups/480ml oil for frying

These spicy chickpea balls, popular around the Persian Gulf port of Bandar Abbas, show the influence of Indian cooking more than that of mainland Iran. I adapted this recipe from a street vendor in the Chabahar market.

1. **To prepare the yeast:** In a small bowl, place the yeast, sugar, and 1 cup/240ml of warm water, and allow to rest for 10 minutes undisturbed. Place a wire rack in a rimmed sheet pan and set aside.

2. **To make the batter:** In a food processor, place the onion, garlic, and serrano peppers and pulse until grainy. Add the rest of the ingredients for the batter and mix until you have a smooth batter.

3. Add the dissolved yeast and mix until you have a thick batter.

4. Cover with plastic wrap and allow to rest undisturbed at room temperature for 1 hour.

5. **To cook the balls:** In a small saucepan heat 2 cups/480ml oil over medium heat until hot but not smoking.

6. Scoop up a spoonful of batter (use an ice-cream scoop for best results) and gently drop it into the hot oil. Cook in batches, 3 or 4 balls at a time (beware that they don't stick together) until golden on the outer edges. Gently turn and cook until golden brown all over and crispy (about 4 minutes).

7. Use tongs to transfer the balls onto the rack in the sheet pan. Serve hot with Black Carrot Pickle (page 671) and Onion Cucumber and Coriander Pickle (page 675) and a green salad. *Nush-e joon!*

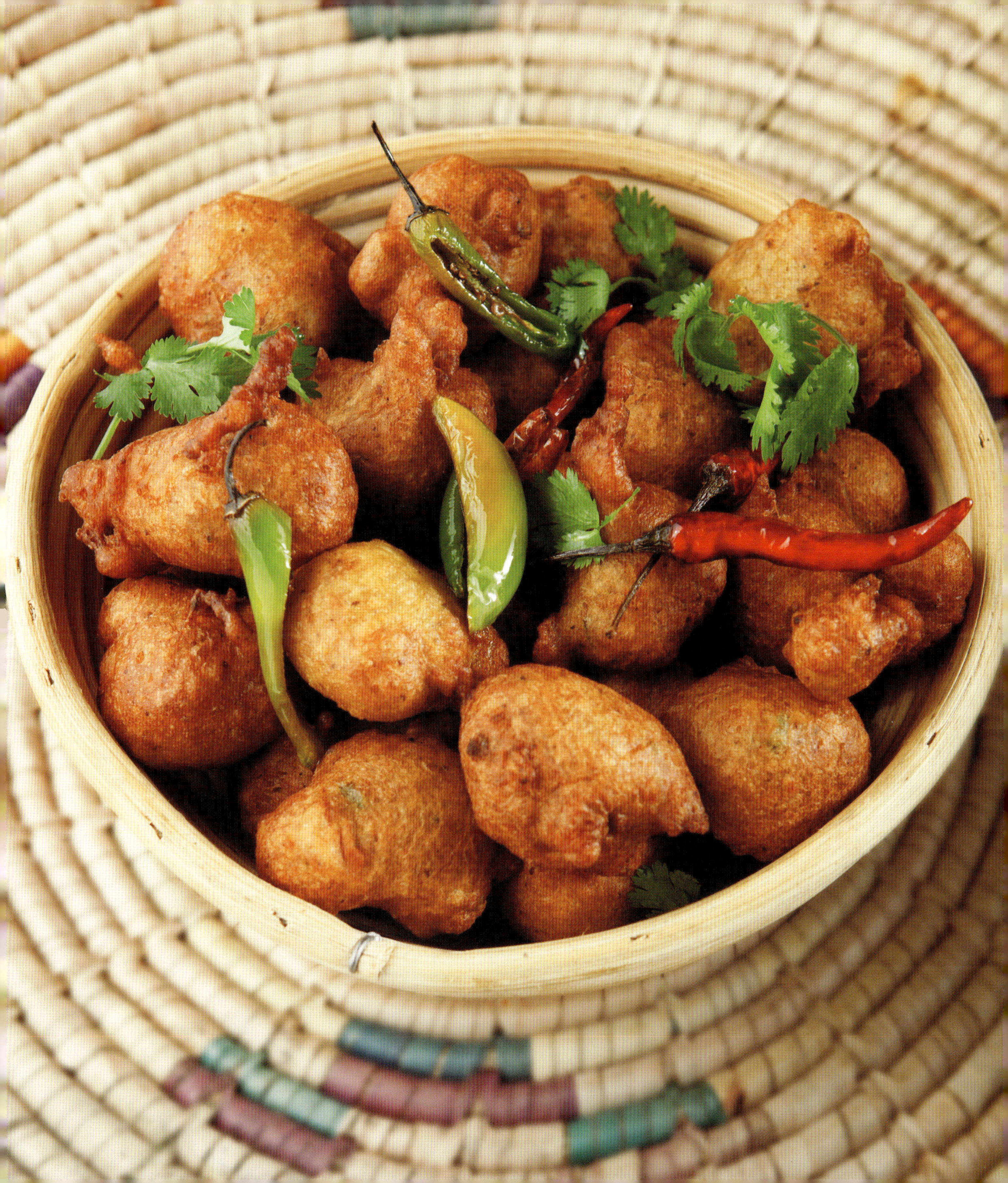

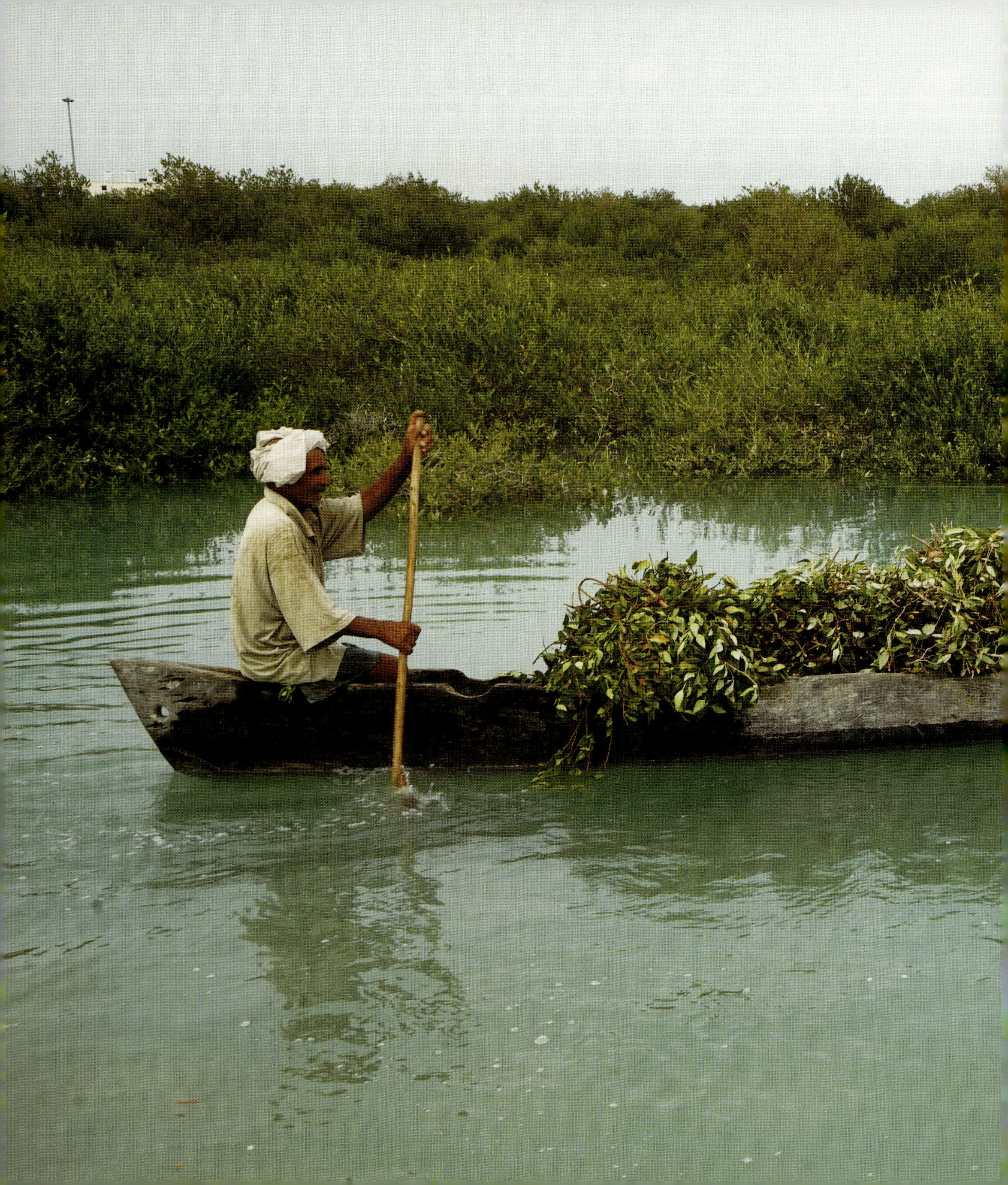

The hara trees that dominate the mangrove forests of Qeshm island in the Persian Gulf are hardy and grow in saltwater. They flower in late summer and produce a sweet, almond-like fruit. Traditionally, the nutritious leaves (equivalent to alfalfa or barley) were used as feed stock, but these days the forests are protected and in winter serve as a major habitat for migratory birds, which include herons, flamingos, and eagles. These groves also provide a suitable seabed for the ovulation of fish in the Persian Gulf.

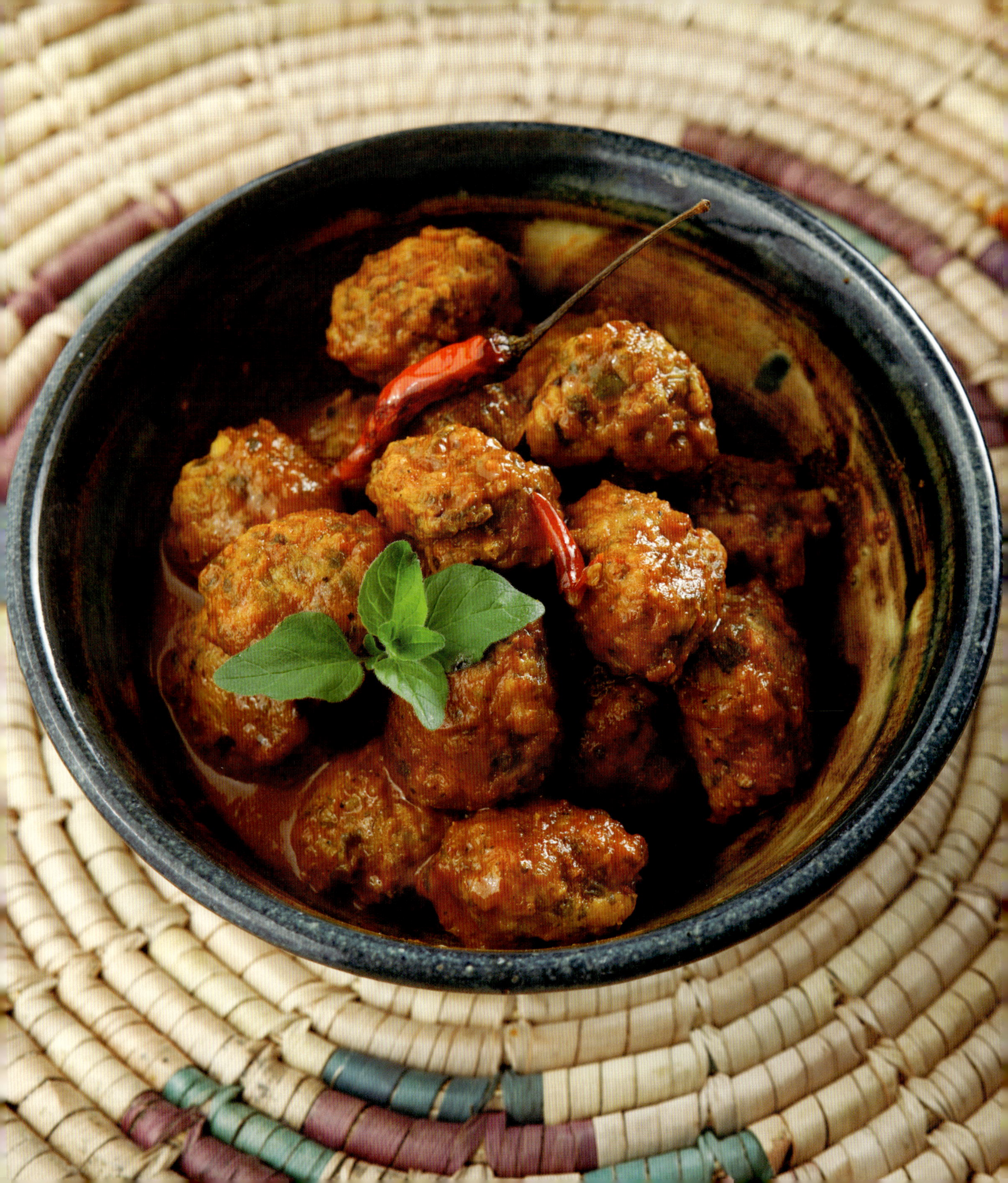

Shrimp Balls in Spicy Sauce

chubeh

Serves 4
Prep: 20 minutes
Cooking: 45 minutes

SHRIMP PASTE

1 small onion, peeled and quartered
4 cloves garlic, peeled
1 serrano chili, stem removed, or ½ teaspoon red pepper flakes
1 teaspoon fine sea salt
½ teaspoon freshly ground pepper
1 tablespoon dried Persian lime powder
1 cup/85g chopped fresh cilantro
1 tablespoon dried fenugreek leaves
2 tablespoons rice flour
1lb/450g shrimp, peeled, deveined, rinsed and patted dry

¼ cup/60ml oil (for sautéing the shrimp)

BROTH

1 teaspoon Bandari seven-spice *advieh*
1 teaspoon fine sea salt
¼ teaspoon freshly ground pepper
½ teaspoon turmeric
1 tablespoon ground hearts of dried Persian limes
5 medium tomatoes (about 2½ cups/500g), peeled and finely diced

GARNISH

1 cup/85g chopped fresh cilantro or your favorite herbs

I was totally surprised to find out how delicious the combination of fenugreek and shrimp could be. These shrimp balls are very easy to make and wonderfully tasty.

1. **To make the shrimp paste:** In a food processor, combine all the ingredients for the shrimp paste and pulse until you have a grainy paste.

2. In a medium-sized sauté pan, heat the oil over low heat until hot. Shape the shrimp paste into walnut-sized balls and add them to the pan as you make them.

3. Sauté the shrimp balls over low heat by shaking the pan back and forth until they are golden brown on all sides.

4. **To make the broth:** Add the *advieh*, salt, pepper, turmeric, and dried limes and sauté for 1 minute longer.

5. Add the tomatoes and give it a gentle stir. Bring to a boil. Reduce heat to low, cover, and simmer for 30 to 35 minutes until the sauce is reduced. Adjust seasoning to taste and garnish. I like to serve these shrimp balls with lettuce or tortillas and eat them as wraps. *Nush-e joon!*

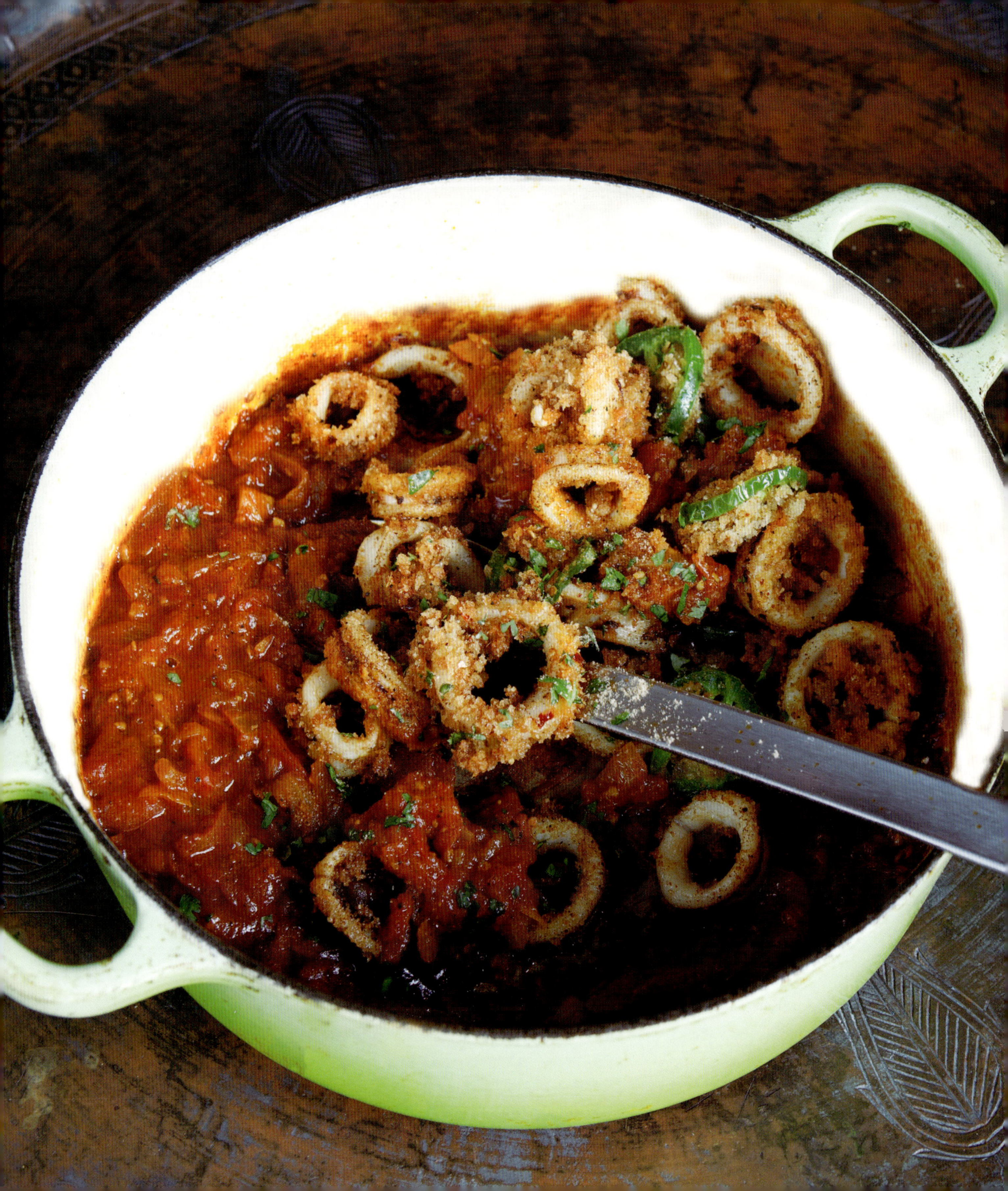

Calamari in Tomato Sauce
khoresh-e hasht pa-ye bandari

Serves 8
Prep: 20 minutes
Cooking: 1 hour

TOMATO SAUCE

4 tablespoons oil
1 medium onion, peeled and thinly sliced
2 cloves garlic, peeled and chopped
1 teaspoon fine sea salt
½ teaspoon freshly ground pepper
½ teaspoon ground turmeric
2 teaspoons Bandari seven-spice *advieh*
1 tablespoon tomato paste
2 cups/400g fresh tomatoes, peeled and finely chopped
1 cup/240ml water

DUSTING

1 cup/100g chickpea flour
1 teaspoon fine sea salt
1 teaspoon ground black pepper
1 teaspoon ground turmeric
1 tablespoon Bandari seven-spice *advieh*

CALAMARI

8 calamari, cut lengthwise, sides trimmed and scored with a fine diamond pattern on the inner surface, then cut in rings, rinsed, and patted dry
2 jalapeño peppers, ¼ inch/6mm rings

2 eggs beaten with ½ teaspoon turmeric

2 cup/480ml oil for frying

GARNISH

1 tablespoon ground hearts of dried Persian limes
1 cup/85g chopped fresh cilantro leaves

There were plenty of locally caught squid, octopus, and cuttlefish in the markets but rarely on any restaurant menu in Bushehr and Bandar Abbas. They are mostly eaten by the locals at home and often in a tomato sauce. You can also use this sauce with fish instead of calamari.

1. **To make the tomato sauce:** Heat the oil in a laminated cast-iron pot over medium heat. Add the onion and garlic, and sauté for 10 to 15 minutes until lightly golden brown.

2. Add all the spices and the tomato paste, and stir-fry for 1 minute. Add the fresh tomatoes and water, and bring to a boil. Reduce heat to low, cover, and simmer for 20 minutes. Keep warm.

3. **To make the dusting:** In a small bowl, combine all the ingredients for the dusting and mix well.

4. **To cook the calamari:** Heat 2 cups oil in a small saucepan over medium heat until hot but not smoking.

5. Dip the calamari and jalapeño pepper rings in the beaten eggs, and dredge them in the dusting. Gently drop them in the hot oil and fry until golden brown on all sides.

6. Place the sauce in a shallow serving platter and arrange the fried calamari on top. Sprinkle with lime powder and cilantro leaves. Serve with bread or plain rice. *Nush-e joon!*

VARIATION

Replace the calamari with 2lb/900g fish fillets, skin removed.

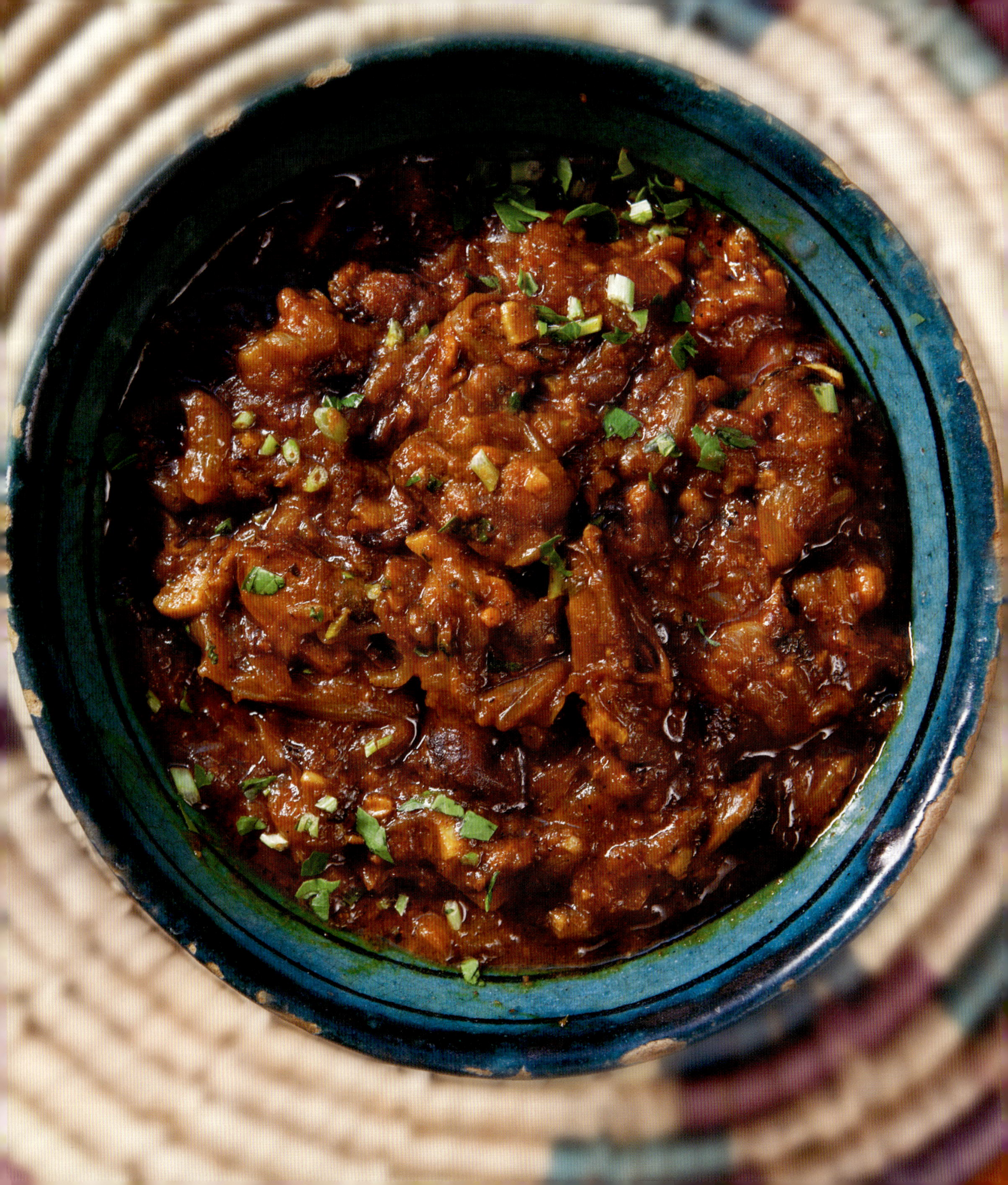

Mussel + Tamarind Braise
kategh muluk /sadaf-e do kafeh

Serves 4
Prep: 15 minutes
Cooking: 15 minutes

TAMARIND + TOMATO SAUCE

¼ cup/60ml oil
4 medium onions, thinly sliced
5 cloves garlic, peeled and sliced
¼ teaspoon fine sea salt
½ teaspoon freshly ground pepper
½ teaspoon turmeric
½ teaspoon cinnamon
½ teaspoon ground cardamom
1 tablespoon Bandari seven-spice *advieh*
1 tablespoon tomato paste
2 tablespoons tamarind paste

MUSSELS

½lb/225g shucked mussels

GARNISH

2 tablespoons chopped fresh cilantro

I adapted this recipe from Raviyeh Daryanavardi in Qeshm.

1. **To make the sauce:** In a medium-sized laminated cast-iron braiser, heat the oil over medium heat, and sauté the onions and garlic until golden brown.

2. Add the salt, pepper, turmeric, cinnamon, cardamom, *advieh*, tomato paste, and tamarind paste, and sauté for 1 minute.

3. Add 1½ cups/360ml water and bring to a boil.

4. **To cook the mussels:** Add the mussels, reduce heat to low, cover partially, and cook for 10 to 15 minutes until the mussels are tender and the sauce is reduced.

4. Adjust seasoning to taste, garnish with cilantro, and serve with bread. *Nush-e joon!*

Poached Lobster or Crab with Dried Limes

khorak-e singu/kharchang

Serves 4
Prep: 15 minutes
Cooking: 30 minutes

¼ cup/60ml oil
2 medium onions, peeled and thinly sliced
1 teaspoon fine sea salt
½ teaspoon freshly ground pepper
½ teaspoon turmeric
1 teaspoon Bandari seven-spice *advieh*
1 tablespoon ground hearts of dried Persian limes
1 tablespoon tomato paste
1 cup/240ml water
½lb (about 2 cups/225g) poached lobster or crab meat

GARNISH

¼ cup/20g chop fresh cilantro leaves

1. Heat the oil in a medium saucepan over medium heat. Sauté the onions until golden brown. Add the salt, pepper, turmeric, *advieh*, hearts of dried lime, and tomato paste. Stir-fry for 1 minute.

2. Add the water and bring to a boil. Add the lobster meat. Reduce heat to low, cover, and simmer for 2 to 3 minutes until all the juices have been absorbed. Adjust seasoning to taste. Garnish with cilantro. *Nush-e joon!*

You can either poach or grill the crab or lobster:

POACHING CRAB OR LOBSTER

To poach: Fill a large pot with 2in/5cm water and add 2 tablespoons fine sea salt, and bring to a boil over high heat. Add the lobster (using gloves and tongs), cover immediately and bring back to a boil. Reduce heat to medium, cover tightly, and boil for 15 to 20 minutes until the color turns orange. Drain and allow to cool. Remove the meat using nut crackers and thin forks.

GRILLING LOBSTER OR CRAB

To grill: Wash the lobster, sprinkle with ½ cup/130g fine sea salt all over and allow to rest for 30 minutes. Grill over hot charcoal. Allow to cool, break shell, and separate the meat from the shell.

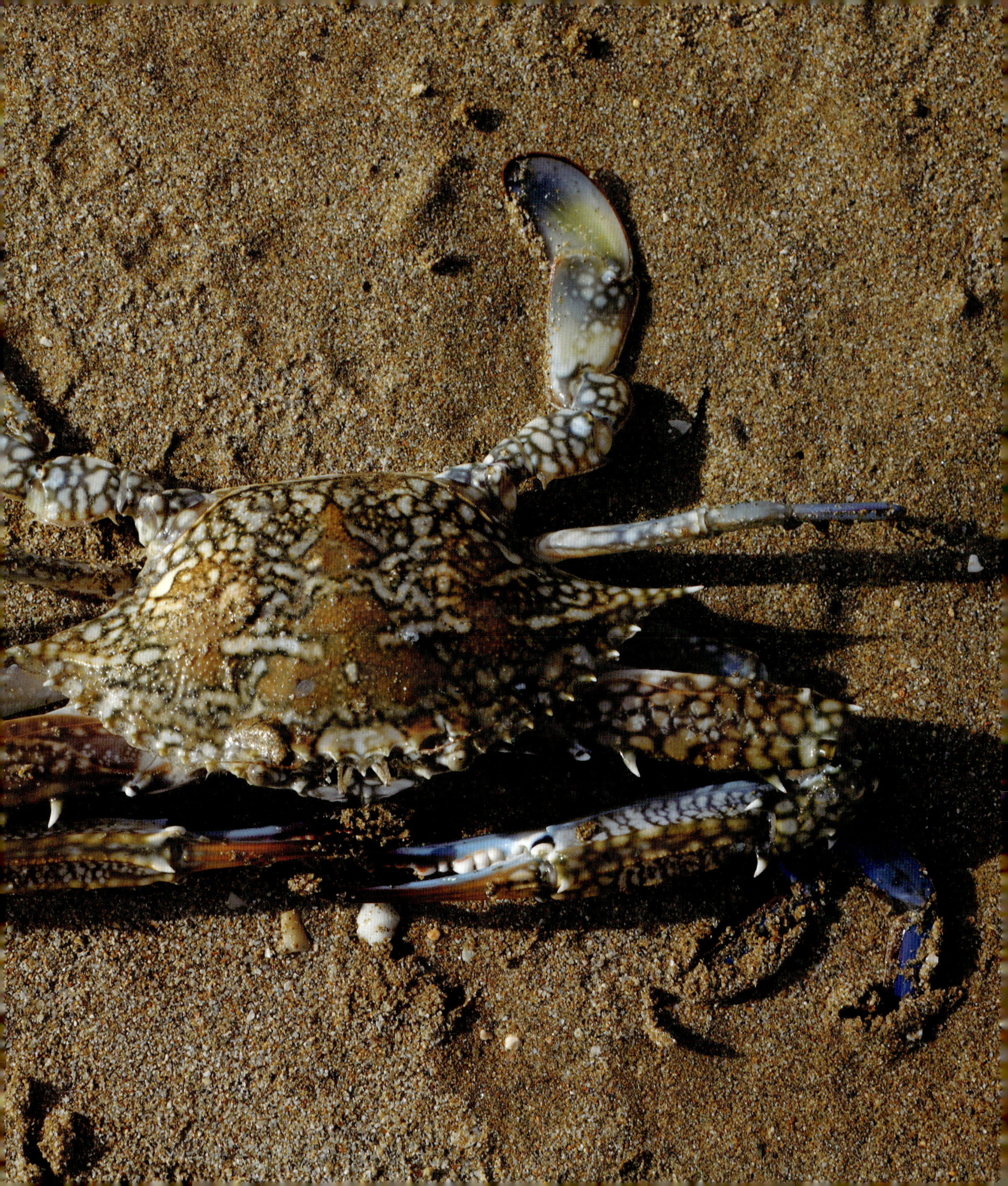

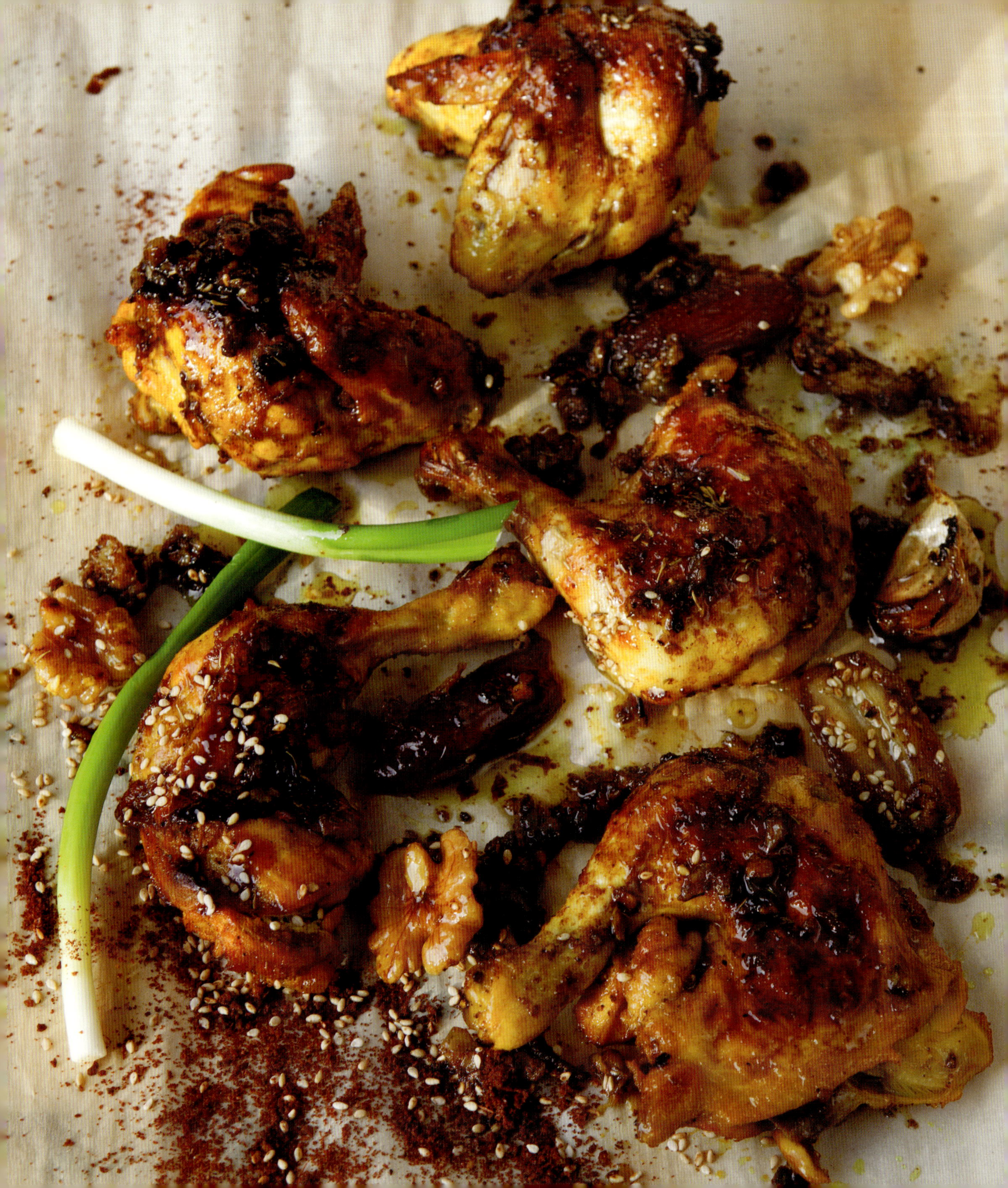

Roast Chicken with Dates, Walnuts + Sumac

morgh-e beryan ba somaq-o khorma

Serves 4 to 6
Prep: 30 minutes
Cooking: 1½ hours

DRY RUB

1 tablespoon fine sea salt
1 teaspoon freshly ground pepper
1 tablespoon turmeric

CHICKEN

1 chicken or 2 Cornish hens (about 4lb/1.8kg), spine removed, quartered, rinsed and patted dry

WET RUB

1 cup/125g walnuts
1 small onion, peeled and quartered
6 cloves garlic, peeled
1 teaspoon fine sea salt
1 teaspoon freshly ground black pepper
3 tablespoons sumac powder
1 tablespoon dry thyme
1 tablespoon raw sesame seeds
½ cup/80g pitted dates
¼ cup/60ml fresh lime juice or vinegar
1/4 cup/60ml raw sesame oil

BASTE

¼ cup/60ml oil or ghee
2 tablespoons date molasses
2 cloves garlic, peeled and grated

The date molasses baste brings about an interesting texture and an unexpected taste to this roast.

1. **Dry rub:** Place all the ingredients for the dry rub in small bowl and mix well. Rub the chicken pieces all over with the dry rub. Allow to rest in the fridge for 1 hour or up to 24 hours.

2. Preheat oven to 450°F/230°C. Line a rimed sheet pan with parchment paper.

3. **Wet rub:** In a food processor combine all ingredients for the wet rub and pulse until you have a coarsely chopped mixture. Rub it all over the chicken and push some under the skins. Arrange the chicken pieces on the sheet pan.

4. Cover with a layer of oiled parchment paper and bake in the preheated oven for 1¼ hours.

5. In a small saucepan, mix all the ingredients for the baste and keep warm.

6. Uncover and continue to bake for another 15 minutes until crispy.

7. Transfer to a serving platter and baste the chicken. .Serve with bread and a green salad. *Nush-e joon!*

The Persian Gulf

Chicken Kabab with Dried Lime + Mint

jujeh kabab-e bandari

Serves 6 to 8
Prep: 20 minutes + overnight marinating
Cooking: 15 minutes

MARINADE

4 teaspoons fine sea salt
2 teaspoons freshly ground pepper
1 teaspoon turmeric
2 teaspoons ground cardamom
3 tablespoons ground hearts of dried Persian limes
1 tablespoon red chili flakes
2 tablespoons dried mint
1 medium onion, coarsely sliced
6 cloves garlic, peeled and sliced
½ cup/120ml fresh lime juice
½ cup/120ml apple cider vinegar
¾ cup/180ml olive oil

CHICKEN

1 chicken, cut up into 10 pieces (about 4lb/1.8kg), or 2½ pounds/1.1kg boneless chicken thighs, rinsed, patted dry, and cut into 3 x 2in/75 x 50mm strips

BASTE

½ cup/110g butter or oil
Juice of one lime
2 cups/170g chopped fresh mint or ¼ cup/20g dried

GARNISH

1 package (12oz/340g) lavash bread
1 tablespoon ground hearts of dried Persian limes
3 bunches fresh basil leaves

SKEWERS

12 flat ½in/1cm sword-like metal skewers or 16 wooden skewers

This chicken kabab tastes quite different from the standard one served in Tehran or Tabriz. The combination of cardamom, dried lime, chili, and mint give it a rare flavor, especially if you marinate your chicken for 3 days and cook it over charcoal.

1. **To marinate:** In a 4qt/3.7l non-reactive container, combine all the ingredients for the marinade and mix well. Add the chicken and toss well. Cover and allow to marinate overnight and up to 3 days in the refrigerator. Turn the chicken twice during this period (best results are with 3 days of marination).

2. **To prepare the grill:** Start a bed of charcoal 30 minutes before you want to cook and let it burn until the coals glow evenly, or preheat the oven broiler. Keep in mind that the success of a good kabab depends on a very hot grill.

3. **Meanwhile, to skewer the chicken:** Skewer the wings, breasts, and legs onto different skewers (they require different cooking times). Place the skewers on a sheet pan next to you.

4. **To prepare the baste:** In a small saucepan, heat the butter, lime juice, and mint over low heat, and keep warm.

5. **To cook the chicken:** Grill the chicken for 8 to 15 minutes, turning frequently until done. The chicken is done when the juice that runs out is yellow rather than pink. Baste the chicken.

6. Spread a lavash bread on a flat serving platter. Remove the chicken from the grill and place on the lavash bread. Keep chicken on the skewers until just before serving—this helps to keep it warm.

7. To remove the chicken from skewers steady them on the platter with a piece of bread and pull out the skewers. Sprinkle dried lime over the chicken and garnish with basil. *Nush-e joon!*

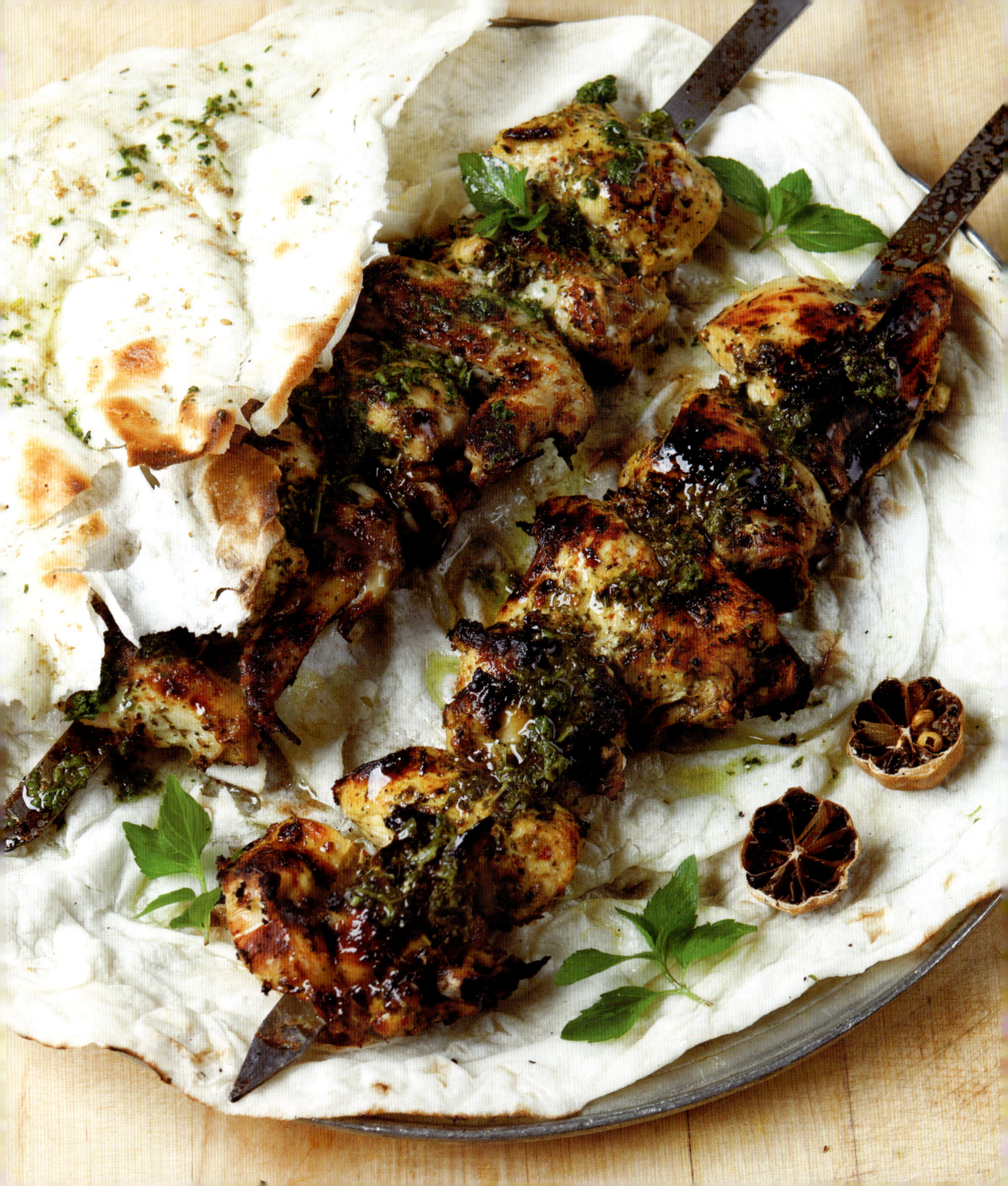

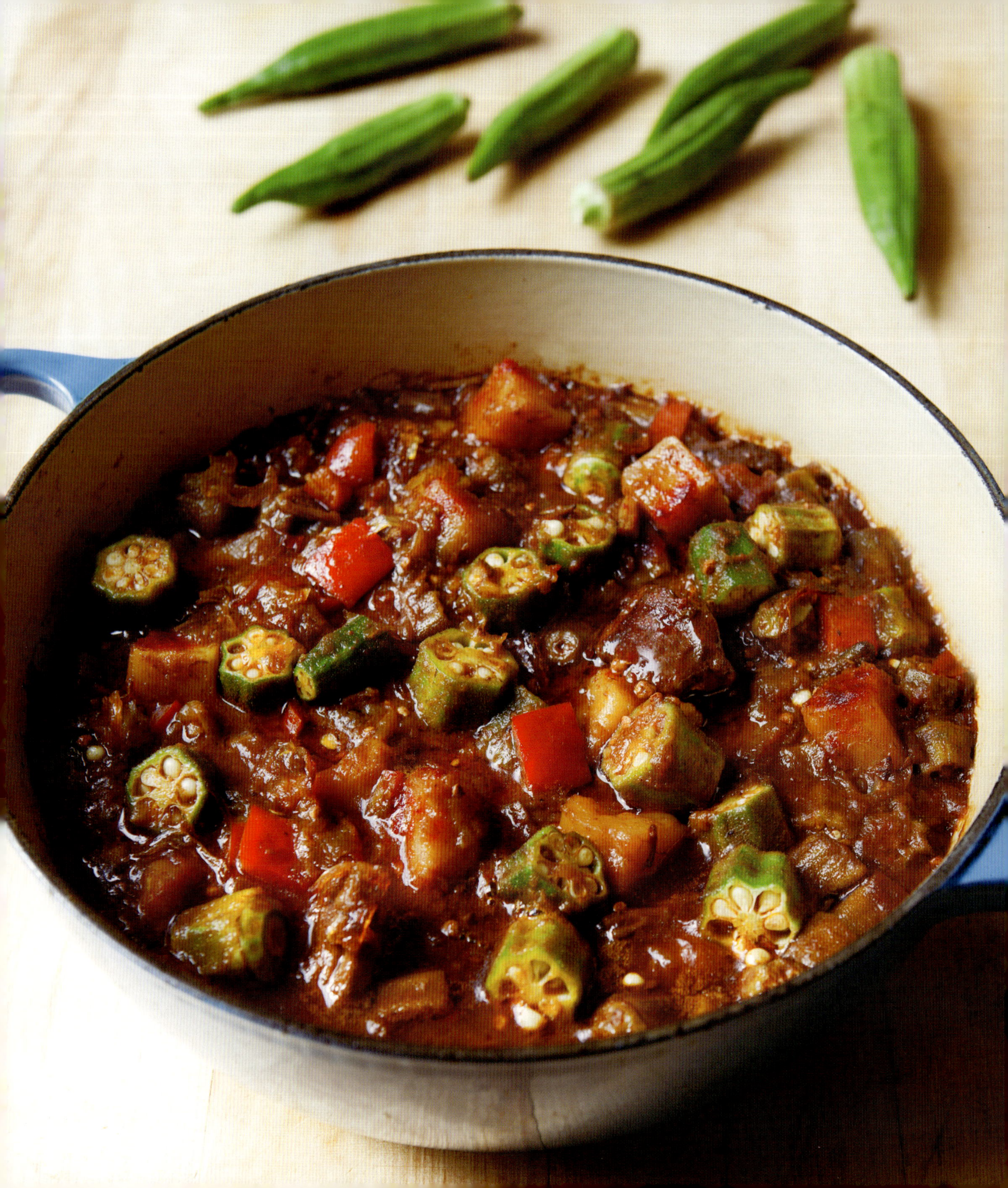

Spicy Okra, Lamb + Potato Braise

khoresh-e bamieh ba sibzamini

Serves 4
Prep: 30 minutes
Cooking: 2½ hours

LAMB

2 tablespoons oil
2 medium onions, peeled and thinly sliced
2 teaspoons fine sea salt
½ teaspoon freshly ground pepper
1 teaspoon turmeric
1lb/450g boneless leg of lamb cut into 2in/5cm pieces
4 cloves garlic, peeled and grated
1 jalapeño pepper, chopped, or 1 teaspoon red pepper flakes
1in/2.5cm fresh ginger, peeled and grated, or 1 teaspoon ginger powder
2 tablespoons tomato paste
2 fresh tomatoes, peeled and chopped

POTATO + OKRA

2 tablespoons oil
1lb/450g russet potatoes, peeled and cut into 1in/2.5cm cubes.
1 red bell pepper, seeded and chopped
1lb/450g fresh or frozen okra, cut into ½in/6mm lengths (if using baby okra, no need to cut them)
2 tablespoons tamarind paste
1 teaspoon date molasses

Okra originated somewhere around the Horn of Africa, on the sea routes of the Persian Gulf. It has been popular in Indian and Persian Gulf cooking from ancient times. These days, in the American South, it's a popular ingredient in gumbo.

1. **To cook the lamb:** Heat 2 tablespoons of oil in a laminated cast-iron pot over medium heat. Sauté the onions until golden. Add the salt, pepper, turmeric, and lamb, and sauté until golden brown.

2. Add the garlic, jalapeno, ginger, and tomato paste, and sauté for 2 minutes longer. Add the fresh tomatoes, 2½ cups/600ml of water, and bring to a boil. Reduce heat to low, cover, and simmer for 1½ hours, stirring occasionally.

3. **To cook the okra:** Heat 2 tablespoons of oil in a wide skillet over medium heat. Sauté the potato and bell pepper for 5 minutes. Add the okra and sauté for another 5 minutes. Transfer to the pot

4. Add the tamarind and date molasses. Cover and simmer over low heat for 25 to 35 minutes until the potato and okra are tender.

5. Adjust the seasoning to taste by adding more tamarind paste or salt. Serve with bread or rice. *Nush-e joon!*

Grouper, Cilantro, Garlic + Tamarind Braise
qaliyeh-ye mahi

Serves 6
Prep: 25 minutes
Cooking: 1½ hours

HERB SAUCE

¼ cup/60ml oil
1 small onion, peeled and quartered
6 cloves garlic, peeled
6 cups/510g roughly chopped fresh cilantro (leaves and stems)
3 tablespoons dried fenugreek leaves
2 teaspoons fine sea salt
½ teaspoon freshly ground pepper
2 teaspoons turmeric
1 teaspoon ground coriander seeds
1 serrano chili, finely chopped, or ½ teaspoon red pepper flakes
3 tablespoons rice flour

2 tablespoons tamarind paste dissolved in 3 cups/720ml water
1 teaspoon date molasses

DUSTING

1 teaspoon fine sea salt
½ teaspoon freshly ground pepper
½ teaspoon turmeric
1 tablespoon Bandari seven-spice *advieh*

FISH

2lb/900g grouper or halibut fillets, skins and any small bones removed, cut into 3in/75mm lengths
2 tablespoons oil

This is one of the most cherished dishes in every part of southern Iran. Served over plain rice, it is also one of my favorites. I tried it in every southern region. In each place they claimed that their version was the superior—a cute rivalry. For me, the best was the one we made with Dowlat Khabarkhosh using a grouper/hamur, which we bought fresh from the fish market that day. We made it with cilantro and fresh green garlic. The fish, cooked with its bone, was spicy and delectable. I loved it. If you feel adventurous, make it with a whole fish, cut up, but I'm giving you a recipe here that's simpler to make and simpler to eat using fish fillets.

1. **To make the herb sauce:** In a food processor, place all the ingredients for the sauce except the tamarind water and date molasses, and pulse until you have a smooth, green paste.

2. **To cook the braise:** Heat ¼ cup/60ml oil in a medium-sized sauté pan over low heat and stir-fry the green paste for 10 to 15 minutes until the aroma begins to rise.

3. Add the tamarind water and date molasses. Stir well and bring to a boil. Reduce heat to low. Cover and simmer for 30 minutes.

4. **To cook the fish:** In a small bowl, mix together all the dusting ingredients. Dust both sides of the fish fillets and set aside.

5. In a wide iron skillet, heat the oil over medium-high heat until very hot but not smoking. Sear the fish fillets on both sides until golden brown.

6. Add the fish to the braise, bring to a simmer, cover, and cook over low heat for 30 minutes. Adjust seasoning to taste by adding more tamarind paste or salt. Cover and keep warm until ready to serve. Serve with plain rice. *Nush-e joon!*

VARIATION

In step 4, you can replace the fish fillets with 1½lb/675g large tiger prawns, shelled, heads and tails removed, butterflied, deveined, rinsed, and patted dry. Everything else remains the same

The Persian Gulf grouper/*hamur* at the fish market in Bushehr. It is the preferred fish for making the tamarind and cilantro braise/*qaliyeh-ye mahi* (recipe on the facing page).

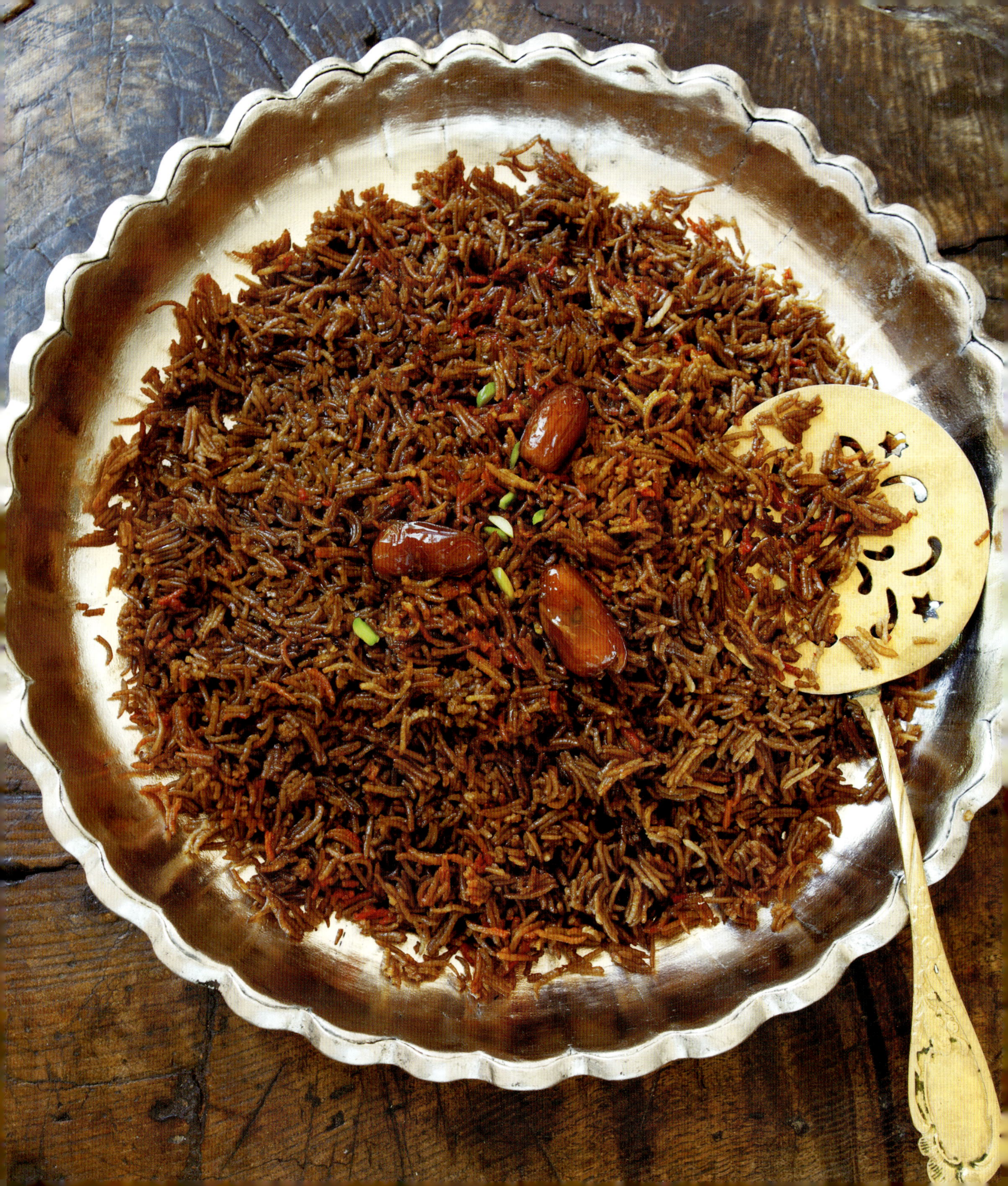

Rice Steamed in Date Molasses
shireh-ye khorma polow

Serves 6
Prep: 5 minutes
Cooking: 40 minutes

2 cups/400g basmati rice
4 cups/960ml water
½ teaspoon fine sea salt
½ cup/120g date molasses
¼ cup/60ml oil or ghee
¼ teaspoon ground saffron threads dissolved in 2 tablespoons rose water (optional)

GARNISH

2 tablespoons slivered pistachio kernels
2 tablespoons slivered almonds

I tried this wonderful, sweet rice for the the first time in Bandar Abbas. It was served with a spicy seared fish (p.112, variation).

1. Wash the rice by placing it in a large container, cover it with water, agitate gently with your hand, then pour off the water. Repeat 4 to 5 times until the water is clear.

2. Place the water, salt, and date molasses in a medium-sized non-stick pot and bring to a boil over high heat.

3. Add the rice, give it a few gentle stirs with a wooden spoon, reduce heat to medium, cover and simmer for 15 to 20 minutes until the rice has absorbed all the water.

4. Swirl the oil and saffron-rose water over the rice. Wrap the lid of the pot with a clean dish towel and cover firmly to prevent steam from escaping. Steam the rice for 20 minutes over low heat.

5. Remove the pot from heat and allow to cool for 5 minutes on a damp surface without uncovering.

6. Gently take one spatula full of rice at a time and mound the rice on a serving platter. *Nush-e joon!*

VARIATION

Rice Cooked in Date Juice
ab-e khorma polow

In a medium-sized saucepan, bring 1lb/450g pitted dates and 4 cups/960ml water to a boil. Reduce heat to medium, cover, and simmer for 5 to 6 minutes until the dates are soft. Strain through a fine-mesh colander into a non-stick pot. Use a masher to press down on the dates to get as much of the juice as possible. Keep the juice and discard the pulp. Add the rice and salt to the pot and bring to a boil. Reduce heat to medium and cook for 15 to 20 minutes until the rice has absorbed all the date juice. Drizzle the oil and saffron-rose water on top. Cover tightly and cook for another 20 minutes over low heat.

The Persian Gulf

Spicy Shrimp + Rice
havari-ye maygu

Serves 6
Prep: 20 minutes
Cooking: 30 minutes

RICE

2 cups/400g basmati rice
½ teaspoon ground saffron threads dissolved in 2 tablespoons water

ONION AND SPICES

¾ cup/180ml oil or ghee
2 medium onions, thinly sliced
1 tablespoon fine sea salt
½ teaspoon freshly ground pepper
½ teaspoon red pepper flakes
1 teaspoon turmeric
1 teaspoon ground cardamom
½ teaspoon ground cinnamon
1 tablespoon cumin seeds
2 tablespoons ground hearts of dried Persian limes
1 cup chopped fresh cilantro
1 tablespoon dried fenugreek leaves
2 tablespoons tamarind paste (optional)
½ cup/75g raisins

SHRIMP

1lb/450g peeled and deveined shrimp, rinsed and patted dry

GARNISH

1 cup/85g chopped fresh cilantro
1 serrano pepper, thinly sliced

Growing up in Tehran, I was not familiar with spicy rice from this part of Iran, but I love the flavor. I adapted this recipe from Raviyeh Daryanavardi in Qeshm, where we made this dish together.

1. Wash the rice by placing it in a large container and covering it with water. Agitate gently with your hand and then pour off the water. Repeat 4 to 5 times until the water is clear.

2. **To cook the rice:** In a large non-stick pot, bring 8 cups/1.9l water and 2 tablespoons fine sea salt to a boil. Add the rice and boil briskly for 7 to 10 minutes, stirring gently with a wooden spoon to loosen any stuck grains. Drain the rice in a large fine-mesh colander. Set aside.

3. **To cook the onion and spices:** In a wide skillet heat ½ cup/120ml oil over medium heat and sauté the onions until golden brown. Add the rest of the ingredients and sauté for 1 minute. Add 1 cup/240ml water and bring to a boil. Add the shrimp, cover, and cook for 1 to 2 minutes until they start to change color (do not overcook the shrimp as it will continue cooking in the rice). Remove from heat and set aside.

4. **To assemble the rice and shrimp:** In the non-stick pot, place 2 tablespoons oil and mound alternating layers of rice and shrimp mixture to form a pyramid.

5. Pour the remaining oil and ½ cup water over the rice. Drizzle the saffron water on top. Wrap the lid of the pot with a clean dish towel and cover firmly to prevent steam from escaping. Steam the rice for 20 minutes over medium heat.

6. Remove from heat. Uncover the pot and gently taking one spatula of rice at a time, mound it on a serving dish. Garnish with the cilantro and sliced serrano pepper. Serve with a salad. *Nush-e joon!*

VARIATIONS

Spicy Fish + Rice
havari-e mahi

Replace the shrimp with 2lb/900g fish fillets, skins removed and cut into 3in/7.5cm strips. Everything else remains the same.

Fish Crusted Rice
tahandaz-e mahi

Replace the shrimp with 2lb/900g fish fillets, skins removed and cut into 3in/7.5cm strips. In step 4 place 2 tablespoons oil in the pot then arrange the fish fillets side by side on the bottom of the pot. Place the rice on top. Add the sauces from cooking the fish on top of the rice. In step 5, cook for 50 minutes over low heat.

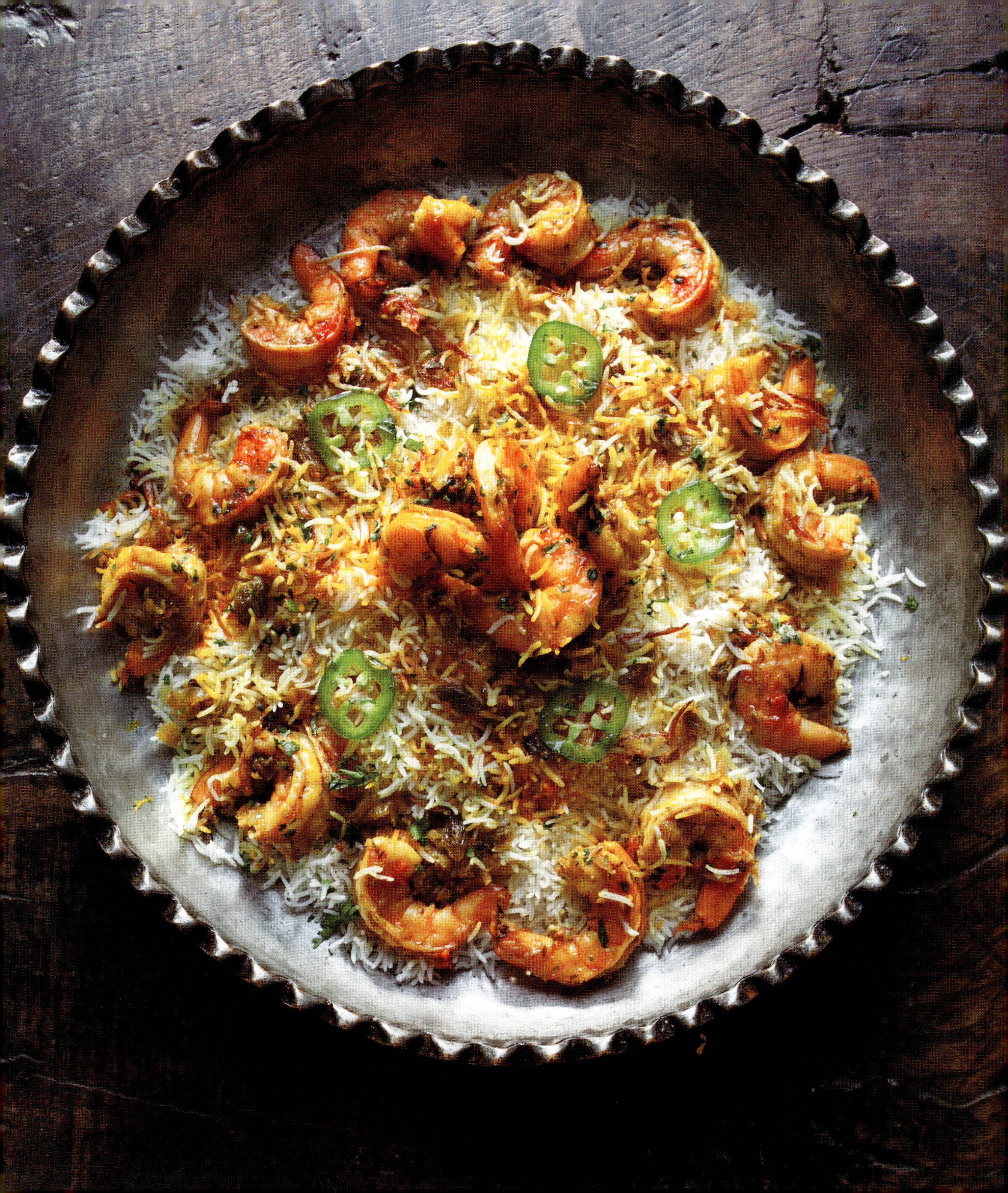

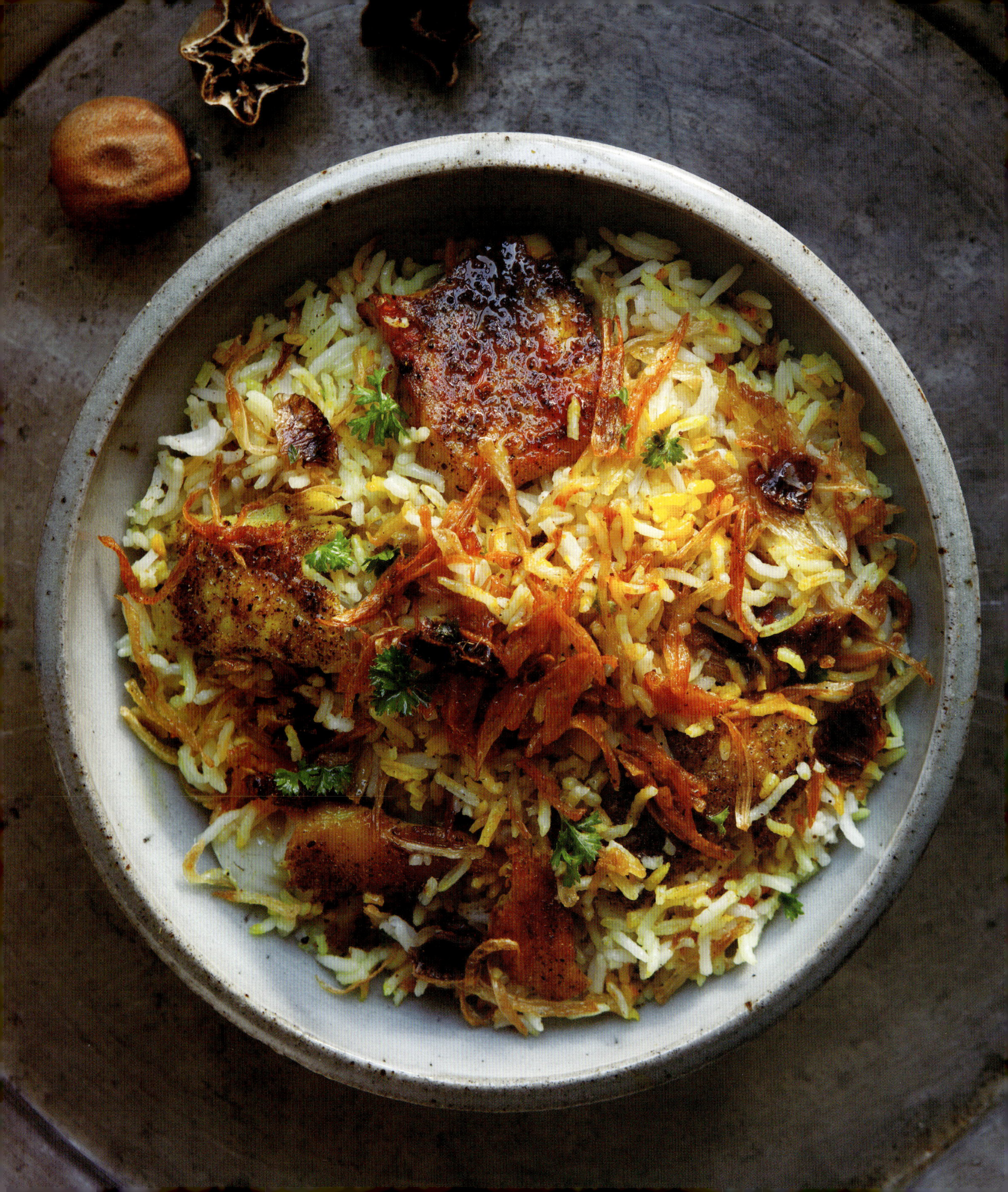

Fish + Dried Lime Rice
dami-e lakh lakh-e bushehri

Serves 6
Prep: 15 minutes + 1 hour in fridge
Cooking: 30 minutes

DUSTING

2 teaspoons fine sea salt
1 teaspoon freshly ground pepper
1 teaspoon turmeric
2 teaspoons Bandari seven-spice *advieh*

FISH

1lb/450g fish fillets, bones removed and cut into 2in/5cm pieces

RICE

½ cup/120ml oil or ghee
2 medium size onions, thinly sliced
2 cloves garlic, grated
1 teaspoon turmeric
2 cups/400g basmati rice, soaked for at least 15 minutes, drained, and rinsed
1 teaspoon fine sea salt
4 cardamom pods, crushed
One 4in/10cm cinnamon stick
1 teaspoon coriander seeds
2 cloves
3 cups/720ml water
2 tablespoons ground hearts of dried Persian limes (about 4 limes)

GARNISH

¼ cup/20g chopped fresh cilantro or dill
½ teaspoon ground saffron threads dissolved in 2 tablespoons warm water (optional)

This recipe is a good example of how Iranian cuisine uses dried limes in surprising and exciting ways.

1. **To prepare the dusting:** Place salt, pepper, turmeric, and *advieh* in a small bowl. Mix well and set aside.

2. Rinse, and pat dry the fish. Rub fish all over with the dusting, cover, and place in the fridge for at least 1 hour and up to 8 hours

3. **To sear the fish:** In a large non-stick pot, heat the oil over medium-high heat until hot but not smoking. Sear the fish on both sides until golden brown. Remove the fish from the pot and set aside.

4. **To cook the rice:** In the same pot heat ½ cup/120ml oil and sauté the onions until golden brown. Add the garlic, turmeric, rice, salt, cardamom, cinnamon, coriander, and cloves, and stir-fry for 1 minute.

5. Add the water and dried lime and bring to a boil. Reduce heat to medium, cover and cook for 10 minutes.

6. Return the fish to the pot. Reduce heat to low, cover tightly, and cook for 15 to 20 minutes until all the liquid has been absorbed. Sprinkle the cilantro and drizzle the saffron water over the rice. Serve with a herb platter and green salad. *Nush-e joon!*

Lamb + Rice with Potato, Onion + Turmeric

goboli pilau-ye bandar-e lengeh

Serves 6 to 8
Prep: 15 minutes + soaking overnight
Cooking: 2½ hour

MEAT

- ½ cup /100g dried chickpeas, soaked overnight in water with ½ teaspoon baking soda, drained and rinsed
- 2lb/900g shoulder of lamb or whole chicken, butterflied and spine removed, rinsed
- 1 tablespoons salt
- 1 teaspoon whole pepper corns
- 1 tablespoon turmeric
- 1 tablespoon ground cardamom
- 1 tablespoon dried rose petals
- 1 tablespoon Bandari *advieh*/abzar
- 2 tablespoons tomato paste
- One 4in/10cm cinnamon stick
- 6 cups /1.4ml water

RICE

- 2 cups/400g white basmati rice, soaked in water for 15 minutes, drained and rinsed

GARNISH/*HASHU*

- ½ cup/110g oil or ghee
- 1lb/450g russet potatoes, peeled and diced into 1in cubes
- 4 medium onions, peeled and thinly sliced
- ½ teaspoon fine sea salt
- 1 teaspoon turmeric
- 2 tablespoons ground hearts of dried Persian limes
- 1 tablespoon dried organic rose petals
- ½ cup/75g currants, soaked in water for 10 minutes and drained

I have adapted this recipe from Ebrahim Mahmoodian, who is from Bandar-e Lengeh. You can make it with lamb or chicken (or even with fish, which you have to boil for 10 minutes). Locally, they usually cook the chickpeas separately, but here I am cooking them with the meat so they can absorb the flavor of the broth. What I love most about this dish is my discovery of turmeric flavored fried onion garnish/hashu.

1. *To cook the lamb:* In a large non-stick pot, place all the ingredients for the meat and bring to a boil. Reduce heat to low, cover, and cook for 1½ to 2 hours for lamb—1 hour for chicken—until the lamb is tender. Place a sieve over a large bowl and drain the lamb. Return the broth to the pot and set the lamb and chickpeas aside to use later.

2. *To cook the rice:* Add the rice to the broth. Give it a gentle stir with a wooden spoon and bring back to a boil. Cover and simmer over low heat for 30 to 40 minutes until the rice is tender and all the broth has been absorbed.

3. *Meanwhile, to make the garnish/hashsu:* In a wide skillet, heat 2 tablespoons oil over medium heat. Add the potatoes and sauté until golden brown. Remove the potatoes from the skillet and set aside.

4. Add the remaining oil to the same skillet and sauté the onion over medium-low heat for 30 minutes or until golden brown. Add the salt, turmeric, dried lime, rose petals, currants, and potato, and sauté for 1 minute longer.

5. Just before serving, heat 2 tablespoons oil in a wide cast-iron skillet over medium heat until hot. Sauté the lamb and chickpeas until golden.

6. *To serve:* Remove the rice from heat and transfer it to a serving platter. Arrange the lamb and garnish/*hashu* on top. *Nush-e joon!*

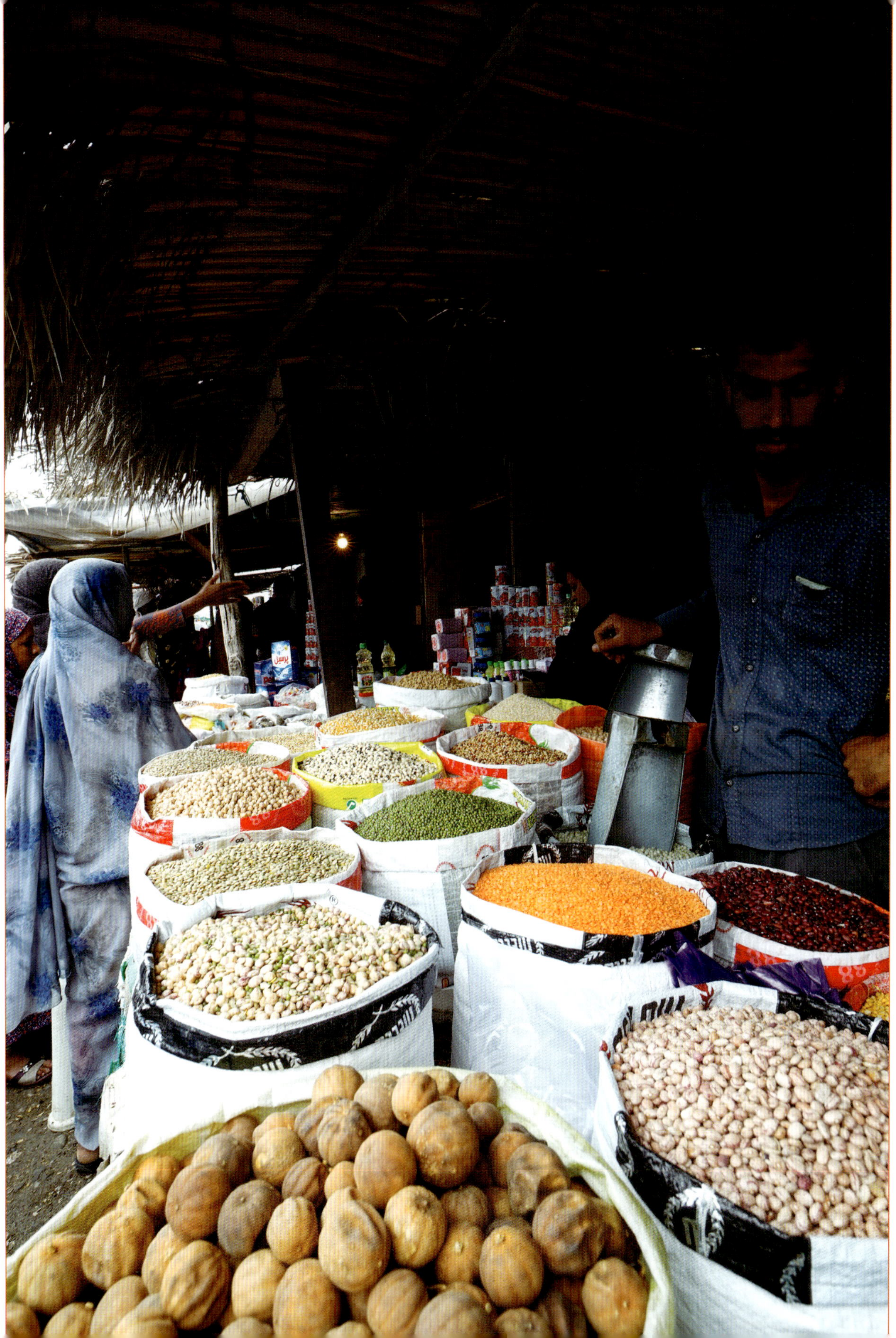

Dried Shrimp with Lentils + Rice
havari-e maygu-e khoshk ba adas

Serves 6
Prep: 20 minutes + soaking overnight
Cooking: 1 hour

RICE + LENTILS

1½ cups/300g basmati rice
½ cup/100g brown lentils, soaked overnight and drained

SHRIMP

½ cup/120ml oil or ghee
2 onions, peeled and sliced
¼lb/110g dried shrimp, soaked in cold water for one hour and drained
1½ teaspoons fine sea salt
½ teaspoon freshly ground pepper
1/2 teaspoon red pepper flakes
1 teaspoons turmeric
1 teaspoon Bandari seven-spice *advieh*
2 tablespoons ground hearts of dried Persian limes
2 teaspoons tomato paste
½lb/225g russet potato (about 1 of them), peeled and diced into 1in/25mm cubes
1 large fresh tomato, peeled and diced
½ cup/60g currants
½ teaspoon cinnamon

GARNISH

⅛ teaspoon ground saffron threads dissolved in 1 tablespoon water
2 tablespoons chopped fresh cilantro

Using dried shrimp in this rice and lentil dish gives it a deeper taste than you might expect—a kind of umami. Locals told me that in the old days they used dried grasshopper/malakh for the dish.

1. Wash the rice by placing it in a large container, cover it with water, agitate gently with your hand, then pour off the water. Repeat 2 to 3 times until the water is clear.

2. **To cook the rice and lentils:** In a large non-stick pot, bring 8 cups/1.9l water and 2 tablespoons fine sea salt to a boil. Add the rice and lentils to the pot. Boil briskly for 10 minutes, stirring gently with a wooden spoon to loosen any grains stuck to the bottom. Drain the rice and lentil mixture in a large fine-mesh colander. Set aside.

3. Meanwhile heat the oil in a wide skillet over medium heat and sauté the onions until golden brown. Add the shrimp, salt, pepper, red pepper flakes, turmeric, *advieh*, dried lime hearts, and tomato paste, and sauté for 20 seconds. Add the potato and sauté for 4 minutes.

4. Add the fresh tomato and ½ cup/120ml water and bring to a boil. Reduce heat to low, cover, and simmer for 10 to 15 minutes until all the juice has been absorbed. Add the currants and cinnamon and set aside.

5. In the same non-stick pot, place 2 tablespoons oil and 2 tablespoons water. Add 1 spatula of rice to the pot, alternating with layers of the shrimp and spice mixture, to form a pyramid.

6. Pour ¼ cup/60ml oil and ½ cup/120ml water over the rice and drizzle the saffron water on top. Wrap the lid of the pot with a clean dish towel and cover firmly to prevent steam from escaping. Cook for 30 minutes over medium heat.

7. Remove from heat and allow to cool for 5 minutes on a damp surface without uncovering it.

8. Uncover the pot and gently taking one spatula of rice at a time, mound it on a serving dish. Garnish with saffron water and cilantro. *Nush-e joon!*

VARIATION

You can replace the dried shrimp with 1/2lb/225g fresh shrimp, deveined and cut up. You can also replace the lentils with mung beans.

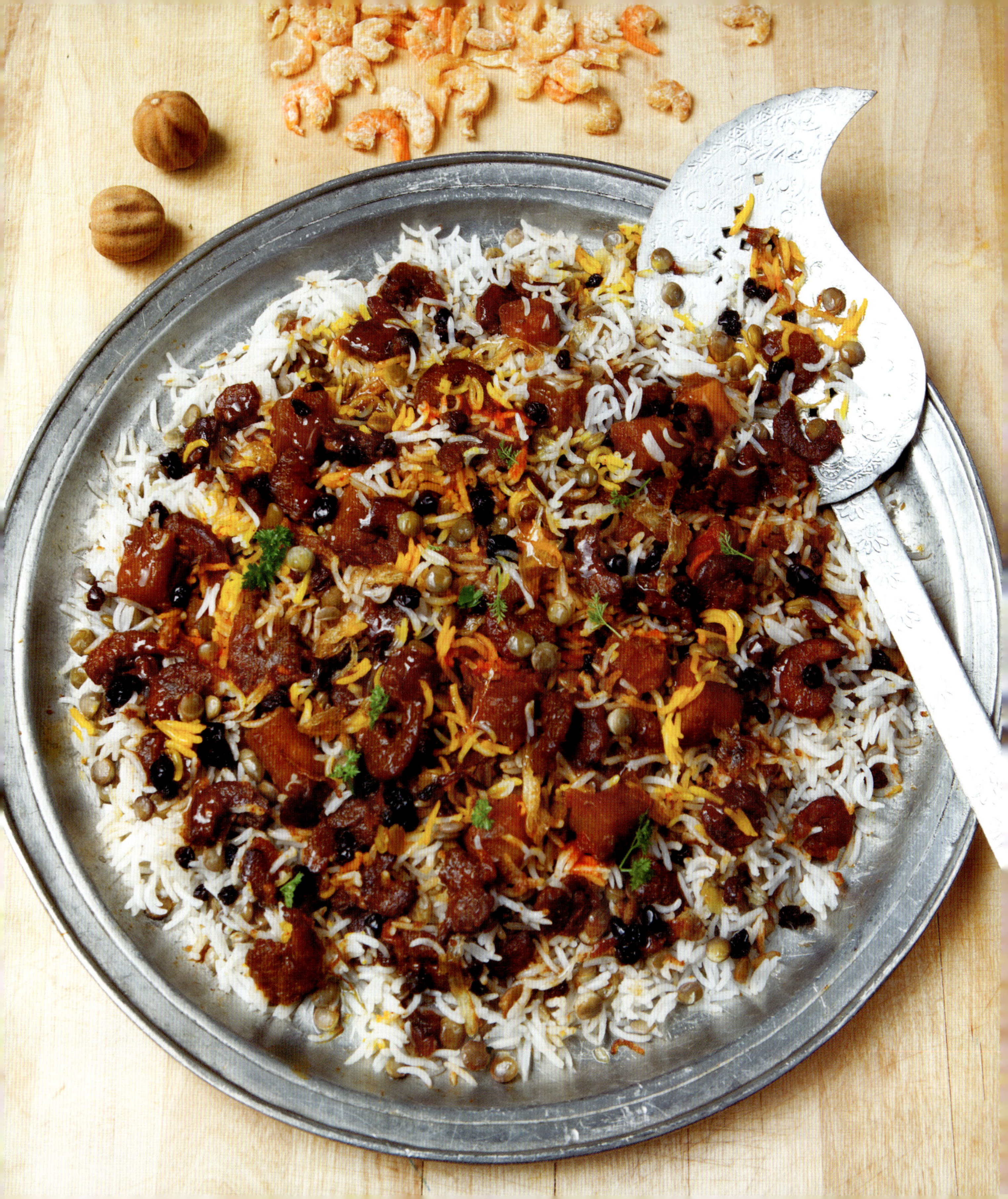

Chicken Briyani with Rice + Potato
beriyani-e morgh

Serves 6
Prep: 55 minutes
Cooking: 2 hours

CHICKEN

2 tablespoons oil, butter, or ghee
1 chickens (4lb/1.8kg), remove the spine and cut up into 6 pieces
2 medium onions, peeled and thinly sliced
2 garlic cloves, peeled and thinly sliced
2 teaspoons fine sea salt
1 teaspoon freshly ground black pepper
½ teaspoon turmeric
2 tablespoons Bandari seven-spice *advieh*
2 serrano chillies, finely chopped, or 1 teaspoon red chili flakes
1in/25mm ginger, peeled and grated
2 large tomatoes, peeled and diced

YOGURT

1 cup/240g plain whole milk yogurt
1 teaspoon saffron dissolved in ¼ cup/60ml rose water

CARAMELIZED ONIONS + NUTS/*HASHU*

2 tablespoons oil or ghee
2 medium onions, thinly sliced
½ teaspoon turmeric
1 cup/170g raw whole cashews or almonds
1 cup/150g currents, soaked for 10 minutes and drained

RICE

2 cups/400g long-grain basmati rice

POTATO CRUST/*TAH-DIG-E SIB ZAMINI*

½ cup/120ml oil or melted butter
2 russet potatoes, peeled and cut into ¼in/6mm-thick round slices
½ teaspoon fine sea salt
½ teaspoon Bandari seven-spice *advieh*

In Persian, briyan *means "roast." These days we associate* briyani *with Indian cooking, but it's actually an ancient Persian cooking technique. Traditionally, lamb and yogurt are arranged on the bottom of the pot, then fried onions and rice are added, covered tightly and cooked over low heat.*

1. *To cook the chicken:* Heat 2 tablespoons oil in a medium-sized pot over medium heat and sauté the chicken. Add the onions and garlic, and sauté until golden brown. Add the rest of the ingredients for the chicken and give it a gentle stir. Cover and cook over low heat for 1 hour.

2. *To prepare the yogurt:* Beat the yogurt with 3 tablespoons of the saffron-rose water for 5 minutes. Add it to the chicken and stir gently. Remove from heat.

3. *To prepare the caramelized onion and nut mixture:* In a wide skillet, heat 2 tablespoons oil over low heat, add the onions, and sauté until golden brown. Add ½ teaspoon turmeric and the cashews, and stir-fry for 1 minute. Add the currents and stir-fry for 20 seconds. Remove from heat and set aside.

4. *To cook the rice:* Wash the rice by placing it in a large container, cover it with water, agitate gently with your hand, then pour off the water. Repeat 2 to 3 times until the water is clear. Bring 8 cups/1.9l water and 2 tablespoons fine sea salt to a boil in a large non-stick pot. Add the rice and boil briskly for 6 to 10 minutes, gently stirring twice to loosen any grains that may have stuck to the bottom. When all the rice has risen to the surface, it is ready to be drained. Drain in a large fine-mesh colander and rinse with 3 cups/720ml cold water.

5. *For the potato crust:* In the same pot heat ¼ cup oil/60ml and 1 tablespoon saffron-rose water, and arrange a layer of the potato slices side by side to fit the bottom of the pot. Sprinkle the salt and *advieh* on top. Place 2 spatulas of rice and some of the caramelized onion and nut mixture on top. Place the chicken over it. Alternate layers of the rice with the onion and nut mixture, and mound the layers to form a pyramid. Cover and cook over medium heat for 10 minutes.

6. Drizzle ¼ cup/60ml oil and ½ cup/120ml water on top of the rice. Wrap the lid with a clean dish towel and cover the pot firmly to prevent steam from escaping. Cook for 50 minutes over low heat. Remove from heat and place on a damp cloth. Allow to cool for 5 minutes without uncovering.

7. Place a serving platter over the uncovered pot and hold the two together tightly. Quickly invert the two together, unmolding the entire mound onto the platter. *Nush-e joon!*

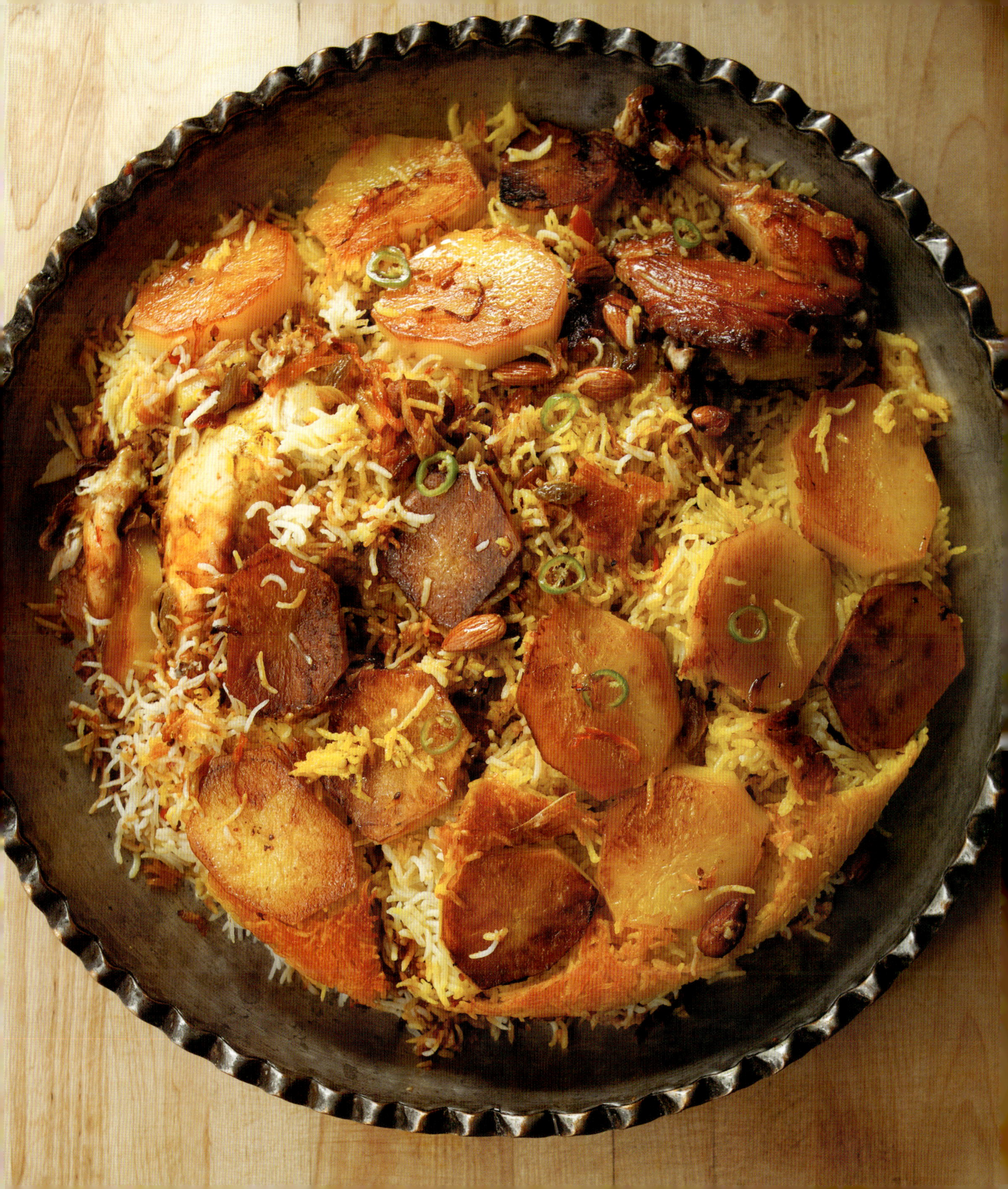

Persian Gulf Date Molasses Halva with Hazelnuts
aseda

Serves 6 to 8
Prep: 20 minutes
Cooking: 20 minutes

GARNISH

¼ cup/30g hazelnuts
1 tablespoon ground pistachio kernels
¼ teaspoon ground cinnamon

HALVA

2 cups/240g unbleached all-purpose flour
1 cup/240g date molasses
¾ cup/180ml oil
½ cup/120ml rose water

This halva, which is very simple to make, is wonderful with some good, strong, Persian Gulf coffee. It's interesting that in Tabriz they make the same halva but use grape molasses instead of date molasses and call it black halva. Another variation is to replace the date molasses with 2 cups/350g pitted dates soaked in 1 cup water for 30 minutes and pureed in the food processor.

1. **To make the garnish:** In a wide skillet over medium heat, toast the hazelnuts by shaking the skillet back and forth for a few minutes. Remove from heat and coarsely chop. Set aside to use as a garnish.

2. **To make the halva:** In a large non-stick pot, toast the flour over medium heat, stirring constantly with a long wooden spoon, for 15 to 20 minutes until the flour is golden brown and has a smoky fragrance. (**This step is very important:** The flour should be neither over- nor under-toasted.)

3. Wear mittens to carefully and gradually add the date molasses to the hot flour, stirring quickly and constantly for 1 minute.

4. Add the oil and continue stirring for 2 minutes until the oil has been absorbed. Add the rose water and continue to stir for 5 minutes until you have a thick smooth paste.

5. Remove from heat and transfer to a flat serving dish. Pack down firmly and quickly with a wooden spoon. Sprinkle the hazelnuts, pistachios, and cinnamon on top. *Nush-e joon!*

Black Carrot Halva
halva-ye havij-e siah

1. In a medium-sized laminated cast-iron pot, place 1lb/450g peeled and grated black carrots, and 4 cups/960ml water. Bring to a boil. Reduce heat to low, cover and cook for 45 to 55 minutes, stirring frequently until carrots are soft.

2. Add ½ cup/120ml oil, ½ cup/120ml date molasses, and 1 teaspoon ground cardamom. Stirring constantly over low heat until you have a soft paste.

3. Transfer the paste to a serving platter and garnish with 1 tablespoon ground pistachio kernels and 2 tablespoons shredded coconut. Allow to cool. *Nush-e joon!*

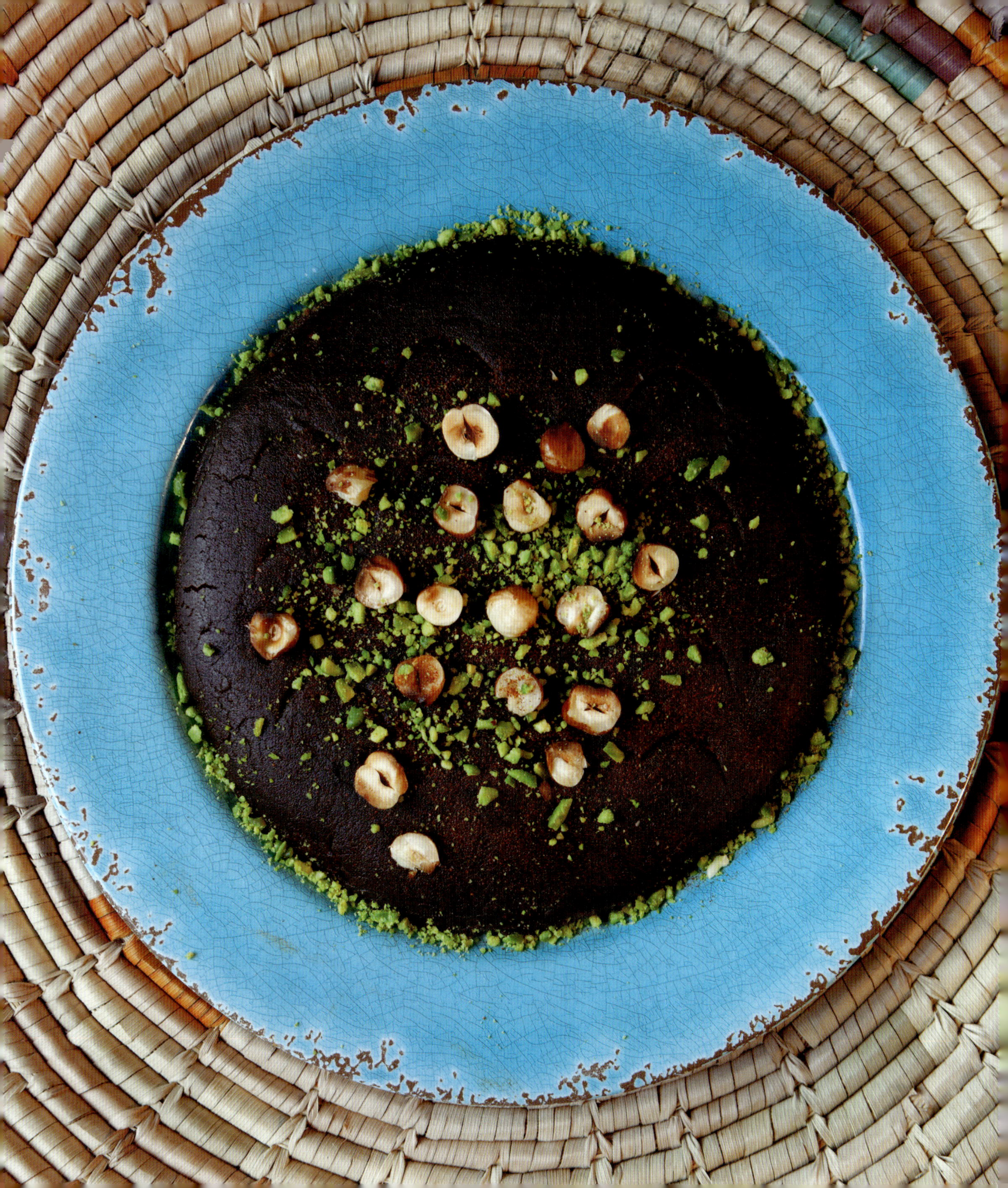

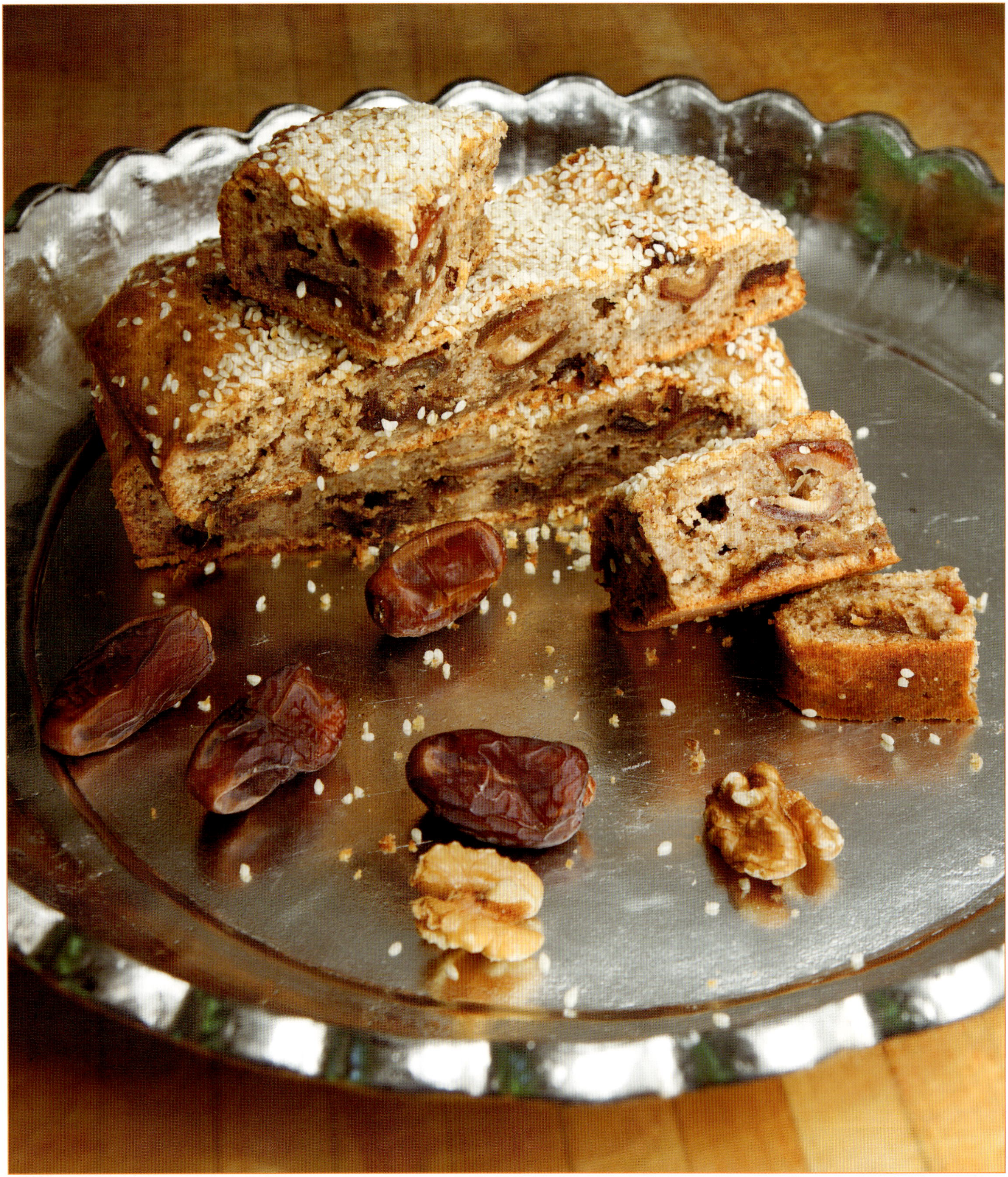

Date, Walnut + Orange Cake

cayk-e ranginak

Makes one 8in/20cm cake
Prep: 20 minutes
Cooking: 40 minutes

DATE

2 cups/350g dates

EGG MIXTURE

½ cup/120ml oil
Zest of 1 orange
½ cup/120ml orange juice
1 teaspoon vanilla extract
1 teaspoon orange blossom water
5 eggs, room temperature

FLOUR AND WALNUT MIXTURE

1 cup/120g unbleached all-purpose flour
½ teaspoon fine sea salt
1 teaspoon baking powder
2 cups/250g walnuts, ground

GARNISH

¼ cup/40g raw sesame seeds

OPTIONAL GLAZE

2 tablespoons grape molasses
2 tablespoons orange juice
1 tablespoon oil

I was served this cake with very strong coffee in Bushehr—a marriage made in heaven! However, when testing the recipe, I found that orange flavor works much better than milk.

1. **To prepare the dates:** Pit and cut the dates into ½in/1cm slices, and chill in the freezer for 30 minutes.

2. Place the oven rack in the center and preheat oven to 350°F/180°C.

3. Butter an 8in/20cm cake pan and line the base with parchment paper. Butter and dust the top of the parchment paper with flour.

4. **To make the egg mixture:** In a large mixing bowl, whisk together all the ingredients for the egg mixture until creamy.

5. **To prepare the flour and walnut mixture:** In another mixing bowl, whisk together the flour, salt, baking powder, and walnuts.

6. Use a rubber spatula to fold the egg mixture into the flour and walnut mixture.

7. Fold in the dates until you have a batter.

8. Gently pour the batter into the cake pan. Garnish the top with sesame seeds. Bake in the preheated oven for 35 to 40 minutes until a tester comes out clean.

9. Remove from the oven and allow to cool on a rack for 10 minutes. Tap the pan to release the cake. Turn the cake out onto the rack, remove the mold, peel off the parchment paper, and turn the cake over. Allow to cool completely. Transfer to a serving platter. *Nush-e joon!*

OPTIONAL GLAZE

In a small sauce pan combine all the ingredients for the glaze and bring to a boil over low heat. Remove from heat and pour the hot glaze over the cake after it has cooled. Allow for the glaze to be thoroughly absorbed while it cools.

The cake with the optional glaze

Upside-Down Mango Cake

cayk-e anbeh

Makes one 10in/25cm cake
Prep: 20 minutes
Cooking: 40 minutes

FLOUR MIXTURE

⅛ teaspoon fine sea salt
2 teaspoons baking powder
½ teaspoon baking soda
1½ cups/180g unbleached all-purpose flour
½ cup/60g almond flour

BATTER:

½ cup/100g sugar
½ cup/110g ghee or oil (120ml)
1 teaspoon vanilla extract
Zest of 1 orange
½ cup/120ml almond milk
3 eggs (room temperature)

MANGO

2 tablespoons sugar
1 tablespoon butter
4 to 5 mangoes, peeled and cut lengthwise into 1in/25mm thick slices

Mangoes are the national fruit of India, where they have been cultivated for at least four thousand years. Their cultivation had spread to southern Persia by the tenth century. By the time of the Mughal ruler Akbar in the sixteenth century, mangoes had become a status symbol. These days they are mostly imported to Iran from India and Pakistan and continue to be popular both as fresh fruit and in the form of chutneys and pickles. You can replace the mangoes with guava (locals call them zaytan)—in which case don't peel the guavas, just slice them.

1. Place the oven rack in the center and preheat oven to 375°F/190°C.

2. **To make the flour mixture:** In a mixing bowl, whisk together the salt, baking powder, baking soda, flour, and almond flour. Set aside.

3. **To make the batter:** In a food processor pulse together the sugar, ghee, vanilla, orange zest, and almond milk. Add the eggs, one by one, and pulse until creamy.

4. Gradually add the egg to the flour mixture and fold until you have a smooth batter.

5. **To bake the cake:** Sprinkle the sugar, evenly, in a 10in/25cm cast-iron skillet over medium heat. Caramelize the sugar over medium heat (about 4 minutes). Add 1 tablespoon butter and use a rubber spatula to mix it with the sugar. Arrange the mango slices side by side, overlapping, on the skillet. Cook for 7 minutes.

6. Gently pour the batter into the skillet and even out to cover the mangoes. Bake in the oven for 25 to 30 minutes until the cake edges are separating from the skillet.

7. Remove from the oven and allow to cool on a rack for 3 minutes. Use a rubber spatula to go around between the cake and skillet to ensure it's not sticking to the edge of the skillet.

8. Place a large serving platter on top, hold the skillet and the platter together, turn over in a single motion, and tap it on the counter. Lift up the skillet gently and ensure that all the mangoes have come down. *Nush-e joon!*

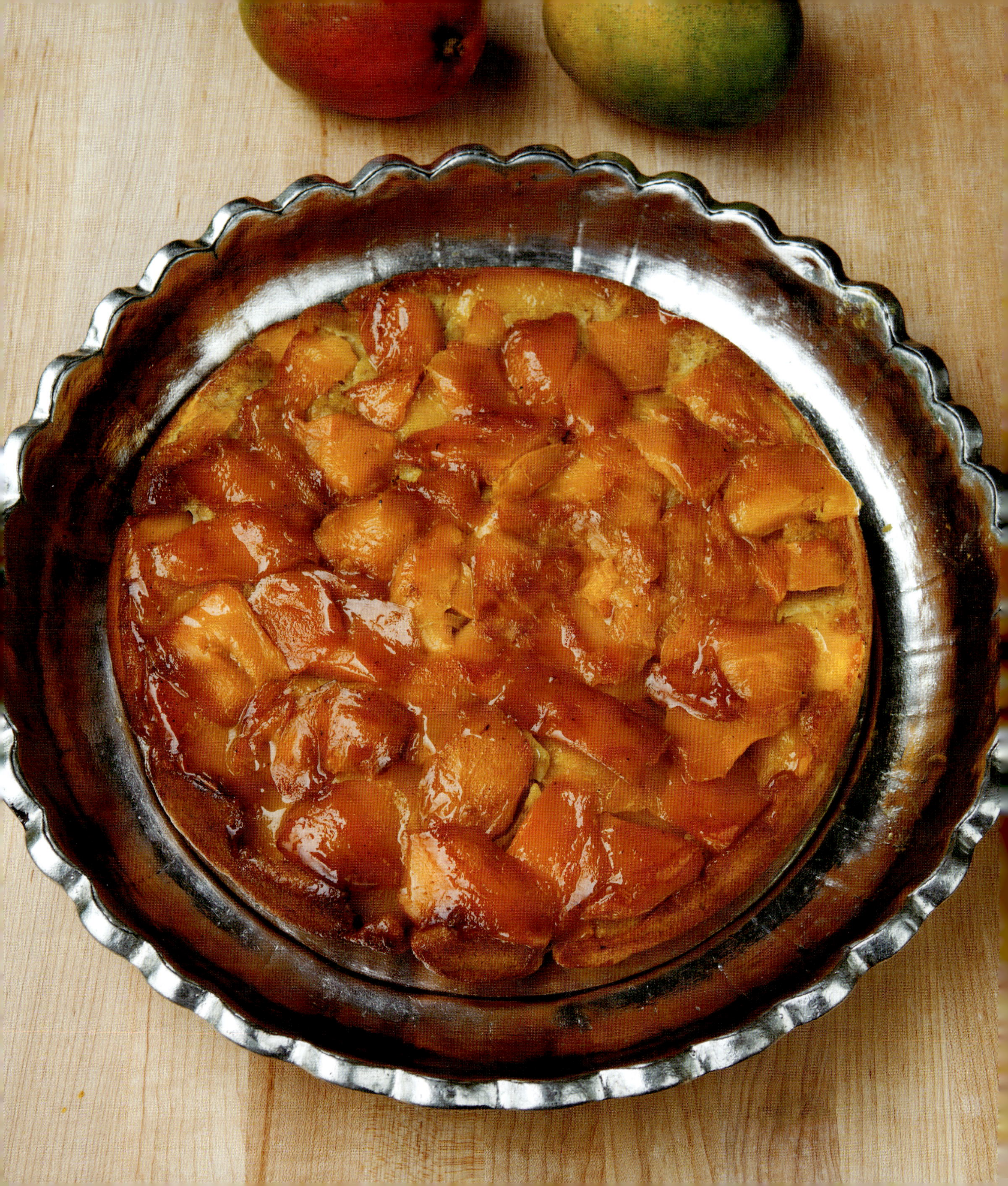

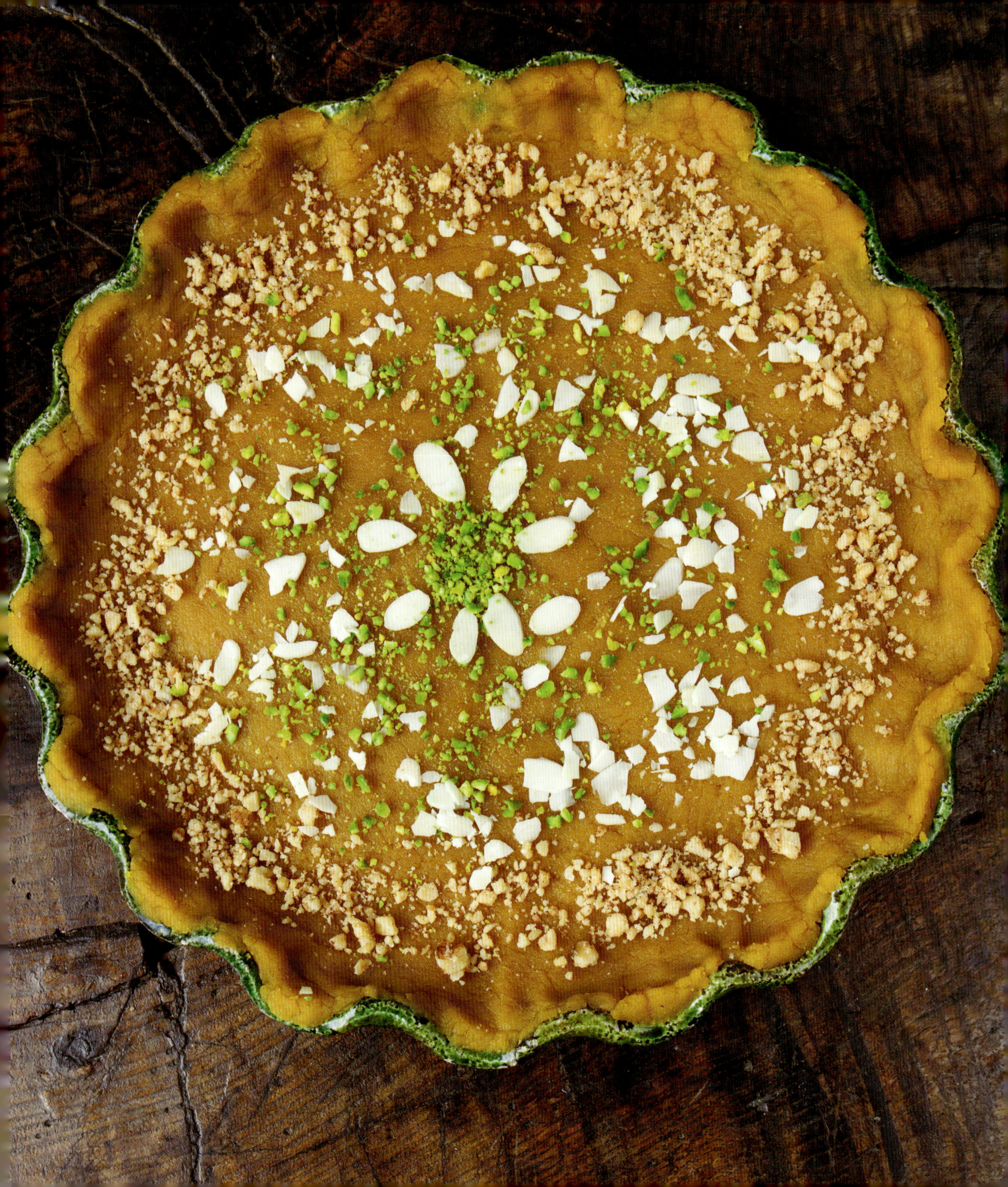

Sesame Halva

halva ardeh

Serves 6
Prep: 20 minutes
Cooking: 30 minutes + 2 hours of chilling

SYRUP

1½ cups/300g sugar
½ cup/120ml water
½ teaspoon ground saffron threads dissolved in ½ cup/120ml rose water

PASTE

2 cups/570g tahini
1½ cups/180g all-purpose wheat flour

GARNISH

¼ cup/30g ground walnuts
2 tablespoons sliced pistachio kernels
2 tablespoons sliced almonds

1. *To make the syrup:* In a small saucepan, whisks together the sugar, water and saffron rose water until the sugar has dissolved. Bring to a boil, remove from heat, cover and keep warm.

2. *To make the paste:* In a small saucepan heat the tahini paste until warm and smooth. Remove from heat.

3. In a wide skillet over medium heat, add the flour, and toast, stirring constantly with a long wooden spoon, for 15 to 20 minutes until lightly golden.

4. Gradually add the tahini to the toasted flour, stirring constantly for 2 minutes, to prevent sticking and lumping until the mixture has a smooth consistency. Remove from Heat.

5. Add the warm syrup gradually and carefully to the flour and tahini mixture. Stir constantly, for 5 to 7 minutes until all the syrup has been absorbed and the mixture has a smooth, thick consistency.

6. Immediately transfer to a serving dish while the halva is still hot. Garnish and allow to cool to room temperature. Cover and chill for at least 2 hours. *Nush-e joon!*

Sweet Potato Halva

Halva-ye pendal/sibzamini-e shirin

Serves 6
Prep: 10 minutes
Cooking: 40 minutes

2lb/900g sweet potatoes
2 tablespoons oil or ghee
½ cup/120g date molasses
1 teaspoon ground cardamom
½ teaspoon ground saffron threads dissolved in ½ cup rose water

GARNISH:

2 tablespoons ground pistachio kernels

1. *To cook the sweet potatoes:* Place the sweet potatoes in a medium-sized saucepan, cover with 4 cups/960ml water, and bring to a boil. Reduce heat to medium, cover, and cook for 20 to 30 minutes until tender. Drain. Allow to cool, peel, grate, and set aside.

2. In a wide skillet, heat 2 tablespoons oil and sauté the grated sweet potatoes for 5 minutes. Add the rest of the ingredients and cook for 2 to 4 minutes, stirring constantly, until you have a smooth paste.

3. Transfer to a serving platter and garnish with the ground pistachio kernels. *Nush-e joon!*

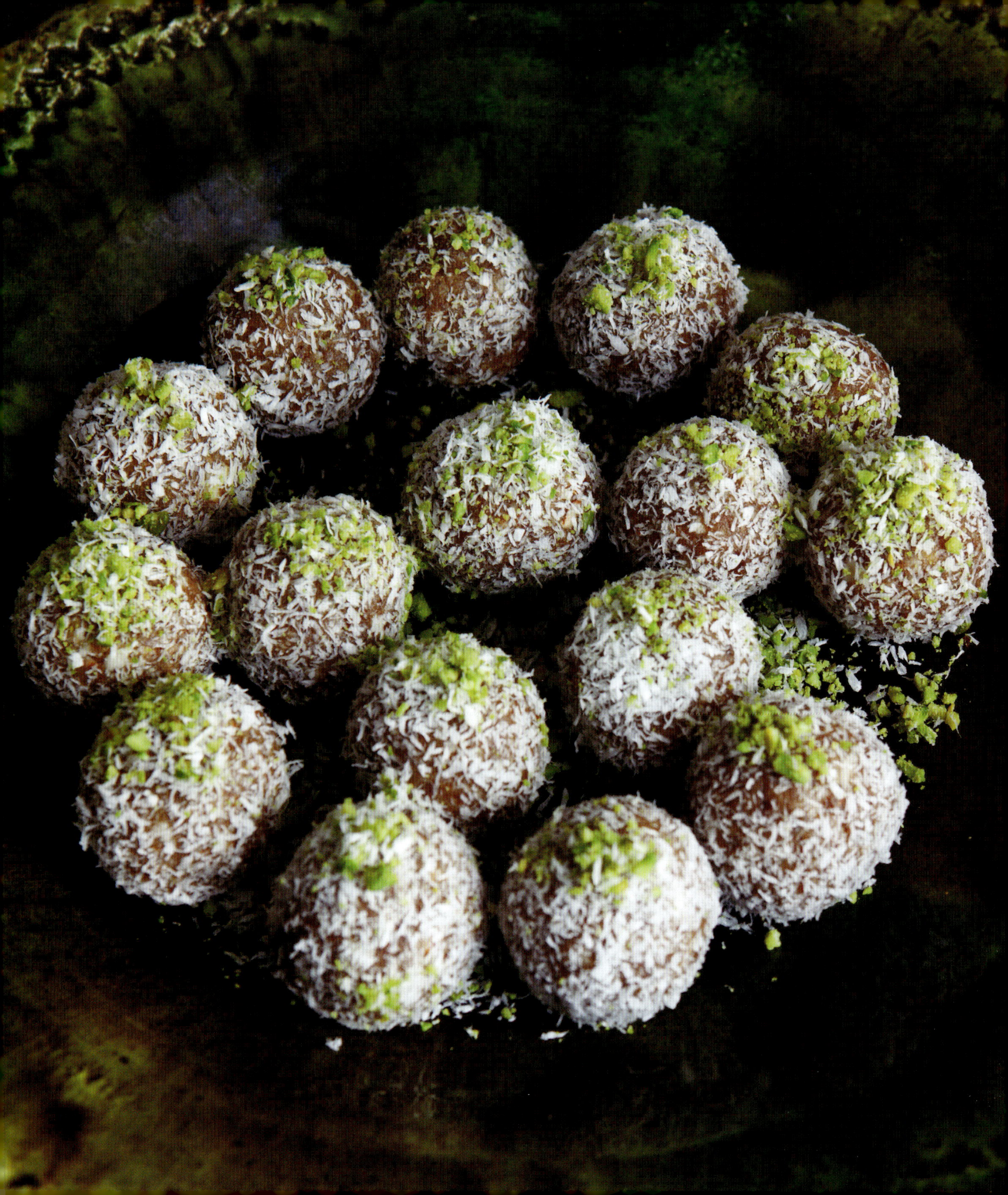

Persian Gulf Date + Coconut Balls
bontu

Makes 25 coconut balls
Prep: 20 minutes
Cooking: 10 minutes

COATING:

1 cup/60g shredded coconuts
2 tablespoons ground pistachio kernels

DATE PASTE

2 tablespoons oil or ghee
2 cups/350g dates, pitted and sliced
½ teaspoon ground cardamom
¼ teaspoon ground cinnamon
2 tablespoons tahini paste
1 cup/120g raw almonds
1 cup/125g walnuts

1 teaspoon orange blossom water

This combination of dates, coconuts, pistachios, and a dash of orange blossom water makes a delicious vegan dessert.

1. **To prepare the coating:** Line 2 sheet pans each with a layer of parchment paper. Sprinkle the shredded coconuts and ground pistachio evenly over them. Set aside.

2. **To make the date paste:** Heat the oil in a wide skillet over medium heat. Add the dates and stir-fry for 3 to 4 minutes until they are soft. Add the rest of the ingredients for the paste and stir-fry for 1 minute.

3. Transfer the date mixture to a food processor and pulse until you have a grainy paste.

4. Use a 2in/5cm ice-cream scoop to pick up a portion of the paste. Moisten the palms of your hands with orange blossom water and shape each portion into bite-sized balls.

5. Roll the date balls in the coconut mixture on the sheet pan until they are covered evenly with the shredded coconuts. Serve as needed or store in a tightly covered glass container. *Nush-e joon!*

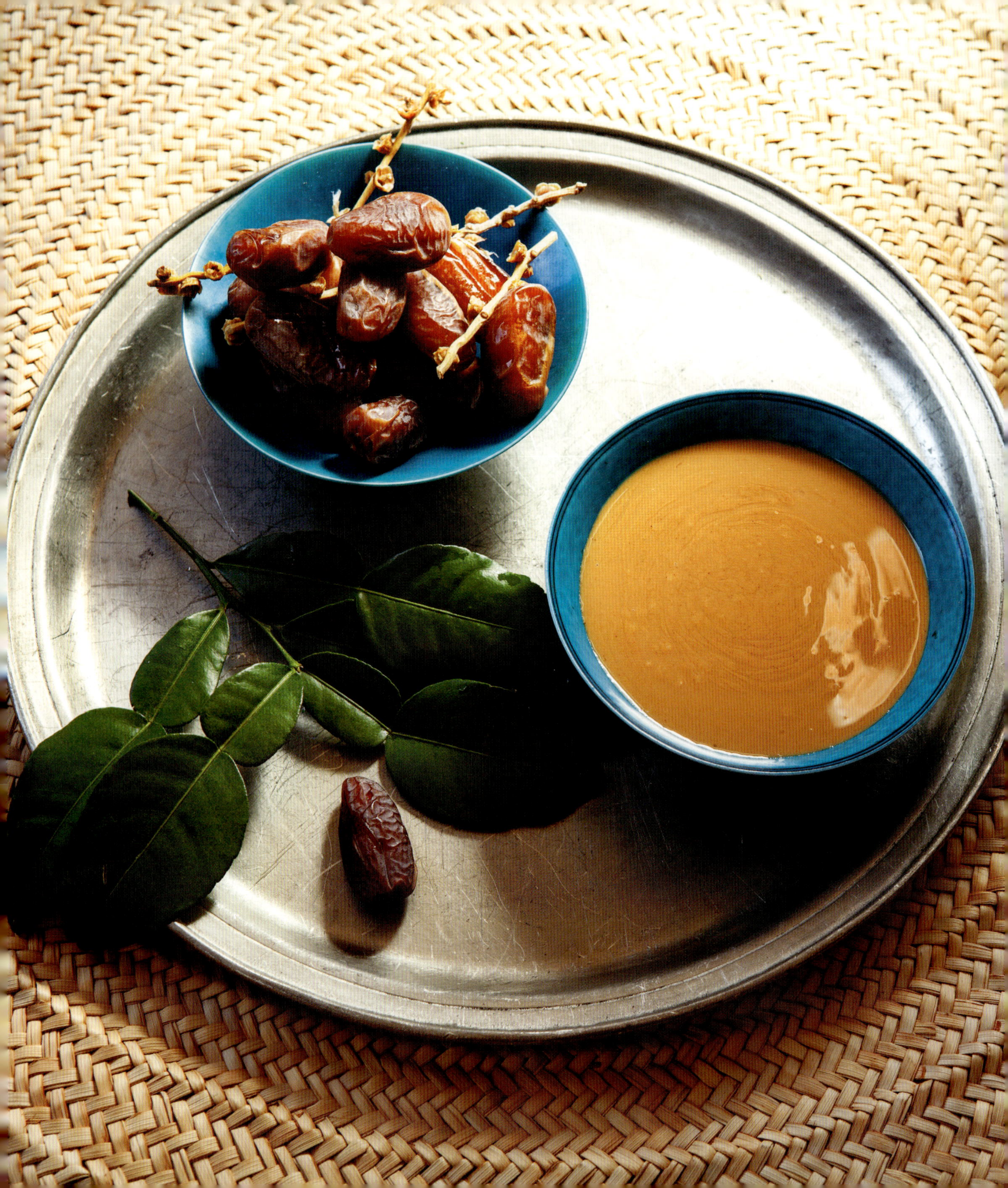

Date, Pistachio + Lime Leaf Dessert
khorma shireh

Serves 6 to 8
Prep: 15 minutes

¼ cup/40g black cumin seeds
1lb/450g dates, pitted and sliced
5 kaffir lime leaves
½ cup/100g wild pistachios/kosudang/baneh, or, if you can't find wild pistachios (the terebinth family), regular pistachio kernels, slivered
1½ cup/360g date molasses

This dish is traditionally made with kosudang (also called baneh), a wild mountain pistachio only available in some regions of Iran. I am replacing them with regularly available pistachio kernels for this recipe. I adapted this recipe from Dowlat Khoshkhabar.

1. Place the cumin seeds in a wide skillet and toast over medium heat, shaking the skillet back and forth until the aroma begins to rise. Remove from heat and set aside.

2. In a wide glass container, place alternating layers of the dates, cumin seeds, kaffir lime leaves, and pistachios.

3. In a small saucepan, warm up the date molasses and pour over the date mixture.

4. Cover the bowl and allow to macerate for 30 minutes. Store in an airtight glass container in a cool place and serve as needed.

5. Serve as a sweet with tea or coffee. *Nush-e joon!*

Date + Tahini Dessert

I was impressed with this simple yet delicious dessert often served at the end of a meal throughout the Persian Gulf. It consists of a bowl of dates and a bowl of toasted tahini (Iranian tahini is more liquid than what's available in the U.S. You can add 2 tablespoons warm water and blend until smooth). At the end of the meal (usually some fish dish) you help yourself by picking up a date and dipping it into the tahini. The resulting mouthful is very satisfying and a perfect end to a meal. According to the Iranian concept of the Yin and Yang of food, *garmi-o sardi*, the "hot/*garmi*" date and tahini help to balance the "cold/*sardi*" of the fish dish.

Photo of the Date + Tahini Dessert.

Persian Gulf Coffee
ghawah

Serves 6
Prep: 10 minutes
Cooking: 1 minute

COFFEE

4 cups/960ml water
3 tablespoons finely ground roasted coffee

FLAVORING

1 teaspoon finely ground cardamom seeds
2 cloves
½ teaspoon ground saffron threads
1 tablespoon rose water

Coffee berries traveled from Ethiopia to Yemen—they are first mentioned by an eleventh-century Arab physician—where the practice of extracting, roasting, and grinding their beans seems to have appeared during the thirteenth century. Yemenis, who made an infusion from the drink, named it qahwah, a poetic word for "wine." The first cafés appeared in 1554 in Istanbul; a few years later, the drink had arrived, via Venice, in Italy. Everywhere they appeared, coffee houses flourished as convivial meeting places for no-doubt-overstimulated poets, writers, and revolutionaries, and as entertainment venues for storytellers, puppeteers, and musicians. So popular were they, and such wellsprings of sedition, that the authorities of every country, Christian or Muslim, complained. Nowadays, tea is the favorite drink in Iran, except perhaps around the Persian Gulf, where coffee is preferred. It is usually amber colored and perfumed with cardamom and saffron. This style of coffee is different from Turkish or Armenian coffee because it is much lighter and usually not sweetened. The coffee is poured from a dallah—a coffee pot with a long, curved spout—into small enameled cups. The drinker takes the cup in his right hand, and the cup is only partially filled each time until he signals that he doesn't want anymore by shaking the empty cup slightly from side to side.

1. In a small saucepan/*ibrik*, add the water and coffee, and bring to a boil over medium heat. Cook for 1 minute.

2. In a spouted coffee pot/*dallah*, mix together the cardamom, cloves, saffron, and rose water.

3. Carefully pour the coffee liquid, not the residue or dregs, into the *dallah* and allow to infuse for 10 minutes before pouring. Do not shake the coffee pot as this will stir the grains and bring them to the top.

4. Pour the flavored coffee into demitasse cups and serve with dates. *Nush-e joon!*

The Persian Gulf

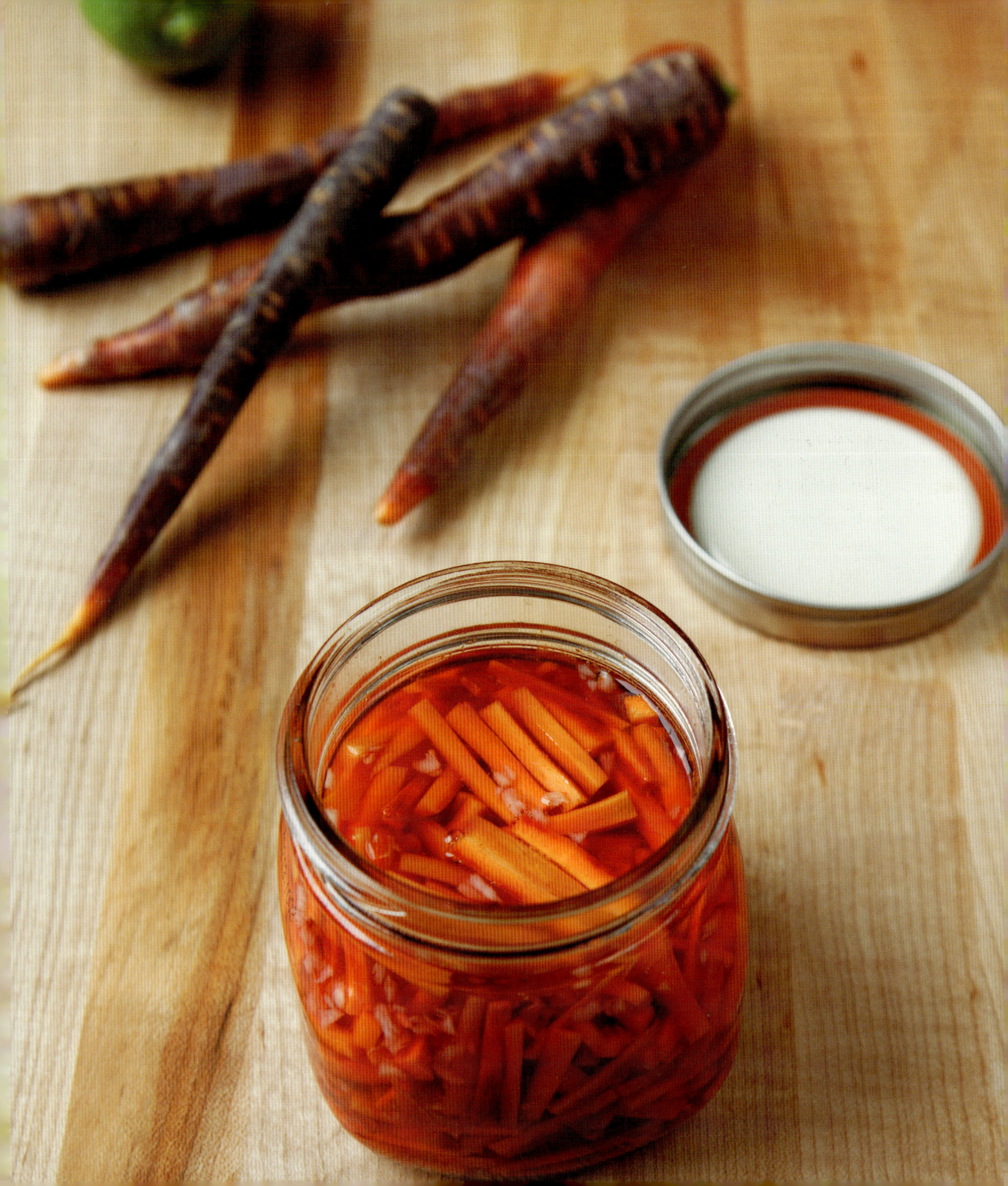

Black Carrot Pickle
torshi-e gazar

Makes 1pt/480g
Prep: 30 minutes
Pickling: 30 minutes and up to 1 week

2lb/900g black carrots, peeled and cut into 1in/2.5cm pieces
4 teaspoons pickling or coarse sea salt
1 tablespoon sugar or date molasses
10 cloves garlic, grated
1 teaspoon freshly ground black pepper
2 tablespoons cilantro leaves
¾ cup/180ml freshly squeezed lime juice or apple cider vinegar

Wild carrots probably originated in northeastern Iran. The roots were black or purple, but they were cultivated mainly for their leaves and seeds. Today we don't eat carrot leaves or seeds, but we love to cook with the leaves and seeds of the carrot family: parsley, cilantro, coriander, fennel, anise, and cumin. The modern carrot with an orange root was also probably first cultivated in this region around the eighth century CE and introduced to Spain by the Arabs. The carrot was brought to colonial America in the seventeenth century by European settlers. I found these carrots at my local farmers' market in Washington, DC. They are black/purple on the outside, but orange on the inside.

1. Place all the ingredients in a food processor and pulse until finely chopped. Adjust seasoning to taste.

2. Transfer to a glass container or jar. Cover tightly and allow to sit for 30 minutes before serving. Store in the fridge for up to 1 week. Use as needed. *Nush-e joon!*

VARIATION

You can replace the carrots with beets or cabbage. Everything else remains the same.

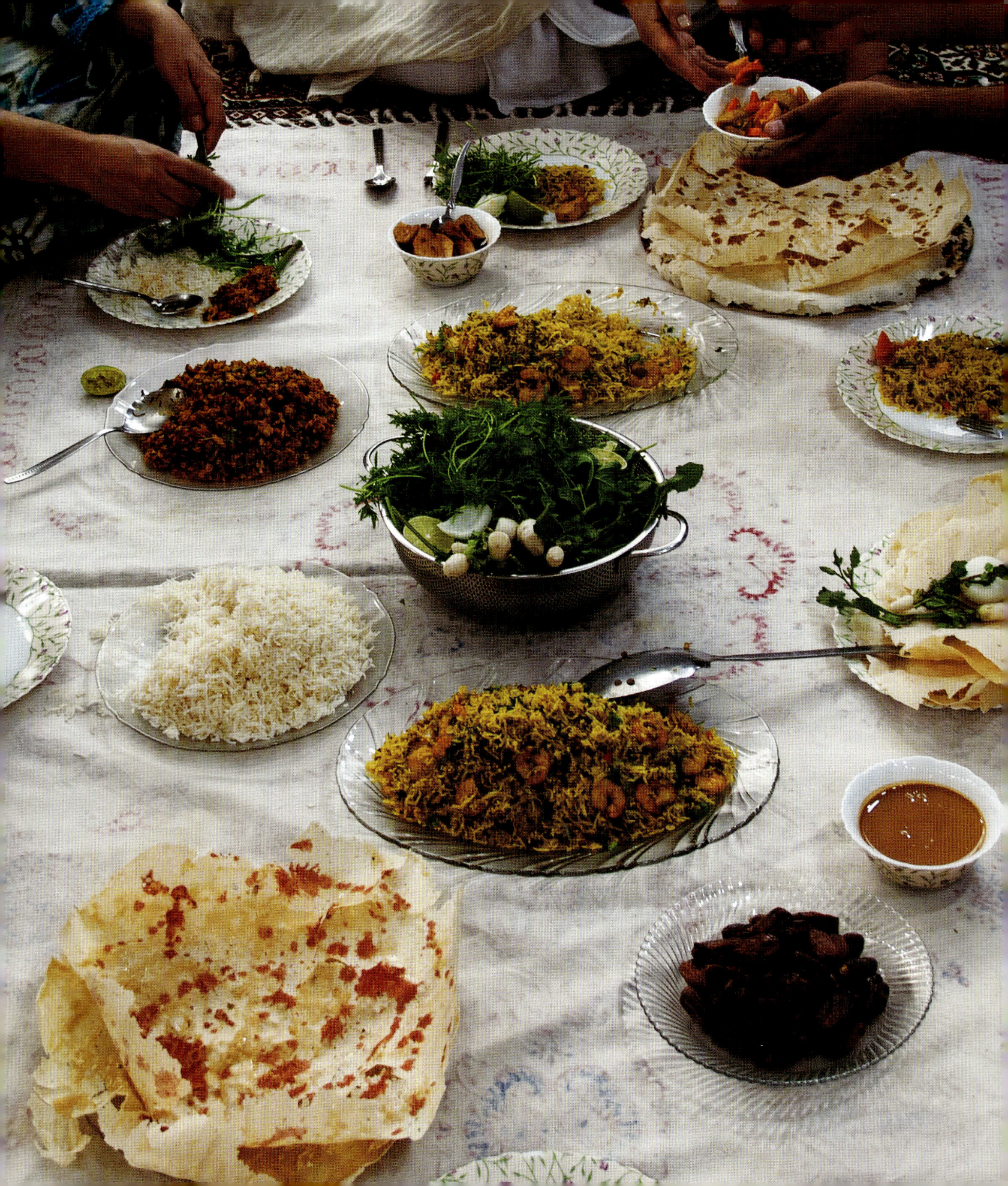

Spicy Oily Lime Pickle
torshi-e limu ba roghan

Makes 1pt/480g
Prep: 25 minutes
Pickling: 10 days

LIMES

2lb/900g limes
½ cup/140g fine sea salt

SPICES

1 bulb garlic, finely chopped
1 tablespoon nigella seeds
1 tablespoon cumin seeds
1 teaspoon mustard seeds
1 tablespoon coriander seeds
1 teaspoon fenugreek seeds
½ cup/120ml oil
1 teaspoon turmeric
1 tablespoon red pepper flakes

1 cup/240ml fresh lime juice

Pickled lemons are generally associated with Morocco, but these spicy pickles are popular in southern Iran as well. The story of the lemon and lime is interesting. The lemon probably originated somewhere in northern India. It is thought to be a hybrid of the sour orange/narenj and the citron/toranj (Citrus medica) not lime. The Persian lime/limu shirazi is the large lime we are used to today (C. latifolia). It is a cross between the lemon and the key lime. The small limes, also called key limes (C. aurantifolia), need a much hotter climate and thrive around the Persian Gulf. They are called Omani limes/limu omani in Iran, loomi in Oman, and noomi-e basra in Iraq. These are the limes that are dried in the sun and used in the cooking of the Persian Gulf to give dishes an earthy, tangy, sour flavor. They start as pale brown, but the older they get the darker they become until they are black, which is also an English name for them—black limes. These dried limes are usually used whole and pierced or ground in Persian cooking, but when I cooked with local cooks around the Persian Gulf, I was fascinated to see that they would open up the limes, seed them, and use the hearts, which made them much more potent. I adapted this pickle recipe from Raviyeh Daryanavardi in Qeshm. The photo on the facing page shows one of our spreads in Qeshm.

1. Wash and scrub the limes. Cut each lime vertically into quarters. Remove the seeds, cut into 1in/2.5cm cubes, and rub all over with salt. Arrange the lime cubes and the garlic in the jar in alternate layers.

2. Heat a wide skillet over low heat. Add the nigella, cumin, mustard, coriander, and fenugreek seeds, and toast them, moving the skillet back and forth for 2 minutes.

3. Add the oil, turmeric, and red pepper flakes and stir-fry for 1 minute longer. Fill the jar to within ½in/12mm of the top with lime juice.

4. Seal the jar and leave undisturbed for 10 days in a cool dark place before serving. *Nush-e joon!*

VARIATION

Turnip Pickle
torshi-e shalqam

Replace the limes with 2lb/900g turnips cut into 1in/2.5cm cubes. Reduce the salt to 1 tablespoon. Instead of lime juice, fill the jar with a mixture of 1 cup/240ml vinegar and 1 cup/240g date molasses. Everything else remains the same.

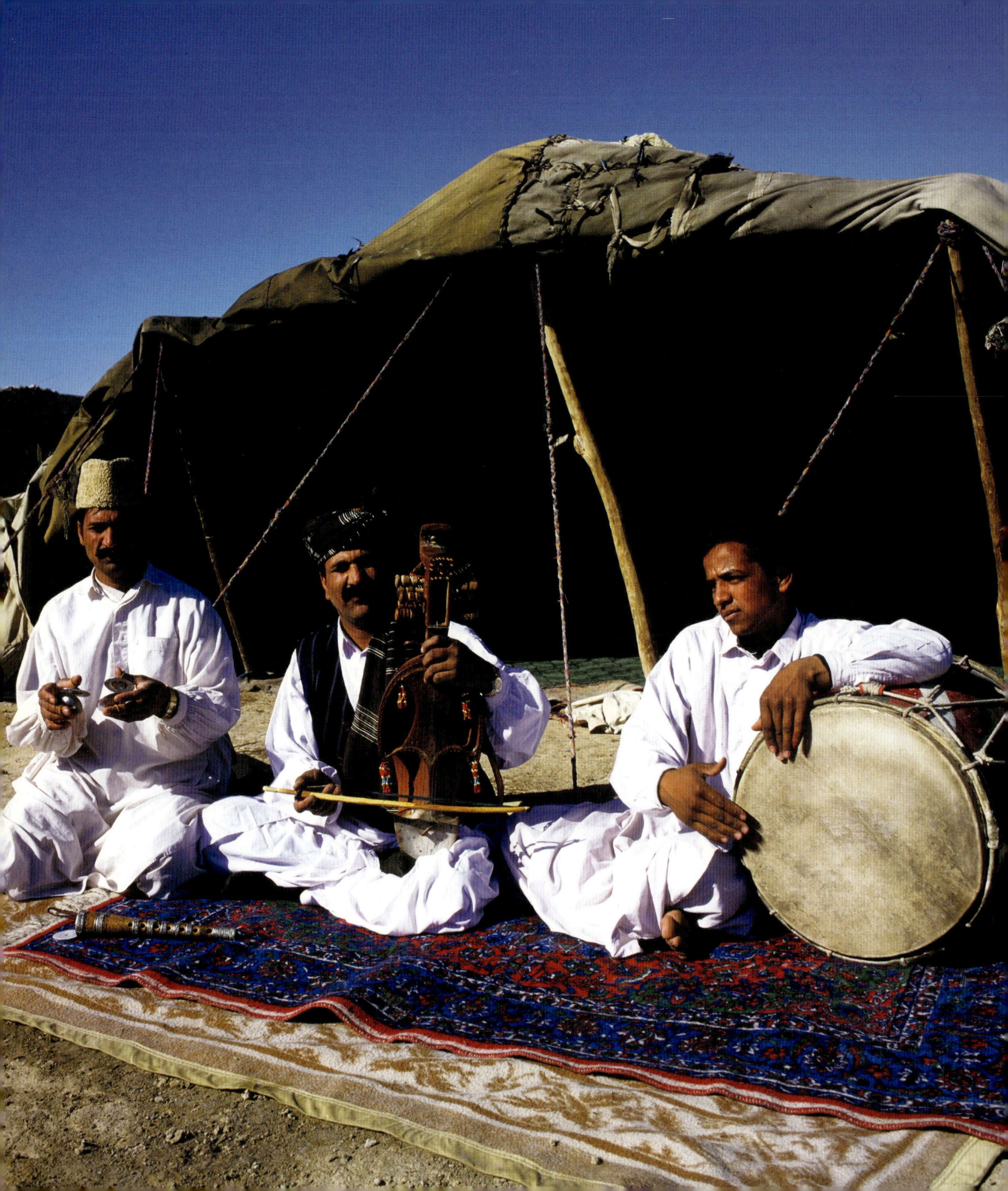

Onion, Cucumber + Coriander Pickle

torshi-e piaz-e hormozgan

Makes ½pt/240g
Prep and cooking: 20 minutes

1lb /450g (1 large) red onion
4 teaspoons fine sea salt
½ teaspoon red pepper flakes
1 tablespoon coriander seeds
12 Persian cucumbers, thinly sliced
1 cup/240ml apple cider vinegar

This quick and easy-to-make pickled onion and toasted coriander relish has an earthy, aromatic flavor. It goes well with everything—fish, chicken, or lamb. Traditionally, cucumbers are not added to it, but I find they provide a very refreshing condiment on the table. The Kurds also add barberries and dried mint.

1. In a medium-sized skillet over low heat, toast the coriander seeds, shaking the skillet constantly until the aroma rises. Remove from heat and set aside.

2. Peel the onion and thinly slice, with the grain, into ⅜in/9mm strips.

3. In a large mixing bowl, place the onion, salt, red pepper flakes, and coriander seeds and massage for 1 minute. Add the cucumber and pour the vinegar over it.

4. Serve as a condiment. You can store any leftover pickle in the fridge in a covered glass container for up to a week. *Nush-e joon!*

Lasura Pickle

torshi-e anbook/sepestan

Makes 1pt/480g
Prep: 20 mintues
Cooking: 5 minutes
Pickling: 2 weeks before using

LASURA

1lb/450g lasura
¼ teaspoon turmeric
1½ cups/360ml water

SPICES

1 tablespoon pickling salt (or sea salt)
½ teaspoon red pepper flakes
1 teaspoon fennel seeds
1½ teaspoons coriander seeds
1½ teaspoons nigella seeds
3 cloves garlic, grated

¼ cup/60ml apple cider vinegar

Lasura (Cordia myxa) is also known in English as Assyrian plum. The locals in this region call it anbook, but in the rest of Iran it is known as sepestan. I remember it as a sweet and sour fruit somewhat similar to greengages. It makes an excellent pickle. Its popularity in the Persian Gulf may be due to the influence of India, where it is very popular.

1. Sterilize canning jars in boiling water. Drain and allow to dry thoroughly.

2. Remove the small crowns on the lasura and place them in a drainer and rinse thoroughly.

3. Combine all the spices in a small bowl, mix well, and set aside.

4. In a medium saucepan, place the lasura and add the turmeric and water. Bring to a boil, reduce heat to medium, and simmer for 5 minutes. Drain and set aside.

5. Fill the jar nearly to the top with the lasura, alternating with layers of the spices. Cover with the vinegar up to ½in/12mm from the top. Sprinkle with some salt on top. Seal the jar and keep in a cool, dark place. Store for at least 2 weeks before using. *Nush-e joon!*

Saffroned Mango Pickle
torshi-e mango-o zaferan

Makes 1pt/480g
Prep and cooking: 1 hour
Picking: 2 weeks before using

MANGOES

2lb/900g firm mangoes, peeled and coarsely diced
4 teaspoons pickling salt (or sea salt)
5 peppercorns
1 teaspoon red pepper flakes
½ teaspoon turmeric
½ teaspoon ground saffron treads

SPICES

1 tablespoon nigella seeds, toasted
1 teaspoon mustard seeds, toasted
1 tablespoon coriander seeds, toasted
1 teaspoon ground Persian hogweed seeds/*golpar*

VINEGAR

¾ cup/180ml apple cider vinegar

For this pickle, it is best to use firm, unripe mangoes. This helps the fruit keep its shape as it ferments.

1. Sterilize canning jar in boiling water. Drain and allow to dry thoroughly.

2. In mixing bowl, place the mango, salt, peppercorns, red pepper flakes, turmeric, and saffron. Mix well, cover, and allow to macerate for 8 hours at room temperature.

3. In a wide skillet over low heat, place the nigella, mustard and coriander seeds. Cover, and toast by shaking the skillet back and forth for a few minutes. Add them to the mangoes. Add the *golpar*. Stir well to combine.

4. Fill the jar with the mangoes. Cover with vinegar to within ½in/12mm of the top and seal. Store the jar in a cool, dark place for at least 2 weeks before serving. *Nush-e joon!*

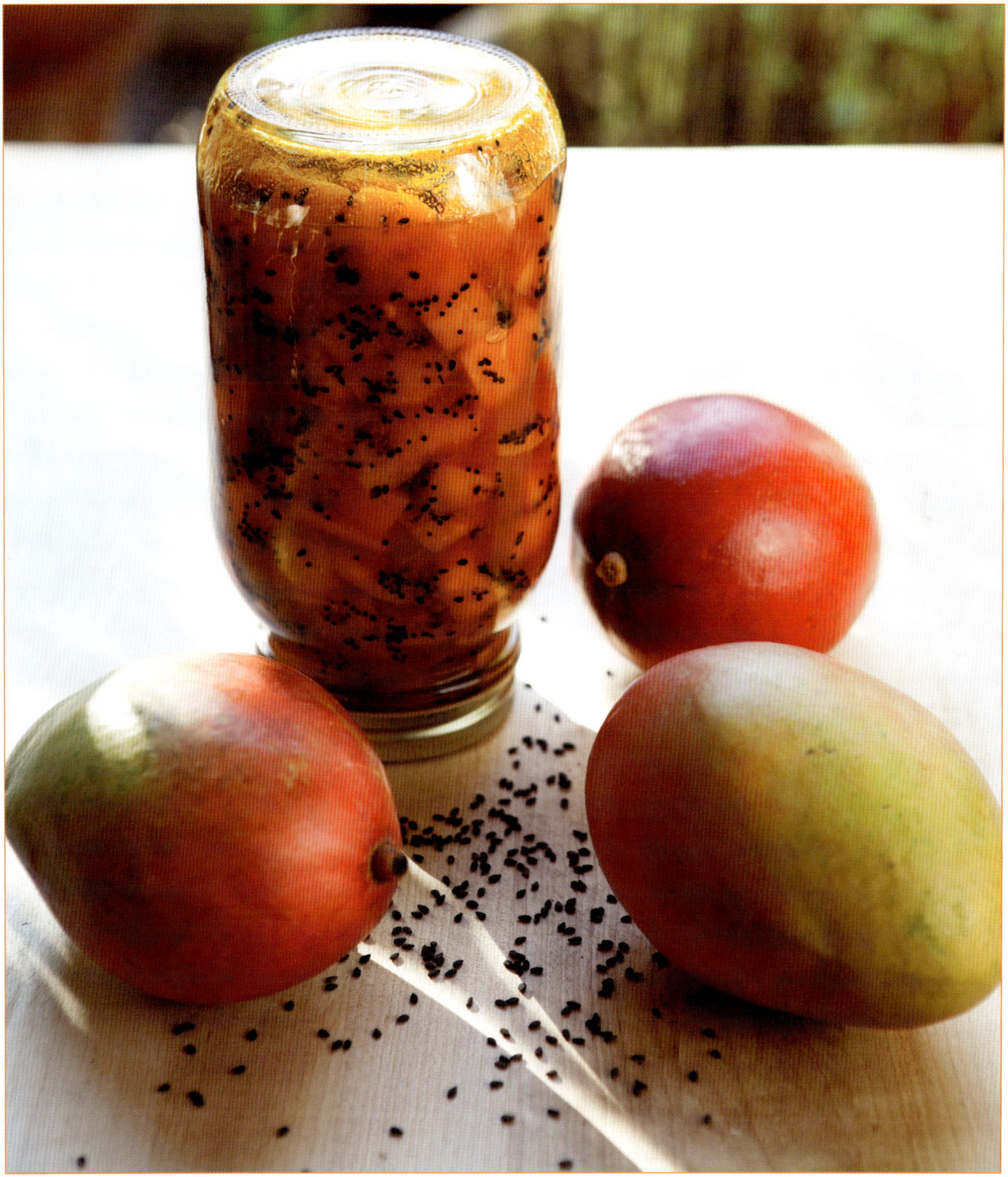

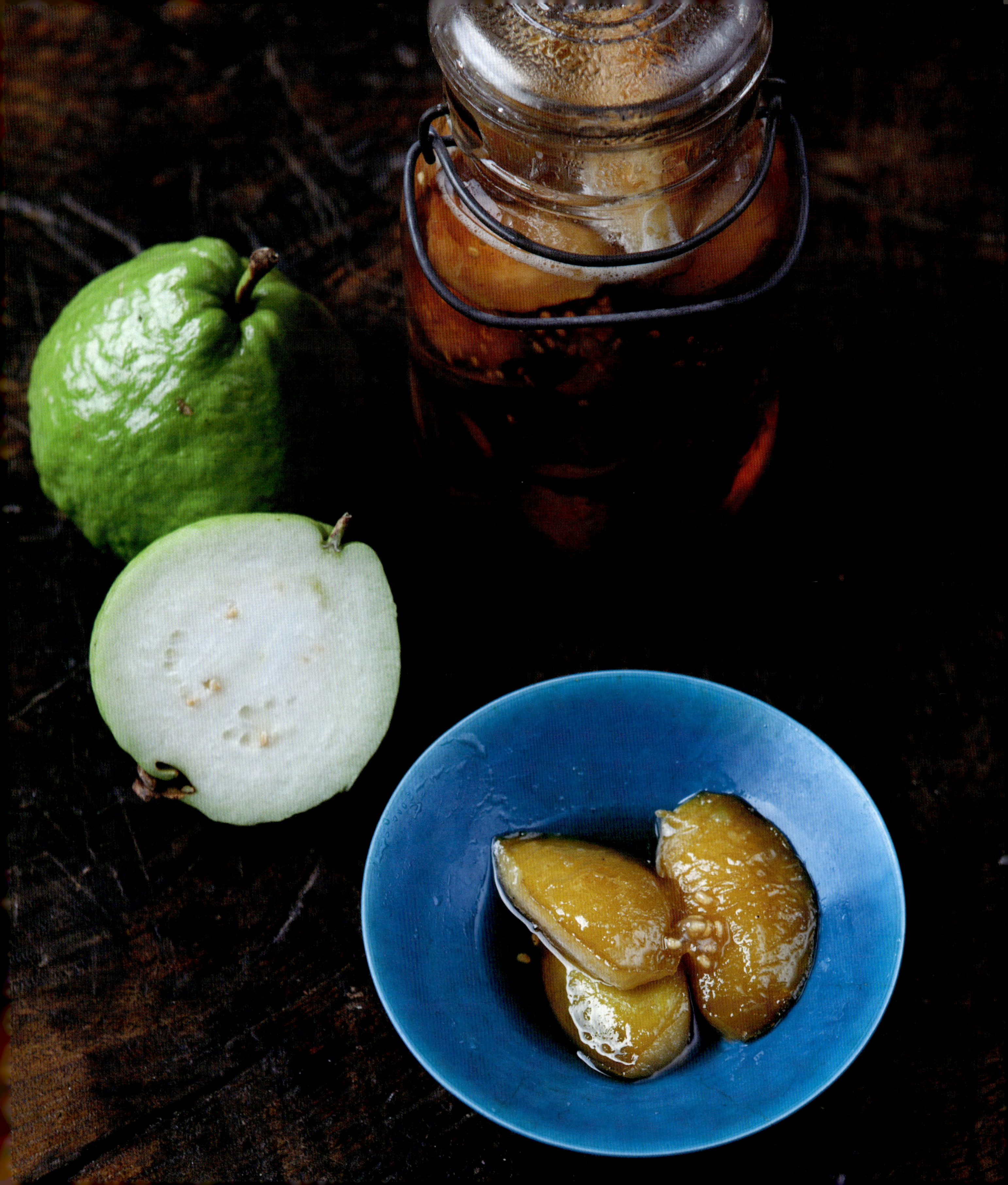

Guava Preserve
moraba-ye guava

Makes 1pt/480g
Prep and cooking: 1 hour
Pickling: 2 weeks before using

SYRUP

4½ cups/900g sugar
2 cups/480ml water

GUAVA

4lb/1.8kg guava, cut into quarters
½ teaspoon ground cardamom
½ teaspoon vanilla extract
2 tablespoons fresh lime juice

Around the Persian Gulf these tropical and subtropical winter fruits have perfume similar to lemon skin, and you can eat them raw like apples, with or without skin. Their high pectin count make them an excellent preserve.

1. Sterilize a jar in boiling water. Drain and allow to dry thoroughly.

2. **To make the syrup:** Place the sugar and water in a heavy-bottomed saucepan and bring to a boil. Reduce heat to low and simmer for 25 minutes, occasionally stirring gently.

3. Add the guava, cardamom, and vanilla, and simmer for 25 to 30 minutes until the syrup has thickened enough to coat the back of a spoon. Add the lime juice and remove from heat.

4. Fill the jar with hot preserve and seal tightly. Store in a cool, dark place. *Nush-e joon!*

VARIATION

Guava Jelly

1. In the saucepan, place guava and water. Cover and cook over medium heat for 30 to 40 minutes or until soft.

2. Strain the guava through 3 layers of cheesecloth, bundle the cheesecloth, and squeeze out all the juice. Return the juice to the saucepan.

3. Add the sugar, cardamom, and vanilla and bring to a boil. Reduce heat to medium and cook for 20 to 40 minutes until the syrup has thickened enough to coat the back of a spoon. Add the lime juice and store.

(For every 2½ cup/600ml juice use 1¾ cups/350g sugar and 1 tablespoon lime juice.)

The Persian Gulf

Sistan + Baluchistan

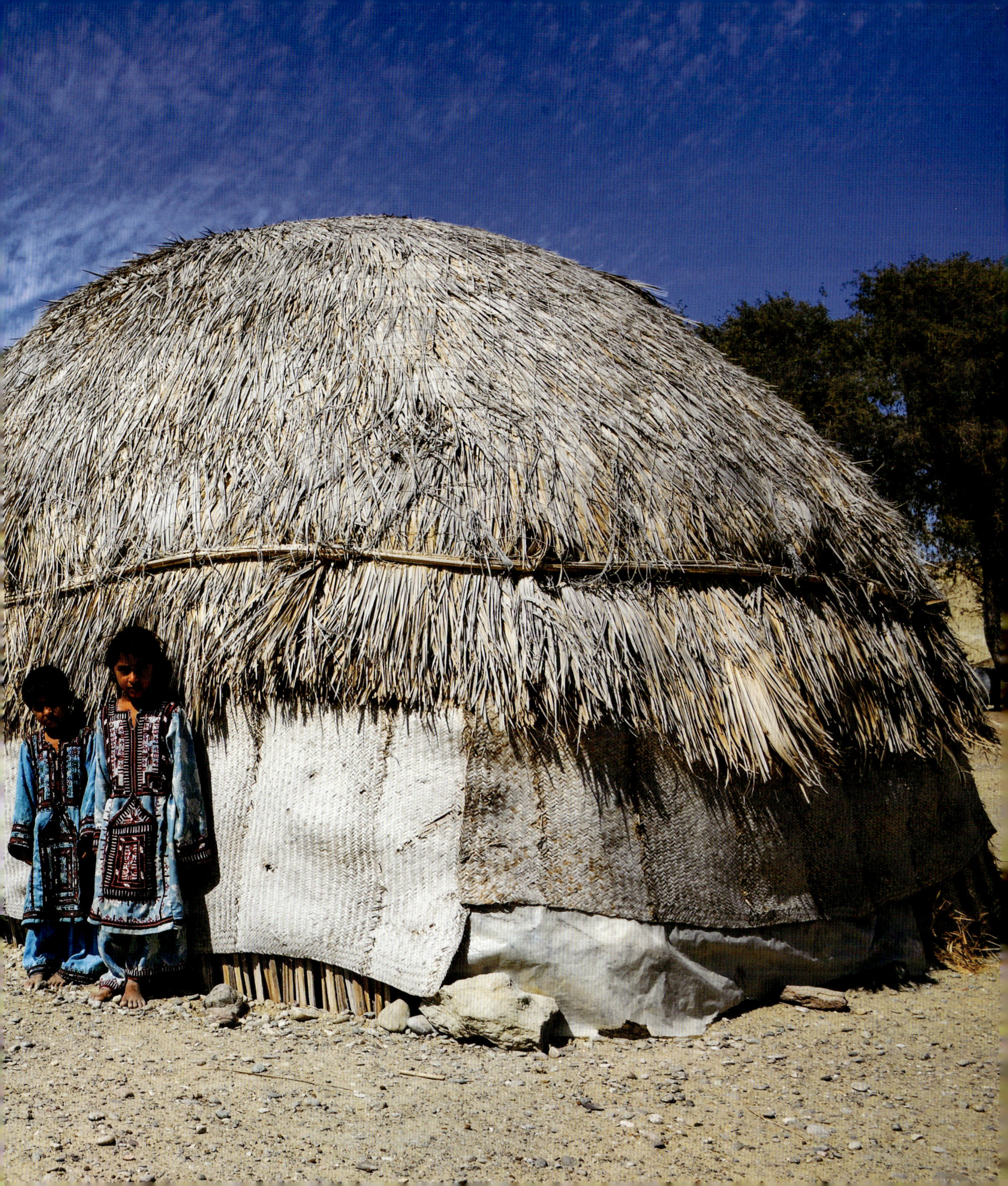

A Little History

Sistan and Baluchistan, two traditionally distinct regions now combined for administrative reasons into one province, is one of the largest and the driest of Iranian provinces. In the *Shahnameh*, the Iranian national epic written by Ferdowsi in 1010, Sistan was the homeland of the great Iranian hero Rostam. Zahedan is the capital of the province and has a wonderful weekly farmers' market/*doshanbeh bazar*. Chabahar is the southernmost city in Iran. Its bay opens out onto the Gulf of Oman and the Indian Ocean.

I was touched by the people of Sistan and Baluchistan, particularly in Chabahar. I had been told to beware of traveling in this region and I was a little anxious. But when I asked around in Bandar Abbas, I was told, "These are all rumors/*in ha hameh shaye ast*" And that was right. I found the people of this region to be calm and easygoing. Not only were our hosts Solmaz Khanezaei and her brother Akram, who were from Dashtiari Fath Ali Kalat village near Chabahar, knowledgeable, generous, and kind, but cooks, fishermen, and vendors in the markets and bazaars were welcoming and laid-back. Wheat, barley, dates, yogurt, and goat are the main ingredients of the cuisine of this region. But it's interesting that dishes are not particularly spicy in this region.

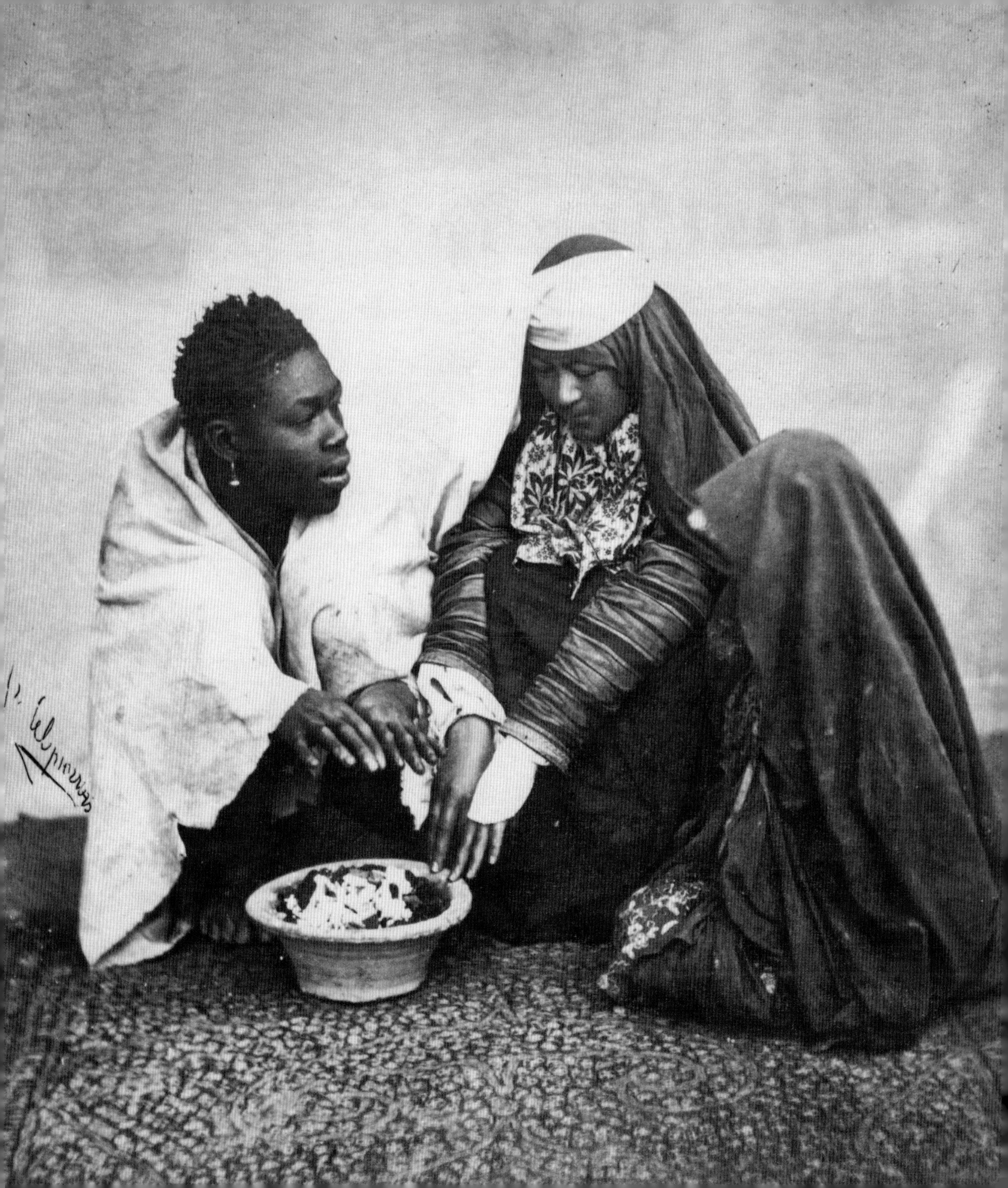

Baluchi Meat Advieh

masaleh-ye gusht

Makes 1 cup/100g
Prep: 20 minutes

2 tablespoons green cardamom pods
2 tablespoons dried ginger
2 tablespoons coriander seeds
2 tablespoons pepper corns
2 tablespoons black cumin seeds
1 tablespoon whole cloves
1 tablespoon ground nutmeg
Two 4in/10cm cinnamon sticks broken into small pieces
10 dried bay leaves

Baluchi Fish Advieh

masaleh-ye mahi

Makes 1½ cups/150g
Prep: 20 minutes

2 tablespoons ground turmeric
2 tablespoons green cardamom pods
2 tablespoons coriander seeds
2 tablespoons pepper corns
2 tablespoon red pepper flakes
2 tablespoons black cumin seeds
2 tablespoons caraway seeds
2 tablespoons safflower petals
1 tablespoon whole cloves
1 tablespoon fenugreek seeds
1 tablespoon fenugreek leaves
1 tablespoon ground nutmeg
10 dried bay leaves

The photo on the right shows the Damani Brothers' spice shop in Chabahar, renowned, reputable, and well organized—a real apothecary. As you enter, all your senses are brought to life by the colors and captivating aromas of the spices. But the old fashioned feel of the shop was countered by the staff who were not only very kind and helpful but also informed and computer-savvy. What was unique for me here compared to other spice shops in Iran was that they not only sold ground spice mixes but also mixes that kept the seeds whole for you to grind later. They also had spice mixes specifically for meats, seafood, and rice. This was my "candy store."

1. Grind the spices, each separately, in a spice grinder.

2. Transfer them to a small bowl as you grind them and use a spoon to mix well.

3. Transfer to an airtight glass jar, label, and keep in a cool place to use as needed. *Nush-e joon!*

1. Grind the spices, each separately, in a spice grinder.

2. Transfer them to a small bowl as you grind them and mix well.

3. Transfer to an airtight glass jar, label and keep in a cool place to use as needed. *Nush-e joon!*

Sistan + Baluchistan

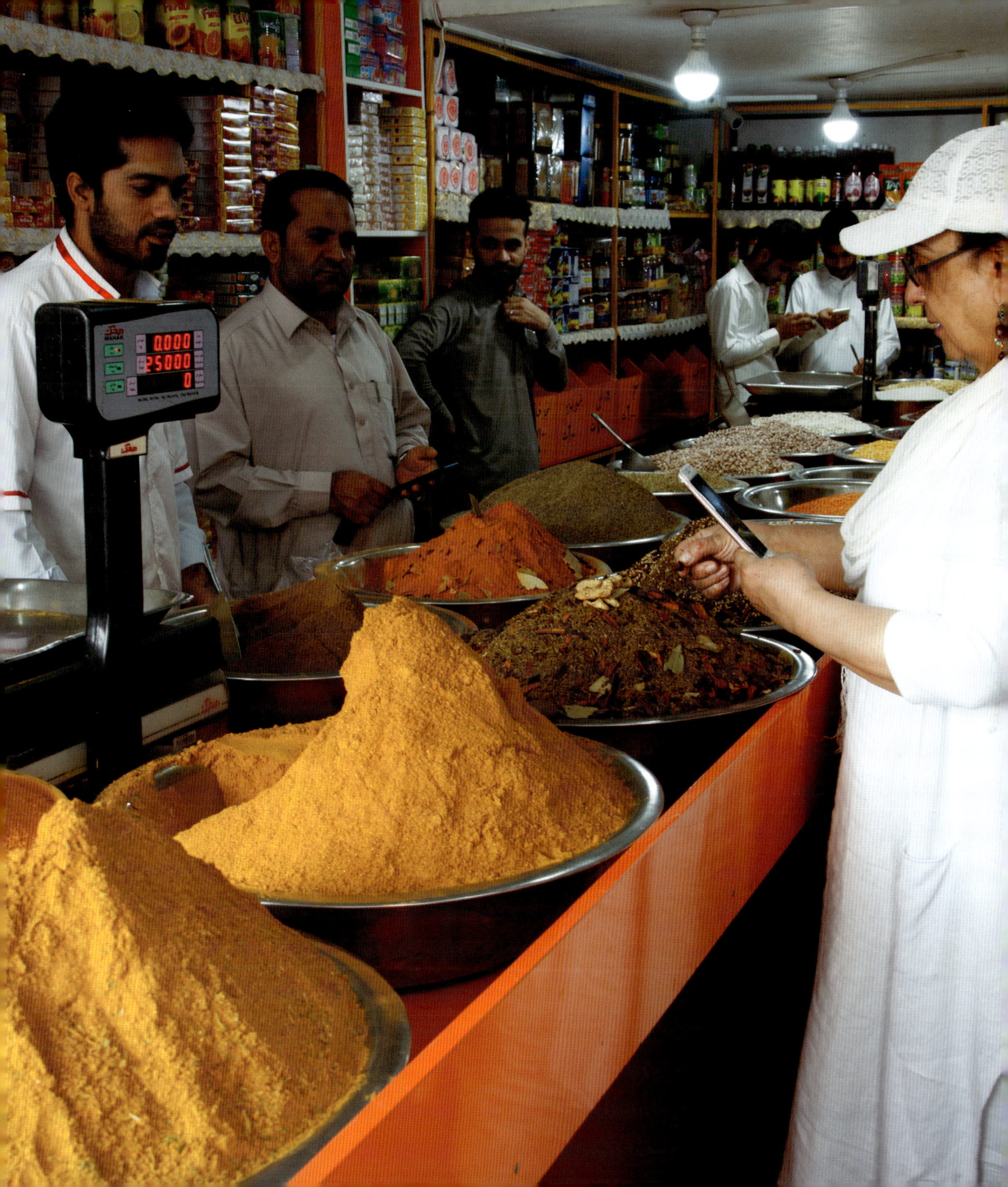
0.000
25000
0

Yellow Kashk Porridge

kashk-e zardeh-ye sistani

Serves 4
Prep: 10 minutes
Cooking: 40 minutes

- 2 tablespoons sheep-tail fat or oil
- 1 medium onion, thinly sliced
- ½ teaspoon fine sea salt
- 4 tablespoons *kashk-e zard* powder
- 4 cups/960ml broth or water
- 2 cups/30g flat bread croutons

This nutritious combination of fermented yogurt and bulgur is very popular in Sistan. It is quite similar to the Kurdish *tarkhineh*. Locals combine bulgur, garlic, green cumin seeds, nigella seeds, turmeric, coriander seeds, and salt with yogurt in a cotton sac and hang it outside for 20 days to ferment. It is then kneaded into a fine powder. You can buy it prepackaged as kashk-e zard in some Iranian markets. I adapted this yellow kashk porridge recipe from Mahsa Behjati in Zabol.

1. Heat the fat in a medium-sized laminated cast-iron pot and sauté the onion until golden brown.

2. Add the salt and *kashk,* and stir-fry for 1 minute. Gradually add the broth, while whisking constantly until it comes to a boil (this prevents curdling). Reduce heat to low, cover, and simmer for 40 minutes.

3. Adjust seasoning to taste.

4. To serve, pour into individual serving bowls and top with croutons. *Nush-e joon!*

Sistani Three-Spice Advieh

achareh

Makes 22 1½–inch/4cm patties
Prep: 20 minutes plus 2 hours of dehydration

- 1 medium yellow onion, peeled and quartered
- 3 tablespoons ground turmeric
- 2 cups/480g unbleached all-purpose wheat flour

Even though much of Iran's Sistan and Baluchistan province borders Pakistan, its food is not peppery but rather delicately spiced much like the food of Kerman on its other border. This fascinating advieh not only adds a distinctive flavor, but it also acts as a bonding agent. These patties are traditionally dehydrated in the sun, but I am drying them in a 200°F/95°C oven for 2 hours.

1. Puree the onion in a food processor. Add the turmeric and mix well.

2. Gradually add the flour and continue to mix until you have a soft dough.

3. Transfer the dough to a mixing bowl and knead until you have a firm dough (add more flour if needed).

4. Shape pieces of the dough into small patties.

5. Arrange the patties on a sheet pan lined with parchment paper and place it in a 200°F/95°C oven for 2 hours to dry.

6. Store in airtight glass jars in the fridge. Use as needed. *Nush-e joon!*

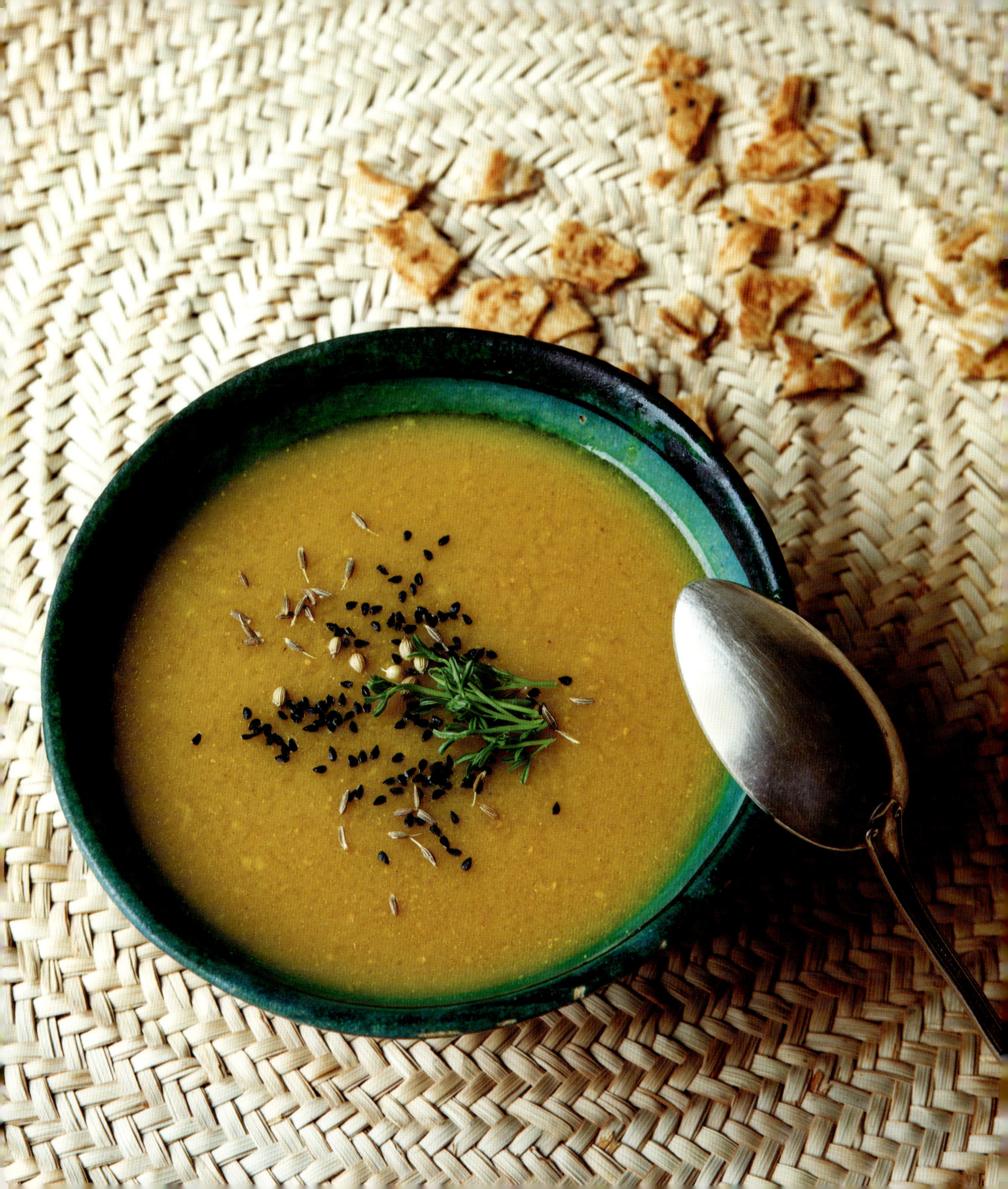

Yogurt + Tomato Fish Soup
lanju/mahi dughi

Serves 4
Prep: 20 minutes
Cooking: 45 minutes

- 2 tablespoons sheep fat tail or oil
- 1 medium onion, peeled and thinly sliced
- 2 cloves garlic, peeled and grated
- 1 teaspoon fine sea salt
- ½ teaspoon freshly ground pepper
- 2 tablespoons Sistani three-spice *advieh/achar*
- 2 medium tomatoes, peeled and finely chopped

DILUTED YOGURT/DUGH

- 1½ cups/360g yogurt
- 1½ cups/360 ml water

FISH

- 2lb/900g fish fillets cut into 2in/5cm strips

At the market in Chabahar, I shopped for seasonal vegetables with my wonderful host and guide Solmaz Khanezaei.

1. Heat the fat in a medium-sized laminated cast-iron pot and sauté the onion until golden brown. Add the garlic, salt, pepper, and *advieh*, and sauté for 1 minute. Add the tomatoes and sauté for 2 minutes.

2. **To cook the yogurt:** In a large mixing bowl, whisk together the yogurt and water for 5 minutes (beating the yogurt prevents curdling when cooking). Add it to the pot and bring to a boil over low heat, stirring constantly.

3. Add the fish and cook for 15 to 20 minutes over low heat until done. Adjust seasoning to taste. *Nush-e joon!*

Sistan + Baluchistan

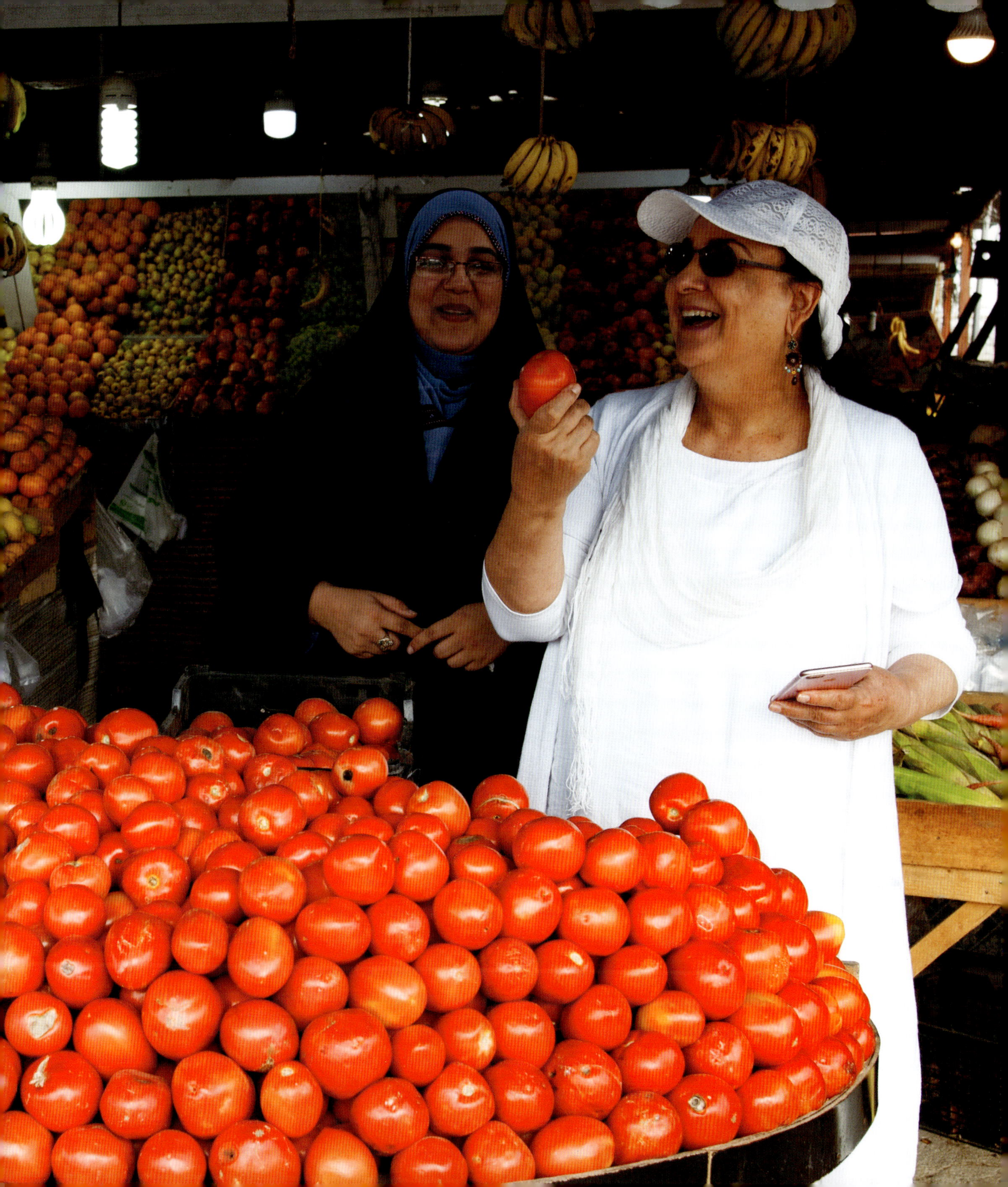

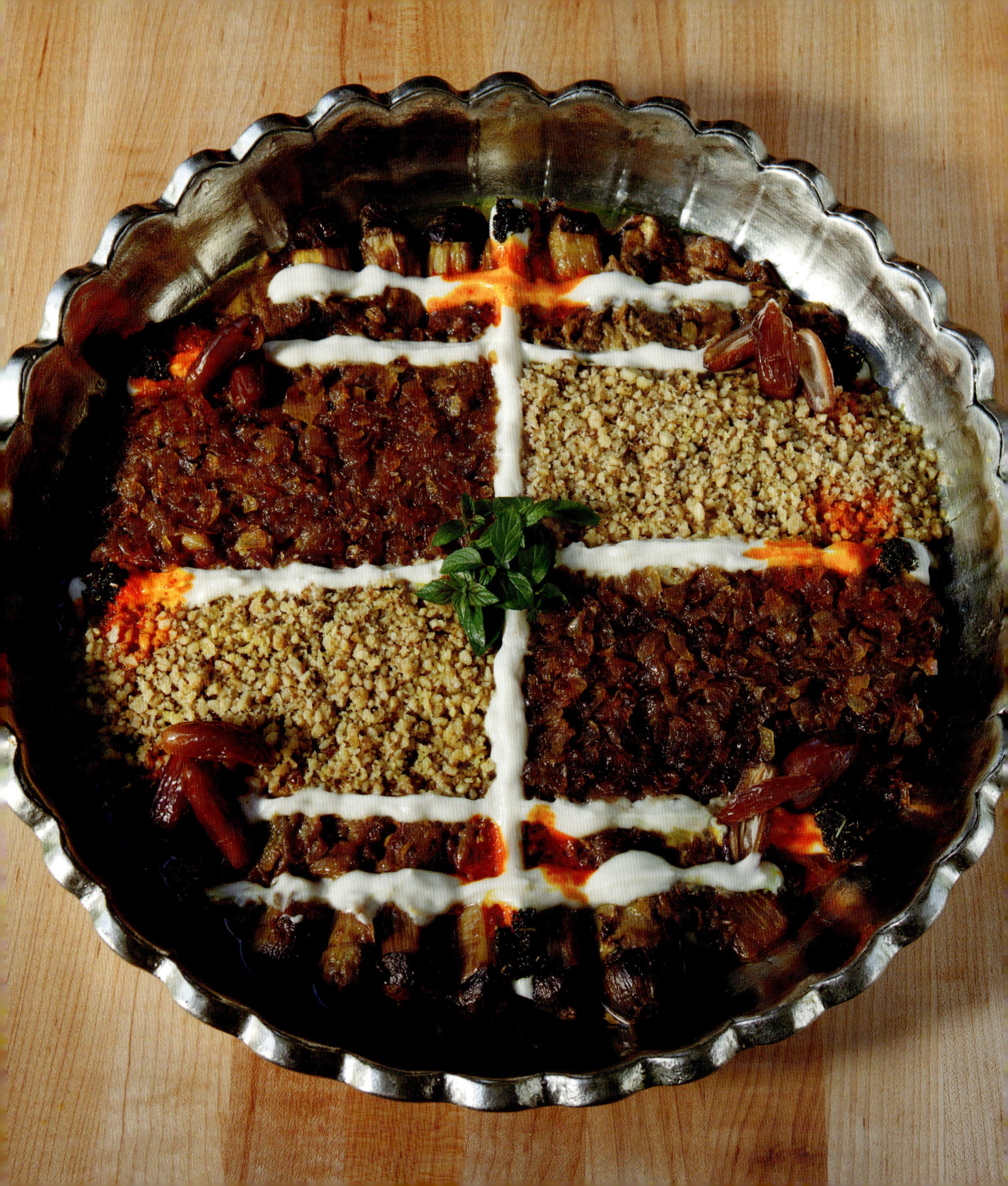

Minty Kashk with Baked Eggplant + Caramelized Onions
kashk-o bademjan-e Baluchi

Serves 6 to 8
Prep: 25 minutes
Cooking: 1½ hours

EGGPLANTS

12 Chinese eggplants (about 5lb/2.2kg)
¼ cup/60ml oil

CARAMELIZED ONION AND GARLIC/NA`NA DAGH

¼ cup/60ml oil
4 medium onions, peeled and thinly sliced
10 cloves garlic, peeled and thinly sliced
1½ teaspoons fine sea salt
1 teaspoon freshly ground black pepper
1 teaspoon turmeric
2 medjool dates, pitted and chopped
3 tablespoons dried mint flakes

KASHK

1 cup/240g liquid *kashk* diluted with 1 cup/240ml water

GARNISH

¼ cup/30g coarsely ground walnuts
4 medjool dates, sliced
¼ cup/30g crispy fried onions (optional)
2 tablespoons liquid *kashk*
¼ teaspoon ground saffron threads dissolved in 1 tablespoon warm water (optional)
¼ cup/20g fresh mint leaves

Many regions of Iran claim that this eggplant dish/kashk-e bademjan belongs to them. The beautifully decorative Baluchi version tastes as good as it looks. The combination of eggplant, garlic, and date makes it mouth-wateringly delicious. Traditionally the eggplant is fried, but I'm giving you a healthy shortcut by baking them.

1. ***To cook eggplant:*** Preheat the oven to 400°F/200°C and line a sheet pan with parchment paper.

2. Peel and cut each eggplant into 4 equal lengths and place them, side by side, on the lined sheet pan. Generously paint the eggplant with oil. Bake in the preheated oven for 40 to 45 minutes until golden brown.

3. ***Meanwhile, to caramelize the onion, garlic, and mint:*** Heat ¼ cup/60ml oil in a wide sauté pan over medium heat, and sauté the onions and garlic until golden brown. Add the salt, pepper, turmeric, and date. Sauté for 1 minute. Add the mint flakes and give it a stir.

4. Gently arrange the eggplants in the sauté pan and drizzle the diluted *kashk* over them. Cover tightly and cook over **low heat** for 30 to 35 minutes until the eggplants are tender. Keep warm until ready to serve.

5. Just before serving garnish the top with walnuts, dates, crispy onions, *kashk*, saffron water, and fresh mint leaves. *Nush-e joon!*

How to Make Crispy Fried Onions

1. Line a sheet pan with parchment paper.

2. Peel and thinly slice, along the grain, 4 medium yellow onions.

3. Fill a medium-sized saucepan with water and bring it to a boil. Add the onions, stir twice, and bring back to a boil. Drain in a sieve and allow to sit for 10 minutes.

4. Meanwhile, heat 4 cups/960ml oil in the saucepan over medium-high heat and gently add the onions (in 2 batches), stirring frequently to ensure the onions cook evenly until golden. Add ¼ teaspoon ground saffron threads and give it a stir.

5. Use a slotted spoon to remove the onions, drain, and spread them on the lined sheet pan. This type of fried onion is excellent for all Iranian cooking that uses fried onions. You can use immediately or allow to cook and store (for up to 2 weeks) in a covered glass container in the fridge and use as needed.

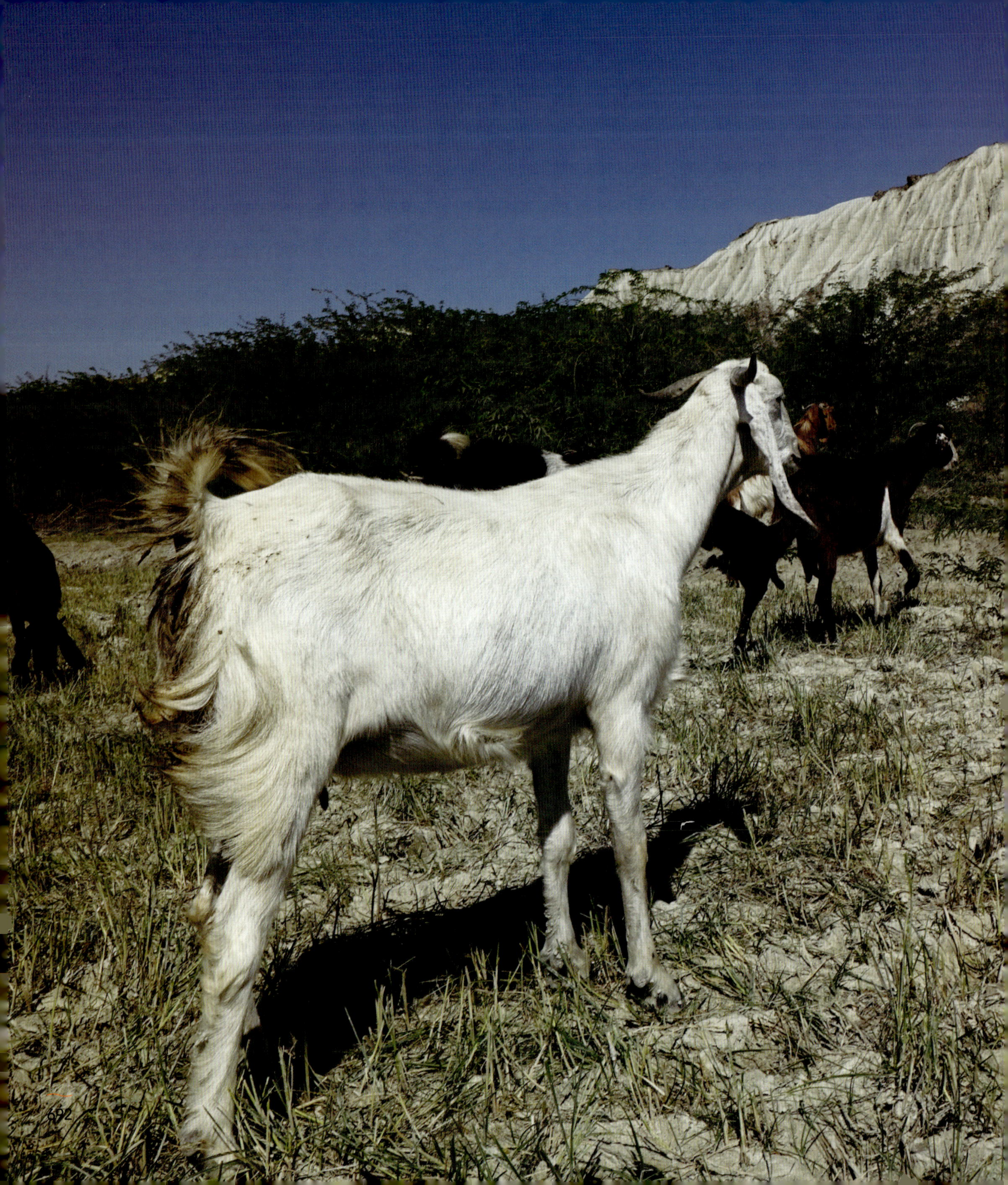

Goat, Yogurt + Split Pea Braise

dugh pa-ye sistani

Serves 6
Prep: 20 minutes
Cooking: 2¼ hours

- ¼ cup/55g sheep tail fat or 60ml oil
- 2 medium onions, thinly sliced
- 1lb/450g goat meat, cut into 1in/2.5cm
- 2 teaspoons fine sea salt
- 1 teaspoon freshly ground pepper
- 1 teaspoon turmeric
- 4 dried Persian limes, pierced
- 1 cup/150g split yellow peas, rinsed and drained
- 2 cups/480g yogurt beaten with ½ cup/120ml water for 5 minutes (to prevent curdling when cooked)
- ½ teaspoon ground saffron dissolved in 2 tablespoons water (optional)

This is an interesting and tasty variation on the renowned braise, khoresh-e qeymeh. The Sistanis, however, cook it in diluted yogurt/dugh, whereas elsewhere in Iran, they use tomatoes, which makes me wonder if this is the more original version. Tomatoes, a New World plant, reached Iran in the seventeenth century.

1. **To make the braise:** Heat 2 tablespoons fat in a medium-sized laminated cast-iron braiser over medium heat, and sauté the onions and goat until golden brown and all the juice has been absorbed. Add the salt, pepper, turmeric, and dried Persian limes, and sauté for 2 minutes longer.

2. Pour in 3 cups/720ml water and bring to a boil. Reduce heat to low, cover, and simmer for 2½ to 3 hours, stirring occasionally, until cooked.

3. Meanwhile, place the split peas in a small saucepan, add 4 cups/960ml water, and bring to a boil. Reduce heat to medium, cover and simmer for 30 to minutes, until the split peas are tender (various types of split peas take more or less time to cook). Drain.

4. **To assemble the braise:** Add the split peas, yogurt, dried limes, and saffron water. to the goat. Bring back to a boil, reduce heat to low, cover and simmer for 10 minutes.

5. Adjust seasoning to taste. Cover and keep warm until ready to serve.

6. Serve with rice/*kateh*, pickles/*torshi*, and a fresh herb platter/*sabzi-khordan*. Nush-e joon!

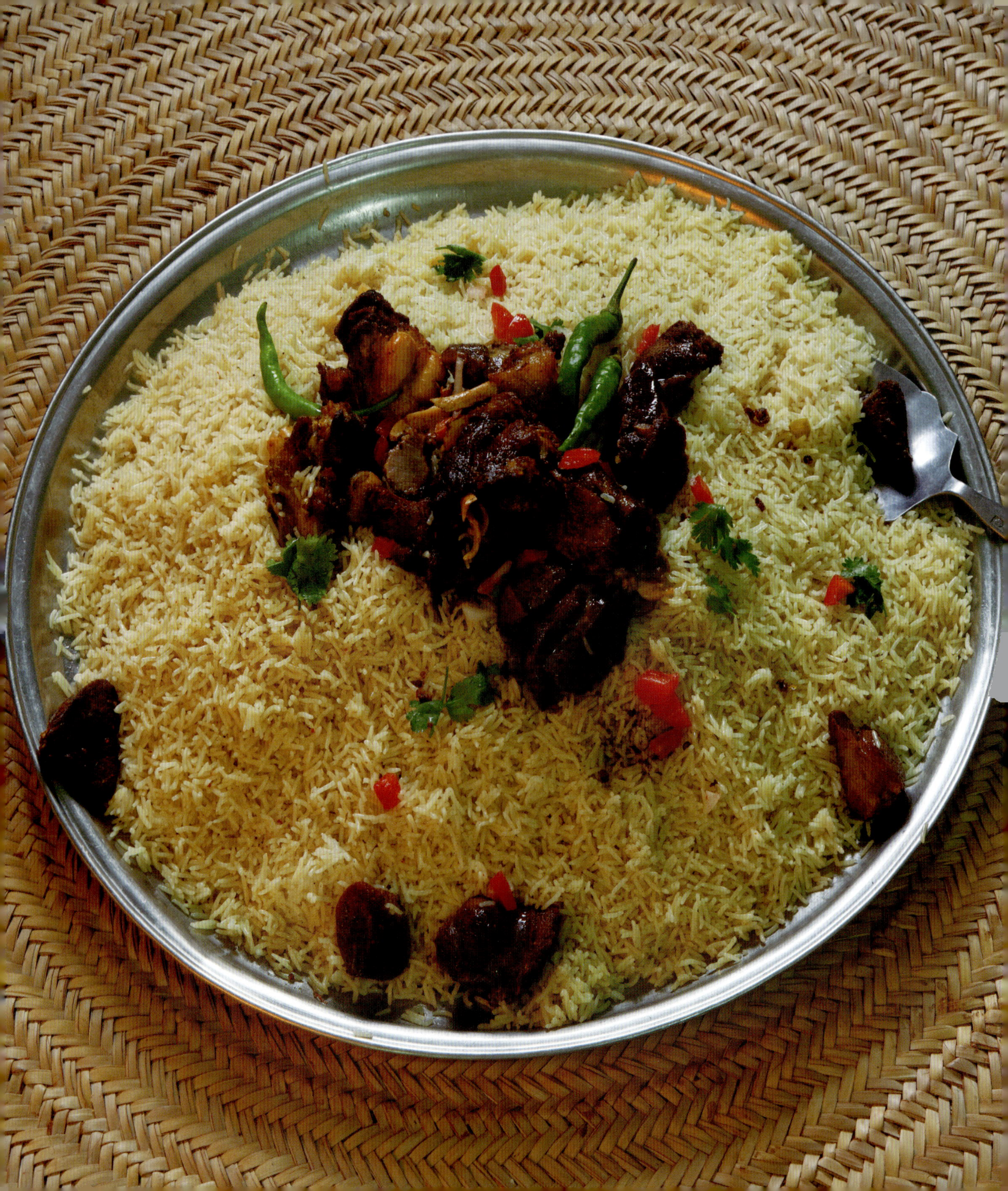

Rice Cooked in Dried Goat + Pomegranate Broth
tabahag

Serves 6 to 8
Prep: 10 minutes
Cooking: 3 hours

BROTH

2lb/900g dried shoulder or leg of goat on the bone
2 medium onions, peeled and thinly sliced
1 cup/120g walnuts
5 cups/1.2l water

RICE

2 cups/400g rice
2 tablespoons sheep-tail fat or ghee

The goat is cut up (keeping the bones), heavily dusted with salt and ground dried pomegranate arils, and hung on a clothesline under the sun for several days to dry completely. It is then used to make a broth in which the rice is cooked. The result is a very tasty rice eaten with the braised meat on the side.

1. **To prepare the meat broth:** In a saucepan, place the meat, onion, and walnuts, and add the water. Bring to a boil, reduce heat to low, cover and cook for 2½ to 3 hours until the meat is tender.

2. Drain, through a sieve into large non-stick pot. Set the meat and onion aside.

3. **To cook the rice:** Wash the rice by placing it in a large container and covering it with water. Agitate gently with your hand and then pour off the water. Repeat 4 to 5 times until the water is clear.

4. Add the rice to the broth and give it a gentle stir. Cover and cook over low heat for 45 to 55 minutes until the rice is cooked and all the juices have been absorbed. Keep warm until ready to serve.

5. **Meanwhile, to sauté the goat:** Heat the tail fat in a wide skillet over medium heat, add the meat and onion mixture, and sauté the for 5 minutes. Cover and keep warm.

6. Transfer the rice to a serving platter with the goat and onion mixture on the side. Serve with pickles. *Nush-e joon!*

VARIATION

To use fresh goat meat without sun-drying: In a mixing bowl, place 1lb/450g deboned goat meat, which has been cut up. Add 1 tablespoon fine sea salt and ¼ cup/25g ground dried pomegranate arils (available at Iranian or Indian stores by the name *anar-daneh*), and 2 tablespoons pomegranate molasses. Toss well, cover, and allow to marinate in the fridge overnight. Continue with step 1 above as you would with dried meat.

Sistan + Baluchistan

Preparing large sardines/*kashuk* before wrapping them in date palm leaves for grilling. Recipe on page 698.

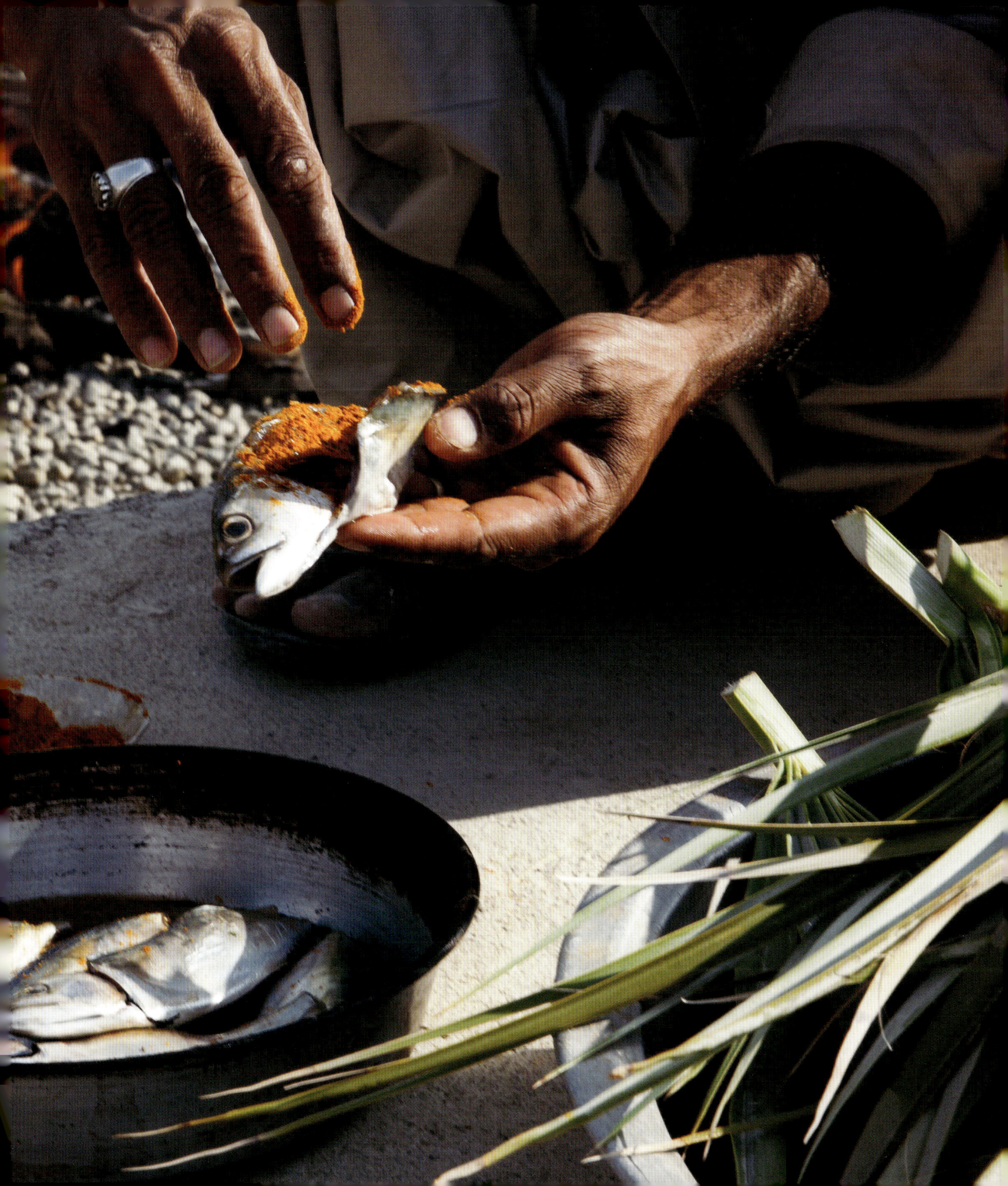

Fish in Wild Date Palm Leaf

mahiag-e pach-e baluchi

Serves 6
Prep: 20 minutes
Cooking: 10 minutes

FISH

6 whole, fish (branzino sea bass are a good size for this), scaled, gutted and rinsed, or 2.5lb/1.1kg fish fillets cut into 6 pieces, all small bones removed
1 tablespoon fine sea salt

DUSTING

1 tablespoon Baluchi fish *advieh*
1 teaspoon freshly ground pepper
1 teaspoon turmeric

WRAP

½ cup sesame oil
6 wild date palm or banana leaves

I made this with Usta Musa in Chabahar. We picked our wild date palm leaves/daz in the backyard. After washing and thoroughly drying the leaves, we wrapped the fresh fish we'd bought at the local market in them. This dish is traditionally made outdoors at picnics.

1. **To prepare the fish:** Salt the fish, inside and outside and set aside.

2. **To grill the fish:** Prepare the grill. Line a sheet pan with parchment paper.

3. Combine all the ingredients for the dusting in a small bowl then dust the fish on all sides inside and outside. Place them on the sheet pan.

4. Spread a layer of date palm leaves on a wooden board, paint the leave with oil and place the fish on it. Drizzle oil over the fish. Wrap the palm leaves around and the fish and tie using strips of the leaf.

5. Once the grill is ready, grill all sides, turning frequently, for 5 to 10 minutes.

6. Serve the fish, still inside the leaf on individual plates for each person to open their own. Serve with Rice Steamed in Date Molasses (page 645). *Nush-e joon!*

Sistan + Baluchistan

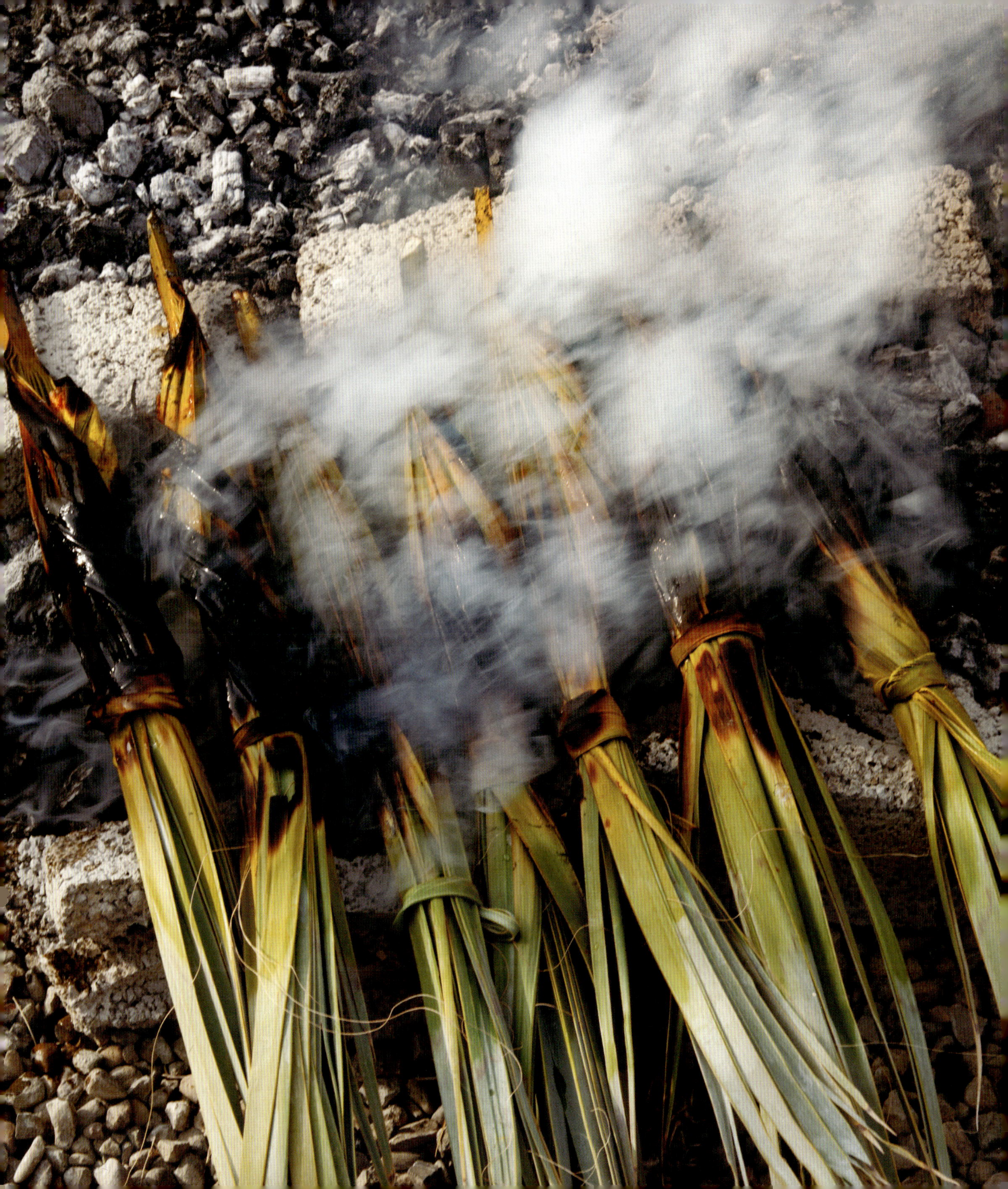

Goat Cooked in Fire Pit
kabab-e tanurcheh

Serves 6
Prep: 20 minutes
Cooking: 6 to 8 hours, or overnight

GOAT

6lb/2.7kg goat meat pieces on the bone, rised and patted dry
1 cup/240ml fresh lime juice

DUSTING

¼ cup Baluchi meat *advieh*
1 tablespoon freshly ground pepper
1 tablespoon turmeric
3 tablespoons fine sea salt

SPECIAL EQUIPMENT

48in/120cm steel rod
Steel wire
Large pan
Clay for sealing pit

This all-day or overnight style of cooking meat is common in Baluchistan.

1. **To prepare the pit:** Dig a round pit, 24in/60cm wide by 48in/120cm deep. Pour charcoal into the pit and light it.

2. **To prepare the meat:** Rub the goat all over with lime juice. Combine all the ingredients for the dusting in a small bowl then dust the meat all over, rubbing it into the meat with your hands. Set aside.

3. Once the charcoal is lit and glowing all over, use the steel wire to attach the pieces of meat to the rod. With the help of another person, lower the rod with the meat dangling from it into the pit.

4. Cover the pit with a large pan, and use wet clay to seal around the pan. Place bricks or a block over the pan to further secure it.

5. Allow the meat to cook in this way for 6 to 8 hours, or overnight. The meat should be well cooked, falling off the bone, and eaten right away. *Nush-e joon!*

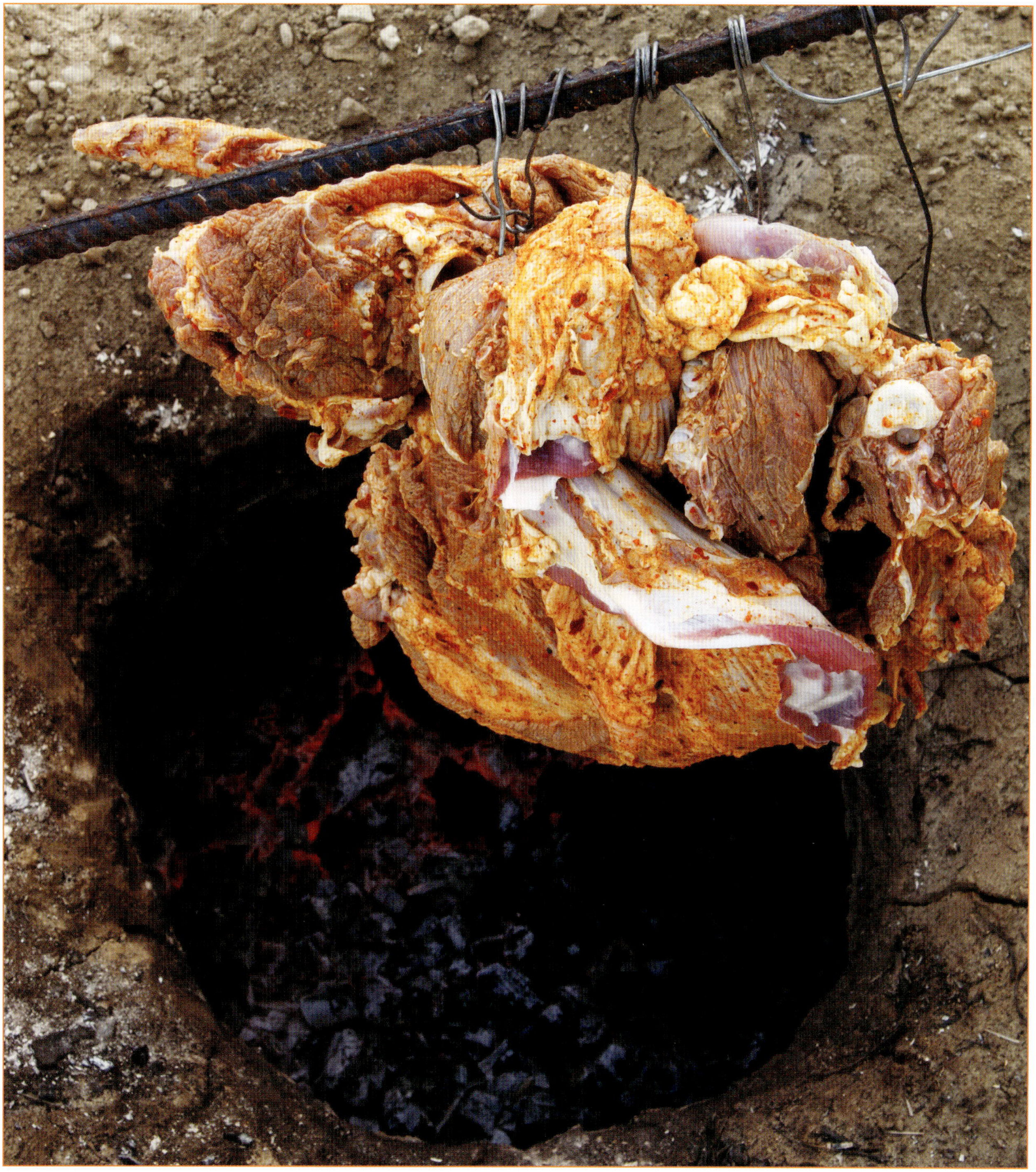

A Visual Glossary of an Iranian Pantry

- unripe grapes
- raisins
- pomegranate
- walnuts
- baby almonds
- pistachios
- sesame seeds
- unripe greengages
- lime
- Persian shallots
- zest of orange
- basmati rice
- fava beans
- rose petals
- dried Persian lime
- Persian cucumber
- sumac
- orange blossom water
- barberries
- rose water
- liquid *kashk*
- saffron threads
- Italian eggplant
- Chinese eggplant
- pomegranate molasses
- grape molasses

- star anise
- Persian hogweed seed/*golpar*
- fennel seeds
- sour orange
- dried Persian lime and hearts of lime
- date molasses
- green + black cardamom
- ground turmeric
- slivered sour orange peel
- yellow *kashk*
- date
- kefir lime leaf
- Sistani three-spice
- smoked rice
- dried terebinth fruit/*pesteh baneh*
- tamarind
- pickled terebinth fruit/*baneh*
- black *kashk*
- tahini
- white *kashk*
- dried pomegranate seeds/*anar daneh*

Acknowledgements

First and foremost, I'd like to thank my dear cousins Mansoureh and Ferdows Manuchehrian in Iran without whose support and guidance I would not have been able to make this journey. I'd also like to thank: Mojdeh Khalili; Naz, Raz, Marjan and Bahram Ebrahimi who were always there for me during my visits. Many thanks to Marjan Khalili, who accompanied me on my trips and assisted me with everything; as well as her sister, Mojan Khalili, who helped me understand Hamadan and took the photographs there.

I am grateful to Mahmood Yassavoli—my publisher in Iran, and his wife Maryam, who guided me and supported this project. Afshin Bakhtiar, has been my wonderful photographer for all my trips in Iran, he is a very sensitive man who loves Iran dearly. I also owe a special thanks to Jahangir Asgharzadeh—our driver and my protector—who drove us tens of thousands of miles across Iran without a single accident or breakdown. I am very grateful to him for his cool and calm attitude, which made every situation easier to deal with. Also in Iran, my sincere thanks to Fati Fereydouni for her help organizing my trips; and Maryam Bahar and her husband Richie Boroumand for their help with photography in Tehran.

A number of people were wonderfully kind and generous in various towns and villages in Iran, I am grateful to them; they add light to this world: Pooya Alaedini, Mr. Aqdassy, Golnessa and Hossein Mozaffari, Dowlat Khabarkhosh, Ebrahim Samanipour, Hamid Qanadour, Dr. Dashtizadeh, Hossein Hedri, Mr. and Mrs. Alizadeh; Shahin and Homayoun Sarlati; Mr. Alaghband; Reza Rasoulian; Nima Safa; Solmaz Khanezaei; and last but not least, the Amin family in Kerman.

In America, I owe heartfelt thanks to many people: Maria Rodrigues, who has been my cooking assistant for the past 25 years; Christol Vincent, my Georgetown graduate student assistant, who loved to cook and who tested all the recipes in this book; Gabriela Sotoro de Mensies, who helped with the mise en place of the recipes for the testing and who also showed a flair for organizing the kitchen. Gerry and Elise Cervenka brought us the pot used on the cover photo. It was made by Elise's father Ken Cassie. Many others passed through my kitchen and cooking classes during the making of this book. I'd like to thank them all for their help: Chefs Chris Morgan and Gerlad Addison of Maydan Restaurant; Ariel Pasternak; Anika Floor; my niece Mojdeh Bahar; Hanif Sadr; and our scholar friends Willem Floor, Hasan Javadi, and Houchang Chehabi. A big thank you to Massumeh Farhad at the Freer and Sackler galleries who encouraged me and generously made their archives of photographs of old Iran available to us. George Constable has been a friend and neighbor and my editor for more than 20 years. I'd like to thank him for all his help and editorial expertise.

I want to thank my sons Zal and Rostam, who took time out of their busy schedules to make valuable recommendations to improve the book in both content and design. My thanks to them knows no bounds. Finally to my husband, my publisher, and my love. I could not even imagine writing a book without his help and support—he is the cheese, walnut and Persian basil to my *sangak* bread.

Our team, from left to right: Afshin Bakhtiar, me, Marjan Khalili, and Jahangir Asgharzadeh.

Credits

All photos © copyrighted by Mage Publishers unless provided under license by institutions listed here.

AFSHIN BAKHTIAR: 2, 8, 10, 12, 14, 15, 18–19, 22, 23, 24, 26, 27, 29, 30–31, 35, 37, 38, 39, 41, 45, 53, 55, 57, 61, 62, 68, 69, 74, 78, 79, 81, 82, 93, 94, 95, 100, 102, 104, 105, 107, 113, 115, 117, 119, 123, 124, 125, 128, 129, 134, 135, 139, 142, 143, 146, 147, 153, 156–157, 158, 161, 162, 165, 166, 167, 171, 177, 179, 180–181, 182, 191, 192, 195, 201, 203, 205, 212, 214–215, 218, 220, 221, 223, 225, 228, 232, 233, 251, 268, 269, 273, 277, 282–283, 288, 289 (bottom), 291, 304, 306, 308, 309, 310, 311, 312, 313, 314, 339, 347, 352, 353, 355, 359–360, 363, 377, 380, 381, 382, 428, 429, 430, 434, 436, 439, 440, 441, 442, 444, 446, 453, 454, 455, 456, 457, 458, 459, 460, 461, 462, 464, 465, 466, 467, 468, 469, 471, 477, 479, 508, 510, 516, 517, 519, 521, 529, 531 (bottom), 537, 541, 544, 545, 548, 550, 551, 553, 554, 555, 556, 561, 562, 563, 564, 566, 567, 568, 574, 575, 576–577, 578, 580, 582, 583, 584, 587, 588, 590, 591, 592-593, 600, 601, 602, 604, 618, 621, 626, 627, 634–635, 643, 651, 672, 674, 680, 681, 683, 685, 689, 692, 694, 696–697, 699, 700, 701, 705, 707, 709, 726–727.

NADER SOURI: 5, 286, 297, 388, 390, 391, 392, 393, 416, 417, 419, 422, 425, 4.

MOJAN KHALILI: 249, 257, 263, 265, 284–285, 289, 292, 293, 298.

MARYAM ZANDI: 155, 384.

ROYA NOURIZADEH: 6–7.

HOSSEIN MOZAFFARI: 306, 589.

HANIF SADR: 168.

KAREN RASMUSSEN/ARCHEOGRAPHICS (MAPS): 11, 70, 229, 313, 389, 462, 518, 565, 575.

HOUCHANG CHEHABI: 33, 261, 415.

FERDOWS MANUCHEHRIAN: 17.

SHOHREH AMIN: 505.

PHILIPE LEROY: 289 (top).

ROLOFF BENY: 176.

MAGE PUBLISHERS: 38, 47, 49, 51, 85, 87, 89, 91, 99, 108, 111, 120, 127, 133, 137, 141, 148, 151, 185, 187, 189, 197, 271, 281, 295, 301, 303, 315, 317, 321, 323, 324, 327, 329, 531 (top), 334, 341, 343, 344, 345, 348, 350, 356, 365, 367, 369, 371, 373, 375, 387, 395, 397, 399, 401, 403, 405, 407, 409, 411, 412, 427, 433, 449, 451, 473, 481, 483, 484, 487, 489, 491, 493, 495, 497, 499, 501, 503, 507, 513, 515, 522, 524, 527, 532, 535, 539, 543, 547, 571, 573, 595, 597, 598, 607, 608, 610, 616, 623, 625, 628, 630, 632, 636, 639, 640, 644, 647, 648, 653, 655, 657, 658, 661, 662, 664, 666, 670, 677, 678, 687, 690, 694, 702, 703.

FREER GALLERY OF ART AND ARTHUR M. SACKLER GALLERY

Album of Persian Photographs. Freer Gallery of Art and Arthur M. Sackler Gallery Archives. Smithsonian Institution, Washington D.C, FSA_A2015.09_087b, 43; FSA_A2015.09_084b: 275; FSA_A2015.09_044, 361; FSA_A2015.09_091b, 420; FSA_A2015.09_073b; 613; FSA_A2015.09_072b, 683.

Myron Bement Smith Collection: Antoin Sevruguin Photographs. Freer Gallery of Art and Arthur M. Sackler Gallery Archives. Smithsonian Institution, Washington D.C. Gift of Katherine Dennis Smith, 1973-1985, FSA_A.4_2.12.Up.09, 65; FSA A.04 2.12.Up.58, 252–253.

Stephen Arpee Collection of Sevruguin Photographs. Freer Gallery of Art and Arthur M. Sackler Gallery Archives. Smithsonian Institution, Washington D.C., 2011, FSA_A2011.03_B.39, 20; FSA_A2011.03_B.40, 331; FSA_A2011.03_B.51, 378–379.

SHUTTERSTOCK.COM

Tappasan Phurisamrit 204–205; Mina Dastjerdi 174–175; Spumador 83.; Martin Canek 172–173

NATIONAL GEOGRAPHIC CREATIVE

Thomas J. Abercrombie 72–73

GEORGE GERSTER: 244–245.

THREE LIONS/HULTON ARCHIVE/GETTY IMAGES: 336.

TRANSLATIONS

DICK DAVIS (TRANSLATIONS): 385, 509, 520, 559.

WILLEM FLOOR (TRANSLATION): 413.

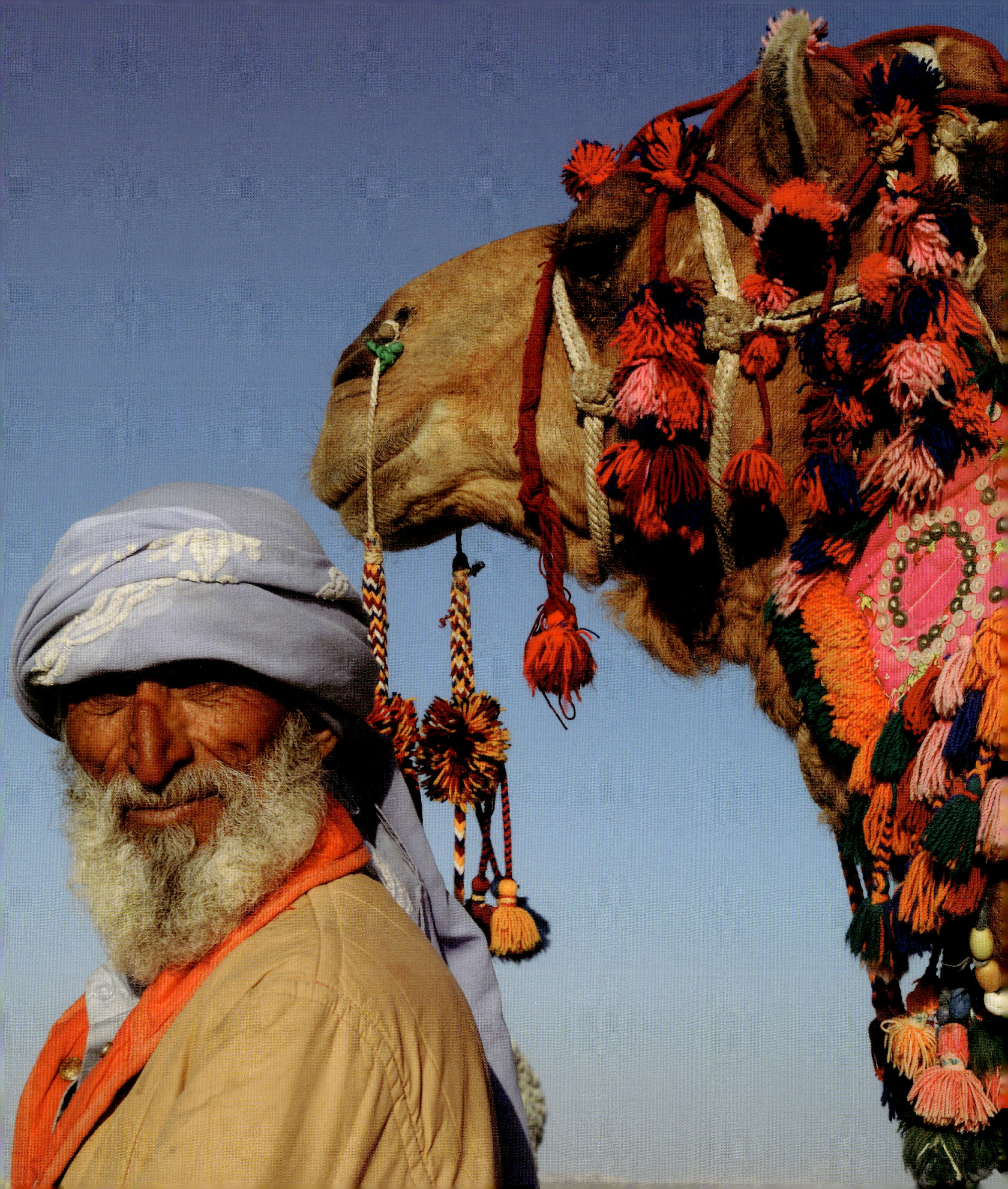

Recipe Contents

Tehran

- Lamb Shank, Chickpea + Kidney Bean Soup 39
  Abgusht-e nokhod lubia, Dizzy
- Lamb's Head, Feet + Tripe Soup 44
  kaleh pacheh-o sirab shirdun
- Onion, Egg + Spinach Soup 46
  eshkeneh-ye tehrani
- Ramp Polow 48
  valak polow
- Darbandi Chicken Kabab 52
  Jujeh kabab-e darband
- Fresh Herb Braise 54
  khoresh-e qormeh sabzi
- Wheat and Turkey Breakfast Porridge 58
  halim-e gandom
- Savory Mushroom Pie 60
  pirashki-e khosravi
- Tongue Sandwich 63
  sandwich-e zaban-e andré
- Cream Puffs 64
  nun-e khamei

Caspian

- Sweet + Sour Patties 76
  shami-e torsh-e rudbar
- Caspian Green Salt 84
  dalar
- Apple + Caspian Green Salt Salad 84
  sibtorsh dalar
- Olive Tapenade 86
  zaytun parvardeh
- Tomato, Egg + Garlic Omelet 88
  cheghertemeh-ye pomodor gilaki
- Smoked Eggplant, Tomato + Walnut Spread 91
  aghuz tareh
- Eggplant Tapenade 91
  kaleh kabab/dokhtar naz
- Smoked Eggplant with Eggs + Garlic 92
  mirza qasemi
- Garlic-Chive Omelet 96
  sir-abij
- Cheese + Dill Omelet 96
  panir abij ba shivid
- Butternut Squash with Rice Flour Patties 98
  kui kaka
- Butternut Squash Osh 101
  osh-e kuhi
- Caviar 106
  khaviar
- Sturgeon Patties 109
  kotlet-e uzunburun
- Fish Roe Omelet 109
  ashpal-e gilaki
- Fish Head Soup 110
  mahi kaleh ab
- Seared Fish with Garlic + Vinegar Glaze 112
  mahi-e kapur-e torsh-o shirin
- Sturgeon Kabab with Sour Orange 114
  kabab-e uzunburun ba narenj
- Sweet + Sour Kabab 116
  kabab-e torsh
- Duck Kabab 118
  kabab-e ordak
- Quail Kabab 121
  kabab-e belderchin
- Plain Rice 122
  kateh
  kateh-ye berenj-e dudi
- Duck Eggs + Fava Beans Braise 126
  baqala qataq
- Eggs, Herbs, Garlic + Sour Orange Braise 130
  torsh tareh
- Duck + Pomegranate Braise 132
  khoresh-e fesenjun-e gilaki ba morqabi
- Eggplant, Walnut + Herb Braise with Meatballs 134
  khoresh-e anar abij/sangeh khoresh
- Butternut Squash, Walnut + Pomegranate Braise 136
  khoresh-e kui-e tar
- Medlar, Walnut, Pomegranate + Chicken Casserole . . . 138
  lavangi
- Sour Cherry Braise 140
  khoresh-e albalu-ye gorgani
- Rice Lace Pancakes 144
  reshteh-ye khoshkar
- Fuman Bun 145
  kolucheh-ye fuman
- Saffroned Rice Flour Cookies 149
  shekam por/shirini-e sam-e pusteh
- Rose Petal Rice Pudding 150
  gol-e paludeh/gol-e qand
- Grape Molasses 152
  dushab-e angur
- Verjuice Molasses 152
  rob-e ab ghureh
- Sour Apple Molasses 152
  rob-e sib-e torsh
- Rose Petal Preserve 154
  moraba-ye gol-e mohammadi
- Fig Jam 154
  khams-e anjir

Wild Parsnip Preserve 159
   moraba-ye shaqaqol
Greengage Molasses 159
   rob-e alucheh
Cornelian Cherry Chutney 160
   khams-e akhteh
Blackberry Preserve 160
   moraba-ye tameshk/velash
Black Garlic Pickle 163
   sir torshi-e shomali
Medlar Pickle 164
   ab konus-e azgil
Borage + Valerian Tea 169
   dam nush-e gol gav zabun va sombolative
Jujub Panacea Tea 169
   dam nush-e annab
Saffron Love Tea 169
   dam nush-e zaferun
Hogweed Seed Tea 170
   dam nush-e golpar
Chabahar Milk Tea 170
   shir chai-ye chabahar
Dried Persian Lime Tea 170
   dam nush-e limu omani

Azarbaijan

Azari Three-Spice Advieh 184
   advieh-ye azari
Tabrizi Cheese, Walnut + Herb Balls 186
   doymaj
Saffron Omelet with Rose Petals 188
   khagineh-ye tabrizi
Stuffed Grape Leaves 190
   dolmeh-ye balg-e mo-tabrizi
Pasta Pellet Osh 194
   osh-e omaj-e tabrizi
Yogurt + Chickpea Osh 196
   osh-e dugh-e ardebili
Azarbaijani Dumpling Soup 198
   gush bareh-ye azarbaijani
Barley Soup 200
   sup-e jow
Tabrizi Meatballs with Split Peas + Tomatoes 202
   kufteh tabrizi
Vegetable + Fruit Casserole 206
   tas kabab-e ardabil
Saffron Steamed Rice 209
   chelow
Fillet Kabab 213
   kabab-e barg
   kabab-e bonab 215
Ground Lamb Kabab 216
   kabab-e kubideh-ye gusfand-e tabrizi
Caucasian Fillet Kabab 217
   kabab-e qafqazi-e urumia

Lamb Liver Kabab 219
   kabab-e jigar
Lamb Fries Kabab 219
   kabab-e donbalan
Carrot + Walnut Halva 222
   halva-ye havij-o gerdu-ye azarbaijani
Black Walnut Halva 224
   halva-ye siah-e ardebili

Qom

Spicy Meatballs with Verjuice 230
   kufteh-ye qomi

Qazvin

Qazvini Four-Spice Advieh 234
   advieh-ye gheymeh nesar
Rice, Lamb, Rose Petals + Barberries 236
   qeymeh nesar-e qazvini
Lentil, Lamb + Prune Braise 238
   marju khoresh-e qazvini
Saffroned Almond + Pistachio Baklava 242
   baqlava-ye do rangeh-ye qazvini

Hamadan

Hamadani Seven-Spice Advieh 246
   advieh-ye hamadani
Cheese, Walnut + Herb Balls 248
   qut-e hamadani
Dried Fruit + Noodles Osh 250
   osh-e khoshkbar-e hamadani
Carrot + Bulgur Osh 254
   osh-e halim-o havij-e hamedani
Bulgur + Curly Cucumber Osh 255
   osh-e khiyar chambar-e hamadani
Bulgur, Noodle + Currant Pilaf 256
   petleh polow-ye hamadani
Pumpkin Preserve 258
   moraba-ye kadu halvai-ye hamadani
Roasted Butternut Squash + Grape Molasses 260
   kadu halvai-o gerdu-o shireh-ye angur-e hamadani
Sweet Sesame Bun 262
   nan-e komaj-e hamadani
Finger Twist Spread 264
   angusht pich-e hamadani
Egg + Saffron Spread 264
   halva zardeh-ye hamadani
Apricot + Nut Pickle 266
   torshi-e ajil-e hamadani

Arak

Tomato + Lime Broth with Tiny Meatballs 270
    gushtabeh/kufteh-ye kaleh gonjishki-e araki
Split Pea, Bulgur + Yogurt Osh 272
    osh-e mast-e araki
    osh-e jow-e araki
Sautéed Liver + Kidney with Black Kashk 274
    jaghurbaghur-e araki ba qareh qurut
Kashk 276
    kashk, also Black Kashk/qorut
Rice with Mung Beans + Caramelized Onions 278
    dami-e mash-e araki/polow mashak
    dampokhtak-e baqali zard/dami-e cheshm bolboli
Walnut + Sumac Meatballs 280
    kufteh-ye somaq-e araki

Bread

Urmia Chorayi Bread 294
    yaghli al choraki/nan-e roghani-e urumia
Tribal Pan-Flat Bread 296
    nan-e saj-e kordi
Khorasani Taftun Bread 299
    nan-e taftun-e khorasani
Deep-Fried Flat Bread 300
    chozmeh-e bojnurdi
Sweet Gingerbread Crackers 302
    nan-e qandi
Twice-Cooked Semi-Sweet Bread 305
    nan-e sokhari
Date + Sesame Bread 307
    gerdeh-ye bushehr
Bread Cooked in Ashes 308
    nan-e purani
Acorn Pan Bread 311
    nan-e balut/kalak-e chahar mahal-e bakhtiari

Kurdistan + Tribal Region

Kurdish Seven-Spice Advieh 314
    advieh-ye haft chanshni-e kordi
Lettuce + Yogurt Salad 316
    borani-e kahu-ye kordi
    borani-e karafs/borani-e khiar-o somaq
Barley, Nettle, Yogurt + Kashk Osh 318
    osh-e gazing
Tarkhineh Osh 320
    osh-e tarkhineh-ye kordi/tarkhineh
Baked Onions Filled with Rice + Herbs 322
    dolmeh-ye piaz-e kordi
Bulgur Meatballs Filled with Caramelized Onion . . . 325
    kabab-e balghur-e kordi/halow kabab
Bulgur Meatballs in a Vegetable Broth 326
    kufteh savara-ye kordi

Saffron Rice + Potato Croquettes 328
    kobeh-ye kordi/ kefteh halab
Chive + White Bean Braise 330
    khoresh-e tareh-ye kordi
Rice with Lamb Rib Chops 333
    dandeh polow-ye ilamati
Saffroned Lamb + Barberry Braise 334
    qeymeh zereshk-e kordi
Almond, Lamb, Saffron + Rose Water Braise 337
    khoresh-e khalal-e badam-e kermanshahi
Rice with Mushrooms + Barberries 338
    qarchak/qarch polow-ye kordi
Bulgur + Lamb Pilaf 340
    savar pilau-ye kordi
Walnut, Pomegranate + Herb Patties 342
    shami kabab-e khorramabad/lori
Lace-Fat-Wrapped Lamb Liver Kabab 344
    jigar vaz-e lorestan
Saffron Rice Cookies 346
    nan-e berenji-e kordi/qors-e khorshidi
Almond Pudding 349
    fereni-e badum/kashkul-e kordi
Rose + Yogurt Love Cake 351
    cayk-e eshq-e kordi

Isfahan

Isfahani Seven-Spice Advieh 357
    advieh-ye esfahani
Sumac Soup 360
    sup-e somaq-e esfahani
Lamb, Prune, Apricot + Quince Spread 362
    yakhmeh-ye torsh-e esfahani
Mung Beans + Kohlrabi Spread 364
    halim-e maush qomry-e esfahani
Chickpea Meatballs in Aromatic Tomato Sauce 366
    khoresh-e ghermez-e nokodchi-e esfahani
Isfahani Lamb Briyani Wrap 368
    kabab-e beriyani-e esfahan
Sweet + Sour Glazed Chickpea + Carrot Patties . . . 370
    kabab-e moshti-e esfahani
Lamb, Quince + Plumb Braise 372
    khoresh-e beh-o alu
Saffroned Yogurt + Lamb Neck Braise with Barberries 374
    khoresh-e mast-e esfahani ba garden-e gusfand
Saffroned Chicken + Yogurt Braise 376
    khoresh-e mast-e esfahani ba morgh
Isfahani Nougat 380
    gaz-e esfahani
Lamb + White Bean Braise with Dill Rice 386
    gusht-o lubia-o shivid polow-ye kashani

Khorasan

Khorasani Seven-Spice Advieh 394
   advieh-ye haft qalami-e khorasan
   advieh-ye haft qalami-e khorasan
Potato Kuku with Saffron Syrup Glaze 396
   kuku-ye shirin-e mashhadi
Barberry Osh 398
   osh-e zershk-e khorasani
Wild Pistachio + Cucumber Soup 400
   pesteh baneh-ye birjandi
Spinach + Dumpling Osh 402
   osh-e jushvareh-ye sabzevari
Turnip Osh 404
   osh-e shalqam-e khorasani
Walnut + Kashk Soup 406
   kaleh jush-e khorasan
   kaleh jush-e sabzevari/komeh jush ba gojefarangi
Lamb Neck, Bulgur + Bean Porridge 408
   sholeh-ye mashhadi
Roasted Vegetables with Garlic Kashk 410
   quruti-e birjand
Twice-Cooked Lamb in Tail-Fat with Fried Bread 412
   Bojnordi qormeh ba nan-e roghani
Rice with Legumes + Butternut Squash 414
   qaboli polow-ye bojnurdi
Barberry Rice 418
   zereshk polow-ye khorasani
Barberry Preserve 421
   moraba-ye zereshk
Barberry Pickle 423
   torshi-ye zereshk
Saffroned Rice Flour Pudding with Cumin 424
   zireh katchi-e bojnurdi
Mashhadi Rice + Milk Cake 426
   digcheh-ye mashhadi

Yazd

Spinach + Beet Osh 432
   osh-e shuly-e yazdi
Saffroned Lamb Braise with Potato Fries 438
   qeymeh-ye yazdi
Iced Starch Drops Sorbet 447
   faludeh/paludeh-ye yazdi
Saffroned Almond Paste 448
   loz-e badam-e yazdi
Mint, Vinegar + Flixweed Shrub 450
   khak-e shir-o sekanjebin/yakhmal-e yazdi
Yazdi Cupcakes 457
   cayk-e yazdi

Kerman

Kermani Seven-Spice Bread Advieh 472
   advieh-ye nan-e kermani
Kermani Pastry Advieh 472
   advieh-ye shirini-e kermani
Brown Butter/Ghee 472
   masskeh/roghan-e gusfand-e kermani
Pistachio, Saffron + Sour Orange Soup 475
   sup-e pesteh ba za'ferun-o narenj-e kermani
Camomile Flowers, Egg + Onion Soup 476
   eshkeneh-ye gol-e babuneh-ye kermani
Kermani Wheat Osh 478
   osh-e gandom-e kermani
Pistachio, Fresh Herbs + Cardamom Kuku 480
   kuku-ye pesteh-ye kermani
Skillet Kabab 482
   kabab-e tabe'-ye kermani
Steamed Rice with Cumin + Potatoes 485
   zireh polow-ye kermani
Milk-Steamed Rice with Dates + Raisins 486
   shir pilau-e kermani
Pistachio + Dill Rice with Lamb Poached in Saffron . . 488
   pesteh polow ba bareh
Pistachio + Pomegranate Braise with Meatballs 490
   fesenjun-e pesteh-o kufteh-ye kermani
Lamb, Pistachio, Dill + Verjuice Braise 492
   khoresh-e pesteh-o ab ghureh
Goat Braised in Kashk + Served with Flat Bread Croutons . . 494
   boz qormeh-ye kermani
Pistachio Cake 496
   cayk-e pesteh-ye kermani
Wheat Sprout Flour Date + Walnut Pie 498
   komaj-e sen-e kermani
Date + Walnut Cookies 500
   kolombeh-ye kermani
Bread + Date Paste 502
   changmal
Turmeric, Cumin + Date Bun 504
   nan-e komaj-e mahan
Power Shake 505
   qovat'tu
Rose Water + Apple Shrub 506
   faludeh-ye sib-e kermani
Pistachio Skin Jam 511
   moraba-ye pust surati-ye pesteh
Baby Green Pistachio Pickle 512
   torshi-e chaghaleh-ye pesteh-ye kermani
Baby Pistachio Preserve 512
   moraba-ye chaghaleh-ye pesteh
Saffron + Lime Roasted Pistachios 514
   pesteh-ye bu dadeh ba zaferun-o limu-ye kermani

Shiraz

- Tomato, Cucumber + Herb Salad 523
  salad-e gojeh khiar-e shirazi
- Red Onion + Pomegranate Salad 523
  omar piyaz-e ahvazi
- Green Herb Osh 525
  osh-e sabz-e shirazi
- Lemony Potato Snack 526
  dopiyazeh alu-ye shirazi
- Desert-Truffle Kuku 528
  kuku-ye aghar/donblan-e zamini
- All Green Shirazi Meatballs 530
  kufteh-ye sabzi-e shirazi
- Pan-Cooked Lamb Kababs Shirazi-Style 533
  kabab digi-e shirazi
- Bakhtiari Mixed Grill. 534
  kabab-e bakhtiari
- Lari Kabab. 536
  kabab-e kenjeh-ye lari
- Rice with Pistachios + Pomegranates 538
  anar polow-ye shirazi
- Caramelized Onion, Walnut + Raisin Rice
  with Pomegranate Syrup 538
  rob polow-ye shirazi
- Rice with Sugar, Rose Water, Saffron + Tangerine Peel Syrup . 539
  shekar polow-ye shirazi
- Kohlrabi + Herb Rice with Meatballs 540
  kalam polow-ye shirazi
- Carrot + Mung Bean Rice 541
  qanbar polow-ye shirazi
- Oven-Baked Chicken, Eggplant + Barberry Rice . . . 542
  tachin-e shirazi/polow qalebi
- Pastry Roll Filled with Almond + Cardamom 545
  kaak /yokheh-ye shiraz
- Shirazi Rose Water Custard 546
  masqati-ye kasehi
- Date + Walnut Pie. 549
  ranginak-e shirazi
  qisava-ye khorma (Crustless Date + Walnut Pie variation)
  khorma beriz-e baluchi ; halva-ye khorma; chingal;
  halegh/charoset
- Three-Nut Starch Halva 550
  halva-ye masqati-e lari
- Tahini Halva 552
  halvardeh/halvardeh-ye khorma
- Rice Noodle Sorbet with a Squeeze of Lime 557
  paludeh-ye shirazi
- Gelatin + Walnut Roll 558
  basloq-e shirazi
- Shrubs 560
  sharbat-ha

Khuzestan

- Crispy Falafel with Garlicky Tahini Sauce 569
  falafel-e abadani
- Turnip + Cilantro Braise 570
  khoresh-e shalgham-o gishniz-e khoramshahr
- Grilled Saboor Fish with Tamarind + Cilantro Stuffing 572
  mahi-e tanuri-e saboor

The Persian Gulf

- Bandari Seven-Spice Advieh 594
  haft advieh-ye bandari/abzar
- Spicy, Lemony Shrimp with Caramelized Onions 596
  dopiyazeh maygu-e bushehri
- Fish with Fenugreek + Tomato Spread 599
  pudini
- Pickled Sardine + Red Earth Sauce 600
  suraq
- Fist Pancakes 603
  nan-e tu moshi/tu moshti
- Spiced Pickled Fish Sauce. 605
  mahyaveh/mahi abeh
- Fried Eggs with Fresh Ginger, Dates + Saffron 606
  khagineh-ye khorma
- Angel Hair Noodle, Egg, Saffron + Cardamom 609
  ballalat
- Red Lentil Soup 611
  dal
- Barley + Tahini Soup 612
  sup-e ardeh
- Fisherman's Soup 614
  sup-e daryai-e bandari
- Onion Soup with Salted Fish 615
  shur piyaz
- Spicy Sweet + Sour Fish with Dates 617
  qaliyeh-ye khorma
  qaliyeh-ye ardeh
- Tiger Prawn Tempura in Spicy Chickpea Batter 619
  maygu-e pofaki
- Fish Kabab with Dried Lime + Coriander 620
  kabab-e mahi bushehri/kabab-e maygu-e bushehri
- Fish Patties Glazed with Tamarind + Date Molasses 622
  kotlet-e mahi ba khorma-o tamr-e hendi
  kotlet-e maygu
- Spicy Chickpea + Wheat Flour Balls. 624
  pakurah
- Shrimp Balls in Spicy Sauce 629
  chubeh
- Calamari in Tomato Sauce 631
  khoresh-e hasht pa-ye bandari
- Mussel + Tamarind Braise 633
  kategh muluk /sadaf-e do kafeh

Poached Lobster or Crab with Dried Limes 634
    khorak-e singu/kharchang
Roast Chicken with Dates, Walnuts + Sumac 637
    morgh-e beryan ba somaq-o khorma
Chicken Kabab with Dried Lime + Mint 638
    jujeh kabab-e bandari
Spicy Okra, Lamb + Potato Braise 641
    khoresh-e bamieh ba sibzamini
Grouper, Cilantro, Garlic + Tamarind Braise 642
    qaliyeh-ye mahi
Rice Steamed in Date Molasses 645
    shireh-ye khorma polow
    ab-e khorma polow
Spicy Shrimp + Rice 646
    havari-ye maygu/havari-e mahi/tahandaz-e mahi
Fish + Dried Lime Rice 649
    dami-e lakh lakh-e bushehri
Lamb + Rice with Potato, Onion + Turmeric 650
    goboli pilau-ye bandar-e lengeh
Dried Shrimp with Lentils + Rice 652
    havari-e maygu-e khoshk ba adas
Chicken Briyani with Rice + Potato 654
    beriyani-e morgh
Persian Gulf Date Molasses Halva with Hazelnuts 656
    aseda
Black Carrot Halva 656
    halva-ye havij-e siah
Date, Walnut + Orange Cake 659
    cayk-e ranginak
Upside-Down Mango Cake 660
    cayk-e anbeh
Sesame Halva 663
    Halva-ye ardeh
Sweet Potato Halva 663
    Halva-ye pendal/sibzamini-e shirin
Persian Gulf Date + Coconut Balls 665
    bontu
Date, Pistachio + Lime Leaf Dessert 667
    khorma shireh
Persian Gulf Coffee 668
    ghawah
Black Carrot Pickle 671
    torshi-e gazar
Spicy Oily Lime Pickle 673
    torshi-e limu ba roghan/torshi-e shalqam
Onion, Cucumber + Coriander Pickle 675
    torshi-e piaz-e hormozgan
Lasura Pickle 675
    torshi-e anbook/sepestan
Saffroned Mango Pickle 676
    torshi-e mango-o zaferan
Guava Preserve 679
    moraba-ye guava

Sistan + Baluchistan

Baluchi Meat Advieh 684
    masaleh-ye gusht
Baluchi Fish Advieh 684
    masaleh-ye mahi
Yellow Kashk Porridge 686
    kashk-e zardeh-ye sistani
Sistani Three-Spice Advieh 686
    achareh
Yogurt + Tomato Fish Soup 688
    lanju/mahi dughi
Minty Kashk with Baked Eggplant + Caramelized Onions . . 691
    kashk-o bademjan-e Baluchi
Goat, Yogurt + Split Pea Braise 693
    dugh pa-ye sistani
Rice Cooked in Dried Goat + Pomegranate Broth 695
    tabahag
Fish in Wild Date Palm Leaf 698
    mahiag-e pach-e baluchi
Goat Cooked in Fire Pit 700
    kabab-e tanurcheh

Index

Page numbers in italics indicate illustrations.

A

Acorn Pan Bread, 311
Advieh (Persian spice mix)
    Azari Three-Spice Advieh, 184, *185*
    Baluchi Meat Advieh, 684
    Bandari Seven-Spice Advieh, 594, *595*
    Hamadani Seven-Spice Advieh, 246, *247*
    Isfahani Seven-Spice Advieh, 356, *357*
    Kermani Pastry Advieh, 472
    Kermani Seven-Spice Bread Advieh, 472, *473*
    Khorasani Seven-Spice Advieh, 394, *395*
    Khorasani Seven-Spice Rice Advieh, 394
    Kurdish Seven-Spice Advieh, 314, *315*
    Qazvini Four-Spice Advieh, 234, *235*, 236, 238
    Sistani Three-Spice Advieh, 686, *703*
Almonds, *702*
    Almond, lamb, Saffron + Rose Water Braise, 337
    Almond Pudding, *348*, 349
    Pastry Roll Filled with Almond + Cardamom, *544–545*, 545
    Saffroned Almond + Pistachio Baklava, 242–243
    Saffroned Almond Paste, 448, *449*
    Saffroned Lamb + Barberry Braise, 334
Apples. *See also* Sour Apples
    Apple + Caspian Green Salt Salad, 84, *85*
    Rose Water + Apple Shrub, 506, *507*
Apricots
    Apricot + Nut Pickle, 266, *267*
    Lamb, Prune, Apricot + Quince Spread, 362
Arak (city), *268–269*, 269
Ardabil (city), 177, *177*
Armenian Cucumbers, 255
Armenians, 354, *378–379*, 379, 577
Azarbaijan, *172–174*, *172–175*, *227*

B

Baklava. *See* Desserts
Baluchistan. *See* Sistan + Baluchistan
Barbari, 289, *289*, 292
Barberries, *416–417*, 417, 419, *702*
    Barberry Lamb + Split Pea Khoresh, 334
    Barberry Osh, 398, *399*
    Barberry Pickle, 423
    Barberry Preserve, 421
    Barberry Rice, 418, 542–543
    Barberry Shrub, 560
    Bulgur Meatballs Filled with Caramelized Onion + Barberries, *324*, 325
    Oven-Baked Chicken, Eggplant + Barberry Rice, 542–543, *543*
    Rice, Lamb, Rose Petals + Barberries, 236, *237*
    Rice with Mushrooms + Barberries, 338
    Saffroned Lamb + Barberry Braise, 334, *335*
    Saffroned Yogurt + Lamb Neck Braise with Barberries, 374, *375*
    Tabrizi Meatballs with Split Peas + Tomatoes (barberry filling), 202, *203*
Barley
    Araki Barley Osh, 272
    Barley, Nettle, Yogurt + Kashk Osh, 318
    Barley + Tahini Soup, 612
    Barley Soup, 200
Basil
    Basil + Mint Garnish, 412
    Basil + Mint to replace *Khalvash*, 76, 86, 130
    Basil Seed Shrub, 560
Beans. *See specific types*
Beef
    Bakhtiari Mixed Grill, 534, *535*
    Calf Liver Kabab, *218*, 219
    Caucasian Fillet Kabab, 217
    Fillet Kabab, *212*, 213
    Lari Kabab, 536, *537*
    Skillet Kabab, 482, *483*
    Sweet + Sour Kabab, 116
Beets
    Barley, Beets, Yogurt + Kashk Osh, 318
    Beet Pickle, 671
    Roasted Beets with Grape Molasses + Walnuts, 260
    Spinach + Beet Osh, 432, *433*
Bonab (town), 215
Borage + Valerian Tea, 169, *171*
Braises (*khoreshes*)
    Almond, Lamb, Saffron + Rose Water Braise, 337
    Butternut Squash, Walnut + Pomegranate Braise, 136
    Chive + White Bean Braise, 330
    Duck + Pomegranate Braise, 132
    Duck Eggs + Fava Beans Braise, 26
    Eggs, Herbs, Garlic + Sour Orange Braise, 130
    Fresh Herb Braise, 54
    Grouper, Cilantro, Garlic + Tamarind Braise, 642
    Lamb, Pistachio, Dill + Verjuice Braise, 492
    Lamb, Quince + Plum Braise, 372
    Lentil, Lamb + Prune Braise, 238
    Mussel + Tamarind Braise, 633
    Pistachio + Pomegranate Braise with Meatballs, 490
    Saffroned Chicken + Yogurt Braise, 376
    Saffroned Lamb + Barberry Braise, 334
    Saffroned Lamb Braise with Potato Fries, 438

Saffroned Yogurt + Lamb Neck Braise with Barberries, 374
Sour Cherry Braise, 140
Spicy Okra, Lamb + Potato Braise, 641
Turnip + Cilantro Braise, 570

Bread, 284–293, *284–286, 288–289, 291–293*. *See also* Buns
Acorn Pan Bread, 311
Barbari, 289, *289*, 292
Bread + Date Paste, 502, *503*
Bread Cooked in Ashes, *308–309*, 309
Date + Sesame Bread, *306*, 307
Deep-Fried Flat Bread, 300, *301*
Flat Bread, 287–293
Flat Bread Croutons, Served with Goat Braised in Kashk, 494, *495*
Fried Bread, Served with Twice-Cooked Lamb in Tail-Fat, 412, *412*
Khorasani Taftun Bread, 299, *299*
Lavash, 288, *289*, 292
Nan-e gerdeh, 245
Sangak, 289, *289*, 292
Taftun, 289, 292
Tribal Pan-Flat Bread, 296, *297–298*
Twice-Cooked Semi-Sweet Bread, *304*, 305
Urmia Chorayi Bread, 294, *295*

Breakfast
Angel Hair Noodles, Egg, Saffron + Cardamom, *608*, 609
Cheese + Dill Omelet, 96
Egg + Saffron Spread, 264
Finger Twist Spread, 264, *265*
Fish Roe Omelet, 109
Fried Eggs with Fresh Ginger, Dates + Saffron, 606, *607*
Garlic-Chive Omelet, 96, *97*
Saffron Omelet with Rose Petals, 188, *189*
Tabrizi Cheese, Walnut + Herb Balls, 186, *187*
Tomato, Egg + Garlic Omelet, 88, *89*
Urmia Chorayi Bread, 294, *295*
Wheat and Turkey Breakfast Porridge, 58, *59*

Briyani
Chicken Briyani with Rice + Potato, 654, *655*
Isfahani Lamb Briyani Wrap, 368

Bulgur
Baked Onion Stuffed with Bulgur, 322
Bulgur, Legumes + Verjuice Soup, 254
Bulgur, Noodle + Currant Pilaf, 256, *257*
Bulgur + Curly Cucumber Osh, 255
Bulgur + Lamb Pilaf, 340, *341*
Bulgur Meatballs Filled with Caramelized Onion + Barberries, *324*, 325
Bulgur Meatballs in a Vegetable Broth, 326, *327*
Carrot + Bulgur Osh, 254
Homemade Bulgur + Yogurt Patties, 320
Lamb Neck, Bulgur + Bean Porridge, 408, *409*
Split Pea, Bulgur + Yogurt Osh, 272

Tarkhineh Osh, 320, *321*
Buns
Fuman Bun, 145, *146–147*
Sweet Sesame Bun, 262, *263*
Turmeric, Cumin + Date Bun, 504
Bushehr (port city), 579, *580*, 597
Butter/Ghee, 472
Buttermilk. *See Kashk*
Butternut Squash. *See Squash*

C

Cabbage Pickle, 671
Cakes. *See Desserts*
Camomile Flowers, Egg + Onion Soup, 476, *477*
Candies and Sweets. *See Desserts*
Cardamom, *703*
Angel Hair Noodles, Egg, Saffron + Cardamom, *608*, 609
Pastry Roll Filled with Almond + Cardamom, *544–545*, 545
Pistachio, Fresh Herbs + Cardamom Kuku, 480, *481*
Saffroned Rice Flour Cookies with a Walnut + Cardamom Filling, *148*, 149
Cardoons, 25, *25*
Carrots
Black Carrot Pickle, *670*, 671
Carrot + Bulgur Osh, 254
Carrot + Mung Bean Rice, 541
Carrot + Walnut Halva, 222, *223*
Sweet + Sour Glazed Chickpea + Carrot Patties, 370, *371*
The Caspian, *68–74, 68–76*, 106
Caviar, 106, *106*
Fish Rose Omelet, 109
Celery, Walnut + Yogurt Salad, 316
Cheese
Cheese, Walnut + Herb Balls, 248, *249*
Cheese + Dill Omelet, 96
Tabrizi Cheese, Walnut + Herb Balls, 186, *187*
Cherries. *See also* Sour Cherries
Cornelian Cherry Chutney, 160
Chicken
Bakhtiari Mixed Grill, 534, *535*
Barley, Nettle, Yogurt + Kashk Osh, 318
Bulgur Meatballs Filled with Caramelized Onion + Barberries, *324*, 325
Bulgur Meatballs in a Vegetable Broth, 326, *327*
Chicken + Rice with Potato, Onion + Turmeric, 650
Chicken Briyani with Rice + Potato, 654, *655*
Chicken Kabab with Dried Lime + Mint, 638, *639*
Chickpea Meatballs in Aromatic Tomato Sauce, 366, *367*
Darbandi Chicken Kabab, 52, *53*
Eggplant, Walnut + Herb Braise with Meatballs, 134
Ground Chicken Kabab, 216
Kohlrabi + Herb Rice with Meatballs, 540, *541*
Lari Kabab, 536, *537*
Medlar, Walnut, Pomegranate + Chicken Casserole, 138

715

Oven-Baked Chicken, Eggplant + Barberry Rice, 542–543, *543*
Pistachio + Dill Rice with Chicken Poached in Saffron-Rose Water, 488, *489*
Roast Chicken with Dates, Walnuts + Sumac, 636, *637*
Saffroned Chicken + Yogurt Braise, 376
Skillet Kabab, 482, *483*
Sour Cherry Braise, 140, *141*
Spicy Meatballs with Verjuice, 230, *231*
Split Pea Meatballs, 325
Sumac Soup, 360
Sweet + Sour Glazed Chickpea + Carrot Patties, 370, *371*
Sweet + Sour Kabab, 116
Sweet + Sour Patties, 76, *77*
Vegetable + Fruit Casserole, 206, *207*
Walnut, Pomegranate + Herb Patties, 342, *343*

Chickpeas
    Chickpea Meatballs in Aromatic Tomato Sauce, 366, *367*
    Crispy Falafel with Garlicky Tahini Sauce, 568, *569*
    Goat Braised in Kashk + Served with Flat Bread Croutons, 494
    Hamadan Meatballs with Chickpeas + Vinegar and Grape Molasses, 202
    Lamb Shank, Chickpea + Kidney Bean Soup (*dizzy*), 38, *39*
    Spicy Chickpea + Wheat Flour Balls, 624, *625*
    Sweet + Sour Glazed Chickpea + Carrot Patties, 370, *371*
    Tiger Prawn Tempura in Spicy Chickpea Batter, 619
    Yogurt + Chickpea Osh, 196, *197*

Chives
    Chive + Split Pea Khoresh, 330
    Chive + White Bean Braise, 330, *331*
    Garlic-Chive Omelet, 96, *97*

Chochaq Leaves, 84, 86, 116, *134*
Chutney, Cornelian Cherry, 160

Cilantro
    Grilled Saboor Fish with Tamarind + Cilantro Stuffing, 572, *573*
    Grouper, Cilantro, Garlic + Tamarind Braise, 642
    Turnip + Cilantro Braise, 570, *571*

Coconut + Persian Gulf Date Balls, 664, *665*
Coffee, Persian Gulf, 668, *669*
Cookies. *See* Desserts

Coriander
    Fish Kabab with Dried Lime + Coriander, 620
    Onion, Cucumber + Coriander Pickle, 675

Cucumbers
    Bulgur + Curly Cucumber Osh, 255
    Cucumber, Sumac + Yogurt Salad, 316
    Persian, *702*
    Tomato, Cucumber + Herb Salad, *522*, 523
    Wild Pistachio + Cucumber Soup, 400, *401*

Cumin
    Saffroned Rice Flour Pudding with Cumin, 424
    Steamed Rice with Cumin + Potatoes, 484, *485*
    Turmeric, Cumin + Date Bun, 504

Curly Cucumber + Bulgur Osh, 255
Currant, Bulgur + Noodle Pilaf, 256, *257*
Cyrus the Great, 253, 465, 519, *519*, 565, 577

D

Dalar. See Salt
Darakeh (part of Tehran), 56, *56–57*
Darband (village), 50, *51*
Date molasses, *703*
    Almond Pudding, 348, *349*
    Date Tahini Halva, 552
    Fish Patties Glazed with Tamarind + Date Molasses, 622, *623*
    Grilled Saboor Fish with Tamarind + Cilantro Stuffing, 572, *573*
    Grouper, Cilantro, Garlic + Tamarind Braise, 642
    Persian Gulf Date Molasses Halva with Hazelnuts, 656, *657*
    Pistachio + Pomegranate Braise with Meatballs, 490, *491*
    Rice Steamed in Date Molasses, 644, *645*
    Seared Fish with Garlic + Vinegar Glaze, 112
    Spicy Oily Lime Pickle, 673
    Spicy Okra, Lamb + Potato Braise, 640, *641*
    Sweet Potato Halva, 663
    Turnip + Cilantro Braise, 570, *571*

Date palms, 584, 585–590, *587–591*
    Date Palm and the Goat, 593
    Fish in Wild Date Palm Leaf, 696–697, 698, *699*

Dates, *703*
    Bread + Date Paste, 502, *503*
    Date, Pistachio + Lime Leaf Dessert, 666, *667*
    Date + Sesame Bread, *306*, 307
    Date + Tahini Dessert, 667
    Date, Walnut + Orange Cake, 658, *659*
    Date + Walnut Cookies, 500, *501*
    Date + Walnut Pie, 549
    Crustless Date + Walnut Pie variation, 549
    Date Tahini Halva, 552
    Fried Eggs with Fresh Ginger, Dates + Saffron, 606, *607*
    Milk-Steamed Rice with Dates + Raisins, 486, *487*
    Persian Gulf Date + Coconut Balls, 664, *665*
    Rice Cooked in Date Juice, 645
    Roast Chicken with Dates, Walnuts + Sumac, 636, *637*
    Spicy Sweet + Sour Fish with Dates, 617
    Turmeric, Cumin + Date Bun, 504
    Wheat Sprout Flour Date + Walnut Pie, 498, *499*

Desserts, 241
    Almond Pudding, *348*, 349
    Bread + Date Paste, 502, *503*
    Carrot + Walnut Halva, 222, *223*
    Cream Puffs, 64
    Date, Pistachio + Lime Leaf Dessert, 666, *667*
    Date + Tahini Dessert, 667
    Date, Walnut + Orange Cake, 658, *659*
    Date + Walnut Cookies, 500, *501*

Date + Walnut Pie, 549
Gelatin + Walnut Roll, 558
Iced Starch Drops Sorbet, 447
Isfahani Nougat, 380, *380–381*
Kermani Pastry Advieh, 472
Mashhadi Rice + Milk Cake, 426, *427*
Pastry Roll Filled with Almond + Cardamom, *544–545*, 545
Persian Gulf Date + Coconut Balls, *664*, 665
Persian Gulf Date Molasses Halva with Hazelnuts, 656, *657*
Pistachio Cake, 496, *497*
Rice Lace Pancakes, *142–143*, 144
Rice Noodle Sorbet with a Squeeze of Lime, 556, *557*
Roasted Beets with Grape Molasses + Walnuts, 260
Roasted Butternut Squash + Grape Molasses, 260
Rose + Yogurt Love Cake, *350*, 351
Rose Petal Rice Pudding, 150, *151*
Saffroned Almond + Pistachio Baklava, 242–243
Saffroned Almond Paste, 448, *449*
Saffroned Rice Flour Cookies with a Walnut + Cardamom Filling, *148*, 149
Saffroned Yogurt + Lamb Neck Braise with Barberries, 374, *375*
Saffron Rice Cookies, 346, *347*
Sesame Halva, *662*, 663
Shirazi Rose Water Custard, 546, *547*
Sweet Potato Halva, 663
Tahini Halva, 552, *553*
Three-Nut Starch Halva, 550, *550–551*
Upside-Down Mango Cake, 660, *661*
Wheat Sprout Flour Date + Walnut Pie, 498, *499*
Yazdi Cupcakes, *456–457*, 457

Dill
Cheese + Dill Omelet, 96
Lamb, Pistachio, Dill + Verjuice Braise, 492, *493*
Lamb + White Bean Braise with Dill Rice, 386, *387*
Pistachio + Dill Rice with Lamb Poached in Saffron-Rose Water, 488, *489*

Dizzy (Lamb Shank Soup), 37

Drinks
Borage + Valerian Tea, 169, *171*
Chabahar Milk Tea, 170
Dried Persian Lime Tea, 170
Hogweed Seed Tea, 170, *171*
Jujub Panacea Tea, 169
Mint, Vinegar + Flixweed Shrub, 450, *451*
Persian Gulf Coffee, 668, *669*
Rose Water + Apple Shrub, 506, *507*
Saffron Love Tea, 169
Shrubs, 560, *561*
Tea, 166, *166–168*

Duck
Duck + Pomegranate Braise, 132, *133*
Duck Eggs + Fava Beans Braise, 126, *127*
Duck Kabab, 118

Dumplings
Azarbaijani Dumpling Soup, 198, *199*
Spinach + Dumpling Osh, 402, *403*

E

Eggplants
Chinese, *702*
Eggplant Tapenade, 91
Eggplant, Walnut + Herb Braise with Meatballs, 134
Eggplant with Garlic + Verjuice, 91
Italian, *702*
Minty Kashk with Baked Eggplant + Caramelized Onions, 690, *691*
Oven-Baked Chicken, Eggplant + Barberry Rice, 542–543, *543*
Roasting, 80
Smoked Eggplant, Tomato + Walnut Spread, *90*, 91
Smoked Eggplant with Eggs + Garlic, 92, *93*
Vegetable + Fruit Casserole, 206, *207*

Eggs
Angel Hair Noodles, Egg, Saffron + Cardamom, 608, *609*
Camomile Flowers, Egg + Onion Soup, 476, *477*
Cheese + Dill Omelet, 96
Chelow Egg Crust, 210
Duck Eggs + Fava Beans Braise, 126, *127*
Egg + Saffron Spread, 264
Eggs, Herbs, Garlic + Sour Orange Braise, 130, *131*
Fried Eggs with Fresh Ginger, Dates + Saffron, 606, *607*
Onion, Egg + Spinach Soup, 46, *47*
Saffron Omelet with Rose Petals, 188, *189*
Smoked Eggplant with Eggs + Garlic, 92, *93*
Tomato, Egg + Garlic Omelet, 88, *89*

F

Falafel with Garlicky Tahini Sauce, 568, *569*
Fars region. *See* Shiraz
Fava beans, *125*, *702*
Duck Eggs + Fava Beans Braise, 126, *127*
Yellow Fava Bean Rice, 278
Fennel seeds, *703*
Fenugreek
Baluchi Fish Advieh, 684
Fish Patties Glazed with Tamarind + Date Molasses, 622, *623*
Fish with Fenugreek + Tomato Spread, 598, *599*
Grilled Saboor Fish with Tamarind + Cilantro Stuffing, 572, *573*
Grouper, Cilantro, Garlic + Tamarind Braise, 642
Kermani Seven-Spice Bread Advieh, 472, *473*
Khorasani Taftun Bread, 299, *299*
Lemony Potato Snack, 526
Mung Beans + Kohlrabi Spread, 364, *365*
Onion, Egg + Spinach Soup, 46, *47*
Pistachio, Fresh Herbs + Cardamom Kuku, 480, *481*
Red Lentil Soup, 610–611, *611*

Saffroned Rice Flour Pudding with Cumin, 424
Seared Fish with Garlic + Vinegar Glaze, 112
Shrimp Balls in Spicy Sauce, *628*, *629*
Spicy Meatballs with Verjuice, 230, *231*
Spicy Oily Lime Pickle, 673
Spicy Shrimp + Rice, *646*, *647*
Spinach + Beet Osh, 432, *433*
Fig Jam, 154
Fish, *580*, *581*
    Chickpea Meatballs in Aromatic Tomato Sauce, 366, *367*
    Fish + Dried Lime Rice, *648*, *649*
    Fish Crusted Rice, 646
    Fisherman's Soup, 614
    Fish Fillets in Tomato Sauce, 631
    Fish Head Soup, 110, *111*
    Fish in Wild Date Palm Leaf, 696–697, *698*, *699*
    Fish Kabab with Dried Lime + Coriander, 620
    Fish Patties Glazed with Tamarind + Date Molasses, 622, *623*
    Fish Roe Omelet, 109
    Fish with Fenugreek + Tomato Spread, *598*, *599*
    Grilled Saboor Fish with Tamarind + Cilantro Stuffing, 572, *573*
    Grouper, Cilantro, Garlic + Tamarind Braise, 642
    Onion Soup with Salted Fish, *615*, 615
    Pickled Sardine + Red Earth Sauce, 600
    Seared Fish with Garlic + Vinegar Glaze, 112
    Spiced Pickled Fish Sauce, 605
    Spicy Fish + Rice, 646
    Spicy Sweet + Sour Fish with Dates, 617
    Sturgeon Kabab with Sour Orange, 114
    Sturgeon Patties, *108*, 109
    Sweet + Sour Glazed Chickpea + Carrot Patties, 370, *371*
    Walnut + Sumac Meatballs, 280, *281*
    Yogurt + Tomato Fish Soup, 688
Flixweed Shrub with Mint and Vinegar, 450, *451*
Fruit. *See also specific types*
    Dried Fruit + Noodles Osh, 250
    Vegetable + Fruit Casserole, 206, *207*

G

Garlic, *161*
    Black Garlic Pickle, *162*, 163
    Crispy Falafel with Garlicky Tahini Sauce, *568*, 569
    Duck Egg with Garlic + Roasted Eggplants, 80
    Eggplant with Garlic + Verjuice, 91
    Eggs, Herbs, Garlic + Sour Orange Braise, 130, *131*
    Garlic-Chive Omelet, *96*, 97
    Grouper, Cilantro, Garlic + Tamarind Braise, 642
    Roasted Vegetables with Garlic Kashk, 410, *411*
    Seared Fish with Garlic + Vinegar Glaze, 112
    Smoked Eggplant with Eggs + Garlic, *92*, *93*
    Tomato, Egg + Garlic Omelet, 88, *89*
Gata (pastry), 34

Ghee/Brown Butter, 472
Ginger. *See also* Advieh
    Fried Eggs with Fresh Ginger, Dates + Saffron, *606*, *607*
Gingerbread Crackers, 302, *303*
Goat
    Date Palm and the Goat, 593
    Goat, Yogurt + Split Pea Braise, 693
    Goat Braised in Kashk + Served with Flat Bread Croutons, *494*, *495*
    Goat Cooked in Fire Pit, *700*, *700–701*
    Rice Cooked in Dried Goat + Pomegranate Broth, *694*, *695*
Golpar. *See* Hogweed Seed
Grape Leaves, Stuffed, 190, *191–192*
Grape Molasses, 152, *153*, *702*
    Barberry Osh, 398, *399*
    Black Walnut Halva, 224, *225*
    Bulgur Meatballs Filled with Caramelized Onion + Barberries, *324*, 325
    Butternut Squash with Rice Flour Patties, 98
    Dried Fruit + Noodles Osh, 250
    Persian Gulf Date Molasses Halva with Hazelnuts, *656*, *657*
    Roasted Beets with Grape Molasses + Walnuts, 260
    Roasted Butternut Squash + Grape Molasses, 260
    Saffron Rice + Potato Croquettes, 328, *329*
    Sautéed Liver + Kidney with Black Kashk, 274
    Seared Fish with Garlic + Vinegar Glaze, 112
    Skillet Kabab, *482*, *483*
    Sumac Soup, 360
    Sweet + Sour Glazed Chickpea + Carrot Patties, 370, *371*
    Tabrizi Meatballs with Split Peas + Tomatoes, 202, *203*
    Walnut, Pomegranate + Herb Patties, 342, *343*
    Walnut + Sumac Meatballs, 280, *281*
Grapes, *702*
Greengages, *702*
    Greengage Molasses, 159
    Lamb, Quince + Plum Braise, 372, *373*
Grilling. *See* Kabobs
Guavas
    Guava Jelly, 679
    Guava Preserve, *678*, 679
    Upside-Down Guava Cake, 660, *661*

H

Halva, 555
    Black Walnut Halva, 224, *225*
    Carrot + Walnut Halva, 222, *223*
    Date Tahini Halva, 552
    Persian Gulf Date Molasses Halva with Hazelnuts, *656*, *657*
    Sesame Halva, *662*, *663*
    Sweet Potato Halva, 663
    Tahini Halva, 552, *553*
    Three-Nut Starch Halva, 550, *550–551*
Hamadan (city), *244–245*, 245
Hazaras (ethnic group), 289

Hazelnuts
    Apricot + Nut Pickle, 266, *267*
    Persian Gulf Date Molasses Halva with Hazelnuts, 656, *657*
Herbs, *55*, *124*. *See also specific types*
    Baked Onions Filled with Rice + Herbs, 322, *323*
    Cheese, Walnut + Herb Balls, 248, *249*
    Eggs, Herbs, Garlic + Sour Orange Braise, 130, *131*
    Eggplant, Walnut + Herb Braise with Meatballs, 134
    Fresh Herb Braise, 54
    Green Herb Osh, *524*, 525
    Kohlrabi + Herb Rice with Meatballs, 540, *541*
    Pistachio, Fresh Herbs + Cardamom Kuku, 480, *481*
    Tabrizi Cheese, Walnut + Herb Balls, 186, *187*
    Tomato, Cucumber + Herb Salad, *522*, 523
    Walnut, Pomegranate + Herb Patties, 342, *343*
Hogweed Seed (*golpar*), 103, 112, *703*
    Hogweed Seed Tea, 170, *171*

I

Ice-Cream, 65. *See also* Desserts
    Roasted Butternut Squash + Grape Molasses, 260
Isfahan (city), 352–354, *352–354*, *358–359*, *361*, *377*

J

Jam and Jelly. *See* Preserves
Jews and Judaism, 193, 245, *252–253*, 253, 354, 577

K

Kababs
    Caucasian Fillet Kabab, 217
    Chelow, *33*, 208
    Chicken Kabab with Dried Lime + Mint, 638, *639*
    Darbandi Chicken Kabab, 52, *53*
    Duck Kabab, 118
    Fillet Kabab, *33*, *212*, 213
    Fish Kabab with Dried Lime + Coriander, 620
    Ground Chicken Kabab, 216
    Ground Lamb Kabab, 216
    Lace-Fat-Wrapped Lamb Liver Kabab, 344, *344–345*
    Lamb Fries Kabab, 219
    Lamb Liver Kabab, *218*, 219
    Lari Kabab, 536, *537*
    Minced, *214–215*, 215
    Pan-Cooked Lamb Kababs Shirazi-Style, *532*, 533
    Quail Kabab, *120*, 121
    Skillet Kabab, 482, *483*
    Sturgeon Kabab with Sour Orange, 114
    Sweet + Sour Kabab, 116, *117*
    Tiger Prawn Kabab, 620
    Kashan (city), *382*, 382–383
Kashk (dried buttermilk), 276, *277*
    Barley, Nettle, Yogurt + Kashk Osh, 318
    Black, 276, *277*, *703*
    Goat Braised in Kashk + Served with Flat Bread Croutons, 494, *495*
    Liquid, *702*
    Minty Kashk with Baked Eggplant + Caramelized Onions, *690*, 691
    Roasted Vegetables with Garlic Kashk, 410, *411*
    Sautéed Liver + Kidney with Black Kashk, 274
    Spinach + Beet Osh, 432, *433*
    Walnut + Kashk Soup, 406, *407*
    White, *703*
    Yellow, *703*
    Yellow Kashk Porridge, 686, *687*
Kerman (city and province), 460–462, *463*, *474*
Khalvash (wild mint) Leaves, 76, 84, 86, 88, 91, 116, 130, 134, *134*
Khorasan (region), 388–391, *391*
Khorma beriz (Date + Walnut Pie variant), 548, *549*
Khuzestan (region), 562–567, *565*
Kidney Beans
    Fresh Herb Braise, 54
    Lamb Shank, Chickpea + Kidney Bean Soup (*dizzy*), 38, *39*
Kohlrabi
    Kohlrabi + Herb Rice with Meatballs, 540, *541*
    Mung Beans + Kohlrabi Spread, 364, *365*
Kukus
    Desert Truffle Kuku, 528
    Pistachio, Fresh Herbs + Cardamom Kuku, 480, *481*
    Potato Kuku with Saffron Syrup Glaze, 396, *397*
Kurds, 313, 577

L

Labneh (creamy yogurt), 374, 376, 531, 533, 536, 542
Lamb
    All Green Shirazi Meatballs, 530–531, *531*
    Bakhtiari Mixed Grill, 534, *535*
    Barberry Lamb + Split Pea Khoresh, 334
    Barley, Nettle, Yogurt + Kashk Osh, 318
    Bulgur + Curly Cucumber Osh, 255
    Bulgur + Lamb Pilaf, 340, *341*
    Bulgur Meatballs Filled with Caramelized Onion + Barberries, *324*, 325
    Bulgur Meatballs in a Vegetable Broth, 326, *327*
    Caucasian Fillet Kabab, 217
    Chickpea Meatballs in Aromatic Tomato Sauce, 366, *367*
    Eggplant, Walnut + Herb Braise with Meatballs, 134
    Fillet Kabab, *212*, 213
    Green Herb Osh, *524*, 525
    Ground Lamb Kabab, 216
    Isfahani Lamb Briyani Wrap, 368, *369*
    Kermani Wheat Osh, 478
    Kohlrabi + Herb Rice with Meatballs, 540, *541*
    Lace-Fat-Wrapped Lamb Liver Kabab, 344, *344–345*
    Lamb, Pistachio, Dill + Verjuice Braise, 492, *493*
    Lamb, Prune, Apricot + Quince Spread, 362

Lamb, Quince + Plum Braise, 372, *373*
Lamb + Rice with Potato, Onion + Turmeric, 650
Lamb + White Bean Braise with Dill Rice, 386, *387*
Lamb Fries Kabab, 219
Lamb Liver Kabab, *218*, 219
Lamb Neck, Bulgur + Bean Porridge, 408, *409*
Lamb Shank, Chickpea + Kidney Bean Soup (*dizzy*), 37, *38, 39*
Lamb's Head, Feet + Tripe Soup, 44, *44–45*
Lari Kabab, 536, *537*
Lentil, Lamb + Prune Braise, 238, *239*
Mung Beans + Kohlrabi Spread, 364, *365*
Oven-Baked Lamb, Eggplant + Barberry Rice, 542–543
Pan-Cooked Lamb Kababs Shirazi-Style, *532*, 533
Pistachio + Dill Rice with Lamb Poached in Saffron-Rose Water, 488, *489*
Pistachio + Pomegranate Braise with Meatballs, 490, *491*
Rice, Lamb, Rose Petals + Barberries, 236, *237*
Rice with Lamb Rib Chops, 333
Saffroned Lamb + Barberry Braise, 334, *335*
Saffroned Lamb Braise with Potato Fries (or Baking Potatoes), 438, *439*
Saffroned Yogurt + Lamb Neck Braise with Barberries, 374, *375*
Sautéed Liver + Kidney with Black Kashk, 274
Skillet Kabab, *482*, 483
Spicy Meatballs with Verjuice, 230, *231*
Spicy Okra, Lamb + Potato Braise, *640*, 641
Split Pea Meatballs, 325
Sumac Soup, 360
Sweet + Sour Glazed Chickpea + Carrot Patties, 370, *371*
Sweet + Sour Kabab, 116
Sweet + Sour Patties, 76, *77*
Tabrizi Meatballs with Split Peas + Tomatoes, 202, *203*
Tomato + Lime Broth with Tiny Meatballs, 270, *271*
Tongue Sandwich, 62, *63*
Twice-Cooked Lamb in Tail-Fat with Fried Bread, 412, *412*
Vegetable + Fruit Casserole, 206, *207*
Walnut, Pomegranate + Herb Patties, 342, *343*
Walnut + Sumac Meatballs, 280, *281*
Wheat and Lamb Breakfast Porridge, 58, *59*
Lanjeen (earthenware container), 245
Lasura Pickle, 675
Lavash, 289, *289*, 292
Chelow Lavash Crust, 210
Leeks
Barley + Tahini Soup, 612
Ramp Polow, 48, *49*
Legumes
Bulgur, Legumes + Verjuice Soup, 254
Rice with Legumes + Butternut Squash, 414
Lemons. *See* Limes and Lemons
Lentils
Dried Shrimp with Lentils + Rice, 652, *653*
Lentil, Lamb + Prune Braise, 238, *239*
Red Lentil Soup, 610–611, *611*
Lettuce + Yogurt Salad, 316, *317*
Lime Leaf, 703
Date, Pistachio + Lime Leaf Dessert, 666, *667*
Limes and Lemons, 702
Chicken Kabab with Dried Lime + Mint, 638, *639*
dried Persian, 702–703
Dried Persian Lime Tea, 170
Fish + Dried Lime Rice, 648, *649*
Fish Kabab with Dried Lime + Coriander, 620
Lemony Potato Snack, 526
Poached Lobster or Crab with Dried Limes, 634
Rice Noodle Sorbet with a Squeeze of Lime, 556, *557*
Saffron + Lime Roasted Pistachios, 514, *515*
Shrimp Balls in Spicy Sauce, 628, *629*
Spicy, Lemony Shrimp with Caramelized Onions, 596
Spicy Oily Lime Pickle, 673
Tomato + Lime Broth with Tiny Meatballs, 270, *271*

M

Mangoes
Saffroned Mango Pickle, 676, *677*
Upside-Down Mango Cake, 660, *661*
Maps
Azarbaijan, *175*
Bushehr, *575*
Caspian Sea, *106*
Fars/Shiraz, *518*
Iran, *11*
Isfahan, *354*
Kashan, *354*
Kerman, *462*
Khorasan, *389*
Khuzestan, *565*
Persian Gulf, *575*
Qazvin, *229*
Qom, *229*
Sistan + Baluchistan, *682*
Tribal Region, *313*
Yazd, *431*
Masouleh (village), *102–103*, 103
Meatballs
All Green Shirazi Meatballs, 530–531, *531*
Bulgur Meatballs Filled with Caramelized Onion + Barberries, *324*, 325
Bulgur Meatballs in a Vegetable Broth, 326, *327*
Chickpea Meatballs in Aromatic Tomato Sauce, 366, *367*
Eggplant, Walnut + Herb Braise with Meatballs, 134
Kohlrabi + Herb Rice with Meatballs, 540, *541*
Pistachio + Pomegranate Braise with Meatballs, 490, *491*
Spicy Meatballs with Verjuice, 230, *231*
Split Pea Meatballs, 325
Tabrizi Meatballs with Split Peas + Tomatoes, 202, *203*
Tomato + Lime Broth with Tiny Meatballs, 270, *271*

Walnut + Sumac Meatballs, 280, *281*
Medlar (fruit)
  Medlar, Walnut, Pomegranate + Chicken Casserole, 138
  Medlar Pickle, 164
Milk
  Chabahar Milk Tea, 170
  Chelow Milk Crust, 210
  Mashhadi Rice + Milk Cake, 426, *427*
  Milk-Steamed Rice with Dates + Raisins, 486, *487*
  Power Shake, 505
Mint. *See also* Khalvash
  Basil + Mint Garnish, 412
  Basil + Mint to replace *Khalvash*, 76, 86, 130
  Chicken Kabab with Dried Lime + Mint, 638, *639*
  Mint, Vinegar + Flixweed Shrub, 450, *451*
  Mint Leaf Shrub, 560
  Minty Kashk with Baked Eggplant + Caramelized Onions, 690, *691*
Molasses. *See also specific types*
  Greengage Molasses, 159
  Sour Apple Molasses, 152, *153*
  Spicy Sweet + Sour Fish with Dates, 617
  Verjuice Molasses, 152
Mongols, 21, 46, 229, 289
Mung Beans
  Bushehri-Style Mung Bean Rice, 278
  Carrot + Mung Bean Rice, 541
  Dried Shrimp with Lentils + Rice, 652, *653*
  Lamb Neck, Bulgur + Bean Porridge, 408, *409*
  Mung Beans + Kohlrabi Spread, 364, *365*
  Rice with Mung Beans + Caramelized Onions, 278, *279*
Mushrooms
  Rice with Mushrooms + Barberries, 338
  Savory Mushroom Pie, 60, *61*

N

Nan. *See* Bread
Nettle, Barley, Yogurt + Kashk Osh, 318
Nigella Seeds, 294, 296, 299, 300, 394, 673
Noodles
  Angel Hair Noodles, Egg, Saffron + Cardamom, *608*, 609
  Bulgur, Noodle + Currant Pilaf, 256, *257*
  Dried Fruit + Noodles Osh, 250
  Rice Noodle Sorbet with a Squeeze of Lime, *556*, 557
Nougat, Isfahani, 380, *380–381*
Nuts. *See specific types*

O

Okra, Lamb + Potato Braise, *640*, 641
Olive Tapenade, 86, *87*
Omaj (pellets of dough for soup), 193
Omelets. *See* Eggs
Onions
  Baked Onions Filled with Rice + Herbs, 322, *323*
  Baked Onion Stuffed with Bulgur, 322
  Bulgur Meatballs Filled with Caramelized Onion + Barberries, *324*, 325
  Camomile Flowers, Egg + Onion Soup, 476, *477*
  Crispy Fried Onions, 691
  Lamb + Rice with Potato, Onion + Turmeric, 650
  Minty Kashk with Baked Eggplant + Caramelized Onions, *690*, 691
  Onion, Egg + Spinach Soup, 46, *47*
  Onion Soup with Salted Fish, *615*, 615
  Onion, Cucumber + Coriander Pickle, 675
  Red Onion + Pomegranate Salad, 523
  Rice with Mung Beans + Caramelized Onions, 278, *279*
  Spicy, Lemony Shrimp with Caramelized Onions, 596
Oranges, *702*. *See also* Sour Oranges
  Blossom Water, *702*
  Orange Blossom Shrub, 560
Osh (porridge). *See also* Soup
  Araki Barley Osh, 272
  Barberry Osh, 398, *399*
  Barley, Nettle, Yogurt + Kashk Osh, 318
  Bulgur + Curly Cucumber Osh, 255
  Butternut Squash Osh, 101
  Carrot + Bulgur Osh, 254
  Dried Fruit + Noodles Osh, 250
  Green Herb Osh, *524*, 525
  Kermani Wheat Osh, 478, *479*
  Lamb Neck, Bulgur + Bean Porridge, 408, *409*
  Pasta Pellet Osh, 194, *195*
  Spinach + Beet Osh, 432, *433*
  Spinach + Dumpling Osh, 402, *403*
  Split Pea, Bulgur + Yogurt Osh, 272
  Tarkhineh Osh, 320, *321*
  Turnip Osh, 404, *405*
  Wheat and Turkey Breakfast Porridge, 58, *59*
  Yellow Kashk Porridge, 686, *687*
  Yogurt + Chickpea Osh, 196, *197*

P

Pancakes
  Fist Pancakes, *602*, 603
  Rice Lace Pancakes, *142–143*, 144
Parsnips: Wild Parsnip Preserve, 159
Persian Gulf, 574–578, *577*, *582–584*, 597, 604, *626–627*
Persian Pantry, ingredients of, *702–703*
Pickle
  Apricot + Nut Pickle, 266, *267*
  Baby Green Pistachio Pickle, 512, *513*
  Barberry Pickle, 423
  Beet Pickle, 671
  Black Carrot Pickle, *670*, 671
  Black Garlic Pickle, *162*, 163
  Cabbage Pickle, 671
  Lasura Pickle, 675

Index

721

Medlar Pickle, 164
Saffroned Mango Pickle, 676, *677*
Spicy Oily Lime Pickle, 673
Spicy Oily Turnip Pickle, 673

Pies
Date + Walnut Pie, 549
Khorma beriz (Date + Walnut Pie variant), 549
Savory Mushroom Pie, 60, *61*
Wheat Sprout Flour Date + Walnut Pie, 498, *499*

Pinto Beans
Araki Barley Osh, 272
Bulgur, Legumes + Verjuice Soup, 254
Lamb Neck, Bulgur + Bean Porridge, 408, *409*
Shirazi-Style Pinto Beans and Rice, 278

Pistachios, 464–469, *465–470*, *471*, *702*
Baby Green Pistachio Pickle, 512, *513*
Baby Pistachio Preserve, 512
Date, Pistachio + Lime Leaf Dessert, 666, *667*
Lamb, Pistachio, Dill + Verjuice Braise, 492, *493*
Pistachio, Fresh Herbs + Cardamom Kuku, 480, *481*
Pistachio, Saffron + Sour Orange Soup, 475
Pistachio + Dill Rice with Lamb Poached in Saffron-Rose Water, 488, *489*
Pistachio + Pomegranate Braise with Meatballs, 490, *491*
Pistachio Cake, 496, *497*
Pistachio Skin Jam, 511
Rice with Pistachios + Pomegranates, 538, *539*
Saffron + Lime Roasted Pistachios, 514, *515*
Saffroned Almond + Pistachio Baklava, 242–243
Wild Pistachio + Cucumber Soup, 400, *401*
Plums in Lamb, Quince + Plum Braise, 372, *373*

Polow. See Rice

Pomegranate Molasses, 445, *702*
Bulgur Meatballs Filled with Caramelized Onion + Barberries, *324*, 325
Caramelized Onion, Walnut + Raisin Rice with Pomegranate Syrup, 538
Duck Kabab, 118
Lamb Liver Kabab, *218*, 219
Sweet + Sour Kabab, 116
Sweet + Sour Patties, 76, *77*
Tomato, Cucumber + Herb Salad, *522*, 523
Walnut + Sumac Meatballs, 280, *281*

Pomegranates, *135*, 440–442, *443–445*, *444*, *702*
Butternut Squash, Walnut + Pomegranate Braise, 136, *137*
Dried Seeds, *703*
Duck + Pomegranate Braise, 132, *133*
Medlar, Walnut, Pomegranate + Chicken Casserole, 138
Pistachio + Pomegranate Braise with Meatballs, 490, *491*
Red Onion + Pomegranate Salad, 523
Rice Cooked in Dried Goat + Pomegranate Broth, 694, *695*
Rice with Pistachios + Pomegranates, 538, *539*
Tomato, Cucumber + Herb Salad, *522*, 523
Walnut, Pomegranate + Herb Patties, 342, *343*

Porridge. *See Osh*

Potatoes
Chelow Potato Crust, 210
Chicken Briyani with Rice + Potato, 654, *655*
Lamb + Rice with Potato, Onion + Turmeric, 650
Lemony Potato Snack, 526
Potato Kuku with Saffron Syrup Glaze, 396, *397*
Saffroned Lamb Braise with Potato Fries (or Baking Potatoes), 438, *439*
Saffron Rice + Potato Croquettes, 328, *329*
Spicy Okra, Lamb + Potato Braise, 640, *641*
Steamed Rice with Cumin + Potatoes, *484*, 485
Sweet Potato Halva, 663

Poultry. *See* Chicken; Quail; Turkey
Power Shake, 505
Prawns. *See* Shrimp and Prawns

Preserves
Azari Tomato Preserve, 258
Baby Pistachio Preserve, 512
Barberry Preserve, 421
Blackberry Preserve, 160
Cornelian Cherry Chutney, 160
Fig Jam, 154
Guava Jelly, 679
Guava Preserve, *678*, 679
Pistachio Skin Jam, 511
Pumpkin Preserve, 258, *259*
Rose Petal Preserve, 154, *155*
Wild Parsnip Preserve, 159

Prunes
Lamb, Prune, Apricot + Quince Spread, 362
Lamb, Quince + Plum Braise, 372, *373*
Lentil, Lamb + Prune Braise, 238, *239*
Tabrizi Meatballs with Split Peas + Tomatoes, 202, *203*

Pumpkin Preserve, 258, *259*

Q

Qazvin (city), *232*, 232–233
qisava-ye khorma (Crustless Date + Walnut Pie), 549
Qom (holy city), 228–229, *228–229*

Quail
Deep-Fried Quail, 121
Pan-Roasted Quail, 121
Quail Kabab, *120*, 121

Quince
Chelow Quince Crust, 210
Lamb, Prune, Apricot + Quince Spread, 362
Lamb, Quince + Plum Braise, 372, *373*

R

Raisins, *702*
Milk-Steamed Rice with Dates + Raisins, 486, *487*
Caramelized Onion, Walnut + Raisin Rice with Pomegranate Syrup, 538
Ramadan (holy month), 144, 294, 426, 525
Ramp Polow, 48, *49*

Index

722

Ramsar (city), *94–95*, 115
Rasht (city), *79*, *80*, *82*, *104–105*
Ray (Raghes/Ragha, part of Tehran), 21, 46
Red earth, *600–601*
    Pickled Sardine + Red Earth Sauce, 600
Rice, *702*
    Baked Onions Filled with Rice + Herbs, 322, *323*
    Barberry Rice, 418
    Brown Basmati Rice, 122
    Bulgur, Noodle + Currant Pilaf, 256, *257*
    Bushehri-Style Mung Bean Rice, 278
    Caramelized Onion, Walnut + Raisin Rice with Pomegranate Syrup, 538
    Carrot + Mung Bean Rice, 541
    Chicken Briyani with Rice + Potato, 654, *655*
    Dried Shrimp with Lentils + Rice, 652, *653*
    Fish + Dried Lime Rice, *648*, 649
    Fish Crusted Rice, 646
    Khorasani Seven-Spice Rice Advieh, 394
    Kohlrabi + Herb Rice with Meatballs, 540, *541*
    Lamb + Rice with Potato, Onion + Turmeric, 650
    Lamb + White Bean Braise with Dill Rice, 386, *387*
    Mashhadi Rice + Milk Cake, 426, *427*
    Milk-Steamed Rice with Dates + Raisins, 486, *487*
    Oven-Baked Chicken, Eggplant + Barberry Rice, 542–543, *543*
    Pistachio + Dill Rice with Lamb Poached in Saffron-Rose Water, 488, *489*
    Plain Rice, 122
    Ramp Polow, 48, *49*
    Rice, Lamb, Rose Petals + Barberries, 236, *237*
    Rice Cooked in Date Juice, 645
    Rice Cooked in Dried Goat + Pomegranate Broth, *694*, 695
    Rice Steamed in Date Molasses, *644*, 645
    Rice with Lamb Rib Chops, 333
    Rice with Legumes + Butternut Squash, 414
    Rice with Mung Beans + Caramelized Onions, 278, *279*
    Rice with Mushrooms + Barberries, 338
    Rice with Pistachios + Pomegranates, 538, *539*
    Rice with Sugar, Rose Water, Saffron + Tangerine Peel Syrup, 539
    Rose Petal Rice Pudding, 150, *151*
    Saffron Rice + Potato Croquettes, 328, *329*
    Saffron Steamed Rice, 209–210, *211*
    Smoked, 122, *703*
    Spicy Fish + Rice, 646
    Spicy Shrimp + Rice, 646, *647*
    Steamed Rice with Cumin + Potatoes, 484, *485*
    Yellow Fava Bean Rice, 278
Rice Flour
    Butternut Squash with Rice Flour Patties, 98, *99*
    Rice Lace Pancakes, *142–143*, 144
    Rice Noodle Sorbet with a Squeeze of Lime, *556*, 557
    Saffroned Rice Flour Cookies with a Walnut + Cardamom Filling, *148*, 149

Saffroned Rice Flour Pudding with Cumin, 424
Saffron Rice Cookies, 346, *347*
Rose Water or Rose Petals, *702*
    Almond, Lamb, Saffron + Rose Water Braise, 337
    Damask, 383, *384*
    Pistachio + Dill Rice with Lamb Poached in Saffron-Rose Water, 488, *489*
    Rice, Lamb, Rose Petals + Barberries, 236, *237*
    Rice with Sugar, Rose Water, Saffron + Tangerine Peel Syrup, 539
    Rose + Yogurt Love Cake, *350*, 351
    Rose Petal Preserve, 154, *155*
    Rose Petal Rice Pudding, 150, *151*
    Rose Petal Sugar, 150
    Rose Water + Apple Shrub, 506, *507*
    Rose Water Shrub, 560
    Saffron Omelet with Rose Petals, 188, *189*
    Shirazi Rose Water Custard, 546, *547*

S

Saffron, *391–393*, *393*, *425*, *702*
    Almond, Lamb, Saffron + Rose Water Braise, 337
    Angel Hair Noodles, Egg, Saffron + Cardamom, *608*, 609
    Egg + Saffron Spread, 264
    Fried Eggs with Fresh Ginger, Dates + Saffron, *606*, 607
    Pistachio, Saffron + Sour Orange Soup, 475
    Pistachio + Dill Rice with Lamb Poached in Saffron-Rose Water, 488, *489*
    Potato Kuku with Saffron Syrup Glaze, 396, *397*
    Rice with Sugar, Rose Water, Saffron + Tangerine Peel Syrup, 539
    Saffron + Lime Roasted Pistachios, 514, *515*
    Saffroned Almond + Pistachio Baklava, 242–243
    Saffroned Almond Paste, 448, *449*
    Saffroned Chicken + Yogurt Braise, 376
    Saffroned Lamb + Barberry Braise, 334, *335*
    Saffroned Lamb Braise with Potato Fries (or Baking Potatoes), 438, *439*
    Saffroned Mango Pickle, *676*, 677
    Saffroned Rice Flour Cookies with a Walnut + Cardamom Filling, *148*, 149
    Saffroned Rice Flour Pudding with Cumin, 424
    Saffroned Yogurt + Lamb Neck Braise with Barberries, 374, *375*
    Saffron Love Tea, 169
    Saffron Omelet with Rose Petals, 188, *189*
    Saffron Rice + Potato Croquettes, 328, *329*
    Saffron Rice Cookies, 346, *347*
    Saffron Shrub, 560
    Saffron Steamed Rice, 209–210, *211*
Salads
    Apple + Caspian Green Salt Salad, 84, *85*
    Celery, Walnut + Yogurt Salad, 316
    Cucumber, Sumac + Yogurt Salad, 316

Lettuce + Yogurt Salad, 316, *317*
Red Onion + Pomegranate Salad, 523
Tomato, Cucumber + Herb Salad, *522*, 523
Salt, Caspian Green, 84
Sangak. See Bread
Seafood, 581. *See also* Shrimp and Prawns
Calamari in Tomato Sauce, *630*, 631
Crabs, Poached, with Dried Limes, 634
Lobsters, Poached, with Dried Limes, 634
Mussel + Tamarind Braise, *632*, 633
Sesame Seeds, 552, *554–555*, 555, *702. See also* Halva
Date + Sesame Bread, *306*, 307
Sesame Halva, *662*, 663
Sweet Sesame Bun, *262*, 263
Shakes, 505
Shallots, *702*
Shiraz (city), *516–519*, 518, *527*, *529*
Shrimp and Prawns
Dried Shrimp with Lentils + Rice, *652*, *653*
Fisherman's Soup, 614
Prawns, Cilantro, Garlic + Tamarind Braise, 642
Shrimp Balls in Spicy Sauce, *628*, 629
Shrimp Patties, 622
Spicy, Lemony Shrimp with Caramelized Onions, 596
Spicy Shrimp + Rice, *646*, 647
Tiger Prawn Kabab, 620
Tiger Prawn Tempura in Spicy Chickpea Batter, 619
Shrubs, *560*, *561*
Mint, Vinegar + Flixweed Shrub, *450*, 451
Rose Water + Apple Shrub, *506*, *507*
Sibtorsh. See Sour Apples
Sistan + Baluchistan (region), *680–683*, *682*
Sorbets. *See* Desserts
Soup, 37. *See also* Osh
Azarbaijani Dumpling Soup, 198, *199*
Barley + Tahini Soup, 612
Barley Soup, 200
Bulgur, Legumes + Verjuice Soup, 254
Camomile Flowers, Egg + Onion Soup, *476*, 477
Fisherman's Soup, 614
Fish Head Soup, 110, *111*
Lamb Shank, Chickpea + Kidney Bean Soup (*dizzy*), 38, *39*
Lamb's Head, Feet + Tripe Soup, 44, *44–45*
Onion, Egg + Spinach Soup, 46, *47*
Onion Soup with Salted Fish, *615*, 615
Pistachio, Saffron + Sour Orange Soup, 475
Red Lentil Soup, *610–611*, 611
Sumac Soup, 360
Walnut + Kashk Soup, *406*, *407*
Wild Pistachio + Cucumber Soup, *400*, *401*
Yogurt + Tomato Fish Soup, 688
Yogurt Walnut + Tomato Soup, 406
Sour Apples
Apple + Caspian Green Salt Salad, 84, *85*
Sour Apple Molasses, 152, *153*

Sour Cherries, *161*
Onion, Egg + Spinach Soup, 46, *47*
Sour Cherry Braise, 140, *141*
Sour Oranges, *703*
Eggs, Herbs, Garlic + Sour Orange Braise, 130, *131*
Pistachio, Saffron + Sour Orange Soup, 475
Seared Fish with Garlic + Vinegar Glaze, 112
Sturgeon Kabab with Sour Orange, 114
Sour Plums, in Apple + Caspian Green Salt Salad, 84, *85*
Spices. *See* Advieh; Persian Pantry, ingredients of; *specific spices*
Spinach
Barley, Nettle, Yogurt + Kashk Osh, 318
Bulgur + Curly Cucumber Osh, 255
Onion, Egg + Spinach Soup, 46, *47*
Roasted Vegetables with Garlic Kashk, 410, *411*
Spinach + Beet Osh, 432, *433*
Spinach + Dumpling Osh, 402, *403*
Split Peas
Barberry Lamb + Split Pea Khoresh, 334
Chive + Split Pea Khoresh, 330
Goat, Yogurt + Split Pea Braise, 693
Lamb, Quince + Plum Braise, 372, *373*
Spinach + Beet Osh, 432, *433*
Split Pea, Bulgur + Yogurt Osh, 272
Split Pea Meatballs, 325
Tabrizi Meatballs with Split Peas + Tomatoes, 202, *203*
Spreads. *See also* Preserves
Caspian, 83
Caspian Green Salt, 84
Egg + Saffron Spread, 264
Eggplant Tapenade, 91
Finger Twist Spread, 264, *265*
Fish with Fenugreek + Tomato Spread, *598*, 599
Lamb, Prune, Apricot + Quince Spread, 362
Mung Beans + Kohlrabi Spread, 364, *365*
Olive Tapenade, 86, *87*
Smoked Eggplant, Tomato + Walnut Spread, *90*, 91
Smoked Eggplant with Eggs + Garlic, 92, *93*
Squash
Butternut Squash, Walnut + Pomegranate Braise, 136, *137*
Butternut Squash Osh, 101
Butternut Squash with Rice Flour Patties, 98, *99*
Rice with Legumes + Butternut Squash, 414
Roasted Butternut Squash + Grape Molasses, 260
Squid. *See* Calamari
Star Anise, *703*
Sugar, *220–221*
Rose Petal, 150
Sumac, *702*
Cucumber, Sumac + Yogurt Salad, 316
Roast Chicken with Dates, Walnuts + Sumac, *636*, 637
Sumac Soup, 360
Tomato, Cucumber + Herb Salad, *522*, 523
Walnut + Sumac Meatballs, *280*, 281

Sweet + Sour Glazed Chickpea + Carrot Patties, 370, *371*
Sweet + Sour Kabab, 116
Sweet + Sour Patties, 76, *77*
Sweet Potatoes, *201*
Sweet Potato Halva, 663

T

Ta'arof (politeness), 33
Tabriz (city) and Tabriz Bazaar, 178, *179–182*, 183, *205*
Taftun. See Bread
Tahini, *703*
　　Barley + Tahini Soup, 612
　　Crispy Falafel with Garlicky Tahini Sauce, *568*, 569
　　Date and Tahini Dessert, 667
　　Date Tahini Halva, 552
　　Spicy Sweet and Sour Fish with Dates and Tahini, 617
　　Tahini Halva, 552, *553*
Tajrish Bazaar (Tehran), 25, *25–29*, *28*
Tamarind, *703*
　　Fish Patties Glazed with Tamarind + Date Molasses, 622, *623*
　　Grilled Saboor Fish with Tamarind + Cilantro Stuffing, 572, *573*
　　Grouper, Cilantro, Garlic + Tamarind Braise, 642
　　Mussel + Tamarind Braise, *632*, 633
　　Tamarind Shrub, 560
Tapenades. See Spreads
Tea, 166, *166–168*
　　Borage + Valerian Tea, 169, *171*
　　Chabahar Milk Tea, 170
　　Dried Persian Lime Tea, 170
　　Hogweed Seed Tea, 170, *171*
　　Jujub Panacea Tea, 169
　　Saffron Love Tea, 169
　　Service Setup, *35*
Tehran, 14–24, 33–34, 42. See also Tajrish Bazaar; *specific locations within*
Tempura, Tiger Prawn, in Spicy Chickpea Batter, 619
Terebinth Fruit. See also Pistachios
　　Dried, *703*
　　Pickled, *703*
Tomatoes
　　Azari Tomato Preserve, 258
　　Calamari in Tomato Sauce, *630*, 631
　　Chickpea Meatballs in Aromatic Tomato Sauce, 366, *367*
　　Fish with Fenugreek + Tomato Spread, *598*, 599
　　Persian Gulf Rice and Tomatoes, 485
　　Smoked Eggplant, Tomato + Walnut Spread, *90*, 91
　　Steamed Rice with Cumin + Potatoes, 485
　　Tabrizi Meatballs with Split Peas + Tomatoes, 202, *203*
　　Tomato, Cucumber + Herb Salad, *522*, 523
　　Tomato, Egg + Garlic Omelet, *88*, 89
　　Tomato + Lime Broth with Tiny Meatballs, 270, *271*
　　Yogurt + Tomato Fish Soup, 688
　　Yogurt Walnut + Tomato Soup, 406
Tribal Region, 312–313, *312–313*
Truffle Kuku, 528
Turkey
　　Eggplant, Walnut + Herb Braise with Meatballs, 134
　　Kermani Wheat Osh, 478
　　Pistachio + Pomegranate Braise with Meatballs, 490, *491*
　　Walnut + Sumac Meatballs, 280, *281*
　　Wheat and Turkey Breakfast Porridge, 58, *59*
Turmeric, *703*
　　Lamb + Rice with Potato, Onion + Turmeric, 650
　　Turmeric, Cumin + Date Bun, 504
Turnips
　　Spicy Oily Turnip Pickle, 673
　　Spinach + Beet Osh, 432, *433*
　　Turnip + Cilantro Braise, 570, *571*
　　Turnip Osh, 404, *405*

V

Veal
Caucasian Fillet Kabab, 217
Fillet Kabab, *212*, 213
Vegetables. *See also specific vegetables*
　　Bulgur Meatballs in a Vegetable Broth, 326, *327*
　　Roasted Vegetables with Garlic Kashk, 410, *411*
　　Vegetable + Fruit Casserole, 206, *207*
Vegan and Vegetarian Dishes
　　Angel Hair Noodles, Egg, Saffron + Cardamom, *608*, 609
　　Apple + Caspian Green Salt Salad, *84*, *85*
　　Baked Onion Stuffed with Bulgur, 322
　　Barley, Nettle, Yogurt + Kashk Osh, 318
　　Barley Soup, 200
　　Barley + Tahini Soup, 612
　　Brown Basmati Rice, 122
　　Bulgur + Curly Cucumber Osh, 255
　　Busheri-Style Mung Bean Rice, 278
　　Butternut Squash, Walnut + Pomegranate Braise, 136, *137*
　　Butternut Squash Osh, 101
　　Butternut Squash with Rice Flour Patties, *98*, 99
　　Camomile Flowers, Egg + Onion Soup, 476
　　Carrot + Bulgur Osh, 254
　　Cheese, Walnut + Herb Balls, 248, *249*
　　Cheese + Dill Omelet, 96
　　Chive + White Bean Braise, 330, *331*
　　Crispy Falafel with Garlicky Tahini Sauce, *568*, 569
　　Desert-Truffle Kuku, 528
　　Dried Fruit + Noodles Osh, 250
　　Eggplant Tapenade, 91
　　Eggs, Herbs, Garlic + Sour Orange Braise, 130, *131*
　　Fist Pancakes, *602*, 603
　　Fried Eggs with Fresh Ginger, Dates + Saffron, *606*, 607
　　Lemony Potato Snack, 526
　　Lentil + Prune Braise, 238
　　Lettuce + Yogurt Salad, 316, *317*

725

Milk-Steamed Rice with Dates + Raisins, 486, *487*
Minty Kashk with Baked Eggplant + Caramelized Onions, 690, *691*
Olive Tapenade, 86, *87*
Onion, Egg + Spinach Soup, 46, *47*
Pasta Pellet Osh, 194, *195*
Pistachio + Dill Rice in Saffron-Rose Water, 488, *489*
Pistachio, Fresh Herbs + Cardamom Kuku, 480, *481*
Pistachio, Saffron + Sour Orange Soup, 475
Plain Rice, 122
Ramp Polow, 48, *49*
Red Lentil Soup, *610–611*, 611
Rice Steamed in Date Molasses, *644*, 645,
Rice with Legumes + Butternut Squash, 414
Rice with Mushrooms + Barberries, 338
Rice with Pistachios + Pomegranates, 538, *539*
Saffron + Barberry Braise, 334, *335*
Saffron Omelet with Rose Petals, 188, *189*
Saffron Rice + Potato Croquettes, 328, *329*
Savory Mushroom Pie, 60, *61*
Smoked Eggplant, Tomato + Walnut Spread, *90*, 91
Smoked Eggplant with Eggs + Garlic, 92, *93*
Smoked Rice, 122
Spinach + Beet Dumpling, 432, *433*
Spinach + Dumpling Osh, 402, *403*
Split Pea, Bulgur + Yogurt Osh, 272
Steamed Rice with Cumin + Potatoes, *484*, 485
Stuffed Grape Leaves, 190, *191–192*
Sumac Soup, 360
Tabrizi Cheese, Walnut + Herb Balls, 186, *187*
Tarkhineh Osh, 320, *321*
Tomato, Cucumber + Herb Salad, *522*, 523
Tomato, Egg + Garlic Omelet, 88, *89*
Verjuice
　Bulgur, Legumes + Verjuice Soup, 254
　Eggplant with Garlic + Verjuice, 91
　Lamb, Pistachio, Dill + Verjuice Braise, 492, *493*
　Spicy Meatballs with Verjuice, 230, *231*
　Verjuice Molasses, 152
Vinegar
　Mint, Vinegar + Flixweed Shrub, 450, *451*
　Seared Fish with Garlic + Vinegar Glaze, 112
　Spicy Sweet + Sour Fish with Dates, 617

W

Walnuts, *702*
　Black Walnut Halva, 224, *225*
　Butternut Squash, Walnut + Pomegranate Braise, 136, *137*
　Caramelized Onion, Walnut + Raisin Rice with Pomegranate Syrup, 538
　Carrot + Walnut Halva, 222, *223*
　Celery, Walnut + Yogurt Salad, 316
　Cheese, Walnut + Herb Balls, 248, *249*
　Date, Walnut + Orange Cake, *658*, 659
　Date + Walnut Cookies, 500, *501*
　Date + Walnut Pie, 549
　Eggplant, Walnut + Herb Braise with Meatballs, 134
　Gelatin + Walnut Roll, 558
　Medlar, Walnut, Pomegranate + Chicken Casserole, 138
　Pistachio, Fresh Herbs + Cardamom Kuku, 480, *481*
　Roast Chicken with Dates, Walnuts + Sumac, 636, *637*
　Roasted Beets with Grape Molasses + Walnuts, 260
　Saffroned Rice Flour Cookies with a Walnut + Cardamom Filling, *148*, 149
　Smoked Eggplant, Tomato + Walnut Spread, *90*, 91
　Tabrizi Cheese, Walnut + Herb Balls, 186, *187*
　Walnut, Pomegranate + Herb Patties, 342, *343*
　Walnut + Kashk Soup, 406, *407*
　Walnut + Sumac Meatballs, 280, *281*
　Wheat Sprout Flour Date + Walnut Pie, 498, *499*
　Yogurt Walnut + Tomato Soup, 406
Wheat
　Kermani Wheat Osh, 478, *479*
　Spicy Chickpea + Wheat Flour Balls, 624, *625*
　Wheat and Turkey Breakfast Porridge, 58, *59*
　Wheat Sprout Flour Date + Walnut Pie, 498, *499*
White Beans
　Chive + White Bean Braise, 330, *331*
　Lamb + White Bean Braise with Dill Rice, 386, *387*
　Lamb Neck, Bulgur + Bean Porridge, 408, *409*
Wine, 227

Y

Yazd (city), *428–431*, 431, 435, *440–441*, 446, 452, *453–455*, 458, *459*
Yogurt
　Barley, Nettle, Yogurt + Kashk Osh, 318
　Bulgur + Curly Cucumber Osh, 255
　Celery, Walnut + Yogurt Salad, 316
　Chelow Yogurt Crust, 210
　Cucumber, Sumac + Yogurt Salad, 316
　Goat, Yogurt + Split Pea Braise, 693
　Homemade Bulgur + Yogurt Patties, 320
　Lettuce + Yogurt Salad, 316, *317*
　Rose + Yogurt Love Cake, *350*, 351
　Saffroned Chicken + Yogurt Braise, 376
　Saffroned Yogurt + Lamb Neck Braise with Barberries, 374, *375*
　Split Pea, Bulgur + Yogurt Osh, 272
　Tarkhineh Osh, 320, *321*
　Yogurt + Chickpea Osh, 196, *197*
　Yogurt + Tomato Fish Soup, 688
　Yogurt Walnut + Tomato Soup, 406

Z

Zoroastrians and Zoroastrianism, 253, 287, 435, *436*, 437, 463

NAJMIEH BATMANGLIJ is a member of Les Dames d'Escoffier and lives in Washington, DC, where she teaches Persian cooking, and consults with restaurants around the world.